Announcing the new *Cooking Light* Annual Recipes

Internet Recipe Finder

myclar2003.com

http://www.myclar2003.com   temporary password: search

Now there's a great new reason to own *Cooking Light* Annual Recipes 2003…access to its Internet companion! Exclusively for *Cooking Light* Annual Recipes buyers, this new site lets you search and rate recipes, see over 200 additional recipe photographs, find quick and easy recipes in an instant, and much more.

Search recipes by categories like "Type of Dish"

Gather your favorite recipes in one handy place

Search recipes by keywords

Search Cooking Tips by keyword or "A to Z" list of topics, or see "Tip of the Day"

Tell us what's in your pantry and get recipes that won't require a trip to the store

Find ingredient substitutions in a flash

Rate recipes and see ratings from other visitors

See over 200 additional recipe photographs

Get Superfast and Dinner Tonight recipes in an instant

Search menus for every occasion

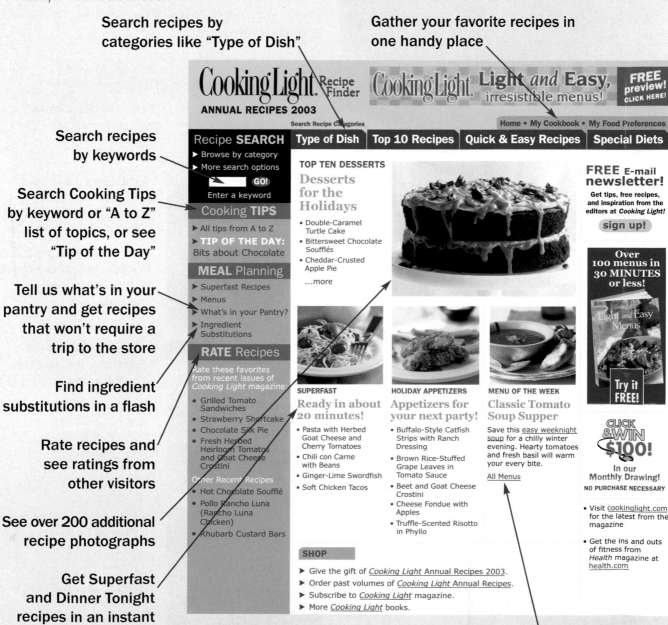

Go to www.myclar2003.com....Enter this temporary password to sign up to use the site: search

Our Favorite Recipes

Not all recipes are created equal. At *Cooking Light*, only those recipes that have passed muster with our Test Kitchens staff and food editors—not an easy crowd—make it onto our pages. We test each recipe at least twice, often three or four times, to ensure that all are not only supremely healthy, tasty, and easy to prepare, but that they also have the all-important "yum factor." So which of our recipes pack the most yum? They're the ones readers keep calling about, the ones our staff whip up for their own families and friends. They're the most delicious of the delicious, and we've listed them for you here.

◄ **Crispy Salmon with Risotto and Slow-Roasted Tomatoes** (page 248):

Refined enough for any dinner party, this dish combines sweet, meaty slow-roasted tomatoes, creamy risotto, and crisp-cooked salmon.

◄ **Bittersweet Chocolate Soufflés** (page 33):

These airy and elegant soufflés are a foolproof, impressive dessert for entertaining.

◄ **Balsamic-Braised Short Ribs with Horseradish Mashed Potatoes** (page 233):

Slow-simmered ribs nestle in mashed potatoes flavored with the slight bite of horseradish.

◄ **Cilantro Rice with Chicken** (page 67):

A puree of cilantro, green onions, ginger, and garlic gives a simple baked rice dish tons of robust flavor. The sautéed cherry tomato topping adds color and a touch of acidity.

◄ **Tenderloin with Grilled Antipasto Vegetables** (page 213):

Meltingly tender beef tenderloin tops grilled vegetables on an arugula-lined platter.

◄ **Garlic Fries** (page 73):

You'll never settle for fast-food fries after tasting these. Oven-baked potatoes tossed with garlic butter just before serving taste rich and savory.

◄ **Rosemary-Scented Flatbread with Black Grapes** (page 240):

Fragrant and savory fresh rosemary enlivens focaccia; black grapes and sugar lend a sweet note.

▲ Lemonade Layer Cake *(page 92)*:

This zesty dessert has moist, lemony cake layers and just the right blend of fruit and creamy frosting. **It's a top-rated recipe on our Internet Recipe Finder.**

◄ Crisp Pecan Cookies *(page 268)*:

If you have a weakness for pecan sandies, these are sure to become a staple in your cookie jar.

◄ Potato Cod Cakes with Dijon Tartar Sauce *(page 262)*:

Mildly sweet cod and mashed potatoes create a hearty fish cake that's paired with a tangy low-fat tartar sauce.

◄ Caramel Popcorn *(page 403)*:

It's easier to make than you'd think. You'll need to make more than one batch if you plan to give bags of this treat as gifts, because you won't be able to resist nibbling.

◄ Crispy Phyllo Napoleons with Berkshire Blue Cheese, Nectarines, and Pears *(page 253)*:

Blue cheese and fruit compote are stacked between crisp phyllo layers and embellished with a drizzle of caramel syrup.

◄ Brined Maple Turkey with Cream Gravy *(page 333)*:

A simple brining procedure produces a moist, tender bird with a subtle touch of maple flavor. Cola and herbs give the gravy a sweet-savory flavor.

◄ Pennsylvania Dutch Tea Rolls *(page 371)*:

The height of these rolls when they come out of the oven will amaze you. It's virtually impossible to eat just one, as our staff discovered.

◄ Apricot-Cream Cheese Braid *(page 402)*:

With a swirl of cream cheese and fruit throughout, this yeasty coffee bread is reminiscent of a Danish pastry minus the fat.

Herbed Cheese Pizza (*Labmacun*)
(*page 82*):

You'll throw out your old pizza dough recipe
once you try this soft, fluffy crust. Salty kasseri
cheese pairs excellently with the cumin, oregano,
and parsley-flavored tomato topping.

Cooking Light.

ANNUAL RECIPES 2003

Oxmoor House.

ISBN: 0-8487-2546-8
ISSN: 1091-3645

Printed in the United States of America
First printing 2002

Be sure to check with your health-care provider
before making any changes in your diet.

Oxmoor House, Inc.
Editor-in-Chief: Nancy Fitzpatrick Wyatt
Executive Editor: Katherine M. Eakin
Art Director: Cynthia R. Cooper
Copy Chief: Catherine Ritter Scholl

Cooking Light® Annual Recipes 2003
Editor: Heather Averett
Copy Editor: Jacqueline B. Giovanelli
Editorial Assistant: Dawn Russell
Publishing Systems Administrator: Rick Tucker
Director, Production and Distribution: Phillip Lee
Books Production Manager: Greg Amason
Production Assistant: Faye Porter Bonner

Contributors:
Designer: Carol Damsky
Indexer: Mary Ann Laurens
Editorial Intern: Sarah Miller

To order additional publications, call 1-800-633-4910.

For more books to enrich your life, visit
oxmoorhouse.com

Cover: *Peanut Butter-Banana Cream Pie (page 164)*

Cooking Light ®

Vice President, Editor: Mary Kay Culpepper
Executive Editor: Billy R. Sims
Managing Editor: Hillari Dowdle
Senior Food Editor: Jill G. Melton, M.S., R.D.
Senior Writer: Robin Mather Jenkins
Projects Editor: Mary Simpson Creel, M.S., R.D.
Editorial Coordinator: Carol C. Noe
Associate Editor: Phillip Rhodes
Associate Food Editor: Krista Ackerbloom Montgomery, M.S., R.D.
Assistant Food Editors: Julie Grimes, Ann Taylor Pittman
Contributing Beauty Editor: Linda Mooney
Senior Editor/Food Development Director: Ellen Templeton
    Carroll, M.S., R.D.
Art Director: Susan Waldrip Dendy
Assistant Art Director: Maya Metz Logue
Designers: Fernande Bondarenko, J. Shay McNamee
Assistant Designer: Brigette Mayer
Senior Photographer: Becky Luigart-Stayner
Photographer: Randy Mayor
Senior Photo Stylist: Lydia DeGaris-Pursell
Photo Stylists: Melanie J. Clarke, Jan Gautro
Photography Assistant: Karry Hosford
Studio Assistant: Kiersten Atkinson
Test Kitchens Director: Vanessa Taylor Johnson
Food Stylist: Kellie Gerber Kelley
Assistant Food Stylist: M. Kathleen Kanen
Test Kitchens Staff: Sam Brannock, Kathryn Conrad,
    John Kirkpatrick, Tiffany Vickers, Mike Wilson
Copy Chief: Maria Parker Hopkins
Copy Editor: Jennifer Southall
Assistant Copy Editor: Leah Griffin
Production Manager: Liz Rhoades
Production Editor: Hazel R. Eddins
Production Assistant: Joanne McCrary
Research Assistant: Dani Leigh Clemmons
Office Manager: Rita K. Jackson
Editorial Assistants: Cindy Hatcher, Heather W. Johnson
Correspondence Editor: Michelle Gibson Daniels
Interns: Jessica Brown, Virginia Odell

CookingLight.com
Editor: Maelynn Cheung
Managing Editor: Jason Burnett
Assistant Editor: Jennifer Middleton

contents

Our Year at Cooking Light®

Dear Reader,

If a great recipe is a wonderful thing, then a year's worth of great recipes is a treasure. And a treasure is what you have before you now. *Cooking Light* Annual Recipes 2003 reprises every recipe that appears on the pages of *Cooking Light* magazine during the past year.

And it's been quite a year for the magazine and its staff. *Cooking Light* made *AdWeek* magazine's prestigious "Hot List," a roster of the top 10 magazines in the country. We redesigned our Web site, CookingLight.com; its handsome new look attracts more than a million visitors each month. Midyear, we discovered that the magazine's readership has grown to more than 10 million strong, and *Cooking Light* celebrated its 15th anniversary in July.

Best of all, we published over 900 recipes in 2002. That means that no matter the season or occasion, you'll certainly find just the dish you're looking for in this book.

Here are some of the stories we've loved working on:

- Our Cooking Class series this year went back to basics and explored familiar foods. That in-depth approach to single topics such as chocolate, fish, and grains can help you move from novice to knowledgeable in no time.

- Award-winning cookbook author Peter Berley brought his passion for artful vegetarian cuisine to our Inspired Vegetarian column.

- The popularity of *Cooking Light* Supper Clubs across the country and on our Web site inspired a complement of stories in our September issue, which was full of sociable menus and game plans for entertaining.

- The overwhelming response to last December's holiday cookbook section convinced us to do it again—bigger and even better—this year.

- Several members of the food staff enjoyed the spotlight in a variety of memorable features. Test Kitchens' staffer John Kirkpatrick devised May's menu for "One Great Grilled Dinner." In June, Mike Wilson, another TK veteran, participated in a community-supported agriculture venture documented in "Common Ground." That same month, Assistant Food Editor Julie Grimes masterminded "Deconstructing the Cream Pie," and Associate Food Editor Krista Ackerbloom Montgomery developed "Sushi Party." Assistant Food Editor Ann Taylor Pittman created "A Month of Sundaes" in August. In September, Food Stylist Kellie Gerber Kelley and TK Staffer Sam Brannock came up with "A Feast for the Eyes." In that same issue, TK staffer Kathryn Conrad and Senior Photo Stylist Lydia DeGaris-Pursell collaborated on "A Party with Style."

Even with these new developments, one thing hasn't changed: If you like to eat smart, be fit, and live well, this is the cookbook for you. My colleagues and I hope you enjoy this new, vibrant edition of *Cooking Light* Annual Recipes 2003.

Very truly yours,

Mary Kay Culpepper

Vice President, Editor

january ◆ february

New Year's Anew

Celebrate the New Year with a traditional—and flavorful—Chinese feast.

The Chinese New Year is the most important holiday in China and is determined by the lunar calendar. Food is integral to the celebration and to a healthy, happy new year in Chinese tradition, and certain foods are considered especially auspicious: Chicken stands for prosperity and joy, while dumplings represent togetherness and heavenly blessings. Pork and beef symbolize wealth and strength, while vegetables and tofu bring harmony and prosperity. Noodles stand for a long, happy life, while shrimp represents happiness and good fortune. A whole fish symbolizes surplus and prosperity, and sweet rice cake brings safety, good fortune, and a sweet New Year.

Chinese New Year's Feast for Eight

Serve all or part of this menu to celebrate the New Year. Just make sure you serve an even number of dishes—an odd number is considered bad luck.

New Year's Dumpling Delight

Longevity Noodles

Lion's Head Meatballs in Spicy Coconut Sauce

Chicken-Ginseng Soup

Orange-Ginger Shrimp Skewers

Steamed Fish with Ginger-Wine Sauce

Vegetarians' Delight

New Year's Rice Cake

search myclar2003.com for all our menus

New Year's Dumpling Delight
(pictured on page 22)

Coat the steamer basket with oil to keep the dumplings from sticking or place each dumpling on a thinly sliced carrot 'disk.' When the dumplings come out of the steamer, each has its own little serving tray. You can also make these dumplings ahead and freeze them.

CHILI-GARLIC DIPPING SAUCE:
- ½ cup low-sodium soy sauce
- 2 tablespoons rice vinegar
- 2 tablespoons lemon juice
- 1 teaspoon sesame oil
- 2 tablespoons green onions, minced
- 2 garlic cloves, minced
- 1 hot red chile, minced

DUMPLINGS:
- 10 ounces ground pork
- 3½ cups shredded Napa (Chinese) cabbage
- 1¼ cups thinly sliced leek (about 1 large)
- 1 cup thinly sliced shiitake mushroom caps (about 3 ounces)
- ¾ cup minced green onions
- 1 tablespoon minced peeled fresh ginger
- 1 tablespoon low-sodium soy sauce
- 1 tablespoon sake (rice wine) or sherry
- 1 teaspoon sesame oil
- ¼ teaspoon salt
- ¼ teaspoon black pepper
- 40 won ton wrappers
- 2 large carrots, thinly sliced

1. To prepare dipping sauce, combine first 7 ingredients. Cover and refrigerate.

2. To prepare dumplings, combine pork and next 10 ingredients in a large bowl.

3. Working with 1 won ton wrapper at a time (cover remaining wrappers with a damp towel to keep from drying), spoon about 2 teaspoons pork mixture into center of each wrapper. Moisten edges of wrapper with water; bring 2 opposite corners to center, pinching points to seal. Bring remaining 2 corners to center, pinching points to seal. Pinch 4 edges together to seal. Place dumplings, seam sides up, on carrot slices (cover loosely with a damp towel to keep from drying).

4. Arrange half of dumplings in a single layer in a bamboo or vegetable steamer. Steam dumplings, covered, for 10 minutes. Remove dumplings from steamer; place on a platter. Keep warm. Repeat procedure with remaining dumplings. Serve with dipping sauce. Yield: 8 servings (serving size: 5 dumplings and about 2 tablespoons dipping sauce).

NOTE: If you don't have a steamer, use a heat-proof plate. Set it on top of a heat-proof bowl placed in the bottom of a pot filled with 2 inches of water. Cover and steam.

CALORIES 284 (30% from fat); FAT 9.5g (sat 3.1g, mono 3.9g, poly 1.5g); PROTEIN 12.6g; CARB 35.6g; FIBER 2.7g; CHOL 30mg; IRON 2.9mg; SODIUM 973mg; CALC 70mg

---

Longevity Noodles

Use the longest noodles you can find for this recipe; the length represents a wish for a long and happy life. The Chinese show respect to their elders at celebrations by serving them extralong noodles. Remember to serve the elders first.

PEANUT SAUCE:
- 2 teaspoons vegetable oil
- 2 tablespoons minced fresh onion
- 1 teaspoon grated peeled fresh ginger
- 1 garlic clove, minced
- ½ cup soy milk
- ¼ cup creamy peanut butter
- 1 teaspoon lemon juice

MARINADE:

- 1 tablespoon dry white wine
- 1 tablespoon low-sodium soy sauce
- 2 teaspoons grated peeled fresh ginger
- 2 teaspoons cornstarch
- ½ teaspoon black pepper
- 8 ounces skinless, boneless chicken breast, cut into thin strips

NOODLES:

- 8 ounces uncooked thin spaghetti
- Cooking spray
- ½ cup snow peas, trimmed
- ½ cup thinly sliced carrot
- ¼ teaspoon salt
- ¼ teaspoon freshly ground black pepper
- ½ cup diagonally sliced green onions

1. To prepare sauce, heat oil in a saucepan over medium-high heat. Add minced onion, 1 teaspoon ginger, and garlic; sauté 5 minutes or until onion is tender. Stir in soy milk, peanut butter, and juice; cook 3 minutes or until peanut butter is completely melted, stirring constantly. Remove from heat; cool completely.

2. To prepare marinade, combine wine and next 4 ingredients in a medium bowl. Add chicken; toss to coat. Cover and marinate in refrigerator 30 minutes.

3. To prepare noodles, cook pasta according to package directions, omitting salt and fat. Drain and rinse. Set aside.

4. Heat a large nonstick skillet coated with cooking spray over medium-high heat. Add chicken mixture; sauté 2 minutes or until done. Add snow peas and carrot; sauté 4 minutes or until crisp-tender. Stir in peanut sauce, salt, and ¼ teaspoon black pepper. Add noodles; toss well. Sprinkle with green onions. Yield: 8 servings (serving size: ½ cup).

WINE NOTE: Peanut sauce and ginger don't rank among wine's traditional partners, but there are many that pair well with this dish—especially those that are white, crisp, and have snappy acidity. An excellent choice is Chateau St. Jean Fumé Blanc (about $12). Its fresh, herbal, limey character is sensational as a juxtaposition to the peanut sauce.

CALORIES 213 (27% from fat); FAT 6.3g (sat 1.2g, mono 2.4g, poly 2.2g); PROTEIN 13.2g; CARB 26g; FIBER 1.8g; CHOL 16mg; IRON 1.8mg; SODIUM 153mg; CALC 27mg

Lion's Head Meatballs in Spicy Coconut Sauce

These spicy meatballs are called "Lion's Head" because of their large size. Also, lions are believed to ward off evil. You can make and cook the meatballs a day or two ahead, store them covered in the refrigerator, and reheat them in the sauce before serving. Decrease the red pepper for a milder flavor.

SPICY COCONUT SAUCE:

- ½ cup light coconut milk
- ½ cup soy milk
- 2 tablespoons Thai fish sauce
- 2 tablespoons minced peeled fresh ginger
- 1 tablespoon chopped green onions
- 2 teaspoons minced hot red chile

MEATBALLS:

- 1 pound ground round or ground pork
- ⅓ cup chopped green onions
- ¼ cup chopped water chestnuts
- 2 tablespoons cornstarch
- 1 tablespoon all-purpose flour
- 1 tablespoon minced peeled fresh ginger
- 1 tablespoon low-sodium soy sauce
- 1 tablespoon dark sesame oil
- 1 teaspoon minced hot red chile
- ¼ teaspoon salt
- 1 tablespoon vegetable oil
- ¼ cup chopped fresh basil
- 1 tablespoon grated lemon rind

1. To prepare sauce, combine first 6 ingredients in a small bowl.

2. To prepare meatballs, combine ground pork and next 9 ingredients in a large bowl, and shape mixture into 8 meatballs. Heat vegetable oil in a large nonstick skillet over medium-high heat. Add meatballs; cook 7 minutes, browning on all sides. Drain well.

3. Place sauce in a large saucepan; bring to a boil over medium-high heat. Add meatballs; cover, reduce heat, and simmer 8 minutes. Garnish with basil and rind. Yield: 8 servings (serving size: 1 meatball and 3 tablespoons sauce).

WINE NOTE: With their gingery spiciness, these meatballs are just waiting for a superfruity red wine that's low in tannin. Zinfandel fits the bill beautifully. Try Dry Creek Vineyard's Reserve Zinfandel (about $30). It's a big, mouth-filling fruit bomb with loads of blackberry, blueberry, and boysenberry flavors. Dry Creek's less expensive Zin, Old Vines, is a great bet at about $21.

CALORIES 297 (20% from fat); FAT 6.5g (sat 1.8g, mono 2g, poly 2.1g); PROTEIN 13.2g; CARB 38.7g; FIBER 17g; CHOL 30mg; IRON 1.4mg; SODIUM 616mg; CALC 12mg

Ways to Greet the New Year

Here are some Chinese traditions. Try a few of them for good luck.

- Clean your house and get rid of old, unused items to make room for the new.
- Pay bills and collect debts.
- Children should finish homework, wash hair, get a haircut, and have a set of new clothes ready for New Year's Day.
- Put out a red tablecloth and cushion covers. Hang red and gold banners and lanterns with Chinese good wishes written on them. Display Chinese dragons to ward off evil spirits.
- Children should bow to pay respect to elders. In return, give children red bags containing money—for prosperity in the year ahead.
- Exchange treats and fruit with loved ones. Candies are for a sweet New Year. Melon seeds and candied melon represent growth and prosperity. Oranges and tangerines stand for instant wealth and health.
- Set off firecrackers to frighten away evil spirits.

Chicken-Ginseng Soup

The Chinese believe cold drinks are harmful to the digestive system, so soup is served not as a first course but as a beverage with the meal. Because it's more readily available than fresh ginseng, we tested the recipe with ginseng tea.

- 2 tablespoons vegetable oil
- 2 cups chopped onion
- 2 tablespoons diced peeled fresh ginger
- 6 garlic cloves, minced
- 1 pound skinless, boneless chicken breast, cut into 1-inch pieces
- 3 cups water
- 3 (14-ounce) cans fat-free, less-sodium chicken broth
- 3 cups fresh or frozen yellow corn
- 4 bags ginseng tea or 2 sliced ginseng roots
- ¼ teaspoon salt
- ⅛ teaspoon white pepper

1. Heat oil in a Dutch oven over medium-high heat. Add onion, ginger, and garlic; sauté 2 minutes. Add chicken; sauté 4 minutes. Add water and broth; bring to a boil. Stir in corn and ginseng tea; bring to a boil. Reduce heat; simmer 20 minutes. Remove and discard tea bags. Sprinkle with salt and pepper. Yield: 8 servings (serving size: 1½ cups).

CALORIES 188 (29% from fat); FAT 6.1g (sat 1.4g, mono 1.2g, poly 2.5g); PROTEIN 18.2g; CARB 16.9g; FIBER 2.4g; CHOL 36mg; IRON 0.9mg; SODIUM 209mg; CALC 33mg

Orange-Ginger Shrimp Skewers

In Southern China, visitors traditionally bring oranges to their hosts. Instead of grilling this recipe in a pan, you can cook the skewers under the broiler.

- ½ cup fresh orange juice (about 2 oranges)
- 2 tablespoons rice vinegar
- 2 tablespoons low-sodium soy sauce
- 2 tablespoons minced green onions
- 1 tablespoon minced peeled fresh ginger
- 1 tablespoon minced fresh cilantro
- 1 tablespoon vegetable oil
- 2 teaspoons grated orange rind
- 1 minced hot red chile (optional)
- 1 pound large shrimp, peeled and deveined
- 2 oranges, peeled, cut in half, and quartered

Cooking spray

1. Combine first 9 ingredients in a bowl. Add shrimp; toss to coat. Cover and marinate in refrigerator 15 minutes.

2. Remove shrimp from dish, reserving marinade. Thread shrimp and orange quarters alternately onto 8 (8-inch) skewers.

3. Heat a large grill pan coated with cooking spray over medium-high heat. Cook skewers 4 minutes on each side or until done, basting with reserved marinade. Yield: 8 servings (serving size: 1 skewer).

CALORIES 104 (24% from fat); FAT 2.8g (sat 0.4g, mono 0.6g, poly 1.4g); PROTEIN 12.2g; CARB 7.4g; FIBER 1g; CHOL 86mg; IRON 1.5mg; SODIUM 218mg; CALC 46mg

Steamed Fish with Ginger-Wine Sauce

Fish is traditionally the last entrée served before dessert. The Chinese word for fish, 'yu,' sounds the same as a word that means 'plenty' or 'more than enough.' Leaving some of the fish at the end of the meal is a wish for the family's prosperity in the New Year.

- 1½ cups thinly sliced green onions
- ½ cup fresh orange juice
- ⅓ cup minced peeled fresh ginger
- 4 tablespoons sake (rice wine)
- 3 tablespoons fish sauce
- 2 tablespoons finely chopped peeled fresh lemon grass
- 1 teaspoon dark sesame oil
- 1 teaspoon finely chopped hot red chile
- ½ teaspoon salt
- ½ teaspoon white pepper
- 8 (6-ounce) trout fillets
- ½ cup red bell pepper, cut into ⅛-inch strips
- 8 cilantro sprigs

1. Combine first 10 ingredients in a 13 x 9-inch baking dish. Add fish; cover and marinate fish in refrigerator 2 hours, turning occasionally.

2. Preheat oven to 350°.

3. Bake fish mixture (including marinade), uncovered, at 350° for 17 minutes or until fish flakes easily when tested with a fork. Garnish with bell pepper and cilantro. Yield: 8 servings.

CALORIES 226 (37% from fat); FAT 9.2g (sat 1.6g, mono 4.4g, poly 2.2g); PROTEIN 27.6g; CARB 5.0g; FIBER 0.8g; CHOL 74mg; IRON 2.4mg; SODIUM 738mg; CALC 76mg

Vegetarians' Delight

Cooking spray
- 2 teaspoons minced peeled fresh ginger
- 2 garlic cloves, minced
- 1 cup diced oyster mushroom caps (about 3 ounces)
- 1 (8-ounce) package Thai-style flavored baked tofu, julienned
- ½ cup (3-inch) julienne-cut carrot
- ½ cup frozen whole-kernel corn
- ½ cup canned whole water chestnuts
- 1 tablespoon low-sodium soy sauce
- 1½ teaspoons rice vinegar
- ⅔ cup (3-inch) julienne-cut green onions
- 1 teaspoon dark sesame oil
- ¼ teaspoon black pepper
- ⅛ teaspoon salt

1. Heat a large skillet or wok coated with cooking spray over medium-high heat. Add ginger and garlic; stir-fry 30 seconds. Add mushrooms and tofu; stir-fry 2 minutes. Add carrot, corn, and water chestnuts; stir-fry 1 minute. Stir in soy sauce and vinegar; cook 2 minutes. Stir in green onions, sesame oil, pepper, and salt. Yield: 8 servings (serving size: ½ cup).

CALORIES 91 (38% from fat); FAT 3.8g (sat 0.5g, mono 0.6g, poly 1.8g); PROTEIN 7.5g; CARB 7.2g; FIBER 1.9g; CHOL 0mg; IRON 1.2mg; SODIUM 233mg; CALC 25mg

New Year's Rice Cake

Children will enjoy helping prepare this simple, yummy delight. You can find rice flour in Asian markets.

3½ cups glutinous rice flour (sweet rice flour), about 1 pound
1½ cups sugar
¼ cup dried tart cherries
¼ cup candied pineapple, chopped
¼ cup chopped pitted dates
¼ cup slivered almonds
1 tablespoon baking powder
1½ cups water
½ cup canola or vegetable oil
3 large eggs
Cooking spray

1. Preheat oven to 375°.
2. Lightly spoon flour into dry measuring cups; level with a knife. Combine flour and next 6 ingredients in a bowl.
3. Combine water, oil, and eggs; add to flour mixture, stirring by hand just until moist.
4. Spoon batter into a 9-inch round cake pan coated with cooking spray. Bake at 375° for 50 minutes or until a wooden pick inserted in center comes out clean. Cool rice cake 15 minutes in pan on a wire rack; remove from pan. Cool completely on wire rack. Yield: 12 servings (serving size: 1 wedge).

CALORIES 389 (28% from fat); FAT 12.1g (sat 1.1g, mono 6.6g, poly 3.1g); PROTEIN 4.5g; CARB 66.2g; FIBER 1.8g; CHOL 53mg; IRON 0.6mg; SODIUM 138mg; CALC 84mg

superfast

. . . And Ready in Just About 20 Minutes

Sometimes a few simple ingredients bring a dish to life.

Stir ginger, cinnamon, and cloves into honey, and discover a sweet and spicy glaze for pork. Or combine hot jalapeños and sweet yellow bell peppers with the tang of tomatoes for a sauce that lends sass to tender, mild shrimp. Balance—between sweet, salty, and spicy—is the key. Here are several combinations to please everyone.

Italian Sausage and White Beans

Serve with warm Italian bread.

12 ounces sweet Italian turkey sausage
Cooking spray
½ cup chopped green bell pepper
½ cup chopped onion
½ teaspoon bottled minced garlic
1 teaspoon dried oregano
1 teaspoon dried basil
1 (19-ounce) can cannellini beans or other white beans, drained
1 (14.5-ounce) can diced Italian-style tomatoes, undrained

1. Remove casings from sausage.
2. Heat a large nonstick skillet coated with cooking spray over medium-high heat. Add bell pepper, onion, and garlic; sauté 3 minutes. Add sausage, and cook 8 minutes, or until browned, stirring to crumble. Stir in oregano and remaining ingredients; reduce heat to medium-low. Cook 5 minutes or until thoroughly heated. Yield: 4 servings (serving size: 1 cup).

CALORIES 266 (29% from fat); FAT 8.5g (sat 2.4g, mono 3.1g, poly 2.8g); PROTEIN 21.4g; CARB 24.9g; FIBER 6.7g; CHOL 72mg; IRON 4.3mg; SODIUM 851mg; CALC 85mg

Ginger-Lime Swordfish

Serve with broiled pineapple wedges.

2 teaspoons grated lime rind
½ cup fresh lime juice (about 2 limes)
¼ cup honey
2 tablespoons bottled fresh ground ginger
2 tablespoons minced green onions
1 tablespoon low-sodium soy sauce
2 teaspoons bottled minced garlic
4 (6-ounce) swordfish steaks (about ¾ inch thick)
Cooking spray
¼ teaspoon salt
¼ teaspoon black pepper

1. Preheat broiler.
2. Combine first 7 ingredients in a small saucepan. Dip each steak into lime mixture to coat.
3. Place fish on a broiler pan coated with cooking spray. Sprinkle with salt and pepper. Broil 10 minutes or until fish flakes easily when tested with a fork.
4. While fish cooks, place lime juice mixture over medium heat; cook until reduced by half (about 8 minutes). Serve sauce with fish. Yield: 4 servings (serving size: 1 swordfish steak and 2 tablespoons sauce).

CALORIES 235 (20% from fat); FAT 5.2g (sat 1.4g, mono 2g, poly 1.2g); PROTEIN 25.8g; CARB 22g; FIBER 0.6g; CHOL 50mg; IRON 1.3mg; SODIUM 397mg; CALC 15mg

Honey and Spice-Glazed Pork Chops

Serve with mashed potatoes.

¼ cup honey
2 tablespoons Dijon mustard
½ teaspoon ground ginger
¼ teaspoon ground cinnamon
⅛ teaspoon ground cloves
Cooking spray
4 (4-ounce) boneless center-cut loin pork chops (about ½ inch thick)
½ teaspoon salt
¼ teaspoon freshly ground black pepper

Continued

1. Combine first 5 ingredients in a bowl.
2. Heat a large nonstick skillet coated with cooking spray over medium-high heat. Sprinkle pork with salt and pepper; cook 2 minutes on each side or until browned. Reduce heat to medium-low; add honey mixture. Cook 10 minutes or until done, turning pork once. Yield: 4 servings (serving size: 1 pork chop and 1 tablespoon glaze).

CALORIES 321 (34% from fat); FAT 12.1g (sat 4.1g, mono 5.5g, poly 0.9g); PROTEIN 34g; CARB 18.7g; FIBER 0.3g; CHOL 92mg; IRON 1.3mg; SODIUM 557mg; CALC 50mg

Spicy Pepper Shrimp

Have shrimp peeled and deveined at the grocery store to save time.

1 (3½-ounce) bag boil-in-bag long-grain rice
1 tablespoon olive oil
1 cup chopped yellow bell pepper
1 tablespoon chopped, seeded jalapeño pepper
¼ teaspoon salt
¼ teaspoon freshly ground black pepper
¼ teaspoon crushed red pepper
1½ pounds peeled and deveined medium shrimp
1 tablespoon lime juice
1 (14.5-ounce) can no-salt-added diced tomatoes, drained

1. Cook rice according to package directions.
2. While rice cooks, heat oil in a large nonstick skillet over medium-high heat. Add bell pepper and jalapeño; sauté 4 minutes. Add salt, black pepper, red pepper, and shrimp; cook 2 minutes or until shrimp are done. Stir in juice and tomatoes; cook 2 minutes or until thoroughly heated. Serve over rice. Yield: 4 servings (serving size: 1½ cups shrimp mixture and ½ cup rice).

CALORIES 324 (18% from fat); FAT 6.6g (sat 1.1g, mono 3g, poly 1.5g); PROTEIN 37.4g; CARB 26.9g; FIBER 1.8g; CHOL 259mg; IRON 5.7mg; SODIUM 409mg; CALC 120mg

Linguine with Pancetta and Parmesan

Serve with a salad of tomato and thinly sliced red onion.

1 (9-ounce) package fresh linguine
Cooking spray
1 cup chopped onion
⅔ cup chopped pancetta or ham (about 2 ounces)
½ teaspoon bottled minced garlic
1 (26-ounce) bottle fat-free Italian herb pasta sauce (such as Muir Glen Organic)
¼ cup chopped ripe olives
1 tablespoon capers, drained
¼ cup (1 ounce) shredded fresh Parmesan cheese

1. Cook pasta according to package directions, omitting salt and fat.
2. While pasta cooks, heat a large nonstick skillet coated with cooking spray over medium-high heat. Add onion, pancetta, and garlic; sauté 5 minutes. Add pasta sauce; cook 5 minutes. Stir in olives and capers. Add pasta; toss to combine. Sprinkle with cheese. Yield: 4 servings (serving size: 1½ cups pasta mixture and 1 tablespoon cheese).

CALORIES 381 (30% from fat); FAT 12.5g (sat 4.5g, mono 5.1g, poly 1.7g); PROTEIN 14.1g; CARB 53g; FIBER 5.2g; CHOL 61mg; IRON 3.5mg; SODIUM 626mg; CALC 237mg

Caramelized Onion Chicken

Sautéed green beans make a great side dish for this sweet, spicy chicken.

1 pound chicken breast tenders
½ teaspoon salt
¼ teaspoon freshly ground black pepper
1 teaspoon olive oil
½ cup sliced onion
½ cup seedless raspberry jam
1 tablespoon red wine vinegar
1 tablespoon low-sodium soy sauce
1 teaspoon bottled minced ginger
½ teaspoon dried rosemary

1. Sprinkle chicken with salt and pepper. Heat oil in a large nonstick skillet over medium-high heat. Add onion, and sauté 2 minutes. Add chicken to pan; sauté 8 minutes or until chicken is done. Remove onion and chicken from pan.
2. Add jam and remaining 4 ingredients to pan; cook 2 minutes, stirring constantly with a whisk. Return chicken mixture to pan; cook 4 minutes, stirring occasionally. Yield: 4 servings (serving size: 3 ounces chicken and 1 tablespoon sauce).

CALORIES 246 (10% from fat); FAT 2.6g (sat 0.5g, mono 1.2g, poly 0.4g); PROTEIN 26.6g; CARB 28.5g; FIBER 0.5g; CHOL 66mg; IRON 1.1mg; SODIUM 521mg; CALC 19mg

Quick Curried Beef

Serve with roasted butternut squash or Brussels sprouts.

1 (3½-ounce) bag boil-in-bag long-grain rice
1 pound flank steak, trimmed
Cooking spray
½ cup (1-inch) sliced green onions
1 teaspoon bottled minced garlic
1 tablespoon ground coriander
1 teaspoon ground cumin
½ teaspoon salt
¼ teaspoon ground turmeric
1 (14.5-ounce) can diced tomatoes, drained

1. Cook rice according to package directions.
2. While rice cooks, cut steak diagonally across grain into thin slices.
3. Heat a large nonstick skillet coated with cooking spray over medium-high heat. Add onions and garlic; sauté 2 minutes. Add coriander, cumin, salt, and turmeric; sauté 1 minute.
4. Add steak; sauté 6 minutes or until done. Add tomatoes, and reduce heat to low. Cook 3 minutes or until thoroughly heated. Serve over rice. Yield: 4 servings (serving size: 1 cup beef mixture and ½ cup rice).

CALORIES 394 (27% from fat); FAT 12g (sat 5g, mono 4.7g, poly 0.5g); PROTEIN 34.3g; CARB 34.4g; FIBER 2.6g; CHOL 76mg; IRON 3.6mg; SODIUM 490mg; CALC 40mg

Hearty Winter Buffet

Tap into some buried treasures for a meal that will warm you even on the season's coldest days.

Being a vegetarian can be challenging. Those new to the lifestyle often find it daunting. Even longtime vegetarians too often fall back on trusted bean-and-rice standbys.

Here's an ambitious spread that makes delicious use of root vegetables, winter's buried treasures. Beets, turnips, carrots, parsnips, onions, and shallots are all featured. Try some appetizers: a bright Lemon-Soy Aïoli served as a dip with crisp vegetables, or Beet and Goat Cheese Crostini. Both can be prepared ahead and assembled at the last minute.

The main event features earthy dishes like sage-toned wild mushroom risotto with the creamy consistency of the classic rice dish, though the recipe calls for barley. The Smothered Beans with Leeks and Collard Greens just may be the tastiest beans you've ever eaten. A refreshing salad of peppery greens tamed with citrus tang balances the deeper flavors. And a sweet and tart Apple-Cranberry-Walnut Crisp rounds out the meal.

Get together with friends and share the warmth with this Hearty Winter Buffet.

Hearty Winter Buffet Menu

Lemon-Soy Aïoli with vegetables

Beet and Goat Cheese Crostini

Wine-Glazed Winter Vegetables

Wild Mushroom-Barley "Risotto" with Sage

Smothered Beans with Leeks and Collard Greens

Watercress Salad with Fennel and Citrus

Apple-Cranberry-Walnut Crisp

search myclar2003.com for all our menus

Lemon-Soy Aïoli

We've pureed tofu for a low-fat, nutritious take on the traditional garlic mayonnaise. Use the leftovers as a sandwich spread.

  2 cups water
  2 garlic cloves, peeled
  8 ounces soft tofu, drained
  3 tablespoons fresh lemon juice
  1½ tablespoons olive oil
  ¾ teaspoon sea salt

1. Bring 2 cups water to a boil in a small saucepan. Add garlic, and cook 10 minutes. Drain.

2. Place tofu on several layers of paper towels; cover with additional paper towels. Let stand 10 minutes.

3. Combine garlic, tofu, and remaining ingredients in a blender or food processor; process until smooth. Serve with fresh vegetables. Yield: 14 servings (serving size: 1 tablespoon).

CALORIES 23 (74% from fat); FAT 1.9g (sat 0.3g, mono 1.2g, poly 0.4g); PROTEIN 0.8g; CARB 0.9g; FIBER 0g; CHOL 0mg; IRON 0.2mg; SODIUM 124mg; CALC 6mg

---

Beet and Goat Cheese Crostini

Prepare the components of this recipe ahead, and assemble it at the last minute.

BEETS:

  ¾ pound beets (about 2 medium)
  1 cup water
  1 tablespoon balsamic vinegar
  1 teaspoon grated lemon rind
  1 teaspoon fresh lemon juice
  ¼ teaspoon sea salt
  ¼ teaspoon freshly ground black pepper

CHEESE SPREAD:

  1 (5-ounce) package goat cheese
  1 tablespoon light mayonnaise
  2 teaspoons minced fresh tarragon
  ⅛ teaspoon freshly ground black pepper
  1 garlic clove, minced
  24 (½-inch-thick) slices diagonally cut French bread baguette, toasted

1. Preheat oven to 375°.

2. To prepare beets, leave root and 1 inch of stem on beets; scrub with a brush. Place beets in an 11 x 7-inch baking dish; add 1 cup water to dish. Cover and bake at 375° for 45 minutes or until tender. Drain and cool. Trim off beet roots; rub off skins. Cut beets lengthwise into quarters, and cut each quarter crosswise into 9 (⅛-inch) slices.

3. Combine vinegar, rind, juice, salt and ¼ teaspoon pepper in a medium bowl. Add beets; toss gently to coat.

4. To prepare cheese spread, combine goat cheese, mayonnaise, tarragon, ⅛ teaspoon pepper, and garlic in a small bowl. Spread each baguette slice with 1 teaspoon cheese mixture; top with 3 slightly overlapping slices of beet. Yield: 12 servings (serving size: 2 crostini).

CALORIES 127 (27% from fat); FAT 3.8g (sat 2g, mono 0.9g, poly 0.3g); PROTEIN 5.2g; CARB 18g; FIBER 1.4g; CHOL 6mg; IRON 1.2mg; SODIUM 297mg; CALC 44mg

---

Wine-Glazed Winter Vegetables

Use Riesling wine for a sweeter flavor.

  10 cups (1-inch) cubed peeled turnip
  2 cups (1-inch) sliced peeled carrot
  1½ cups (1-inch) cubed peeled parsnip
  8 cups water
  1 cup Sauvignon Blanc or other white wine
  2 tablespoons honey
  2 tablespoons butter
  ½ teaspoon sea salt
  ¼ cup chopped fresh parsley

1. Combine first 4 ingredients in a Dutch oven. Bring to a boil; cover, reduce heat, and simmer 15 minutes or until tender. Drain; return vegetables to pan. Add wine, honey, butter, and salt; bring to a boil. Cook 9 minutes or until liquid evaporates, stirring occasionally. Sprinkle with parsley. Yield: 8 servings (serving size: about 1¼ cups).

CALORIES 138 (21% from fat); FAT 3.2g (sat 1.8g, mono 0.9g, poly 0.2g); PROTEIN 2.2g; CARB 22.4g; FIBER 5.1g; CHOL 8mg; IRON 1mg; SODIUM 272mg; CALC 72mg

Wild Mushroom-Barley "Risotto" with Sage

This creamy dish is similar to regular risotto, but it's easier to make.

 1 cup uncooked pearl barley
 2 cups water
 4 cups Rich Porcini Stock
 1 tablespoon olive oil
 1 cup finely chopped onion
 8 cups thinly sliced shiitake
   mushroom caps (about 1 pound)
 1½ teaspoons sea salt
 2 teaspoons chopped fresh sage
 ⅓ cup (about 1½ ounces) grated
   fresh Parmesan cheese
 1 tablespoon butter
 ⅛ teaspoon freshly ground black
   pepper

1. Combine barley and water in a bowl. Let stand 2 hours; drain.
2. Bring Rich Porcini Stock to a simmer in a saucepan. Heat oil in a Dutch oven over medium heat. Add onion; cook 5 minutes or until tender. Add mushrooms and salt; cook 3 minutes.
3. Add barley, Rich Porcini Stock, and sage to onion mixture. Bring to a boil over medium heat; reduce heat, and simmer 30 minutes or until most of liquid is absorbed. Remove from heat; stir in cheese, butter, and pepper. Yield: 8 servings (serving size: about ⅔ cup).

CALORIES 191 (22% from fat); FAT 4.7g (sat 2g, mono 2.1g, poly 0.4g); PROTEIN 6.1g; CARB 26g; FIBER 5.1g; CHOL 7mg; IRON 2mg; SODIUM 448mg; CALC 75mg

RICH PORCINI STOCK:

Refrigerate this easy stock for up to three days, or freeze it for up to two months.

 1 cup dried porcini mushrooms
   (about 2 ounces)
 5 cups warm water, divided
 1½ cups coarsely chopped red onion
 1 cup dry red wine
 ½ cup coarsely chopped celery
 ½ cup chopped shallots
 ⅓ cup chopped carrot
 1 whole garlic head, halved
 2 thyme sprigs
 1 flat-leaf parsley sprig
 1 sage sprig

1. Combine mushrooms and 2 cups water in a bowl; cover and let stand 20 minutes. Drain mushrooms in a colander over a bowl, reserving liquid. Rinse mushrooms. Place in a 3-quart saucepan; strain reserved liquid into pan. Add 3 cups water, red onion, and remaining ingredients.
2. Bring to a boil over medium heat; reduce heat, and simmer, partially covered, 1 hour. Strain. Yield: 4 cups stock (serving size: 1 cup).

CALORIES 53 (2% from fat); FAT 0.1g (sat 0g, mono 0.1g, poly 0g); PROTEIN 0.8g; CARB 3g; FIBER 0.4g; CHOL 0mg; IRON 0.6mg; SODIUM 6mg; CALC 10mg

Smothered Beans with Leeks and Collard Greens

Layering the beans and aromatic vegetables distributes the flavor evenly.

 1 cup dried Great Northern beans
 ¼ cup dried pinto beans
 1 quart water
 2 tablespoons olive oil
 2 cups thinly sliced leeks (about 2
   large)
 1 tablespoon chopped fresh or 1
   teaspoon dried oregano
 1½ teaspoons sea salt, divided
 3 garlic cloves, thinly sliced
 1 pound collard greens, chopped
 ½ teaspoon freshly ground black
   pepper
 1 (14.5-ounce) can no-salt-added
   whole tomatoes, undrained and
   chopped

1. Sort and wash beans; place in a large saucepan. Cover with water to 2 inches above beans; cover and let stand 8 hours. Drain beans. Return beans to pan; add 1 quart water. Bring to a boil over medium heat. Reduce heat, and simmer, partially covered, 30 minutes. Cool. Drain beans in a colander over a bowl, reserving cooking liquid; set beans aside. Add enough water to cooking liquid to equal 3 cups; set aside.
2. Heat oil in a Dutch oven over medium-high heat. Add leeks, oregano, 1 teaspoon salt, and garlic; sauté 5 minutes or until leeks are tender. Reduce heat to low; cover and cook 10 minutes, stirring occasionally. Transfer leek mixture to a large bowl; add greens. Toss well to combine.
3. Place half of greens mixture in bottom of Dutch oven; top with beans. Spread remaining greens mixture over beans. Sprinkle with ½ teaspoon salt and pepper. Pour reserved liquid over greens. Cover and simmer over medium heat 1 hour or until beans are tender, stirring once. Uncover and stir in tomatoes; simmer 10 minutes. Yield: 8 servings (serving size: about ¾ cup).

CALORIES 153 (24% from fat); FAT 4.1g (sat 0.6g, mono 2.5g, poly 0.6g); PROTEIN 7.5g; CARB 24g; FIBER 7.8g; CHOL 0mg; IRON 2.3mg; SODIUM 382mg; CALC 158mg

Simple Supper Menu
serves 8

Citrus is the star of this meal, which can be pulled together in less than an hour. Use a grill pan to brown and cook the chicken while making the couscous and tossing the salad.

Watercress Salad with Fennel and Citrus

Lemon couscous*

Pan-grilled chicken breast

Orange sherbet

*Cook 1½ cups couscous according to package directions; fluff with a fork. Toss with 1 tablespoon grated fresh lemon rind and ¼ cup chopped fresh parsley.

search myclar2003.com for all our menus

Watercress Salad with Fennel and Citrus

The flavors of fennel and sweet oranges balance the peppery notes of the watercress and radishes.

SALAD:
 4 cups trimmed watercress (about 1
   bunch)
 1½ cups thinly sliced fennel bulb
   (about 1 small bulb)
 ½ cup thinly sliced radishes
 3 navel oranges, sectioned

DRESSING:

  2 tablespoons fresh lemon juice
1½ tablespoons extra-virgin olive oil
  1 teaspoon Dijon mustard
  ½ teaspoon maple syrup
     Dash of sea salt
     Dash of freshly ground black pepper

1. To prepare salad, combine first 4 ingredients in a bowl.
2. To prepare dressing, combine juice and remaining 5 ingredients in a small bowl, stirring with a whisk. Drizzle over watercress mixture; toss gently to coat. Yield: 8 servings (serving size: ⅔ cup).

CALORIES 58 (42% from fat); FAT 2.7g (sat 0.4g, mono 1.9g, poly 0.3g); PROTEIN 1.2g; CARB 8.5g; FIBER 2.1g; CHOL 0mg; IRON 0.3mg; SODIUM 52mg; CALC 52mg

Apple-Cranberry-Walnut Crisp

The combination of oats, whole wheat pastry flour, and walnuts makes the topping taste like a granola bar. This dish can be made ahead and warmed in a 250° oven. It's great served with low-fat vanilla ice cream.

FILLING:

  9 cups sliced peeled Gala apples
     (about 3 pounds)
  ½ cup fresh cranberries
  ½ cup apple cider or juice
  ¼ cup maple syrup
1½ teaspoons cornstarch
  1 teaspoon ground cinnamon
  1 teaspoon vanilla extract
     Dash of salt
     Cooking spray

TOPPING:

  1 cup regular oats
  1 cup whole wheat pastry flour
  ⅓ cup coarsely chopped walnuts
  ⅓ cup maple syrup
  ¼ cup unsalted butter, softened
  1 teaspoon ground cinnamon
  1 teaspoon vanilla extract
  ½ teaspoon salt

1. Preheat oven to 375°.
2. To prepare filling, combine first 8 ingredients. Spoon apple mixture into a 13 x 9-inch baking dish coated with cooking spray.
3. To prepare topping, combine oats and remaining 7 ingredients. Sprinkle over apple mixture. Cover with foil; bake at 375° for 40 minutes. Uncover; bake an additional 20 minutes or until topping is crisp and juices are thick and bubbly. Yield: 10 servings.

CALORIES 282 (27% from fat); FAT 8.5g (sat 3.3g, mono 1.9g, poly 2.4g); PROTEIN 4.5g; CARB 50g; FIBER 6g; CHOL 12mg; IRON 1.6mg; SODIUM 140mg; CALC 32mg

cooking light profile

Exchange Policy

Until her mid-40s JoAnna Lund—Middle America's Martha Stewart—had never created a recipe or spoken in public. Now, at 57, she is a success at both.

After decades of dieting, and a particularly stressful year with the loss of her mother and sending her son-in-law and daughter to the Persian Gulf War, JoAnna Lund was inspired to make some changes. Rather than turning to food to cope, JoAnna changed her goal from losing weight to recapturing health.

So JoAnna began to develop recipes. As a guide, she used the exchange plan, a flexible system of food exchanges upon which many special diets are based. JoAnna felt it provided a clear-cut way of establishing portion control.

Speed, convenience, taste, low fat, and low sugar characterize her recipes, which she describes as "common-folk" meals.

People certainly respond favorably to her utilitarian style. Over the past seven years JoAnna has gone on to author more than two dozen cookbooks that have sold three million-plus copies.

Today her thriving business concerns are a monthly newsletter, speaking engagements, and continued recipe development. JoAnna is particularly pleased that she has been able to help so many people. "What's most important to me is that when I solved a problem for my family, I solved it for other families, too."

Turkey Tetrazzini

Although this dish is one of JoAnna Lund's first culinary creations, she and her grandson still love the combination of turkey and the cheesy sauce.

     Cooking spray
1½ cups diced deli, lower-salt turkey
     breast (about ½ pound)
  ½ cup chopped onion
  ¼ cup water
  1 (10¾-ounce) can condensed
     reduced-fat, reduced-sodium cream
     of mushroom soup, undiluted
  ¾ cup (3 ounces) shredded reduced-
     fat sharp cheddar cheese
  2 cups hot cooked spaghetti (about 4
     ounces uncooked)
  2 tablespoons chopped fresh parsley
  ⅛ teaspoon black pepper
  1 (2-ounce) jar diced pimiento
     Parsley sprigs (optional)

1. Heat a large nonstick skillet or saucepan coated with cooking spray over medium-high heat. Add turkey and onion; sauté 3 minutes or until onion is tender. Stir in water, soup, and cheese; reduce heat to low, and cook 4 minutes or until cheese melts, stirring until mixture is smooth. Stir in pasta and next 3 ingredients; cook until thoroughly heated. Garnish with parsley sprigs, if desired. Yield: 2 servings (serving size: about 1½ cups).

CALORIES 500 (16% from fat); FAT 8.8g (sat 3.7g, mono 1.6g, poly 1g); PROTEIN 25.7g; CARB 77.7g; FIBER 4.9g; CHOL 31mg; IRON 3.5mg; SODIUM 1,077mg; CALC 349mg

A Fettuccine Affair

A Seattle reader's heart belongs to a creamy seafood pasta dish.

For as long as she can remember, Carmen Thrower, 25, has been in love. The object of her affection? Fettuccine with loads of seafood tossed in an Alfredo-like cream sauce.

As a student in naturopathic medicine at Bastyr University, Carmen studies nutrition. That's why she feels guilty every time she prepares the recipe, which is made with a mountain of grated cheese, a pint of heavy cream, and a quarter-cup of butter.

After receiving her letter pleading for help, we set out to lighten her recipe. We started by using less butter to sauté the seafood, since a little goes a long way in a nonstick skillet. That alone shaved about 29 grams of fat from the recipe. Because fresh Parmesan has such intense flavor, we were able to reduce the cheese by three-fourths and save another 66 grams of fat. Finally, we trimmed an additional 120 fat grams when we switched from whipping cream to half-and-half. The dish remained rich and creamy, but with only about a third of the fat of the original. And reducing the quantities of Parmesan and butter decreased the sodium by about a third, too. As for Carmen...she's still in love.

BEFORE	AFTER
SERVING SIZE	
1½ cups	
CALORIES PER SERVING	
721	438
FAT	
41.7g	14.8g
PERCENT OF TOTAL CALORIES	
52%	30%
SODIUM	
1,145mg	747mg

Seafood Fettuccine

The sauce is like a traditional Alfredo, with no flour or other thickener. Don't worry if it looks thin. It's the perfect consistency for coating the pasta. Pat the shrimp and scallops dry with paper towels before cooking so they don't dilute the sauce.

- 1½ tablespoons butter
- 1 cup chopped green onions
- 4 garlic cloves, minced
- 1 pound medium shrimp, peeled
- 1 pound sea scallops
- 2 cups half-and-half
- ½ teaspoon salt
- ¼ teaspoon black pepper
- ½ pound lump crabmeat, shell pieces removed
- ¾ cup (3 ounces) grated fresh Parmesan cheese, divided
- 8 cups hot cooked fettuccine (about 1 pound uncooked pasta)
- ¼ cup chopped fresh parsley

1. Melt butter in a 12-inch nonstick skillet over medium-high heat. Add onions and garlic; sauté 1 minute or until tender. Add shrimp and scallops; sauté 3 minutes or until done. Reduce heat to medium-low.
2. Add half-and-half, salt, pepper, and crabmeat; cook 3 minutes or until thoroughly heated, stirring constantly (do not boil). Gradually sprinkle ½ cup cheese over seafood mixture, stirring constantly; cook 1 minute, stirring constantly. Remove from heat. Combine pasta and seafood mixture in a large bowl. Top each serving with 1½ teaspoons cheese and 1½ teaspoons parsley. Yield: 8 servings (serving size: 1½ cups).

CALORIES 438 (30% from fat); FAT 14.8g (sat 7.7g, mono 3.6g, poly 0.9g); PROTEIN 38.5g; CARB 38g; FIBER 2.2g; CHOL 160mg; IRON 3.4mg; SODIUM 747mg; CALC 257mg

Gratin Dauphinois

Along with the Statue of Liberty, Gratin Dauphinois (grah-TAN doh-feen-wah) is among our favorite French imports, and rightly so.

Easy and satisfying, this sophisticated take on scalloped potatoes is an excellent accompaniment for roasted, grilled, baked, or broiled meat.

What we love best about this dish, which debuted in a story on French cooking in the May/June 1992 issue of *Cooking Light* magazine, is its simplicity. Slice potatoes, layer with cheese and butter, drizzle with milk, and bake.

Gratin Dauphinois
Scalloped Potatoes with Cheese
(pictured on page 21)

- 1 garlic clove, halved
- Cooking spray
- 6 peeled red potatoes, cut into ⅛-inch slices (about 2 pounds)
- 2 tablespoons butter, melted
- ½ teaspoon salt
- ⅛ teaspoon black pepper
- ½ cup (2 ounces) shredded Gruyère cheese
- 1 cup fat-free milk

1. Preheat oven to 425°.
2. Rub an 11 x 7-inch baking dish with cut sides of garlic halves; discard garlic. Coat dish with cooking spray.
3. Arrange half of potatoes in dish, and drizzle with half of butter. Sprinkle with half of salt and half of pepper, and top with half of cheese. Repeat layers once.
4. Bring milk to a boil over low heat in a small saucepan; pour over potato mixture. Bake at 425° for 40 minutes or until tender. Yield: 7 servings (serving size: 1 cup).

CALORIES 228 (24% from fat); FAT 6.7g (sat 2.3g, mono 2.1g, poly 1.2g); PROTEIN 7.6g; CARB 36.6g; FIBER 3.2g; CHOL 10mg; IRON 1.4mg; SODIUM 262mg; CALC 142mg

Tomato and Roasted Pepper
Salad, page 38

Gratin Dauphinois
Scalloped Potatoes with Cheese,
page 20

New Year's Dumpling Delight, page 12

Red Wine-Braised Chicken with Couscous, page 35

Baked Compote of Winter Fruit,
page 26

Lentil Stew with Ham and Greens, page 26

Chocolate Bundt Cake, with Rich Chocolate Sauce, page 32

Cold Medicine

Simple, soul-soothing recipes provide sustenance for the season.

Give your body what it craves with food that's simple, yet hearty enough to thaw winter's chill. These are the kinds of dishes you'll find here. Think of them as cold medicine—nourishment for the body as well as the soul.

Fisherman's Seafood Stew

This stew is brimming with fish and mussels.

- 2 tablespoons olive oil
- ½ cup minced shallots or onion
- ½ cup finely chopped red bell pepper
- ¾ cup dry white wine
- ½ teaspoon salt
- ½ teaspoon dried basil
- ¼ teaspoon black pepper
- 2 garlic cloves, minced
- 1 (14.5-ounce) can diced tomatoes, undrained
- 1 bay leaf
- 1 pound grouper or other firm whitefish fillets, cut into 5 pieces
- 1½ pounds small mussels, scrubbed and debearded
- 2 tablespoons chopped fresh flat-leaf parsley

1. Heat oil in a large Dutch oven over medium heat. Add shallots and bell pepper; cook 5 minutes. Add wine and next 6 ingredients; bring to a boil. Reduce heat; simmer 5 minutes, stirring occasionally.

2. Nestle fish into tomato mixture; top with mussels. Cover and cook 8 minutes; gently shake pan twice to stir mussels (do not lift cover). Discard any unopened shells and bay leaf. Sprinkle with parsley. Yield: 5 servings (serving size: about 2 ounces fish, ⅔ cup tomato mixture, and 8 mussels).

CALORIES 284 (30% from fat); FAT 9.6g (sat 1.6g, mono 4.9g, poly 1.6g); PROTEIN 35.3g; CARB 13.4g; FIBER 1.4g; CHOL 72mg; IRON 7.3mg; SODIUM 799mg; CALC 102mg

Cucumbers Vinaigrette

Chilled cucumbers provide a tangy, crisp complement to a hearty, hot bowl of soup.

- 3 cucumbers, peeled, halved lengthwise, seeded, and thinly sliced (about 3½ cups)
- ½ cup vertically sliced red onion
- 2 tablespoons red wine vinegar
- 1 tablespoon olive oil
- 1 tablespoon chopped fresh or 1 teaspoon dried basil
- 1 tablespoon chopped fresh or 1 teaspoon dried parsley
- 2½ teaspoons Dijon mustard
- ¼ teaspoon salt

1. Place cucumbers and onion in a bowl. Combine wine vinegar and remaining 5 ingredients; pour over cucumber mixture.

Toss gently. Cover and chill. Yield: 6 servings (serving size: ½ cup).

CALORIES 35 (67% from fat); FAT 2.6g (sat 0.4g, mono 1.7g, poly 0.3g); PROTEIN 0.7g; CARB 2.9g; FIBER 0.7g; CHOL 0mg; IRON 0.3mg; SODIUM 153mg; CALC 16mg

Ugly Bread

Ugly is a term of endearment here, as well as a reference to the free-form shape of the dough. Extra rising gives this bread a wonderfully coarse texture.

- 1 package dry yeast (about 2¼ teaspoons)
- 1 teaspoon sugar
- 1 cup warm water (100° to 110°)
- 3½ cups all-purpose flour, divided
- ¼ cup whole wheat flour
- ½ cup 1% low-fat milk
- 2 teaspoons olive oil
- 1 teaspoon salt
- Cooking spray
- 1 tablespoon cornmeal

1. Dissolve yeast and sugar in warm water in a large bowl; let stand 5 minutes. Lightly spoon flours into dry measuring cups; level with a knife. Add 3 cups all-purpose flour, whole wheat flour, milk, oil, and salt to yeast mixture; stir with a wooden spoon until smooth. Turn dough out onto a floured surface. Knead until smooth and elastic (about 10 minutes); add enough of remaining all-purpose flour, 1 tablespoon at a time, to prevent dough from sticking to hands (dough will feel tacky).

2. Place dough in a large bowl coated with cooking spray, turning to coat top. Cover and let rise in a warm place (85°), free from drafts, 1 hour or until doubled in size. (Press two fingers into dough. If indentation remains, dough has risen enough.) Punch dough down; cover and let rest 5 minutes. Divide dough in half.

3. Working with one portion at a time (cover remaining dough to keep from drying), shape each portion into a 6-inch oval on a floured surface. Cover with a slightly damp towel; let rise 20 minutes (dough will not double in size).

Continued

4. Working with one portion at a time, stretch each portion into a 15-inch-long loaf (loaf will be flat); place on a baking sheet coated with cooking spray and sprinkled with cornmeal. Cover with a slightly damp towel; let rise 30 minutes (dough will not double in size). Lightly dust each loaf with all-purpose flour.

5. Preheat oven to 425°.

6. Bake at 425° for 25 minutes or until loaves are browned on bottom and sound hollow when tapped. Remove from pan; cool on wire racks. Yield: 2 loaves, 12 slices per loaf (serving size: 1 [1-inch] slice).

CALORIES 79 (8% from fat); FAT 0.7g (sat 0.1g, mono 0.3g, poly 0.1g); PROTEIN 2.4g; CARB 15.6g; FIBER 0.7g; CHOL 0mg; IRON 1mg; SODIUM 101mg; CALC 10mg

Lentil Stew with Ham and Greens

(pictured on page 24)

One of the best things about this supper—besides its great flavor—is that it can be ready in less than an hour, start to finish.

1½ tablespoons olive oil
1 cup chopped onion
3 garlic cloves, minced
5 cups fat-free, less-sodium chicken broth
1 cup dried lentils
½ cup chopped carrot
2 bay leaves
3 cups chopped Swiss chard, collard greens, or spinach
1½ cups chopped baking potato
1 cup chopped smoked ham
1 (14.5-ounce) can diced tomatoes, drained
1 teaspoon dried basil
½ teaspoon dried thyme
½ teaspoon black pepper
3 tablespoons chopped fresh parsley

1. Heat oil in a Dutch oven over medium-high heat. Add onion and garlic; sauté 5 minutes. Add broth, lentils, carrot, and bay leaves; bring to a boil. Partially cover, reduce heat, and simmer 20 minutes. Add Swiss chard, potato, and ham; bring to a boil. Reduce heat; simmer 15 minutes or until potato is tender. Stir in tomatoes, basil, thyme, and pepper; simmer 10 minutes. Discard bay leaves. Sprinkle with parsley. Yield: 5 servings (serving size: about 1½ cups).

WINE NOTE: This dish recalls many of the casseroles of Northern Europe, where ham and lentils often appear on the menu. What would Northern Europeans drink with such fare? Usually Riesling. Riesling's tingling acidity is a terrific counterpoint to the sweetness and smokiness of the ham and the earthiness of the lentils. A Riesling from Alsace, France, (try Trimbach or Hugel) would be lovely. Closer to home, Trefethen's Dry Riesling from the Napa Valley is about $15.

CALORIES 320 (24% from fat); FAT 8.6g (sat 2g, mono 5g, poly 1.1g); PROTEIN 20.4g; CARB 41.7g; FIBER 15.1g; CHOL 12mg; IRON 5.6mg; SODIUM 943mg; CALC 84mg

Baked Compote of Winter Fruit

(pictured on page 23)

This simple compote of pears, apples, and cranberries smells wonderful while it bakes. Applesauce adds body to the syrup.

½ cup applesauce
1½ cups fresh cranberries
½ cup ruby port or other sweet red wine
½ cup apple cider
⅓ cup sugar
1 (1-inch) slice lemon rind strip
4 cups sliced peeled Golden Delicious apple (about 1¼ pounds)
2 cups firm Anjou pear, cored and cut into ¼-inch-thick wedges (about ¾ pound)
Cooking spray
3 cups vanilla low-fat ice cream

1. Preheat oven to 400°.

2. Spoon applesauce onto several layers of heavy-duty paper towels; spread to ½-inch thickness. Cover with additional paper towels; let stand 5 minutes. Scrape into a bowl using a rubber spatula.

3. Combine cranberries, wine, cider, sugar, and rind in a small saucepan; bring to a simmer over medium heat, stirring occasionally. Remove from heat; stir in applesauce.

4. Combine apple and pear in an 11 x 7-inch baking dish coated with cooking spray. Pour cranberry mixture over apple mixture. Cover and bake at 400° for 25 minutes. Uncover and bake an additional 10 minutes or until fruit is tender, basting occasionally with liquid from dish. Remove rind. Serve compote with ice cream. Yield: 6 servings (serving size: 1 cup compote and ½ cup ice cream).

CALORIES 260 (9% from fat); FAT 2.5g (sat 1.1g, mono 0.7g, poly 0.2g); PROTEIN 3.6g; CARB 57.6g; FIBER 5g; CHOL 5mg; IRON 0.4mg; SODIUM 49mg; CALC 115mg

Braised Cabbage and Leeks with Turkey Sausage

Serve this unpretentious dish with Ugly Bread (recipe on page 25) for a simple supper.

Cooking spray
8 cups thinly sliced green cabbage (about 2 pounds), divided
1½ cups sliced leek (about 3 small)
¼ teaspoon black pepper
½ cup fat-free, less-sodium chicken broth
1 pound smoked turkey sausage, cut into 6 pieces
¼ cup Dijon mustard

1. Heat a large nonstick skillet coated with cooking spray over medium heat. Add 4 cups cabbage and leek. Cover and cook 5 minutes. Stir in remaining cabbage and pepper. Cover and cook 5 minutes; stir in broth.

2. Add sausage to pan, nestling pieces into vegetable mixture. Cover and cook 10 minutes or until sausage is heated. Serve with mustard. Yield: 6 servings (serving size: ¾ cup vegetable mixture, 1 sausage piece, and 2 teaspoons mustard).

CALORIES 187 (41% from fat); FAT 8.6g (sat 2.1g, mono 3.1g, poly 2.5g); PROTEIN 14.3g; CARB 15.6g; FIBER 4g; CHOL 48mg; IRON 2.7mg; SODIUM 927mg; CALC 118mg

Braised Root Vegetables and Chicken Thighs

Winter is the peak season for rutabagas, turnips, and parsnips. Their strong flavors mellow with cooking.

- ¼ cup all-purpose flour
- 8 chicken thighs (about 2 pounds), skinned
- 5 teaspoons olive oil, divided
- 2 cups chopped onion
- 2 cups (¾-inch) cubed peeled rutabaga
- 2 cups (¾-inch) cubed peeled turnip (about 1 pound)
- 2 cups (¾-inch) cubed peeled butternut squash
- 1 cup (¼-inch-thick) slices parsnip
- 1 garlic clove, minced
- ½ cup fat-free, less-sodium chicken broth
- 1 teaspoon chopped fresh or ¼ teaspoon dried thyme
- 1 teaspoon chopped fresh or ¼ teaspoon dried rubbed sage
- ½ teaspoon salt
- ¼ teaspoon black pepper
- 1 bay leaf

1. Place flour in a shallow dish; dredge chicken in flour.
2. Heat 1 tablespoon oil in a large nonstick skillet over medium-high heat. Add chicken; sauté 5 minutes, turning once. Remove chicken from pan, and keep warm.
3. Heat 2 teaspoons oil in pan. Add onion; sauté 3 minutes. Add rutabaga, turnip, squash, parsnip, and garlic; sauté 3 minutes. Stir in broth and remaining 5 ingredients; nestle chicken into vegetable mixture. Bring to a boil; cover, reduce heat, and simmer 20 minutes or until chicken is done. Uncover and simmer 3 minutes or until thick. Remove bay leaf. Yield: 4 servings (serving size: 2 thighs and 1¼ cups vegetable mixture).

CALORIES 355 (29% from fat); FAT 11.3g (sat 2.2g, mono 5.8g, poly 2g); PROTEIN 30.2g; CARB 34g; FIBER 7.5g; CHOL 107mg; IRON 3.1mg; SODIUM 522mg; CALC 114mg

Ham and White Bean Soup

A touch of vinegar added at the end brightens the flavor of this amiable stew.

- 2 cups coarsely chopped yellow onion
- ¾ cup coarsely chopped celery
- ½ cup coarsely chopped carrot
- 2 teaspoons vegetable oil
- ½ cup chopped cooked ham
- 1 bay leaf
- 1 (15.8-ounce) can Great Northern beans, rinsed and drained
- 2 (14-ounce) cans fat-free, less-sodium chicken broth
- 1 teaspoon white wine vinegar
- ¼ teaspoon black pepper

1. Combine first 3 ingredients in a food processor; pulse 10 times or until finely chopped. Heat oil in a Dutch oven over medium-high heat. Add onion mixture; sauté 5 minutes, stirring occasionally. Add ham, bay leaf, beans, and broth; bring to a boil. Reduce heat; simmer 12 minutes or until vegetables are tender. Remove from heat; stir in vinegar and pepper. Discard bay leaf. Yield: 4 servings (serving size: 1 cup).

CALORIES 230 (14% from fat); FAT 3.6g (sat 0.8g, mono 0.9g, poly 1.6g); PROTEIN 15.7g; CARB 34.9g; FIBER 7.9g; CHOL 9mg; IRON 2.4mg; SODIUM 591mg; CALC 92mg

Cauliflower, Olive, and Sun-Dried Tomato Salad

Paired with Ugly Bread (recipe on page 25), this side can double as an appetizer.

- 1 ounce sun-dried tomatoes, packed without oil (about 12)
- ⅓ cup pitted green olives
- ¼ cup fresh parsley leaves
- 2 tablespoons white wine vinegar
- 1 tablespoon olive oil
- 2 garlic cloves, peeled
- 6 cups cauliflower florets
- ¼ cup finely chopped red onion
- ½ teaspoon salt
- ¼ teaspoon black pepper

1. Combine sun-dried tomatoes and enough boiling water to cover tomatoes in a bowl; let stand 30 minutes or until soft. Drain and chop. Combine tomato, olives, and next 4 ingredients in a food processor; process until finely chopped, scraping sides of bowl once.
2. Cook cauliflower in boiling water 2 minutes. Drain and rinse cauliflower with cold water. Combine tomato mixture, cauliflower, onion, salt, and pepper in a bowl; toss well. Yield: 6 servings (serving size: 1 cup).

CALORIES 71 (43% from fat); FAT 3.4g (sat 0.5g, mono 2.3g, poly 0.4g); PROTEIN 2.9g; CARB 9.4g; FIBER 3.6g; CHOL 0mg; IRON 1.4mg; SODIUM 392mg; CALC 41mg

dinner tonight

Soup It Up

No matter how cold it may be, you can warm up with these easy weeknight soups.

Indian-Seasoned Soup Menu
serves 4

Spicy Mulligatawny

Pita wedges

Ice cream with sautéed pears*

*Toss 2 cups sliced peeled pear with 1 teaspoon lemon juice. Heat 1 tablespoon butter in a nonstick skillet over medium-high heat. Add pear; sauté 6 minutes or until tender. Stir in 2 tablespoons brown sugar. Serve pear over vanilla low-fat ice cream; top with crushed gingersnaps.

Game Plan

1. Chop and measure ingredients for soup
2. While soup simmers:
- Sauté pear for dessert; keep warm
- Crush gingersnaps for dessert
- Cut pitas into wedges

search myclar2003.com for all our menus

Continued

Spicy Mulligatawny

The name of this highly seasoned Indian soup means "pepper water." It gets quite a kick from the combination of curry powder, ground ginger, and crushed red pepper, but you can halve those ingredients if you don't like spicy foods.

TOTAL TIME: 35 MINUTES

QUICK TIP: Slightly frozen chicken cuts quickly and easily. Place raw chicken in the freezer 20 minutes before cutting into bite-sized pieces.

    1   tablespoon vegetable oil, divided
    ½   pound skinless, boneless chicken
        breast, cut into bite-sized pieces
    1   cup chopped peeled Gala or
        Braeburn apple
    ¾   cup chopped onion
    ½   cup chopped carrot
    ½   cup chopped celery
    ½   cup chopped green bell pepper
    2   tablespoons all-purpose flour
    1   tablespoon curry powder
    1   teaspoon ground ginger
    ½   teaspoon crushed red pepper
    ¼   teaspoon salt
    2   (14-ounce) cans fat-free,
        less-sodium chicken broth
    ⅓   cup mango chutney
    ¼   cup tomato paste
        Chopped fresh parsley (optional)

1. Heat 1 teaspoon oil in a Dutch oven over medium-high heat. Add chicken, and sauté 3 minutes. Remove from pan; set aside.

2. Heat 2 teaspoons oil in pan. Add apple and next 4 ingredients; sauté 5 minutes, stirring frequently. Stir in flour and next 4 ingredients; cook 1 minute. Stir in broth, chutney, and tomato paste; bring to a boil.

3. Reduce heat; simmer 8 minutes. Return chicken to pan; cook 2 minutes or until mixture is thoroughly heated. Sprinkle with parsley, if desired. Yield: 4 servings (serving size: 1¼ cups).

CALORIES 236 (18% from fat); FAT 4.8g (sat 0.8g, mono 1.1g, poly 2.3g); PROTEIN 18g; CARB 31g; FIBER 4.9g; CHOL 33mg; IRON 1.9mg; SODIUM 599mg; CALC 42mg

---

Bean Soup Supper
serves 5

North Woods Bean Soup

Country apple coleslaw*

Pumpernickel bread with honey butter

*Combine ¼ cup red wine vinegar, 3 tablespoons brown sugar, 1 teaspoon vegetable oil, and ¼ teaspoon salt in a microwave-safe bowl. Microwave at HIGH 1 minute. Add 1 (10-ounce) package coleslaw, 2 cups chopped apple, and ½ cup raisins; toss well to coat. Serve chilled or at room temperature.

Game Plan

1. Cut kielbasa and vegetables for soup
2. While kielbasa and vegetables cook, microwave dressing for slaw
3. While soup simmers, chop apple for slaw

North Woods Bean Soup

Pureeing some of the soup lends body to the dish. Stir in fresh spinach after the soup is removed from the heat so it won't overcook and lose its bright color.

TOTAL TIME: 27 MINUTES

QUICK TIP: Baby carrots work well for fast dinners—they're already peeled, and they cook in a flash.

        Cooking spray
    1   cup baby carrots, halved
    1   cup chopped onion
    2   garlic cloves, minced
    7   ounces turkey kielbasa, halved
        lengthwise and cut into ½-inch
        pieces
    4   cups fat-free, less-sodium chicken
        broth
    ½   teaspoon dried Italian seasoning
    ½   teaspoon black pepper
    2   (15.8-ounce) cans Great Northern
        beans, drained and rinsed
    1   (6-ounce) bag fresh baby spinach
        leaves

1. Heat a large saucepan coated with cooking spray over medium-high heat. Add carrots, onion, garlic, and kielbasa; sauté 3 minutes, stirring occasionally. Reduce heat to medium; cook 5 minutes. Add broth, Italian seasoning, pepper, and beans. Bring to a boil; reduce heat, and simmer 5 minutes.

2. Place 2 cups of soup in a food processor or blender, and process until smooth. Return pureed mixture to pan. Simmer 5 minutes. Remove soup from heat. Add spinach, stirring until spinach wilts. Yield: 5 servings (serving size: about 1½ cups).

CALORIES 227 (15% from fat); FAT 3.9g (sat 1.2g, mono 1.3g, poly 1.2g); PROTEIN 18.1g; CARB 30.8g; FIBER 6.7g; CHOL 26mg; IRON 3.5mg; SODIUM 750mg; CALC 112mg

---

Quick and Cheesy Soup Menu
serves 6

Broccoli and Cheese Soup

Broiled plum tomatoes*

Baked potatoes

*Preheat broiler. Cut 9 plum tomatoes in half lengthwise. Scoop out and discard seeds. Place tomato halves on a jelly roll pan coated with cooking spray. Sprinkle ½ teaspoon seasoned dry breadcrumbs over each tomato half, and top with 1 teaspoon shredded part-skim mozzarella cheese. Coat tomatoes lightly with cooking spray. Broil 2 to 3 minutes or until cheese bubbles.

Game Plan

1. Preheat broiler for tomatoes
2. While broth for soup comes to a boil, prepare tomatoes
3. While broccoli boils:
  • Microwave potatoes
  • Combine milk and flour for soup
  • Cube cheese for soup
  • Broil tomatoes

Broccoli and Cheese Soup

Processed cheese melts beautifully, giving this soup a smooth texture and mild flavor.

TOTAL TIME: 33 MINUTES

QUICK TIP: Packaged broccoli florets, found with bagged salads in the produce section, eliminate cutting and cleanup.

    Cooking spray
    1   cup chopped onion
    2   garlic cloves, minced
    3   cups fat-free, less-sodium chicken broth
    1   (16-ounce) package broccoli florets
    2½ cups 2% reduced-fat milk
    ⅓   cup all-purpose flour
    ¼   teaspoon black pepper
    8   ounces light processed cheese, cubed (such as Velveeta Light)

1. Heat a large nonstick saucepan coated with cooking spray over medium-high heat. Add onion and garlic; sauté 3 minutes or until tender. Add broth and broccoli. Bring broccoli mixture to a boil over medium-high heat. Reduce heat to medium; cook 10 minutes.

2. Combine milk and flour, stirring with a whisk until well blended. Add milk mixture to broccoli mixture. Cook 5 minutes or until slightly thick, stirring constantly. Stir in pepper. Remove from heat; add cheese, stirring until cheese melts.

3. Place one-third of soup in a blender or food processor, and process until smooth. Return pureed soup mixture to pan. Yield: 6 servings (serving size: 1⅓ cups).

CALORIES 203 (28% from fat); FAT 6.3g (sat 4g, mono 1.8g, poly 0.4g); PROTEIN 15.6g; CARB 21.7g; FIBER 2.9g; CHOL 24mg; IRON 1.2mg; SODIUM 897mg; CALC 385mg

---

Classic Soup Supper Menu
serves 4

Tomato-Basil Soup

Cheese toast*

Green salad

*Preheat broiler. Spread each of 8 (½-inch-thick) slices French bread baguette with 1 teaspoon light Boursin cheese. Broil 2 minutes or until lightly browned.

Game Plan

1. Slice basil and mince garlic for soup
2. Preheat broiler for cheese toast
3. While soup simmers:
  • Prepare salad
  • Broil cheese toast

search myclar2003.com for all our menus

Tomato-Basil Soup

This quick version of the classic soup makes a refreshingly light supper. Toasted French bread spread with light Boursin cheese is a tasty stand-in for the standard grilled cheese sandwich.

TOTAL TIME: 30 MINUTES

QUICK TIP: To easily slice the basil, stack several leaves on top of one another. Roll the leaves together tightly, and slice the roll thinly. The ribbonlike slices are called chiffonade.

    2   teaspoons olive oil
    3   garlic cloves, minced
    3   cups fat-free, less-sodium chicken broth
    ¾   teaspoon salt
    3   (14.5-ounce) cans no-salt-added diced tomatoes, undrained
    2   cups fresh basil leaves, thinly sliced
    Basil leaves (optional)

1. Heat oil in a large saucepan over medium heat. Add garlic; cook 30 seconds, stirring constantly. Stir in broth, salt, and tomatoes; bring to a boil. Reduce heat; simmer 20 minutes. Stir in sliced basil.

2. Place half of soup in a blender, and process until smooth. Pour pureed soup into a bowl, and repeat procedure with remaining soup. Garnish with basil leaves, if desired. Yield: 4 servings (serving size: 1½ cups).

CALORIES 103 (24% from fat); FAT 2.8g (sat 0.4g, mono 1.7g, poly 0.4g); PROTEIN 5.8g; CARB 15.9g; FIBER 4g; CHOL 0mg; IRON 2.4mg; SODIUM 809mg; CALC 129mg

---

reader recipes

Indian Inspiration

You'll love this spicy combination of potatoes and green beans as a main dish or as a vegetable side.

Indian-Style Potatoes

—Kay Bozich-Owens, Raleigh, North Carolina

    1   tablespoon canola oil
    1   teaspoon brown mustard seeds
    ¾   teaspoon salt
    ¾   teaspoon crushed red pepper
    ½   teaspoon turmeric
    ½   teaspoon dry mustard
    2   garlic cloves, minced
    1   pound green beans, trimmed
    1   large baking potato, peeled and cut into ¼-inch strips (about 4 cups)
    ¼   cup water
    2   teaspoons fresh lemon juice
    ½   teaspoon grated lemon rind (optional)

1. Heat oil in a Dutch oven over medium-high heat. Add mustard seeds and next 5 ingredients; sauté 1 minute (mustard seeds will pop). Stir in green beans and potato; cook 5 minutes, stirring occasionally. Add water and lemon juice; cover, reduce heat to low, and cook 10 minutes or until potato is tender. Garnish with lemon rind, if desired. Yield: 3 servings (serving size: about 2 cups).

CALORIES 246 (20% from fat); FAT 5.4g (sat 0.4g, mono 2.7g, poly 1.5g); PROTEIN 6.4g; CARB 46.7g; FIBER 8.1g; CHOL 0mg; IRON 2.4mg; SODIUM 604mg; CALC 72mg

White Cheese and Sausage Pasta

"This recipe is definitely a family favorite. My daughter, Julie, and I invented it 10 years ago because she loves cheese. Now it is her husband's favorite meal. It is very easy, and if you like cheese, you'll love this."

—Vicki Koessl, Edina, Minnesota

½ pound mild Italian turkey sausage
Cooking spray
2 tablespoons butter
3 tablespoons all-purpose flour
2 cups 1% low-fat milk
6 cups hot cooked ziti (about 4 cups uncooked short tube-shaped pasta)
¾ cup (3 ounces) grated fresh Parmesan cheese
¼ teaspoon salt
½ cup (2 ounces) shredded part-skim mozzarella cheese

1. Preheat oven to 400°.
2. Remove sausage from casings. Place a large skillet coated with cooking spray over medium heat; cook sausage until browned, stirring to crumble. Drain well; set aside. Wipe drippings from pan with a paper towel.
3. Melt butter in pan over medium heat. Add flour; stir with a whisk. Gradually add milk, stirring with a whisk until smooth. Cook until thick (about 8 minutes); remove from heat. Combine milk mixture, sausage, pasta, Parmesan, and salt in a large bowl. Spoon mixture into an 11 x 7-inch baking dish coated with cooking spray. Sprinkle with mozzarella. Bake at 400° for 20 minutes or until lightly browned. Yield: 4 servings (serving size: about 1½ cups).

CALORIES 577 (29% from fat); FAT 18.4g (sat 10.1g, mono 4.4g, poly 1.3g); PROTEIN 31.3g; CARB 71.4g; FIBER 2.7g; CHOL 56mg; IRON 3.7mg; SODIUM 907mg; CALC 562mg

Adobo Pork Tenderloin

"Through *Cooking Light* I have discovered chipotle chiles in adobo sauce and bottled roasted red pepper, two amazing ingredients that can spice up any recipe. Not only is this quick and easy (no 24-hour marinade), but it is tasty as well."

—Erin Kaese, Chicago, Illinois

1 (1-pound) pork tenderloin, trimmed
1 (7-ounce) can chipotle chiles in adobo sauce
½ cup finely chopped green bell pepper
½ cup chopped bottled roasted red bell peppers
2 tablespoons grated fresh Parmesan cheese
1 tablespoon brown sugar
4 garlic cloves, minced

1. Preheat oven to 375°.
2. Slice pork lengthwise, cutting to, but not through, other side. Open halves, laying pork flat. Slice each half lengthwise, cutting to, but not through, other side; open flat. Place plastic wrap over pork; pound to an even thickness using a meat mallet or rolling pin.
3. Remove 1 chile and 1 teaspoon sauce from can; reserve remaining chiles and sauce for another use. Finely chop chile. Combine chopped chile, 1 teaspoon sauce, and remaining 5 ingredients in a small bowl. Spread chile mixture over pork, leaving a ½-inch border around edges. Roll up pork, jelly roll fashion, starting with short side. Secure at 2-inch intervals with twine. Place pork on a baking sheet.
4. Bake at 375° for 30 minutes or until a meat thermometer registers 160°. Cover lightly with foil; let stand 5 minutes. Remove twine, and cut pork into ½-inch-thick slices. Yield: 4 servings (serving size: 3 ounces pork).

CALORIES 175 (25% from fat); FAT 4.9g (sat 1.9g, mono 1.8g, poly 0.5g); PROTEIN 25.3g; CARB 6.6g; FIBER 0.5g; CHOL 76mg; IRON 1.7mg; SODIUM 145mg; CALC 49mg

Brown-Bag Lunch Menu
serves 6

Serve Cuban Beans and Rice Salad as a side for dinner, and take leftovers to work. You can make the salsa ahead and keep refrigerated, but since it may become hotter as it sits overnight, you may want to cut back on the jalapeño. Use fresh pineapple for the best flavor.

Cuban Beans and Rice Salad

Pineapple salsa*

Baked tortilla chips

*Place 3 cups chopped pineapple, 2 tablespoons chopped green onions, 2 teaspoons chopped fresh jalapeño pepper, 2 teaspoons chopped fresh mint, 1 teaspoon chopped fresh cilantro, 1 teaspoon fresh lime juice, ¼ teaspoon ground cumin, and ⅛ teaspoon salt in a medium bowl. Toss to combine.

search myclar2003.com for all our menus

Cuban Beans and Rice Salad

"This recipe can be assembled in a hurry—I usually cook the rice the night before."
—Linda Lum, Steilacoom, Washington

½ cup diced peeled avocado
2 tablespoons balsamic vinegar
1 tablespoon olive oil
1 teaspoon ground cumin
½ teaspoon salt
¼ teaspoon black pepper
3 cups cooked white rice
1 cup chopped, seeded plum tomato (about 3 tomatoes)
¼ cup minced fresh parsley
1 (15-ounce) can black beans, rinsed and drained
2 tablespoons minced fresh cilantro (optional)

1. Combine first 6 ingredients in a bowl, and toss gently. Add rice, next 3 ingredients, and cilantro, if desired; toss well. Serve chilled or at room temperature. Yield: 6 servings (serving size: 1 cup).

CALORIES 184 (23% from fat); FAT 4.6g (sat 0.7g, mono 3g, poly 0.5g); PROTEIN 4.9g; CARB 32.8g; FIBER 4g; CHOL 0mg; IRON 2.3mg; SODIUM 421mg; CALC 36mg

Spicy Green and Red Pork Loin Tostadas

"The pork roast can be cooked and shredded a day ahead. Simply reheat it before serving. I like to offer a variety of toppings for these tostadas, such as shredded lettuce, chopped tomato, grated cheese, salsa, and light sour cream."

—Christine Datian, Las Vegas, Nevada

PORK:
- 1 tablespoon ground red pepper
- 1 tablespoon dried oregano
- 1 teaspoon salt
- 1 teaspoon black pepper
- 1 (1½-pound) boneless pork loin roast, trimmed
- Cooking spray

SALSA:
- 3 cups chopped yellow onion
- 3 garlic cloves, minced
- 1 cup chopped red bell pepper
- 1 cup green salsa
- ½ cup frozen corn kernels, thawed
- ½ cup canned black beans, drained and rinsed
- 1 teaspoon crushed red pepper
- 1 teaspoon hot sauce
- ½ cup diced red apple
- ½ cup chopped fresh cilantro

ADDITIONAL INGREDIENTS:
- 8 (6-inch) corn tortillas
- ½ cup (2 ounces) shredded Monterey Jack cheese

1. Preheat oven to 350°.
2. To prepare pork, combine first 4 ingredients in a small bowl. Rub pork loin with pepper mixture. Place pork on a broiler pan coated with cooking spray. Bake at 350° for 1 hour or until meat thermometer registers 155°; cool and shred with 2 forks.
3. To prepare salsa, heat a nonstick skillet coated with cooking spray over medium-high heat. Sauté onion and garlic 2 minutes; add red bell pepper and next 5 ingredients. Reduce heat to low; cook 20 minutes, stirring occasionally. Stir in apple and cilantro, and cook 5 minutes.

4. Warm tortillas according to package directions. Place ½ cup pork and ½ cup salsa on each tortilla; sprinkle each with 1 tablespoon cheese, and top with desired toppings. Yield: 8 servings (serving size: 1 tostada).

CALORIES 286 (31% from fat); FAT 9.9g (sat 3.7g, mono 3g, poly 0.9g); PROTEIN 23.9g; CARB 26.6g; FIBER 4.9g; CHOL 59mg; IRON 2.1mg; SODIUM 667mg; CALC 144mg

Tarragon Turkey Burgers

"Whenever I serve these to my hard-to-impress teenagers, they exclaim, 'Oh boy! Turkey burgers!' At my house, the eight patties the recipe makes serve five. These burgers are the main reason I grow tarragon."

—Freda Briggs, El Dorado, Kansas

- 2 pounds ground turkey
- ½ cup dry breadcrumbs
- ½ cup finely shredded zucchini
- ¼ cup chopped onion
- 1 tablespoon chopped fresh or 1 teaspoon dried tarragon
- ½ teaspoon garlic salt
- ½ teaspoon black pepper
- Cooking spray
- 8 (1½-ounce) hamburger buns

1. Preheat broiler.
2. Combine first 7 ingredients in a large bowl. Divide turkey mixture into 8 equal portions, shaping each into a ½-inch-thick patty. Place patties on a broiler pan coated with cooking spray; broil 6 minutes on each side or until thoroughly cooked. Serve on hamburger buns with desired toppings. Yield: 8 servings.

CALORIES 275 (30% from fat); FAT 9.2g (sat 2.4g, mono 3.2g, poly 2.7g); PROTEIN 19.4g; CARB 27.7g; FIBER 1.5g; CHOL 67mg; IRON 2.5mg; SODIUM 508mg; CALC 68mg

Super Simple Peanut Soup with Vegetables

For me, peanut salad dressing mix is a necessity. This recipe is ridiculously easy, and everything except the dressing mix can be substituted. Leftover pork chops or chicken tastes great in place of tofu, and almost any fresh or frozen veggie tastes great."

—Sloan Anderson, Morehead City, North Carolina

- 2 (14-ounce) cans fat-free, less-sodium chicken broth
- 1 (2.9-ounce) packet peanut salad dressing mix (such as Taste of Thai)
- 4 cups small broccoli florets
- 1 cup chopped red bell pepper
- 1 (12.3-ounce) package extra-firm tofu, drained and cubed
- 4 cups hot cooked basmati rice
- 2 tablespoons chopped fresh cilantro (optional)

1. Combine broth and dressing mix in a large saucepan; bring to a boil. Add broccoli, bell pepper, and tofu. Reduce heat; simmer 10 minutes. Serve over rice; garnish each serving with 1 teaspoon cilantro, if desired. Yield: 6 servings (serving size: 1 cup soup and ⅔ cup rice).

CALORIES 318 (25% from fat); FAT 8.8g (sat 2.1g, mono 1.2g, poly 3g); PROTEIN 17.3g; CARB 47g; FIBER 3.6g; CHOL 3mg; IRON 7.9mg; SODIUM 567mg; CALC 499mg

All About Chocolate

Here's how to get maximum chocolate goodness with minimal effort.

The best ingredients, good technique, and a little bit of knowledge are all you need to make magnificent light chocolate desserts. Follow the simple tips below.

• Choose the best-tasting and freshest ingredients. Low-fat baking is like wearing a bikini—you can't hide much.

• Use small amounts of the real thing. Rarely use light or fat-free versions of anything, with the exception of some low-fat dairy products.

• Cocoa powder delivers a strong punch of flavor, alone or used in conjunction with other forms of chocolate.

• Oven temperatures can vary, and low-fat baked goods dry out easily. Always check the dessert five minutes before the recipe directs.

Combine these tips with the techniques and recipes that follow, and you can have chocolate goodness with minimal effort.

Chocolate Bundt Cake

(pictured on page 24)

A 6-cup Bundt pan is smaller than the standard size. You can also use a 9-inch round cake pan; reduce the bake time to 20 minutes.

  1 cup all-purpose flour
  1 cup sugar
  ½ cup unsweetened natural cocoa
  ½ teaspoon baking soda
  ¼ teaspoon salt
  ¼ cup butter, softened
  2 large egg whites
  1 large egg
  ½ cup 1% low-fat milk
  2 teaspoons instant espresso granules
 1½ teaspoons vanilla extract
    Cooking spray

1. Preheat oven to 350°.
2. Lightly spoon flour into a dry measuring cup; level with a knife. Combine flour and next 4 ingredients in a large bowl; stir well with a whisk. Add butter, egg whites, and egg; beat with a mixer at low speed 1 minute. Beat at high speed 1 minute. Add milk, espresso granules, and vanilla; beat 1 minute. Pour batter into a 6-cup Bundt pan coated with cooking spray.

3. Bake at 350° for 35 to 40 minutes or until a wooden pick inserted near center comes out clean. Cool in pan 10 minutes. Remove from pan; cool completely on a wire rack. Yield: 10 servings (serving size: 1 piece).

CALORIES 192 (28% from fat); FAT 6g (sat 3.5g, mono 1.8g, poly 0.3g); PROTEIN 4g; CARB 32.8g; FIBER 1.8g; CHOL 34mg; IRON 1.3mg; SODIUM 225mg; CALC 27mg

Rich Chocolate Sauce

(pictured on page 24)

This all-purpose chocolate sauce flavorfully pairs with cake, frozen yogurt, or fresh fruit.

  ½ cup sugar
  ½ cup unsweetened cocoa
  1 cup fat-free milk
  1 tablespoon butter
 1½ ounces semisweet chocolate, chopped
  ½ teaspoon vanilla extract

1. Combine sugar and cocoa in a small saucepan; stir in milk and butter. Bring to a boil over medium heat, stirring constantly. Cook 3 minutes, stirring constantly. Remove from heat; stir in chocolate and vanilla, stirring until chocolate melts. Serve warm or let stand 10 minutes to thicken. Yield: 1½ cups (serving size: 2 tablespoons).

CALORIES 73 (36% from fat); FAT 2.9g (sat 1.7g, mono 1g, poly 0.1g); PROTEIN 1.7g; CARB 12.9g; FIBER 1.3g; CHOL 3mg; IRON 0.7mg; SODIUM 21mg; CALC 32mg

Cocoa Fudge Cookies

You can mix these incredibly easy, fudgy cookies right in the saucepan. When freshly baked, these thin cookies have crisp edges and chewy centers. You can make them with either Dutch process or natural unsweetened cocoa powder; we opted for the latter.

  1 cup all-purpose flour
  ¼ teaspoon baking soda
  ⅛ teaspoon salt
  5 tablespoons butter
  7 tablespoons unsweetened cocoa
  ⅔ cup granulated sugar
  ⅓ cup packed brown sugar
  ⅓ cup plain low-fat yogurt
  1 teaspoon vanilla extract
    Cooking spray

1. Preheat oven to 350°.
2. Lightly spoon flour into a dry measuring cup; level with a knife. Combine flour, soda, and salt; set aside. Melt butter in a large saucepan over medium heat. Remove from heat; stir in cocoa and sugars (mixture will resemble coarse sand). Stir in yogurt and vanilla. Add flour mixture, stirring until moist. Drop by level tablespoons 2 inches apart onto baking sheets coated with cooking spray.
3. Bake at 350° for 8 to 10 minutes or until almost set. Cool on pans 2 to 3 minutes or until firm. Remove cookies from pans; cool on wire racks. Yield: 2 dozen (serving size: 1 cookie).

CALORIES 78 (31% from fat); FAT 2.7g (sat 1.6g, mono 0.8g, poly 0.1g); PROTEIN 1g; CARB 13.4g; FIBER 0.5g; CHOL 7mg; IRON 0.5mg; SODIUM 54mg; CALC 12mg

Chocolate Defined

The amount of chocolate liquor (a.k.a. unsweetened baking chocolate) present defines the various forms of chocolate. Here are the most common:

Unsweetened Baking Chocolate

This is pure chocolate liquor—ground, shelled, and roasted cocoa beans without added sugar or any other ingredients—and despite the reference to liquor, it contains no alcohol. Baking chocolate is quite bitter and isn't meant to be eaten by itself.

Milk Chocolate

America's favorite snacking chocolate, milk chocolate is often used for making candy bars. It's lighter in color and has a milder, creamier flavor than dark chocolate. It must contain at least 10 percent chocolate liquor, at least 12 percent milk solids, and no less than 3.66 percent butter fat. Because of the milk solids, high sugar, and low chocolate liquor, milk chocolate doesn't usually substitute for dark chocolate in recipes.

White Chocolate

White chocolate isn't really chocolate since it contains no chocolate liquor. It may contain cocoa butter, however, which is derived from chocolate liquor. Look for cocoa butter on the ingredient listing for quality white chocolate; if it contains palm kernel oil, it's white confectionery coating.

Sweet Dark Chocolate

This category includes all chocolates, bittersweet and semisweet, that have at least 35 percent chocolate liquor. The terms *bittersweet* and *semisweet* are often used interchangeably since there is no official distinction between them. Generally (but not necessarily), bittersweet chocolate is less sweet than semi-sweet, because bittersweet often contains more chocolate liquor. Semi-sweet and bittersweet chocolate are commonly used in baking, but both are also delicious eaten out of the package.

Sometimes packaging labels prominently indicate the percentage of chocolate liquor. Although 35 percent is the required minimum, American bittersweet and semisweet chocolates found in supermarkets—such as Hershey's or Baker's—usually contain at least 50 percent chocolate liquor. It's not uncommon to find chocolate liquor contents of 60 percent or more in such premium chocolates as Valrhona and Scharffen-Berger. These have intense chocolate flavor and are excellent in low-fat desserts.

Bittersweet Chocolate Soufflés

These chocolaty soufflés, which are airy and elegant, garnered our test kitchens' highest rating.

Cooking spray
- 2 tablespoons granulated sugar
- ¾ cup granulated sugar, divided
- ½ cup Dutch process cocoa
- 2 tablespoons all-purpose flour
- ⅛ teaspoon salt
- ½ cup 1% low-fat milk
- 1 teaspoon vanilla extract
- 2 large egg yolks
- 4 large egg whites
- ⅛ teaspoon cream of tartar
- 3 ounces bittersweet chocolate, finely chopped
- 1 tablespoon powdered sugar

1. Preheat oven to 350°.
2. Coat 8 (4-ounce) ramekins with cooking spray, and sprinkle evenly with 2 tablespoons granulated sugar.
3. Combine ½ cup granulated sugar, cocoa, flour, and salt in a small saucepan. Gradually add milk, stirring with a whisk until blended. Bring to a boil over medium heat; cook until thick (about 3 minutes), stirring constantly. Remove from heat; let stand 3 minutes. Gradually stir in vanilla and egg yolks. Spoon chocolate mixture into a large bowl; cool.
4. Place egg whites in a large bowl; beat with a mixer at high speed until foamy. Gradually add ¼ cup granulated sugar and cream of tartar, beating until stiff peaks form. Gently stir one-fourth of egg white mixture into chocolate mixture; gently fold in remaining egg white mixture and chopped chocolate. Spoon into prepared ramekins.
5. Bake at 350° for 15 minutes or until puffy and set. Sprinkle with powdered sugar. Serve immediately. Yield: 8 servings.

CALORIES 206 (24% from fat); FAT 5.5g (sat 3g, mono 1g, poly 0.3g); PROTEIN 5.2g; CARB 34.1g; FIBER 2.3g; CHOL 55mg; IRON 1mg; SODIUM 75mg; CALC 33mg

Do Brands Make a Difference?

Normally, the *Cooking Light* Test Kitchens use national supermarket brands of chocolate, such as Hershey's, Nestlé, or Baker's. But we wanted to know if premium chocolate would improve top-rated Bittersweet Chocolate Soufflés (recipe at left). The outcome of our side-by-side test? The vote was split. Some *Cooking Light* staffers couldn't detect a difference, while others thought that seeking premium chocolate is well worth the extra time and money.

search myclar2003.com for all our tips

Individual Chocolate Mousse Cakes

1¼ cups sugar, divided
½ cup unsweetened cocoa
2 tablespoons all-purpose flour
⅛ teaspoon salt
¾ cup water
5 ounces bittersweet chocolate, finely chopped
1 tablespoon dark rum
1 teaspoon vanilla extract
2 large eggs
1 large egg white
Cooking spray

1. Preheat oven to 350°.
2. Combine ¾ cup sugar, cocoa, flour, and salt in a small saucepan. Add water;

stir well with a whisk. Bring to a simmer over medium heat; cook 2 minutes, stirring constantly. Place chopped chocolate in a large bowl. Pour hot cocoa mixture over chocolate; stir until chocolate melts. Stir in rum and vanilla.
3. Place ½ cup sugar, eggs, and egg white in a bowl; beat with a mixer at high speed 6 minutes. Gently fold egg mixture into chocolate mixture.
4. Divide chocolate mixture evenly among 10 (4-ounce) ramekins coated with cooking spray. Place ramekins in a 13 x 9-inch baking pan; add hot water to pan to a depth of 1 inch. Bake cakes at 350° for 25 minutes or until puffy and set. Serve warm. Yield: 10 servings.

CALORIES 213 (27% from fat); FAT 6.4g (sat 3.6g, mono 1g, poly 0.2g); PROTEIN 3.6g; CARB 36.8g; FIBER 2.6g; CHOL 43mg; IRON 0.9mg; SODIUM 49mg; CALC 12mg

Chocolate Malt Ice Cream

This tastes just like the frozen malts you may have had at a drugstore soda fountain. Look for malt powder near the powdered milk in the supermarket.

1⅓ cups sugar
1 cup unsweetened cocoa
1 cup boiling water
1 cup malt powder
6 cups whole milk

1. Combine first 3 ingredients in a bowl; stir well with a whisk. Add malt

powder, stirring until dissolved. Stir in milk. Cover and chill. Pour mixture into freezer can of an ice-cream freezer; freeze according to manufacturer's instructions. Yield: 10 servings (serving size: ¾ cup).

CALORIES 223 (25% from fat); FAT 6.2g (sat 3.8g, mono 2g, poly 0.2g); PROTEIN 6.8g; CARB 40.4g; FIBER 2.9g; CHOL 20mg; IRON 1.8mg; SODIUM 85mg; CALC 196mg

White Chocolate-Lemon Biscotti

For a variation, substitute orange for lemon and semisweet chocolate chips for chopped white chocolate. Take time to chop a white chocolate candy bar; white chocolate morsels contain no cocoa butter and will compromise the end result.

¾ cup sugar
2 teaspoons grated lemon rind
1 teaspoon vanilla extract
¼ teaspoon lemon extract
2 large eggs
1⅔ cups all-purpose flour
½ teaspoon baking soda
¼ teaspoon salt
1¼ cups (6-ounce bar) premium white chocolate, chopped
Cooking spray

1. Preheat oven to 300°.
2. Place first 5 ingredients in a large bowl; beat with a mixer at medium speed until well blended. Lightly spoon flour into dry measuring cups; level with a

---

How Chocolate Is Made

Chocolate is grown in the tropics near the equator. The biggest crops of cacao come from Brazil and from Africa's Ivory Coast. Cacao refers to the tree as well as its fruit and seeds. The fruit, colorful grooved pods about 12 inches long, grows directly from the trunk and lower branches of the tree. At harvest, the pods are cut, split open, and emptied of their pulp and the 24 to 40 navy bean-sized seeds. The

seeds and pulp are then heaped into bins and covered to ferment for three to five days, during which time they are shoveled and turned daily. Without proper fermentation, there is no possibility that the seeds, or cocoa beans, can be later transformed into good chocolate.

After fermentation, the seeds are dried before they are bagged and shipped to chocolate factories. At the factories, the

cocoa beans are cleaned, roasted, and winnowed to remove hulls. The process of winnowing also breaks the hulled beans into pieces, called cocoa nibs. Nibs from different varieties and origins are usually blended after roasting to create different chocolates with distinct flavors, just as grapes are blended in making wine. After blending, the nibs are ground into chocolate liquor, which you know as unsweetened baking chocolate.

knife. Combine flour, baking soda, and salt; gradually add to sugar mixture, beating until well blended. Stir in chocolate.

3. Turn dough out onto a baking sheet coated with cooking spray. Shape dough into 2 (12-inch-long) rolls; pat to 2½-inch width.

4. Bake at 300° for 35 minutes. Remove rolls from baking sheet; cool 10 minutes on a wire rack.

5. Cut each roll diagonally into 24 (½-inch) slices. Place, cut sides down, on baking sheet. Bake at 300° for 10 to 12 minutes. Turn cookies over; bake an additional 10 minutes (cookies will be slightly soft in center but will harden as they cool). Remove from baking sheet; cool completely on wire rack. Yield: 48 servings (serving size: 1 biscotto).

CALORIES 55 (28% from fat); FAT 1.7g (sat 0.9g, mono 0.5g, poly 0.1g); PROTEIN 1g; CARB 9.1g; FIBER 0.1g; CHOL 10mg; IRON 0.3mg; SODIUM 32mg; CALC 11mg

Cocoa Powder

Cocoa powder is made from roasted, ground cacao seeds that have had much of their fat removed. There are two types of cocoa: natural (nonalkalized) and Dutch process (alkalized). Both are unsweetened, but their flavors differ.

Natural cocoa tastes fruity, tart, and acidic, and is simply untreated cocoa. Rarely labeled "natural," its package usually reads "cocoa." Dutch process cocoa is named for a Dutchman who invented a method for treating cocoa with an alkali to reduce its harshness and acidity. "Dutching" gives the cocoa a rich, dark color and a mellow, toasted flavor.

If a recipe calls for cocoa and is leavened with baking soda, use the natural variety. Because Dutch process cocoa is more alkaline, it may alter the recipe's chemistry. In recipes with no leaveners, either type may be used successfully.

It's best to store cocoa away from herbs, spices, and other aromatic substances: It picks up other flavors relatively easily.

search myclar2003.com for all our tips

Five Ways to Make Winter Tomatoes Taste Like Summer

Easy techniques revive the missing flavor.

Just because you've dragged your mittens and parkas out of storage doesn't mean the longing for a good tomato has gone away. Use a few tricks, and you can satisfy that craving with a store-bought winter tomato. With a little tender loving care, you can coax it into some semblance of those you remember from summer.

Five simple techniques—marinating, roasting, oven drying, grilling, and braising—improve the mealy texture of winter tomatoes and concentrate the pallid flavor to bring the off-season veggies to life. And with some experimentation, you'll quickly learn how to match the right method to any recipe.

Red Wine-Braised Chicken with Couscous
(pictured on page 22)

Braising (slow cooking in liquid over low heat) causes tomatoes to break down and absorb other flavors in the dish. Capers, olives, tomatoes, and wine create a rich, salty-sweet sauce.

  5 garlic cloves, peeled
  2 chicken breast halves, skinned
  2 chicken drumsticks, skinned
  2 chicken thighs, skinned
  ¼ teaspoon freshly ground black pepper
  2 teaspoons olive oil
  2 cups Merlot or other fruity red wine
1½ cups fat-free, less-sodium chicken broth
  2 cups chopped seeded peeled tomato
  1 tablespoon tomato paste
  ½ cup kalamata olives, pitted
  3 tablespoons capers, rinsed
  2 cups hot cooked couscous
Flat-leaf parsley sprigs (optional)

1. Place garlic in a small saucepan; cover with water. Bring to a boil. Reduce heat; simmer 2 minutes. Drain; set garlic aside.

2. Sprinkle chicken with pepper. Heat oil in a large Dutch oven over medium-high heat. Add chicken; cook 10 minutes or until browned, turning once. Remove chicken from pan.

3. Increase heat to high; add wine to pan. Cook until reduced to 1 cup (about 5 minutes). Remove from heat. Stir in garlic, drumsticks, thighs, broth, tomato, and tomato paste. Bring to a boil. Reduce heat; simmer 5 minutes. Add breast halves; cover and cook 20 minutes, turning chicken after 10 minutes. Remove chicken from pan; keep warm.

4. Increase heat to medium-high; add olives and capers to pan. Cook, uncovered, 10 minutes, stirring occasionally. Return chicken to pan, turning to coat. Cover and let stand 5 minutes. Serve with couscous. Garnish with parsley, if desired. Yield: 4 servings (serving size: 3 ounces chicken, ½ cup sauce, and ½ cup couscous).

CALORIES 466 (27% from fat); FAT 13.8g (sat 2.5g, mono 7.6g, poly 2.4g); PROTEIN 54.3g; CARB 28.8g; FIBER 3g; CHOL 154mg; IRON 3.6mg; SODIUM 946mg; CALC 62mg

Peeling Tomatoes

No matter what time of year, store tomatoes at room temperature, out of direct sunlight. Place them, stem ends up, in a single layer to avoid bruising. Above all, to preserve flavor and texture, keep tomatoes out of the refrigerator.

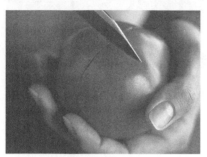

1. *Using a sharp knife, cut a shallow "X" in bottom of each tomato.*

2. *Drop tomatoes into boiling water 15 to 20 seconds; remove with a slotted spoon or tongs.*

3. *Plunge tomato into ice water; remove and discard skins. Or, cut tomato in half and use largest side of a box grater to grate tomato. Skin will stay behind.*

Roasted Tomato Sauce

By leaving the skins on the tomatoes and broiling them on the lower rack, their surfaces gradually blacken while the insides develop a deep caramelized flavor. Serve this sauce over pasta as a substitute for commercial tomato sauce.

- 4 garlic cloves, unpeeled
- 2 small red onions, unpeeled and cut in half horizontally
- 3 pounds tomatoes, cored (about 6)
- 2 tablespoons balsamic vinegar
- 1 tablespoon olive oil
- 1 tablespoon tomato paste
- 1 teaspoon sugar
- 1 teaspoon fresh oregano leaves
- ½ teaspoon salt
- ¼ teaspoon crushed red pepper
- ¼ teaspoon ground black pepper

1. Preheat broiler.
2. Place garlic and onions, skin sides up, on a jelly roll pan. Place pan on lower oven rack. Broil 30 minutes. Add tomatoes to pan, core sides down. Cook 30 minutes or until blackened. Cool 5 minutes. Remove skins from garlic, onion, and tomatoes; discard skins. Place garlic, onion, and tomatoes in a food processor. Add vinegar and remaining ingredients; process until smooth. Yield: 8 servings (serving size: ½ cup).

NOTE: The sauce will keep in the refrigerator for up to a week, or in the freezer for up to a month.

CALORIES 92 (23% from fat); FAT 2.4g (sat 0.3g, mono 1.4g, poly 0.4g); PROTEIN 2.7g; CARB 17.3g; FIBER 3.6g; CHOL 0mg; IRON 1.1mg; SODIUM 182mg; CALC 34mg

Roasted Tomatoes with Shallots and Herbs

Roasting briefly at high heat leaves tomatoes juicy while condensing their flavors. Serve with roasted chicken or grilled fish.

- 4 medium tomatoes, cut in half horizontally (about 2 pounds)
- ½ teaspoon salt, divided
- Cooking spray
- ¼ cup minced shallot
- 1 tablespoon chopped fresh flat-leaf parsley
- 1 teaspoon chopped fresh or ¼ teaspoon dried oregano
- 1 teaspoon chopped fresh or ¼ teaspoon dried thyme
- ½ teaspoon chopped fresh or ⅛ teaspoon dried rosemary
- ¼ teaspoon freshly ground black pepper
- 2 teaspoons olive oil

1. Preheat oven to 350°.
2. Core and seed tomato halves. Sprinkle cut sides of tomato halves with ¼ teaspoon salt. Place tomato halves, cut sides down, on paper towels. Let stand 20 minutes.
3. Place tomato halves, cut sides up, in a 13 x 9-inch baking dish coated with cooking spray. Sprinkle with ¼ teaspoon salt, shallot, and next 5 ingredients. Drizzle with oil. Bake at 350° for 1 hour and 15 minutes or until tomatoes soften. Yield: 8 servings (serving size: 1 tomato half).

CALORIES 38 (36% from fat); FAT 1.5g (sat 0.2g, mono 0.9g, poly 0.3g); PROTEIN 1.1g; CARB 6.2g; FIBER 1.3g; CHOL 0mg; IRON 0.6mg; SODIUM 121mg; CALC 10mg

Indoor Grilling Menu
serves 4

Grilled Steak with Charred Tomato Salsa

Roasted potato wedges*

Green salad

*Cut 2 medium baking potatoes into wedges. Sprinkle wedges with 2 teaspoons crushed rosemary, ½ teaspoon salt, and ⅛ teaspoon ground red pepper; spread evenly on a baking sheet coated with cooking spray. Bake at 450° for 30 minutes or until potatoes are tender.

search myclar2003.com for all our menus

Grilled Steak with Charred Tomato Salsa

The high heat used in grilling quickly caramelizes the natural sugars, producing slightly charred, juicy tomatoes with rich flavor. To make your own basil oil, heat ¼ cup chopped basil and ¼ cup olive oil in a small saucepan over low heat just until the oil sizzles. Remove from heat, and let sit about an hour or until cool. Strain and discard the basil. The basil oil will keep in the refrigerator for up to two weeks.

  1 pound large tomatoes, cored, cut in half horizontally, and seeded (about 2 medium)
Cooking spray
  ½ cup thinly sliced red onion
  1 tablespoon red wine vinegar
  1 teaspoon basil-flavored olive oil
  ¼ teaspoon salt, divided
  ¼ teaspoon freshly ground black pepper, divided
  6 basil leaves, thinly sliced
  1 (1-pound) boneless sirloin steak

1. Place tomato halves, cut sides down, on paper towels. Let stand 30 minutes.
2. Heat a grill pan coated with cooking spray over medium-high heat. Place tomato halves, cut sides down, in pan; grill 5 minutes. Turn tomato halves over; grill 1 minute or until skin is blackened. Remove from pan; cool 5 minutes. Cut tomato halves into 1-inch pieces. Combine tomato, onion, vinegar, oil, ⅛ teaspoon salt, ⅛ teaspoon pepper, and basil.
3. Sprinkle steak with ⅛ teaspoon salt and ⅛ teaspoon pepper. Place steak in pan coated with cooking spray; grill 6 minutes on each side or until desired degree of doneness. Let stand 5 minutes. Cut steak diagonally across grain into thin slices. Serve with tomato salsa. Yield: 4 servings (serving size: 3 ounces steak and about ¼ cup tomato salsa).

CALORIES 206 (35% from fat); FAT 8g (sat 2.8g, mono 3.7g, poly 0.5g); PROTEIN 26.4g; CARB 6.6g; FIBER 1.6g; CHOL 76mg; IRON 3.4mg; SODIUM 213mg; CALC 20mg

Flatbread with Oven-Dried Tomatoes, Rosemary, and Fontina

This bread was a hit in our test kitchens. You can also use basil for the rosemary and provolone for the fontina. Using the tomatoes you've roasted at home gives the bread a heartier taste.

  2 tablespoons olive oil
  4 rosemary sprigs
2¾ cups all-purpose flour, divided
  1 package dry yeast (about 2¼ teaspoons)
  1 cup plus 2 tablespoons very warm water (120° to 130°), divided
  2 teaspoons chopped fresh or ½ teaspoon dried rosemary
  1 teaspoon salt, divided
Cooking spray
  ¾ cup Oven-Dried Tomatoes (recipe on page 38), halved lengthwise
  1 cup (4 ounces) diced fontina cheese

1. Place oil and rosemary sprigs in a small bowl; microwave at HIGH 30 seconds. Let stand 15 minutes. Gently squeeze oil from rosemary; discard sprigs.
2. Lightly spoon flour into dry measuring cups; level with a knife. Combine ½ cup flour and yeast in a large bowl, stirring with a whisk. Add ½ cup warm water; let stand 20 minutes. Add rosemary oil, 2 cups flour, ½ cup plus 2 tablespoons warm water, chopped rosemary, and ¾ teaspoon salt; stir until a soft dough forms. Turn dough out onto a lightly floured surface. Knead until smooth and elastic (about 8 minutes); add enough of remaining flour, 1 tablespoon at a time, to prevent dough from sticking to hands (dough will feel tacky).
3. Place dough in a large bowl coated with cooking spray, turning to coat top. Cover and let rise in a warm place (85°), free from drafts, 1 hour or until doubled in size. (Press two fingers into dough. If indentation remains, dough has risen enough.) Punch dough down; form into a ball. Place on a baking sheet. Let rest 5 minutes.
4. Preheat oven to 500°.
5. Roll dough into a 12-inch circle. Arrange tomatoes on top of flatbread,

Coring and Seeding Tomatoes

Follow these basics for coring and seeding tomatoes.

1. *Using a small knife, cut a small circle around stem end. With tip of paring knife, remove the core.*

2. *Cut tomatoes in half horizontally. Cup each tomato half in the palm of your hand, cut side down; gently squeeze out seeds. You can also scoop out seeds using your fingers.*

leaving a ½-inch border. Sprinkle with cheese; gently press tomatoes into dough. Sprinkle with ¼ teaspoon salt. Bake at 500° for 10 minutes or until golden brown. Yield: 1 flatbread; 12 servings (serving size: 1 wedge).

CALORIES 162 (25% from fat); FAT 4.5g (sat 2g, mono 1.7g, poly 0.4g); PROTEIN 6g; CARB 24.2g; FIBER 1.4g; CHOL 11mg; IRON 1.7mg; SODIUM 335mg; CALC 59mg

Tomato and Roasted Pepper Salad

(pictured on page 21)

Marinating tomatoes in acidic balsamic vinegar and sweet honey enhances the natural flavors of raw tomatoes. Caperberries taste like capers, but are about the size of olives and have stems. Look for them with olives at the grocery store.

    4   medium tomatoes (about 2
        pounds), each cut into 4 slices
    2   tablespoons balsamic vinegar,
        divided
    1   tablespoon honey
    ¼   teaspoon salt
    ¼   teaspoon freshly ground black
        pepper
    1   large red bell pepper
    1   large yellow bell pepper
    1   tablespoon red wine vinegar
    2   teaspoons olive oil
    1   garlic clove, minced
    ½   cup bottled caperberries (about 20)

1. Arrange tomato slices in a single layer on a platter. Combine 1 tablespoon balsamic vinegar and honey in a small bowl, stirring with a whisk. Drizzle mixture evenly over tomato slices. Sprinkle with salt and black pepper; marinate 15 minutes.
2. Preheat broiler.
3. Cut bell peppers in half lengthwise; discard seeds and membranes. Place pepper halves, skin sides up, on a foil-lined baking sheet; flatten pepper halves with hand. Broil 10 minutes or until bell peppers are blackened. Place in a zip-top plastic bag; seal. Let stand 10 minutes. Peel and cut into ¾-inch strips.

4. Combine 1 tablespoon balsamic vinegar, red wine vinegar, oil, and garlic in a medium bowl; stir well with a whisk. Add bell peppers and caperberries; toss gently to coat. Top tomato slices with bell pepper mixture. Yield: 8 servings (serving size: 2 tomato slices and about 2 tablespoons bell pepper mixture).

CALORIES 48 (28% from fat); FAT 1.5g (sat 0.2g, mono 0.9g, poly 0.2g); PROTEIN 1.1g; CARB 9g; FIBER 1.4g; CHOL 0mg; IRON 0.6mg; SODIUM 232mg; CALC 10mg

Oven-Dried Tomatoes

Cooking tomatoes for a long time at a low temperature dehydrates them and concentrates their flavor. These are plumper and softer than commercial sun-dried tomatoes, with a delicate, rich flavor.

    1½ pounds (about 10) plum tomatoes,
        cored and cut in half lengthwise
    1   teaspoon kosher salt

1. Sprinkle cut sides of tomato halves with kosher salt. Place tomato halves, cut sides down, on paper towels. Let stand 1 hour.
2. Preheat oven to 300°.
3. Arrange tomato halves, cut sides up, in a single layer on a baking sheet. Bake at 300° for 3½ to 4 hours or until edges of tomatoes curl (tomatoes will feel dry to the touch). Yield: 1 cup (serving size: ¼ cup).
NOTE: These tomatoes will keep for a week, covered, in the refrigerator, or for up to a month in the freezer in an airtight container.

CALORIES 36 (15% from fat); FAT 0.6g (sat 0.1g, mono 0.1g, poly 0.2g); PROTEIN 1.5g; CARB 7.9g; FIBER 1.9g; CHOL 0mg; IRON 0.8mg; SODIUM 251mg; CALC 9mg

Tomato Salad with Lemon and Honey

Tangy lemon juice and sweet honey brightens the flavor of the tomatoes in this recipe. Serve the dish as a side salad or topping for broiled fish or chicken.

    ½   teaspoon grated lemon rind
    2   tablespoons fresh lemon juice
    1   tablespoon olive oil
    1   tablespoon honey
    ¼   teaspoon salt
    ¼   teaspoon ground black pepper
    4½ cups chopped seeded tomato
    2   teaspoons chopped fresh flat-leaf
        parsley
    1   lemon, thinly sliced (optional)

1. Combine first 6 ingredients in a medium bowl. Add tomato and parsley; toss gently to coat. Marinate 15 minutes. Garnish with lemon slices, if desired. Yield: 9 servings (serving size: ½ cup).

CALORIES 40 (41% from fat); FAT 1.8g (sat 0.2g, mono 1.2g, poly 0.3g); PROTEIN 0.8g; CARB 6.5g; FIBER 1g; CHOL 0mg; IRON 0.5mg; SODIUM 74mg; CALC 6mg

Best Winter Picks

Some tomatoes are better than others in winter. Best bets are vine-ripened, Roma, and cherry tomatoes. Vine-ripened tomatoes are small- to medium-sized, and often sold in clusters still attached to a vine. Oval Roma, or plum, tomatoes have firmer pulp and fewer seeds than other varieties, so they hold their shape well. Cherry and grape tomatoes are always flavorful because their size, shape, and packaging protect them; they have less need to be hybridized to stand up to the rigors of mechanical harvesting and shipping.

march

Home Bistro

Bring comfort foods inspired by the cozy cafés of France into your own home tonight.

The bistro is the embodiment of a centuries-old Gallic love of food. If you've been to one, you'll agree that the entire ambience says conviviality, pleasure—and hearty, rustic fare. Small wonder bistros have migrated so successfully to this side of the Atlantic. The bistro hallmark is comfort food. It's predicated on the slow simmering of local and often humble ingredients—and lends itself well to home cooking and entertaining.

You don't need special pots and pans to get started. The large stockpot you've had for years will do just fine. And don't bother with the good china, either—a bistro meal is most suitably served on plain, heavy white tableware. You'll be serving directly from the oven or stovetop, and carving and ladling from the table. Your guests will love the casual presentation, and as the cook, you'll have found the preparation amenable, too. *C'est la vie* at the bistro.

Sunday Dinner Menu
serves 6

Mussels with Fennel

Quick Coq au Vin

Goat Cheese, Roasted Garlic, and Tomato Croutes

search myclar2003.com for all our menus

Mussels with Fennel

Here's an easy tip to help start your meal: Clean mussels, and prepare broth ahead of time. Before serving, bring broth to a simmer, add mussels, and cook until shells open.

- 2 teaspoons olive oil
- 1½ cups chopped fennel bulb (about 2 small bulbs)
- 1 teaspoon fennel seeds
- 2 garlic cloves, minced
- ¾ cup dry white wine
- ½ cup water
- 2 tablespoons fresh lemon juice
- ½ teaspoon salt
- 2 (14.5-ounce) cans no-salt-added diced tomatoes, undrained
- 42 mussels (about 2 pounds), scrubbed and debearded

1. Heat olive oil in a large skillet over medium-high heat. Add fennel, fennel seeds, and garlic; sauté 3 minutes. Stir in wine, water, juice, salt, and tomatoes; bring to a boil. Reduce heat, and simmer 10 minutes. Add mussels; cover and cook 6 minutes or until shells open. Remove from heat; discard any unopened shells. Yield: 6 servings (serving size: 7 mussels and about ¾ cup broth).

CALORIES 101 (26% from fat); FAT 2.9g (sat 0.5g, mono 1.4g, poly 0.5g); PROTEIN 8.7g; CARB 10.8g; FIBER 0.2g; CHOL 16mg; IRON 3.6mg; SODIUM 383mg; CALC 91mg

---

Hearty Weeknight Menu
serves 6

Quick Coq au Vin

Tarragon red potatoes*

Brussels sprouts

*Combine 2 pounds quartered red potatoes, 2 tablespoons chopped fresh tarragon, 2 teaspoons olive oil, and ¾ teaspoon salt on a baking sheet. Bake at 350° for 30 minutes or until tender.

Quick Coq au Vin

Cooking uncovered over high heat, the liquid reduces and concentrates its flavors in a fraction of the time required for the traditional long-simmered dish.

- ¼ cup all-purpose flour
- 1 teaspoon dried thyme
- ½ teaspoon salt
- 6 (4-ounce) skinless, boneless chicken thighs
- 1 tablespoon olive oil
- 6 cups quartered cremini mushrooms
- 2 cups (¼-inch-thick) slices carrot
- ⅓ cup (¼-inch-thick) slices Canadian bacon
- 1 cup dry red wine
- 1 cup fat-free, less-sodium chicken broth
- 1 tablespoon tomato paste

1. Combine flour, thyme, and salt in a zip-top plastic bag; add chicken. Seal and shake to coat. Remove chicken from bag, shaking off excess flour mixture.
2. Heat oil in a large nonstick skillet over medium-high heat. Add chicken; cook 8 minutes or until browned, turning frequently. Remove chicken from pan.
3. Add mushrooms, carrot, and bacon to pan; sauté 2 minutes. Stir in wine, broth, and tomato paste; cook 9 minutes. Return chicken to pan; cook 8 minutes or until chicken is done. Yield: 6 servings (serving size: about 1¼ cups).

WINE NOTE: In France, coq au vin is served with a medium-bodied earthy red like a Côtes du Rhône. Some quality producers are St. Cosme, Perrin Reserve, and E. Guigal. Count on spending $10-13.

CALORIES 230 (30% from fat); FAT 7.8g (sat 1.7g, mono 3.4g, poly 1.5g); PROTEIN 27.3g; CARB 12.5g; FIBER 2.4g; CHOL 99mg; IRON 3.1mg; SODIUM 527mg; CALC 35mg

Goat Cheese, Roasted Garlic, and Tomato Croutes

For a more authentic approach, roast the garlic and invite guests to rub the cloves on toasted bread themselves. Serve cheese and tomatoes on the side.

    1 whole garlic head
       Cooking spray
    3 plum tomatoes, each cut into 4
       wedges
   ½ cup (2 ounces) crumbled goat
       cheese
   12 (½-inch-thick) slices diagonally
       cut French bread baguette, toasted

1. Preheat oven to 425°.
2. Remove white papery skin from garlic head (do not peel or separate cloves); wrap in foil. Line a baking sheet with foil; coat foil with cooking spray. Arrange tomato wedges in a single layer on foil. Bake garlic and tomatoes at 425° for 40 minutes, turning tomatoes after 20 minutes. Remove tomatoes from oven; bake garlic an additional 5 minutes. Remove garlic from oven; cool 10 minutes. Separate cloves; squeeze to extract garlic pulp. Discard skins. Mash garlic pulp and goat cheese with a fork until blended.
3. Spread 2 teaspoons goat cheese mixture over each bread slice. Top each with 1 tomato wedge. Yield: 6 servings (serving size: 2 croutes).

CALORIES 135 (23% from fat); FAT 3.4g (sat 1.7g, mono 0.9g, poly 0.5g); PROTEIN 5g; CARB 21.4g; FIBER 1.5g; CHOL 8mg; IRON 1.2 mg; SODIUM 298mg; CALC 90mg

---

Casual Company Menu
serves 6

Cabbage Remoulade

Olive Bread

Bouillabaisse

Cabbage Remoulade

   ½ cup plain fat-free yogurt
    3 tablespoons capers
    2 tablespoons minced fresh onion
    2 tablespoons light mayonnaise
    1 tablespoon fresh lemon juice
    1 teaspoon Worcestershire sauce
    6 cups shredded green cabbage
    1 cup shredded carrot

1. Combine first 6 ingredients in a large bowl. Stir in cabbage and carrot; toss to coat. Yield: 6 servings (serving size: 1 cup).

CALORIES 61 (24% from fat); FAT 1.6g (sat 0.3g, mono 0.4g, poly 0.8g); PROTEIN 2.6g; CARB 10.2g; FIBER 2.9g; CHOL 2mg; IRON 0.6mg; SODIUM 420mg; CALC 82mg

---

Olive Bread

    1 (1-pound) loaf frozen white bread
       dough
   ½ cup chopped pitted kalamata
       olives
  1½ teaspoons dried rosemary
       Cooking spray
    1 large egg white, lightly beaten

1. Thaw dough in refrigerator 12 hours.
2. Sprinkle olives and rosemary over dough; gently knead on a lightly floured surface 4 or 5 times or just until olives are incorporated into dough. Cover dough; let rest 10 minutes. Roll dough into a 10 x 8-inch rectangle. Beginning with long side, roll up jelly roll fashion; pinch seam to seal. Place roll, seam side down, on a baking sheet coated with cooking spray. Cover and let rise in a warm place (85°), free from drafts, 1 hour or until doubled in size.
3. Preheat oven to 375°.
4. Uncover dough; cut several 2-inch diagonal slits into top of dough using a sharp knife. Brush with egg white. Bake at 375° for 40 minutes or until loaf sounds hollow when tapped. Remove from baking sheet; cool on a wire rack. Yield: 1 loaf, 12 servings (serving size: 1 slice).

CALORIES 96 (18% from fat); FAT 1.9g (sat 0.5g, mono 0.9g, poly 0.5g); PROTEIN 3.3g; CARB 16.4g; FIBER 0.2g; CHOL 0mg; IRON 1mg; SODIUM 226mg; CALC 27mg

---

Bouillabaisse

The traditional seafood stew of Provence, a bouillabaisse is typically made with tomatoes, onions, wine, olive oil, garlic, herbs, fish, and shellfish. Soak up the flavorful broth with Olive Bread (recipe at left) or a crusty French baguette. While 8 cups of water doesn't seem like much, it's enough to steam the lobsters. If clams are unavailable, substitute an equal weight of mussels.

    8 cups water
    3 (1¼-pound) whole lobsters
    1 tablespoon olive oil
    2 cups chopped onion
    2 cups coarsely chopped celery
  1½ cups coarsely chopped carrot
    4 garlic cloves, minced
    4 cups coarsely chopped tomato
       (about 1½ pounds)
   ½ teaspoon salt
   ½ teaspoon saffron threads, crushed
   ½ teaspoon dried thyme
   ¼ teaspoon black pepper
    2 bay leaves
    1 pound skinned halibut fillets or
       other lean white fish fillets, cut
       into 2-inch pieces
   22 small clams, scrubbed (about 1¾
       pounds)
   30 small mussels, scrubbed and
       debearded (about 1½ pounds)
   ½ pound medium shrimp, peeled and
       deveined

1. Bring water to a boil in an 8-quart stockpot. Plunge lobsters headfirst into water. Return to a boil; cover, reduce heat, and simmer 12 minutes. Remove lobsters from water (do not drain); cool. Remove meat from cooked lobster tails and claws; cut into 1-inch pieces, reserving shells. Cover and refrigerate meat.
2. Return reserved shells to water; bring to a boil. Reduce heat, and simmer 5 minutes. Drain through a colander over a large bowl, reserving broth; discard shells. Wipe pan dry with a paper towel.
3. Heat oil in pan over medium-high heat. Add onion, celery, carrot, and garlic; sauté 5 minutes. Add reserved broth, tomato, and next 5 ingredients; bring to a
Continued

boil. Reduce heat, and simmer 15 minutes; discard bay leaves. Bring to a boil; add fish, reduce heat, and simmer 4 minutes. Add clams; cook 1 minute. Add mussels; cook 2 minutes. Add shrimp; cook 3 minutes. Bring to a boil. Add reserved lobster meat; cook until thoroughly heated. Discard unopened shells. Yield: 6 servings (serving size: about 3 cups).

CALORIES 332 (19% from fat); FAT 7.1g (sat 1g, mono 2.6g, poly 1.7g); PROTEIN 48.2g; CARB 18.5g; FIBER 4.1g; CHOL 146mg; IRON 8.1mg; SODIUM 701mg; CALC 162mg

Saturday Dinner Menu

serves 6

Lamb Shanks on Cannellini Beans

Chicory and Roasted Beet Salad with Blue Cheese Dressing

Lamb Shanks on Cannellini Beans

Cooking the beans and lamb at the same time frees you to work on other recipes. We loved the dry beans, but for a quicker approach, substitute drained canned beans. Just stir them in with the bacon.

    6 (¾-pound) lamb shanks, trimmed
    ½ teaspoon salt
    ¼ teaspoon black pepper
    2 cups finely chopped carrot
    1 cup finely chopped onion
    1 cup finely chopped celery
    1 cup dry red wine
    ½ cup beef broth
    1½ teaspoons dried rosemary
    2 (14.5-ounce) cans diced tomatoes
    2 bay leaves
    1 cup dried cannellini beans or other white beans
    4 bacon slices
    4 garlic cloves, sliced
    Rosemary sprigs (optional)

1. Sprinkle lamb with salt and pepper. Heat a large nonstick skillet over medium-high heat. Add lamb; cook 12 minutes, browning on all sides. Remove from pan. Add carrot, onion, and celery; sauté 3 minutes. Add wine. Bring to a boil; cook 5 minutes. Stir in broth, dried rosemary, tomatoes, and bay leaves. Return lamb to pan (pan will be very full). Cover, reduce heat, and simmer 2 hours or until lamb is very tender, turning lamb once. Remove lamb from pan; bring liquid to a boil; cook 5 minutes. Discard bay leaves.
2. Sort and wash beans; place in a large Dutch oven. Cover with water to 2 inches above beans; bring to a boil, and cook 2 minutes. Remove from heat; cover and let stand 1 hour. Drain beans; place in Dutch oven. Cover with water to 2 inches above beans; bring to a boil. Reduce heat, and simmer 1 hour or until tender. Drain.
3. Cook bacon in Dutch oven over medium-high heat until crisp. Remove bacon from Dutch oven, reserving 2 teaspoons drippings in Dutch oven. Crumble bacon. Heat drippings over medium-high heat. Add garlic; sauté 2 minutes or until golden. Stir in beans and bacon; remove from heat.
4. Divide beans evenly among 6 plates; arrange lamb on beans. Spoon sauce over lamb. Garnish with rosemary sprigs, if desired. Yield: 6 servings (serving size: 1 shank, ⅔ cup beans, and 1⅓ cups sauce).

CALORIES 506 (26% from fat); FAT 14.5g (sat 5.1g, mono 5.9g, poly 1.7g); PROTEIN 60.2g; CARB 32.9g; FIBER 6.3g; CHOL 156mg; IRON 8.3mg; SODIUM 791mg; CALC 130mg

Chicory and Roasted Beet Salad with Blue Cheese Dressing

You can substitute half a (15-ounce) can whole beets (cut into wedges) for the fresh; there's no need to roast the canned beets.

    3 beets (about ¾ pound), trimmed
    2 cups (¾-inch) cubed French bread (about 3 ounces)
    Cooking spray
    6 cups torn chicory (curly endive)
    Blue Cheese Dressing

1. Preheat oven to 425°.
2. Leave root and 1 inch stem on beets; scrub with a brush. Place beets on a baking sheet. Bake at 425° for 1 hour or until tender. Cool slightly. Trim off beet roots; rub off skins. Cut each beet into 8 wedges.
3. Place bread cubes on a jelly roll pan; lightly coat bread cubes with cooking spray. Bake at 425° for 7 minutes or until golden. Combine croutons and chicory in a large bowl. Add dressing; toss to coat. Top with beets. Serve immediately. Yield: 6 servings (serving size: 1 cup salad and 4 beet wedges).

(Totals include Blue Cheese Dressing) CALORIES 164 (29% from fat); FAT 5.3g (sat 2.3g, mono 1.4g, poly 1.2g); PROTEIN 8.4g; CARB 14.9g; FIBER 2.3g; CHOL 9mg; IRON 2.5mg; SODIUM 395mg; CALC 287mg

BLUE CHEESE DRESSING:

    ½ cup (2 ounces) crumbled blue cheese
    ½ cup plain fat-free yogurt
    2 tablespoons light mayonnaise

1. Combine all ingredients in a small bowl. Cover and chill. Yield: ¾ cup (serving size: 1 tablespoon).

CALORIES 29 (64% from fat); FAT 2g (sat 1g, mono 0.6g, poly 0.4g); PROTEIN 1.6g; CARB 1g; FIBER 0g; CHOL 5mg; IRON 0mg; SODIUM 92mg; CALC 44mg

Apple Marzipan Galette

Marzipan (sweetened almond paste) can be found with other baking ingredients in the supermarket. Look for it packaged in a small box or can. This galette makes a nice dessert for any of the home bistro menus.

    Cooking spray
    ½ (15-ounce) package refrigerated pie dough (such as Pillsbury)
    ½ cup marzipan, softened
    4 cups sliced peeled Granny Smith apple (about 2 pounds)
    ¾ cup sugar, divided
    1 tablespoon all-purpose flour
    2 teaspoons lemon juice
    1 teaspoon almond extract, divided
    Dash of salt

1. Preheat oven to 425°.
2. Line a jelly roll pan with foil; coat foil with cooking spray. Roll dough to a 14-inch circle on a lightly floured surface. Place on prepared pan. Roll marzipan to a 9-inch circle on a lightly floured surface. Place marzipan on top of dough.

3. Combine apple, ½ cup sugar, flour, juice, ¾ teaspoon extract, and salt in a large bowl; toss well. Spoon apple mixture over marzipan. Fold 2-inch dough border over apple mixture, pressing gently to seal (dough will only partially cover apple mixture). Bake at 425° for 30 minutes or until lightly browned (filling may leak slightly during cooking).

4. Place ¼ cup sugar in a small heavy saucepan over medium-high heat; cook until sugar dissolves, stirring as needed to dissolve sugar evenly (about 4 minutes). Cook 1 minute or until golden. Remove from heat; carefully stir in ¼ teaspoon almond extract. Drizzle over galette. Yield: 8 servings.

WINE NOTE: Try the lush southern French dessert wine, Muscat Baumes-de-Venise, with this galette. Paul Jaboulet Aîné produces one of the best. It's about $15 for a half bottle (375 milliliters).

CALORIES 291 (29% from fat); FAT 9.4g (sat 3g, mono 4.5g, poly 1.4g); PROTEIN 1.7g; CARB 50.8g; FIBER 1.1g; CHOL 5mg; IRON 0.1mg; SODIUM 119mg; CALC 13mg

Every Home a Bistro

Pottery and wood, lots of candles, and everyday tableware lend an informal French touch to the table with minimal effort. Keep it comfortable and easy.

- Use plain white tableware, not your good china.
- Serve food on platters, or set the pots atop trivets on the table.
- Use candlesticks of different heights on sideboards and mantels. Scatter votive candles on the table for unobtrusive lighting.
- Spread a white linen tablecloth. For napkins, use tea towels or plain white cloths.
- Serve bread on a wooden cutting board; offer a serrated knife for guests to cut their own slices.
- Place a basket filled with fresh produce, such as carrots with their greens, beets, colorful bell peppers, and leafy kale, on the table.

search myclar2003.com for all our tips

superfast

. . . And Ready in Just About 20 Minutes

With a little multitasking and ingenuity, you can streamline procedures without sacrificing quality or taste.

Think Fast

The recipe for Italian Chicken with Chickpeas (recipe below) takes advantage of chicken tenders, the tenderloins from chicken breasts. Tenders are smaller than chicken breasts and are trimmed of fat, so they cook in less time and require minimal preparation—just a rinse under water. For our first testing of Italian Chicken with Chickpeas, we used chicken breasts and cooked them separately from the vegetables. By switching to chicken tenders, we cut the total cook time for the chicken and were able to sauté the vegetables with the chicken, shaving off about 10 minutes.

Italian Chicken with Chickpeas

This simple one-dish meal is also great reheated the next day for lunch.

    1   pound chicken breast tenders
    ¼   teaspoon salt
    ¼   teaspoon black pepper
    1   tablespoon olive oil
    1⅓ cups sliced onion
    1   cup green bell pepper strips
    ½   teaspoon bottled minced garlic
    1   (15½-ounce) can chickpeas, drained
    1   (14.5-ounce) can diced tomatoes with basil, garlic, and oregano, undrained

1. Sprinkle chicken with salt and pepper. Heat oil in a large nonstick skillet over medium-high heat. Add chicken to pan; cook 2 minutes on each side or until browned. Add onion and bell pepper; sauté 4 minutes. Reduce heat to medium. Add garlic, chickpeas, and tomatoes; cover and cook 8 minutes or until thoroughly heated. Yield: 4 servings (serving size: 1½ cups).

CALORIES 296 (19% from fat); FAT 6.1g (sat 1g, mono 3.1g, poly 1.2g); PROTEIN 32g; CARB 28.2g; FIBER 5.6g; CHOL 66mg; IRON 2.9mg; SODIUM 637mg; CALC 79mg

Sea Bass and Confetti Vegetables with Lemon-Butter Sauce

Chop the parsley, spinach, and tomato while the fish cooks. Keep the fish warm by tenting it with aluminum foil.

    2   (6-ounce) sea bass or grouper fillets
    ½   teaspoon salt
    Cooking spray
    ¼   cup dry white wine
    2   teaspoons lemon juice
    1   tablespoon chopped fresh parsley
    1   teaspoon butter
    ½   cup frozen whole-kernel corn
    ½   cup chopped plum tomato
    1   (6-ounce) bag baby spinach, coarsely chopped

1. Sprinkle fillets with salt. Heat a large nonstick skillet coated with cooking spray over medium-high heat. Add fillets to pan; cook 5 minutes on each side or until fish flakes easily when tested with a fork. Remove fillets from pan. Place one fillet on each of 2 plates; keep warm.

2. Add wine and juice to pan; cook over medium-high heat 2 minutes. Remove from heat; stir in parsley and butter. Drizzle sauce over fillets.

3. Add corn to pan; cook 2 minutes. Add tomato and spinach; cook 1 minute or until spinach wilts. Arrange 1 cup vegetables on each plate. Yield: 2 servings.

CALORIES 262 (21% from fat); FAT 6g (sat 2.2g, mono 1.4g, poly 1.6g); PROTEIN 34.4g; CARB 14.6g; FIBER 3.8g; CHOL 73mg; IRON 3.4mg; SODIUM 793mg; CALC 111mg

Curried Coconut Shrimp Stir-Fry

Buy peeled and deveined shrimp at the market; you'll save an appreciable amount of preparation time. Look for bags of broccoli and cauliflower florets on the same aisle as the bagged salad greens.

1 (3½-ounce) bag boil-in-bag long-grain rice
1 tablespoon dark sesame oil
1 tablespoon bottled ground fresh ginger
2 teaspoons curry powder
1 cup chopped red bell pepper
1 (16-ounce) bag broccoli and cauliflower florets
1½ pounds peeled and deveined medium shrimp
1 cup light coconut milk
¼ cup low-sodium soy sauce
1 teaspoon fish sauce

1. Prepare rice according to package directions.
2. While rice cooks, heat oil in a large nonstick skillet over medium-high heat. Add ginger and curry; cook 30 seconds, stirring constantly. Add bell pepper and broccoli and cauliflower florets; cook 5 minutes, stirring frequently.
3. Add shrimp; cook 5 minutes or until shrimp are done, stirring frequently.
4. Add coconut milk, soy sauce, and fish sauce; cook 4 minutes or until sauce is slightly thick. Serve over rice. Yield: 4 servings (serving size: 1½ cups shrimp mixture and ½ cup rice).

CALORIES 392 (23% from fat); FAT 9.9g (sat 3.2g, mono 2g, poly 2.7g); PROTEIN 40.2g; CARB 34.5g; FIBER 4.1g; CHOL 259mg; IRON 6.6mg; SODIUM 957mg; CALC 137mg

Pasta with Watercress, Tomatoes, and Goat Cheese

Hot pasta melts the goat cheese, creating a creamy sauce. Any short pasta will work in this recipe. Chop the tomatoes and watercress while the pasta cooks.

3 cups uncooked tubetti (about 12 ounces short tubular pasta)
4 cups halved cherry tomatoes
4 cups chopped trimmed watercress (about 8 ounces)
4 ounces goat cheese, crumbled (about 1 cup)
¾ teaspoon salt
½ teaspoon pepper

1. Cook pasta according to package directions, omitting salt and fat. Drain. Place pasta in a large bowl. Add tomatoes and remaining 4 ingredients; toss well to coat. Serve immediately. Yield: 6 servings (serving size: 2 cups).

CALORIES 285 (16% from fat); FAT 5.2g (sat 2.9g, mono 1.1g, poly 0.6g); PROTEIN 12.1g; CARB 47.5g; FIBER 3.3g; CHOL 9mg; IRON 3.1mg; SODIUM 382mg; CALC 70mg

Ham and Mushroom Quesadillas

Flip the quesadillas gently so that the filling stays inside. You can keep the quesadillas warm by placing them in the oven at the lowest setting.

Cooking spray
1 cup chopped ham
2 tablespoons canned chopped green chiles
1 (8-ounce) package presliced mushrooms
4 (8-inch) flour tortillas
1 cup (4 ounces) shredded reduced-fat extra-sharp cheddar cheese

1. Heat a large nonstick skillet coated with cooking spray over medium-high heat. Add ham, green chiles, and mushrooms; sauté 5 minutes. Remove from pan. Wipe pan clean with a paper towel.
2. Place 1 tortilla in pan. Sprinkle 2 tablespoons cheese over half of tortilla; arrange ½ cup ham mixture over cheese. Sprinkle with 2 tablespoons cheese; fold in half. Cook 1 minute on each side or until cheese melts. Repeat procedure with remaining tortillas, cheese, and ham mixture. Yield: 4 servings (serving size: 1 quesadilla).

CALORIES 245 (24% from fat); FAT 6.5g (sat 2.3g, mono 2.6g, poly 0.8g); PROTEIN 18.1g; CARB 28.7g; FIBER 0.8g; CHOL 19mg; IRON 2.2mg; SODIUM 802mg; CALC 221mg

Country-Fried Steak with Mushroom Gravy

(pictured on page 57)

You may know country-fried steak as chicken-fried steak, depending on where you live. We call for cubed steak, but you can buy regular sirloin steak and pound it with a rolling pin or meat mallet. For the mashed potatoes, you can't beat the frozen variety for speed.

3 tablespoons fat-free milk
2 large egg whites
⅓ cup all-purpose flour
½ teaspoon onion powder
½ teaspoon salt
¼ teaspoon garlic powder
¼ teaspoon black pepper
4 (4-ounce) sirloin cubed steaks
2 teaspoons vegetable oil
2⅔ cups frozen mashed potatoes (such as Ore Ida)
1⅓ cups fat-free milk
2 cups mushrooms, quartered
2½ tablespoons all-purpose flour
¼ teaspoon salt
1 (14-ounce) can fat-free, low-salt beef broth

1. Combine 3 tablespoons milk and egg whites in a shallow dish, stirring with a whisk. Combine ⅓ cup flour and next 4 ingredients in a shallow dish. Working with 1 steak at a time, dip in egg mixture; dredge in flour mixture. Repeat procedure with remaining steaks, egg mixture, and flour mixture.
2. Heat oil in a large nonstick skillet over medium-high heat. Add steaks; cook 3 minutes on each side or until

browned. Remove steaks from pan, and keep warm.

3. While steaks cook, prepare mashed potatoes according to package directions, using 1⅓ cups milk. Keep warm.

4. Add mushrooms to pan; sauté 3 minutes. Combine 2½ tablespoons flour, ¼ teaspoon salt, and broth, stirring with a whisk. Add broth mixture to pan. Bring to a boil; cook 1 minute, stirring constantly. Spoon over steaks. Serve with mashed potatoes. Yield: 4 servings (serving size: 1 steak, 1 cup potatoes, and about ⅓ cup gravy).

CALORIES 436 (30% from fat); FAT 14.7g (sat 5.1g, mono 4.8g, poly 2.2g); PROTEIN 38.2g; CARB 34.7g; FIBER 1.9g; CHOL 189mg; IRON 4.6mg; SODIUM 759mg; CALC 147mg

Bean and Bacon Soup

  3 bacon slices, chopped
  1 cup chopped onion
  1 tablespoon chili powder
1½ teaspoons dry mustard
1½ cups water
  1 tablespoon dark molasses
  1 tablespoon red wine vinegar
  2 (15-ounce) cans cannellini beans or other white beans, drained
  1 (14.5-ounce) can diced tomatoes with garlic and onions, undrained

1. Cook bacon in a large saucepan over medium-high heat until crisp. Remove bacon from pan, reserving 2 teaspoons drippings in pan.

2. Add onion, chili powder, and mustard to drippings in pan; sauté 3 minutes. Stir in bacon, water, and remaining 4 ingredients; bring to a boil. Reduce heat, and simmer 7 minutes. Partially mash beans with a potato masher. Yield: 4 servings (serving size: 1¼ cups).

CALORIES 361 (28% from fat); FAT 11.2g (sat 3.8g, mono 4.6g, poly 1.7g); PROTEIN 20g; CARB 47.9g; FIBER 2.2g; CHOL 15mg; IRON 6.8mg; SODIUM 804mg; CALC 132mg

Tea Time

An aspiring chef combines two of her favorite flavors to yield one great cake.

As a full-time culinary student living at home in San Gabriel, California, 18-year-old Ling Fong uses her parents' kitchen to perfect her craft. "I love to cook," says Fong, who worked in a school cafeteria before enrolling in the California School of Culinary Arts. An aspiring pastry chef, Fong makes frequent trips to the local Asian markets for special ingredients.

In the recipe Fong submitted, she decided to put a twist on a traditional dessert. When the discriminating young culinarian first tasted honey cake, she says, "It was good, but not special." What could she do to spruce up the recipe? "I always liked the combination of green tea with honey," she says, "so I thought, why not add green tea to the honey cake?"

Excellent idea. Easy to prepare and refreshingly tasty, Fong's Green Tea Honey Cake was a hit with her family and friends. If it's any indication of her talents, we're confident she is well on her way to becoming a successful chef.

Green Tea Honey Cake

If you can't find green tea powder, available at many Asian markets, use a clean coffee grinder to pulverize green tea leaves. We used gunpowder green tea.

    Cooking spray
⅔ cup sugar
4 large eggs
4 large egg yolks
⅓ cup fat-free milk
¼ cup honey
1 cup all-purpose flour
2 tablespoons green tea powder

1. Preheat oven to 350°.
2. Coat a 9-inch round cake pan with cooking spray; line bottom of pan with wax paper. Coat wax paper with cooking spray; set aside.

3. Place sugar, eggs, and yolks in a large bowl; beat with a mixer at medium speed until thick and pale (about 6 minutes).

4. Combine milk and honey in a small bowl; stir well with a whisk. Add milk mixture to egg mixture, stirring well.

5. Lightly spoon flour into a dry measuring cup; level with a knife. Place flour in a mixing bowl; add tea powder, stirring well with a whisk. Fold flour mixture into egg mixture. Pour batter into prepared pan.

6. Bake at 350° for 30 minutes or until a wooden pick inserted in center comes out clean. Cool in pan 10 minutes on a wire rack; remove from pan. Cool completely on wire rack. Yield: 8 servings (serving size: 1 wedge).

CALORIES 218 (21% from fat); FAT 5.1g (sat 1.6g, mono 1.9g, poly 0.7g); PROTEIN 6.4g; CARB 37.9g; FIBER 0.4g; CHOL 213mg; IRON 1.4mg; SODIUM 41mg; CALC 37mg

Mediterranean Muesli

"I discovered a similar dish in Cairo and have been eating my version for breakfast ever since. I prefer to use Irish oatmeal, but non-instant oatmeal is just as good. You can eat it right away, but it also keeps well in the fridge."

—Sandra Conroy,
Fripp Island, South Carolina

1 cup regular oats
1 cup plain low-fat yogurt
1 cup 1% low-fat milk
½ cup coarsely chopped walnuts
⅓ cup honey
¼ cup oat bran
3 tablespoons chopped dried apricots
3 tablespoons chopped dried figs
3 tablespoons chopped pitted dates
Raspberries or other fresh berries (optional)

1. Combine first 9 ingredients in a bowl, stirring well. Chill 2 hours. Garnish with fresh berries, if desired. Yield: 5 servings (serving size: ½ cup).

CALORIES 321 (30% from fat); FAT 10.6g (sat 1.8g, mono 1.9g, poly 6.3g); PROTEIN 10g; CARB 52.6g; FIBER 5.1g; CHOL 5mg; IRON 1.9mg; SODIUM 63mg; CALC 190mg

Asian Barbecue Chicken

"This is a recipe I love to make for family and friends. I usually serve it with roasted sesame asparagus and a sesame-noodle salad. Let the chicken marinate overnight for best results."

—Jen McDonald, Centerville, Virginia

 ¼ cup packed brown sugar
 ¼ cup low-sodium soy sauce
 1 tablespoon fresh lime juice
 ½ teaspoon crushed red pepper
 ¼ teaspoon curry powder
 3 garlic cloves, minced
 8 (6-ounce) chicken thighs, skinned
Cooking spray
Lime wedges (optional)
Green onion tops (optional)

1. Combine first 6 ingredients in a large zip-top plastic bag; stir well, and add chicken. Seal and marinate in refrigerator 4 hours, turning occasionally.
2. Prepare grill.
3. Remove chicken from bag, reserving marinade. Place marinade in a small saucepan. Bring to a boil; cook 1 minute.
4. Place chicken on grill rack coated with cooking spray; grill 20 minutes or until done, turning and basting frequently with marinade. Garnish with lime wedges and green onion tops, if desired. Yield: 4 servings (serving size: 2 thighs).

CALORIES 297 (23% from fat); FAT 7.7g (sat 2g, mono 2.4g, poly 1.9g); PROTEIN 39.2g; CARB 16.1g; FIBER 0.4g; CHOL 161mg; IRON 2.7mg; SODIUM 706mg; CALC 39mg

Brown Rice-Shrimp Jambalaya

"I moved to the South three years ago from New England and tried the first jambalaya recipe I read. It called for ¼ cup bacon drippings and loads of cayenne pepper. Gradually, I devised my own recipe. It's my favorite way to pass off brown rice to my husband, who is a white-rice connoisseur. Non-seafood lovers can substitute cubed and browned chicken breast for the shrimp."

—Cedar Wang, Memphis, Tennessee

 2 teaspoons canola oil
 2 cups finely chopped yellow onion
 ¾ cup chopped green bell pepper
 ½ cup finely diced ham
 ½ cup chopped celery
 4 garlic cloves, minced
 2 teaspoons dried parsley
 ½ teaspoon dried thyme
 ½ teaspoon black pepper
 1 (14.5-ounce) can diced tomatoes, undrained
 1 (10-ounce) can diced tomatoes and green chiles, undrained
 4 cups fat-free, less-sodium chicken broth
 1½ cups uncooked long-grain brown rice
 1½ pounds medium shrimp, peeled and deveined

1. Heat oil in a large Dutch oven over medium-high heat. Add onion, bell pepper, ham, and celery; sauté 5 minutes or until onion is tender. Add garlic; sauté 2 minutes.
2. Stir in parsley and next 4 ingredients. Bring to a boil; reduce heat, and simmer, uncovered, 5 minutes. Add broth and rice; cover and simmer 30 minutes or until rice is tender. Add shrimp; cook 4 minutes. Let stand 5 minutes before serving. Yield: 6 servings (serving size: about 1⅔ cups).

CALORIES 393 (13% from fat); FAT 5.6g (sat 1g, mono 2g, poly 1.8g); PROTEIN 33.4g; CARB 50.8g; FIBER 4.9g; CHOL 178mg; IRON 5mg; SODIUM 940mg; CALC 127mg

Family Night Menu
serves 4

For an easy weeknight dinner, pick up a whole roasted chicken at the supermarket deli and whip up easy side dishes.

Caribbean Vegetables
Buttermilk mashed potatoes*
Whole roasted chicken

*Place 1½ pounds chopped peeled baking potato and 2 minced garlic cloves in a large Dutch oven. Cover with water, and bring to a boil. Cook 15 minutes or until potato is tender. Drain. Return potato to pan. Add ½ cup fat-free buttermilk, ¼ cup low-fat sour cream, 2 tablespoons chopped fresh chives, and ½ teaspoon salt. Mash to desired consistency with a potato masher. Cook over medium heat 1 minute or until thoroughly heated, stirring constantly.

search myclar2003.com for all our menus

Caribbean Vegetables

"I got the idea for this recipe one night when I was determined to cook something Caribbean. This is a colorful and flavorful side dish, great when served with grilled jerked meat, or it can stand alone as a meatless entrée."

—Susan Russell, Lee's Summit, Missouri

 2 teaspoons olive oil
 3 cups chopped peeled sweet potato (about 1 pound)
 ½ cup fat-free, less-sodium chicken broth
 1 tablespoon chopped fresh cilantro
 1 tablespoon grated peeled fresh ginger
 ½ teaspoon chopped fresh parsley
 ½ teaspoon ground coriander seeds
 ⅛ teaspoon ground allspice
 ⅛ teaspoon salt
 ⅛ teaspoon black pepper
 2¼ cups chopped zucchini

1. Heat oil in a large nonstick skillet over medium-high heat. Add sweet potato; sauté 5 minutes. Add chicken broth and next 7 ingredients; cook 15 minutes or until potato is tender. Add zucchini; cook 2 minutes. Yield: 4 servings (serving size: about 1 cup).

CALORIES 187 (14% from fat); FAT 2.9g (sat 0.4g, mono 1.7g, poly 0.4g); PROTEIN 3.6g; CARB 37.8g; FIBER 5.7g; CHOL 0mg; IRON 1.2mg; SODIUM 150mg; CALC 47mg

Stuffed Mushrooms

"I've always loved to prepare stuffed mushrooms and came up with this low-fat version that tastes just as good as my original recipe. When I serve this at dinner parties and for my family, I receive nothing but compliments."

—Lori Smith, Erie, Michigan

  1 tablespoon butter
  ½ cup finely chopped onion
  ½ cup finely chopped green bell pepper
  2 garlic cloves, minced
  ⅔ cup fat-free cottage cheese
  2 teaspoons Worcestershire sauce
  ⅓ cup Italian-seasoned breadcrumbs
  24 button mushroom caps
Cooking spray
  ½ teaspoon paprika
  3 tablespoons grated fresh Parmesan cheese

1. Preheat oven to 350°.
2. Melt butter in a nonstick skillet over medium-high heat. Add onion, bell pepper, and garlic; sauté 5 minutes or until tender. Stir in cottage cheese and Worcestershire sauce, stirring until cheese melts. Remove from heat; stir in breadcrumbs. (Mixture will be thick.) Spoon mixture evenly into mushroom caps.
3. Place mushroom caps in an 11 x 7-inch baking dish coated with cooking spray. Sprinkle mushrooms evenly with paprika. Bake at 350° for 20 minutes or until tender. Sprinkle with Parmesan cheese. Yield: 6 servings (serving size: 4 mushrooms).

CALORIES 104 (29% from fat); FAT 3.4g (sat 1.9g, mono 0.9g, poly 0.3g); PROTEIN 8.2g; CARB 11.4g; FIBER 1.7g; CHOL 10mg; IRON 1.3mg; SODIUM 358mg; CALC 75mg

The World in a Bottle

Oregano, move over; cinnamon, make way.
Wasabi and chipotle powder are here to stay.

Next time you tour the spice aisle of your neighborhood market, look closely: There, next to the allspice, basil, and bay, you're likely to find Mexican ancho and chipotle chile powders. You'll also find Japanese wasabi, Thai red curry, and Indian garam masala. These spices weren't there when you were a child; they probably weren't there 10 years ago.

So what's prompted the change? Apparently, America's newest culinary immigrants are making their mark on our palates. For example, Thai and Vietnamese cuisines have exploded in popularity, and more than two-thirds of us say we're familiar with these foods, reports the National Restaurant Association. A study by Land O' Lakes found that more than half of those surveyed describe themselves as culinarily curious.

Taking note of these statistics, major spice manufacturers such as McCormick's and Spice Island have responded, introducing new spices and spice blends designed to cater to gourmet tastes and to appeal to their customers' hunger for exotic flavors.

Until now, if you wanted to use a true garam masala, you'd have to make a special trip to an ethnic market; ditto dried chiles needed for chile powders, and the wasabi powder called for in genuine Japanese cuisine. Now the world is as close as your corner grocery store.

Chipotle Turkey Cutlets

This recipe uses chipotle chile powder to create a mole, the flavorful Mexican sauce whose hallmark ingredient is chocolate. Usually served with poultry, mole recipes vary but generally include onions, chiles, and ground seeds.

  2 teaspoons sesame seeds
  ½ teaspoon black pepper
  ¼ teaspoon salt
  8 (2-ounce) turkey breast cutlets
  1 tablespoon olive oil, divided
  ¾ cup coarsely chopped onion
  1½ teaspoons ground chipotle chile powder
  ½ teaspoon ground cumin
  ⅔ cup fat-free, less-sodium chicken broth
  2 teaspoons unsweetened cocoa
  1 (14.5-ounce) can Mexican-style stewed tomatoes with jalapeño peppers and spices, undrained

1. Combine first 3 ingredients. Sprinkle turkey with sesame seed mixture.
2. Heat 2 teaspoons oil in a large nonstick skillet over medium-high heat. Add turkey; cook 3 minutes on each side or until browned. Remove from pan.
3. Heat 1 teaspoon oil in pan. Add onion; sauté 5 minutes or until tender. Stir in chipotle powder and cumin; sauté 30 seconds. Stir in broth, cocoa, and tomatoes. Return turkey to pan; bring to a boil. Partially cover, reduce heat, and simmer 20 minutes or until turkey is tender and sauce is slightly thickened. Yield: 4 servings (serving size: 2 turkey cutlets and about ⅓ cup sauce).

CALORIES 267 (28% from fat); FAT 8.2g (sat 1.8g, mono 3.2g, poly 1.3g); PROTEIN 36.3g; CARB 11.5g; FIBER 2.8g; CHOL 79mg; IRON 2.5mg; SODIUM 567mg; CALC 53mg

Mussels in Red Curry Broth

(pictured on page 58)

The Indonesian-style preparation of this dish is a pleasant surprise, since mussels usually receive an Italian or French treatment. Serve with crusty bread to soak up the delicious broth.

    2 teaspoons olive oil
  ⅓ cup chopped shallots
1 ½ teaspoons red curry powder
    1 cup clam juice
  ½ cup dry white wine
  ½ cup light coconut milk
    2 tablespoons finely chopped peeled fresh lemon grass
  ¼ teaspoon crushed red pepper
    3 pounds mussels, scrubbed and debearded
    2 tablespoons chopped fresh cilantro

1. Heat oil in a large Dutch oven over medium heat. Add shallots; sauté 1 minute. Add curry powder; sauté 30 seconds. Stir in clam juice and next 4 ingredients; bring to a simmer. Add mussels; bring to a boil. Cover, reduce heat, and simmer 5 minutes or until shells open; sprinkle with cilantro. Discard any unopened shells. Yield: 6 servings (serving size: about 12 mussels and about ⅓ cup sauce).

CALORIES 191 (30% from fat); FAT 6.3g (sat 1.6g, mono 2g, poly 1.1g); PROTEIN 20.1g; CARB 9.3g; FIBER 0.2g; CHOL 47mg; IRON 6.2mg; SODIUM 400mg; CALC 41mg

Garam Masala Dipping Sauce

This dip is also great with chicken skewers or vegetables.

    1 cup plain low-fat yogurt
  ½ cup chopped seeded plum tomato
  ⅓ cup finely chopped onion
    1 teaspoon garam masala
  ¼ teaspoon salt
    2 (6-inch) pitas, each cut into 10 wedges

1. Combine first 5 ingredients in a bowl. Cover and chill 1 hour. Serve with pita wedges. Yield: 5 servings (serving size: ¼ cup sauce and 4 pita wedges).

CALORIES 105 (9% from fat); FAT 1.1g (sat 0.5g, mono 0.2g, poly 0.2g); PROTEIN 5g; CARB 18.6g; FIBER 0.9g; CHOL 3mg; IRON 0.8mg; SODIUM 282mg; CALC 116mg

Spinach, Walnut, and Curried-Apple Salad

This warm spinach salad is sweet, salty, spicy, and crunchy. Add an extra ½ teaspoon of red curry powder for a spicier dish.

    Cooking spray
1 ½ cups thinly sliced Granny Smith apple
    1 cup thinly sliced red onion
    1 teaspoon red curry powder
    3 tablespoons cider vinegar
    2 tablespoons fat-free, less-sodium chicken broth
    1 tablespoon honey
    8 cups fresh spinach (about ½ pound)
    2 tablespoons chopped walnuts, toasted
    2 bacon slices, cooked and crumbled (drained)

1. Heat a nonstick skillet coated with cooking spray over medium-high heat. Add apple and onion; sauté 3 minutes. Stir in curry powder; sauté 1 minute. Stir in vinegar, broth, and honey. Remove from heat.
2. Place spinach in a large bowl. Pour warm apple mixture over spinach; toss well. Sprinkle with walnuts and bacon. Yield: 6 servings (serving size: about ¾ cup).

CALORIES 74 (35% from fat); FAT 2.9g (sat 0.6g, mono 0.9g, poly 1.2g); PROTEIN 2.5g; CARB 11.3g; FIBER 2.4g; CHOL 2mg; IRON 1.4mg; SODIUM 69mg; CALC 51mg

Sunday Supper Menu
serves 10

Fiery Chipotle Baked Beans

Tangy turnip greens*

Roasted pork tenderloins

Cook beans first, and keep warm. Season 2 (1¼-pound) pork tenderloins with salt and pepper; roast at 450° for 20 minutes or until a meat thermometer registers 155°. Let stand 5 minutes before slicing.

*Sauté 1 bacon slice in a large Dutch oven until crisp. Remove bacon from pan; cool and crumble. Sauté 1 cup chopped onion in bacon drippings over medium-high heat 2 minutes; stir in 2 pounds trimmed turnip greens and 2 (14-ounce) cans fat-free, less-sodium chicken broth. Bring to a boil; cover, reduce heat, and simmer 30 minutes. Stir in 2 tablespoons white vinegar; sprinkle with bacon. Serve immediately.

Fiery Chipotle Baked Beans

If you like hot, smoky flavors, you'll love this version of baked beans. Molasses sweetens the beans, vinegar adds tang, and the chipotle chile powder makes them spicy.

    4 ounces chorizo, thinly sliced
2 ½ cups chopped onion
    1 cup fat-free, less-sodium chicken broth
  ⅓ cup packed brown sugar
  ⅓ cup cider vinegar
  ⅓ cup bottled chili sauce
  ⅓ cup dark molasses
    2 teaspoons dry mustard
    2 teaspoons chipotle chile powder
  ¼ teaspoon salt
  ¼ teaspoon ground cloves
  ¼ teaspoon ground allspice
    1 (15-ounce) can black beans, rinsed and drained
    1 (15-ounce) can kidney beans, rinsed and drained
    1 (15-ounce) can pinto beans, rinsed and drained

1. Preheat oven to 325°.
2. Heat a Dutch oven over medium-high heat. Add chorizo; sauté 2 minutes.

Add onion; sauté 5 minutes, stirring occasionally. Stir in broth and remaining 12 ingredients; bake uncovered at 325° for 1 hour. Yield: 10 servings (serving size: ½ cup).

CALORIES 245 (20% from fat); FAT 5.4g (sat 1.8g, mono 2.2g, poly 0.6g); PROTEIN 10.3g; CARB 40g; FIBER 8g; CHOL 10mg; IRON 3.6mg; SODIUM 639mg; CALC 135mg

Wasabi Cream

Just a little of this low-calorie sauce adds zip to a baked potato, steak, or sandwich.

  1 cup low-fat sour cream
  2 teaspoons wasabi powder
 ¼ teaspoon salt
 ¼ cup chopped fresh chives

1. Combine first 3 ingredients in a bowl. Cover and chill 30 minutes. Stir in chives. Yield: 1 cup (serving size: 2 tablespoons).

CALORIES 42 (54% from fat); FAT 2.5g (sat 2g, mono 0g, poly 0g); PROTEIN 2.1g; CARB 2.5g; FIBER 0.2g; CHOL 10mg; IRON 0mg; SODIUM 95mg; CALC 45mg

Four Tips for Lasting Flavor

1. Ideally, ground spices have a shelf life of about a year. Of course, you probably have spices older than that. A good rule of thumb is the smell test: If ground spices don't emit an aroma when the jar is opened, they'll be dull in food, too.
2. Buy your spices from a store that sells a wide variety of them.
3. Buy spices in the smallest size possible, especially those that you won't use often.
4. Store spices in a cool, dark place, like the freezer. Decorative wall spice racks are just that, since heat and sunlight speed up flavor loss.

search myclar2003.com for all our tips

Kitchen Report, Spice by Spice

Ground Ancho Chile Powder
Ancho chiles are dried poblano peppers. Most chili—note the *i*—powders are a blend of spices, including ancho chiles, cumin, garlic, and oregano. Chile—with an *e*—powders are finely ground dried chiles, nothing else. Tex-Mex dishes use chili powder; true Mexican dishes use chile powder for pure flavor with mild heat.

Ground Chipotle Chile Powder
Chipotle chiles are dried, smoked jalapeño peppers, previously available only in cans with adobo sauce. That packaging presents two problems: The flavor of the tomato-based adobo sauce sometimes takes over, and most recipes use just a single pepper, leaving you the rest of the can to deal with. The powder is much easier to use. Blend it with other ingredients for a pure smoky chipotle flavor.

Garam Masala
The Indian spice blend's ingredients vary from cook to cook, but typically include black pepper, cardamom, cinnamon, cloves, and cumin. As noted in

Cooking Light Annual Recipes 2002, page 321, commercial versions are usually milder than homemade, though they certainly save time.

Wasabi Powder
This intensely hot green powder, made from a ground root, is welcome anywhere horseradish would be. To play off its pungency, combine it with nutty miso and sweet mirin in a marinade for flank steak. Also pair it with low-fat sour cream and chives in a creamy topping for baked potatoes. Like red curry powder, wasabi powder is milder than the pure form you buy in Asian markets, and more versatile.

Red Curry Powder
This complex spice mix is the basis of many memorable Thai and Malaysian dishes. The mainstream version is a touch milder than its ethnic market counterpart. It has a softer edge, making it more versatile and easier to incorporate into a variety of dishes. A dash with coconut milk and wine transforms the flavor of mussels.

Wasabi-Miso Marinated Flank Steak

A few simple ingredients converge for big, bold flavors in this quick and easy dish. Although you may need to make a trip to an Asian market to pick up miso and mirin, look for wasabi powder on your supermarket's spice aisle; it's much milder than the kind found in Japanese markets.

 ¼ cup yellow miso (soybean paste)
 ¼ cup mirin (sweet rice wine)
 ¼ cup dry white wine
  1 tablespoon wasabi powder
  1 tablespoon rice vinegar
  1 (1-pound) flank steak, trimmed
Cooking spray

1. Combine first 5 ingredients in a small bowl; stir well with a whisk. Combine miso mixture and steak in a large zip-top plastic bag. Seal and marinate in refrigerator 2 hours, turning occasionally.
2. Prepare grill or broiler.
3. Remove steak from bag, reserving marinade. Place marinade in a small saucepan. Bring to a boil; cook 1 minute. Place steak on grill rack or broiler pan coated with cooking spray. Grill or broil 6 minutes on each side or until desired degree of doneness, basting occasionally with reserved marinade. Yield: 4 servings (serving size: 3 ounces steak).

CALORIES 252 (34% from fat); FAT 9.5g (sat 3.7g, mono 3.7g, poly 1g); PROTEIN 25.2g; CARB 9g; FIBER 0.9g; CHOL 57mg; IRON 2.4mg; SODIUM 817mg; CALC 20mg

Ancho Pork and Peppers

The ancho chile powder transforms ordinary pork chops into a Mexican-inspired meal.

- 2 teaspoons ancho chile powder
- 1 teaspoon ground cumin
- 1 teaspoon salt, divided
- 4 (4-ounce) boneless center-cut loin pork chops (about ½ inch thick)
- Cooking spray
- 1 teaspoon olive oil
- 3 cups vertically sliced onion
- 1 large red bell pepper, cut into ¼-inch strips
- 1 large green bell pepper, cut into ¼-inch strips
- 2 garlic cloves, minced
- 2 tablespoons fresh lime juice

1. Combine chile powder, cumin, and ½ teaspoon salt in a small bowl. Sprinkle both sides of pork with chile mixture. Heat a large nonstick skillet coated with cooking spray over medium-high heat. Add pork; cook 4 minutes on each side or until done. Remove from pan; keep warm.
2. Heat oil in pan over medium-high heat. Add onion, peppers, and ½ teaspoon salt; sauté 4 minutes. Add garlic; sauté 1 minute. Remove from heat. Stir in juice. Yield: 4 servings (serving size: 1 pork chop and about ¾ cup pepper mixture).

CALORIES 248 (32% from fat); FAT 8.9g (sat 2.8g, mono 4.1g, poly 0.8g); PROTEIN 27.7g; CARB 14.1g; FIBER 3.3g; CHOL 73mg; IRON 1.9mg; SODIUM 675mg; CALC 57mg

Lamb with Garam Masala Crumbs and Curried Mint Sauce

Adding red curry powder to the mint sauce and seasoning the breadcrumbs with garam masala gives this dish an Indian flair.

SAUCE:

- 1 tablespoon water
- ½ teaspoon cornstarch
- ⅔ cup white wine vinegar
- 3 tablespoons sugar
- ¼ cup chopped fresh mint
- ½ teaspoon red curry powder

LAMB:

- 2 (1-ounce) slices day-old white bread
- 2 teaspoons garam masala
- ½ teaspoon salt
- ½ teaspoon freshly ground black pepper
- 12 (4-ounce) French-cut lamb rib chops, trimmed

1. To prepare sauce, combine water and cornstarch in small bowl, stirring with a whisk to form a slurry. Bring vinegar and sugar to a simmer in small saucepan, stirring until sugar dissolves. Add slurry mixture; simmer 2 minutes or until slightly thickened, stirring constantly with a whisk. Remove from heat. Stir in mint and curry powder; steep 30 minutes. Strain and set aside.
2. Preheat oven to 450°.
3. To prepare lamb, place bread in a food processor, and pulse 10 times or until coarse crumbs form to measure 1 cup. Combine breadcrumbs, garam masala, salt, and pepper in a small bowl. Place lamb on a shallow baking sheet. Press breadcrumb mixture evenly onto lamb. Bake at 450° for 15 minutes or until desired degree of doneness. Yield: 6 servings (serving size: 2 chops and about 1½ tablespoons sauce).

CALORIES 381 (33% from fat); FAT 14g (sat 4.9g, mono 5.5g, poly 1.2g); PROTEIN 48.3g; CARB 13.7g; FIBER 0.4g; CHOL 150mg; IRON 4.8mg; SODIUM 405mg; CALC 43mg

inspired vegetarian

Souped Up

These hearty pairs will energize you on gray, chilly days.

The soups and stews featured will keep refrigerated for up to five days and frozen for three months. And you can easily pack a serving in a thermos for lunch.

Although bread is a worthy addition to any of these dishes, creative accompaniments make a more memorable meal. A fluffy quinoa-and-tofu stir-fry complements the light miso soup. Goat Cheese Crostini balance the complex flavors in the White Bean Soup. The hearty Red Onion Focaccia stands up to the robust Roasted-Root Vegetable Stew, and creamy Soft Polenta is a simple, sublime foil to the intense, rich mushroom stew.

Soups and Sides

Roasted-Root Vegetable Stew
&
Red Onion Focaccia

Goat Cheese Crostini
&
White Bean Soup

Wild Mushroom Stew with Gremolata
&
Soft Polenta

Miso Soup with Spring Greens
&
Sesame Quinoa with Tofu

Vegetable Stock

This all-purpose vegetable stock has woodsy undertones from the mushrooms and subtle sweetness from the parsnip.

- 12 cups water
- 1 (8-ounce) package presliced mushrooms
- 1 cup chopped onion
- ¾ cup chopped carrot
- ½ cup coarsely chopped celery
- ½ cup chopped parsnip
- 2 bay leaves
- 2 thyme sprigs
- 1 whole garlic head, halved

1. Combine all ingredients in a Dutch oven; bring to a boil. Reduce heat, and simmer until reduced to 6 cups (about 1 hour). Strain stock through a sieve into a large bowl; discard solids. Refrigerate stock in an airtight container for up to 1 week or freeze for up to 3 months. Yield: 6 cups (serving size: 1 cup).

CALORIES 8 (11% from fat); FAT 0.1g (sat 0g, mono 0g, poly 0.1g); PROTEIN 0.3g; CARB 1.7g; FIBER 0.3g; CHOL 0mg; IRON 0.1mg; SODIUM 2mg; CALC 7mg

Roasted-Root Vegetable Stew

Use large shallots; they're easier to peel.

    2   cups (1-inch-thick) slices carrot
    2   cups (1-inch) cubed peeled beets
    1   cup (1-inch) cubed peeled turnips
  ¾   cup (1-inch-thick) slices parsnip
   12   large shallots, peeled
        (about 8 ounces)
    8   large garlic cloves, peeled
        (about 1 garlic head)
    1   tablespoon olive oil
    2   tablespoons all-purpose flour
    2   teaspoons minced peeled fresh ginger
  1½   teaspoons chopped fresh sage
    3   cups Vegetable Stock (recipe on
        page 50) or water
  ¾   teaspoon salt
  ½   teaspoon black pepper
    2   tablespoons chopped fresh
        flat-leaf parsley
    4   teaspoons crème fraîche or light
        sour cream

1. Preheat oven to 450°.
2. Combine first 7 ingredients in a shallow roasting pan. Bake at 450° for 30 minutes.
3. Place vegetable mixture in a Dutch oven over medium heat. Add flour, ginger, and sage; cook 3 minutes. Add Vegetable Stock, and bring to a boil. Cover, reduce heat, and simmer 30 minutes. Stir in salt and pepper. Sprinkle each serving with 1½ teaspoons parsley, and top with 1 teaspoon crème fraîche. Yield: 4 servings (serving size: about 1⅓ cups).

(Totals include Vegetable Stock) CALORIES 189 (24% from fat); FAT 5.1g (sat 1.4g, mono 2.9g, poly 0.5g); PROTEIN 4.7g; CARB 33.7g; FIBER 6.9g; CHOL 3mg; IRON 2.2mg; SODIUM 540mg; CALC 88mg

---

Brown-Bag Lunch Menu
serves 6
Red Onion Focaccia
Fresh fruit
Spicy chicken salad*

*Combine 6 cups chopped cooked chicken, ½ cup low-fat mayonnaise, ¼ cup chopped fresh basil, 3 tablespoons fresh lime juice, 2 teaspoons Thai chile garlic paste, and 1 teaspoon salt in a large bowl.

Red Onion Focaccia

Resist the urge to add more flour to this dough. A slightly wet dough makes crisp focaccia with a light texture. Starting the bread with a sponge and an overnight rising in the refrigerator helps the yeast develop slowly, so its flavor will be more pronounced. But you can skip the overnight rise if it doesn't suit your schedule.

SPONGE:
    1   package dry yeast (about 2¼
        teaspoons)
    1   teaspoon honey
    2   cups warm water (100° to 110°)
    2   cups all-purpose flour

DOUGH:
    1   cup bread flour
    1   cup whole wheat flour
    4   teaspoons olive oil, divided
    2   teaspoons sea salt

TOPPING:
    1   teaspoon olive oil
    5   cups thinly sliced red onion
    1   tablespoon chopped fresh rosemary
  ¼   teaspoon sea salt
  ¼   teaspoon crushed red pepper

1. To prepare sponge, dissolve yeast and honey in warm water in a large bowl, and let stand 5 minutes. Lightly spoon all-purpose flour into dry measuring cups; level with a knife. Stir all-purpose flour into yeast mixture. Cover and chill overnight.
2. To prepare dough, stir yeast mixture with a spoon; let stand 30 minutes or until it begins to bubble. Lightly spoon

---

bread flour and whole wheat flour into dry measuring cups; level with a knife. Combine yeast mixture, bread flour, whole wheat flour, 1 tablespoon oil, and 2 teaspoons sea salt in a large bowl. Beat with a mixer at medium speed 15 minutes or until dough pulls away from sides of bowl. Cover and let rise in a warm place (85°), free from drafts, 1 hour or until doubled in size (dough will be wet).
3. Spread 1 teaspoon oil evenly over bottom of a 15 x 10-inch jelly roll pan. Pour dough into pan; let stand 5 minutes. Gently press dough to fill pan; let stand 30 minutes.
4. Preheat oven to 425°.
5. While dough is rising, prepare topping by heating 1 teaspoon oil in a large nonstick skillet over medium heat. Add onion and rosemary, and cook 15 minutes or until browned. Arrange onion over top of dough. Sprinkle with ¼ teaspoon sea salt and crushed red pepper. Bake at 425° for 25 minutes or until golden brown. Cool 5 minutes. Yield: 12 servings.

CALORIES 197 (12% from fat); FAT 2.6g (sat 0.4g, mono 1.5g, poly 0.5g); PROTEIN 5.9g; CARB 38g; FIBER 3.4g; CHOL 0mg; IRON 2.1mg; SODIUM 426mg; CALC 23mg

Goat Cheese Crostini

This toasted bread is a tangy companion to White Bean Soup (recipe on page 52).

    1   (3-ounce) package goat cheese
    2   teaspoons fresh lemon juice
    1   teaspoon chopped fresh thyme
    1   garlic clove, minced
    8   (1-ounce) slices sourdough bread

1. Preheat oven to 400°.
2. Combine first 4 ingredients in a bowl.
3. Place bread slices in a single layer on a jelly roll pan. Bake at 400° for 8 minutes or until toasted. Turn slices over; spread cheese mixture evenly over bread. Bake 5 minutes or until toasted. Serve immediately. Yield: 4 servings (serving size: 2 crostini).

CALORIES 214 (26% from fat); FAT 6.2g (sat 3.5g, mono 1.7g, poly 0.5g); PROTEIN 9g; CARB 30.1g; FIBER 1.8g; CHOL 10mg; IRON 1.9mg; SODIUM 424mg; CALC 75mg

White Bean Soup

Roasted garlic adds a robust flavor to this nourishing bean soup. If you're not a fan of kale, try Swiss chard.

     1 whole garlic head
     4 teaspoons olive oil, divided
     1 cup finely chopped onion
    ¾ teaspoon sea salt
    ½ cup finely chopped carrot
    ½ cup finely chopped peeled potato
    ¼ cup finely chopped celery
     2 tablespoons tomato paste
     1 tablespoon chopped fresh rosemary
     6 cups Vegetable Stock (recipe on page 50)
     1 (16-ounce) can cannellini beans or other white beans, drained
     4 cups chopped fresh kale
     2 tablespoons fresh lemon juice
    ¼ teaspoon freshly ground black pepper
Chopped fresh parsley (optional)

1. Preheat oven to 350°.
2. Remove white papery skin from garlic head (do not peel or separate cloves). Brush with 1 teaspoon olive oil; wrap in foil. Bake at 350° for 1 hour; cool 10 minutes. Separate cloves; squeeze to extract garlic pulp. Discard skins.
3. Heat 1 tablespoon oil in a large saucepan over medium-high heat. Add onion and salt; sauté 5 minutes. Add carrot and next 4 ingredients; cook 5 minutes, stirring frequently. Add Vegetable Stock and beans; bring to a boil. Reduce heat; simmer, uncovered, 30 minutes.
4. Stir in garlic and kale; simmer 10 minutes or until kale is tender. Stir in lemon juice and pepper. Garnish with parsley, if desired. Yield: 4 servings (serving size: 2 cups).

(Totals include Vegetable Stock) CALORIES 242 (22% from fat); FAT 5.8g (sat 0.7g, mono 3.4g, poly 1.2g); PROTEIN 9.5g; CARB 40.5g; FIBER 9g; CHOL 0mg; IRON 3.8mg; SODIUM 823mg; CALC 176mg

Wild Mushroom Stew with Gremolata

The Mushroom Stock used here also makes a great base for mushroom barley soup, savory gravy for mashed potatoes, or a braised bean dish.

STEW:
    4½ cups quartered fresh shiitake mushrooms (about 8 ounces)
    4½ cups quartered cremini mushrooms (about 8 ounces)
     1 (8-ounce) package button mushrooms, quartered
    1½ tablespoons olive oil, divided
     2 cups thinly sliced leek (about 2 medium)
     1 cup chopped fennel bulb (about 1 small bulb)
     1 cup (1-inch-thick) slices carrot
    ¾ teaspoon salt, divided
     2 cups Mushroom Stock
     2 tablespoons low-sodium soy sauce
     1 teaspoon minced fresh or ¼ teaspoon dried tarragon
     1 teaspoon chopped fresh or ¼ teaspoon dried thyme
     1 teaspoon chopped fresh or ¼ teaspoon dried sage
     1 teaspoon honey
    ⅛ teaspoon black pepper
     1 (14.5-ounce) can chopped tomatoes, undrained
     1 tablespoon cornstarch
     1 tablespoon water

GREMOLATA:
     2 tablespoons chopped fresh flat-leaf parsley
     1 teaspoon grated lemon rind
     1 garlic clove, minced

1. Preheat oven to 450°.
2. To prepare stew, combine mushrooms and 1 tablespoon oil in a single layer on a jelly roll pan. Bake mushrooms at 450° for 30 minutes, stirring once.
3. Heat 1½ teaspoons oil in a Dutch oven over medium heat. Add leek, fennel, and carrot; cook 5 minutes. Sprinkle leek mixture with ¼ teaspoon salt. Cover, reduce heat, and cook 10 minutes. Uncover; add mushroom mixture, stock, and next 7 ingredients. Bring to a

boil. Reduce heat; simmer 5 minutes. Stir in ½ teaspoon salt. Combine cornstarch and water. Stir cornstarch mixture into mushroom mixture, and cook 1 minute.
4. To prepare gremolata, combine parsley, lemon, and garlic. Serve with stew. Yield: 4 servings (serving size: 2 cups stew and 1½ teaspoons gremolata).

(Totals include Mushroom Stock) CALORIES 228 (28% from fat); FAT 7g (sat 1.7g, mono 4.2g, poly 0.7g); PROTEIN 9.8g; CARB 32.1g; FIBER 7.6g; CHOL 4mg; IRON 5.2mg; SODIUM 953mg; CALC 101mg

MUSHROOM STOCK:
     5 cups water
     1 cup dried porcini mushrooms (about 1 ounce)
    ½ cup chopped celery
    ⅓ cup dry red wine
    ¼ cup dried lentils
     2 fresh thyme sprigs
     1 fresh sage sprig
     1 whole garlic head, halved

1. Combine all ingredients in a large saucepan; bring to a boil. Reduce heat, and simmer until reduced to 2 cups (about 40 minutes). Strain stock through a sieve into a bowl; discard solids. Yield: 2 cups (serving size: 1 cup).

CALORIES 29 (3% from fat); FAT 0.1g (sat 0g, mono 0g, poly 0.1g); PROTEIN 1.8g; CARB 5.1g; FIBER 1.3g; CHOL 0mg; IRON 0.7mg; SODIUM 5mg; CALC 18mg

Soft Polenta

For variations on this recipe, use stock or broth in place of water for a richer dish, or a different cheese for a whole new flavor.

     4 cups boiling water
     1 tablespoon butter
    ¼ teaspoon sea salt
     1 cup whole grain yellow cornmeal (such as Arrowhead Mills)
    ¼ cup (1 ounce) grated fresh Parmesan cheese

1. Combine first 3 ingredients in a medium saucepan. Gradually add cornmeal, stirring with a whisk. Bring cornmeal mixture to a boil, stirring constantly. Reduce heat to low; cook 25

minutes, stirring frequently. Remove from heat; stir in cheese. Serve immediately. Yield: 4 servings (serving size: ¾ cup).

CALORIES 184 (27% from fat); FAT 5.6g (sat 3.2g, mono 1.6g, poly 0.4g); PROTEIN 5.9g; CARB 27.1g; FIBER 2.6g; CHOL 13mg; IRON 0.5mg; SODIUM 306mg; CALC 100mg

Miso Soup with Spring Greens

Dashi—a broth made from kombu seaweed and water—is the base for this traditional Japanese soup. Miso offers a meaty flavor. Substitute arugula or spinach for the watercress, if you wish.

    1   cup dried kombu or other shredded
          seaweed (about 1 ounce)
    4   cups water
    ¼   cup yellow miso (soybean paste)
    1   teaspoon olive oil
  1¼   cups shredded peeled daikon
          radish or sliced radish
    ¼   cup shredded carrot
    2   tablespoons chopped green onion
          bottoms
    2   cups trimmed watercress (about
          1 bunch) or arugula
    2   teaspoons chopped fresh dill
    1   teaspoon fresh lemon juice
    2   tablespoons chopped green onion
          tops

1. Combine kombu and water in a large saucepan; bring to a boil. Reduce heat, and simmer 1 minute. Drain in a colander over a bowl, reserving liquid. Discard kombu. Combine ¼ cup reserved liquid and miso, stirring with a whisk.
2. Heat oil in pan over medium heat. Add daikon, carrot, and onion bottoms; cook 3 minutes. Add remaining reserved liquid; bring to a boil. Reduce heat; simmer 5 minutes. Add watercress and dill; cook 1 minute. Stir in miso mixture, and cook 1 minute. Stir in lemon juice. Sprinkle with green onion tops. Yield: 4 servings (serving size: 1 cup).

CALORIES 52 (35% from fat); FAT 2g (sat 0.2g, mono 1.1g, poly 0.7g); PROTEIN 2.6g; CARB 6.2g; FIBER 1.6g; CHOL 0mg; IRON 0.4mg; SODIUM 757mg; CALC 34mg

Sesame Quinoa with Tofu

The water-packed, extra-firm tofu in this recipe stands up to sautéing.

    8   ounces extra-firm tofu, drained
    1   teaspoon olive oil
    1   tablespoon sesame seeds
    1   cup uncooked quinoa
  1½   cups Vegetable Stock (recipe on
          page 50) or water
    ¼   teaspoon salt
    ½   cup chopped green onions
    1   tablespoon low-sodium soy sauce
    ⅛   teaspoon black pepper

1. Place tofu on several layers of heavy-duty paper towels; let stand 20 minutes. Cut into ½-inch cubes.
2. Heat oil in a medium saucepan over medium heat. Add tofu and seeds; sauté 3 minutes. Remove tofu mixture from pan. Add quinoa to pan; cook 3 minutes, stirring frequently. Add Vegetable Stock and salt; bring to a boil. Cover, reduce heat, and simmer 20 minutes. Place in a large bowl. Add tofu mixture, green onions, soy sauce, and pepper; toss. Yield: 4 servings (serving size: 1 cup).

(Totals include Vegetable Stock) CALORIES 274 (32% from fat); FAT 9.7g (sat 1.3g, mono 3g, poly 4.4g); PROTEIN 15.2g; CARB 34.3g; FIBER 4.7g; CHOL 0mg; IRON 10.4mg; SODIUM 300mg; CALC 438mg

happy endings

Passover Desserts

Elegantly simple sweets delight, defining a special holiday.

Probably humanity's longest continually celebrated holiday, Passover begins with the traditional seder, a feast that commemorates the Jews' exodus from slavery in Egypt to freedom in the land of Israel.

Because many ingredients like flour and baking powder are forbidden during Passover, desserts are a challenge to prepare. Here's an array of recipes to try.

Chocolate and Berry-Covered Meringue
(pictured on page 60)

This is a lower-fat substitute for the traditional Schaum Torte—a large meringue filled with strawberries and topped with whipped cream, and sometimes tiny meringue kisses. It's guaranteed to satisfy every chocoholic in the house.

MERINGUE:

    4   large egg whites
  Dash of salt
    1   teaspoon fresh lemon juice
    ½   teaspoon vanilla extract
    ¾   cup sugar

TOPPING:

    ¼   cup semisweet chocolate,
          chopped
    4   teaspoons water
    2   cups fresh blueberries
    2   cups fresh raspberries
  Mint sprigs (optional)

1. Preheat oven to 200°.
2. To prepare meringue, cover a baking sheet with parchment paper. Draw a 9-inch circle on paper. Turn paper over; secure with masking tape. Place egg whites and salt in a large bowl; beat with a mixer at high speed until foamy. Add juice and vanilla; beat until soft peaks form. Add ¾ cup sugar, 1 tablespoon at a time, beating until stiff peaks form.
3. Spoon egg white mixture into 9-inch circle on prepared baking sheet. Shape meringue into a nest with 1-inch sides using back of a spoon. Bake at 200° for 1 hour. Turn oven off; cool meringue in closed oven 30 minutes. Remove meringue from oven; carefully remove meringue from paper.
4. To prepare topping, place chocolate and water in a microwave-safe bowl. Microwave at HIGH 1 minute or until chocolate melts, stirring every 20 seconds.
5. Arrange berries on top of meringue; drizzle with chocolate sauce. Garnish with mint sprigs, if desired. Yield: 8 servings (serving size: 1 slice).

CALORIES 142 (12% from fat); FAT 1.9g (sat 1g, mono 0.6g, poly 0.2g); PROTEIN 2.5g; CARB 31g; FIBER 3.4g; CHOL 0mg; IRON 0.4mg; SODIUM 67mg; CALC 12mg

Almond-Apricot Macaroons

This is a version of traditional Greek Passover almond macaroons.

    2   tablespoons matzo cake meal
    ¾   cup whole blanched almonds
    ¾   cup matzo cake meal
    ¾   cup sugar
    ½   cup chopped dried apricots
    1   teaspoon grated orange rind
    ¼   teaspoon almond extract
    3   large egg whites

1. Preheat oven to 325°.
2. Line a baking sheet with parchment paper, and sprinkle with 2 tablespoons matzo cake meal.
3. Place almonds in a food processor; pulse 3 or 4 times or until coarsely chopped.
4. Lightly spoon ¾ cup matzo cake meal into dry measuring cups; level with a knife. Add ¾ cup matzo cake meal, sugar, and remaining 4 ingredients to almonds; pulse 3 or 4 times or just until combined. (Mixture will be sticky.)
5. Using hands dusted with matzo cake meal, divide dough into 16 portions. Roll each portion into a ball; pinch tops to form pear shapes. Place on prepared baking sheet. Bake at 325° for 20 minutes or until lightly browned. Cool on a wire rack. Yield: 16 servings (serving size: 1 macaroon).

CALORIES 117 (27% from fat); FAT 3.5g (sat 0.3g, mono 2.2g, poly 0.8g); PROTEIN 3g; CARB 19.8g; FIBER 1.4g; CHOL 0mg; IRON 0.6mg; SODIUM 13mg; CALC 18mg

Almond-Lemon Torte

Nut tortes are nice to have at Passover, and this is a family must. You can grind the almonds in the food processor.

CAKE:
    Cooking spray
    1   tablespoon matzo cake meal
    1   cup matzo cake meal
    1   cup coarsely ground almonds
    1½ teaspoons grated lemon rind
    ⅛   teaspoon salt
    3   large egg yolks, lightly beaten
    8   large egg whites
    ½   cup sugar

GLAZE:
    1½ teaspoons grated lemon rind
    ½   cup fresh lemon juice (about 2 lemons)
    ½   cup sugar
    1   large egg yolk, lightly beaten
    Lemon slices (optional)
    Strawberries (optional)

1. Preheat oven to 325°.
2. To prepare cake, coat a 9-inch springform cake pan with cooking spray; dust with 1 tablespoon matzo cake meal.
3. Lightly spoon 1 cup matzo cake meal into a dry measuring cup; level with a knife. Combine 1 cup matzo cake meal, almonds, 1½ teaspoons lemon rind, and salt in a large bowl; stir with a fork until blended. Stir in 3 egg yolks.
4. Place egg whites in a large bowl; beat with a mixer at high speed until foamy. Gradually add ½ cup sugar to egg whites, 1 tablespoon at a time, beating until stiff peaks form. Gently stir one-fourth of egg white mixture into matzo mixture; gently fold in remaining egg white mixture.
5. Spoon batter into prepared pan. Bake at 325° for 1 hour or until golden. Cool in pan on a wire rack 5 minutes. Pierce top of torte with a wooden skewer in several places.
6. To prepare glaze, combine 1½ teaspoons lemon rind, juice, ½ cup sugar, and 1 egg yolk in a small saucepan; stir well with a whisk. Bring to a boil over medium heat; cook 3 minutes or until thick, stirring constantly. Pour glaze

over cake in pan; let stand 10 minutes. Remove from pan, and cool completely on a wire rack. Garnish with lemon slices and strawberries, if desired. Yield: 10 servings (serving size: 1 slice).

CALORIES 238 (27% from fat); FAT 7.1g (sat 1g, mono 3.8g, poly 1.5g); PROTEIN 7.4g; CARB 37.1g; FIBER 1.9g; CHOL 85mg; IRON 1.2mg; SODIUM 77mg; CALC 44mg

Frozen Strawberry Swirl

This dessert tastes and looks great. And it can be made and frozen in advance. You can substitute 2 (16-ounce) packages frozen unsweetened strawberries, slightly thawed, for the 8 cups of fresh strawberries, if you prefer.

    2   large egg whites
    ½   cup sugar
    ¼   cup water
    8   cups sliced fresh strawberries (about 6 pints), divided
    1   tablespoon fresh lemon juice
    1   teaspoon vanilla extract
    3   tablespoons orange marmalade
    2   tablespoons orange-flavored liqueur
    1   cup sliced fresh strawberries

1. Place egg whites in a large bowl; beat with a mixer at high speed until stiff peaks form. Combine sugar and water in a saucepan; bring to a boil. Cook, without stirring, until candy thermometer registers 238°. Pour hot sugar syrup in a thin stream over egg whites, beating at high speed.
2. Place 4 cups strawberries, lemon juice, and vanilla in a food processor or blender; process 1 minute or until smooth. Strain strawberry mixture through a sieve over a large bowl; discard seeds. Gently stir one-fourth of egg white mixture into strawberry mixture; gently fold in remaining egg white mixture.
3. Place 4 cups strawberries, marmalade, and liqueur in a food processor or blender; process 1 minute or until smooth. Reserve 1½ cups sauce. Drizzle remaining ½ cup sauce over egg white mixture, and swirl sauce into mixture using tip of a knife. Cover; freeze until

firm. Serve with reserved sauce and 1 cup sliced strawberries. Yield: 5 servings (serving size: 1 cup swirl, about ⅓ cup sauce, and about ¼ cup strawberries). **NOTE:** Store swirl in freezer for up to 2 days.

CALORIES 220 (2% from fat); FAT 0.6g (sat 0g, mono 0.2g, poly 0.4g); PROTEIN 2.8g; CARB 50.2g; FIBER 5g; CHOL 0mg; IRON 1.4mg; SODIUM 32mg; CALC 42mg

Passover Chremslach with Mixed Fruit Compote

These fritters, which are traditionally deep-fried, still work well when panfried briefly and then baked. You can crisp any leftovers in a warm oven and sprinkle them with cinnamon sugar for breakfast.

    1   cup matzo cake meal
    ¼   cup dried currants
    ¼   cup coarsely chopped walnuts
    1½ teaspoons grated lemon rind
    ½   teaspoon ground cinnamon
    ⅛   teaspoon salt
    1   cup water
    1   tablespoon fresh lemon juice
    ½   teaspoon vanilla extract
    3   large egg yolks
    3   large egg whites
    ¼   cup sugar
        Cooking spray
        Mixed Fruit Compote

1. Preheat oven to 350°.
2. Lightly spoon matzo cake meal into a dry measuring cup; level with a knife. Combine matzo cake meal and next 5 ingredients in a large bowl; stir well. Add water, juice, vanilla, and egg yolks; stir with a fork until blended.
3. Beat egg whites with a mixer at high speed until foamy. Gradually add sugar, 1 tablespoon at a time, beating until stiff peaks form. Gently stir one-fourth of egg white mixture into matzo mixture; gently fold in remaining egg white mixture. Cover and chill 15 minutes.
4. Heat a large nonstick skillet coated with cooking spray over medium-high heat. Drop dough by tablespoons into pan; cook 1 minute on each side or until lightly browned.

5. Place chremslach on a baking sheet; bake at 350° for 10 minutes. Serve with Mixed Fruit Compote. Yield: 8 servings (serving size: 2 chremslach and about ½ cup compote).

(Totals include Mixed Fruit Compote) CALORIES 317 (14% from fat); FAT 5g (sat 0.8g, mono 1.1g, poly 2.1g); PROTEIN 6.4g; CARB 62.6g; FIBER 4.8g; CHOL 80mg; IRON 2.9mg; SODIUM 70mg; CALC 48mg

MIXED FRUIT COMPOTE:

    ½   teaspoon grated orange rind
    2   cups fresh orange juice (about 6 oranges)
    3   tablespoons brandy
    ¼   teaspoon whole cloves
    2   (7-ounce) packages dried mixed fruit
    2   (3-inch) cinnamon sticks
    1   lemon, quartered

1. Place all ingredients in a medium saucepan; bring to a boil. Reduce heat, cover, and simmer 20 minutes. Cool. Discard cloves, cinnamon, and lemon. Serve with chremslach. Yield: 8 servings (serving size: ½ cup).
NOTE: Store compote in refrigerator for up to a week.

CALORIES 160 (2% from fat); FAT 0.4g (sat 0g, mono 0.1g, poly 0.1g); PROTEIN 1.7g; CARB 38.3g; FIBER 4g; CHOL 0mg; IRON 1.5mg; SODIUM 10mg; CALC 28mg

---

Keeping It Kosher

To make sure your desserts are kosher, look for the words *kosher for Passover* on the labels of the following ingredients or consult a local rabbi:

- Brown sugar
- Butter
- Chocolate
- Dried fruit
- Granulated sugar
- Liqueur
- Matzo cake meal
- Nuts
- Oils
- Powdered sugar
- Vanilla extract

search myclar2003.com for all our tips

Passover Pear-Ginger Crisp

Matzo cake meal has been substituted for flour in this crisp to make a scrumptious Passover dessert.

FILLING:

    ¼   cup sugar
    1½ teaspoons grated lemon rind
    1   tablespoon fresh lemon juice
    1½ teaspoons grated peeled fresh ginger
    ½   teaspoon ground cinnamon
    10 peeled Bosc or Bartlett pears, cored and coarsely chopped (about 3¾ pounds)
        Cooking spray

TOPPING:

    1   cup matzo cake meal
    ¾   cup packed brown sugar
    ¼   teaspoon ground ginger
    ⅛   teaspoon salt
    ⅛   teaspoon ground nutmeg
    ⅛   teaspoon ground allspice
    1   large egg white
    6   tablespoons chilled butter, cut into small pieces

1. Preheat oven to 400°.
2. To prepare filling, combine first 6 ingredients in a large bowl; toss well. Spoon filling into a 13 x 9-inch baking dish coated with cooking spray.
3. To prepare topping, combine matzo cake meal and next 5 ingredients in a medium bowl, stirring with a whisk. Add egg white; stir well with a whisk. Cut in butter with a pastry blender or 2 knives until mixture resembles coarse meal; sprinkle topping over filling.
4. Bake at 400° for 30 minutes or until pears are soft and topping is golden. Yield: 10 servings.

CALORIES 270 (25% from fat); FAT 7.5g (sat 4.3g, mono 2.1g, poly 0.4g); PROTEIN 2.5g; CARB 50.5g; FIBER 0.2g; CHOL 19mg; IRON 1.1mg; SODIUM 112mg; CALC 26mg

Mom's Banana Bread

Mom always told you to eat plenty of fruits and veggies, and we have just the right recipe for sneaking in an extra serving—Mom's Banana Bread.

Originally published as a reader recipe from Stacey A. Johnson of Arlington, Washington, in December 1996, this bread quickly became a staple in our own kitchens. We've run a number of banana bread recipes in the past, but we're partial to this one because it's the quintessential banana bread: fast, easy, and delicious. Bake the other recipes when you want to wow someone, but when you want a simple little something that tastes oh-so-familiar, this is the best bet.

Mom's Banana Bread

 1 cup sugar
 ¼ cup light butter, softened
1⅔ cups mashed ripe banana (about 3 bananas)
 ¼ cup fat-free milk
 ¼ cup low-fat sour cream
 2 large egg whites
 2 cups all-purpose flour
 1 teaspoon baking soda
 ½ teaspoon salt
 Cooking spray

1. Preheat oven to 350°.
2. Combine sugar and butter in a bowl; beat with a mixer at medium speed until well blended. Add banana, milk, sour cream, and egg whites; beat well.
3. Lightly spoon flour into dry measuring cups; level with a knife. Combine flour, baking soda, and salt; stir well. Add flour mixture to banana mixture, beating until blended.
4. Spoon batter into 4 (5 x 2½-inch) mini-loaf pans coated with cooking spray. Bake at 350° for 45 minutes or until a wooden pick inserted in center comes out clean. Cool in pans 10 minutes on a wire rack; remove from pans. Cool completely on wire rack. Yield: 4 loaves, 4 servings per loaf (serving size: 1 slice).

NOTE: To make a 9-inch loaf, spoon batter into a 9 x 5-inch loaf pan coated with cooking spray; bake at 350° for 1 hour and 10 minutes or until a wooden pick inserted in center comes out clean. Yield: 1 loaf, 16 servings (serving size: 1 slice).

CALORIES 147 (14% from fat); FAT 2.2g (sat 1.4g, mono 0.2g, poly 0.1g); PROTEIN 2.5g; CARB 30.2g; FIBER 1.1g; CHOL 7mg; IRON 0.8mg; SODIUM 180mg; CALC 13mg

Beset by Broccoli Bread

We answer a call for help from an Oklahoma family obsessed with this easy, hearty recipe.

Melissa DuPont, a psychology major at Oklahoma State, admits she and her family were addicted to Broccoli Bread. It was hard to resist on cold, snowy nights when the taste and texture made it the DuPonts' favorite companion for a steaming bowl of soup. (Try it with one of our vegetarian soups; recipes begin on page 50.)

As a student of human behavior, Melissa realized her obsession with Broccoli Bread could have consequences and asked for our help.

Our first step was to cut back on the butter without sacrificing the tender texture of the bread. We reduced the butter to two tablespoons while adding a half-cup of fat-free sour cream, which kept the bread moist, yet shaved 69 grams of fat from the recipe. Then we switched from whole eggs to egg substitute. This substitution was undetectable—and it slashed another 20 grams of fat from the recipe. Finally, we used fat-free cottage cheese, reducing the total by another 7.5 grams of fat.

The new, slimmer bread still has great broccoli and onion flavor, but with about one-third the fat of the original.

Broccoli Bread
(pictured on page 57)

Packaged corn muffin mix gives this bread a touch of sweetness. If you make this corn bread-type recipe in a glass baking dish instead of a metal pan, decrease the oven temperature by 25 degrees.

 1 cup egg substitute
 ¾ cup fat-free cottage cheese
 ½ cup fat-free sour cream
 2 tablespoons butter, melted
 ¾ teaspoon salt
1½ cups finely chopped onion
 1 (10-ounce) package frozen chopped broccoli, thawed and drained
 1 (8½-ounce) package corn muffin mix (such as Jiffy)
 Cooking spray

1. Preheat oven to 400°.
2. Combine first 5 ingredients in a large bowl. Stir in onion, broccoli, and muffin mix; stir until well blended. Pour into a 13 x 9-inch baking pan coated with cooking spray. Bake at 400° for 27 minutes or until set. Yield: 12 servings.

CALORIES 146 (28% from fat); FAT 4.5g (sat 1.8g, mono 1.9g, poly 0.5g); PROTEIN 6.7g; CARB 19.8g; FIBER 2.4g; CHOL 8mg; IRON 0.7mg; SODIUM 497mg; CALC 62mg

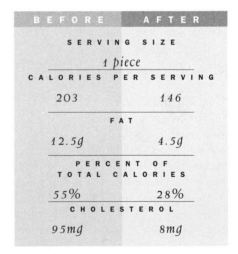

BEFORE	AFTER
SERVING SIZE	
1 piece	
CALORIES PER SERVING	
203	146
FAT	
12.5g	4.5g
PERCENT OF TOTAL CALORIES	
55%	28%
CHOLESTEROL	
95mg	8mg

Broccoli Bread, page 56

Country-Fried Steak with Mushroom Gravy, page 44

Mussels in Red Curry Broth, page 48

Roasted Asparagus with Balsamic
Browned Butter, page 63

Spicy Pork and Sauerkraut Sandwiches,
page 70

Cilantro Rice with Chicken, page 67

Chocolate and Berry-Covered Meringue,
page 53

Three's a Charm

Take a behind-the-scenes look at last year's best recipes.

Every Tuesday through Friday, members of the *Cooking Light* editorial team assemble in our kitchens to rate the recipes tested that day. All told, we test more than 4,000 recipes a year. To do that, we use a simple yet rigorous system: Some dishes simply fail, while those that pass receive a numerical rating: 1 is defined as an OK recipe; 1+ is good overall; 2 is very good overall; 2+ is a high-quality recipe; and 3 is superior in all aspects. Here, a rating of "3" means a recipe is the best it can be.

We're a demanding crew, and 3s are rare. In 2001, *Cooking Light* published just 11 recipes that gained our highest rating. Here are eight of the 11 recipes and some brief glimpses at how they became stars.

A Three Is Born

There are many indications that a recipe deserves a 3. One is that there's not much left by the time taste testing starts around noon. The first of each day's recipes begin to appear at 7 a.m., so when one of them is outstanding, it's usually nibbled on all morning, leaving just enough for the group to sample.

Cooking Light staffers say they also ask themselves a variety of questions about each dish they taste:

- How could we make this better?
- If I had this at a restaurant, would I think it was superb?
- Would I make this tonight? Would I make it again and again?
- Is it better than other versions of the dish I've had?
- Can I tell it's light?
- Will I tell all my friends to make this?
- Would I be proud to serve this to guests?

Chambord Granita

The original recipe for Chambord Granita (July 2001) called for crème de framboise, but it was hard to find. So we tested with raspberry schnapps. We weren't crazy about the results, but knew a liqueur change could make the difference. For such a simple recipe, quality is key. It had to be Chambord, a French black raspberry liqueur. At the second testing, we all liked the granita immediately. It was beautiful and used just four ingredients.

—Martha Condra, former test kitchens staffer

- 3 cups water, divided
- 1 cup sugar
- 4 cups fresh raspberries (about 1½ pounds)
- 1 cup Chambord (black raspberry liqueur)

1. Combine 1 cup water and sugar in a saucepan; bring to a boil, stirring until sugar dissolves. Remove from heat; cool completely.

2. Place raspberries in a blender; process until smooth. Press raspberry puree through a sieve into a medium bowl; discard seeds. Stir in sugar syrup, 2 cups water, and liqueur. Pour mixture into an 11 x 7-inch baking dish. Cover and freeze 8 hours or until firm. Remove mixture from freezer; let stand 10 minutes. Scrape entire mixture with a fork until fluffy. Yield: 8 cups (serving size: ½ cup).

CALORIES 105 (2% from fat); FAT 0.2g (sat 0g, mono 0g, poly 0.1g); PROTEIN 0.3g; CARB 21.3g; FIBER 0g; CHOL 0mg; IRON 0.2mg; SODIUM 0mg; CALC 7mg

---

Chocolate Mousse

Chocolate Mousse (May 2001) beckoned from across the table, looking so adorably scrumptious in its little whipped-topping beret. This was a dish that would make me pick up a magazine, I declared to the group gathered around to select the perfect May cover. This wasn't just incredible for a lightened mousse, but for any mousse—any dessert, really—anywhere. One bite demanded another and another, and before cover preview was over, the mousse was gone, and the decision was made (perhaps in part) based on the smile on my face.

—Hillari Dowdle, Managing Editor

- ¾ cup semisweet chocolate chips, melted
- 1 (12.3-ounce) package light extra-firm tofu
- ¼ teaspoon salt
- 3 large egg whites
- ½ cup sugar
- ¼ cup water
- Fat-free whipped topping, thawed (optional)
- Grated chocolate (optional)

1. Place melted chocolate chips and tofu in a food processor or blender; process 2 minutes or until smooth.

2. Place salt and egg whites in a medium bowl; beat with a mixer at high speed until stiff peaks form.

3. Combine sugar and water in a small saucepan; bring to a boil. Cook, without stirring, until candy thermometer registers 238°. Pour hot sugar syrup in a thin stream over egg whites, beating at high speed. Gently stir one-fourth of meringue into tofu mixture; gently fold in remaining meringue. Spoon ½ cup mousse into each of 8 (6-ounce) custard cups. Cover and chill at least 4 hours. Garnish with whipped topping and grated chocolate, if desired. Yield: 8 servings.

NOTE: Pouring hot sugar syrup over beaten egg whites brings them up to 238°, which renders them safe to eat.

CALORIES 147 (34% from fat); FAT 5.6g (sat 3.3g, mono 1.8g, poly 0.5g); PROTEIN 5.2g; CARB 22.5g; FIBER 0.2g; CHOL 0mg; IRON 0.9mg; SODIUM 134mg; CALC 26mg

Quick Vegetarian Chili with Avocado Salsa

Quick Vegetarian Chili with Avocado Salsa (April 2001) appeared in "The Good Fats," a story proclaiming the health benefits of getting certain fats in your diet. The chili calls for canola oil, which provides omega-3 fatty acids, and is topped with an avocado salsa, which contains "good" monounsaturated fat. The ingredients themselves are unremarkable, but when several of us were huddled around a kitchen island eating the finished product on a rainy, cold Friday, we couldn't stop. The chili's flavor, considering its humble ingredients and quick prep time, was comforting and good. We simply couldn't find fault, and we all rated it a 3.

—Krista Ackerbloom, Associate Food Editor

2 teaspoons canola oil
1 cup chopped onion
1 cup chopped red bell pepper
2 teaspoons chili powder
1 teaspoon ground cumin
1 teaspoon dried oregano
3 garlic cloves, minced
1 (4.5-ounce) can chopped green chiles
⅔ cup uncooked quick-cooking barley
¼ cup water
1 (15-ounce) can black beans, drained
1 (14.5-ounce) can no-salt-added diced tomatoes, undrained
1 (14½-ounce) can vegetable broth
3 tablespoons chopped fresh cilantro
6 tablespoons reduced-fat sour cream
6 lime wedges
18 baked tortilla chips
Avocado Salsa

1. Heat oil in a Dutch oven over medium-high heat. Add onion and bell pepper; sauté 3 minutes. Add chili powder and next 4 ingredients; cook 1 minute. Stir in barley and next 4 ingredients; bring to a boil. Cover, reduce heat, and simmer 20 minutes or until barley is tender. Stir in cilantro. Serve with sour cream, lime wedges, chips, and Avocado Salsa. Yield: 6 servings (serving size: 1 cup chili, 1 tablespoon sour cream, 1 lime wedge, 3 chips, and about 2½ tablespoons Avocado Salsa).

NOTE: Store chili in an airtight container in the refrigerator for up to 2 days.

(Totals include Avocado Salsa) CALORIES 313 (29% from fat); FAT 10.1g (sat 2.2g, mono 4.8g, poly 1.6g); PROTEIN 9.6g; CARB 50.4g; FIBER 9.5g; CHOL 6mg; IRON 3.4mg; SODIUM 814mg; CALC 100mg

AVOCADO SALSA:

½ cup finely chopped peeled avocado
⅓ cup chopped seeded tomato
2 tablespoons finely chopped onion
1 tablespoon finely chopped seeded jalapeño pepper
1 tablespoon chopped fresh cilantro
1 tablespoon fresh lime juice
⅛ teaspoon salt

1. Combine all ingredients; toss mixture gently. Serve salsa immediately. Yield: 1 cup (serving size: about 2½ tablespoons).

CALORIES 59 (79% from fat); FAT 5.2g (sat 0.8g, mono 3.2g, poly 0.7g); PROTEIN 0.8g; CARB 3.7g; FIBER 1.9g; CHOL 0mg; IRON 0.5mg; SODIUM 54mg; CALC 6mg

Lombo di Maiale Coi Porri
Pan-Roasted Pork Loin with Leeks

As the magazine's senior food editor, it's sometimes hard for me to be objective. I frequently say that I wish I could step back and, just for a day, see the magazine as a regular reader. Well, I got my wish. Lombo di Maiale Coi Porri (March 2001) went through the test kitchens while I was on maternity leave. When the story arrived at my door weeks later for editing, my first thought was, "How can a dish with only four simple ingredients (not counting water, salt, and pepper) be so outstanding?" So I made it, and it truly was. Part of its goodness lies in the cooking technique: The leeks are braised and take on an almost buttery consistency.

—Jill Melton, Senior Food Editor

4 large leeks (about 2¼ pounds)
½ cup water
1 tablespoon butter, divided
½ teaspoon salt, divided
½ teaspoon black pepper, divided
1 (2-pound) boneless pork loin, trimmed
½ cup dry white wine
Chopped fresh parsley (optional)

1. Remove roots and tough upper leaves from leeks. Cut each leek in half lengthwise. Cut each half crosswise into ½-inch-thick slices (you should have about 6 cups). Soak in cold water to loosen dirt; rinse and drain.
2. Heat sliced leek, ½ cup water, 1 teaspoon butter, ¼ teaspoon salt, and ¼ teaspoon pepper in a large Dutch oven or deep sauté pan over medium-high heat. Cook 10 minutes or until leek has wilted. Pour into a bowl.
3. Heat 2 teaspoons butter in pan over medium-high heat. Add pork; cook 5 minutes, browning on all sides. Add ¼ teaspoon salt, ¼ teaspoon pepper, and wine; cook 15 seconds, scraping pan to loosen browned bits. Return leek mixture to pan. Cover, reduce heat, and simmer 2 hours or until pork is tender. Remove pork from pan; increase heat to reduce leek sauce if it's too watery. Cut pork into ¼-inch-thick slices. Serve with leek mixture; garnish with parsley, if desired. Yield: 6 servings (serving size: about 3 ounces pork and about 2½ tablespoons leek mixture).

WINE NOTE: Pork matches well with both white and red wines, but the leeks in this dish suggest a vibrant, herbal white wine. Go for a Pinot Grigio from the north of Italy. Zenato ($10) is an affordable favorite.

CALORIES 246 (39% from fat); FAT 10.7g (sat 4.2g, mono 4.4g, poly 1.1g); PROTEIN 24.8g; CARB 12.1g; FIBER 1g; CHOL 73mg; IRON 2.8mg; SODIUM 306mg; CALC 60mg

Anticuchos with Roasted Yellow Pepper Sauce
Peruvian Beef Kebabs

For me, taste testing starts as I walk down the hallway to the test kitchens. The good smells of cumin, onions, roasted peppers, garlic, and grilled beef wafted out to meet me this day. As I moved through the buffet line, I kept sniffing. I followed my nose to these grill-charred kebabs with their sunny yellow sauce. Here was a dish with all the things I love: big-bang flavors, unsubtle scents, beautifully grilled beef, brilliant color contrast. Wow! I thought. How long has this been going on? How long will it take to move to Peru, and how can I earn enough money when I get there to eat these kebabs every single day? The Anticuchos with Roasted Yellow Pepper Sauce (September 2001) got instant, unanimous praise. But I don't think our test kitchens director believed me when I gave it a rating of 50,000+.

—Robin Mather Jenkins, Senior Writer

BEEF:

1½ pounds boneless sirloin steak, trimmed and cut into ½-inch pieces
3 tablespoons red wine vinegar
2 teaspoons ground aji amarillo or hot paprika
1 teaspoon salt
1 teaspoon freshly ground black pepper
½ teaspoon ground cumin
½ teaspoon ground turmeric

FIERY RUB:

3 tablespoons chopped fresh flat-leaf parsley
1 teaspoon salt
1 teaspoon ground aji amarillo or hot paprika
½ teaspoon freshly ground black pepper
¼ teaspoon ground turmeric

REMAINING INGREDIENTS:

Cooking spray
Roasted Yellow Pepper Sauce

1. To prepare beef, combine first 7 ingredients in a large bowl; toss well. Cover and chill 3 hours.

2. To prepare fiery rub, combine parsley and next 4 ingredients.

3. Prepare grill.

4. Remove beef from bowl; thread beef onto 6 (10-inch) skewers. Press fiery rub onto beef. Place kebabs on a grill rack coated with cooking spray; grill 6 minutes or until desired degree of doneness, turning once. Serve with Roasted Yellow Pepper Sauce. Yield: 6 servings (serving size: 3 ounces meat and about 2½ tablespoons sauce).

NOTE: Look for aji amarillo, a fiery yellow chile, in Latin food markets.

(Totals include Roasted Yellow Pepper Sauce) CALORIES 188 (34% from fat); FAT 7g (sat 2.7g, mono 3g, poly 0.3g); PROTEIN 26.3g; CARB 3.4g; FIBER 0.8g; CHOL 76mg; IRON 3.6mg; SODIUM 809mg; CALC 23mg

ROASTED YELLOW PEPPER SAUCE:

1 large yellow bell pepper (about 10 ounces)
¼ cup finely chopped green onions
2 tablespoons white vinegar
1 tablespoon water
1 tablespoon olive oil
1 tablespoon fresh lemon juice
1 teaspoon ground cumin
1 teaspoon ground aji amarillo or hot paprika
½ teaspoon ground turmeric
¼ teaspoon salt
¼ teaspoon black pepper
1 garlic clove, minced

1. Preheat broiler.

2. Cut bell pepper in half lengthwise, discarding seeds and membranes. Place pepper halves, skin sides up, on a foil-lined baking sheet; flatten pepper with hand. Broil 15 minutes or until blackened. Place in a zip-top plastic bag; seal. Let stand 15 minutes. Peel and coarsely chop. Place bell pepper and remaining 11 ingredients in a blender; process until smooth. Yield: about 1 cup (serving size: 2½ tablespoons).

CALORIES 55 (39% from fat); FAT 2.4g (sat 0.3g, mono 1.7g, poly 0.3g); PROTEIN 0.7g; CARB 8.1g; FIBER 0.8g; CHOL 0mg; IRON 0.5mg; SODIUM 203mg; CALC 12mg

Roasted Asparagus with Balsamic Browned Butter
(pictured on page 59)

Side dishes have tough going at our taste testings. We want something beyond steamed veggies, but not as labor intensive as an entrée. Roasted Asparagus with Balsamic Browned Butter (September 2001) is made from ingredients everyone has on hand, but involves a bit of skill. Browning the butter takes a watchful eye. Yet it's the touch that makes this dish sing. How could this recipe go wrong? It's sweet, sour, salty, smoky, and rich—all while being hearty and elegant. We unanimously agreed that this dish tops any asparagus recipe we've ever done.

—John Kirkpatrick, test kitchens staffer

40 asparagus spears, trimmed (about 2 pounds)
Cooking spray
¼ teaspoon kosher salt
⅛ teaspoon black pepper
2 tablespoons butter
2 teaspoons low-sodium soy sauce
1 teaspoon balsamic vinegar

1. Preheat oven to 400°.

2. Arrange asparagus in a single layer on baking sheet; coat with cooking spray. Sprinkle with salt and pepper. Bake at 400° for 12 minutes or until tender.

3. Melt butter in a small skillet over medium heat; cook 3 minutes or until lightly browned, shaking pan occasionally. Remove from heat; stir in soy sauce and vinegar. Drizzle over asparagus, tossing well to coat. Serve immediately. Yield: 8 servings (serving size: 5 spears).

WINE NOTE: Asparagus has been called wine's worst enemy, but grilled or roasted asparagus is wine-friendly. The best wine for this flavorful recipe? Pinot Gris (known as Pinot Grigio in Italy). Try a Pinot Gris from California, like the one from J (about $17).

CALORIES 45 (60% from fat); FAT 3g (sat 1.8g, mono 0.9g, poly 0.2g); PROTEIN 1.9g; CARB 3.9g; FIBER 1.7g; CHOL 8mg; IRON 0.7mg; SODIUM 134mg; CALC 18mg

Pommes Anna
Potatoes Anna

In putting together the magazine, we shoot a lot of photography. Usually, I look at the food only as another prop in the shot; I rarely eat when we're working. But when Food Stylist Kellie Gerber Kelley unveiled Pommes Anna (April 2001) at a photo shoot, I simply had to taste it! It has everything—it's beautiful, easy to make, and has a wonderfully sophisticated taste. And who wouldn't love the completely addictive chips that form the top of the dish? The day of the photo shoot, I even took some of it home to my husband.

—Maya Metz Logue,
Assistant Art Director

    1 teaspoon kosher or sea salt
    ½ teaspoon black pepper
    2½ tablespoons unsalted butter
    3 pounds peeled baking potatoes,
       cut into ⅛-inch-thick slices
    1 tablespoon unsalted butter, melted
       and divided
    1 tablespoon chopped fresh flat-leaf
       parsley (optional)

1. Preheat oven to 450°.
2. Combine salt and pepper in a small bowl.
3. Melt 2½ tablespoons butter in a 10-inch cast iron or ovenproof heavy skillet over medium heat. Arrange a single layer of potato slices, slightly overlapping, in a circular pattern in pan; sprinkle with ¼ teaspoon salt mixture. Drizzle ½ teaspoon melted butter over potatoes. Repeat layers 5 times, ending with butter. Press firmly to pack. Cover and bake at 450° for 20 minutes.
4. Uncover and bake an additional 25 minutes or until potatoes are golden. Loosen edges of potatoes with a spatula. Place a plate upside down on top of pan; invert potatoes onto plate. Sprinkle with parsley, if desired. Yield: 8 servings (serving size: 1 wedge).

CALORIES 208 (23% from fat); FAT 5.2g (sat 3.2g, mono 1.5g, poly 0.3g); PROTEIN 3.4g; CARB 36.7g; FIBER 2.6g; CHOL 14mg; IRON 0.7mg; SODIUM 353mg; CALC 11mg

Sichuan-Style Stir-Fried Chicken with Peanuts

When we first sampled Sichuan-Style Stir-Fried Chicken with Peanuts (January/February 2001) at taste testing, I loved it. But it was months later that I realized its staying power—which is the real benchmark of a great recipe. I don't clip recipes from the magazine (I know where to find them), but this one is taped into my personal spiral-bound recipe book. Although my husband sometimes tires of exotic, ethnic flavors, this dish is a comfort because of its familiar tastes and ingredients.

—Jill Melton, Senior Food Editor

MARINADE:
    2 tablespoons low-sodium soy sauce
    2 tablespoons rice wine or sake
    1 teaspoon cornstarch
    1 teaspoon dark sesame oil
    1½ pounds skinless, boneless chicken
       breast, cut into bite-sized pieces

STIR-FRYING OIL:
    2 tablespoons vegetable oil, divided

SAUCE:
    ½ cup fat-free, less-sodium chicken
       broth
    2½ tablespoons low-sodium soy sauce
    2 tablespoons rice wine or sake
    2 tablespoons sugar
    1 tablespoon Chinese black vinegar
       or Worcestershire sauce
    1¼ teaspoons cornstarch
    1 teaspoon dark sesame oil
    2 tablespoons minced green onions
    1½ tablespoons minced peeled fresh
       ginger
    1½ tablespoons minced garlic (about
       7 cloves)
    1 teaspoon chile paste with garlic

REMAINING INGREDIENTS:
    1½ cups drained sliced water chestnuts
    1 cup (½-inch) sliced green onion
       tops
    ¾ cup unsalted, dry-roasted peanuts
    6 cups hot cooked long-grain rice

1. To prepare marinade, combine first 4 ingredients in a medium bowl, and add chicken; cover and chill 20 minutes.

2. Heat 1 tablespoon vegetable oil in a wok or large nonstick skillet over medium-high heat. Add chicken mixture; stir-fry 4 minutes or until chicken is done. Remove from pan; set aside.
3. To prepare sauce, combine broth and next 6 ingredients; stir well with a whisk. Heat 1 tablespoon vegetable oil in pan. Add minced green onions, ginger, garlic, and chile paste; stir-fry 15 seconds. Add broth mixture; cook 1 minute or until thick, stirring constantly.
4. Stir in cooked chicken, water chestnuts, green onion tops, and peanuts; cook 1 minute or until thoroughly heated. Serve over rice. Yield: 6 servings (serving size: ¾ cup stir-fry and 1 cup rice).

WINE NOTE: Though it's wildly cross-cultural, the best wine with this dish is a sparkling wine. A sparkler's crisp acidity and tingling bubbles balance the soy sauce, sesame oil, chile paste, and peanuts beautifully. If your pocketbook allows, spring for a Champagne labeled "extra dry." Mumm, Moët and Chandon, and numerous other producers offer extra dry Champagnes for about $30, but remember that Champagne is often on sale. Domaine Ste. Michelle's extra-dry sparkling wine from Washington State is a good buy at $11.

CALORIES 590 (25% from fat); FAT 16.7g (sat 2.7g, mono 6.8g, poly 6g); PROTEIN 36.9g; CARB 71.4g; FIBER 3.3g; CHOL 66mg; IRON 3.8mg; SODIUM 591mg; CALC 75mg

All About Rice

Much of the world relies on rice. Now you can, too.

Most people grow up eating some kind of basic rice dish: maybe chicken and rice, Spanish rice, fried rice, rice pilaf, or rice and gravy. Those dishes are still pleasing, but you may be ready to expand your horizons. To help, we've developed a guide so you can choose the right rice for anything you wish to cook.

Brown Rice-Stuffed Grape Leaves in Tomato Sauce

This appetizer is a version of classic Greek *dolmades*, flavored here with dill, parsley, and savory. You can stuff leaves ahead and reheat in tomato sauce just before serving. Look for bottled grape leaves in Greek or Italian markets, or with the Mediterranean foods or olives in supermarkets. To assemble the grape leaves, mound a rounded tablespoon of the rice filling onto the center of each leaf. Fold the sides over the filling, then roll up from the bottom of the leaf.

4	cups water
1	cup uncooked long-grain brown rice
½	teaspoon salt
2	teaspoons vegetable oil
1	cup thinly sliced leek (about 1 large)
1	garlic clove, minced
2	tablespoons chopped fresh flat-leaf parsley
2	tablespoons chopped toasted pine nuts
2	tablespoons dried currants
1	tablespoon chopped fresh dill
1	tablespoon fresh lemon juice
½	teaspoon grated fresh lemon rind
½	teaspoon dried savory
⅛	teaspoon salt
¼	teaspoon black pepper, divided
1	(14.5-ounce) can crushed tomatoes, undrained
24	bottled large grape leaves

1. Bring water to a boil in a medium saucepan; add rice and ½ teaspoon salt. Cover, reduce heat, and simmer 40 minutes or until liquid is absorbed. Remove from heat; uncover and cool to room temperature.

2. Heat oil in a large nonstick skillet over medium-low heat. Add leek; cook 10 minutes or until tender, stirring frequently (do not brown). Add garlic; cook 1 minute. Reserve ¼ cup leek mixture; stir remaining leek mixture into rice. Stir parsley and next 7 ingredients into rice mixture. Add ⅛ teaspoon pepper.

3. Combine reserved ¼ cup leek mixture, ⅛ teaspoon pepper, and tomatoes in skillet; bring to a boil. Reduce heat, and simmer 10 minutes. Remove from heat.

4. Rinse grape leaves with cold water; drain well. Pat dry with paper towels. Remove and discard stems. Select 24 large leaves; reserve remaining leaves for another use. Spoon 1 rounded tablespoon of rice mixture onto center of each grape leaf. Working with one leaf at a time, bring 2 opposite points of leaf to center; fold over filling. Beginning at 1 short side, roll up leaf tightly, jelly roll fashion. Repeat procedure with remaining leaves.

5. Nestle stuffed grape leaves, seam sides down, in tomato sauce. Cover and cook over medium-low heat 20 minutes or until thoroughly heated. Yield: 8 servings (serving size: 3 stuffed leaves and about ¼ cup sauce).

CALORIES 148 (19% from fat); FAT 3.2g (sat 0.4g, mono 1.3g, poly 1.2g); PROTEIN 4g; CARB 26.7g; FIBER 2.2g; CHOL 0mg; IRON 1.9mg; SODIUM 498mg; CALC 71mg

How to Cook Basic White Rice

Cooking flawless long-grain white rice is not difficult, if you follow these directions:

1. Select a broad, shallow saucepan; deep skillet; or sauté pan with a snug-fitting lid.

2. Heat water to boiling.
- For soft, tender rice, use 2 cups water per 1 cup rice.
- For dry, separate grains, use 1¾ cups water per 1 cup rice.
- One cup uncooked rice will yield about 3 cups cooked.

3. Add rice and salt; stir once.

4. Return to boiling; stir once.

5. Cover and reduce heat to low.

6. Cook for 15 minutes or until all the water is absorbed. Don't lift the lid or stir. Lifting the lid allows steam to escape, and stirring the rice will release more starch, causing the grains to stick together in lumps.

7. Remove lid carefully (try not to let the condensation on lid drip onto the rice).

Baked Mushroom Rice

Rice cooks beautifully in the oven—and removes the temptation to lift the lid and peek as it cooks.

1	tablespoon olive oil
1	cup sliced cremini mushrooms
1½	cups fat-free, less-sodium chicken broth
1	cup uncooked medium-grain rice
¼	teaspoon salt

1. Preheat oven to 400°.

2. Heat oil in a medium nonstick skillet over medium-high heat. Add mushrooms; sauté 5 minutes. Stir in broth, rice, and salt; bring to a boil. Wrap handle of skillet with foil; cover and bake at 400° for 20 minutes. Uncover; let stand 3 minutes. Yield: 4 servings (serving size: about ¾ cup).

CALORIES 212 (16% from fat); FAT 3.7g (sat 0.5g, mono 2.6g, poly 0.4g); PROTEIN 5.1g; CARB 38.5g; FIBER 0.8g; CHOL 0mg; IRON 2.1mg; SODIUM 319mg; CALC 18mg

Rice Defined

Arborio

This popular Italian rice is used to make risotto. Each medium-length grain has a white "eye" that remains firm to the bite, while the rest of the grain softens and lends creaminess. Once grown exclusively in Italy, Arborio is now also grown in California and Texas. Other Italian rices used to make risotto are *carnaroli* and *vialone nano*.

Basmati

Sometimes called "popcorn rice," this long-grain variety is highly regarded for its fragrance, taste, and slender shape. True basmati is grown in India and Pakistan, although many hybrids are grown elsewhere, including the United States. Texmati, for example, is grown in Texas.

Black

Both medium- and short-grain, this rice is grown mostly in Southeast Asia and in limited quantity in California. It gets its color from the black bran that surrounds the endosperm, or kernel. When cooked, the rice might turn purple or lavender—the bran dyes the white kernel inside. Look for Black Japonica or Forbidden Rice.

Brown

This is rice that has been hulled with bran intact. The bran lends chewy texture and nutty flavor, and contains vitamins, minerals, and fiber. It requires a longer cooking time because the bran is a barrier to water.

Glutinous

This word describes sticky rice. The term is confusing, however, because rice doesn't contain gluten, a protein found in wheat.

Instant

Also called precooked, this rice has been partially or completely cooked and dried; it takes only a few minutes to prepare.

Jasmine

Thailand's favorite, this aromatic rice has more amylopectin, or sticky starch, than other long-grain rice, so it's moist and tender. It's grown in Asia and the United States.

Parboiled

Steam-pressure treatment before milling produces this tan grain that is firm and stays separate when cooked. Don't confuse it with instant rice—parboiled rice takes longer to cook. Look for Uncle Ben's version, called converted rice.

Red

This aromatic rice with reddish-brown bran has a nutty flavor and chewy consistency. Look for Wehani (American grown), Bhutanese Red Rice (imported), and Camargue (imported from France's Provence region) in specialty markets. Red rice is great with hearty foods like pork or butternut squash.

Sushi

This short-grain sticky rice is glassy and smooth. It grows throughout Asia and in California.

Wild

The only rice native to North America, this is actually an aquatic grass. It's often sold mixed with long-grain white rice.

Lemon Risotto with Asparagus

Risotto is traditionally made with Arborio rice because of its high starch content and firm texture. Constant stirring helps release the rice's starches, creating a creamy texture with separate grains. A large skillet or sauté pan provides a broad surface to help the rice cook evenly.

  3 (14-ounce) cans fat-free, less-sodium chicken broth
  1 tablespoon olive oil
  ½ cup finely chopped onion
1½ cups uncooked Arborio rice
  2 teaspoons grated lemon rind
  ½ cup dry white wine
  3 cups (1-inch) diagonally cut asparagus (about 1 pound)
  ½ cup (2 ounces) grated Parmigiano-Reggiano cheese
  2 tablespoons fresh lemon juice
  2 teaspoons fresh thyme leaves

1. Bring broth to a simmer in a large saucepan (do not boil). Keep warm over low heat.
2. Heat oil in a large nonstick skillet over medium heat. Add onion; cook 5 minutes or until tender, stirring frequently. Add rice and rind; cook 2 minutes, stirring constantly. Stir in wine, and cook 3 minutes or until liquid is nearly absorbed, stirring constantly.
3. Add 3½ cups warm broth, ½ cup at a time, stirring constantly until each portion of broth is absorbed before adding next (about 20 minutes). Stir in asparagus. Add remaining broth, ½ cup at a time, stirring constantly until each portion of broth is absorbed before adding next (about 10 minutes). Remove from heat; stir in cheese and juice. Sprinkle with thyme. Yield: 6 servings (serving size: about 1¼ cups).

CALORIES 307 (14% from fat); FAT 4.9g (sat 1.9g, mono 2.4g, poly 0.3g); PROTEIN 11.7g; CARB 51.2g; FIBER 2.7g; CHOL 6mg; IRON 1.2mg; SODIUM 532mg; CALC 154mg

---

Leftover Rice

Store cooked rice, tightly covered and refrigerated, for up to six days. To use leftovers, consider these simple ideas:

Rice salad

Add bottled vinaigrette to room-temperature rice. Stir in feta cheese, chopped red onion, carrot, celery, and bell pepper.

Frittata

Sauté bell pepper, onion, and garlic in olive oil until tender. Stir in cold rice, and cook until heated. Add 4 beaten eggs; cover, reduce heat, and cook until set. Sprinkle with Parmesan cheese.

Soup

Add rice and your favorite vegetables to any kind of stock.

Marinara

Reheat rice in microwave (1 cup takes about 1 minute); serve with hot marinara sauce and grated cheese.

search myclar2003.com for all our tips

Cilantro Rice with Chicken

(pictured on page 60)

A sauce of fresh cilantro, green onions, ginger, and garlic gives the rice intense fragrance and flavor. Shiitake mushrooms add an earthy, smoky flavor.

RICE:

- 1 tablespoon olive oil
- 2 cups quartered shiitake mushroom caps (about 6 ounces)
- ¼ cup chopped green onion bottoms
- 1 (½-inch) piece peeled fresh ginger
- 1 garlic clove, crushed
- 2 cups uncooked long-grain rice
- 2 teaspoons ground cumin
- 6 skinless, boneless chicken thighs (about 1¾ pounds), cut into bite-sized pieces
- 3 cups fat-free, less-sodium chicken broth

SAUCE:

- 2 cups loosely packed cilantro leaves
- ½ cup fat-free, less-sodium chicken broth
- 2 tablespoons chopped green onion tops
- 1 teaspoon chopped peeled fresh ginger
- ½ teaspoon kosher salt
- 1 garlic clove, peeled

TOPPING:

- 1 teaspoon olive oil
- 2 cups grape or cherry tomatoes, halved
- 2 tablespoons chopped green onion tops

Cilantro sprigs (optional)

1. Preheat oven to 350°.
2. To prepare rice, heat 1 tablespoon oil in a Dutch oven over medium heat. Add mushrooms and next 3 ingredients; cook 5 minutes, stirring frequently. Stir in rice, cumin, and chicken; cook 1 minute. Stir in 3 cups broth; bring to a boil. Cover and bake at 350° for 25 minutes. Remove from oven; let stand, covered, 10 minutes.
3. To prepare sauce, place cilantro leaves and next 5 ingredients in a food processor or blender; process until smooth. Stir into rice mixture.

4. To prepare topping, heat 1 teaspoon oil in a medium skillet over medium-low heat. Add tomatoes; cook 2 minutes. Stir in 2 tablespoons green onion tops. Place rice mixture in a large bowl; spoon tomato topping over rice. Garnish with cilantro sprigs, if desired. Yield: 8 servings (serving size: about 1 cup rice mixture and about ¼ cup tomato topping).

CALORIES 339 (18% from fat); FAT 6.8g (sat 1.4g, mono 3g, poly 1.3g); PROTEIN 25.3g; CARB 41.5g; FIBER 1.8g; CHOL 82mg; IRON 3.9mg; SODIUM 416mg; CALC 44mg

Sushi-Rice Salad

This side salad pairs well with seared tuna or soy-glazed salmon.

RICE:

- 2 cups uncooked sushi rice
- 2 cups water
- 1 teaspoon kosher salt

DRESSING:

- ½ cup rice vinegar
- 1 tablespoon vegetable oil
- 1 tablespoon dark sesame oil
- 1 tablespoon low-sodium soy sauce
- 1 teaspoon grated peeled fresh ginger
- 1 garlic clove, minced
- ¼ to ¾ teaspoon prepared wasabi or Japanese horseradish (optional)

REMAINING INGREDIENTS:

- 1 cup (2-inch) julienne-cut peeled English cucumber
- ¼ cup minced red onion
- 1 tablespoon sesame seeds, toasted
- 1 sheet nori (seaweed), cut into 2-inch julienne strips

1. To prepare rice, rinse rice thoroughly in a sieve. Drain well. Bring 2 cups water to a boil in a medium saucepan; add rice and salt. Cover, reduce heat, and simmer 20 minutes or until liquid is absorbed. Remove from heat; uncover and cool to room temperature.
2. To prepare dressing, combine vinegar and next 5 ingredients in a small bowl. Add wasabi, if desired. Combine cooled rice, dressing, cucumber, onion, and sesame seeds in a large bowl. Sprinkle

evenly with nori. Yield: 7 servings (serving size: 1 cup).

CALORIES 256 (15% from fat); FAT 4.3g (sat 0.5g, mono 2g, poly 1.5g); PROTEIN 4.2g; CARB 46.7g; FIBER 2g; CHOL 0mg; IRON 4.4mg; SODIUM 346mg; CALC 9mg

Fried Rice with Broccoli and Eggs

Stir-frying rice is a great way to turn leftover rice into a quick and easy meal. It's important that the rice is cold so it won't become sticky while cooking; the oil coats the chilled grains and prevents clumping.

- 3 cups small broccoli florets
- 4 large eggs
- 2 tablespoons water
- 1 tablespoon vegetable oil, divided
- 1 tablespoon minced peeled fresh ginger
- 2 garlic cloves, minced
- 4 cups cooked long-grain rice, chilled
- ½ cup shredded carrot
- ¼ cup fat-free, less-sodium chicken broth
- 2 tablespoons low-sodium soy sauce
- 2 teaspoons dark sesame oil
- ¼ teaspoon salt
- ¼ cup thinly sliced green onions

1. Steam broccoli, covered, 2 minutes or until crisp-tender; rinse with cold water. Drain; cool.
2. Combine eggs and 2 tablespoons water. Heat 1 teaspoon vegetable oil in a large nonstick skillet or wok over medium-high heat. Add egg mixture; stir-fry 30 seconds or until soft-scrambled, stirring constantly. Remove egg mixture from pan.
3. Add 2 teaspoons vegetable oil to pan. Add ginger and garlic; stir-fry 30 seconds. Add rice; stir-fry 3 minutes. Add broccoli, carrot, and broth; cook 1 minute. Add egg mixture, soy sauce, sesame oil, and salt; stir-fry 1 minute or until thoroughly heated. Sprinkle with green onions. Yield: 6 servings (serving size: 1⅓ cups).

CALORIES 254 (28% from fat); FAT 7.8g (sat 1.6g, mono 3.4g, poly 2g); PROTEIN 9.9g; CARB 36.4g; FIBER 3.2g; CHOL 142mg; IRON 2.6mg; SODIUM 362mg; CALC 69mg

Rice and Black Bean Salad with Cumin Dressing

Parboiled rice is treated so that the starch in the grain is gelatinized, resulting in separate grains. Don't use instant, or precooked, rice in its place.

RICE:

1 teaspoon vegetable oil
1½ cups uncooked long-grain parboiled rice (such as Uncle Ben's converted rice)
½ teaspoon ground turmeric
½ teaspoon ground cumin
3⅓ cups water
½ teaspoon kosher salt
1 cup frozen whole-kernel corn, thawed
½ cup finely chopped seeded peeled cucumber
½ cup finely chopped red bell pepper
½ cup finely chopped green onions
¼ cup chopped cilantro
1 tablespoon minced seeded jalapeño pepper
1 (15-ounce) can black beans, rinsed and drained

DRESSING:

1 teaspoon ground cumin
6 tablespoons fresh lime juice
3 tablespoons vegetable oil
2 tablespoons water
½ teaspoon kosher salt
1 garlic clove, minced

TOPPING:

2 cups thin wedges plum tomato (about 4 tomatoes)
1 tablespoon fresh lime juice
⅛ teaspoon kosher salt

1. To prepare rice, heat 1 teaspoon oil in a large nonstick skillet over medium heat. Add rice; cook 1 minute. Stir in turmeric and ½ teaspoon cumin. Add 3⅓ cups water and ½ teaspoon salt; bring to a boil. Cover, reduce heat, and simmer 25 minutes or until liquid is absorbed. Remove from heat; uncover and cool to room temperature. Add corn and next 6 ingredients.
2. To prepare dressing, heat 1 teaspoon cumin in a small nonstick skillet over low heat 30 seconds or just until fragrant. Remove from heat. Stir in 6 tablespoons lime juice and next 4 ingredients. Stir into rice mixture.
3. To prepare topping, combine tomato, 1 tablespoon lime juice, and ⅛ teaspoon salt. Place rice mixture on a serving platter; spoon tomato topping over rice. Yield: 6 servings (serving size: 1⅓ cups).

CALORIES 365 (22% from fat); FAT 8.9g (sat 0.8g, mono 4.7g, poly 2.7g); PROTEIN 9.3g; CARB 63.3g; FIBER 6.7g; CHOL 0mg; IRON 3.5mg; SODIUM 468mg; CALC 57mg

Cinnamon Rice Pudding with Dried-Cherry Sauce

Aromatic jasmine rice cooks to a moist texture, which makes it perfect for rice pudding. Use a pan that has a thick bottom surface to prevent scorching.

PUDDING:

6 cups water
1½ cups uncooked jasmine rice
1 teaspoon kosher salt
1 (3-inch) cinnamon stick
3 cups 2% reduced-fat milk
½ cup sugar
1 teaspoon ground cinnamon
1 teaspoon vanilla extract
½ teaspoon almond extract

SAUCE:

1 cup dried tart cherries
1½ cups water
2 tablespoons sugar
1 tablespoon water
1 teaspoon cornstarch
½ teaspoon vanilla extract
¼ teaspoon almond extract

1. To prepare pudding, combine first 4 ingredients in a large, heavy saucepan; bring to a boil. Reduce heat, and simmer, uncovered, 20 minutes or until rice is tender. Drain.
2. Return rice and cinnamon stick to pan; stir in milk, ½ cup sugar, and ground cinnamon. Bring to a simmer over medium heat, stirring constantly. Reduce heat to medium-low; cook 30 minutes or until thick, stirring frequently. Discard cinnamon stick. Remove from heat; stir in 1 teaspoon vanilla extract and ½ teaspoon almond extract.
3. To prepare sauce, combine cherries and 1½ cups water in a medium saucepan; bring to a boil. Reduce heat, and simmer 20 minutes. Stir in 2 tablespoons sugar; cook 5 minutes. Combine 1 tablespoon water and cornstarch. Add to cherry mixture; bring to a boil. Cook 1 minute or until slightly thick, stirring constantly. Remove from heat; stir in ½ teaspoon vanilla extract and ¼ teaspoon almond extract. Serve with sauce. Yield: 8 servings (serving size: ¾ cup pudding and about 2½ tablespoons sauce).

CALORIES 290 (7% from fat); FAT 2.1g (sat 1.1g, mono 0.5g, poly 0.1g); PROTEIN 6.2g; CARB 61.4g; FIBER 1.2g; CHOL 7mg; IRON 1.1mg; SODIUM 126mg; CALC 127mg

Spiced Brown Basmati Pilaf

This is an excellent accompaniment to roasted chicken. Brown rice lends nutty flavor and a slightly chewy bite; red rice is also a good choice for this dish.

1 tablespoon vegetable oil
1 cup chopped onion
2 cups uncooked brown basmati rice
½ cup golden raisins
3 whole cloves
1 (3-inch) cinnamon stick
1 cup water
2 tablespoons tomato paste
1 teaspoon salt
2 (14-ounce) cans fat-free, less-sodium chicken broth
¼ cup chopped pistachios

1. Heat oil in a large nonstick skillet over medium heat. Add onion; cook 10 minutes or until golden, stirring frequently. Add rice, raisins, cloves, and cinnamon stick; stir well. Stir in water, tomato paste, salt, and broth; bring to a boil. Cover, reduce heat, and simmer 45 minutes. Let stand 5 minutes. Discard cloves and cinnamon stick. Sprinkle with pistachios. Yield: 10 servings (serving size: about ¾ cup).

CALORIES 205 (19% from fat); FAT 4.3g (sat 0.6g, mono 2.1g, poly 1.3g); PROTEIN 5.2g; CARB 39.3g; FIBER 3g; CHOL 0mg; IRON 0.8mg; SODIUM 392mg; CALC 15mg

Around the World

These robust dishes bring world flavors to your weeknight dinner table.

Hungarian Menu
serves 4

Chicken Paprikash-Topped Potatoes

Garlic breadsticks

Roasted Brussels sprouts*

*Combine 4 cups trimmed, halved Brussels sprouts, 2 teaspoons melted butter, ½ teaspoon salt, and ¼ teaspoon black pepper on a jelly roll pan coated with cooking spray. Bake at 425° for 25 minutes or until crisp-tender.

Game Plan

1. Preheat oven for Brussels sprouts
2. While Brussels sprouts roast:
- Microwave potatoes
- Prepare chicken mixture for potatoes
- Warm breadsticks

Chicken Paprikash-Topped Potatoes

TOTAL TIME: 30 MINUTES

- 4 baking potatoes (about 1½ pounds)
- 4 skinless, boneless chicken thighs (about 12 ounces), cut into bite-sized pieces
- 2 tablespoons all-purpose flour
- 2 teaspoons paprika
- ¾ teaspoon salt
- ¼ teaspoon ground red pepper
- 1 tablespoon butter
- ½ cup coarsely chopped onion
- 1 (8-ounce) package presliced mushrooms
- 2 garlic cloves, minced
- ½ cup fat-free, less-sodium chicken broth
- ¼ cup reduced-fat sour cream
- 2 tablespoons chopped fresh parsley

1. Pierce potatoes with a fork; arrange in a circle on paper towels in microwave oven. Microwave at HIGH 16 minutes or until done, rearranging potatoes after 8 minutes. Let stand 5 minutes.

2. Combine chicken, flour, paprika, salt, and pepper in a large zip-top plastic bag; seal and shake to coat.

3. Melt butter in a large nonstick skillet over medium-high heat. Add chicken mixture, onion, mushrooms, and garlic; sauté 5 minutes. Add broth; bring to a boil. Cook 6 minutes or until chicken is done and sauce thickens, stirring frequently. Remove from heat; stir in sour cream.

4. Split potatoes open with fork; fluff pulp. Divide chicken mixture evenly over potatoes; sprinkle with parsley. Yield: 4 servings (serving size: 1 potato and ½ cup chicken mixture).

CALORIES 311 (25% from fat); FAT 8.6g (sat 3.9g, mono 1.9g, poly 1.2g); PROTEIN 22.9g; CARB 36.3g; FIBER 3.4g; CHOL 86mg; IRON 2.6mg; SODIUM 619mg; CALC 56mg

French Menu
serves 4

Tarragon Chicken-in-a-Pot Pies

Green salad

Caramel-coconut sundaes*

*Sprinkle ¼ cup flaked sweetened coconut on a jelly roll pan. Bake at 325° for 10 minutes or until golden brown, stirring occasionally. Scoop ½ cup vanilla low-fat ice cream into each of 4 dessert bowls; top each serving with 1 tablespoon fat-free caramel sundae syrup and about 1 tablespoon toasted coconut flakes.

Game Plan

1. Preheat oven for coconut
2. While coconut bakes:
- Chop onion; slice carrot and zucchini
- Cut chicken into bite-sized pieces
3. While chicken mixture cooks:
- Hollow out bread
- Prepare salad

search myclar2003.com for all our menus

Tarragon Chicken-in-a-Pot Pies

Popular in French cooking, tarragon adds anise flavor to the creamy chicken mixture. Hollowed-out rolls serve as edible, individual vessels that soak up the sauce.

TOTAL TIME: 36 MINUTES

QUICK TIP: Make breadcrumbs for future use with the bread you remove from the rolls. Place the bread scraps in a food processor, and pulse 5 to 10 times. Freeze the breadcrumbs in a heavy-duty zip-top plastic bag for up to 6 months.

- 2 tablespoons all-purpose flour
- 1 cup 1% low-fat milk
- ½ cup fat-free, less-sodium chicken broth
- ½ cup dry white wine
- 1 tablespoon olive oil
- ⅔ cup chopped sweet onion
- 1 pound skinless, boneless chicken breast, cut into bite-sized pieces
- 1 cup sliced carrot
- 1 cup (⅛-inch-thick) slices zucchini
- ½ teaspoon salt
- ½ teaspoon dried tarragon
- ½ teaspoon black pepper
- 4 (4.5-ounce) country or peasant rolls

1. Place flour in a small bowl; slowly add milk, stirring with a whisk until well blended to form a slurry. Add broth and wine.

2. Heat oil in a large saucepan over medium-high heat; add onion and chicken. Sauté 2 minutes; stir in carrot and next 4 ingredients. Cover, reduce heat, and cook 4 minutes. Stir slurry into chicken mixture. Bring to a boil; cover, reduce heat, and simmer until thick (about 10 minutes), stirring occasionally.

3. Cut rolls horizontally, 1 inch from tops. Hollow out bottoms of rolls, leaving ¼-inch-thick shells; reserve torn bread and bread tops for another use. Spoon 1¼ cups chicken mixture into each bread shell. Yield: 4 servings.

CALORIES 413 (17% from fat); FAT 7.8g (sat 2.7g, mono 3g, poly 0.7g); PROTEIN 35.7g; CARB 48.8g; FIBER 3.5g; CHOL 68mg; IRON 4.2mg; SODIUM 865mg; CALC 199mg

Dilled Pork Stroganoff

This version of the Russian classic uses pork instead of the traditional beef and gives the sour cream sauce a touch of dill flavor.

TOTAL TIME: 30 MINUTES

    3   cups uncooked medium egg noodles (about 6 ounces)
    1   (1-pound) pork tenderloin, trimmed and cut into ½-inch strips
    ½   teaspoon salt, divided
    ¼   teaspoon black pepper
    2½ teaspoons butter, divided
        Cooking spray
    ½   cup fat-free, less-sodium chicken broth
    2   cups chopped Walla Walla or other sweet onion
    1   (8-ounce) package presliced mushrooms
    1   cup low-fat sour cream
    1   tablespoon chopped fresh dill
    1   tablespoon Dijon mustard
    1   teaspoon all-purpose flour
        Dill sprigs (optional)

1. Cook pasta according to package directions, omitting salt and fat.

2. Sprinkle pork with ¼ teaspoon salt and pepper. Melt 1½ teaspoons butter in a large nonstick skillet coated with cooking spray over medium-high heat. Add pork; sauté 4 minutes or until pork loses pink color. Remove pork from pan; keep warm.

3. Add broth to pan; cook 30 seconds. Add 1 teaspoon butter, ¼ teaspoon salt, onion, and mushrooms; cook 8 minutes or until vegetables are lightly browned. Remove from heat.

4. Combine sour cream, chopped dill, mustard, and flour in a small bowl. Add pork and sour cream mixture to pan; stir well. Serve pork mixture immediately over noodles. Garnish with dill sprigs, if desired. Yield: 4 servings (serving size: 1 cup pork mixture and 1 cup noodles).

CALORIES 384 (30% from fat); FAT 13g (sat 7.1g, mono 2.9g, poly 1g); PROTEIN 34.4g; CARB 31.6g; FIBER 3g; CHOL 123mg; IRON 3.5mg; SODIUM 585mg; CALC 120mg

Spicy Pork and Sauerkraut Sandwiches

(pictured on page 59)

Packaged coleslaw mix creates easy, speedy "sauerkraut" that's more colorful and less salty than the traditional recipe.

TOTAL TIME: 27 MINUTES

    ½   teaspoon salt, divided
    ½   teaspoon dried oregano
    ½   teaspoon dried thyme
    ½   teaspoon black pepper
    1   pound pork tenderloin, trimmed and cut crosswise into ¼-inch-thick slices
    1   tablespoon vegetable oil, divided
        Cooking spray
    4   cups packaged cabbage-and-carrot coleslaw (about 8 ounces)
    1   tablespoon prepared horseradish
    1   tablespoon red wine vinegar
    1½ teaspoons Worcestershire sauce
    ½   teaspoon crushed red pepper
    ⅓   cup fat-free mayonnaise
    1   tablespoon Dijon mustard
    4   (2-ounce) Kaiser rolls or hamburger buns
    16 (⅛-inch-thick) slices cucumber

1. Combine ¼ teaspoon salt, oregano, thyme, and black pepper; sprinkle pork with spice mixture. Heat 1½ teaspoons oil in a large nonstick skillet coated with cooking spray over medium-high heat. Add pork; cook 2 minutes on each side or until done. Remove pork from pan; keep warm.

2. Heat 1½ teaspoons oil in pan over medium-high heat. Add ¼ teaspoon salt, coleslaw, and next 4 ingredients; cook 2 minutes, stirring frequently. Remove from heat.

3. Combine mayonnaise and mustard; spread mixture evenly over cut sides of rolls. Divide coleslaw mixture, pork, and cucumber slices evenly among bottom halves of rolls. Cover with top halves of rolls. Yield: 4 servings.

CALORIES 366 (27% from fat); FAT 10.8g (sat 2.6g, mono 3.2g, poly 3.8g); PROTEIN 29.9g; CARB 37.5g; FIBER 4.1g; CHOL 76mg; IRON 3.7mg; SODIUM 989mg; CALC 108mg

april

Out of the Frying Pan Into the Oven

It's not only possible to lighten your favorite fried foods—it's deliciously simple.

The popularity of fried food has much to do with its texture. The crisp exterior, contrasted with the moist, tender interior, is a large part of the appeal. But how can we reconcile what we want with what we ought to have? Is there a way to duplicate what we love about fried food without its hefty nutritional price tag?

After much experimentation, we've found that creating crisp, crunchy faux-fried food in the oven *is* possible and comes down to three simple techniques:

Bread it. With the exception of french fries, most foods are well served by a double dip—sometimes even a triple dip—in flour or some other breading to create a substantial crunchy coating.

Oil it. Give the food a shot of cooking spray after breading it, just before it goes in the oven. This helps brown and crisp the surface.

Heat it. The higher the heat, the browner and crispier the coating will get.

Now you can have the crisp, the crunch, the chewy satisfaction of fried food—and guilt-free pleasure as well.

Oven-Fried Chicken

FAT COMPARISON:	
Oven-Fried Chicken	4.4 g
Fast food fried chicken breast	24 g

Marinating in buttermilk results in tender, juicy chicken, and double breading gives a crisp crust. For a smoky taste, use ground chipotle pepper in place of the ground red pepper.

- ¾ cup low-fat buttermilk
- 2 chicken breast halves (about 1 pound), skinned
- 2 chicken drumsticks (about ½ pound), skinned
- 2 chicken thighs (about ½ pound), skinned
- ½ cup all-purpose flour
- 1 teaspoon salt
- ½ teaspoon ground red pepper
- ¼ teaspoon white pepper
- ¼ teaspoon ground cumin
- Cooking spray

1. Combine first 4 ingredients in a large zip-top plastic bag; seal. Marinate in refrigerator 1 hour, turning occasionally.

2. Preheat oven to 450°.

3. Combine flour, salt, peppers, and cumin in a second large zip-top plastic bag. Remove chicken from first bag, discarding marinade. Add chicken, one piece at a time, to flour mixture, shaking bag to coat chicken. Remove chicken from bag, shaking off excess flour; lightly coat each chicken piece with cooking spray. Return chicken, one piece at a time, to flour mixture, shaking bag to coat chicken. Remove chicken from bag, shaking off excess flour.

4. Place chicken on a baking sheet lined with parchment paper. Lightly coat chicken with cooking spray. Bake at 450° for 35 minutes or until done, turning after 20 minutes. Yield: 4 servings (serving size: 1 breast half or 1 thigh and 1 drumstick).

CALORIES 263 (15% from fat); FAT 4.4g (sat 1.2g, mono 1.1g, poly 0.9g); PROTEIN 38.4g; CARB 14.9g; FIBER 0.8g; CHOL 110mg; IRON 2.2mg; SODIUM 754mg; CALC 73mg

Savory Stuffed Mushrooms

FAT COMPARISON:	
Savory Stuffed Mushrooms	4.2 g
Fried mushrooms	9 g

If you can't find whole portobello mushrooms, use about 24 cremini or large button mushrooms instead.

- 6 (4-inch) whole portobello mushrooms
- Cooking spray
- 1 garlic clove, minced
- ¼ cup dry white wine
- ¼ cup chopped green onions
- ¼ cup (2 ounces) ⅓-less-fat cream cheese
- 2 tablespoons grated fresh Parmesan cheese
- ¼ teaspoon black pepper
- ⅛ teaspoon ground red pepper
- ½ cup egg substitute
- 1 tablespoon all-purpose flour
- ⅔ cup dry breadcrumbs

1. Preheat oven to 450°.

2. Remove mushroom stems from caps; finely chop stems to measure ½ cup. Set caps aside.

3. Heat a large nonstick skillet coated with cooking spray over medium-high heat. Add chopped mushroom stems and garlic; sauté 3 minutes. Add wine; cook 2 minutes or until liquid evaporates. Remove from heat; cool 3 minutes. Add onions, cheeses, and peppers; stir until smooth. Spread evenly into mushroom caps.

4. Combine egg substitute and flour in a small bowl; stir well with a whisk. Place breadcrumbs in a shallow dish. Working with one mushroom cap at a time, dip each cap, cheese side up, into egg mixture; dredge in breadcrumbs, coating only the mushroom cap. Place mushroom cap, cheese side up, on a baking sheet coated with cooking spray. Lightly coat stuffed mushrooms with cooking spray. Bake at 450° for 25 minutes or until tender and lightly browned. Yield: 6 servings (serving size: 1 mushroom).

CALORIES 127 (30% from fat); FAT 4.2g (sat 2.1g, mono 1.3g, poly 0.6g); PROTEIN 6.5g; CARB 12.3g; FIBER 1g; CHOL 9mg; IRON 1.4mg; SODIUM 222mg; CALC 77mg

Coconut Shrimp with Pineapple Salsa

FAT COMPARISON:

Coconut Shrimp	11.4 g
Fried shrimp	25 g

Eat this shrimp with a fork to ensure that you get some salsa with every bite.

SHRIMP:
- 28 large shrimp (about 1½ pounds)
- ⅓ cup cornstarch
- ¾ teaspoon salt
- ½ to ¾ teaspoon ground red pepper
- 3 large egg whites
- 1½ cups flaked sweetened coconut
- Cooking spray

SALSA:
- 1 cup finely chopped fresh pineapple
- ⅓ cup finely chopped red onion
- ¼ cup finely chopped fresh cilantro
- ¼ cup pineapple preserves
- 1½ tablespoons fresh lime juice
- 1 tablespoon finely chopped seeded jalapeño pepper
- ¼ teaspoon black pepper

1. Preheat oven to 400°.
2. To prepare shrimp, peel and devein shrimp, leaving tails intact. Rinse shrimp with cold water; drain on paper towels until dry.
3. Combine cornstarch, salt, and red pepper in a shallow dish; stir with a whisk. Place egg whites in a medium bowl, and beat with a mixer at medium-high speed until frothy (about 2 minutes). Place coconut in a shallow dish.
4. Working with one shrimp at a time, dredge each shrimp in cornstarch mixture. Dip in egg white; dredge in coconut, pressing gently with fingers. Place shrimp on a baking sheet coated with cooking spray. Lightly coat shrimp with cooking spray. Bake at 400° for 20 minutes or until shrimp are done, turning after 10 minutes.
5. To prepare salsa, combine pineapple and remaining 6 ingredients. Yield: 4 servings (serving size: 7 shrimp and about ¼ cup salsa).

CALORIES 397 (26% from fat); FAT 11.4g (sat 8.4g, mono 0.7g, poly 1g); PROTEIN 29.9g; CARB 45g; FIBER 2.2g; CHOL 194mg; IRON 3.9mg; SODIUM 753mg; CALC 80mg

Beer-Battered Fish

FAT COMPARISON:

Beer-Battered Fish	5.1 g
Fried fish sticks	15 g

Serve with malt vinegar and Garlic Fries (recipe at right) for a healthier version of fish and chips.

- 1½ tablespoons vegetable oil
- 1 cup all-purpose flour
- ½ teaspoon black pepper
- ¼ teaspoon garlic salt
- ⅔ cup beer
- 2 large egg whites
- 2 cups dry breadcrumbs
- ½ cup chopped fresh parsley
- 1½ pounds grouper or other firm white fish fillets, such as catfish or tilapia, cut into 4- x 1-inch strips
- Cooking spray
- Malt vinegar (optional)

1. Preheat oven to 450°.
2. Coat bottom of a jelly roll pan with oil.
3. Lightly spoon flour into a dry measuring cup; level with a knife. Combine flour, pepper, and garlic salt in a large bowl. Add beer; stir well. Beat egg whites with a mixer at high speed until stiff peaks form. Gently fold egg white mixture into flour mixture.
4. Combine breadcrumbs and parsley in a shallow dish. Working with one fish strip at a time, dip each strip in flour mixture; dredge in breadcrumb mixture. Place on prepared baking sheet. Lightly coat strips with cooking spray.
5. Bake at 450° for 15 minutes or until fish flakes easily when tested with a fork. Remove from oven.
6. Preheat broiler.
7. Broil fish sticks 1 minute or until tops are lightly browned. Serve with malt vinegar, if desired. Yield: 4 servings.

CALORIES 351 (13% from fat); FAT 5.1g (sat 1g, mono 1.4g, poly 1.9g); PROTEIN 39.1g; CARB 32.9g; FIBER 1.4g; CHOL 63mg; IRON 4.4mg; SODIUM 371mg; CALC 122mg

Garlic Fries

(pictured on page 95)

FAT COMPARISON:

Garlic Fries	7.7 g
Fast food large fries	22 g

Tossing the fries in butter and garlic after cooking makes them unbelievably rich.

- 3 pounds peeled baking potatoes, cut into ¼-inch-thick strips
- 4 teaspoons vegetable oil
- ¾ teaspoon salt
- Cooking spray
- 2 tablespoons butter
- 8 garlic cloves, minced (about 5 teaspoons)
- 2 tablespoons finely chopped fresh parsley
- 2 tablespoons freshly grated Parmesan cheese

1. Preheat oven to 400°.
2. Combine first 3 ingredients in a large zip-top plastic bag, tossing to coat.
3. Arrange potatoes in a single layer on a baking sheet coated with cooking spray. Bake at 400° for 50 minutes or until potatoes are tender and golden brown, turning after 20 minutes.
4. Place butter and garlic in a large non-stick skillet; cook over low heat 2 minutes, stirring constantly. Add potatoes, parsley, and cheese to pan; toss to coat. Serve immediately. Yield: 6 servings.

CALORIES 256 (27% from fat); FAT 7.7g (sat 3.3g, mono 2g, poly 2g); PROTEIN 5.9g; CARB 42.3g; FIBER 3.5g; CHOL 12mg; IRON 1.9mg; SODIUM 386mg; CALC 55mg

Jalapeño Chile Poppers

FAT COMPARISON:

Jalapeño Chile Poppers	4.5 g
Fried chile poppers	7.3 g

Each pepper gets a double dip in the egg and breadcrumbs for an extracrisp coating. The tip of a paring knife works well for removing the membranes and seeds from peppers.

- 12 pickled whole jalapeño peppers (about 2 [12-ounce] jars)
- ½ cup (2 ounces) shredded reduced-fat sharp cheddar cheese
- ½ cup (4 ounces) ⅓-less-fat cream cheese, softened
- ½ cup egg substitute
- 2 tablespoons all-purpose flour
- ⅔ cup dry breadcrumbs
- ¾ teaspoon garlic powder
- ½ teaspoon salt
- ¼ teaspoon paprika
- Cooking spray

1. Preheat oven to 400°.

2. Drain jalapeños. Cut ¼ inch off stem ends of peppers, reserving stem ends. Carefully remove membranes and seeds, leaving peppers intact.

3. Combine cheeses in a small bowl. Spoon cheese mixture into a zip-top plastic bag; seal. Carefully snip off one bottom corner of bag. Pipe cheese mixture evenly into peppers; replace stem ends, pressing gently to seal.

4. Combine egg substitute and flour in a small bowl, stirring with a whisk. Combine breadcrumbs, garlic powder, salt, and paprika in a shallow bowl.

5. Working with one pepper at a time, dip each pepper in egg mixture; dredge in breadcrumb mixture. Return peppers, one at a time, to egg mixture; dredge in breadcrumb mixture. Place peppers on a baking sheet coated with cooking spray. Lightly coat peppers with cooking spray.

6. Bake peppers at 400° for 15 minutes or until lightly browned. Yield: 6 servings (serving size: 2 poppers).

CALORIES 153 (26% from fat); FAT 4.5g (sat 1.8g, mono 0.2g, poly 0.4g); PROTEIN 9g; CARB 18.8g; FIBER 1.9g; CHOL 14mg; IRON 1.4mg; SODIUM 532mg; CALC 216mg

---

superfast

. . . And Ready in Just About 20 Minutes

Homemade chicken stock may be the best way to go if you're making soup and have plenty of time on your hands, but canned chicken broth certainly has its virtues.

Three recipes featured here show how canned broth can help get a speedy supper on the table.

Broth thins a sweet sauce made with apricot preserves for Apricot-Hoisin Pork Chops with Somen. In Chicken with Rosemary Sauce it provides the foundation for a silky sauce finished with half-and-half. Finally, broth provides an extra fillip of flavor when it's used to rehydrate sun-dried tomatoes for Chicken with Sun-Dried Tomato-Mushroom Sauce.

Chicken with Sun-Dried Tomato-Mushroom Sauce

Serve over orzo or bow tie pasta. If you can't find sun-dried tomato sprinkles, you can chop whole sun-dried tomatoes with a knife or kitchen shears.

- 4 teaspoons olive oil, divided
- 4 (4-ounce) skinless, boneless chicken breast halves
- ½ teaspoon salt
- ¼ teaspoon black pepper
- 2 cups presliced mushrooms
- ⅓ cup finely chopped shallots
- ¾ cup fat-free, less-sodium chicken broth
- ¼ cup sun-dried tomato sprinkles
- ¼ cup dry white wine
- 1 tablespoon chopped fresh parsley

1. Heat 2 teaspoons oil in a large non-stick skillet over medium-high heat. Sprinkle chicken with salt and pepper. Add chicken to pan; cook 4 minutes on each side or until done. Remove from pan; keep warm.

2. Reduce heat to medium. Add 2 teaspoons oil, mushrooms, and shallots; cook 2 minutes, stirring frequently. Stir in broth, tomato sprinkles, and wine; cook 1 minute. Spoon sauce over chicken; sprinkle with parsley. Yield: 4 servings (serving size: 1 chicken breast half and ½ cup sauce).

CALORIES 206 (28% from fat); FAT 6.3g (sat 1g, mono 3.7g, poly 0.8g); PROTEIN 29.2g; CARB 8.2g; FIBER 1.5g; CHOL 66mg; IRON 2.2mg; SODIUM 604mg; CALC 30mg

Baked Grouper with Chunky Tomato Sauce

The grouper is seared to give it a slightly crisp crust that can hold up to the moisture from the tomato topping. Use a heavy oven-proof skillet that can go from stove-top to oven. To seed a tomato, cut it in half, hold each half in the palm of your hand, and squeeze gently.

- 3½ cups chopped seeded tomato (about 4 medium)
- ¼ cup chopped green onions
- ¼ cup dry white wine
- 1 tablespoon chopped fresh basil
- 1 teaspoon capers
- 1 teaspoon bottled minced garlic
- 1 teaspoon fresh lemon juice
- ½ teaspoon salt
- ¼ teaspoon crushed red pepper
- ¼ teaspoon black pepper
- 2 teaspoons olive oil
- 4 (6-ounce) grouper fillets

1. Preheat oven to 425°.

2. Combine first 10 ingredients in a medium bowl.

3. Heat oil in a large heavy skillet over high heat. Place fish, skin sides up, in pan; cook 2 minutes. Turn fish over; top with tomato mixture. Bring to a boil. Place pan in oven; bake at 425° for 8 minutes or until fish flakes easily when tested with a fork. Yield: 4 servings (serving size: 1 grouper fillet and ½ cup tomato mixture).

CALORIES 200 (26% from fat); FAT 5.7g (sat 0.8g, mono 2.7g, poly 1.3g); PROTEIN 28g; CARB 8.6g; FIBER 2.2g; CHOL 41mg; IRON 2mg; SODIUM 400mg; CALC 73mg

Grilled Turkey and Swiss Sandwiches

Serve with bowls of tomato soup.

¼ cup mango chutney
8 (1½-ounce) slices hearty white bread
4 (1-ounce) slices reduced-fat Jarlsberg cheese
4 ounces thinly sliced smoked turkey breast
⅓ cup fat-free milk
1 large egg
Cooking spray

1. Spread about 1 teaspoon mango chutney over each bread slice. Place 1 cheese slice on each of 4 bread slices. Divide turkey evenly over cheese. Top with remaining 4 bread slices, chutney side down. Combine milk and egg in a shallow dish. Dip both sides of each sandwich into milk mixture.
2. Heat a large nonstick skillet coated with cooking spray over medium heat. Cook sandwiches 3 minutes on each side or until lightly browned. Yield: 4 servings (serving size: 1 sandwich).

CALORIES 466 (26% from fat); FAT 13.3g (sat 4.7g, mono 4.4g, poly 1.7g); PROTEIN 22.4g; CARB 59g; FIBER 2g; CHOL 87mg; IRON 3.2mg; SODIUM 1,020mg; CALC 353mg

Apricot-Hoisin Pork Chops with Somen

Serve with steamed snow peas or broccoli florets.

4 ounces uncooked somen (wheat noodles) or angel hair pasta
½ cup fat-free, less-sodium chicken broth
½ cup apricot preserves
1 tablespoon hoisin sauce
2 teaspoons dark sesame oil
4 (4-ounce) boneless center-cut loin pork chops (about ½ inch thick)
¼ teaspoon salt
¼ teaspoon black pepper

1. Cook noodles according to package directions.

2. While noodles cook, combine broth, preserves, and hoisin sauce in a medium bowl, stirring with a whisk.
3. Heat oil in a large skillet over medium-high heat. Sprinkle pork chops with salt and pepper. Add pork to pan; cook 2 minutes on each side or until browned. Add broth mixture; bring to a boil, and cook until sauce is reduced to ½ cup (about 8 minutes). Serve over noodles. Yield: 4 servings (serving size: 1 pork chop, 2 tablespoons sauce, and ½ cup noodles).

CALORIES 446 (24% from fat); FAT 12g (sat 3.8g, mono 5.2g, poly 1.8g); PROTEIN 25.8g; CARB 58.4g; FIBER 2.4g; CHOL 59mg; IRON 1.4mg; SODIUM 505mg; CALC 42mg

Cilantro Turkey Burgers with Chipotle Ketchup

Smoky chipotle and cilantro give this burger Latin flair. Serve with baked potato chips or oven-baked fries.

⅓ cup dry breadcrumbs
¼ cup minced fresh cilantro
¼ cup (1 ounce) preshredded Parmesan cheese
¼ teaspoon salt
¼ teaspoon black pepper
1 pound ground turkey
Cooking spray
1 (7-ounce) can chipotle chiles in adobo sauce
¼ cup ketchup
4 (2½-ounce) whole wheat hamburger buns
4 red leaf lettuce leaves

1. Combine first 6 ingredients in a large bowl. Divide turkey mixture into 4 equal portions, shaping each into a ⅓-inch-thick patty.
2. Heat a large grill pan or large nonstick skillet coated with cooking spray over medium-high heat. Add turkey patties, and cook 5 minutes on each side or until done.
3. Remove 1 chile and 1 teaspoon adobo sauce from can. Reserve remaining chiles and sauce for another use. Mince chile. Combine chile, adobo sauce, and ketchup.

4. Place 1 patty on bottom half of each bun; top each patty with 1 tablespoon chipotle ketchup and 1 lettuce leaf. Cover with top halves of buns. Yield: 4 servings (serving size: 1 burger).

CALORIES 406 (30% from fat); FAT 13.6g (sat 4.3g, mono 4g, poly 3.7g); PROTEIN 26.6g; CARB 44.5g; FIBER 1.5g; CHOL 73mg; IRON 4.4mg; SODIUM 977mg; CALC 229mg

Chinese Five-Spice Steak with Rice Noodles

The delicate flavor and texture of rice sticks balances the highly seasoned beef. You can also serve the steak with basmati rice. As the tomatoes are heated, they will start to soften; stir gently so they don't lose their shape.

4 ounces uncooked wide rice stick noodles (bánh pho)
¼ cup hoisin sauce
3 tablespoons low-sodium soy sauce
1 teaspoon five-spice powder
1 (1-pound) flank steak, trimmed and cut into ¼-inch strips
2 teaspoons vegetable oil
2 tablespoons minced green onions
2 teaspoons bottled minced garlic
2 medium tomatoes, each cut into 6 wedges
2 green onions, cut into 2-inch pieces
1 tablespoon chopped fresh basil

1. Cook noodles according to package directions.
2. While noodles cook, combine hoisin sauce, soy sauce, five-spice powder, and steak in a large bowl. Heat oil in a large nonstick skillet over medium-high heat. Add minced green onions and garlic; sauté 30 seconds. Add beef mixture; cook 5 minutes, stirring frequently. Stir in tomato, green onion pieces, and basil; cook 2 minutes, stirring occasionally. Yield: 4 servings (serving size: 1½ cups beef mixture and 1 cup noodles).

CALORIES 374 (29% from fat); FAT 12.1g (sat 4.3g, mono 4.3g, poly 2.1g); PROTEIN 28.2g; CARB 36.6g; FIBER 2.3g; CHOL 59mg; IRON 4.1mg; SODIUM 744mg; CALC 32mg

Almond-Crusted Chicken with Scallion Rice

Brown the chicken quickly over high heat, then finish it in the oven to give the chicken a golden crust without burning the almonds.

> 1 (3½-ounce) bag boil-in-bag brown rice
> 4 (4-ounce) skinless, boneless chicken breast halves
> ¾ teaspoon salt, divided
> ¼ teaspoon black pepper
> ¼ cup all-purpose flour
> ½ cup low-fat buttermilk
> 2 tablespoons honey mustard
> ⅔ cup sliced almonds
> ½ cup dry breadcrumbs
> Cooking spray
> ¼ cup chopped green onions

1. Preheat oven to 450°.

2. Prepare rice according to package directions; keep warm.

3. Place each chicken breast half between 2 sheets of heavy-duty plastic wrap; pound to ½-inch thickness using a meat mallet or rolling pin. Sprinkle both sides of chicken with ¼ teaspoon salt and pepper.

4. Place flour in a zip-top plastic bag. Working with one piece at a time, add each chicken piece to bag; seal and shake to coat. Remove chicken from bag, shaking off excess flour. Combine buttermilk and honey mustard in a shallow bowl. Combine almonds and breadcrumbs in a shallow bowl. Dip chicken in buttermilk mixture; dredge in almond mixture.

5. Heat a large skillet coated with cooking spray over high heat. Add chicken; cook 1 minute. Turn chicken over. Wrap handle of pan with foil. Place pan in oven; bake at 450° for 9 minutes or until chicken is done. Add ½ teaspoon salt and green onions to rice; serve with chicken. Yield: 4 servings (serving size: 1 chicken breast half and ½ cup rice).

CALORIES 408 (24% from fat); FAT 10.7g (sat 1.4g, mono 5.9g, poly 2.5g); PROTEIN 35g; CARB 41.4g; FIBER 3.4g; CHOL 68mg; IRON 3.3mg; SODIUM 749mg; CALC 125mg

Chicken with Rosemary Sauce

In this dish chicken breasts are enveloped in an herb sauce enriched with wine and half-and-half.

> 1 teaspoon olive oil
> 4 (4-ounce) skinless, boneless chicken breast halves
> ¼ teaspoon salt
> ⅛ teaspoon black pepper
> ½ cup chopped green onions
> ¼ cup dry white wine
> 1 teaspoon minced fresh rosemary
> ½ cup fat-free, less-sodium chicken broth
> ½ cup half-and-half

1. Heat oil in a large nonstick skillet over medium-high heat. Sprinkle chicken with salt and pepper. Add chicken to pan; cook 3 minutes on each side. Add green onions, wine, and rosemary; cook 30 seconds. Stir in broth; cook 2 minutes. Add half-and-half; cook 2 minutes. Yield: 4 servings (serving size: 1 chicken breast half and about 3 tablespoons sauce).

CALORIES 183 (30% from fat); FAT 6g (sat 2.7g, mono 2.2g, poly 0.5g); PROTEIN 27.5g; CARB 2.7g; FIBER 0.5g; CHOL 77mg; IRON 0.9mg; SODIUM 293mg; CALC 46mg

inspired vegetarian

The Meaty Olive

One of the world's greatest delicacies makes even the simplest fare exquisite.

Cured olives—steeped in oil, salted, or brined—are the vegetarian cousins of the cured pork and preserved anchovies of the Mediterranean. Generations of cooks have discovered ways to preserve and transform the olive—an acrid and bitter fruit—into salty, sour, pungent condiments that turn humble fare into cuisine ripe with vivid flavors. The olive contributes dimension to vegetarian dishes that won't leave you feeling deprived.

Zesty Tofu Wraps with Olive Tapenade

Refrigerate the tapenade for up to a week. Make extra to use as a sandwich spread or as an appetizer served with bread.

TAPENADE:

> ½ cup kalamata olives, pitted
> ¼ cup oil-cured black olives, pitted
> 1 teaspoon grated lemon rind
> 1 teaspoon olive oil

WRAPS:

> 1 cup sun-dried tomatoes, packed without oil
> 1 pound extra-firm tofu, drained
> Cooking spray
> 1⅓ cups (¼-inch-thick) slices red onion, separated into rings
> 3 tablespoons balsamic vinegar
> 2 tablespoons fresh lemon juice
> 1 tablespoon red wine vinegar
> 1 tablespoon honey
> 2 teaspoons Dijon mustard
> 1 teaspoon chopped fresh rosemary
> ¼ teaspoon sea salt
> 1 garlic clove, minced
> 4 (10-inch) flour tortillas
> 4 cups trimmed watercress (about 1 bunch)

1. To prepare tapenade, place first 4 ingredients in a food processor; pulse 2 or 3 times or until minced. Set aside.

2. To prepare wraps, combine 2 cups boiling water and sun-dried tomatoes in a bowl; let stand 30 minutes or until soft. Drain and chop. Set aside.

3. Cut tofu lengthwise into quarters. Place tofu slices on several layers of paper towels; cover with additional paper towels. Let stand about 20 minutes or until barely moist.

4. Heat a large nonstick skillet coated with cooking spray over medium-high heat. Add onion; sauté 5 minutes or until lightly browned. Place in a bowl; stir in balsamic vinegar.

5. Combine lemon juice and next 6 ingredients. Heat pan coated with cooking spray over medium-high heat. Add tofu; cook 6 minutes, browning on all sides. Stir in lemon juice mixture; cook 1 minute or until sauce thickens.

6. Warm tortillas according to package directions. Spread 2 tablespoons tapenade evenly over each tortilla. Top each tortilla with 1 tofu piece, about ¼ cup sun-dried tomatoes, ⅓ cup onion mixture, and 1 cup watercress; roll up. Yield: 4 servings (serving size: 1 wrap).

CALORIES 312 (29% from fat); FAT 9.9g (sat 1g, mono 4.5g, poly 1.4g); PROTEIN 14.7g; CARB 44g; FIBER 4.4g; CHOL 0mg; IRON 3.6mg; SODIUM 960mg; CALC 199mg

---

It's the Pits

To quickly dislodge pits, place a few olives on a cutting surface. Lay the wide, flat side of a heavy chef's knife on top and give a good, sharp whack to the blade. The olives will pop open, exposing the pits for easy removal. To pit a large volume of olives, wrap them in a cloth towel and smack them with a rolling pin or the bottom of a heavy skillet.

search myclar2003.com for all our tips

Tempeh Stew Niçoise

Baking the tempeh in the juice mixture helps it hold its shape in this hearty stew.

    3   tablespoons fresh lemon juice
    1   teaspoon sugar
    1   teaspoon ground red pepper
    1   teaspoon sea salt
    1   pound tempeh, cut into 1-inch
        cubes
    Cooking spray
    4   cups chopped onion
    2   teaspoons chopped fresh thyme
    1   teaspoon chopped fresh rosemary
    4   garlic cloves, thinly sliced
    ½   cup dry white wine
    2   (14.5-ounce) cans no-salt-added
        diced tomatoes, undrained
    1   (3-inch) orange rind strip
    ½   cup niçoise olives, pitted
    2   tablespoons finely chopped fresh
        parsley
    3   cups hot cooked rice

1. Preheat oven to 375°.
2. Combine first 4 ingredients in a medium bowl. Add tempeh; toss gently.

Arrange tempeh mixture in a single layer in a 11 x 7-inch baking dish. Bake at 375° for 30 minutes.
3. Heat a Dutch oven coated with cooking spray over medium heat. Add onion; cook 7 minutes or until tender, stirring frequently. Add thyme, rosemary, and garlic; cook 1 minute, stirring constantly. Add wine; bring to a boil. Stir in tomatoes and rind; cover, reduce heat, and simmer 15 minutes. Stir in tempeh and olives; cook 5 minutes. Discard rind. Sprinkle with parsley; serve over rice. Yield: 6 servings (serving size: 1 cup stew and ½ cup rice).

CALORIES 407 (21% from fat); FAT 9.7g (sat 1.4g, mono 3.8g, poly 3.8g); PROTEIN 20.1g; CARB 61.3g; FIBER 4.9g; CHOL 0mg; IRON 4.1mg; SODIUM 664mg; CALC 179mg

---

Pan-Roasted Shallots with Olives and Sage

The slightly sweet caramelized shallots and pungent, oil-cured black olives combine to make this a hearty side dish. Buy large shallots, so you'll have fewer to peel.

    1   tablespoon butter
    5   cups shallots, peeled (about 2½
        pounds)
    ¾   cup dry red wine
    1   tablespoon chopped fresh sage
    1   tablespoon honey
    ¾   teaspoon sea salt
    ½   teaspoon freshly ground black
        pepper
    12 garlic cloves, peeled
    2   bay leaves
    2   tablespoons oil-cured black olives,
        pitted and chopped
    2   tablespoons chopped fresh
        parsley

1. Preheat oven to 400°.
2. Melt butter in a 12-inch cast iron skillet over medium-high heat. Add shallots; sauté 10 minutes or until lightly browned. Stir in wine and next 6 ingredients. Cover and bake at 400° for 30 minutes. Uncover and bake 40 minutes or until sauce thickens. Remove bay leaves. Stir in olives; sprinkle with

parsley. Yield: 6 servings (serving size: about ½ cup).

CALORIES 162 (21% from fat); FAT 3.7g (sat 1.3g, mono 1.5g, poly 0.2g); PROTEIN 4.2g; CARB 24.2g; FIBER 2.7g; CHOL 5mg; IRON 1.7mg; SODIUM 397mg; CALC 69mg

---

Fennel Salad with Green Olive Vinaigrette

The licorice-flavored fennel, the tart apples, and the slightly sweet, tangy olives combine to make a refreshingly crisp salad—a creative alternative to traditional cabbage slaw.

    1   teaspoon fennel seeds
    3   tablespoons fresh lemon juice
    2   tablespoons picholine olives,
        pitted and minced
    1   tablespoon olive oil
    ¼   teaspoon black pepper
    ⅛   teaspoon sea salt
    5   cups thinly sliced fennel bulb
        (about 2 medium bulbs)
    2   cups thinly sliced Granny Smith
        apple (about 2 apples)
    1   tablespoon chopped fennel fronds
    2   tablespoons grated fresh Parmesan
        cheese
    Fennel fronds (optional)

1. Place fennel seeds in a small nonstick skillet, and cook over medium heat 1 minute or until toasted. Place fennel seeds in a spice or coffee grinder; process until finely ground.
2. Combine ground seeds, lemon juice, olives, oil, pepper, and salt in a large bowl; stir with a whisk. Add fennel bulb and apple, tossing to coat. Sprinkle with chopped fennel fronds; top with cheese. Garnish with fennel fronds, if desired. Yield: 7 servings (serving size: about 1 cup).

CALORIES 85 (35% from fat); FAT 3.3g (sat 0.6g, mono 1.9g, poly 0.3g); PROTEIN 2g; CARB 14.1g; FIBER 0.8g; CHOL 1mg; IRON 0.9mg; SODIUM 144mg; CALC 72mg

Pasta and Greens with Olives and Feta

Radicchio is a bitter green, so it holds its own with the briny olives. Substitute Swiss chard or broccoli rabe in its place.

- 1 (1-ounce) slice white bread
- 3 cups uncooked fusilli or cavatappi (about 8 ounces)
- 1 teaspoon olive oil
- 4 cups torn radicchio
- ½ teaspoon crushed red pepper
- 3 garlic cloves, chopped
- 10 cups chopped spinach
- ¾ cup picholine olives, pitted and chopped
- 1 tablespoon chopped fresh or 1 teaspoon dried oregano
- ⅔ cup (about 2½ ounces) crumbled feta cheese
- ¼ teaspoon sea salt
- ⅛ teaspoon black pepper
- 4 lemon wedges

1. Preheat oven to 350°.

2. Place bread in a food processor; pulse 5 times or until coarse crumbs form to measure ½ cup. Place crumbs on a baking sheet. Bake at 350° for 7 minutes or until golden. Set aside.

3. Cook pasta according to package directions, omitting salt and fat. Drain, reserving ½ cup pasta water.

4. Heat oil in a large Dutch oven over medium-high heat. Add radicchio, red pepper, and garlic; sauté 1 minute. Add spinach, olives, and oregano; toss 2 minutes or until spinach wilts. Add pasta and reserved pasta water; cook 1 minute. Remove from heat; stir in cheese, salt, and black pepper. Sprinkle each serving with 2 tablespoons breadcrumbs. Serve with lemon wedges. Yield: 4 servings (serving size: 2 cups).

CALORIES 394 (30% from fat); FAT 13.1g (sat 3.9g, mono 6.4g, poly 2g); PROTEIN 16.3g; CARB 59.8g; FIBER 8.8g; CHOL 16mg; IRON 6.4mg; SODIUM 868mg; CALC 291mg

Spiced Braised Carrots with Olives and Mint

Although carrots, olives, and mint may seem like an unlikely combination, you'll love the rich flavor of this dish. The cooking liquid is reduced to concentrate the flavor.

- 2 cups water
- 5 cups (1-inch) sliced carrot (about 2 pounds)
- 1½ tablespoons honey
- 1 tablespoon fresh lemon juice
- ½ teaspoon sea salt
- ½ teaspoon coriander seeds
- ¼ teaspoon crushed red pepper
- 1 (5-inch) mint sprig
- 1 (2-inch) cinnamon stick
- 1 garlic clove, minced
- ¼ cup oil-cured black olives, pitted and coarsely chopped
- 1 teaspoon rice vinegar
- 1 teaspoon extra-virgin olive oil
- 1 teaspoon chopped fresh mint
- Mint sprigs (optional)

1. Bring water to a simmer in a large saucepan. Stir in carrot and next 8 ingredients; cover and simmer 15 minutes or until carrot is tender. Remove carrot with a slotted spoon, reserving liquid.

2. Bring liquid to a boil; cook until reduced to ¼ cup (about 10 minutes). Discard mint sprig and cinnamon stick. Return carrot to pan; stir in olives, vinegar, and oil. Cook 1 minute or until heated. Sprinkle with chopped mint. Garnish with mint sprigs, if desired. Yield: 5 servings (serving size: about 1 cup).

CALORIES 139 (27% from fat); FAT 4.1g (sat 0.5g, mono 2.8g, poly 0.5g); PROTEIN 2.2g; CARB 25.7g; FIBER 5.7g; CHOL 0mg; IRON 1.1mg; SODIUM 470mg; CALC 57mg

Stuffed Portobello Mushrooms with Olives and Caramelized Onions

Bake the mushrooms on a rack over a pan to catch breadcrumbs that may fall. Serve with a green salad for a complete meal.

    4   (4-inch) portobello mushrooms
    Cooking spray
    2   teaspoons olive oil
    4   cups finely chopped Vidalia or
        other sweet onion
    ½   cup dry red wine
    1   tablespoon balsamic vinegar
    2   teaspoons finely chopped fresh
        thyme, divided
    ½   teaspoon sea salt
    ¾   cup chopped pitted kalamata olives
    1   teaspoon grated lemon rind
    ¼   teaspoon black pepper
    3   (1-ounce) slices white bread
    ⅓   cup (about 1½ ounces) grated
        fresh Parmesan cheese
    ¼   cup finely chopped fresh flat-leaf
        parsley

1. Preheat oven to 350°.
2. Remove stem and brown gills from undersides of mushrooms using a spoon; discard gills. Place mushrooms, stem side down, on a baking sheet coated with cooking spray. Bake at 350° for 10 minutes; cool mushrooms on a wire rack.
3. Heat oil in a large nonstick skillet over medium-high heat. Add onion; sauté 12 minutes. Stir in wine, vinegar, 1 teaspoon thyme, and salt; bring to a boil. Cover, reduce heat, and simmer 25 minutes. Uncover and increase heat to medium-high; cook 5 minutes or until liquid evaporates. Stir in olives, rind, and pepper.
4. Place bread in a food processor; pulse 10 times or until coarse crumbs form to measure 1½ cups. Combine 1 teaspoon thyme, crumbs, cheese, and parsley. Spoon ½ cup olive mixture into each mushroom; top with about ¾ cup cheese mixture. Bake at 350° for 25 minutes or until golden brown. Yield: 4 servings (serving size: 1 stuffed mushroom).

CALORIES 246 (30% from fat); FAT 8.1g (sat 2.2g, mono 4.2g, poly 0.8g); PROTEIN 7.6g; CARB 27.6g; FIBER 4.4g; CHOL 7mg; IRON 1.3mg; SODIUM 700mg; CALC 134mg

---

Breakfast for Dinner

Having a topsy-turvy day? Turn it sunny-side up with breakfast for dinner.

Diner-Style Breakfast
serves 4

Lumberjack Hash

Honeyed citrus salad*

Corn bread twists
(such as Pillsbury)

*Place 2 cups grapefruit sections and 2 cups orange sections in a large bowl. Combine 1 tablespoon chopped fresh mint, 1 tablespoon fresh lime juice, and 2 tablespoons honey in a small bowl; stir well with a whisk. Pour dressing over fruit; toss gently to coat.

Game Plan

1. Preheat oven for corn bread twists
2. While oven heats, prepare citrus salad; refrigerate until serving time
3. While twists bake, prepare hash

Lumberjack Hash

TOTAL TIME: 28 MINUTES

    2   teaspoons vegetable oil
    2   teaspoons butter
    1   cup chopped onion
    1   cup chopped green bell pepper
    2   garlic cloves, minced
    8   cups frozen shredded hash brown
        potatoes, thawed (about 1 pound)
    ½   teaspoon salt
    ½   teaspoon black pepper
    4   ounces 33%-less-sodium ham, diced
    ¾   cup (3 ounces) shredded reduced-
        fat cheddar cheese

1. Heat oil and butter in a large nonstick skillet over medium heat. Add onion; cook 5 minutes. Add bell pepper and garlic; cook 3 minutes. Add potatoes, salt,

---

pepper, and ham; cook 16 minutes or until potatoes are golden brown, stirring occasionally. Top with cheese; cook 2 minutes or until cheese melts. Yield: 4 servings (serving size: 1¼ cups).

CALORIES 276 (30% from fat); FAT 9.1g (sat 4.2g, mono 1.6g, poly 1.6g); PROTEIN 16.5g; CARB 33.7g; FIBER 3.5g; CHOL 33mg; IRON 0.8mg; SODIUM 738mg; CALC 208mg

Pancake Breakfast Menu
serves 6

Whole Wheat Buttermilk Pancakes

Fresh fruit salad*

Chai tea

*Combine 3 cups sliced strawberries, 1 cup blueberries, and 1 cup sliced banana in a large bowl. Sprinkle fruit with 1 tablespoon sugar; toss well to combine. Chill until ready to serve.

Game Plan

1. Prepare fruit salad; refrigerate until serving time
2. Prepare pancake batter
3. While pancakes cook, boil water and steep tea

Whole Wheat Buttermilk Pancakes
(pictured on page 94)

Keep cooked pancakes warm in a 200° oven while preparing remaining pancakes.

TOTAL TIME: 20 MINUTES

    ¾   cup all-purpose flour
    ¾   cup whole wheat flour
    3   tablespoons sugar
    1½   teaspoons baking powder
    ½   teaspoon baking soda
    ½   teaspoon salt
    1½   cups low-fat buttermilk
    1   tablespoon vegetable oil
    1   large egg
    1   large egg white
    Cooking spray
    ¾   cup maple syrup
    3   tablespoons butter

Continued

1. Lightly spoon flours into dry measuring cups; level with a knife. Combine flours, sugar, baking powder, baking soda, and salt in a large bowl, stirring with a whisk. Combine buttermilk, oil, egg, and egg white, stirring with a whisk; add to flour mixture, stirring just until moist.

2. Heat a nonstick griddle or nonstick skillet coated with cooking spray over medium heat. Spoon about ¼ cup batter for each pancake onto griddle. Turn pancakes when tops are covered with bubbles and edges look cooked. Serve with syrup and butter. Yield: 6 servings (serving size: 2 pancakes, 2 tablespoons syrup, and 1½ teaspoons butter).

CALORIES 351 (26% from fat); FAT 10g (sat 4.6g, mono 2.8g, poly 1.9g); PROTEIN 7.6g; CARB 59.7g; FIBER 2.3g; CHOL 55mg; IRON 2.1mg; SODIUM 570mg; CALC 176mg

---

Southwestern Breakfast Menu
serves 2

Southwestern Omelet

Quick quesadillas*

Pineapple juice

*Preheat broiler. Coat 4 (6-inch) corn tortillas with cooking spray. Place 2 tortillas, coated sides down, on a baking sheet. Top each tortilla with 2 tablespoons shredded reduced-fat cheddar cheese and 2 teaspoons chopped green onions. Top with remaining tortillas, coated sides up. Broil 2 minutes or until golden. Turn quesadillas over; broil 2 minutes or until tops are golden and cheese is melted. Cut each quesadilla into quarters; serve with salsa and fat-free sour cream.

Game Plan

1. Preheat broiler for quesadillas
2. While oven heats, chop and measure ingredients for quesadillas and omelet
3. Assemble quesadillas
4. While quesadillas cook, prepare omelet

search myclar2003.com for all our menus

Southwestern Omelet

To vary this omelet, use kidney beans and Monterey Jack cheese with jalapeños.

TOTAL TIME: 10 MINUTES

　2　tablespoons chopped fresh cilantro
　¼　teaspoon salt
　4　large egg whites
　1　large egg
　½　cup canned black beans, rinsed
　　　and drained
　¼　cup chopped green onions
　¼　cup (1 ounce) shredded reduced-
　　　fat cheddar cheese
　¼　cup bottled salsa
Cooking spray

1. Combine first 4 ingredients in a medium bowl, stirring with a whisk. Combine beans, onions, cheese, and salsa.
2. Heat a medium nonstick skillet coated with cooking spray over medium heat. Pour egg mixture into pan; let egg mixture set slightly. Tilt pan, and carefully lift edges of omelet with a spatula; allow uncooked portion to flow underneath cooked portion. Cook 3 minutes; flip omelet. Spoon bean mixture onto half of omelet. Carefully loosen omelet with a spatula; fold in half. Cook 1 minute or until cheese melts. Slide omelet onto a plate; cut in half. Yield: 2 servings.

CALORIES 181 (27% from fat); FAT 5.5g (sat 2.3g, mono 1g, poly 0.8g); PROTEIN 20.2g; CARB 13.8g; FIBER 6g; CHOL 116mg; IRON 2.1mg; SODIUM 822mg; CALC 184mg

---

French-Style Breakfast
serves 4

Croque Monsieur

Berry smoothies*

*Place 2 cups fat-free milk, 1 cup frozen raspberries, 1 cup raspberry sorbet, and 1 (8-ounce) carton vanilla low-fat yogurt in a blender; process until smooth. Serve in chilled glasses.

Game Plan

1. Chill glasses for smoothies
2. Prepare sandwiches
3. While sandwiches cook, prepare smoothies

Croque Monsieur

Similar to a Monte Cristo, a croque monsieur is a French-style grilled ham and cheese sandwich that is dipped in egg batter and then cooked in a skillet. Our version is more like stuffed French toast than a sandwich, though. Keep the finished ones warm in a 200° oven while cooking the others.

TOTAL TIME: 20 MINUTES

　4　(1½-ounce) slices French bread
　4　teaspoons honey mustard
　6　ounces reduced-fat deli ham,
　　　thinly sliced
　4　(1-ounce) slices reduced-fat Swiss
　　　cheese
　½　cup fat-free milk
　3　large egg whites
Cooking spray

1. Cut a slit in each bread slice to form a pocket. Spread 1 teaspoon honey mustard into each bread pocket. Divide ham and cheese evenly among bread pockets.
2. Combine milk and egg whites in a shallow bowl, stirring with a whisk. Dip sandwiches, 1 at a time, in milk mixture, turning to coat.
3. Heat a large nonstick skillet coated with cooking spray over medium-high heat. Add 2 sandwiches; cook 3 minutes on each side or until golden brown. Repeat procedure with remaining sandwiches. Yield: 4 servings (serving size: 1 sandwich).

CALORIES 293 (30% from fat); FAT 9.8g (sat 5.2g, mono 0.8g, poly 0.8g); PROTEIN 22.3g; CARB 27.9g; FIBER 1.3g; CHOL 40mg; IRON 1.6mg; SODIUM 649mg; CALC 475mg

Turkish Delights

Let the tastes and flavors of Istanbul's street food transport you to that magical city.

In this vibrant, sprawling city of 12 million, every neighborhood is dotted with *hazir yemek*, or "ready food" establishments.

Street vendors prepare the food in their home kitchens, load their baskets and carts, and wander the neighborhoods, setting up portable shops in the streets and public gardens. Each trader specializes in a particular type of food. One makes Turkish delight and other candies; another, meatballs; yet another, *lahmacun*, the pizza-like flatbread. The recipes that follow re-create the city's flavors and essences. Through them, Istanbul can live in your heart and in your kitchen.

Noah's Pudding

Also known as *asure*, this unique Turkish dessert is made with barley, legumes, dried fruits, and nuts. Traditional folklore holds that Noah gathered all of the remaining foodstuffs to make this sweet pudding when he and his family left the ark. Today it is customary to share the dish with others.

½ cup uncooked pearl barley
1 tablespoon long-grain rice
4 cups water
¼ teaspoon salt
½ cup sugar
½ cup canned chickpeas, rinsed and drained
½ cup canned kidney beans, rinsed and drained
¼ cup raisins
¼ cup dried apricots, finely chopped
¼ cup dried figs, finely chopped
1 tablespoon rose water
3 tablespoons chopped almonds
3 tablespoons chopped pistachios
3 tablespoons pomegranate seeds

1. Place barley and rice in a medium bowl, and cover with water to 2 inches above barley mixture. Cover and soak overnight. Drain.

2. Place barley mixture, 4 cups water, and salt in a large saucepan; bring to a boil. Cover, reduce heat, and simmer 25 minutes. Remove from heat, and drain in a colander over a bowl, reserving 2¼ cups cooking liquid.

3. Place 1½ cups barley mixture and ¼ cup reserved liquid in a food processor; process 2 minutes. Return pureed mixture to saucepan; stir in remaining barley mixture, remaining 2 cups reserved liquid, sugar, and next 5 ingredients. Bring to a boil. Reduce heat; simmer 30 minutes. Remove from heat; stir in rose water, and sprinkle with nuts and pomegranate seeds. Yield: 6 servings (serving size: about 1 cup).

CALORIES 329 (16% from fat); FAT 6g (sat 0.6g, mono 3g, poly 1.2g); PROTEIN 9.9g; CARB 62.6g; FIBER 6.6g; CHOL 0mg; IRON 3.3mg; SODIUM 107mg; CALC 70mg

Fish Sandwiches

Fish sandwiches—sold from small fishing boats and stands by the ferry terminal at the Galata Bridge—are classic Turkish street food. The traditional fish used is the local *lufer;* we used grouper.

4 (6-ounce) grouper fillets (¾ inch thick)
2 teaspoons olive oil
½ teaspoon salt
½ teaspoon freshly ground black pepper
Cooking spray
1 (6-ounce) French bread baguette
4 tablespoons Muhammara (recipe on page 83)
1 teaspoon fresh lemon juice
1 cup thinly sliced onion
1 cup thinly sliced poblano chile
1 cup chopped tomato

1. Prepare grill.

2. Brush both sides of fillets with olive oil. Sprinkle with salt and pepper. Place on grill rack coated with cooking spray; grill 5 minutes on each side or until fish flakes easily when tested with a fork.

3. Cut bread into 4 (1½-ounce) pieces; cut each in half horizontally. Spread Muhammara evenly over top halves of bread. Arrange fish on bottom halves. Sprinkle each fillet with ¼ teaspoon juice; top with ¼ cup onion, ¼ cup poblano, ¼ cup tomato, and top half of bread. Serve immediately. Yield: 4 servings.

(Totals include Muhammara) CALORIES 336 (20% from fat); FAT 7.5g (sat 1.2g, mono 3.4g, poly 2.1g); PROTEIN 31.2g; CARB 35.8g; FIBER 3.7g; CHOL 47mg; IRON 3.5mg; SODIUM 814mg; CALC 100mg

Spicy Kofte

This meat on a skewer is a specialty of the Mediterranean coast of Turkey. Processing the lamb together with all the ingredients and refrigerating allows the flavors to mingle. Though traditionally cooked over an open fire, the skewers can also be cooked in a 450° oven. Serve with pita bread.

1 pound leg of lamb, trimmed and cut into 1-inch cubes
¾ cup chopped fresh parsley
½ cup chopped onion
½ cup chopped fresh mint
2 teaspoons white vinegar
1 teaspoon salt
½ teaspoon chili powder
½ teaspoon freshly ground black pepper
3 garlic cloves
2 (2-ounce) slices whole wheat nut bread (such as Arnold Health Nut)
Cooking spray

1. Place all ingredients except cooking spray in a food processor; process until smooth. Cover and refrigerate 2 hours.

2. Prepare grill.

3. Divide meat mixture into 6 equal portions. Roll each portion into a 6-inch rope. Insert an 8-inch skewer lengthwise through center of each rope.

4. Place kebabs on grill rack coated with cooking spray; grill 4 minutes on each side or until done. Yield: 6 servings.

CALORIES 180 (28% from fat); FAT 5.6g (sat 1.8g, mono 2.2g, poly 0.7g); PROTEIN 18.6g; CARB 14.1g; FIBER 2.6g; CHOL 50mg; IRON 3.6mg; SODIUM 565mg; CALC 57mg

Swordfish Kebabs

This is just one of the many varieties of kebabs available on the streets of Istanbul, where they are often served wrapped in a warm *pide* (flatbread). At home, they can be served with rice pilaf or wrapped in warm pita bread.

  1 cup chopped onion
 ¼ cup fresh lemon juice (about 2 lemons)
  2 tablespoons olive oil
  1 tablespoon minced garlic
  1 teaspoon salt
  1 teaspoon ground cumin
  1 teaspoon paprika
 ½ teaspoon black peppercorns
 ¼ teaspoon crushed red pepper
  1 pound swordfish, cut into (½-inch) cubes
  1 pint large cherry tomatoes
  4 poblano chiles, seeded and cut into 1-inch pieces
Cooking spray

1. Place first 9 ingredients in a food processor; process until smooth. Combine onion mixture and swordfish in a bowl. Cover and refrigerate 30 minutes.

2. Prepare grill.

3. Remove fish from bowl, reserving marinade. Thread fish, cherry tomatoes, and poblano pieces alternately onto each of 8 (12-inch) skewers. Place kebabs on grill rack coated with cooking spray. Cook 10 minutes or until fish flakes easily when tested with a fork, turning and basting frequently with reserved marinade. Yield: 4 servings (serving size: 2 kebabs).

CALORIES 245 (28% from fat); FAT 7.7g (sat 1.7g, mono 3.5g, poly 1.6g); PROTEIN 25.4g; CARB 20.3g; FIBER 5.1g; CHOL 44mg; IRON 2.6mg; SODIUM 702mg; CALC 43mg

Herbed Cheese Pizza
Labmacun

This is Turkey's version of pizza. Kasseri, a semi-hard sheep's milk cheese, is used here, but provolone or manchego are good substitutes. If you are short on time, you can use prepared individual 6-inch pizza crusts or 2 (12-inch) pizza crusts.

DOUGH:

  2 cups bread flour, divided
  1 teaspoon sugar
  2 packages dry yeast (about 4½ teaspoons)
  2 cups warm water (100° to 110°), divided
2½ cups all-purpose flour, divided
  1 teaspoon salt
  2 teaspoons olive oil
Cooking spray

TOPPING:

  2 teaspoons dried oregano
  2 teaspoons ground cumin
  1 teaspoon hot paprika
 ¾ teaspoon coarsely ground black pepper, divided
  1 teaspoon olive oil
  1 cup finely chopped onion
 ½ teaspoon salt
  5 garlic cloves, minced
  1 bay leaf
  1 (28-ounce) can diced tomatoes, undrained
10 ounces thinly sliced kasseri cheese
  3 tablespoons minced fresh parsley

1. To prepare dough, lightly spoon bread flour into dry measuring cups; level with a knife. Combine 1 cup bread flour, sugar, yeast, and 1 cup warm water in a large bowl; let yeast mixture stand 15 minutes.

2. Lightly spoon all-purpose flour into dry measuring cups; level with a knife. Combine 2 cups all-purpose flour, 1 cup bread flour, and 1 teaspoon salt in a large bowl; make a well in center of mixture. Add yeast mixture, 1 cup warm water, and 2 teaspoons oil to flour mixture; stir well. Turn dough out onto a floured surface. Knead until smooth and elastic (about 10 minutes); add enough of remaining all-purpose flour, 1 tablespoon at a time, to prevent dough from sticking to hands (dough will feel tacky).

3. Place dough in a large bowl coated with cooking spray, turning to coat top. Cover and let rise in a warm place (85°), free from drafts, 45 minutes or until doubled in size. (Press two fingers into dough. If indentation remains, dough has risen enough.) Punch dough down; divide dough into 8 equal portions. Cover and let rest 20 minutes.

4. To prepare topping, combine oregano, cumin, paprika, and ½ teaspoon pepper; set aside. Heat 1 teaspoon oil in a large nonstick skillet over medium-high heat. Add onion; sauté 3 minutes. Add ¼ teaspoon pepper, ½ teaspoon salt, garlic, bay leaf, and tomatoes; bring to a boil. Reduce heat to medium; simmer 15 minutes or until thick. Remove from heat; discard bay leaf.

5. Preheat oven to 450°.

6. Working with one portion of dough at a time (cover remaining dough to keep from drying), roll each portion into a 6-inch circle on a lightly floured surface; place circles on a baking sheet coated with cooking spray.

7. Top each crust with ¼ cup tomato mixture, 1¼ ounces cheese, and ½ teaspoon oregano mixture. Bake at 450° for 12 minutes or until crusts are lightly browned. Sprinkle evenly with minced parsley. Yield: 8 servings (serving size: 1 [6-inch] pizza).

CALORIES 434 (28% from fat); FAT 13.4g (sat 6.6g, mono 1.3g, poly 0.2g); PROTEIN 19.7g; CARB 62.6g; FIBER 4.6g; CHOL 35mg; IRON 5.6mg; SODIUM 934mg; CALC 308mg

Muhammara

This pepper puree complements the Spicy Kofte (recipe on page 81) and the Swordfish Kebabs (recipe on page 82) and adds interest to the Fish Sandwiches (recipe on page 81). Originally from southeast Turkey, it has become ubiquitous in Istanbul, where it's used in restaurants as a condiment with just about everything. You can also serve it as a dip with pita or flatbread.

  2   red bell peppers
  2   tablespoons water
  1   tablespoon olive oil
  2   teaspoons balsamic vinegar
  2   teaspoons pomegranate molasses
        or molasses
  1   teaspoon salt
  1   teaspoon cumin seeds
  ¼   teaspoon crushed red pepper
  3   garlic cloves
  2   (2-ounce) slices whole wheat nut
        bread (such as Arnold Health Nut)
  1   habanero pepper, seeded
  ⅓   cup walnuts, toasted

1. Preheat broiler.
2. Cut bell peppers in half lengthwise; discard seeds and membranes. Place pepper halves, skin sides up, on a foil-lined baking sheet; flatten with hand. Broil 15 minutes or until blackened. Place in a zip-top plastic bag; seal. Let stand 20 minutes. Peel.
3. Place bell pepper halves and next 10 ingredients in a food processor; process

until smooth. Add walnuts, and pulse 5 times or until walnuts are coarsely chopped. Yield: 2 cups (serving size: 2 tablespoons).

CALORIES 50 (49% from fat); FAT 2.7g (sat 0.3g, mono 1.1g, poly 1.2g); PROTEIN 1.5g; CARB 5.4g; FIBER 0.9g; CHOL 0mg; IRON 0.5mg; SODIUM 182mg; CALC 11mg

cooking light profile

The Gospel of Good Fish

Chef Dave Pasternack spreads the word about the joys of dining on fish.

Visiting Fulton Fish Market with Dave Pasternack—chef/partner at Esca, the upscale Italian restaurant causing a sensation in New York's theater district—at 3 a.m. is an educational experience. Dave knows fish—where they come from, what they feed on, and how they're caught. He knows the people who cook them, who sell them, and who pull in the nets.

Not only does Dave know fish, he loves fish. In fact, when you consider that he cuts and serves them at his restaurant six days a week, then spends his days off reeling them in, you might say he is obsessed.

Although trained in French cooking technique, Dave has made a name for himself reinventing Italian seafood, with the aim of bringing out natural complexities and flavors. His straightforward approach relies strictly on fresh herbs—some of which he grows himself—a variety of unprocessed sea salts, extra-virgin olive oils from every corner of Italy, and the finest seafood.

His dishes are simple and give diners the sense they could make them at home.

At home, Dave tends to approach his meals the same way that he does at work. A typical at-home dinner for him and his wife might include some homegrown broccoli with garlic, couscous, Dave's "killer" salad, and of course, fresh fish. "Nothing fancy, just bread the fish, chop some herbs, bake it, and finish with a little olive oil," Dave says. "It's the best and the simplest way to eat fish—the best."

Seared Tuna with Arugula Salad

When Dave Pasternack serves this recipe in his restaurant, he cooks fresh artichokes, chops the hearts, and tosses them with the salad.

  4   (6-ounce) Yellowfin tuna steaks
          (about ¾ inch thick)
  1½   teaspoons freshly ground black
          pepper, divided
  ¾   teaspoon kosher salt, divided
  2   tablespoons olive oil, divided
  2   tablespoons fresh lemon juice
  8   cups arugula leaves
  2   cups thinly sliced fennel bulb
          (about 1 small bulb)

1. Sprinkle tuna steaks with 1 teaspoon pepper and ¼ teaspoon salt. Heat 1 tablespoon oil in a large nonstick skillet over medium-high heat. Add tuna steaks; cook 2 minutes on each side or until desired degree of doneness.
2. Combine ½ teaspoon pepper, ½ teaspoon salt, 1 tablespoon oil, and juice in a large bowl; stir with a whisk. Add arugula and fennel; toss well. Place about 2 cups salad on each of 4 plates; top each serving with 1 tuna steak. Yield: 4 servings.

CALORIES 276 (29% from fat); FAT 8.8g (sat 1.3g, mono 5.2g, poly 1.1g); PROTEIN 41.7g; CARB 6.9g; FIBER 2g; CHOL 77mg; IRON 2.3mg; SODIUM 544mg; CALC 124mg

Spring Collection

The chic vary their wardrobes of classics simply by changing accessories. You can do the same with these timeless dishes.

Our spring collection features the familiar pastels of this time of year—pale greens and butter yellows—using seasonal produce to lend freshness and variety to classic kitchen standbys. These six recipes are fabulously adaptable. To demonstrate, we've provided two variations on each recipe's theme. Some are ideal for company, others for Thursday dinners when everyone's bushed. Master the main recipe and you can create your own new variations, as well.

Pasta Primavera

This harbinger of spring is colorful, fragrant, and fresh tasting.

1½ cups baby carrots, trimmed (about 6 ounces)
3 cups uncooked cavatappi or penne pasta (about 8 ounces)
1 teaspoon olive oil
2 cups pattypan squash, halved (about 8 ounces)
¾ cup shelled green peas
1 teaspoon salt
¼ teaspoon freshly ground black pepper
2 garlic cloves, minced
¼ cup dry white wine
⅓ cup whipping cream
1 tablespoon fresh lemon juice
¼ cup (1 ounce) grated fresh Parmesan cheese
¼ cup thinly sliced fresh basil
¼ cup chopped fresh parsley

1. Bring 2 quarts of water to a boil in a stockpot. Add carrots; cook 3 minutes. Remove with a slotted spoon. Add pasta to boiling water; cook according to package directions, omitting salt and fat. Drain.
2. Heat oil in a large nonstick skillet over medium-high heat. Add squash; sauté 3 minutes. Add carrots, peas, salt, pepper, and garlic; sauté 2 minutes. Stir in wine, scraping pan to loosen browned bits. Stir in cream and juice; cook 1 minute. Add pasta and cheese; stir well to coat. Remove from heat; stir in basil and parsley. Yield: 4 servings (serving size: 2 cups).

WINE NOTE: Squash, peas, carrots, and an ample amount of herbs give this pasta a satisfying freshness that's made luxurious by cream and Parmesan. A crisp Sauvignon Blanc would be perfect—especially one that's refined and effortless to drink. Try Robert Mondavi Fumé Blanc from the Napa Valley (about $18).
NOTE: Fumé Blanc is just another name for Sauvignon Blanc.

CALORIES 373 (28% from fat); FAT 11.8g (sat 6.1g, mono 3.6g, poly 1.1g); PROTEIN 13.9g; CARB 53.8g; FIBER 4.5g; CHOL 32mg; IRON 3.9mg; SODIUM 731mg; CALC 150mg

Variations:

PASTA PRIMAVERA WITH SHRIMP AND SUGAR SNAP PEAS:

Substitute 2 cups sugar snap peas for green peas; cook sugar snap peas in boiling water with carrots. Substitute 1 pound peeled and deveined medium shrimp for pattypan squash; sauté 2 minutes. Stir in 2 cups trimmed arugula and 2 tablespoons chopped green onions with basil and parsley. Yield: 4 servings (serving size: 2¼ cups).

CALORIES 501 (24% from fat); FAT 13.5g (sat 6.4g, mono 3.9g, poly 1.7g); PROTEIN 36.4g; CARB 57.3g; FIBER 5g; CHOL 204mg; IRON 6.5mg; SODIUM 972mg; CALC 252mg

PASTA PRIMAVERA WITH CHICKEN AND ASPARAGUS:

Substitute 2 cups (1-inch) sliced asparagus for carrot. Substitute 12 ounces skinless, boneless chicken breast for pattypan squash. Cut chicken crosswise into ¼-inch-wide strips; sauté 5 minutes. Increase green peas to 1 cup. Stir in 2 tablespoons chopped green onions with basil and parsley. Yield: 4 servings (serving size: 2 cups).

CALORIES 463 (24% from fat); FAT 12.6g (sat 6.4g, mono 3.9g, poly 1.2g); PROTEIN 33.6g; CARB 53.1g; FIBER 5.1g; CHOL 81mg; IRON 4.4mg; SODIUM 773mg; CALC 154mg

Arugula and Fontina Soufflé

Serve this light, savory soufflé at brunch or at dinner as a side for beef or chicken.

Cooking spray
½ cup dry breadcrumbs
6 ounces trimmed arugula (about 9 cups)
⅓ cup all-purpose flour
½ teaspoon salt
⅛ teaspoon ground nutmeg
⅛ teaspoon ground red pepper
⅛ teaspoon freshly ground black pepper
1¼ cups 1% low-fat milk
1 large egg yolk, lightly beaten
½ cup (2 ounces) shredded fontina cheese
6 large egg whites
Dash of cream of tartar

1. Preheat oven to 350°.
2. Coat a 2-quart soufflé dish with cooking spray; sprinkle breadcrumbs over bottom and sides of dish.
3. Cook arugula in boiling water 15 seconds or until wilted, and drain in a sieve, pressing until barely moist. Finely chop; place in a large bowl.
4. Lightly spoon flour into a dry measuring cup; level with a knife. Place flour, salt, nutmeg, red pepper, and black pepper in a medium saucepan. Gradually add milk, stirring with a whisk until blended. Bring to a boil over medium heat, stirring constantly. Cook 1 minute or until thick.
5. Gradually stir about one-fourth of hot

milk mixture into egg yolk, stirring constantly with a whisk, and add to remaining hot milk mixture, stirring constantly. Cook 30 seconds, and remove from heat. Stir in arugula and cheese. Cool slightly.

6. Place egg whites and cream of tartar in a large bowl, and beat with a mixer at high speed until stiff peaks form. Gently stir one-fourth of egg white mixture into arugula mixture; gently fold in remaining egg white mixture. Spoon into prepared soufflé dish. Bake at 350° for 45 minutes or until puffed, golden, and set. Serve immediately. Yield: 6 servings.

WINE NOTE: In France the choice for this dish would be a Sancerre or Pouilly Fumé, both of which are light, crisp wines made with Sauvignon Blanc grapes. Of course, there are dozens of fabulous Sauvignon Blancs made in the United States, too. A sassy light one that would be terrific here: Geyser Peak's Sauvignon Blanc from Sonoma County (about $10).

CALORIES 154 (30% from fat); FAT 5.1g (sat 2.5g, mono 1.5g, poly 0.5g); PROTEIN 10.8g; CARB 16g; FIBER 0.9g; CHOL 50mg; IRON 1.4mg; SODIUM 437mg; CALC 178mg

Variations:

ASPARAGUS AND GRUYÈRE SOUFFLÉ:

Substitute ¾ pound asparagus for arugula. Cook asparagus in boiling water 4 minutes; drain and rinse with cold water. Cut a 1-inch tip from each asparagus spear; finely chop stalks. Substitute 1 teaspoon dry mustard for ground red pepper. Substitute ½ cup (2 ounces) shredded Gruyère for fontina. Stir in asparagus tips and chopped asparagus with cheese. Yield: 6 servings.

CALORIES 165 (29% from fat); FAT 5.3g (sat 2.5g, mono 1.6g, poly 0.4g); PROTEIN 11.9g; CARB 17.5g; FIBER 1.7g; CHOL 49mg; IRON 1.6mg; SODIUM 387mg; CALC 191mg

SPINACH AND FETA SOUFFLÉ:

Substitute 10 ounces baby spinach (about 8 cups) for arugula. Substitute ½ cup (2 ounces) crumbled feta cheese for fontina. Stir in spinach and 2 teaspoons chopped fresh dill with cheese. Yield: 6 servings.

CALORIES 143 (26% from fat); FAT 4.1g (sat 2.1g, mono 1.1g, poly 0.3g); PROTEIN 10.1g; CARB 16.5g; FIBER 1.5g; CHOL 47mg; IRON 2.1mg; SODIUM 490mg; CALC 167mg

White Bean Salad with Shrimp and Asparagus

(pictured on page 93)

Warm bacon vinaigrette wilts the fresh spinach. This salad is best eaten immediately after tossing.

 2 cups (1-inch) sliced asparagus (about ½ pound)
 ¾ pound medium shrimp, peeled and deveined
 ½ teaspoon freshly ground black pepper, divided
 ¼ teaspoon salt, divided
 1 teaspoon vegetable oil
 2 cups torn spinach
 1 (19-ounce) can cannellini beans, rinsed and drained
 3 bacon slices
 ½ cup chopped Vidalia green onions
 1 garlic clove, minced
 ¼ cup fat-free, less-sodium chicken broth
 1 tablespoon chopped fresh parsley
 2 tablespoons fresh lemon juice
 1 tablespoon cider vinegar

1. Steam asparagus, covered, 3 minutes. Drain and rinse with cold water.
2. Sprinkle shrimp with ⅛ teaspoon pepper and ⅛ teaspoon salt. Heat oil in a medium nonstick skillet over medium-high heat. Add shrimp; sauté 4 minutes. Remove from pan; place in a large bowl. Add asparagus, spinach, and beans to shrimp; toss well.
3. Add bacon to pan; cook over medium heat until crisp. Remove bacon from pan; crumble. Reserve 2 teaspoons drippings in pan. Add onions and garlic; cook 3 minutes or until soft, stirring frequently. Remove from heat; add remaining pepper, ⅛ teaspoon salt, bacon, broth, and remaining 3 ingredients. Drizzle dressing over salad; toss to coat. Serve immediately. Yield: 4 servings (serving size: 1¾ cups).

CALORIES 245 (29% from fat); FAT 7.8g (sat 2.4g, mono 2.6g, poly 2.1g); PROTEIN 24.5g; CARB 19.1g; FIBER 5.5g; CHOL 136mg; IRON 4.5mg; SODIUM 578mg; CALC 108mg

Variations:

WHITE BEAN SALAD WITH CHICKEN AND SUGAR SNAP PEAS:

Substitute 2 cups sugar snap peas for asparagus. Substitute ½ pound boneless, skinless chicken breast for shrimp; cook 4 minutes on each side or until done. Shred cooked chicken. Substitute 2 cups arugula for spinach. Yield: 4 servings (serving size: 1¼ cups).

CALORIES 229 (23% from fat); FAT 5.8g (sat 2.1g, mono 2.3g, poly 1g); PROTEIN 20.8g; CARB 22.7g; FIBER 6.2g; CHOL 39mg; IRON 2.6mg; SODIUM 550mg; CALC 103mg

WHITE BEAN SALAD WITH TUNA AND HARICOTS VERTS:

Substitute 2 cups haricots verts for asparagus. Substitute 1 (8-ounce) tuna steak for shrimp; cook 3 minutes on each side or until desired degree of doneness. Cut into bite-sized pieces. Substitute 2 cups torn radicchio for spinach. Yield: 4 servings (serving size: 1½ cups).

CALORIES 221 (28% from fat); FAT 6.8g (sat 2.2g, mono 2.5g, poly 1.7g); PROTEIN 19.9g; CARB 20g; FIBER 5.9g; CHOL 32mg; IRON 2.6mg; SODIUM 469mg; CALC 70mg

Cream of Asparagus Soup

For a vegetarian version, use vegetable broth in place of chicken broth. Garnish with thin asparagus spears for a graceful presentation.

 3 cups (½-inch) sliced asparagus (about 1 pound)
 2 cups fat-free, less-sodium chicken broth
 ¾ teaspoon fresh thyme, divided
 1 bay leaf
 1 garlic clove, crushed
 1 tablespoon all-purpose flour
 2 cups 1% low-fat milk
 Dash of ground nutmeg
 2 teaspoons butter
 ¾ teaspoon salt
 ¼ teaspoon grated lemon rind

1. Combine asparagus, broth, ½ teaspoon thyme, bay leaf, and garlic in a large saucepan over medium-high heat; bring to a boil. Reduce heat, cover, and
Continued

simmer 10 minutes. Discard bay leaf. Place asparagus mixture in a blender; process until smooth.

2. Place flour in pan. Gradually add milk, stirring with a whisk until blended. Stir in pureed asparagus and ground nutmeg. Bring to a boil. Reduce heat; simmer 5 minutes, stirring constantly. Remove from heat, and stir in ¼ teaspoon thyme, butter, salt, and lemon rind. Yield 4 servings (serving size: 1¼ cups).

CALORIES 117 (27% from fat); FAT 3.5g (sat 2g, mono 0.8g, poly 0.2g); PROTEIN 8.9g; CARB 14g; FIBER 2.5g; CHOL 13mg; IRON 1.1mg; SODIUM 748mg; CALC 163mg

Variations:

CREAM OF CARROT SOUP:

Substitute 2 cups baby carrots for asparagus. Omit bay leaf. Yield: 4 servings (serving size: 1 cup).

CALORIES 112 (28% from fat); FAT 3.5g (sat 2g, mono 0.8g, poly 0.2g); PROTEIN 6.7g; CARB 13.4g; FIBER 1.1g; CHOL 13mg; IRON 0.6mg; SODIUM 765mg; CALC 152mg

CREAM OF LEEK SOUP:

Substitute 3 cups sliced leek for asparagus. Substitute ¾ teaspoon rosemary for thyme. Omit bay leaf. Yield: 4 servings (serving size: 1 cup).

CALORIES 131 (23% from fat); FAT 3.4g (sat 2g, mono 0.8g, poly 0.2g); PROTEIN 7.3g; CARB 18.3g; FIBER 1.3g; CHOL 13mg; IRON 1.5mg; SODIUM 759mg; CALC 178mg

Eats for Eight Menu
serves 8

Brush the salmon fillets with a mixture of equal parts molasses and lime juice halfway through the cooking time for added flavor.

Broiled salmon fillets

Potato Gratin with Baby Carrots and Asiago

Arugula-apple salad with pecorino*

*Combine 8 cups baby spinach and 4 cups trimmed arugula in a large bowl. Arrange 1½ cups greens on each of 8 salad plates. Top each serving with ½ cup sliced Granny Smith apple and 2 tablespoons shaved pecorino or Parmesan cheese. Drizzle each serving with 1½ tablespoons bottled low-fat balsamic dressing.

search myclar2003.com for all our menus

Potato Gratin with Haricots Verts and Ham

Haricots verts is French for green beans. The key to making these potatoes rich and flavorful without adding lots of butter is simmering them in milk before baking.

    3   cups 2% low-fat milk
    2   pounds small red potatoes, thinly
        sliced
    2   garlic cloves, thinly sliced
    2   bay leaves
    4   ounces haricots verts, trimmed
Cooking spray
    ½   cup thinly sliced deli smoked ham,
        chopped
    1   cup (4 ounces) shredded Gruyère
        cheese
    ½   teaspoon salt
    ¼   teaspoon freshly ground black
        pepper
    ⅛   teaspoon ground nutmeg

1. Preheat oven to 400°.
2. Combine first 4 ingredients in a large saucepan over medium heat; bring to a boil, stirring constantly. Reduce heat; simmer 10 minutes, stirring frequently. Remove from heat, and let stand 10 minutes. Drain potatoes in a colander over a bowl, reserving 1 cup milk mixture. Discard bay leaves.
3. Cook haricots verts in boiling water 2 minutes or until crisp-tender. Rinse with cold water; drain.
4. Arrange half of potatoes in bottom of a 13 x 9-inch baking dish coated with cooking spray. Arrange haricots verts and ham over potatoes. Sprinkle with half of cheese, salt, and pepper. Top with remaining potatoes. Sprinkle with remaining cheese, salt, and pepper. Stir nutmeg into reserved milk mixture; pour over potatoes.
5. Cover with foil; cut 3 (1-inch) slits in foil. Bake at 400° for 20 minutes. Uncover and bake an additional 20 minutes or until cheese begins to brown. Let stand 10 minutes before serving. Yield: 8 servings.

CALORIES 208 (29% from fat); FAT 6.8g (sat 3.9g, mono 1.9g, poly 0.4g); PROTEIN 11.5g; CARB 26.2g; FIBER 2.3g; CHOL 27mg; IRON 1.2mg; SODIUM 352mg; CALC 270mg

Variations:

POTATO GRATIN WITH BABY CARROTS AND ASIAGO:

Substitute 6 fresh thyme sprigs for bay leaves. Substitute 6 ounces baby carrots (about 1½ cups) for haricots verts. Substitute 1 cup (4 ounces) shredded Asiago cheese for Gruyère. Yield: 8 servings.

CALORIES 206 (27% from fat); FAT 6.2g (sat 3.8g, mono 1.6g, poly 0.3g); PROTEIN 11.2g; CARB 27.3g; FIBER 2.2g; CHOL 24mg; IRON 1.3mg; SODIUM 348mg; CALC 262mg

POTATO GRATIN WITH BABY SPINACH, TURKEY, AND WHITE CHEDDAR:

Substitute 8 ounces baby spinach for haricots verts; cook 30 seconds. Substitute ½ cup chopped deli smoked turkey for smoked ham. Substitute 1 cup (4 ounces) shredded sharp white cheddar cheese for Gruyère. Yield: 8 servings.

CALORIES 208 (30% from fat); FAT 7g (sat 4.2g, mono 1.8g, poly 0.3g); PROTEIN 11.3g; CARB 26.3g; FIBER 2.1g; CHOL 26mg; IRON 1.9mg; SODIUM 414mg; CALC 251mg

Risotto with Sugar Snap Peas and Spring Leeks

Use both the white and light green portions of the leek.

    4   cups fat-free, less-sodium chicken
        broth
    1½ cups sugar snap peas, trimmed
    1   tablespoon olive oil
    1½ cups (½-inch-thick) sliced leek
    ½   cup chopped carrot
    1   cup Arborio rice
    ¼   cup dry vermouth
    ¼   teaspoon salt
    ¼   teaspoon dried oregano
    ½   cup (2 ounces) grated fresh
        Parmesan cheese
    1   teaspoon butter
    ½   teaspoon fresh lemon juice
    ⅛   teaspoon freshly ground black
        pepper

1. Bring broth to a simmer in a medium saucepan (do not boil). Keep warm over low heat.
2. Cook peas in boiling water 3 minutes or until crisp-tender. Drain and rinse with cold water; drain.

3. Heat oil in a large nonstick skillet over medium-high heat. Add leek and carrot; sauté 5 minutes or until tender. Add rice; cook 3 minutes, stirring constantly. Stir in 1 cup broth; cook 5 minutes or until liquid is nearly absorbed, stirring frequently. Stir in ½ cup broth, vermouth, salt, and oregano, stirring until broth is absorbed. Add remaining broth, ½ cup at a time, stirring frequently until each portion of broth is absorbed before adding next (about 25 minutes). Add peas; cook 4 minutes. Stir in cheese and remaining ingredients. Yield: 4 servings (serving size: 1¼ cups).

WINE NOTE: Why not mirror all the greenness of the sugar snap peas and leeks with a wine that's got its own green drama going on? A great bet, and a steal: Brancott Vineyards Sauvignon Blanc from Marlborough, New Zealand (about $10).

CALORIES 400 (20% from fat); FAT 8.7g (sat 3.7g, mono 4g, poly 0.5g); PROTEIN 15.3g; CARB 59.6g; FIBER 3.8g; CHOL 13mg; IRON 1.8mg; SODIUM 936mg; CALC 275mg

Variations:

RISOTTO WITH SHRIMP AND ASPARAGUS:

Substitute 3 cups (1-inch) sliced asparagus for sugar snap peas. Substitute 1 cup chopped onion for leek. Omit carrot and oregano. Stir in ½ pound peeled and deveined medium shrimp with blanched asparagus for last 4 minutes of cooking. Yield: 4 servings (serving size: 1¼ cups).

CALORIES 443 (20% from fat); FAT 9.8g (sat 4g, mono 4.2g, poly 1g); PROTEIN 27.1g; CARB 56g; FIBER 3.9g; CHOL 100mg; IRON 2.9mg; SODIUM 957mg; CALC 274mg

RISOTTO WITH VIDALIA GREEN ONIONS AND BLUE CHEESE:

Omit sugar snap peas. Substitute 1½ cups thinly sliced Vidalia green onions for leeks. (Vidalia green onions have a rounded bulb and are sweeter than regular green onions, but you can also use green onions or leeks.) Stir in 1 teaspoon minced garlic and 1 bay leaf with rice. Substitute ¼ cup (1 ounce) crumbled blue cheese for Parmesan. Stir in ¼ cup chopped fresh parsley when risotto is done. Serve with roast chicken, ham, or pork. Yield: 4 servings (serving size: ¾ cup).

CALORIES 366 (22% from fat); FAT 8.8g (sat 3.9g, mono 4g, poly 0.5g); PROTEIN 12.2g; CARB 52.6g; FIBER 3.2g; CHOL 14mg; IRON 0.9mg; SODIUM 869mg; CALC 181mg

Cultural Fusion

From musical choices to supper selections, these newlyweds create a world beat all their own.

Emi Ponce de Souza and her husband, Eric, have mastered the art of blending cultures—from cooking to musical styles. Emi, 23, is from Mexico City, and Eric, 28, is from San Francisco; they now live in Dallas. The Souzas used to sing and play guitar at local spots, merging modern sounds with traditional ones. That same fusion is now taking place in their kitchen.

"We started experimenting together with all sorts of recipes," Emi says. "Among those recipes are very traditional, typical Mexican dishes. Rajas Poblanos is one of those recipes that simply evokes home to me."

"The dish is a practical way to bring the traditional warmth and flavor of old Mexican food to everyday life," Emi says. "*Rajas* is a term that refers to both roasted, sliced chiles and the creamy dish in which they are used. Although the degree of heat from the chiles can vary, their warm flavors are unmistakably Mexican."

This dish, great for a crowd, is usually served buffet-style in large clay bowls. Guests help themselves to the warm tortillas and spoon the rajas onto them. Emi and Eric substitute chicken breasts for the flank steak when it's just the two of them.

Rajas Poblanos

6 poblano chiles (about 1¼ pounds)
1 teaspoon olive oil
1 pound flank steak, trimmed and cut into ¼-inch strips
1 cup chopped onion
2 garlic cloves, minced
¾ cup plain fat-free yogurt
½ cup (4 ounces) ⅓-less-fat cream cheese, softened
1½ cups fresh corn kernels (about 3 ears)
1 teaspoon chicken-flavored bouillon granules
½ teaspoon black pepper
½ teaspoon ground cumin
⅓ cup chopped fresh cilantro (optional)
16 (6-inch) corn tortillas
Cilantro sprigs (optional)

1. Preheat broiler.
2. Cut chiles in half lengthwise, and discard seeds and membranes. Place chile halves, skin sides up, on a foil-lined baking sheet; flatten with hand. Broil 10 minutes or until blackened. Place chiles in a zip-top plastic bag, and seal. Let stand 10 minutes. Peel and cut into ¼-inch strips.
3. Heat oil in a large nonstick skillet over medium-high heat. Add steak, onion, and garlic; sauté 6 minutes. Add chiles, and sauté 2 minutes. Add yogurt and cream cheese; stir until cheese melts. Stir in corn, bouillon, black pepper, and cumin. Cover and cook over low heat 10 minutes. Stir in chopped cilantro, if desired. Spoon about ¼ cup steak mixture into center of each tortilla, and fold in half. Garnish with cilantro sprigs, if desired. Yield: 8 servings (serving size: 2 tortillas).

CALORIES 350 (24% from fat); FAT 9.2g (sat 3.4g, mono 3g, poly 1.2g); PROTEIN 23.7g; CARB 46.9g; FIBER 6g; CHOL 40mg; IRON 3.9mg; SODIUM 343mg; CALC 188mg

Cambodian Summer Rolls

"While the rolling can take a while, the result is worth it. I usually have all the ingredients ready and prepare the rolls for my guests while they gather around the kitchen."

—Cathy Jo Belford, Novato, California

ROLLS:

- 6 cups water
- 1 pound medium shrimp
- 6 ounces uncooked rice noodles
- 12 (8-inch) round sheets rice paper
- ¼ cup hoisin sauce
- 3 cups shredded red leaf lettuce
- ¼ cup thinly sliced fresh basil
- ¼ cup thinly sliced fresh mint

DIPPING SAUCE:

- ⅓ cup low-sodium soy sauce
- ¼ cup water
- 2 tablespoons sugar
- 2 tablespoons chopped fresh cilantro
- 2 tablespoons fresh lime juice
- 1 teaspoon minced peeled fresh ginger
- 1 teaspoon chile paste with garlic
- 1 garlic clove, minced

1. To prepare rolls, bring 6 cups water to a boil in a large saucepan. Add shrimp; cook 3 minutes or until done. Drain and rinse with cold water. Peel shrimp; chill.
2. Place rice noodles in a large bowl; cover with boiling water. Let stand 8 minutes; drain.
3. Add cold water to a large, shallow dish to a depth of 1 inch. Place 1 rice paper sheet in water. Let stand 2 minutes or until soft. Place rice paper sheet on a flat surface.
4. Spread 1 teaspoon hoisin sauce in center of sheet; top with 2 or 3 shrimp, ¼ cup lettuce, about ¼ cup rice noodles, 1 teaspoon basil, and 1 teaspoon mint. Fold sides of sheet over filling, roll up jelly roll fashion, and gently press seam to seal. Place roll, seam side down, on a serving platter; cover to keep from drying. Repeat procedure with remaining rice paper, hoisin sauce, shrimp, lettuce, rice noodles, basil, and mint.
5. To prepare dipping sauce, combine soy sauce and remaining 7 ingredients in a small bowl; stir with a whisk. Yield: 12 servings (serving size: 1 roll and about 1½ tablespoons sauce).

CALORIES 140 (5% from fat); FAT 0.8g (sat 0.1g, mono 0.1g, poly 0.3g); PROTEIN 9g; CARB 23.5g; FIBER 0.7g; CHOL 47mg; IRON 1.3mg; SODIUM 385mg; CALC 32mg

Lettuce Wraps

"I love eating lettuce wraps in restaurants, but they can be too hot for my husband and daughter. These are milder, really fast to prepare, and even my two-year-old loves them."

—Sarah Parslow, South Providence, Utah

- 2 teaspoons olive oil
- 2 (4-ounce) skinless, boneless chicken breast halves, cut into thin strips
- 2 tablespoons grated peeled fresh ginger
- 2 tablespoons teriyaki sauce
- 2 tablespoons rice vinegar
- 1 tablespoon honey
- ½ to 1 teaspoon crushed red pepper
- ½ teaspoon cornstarch
- 1½ cups grated carrot
- 1 cup fresh bean sprouts
- 1 cup snow peas, trimmed and cut lengthwise into thin strips
- ½ cup sliced green onions
- ¼ cup sliced almonds, toasted
- 12 Bibb lettuce leaves

1. Heat oil in a wok or large nonstick skillet over medium-high heat. Add chicken and ginger; sauté 5 minutes or until chicken is done.
2. Combine teriyaki sauce, rice vinegar, honey, red pepper, and cornstarch in a small bowl; stir with a whisk. Add teriyaki mixture to chicken mixture in wok; stir in carrot, bean sprouts, snow peas, and onions. Cook 3 minutes or until sauce thickens slightly, stirring often. Stir in almonds.
3. Spoon ¼ cup chicken mixture onto each lettuce leaf; roll up. Yield: 4 servings (serving size: 3 wraps).

CALORIES 189 (30% from fat); FAT 6.2g (sat 0.8g, mono 3.8g, poly 1.2g); PROTEIN 17g; CARB 17.3g; FIBER 3.8g; CHOL 33mg; IRON 1.8mg; SODIUM 403mg; CALC 53mg

Japanese Chicken Salad

"I like to eat this during the warm months and serve it with a cold fruit salad of kiwi, mandarin oranges, and a little shredded coconut."

—Jan Hughes, Fort Worth, Texas

- 2 cups water
- 2 chicken-flavored bouillon cubes
- 1 pound skinless, boneless chicken breast
- 1 (2-inch) piece peeled fresh ginger, sliced
- ¼ cup sugar
- ¼ cup fresh lemon juice
- 2 teaspoons vegetable oil
- ¼ teaspoon salt
- ¼ teaspoon black pepper
- 12 cups torn iceberg lettuce (1 head)
- ½ cup chow mein noodles
- ⅓ cup sliced green onions
- ¼ cup sliced almonds, toasted
- 2 tablespoons sesame seeds, toasted

1. Combine water and bouillon cubes in a large, heavy saucepan over medium-high heat; stir until bouillon cubes dissolve. Add chicken and ginger; bring to a boil. Reduce heat to low; simmer 20 minutes or until chicken is done. Cool chicken in broth; discard broth. Shred chicken with 2 forks.
2. Combine sugar, lemon juice, oil, salt, and pepper in a small bowl; stir with a whisk.
3. Combine lettuce and remaining 4 ingredients in a large bowl. Add chicken and dressing, tossing to coat. Serve immediately. Yield: 5 servings (serving size: 2 cups).

CALORIES 248 (29% from fat); FAT 8.1g (sat 1.2g, mono 3g, poly 3.2g); PROTEIN 24.5g; CARB 19.6g; FIBER 3.2g; CHOL 53mg; IRON 1.8mg; SODIUM 737mg; CALC 71mg

Tortilla Chicken Soup

"Our family always spends Christmas in Mexico, where we discovered this recipe. I like to serve the soup over hot cooked rice along with some bread for an entire meal. We usually make a big pot, freeze it in small batches, and heat it up as needed."

—Lisa Revelli, Oakland, California

```
1   teaspoon vegetable oil
1   cup finely chopped onion
2   garlic cloves, minced
1   tablespoon chili powder
1   teaspoon ground cumin
1   teaspoon dried oregano
2   (14-ounce) cans fat-free,
    less-sodium chicken broth
2   (14.5-ounce) cans no-salt-added
    diced tomatoes, undrained
1   (16-ounce) can fat-free refried
    beans
1   bay leaf
2   ounces baked tortilla chips,
    crushed (about 2 cups)
```

1. Heat oil in a large saucepan over medium heat. Add onion and garlic; sauté 3 minutes. Add chili powder and next 6 ingredients. Bring to a boil; reduce heat, and simmer 45 minutes. Remove from heat; discard bay leaf. Ladle into bowls; top with chips. Yield: 4 servings (serving size: 2 cups soup and about ½ cup chips).

CALORIES 256 (14% from fat); FAT 4.1g (sat 1.1g, mono 0.5g, poly 1.3g); PROTEIN 12.6g; CARB 44.5g; FIBER 10.1g; CHOL 4mg; IRON 3.5mg; SODIUM 700mg; CALC 155mg

Candy Clouds

"These desserts fulfill the craving for something sweet without the guilt."

—Ellen Siegel, Hastings-on-Hudson, New York

```
3   large egg whites
⅛   teaspoon cream of tartar
⅓   cup sugar
¼   teaspoon almond extract
2   tablespoons unsweetened cocoa
```

1. Preheat oven to 200°.
2. Cover a baking sheet with parchment paper; secure with masking tape.

3. Place egg whites and cream of tartar in a large bowl; beat with a mixer at high speed until foamy. Add sugar, 1 tablespoon at a time, beating until stiff peaks form. Beat in extract.
4. Spoon mixture into a pastry bag fitted with a ¼-inch round tip or into a large zip-top plastic bag with 1 corner snipped to a ¼-inch opening. Pipe 40 (1-inch-round) mounds ¼ inch apart onto prepared baking sheet. Bake at 200° for 2 hours.
5. Turn oven off; cool meringues in closed oven at least 1 hour. Carefully remove meringues from paper. Combine meringues and cocoa in a large zip-top plastic bag; seal and shake to coat. Yield: 10 servings (serving size: 4 clouds).

CALORIES 35 (3% from fat); FAT 0.1g (sat 0.1g, mono 0g, poly 0g); PROTEIN 1.3g; CARB 7.3g; FIBER 0.3g; CHOL 0mg; IRON 0.2mg; SODIUM 17mg; CALC 2mg

back to the best

Sour Cream Pound Cake

Readers never get enough of this Sour Cream Pound Cake. Frankly, neither do we. In fact, we love it so much that we named it one of our 10 best recipes ever in Cooking Light Annual Recipes 1998.

Over the years, this cake has become a staff standby for birthdays, showers, and holidays. And in all the times we've made it, we've come to admire its versatility. Varying the flavor is easy:

• Lemon: Add 1 teaspoon grated lemon rind
• Coconut: Decrease vanilla to 1 teaspoon; add 1 teaspoon coconut extract
• Almond: Decrease vanilla to 1 teaspoon; add 1 teaspoon almond extract

Any way you want it, try making it when you crave something simple and delicious. That's exactly what we do.

Sour Cream Pound Cake

This cake can also be baked in a Bundt pan at 300° for 1 hour and 35 minutes.

```
3    cups sugar
¾    cup butter, softened
1⅓   cups egg substitute
1½   cups low-fat sour cream
1    teaspoon baking soda
4½   cups sifted cake flour
¼    teaspoon salt
2    teaspoons vanilla extract
     Cooking spray
     Fresh blackberries (optional)
     Mint sprigs (optional)
```

1. Preheat oven to 325°.
2. Place sugar and butter in a large bowl; beat with a mixer at medium speed until well blended (about 5 minutes). Gradually add egg substitute, beating well.
3. Combine sour cream and baking soda. Stir well. Combine flour and salt. Add flour mixture to sugar mixture alternately with sour cream mixture, beginning and ending with flour mixture. Stir in vanilla.
4. Pour batter into a 10-inch tube pan coated with cooking spray. Bake at 325° for 1 hour and 35 minutes or until a wooden pick inserted in center comes out clean. Cool in pan 10 minutes on wire rack; remove from pan. Cool completely on wire rack. Garnish with blackberries and mint, if desired. Yield: 24 servings (serving size: 1 slice).
NOTE: Eight egg whites can be used in place of egg substitute, if desired. Add one at a time to sugar mixture.

CALORIES 250 (28% from fat); FAT 7.7g (sat 2.3g, mono 3.1g, poly 1.9g); PROTEIN 3.5g; CARB 41.9g; FIBER 0g; CHOL 6mg; IRON 1.8mg; SODIUM 170mg; CALC 25mg

A Fancy for Sandwiches

Tempt and satisfy your guests with these dressed-up sandwiches.

A sun-splashed Saturday can be all the reason you need to ring up a friend or two for an impromptu midday celebration. These sandwiches—considerably more interesting than plain old turkey breast on whole wheat—are intriguing enough to pique your guests' interest, yet light enough that they won't spoil anyone's appetite for supper.

With these at the center of the meal, you're free to slide by with a simple salad as an accompaniment and fresh fruit for dessert, if such low-key fare suits your mood. Or you can check out the gourmet deli counter, and choose your sides there before you pick up something sweet at the bakery. In other words, you don't—and shouldn't—have to do all the work to make a festively appetizing meal. After all, you're supposed to enjoy the day as much as your guests.

Dressing Up Sandwiches

- Instead of iceberg lettuce, try using greens such as peppery endive, colorful radicchio, baby spinach leaves, or arugula.
- Spread your bread with prepared pesto, olive tapenade, honey mustard, or cream cheese mixed with fresh herbs.
- Add extra flavor with jarred roasted red peppers, pepperoncini peppers, sweet and hot jalapeños, rehydrated sun-dried tomatoes, grilled pineapple slices, or grilled avocado slices.
- Use hearty or flavored breads, and toast them first so they'll stand up to the ingredients.

search myclar2003.com for all our tips

Open-Faced Roast Beef Reuben with Spicy Slaw and Melted Swiss

- 1 (7-ounce) can chipotle chiles in adobo sauce
- ⅓ cup fat-free mayonnaise
- 2 cups packaged cabbage-and-carrot coleslaw
- 4 (1¼-ounce) slices rye bread
- 12 ounces thinly sliced deli roast beef
- 1 cup (4 ounces) shredded reduced-fat Swiss cheese

1. Preheat broiler.
2. Drain chipotles in a colander over a bowl, reserving 1 chile. Reserve remaining chiles and sauce for another use. Finely chop 1 chile. Place 2 teaspoons finely chopped chile in a large bowl, and discard remaining finely chopped chile. Add mayonnaise, and stir well with a whisk. Add slaw; toss gently.
3. Spoon ¼ cup slaw mixture onto each bread slice, and top each slice with 3 ounces roast beef and ¼ cup cheese. Place sandwiches on a baking sheet, and broil 3 minutes or until cheese melts. Yield: 4 servings (serving size: 1 sandwich).

CALORIES 333 (29% from fat); FAT 10.9g (sat 4.9g, mono 2.6g, poly 0.7g); PROTEIN 31.3g; CARB 25.8g; FIBER 3.1g; CHOL 73mg; IRON 3.5mg; SODIUM 1,440mg; CALC 380mg

---

Smoked Salmon with Mango Chutney and Pumpernickel

(pictured on page 94)

- 2 cups diced peeled mango
- ⅓ cup finely chopped shallots
- ¼ cup dried currants
- ¼ cup water
- 2 tablespoons brown sugar
- 2 tablespoons cider vinegar
- 1 tablespoon minced seeded habanero pepper
- 2 teaspoons minced peeled fresh ginger
- 8 (1-ounce) slices pumpernickel bread, toasted
- 12 ounces thinly sliced smoked salmon
- 16 baby spinach leaves

1. Combine first 8 ingredients in a medium saucepan over medium heat; bring to a simmer. Cover and cook 5 minutes. Uncover and cook 15 minutes or until liquid almost evaporates, stirring frequently.
2. Spread about ⅓ cup mango mixture over each of 4 bread slices; top each with 3 ounces salmon and 4 spinach leaves. Top with remaining bread slices. Yield: 4 servings (serving size: 1 sandwich).

CALORIES 329 (16% from fat); FAT 5.7g (sat 1.1g, mono 2.3g, poly 1.6g); PROTEIN 21.5g; CARB 49.5g; FIBER 5.4g; CHOL 20mg; IRON 2.9mg; SODIUM 1,055mg; CALC 72mg

---

Broiled Salmon Sandwich with Wasabi Mayonnaise

Wasabi is a green Japanese version of horseradish that gives the salmon a sharp, fiery flavor. Wasabi powder is found in the Asian sections of supermarkets.

- 1 (1-pound) salmon fillet, skinned
- ¼ teaspoon salt
- ¼ teaspoon black pepper
- Cooking spray
- ½ teaspoon wasabi powder
- ½ teaspoon water
- ⅓ cup fat-free mayonnaise
- ¼ cup chopped green onions
- 1 teaspoon low-sodium soy sauce
- ¼ teaspoon dark sesame oil
- 4 curly leaf lettuce leaves
- 8 (1-ounce) slices multigrain bread

1. Preheat broiler.
2. Sprinkle fish with salt and pepper. Place fish on a broiler pan coated with cooking spray; broil 8 minutes or until fish flakes easily when tested with a fork. Cut fish into 1-inch pieces. Cool.
3. Combine wasabi and water in a small bowl. Add mayonnaise, onion, soy sauce, and oil, stirring to combine. Add fish, and toss gently. Arrange 1 lettuce leaf on each of 4 bread slices. Divide fish mixture evenly over lettuce; top with remaining bread slices. Yield: 4 servings (serving size: 1 sandwich).

CALORIES 357 (30% from fat); FAT 11.9g (sat 2.2g, mono 5.7g, poly 2.6g); PROTEIN 28.6g; CARB 33.5g; FIBER 3.5g; CHOL 74mg; IRON 2.3mg; SODIUM 820mg; CALC 40mg

Barbecue Pulled Chicken with Marinated Cucumbers

You can also serve this on barbecue bread or Texas toast. The marinated cucumbers are so good you might want to make a double batch.

CHICKEN:
- ¼ cup light brown sugar
- 1 tablespoon chili powder
- 2 teaspoons ground cumin
- ½ teaspoon salt
- ½ teaspoon paprika
- ¼ teaspoon black pepper
- 1 pound skinless, boneless chicken breast
- 2 teaspoons olive oil
- 1 cup thinly sliced onion
- 1 cup fat-free, less-sodium chicken broth
- 1 tablespoon balsamic vinegar

CUCUMBERS:
- ¼ cup cider vinegar
- 2 tablespoons light brown sugar
- ¼ teaspoon salt
- 1 cucumber, peeled and sliced

REMAINING INGREDIENT:
- 4 (2-ounce) hamburger buns

1. To prepare chicken, combine first 6 ingredients. Rub surface of chicken with brown sugar mixture. Heat oil in a large nonstick skillet over medium-high heat. Add chicken; cook 2 minutes on each side. Remove from pan. Add onion to pan; cook 2 minutes or until tender, stirring constantly.

2. Return chicken to pan; add broth. Bring to a boil; cover, reduce heat, and simmer 30 minutes or until chicken is done. Remove from heat. Remove chicken from pan; shred with 2 forks. Return chicken to pan. Bring to a boil; reduce heat, and simmer, uncovered, 15 minutes or until liquid evaporates. Stir in balsamic vinegar.

3. To prepare cucumbers, combine cider vinegar and next 3 ingredients in a large zip-top plastic bag; seal and marinate in refrigerator 10 minutes. Remove cucumber from bag; discard marinade.

4. Spoon 1 cup chicken mixture onto bottom half of each bun. Top each with ¼ cup cucumber mixture and top half of bun. Yield: 4 servings (serving size: 1 sandwich).

CALORIES 373 (15% from fat); FAT 6.4g (sat 1.3g, mono 3.1g, poly 1.2g); PROTEIN 32.7g; CARB 45.3g; FIBER 3g; CHOL 66mg; IRON 4mg; SODIUM 892mg; CALC 113mg

Turkey Sandwich with Red Pepper-Pine Nut Pesto and Caramelized Onions

Ciabatta is crunchy on the outside and soft in the middle. Since it is a thin loaf, focaccia would be a good substitute.

- ¼ cup chopped fresh basil
- 2 tablespoons grated fresh Parmesan cheese
- 1 tablespoon pine nuts, toasted
- 1 tablespoon water
- 2 garlic cloves, halved
- 1 (7-ounce) bottle roasted red bell peppers, drained
- 2 teaspoons olive oil
- 2 cups vertically sliced onion
- 2 teaspoons sugar
- 1 (8-ounce) loaf ciabatta
- 12 (1-ounce) slices cooked turkey breast
- 2 (1-ounce) slices fontina cheese
- 2 cups trimmed watercress

1. Place first 6 ingredients in a blender; process until smooth.

2. Heat oil in a large nonstick skillet over medium-high heat. Add onion and sugar; cook 8 minutes or until onion is browned, stirring occasionally.

3. Cut bread loaf in half horizontally; spread pepper mixture evenly over cut sides of bread. Layer turkey, fontina cheese, onion, and watercress over bottom half of loaf; top with remaining loaf half. Cut loaf into 4 pieces. Serve immediately. Yield: 4 servings.

CALORIES 416 (25% from fat); FAT 11.5g (sat 4.4g, mono 4.5g, poly 1.6g); PROTEIN 37.5g; CARB 39.9g; FIBER 3.6g; CHOL 90mg; IRON 3.4mg; SODIUM 572mg; CALC 217mg

Curried Crab Salad with Coriander-Dusted Flatbread

We used refrigerated pizza crust and added seasonings to make a unique flatbread that's a snap to prepare.

- 1 (10-ounce) can refrigerated pizza crust dough
- Cooking spray
- ½ teaspoon salt
- ½ teaspoon ground coriander
- ⅛ teaspoon black pepper
- ½ cup fat-free sour cream
- 2 tablespoons chopped fresh cilantro
- 1 teaspoon curry powder
- ⅛ teaspoon ground red pepper
- ¾ pound crabmeat, shell pieces removed
- 4 romaine lettuce leaves

1. Preheat oven to 425°.

2. Unroll dough onto a baking sheet coated with cooking spray, and pat into a 12 x 9-inch rectangle. Lightly coat dough with cooking spray; sprinkle with salt, coriander, and black pepper. Bake at 425° for 13 minutes or until lightly browned. Remove from pan; cool on a wire rack. Cut bread into quarters. Cut each portion in half lengthwise.

3. Combine sour cream, cilantro, curry powder, and red pepper in a medium bowl. Add crabmeat, and stir gently. Place 1 lettuce leaf on each of 4 bread slices. Divide crabmeat mixture evenly over lettuce, and top with remaining bread slices. Yield: 4 servings (serving size: 1 sandwich).

CALORIES 304 (14% from fat); FAT 4.6g (sat 0.8g, mono 1.1g, poly 1.6g); PROTEIN 25.8g; CARB 36.6g; FIBER 1.1g; CHOL 85mg; IRON 3mg; SODIUM 1,029mg; CALC 98mg

Hummus-Stuffed Pita with Roasted Vegetables

Make the hummus while the vegetables are roasting or prepare it a couple days ahead and store it in the refrigerator.

ROASTED VEGETABLES:

- 5 cups (1-inch) cubed peeled eggplant (about 1 pound)
- 2 cups coarsely chopped red onion
- 1½ cups coarsely chopped tomato
- 1 cup (1-inch) pieces green bell pepper
- 1 tablespoon chopped fresh or 1 teaspoon dried thyme
- 1 tablespoon chopped fresh parsley
- 2 teaspoons chopped fresh or ½ teaspoon dried rosemary
- ¼ teaspoon salt
- ¼ teaspoon black pepper
- Cooking spray

HUMMUS:

- ¼ cup tahini (sesame-seed paste)
- ¼ cup fresh lemon juice
- 1 tablespoon warm water
- 1 teaspoon ground cumin
- ½ teaspoon salt
- ¼ teaspoon black pepper
- 2 garlic cloves, chopped
- 1 (19-ounce) can chickpeas (garbanzo beans), drained

REMAINING INGREDIENT:

- 4 (6-inch) whole wheat pitas, cut in half

1. Preheat oven to 350°.

2. To prepare roasted vegetables, combine first 9 ingredients in a large shallow roasting pan coated with cooking spray. Bake at 350° for 30 minutes or until vegetables are tender, stirring occasionally.

3. To prepare hummus, combine tahini and next 7 ingredients in a food processor, and process until smooth. Spread ¼ cup hummus in each pita half, and fill each with ½ cup roasted vegetable mixture. Yield: 8 servings (serving size: 1 pita half).

CALORIES 261 (23% from fat); FAT 6.8g (sat 0.9g, mono 2g, poly 2.8g); PROTEIN 10.5g; CARB 43.8g; FIBER 7.9g; CHOL 0mg; IRON 4.1mg; SODIUM 508mg; CALC 87mg

lighten up

Luscious Lemon Cake

Our lightened version of a refreshingly tangy cake is enough to turn a chocoholic's head.

Melissa Crawford Mazeo of Chicago discovered this zesty cake on the Internet. For the first time, her husband Michael would eat a dessert other than chocolate. The only problem then was the high fat. So, we lightened it. While the lightened cake was still as moist and lemony as the original, calories per serving had dropped from 468 to a more reasonable 322, and the fat was reduced by almost two-thirds.

Lemonade Layer Cake
(pictured on page 93)

When making the frosting, be sure the cream cheese is cold; when warm, it's softer, which makes the frosting too thin. We loved this cake chilled, but it's also good at room temperature.

CAKE:

- 1⅓ cups granulated sugar
- 6 tablespoons butter, softened
- 1 tablespoon grated lemon rind
- 3 tablespoons thawed lemonade concentrate
- 2 teaspoons vanilla extract
- 2 large eggs
- 2 large egg whites
- 2 cups all-purpose flour
- 1 teaspoon baking powder
- ½ teaspoon salt
- ½ teaspoon baking soda
- 1¼ cups fat-free buttermilk
- Cooking spray

FROSTING:

- 2 tablespoons butter, softened
- 2 teaspoons grated lemon rind
- 2 teaspoons thawed lemonade concentrate
- ½ teaspoon vanilla extract
- 8 ounces ⅓-less-fat cream cheese
- 3½ cups powdered sugar

1. Preheat oven to 350°.

2. To prepare cake, place first 5 ingredients in a large bowl; beat with a mixer at medium speed until well blended (about 5 minutes). Add eggs and egg whites, 1 at a time, beating well after each addition. Lightly spoon flour into dry measuring cups; level with a knife. Combine flour, baking powder, salt, and baking soda; stir well with a whisk. Add flour mixture to sugar mixture alternately with buttermilk, beginning and ending with flour mixture; beat well after each addition.

3. Pour batter into 2 (9-inch) round cake pans coated with cooking spray; sharply tap pans once on counter to remove air bubbles. Bake at 350° for 20 minutes or until a wooden pick inserted in center comes out clean. Cool in pans 10 minutes on a wire rack; remove from pans. Cool completely on wire rack.

4. To prepare frosting, place 2 tablespoons butter and next 4 ingredients in a large bowl; beat with a mixer at high speed until fluffy. Add powdered sugar, and beat at low speed just until blended (do not overbeat). Chill 1 hour.

5. Place 1 cake layer on a plate; spread with ½ cup frosting. Top with remaining cake layer. Spread remaining frosting over top and sides of cake. Store cake loosely covered in refrigerator. Yield: 16 servings (serving size: 1 slice).

CALORIES 322 (28% from fat); FAT 9.9g (sat 5.9g, mono 2.9g, poly 0.5g); PROTEIN 5g; CARB 54.1g; FIBER 0.5g; CHOL 53mg; IRON 1mg; SODIUM 293mg; CALC 60mg

BEFORE	AFTER
SERVING SIZE	
1 slice	
CALORIES PER SERVING	
468	322
FAT	
27.8g	9.9g
PERCENT OF TOTAL CALORIES	
53%	28%
CHOLESTEROL	
129mg	53mg

Lemonade Layer Cake,
page 92

White Bean Salad with Shrimp
and Asparagus, page 85

Smoked Salmon with Mango Chutney
and Pumpernickel, page 90

Whole Wheat Buttermilk Pancakes,
page 79

Garlic Fries, page 73

Gramercy Crawfish Gumbo,
page 97

Celebrate with Crawfish

In Louisiana, a pretty spring day is reason enough to host a crawfish boil.

Early spring is the peak of the crawfish season, and the perfect time for a crawfish boil. By the end of May, the crawfish will be gone until December, snug in their underground tunnels, hiding from summer's heat.

Some grumble that crawfish pose a lot of work for little reward: All the meat's in the tail, and there's not much there. You have to peel a whole pound of crawfish to get just 2½ ounces of meat. But those who love crawfish remark that speed isn't the point. They know that the leisurely work of peeling crawfish leaves plenty of time to get to know the stranger standing beside you, and to renew ties with that old pal you just never see enough. They recognize—and cherish—chances to hear new jokes and tell silly stories. Perhaps best of all, they believe there's no point in trying to do a crawfish boil for just one or two. Like barbecue, it's the same amount of work to feed 20 as it is to feed a few, so you might as well invite 20.

Hosting a Crawfish Boil

For an authentic Louisiana-style crawfish boil, estimate how many people you expect to serve and how much you expect them to eat. Some sources suggest two pounds per person, but most Louisiana cooks figure five pounds per person—that allows light eaters and heavy eaters to have their fill, but leaves plenty left over for the freezer.

Live crawfish should be purged before cooking. Here's how: Empty the crawfish into a large cooler or ice chest with a drain. Cover them with cool water, then pour in half a box of salt. Let the crawfish stand for 5 to 10 minutes; drain, rinse, and repeat twice.

To cook crawfish outside, you'll need a gas or propane-fired cooker (available at hardware stores). You'll also need a big pot with a lid and a basket that fits inside. Forty pounds of crawfish need an 80-quart pot. Follow these steps:
- Fill pot halfway with water and place it on the cooker. Add 8 to 10 garlic heads; add halved onions and halved lemons (about 28 of each for 40 pounds of crawfish). Bring water to a boil.
- Add crab boil seasoning. Our All That Jazz Seasoning (recipe on page 98) is featured in these recipes. Zatarain's is the traditional commercial brand in Louisiana, and is available nationally; it comes in both liquid and dry forms. For 40 pounds of crawfish, you'll need 4 (8-ounce) bottles or 2 (3-ounce) bags. Allow the water to boil for a few minutes so the seasoning can mix well.
- Add whole new potatoes (2 per person), and let boil 10 to 15 minutes.
- Add halved corn ears (2 per person) and crawfish; stir gently. Cover and return to a boil for 15 minutes.
- Gently stir again. Turn off the fire, and let the crawfish soak for 30 minutes. The longer you soak the crawfish, the spicier they will be.
- Remove basket and tip the contents onto a newspaper-lined table.

search myclar2003.com for all our tips

Gramercy Crawfish Gumbo
(pictured on page 96)

Traditionally gumbo starts with a roux—a mixture of flour and fat that's cooked slowly until browned. In this recipe, named for a small town in Louisiana, you brown the flour in the oven. This technique provides a deep, nutty flavor without the fat.

½ cup all-purpose flour
¼ cup vegetable oil
1 cup finely chopped onion
8 cups water
1½ cups sliced okra pods (about 6 ounces)
¼ cup finely chopped green bell pepper
¼ cup chopped fresh parsley
¼ cup chopped celery leaves
2 to 3 tablespoons All That Jazz Seasoning (recipe on page 98)
2 teaspoons salt
8 garlic cloves, minced
1 (14.5-ounce) can stewed tomatoes, undrained
2 cups cooked crawfish tail meat (about 12 ounces)
1 cup lump crabmeat, shell pieces removed (about ⅓ pound)
1 teaspoon hot sauce
6 cups hot cooked rice
Chopped fresh parsley (optional)

1. Preheat oven to 350°.
2. Lightly spoon flour into a dry measuring cup; level with a knife. Place flour in a 9-inch pie plate; bake at 350° for 45 minutes or until lightly browned, stirring frequently. Cool on a wire rack.
3. Heat oil in a large Dutch oven over medium-high heat. Add onion; sauté 4 minutes. Stir in browned flour; cook 1 minute, stirring constantly. Gradually stir in water and next 8 ingredients; bring to a boil. Reduce heat; simmer 1 hour.
4. Stir in crawfish, crabmeat, and sauce. Bring to a boil; reduce heat, and simmer 25 minutes. Serve with rice; sprinkle with parsley, if desired. Yield: 8 servings (serving size: 1⅓ cups gumbo and ¾ cup rice).

CALORIES 334 (22% from fat); FAT 8.2g (sat 1.2g, mono 1.9g, poly 4.4g); PROTEIN 15.8g; CARB 48.8g; FIBER 2.8g; CHOL 71mg; IRON 3.2mg; SODIUM 838mg; CALC 107mg

All That Jazz Seasoning

This spice blend has all the flavors of traditional Cajun seasoning, but with less salt than commercial brands. Store in an airtight container.

¼ cup garlic powder
¼ cup onion powder
2 tablespoons paprika
1 tablespoon ground red pepper
1 tablespoon black pepper
1½ teaspoons celery seeds
1½ teaspoons chili powder
1 teaspoon salt
1 teaspoon lemon pepper
½ teaspoon ground nutmeg

1. Combine all ingredients. Yield: 1 cup (serving size: 1 tablespoon).

CALORIES 20 (14% from fat); FAT 0.3g (sat 0.1g, mono 0.1g, poly 0.1g); PROTEIN 0.8g; CARB 4.3g; FIBER 1.1g; CHOL 0mg; IRON 0.6mg; SODIUM 177mg; CALC 18mg

"Bayou-Self" Crawfish Boil

Here's a manageably sized crawfish boil that you can do on the stovetop.

¼ cup mustard seeds
3 tablespoons coriander seeds
2 tablespoons whole allspice
2 teaspoons crushed red pepper
2 teaspoons whole cloves
¼ teaspoon black peppercorns
6 bay leaves, crumbled
2 gallons water
¾ cup salt
¼ cup All That Jazz Seasoning (recipe at bottom left)
3 tablespoons paprika
2 tablespoons ground red pepper
12 small red potatoes (about 12 ounces)
4 onions, halved
4 lemons, halved
4 whole garlic heads
4 ears shucked corn, halved crosswise
6 pounds live crawfish

1. Place first 7 ingredients on a double layer of cheesecloth. Gather edges of cheesecloth together; tie securely.
2. Combine cheesecloth bag, water, salt, All That Jazz Seasoning, paprika, and ground red pepper in an extra-large stockpot, and bring to a boil. Cover, reduce heat, and simmer 15 minutes.
3. Add potatoes, onions, lemons, and garlic. Cover and return to a boil; cook 10 minutes. Add corn and crawfish. Cover and return to a boil; cook 15 minutes or until done. Let stand 30 minutes. Drain; discard cheesecloth bag. Yield: 4 servings (serving size: 1½ pounds crawfish, 3 potatoes, and 2 corn halves).

CALORIES 346 (8% from fat); FAT 3.2g (sat 0.5g, mono 0.7g, poly 1.2g); PROTEIN 35.3g; CARB 46.7g; FIBER 6.9g; CHOL 226mg; IRON 3mg; SODIUM 777mg; CALC 151mg

Crawfish-Stuffed Mirlitons

Mirlitons, also known as chayotes, are pear-shaped squashes with light green skin and mild pulp. Serve as an appetizer or side dish.

4 mirlitons
1 tablespoon butter
1 cup finely chopped onion
2 garlic cloves, minced
2¼ cups cooked crawfish tail meat (about 14 ounces)
½ cup dry breadcrumbs
1 tablespoon chopped fresh parsley
1 teaspoon salt
¾ teaspoon hot sauce
½ teaspoon ground thyme
1 large egg, lightly beaten

1. Pierce mirlitons with a fork. Place in a Dutch oven; cover with water. Bring to a boil over high heat; reduce heat, and simmer 30 minutes or until tender. Drain and cool. Cut mirlitons in half lengthwise; discard seeds. Scoop out pulp, leaving ¼-inch-thick shells. Chop pulp; place in a large bowl.
2. Preheat oven to 375°.
3. Melt butter in a medium nonstick skillet over medium heat. Add onion and garlic; cook 6 minutes or until onion is tender. Add onion mixture, crawfish, and remaining 6 ingredients to chopped pulp; stir to combine.
4. Spoon about ½ cup crawfish mixture into each shell; place stuffed mirlitons on a baking sheet. Bake at 375° for 30 minutes or until crawfish mixture is thoroughly heated and golden. Yield: 8 servings (serving size: 1 mirliton half).

CALORIES 124 (24% from fat); FAT 3.3g (sat 1.3g, mono 1g, poly 0.5g); PROTEIN 12.3g; CARB 11.6g; FIBER 2.3g; CHOL 106mg; IRON 1.5mg; SODIUM 433mg; CALC 78mg

Crawfish Jambalaya

This Creole classic also includes peppers, celery, onions, and rice.

- 2 tablespoons vegetable oil
- 1 tablespoon all-purpose flour
- 1 cup finely chopped onion
- 3½ cups water, divided
- 2 cups cooked crawfish tail meat (about 12 ounces)
- ½ cup diced reduced-fat ham (3 ounces)
- 1¼ cups uncooked long-grain rice
- ½ cup chopped red bell pepper
- ½ cup chopped celery
- ½ cup chopped green onions
- 2 teaspoons chopped fresh parsley
- 1 teaspoon All That Jazz Seasoning (recipe on page 98)
- ½ teaspoon salt
- ¼ teaspoon ground black pepper
- ¼ teaspoon ground red pepper

1. Heat oil in a large Dutch oven over medium heat. Add flour; cook 1 minute, stirring constantly. Add onion; cook 4 minutes. Add 1½ cups water; bring to a simmer. Simmer 30 minutes. Stir in crawfish and ham; cook 5 minutes. Add 2 cups water, and bring to a boil. Stir in rice and remaining ingredients; cover and simmer 30 minutes, stirring occasionally. Yield: 4 servings (serving size: 1¾ cups).

WINE NOTE: Bell peppers, onions, and a dash of peppery spice make this dish a bit of a challenge winewise. Steer away from wines with a lot of tannin (like Cabernet Sauvignon and Merlot); they'll probably taste harsh. But a fruity red is just the ticket. A great bet: Georges Duboeuf Beaujolais from any one of the top villages in the Beaujolais region—Morgon, Moulin-a-Vent, or Fleurie, for example (about $8).

CALORIES 404 (21% from fat); FAT 9.4g (sat 1.6g, mono 2.4g, poly 4.5g); PROTEIN 23.1g; CARB 54.7g; FIBER 2.8g; CHOL 122mg; IRON 3.9mg; SODIUM 619mg; CALC 88mg

How to Shell Crawfish

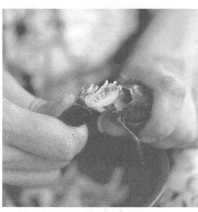

1. *Before you peel the shell, separate the tail from the head. Begin by holding the head in one hand and the tail in the other.*

2. *Gently twist your hands in opposite directions until crawfish splits in half.*

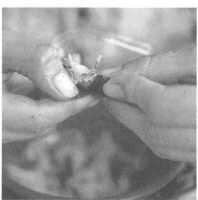

3. *Gently squeeze the sides of the tail until you hear the shell crack. Beginning at the top, peel away a few segments of the shell until there is enough exposed meat for you to grasp securely.*

4. *Holding the fan of the tail in one hand, pull the meat away from the shell. Tip: If the meat breaks apart, peel away the remaining shell segments.*

5. *Now, you're ready to eat. For a more authentic Cajun experience: After you remove the head, suck the seasoned cooking liquid before discarding. Also, you can use your teeth rather than your fingers to remove the crawfish meat from the cracked shell.*

Fleur-de-Lis Chicken

Extra crawfish meat is used to make elegant stuffed chicken breasts. The fleur-de-lis, three stylized iris segments tied by a decorative band, was the favorite adornment of Louis XIV, for whom Louisiana is named. Turn the chicken carefully so the filling doesn't spill out.

    1   cup cooked crawfish tail meat
        (about 6 ounces)
    1   cup chopped spinach
    ¼   cup finely chopped mushrooms
    ¼   cup chopped green onions
    ¼   cup part-skim ricotta cheese
    2   tablespoons grated fresh Parmesan
        cheese
    1½ teaspoons chopped fresh oregano
    ½   teaspoon salt
    ½   teaspoon black pepper
    2   garlic cloves, minced
    6   (4-ounce) skinless, boneless
        chicken breast halves
    1   tablespoon butter

1. Preheat oven to 350°.
2. Combine first 10 ingredients in a medium bowl. Cut a horizontal slit through thickest portion of each breast half to form a pocket. Stuff ⅓ cup crawfish mixture into each pocket.
3. Melt butter in a large nonstick skillet over medium-high heat. Add chicken; cook 4 minutes on each side or until

browned. Wrap handle of pan with foil; bake at 350° for 35 minutes or until chicken is done. Yield: 6 servings (serving size: 1 breast half).

CALORIES 206 (29% from fat); FAT 6.7g (sat 3g, mono 2.1g, poly 0.9g); PROTEIN 32.7g; CARB 1.7g; FIBER 0.4g; CHOL 114mg; IRON 1.4mg; SODIUM 356mg; CALC 93mg

Crawfish Salad with Creole Honey-Mustard Dressing

Creole mustard and All That Jazz Seasoning make a spicy-sweet salad dressing. Serve with a sandwich for lunch or to start a Cajun meal.

DRESSING:

    6   tablespoons Creole mustard
    1½ tablespoons fresh lemon juice
    1½ tablespoons honey
    1   teaspoon All That Jazz Seasoning
        (recipe on page 98)
    1   teaspoon olive oil

SALAD:

    6   cups thinly sliced romaine lettuce
    3¾ cups sliced mushrooms
    2   cups cooked crawfish tail meat
        (about 12 ounces)
    ⅓   cup sliced green onions
    ¼   cup sliced bottled roasted red bell
        peppers
    2   tablespoons sunflower seed
        kernels, toasted
    1   (2¼-ounce) can sliced ripe olives,
        drained
    1   hard-cooked large egg, sliced

1. To prepare dressing, combine first 5 ingredients in a small bowl; stir well with a whisk.
2. To prepare salad, combine lettuce and remaining 7 ingredients in a large bowl. Add dressing; toss well. Yield: 6 servings (serving size: about 2 cups).

CALORIES 148 (30% from fat); FAT 4.9g (sat 0.8g, mono 2g, poly 1.5g); PROTEIN 13.7g; CARB 10.4g; FIBER 2.4g; CHOL 111mg; IRON 2.1mg; SODIUM 461mg; CALC 72mg

Crawfish Enchiladas

    1   tablespoon butter
    1   cup chopped green onions
    ½   cup chopped red onion
    ¼   cup chopped red bell pepper
    ¼   cup chopped green bell pepper
    ¼   cup chopped yellow bell pepper
    ¼   cup chopped seeded jalapeño
        pepper
    3   garlic cloves, minced
    2   teaspoons all-purpose flour
    1   cup 1% low-fat milk
    ½   teaspoon salt
    ½   teaspoon dried oregano
    ½   teaspoon chili powder
    ½   teaspoon paprika
    ¼   teaspoon black pepper
    1   cup (4 ounces) shredded
        reduced-fat sharp cheddar
        cheese
    ½   cup fat-free sour cream
    2   cups cooked crawfish tail meat
        (about 12 ounces)
    12 (6-inch) corn tortillas
        Cooking spray
    ½   cup (2 ounces) shredded Monterey
        Jack cheese

1. Melt butter in a large nonstick skillet over medium-high heat. Add green onions and next 6 ingredients; sauté 5 minutes or until tender. Sprinkle flour over vegetables; cook 1 minute, stirring constantly. Gradually add milk, stirring with a whisk. Cook over medium heat until thick (about 8 minutes), stirring constantly. Stir in salt and next 4 ingredients. Remove from heat; let stand 3 minutes. Add cheddar cheese and sour cream, stirring until cheese melts. Stir in crawfish.
2. Preheat oven to 325°.

3. Add water to a medium skillet to a depth of 1 inch; bring to a simmer. Dip 1 tortilla in water using tongs. Spoon ¼ cup crawfish mixture into center of 1 tortilla; roll tightly, and place in a 13 x 9-inch baking dish coated with cooking spray. Repeat procedure with remaining tortillas and 2¾ cups crawfish mixture. Spread remaining crawfish mixture over tortillas; sprinkle with Monterey Jack cheese.

4. Cover and bake at 325° for 10 minutes or until thoroughly heated. Yield: 6 servings (serving size: 2 enchiladas).

CALORIES 332 (30% from fat); FAT 11g (sat 5.8g, mono 2g, poly 1g); PROTEIN 24g; CARB 35.7g; FIBER 4.3g; CHOL 106mg; IRON 1.7mg; SODIUM 594mg; CALC 457mg

The Big Easy Crawfish Omelet

For a New Orleans-style Sunday brunch, serve with Bloody Marys and hash browns.

- 1 tablespoon chopped fresh chives
- 1 tablespoon water
- ¼ teaspoon hot sauce
- 4 large egg whites
- 2 large eggs
- ¼ cup cooked crawfish tail meat, chopped
- 1 tablespoon All That Jazz Seasoning (recipe on page 98)
- 1 teaspoon fat-free sour cream
- Cooking spray
- ⅓ cup sliced mushrooms
- ¼ cup finely diced reduced-fat ham (1½ ounces)
- 2 tablespoons shredded light processed cheese (such as Velveeta Light)

1. Combine first 5 ingredients, stirring with a whisk.

2. Combine crawfish, All That Jazz Seasoning, and sour cream.

3. Heat a small nonstick skillet coated with cooking spray over medium-high heat. Add mushrooms and ham; sauté 3 minutes. Pour egg mixture into pan; let egg mixture set slightly. Tilt pan, and carefully lift edges of omelet with a spatula; allow uncooked portion to flow underneath cooked portion. Cook 3 minutes; flip omelet. Spoon crawfish mixture onto half of omelet. Carefully loosen omelet with a spatula; fold in half. Gently slide omelet onto a plate; top with cheese. Cut omelet in half. Yield: 2 servings.

CALORIES 185 (36% from fat); FAT 7.3g (sat 2.5g, mono 2.5g, poly 1g); PROTEIN 23.3g; CARB 5.4g; FIBER 0.7g; CHOL 254mg; IRON 1.6mg; SODIUM 703mg; CALC 98mg

Cajun Crawfish Corn Bread

Cooking spray
- ½ cup all-purpose flour
- 1½ cups yellow cornmeal
- 1 tablespoon baking powder
- 2 teaspoons All That Jazz Seasoning (recipe on page 98)
- ½ teaspoon salt
- 1½ cups cooked crawfish tail meat, coarsely chopped (about 9 ounces)
- 1 cup (4 ounces) shredded sharp cheddar cheese
- 1 cup low-fat buttermilk
- 1 tablespoon butter, melted
- 1 large egg white, lightly beaten
- 1 large egg, lightly beaten
- 1 (8¾-ounce) can cream-style corn

1. Preheat oven to 375°.

2. Coat a 9-inch cast iron skillet with cooking spray. Place in a 375° oven for 10 minutes.

3. Lightly spoon flour into a dry measuring cup; level with a knife. Combine flour and next 4 ingredients in a large bowl. Combine crawfish and remaining 6 ingredients in a medium bowl; stir well with a whisk. Add to flour mixture, stirring until moist. Pour batter into preheated pan. Bake at 375° for 35 minutes or until a wooden pick inserted in center comes out clean. Yield: 12 servings (serving size: 1 wedge).

CALORIES 179 (27% from fat); FAT 5.3g (sat 2.6g, mono 0.6g, poly 0.4g); PROTEIN 9.9g; CARB 22.8g; FIBER 1.7g; CHOL 60mg; IRON 0.9mg; SODIUM 411mg; CALC 176mg

Going to the Source

In the heart of South Louisiana's Cajun country lies Breaux Bridge, home to the Breaux Bridge Crawfish Festival. Each May, thousands of natives and tourists gather there to celebrate the humble crawfish.

Townsfolk strive to keep the festival a genuine depiction of their Cajun heritage, with authentic music, arts and crafts, cooking demonstrations, and an endless supply of crawfish. Hungry festivalgoers enjoy every conceivable crawfish creation: boiled crawfish, fried crawfish, crawfish bisque, crawfish étouffée, crawfish jambalaya, crawfish boudin, crawfish dogs, crawfish pies, crawfish fettuccine, crawfish gumbo, and more.

You might decide to enter the crawfish eating contest. Nick Stipelcovich of Metairie, Louisiana, who downed almost 56 pounds in one sitting, holds the record.

The festival is one of the nation's largest gatherings of Cajun musicians. Cajun, zydeco, and swamp pop complement the food. Three dozen bands perform during the three-day event. Watch the Cajun dance contests, and if you're not shy, join in.

For more information, call the Breaux Bridge Crawfish Festival Association at 318-332-6655, or visit www.louisianatravel.com/crawfish_festival.

All About Mushrooms

Whether farmed or foraged, mushrooms lend unique texture and aroma to any dish they grace.

S ome dishes that showcase mushrooms are ethereal and exotic, others are down-to-earth good. Whether you're taking your menu uptown or down-home, a tantalizing variety of fresh mushrooms is ready to be a part of it.

More than 2,500 varieties of mushrooms grow around the world. Just take one glance at any upscale market's produce aisle—you'll find mushrooms in many sizes, shapes, colors, textures, and flavors.

Of course, not everyone lives near an upscale grocery store or a mushroom-filled forest. But you can also find mushrooms at farmers' markets, Asian groceries, and mail-order sources. Wherever you find them, the information and recipes that follow will help you put them to good use.

Portobello Quesadillas with Pico de Gallo

Meaty portobellos are paired with flavorful pancetta in this appetizer. Keep the cooked quesadillas warm in an oven set to low heat while you're preparing the rest.

PICO DE GALLO:

1½ cups chopped plum tomato
⅓ cup chopped red onion
¼ cup chopped fresh cilantro
2 tablespoons finely chopped seeded jalapeño pepper
1 tablespoon fresh lime juice
¼ teaspoon kosher salt
¼ teaspoon freshly ground black pepper
2 garlic cloves, minced

QUESADILLAS:

2 ounces chopped pancetta or bacon
8 cups (¼-inch-thick) sliced portobello mushrooms (about 1 pound)
1 cup (4 ounces) shredded reduced-fat cheddar cheese
8 (8-inch) fat-free flour tortillas
Cooking spray
¾ cup fat-free sour cream

1. To prepare pico de gallo, combine first 8 ingredients in a medium bowl.
2. To prepare quesadillas, cook pancetta in a large nonstick skillet over medium-high heat until crisp. Remove pancetta from pan with a slotted spoon; place in a medium bowl. Add mushrooms to drippings in pan; sauté 6 minutes or until tender. Add mushrooms to pancetta in bowl; toss well.
3. Wipe pan clean with paper towels. Sprinkle 2 tablespoons cheese over each of 4 tortillas; top each with ½ cup mushroom mixture, 2 tablespoons cheese, and 1 tortilla. Lightly coat top tortillas with cooking spray. Heat pan coated with cooking spray over medium-high heat. Place 1 quesadilla in pan; cook 2 minutes on each side or until tortillas are lightly browned. Set aside, and keep warm. Repeat procedure with remaining quesadillas. Cut each quesadilla into 6 wedges. Serve with pico de gallo and sour cream. Yield: 12 servings (serving size: 2 quesadilla wedges, 2 tablespoons pico de gallo, and 1 tablespoon sour cream).

CALORIES 163 (27% from fat); FAT 4.8g (sat 2.2g, mono 1.3g, poly 0.4g); PROTEIN 7g; CARB 17.5g; FIBER 3.1g; CHOL 12mg; IRON 0.4mg; SODIUM 309mg; CALC 132mg

Chicken Scallopine with Morels and Spring Vegetables

Morels have a spongy texture that's perfect for soaking up the sherry-cream sauce. After rehydrating, be sure to rinse the mushrooms well to remove any grit or dirt.

1 cup fat-free, less-sodium chicken broth
½ cup dry sherry
1 ounce dried morels
4 (4-ounce) skinless, boneless chicken breast halves
½ teaspoon kosher salt
½ teaspoon freshly ground black pepper
2 tablespoons all-purpose flour
1 tablespoon Porcini Powder (recipe on page 104)
1 tablespoon butter
1 cup (1-inch) sliced asparagus
1 cup fresh or frozen petite green peas, thawed
¼ cup whipping cream
2 tablespoons chopped fresh parsley
2 tablespoons chopped fresh chives
1 teaspoon chopped fresh tarragon

1. Bring chicken broth and sherry to a boil in a small saucepan; add morels. Remove from heat; cover and let stand 30 minutes. Drain mushrooms in a cheesecloth-lined sieve over a bowl, reserving soaking liquid. Rinse mushrooms; drain.
2. Place each chicken breast half between 2 sheets of heavy-duty plastic wrap; pound to ¼-inch thickness using a meat mallet. Sprinkle chicken with salt and pepper. Combine flour and Porcini Powder in a shallow dish. Dredge chicken in flour mixture. Melt butter in a large nonstick skillet over medium-high heat. Add chicken; cook 1 minute on each side or until golden. Remove from pan.
3. Add mushrooms, soaking liquid, and asparagus to pan; cook until liquid is reduced to ¼ cup (about 5 minutes). Add chicken, peas, and remaining ingredients to pan; cook 5 minutes or until sauce thickens. Yield: 4 servings.

CALORIES 310 (30% from fat); FAT 10.5g (sat 5.7g, mono 3.1g, poly 0.8g); PROTEIN 33g; CARB 15.4g; FIBER 3.9g; CHOL 94mg; IRON 4.1mg; SODIUM 504mg; CALC 52mg

Mushroom Varieties

Button For practicality, this familiar mushroom can't be beat. Its subtle scent is distinctive in simple preparations such as sautéed mushrooms, but the button also stands up to spices—think curry, cumin, and chipotle. Lemon brings out its assertiveness, while onions lend a sweet note. The button's comparatively low price makes it a good budget stretcher, too. Substitute button mushrooms for half the wild mushrooms called for in any recipe—they'll adopt the flavor of the wild variety and add crunch.

Chanterelle The pumpkin-colored, flower-shaped chanterelle is a head turner. Its intoxicating, fruity aroma is well-matched with chives, tarragon, and chervil, and it combines well with ham, corn, apricot-laced stuffing, and poached salmon. Moderately expensive, this mushroom comes from eastern Canada, the Pacific Northwest, and Europe. It ranges in size from fingernail-tiny to a sprawling four inches. Pine needles and sand often hitch a ride in the cap's hollow and under its gills, so clean well before cooking. Sautéing coaxes the best flavor from chanterelles, but they're also great roasted. The chanterelle dries well, although doing so renders a crunchy texture.

Cremini When you want the juiciness and crunchy bite of the button but also want rich flavor, the cremini is the way to go. It's shaped like a button, with a beige to brown cap. Whether speedily sautéed or slowly roasted, the cremini stays plump and juicy. Garlic, thyme, and balsamic vinegar bring the cremini's flavor to the fore. This is one of the few mushroom varieties that is as good eaten raw as cooked, and it marinates well.

Enoki Shaped like a cotton swab, the enoki has a slender, edible stem. They usually come in clumps, attached by roots at the bottom. Trim off the root end of the cluster and separate. The enoki adds crunch, mild flavor, and bulk to any dish—from aromatic Asian soups to quick stir-fries and salads.

Morels This is an expensive mushroom. Its deep-woods flavor, springy texture, and little cream-catching pits invite you to sauté, stuff, and simmer. Morels are hollow, cone-shaped, and covered with ridges. They come in shades from light beige to gray to black. Smoky, earthy morels hold their own paired with hearty red meats and rich wine sauces. They transform eggs and pasta into elegant meals, and become heavenly with a little cream. Fresh morels are available in spring and summer; dried varieties can be found year-round and perform admirably. The morel's cavity is a natural sand collector, so slice it lengthwise to wipe out the interior before cooking.

Oyster The fan-shaped oyster mushroom, with its namesake's mild flavor, is fabulous with fish, seafood, red meat, and poultry. The creamy white, beige, or gray caps grow in a cluster, which is stunning when roasted whole. Mushroom farmers have had a lot of success growing yellow, pink, and blue oysters, which can be substituted for the white ones in most recipes (the colors fade when cooked, however). They make a great accompaniment to a simple fish fillet when quickly sautéed and then simmered in fish stock and herbs. Yet there's nothing like sinking your teeth into roasted oyster mushrooms, especially when they're mingled with more assertive varieties, such as shiitakes or chanterelles.

Porcini The pricey porcini (its Italian name) or cèpe (as it's known in France) is one of the most sought after wild mushrooms. Its essence-of-forest flavor is combined with a juicy, slippery-soft texture. Porcini come from the woods, so you need to wipe them with a damp paper towel. The stems can be sautéed and are delicious tucked into highly seasoned omelets. The caps can go a number of directions—sauté, roast, and grill, for starters. Serve over pasta or use them to garnish strongly flavored meats and game.

The most easily obtained form of porcini is dried. But be careful when purchasing them: Less flavorful varieties are sometimes substituted for the real thing, so buy from a trusted source and check that the mushroom's botanical name is listed as *Boletus edulis*. Once reconstituted, dried porcini yield a strong, earthy, smoky flavor. Use them to flavor soups, stews, sauces, and stuffings. To get around dried mushrooms' chewy texture, chop them finely after reconstituting and rinsing them.

Frozen porcini are a terrific substitute for fresh, as they retain nearly the same texture and are actually juicier. Don't defrost before using; roast them whole in a moderate oven for an hour, or slice and toss right into the skillet. With the juices they produce, frozen porcini make a great pasta sauce.

Portobello Let a cremini grow a few days longer, and you end up with a portobello. This flying saucer-like disk, which often measures from three to six inches across, is firm, meaty, and intensely flavorful. The portobello stands up to such gutsy flavors as acidic marinades, fresh rosemary and basil, and chile peppers. Grilling or roasting best preserves the mushroom's steaklike texture, but other cooking methods work just as well. When sautéing, remove the black gills on the underside of the cap to prevent the mushrooms from blackening. Sautéed portobellos are delicious in ragoût, as a topping for polenta or pizza, or as a filling for fajitas, quesadillas, or tacos.

Shiitake This Asian import came to America years ago. The soft, brown, open cap lends itself to several cooking styles. Sautéing brings out the shiitake's strong smoky flavor, softens the texture to velvety smoothness, and provides an easy mingling with other ingredients. Combined with crunchy vegetables, the shiitake takes naturally to the wok; with leeks and cream, it goes French and fancy. For maximum flavor, use dried shiitakes—they are chewier and more intense. Discard the thin, tough stalks, or use them to flavor stock.

Where Do Mushrooms Come From?

Cultivation As the market for mushrooms evolved in the 1980s, farmers converted button mushroom bunkers, which produced the first commercially viable mushrooms for the American market, into growing rooms for exotic mushrooms, such as shiitake, cremini, and oyster. These long, windowless buildings are lined with wood shelves stacked like bunk beds. Plastic bags filled with growing mediums—such as sawdust, corncobs, and hay—are inoculated with mycelium, or spawn. Moisture is high, light low. Workers wearing miners' lamps move from bag to bag, monitoring the growth of the mushrooms that pop out of holes in the bags.

Wild/Forest Because cultivated mushrooms are available year-round, you can always count on finding them for your favorite recipes. Some folks still like to take a walk on the wild side, substituting foraged mushrooms for the good old standards. In mid-summer, chanterelles—those glorious, orange, flower-shaped mushrooms—arrive by the truckload. Autumn heralds the arrival of dewy, earthy porcini, and winter brings over-the-top, aromatic truffles. And there is no better indication that spring has arrived than the appearance of the spade-shaped morel, with its delightful aroma of freshly dug earth. Wild mushrooms are available in some local markets or through on-line mushroom purveyors.

Mail-Order Sources

To order fresh or dried mushrooms, try these sources:
- Earthy Delights
800-367-4709, www.earthy.com
- Marché aux Delices
888-547-5471, www.auxdelices.com
- Oyster Creek Mushroom Company
207-563-1076,
www.oystercreekmushroom.com

Porcini Powder

Use this powder to flavor sauces, soups, and breads, or for dusting chicken or fish before sautéing. Refrigerate in a zip-top plastic bag for up to six months. Sift pulverized mushrooms so you can discard any big pieces.

1　cup dried porcini mushrooms (about 1 ounce)

1. Place mushrooms in a food processor; process 3 minutes or until finely ground. Sift mushroom powder into a bowl. Yield: 3 tablespoons.

CALORIES 100 (10% from fat); FAT 1.1g (sat 0.1g, mono 0.5g, poly 0.4g); PROTEIN 8.7g; CARB 13.9g; FIBER 4.6g; CHOL 0mg; IRON 5.9mg; SODIUM 11mg; CALC 8mg

Mushroom Duxelles on Bruschetta

Duxelles (dook-SEHL) is a mixture of finely chopped mushrooms cooked to the consistency of pâté. This version uses shiitakes and creminis, but you can use any combination.

16　(½-inch-thick) slices diagonally cut French bread baguette
4　cups cremini mushrooms (about 8 ounces)
4　cups shiitake mushroom caps (about 8 ounces)
Cooking spray
3　garlic cloves, minced
3　tablespoons whipping cream
2　tablespoons chopped fresh parsley
2　teaspoons chopped fresh thyme
½　teaspoon kosher salt
¼　teaspoon ground black pepper

1. Prepare grill or broiler.
2. Place bread on a grill rack or baking sheet; cook 1 minute on each side or until toasted.
3. Place mushrooms in a food processor; pulse 10 times or until finely chopped.
4. Heat a large nonstick skillet coated with cooking spray over medium-high heat. Add mushrooms and garlic; sauté 10 minutes or until most of liquid evaporates. Add cream and remaining 4 ingredients; cook 2 minutes, stirring

occasionally. Spoon 1 tablespoon duxelles onto each bread slice. Serve immediately. Yield: 8 servings (serving size: 2 bread slices and 2 tablespoons duxelles).

CALORIES 117 (30% from fat); FAT 3.9g (sat 1.6g, mono 1.1g, poly 1g); PROTEIN 3.7g; CARB 16.4g; FIBER 2.1g; CHOL 8mg; IRON 1.1mg; SODIUM 244mg; CALC 12mg

Wild Mushroom-and-Sweet Potato Gratin

Chanterelle mushrooms and fontina cheese contribute a delicate, nutty flavor that contrasts nicely with sweet potatoes. Serve with roasted pork loin or ham.

2　teaspoons olive oil
4　cups (¼-inch-thick) sliced cremini mushrooms (about 8 ounces)
3½　cups (¼-inch-thick) sliced chanterelle mushrooms (about 8 ounces)
⅓　cup finely chopped shallots
½　teaspoon kosher salt, divided
½　teaspoon black pepper, divided
1½　tablespoons finely chopped fresh parsley, divided
1½　tablespoons chopped fresh chives, divided
4　cups peeled sweet potatoes, cut into ¼-inch-thick slices (about 1½ pounds)
Cooking spray
1　cup (4 ounces) shredded fontina cheese
½　cup fat-free, less-sodium chicken broth

1. Preheat oven to 425°.
2. Heat oil in a large skillet over medium-high heat. Add mushrooms, shallots, ¼ teaspoon salt, and ¼ teaspoon pepper; sauté 5 minutes or until moisture evaporates. Remove from heat; stir in 1 tablespoon parsley and 1 tablespoon chives.
3. Arrange half of potato slices in a single layer in an 11 x 7-inch baking dish coated with cooking spray; sprinkle with ⅛ teaspoon salt and ⅛ teaspoon pepper. Spoon half of mushroom mixture over potato slices; sprinkle with half of cheese. Repeat layers, ending with cheese; add broth to dish. Cover and

bake at 425° for 30 minutes. Uncover and bake 20 minutes or until potatoes are tender. Sprinkle with 1½ teaspoons parsley and 1½ teaspoons chives. Yield: 8 servings.

CALORIES 193 (28% from fat); FAT 6.1g (sat 3g, mono 2.3g, poly 0.6g); PROTEIN 8g; CARB 26.8g; FIBER 4.7g; CHOL 17mg; IRON 1.6mg; SODIUM 282mg; CALC 110mg

Spring Lamb Chops on Oyster Mushrooms

This entrée is so easy that you might want to serve it for company—just double or triple the recipe as needed. Roasting the lamb over the mushrooms allows them to soak up the flavorful drippings. Serve with couscous to ensure that none of the sauce goes to waste.

    2 (8-ounce) lamb rib chops, trimmed
       (about 2 inches thick)
    ½ teaspoon kosher salt, divided
    ½ teaspoon freshly ground black
       pepper, divided
    2 tablespoons stone-ground mustard
    1 tablespoon finely chopped fresh
       rosemary
    1 teaspoon chopped fresh or ¼
       teaspoon dried thyme
    3 tablespoons dry red wine
    1 tablespoon olive oil
    1 pound oyster mushrooms, trimmed
       and cut into ½-inch-wide strips
       Cooking spray
    ½ cup fat-free, less-sodium chicken
       broth
  1½ cups hot cooked couscous

1. Preheat oven to 425°.
2. Sprinkle lamb with ¼ teaspoon salt and ¼ teaspoon pepper. Combine mustard, rosemary, and thyme. Rub lamb with half of mustard mixture. Combine ¼ teaspoon salt, ¼ teaspoon pepper, remaining mustard mixture, wine, and oil in a large bowl. Add mushrooms; toss well.
3. Place lamb on rack of a broiler pan or roasting pan coated with cooking spray. Spoon mushroom mixture into bottom of pan coated with cooking spray; place rack in pan over mushrooms. Insert a meat thermometer into thickest part of 1 chop.

4. Bake at 425° for 25 minutes or until thermometer registers 140°, stirring mushroom mixture after 12 minutes. Place 1 lamb chop on each of 2 plates; keep warm. Remove rack from pan; add broth to mushroom mixture in pan. Place pan over medium-high heat; cook 5 minutes or until liquid almost evaporates. Serve lamb with mushroom mixture and couscous. Yield: 2 servings (serving size: 1 lamb chop, 1 cup mushroom mixture, and ¾ cup couscous).

CALORIES 494 (27% from fat); FAT 14.6g (sat 3.6g, mono 7.9g, poly 1.3g); PROTEIN 41.9g; CARB 39.7g; FIBER 6.1g; CHOL 81mg; IRON 7.2mg; SODIUM 987mg; CALC 62mg

---

Mushroom Know-How

Choosing Mushrooms should, above all, have a mushroomy aroma. If they don't smell good, chances are they won't taste much better. Avoid wet spots; dry, cracking edges; flattened gills (under the cap); splayed-out caps; wrinkled flesh; telltale insect holes; and white mold.

Storing Place mushrooms in a wicker basket lined with a paper towel, cover with a slightly dampened paper towel, and store in the fridge. Avoid the vegetable bin, as well as any plastic—high humidity is death for mushrooms. Most mushrooms will hold well for three to seven days, but it really depends on when they were harvested and how well they were transported.

Cleaning Some mushrooms carry little sand or dirt and only need a quick wipe with a damp paper towel to clean; others—especially wild varieties—attract ferns, pine needles, dirt, and other cling-ons. Figure in extra time to clean wild mushrooms. Remove the stems, discarding or saving for later use (keep a plastic container in the freezer for such trimmings, to be turned into duxelles, soup, or mushroom stock). Use a damp paper towel or soft brush to clean both sides of the cap. If there are little holes, check to make sure insects have not embedded themselves in the cap.

Curried Mushroom and Chicken Brochettes

These brochettes (French for *skewers*) make wonderful appetizers.

   24 button mushrooms (about 2
       [8-ounce] packages)
  1½ tablespoons curry powder
  1½ tablespoons vegetable oil
  2½ tablespoons lime juice
  1½ tablespoons honey
    1 teaspoon kosher salt
    ½ teaspoon freshly ground black
       pepper
    1 pound skinless, boneless chicken
       breast, cut into 24 pieces
       Cooking spray

1. Remove stems from mushrooms; discard stems.
2. Cook curry powder and oil in a small skillet over medium-low heat 1 minute or until fragrant, stirring constantly. Remove from heat; cool 5 minutes. Stir in lime juice, honey, salt, and pepper. Place mushrooms and half of curry mixture in a large zip-top plastic bag. Place chicken and remaining curry mixture in another large zip-top plastic bag. Seal bags, and marinate in refrigerator 1 hour, turning bags occasionally. Remove mushrooms and chicken from bags, discarding marinades.
3. Prepare grill or broiler.
4. Thread 4 mushrooms onto each of 6 (8-inch) skewers. Thread 4 chicken pieces onto each of 6 (8-inch) skewers. Place chicken brochettes on grill rack or broiler pan coated with cooking spray; cook 5 minutes or until done. Place mushroom brochettes on grill rack or broiler pan coated with cooking spray; cook 3 minutes or until tender. Yield: 6 servings (serving size: 1 mushroom brochette and 1 chicken brochette).

WINE NOTE: The curry powder mingled with lime in this terrific appetizer gives it a slightly exotic flavor. Serve these with an inexpensive sparkling wine, something fresh, light, and—like the curry—tingly. Korbel Brut nonvintage is a great match at just $12.99.

CALORIES 156 (28% from fat); FAT 4.8g (sat 0.8g, mono 1.1g, poly 2.3g); PROTEIN 19.9g; CARB 9.1g; FIBER 1.5g; CHOL 44mg; IRON 1.9mg; SODIUM 367mg; CALC 21mg

Whole Wheat Mushroom Croutons

These crispy croutons add crunch and earthiness to soups and salads. Any firm bread will work here. Store in an airtight container for up to a week.

 2 cups (½-inch) cubed whole wheat bread (about 3½ ounces)
 2 teaspoons Porcini Powder (recipe on page 104)
 1 teaspoon olive oil
 ¼ teaspoon kosher salt
 1 tablespoon grated fresh Parmesan cheese

1. Preheat oven to 350°.
2. Combine first 4 ingredients on a jelly roll pan, tossing gently to coat; arrange in a single layer. Bake at 350° for 15 minutes or until toasted, stirring after 8 minutes; toss with cheese. Yield: 2 cups (serving size: ¼ cup).

CALORIES 56 (29% from fat); FAT 1.8g (sat 0.5g, mono 0.9g, poly 0.3g); PROTEIN 2.4g; CARB 8.2g; FIBER 1.3g; CHOL 1mg; IRON 0.8mg; SODIUM 185mg; CALC 27mg

Spicy Noodle Bowl with Mushrooms and Spinach

This clear, aromatic soup is the perfect antidote to heavy or complicated meals. Somen—thin, quick-cooking Japanese wheat noodles—can be found in Asian markets or in the Asian section of large supermarkets. Use grilled or sautéed pork chops for this recipe.

 6 (2-ounce) boneless center-cut loin pork chops (¼ inch thick), cooked
 8 cups low-salt beef broth
 2 cups water
 1 teaspoon grated peeled fresh ginger
 ½ teaspoon crushed red pepper
 6 cups thinly sliced shiitake mushroom caps (about ½ pound)
 4 ounces somen (wheat noodles) or angel hair pasta
 3 cups chopped spinach
 1¾ cups enoki mushrooms (about 3½ ounces)
 ½ cup thinly sliced green onions
 ½ teaspoon kosher salt
 ¼ cup chopped fresh cilantro

1. Thinly slice pork chops.
2. Bring broth, water, ginger, and pepper to a simmer in a large Dutch oven. Stir in shiitakes; simmer 10 minutes. Stir in noodles; cook 2 minutes or until tender. Stir in pork, spinach, enoki mushrooms, green onions, and salt; cook 1 minute or until spinach wilts. Sprinkle with cilantro. Yield: 6 servings (serving size: about 1¾ cups).

CALORIES 232 (21% from fat); FAT 5.5g (sat 1.8g, mono 2.4g, poly 0.7g); PROTEIN 23.5g; CARB 20g; FIBER 2.5g; CHOL 34mg; IRON 2.5mg; SODIUM 651mg; CALC 46mg

Dried Mushrooms

Dried mushrooms are used differently than fresh. The best varieties to use in dried form are porcini, shiitakes, and morels, although many other kinds also pack a flavorful punch. When mushrooms are dried, they shrivel and their flavor concentrates. Look inside the package of dried mushrooms to see how big the pieces are; if they've crumbled to dust, don't buy them.

Check the package for Latin names. The choicest morels are *Morchella esculaenta*, *Morchella conica*, and *Morchella deliciosa*, which are all delicious when cooked. The porcini/cèpe is called *Boletus edulis*; others in the same family are *Boletus luteus* and *Boletus barrosii*, which are still fine to eat but may have a bitter, unpleasant aftertaste. Also, look for countries of origin, if any. Morels from the United States are often shipped to Europe, dried, packaged, and reshipped here to capitalize on a French or Swiss name, which means you pay more for the cachet but not necessarily for better quality.

Soak dried mushrooms in hot liquid, such as water or heated chicken broth. They should reconstitute in about 30 minutes. Drain mushrooms into a fine sieve lined with paper towels or cheesecloth placed over a bowl, reserving the liquid (which makes a flavorful sauce). To get rid of any remaining sand, rinse and drain the mushrooms again. Then proceed with the recipe.

search myclar2003.com for all our tips

may

One Great Grilled Dinner

Here's an all-purpose menu you'll roll out time and again, no sweat.

If grilling for guests provokes high anxiety in your home, this menu is for you. By front-loading most of the work before guests arrive, you can show off grill mastery without standing over searing coals while everyone else sips ice-cold beer.

Because there is a proportional ratio of how long it takes to grill chicken to the number of guests waiting for it, chicken is out. Instead, caramel overtones of bourbon and maple influence a hoisin baste for either tuna or pork. And since it wouldn't be a barbecue without the bugs, finish off with refreshing Grasshopper Ice Cream Pie.

Great Grilled Menu

Téo's Punch

Bruschetta Gorgonzola and Apples

Hoisin and Bourbon-Glazed Pork Tenderloin with Three-Fruit Salsa
or
Hoisin and Bourbon-Glazed Tuna with Tomato Relish

Spring Giardiniera

Rosemary-Roasted Mashed Potatoes

Grasshopper Ice Cream Pie

search myclar2003.com for all our menus

Téo's Punch

For a decidedly adult enhancement, add 1 ounce of rum per individual serving; add 10 ounces for the whole recipe.

- 2 cups apple juice
- 2 (6-ounce) cans pineapple juice
- 1 (12-ounce) can thawed cranberry juice concentrate, undiluted
- 1 (6-ounce) can thawed orange juice concentrate, undiluted
- 4 cups club soda, chilled

1. Combine first 4 ingredients; stir until blended. Add soda just before serving.

Serve over ice. Yield: 10 servings (serving size: about 1 cup).

CALORIES 134 (1% from fat); FAT 0.1g (sat 0g, mono 0g, poly 0.1g); PROTEIN 0.6g; CARB 33.4g; FIBER 0.3g; CHOL 0mg; IRON 0.4mg; SODIUM 23mg; CALC 23mg

Bruschetta Gorgonzola and Apples

For this classic Italian appetizer, we suggest Gorgonzola for its sweet creaminess, but any quality blue cheese will do. A slice of tart apple is a nice foil to the garlic and cheese.

- 1/3 cup (about 1 1/2 ounces) crumbled Gorgonzola cheese
- 2 tablespoons butter, softened
- 1 tablespoon brandy or cognac
- 1/8 teaspoon black pepper
- 12 (1-ounce) slices diagonally cut French bread (about 1 inch thick)
Cooking spray
- 6 garlic cloves, halved
- 3 Granny Smith apples, each cut into 8 wedges (about 18 ounces)

1. Prepare grill.
2. Combine first 4 ingredients in a small bowl, stirring until blended.
3. Place bread slices on grill rack coated with cooking spray; cook 2 minutes on each side or until lightly browned. Remove from grill. Rub cut sides of garlic over one side of each bread slice. Spread 2 teaspoons cheese mixture over each bread slice. Serve with apple wedges. Yield: 12 servings (serving size: 1 bruschetta and 2 apple wedges).

CALORIES 148 (30% from fat); FAT 5g (sat 2.7g, mono 0.9g, poly 0.3g); PROTEIN 4.1g; CARB 21.4g; FIBER 1.7g; CHOL 13mg; IRON 0.9mg; SODIUM 263mg; CALC 68mg

Hoisin and Bourbon-Glazed Pork Tenderloin
(pictured on page 131)

The baste in this recipe has a range of flavors—sweet, sour, salty, woody, and spicy. Because it's butterflied, the pork picks up more flavor and cooks more quickly. Soaking wood chips in water prevents flare-ups on the grill, and butterflying the tenderloin exposes more surface area. This allows the pork to absorb more of the smoky flavor and creates a nice caramelized exterior.

- 1 cup hickory wood chips
- 1/3 cup hoisin sauce
- 2 tablespoons seasoned rice vinegar
- 2 tablespoons bourbon
- 2 tablespoons maple syrup
- 1 1/2 teaspoons grated peeled fresh ginger
- 1 1/2 teaspoons fresh lime juice
- 1/2 teaspoon chile paste with garlic
- 1 garlic clove, minced
- 2 (1-pound) pork tenderloins, trimmed
- 1/2 teaspoon salt
- 1/2 teaspoon freshly ground black pepper
Cooking spray

1. Soak wood chips in water 30 minutes; drain well.
2. Prepare grill.
3. Combine hoisin sauce and next 7 ingredients in a small bowl; stir with a whisk.
4. Slice pork lengthwise, cutting to, but not through, other side. Open halves, laying pork flat. Sprinkle pork with salt and pepper. Add wood chips to grill.

Place pork on grill rack coated with cooking spray; cook 5 minutes. Turn and baste pork with hoisin mixture; cook 5 minutes. Turn and baste pork with hoisin mixture; cook 5 minutes or until pork reaches 155° or desired degree of doneness. Let stand 5 minutes; cut pork into ½-inch slices. Yield: 8 servings (serving size: 3 ounces pork).

CALORIES 209 (25% from fat); FAT 5.8g (sat 2g, mono 2.3g, poly 0.7g); PROTEIN 26.3g; CARB 9.2g; FIBER 0.4g; CHOL 80mg; IRON 1.4mg; SODIUM 452mg; CALC 13mg

HOISIN AND BOURBON-GLAZED TUNA:
Follow steps 1 through 3 above. Sprinkle 6 (6-ounce) tuna steaks with ¼ teaspoon salt and ⅛ teaspoon freshly ground black pepper. Add wood chips to grill. Place tuna steaks on grill rack coated with cooking spray; cook 5 minutes. Turn and baste tuna with hoisin mixture; cook 5 minutes. Turn and baste tuna with hoisin mixture; cook 2 minutes or until tuna flakes easily when tested with a fork. Yield: 6 servings (serving size: 1 tuna steak).

CALORIES 328 (26% from fat); FAT 9.4g (sat 2.4g, mono 3.1g, poly 2.9g); PROTEIN 42.9g; CARB 12.2g; FIBER 0.4g; CHOL 70mg; IRON 2.1mg; SODIUM 502mg; CALC 25mg

Three-Fruit Salsa

(pictured on page 131)

This salsa, takes on a tropical appeal with its Thai-inspired notes.

     1   cup finely chopped peeled
         cantaloupe
     1   cup finely chopped peeled mango
     1   cup sliced small strawberries
     ½   cup finely chopped seeded peeled
         cucumber
     ½   cup finely chopped green bell pepper
     ½   cup finely chopped red onion
     2   tablespoons finely chopped seeded
         jalapeño pepper
    1½   tablespoons chopped fresh mint
     1   tablespoon chopped fresh basil
     2   tablespoons fresh lime juice
     1   tablespoon honey
     ¼   teaspoon salt

1. Combine all ingredients in a bowl; toss to combine. Serve salsa with a slotted spoon. Yield: 6 servings (serving size: about ¾ cup).

CALORIES 59 (6% from fat); FAT 0.4g (sat 0.1g, mono 0.1g, poly 0.1g); PROTEIN 1g; CARB 14.7g; FIBER 2.1g; CHOL 0mg; IRON 0.5mg; SODIUM 103mg; CALC 19mg

Tomato Relish

Cucumbers and mint enhance this easy relish, which will be as familiar as salsa.

     2   cups chopped tomato
     1   cup chopped yellow tomato
     ½   cup finely chopped seeded peeled
         cucumber
     ½   cup finely chopped green bell
         pepper
     ½   cup finely chopped red onion
     3   tablespoons chopped fresh
         basil
     2   tablespoons fresh lime juice
    1½   teaspoons chopped fresh mint
     ½   teaspoon salt
     ½   teaspoon sugar
     ½   teaspoon crushed red pepper

1. Combine all ingredients in a bowl; toss to combine. Serve with a slotted spoon. Yield: 6 servings (serving size: ⅔ cup).

CALORIES 33 (11% from fat); FAT 0.4g (sat 0.1g, mono 0.1g, poly 0.2g); PROTEIN 1.2g; CARB 7.5g; FIBER 1.8g; CHOL 0mg; IRON 0.8mg; SODIUM 205mg; CALC 16mg

Spring Giardiniera

(pictured on page 130)

Giardiniera is great to prepare ahead and have available. It can be a perfect vegetable side or a fabulous snack.

    1½   cups cider vinegar
     ½   cup water
     2   tablespoons sugar
     1   tablespoon salt
     1   teaspoon black peppercorns
     ½   teaspoon mustard seeds
     ½   teaspoon dried dill
     2   bay leaves
     2   cups small cauliflower florets
     2   cups (3-inch) diagonally cut
         asparagus
    1½   cups green beans, trimmed (about
         8 ounces)
     1   cup (¼-inch) diagonally cut
         carrot
     1   cup red bell pepper strips
     6   green onion bottoms, trimmed
     4   garlic cloves, halved

Continued

+--+
| Timetable |
| |
Day Before:	**45 minutes ahead:**
• Trim and butterfly pork	• Prepare and preheat grill
• Prepare Spring Giardiniera	• Roast potatoes
• Prepare Gorgonzola spread	• Soak wood chips
• Prepare Grasshopper Ice Cream Pie	
	15 minutes ahead:
Morning of:	• Check grill; add additional charcoal as
• Buy tuna	needed
• Ice beer	• Grill bread and slice apples for
• Mix hoisin sauce	appetizer
• Prepare Téo's Punch without soda; chill	• Prepare mashed potatoes; keep warm
• Chop vegetables for Tomato Relish or	• Add soda to punch
fruit for Three-Fruit Salsa	
	As guests arrive:
Two hours ahead:	• Add wood chips to grill
• Set up buffet area or dinner table	• Prepare entrée
• Cut up potatoes	• Temper pie in refrigerator
	• Sit back and relax; you're all done—
One hour ahead:	except for the eating
• Assemble Tomato Relish or Three-Fruit Salsa	
• Preheat oven for potatoes	
+--+

1. Combine first 8 ingredients in a large Dutch oven. Bring to a boil; reduce heat, and simmer 3 minutes. Arrange cauliflower and remaining 6 ingredients in a large heavy-duty zip-top plastic bag. Carefully pour vinegar mixture over cauliflower mixture.

2. Seal bag; refrigerate 8 hours or overnight, turning occasionally. Discard bay leaves. Serve with a slotted spoon. Yield: 6 servings (serving size: 1 cup).

CALORIES 57 (5% from fat); FAT 0.3g (sat 0.1g, mono 0g, poly 0.2g); PROTEIN 3.2g; CARB 12.8g; FIBER 4.7g; CHOL 0mg; IRON 1.5mg; SODIUM 141mg; CALC 55mg

Rosemary-Roasted Mashed Potatoes

Roasting the potatoes for these mashers mimics a grilled quality. If the appetizer course goes long, just stir in a little hot water to revive the creamy texture; the seasonings will remain just as robust.

    8   cups baking potato, cut into
          1-inch pieces (about 2 pounds)
    1   tablespoon olive oil
   ½   teaspoon dried rosemary, crushed
   ½   teaspoon salt
   ½   teaspoon freshly ground black
          pepper
   Cooking spray
   ¾   cup hot water
   ¼   cup chopped green onions
   ¼   cup (1 ounce) grated fresh
          Parmesan cheese
   ¼   teaspoon garlic powder
    1   (8-ounce) container low-fat sour
          cream

1. Preheat oven to 425°.
2. Combine first 5 ingredients in a shallow roasting pan coated with cooking spray; toss well to coat. Bake at 425° for 30 minutes or until tender.
3. Combine water and remaining 4 ingredients in a large bowl; add potato mixture. Mash with a potato masher to desired consistency. Serve immediately. Yield: 6 servings (serving size: ¾ cup).

CALORIES 231 (26% from fat); FAT 6.7g (sat 3.6g, mono 2g, poly 0.3g); PROTEIN 7.1g; CARB 35.8g; FIBER 2.5g; CHOL 15mg; IRON 0.7mg; SODIUM 304mg; CALC 115mg

Grasshopper Ice Cream Pie

    1   cup chocolate wafer crumbs (about
          20 cookies; such as Nabisco's
          Famous Chocolate Wafers)
    2   tablespoons butter, melted
    2   tablespoons 1% low-fat milk
    1   (7-ounce) jar marshmallow creme
   ¼   cup green crème de menthe
    2   tablespoons white crème de cacao
    1   (8-ounce) container frozen fat-free
          whipped topping, thawed
    3   cups vanilla low-fat ice cream,
          softened
    2   teaspoons chocolate syrup

1. Combine crumbs and butter in a small bowl; stir with a fork until moist. Press into bottom of a 9-inch springform pan. Chill.
2. Combine milk and marshmallow creme in a microwave-safe bowl; microwave at HIGH 1 minute, stirring once. Add crème de menthe, crème de cacao, and whipped topping, stirring until blended. Spread ice cream into prepared pan; top with marshmallow mixture. Freeze at least 6 hours. Drizzle with chocolate syrup before serving. Yield: 12 servings.

CALORIES 234 (17% from fat); FAT 4.4g (sat 2.2g, mono 1.1g, poly 0.3g); PROTEIN 2.4g; CARB 40.6g; FIBER 0.9g; CHOL 9mg; IRON 0.4mg; SODIUM 139mg; CALC 54mg

great starts

Mother's Day Brunch

Whether you're honoring Mom or seeking respite from a hectic week, try this menu.

Brunch Menu

Raspberry-Orange Sunrises

Apple-Oat Muffins

Sliced Mangoes with Crystallized Ginger

Spinach and Tomato Strata or **Tofu Breakfast Burritos**

Raspberry-Orange Sunrises

(pictured on page 130)

    4   cups fresh orange juice (about 8
          oranges)
    1   cup frozen unsweetened raspberries
   1½   cups semisweet sparkling wine
    3   orange slices, halved (optional)

1. Place orange juice and raspberries in a blender; process until smooth. Pour orange juice mixture into a pitcher and stir in wine. Serve over ice. Garnish with orange slices, if desired. Yield: 6 servings (serving size: 1 cup).

CALORIES 178 (1% from fat); FAT 0.2g (sat 0g, mono 0g, poly 0.1g); PROTEIN 1.6g; CARB 33.2g; FIBER 2.5g; CHOL 0mg; IRON 0.8mg; SODIUM 10mg; CALC 33mg

Apple-Oat Muffins

The shredded apple adds moisture to the muffins. You'll find that the batter fills the muffin cups more than most recipes, but it shouldn't overflow in the oven.

    2   cups shredded peeled McIntosh
          apple (about ¾ pound)
   1½   cups all-purpose flour
    1   cup quick-cooking oats
   ⅔   cup packed brown sugar
   1½   teaspoons baking powder
   ½   teaspoon baking soda
   ½   teaspoon salt
   ½   teaspoon ground cinnamon
   ¼   cup fat-free milk
    2   tablespoons vegetable oil
    1   teaspoon vanilla extract
    1   (8-ounce) carton plain low-fat yogurt
    1   large egg
   Cooking spray

1. Preheat oven to 400°.
2. Place apple on paper towels; squeeze until barely moist. Lightly spoon flour into dry measuring cups; level with a knife. Combine flour and next 6 ingredients in a medium bowl; stir with a whisk. Make a well in center of mixture. Combine milk, oil, vanilla, yogurt, and egg; stir well with a whisk. Add to flour mixture, stirring just until moist. Stir in apple.

3. Spoon batter into 12 muffin cups coated with cooking spray. Bake at 400° for 20 minutes or until muffins spring back when touched lightly in center. Remove muffins from pans immediately; place on a wire rack. Yield: 1 dozen (serving size: 1 muffin).

CALORIES 190 (19% from fat); FAT 3.9g (sat 0.9g, mono 1.1g, poly 1.5g); PROTEIN 4.5g; CARB 34.6g; FIBER 1.9g; CHOL 20mg; IRON 1.5mg; SODIUM 238mg; CALC 96mg

Sliced Mangoes with Crystallized Ginger

Garnish the serving platter with a handful of fresh raspberries or blackberries.

    4 cups sliced peeled mango (about 3
       pounds)
    2 tablespoons finely chopped
       crystallized ginger
    1 tablespoon thinly sliced fresh mint
    1 tablespoon fresh lime juice
    1 tablespoon honey

1. Place all ingredients in a large bowl, and toss gently to combine. Cover and chill 1 hour. Yield: 8 servings (serving size: ½ cup).

CALORIES 114 (3% from fat); FAT 0.4g (sat 0.1g, mono 0.2g, poly 0.1g); PROTEIN 0.8g; CARB 29.9g; FIBER 2.3g; CHOL 0mg; IRON 0.6mg; SODIUM 4mg; CALC 20mg

Spinach and Tomato Strata

Use a dense, chewy bread for best results.

    1 teaspoon olive oil
    3 garlic cloves, minced
    1 (10-ounce) package fresh spinach
    2 (14.5-ounce) cans diced tomatoes,
       drained
       Cooking spray
   16 (1-ounce) slices sturdy white
       bread, cut in half
   2½ cups 1% low-fat milk
    ¼ teaspoon salt
    ¼ teaspoon black pepper
    5 large eggs
    ¾ cup (3 ounces) shredded reduced-
       fat Jarlsberg cheese

1. Heat oil in a Dutch oven over medium heat. Add garlic and spinach; cook 3 minutes or until spinach wilts and liquid almost evaporates. Cool.
2. Spread half of tomatoes over bottom of a 13 x 9-inch baking dish coated with cooking spray. Arrange half of bread slices over tomatoes; top with remaining tomatoes, spinach mixture, and remaining bread slices. Combine milk, salt, pepper, and eggs, stirring with a whisk. Pour over bread slices; sprinkle with cheese. Cover and refrigerate 8 hours.
3. Preheat oven to 375°.
4. Uncover strata. Bake at 375° for 50 minutes or until set. Yield: 9 servings.

CALORIES 271 (26% from fat); FAT 7.8g (sat 2.7g, mono 2.8g, poly 1.1g); PROTEIN 15.3g; CARB 35.3g; FIBER 3.4g; CHOL 131mg; IRON 3.2mg; SODIUM 631mg; CALC 304mg

Tofu Breakfast Burritos

This recipe can be doubled; just use a large nonstick skillet.

    1 teaspoon vegetable oil
    1 teaspoon chili powder
    ½ teaspoon ground cumin
    1 (12.3-ounce) package reduced-fat
       firm tofu, drained and crumbled
    ¼ cup (1 ounce) shredded reduced-
       fat cheddar cheese
    2 tablespoons minced fresh cilantro
    ⅛ teaspoon salt
    4 (8-inch) flour tortillas
    2 cups baby spinach leaves
    1 cup bottled salsa

1. Heat oil in a medium nonstick skillet over medium-high heat. Add chili powder and cumin; cook 10 seconds. Add tofu; cook 1½ minutes, stirring frequently. Stir in cheese, cilantro, and salt. Remove from heat.
2. Warm tortillas according to package directions. Arrange ½ cup spinach over each tortilla; top each with ¼ cup tofu mixture. Roll up. Serve with salsa. Yield: 4 servings (serving size: 1 burrito and ¼ cup salsa).

CALORIES 209 (28% from fat); FAT 6.4g (sat 1.6g, mono 2g, poly 2.4g); PROTEIN 12g; CARB 26.4g; FIBER 3.6g; CHOL 5mg; IRON 3.6mg; SODIUM 674mg; CALC 191mg

. . . And Ready in Just about 20 Minutes

In sync with May's milder weather, these speedy suppers will give you more time on your deck to watch the sunset.

Shrimp and kiwi pair in a fresh, satisfying salad, lamb chops team up with tomato and onion for an easy grilled dinner, and turkey cutlets get the Marsala treatment.

Shrimp and Kiwi Salad

    1 tablespoon olive oil, divided
   12 peeled and deveined large shrimp
       (about ¾ pound)
    1 tablespoon chopped green onions
    1 tablespoon chopped fresh cilantro
    1 tablespoon rice vinegar
    1 teaspoon grated lime rind
    1 tablespoon fresh lime juice
    ⅛ teaspoon salt
    ⅛ teaspoon crushed red pepper
    ⅛ teaspoon black pepper
    2 cups torn red leaf lettuce leaves
    1 cup cubed peeled kiwifruit (about
       3 kiwifruit)

1. Heat 1 teaspoon oil in a large nonstick skillet over medium-high heat. Add shrimp; sauté 4 minutes or until done. Remove from heat.
2. Combine 2 teaspoons oil, onions, and next 7 ingredients in a bowl. Add shrimp; toss to coat. Spoon mixture over lettuce; top with kiwi. Yield: 2 servings (serving size: 6 shrimp, 1 cup lettuce, and ½ cup kiwi).

CALORIES 330 (29% from fat); FAT 10.7g (sat 1.5g, mono 5.4g, poly 1.8g); PROTEIN 36.9g; CARB 22.8g; FIBER 4.4g; CHOL 259mg; IRON 5.5mg; SODIUM 405mg; CALC 175mg

Fruited Pork Tenderloin

1 (1-pound) pork tenderloin, trimmed
½ teaspoon salt, divided
⅛ teaspoon black pepper
2 teaspoons olive oil
Cooking spray
¼ cup chopped pitted dates
¼ cup golden raisins
¼ cup water
¼ cup apple juice
¼ cup tawny port or other sweet red wine
1 teaspoon Dijon mustard
2 whole cloves
Parsley sprigs (optional)

1. Cut pork crosswise into 8 slices; sprinkle with ¼ teaspoon salt and pepper. Heat oil in a large nonstick skillet coated with cooking spray over medium-high heat. Add pork; cook 2 minutes on each side or until browned.
2. Add ¼ teaspoon salt, dates, and next 6 ingredients. Cover; simmer 2 minutes or until pork is done. Remove pork from pan. Bring date mixture to a boil; cook until reduced to ⅔ cup (about 5 minutes). Remove cloves; discard. Garnish with parsley sprigs, if desired. Yield: 4 servings (serving size: 3 ounces pork and about 2½ tablespoons sauce).

CALORIES 265 (29% from fat); FAT 8.6g (sat 2.5g, mono 4.5g, poly 0.9g); PROTEIN 23.9g; CARB 19.7g; FIBER 1.6g; CHOL 75mg; IRON 1.9mg; SODIUM 382mg; CALC 16mg

Grilled Lamb Chops with Tomato and Onion

Cooking spray
⅛ teaspoon salt
⅛ teaspoon dried basil
⅛ teaspoon black pepper
2 (¼-inch-thick) slices tomato
2 (⅛-inch-thick) slices onion
4 (4-ounce) lamb loin chops, trimmed

1. Heat a grill pan coated with cooking spray over medium-high heat.
2. Combine salt, basil, and pepper in a small bowl. Sprinkle half of basil mixture

over tomato and onion; rub lamb with remaining basil mixture. Add tomato, onion, and lamb to pan. Cook vegetables 2 minutes on each side or until lightly browned. Cook lamb 8 minutes on each side or until desired degree of doneness Yield: 2 servings (serving size: 2 chops, 1 tomato slice, and 1 onion slice).

CALORIES 264 (38% from fat); FAT 11.2g (sat 4g, mono 4.9g, poly 0.8g); PROTEIN 34.7g; CARB 4.3g; FIBER 1g; CHOL 108mg; IRON 2.5mg; SODIUM 244mg; CALC 32mg

Turkey Marsala

2 tablespoons olive oil, divided
1 tablespoon chopped fresh basil
3 garlic cloves, crushed
1 (8-ounce) package presliced mushrooms
¾ cup fat-free, less-sodium chicken broth, divided
1 tablespoon cornstarch
½ cup dry Marsala wine
½ teaspoon salt
¼ teaspoon garlic powder
¼ teaspoon black pepper
4 (4-ounce) turkey cutlets
Basil sprigs (optional)

1. Heat 1 tablespoon oil in a large nonstick skillet over medium-high heat. Add chopped basil, garlic, and mushrooms; cook 5 minutes, stirring frequently.
2. Combine chicken broth and cornstarch in a small bowl. Add broth mixture and Marsala to mushroom mixture. Bring to a boil; cook 1 minute, stirring constantly. Reduce heat to medium-low; cook 5 minutes, stirring frequently.
3. While sauce cooks, combine salt, garlic powder, and pepper; sprinkle over turkey. Heat 1 tablespoon oil in a large nonstick skillet over medium-high heat. Add turkey; cook 2 minutes on each side or until done. Serve with sauce. Garnish with basil sprigs, if desired. Yield: 4 servings (serving size: 1 turkey cutlet and ½ cup sauce).

CALORIES 245 (29% from fat); FAT 7.8g (sat 1.2g, mono 5.1g, poly 0.9g); PROTEIN 36.6g; CARB 5.8g; FIBER 0.9g; CHOL 94mg; IRON 2.6mg; SODIUM 439mg; CALC 25mg

Shrimp with Feta

1 (3½-ounce) bag boil-in-bag long-grain rice
2 teaspoons olive oil
Cooking spray
¼ cup coarsely chopped Vidalia or other sweet onion
¼ cup chopped fresh parsley
½ teaspoon salt
½ teaspoon dried basil
½ teaspoon dried oregano
¼ teaspoon dried dill
¼ teaspoon crushed red pepper
2 (14.5-ounce) cans no-salt-added diced tomatoes, undrained
1 garlic clove, crushed
⅓ cup dry white wine
1½ pounds peeled and deveined large shrimp
1 (4-ounce) package crumbled feta cheese
Chopped parsley (optional)

1. Cook rice according to package directions.
2. While rice cooks, heat oil in a nonstick skillet coated with cooking spray over medium-high heat. Add onion; sauté 4 minutes. Stir in ¼ cup parsley and next 7 ingredients; cook 3 minutes. Stir in wine and shrimp. Cover; cook 3 minutes or until shrimp are done. Remove from heat; sprinkle with cheese. Serve over rice. Garnish with parsley, if desired. Yield: 4 servings (serving size: 1¾ cups shrimp mixture and ½ cup rice).

CALORIES 457 (23% from fat); FAT 11.9g (sat 5.2g, mono 3.6g, poly 1.7g); PROTEIN 43.6g; CARB 42.5g; FIBER 3g; CHOL 284mg; IRON 6.2mg; SODIUM 887mg; CALC 321mg

Flatbreads and Spreads

These classic flavor combinations are perfect for nibbling now.

Flatbreads—the most ancient and primitive breads—have recently enjoyed a revival among sophisticates and the mass market alike.

The advantage of flatbreads over loaves is their affinity for dips, spreads, and fillings. A great counterpoint to spicy foods, each bread in the following recipes pairs with a traditional dip or spread, all of which can be prepared ahead.

International Pairs

Naan & Red Pepper Relish

Pitas & Garlicky Red Lentil Dal

Chapatis & Spiced Yogurt Dip

Dosas & Fig and Pistachio Chutney

Arepas & Tomatillo Salsa

Naan

Naan, one of the daily breads of India, is dense and chewy, almost like focaccia but thinner. If you don't have a pizza peel, use the back of a baking sheet to transfer the dough to a hot pizza stone. You can also bake naan on a heavy baking sheet lined with parchment paper.

    1   teaspoon dry yeast
    ¾   cup warm water (100° to 110°)
    ½   cup plain low-fat yogurt
    2¼ cups bread flour, divided
    1   cup whole wheat flour
    1¼ teaspoons sea salt
    1   tablespoon olive oil
        Cooking spray
    4   tablespoons cornmeal, divided

1. Dissolve yeast in warm water in a large bowl; let stand 5 minutes. Stir in yogurt. Lightly spoon flours into dry measuring cups; level with a knife. Add ½ cup bread flour and whole wheat flour to yeast mixture; stir with a whisk until smooth. Cover and let rise in a warm place (85°), free from drafts, 2 hours (batter will be bubbly, lacy, and weblike).
2. Stir in salt and oil. Add 1½ cups bread flour (½ cup at a time); stir with a wooden spoon (dough will become very difficult to stir).
3. Turn dough out onto a lightly floured surface. Knead until smooth and elastic (about 10 minutes); add enough of remaining bread flour, 1 tablespoon at a time, to prevent dough from sticking to hands (dough will feel tacky). Place dough in a large bowl coated with cooking spray, turning to coat top. Cover and let rise in a warm place (85°), free from drafts, 2 hours or until doubled in size. (Press 2 fingers into dough. If indentation remains, dough has risen enough.)
4. Place pizza stone on bottom rack in oven. Preheat oven to 500°.
5. Punch dough down; turn out onto a lightly floured surface. Cover and let rest 5 minutes.
6. Divide dough into 8 equal portions. Working with 1 portion at a time, (cover remaining dough to keep from drying), stretch each portion into a 6-inch oval. Cover and let rest 5 minutes.
7. Make indentations in top of dough portions using handle of a wooden spoon or your fingertips; cover and let rise 20 minutes.
8. Place 2 dough portions on back of a pizza peel dusted with 1 tablespoon cornmeal. Slide onto preheated pizza stone or baking sheet lined with parchment. Bake at 500° for 6 minutes or until lightly browned. Repeat with remaining dough and cornmeal. Serve immediately. Yield: 8 servings.

CALORIES 216 (12% from fat); FAT 2.9g (sat 0.5g, mono 1.4g, poly 0.6g); PROTEIN 7.5g; CARB 40.4g; FIBER 3.1g; CHOL 1mg; IRON 2.4mg; SODIUM 371mg; CALC 39mg

Red Pepper Relish

Try this slightly sweet, tangy relish on a veggie sandwich.

    4   large red bell peppers
    ½   teaspoon coriander seeds
    1   teaspoon olive oil
    2   cups finely chopped Vidalia or
        other sweet onion
    ½   teaspoon crushed red pepper
    4   garlic cloves, thinly sliced
    2   tablespoons red wine vinegar
    1   teaspoon sugar
    1   teaspoon fresh lemon juice
    ½   teaspoon salt
    ¼   teaspoon freshly ground black
        pepper
    2   tablespoons chopped fresh cilantro

1. Preheat broiler.
2. Cut bell peppers in half lengthwise; discard seeds and membranes. Place pepper halves, skin sides up, on a foil-lined baking sheet; flatten with hand. Broil 15 minutes or until blackened. Place in a zip-top plastic bag; seal. Let stand 15 minutes. Peel and finely chop.
3. Place coriander seeds in a small skillet; cook over medium heat 3 minutes or until seeds are lightly browned and fragrant, shaking pan frequently. Transfer seeds to a spice or coffee grinder, and process until finely ground.
4. Heat oil in a medium nonstick skillet over medium heat. Add onion; sauté 8 minutes or until translucent. Add coriander, crushed red pepper, and garlic; sauté 3 minutes.
5. Combine onion mixture and roasted bell pepper in a medium bowl. Stir in red wine vinegar and next 4 ingredients. Cover and refrigerate 30 minutes. Stir in cilantro. Yield: 6 servings (serving size: ⅓ cup).

CALORIES 66 (15% from fat); FAT 1.1g (sat 0.2g, mono 0.6g, poly 0.2g); PROTEIN 1.8g; CARB 13.9g; FIBER 3.4g; CHOL 0mg; IRON 0.7mg; SODIUM 201mg; CALC 27mg

Pitas

A pizza stone yields puffier bread. If you don't have one, use the back of a heavy jelly roll pan to bake these. After it has risen, you can keep the dough refrigerated for three days.

½ teaspoon dry yeast
1¼ cups warm water (100° to 110°)
1¼ cups whole wheat flour, divided
1½ teaspoons fine sea salt
½ teaspoon olive oil
1¾ cups bread flour
Cooking spray

1. Dissolve yeast in warm water in a large bowl; let stand 5 minutes. Lightly spoon whole wheat flour into dry measuring cups; level with a knife. Add 1 cup whole wheat flour to yeast mixture, stirring with a whisk. Cover and let rise in a warm place (85°), free from drafts, 2 hours (batter will be bubbly).
2. Stir in salt and oil. Lightly spoon bread flour into dry measuring cups; level with a knife. Add bread flour to yeast mixture, stirring with a spoon. Turn dough out onto a lightly floured surface. Knead until smooth and elastic (about 10 minutes); add enough of remaining whole wheat flour, 1 tablespoon at a time, to prevent dough from sticking to hands (dough will feel tacky). Coat inside of a large zip-top plastic bag with cooking spray; add dough. Seal and refrigerate 12 hours or overnight.
3. Place pizza stone on bottom rack in oven. Preheat oven to 500°.
4. Turn dough out onto a lightly floured surface; shape into a 12-inch log. Divide dough into 6 equal portions. Working with 1 portion at a time (cover remaining dough to keep from drying), shape each portion into a ball. Cover; let rest 1 hour.
5. Roll each ball into a 6-inch circle. Place 3 circles on pizza stone. Bake at 500° for 5 minutes. Transfer pitas to top rack; bake an additional 2 minutes. Cool on a wire rack. Repeat with remaining dough. Yield: 6 servings.

CALORIES 233 (6% from fat); FAT 1.5g (sat 0.2g, mono 0.4g, poly 0.5g); PROTEIN 8.3g; CARB 47.3g; FIBER 4.1g; CHOL 0mg; IRON 2.8mg; SODIUM 578mg; CALC 15mg

---

Brown-Bag Lunch Menu
serves 9

Garlicky Red Lentil Dal

Pitas

Chickpea, olive, and feta salad*

*Drain 4 cans chickpeas; combine with ½ cup chopped fresh parsley, ⅓ cup fresh lemon juice, ¼ cup chopped pitted kalamata olives, 2 teaspoons extra-virgin olive oil, ½ teaspoon salt, ¼ teaspoon ground red pepper, and 1 ounce crumbled feta cheese. Toss and chill.

search myclar2003.com for all our menus

Garlicky Red Lentil Dal

This dip tastes best at room temperature. If you can't find red lentils, use brown or green instead.

2½ cups water
1 cup dried small red lentils
1 bay leaf
1½ teaspoons cumin seeds, divided
1 teaspoon salt
½ teaspoon ground turmeric
½ teaspoon Hungarian sweet paprika
½ teaspoon ground red pepper
4 teaspoons olive oil, divided
¼ cup chopped onion
½ cup chopped seeded tomato
1 garlic clove, chopped
2 tablespoons fresh lemon juice
¼ teaspoon freshly ground black pepper
1 teaspoon chopped fresh mint

1. Combine first 3 ingredients in a medium saucepan; bring to a boil. Cover, reduce heat, and simmer 10 minutes or until tender. Drain; discard bay leaf. Place lentils in a small bowl.
2. Combine 1 teaspoon cumin seeds, salt, turmeric, paprika, and red pepper in a spice or coffee grinder; process until finely ground.
3. Heat 1 tablespoon oil in a medium nonstick skillet over medium-high heat. Add onion; sauté 2 minutes or until tender. Stir in spice mixture, tomato, and garlic; cook 2 minutes or until slightly

thick. Remove pan from heat; stir in lentils, lemon juice, and black pepper. Place lentil mixture in a food processor; process until smooth. Place in a bowl.
4. Heat 1 teaspoon oil in a small saucepan over medium heat, and add ½ teaspoon cumin seeds. Sauté seeds 15 seconds, and drizzle over dal. Sprinkle with fresh mint. Yield: 9 servings (serving size: ¼ cup).

CALORIES 97 (22% from fat); FAT 2.4g (sat 0.3g, mono 1.6g, poly 0.3g); PROTEIN 6.3g; CARB 13.8g; FIBER 6.8g; CHOL 0mg; IRON 2.3mg; SODIUM 265mg; CALC 17mg

---

Chapatis

If you want to mix and shape these ahead, keep them moist and pliable under a damp towel.

1 cup whole wheat flour
¾ cup bread flour
1 teaspoon fine sea salt
¾ cup warm water (100° to 110°)
2 tablespoons olive oil

1. Lightly spoon flours into dry measuring cups; level with a knife. Combine flours and salt in large bowl. Stir in water and oil to form a thick dough; mix well.
2. Turn dough out onto a lightly floured surface. Knead until smooth and elastic (about 10 minutes). Cover and let rise at room temperature 1 hour.
3. Divide dough into 8 equal portions. Working with 1 portion at a time (cover remaining dough to keep from drying), shape each portion into a ball. Let rest 5 minutes.
4. Roll each ball into a 6-inch circle on a lightly floured surface.
5. Heat a large cast iron skillet over medium-high heat. Working with 1 portion at a time, cook 4 minutes on each side or until lightly browned with dark spots. Yield: 8 servings.

CALORIES 127 (26% from fat); FAT 3.6g (sat 0.5g, mono 2.5g, poly 0.3g); PROTEIN 4g; CARB 20.3g; FIBER 2.3g; CHOL 0mg; IRON 1.3mg; SODIUM 288mg; CALC 0mg

Spiced Yogurt Dip

You can make the dip ahead, but add the green onions just before serving.

  2 teaspoons coriander seeds
  1 teaspoon cumin seeds
  1 teaspoon caraway seeds
  1 teaspoon ground turmeric
  1 teaspoon ground red pepper
  2 cups plain fat-free yogurt
  3 tablespoons fresh lime juice
  1 tablespoon thinly sliced green
     onions
  ½ teaspoon honey
  ¼ teaspoon sea salt

1. Place first 3 ingredients in a spice or coffee grinder; process until finely ground.
2. Place spice mixture, turmeric, and pepper in a small skillet over medium heat; cook 1 minute or until fragrant.
3. Combine spice mixture, yogurt, and remaining ingredients in a medium bowl. Yield: 2 cups (serving size: ¼ cup).

CALORIES 33 (5% from fat); FAT 0.2g (sat 0g, mono 0.1g, poly 0.1g); PROTEIN 2.7g; CARB 6.5g; FIBER 0.2g; CHOL 1mg; IRON 0.4mg; SODIUM 179mg; CALC 84mg

Dosas
Indian Rice and Lentil Pancakes

In this classic Indian recipe the lentils and rice are not cooked, but soaked overnight in water, which softens and ferments them. Then they are pureed. The chlorine in tap water can inhibit the softening of the lentils, so it is best to use bottled spring water. *Urad dal* are skinned, split lentils that are available in Indian groceries. Typical lentils found in the supermarket will not substitute in this recipe.

7¼ cups bottled spring water, divided
1½ cups white basmati rice
  ½ cup urad dal (skinned, split lentils)
  1 tablespoon sugar
  2 teaspoons sea salt
  4 teaspoons vegetable oil, divided

1. Combine 6 cups water, rice, and lentils in a large bowl. Cover and let stand 8 hours. Drain and rinse.

2. Place rice mixture, 1¼ cups water, and sugar in a food processor; puree until smooth (about 1 minute).
3. Spoon batter into a clean bowl. Cover and let stand in a warm place (85°), free from drafts, 12 hours or overnight. Stir in salt.
4. Heat ½ teaspoon oil in a medium cast iron skillet over medium heat. Spoon about ⅓ cup batter into pan. Turn pancake when top is covered with bubbles and edges look cooked (about 1 minute). Repeat with remaining oil and batter. Yield: 8 servings.

CALORIES 197 (13% from fat); FAT 2.9g (sat 0.3g, mono 0.6g, poly 1.3g); PROTEIN 5.5g; CARB 37.3g; FIBER 0.9g; CHOL 0mg; IRON 1.2mg; SODIUM 583mg; CALC 20mg

Fig and Pistachio Chutney

Pistachios create an unusual and interesting take on chutney—a condiment with fruit, vinegar, and spices.

  3 cups water
1¾ cups dried figs, chopped
  ⅓ cup cider vinegar
  3 tablespoons honey
  2 tablespoons chopped peeled fresh
     ginger
  ¼ teaspoon salt
  ¼ teaspoon fennel seeds
  ¼ teaspoon coriander seeds
  ¼ teaspoon crushed red pepper
  ¼ teaspoon black peppercorns
  2 (2-inch) orange rind strips
  ¼ cup chopped unsalted pistachios

1. Combine first 11 ingredients in a medium saucepan over medium heat. Bring mixture to a simmer; cover, reduce heat, and simmer 30 minutes. Uncover and simmer an additional 30 minutes or until fruit is tender and liquid is slightly syrupy, stirring occasionally. Discard orange rind; cool. Stir in pistachios. Yield: 6 servings (serving size: ¼ cup).

CALORIES 165 (17% from fat); FAT 3.1g (sat 0.4g, mono 1.9g, poly 0.6g); PROTEIN 2.4g; CARB 35.9g; FIBER 4.4g; CHOL 0mg; IRON 1.4mg; SODIUM 106mg; CALC 68mg

Arepas

These thick corn cakes taste like tortillas.

2¼ cups water
  1 teaspoon sea salt
  5 teaspoons olive oil
  2 cups masa harina
Cooking spray

1. Combine first 3 ingredients in a medium saucepan; bring to a boil. Place masa harina in a large bowl; add boiling mixture, stirring with a wooden spoon. Cover; let stand 15 minutes.
2. Divide dough into 12 equal portions. Working with 1 portion at a time, shape each portion into a ball with moist hands. Shape balls into ½-inch-thick patties. Coat top of each patty with cooking spray.
3. Heat a 10-inch cast iron skillet over medium heat until hot. Place 4 arepas, cooking spray sides down, in pan. Press arepas lightly with a spatula to flatten slightly; cook 5 minutes on each side or until crispy and speckled brown. Repeat with remaining arepas. Yield: 12 servings.

CALORIES 90 (28% from fat); FAT 2.8g (sat 0.4g, mono 1.6g, poly 0.7g); PROTEIN 1.9g; CARB 15.9g; FIBER 1.7g; CHOL 0mg; IRON 0.6mg; SODIUM 193mg; CALC 38mg

Tomatillo Salsa

This salsa is also a great accompaniment to black bean burritos, quesadillas, or soft tacos. Although available canned, fresh tomatillos taste better in this recipe.

  1 teaspoon cumin seeds
  2 jalapeño peppers
  1 pound tomatillos, husks removed
  2 tablespoons chopped Vidalia or
     other sweet onion
  ¼ cup chopped fresh cilantro
  1 tablespoon fresh lime juice
  ¾ teaspoon sea salt

1. Place cumin seeds in a cast iron skillet over medium heat; cook 2 minutes or until toasted. Transfer to a spice or coffee grinder; process until finely ground.
Continued

2. Cut ¼ inch off stem ends of peppers; discard stem ends. Using tip of a paring knife, carefully remove and discard membranes and seeds, leaving peppers intact.
3. Heat skillet over medium heat. Add peppers and tomatillos. Cook 15 minutes, turning frequently (peppers and tomatillos will become speckled with black marks).
4. Transfer pepper mixture to a food processor, and puree until smooth. Add onion, and pulse 5 times or until blended. Pour pepper mixture into a medium bowl. Stir in cumin, cilantro, lime juice, and salt. Yield: 8 servings (serving size: ¼ cup).

CALORIES 22 (29% from fat); FAT 0.7g (sat 0.1g, mono 0.1g, poly 0.3g); PROTEIN 0.7g; CARB 4g; FIBER 1.3g; CHOL 0mg; IRON 0.6mg; SODIUM 217mg; CALC 8mg

reader recipes

Home Is Where the Heart Is

An English expatriate begins a new tradition with her American family.

Florida resident Jane Jordan—a native of Great Britain—has adapted her mums rhubarb dessert to include more typical American fruits. Her children enjoy this apple and blackberry crumble as much as she loved her mother's offering. Jane serves it with hot custard or vanilla ice cream.

Apple and Blackberry Crumble

6   cups sliced peeled Rome apples
    (about 1½ pounds)
⅓   cup packed brown sugar
1   tablespoon lemon juice
1   tablespoon water
1   cup blackberries
1¼ cups all-purpose flour
6   tablespoons chilled butter, cut
    into small pieces
½   cup granulated sugar
¼   teaspoon ground ginger

1. Preheat oven to 350°.
2. Combine first 4 ingredients in a medium saucepan; cook 10 minutes over medium heat or until apples are soft. Place apple mixture in an 8-inch pie plate. Sprinkle blackberries over apple mixture.
3. Lightly spoon flour into dry measuring cups; level with a knife. Place flour in a medium bowl; cut in butter with a pastry blender or 2 knives until mixture resembles coarse meal. Add granulated sugar and ginger; toss well. Sprinkle flour mixture over fruit. Bake at 350° for 30 minutes or until bubbly.
4. Preheat broiler.
5. Broil crumble 1 minute or until lightly browned. Yield: 8 servings.

CALORIES 287 (29% from fat); FAT 9.2g (sat 5.5g, mono 2.6g, poly 0.5g); PROTEIN 2.4g; CARB 51.1g; FIBER 3.1g; CHOL 23mg; IRON 1.3mg; SODIUM 92mg; CALC 23mg

South of the Border Menu
serves 5

If your family does not like spicy food, use 2 tablespoons chopped green bell pepper instead of jalapeño pepper in the enchiladas, and look for the milder tomatoes and green chiles for the rice.

Creamy Spinach and Mushroom Enchiladas

Spanish rice*

Black beans

*Melt 2 teaspoons butter in a large nonstick skillet over medium-high heat; add ½ cup chopped onion and 2 minced garlic cloves. Sauté 5 minutes. Stir in 1¼ cups long-grain white rice; sauté 1 minute. Add 1 (10½-ounce) can diced tomatoes and green chiles and 1 (14½-ounce) can fat-free, less-sodium chicken broth. Bring mixture to a boil; cover, reduce heat, and simmer 20 minutes.

search myclar2003.com for all our menus

Creamy Spinach and Mushroom Enchiladas

"I love and never grow tired of Mexican-style food. At home, I like to make a variety of enchiladas. Over the years I have mixed and matched recipes and added my own twists. The favorite in our home is this recipe."

—Eva Marie Duran, Madison, Wisconsin

SAUCE:
1   teaspoon garlic powder
1   (10-ounce) can condensed reduced-fat cream of chicken soup, undiluted
1   (8-ounce carton) fat-free sour cream
1   (4.5-ounce) can chopped green chiles, undrained

ENCHILADAS:
Cooking spray
1   cup chopped onion
1   jalapeño pepper, seeded and chopped
2   cups sliced mushrooms
1   teaspoon garlic powder
1   teaspoon ground cumin
½   teaspoon salt
2   (10-ounce) packages frozen chopped spinach, thawed and drained
1   cup (4 ounces) shredded Monterey Jack cheese, divided
10 (6-inch) corn tortillas

GARNISH:
½   cup chopped seeded plum tomato
¼   cup chopped green onion tops

1. Preheat oven to 350°.
2. To prepare sauce, combine first 4 ingredients; stir well.
3. To prepare enchiladas, heat a large nonstick skillet coated with cooking spray over medium-high heat. Add 1 cup onion and jalapeño; sauté 5 minutes or until tender, stirring frequently. Add mushrooms; sauté 3 minutes or until tender. Stir in 1 teaspoon garlic powder, cumin, salt, and spinach; cook 5 minutes or until heated. Combine spinach mixture and ¼ cup cheese in a large bowl.
4. Spoon ½ cup sauce into a 13 x 9-inch baking dish coated with cooking spray. Warm tortillas according to package

directions. Spoon about ⅓ cup spinach mixture down center of each tortilla; roll up. Place filled tortillas seam sides down in baking dish. Spread remaining sauce evenly over tortillas; top with ¾ cup cheese.

5. Bake at 350° for 20 minutes. Top with tomato and green onion. Yield: 5 servings (serving size: 2 enchiladas).

CALORIES 356 (26% from fat); FAT 10.2g (sat 5.6g, mono 2.8g, poly 1.3g); PROTEIN 17.8g; CARB 50.4g; FIBER 8g; CHOL 33mg; IRON 4.1mg; SODIUM 874mg; CALC 475mg

Stuffed Bok Choy

"Stuffed cabbage was an enormous part of my Hungarian and Slovak upbringing. I was pleasantly surprised with the results of this adaptation. The filling is moist, tasty, and—most important—low in fat."

—Steve Gdula, Washington, D.C.

BOK CHOY:
- 28 bok choy leaves (about 2 heads bok choy)
- 1 (14½-ounce) can fat-free, less-sodium chicken broth

STUFFING:
- 1 pound ground turkey
- ⅔ cup uncooked long-grain rice
- ½ cup finely chopped sweet onion
- ¼ cup chopped fresh cilantro
- 1 tablespoon curry powder
- 1 tablespoon minced peeled fresh ginger
- 2 tablespoons rice vinegar
- 2 teaspoons sesame oil
- ¼ teaspoon salt
- ¼ teaspoon ground red pepper
- ¼ teaspoon black pepper

DIPPING SAUCE:
- ½ cup low-sodium soy sauce
- ¼ cup fat-free, less-sodium chicken broth
- ¼ cup rice vinegar
- 1½ tablespoons brown sugar
- 1 tablespoon finely chopped seeded jalapeño pepper
- 1 tablespoon fresh lime juice
- 1 garlic clove, minced

1. To prepare bok choy, remove stems and center ribs from bok choy; cut large leaves in half lengthwise. Heat 1 can of broth in a large skillet over medium-high heat; bring to a boil. Reduce heat, and simmer. Place 3 bok choy leaves in broth; cook 15 seconds or until wilted. Remove leaves from pan; cool. Repeat procedure with remaining leaves. Reserve broth in pan.

2. To prepare stuffing, combine turkey and next 10 ingredients in a large bowl. Spoon 1 rounded tablespoon turkey mixture onto center of each leaf. Bring 2 opposite points of leaf to center, and fold over filling. Beginning at 1 short side of leaf, roll up each leaf tightly, jelly roll fashion.

3. Carefully arrange stuffed leaves, seam sides down, in a single layer in broth. Bring to a boil. Cover, reduce heat to medium-low, and cook 30 minutes.

4. To prepare dipping sauce, combine soy sauce and remaining 7 ingredients. Serve with stuffed leaves. Yield: 7 servings (serving size: 4 stuffed leaves and about 2 tablespoons sauce).

CALORIES 248 (29% from fat); FAT 8g (sat 2g, mono 2.1g, poly 1.6g); PROTEIN 18.8g; CARB 26.1g; FIBER 3.2g; CHOL 53mg; IRON 3.3mg; SODIUM 1,034mg; CALC 283mg

Baba Gha-Hummus

"I noticed, when looking at my favorite recipes for hummus and baba ghanoush, that they were quite similar, so I combined the two, making a large amount of dip with half the work. I make this dish for parties. Leftovers are great for snacks and sandwiches (especially served in a pita with lettuce and roasted peppers)."

—Helena Scheffer, Beaconsfield, Quebec

- 1 large eggplant
- 3 tablespoons tahini (sesame-seed paste)
- 1½ teaspoons ground cumin
- 1 teaspoon ground coriander
- ¾ teaspoon salt
- ⅛ teaspoon ground red pepper
- 2 garlic cloves, chopped
- 1 (15-ounce) can chickpeas (garbanzo beans), rinsed and drained

1. Preheat oven to 375°.

2. Pierce eggplant with a fork. Place eggplant on a jelly roll pan. Bake at 375° for 30 minutes or until tender. Cool and peel; discard skin.

3. Combine eggplant, tahini, and remaining ingredients in a food processor; process until smooth. Yield: 2 cups (serving size: ¼ cup).

CALORIES 114 (30% from fat); FAT 3.8g (sat 0.5g, mono 1.3g, poly 1.6g); PROTEIN 4.3g; CARB 17.3g; FIBER 5g; CHOL 0mg; IRON 1.5mg; SODIUM 368mg; CALC 51mg

Baked Risotto with Asparagus, Spinach, and Parmesan

"I like this dish because it's quick and easy to prepare—just throw it in the oven, and it's done. I usually serve this with a spinach salad, and sometimes fish or chicken. It reheats and freezes well."

—Erin Corry, Victoria, British Columbia

- 1 tablespoon olive oil
- 1 cup finely chopped onion
- 1 cup uncooked Arborio rice
- 8 cups spinach leaves (about 4 ounces)
- 2 cups fat-free, less-sodium chicken broth
- ¼ teaspoon salt
- ¼ teaspoon ground nutmeg
- ½ cup (2 ounces) grated fresh Parmesan cheese, divided
- 1½ cups (1-inch) diagonally sliced asparagus

1. Preheat oven to 400°.

2. Heat oil in a Dutch oven over medium heat. Add onion; cook 4 minutes or until tender. Add rice; stir well. Stir in spinach, broth, salt, and nutmeg. Bring to a simmer; cook 7 minutes. Stir in ¼ cup cheese.

3. Cover and bake at 400° for 15 minutes. Stir in asparagus; sprinkle with ¼ cup cheese. Cover and bake an additional 15 minutes or until liquid is almost absorbed. Yield: 4 servings (serving size: 1 cup).

CALORIES 309 (22% from fat); FAT 7.6g (sat 2.9g, mono 3.7g, poly 0.6g); PROTEIN 12.3g; CARB 47.6g; FIBER 3.7g; CHOL 10mg; IRON 3.5mg; SODIUM 639mg; CALC 217mg

The Art of Low-Fat Baking

Answers to frequently asked questions and recipes that hit the sweet spot.

Most cooks can easily figure out ways to decrease fat in certain dishes: Use less oil in your pasta. Substitute fat-free or reduced-fat dairy items for their full-fat counterparts. But baking is different. Many cooks quake at the thought of attempting to change the chemistry of a cake or pastry. Less-than-precise baking can leave you with a doughy mess and a mass of disappointment.

Here, we offer answers to some of the most common questions we receive on the topic, along with helpful advice from *Cooking Light* Test Kitchens Director Vanessa Johnson and food scientist Shirley Corriher, author of *Cookwise*. They explain which changes you can easily make and which need more careful consideration. The recipes that follow demonstrate that low-fat baking is indeed an art.

Blackberry Jam Cake

This classic butter cake is infused with spices and topped with blackberry jam. It's also good with the caramel frosting used in the Double-Caramel Turtle Cake (recipe on page 121).

Cooking spray
- 1 tablespoon all-purpose flour
- 1 cup granulated sugar
- ½ cup butter, softened
- 1 tablespoon vanilla extract
- 3 large eggs
- 2¼ cups all-purpose flour (10 ounces)
- 2½ teaspoons baking powder
- ½ teaspoon salt
- ½ teaspoon ground cinnamon
- ⅛ teaspoon ground nutmeg
- 1¼ cups fat-free milk
- 1 cup seedless blackberry jam, divided
- 1 tablespoon powdered sugar

1. Preheat oven to 350°.
2. Coat bottoms of 2 (9-inch) round cake pans with cooking spray (do not coat sides of pans); line bottoms with wax paper. Coat wax paper with cooking spray; dust with 1 tablespoon flour.

3. Place granulated sugar, butter, and vanilla in a large bowl; beat with a mixer at medium speed until well blended (about 5 minutes). Add eggs, 1 at a time, beating well after each addition. Lightly spoon 2¼ cups flour into dry measuring cups; level with a knife. Combine 2¼ cups flour and next 4 ingredients, stirring well with a whisk. Add flour mixture and milk alternately to sugar mixture, beginning and ending with flour mixture.
4. Pour batter into prepared pans; sharply tap pans once on counter to remove air bubbles. Bake at 350° for 25 minutes or until a wooden pick inserted in center comes out clean. Cool in pans 10 minutes on a wire rack; remove from pans. Cool completely on wire rack.
5. Place jam in a small bowl, and stir with a whisk until smooth. Place 1 cake layer on a plate; spread with ½ cup jam. Top with other cake layer; spread ½ cup jam over top of cake. Sprinkle with powdered sugar. Yield: 16 servings.

CALORIES 240 (26% from fat); FAT 6.9g (sat 3.9g, mono 2.1g, poly 0.4g); PROTEIN 3.8g; CARB 41.1g; FIBER 0.5g; CHOL 56mg; IRON 1.1mg; SODIUM 240mg; CALC 76mg

Cinnamon Cookies

These not-too-sweet rolled cookies are a tasty accompaniment to tea.

- 6 tablespoons granulated sugar
- ⅓ cup butter, softened
- 2 tablespoons light brown sugar
- 2 teaspoons vanilla extract
- 2 large egg whites
- 1½ cups all-purpose flour (6¾ ounces)
- ¼ cup cornstarch
- ½ teaspoon baking powder
- ¼ teaspoon baking soda
- ¼ teaspoon salt
- ¼ teaspoon ground cinnamon
- ⅔ cup powdered sugar
- 2 teaspoons fat-free milk
- ⅛ teaspoon ground cinnamon
- 2 tablespoons sliced almonds

1. Place first 4 ingredients in a large bowl; beat with a mixer at medium speed until well blended (about 5 minutes). Add egg whites, 1 at a time, beating well after each addition.
2. Lightly spoon flour into dry measuring cups; level with a knife. Combine flour and next 5 ingredients, stirring well with a whisk. Add to butter mixture; beat well. Divide dough into 4 equal portions. Roll each portion to a ⅛-inch thickness between 2 sheets of plastic wrap. Freeze dough 20 minutes or until plastic wrap can be easily removed.
3. Preheat oven to 375°.
4. Working with 1 portion of dough at a time (keep remaining dough in freezer), remove top sheet of plastic wrap. Cut dough with a 2-inch round cookie cutter; place cookies on baking sheets. Discard bottom sheet of plastic wrap.
5. Bake at 375° for 8 minutes or until lightly browned. Remove from baking sheet; cool on a wire rack. Combine powdered sugar, milk, and ⅛ teaspoon cinnamon; drizzle mixture over cookies. Sprinkle with almonds. Yield: 4 dozen (serving size: 1 cookie).

CALORIES 45 (28% from fat); FAT 1.4g (sat 0.8g, mono 0.4g, poly 0.1g); PROTEIN 0.6g; CARB 7.5g; FIBER 0.2g; CHOL 3mg; IRON 0.2mg; SODIUM 39mg; CALC 6mg

Answers to Frequently Asked Baking Questions

What does sugar do in baked goods?

Shirley Corriher: Sugar prevents the flour proteins from joining and making gluten; gluten development would make a cake or cookie tough. In this way sugar acts as a tenderizer and can replace some of the fat in the recipe. When sugar is present in amounts above 2 tablespoons per cup of flour, the two proteins in flour that normally join with each other and water to form gluten join with the sugar instead.

Sugar also caramelizes in baking, which enriches flavors. Substituting as little as a tablespoon of corn syrup for sugar can make cookies much browner, because corn syrup browns at a lower temperature than sugar. Some sugars, like honey and brown sugar, absorb moisture from the atmosphere, which means that things baked with them will stay soft and moist longer.

Why does butter make cookies crisp, and how can you lighten cookies?

Corriher: Cookies made with butter spread during baking, which means they're thinner. Trimming the amount of fat just a little will limit their spread. If you want to reduce the amount of butter but preserve the crispness, add a little corn syrup to the cookie dough. If you want a puffy cookie that stays soft, use shortening to limit the spread in baking.

Vanessa Johnson: Of all the desserts, cookies are truly the hardest for us to lighten. Because we use less butter, our cookies generally err on the chewy, fudgy side rather than the crisp side. However, small amounts of yogurt, applesauce, or egg whites can help give lower-fat cookies the texture of high-fat ones, as in our Cinnamon Cookies (recipe on page 118).

Why are butter and eggs necessary in cakes?

Corriher: Butter has three roles in cakes: to make the cake light and delicate by holding air bubbles produced by leaveners like baking powder or soda; to make the cake tender by coating the flour protein; and to carry rich flavors.

Stick margarine and shortening can substitute for butter; in fact, shortening is already aerated before you buy it, so it can produce a fine, tender cake. A margarine spread that is soft at room temperature can't substitute for butter, though.

Eggs have two parts, whites and yolks, which do two different things. Whites are an incredible drying and leavening agent, and yolks are nature's great emulsifiers for creamy texture.

Why can't you replace all the eggs in baking with egg substitute?

Corriher: Egg substitutes are usually composed of egg whites and oil, along with other ingredients like coloring and stabilizer. Because they don't have yolks, they can't serve as emulsifiers; it's the natural lecithin in the yolks that helps make an emulsion.

The lack of yolks is the reason you can't use egg substitute to make custards, either. With no yolks, custards wouldn't be smooth and creamy.

Johnson: We generally use fewer yolks and more whites than an equal amount of egg substitute simply from a practicality standpoint: Everyone usually has eggs in the fridge, but not necessarily egg substitute.

What difference does the way you measure flour make?

Johnson: It can make a terrific difference—as much as an ounce per cup of flour!

When fat is reduced in baking, the exact and precise measurement of flour becomes crucial. When a reader says she's had a problem with one of our recipes, one of the first things we suspect is that she's used the measuring cup to scoop flour out of the canister.

We advise readers to use the spoon-and-measure method: Stir the flour to aerate it, then lightly spoon into a dry measuring cup and level with a knife. By this method, a cup of all-purpose flour will weigh four and a half ounces. For more precise measurements, we've included cup and weight measures in these recipes.

Why doesn't *Cooking Light* use applesauce or fruit puree to replace fat?

Johnson: Because it generally doesn't work to do so. In our opinion, baked products made with fruit purees have an inferior texture and taste. We get far better results by simply reducing the fat.

Why does *Cooking Light* use sugar instead of sugar substitutes?

Johnson: Sugar is a key ingredient in baking, providing structure and mass in many desserts. Consider a cake: If you substituted artificial sweetener for sugar, you would lose the volume that sugar contributes, and the cake batter would not have enough substance to become a cake. Also, the tastes and textures of sugar substitutes may change when they're heated.

Because sugar also acts as a tenderizer in baking, it can actually replace some of the fat in reduced-fat baked goods. Sugar substitutes don't tenderize like sugar does.

Hot Chocolate Soufflé

Beaten egg whites give this soufflé volume. Softened ice cream makes a great, quick sauce.

Cooking spray
1 tablespoon granulated sugar
¾ cup 1% low-fat milk
¼ cup granulated sugar
4 teaspoons cornstarch
1 teaspoon instant coffee granules
⅛ teaspoon salt
1 large egg yolk
1 teaspoon vanilla extract
4 ounces bittersweet chocolate, coarsely chopped
4 large egg whites
3 tablespoons light brown sugar
¾ cup coffee low-fat ice cream, softened

1. Preheat oven to 375°.
2. Coat a 1½-quart soufflé dish with cooking spray; sprinkle with 1 tablespoon granulated sugar. Set dish aside.
3. Combine milk and next 4 ingredients in a small saucepan, stirring with a whisk until blended. Bring to a boil over medium heat; cook 1 minute or until thick, stirring constantly. Remove from heat.
4. Gradually add hot milk mixture to egg yolk, stirring constantly with a whisk. Return milk mixture to pan. Cook over medium heat until thick (about 2 minutes), stirring constantly. Remove from heat. Add vanilla and chocolate, stirring until chocolate melts.
5. Place egg whites in a large bowl; beat with a mixer at high speed until soft peaks form. Gradually add 3 tablespoons brown sugar, 1 tablespoon at a time, beating until stiff peaks form.
6. Gently stir one-fourth of egg white mixture into chocolate mixture; gently fold in remaining egg white mixture. Spoon into prepared soufflé dish.
7. Bake at 375° for 25 minutes or until puffy and set. Serve immediately topped with ice cream. Yield: 6 servings (serving size: about ⅔ cup soufflé and 2 tablespoons ice cream).

CALORIES 253 (29% from fat); FAT 8.2g (sat 4.6g, mono 2.7g, poly 0.4g); PROTEIN 6g; CARB 41.4g; FIBER 1.3g; CHOL 39mg; IRON 0.9mg; SODIUM 122mg; CALC 81mg

Coconut Crème Caramel with Pineapple Concassé

A water bath insulates the delicate egg custard to ensure a creamy texture. This is a great make-ahead dessert, because both the crème caramel and the *concassé* (a coarsely chopped mixture) need to chill for at least four hours.

⅓ cup sugar
3 tablespoons water
Cooking spray
3 large eggs
1 large egg white
1⅔ cups 2% reduced-fat milk
½ cup sugar
⅓ cup cream of coconut
2 teaspoons vanilla extract
⅛ teaspoon salt
Pineapple Concassé

1. Preheat oven to 325°.
2. Combine ⅓ cup sugar and water in a small, heavy saucepan over medium-high heat; cook until sugar dissolves, stirring frequently. Continue cooking until golden (about 10 minutes). Immediately pour into 6 (6-ounce) ramekins or custard cups coated with cooking spray, tilting each ramekin quickly until caramelized sugar coats bottom of cup.
3. Place eggs and egg white in a medium bowl; stir well with a whisk. Add milk and next 4 ingredients, stirring until well blended. Divide egg mixture evenly among prepared ramekins. Place ramekins in a 13 x 9-inch baking pan; add hot water to pan to a depth of 1 inch. Bake at 325° for 50 minutes or until a knife inserted in center comes out clean. Remove ramekins from pan. Cover and chill at least 4 hours.
4. Loosen edges of custards with a knife or rubber spatula. Place a dessert plate, upside down, on top of each ramekin; invert onto plate. Serve with Pineapple Concassé. Yield: 6 servings (serving size: 1 custard and ¼ cup Pineapple Concassé).

(Totals include Pineapple Concassé) CALORIES 239 (26% from fat); FAT 6.9g (sat 4.2g, mono 1.5g, poly 0.5g); PROTEIN 6.6g; CARB 38.5g; FIBER 0.9g; CHOL 111mg; IRON 0.7mg; SODIUM 132mg; CALC 99mg

PINEAPPLE CONCASSÉ:
Basil adds an interesting, fresh flavor to the concassé, but it can be omitted.

1½ cups finely chopped pineapple
1 tablespoon thinly sliced fresh basil
1 teaspoon sugar
1 teaspoon fresh lime juice

1. Combine all ingredients in a small bowl. Cover and chill at least 4 hours. Yield: 6 servings (serving size: ¼ cup).

CALORIES 22 (8% from fat); FAT 0.2g (sat 0g, mono 0g, poly 0.1g); PROTEIN 0.2g; CARB 5.6g; FIBER 0.5g; CHOL 0mg; IRON 0.2mg; SODIUM 0mg; CALC 3mg

Triple-Fruit Shortcakes

Blueberries and orange sections are welcome additions to the more traditional strawberries-only version. Sugar tenderizes these sweet, biscuitlike shortcakes and allows for caramelization, which creates a rich, sugary crust.

FILLING:
4 cups sliced strawberries
2 cups blueberries
½ cup orange sections
⅓ cup sugar
¼ cup fresh orange juice

SHORTCAKES:
2 cups all-purpose flour (9 ounces)
½ cup sugar
2 teaspoons baking powder
½ teaspoon salt
½ cup chilled butter, cut into small pieces
¾ cup fat-free buttermilk
Cooking spray
2 teaspoons water
1 large egg white
2 teaspoons sugar

1. To prepare filling, combine first 5 ingredients in a bowl. Cover and chill 2 hours.
2. Preheat oven to 400°.
3. To prepare shortcakes, lightly spoon flour into dry measuring cups; level with a knife. Combine flour, ½ cup sugar, baking powder, and salt in a large bowl;

stir well with a whisk. Cut in butter with a pastry blender or 2 knives until mixture resembles coarse meal. Add buttermilk; stir just until moist.

4. Turn dough out onto a lightly floured surface; knead lightly 4 or 5 times. Pat dough into a 9-inch round cake pan coated with cooking spray. Cut dough into 10 wedges, cutting into but not through dough. Combine water and egg white; brush egg white mixture over dough. Sprinkle 2 teaspoons sugar over dough.

5. Bake at 400° for 25 minutes or until golden. Cool in pan 5 minutes on a wire rack; remove from pan. Cool completely on wire rack. Cut shortcake into 10 wedges. Split each wedge in half horizontally. Fill each wedge with ½ cup filling. Yield: 10 servings.

CALORIES 292 (30% from fat); FAT 9.8g (sat 5.8g, mono 2.8g, poly 0.6g); PROTEIN 4.4g; CARB 48.3g; FIBER 3.2g; CHOL 25mg; IRON 1.6mg; SODIUM 335mg; CALC 99mg

Sugar Spot Banana Muffins

Those tiny brown spots on ripe bananas are called sugar spots; fruits that have them make the sweetest muffins. Vegetable oil makes these muffins tender and keeps them from becoming dry.

  ⅔ cup packed light brown sugar
  ¼ cup vegetable oil
  1 large egg
  1 large egg white
  ¾ cup mashed ripe banana
  ⅓ cup fat-free milk
  1⅓ cups all-purpose flour (6 ounces)
  ⅔ cup honey-crunch wheat germ
  1½ teaspoons baking powder
  ¼ teaspoon baking soda
  ¼ teaspoon salt
  Cooking spray

1. Preheat oven to 350°.

2. Combine first 4 ingredients in a large bowl; beat with a mixer at medium speed until well blended. Add banana and milk; beat well.

3. Lightly spoon flour into dry measuring cups; level with a knife. Combine flour and next 4 ingredients in a medium

bowl, stirring well with a whisk. Add to sugar mixture; beat just until moist.

4. Spoon batter evenly into 12 muffin cups coated with cooking spray. Bake at 350° for 22 minutes or until muffins spring back when touched lightly in center. Cool in pan 5 minutes on a wire rack; remove from pan. Cool on wire rack. Yield: 12 servings (serving size: 1 muffin).

CALORIES 183 (28% from fat); FAT 5.7g (sat 0.9g, mono 1.3g, poly 3.1g); PROTEIN 4.3g; CARB 30g; FIBER 1.4g; CHOL 18mg; IRON 1.6mg; SODIUM 155mg; CALC 61mg

Double-Caramel Turtle Cake

(pictured on page 132)

It's hard to believe this decadent cake, which plays off the popular Turtle candies, is light. Butter and eggs keep the cake layers moist.

CAKE:
  Cooking spray
  1 tablespoon all-purpose flour
  1½ cups boiling water
  ¾ cup unsweetened cocoa
  1½ cups granulated sugar
  6 tablespoons butter, softened
  1 teaspoon vanilla extract
  2 large eggs
  1⅔ cups all-purpose flour (7½ ounces)
  1 teaspoon baking soda
  ¾ teaspoon baking powder
  ¼ teaspoon salt

FROSTING:
  2 tablespoons butter
  ¼ cup packed dark brown sugar
  2 to 3 tablespoons fat-free milk, divided
  2 teaspoons vanilla extract
  2 cups sifted powdered sugar

TOPPING:
  ⅔ cup fat-free caramel apple dip (such as T. Marzetti's)
  ¼ cup finely chopped pecans, toasted

1. Preheat oven to 350°.
2. To prepare cake, coat bottoms of 2 (8-inch) round cake pans with cooking

spray (do not coat sides of pans); line bottoms with wax paper. Coat wax paper with cooking spray; dust with 1 tablespoon flour.

3. Combine boiling water and cocoa, stirring well with a whisk. Cool completely.

4. Place granulated sugar, 6 tablespoons butter, and vanilla in a large bowl; beat with a mixer at medium speed until well blended (about 5 minutes). Add eggs, 1 at a time, beating well after each addition. Lightly spoon 1⅔ cups flour into dry measuring cups; level with a knife. Combine 1⅔ cups flour, baking soda, baking powder, and salt, stirring well with a whisk. Add flour mixture and cocoa mixture alternately to sugar mixture, beginning and ending with flour mixture.

5. Pour batter into prepared pans; sharply tap pans once on counter to remove air bubbles. Bake at 350° for 30 minutes or until a wooden pick inserted in center comes out clean. Cool in pans 10 minutes on a wire rack; remove from pans. Cool completely on wire rack.

6. To prepare frosting, melt 2 tablespoons butter in a small saucepan over medium heat. Add brown sugar and 2 tablespoons milk; cook 1 minute or until sugar melts. Remove from heat; cool slightly. Combine butter mixture and 2 teaspoons vanilla in a large bowl. Gradually add powdered sugar; beat with a mixer at medium speed until smooth. Add additional milk, 1 teaspoon at a time, beating until spreading consistency.

7. Place 1 cake layer on a plate; spread top with half of frosting. Place caramel dip in a small zip-top plastic bag. Snip a small hole in 1 corner of bag; drizzle half of caramel dip over frosting. Top with other cake layer. Spread remaining frosting over top of cake; drizzle with remaining caramel dip. Sprinkle with pecans. Yield: 16 servings.

CALORIES 309 (24% from fat); FAT 8.4g (sat 4.3g, mono 2.9g, poly 0.8g); PROTEIN 3.7g; CARB 56.7g; FIBER 1.9g; CHOL 42mg; IRON 1.5mg; SODIUM 249mg; CALC 41mg

Cream Cheese Brownies

These fudgy, dense brownies are topped with a cheesecake-like layer.

BROWNIES:

Cooking spray
½ cup butter, softened
1½ cups sugar
1 teaspoon vanilla extract
2 large egg whites
1 large egg
⅔ cup unsweetened cocoa
½ cup fat-free milk
1½ cups all-purpose flour (6¾ ounces)
½ teaspoon baking powder
¼ teaspoon salt

TOPPING:

1 (8-ounce) block ⅓-less-fat cream cheese
1 tablespoon cornstarch
1 teaspoon vanilla extract
1 (14-ounce) can fat-free sweetened condensed milk
1 large egg

1. Preheat oven to 350°.
2. Coat bottom of a 13 x 9-inch baking pan with cooking spray.
3. To prepare batter, place butter in a large bowl; beat with a mixer at medium speed until fluffy. Add sugar and 1 teaspoon vanilla; beat until well blended (about 5 minutes). Add egg whites and 1 egg, 1 at a time, beating well after each addition. Add cocoa and ½ cup milk; beat well (mixture will appear curdled). Lightly spoon flour into dry measuring cups; level with a knife. Combine flour, baking powder, and salt; stir with a whisk. Add to cocoa mixture; beat at low speed just until blended. Spoon batter into prepared pan.
4. To prepare topping, place cream cheese in a large bowl; beat with a mixer at medium speed until smooth. Gradually add cornstarch and remaining 3 ingredients; beat until smooth. Spread evenly over batter. Bake at 350° for 35 minutes or until set. Cool in pan on a wire rack. Cut into bars. Yield: 36 servings.

CALORIES 131 (29% from fat); FAT 4.2g (sat 2.5g, mono 1.3g, poly 0.2g); PROTEIN 3.2g; CARB 20.7g; FIBER 0.7g; CHOL 23mg; IRON 0.6mg; SODIUM 88mg; CALC 51mg

Back on the Menu

Once nutrition no-no's, eggs, red meat, wine, nuts, shellfish, and butter have a place on your table.

Nutrition news sometimes seems as variable as the wind. One year, research implicates a food as a dietary villain; a few years later, subsequent studies exonerate the food in question. Eggs, shellfish, nuts, and wine are cases in point. Others, such as red meat and butter, have also taken bad raps, but we have learned that in reasonable amounts they, too, have benefits for a healthy body.

"Consumers are in a difficult position," says Walter Willett, Ph.D., head of the nutrition department at Harvard's School of Public Health. "They hear the latest nutrition findings, but those are often not reliable because it's usually more important to know about the third or fourth confirmatory study. Unfortunately, those don't make the headlines because the findings aren't new anymore."

Here's a fresh look at some formerly taboo foods, and how to make the most of them.

Frittata with Smoked Cheese and Canadian Bacon

Four eggs and four egg whites go into this frittata, which makes for a satisfying, quick supper. Potatoes, Canadian bacon, and smoked cheese make this version particularly hearty.

Cooking spray
1½ cups frozen Southern-style hash brown potatoes (such as Ore-Ida)
½ cup chopped onion
⅓ cup diced Canadian bacon (about 2 ounces)
½ teaspoon salt
½ teaspoon hot sauce (such as Tabasco)
⅛ teaspoon black pepper
4 large eggs
4 large egg whites
¼ cup (1 ounce) shredded smoked cheddar or smoked mozzarella cheese
2 tablespoons chopped green onions
Green onion strips (optional)

1. Preheat broiler.
2. Heat a 10-inch nonstick skillet coated with cooking spray over medium-high heat. Add potatoes, onion, and bacon; sauté 8 minutes or until potatoes are golden brown. Remove from pan. Wipe pan clean with paper towels; recoat with cooking spray. Combine salt, hot sauce, pepper, eggs, and egg whites in a medium bowl, stirring with a whisk. Stir in potato mixture, cheese, and chopped green onions.
3. Heat pan over medium heat. Pour in egg mixture. Reduce heat to medium-low; cook 3 minutes or until bottom is lightly browned, lifting edges and tilting skillet as eggs cook to allow uncooked portion to flow underneath cooked portion.
4. Wrap handle of pan with foil. Broil 2 minutes or until top is lightly browned and set. Garnish with green onion strips, if desired. Yield: 4 servings (serving size: 1 wedge).

CALORIES 202 (37% from fat); FAT 8.2g (sat 3.3g, mono 2.9g, poly 0.9g); PROTEIN 15.5g; CARB 16.1g; FIBER 1.9g; CHOL 227mg; IRON 1.8mg; SODIUM 582mg; CALC 93mg

No Longer Forbidden Foods

Foods such as red meat, eggs, and nuts were once thought to be off-limits. But now, research shows that incorporating moderate amounts of these products may in fact contribute to a healthy diet. We've included information below to help you decipher the conflicting reports you may have heard about in regards to the "forbidden foods."

Red Meat

The news about red meat hasn't changed much; it still has saturated fat, and intake of saturated fat should be limited. What's changed is that grocers are offering a greater variety of low-fat cuts. Top round and flank steak, for example, are similar to chicken thighs in fat content. And alternative red meats like buffalo and venison, which are naturally low in fat, are becoming more widely available.

A 3-ounce serving of beef has 30 to 40 percent of the daily recommended value for zinc and 10 to 15 percent of the daily value for iron (the percentages vary based on cut). Beef is also packed with 20 to 25 grams of protein per 3-ounce serving.

Butter

It's not that butter is better; it's that stick margarine is worse. Used to be, margarine was the clear choice because it has no saturated fat. But recent research indicates that the fat in stick margarine—trans fat—can be more harmful than the saturated fat in butter. Not only do trans fats raise the harmful type of cholesterol (LDL), they also lower the good kind (HDL). (Though trans fat-free margarine is fine for spreading on toast, it's not a good substitute in recipes because it has a higher water content than butter.) You still need to use butter with restraint, but there's no health advantage to be gained from using stick margarine. And butter just tastes better.

Shellfish

Shellfish were tainted with cholesterol's bad reputation. The link between dietary cholesterol and heart disease still isn't fully understood, but we now know that cholesterol in food is far less dangerous than saturated fat. "Most shellfish have so little fat that you can pretty much eat it without worry," says Connie Diekman, spokesperson for the American Dietetic Association (ADA). In fact, research indicates that eating fish once a week can reduce the risk of sudden cardiac death by half.

Eggs

Cholesterol is bad; eggs have cholesterol, therefore eggs are bad. So went the public's reasoning when the American Heart Association first warned about the dangers of cholesterol in 1961. Since then, it's been found that the link between the cholesterol you eat and the kind that obstructs your arteries isn't as clear as once thought. "The real villain is saturated fat," says ADA spokesperson Connie Diekman. "That's what fuels the body's cholesterol-making machinery." Although eggs do contain some saturated fat—about 1.5 grams in a large egg—recent research has shown that, for most people, an egg a day doesn't elevate cholesterol levels. Plus, eggs offer great nutritional benefits: They're an excellent source of protein, and they have vitamin B_{12} and folate.

Red Wine

Wine was once nutritionally grouped with beer and liquor and thought to offer only empty calories. With them, it bore the brunt of the nation's concern about alcoholism and drunk driving. No one is trivializing these concerns; they're as important today as ever. But wine—particularly red wine—appears to possess health benefits, and the consensus has shifted in its favor. What brought about the change? Mainly the discovery that wine contains the antioxidant resveratrol, which may help lower cholesterol and reduce the risk of heart disease.

Nuts

With their high fat content—up to 90 percent of their calories come from fat—it's no wonder nuts were taboo for the health and weight conscious. But researchers have discovered that the fat in nuts (monounsaturated and, sometimes, omega-3s) is actually beneficial. Nuts are also rich in antioxidants and phytosterols, both of which can help fight heart disease. (Peanuts have the same compound, resveratrol, that has boosted red wine's reputation.)

Not convinced? Despite their high calorie content, recent research has found that there's something about nuts—the satiety factor, perhaps—that helps dieters stick to weight-loss regimens.

search myclar2003.com for all our tips

1. Heat oil in a large Dutch oven coated with cooking spray over medium heat. Add leek and garlic; cook 4 minutes or until tender, stirring occasionally. Add wine and broth; bring to a simmer. Stir in shrimp and scallops; bring to a boil. Reduce heat; simmer 3 minutes or until shrimp and scallops are done.

2. Remove shrimp and scallops from pan with a slotted spoon; keep warm. Bring broth mixture to a boil; cook 4 minutes. Reduce heat to low. Add butter, stirring constantly with a whisk. Stir in tomato and remaining 5 ingredients.

3. Divide shrimp and scallops evenly among 4 soup bowls; spoon ¾ cup broth mixture into each bowl. Yield: 4 servings.

CALORIES 287 (29% from fat); FAT 9.3g (sat 4.1g, mono 2.8g, poly 1.2g); PROTEIN 34g; CARB 10.8g; FIBER 1.3g; CHOL 173mg; IRON 3.3mg; SODIUM 817mg; CALC 93mg

---

Strawberry-Blueberry Compote in Red Wine Syrup

Infusing red wine with warm spices and herbs creates a fragrant syrup for the distinctive ruby-hued compote. Serve over ice cream, pound cake, or with almond biscotti, and garnish with mint.

    1   cup dry red wine
    ¼   cup sugar
    ½   teaspoon whole black peppercorns
    2   (2½-inch) orange rind strips
    1   cinnamon stick
    1   bay leaf
    4   cups sliced strawberries
    1   cup blueberries

1. Combine first 6 ingredients in a small nonaluminum saucepan; bring to a boil. Reduce heat; simmer, uncovered, 20 minutes or until liquid is reduced to ½ cup. Strain wine mixture through a colander into a large bowl; discard solids. Add berries; toss to coat. Serve warm or chill up to 2 hours. Yield: 8 servings (serving size: ½ cup).

CALORIES 61 (6% from fat); FAT 0.4g (sat 0g, mono 0.1g, poly 0.2g); PROTEIN 0.7g; CARB 15g; FIBER 2.4g; CHOL 0mg; IRON 0.5mg; SODIUM 4mg; CALC 15mg

---

Spring Seafood Stew

Poaching is an excellent way to cook seafood, since the cooking liquid makes a flavorful base for sauce. This recipe features a French technique called *monter au beurre* (to mount with butter), whereby chilled butter is whisked into the cooking liquid at the last minute to ensure a satiny sauce.

    1   teaspoon olive oil
    Cooking spray
    1   cup thinly sliced leek (about 1
          large)
    3   garlic cloves, minced
    1   cup dry white wine
    1   (14-ounce) can fat-free,
          less-sodium chicken broth
    ¾   pound medium shrimp, peeled and
          deveined
    ¾   pound large sea scallops, cut in
          half horizontally
    2   tablespoons chilled butter, cut into
          small pieces
    1½   cups chopped plum tomato
    1   tablespoon minced fresh tarragon
    1   teaspoon grated lemon rind
    ½   teaspoon salt
    ½   teaspoon black pepper
    ¼   teaspoon ground red pepper

Triple Hazelnut Cheesecake

Hazelnuts, hazelnut-chocolate spread, and fat-free cheeses make this dessert lower in saturated fat and higher in heart-healthy monounsaturated fat than most cheese-cakes. Look for hazelnut-chocolate spread near the peanut butter in your supermarket.

    ¼   cup chopped hazelnuts, toasted
    1   tablespoon light brown sugar
    15   chocolate wafers
    1   tablespoon vegetable oil
    Cooking spray
    1   tablespoon instant coffee granules
    1   tablespoon hot water
    1   (16-ounce) container fat-free
          cottage cheese
    1   (8-ounce) block fat-free cream
          cheese
    ¾   cup unsweetened cocoa
    ¾   cup packed brown sugar
    ½   cup granulated sugar
    ½   cup hazelnut-chocolate spread
          (such as Nutella)
    2   tablespoons cornstarch
    2   tablespoons Frangelico (hazelnut-
          flavored liqueur, optional)
    ¼   teaspoon salt
    3   large eggs, lightly beaten
    ¼   cup chopped hazelnuts, toasted

1. Preheat oven to 325°.

2. Place first 3 ingredients in a food processor; process until finely ground. Add oil; process until crumbs are moist. Firmly press crumb mixture into bottom of a 9-inch springform pan coated with cooking spray. Wrap outside of pan with a double layer of aluminum foil.

3. Combine coffee granules and hot water in a small bowl. Place cheeses in food processor; process until smooth. Add coffee mixture, cocoa, and next 6 ingredients; process until well blended. Add eggs; process until smooth. Pour into pan.

4. Place pan in a large baking pan; add hot water to baking pan to a depth of 1 inch. Bake at 325° for 1 hour or until cheesecake center barely moves when pan is touched.

5. Remove cheesecake from oven; run a knife around outside edge. Cool to room temperature. Cover and chill at least 8 hours. Remove cheesecake from springform pan; sprinkle with ¼ cup hazelnuts. Yield: 12 servings.

CALORIES 317 (30% from fat); FAT 10.6g (sat 2.4g, mono 6g, poly 1.7g); PROTEIN 12.3g; CARB 44.8g; FIBER 3.2g; CHOL 58mg; IRON 2mg; SODIUM 354mg; CALC 105mg

Company is Coming Menu
serves 6

This grilled shrimp dish is a simple way to impress guests. Romesco sauce is made from a puree of tomatoes, red bell peppers, spices, and nuts. It can also be served with fish or chicken.

Shrimp Skewers with Romesco Sauce

Salad with goat cheese and Dijon dressing*

Couscous with chopped green onions

*Combine 9 cups torn red leaf lettuce, ¼ cup chopped red onion, and ¼ cup (1 ounce) crumbled goat cheese; toss gently. Combine ¼ cup fresh lemon juice, 1 tablespoon Dijon mustard, and 2 teaspoons olive oil, stirring with a whisk. Toss salad with dressing.

Shrimp Skewers with Romesco Sauce

Substitute walnuts or more almonds for the hazelnuts, if you prefer.

ROMESCO SAUCE:

3 tablespoons slivered almonds, toasted
2 tablespoons chopped hazelnuts, toasted
¼ teaspoon salt
1 (1-ounce) slice French bread, toasted
1 garlic clove, crushed
1 cup chopped plum tomato
1 tablespoon red wine vinegar
1 teaspoon extra-virgin olive oil
½ teaspoon paprika
¼ teaspoon crushed red pepper
¼ teaspoon black pepper
1 (7-ounce) bottle roasted red bell peppers, drained
3 tablespoons chopped fresh flat-leaf parsley

SHRIMP:

2¼ pounds jumbo shrimp, peeled and deveined
1 teaspoon minced garlic
¼ teaspoon salt
¼ teaspoon black pepper
Cooking spray
6 lemon wedges

1. To prepare romesco, place first 5 ingredients in a food processor; process until finely ground. Add tomato and next 6 ingredients; process until smooth. Transfer to a bowl; stir in parsley.

2. Prepare grill or broiler.

3. To prepare shrimp, combine shrimp, minced garlic, ¼ teaspoon salt, and ¼ teaspoon black pepper; toss to coat. Thread shrimp onto 6 (8-inch) skewers. Place skewers on grill rack or broiler pan coated with cooking spray; cook 3 minutes on each side or until shrimp are done. Serve shrimp with sauce and lemon wedges. Yield: 6 servings (serving size: 1 skewer, ¼ cup sauce, and 1 lemon wedge).

WINE NOTE: Given the spiciness, nuttiness, and sweetness of the romesco and the char of the grilled shrimp, a wimpy white won't do. Albarino, Spain's leading white wine, is fresh, snappy, citrusy, and has a hint of almond on the end. Try Lusco Albarino. The 2000 vintage is about $15.

CALORIES 263 (27% from fat); FAT 7.8g (sat 1g, mono 3.6g, poly 2.1g); PROTEIN 37.2g; CARB 9.7g; FIBER 1.7g; CHOL 259mg; IRON 5.1mg; SODIUM 597mg; CALC 118mg

Flank Steak with Cilantro-Almond Pesto

Ground almonds thicken this lively herb sauce. The pesto is also good as a spread for burgers and sandwiches, or as a pizza sauce. Most of the fat here is monounsaturated.

¾ cup fresh cilantro
2 tablespoons slivered almonds, toasted
1 tablespoon chopped seeded jalapeño pepper
⅛ teaspoon salt
⅛ teaspoon black pepper
1 garlic clove, chopped
3 tablespoons plain fat-free yogurt
1½ teaspoons fresh lime juice
1 (1-pound) flank steak, trimmed
Cilantro sprigs (optional)

1. Prepare grill.

2. Combine first 6 ingredients in a blender; process until finely chopped (about 15 seconds). Add yogurt and juice; process until smooth.

3. Grill steak 6 minutes on each side or until desired degree of doneness. Cut steak diagonally across grain into thin slices. Serve steak with pesto. Garnish with cilantro sprigs, if desired. Yield: 4 servings (serving size: 3 ounces steak and about 1 tablespoon pesto).

WINE NOTE: The tangy herbal flavors in the pesto are well suited for Cabernet Franc, which has a light herbal, mintlike underpinning and is sleeker than Cabernet Sauvignon. Try Longoria's "Blues" from California's Santa Ynez Valley. The 1999 vintage is $25.

CALORIES 209 (47% from fat); FAT 10.8g (sat 3.9g, mono 4.9g, poly 0.8g); PROTEIN 24.6g; CARB 2.4g; FIBER 0.6g; CHOL 57mg; IRON 2.5mg; SODIUM 152mg; CALC 36mg

Revved-Up Rhubarb Bars

A creamy rhubarb custard recipe evolves into a healthier incarnation.

Jennifer Otterson, of Milaca, Minnesota, knew that the rhubarb bars recipe that she found on the Internet "must be incredibly high in fat and calories" and asked us for help. Here's our lightened version.

Rhubarb Custard Bars

Rhubarb, which looks like crimson celery, has a short season but freezes beautifully; just store the stalks in a heavy-duty zip-top plastic bag. You can use fresh or frozen rhubarb, but we actually preferred unthawed frozen rhubarb.

CRUST:

1½ cups all-purpose flour
½ cup sugar
⅛ teaspoon salt
9 tablespoons chilled butter, cut into small pieces
Cooking spray

FILLING:

⅓ cup all-purpose flour
1½ cups sugar
1½ cups 1% low-fat milk
3 large eggs
5 cups (½-inch) sliced fresh or frozen rhubarb (unthawed)

TOPPING:

½ cup sugar
½ cup (4 ounces) block-style fat-free cream cheese
½ cup (4 ounces) block-style ⅓-less-fat cream cheese
½ teaspoon vanilla extract
1 cup frozen fat-free whipped topping, thawed
Mint sprigs (optional)

1. Preheat oven to 350°.

2. To prepare crust, lightly spoon 1½ cups flour into dry measuring cups; level with a knife. Combine 1½ cups flour, ½ cup sugar, and salt in a bowl. Cut in butter with a pastry blender or 2 knives until mixture resembles coarse meal. Press mixture into a 13 x 9-inch baking dish coated with cooking spray. Bake at 350° for 15 minutes or until golden brown.

3. To prepare filling, lightly spoon ⅓ cup flour into a dry measuring cup; level with a knife. Combine ⅓ cup flour and 1½ cups sugar in a large bowl; add milk and eggs, stirring with a whisk until well blended. Stir in rhubarb. Pour rhubarb mixture over crust. Bake at 350° for 40 minutes or until set. Cool rhubarb bars to room temperature.

4. To prepare topping, place ½ cup sugar, cheeses, and vanilla in a bowl; beat with a mixer at medium speed until smooth. Gently fold in whipped topping; spread evenly over baked custard. Cover and chill at least 1 hour. Garnish with mint sprigs, if desired. Yield: 36 servings (serving size: 1 bar).

CALORIES 131 (29% from fat); FAT 4.2g (sat 2.5g, mono 1.3g, poly 0.2g); PROTEIN 2.5g; CARB 21g; FIBER 0.5g; CHOL 29mg; IRON 0.4mg; SODIUM 78mg; CALC 42mg

BEFORE	AFTER
SERVING SIZE	
1 bar	
CALORIES PER SERVING	
201	131
FAT	
11g	4.2g
PERCENT OF TOTAL CALORIES	
49%	29%

dinner tonight

Advantageous Asian Noodles

Take advantage of the wide variety of Asian noodles for fast, easy dinners.

Beef Noodle Bowl Menu

serves 5

Udon-Beef Noodle Bowl

Steamed edamame (fresh soybeans)

Gingered won ton chips with ice cream*

*Cut 10 won ton wrappers into thin strips. Combine won ton strips and ½ teaspoon dark sesame oil in a small bowl, tossing to coat. Add 2 teaspoons sugar and ½ teaspoon ground ginger, tossing to coat. Arrange strips on a baking sheet. Bake at 400° for 8 minutes or until crisp, turning once. Serve won ton chips with vanilla low-fat ice cream.

Game Plan

1. Preheat oven for won ton chips
2. While water for noodles and broth mixture come to a boil:
  • Prepare won tons for baking
  • Slice mushrooms, carrot, and beef
3. While noodles cook and broth mixture simmers:
  • Bake won ton chips
  • Steam edamame until tender
  • Sauté vegetables for noodle bowl

Udon-Beef Noodle Bowl

This entrée falls somewhere between a soup and a noodle dish. You can eat it with chopsticks, but be sure to have spoons around to catch the broth.

TOTAL TIME: 35 MINUTES

QUICK TIP: To speed the slicing of the shiitakes, stack a few caps on top of one another, then slice the entire stack.

8 ounces uncooked udon noodles (thick, round fresh Japanese wheat noodles) or spaghetti
1½ teaspoons bottled minced garlic
½ teaspoon crushed red pepper
2 (14¼-ounce) cans low-salt beef broth
3 tablespoons low-sodium soy sauce
3 tablespoons sake (rice wine) or dry sherry
1 tablespoon honey
Cooking spray

2 cups sliced shiitake mushroom caps (about 4 ounces)
½ cup thinly sliced carrot
8 ounces top round, thinly sliced
¾ cup diagonally cut green onions
1 (6-ounce) bag prewashed baby spinach

1. Cook noodles according to package directions; drain.
2. Place garlic, pepper, and broth in a large saucepan. Bring to a boil; reduce heat, and simmer 10 minutes.
3. Combine soy sauce, sake, and honey in a small bowl; stir with a whisk.
4. Heat a large nonstick skillet coated with cooking spray over medium-high heat. Add mushrooms and carrot; sauté 2 minutes. Stir in soy sauce mixture, and cook 2 minutes, stirring constantly. Add vegetable mixture to broth mixture. Stir in beef; cook 2 minutes or until beef loses its pink color. Stir in noodles, green onions, and spinach. Serve immediately. Yield: 5 servings (serving size: about 1½ cups).

CALORIES 306 (16% from fat); FAT 5.6g (sat 1.8g, mono 2g, poly 0.4g); PROTEIN 22.4g; CARB 36.6g; FIBER 2.4g; CHOL 39mg; IRON 3.4mg; SODIUM 707mg; CALC 59mg

---

Thai Noodle Menu
serves 6
Shrimp Pad Thai
Spicy cucumber salad*

Lemon sorbet

*Combine 2 cups thinly sliced seeded peeled cucumber, 1 cup julienne-cut red bell pepper, and ¼ cup thinly sliced red onion in a large bowl. Combine 1 tablespoon sugar, 2 tablespoons fresh lime juice, 1 tablespoon fish sauce, and ½ teaspoon crushed red pepper. Pour dressing over vegetables; toss to combine.

Game Plan

1. While water for noodles heats, prepare cucumber salad
2. While noodles soak:
  • Peel and devein shrimp
  • Combine sauce ingredients
  • Slice green onions
  • Beat eggs

Shrimp Pad Thai

Pad Thai is the most popular noodle dish in Thailand. Pungent fish sauce (also called *nam pla*) is an important flavoring for this dish; you can find it in the Asian foods section of most large supermarkets or in Asian markets. Substitute 4 cups hot cooked linguine for the rice stick noodles if you have trouble finding them.

TOTAL TIME: 30 MINUTES

QUICK TIP: Ask the folks in the seafood department at your supermarket to peel and devein your shrimp.

8 ounces wide rice stick noodles (Banh Pho)
¼ cup ketchup
3 tablespoons fish sauce
2 tablespoons sugar
½ teaspoon crushed red pepper
2 tablespoons vegetable oil, divided
1 pound medium shrimp, peeled and deveined
2 large eggs, lightly beaten
1 cup fresh bean sprouts
¾ cup (1-inch) sliced green onions
1 teaspoon bottled minced garlic
2 tablespoons chopped unsalted, dry-roasted peanuts

1. Place noodles in a large bowl. Add hot water to cover; let stand 12 minutes or until tender. Drain.
2. Combine ketchup, fish sauce, sugar, and pepper in a small bowl.
3. Heat 2 teaspoons oil in a large nonstick skillet over medium-high heat. Add shrimp; sauté 2 minutes or until shrimp are done. Remove shrimp from pan; keep warm.
4. Heat 4 teaspoons oil in pan over medium-high heat. Add eggs; cook 30 seconds or until soft-scrambled, stirring constantly. Add sprouts, green onions, and garlic; cook 1 minute. Add noodles, ketchup mixture, and shrimp; cook 3 minutes or until heated. Sprinkle with peanuts. Yield: 6 servings (serving size: 1½ cups).

CALORIES 343 (24% from fat); FAT 9.2g (sat 1.6g, mono 2.6g, poly 3.9g); PROTEIN 21.3g; CARB 42.4g; FIBER 1.4g; CHOL 186mg; IRON 3mg; SODIUM 912mg; CALC 60mg

---

Asian Flair Menu
serves 5
Chicken and Noodles with Peanut Sauce
Asian slaw*

Steamed broccoli spears

*Combine 1 tablespoon sugar, 3 tablespoons rice vinegar, 1 tablespoon low-sodium soy sauce, and 2 teaspoons dark sesame oil. Pour dressing over 4 cups cabbage-and-carrot coleslaw; toss to coat. Chill until ready to serve.

Game Plan

1. While water comes to a boil:
  • Prepare and refrigerate slaw
  • Combine sauce ingredients for noodles
  • Cut bell pepper into strips
2. While chicken is sautéing, prepare broccoli

Chicken and Noodles with Peanut Sauce

This dish is great served at room temperature or cold; add a touch of warm water to loosen the noodles if serving cold.

TOTAL TIME: 30 MINUTES

QUICK TIP: Chicken breast tenders are ideal for hectic schedules. They don't need to be cut or trimmed, and the smaller pieces cook more quickly than chicken breasts.

5 ounces uncooked Japanese curly noodles (chucka soba)
2 teaspoons dark sesame oil, divided
1 pound chicken breast tenders
1½ cups red bell pepper strips
½ cup fat-free, less-sodium chicken broth
⅓ cup hoisin sauce
¼ cup creamy peanut butter
2 tablespoons rice vinegar
2 tablespoons ketchup
¼ teaspoon crushed red pepper
1 tablespoon bottled ground fresh ginger (such as Spice World)
1 teaspoon bottled minced garlic
½ cup chopped green onions, divided

Continued

1. Cook noodles according to package directions; drain.

2. Heat 1 teaspoon oil in a large non-stick skillet over medium-high heat. Add chicken; sauté 4 minutes. Add bell pepper; sauté 3 minutes. Remove from heat. Combine chicken mixture and noodles in a large bowl.

3. Combine broth and next 5 ingredients in a bowl; stir well with a whisk.

4. Heat 1 teaspoon oil in pan over medium heat. Add ginger and garlic; cook 15 seconds. Stir in broth mixture, and cook 30 seconds, stirring constantly. Add broth mixture and ¼ cup green onions to noodle mixture; toss well. Sprinkle with ¼ cup green onions. Yield: 5 servings (serving size: 1 cup).

CALORIES 353 (28% from fat); FAT 10.9g (sat 2g, mono 4.3g, poly 3.1g); PROTEIN 28.5g; CARB 36g; FIBER 2.3g; CHOL 53mg; IRON 1.5mg; SODIUM 663mg; CALC 21mg

Vegetarian Noodle Menu

serves 4

Curried Noodles with Tofu

Sesame-scented snow peas and carrots*

Green tea

*Cook 1½ cups snow peas and ½ cup diagonally sliced carrot in boiling water 30 seconds; drain. Toss vegetables with 2 teaspoons low-sodium soy sauce, 1 teaspoon dark sesame oil, 1 teaspoon rice vinegar, and ½ teaspoon sugar.

Game Plan

1. While water comes to a boil for snow peas and carrots:
   • Prepare tofu, red bell pepper, cabbage, green onions, and cilantro
   • Combine sauce ingredients for noodles
2. While tofu is sautéing, soak rice sticks in hot water
3. While noodle mixture cooks in sauce, toss snow peas and carrots with seasonings

search myclar2003.com for all our menus

Curried Noodles with Tofu

Look for curry paste in the Asian foods section of your supermarket. Use it conservatively, though—a little goes a long way.

TOTAL TIME: 31 MINUTES

QUICK TIP: You can use the hot water left over from cooking the snow peas and carrots to soak the rice sticks: Remove the vegetables with a slotted spoon, and pour the cooking water over the noodles.

6 ounces uncooked rice sticks (rice-flour noodles), angel hair pasta, or vermicelli
1 cup light coconut milk
2 tablespoons low-sodium soy sauce
1½ tablespoons bottled ground fresh ginger (such as Spice World)
1 tablespoon sugar
2 teaspoons bottled minced garlic
1 teaspoon green curry paste
½ teaspoon salt
Cooking spray
1 (12.3-ounce) package extra-firm tofu, drained and cut into 1-inch cubes
1 cup red bell pepper strips
4 cups shredded napa (Chinese) cabbage
1 cup chopped green onions
3 tablespoons chopped fresh cilantro

1. Place noodles in a large bowl. Add hot water to cover; let stand 5 minutes. Drain.

2. Combine coconut milk and next 6 ingredients in a small bowl.

3. Heat a large nonstick skillet coated with cooking spray over medium-high heat. Add tofu; sauté 10 minutes or until golden brown. Remove tofu from pan; keep warm.

4. Add bell pepper to pan; sauté 1 minute or until crisp-tender. Add cabbage; sauté 30 seconds. Stir in noodles, coconut milk mixture, and tofu; cook 2 minutes or until noodles are tender. Stir in green onions and cilantro. Yield: 4 servings (serving size: 1¼ cups).

CALORIES 300 (15% from fat); FAT 4.9g (sat 2.3g, mono 0.4g, poly 1.1g); PROTEIN 11.5g; CARB 51.4g; FIBER 4.5g; CHOL 0mg; IRON 3.6mg; SODIUM 678mg; CALC 89mg

Around the World on Bikes

A South Dakota couple follows their dream by melding a passion for fitness with a yen for adventurous travel.

Tass Thacker and her husband Bruce Junek—both of whom are approaching 50—are avid and well-traveled cyclists. They've biked on trails all over the world—North America, the Middle East, Europe, Asia, South America, and Australia. And along their journeys they've learned that none of it would have been possible without a commitment to fitness and paying close attention to their diet. They emphasize a diet with vegetables, whole grains, and tofu—and now incorporate fish on occasion for additional protein. Here's one of their recipes.

Mango Salsa

Tass and Bruce first tasted fresh mango more than 20 years ago in Mexico, where they also ate fiery salsa that brought tears to their eyes. Tass didn't combine the two ingredients until years later. Serve with grilled chicken, fish, or baked tortilla chips.

3 cups cubed peeled ripe mango
1 cup chopped green onions
½ cup chopped fresh cilantro
⅓ cup fresh lime juice
3 tablespoons finely chopped seeded jalapeño pepper (about 2 peppers)
1 teaspoon sugar
½ teaspoon salt

1. Combine all ingredients in a bowl; toss well. Cover and chill. Yield: 6 servings (serving size: ½ cup).

CALORIES 68 (4% from fat); FAT 0.3g (sat 0.1g, mono 0.1g, poly 0.1g); PROTEIN 0.6g; CARB 17.5g; FIBER 2.3g; CHOL 0mg; IRON 0.2mg; SODIUM 201mg; CALC 11mg

Pollo Rancho Luna
Rancho Luna Chicken, **page 139**

Cheddar-Crusted Apple Pie,
page 137

Raspberry-Orange Sunrises,
page 110

Spring Giardiniera,
page 109

Hoisin and Bourbon-Glazed Pork Tenderloin
with Three-Fruit Salsa, pages 108 and 109

Double-Caramel Turtle Cake,
page 121

All About Cheese

How to choose and prepare cheeses that please.

Anyone who's visited the dairy department of a local supermarket, eaten at a white-linen restaurant, or gone to a farmers' market recently has noticed this country's most exciting food trend: cheese. From Hispanic cheeses to handcrafted goat cheeses, Americans have more choices now than ever before.

Baked Onions with Feta

Look for feta packed in water; it has a more pronounced flavor and tastes fresher.

  4 Vidalia or other sweet onions
Olive oil-flavored cooking spray
  ½ cup fat-free, less-sodium chicken broth
  ½ cup (2 ounces) crumbled feta cheese
  ¼ cup dry breadcrumbs
  ½ teaspoon chopped fresh or ⅛ teaspoon dried thyme
Dash of black pepper

1. Preheat oven to 450°.
2. Peel onions, leaving root ends intact. Trim top third of each onion; reserve for another use. Arrange onions, cut sides down, in an 8-inch square baking pan coated with cooking spray; add chicken broth. Cover pan with foil; bake at 450° for 30 minutes. Uncover and bake an additional 30 minutes. Carefully turn onions over with a spatula; bake an additional 30 minutes or until onions are soft and liquid has almost evaporated. Remove from oven.
3. Preheat broiler.
4. Combine feta, breadcrumbs, thyme, and pepper; stir with a fork until well blended. Gently pat cheese mixture evenly onto cut sides of onions. Broil onions until cheese mixture begins to brown (about 1 minute). Yield: 4 servings (serving size: 1 onion).

CALORIES 106 (26% from fat); FAT 3.1g (sat 2.5g, mono 0.2g, poly 0.1g); PROTEIN 4.5g; CARB 15.9g; FIBER 3.1g; CHOL 10mg; IRON 0.5mg; SODIUM 306mg; CALC 64mg

Brie Toasts with Eggplant Marmalade

Serve these vegetarian open-faced sandwiches for lunch, a light dinner, or as appetizers.

  6 cups finely chopped eggplant (about 12 ounces)
  3 tablespoons red wine vinegar
1½ tablespoons sugar
  1 teaspoon brown sugar
  ¼ teaspoon freshly ground black pepper
  ⅛ teaspoon salt
  1 (14½-ounce) can vegetable broth
  1 garlic clove, minced
  8 (1½-ounce) slices diagonally cut multigrain bread
  4 ounces Brie cheese, cut into 8 slices
  2 tablespoons chopped fresh parsley

1. Combine first 7 ingredients in a medium saucepan over medium-high heat. Bring to a boil. Reduce heat to low; simmer 30 minutes or until thick, stirring occasionally. Remove from heat; stir in garlic. Cool to room temperature.
2. Preheat broiler.
3. Arrange bread slices in a single layer on a baking sheet; broil 1 minute or until lightly toasted. Top each slice with ¼ cup eggplant mixture and 1 slice Brie. Broil 1 minute or until cheese melts. Sprinkle with parsley. Yield: 4 servings (serving size: 2 toasts).

CALORIES 346 (29% from fat); FAT 11.3g (sat 5.6g, mono 3.5g, poly 0.9g); PROTEIN 16.3g; CARB 59.3g; FIBER 16.9g; CHOL 28mg; IRON 3.6mg; SODIUM 942mg; CALC 231mg

Arugula, Fig, and Blue Cheese Salad

If you're not a fan of blue cheese, use Parmesan shavings.

  2 cups torn red leaf lettuce
1¼ cups fresh figs, quartered
  1 cup trimmed arugula
  2 tablespoons fresh lemon juice
  2 teaspoons olive oil
  ¼ teaspoon salt
  ¼ teaspoon freshly ground black pepper
  3 tablespoons crumbled blue cheese

1. Combine first 3 ingredients in a large bowl. Combine lemon juice, oil, salt, and pepper; stir well with a whisk. Gently toss lettuce mixture with lemon juice mixture. Sprinkle with blue cheese. Yield: 4 servings (serving size: 1 cup).

CALORIES 74 (35% from fat); FAT 2.9g (sat 1.1g, mono 0.9g, poly 0.2g); PROTEIN 2g; CARB 11.6g; FIBER 2.3g; CHOL 4mg; IRON 0.7mg; SODIUM 224mg; CALC 74mg

Casual Supper Menu
serves 8

Polenta with Fontina and Spinach

Balsamic grilled asparagus*

Grilled pork tenderloin

*Combine ¼ cup balsamic vinegar, 1 teaspoon sugar, ½ teaspoon salt, ½ teaspoon ground black pepper, and 2 minced garlic cloves; stir. Trim 2 pounds asparagus; toss with balsamic mixture. Grill 5 minutes, turning once.

Polenta with Fontina and Spinach

Fontina is one of the great cheeses of Italy. It has a mild, creamy flavor and melts well, making it super-versatile. You can use almost any cheese in this side dish, though; try Parmesan for a sharper, nutty flavor.

Olive oil-flavored cooking spray
2　garlic cloves, minced
3　cups chopped spinach (about 3½ ounces)
2　cups water
1　(14-ounce) can fat-free, less-sodium chicken broth
1　cup polenta
½　teaspoon salt
¼　teaspoon black pepper
½　cup (2 ounces) shredded fontina or Parmesan cheese

1. Heat a medium nonstick skillet coated with cooking spray over medium-high heat. Add garlic; sauté 1 minute. Add spinach; cook 1 minute or until spinach wilts. Remove from heat.
2. Combine water and broth in a large saucepan over medium-high heat; bring to a boil. Gradually add polenta, stirring constantly with a whisk. Reduce heat to medium; cook 20 minutes, stirring frequently. Remove from heat; stir in spinach mixture, salt, and pepper.
3. Spoon polenta mixture evenly into a 9-inch springform pan coated with cooking spray. Press plastic wrap onto surface of polenta; chill 2 hours or until firm.
4. Preheat oven to 400°.
5. Remove polenta from pan; place on a baking sheet coated with cooking spray. Sprinkle cheese evenly over polenta. Bake at 400° for 15 minutes or until cheese melts and begins to brown. Remove from oven; cool 5 minutes. Cut polenta into wedges using a sharp knife. Serve immediately. Yield: 8 servings (serving size: 1 wedge).

CALORIES 126 (30% from fat); FAT 4.2g (sat 1.7g, mono 0.6g, poly 0.2g); PROTEIN 5.7g; CARB 16.9g; FIBER 1.9g; CHOL 9mg; IRON 1.8mg; SODIUM 419mg; CALC 106mg

Gruyère and Cherry Compote

This is a great introduction to cheese for dessert. Gruyère is a Swiss cheese that has a rich, sweet, nutty flavor. Domestic Swiss and Emmental also work well.

½　cup sugar
½　cup water
1　pound fresh Bing cherries, pitted
¼　cup fresh lemon juice
5　(1-inch-thick) slices Italian bread (about 5 ounces)
4　ounces Gruyère cheese, cut into 15 thin slices

1. Combine sugar and water in a medium, heavy saucepan over high heat. Bring to a boil; cook 1 minute. Add cherries; cook 1 minute. Reduce heat to medium-low; cook 20 minutes. Remove cherries from pan with a slotted spoon.
2. Cook cherry liquid until reduced to ¼ cup (about 15 minutes). Remove from heat. Add cherries to pan; stir in lemon juice. Cool.
3. Preheat broiler.
4. Cut each bread slice crosswise into 3 strips. Arrange in a single layer on a baking sheet; broil 1 minute on each side or until toasted. Cool completely. Cut each cheese slice in half diagonally. Arrange 3 bread strips on each of 5 plates. Top each bread strip with 2 slices cheese and about 1 tablespoon compote. Yield: 5 servings.

WINE NOTE: Since this dessert is not overly sweet, it might also be considered a cheese course. We suggest two wines, either of which would be excellent. The first is a demi-sec Champagne, a slightly sweet sparkler that's sensational with cheese, and great with desserts like this. A good one is by Veuve Clicquot (about $40). The second is Hungarian Tokay, one of the best known of the trendy dessert wines. The wine offers a flavor like dried fruits and nuts, which makes it an especially good match for a nutty cheese and fruit compote. Try the Royal Tokaji Wine Company's Tokaji ($32).

CALORIES 324 (26% from fat); FAT 9.3g (sat 4.8g, mono 2.8g, poly 1.1g); PROTEIN 10.6g; CARB 51.7g; FIBER 3g; CHOL 25mg; IRON 1.3mg; SODIUM 258mg; CALC 281mg

Shrimp, Tomato, and Basil Linguine with Warm Goat Cheese Rounds

Most goat cheese is soft and creamy, and ideal for molding into patties and baking. Prepare the goat cheese rounds a day ahead and refrigerate to make this recipe extra easy.

   1 (1-ounce) slice white bread
   1 (4-ounce) package log-shaped goat cheese
   1 tablespoon olive oil
   1 cup coarsely chopped onion
   2 garlic cloves, minced
   2½ cups chopped seeded peeled plum tomatoes (about 1½ pounds)
   ¼ cup water
   1½ teaspoons sugar
   ¾ teaspoon crushed red pepper
   ½ pound medium shrimp, peeled and deveined
   ½ teaspoon salt
   6 cups hot cooked linguine (about 12 ounces uncooked pasta)
   ½ cup thinly sliced fresh basil
   Basil sprigs (optional)

1. Preheat oven to 400°.
2. Place bread in a food processor; pulse 10 times or until coarse crumbs measure ½ cup. Sprinkle breadcrumbs on a baking sheet; bake at 400° for 2½ minutes or until golden brown. Transfer to a shallow plate; cool completely. Slice goat cheese crosswise into 4 rounds. Press both sides of each round into breadcrumbs. Arrange in a single layer on a baking sheet; chill.
3. Heat oil in a large nonstick skillet over medium-high heat. Add onion and garlic; sauté 5 minutes. Stir in chopped tomato, water, sugar, and pepper; cook mixture 15 minutes, stirring occasionally. Add shrimp and salt; cook 4 minutes or until shrimp are done. Remove from heat. Cover; keep warm.
4. Bake cheese rounds at 400° for 10 minutes or until soft but still holding their shape.
5. Add pasta and ½ cup basil to tomato mixture; toss to combine. Divide pasta mixture evenly among 4 bowls; top each serving with 1 goat cheese round.

Garnish with basil sprigs, if desired. Yield: 4 servings (serving size: about 2 cups pasta mixture and 1 goat cheese round).

CALORIES 461 (28% from fat); FAT 14.3g (sat 6.7g, mono 4.8g, poly 1.4g); PROTEIN 24.5g; CARB 58.9g; FIBER 4.1g; CHOL 87mg; IRON 4.8mg; SODIUM 562mg; CALC 148mg

Meringues with Fresh Strawberries and Chocolate Mascarpone

Crisp meringues, sweet strawberries, rich chocolate, and creamy mascarpone cheese make one fabulous dessert. Mascarpone is Italian cream cheese, and is available in most large supermarkets and Italian delicatessens. The dessert's components can be made ahead, but assemble at the last minute so the meringues stay crisp.

MERINGUES:
   2 large egg whites
   ¼ teaspoon cream of tartar
   ½ cup sugar

CHOCOLATE MASCARPONE:
   1½ tablespoons sugar
   1 tablespoon unsweetened cocoa
   6 tablespoons (3 ounces) mascarpone cheese, softened
   1 teaspoon fat-free milk
   ¼ teaspoon vanilla extract

STRAWBERRIES:
   3½ cups quartered small strawberries (about 1½ quarts)
   ¼ cup sugar
   Mint sprigs (optional)

1. Preheat oven to 225°.
2. To prepare meringues, cover a baking sheet with parchment paper. Draw 6 (4-inch) circles on paper. Turn paper over; secure with masking tape. Place egg whites and cream of tartar in a large bowl; beat with a mixer at high speed until foamy. Gradually add ½ cup sugar, 1 tablespoon at a time, beating until stiff peaks form (do not underbeat). Divide egg white mixture evenly among 6 drawn circles on baking sheet; spread to fill circles using back of a spoon.
3. Bake at 225° for 1½ hours. Turn oven off; cool meringues in closed oven 30 minutes. Carefully remove meringues from paper. Cool completely. (Meringues can be stored in an airtight container for up to a week.)
4. To prepare chocolate mascarpone, sift together 1½ tablespoons sugar and cocoa. Combine mascarpone, milk, and vanilla in a small bowl; stir just until combined. Stir in cocoa mixture.
5. To prepare strawberries, toss berries with ¼ cup sugar; let stand 15 minutes.
6. Place 1 meringue on each of 6 plates; spread about 1½ tablespoons mascarpone mixture on top of each meringue. Top each serving with about ½ cup strawberry mixture. Garnish with mint sprigs, if desired. Yield: 6 servings.

CALORIES 211 (30% from fat); FAT 7g (sat 3.6g, mono 1.5g, poly 0.4g); PROTEIN 3g; CARB 35.9g; FIBER 2.5g; CHOL 18mg; IRON 0.5mg; SODIUM 28mg; CALC 32mg

---

Cheese Bits

• Save the rind of Parmesan cheese to toss into soups, beans, and chili. It lends savory flavor. When cooked, discard the rind.

• Use unflavored dental floss or a cheese cutter with a wire to cut delicate, soft cheeses.

• Best tools to render cheese ready for cooking or serving? We recommend the Zyliss brand handheld cheese grater. Microplanes, in both coarse and fine textures, are well suited to create hard cheese garnishes in varying shapes; using a vegetable peeler or chocolate shaver gives you thin sheets or shards to change the look of a dish even more.

• For easier grating, place softer cheeses (such as fontina and Monterey Jack) in the freezer for 10 to 15 minutes beforehand.

• Shred cheese for recipes using the larger holes of a box grater or in a food processor. For a finer texture, grate cheese using the smaller holes of a box grater or with the steel knife of a food processor.

Cheese Substitutions

Cheese is one of the most interchangeable ingredients. The most important guideline is to substitute similar textures. Use personal flavor preferences and this chart as your guide.

Fresh cheeses (not aged or ripened)

When a recipe calls for:	You can substitute:
Queso blanco fresco	Feta or goat cheese
Ricotta	Cottage cheese
Mascarpone	Fromage blanc or Quark (yogurt cheese)
Scamorza	Mozzarella or Oaxaca cheese

Soft-ripened

Soft-ripened cheeses are good eating cheeses because of their creamy texture. They are also well suited for cooking and melt smoothly.

When a recipe calls for:	You can substitute:
Brie	Camembert
Saint André	Explorateur

Semisoft

Semisoft cheeses are also good eating cheeses. They make suitable accents for bread, salad, and salad dressings.

When a recipe calls for:	You can substitute:
Roquefort	Gorgonzola, Stilton, or Saga blue
Reblochon	Teleme or Taleggio
Livarot	Muenster, Epoisses, or Havarti
Brick	Limburger

Semihard

Semihard cheeses are excellent cooking cheeses and melt easily. Shred to top pizzas or casseroles.

When a recipe calls for:	You can substitute:
Cantal	Colby or cheddar
Emmental	Jarlsberg, Swiss, or Gruyère
Edam	Gouda or Tilsit
Kasseri	Provolone
Manchego	Monterey Jack

Hard

Often used as grating cheeses, these are good for baked dishes such as gratins and pasta toppings, or for shaving over salads. Generally, with these full-flavored cheeses, only a little bit is needed.

When a recipe calls for:	You can substitute:
Pecorino Romano	Parmigiano-Reggiano
Dry Jack	Aged cheddar
Asiago	Romano

search myclar2003.com for all our tips

Monterey Pizza

Mild Monterey Jack cheese melts well and doesn't overwhelm the mango in this vegetarian pizza. Nonvegetarians can add ham or chicken to the top. Muenster, fontina, or Manchego also works well in this recipe.

- 1 package dry yeast (about 2¼ teaspoons)
- ¾ cup warm water (100° to 110°)
- 1 teaspoon olive oil
- ½ teaspoon salt
- 2 cups all-purpose flour, divided
- Cooking spray
- 1 teaspoon cornmeal
- 1½ cups chopped peeled mango (about 1½ mangoes)
- 1 tablespoon fresh lime juice
- 1½ cups (6 ounces) Monterey Jack cheese, shredded
- ¼ cup chopped fresh cilantro
- 2 finely chopped seeded jalapeño peppers

1. Dissolve yeast in water in a large bowl; let stand 5 minutes. Stir in oil and salt. Lightly spoon flour into dry measuring cups; level with a knife. Add 1¾ cups flour to yeast mixture; stir until a soft dough forms. Turn dough out onto a lightly floured surface. Knead until smooth and elastic (about 5 minutes); add enough of remaining flour, 1 tablespoon at a time, to prevent dough from sticking to hands (dough will feel tacky).

2. Place dough in a large bowl coated with cooking spray, turning to coat top. Cover and let rise in a warm place (85°), free from drafts, 45 minutes or until doubled in size. (Press two fingers into dough. If indentation remains, dough has risen enough.)

3. Preheat oven to 500°.

4. Punch dough down; turn out onto a baking sheet sprinkled with cornmeal. Roll into a 14 x 10-inch rectangle. Lightly coat surface of dough with cooking spray.

5. Combine mango and lime juice in a small bowl; toss well.

6. Combine cheese and cilantro in a small bowl. Sprinkle cheese mixture evenly over dough. Top with jalapeño.

Bake at 500° for 8 minutes or until cheese is bubbly and crust is browned. Top with mango mixture. Yield: 8 servings (serving size: 2 slices).

CALORIES 236 (30% from fat); FAT 7.9g (sat 4g, mono 2.5g, poly 0.5g); PROTEIN 9.3g; CARB 32.9g; FIBER 1.9g; CHOL 23mg; IRON 1.7mg; SODIUM 278mg; CALC 162mg

Cheddar-Crusted Apple Pie

(pictured on page 129)

Granny Smith apples are good for baking, and they add a tart contrast to the sharp cheddar flavor in the crust.

CRUST:
- 1 tablespoon all-purpose flour
- ¾ cup (3 ounces) shredded extra-sharp cheddar cheese
- 2 cups all-purpose flour, divided
- ½ cup ice water
- ½ teaspoon salt
- ¼ cup chilled butter, cut into small pieces

FILLING:
- 10 cups very thinly sliced peeled Granny Smith apple (about 2¾ pounds)
- 2 tablespoons fresh lemon juice
- ⅓ cup packed brown sugar
- ¼ cup granulated sugar
- 3 tablespoons all-purpose flour
- ¼ teaspoon ground cinnamon
- ¼ teaspoon ground nutmeg
- ¼ teaspoon ground ginger
- Dash of salt

REMAINING INGREDIENTS:
- Cooking spray
- 1 large egg white, lightly beaten

1. Preheat oven to 400°.
2. To prepare crust, combine 1 tablespoon flour and cheese in a small bowl; toss well. Place mixture in freezer 10 minutes.
3. Lightly spoon 2 cups flour into dry measuring cups; level with a knife. Combine ¼ cup flour and ½ cup ice water in a small bowl, stirring with a whisk until well blended to form a slurry. Combine 1¾ cups flour and ½ teaspoon salt in a large bowl; cut in butter with a pastry blender or 2 knives until mixture resembles coarse meal. Stir in cheese mixture. Add slurry; toss with a fork. Sprinkle surface with up to 1 tablespoon ice water, tossing with a fork until moist and crumbly (do not form a ball). Mixture will seem slightly dry.
4. Divide dough in half. Gently press each half into a 4-inch circle on 2 sheets of overlapping heavy-duty plastic wrap; cover with 2 additional sheets of overlapping plastic wrap. Roll each dough half, still covered, into a 12-inch circle. Chill 30 minutes or until plastic wrap can be easily removed.
5. To prepare filling, combine apple and lemon juice in a large bowl. Combine brown sugar and next 6 ingredients in a small bowl. Sprinkle brown sugar mixture over apples; toss well to coat.
6. To assemble pie, remove top sheets of plastic wrap from 1 dough circle; fit dough, plastic wrap side up, into a 10-inch deep-dish pie plate coated with cooking spray, letting dough extend over edge of plate. Remove remaining plastic wrap. Spoon filling into crust. Brush edges of crust lightly with water. Remove top sheets of plastic wrap from remaining dough circle; place, plastic wrap side up, on apple mixture. Remove remaining plastic wrap. Press edges of dough together; fold edges under, and flute. Cut 3 (1-inch) slits in top of pastry using a sharp knife.
7. Combine egg white and 1 tablespoon water; brush over top and edges of pie. Place pie on a baking sheet; bake at 400° for 45 minutes or until golden. Cool on a wire rack. Yield: 10 servings (serving size: 1 wedge).

CALORIES 285 (24% from fat); FAT 7.7g (sat 4.5g, mono 1.4g, poly 0.3g); PROTEIN 5.4g; CARB 52g; FIBER 3.1g; CHOL 22mg; IRON 1.6mg; SODIUM 242mg; CALC 75mg

sound bites

Anti Up with a Winning Menu

Power pack your day with plenty of health-boosting antioxidants.

Power-Packed Antioxidant Menu

BREAKFAST:

Toasted whole wheat bagels with peanut butter

Strawberry-Kiwi Smoothie

Green tea

LUNCH:

Turkey, Swiss cheese, and asparagus wrap

Chopped Vegetable Salad with Garlic Dressing

SNACKS:

Carrots, broccoli, and cauliflower with ranch dressing

Pistachios

DINNER:

Wine

Cumin-Dusted Salmon Fillets

Curried Barley with Raisins and Almonds

Spinach sautéed with garlic

Taste of Summer Blueberry and Peach Cobbler

Strawberry-Kiwi Smoothie

You can use frozen blueberries, raspberries, or blackberries in place of the strawberries.

- 1 cup frozen unsweetened whole strawberries
- 1 cup vanilla low-fat soy milk
- 2 teaspoons honey
- ½ teaspoon vanilla extract
- 3 peeled kiwifruit, halved
- 3 firm bananas, peeled and halved

Continued

1. Place all ingredients in a blender; process until smooth. Chill thoroughly. Yield: 4 servings (serving size: 1 cup).

CALORIES 176 (7% from fat); FAT 1.4g (sat 0.2g, mono 0.2g, poly 0.4g); PROTEIN 2.9g; CARB 42.2g; FIBER 3.9g; CHOL 0mg; IRON 1mg; SODIUM 26mg; CALC 57mg

Chopped Vegetable Salad with Garlic Dressing

    2 cups chopped English cucumber
    1 cup chopped red bell pepper
    1 cup chopped yellow bell pepper
    1 cup chopped plum tomato
    ½ cup chopped green onions
    1 tablespoon fresh lemon juice
    1 teaspoon olive oil
    ½ teaspoon salt
    ¼ teaspoon Dijon mustard
    ⅛ teaspoon freshly ground black pepper
    2 garlic cloves, minced
    6 red leaf lettuce leaves (optional)

1. Combine first 5 ingredients in a large bowl. Combine lemon juice and next 5 ingredients in a small bowl; stir well with a whisk. Pour dressing over vegetables; toss gently to coat. Serve salad on lettuce leaves, if desired. Yield: 6 servings (serving size: about 1 cup).

CALORIES 39 (25% from fat); FAT 1.1g (sat 0.2g, mono 0.6g, poly 0.2g); PROTEIN 1.1g; CARB 7.2g; FIBER 1.8g; CHOL 0mg; IRON 0.5mg; SODIUM 208mg; CALC 16mg

Cumin-Dusted Salmon Fillets

Salmon is high in omega-3 fatty acids, which can help lower unhealthful cholesterol. This entrée is ready in less than 20 minutes.

    1 teaspoon ground cumin
    1 teaspoon paprika
    ½ teaspoon salt
    ½ teaspoon freshly ground black pepper
    4 (6-ounce) salmon fillets (about 1 inch thick), skinned
    Cooking spray

1. Combine first 4 ingredients. Sprinkle both sides of fish with spice mixture.

2. Heat a large nonstick skillet coated with cooking spray over medium heat, and add fish. Cook 6 minutes on each side or until fish flakes easily when tested with a fork. Yield: 4 servings.

CALORIES 184 (40% from fat); FAT 8.2g (sat 1.3g, mono 2.7g, poly 3.2g); PROTEIN 25.4g; CARB 0.4g; FIBER 0.3g; CHOL 70mg; IRON 1.3mg; SODIUM 350mg; CALC 21mg

Curried Barley with Raisins and Almonds

Barley, onion, garlic, and almonds provide lots of fiber and antioxidants in this side dish. Serve it with fish, chicken, or beef—any entrée you'd normally have with rice or potatoes. This is also great served with mango chutney.

    1½ teaspoons olive oil, divided
    2½ cups vertically sliced onion
    1 teaspoon minced garlic
    1 teaspoon curry powder
    1½ cups cooked pearl barley
    2 tablespoons raisins
    2 tablespoons chopped fresh flat-leaf parsley
    2 tablespoons slivered almonds, toasted
    ¼ teaspoon salt
    ⅛ teaspoon freshly ground black pepper

1. Heat ½ teaspoon oil in a medium nonstick skillet over medium heat. Add onion; cover and cook 15 minutes or until golden brown, stirring occasionally. Add garlic, and cook 1 minute. Remove from pan.

2. Add 1 teaspoon oil to pan. Add curry powder, and cook 1 minute. Add barley, and toss gently to coat. Stir in onion mixture, raisins, and remaining ingredients. Serve immediately. Yield: 4 servings (serving size: about ⅔ cup).

CALORIES 157 (25% from fat); FAT 4.3g (sat 0.5g, mono 2.7g, poly 0.8g); PROTEIN 3.4g; CARB 27.9g; FIBER 4.4g; CHOL 0mg; IRON 1.5mg; SODIUM 153mg; CALC 41mg

Taste of Summer Blueberry and Peach Cobbler

    1 pound frozen sliced peaches
    1 pound frozen blueberries
    1 teaspoon vanilla extract
    ¾ cup granulated sugar, divided
    1½ tablespoons cornstarch
    ¼ teaspoon ground cinnamon
    ⅛ teaspoon grated whole nutmeg (optional)
    1 cup all-purpose flour
    ¾ teaspoon baking powder
    ¼ teaspoon baking soda
    ¼ cup chilled butter, cut into small pieces
    ½ cup low-fat buttermilk
    1 large egg, lightly beaten
    1 tablespoon turbinado sugar (optional)

1. Preheat oven to 400°.
2. Combine first 3 ingredients in a large bowl. Combine ½ cup granulated sugar, cornstarch, cinnamon, and nutmeg, if desired, in a small bowl. Add sugar mixture to fruit, tossing to coat. Spoon fruit mixture into an 11 x 7-inch baking dish.
3. Lightly spoon flour into a dry measuring cup; level with a knife. Combine flour, ¼ cup granulated sugar, baking powder, and baking soda in a large bowl. Cut in butter with a pastry blender or 2 knives until mixture resembles coarse meal. Combine buttermilk and egg in a small bowl; stir with a whisk. Add buttermilk mixture to flour mixture; stir until moist.
4. Drop dough by spoonfuls onto fruit mixture to form 8 dumplings. Sprinkle with turbinado sugar, if desired. Cover and bake at 400° for 35 minutes; uncover and bake an additional 15 minutes or until browned. Yield: 8 servings.

CALORIES 261 (24% from fat); FAT 7.1g (sat 3.9g, mono 2g, poly 0.5g); PROTEIN 3.7g; CARB 46g; FIBER 2.9g; CHOL 43mg; IRON 1.1mg; SODIUM 172mg; CALC 56mg

Cuban Cooking

Using a few handy shortcuts, you can prepare authentic Cuban cuisine in a snap.

In the following recipes, no flavor or authenticity has been compromised by lightening and simplifying them. They are simple and delicious because they rely on the bright flavors of fresh ingredients. And with the exception of marinating time, all these dishes can be prepared in about an hour.

Pollo Rancho Luna
Rancho Luna Chicken
(pictured on page 129)

In the Havana of the '50s, there was a very popular country restaurant called Rancho Luna. The house specialty: chicken marinated in a secret family recipe. This simple version is a good approximation of the original.

  4 (4-ounce) skinless, boneless
       chicken breast halves
  3 tablespoons commercial mojo
       marinade (such as Goya)
  ½ cup finely chopped onion
  ¼ cup finely chopped fresh parsley
  1 teaspoon vegetable oil
  4 teaspoons fresh lime juice
Lime wedges (optional)

1. Combine chicken and mojo in a large zip-top plastic bag; seal and marinate in refrigerator 2 hours, turning occasionally.
2. Combine chopped onion and parsley in a small bowl.
3. Remove chicken from bag; pat dry. Heat oil in a large nonstick skillet over medium-high heat. Add chicken; cook 4 minutes on each side or until done. Drizzle each breast with 1 teaspoon lime juice; top each serving with 2 tablespoons onion mixture. Serve with lime wedges, if desired. Yield: 4 servings.

CALORIES 149 (16% from fat); FAT 2.6g (sat 0.6g, mono 0.6g, poly 1g); PROTEIN 26.6g; CARB 3.2g; FIBER 0.5g; CHOL 66mg; IRON 1.2mg; SODIUM 279mg; CALC 45mg

Enchilado de Camerones
Deviled Shrimp

This is one of the few dishes in Cuban cooking that is spicy.

  1 tablespoon olive oil
  1 cup chopped onion
  ½ cup chopped red bell pepper
  ½ cup chopped green bell pepper
  ½ to 1 teaspoon crushed red pepper
  ¼ teaspoon salt
  4 garlic cloves, minced
  1 (14.5-ounce) can diced tomatoes,
       undrained
  1 pound medium shrimp, peeled
       and deveined
  ¼ cup light coconut milk
  2 tablespoons chopped fresh cilantro

1. Heat oil in a large nonstick skillet over medium-high heat. Add onion; sauté 2 minutes. Add bell peppers, crushed red pepper, salt, and garlic; sauté 4 minutes. Add tomatoes; cook 6 minutes or until liquid almost evaporates, stirring frequently.
2. Stir in shrimp, and cook 4 minutes or until shrimp are done, stirring frequently. Remove shrimp mixture from heat, and stir in coconut milk. Sprinkle with cilantro. Yield: 4 servings (serving size: ¾ cup).

CALORIES 212 (27% from fat); FAT 6.4g (sat 1.4g, mono 2.8g, poly 1.1g); PROTEIN 25g; CARB 13.7g; FIBER 3.5g; CHOL 172mg; IRON 3.5mg; SODIUM 453mg; CALC 93mg

---

Essentials of Cuban Cooking: A Glossary

Adobo: A seasoning for meats and poultry. The dry version is a rub consisting of salt, pepper, garlic, oregano, and cumin. A wet version, used as a marinade, contains sour orange juice, garlic, seasonings, and various herbs and spices.

Arroz: Rice (plain white is used most often).

Beans: A daily staple, from chickpeas to black beans, or red, white, and pink beans.

Bijol: Bright orange powder used for coloring and made with *achiote* (annatto) seeds and flavorings, often used with saffron.

Bitter orange: A component of marinades and *mojos* with a flavor between lime and orange (also known as *naranja agria*).

Calabaza: Type of pumpkin from the Caribbean with a mild but distinctive flavor. Butternut squash is a good substitute.

Cilantro: Herb used in *sofrito*, as a garnish, or to punch up a dish.

Coconut: Its refreshing juice is used in alcoholic drinks, or taken plain. The white flesh is eaten from the hand or— when harder—used to make sweets. Since getting fresh milk is labor intensive, canned is almost always used.

Mojo: Juice-based (usually bitter orange) sauce served cold or hot. Cold, it is used as a marinade. If hot, garlic is sautéed in olive oil and the juice and flavorings are added to the pan. The sauce is then poured over meats or tuber vegetables.

Plantain: Green or ripe, boiled, mashed, fried, or baked, this is also known as a cooking banana.

Saffron: Its deep, earthy flavor has no substitute, but its color can be reproduced with Bijol.

Sofrito: The linchpin of Caribbean cooking, it's a mix of onion, pepper, garlic, herbs, and seasonings sautéed in olive oil. Tomatoes, tomato sauce, or cilantro may be added.

Picadillo

Although picadillo is traditionally made with ground beef, using ground turkey offers a great lower-fat alternative. Typical accompaniments are white rice and ripe plantains.

 1 teaspoon olive oil
 1 cup finely chopped onion
 1 pound ground turkey
 3 garlic cloves, minced
 1 cup low-salt beef broth
 ⅓ cup raisins
 ⅓ cup coarsely chopped pimiento-stuffed olives
 3 tablespoons capers
 1 tablespoon tomato paste
 ¼ teaspoon freshly ground black pepper
 3 cups hot cooked rice
 Parsley sprigs (optional)

1. Heat oil in a large nonstick skillet over medium-high heat. Add onion; sauté 5 minutes. Add turkey and garlic; cook 5 minutes or until browned, stirring to crumble. Add broth and next 5 ingredients; stir well. Bring to a boil. Cover, reduce heat, and simmer 25 minutes. Serve with rice. Garnish with parsley sprigs, if desired. Yield: 4 servings (serving size: 1 cup picadillo and ¾ cup rice).

CALORIES 423 (29% from fat); FAT 13.5g (sat 3.2g, mono 6.2g, poly 2.8g); PROTEIN 26.1g; CARB 48.9g; FIBER 2.7g; CHOL 90mg; IRON 3.9mg; SODIUM 782mg; CALC 62mg

Frijoles Colorados
Red Beans with Squash

This simplified side uses the convenience of bottled sofrito and canned beans. Look for beans labeled "ready to eat"; they're seasoned and lend more flavor.

 3 cups (½-inch) cubed peeled calabaza or butternut squash (about 1 pound)
 ¼ cup commercial sofrito (such as Goya)
 1 (15-ounce) can small red beans, undrained
 ¼ cup thinly sliced onion

1. Cook squash in boiling water 6 minutes or until tender; drain.
2. Combine sofrito and beans in a small saucepan. Cook over medium heat 10 minutes or until thoroughly heated. Gently stir in squash. Top with onion. Yield: 6 servings (serving size: ⅔ cup).

CALORIES 110 (16% from fat); FAT 1.9g (sat 0.5g, mono 0.8g, poly 0.2g); PROTEIN 4.7g; CARB 20.3g; FIBER 6.1g; CHOL 2mg; IRON 1.4mg; SODIUM 262mg; CALC 61mg

Mojito

The *mojito* is just catching on in the United States, but it has been popular in Cuba since the 1920s. As smooth and potent as a mint julep, it is lively and tasty. The secret to a good mojito is fresh mint muddled with sugar to release the mint's essential oils.

 2 teaspoons sugar
 10 small mint leaves
 ¼ cup white rum
 2 tablespoons fresh lime juice
 1 (6-ounce) bottle club soda, chilled
 1 mint sprig (optional)

1. Place sugar and mint leaves in a tall glass; crush with back of a long spoon. Fill glass with crushed ice. Add rum, juice, and club soda. Garnish with mint sprig, if desired. Yield: 1 serving (serving size: about 1 cup).

CALORIES 169 (0% from fat); FAT 0g; PROTEIN 0.2g; CARB 11.2g; FIBER 0.2g; CHOL 0mg; IRON 0.1mg; SODIUM 37mg; CALC 13mg

Carne con Papas
Stew of Beef and Potatoes

This everyday dish is usually accompanied by white rice. To streamline the preparation process, chop the potatoes and olives while the beef and vegetables simmer.

 1 teaspoon vegetable oil
 Cooking spray
 1½ pounds beef stew meat, trimmed and cut into 1-inch cubes
 1½ cups chopped onion
 ½ cup chopped green bell pepper
 ½ teaspoon salt
 ½ teaspoon freshly ground black pepper
 3 garlic cloves, minced
 ¼ cup water
 1 teaspoon dried oregano
 1 teaspoon paprika
 ⅛ teaspoon ground cumin
 1 bay leaf, crumbled
 1 (14¼-ounce) can low-salt beef broth
 4 cups cubed peeled baking potato (about 2 pounds)
 3 tablespoons raisins
 3 tablespoons coarsely chopped pimiento-stuffed olives
 2 tablespoons capers

1. Heat oil in a large Dutch oven coated with cooking spray over medium-high heat. Add beef, and cook 2 minutes or until browned. Add onion, bell pepper, salt, black pepper, and garlic; sauté 3 minutes. Add water and next 5 ingredients; bring to a boil. Cover, reduce heat, and simmer 30 minutes.
2. Stir in potato and remaining ingredients. Cook, covered, over medium heat 20 minutes or until potato is tender, stirring occasionally. Yield: 5 servings (serving size: about 1½ cups).
WINE NOTE: You'll need a wine that can stand up to the stew's varied flavors. A great bet: Lincourt Vineyards Syrah 2000 from Santa Barbara County (about $20). It's got luscious dark flavors of bitter chocolate, espresso, licorice, and blackberries.

CALORIES 410 (27% from fat); FAT 12.3g (sat 4g, mono 5.3g, poly 1.2g); PROTEIN 31.8g; CARB 43.4g; FIBER 4.9g; CHOL 85mg; IRON 4.5mg; SODIUM 650mg; CALC 57mg

Filete de Cerdo con Adobo
Marinated Pork Tenderloin

Pork is a staple in Cuban cooking. Orange and lemon juices combine to simulate the bitter orange flavor essential to this dish.

1¼ cups fresh orange juice
     (about 2 oranges), divided
  3 tablespoons fresh lemon juice,
     divided
  1 tablespoon olive oil, divided
  1 teaspoon salt
  1 teaspoon chopped fresh oregano
  ½ teaspoon ground cumin
  4 garlic cloves, chopped
  2 (1-pound) pork tenderloins,
     trimmed
     Orange and lemon wedges (optional)
     Oregano sprigs (optional)

1. Place ½ cup orange juice, 2 tablespoons lemon juice, 1½ teaspoons olive oil, salt, oregano, cumin, and garlic cloves in a blender; process until smooth. Combine orange juice mixture and pork in a large zip-top plastic bag; seal and marinate in refrigerator 2 hours, turning occasionally. Remove pork from bag, reserving marinade.
2. Heat 1½ teaspoons oil in a large non-stick skillet over medium-high heat. Add pork; cook 4 minutes on each side or until browned. Add reserved marinade; cover, reduce heat to medium-low, and simmer 20 minutes or until thermometer inserted into thickest portion of pork registers 160° (slightly pink). Remove pork from pan; keep warm.
3. Add ¾ cup orange juice and 1 tablespoon lemon juice to pan. Bring to a boil; cook until reduced to ½ cup (about 5 minutes). Serve sauce with pork. Serve with orange and lemon wedges, if desired. Garnish with oregano sprigs, if desired. Yield: 8 servings (serving size: 3 ounces pork and 1 tablespoon sauce).

CALORIES 173 (30% from fat); FAT 5.7g (sat 1.6g, mono 3g, poly 0.6g); PROTEIN 24.2g; CARB 5.1g; FIBER 0.2g; CHOL 74mg; IRON 1.6mg; SODIUM 351mg; CALC 15mg

Arroz con Pollo
Chicken with Rice

With annatto seeds forming the base, Bijol powder serves mostly as a colorant. You can combine equal parts ground cumin and turmeric to use as a substitute for Bijol seasoning.

CHICKEN:
  ¼ cup fresh lemon juice
  1 teaspoon salt
  1 teaspoon dried oregano
  ⅛ teaspoon Bijol seasoning
  6 chicken drumsticks (about 1½
     pounds), skinned
  6 chicken thighs (about 2 pounds),
     skinned
  4 garlic cloves, minced

RICE:
  2 cups uncooked Valencia rice or
     other short-grain rice
  2 teaspoons olive oil, divided
2½ cups fat-free, less-sodium chicken
     broth
  3 tablespoons commercial sofrito
     (such as Goya)
  ½ teaspoon Bijol seasoning
  ½ teaspoon saffron threads (optional)
  ½ cup frozen petite green peas,
     thawed
  1 (7-ounce) jar sliced pimiento,
     drained

1. To prepare chicken, combine first 7 ingredients in a large zip-top plastic bag; seal and marinate in refrigerator 1 hour, turning bag occasionally. Remove chicken from bag, reserving marinade.
2. To prepare rice, place rice in a colander in a large bowl, and rinse with cold water until water runs clear. Drain well.
3. Heat 1 teaspoon oil in a large Dutch oven over medium-high heat. Add drumsticks, and cook 5 minutes on each side or until browned. Remove from pan; keep warm. Repeat procedure with 1 teaspoon oil and thighs. Remove from pan; keep warm.
4. Add reserved marinade, rice, chicken, chicken broth, sofrito, ½ teaspoon Bijol, and saffron threads, if desired, to pan. Bring to a boil. Cover, reduce heat, and simmer 25 minutes. Stir in peas and pimiento; let stand, covered, 10 minutes. Yield: 6 servings (serving size: 2 chicken pieces and about ⅔ cup rice mixture).

CALORIES 472 (17% from fat); FAT 8.7g (sat 2.1g, mono 3.5g, poly 1.8g); PROTEIN 37.1g; CARB 57.8g; FIBER 3.1g; CHOL 122mg; IRON 5.2mg; SODIUM 773mg; CALC 32mg

Bul

A crisp combination of ingredients makes *bul* (BOOL) a refreshing sipper. It's a popular summer drink often prepared in Cuban homes. It's best made with a pale ale or light-colored beer.

  ⅓ cup fresh lime juice
  1 (12-ounce) bottle beer, chilled
  1 (12-ounce) bottle ginger ale,
     chilled
  4 lime slices (optional)

1. Combine first 3 ingredients in a pitcher. Serve over ice. Garnish with lime slices, if desired. Yield: 4 servings (serving size: about ¾ cup).

CALORIES 69 (0% from fat); FAT 0g; PROTEIN 0.4g; CARB 12.4g; FIBER 0.3g; CHOL 0mg; IRON 0.2mg; SODIUM 10mg; CALC 9mg

Pargo con Salsa de Perejil
Snapper in Parsley Sauce

Serve with cherry tomatoes sautéed with garlic and boiled potatoes or white rice.

  4 (6-ounce) red snapper or other
     firm white fish fillets
     Cooking spray
  2 cups fresh parsley leaves
  1 cup chopped onion
  ½ cup clam juice
  2 tablespoons fresh lime juice
  ¾ teaspoon salt
  3 garlic cloves

1. Preheat oven to 400°.
2. Arrange snapper fillets in a 13 x 9-inch baking dish coated with cooking spray.
3. Place parsley and remaining 5 ingredients in a blender or food processor;

Continued

process until smooth. Pour sauce over fish. Bake at 400° for 18 minutes or until fish flakes easily when tested with a fork. Yield: 4 servings.

CALORIES 147 (12% from fat); FAT 1.9g (sat 0.4g, mono 0.4g, poly 0.6g); PROTEIN 25.2g; CARB 6.8g; FIBER 1.8g; CHOL 43mg; IRON 2.3mg; SODIUM 574mg; CALC 94mg

Machuquillo
Plantain Mash

Use plantains that have mottled skins and are moderately ripe.

 2 medium plantains, peeled and thinly sliced
 1 tablespoon olive oil
½ teaspoon salt
 1 garlic clove, minced

1. Cook plantain slices in boiling water 15 minutes or until tender; drain. Place plantains, oil, salt, and garlic in a bowl; mash with a potato masher until smooth. Serve immediately. Yield: 4 servings (serving size: ½ cup).

CALORIES 140 (24% from fat); FAT 3.7g (sat 0.6g, mono 2.5g, poly 0.4g); PROTEIN 1.2g; CARB 28.8g; FIBER 2.1g; CHOL 0mg; IRON 0.6mg; SODIUM 297mg; CALC 4mg

Batido de Mango
Mango Smoothie

The *batido* is a smoothie made with milk and tropical fruits. Omit the lime juice and substitute frozen *guanábana* pulp for the mango to create a classic Cuban drink. Guanábana is an exotic-tasting, rich, tart-sweet, white-fleshed fruit.

1½ cups chopped peeled mango
1½ cups fat-free milk
¼ cup fresh lime juice
 1 tablespoon brown sugar

1. Place all ingredients in a blender; process until smooth. Serve over ice. Yield: 4 servings (serving size: ¾ cup).

CALORIES 89 (4% from fat); FAT 0.4g (sat 0.2g, mono 0.1g, poly 0g); PROTEIN 3.5g; CARB 19.5g; FIBER 1.2g; CHOL 2mg; IRON 0.1mg; SODIUM 49mg; CALC 121mg

back to the best

Malaysian Chicken Pizza

This favorite first appeared in the September/October 1991 issue.

An exotic peanut-ginger sauce tops a traditional Italian pizza crust. Swiss and mozzarella cheeses finish the pizza.

Malaysian Chicken Pizza

¾ cup rice vinegar
¼ cup packed brown sugar
¼ cup low-sodium soy sauce
 3 tablespoons water
 1 tablespoon minced peeled fresh ginger
 2 tablespoons chunky peanut butter
½ to ¾ teaspoon crushed red pepper
 4 garlic cloves, minced
Cooking spray
½ pound skinless, boneless chicken breast, cut into bite-sized pieces
½ cup (2 ounces) shredded reduced-fat, reduced-sodium Swiss cheese (such as Alpine Lace)
¼ cup (1 ounce) shredded part-skim mozzarella cheese
 1 (12-inch) Basic Pizza Crust (recipe at right)
¼ cup chopped green onions

1. Preheat oven to 500°.
2. Combine first 8 ingredients in a bowl; stir well with a whisk.
3. Heat a nonstick skillet coated with cooking spray over medium heat. Add chicken, and sauté 2 minutes. Remove chicken from pan.
4. Pour rice vinegar mixture into pan, and bring to a boil over medium-high heat. Cook mixture 6 minutes or until slightly thickened. Return chicken to pan; cook 1 minute or until chicken is done. (Mixture will be consistency of thick syrup.)
5. Sprinkle cheeses over prepared crust, leaving a ½-inch border, and top with chicken mixture. Bake at 500° for 12

minutes on bottom rack in oven. Sprinkle with green onions. Place pizza on a cutting board; let stand 5 minutes. Yield: 6 servings.

(Values include Basic Pizza Crust) CALORIES 293 (22% from fat); FAT 7.3g (sat 2.9g, mono 2.6g, poly 1.2g); PROTEIN 18.2g; CARB 38.3g; FIBER 1.8g; CHOL 33mg; IRON 2.4mg; SODIUM 487mg; CALC 151mg

BASIC PIZZA CRUST:

 1 tablespoon sugar
 1 package dry yeast (about 2¼ teaspoons)
 1 cup warm water (100° to 110°)
 3 cups all-purpose flour, divided
¼ teaspoon salt
 1 teaspoon olive oil
Cooking spray
 1 tablespoon cornmeal

1. Dissolve sugar and yeast in water in a large bowl, and let stand 5 minutes. Stir 2¾ cups flour, salt, and oil into yeast mixture to form a soft dough.
2. Turn dough out onto a lightly floured surface. Knead until smooth and elastic (about 5 minutes); add enough of remaining flour, 1 tablespoon at a time, to prevent dough from sticking to hands.
3. Place dough in a bowl coated with cooking spray, turning to coat. Cover; let rise in a warm place (85°), free from drafts, 1 hour or until doubled in size. (Press two fingers into dough. If indentation remains, dough has risen enough.)
4. Punch dough down; divide in half. Roll each half into a 12-inch circle on a lightly floured surface. Place dough on 2 (12-inch) pizza pans or baking sheets each coated with cooking spray and sprinkled with 1½ teaspoons cornmeal. Crimp edges of dough with fingers to form a rim. Cover; let rise in a warm place (85°), free from drafts, 30 minutes. Yield: 2 (12-inch) pizza crusts.
NOTE: To save half of dough for later, wrap in plastic wrap, and store in a heavy-duty zip-top plastic bag in freezer. To thaw, place dough in refrigerator 12 hours or overnight; bring to room temperature, and shape as desired.

(Per Pizza Crust) CALORIES 751 (5% from fat); FAT 4.4g (sat 0.6g, mono 2g, poly 1.0g); PROTEIN 21g; CARB 154g; FIBER 6.1g; CHOL 0mg; IRON 9.4mg; SODIUM 300mg; CALC 31mg

june

Grapes

Beyond beauty and flavor, grapes pack a healthy punch.

A cup of grapes has almost as much fiber as a slice of whole wheat toast, a good amount of potassium, just a trace of fat, and little more than 100 calories. But grapes' most potent benefits lie in their phytonutrients, particularly in the compound resveratrol—found within the skin of grapes of all colors—that may help prevent several kinds of cancer and heart disease. Pluck grapes by the bunch, or one by one. They may well keep the doctor away.

Barbecue Chicken and Grape Salad

Although similar to a Waldorf salad, this recipe uses grapes instead of apples. The rub gives the chicken a barbecue flavor. Rinsing the onions takes away some of their bite.

    1   teaspoon onion powder
    1   teaspoon paprika
    1   teaspoon ancho chili powder
    ¾   teaspoon salt, divided
    1   pound skinless, boneless chicken
        breast
    1   teaspoon olive oil
    ¾   cup seedless green grapes, halved
    ¾   cup seedless red grapes, halved
    ⅔   cup coarsely chopped celery
    ½   cup thinly sliced red onion
    ¼   cup low-fat mayonnaise
    1   tablespoon red wine vinegar
    1   tablespoon fresh orange juice
    ¼   cup coarsely chopped walnuts,
        toasted

1. Preheat oven to 350°.
2. Combine onion powder, paprika, chili powder, and ½ teaspoon salt; sprinkle over chicken.
3. Heat oil in a large nonstick oven-proof skillet over medium-high heat. Add chicken, and sauté 2 minutes on each side or until browned. Wrap handle of skillet in foil; bake chicken at 350° for 10 minutes or until done. Remove from pan; refrigerate until chilled. Chop into bite-sized pieces.
4. Combine ¼ teaspoon salt, green grapes, and next 6 ingredients in a large bowl. Add chopped chicken, and toss to coat. Sprinkle salad with walnuts. Yield: 4 servings (serving size: about 1¼ cups).

CALORIES 266 (29% from fat); FAT 8.5g (sat 1.1g, mono 2.5g, poly 4.1g); PROTEIN 29.1g; CARB 19.1g; FIBER 2g; CHOL 66mg; IRON 1.6mg; SODIUM 676mg; CALC 40mg

Grape Chutney with Grilled Chicken

The grapes retain most of their shape in the thickened syrup. The chutney is also good with pork or beef.

    ½   cup chopped onion
    ½   cup red wine vinegar
    ½   cup dry red wine
    ¼   cup chopped dried figs
    2   tablespoons sugar
    2   teaspoons hot paprika
    1   teaspoon grated peeled fresh ginger
    1   (3-inch) cinnamon stick
    1   cup seedless green grapes, halved
    1   cup seedless red grapes, halved
    4   (4-ounce) skinless, boneless
        chicken breast halves
    2   teaspoons vegetable oil
    ½   teaspoon salt
    ¼   teaspoon freshly ground black
        pepper

1. Prepare grill.
2. Combine first 8 ingredients in a medium saucepan over medium-high heat. Bring to a boil; cook 10 minutes. Stir in grapes; reduce heat, and simmer 20 minutes. Remove cinnamon stick.

3. Coat chicken with oil; sprinkle with salt and pepper. Grill 5 minutes on each side or until done. Serve with chutney. Yield: 4 servings (serving size: 1 chicken breast half and ¼ cup chutney).

CALORIES 271 (15% from fat); FAT 4.5g (sat 0.9g, mono 0.9g, poly 1.9g); PROTEIN 27.6g; CARB 31.6g; FIBER 2.9g; CHOL 66mg; IRON 2mg; SODIUM 376mg; CALC 50mg

---

Easy Roasting Menu
serves 4

Roasted Pork with Honeyed Grape Sauce

Roasted asparagus with feta*

Couscous

*Trim 1 pound asparagus, and arrange in an 11 x 7-inch baking dish. Top with ¼ cup crumbled feta cheese, 2 tablespoons fresh lemon juice, and 1 teaspoon chopped fresh thyme. Cover and bake at 450° for 12 minutes or until asparagus is crisp-tender.

search myclar2003.com for all our menus

Roasted Pork with Honeyed Grape Sauce

A salty-sweet sauce is a delicious match for pan-roasted pork. Serve this dish with roasted red onions and mashed sweet potatoes. You can use green grapes, but the sauce won't be as rich, or as pretty.

    2   teaspoons olive oil, divided
    ⅓   cup chopped shallots
    1   tablespoon minced garlic
    2   cups coarsely chopped seedless red
        grapes
    2   tablespoons tamari sauce or soy
        sauce
    2   tablespoons honey
    1   teaspoon grated peeled fresh ginger
    Dash of five-spice powder
    1¼ pounds pork tenderloin, trimmed
    ½   teaspoon salt
    ½   teaspoon freshly ground black
        pepper

1. Preheat oven to 450°.
2. Heat 1 teaspoon oil in a medium saucepan over medium heat. Add shallots

and garlic; sauté 3 minutes or until tender. Add grapes and next 4 ingredients. Bring to a boil; reduce heat, and simmer 15 minutes. Cool 10 minutes. Place mixture in a blender; process until smooth.

3. Heat 1 teaspoon oil in a large cast iron skillet over medium-high heat. Sprinkle pork with salt and pepper. Add pork to pan; cook 5 minutes, browning on all sides. Insert meat thermometer into thickest portion of pork. Bake pork at 450° for 12 minutes or until thermometer registers 155°. Tent with foil; let stand 10 minutes before slicing. Serve with sauce. Yield: 4 servings (serving size: 3 ounces pork and ¼ cup sauce).

CALORIES 263 (23% from fat); FAT 6.6g (sat 1.8g, mono 3.4g, poly 0.8g); PROTEIN 25.6g; CARB 26.6g; FIBER 1g; CHOL 74mg; IRON 2.1mg; SODIUM 759mg; CALC 27mg

Grape Margarita Slush

This is equally good without the tequila and Triple Sec. Substitute water for the tequila and orange juice for the Triple Sec.

- ¾ cup water
- ⅓ cup sugar
- 1 cup tequila
- ½ cup fresh lime juice (about 3 large limes)
- ⅓ cup Triple Sec
- 3 cups seedless green grapes
- 7 cups ice cubes

1. Combine water and sugar in a small saucepan over medium heat. Cook 3 minutes or until sugar dissolves. Pour into a freezer-safe container; cool completely. Add tequila, juice, and Triple Sec to sugar mixture; stir to combine. Cover and freeze overnight. Place grapes in a large heavy-duty zip-top plastic bag; freeze overnight.

2. Place half of tequila mixture, 1½ cups grapes, and 3½ cups ice in a blender; process until desired consistency. Repeat with remaining tequila mixture, grapes, and ice. Yield: 10 cups (serving size: 1 cup).

CALORIES 149 (2% from fat); FAT 0.3g (sat 0.1g, mono 0g, poly 0.1g); PROTEIN 0.4g; CARB 19.6g; FIBER 0.5g; CHOL 0mg; IRON 0.2mg; SODIUM 2mg; CALC 6mg

Duck with Grape Demi-Glace

Look for veal and duck demi-glace in the frozen foods section or near the butcher's counter of your market.

- 1 teaspoon olive oil
- ⅓ cup chopped fennel bulb
- ⅓ cup chopped shallots
- ⅔ cup coarsely chopped seedless red grapes
- ½ cup red wine
- ½ cup ruby port
- 5 juniper berries, crushed
- 1 (2-inch) thyme sprig
- 1 (1-inch) rosemary sprig
- Cooking spray
- 1½ pounds skinless, boneless duck breast, trimmed
- 1 teaspoon water
- ½ teaspoon cornstarch
- 2 tablespoons veal and duck demi-glace (such as D'Artagnan)
- ½ cup seedless red grapes, halved
- 1 teaspoon balsamic vinegar
- 1 teaspoon butter
- ⅛ teaspoon freshly ground black pepper

1. Heat oil in a medium saucepan over medium-low heat. Add fennel and shallots; cover and cook 3 minutes or until tender. Add ⅔ cup grapes and next 5 ingredients. Bring to a boil; reduce heat, and simmer until liquid is reduced to ¾ cup (about 10 minutes). Strain wine mixture through a fine sieve; discard solids. Return wine mixture to pan.

2. Heat a large skillet coated with cooking spray over medium heat. Add duck; cook 8 minutes on each side or until done. Let stand 5 minutes; cut duck breasts into ¼-inch-thick slices.

3. Combine water and cornstarch. Add cornstarch mixture and demi-glace to wine mixture, stirring constantly with a whisk. Bring to a boil; cook 1 minute. Add ½ cup grapes; cook 30 seconds. Remove from heat; stir in balsamic vinegar, butter, and pepper. Yield: 6 servings (serving size: 3 ounces duck breast and about 2½ tablespoons sauce).

CALORIES 232 (26% from fat); FAT 6.6g (sat 2.1g, mono 2.2g, poly 0.8g); PROTEIN 23.3g; CARB 11.1g; FIBER 0.6g; CHOL 89mg; IRON 5.6mg; SODIUM 120mg; CALC 17mg

Arugula Salad with Shrimp and Grapes

DRESSING:

- ⅓ cup seedless green grapes
- 1 tablespoon Champagne vinegar or white wine vinegar
- 1 teaspoon olive oil
- ¾ teaspoon Dijon mustard
- ½ teaspoon minced fresh Vidalia or sweet onion (optional)
- ⅛ teaspoon salt
- Dash of white pepper

SALAD:

- 4 cups water
- ¾ pound large shrimp, peeled and deveined
- ½ cup diagonally cut celery
- 5 cups trimmed arugula
- 1 cup seedless red grapes, halved
- 1 cup seedless green grapes, halved
- ¼ cup fresh basil leaves, thinly sliced
- 2 tablespoons crumbled Gorgonzola cheese
- 1 tablespoon coarsely chopped walnuts, lightly toasted

1. To prepare dressing, combine first 7 ingredients in a blender; process until smooth.

2. To prepare salad, bring 4 cups water to a boil in a large saucepan. Add shrimp; cook 1 minute. Add celery; cook 1 minute. Drain and rinse with cold water; pat dry.

3. Place shrimp mixture, arugula, halved grapes, and basil in a large bowl. Drizzle with dressing, and toss gently to coat. Top with cheese and walnuts. Yield: 4 servings (serving size: 2 cups).

WINE NOTE: A delicate wine simply wouldn't hold up to the peppery arugula, sweet grapes, and salty Gorgonzola in this dish. Opt for something dramatically green, peppery, and fruity that has good acidity to balance the saltiness of the cheese. Our top choice: the 2000 Brancott Sauvignon Blanc from Marlborough, New Zealand (about $10).

CALORIES 163 (27% from fat); FAT 4.8g (sat 1.3g, mono 1.2g, poly 1.5g); PROTEIN 13.4g; CARB 18.6g; FIBER 1.8g; CHOL 105mg; IRON 2.5mg; SODIUM 271mg; CALC 106mg

Grape and Cucumber Salsa

Increase the jalapeño or leave the seeds in for more kick. Serve with tortilla chips or grilled chicken.

   1 cup seedless green grapes, quartered
   1 cup seedless red grapes, quartered
  ¾ cup finely chopped peeled English cucumber
  ¼ cup finely chopped Vidalia or other sweet onion
   2 tablespoons fresh lime juice
   1 tablespoon chopped fresh cilantro
   1 tablespoon finely chopped seeded jalapeño pepper
  ¼ teaspoon salt

1. Combine all ingredients in a medium bowl. Cover and chill 1 hour, stirring occasionally. Yield: 6 servings (serving size: ½ cup).

CALORIES 22 (8% from fat); FAT 0.2g (sat 0.1g, mono 0g, poly 0.1g); PROTEIN 0.3g; CARB 5.5g; FIBER 0.4g; CHOL 0mg; IRON 0.1mg; SODIUM 50mg; CALC 5mg

Spiced Grapes in Port Dessert Sauce

Serve with vanilla ice cream or pound cake.

   1 cup ruby port
   2 tablespoons sugar
   1 (1-inch) strip lemon rind
   1 star anise
   1 teaspoon balsamic vinegar
  ⅛ teaspoon freshly ground black pepper
 2½ cups seedless red grapes, halved

1. Combine first 4 ingredients in a saucepan. Bring to a boil; cook 2 minutes or until sugar dissolves. Reduce heat; simmer 15 minutes. Remove lemon rind and anise; discard. Add vinegar and pepper to wine mixture; cook until reduced to ¼ cup (about 10 minutes). Remove from heat; stir in grapes. Serve at room temperature or chilled. Yield: 6 servings (serving size: ⅓ cup).

CALORIES 124 (3% from fat); FAT 0.4g (sat 0.1g, mono 0g, poly 0.1g); PROTEIN 0.5g; CARB 20.8g; FIBER 0.7g; CHOL 0mg; IRON 0.3mg; SODIUM 5mg; CALC 11mg

Rustic Grape Tart

CRUST:

   1 cup all-purpose flour
  ¼ cup yellow cornmeal
   3 tablespoons granulated sugar
  ½ teaspoon baking powder
  ½ teaspoon salt
  ¼ cup chilled butter, cut into small pieces
   3 tablespoons orange juice
   1 teaspoon all-purpose flour

FILLING:

 2¼ cups seedless red grapes
 2¼ cups seedless black grapes
   2 tablespoons granulated sugar
   1 tablespoon cornstarch
  ¾ teaspoon vanilla extract
  ¼ teaspoon ground cinnamon

REMAINING INGREDIENTS:

   1 teaspoon water
   1 large egg yolk
   1 teaspoon turbinado sugar (optional)

1. To prepare crust, lightly spoon 1 cup flour into a dry measuring cup; level with a knife. Combine 1 cup flour, cornmeal, 3 tablespoons granulated sugar, baking powder, and salt in a food processor; pulse 4 times or until blended. Add chilled butter; pulse 6 times or until mixture resembles coarse meal. With processor on, slowly pour orange juice through food chute, processing just until blended (do not form a ball).

2. Press mixture gently into a 4-inch circle on plastic wrap; cover. Chill 15 minutes. Slightly overlap 2 lengths of plastic wrap on a slightly damp surface. Unwrap and place chilled dough on plastic wrap. Cover dough with 2 additional lengths of overlapping plastic wrap. Roll dough, still covered, into an 11-inch circle. Remove top sheets of plastic wrap; place dough, plastic wrap side up, on a baking sheet lined with parchment paper. Remove plastic wrap. Sprinkle dough with 1 teaspoon flour.

3. Preheat oven to 400°.

4. To prepare filling, combine red grapes and next 5 ingredients. Spoon grape mixture into center of dough, leaving a 2-inch border. Fold edges of dough toward center, pressing gently to seal (dough will only partially cover grape mixture). Combine water and egg yolk; brush over edges of dough. Sprinkle turbinado sugar over grape mixture and dough, if desired. Bake at 400° for 25 minutes or until crust is brown. Serve warm or at room temperature. Yield: 8 servings (serving size: 1 wedge).

CALORIES 231 (26% from fat); FAT 6.7g (sat 4.4g, mono 0.3g, poly 0.2g); PROTEIN 2.9g; CARB 40.8g; FIBER 1.5g; CHOL 42mg; IRON 1.3mg; SODIUM 180mg; CALC 31mg

dinner tonight

Chop, Chop

Easy salads for busy nights begin with bite-sized ingredients and tasty dressings.

Summer on a Plate Menu
serves 4

Tuscan Panzanella

Eggplant Napoleons*

Lemon sorbet

*Arrange 12 (¼-inch-thick) slices eggplant on a baking sheet coated with cooking spray. Coat eggplant slices with cooking spray; sprinkle with ¼ teaspoon salt. Broil 2 minutes on each side or until tender. Sprinkle 1½ tablespoons shredded part-skim mozzarella cheese on each of 4 eggplant slices; top each with a basil leaf. Repeat layers, ending with eggplant.

Game Plan

1. While oven heats for bread:
  - Prepare bread
  - Rinse and drain beans
2. While bread bakes:
  - Prepare basil, onion, olives, and tomatoes for salad
  - Slice eggplant, and arrange on baking sheet for Napoleons
3. While eggplant broils, prepare dressing for salad
4. Assemble Napoleons

Tuscan Panzanella

This classic bread salad, full of juicy tomatoes, is like summer on a plate. It's best when the toasted bread is still crisp, so serve immediately after tossing.

TOTAL TIME: 40 MINUTES

QUICK TIP: To core tomatoes easily, cut each one into quarters, then slice the core out of each quarter.

4 (1-ounce) slices Italian bread
Cooking spray
1 cup torn fresh basil leaves
½ cup thinly sliced red onion
⅓ cup pitted kalamata olives, halved
2 pounds ripe tomatoes, cored and cut into 1-inch pieces
1 (16-ounce) can cannellini beans or other white beans, rinsed and drained
3 tablespoons red wine vinegar
1 tablespoon water
1 tablespoon extra-virgin olive oil
1 teaspoon bottled minced garlic
½ teaspoon freshly ground black pepper
¼ teaspoon salt

1. Preheat oven to 350°.
2. Trim crusts from bread slices; discard crusts. Cut bread into 1-inch cubes. Arrange bread cubes in a single layer on a baking sheet; coat bread with cooking spray. Bake at 350° for 15 minutes or until toasted.
3. Combine basil and next 4 ingredients in a large bowl. Combine vinegar and remaining 5 ingredients in a small bowl; stir with a whisk. Pour over tomato mixture; toss to coat. Add bread cubes; toss well. Serve immediately. Yield: 4 servings (serving size: 2 cups).

CALORIES 255 (29% from fat); FAT 8.1g (sat 1g, mono 4.9g, poly 1.1g); PROTEIN 9.8g; CARB 39.9g; FIBER 8.2g; CHOL 0mg; IRON 3.4mg; SODIUM 708mg; CALC 83mg

---

Easy Salad Supper Menu
serves 4

Fennel-Grapefruit Salad with Chicken

Peppered fontina breadsticks*

Fresh melon

*Separate dough from 1 (11-ounce) can refrigerated breadstick dough to form 12 breadsticks. Sprinkle dough with ½ cup shredded fontina cheese, gently pressing cheese into dough. Sprinkle with ½ teaspoon freshly ground black pepper. Twist each breadstick, and place on a baking sheet coated with cooking spray. Bake at 375° for 13 minutes or until lightly browned. Refrigerate leftover breadsticks in heavy-duty aluminum foil. Unwrap and place on a baking sheet; reheat at 350° for 5 minutes or until warm.

Game Plan

1. While oven heats for breadsticks:
 • Shred cheese for breadsticks
 • Prepare dressing for salad
2. While breadsticks bake:
 • Prepare salad ingredients
 • Prepare melon

Fennel-Grapefruit Salad with Chicken

The dressing is flavored with miso, Japanese soybean paste. You'll find miso in the refrigerated section of large supermarkets or in Asian markets. Look for bottled grapefruit sections in the produce department.

TOTAL TIME: 40 MINUTES

QUICK TIP: To speed preparation, look for preshredded cooked chicken breast (such as Tyson) in your supermarket.

2 cups thinly sliced fennel bulb
2 cups chopped romaine lettuce
2 cups shredded roasted skinless, boneless chicken breast (about 2 breasts)
2 cups bottled red grapefruit sections
¼ cup thinly sliced red onion
2 tablespoons chopped pitted kalamata olives
1 tablespoon thinly sliced fresh mint

1 tablespoon orange juice
1 tablespoon Champagne vinegar or white wine vinegar
1 tablespoon miso (soybean paste)
2 teaspoons minced shallots
2 teaspoons extra-virgin olive oil
¼ teaspoon kosher salt
¼ teaspoon freshly ground black pepper

1. Combine first 6 ingredients in a large bowl. Combine mint and remaining 7 ingredients in a small bowl; stir well with a whisk. Pour over chicken mixture; toss well. Serve immediately. Yield: 4 servings (serving size: 1½ cups).

CALORIES 200 (29% from fat); FAT 6.5g (sat 1.3g, mono 3.9g, poly 1.1g); PROTEIN 20.8g; CARB 16.7g; FIBER 3.5g; CHOL 49mg; IRON 0.9mg; SODIUM 888mg; CALC 66mg

---

Busy Night Salad Menu
serves 4

Warm Sesame Shrimp and Eggplant Salad

Seasoned jasmine rice*

Mango slices topped with crystallized ginger

*Bring 2 cups water to a boil in a medium saucepan. Add 1 cup uncooked jasmine rice and ½ teaspoon salt; cover, reduce heat, and simmer 20 minutes or until liquid is absorbed. Combine 2 tablespoons chopped green onions, 2 tablespoons rice wine vinegar, and 1 teaspoon bottled ground fresh ginger in a small bowl. Pour vinegar mixture over rice, tossing to combine.

Game Plan

1. While water comes to a boil for rice and oven heats for bell peppers and eggplant:
 • Peel shrimp, and place in marinade
 • Quarter bell peppers, and slice eggplant
2. While rice cooks:
 • Broil bell peppers and eggplant
 • Cook shrimp and bok choy
 • Combine sauce ingredients for salad
 • Prepare mango

search myclar2003.com for all our menus

Continued

Warm Sesame Shrimp and Eggplant Salad

TOTAL TIME: 40 MINUTES

QUICK TIP: To save time, purchase peeled and deveined shrimp at your grocery store.

1 tablespoon peanut oil, divided
1 teaspoon crushed red pepper, divided
2 teaspoons bottled minced garlic, divided
¼ teaspoon salt
1 pound medium shrimp, peeled
2 red bell peppers, seeded and quartered
1 eggplant, cut into ¾-inch-thick slices (about ¾ pound)
Cooking spray
2 tablespoons rice vinegar
1 tablespoon oyster sauce
2 teaspoons chili garlic sauce (such as Lee Kum Kee)
1 teaspoon bottled ground fresh ginger (such as Spice World)
1 tablespoon sesame seeds
6 cups coarsely chopped bok choy
3 tablespoons water
2 tablespoons chopped green onions
2 tablespoons chopped fresh cilantro

1. Preheat broiler.
2. Combine 2 teaspoons oil, ½ teaspoon crushed pepper, 1 teaspoon garlic, salt, and shrimp in a bowl. Cover and marinate in refrigerator 10 minutes.
3. Flatten bell pepper pieces with hand. Place bell pepper and eggplant on a baking sheet. Lightly coat with cooking spray. Broil 10 minutes or until tender, turning pieces occasionally. Cut bell pepper and eggplant into 1-inch pieces.
4. Combine 1 teaspoon oil, ½ teaspoon crushed red pepper, 1 teaspoon garlic, rice vinegar, oyster sauce, chili garlic sauce, and ginger in a small bowl.
5. Sprinkle shrimp with sesame seeds. Heat a large nonstick skillet coated with cooking spray over medium-high heat. Add shrimp, and sauté 2 minutes or until shrimp are done. Place in a large bowl.
6. Add bok choy and water to pan; cover and cook 3 minutes or until bok choy wilts. Add bell pepper, eggplant, bok choy, onions, and cilantro to shrimp. Drizzle shrimp mixture with vinegar mixture; toss. Yield: 4 servings (serving size: 1½ cups).

CALORIES 233 (27% from fat); FAT 7.1g (sat 1.2g, mono 2.3g, poly 2.6g); PROTEIN 26.6g; CARB 16.4g; FIBER 5.1g; CHOL 172mg; IRON 4.5mg; SODIUM 693mg; CALC 207mg

Greek Salad Menu

serves 4

Chicken Souvlaki Salad

Greek pita wedges*

Vanilla low-fat ice cream topped with cinnamon and honey

*Cut each of 2 (6-inch) pitas into 6 wedges; arrange on a baking sheet. Coat pita wedges with olive oil-flavored cooking spray; sprinkle with ¼ teaspoon kosher salt and ¼ teaspoon dried oregano. Bake at 375° for 7 minutes or until golden.

Game Plan

1. While grill heats:
• Combine chicken and lemon mixture
• Prepare dressing for salad
• Preheat oven for pita wedges
2. While chicken cooks:
• Prepare onion, olives, cucumber, and tomatoes for salad
• Bake pita wedges

Chicken Souvlaki Salad

The elements of a classic Greek salad and a chicken souvlaki sandwich combine in this piquant dish. You can also use lamb in place of the chicken.

TOTAL TIME: 40 MINUTES

QUICK TIP: Place the chicken and seasonings in a zip-top plastic bag. A quick shake will coat the chicken, and there's no bowl to wash.

2 teaspoons bottled minced garlic, divided
1 teaspoon fresh lemon juice
1 teaspoon extra-virgin olive oil
½ teaspoon dried oregano
¼ teaspoon salt
¼ teaspoon black pepper
1 pound skinless, boneless chicken breast
3 cups cubed peeled cucumber (about 3 cucumbers)
½ cup vertically sliced red onion
½ cup (2 ounces) crumbled feta cheese
2 tablespoons chopped pitted kalamata olives
2 ripe tomatoes, cored and cut into 1-inch pieces (about 1 pound)
½ cup plain fat-free yogurt
¼ cup grated peeled cucumber
1 teaspoon white wine vinegar
½ teaspoon garlic powder
¼ teaspoon salt
¼ teaspoon ground red pepper
¼ teaspoon black pepper

1. Prepare grill or preheat broiler.
2. Combine 1 teaspoon garlic, lemon juice, and next 5 ingredients in a large zip-top plastic bag. Seal bag; shake to coat. Remove chicken from bag. Cook chicken 5 minutes on each side or until done. Cut into 1-inch pieces.
3. Combine chicken, cubed cucumber, and next 4 ingredients in a large bowl. Combine 1 teaspoon garlic, yogurt, and remaining 6 ingredients in a small bowl. Pour over chicken mixture; toss well. Yield: 4 servings (serving size: 2 cups).

CALORIES 259 (28% from fat); FAT 8.2g (sat 3g, mono 3.4g, poly 1g); PROTEIN 31.8g; CARB 15.3g; FIBER 2.9g; CHOL 79mg; IRON 2mg; SODIUM 679mg; CALC 161mg

Sushi Party

Surprise: Japan's hottest export is fast, easy, and widely sociable.

The thought of making sushi is intimidating at first, but you'll quickly find that it's easy. And it's far less expensive than eating at a sushi bar. Sushi refers to rice, after all, and a few rolls require just a small amount of filling.

Sushi Terms

Anago: conger eel broiled and brushed with a sweet sauce

Bonito: a type of tuna with a strong flavor; often dried and used as the base for soups

Ebi: shrimp

Futomaki: thick sushi rolls

Gari: pickled ginger root that is used to cleanse the palate between bites of different sushi

Gyoku: rolled egg omelette

Hasomaki: thin sushi rolls

Hirame: flounder

Ika: squid

Ikura: salmon roe

Kani: crab

Kappa: cucumber

Maguro: tuna

Maki: sushi that is rolled in nori

Masago: crab roe

Miso: fermented soybean paste that is a basic flavoring in many Japanese dishes

Nigiri: slices of raw or cooked seafood served on a layer of rice

Nori: toasted seaweed sheets used to hold sushi rolls together

Otoro: fatty tuna

Saba: mackerel

Sake: salmon

Sashimi: slices of raw seafood

Short-grain rice: sticks together, unlike long-grain rice that fluffs, so is ideal for sushi

Sushi: refers to seasoned rice, not raw fish

Tako: octopus

Temaki: sushi that is wrapped in nori in a cone shape

Unagi: eel

Uni: sea urchin roe

Wasabi: a potent Japanese horseradish that is served as a condiment for sushi and can be mixed into soy sauce to make a dipping sauce

search myclar2003.com for all our tips

Iceberg Salad with Ginger Dressing

Make the dressing up to two days ahead.

DRESSING:

¼ cup coarsely chopped onion
3 tablespoons rice vinegar
2 tablespoons water
1 tablespoon toasted peanut oil
1 tablespoon low-sodium soy sauce
1 tablespoon grated peeled fresh ginger
1 tablespoon finely chopped celery
2 teaspoons sugar
1 teaspoon fresh lemon juice
1 teaspoon miso (soybean paste)
¼ teaspoon salt
⅛ teaspoon black pepper

SALAD:

9 cups chopped iceberg lettuce
1½ cups cucumber, halved lengthwise and thinly sliced
¾ cup shredded carrot
¾ cup chopped celery
⅓ cup chopped onion
12 cherry tomatoes, halved

1. To prepare dressing, combine first 12 ingredients in a blender, and process until smooth.

2. To prepare salad, combine lettuce and remaining 5 ingredients in a medium bowl. Drizzle dressing over salad; toss gently to coat. Yield: 6 servings (serving size: 1½ cups).

CALORIES 66 (37% from fat); FAT 2.7g (sat 0.5g, mono 1.1g, poly 0.9g); PROTEIN 2.1g; CARB 9.8g; FIBER 2.9g; CHOL 0mg; IRON 0.9mg; SODIUM 259mg; CALC 37mg

Sushi Rice

The rice sticks together better when it's not chilled, so don't make it too far in advance of serving.

4 cups uncooked short-grain rice
4 cups water
½ cup seasoned rice vinegar

1. Bring rice and water to a boil in a medium saucepan. Cover, reduce heat, and simmer 15 minutes. Remove from heat; let stand, covered, 15 minutes.

2. Place rice in a large bowl; gently stir in rice vinegar with a spoon until combined. Cover rice mixture; let rest 30 minutes. Yield: 10 cups (serving size: ½ cup).

CALORIES 137 (1% from fat); FAT 0.2g (sat 0g, mono 0.1g, poly 0.1g); PROTEIN 2.4g; CARB 30.5g; FIBER 1g; CHOL 0mg; IRON 1.5mg; SODIUM 158mg; CALC 1mg

Miso Soup

Bonito stock gives the soup a rich flavor.

6 cups water
1 tablespoon bonito-flavored soup stock
¼ cup white miso (soybean paste)
½ cup cubed firm tofu (about 3 ounces)
⅓ cup sliced green onions

Continued

1. Combine water and soup stock in a large saucepan; bring to a boil. Add miso, and cook until miso is blended, stirring constantly. Ladle soup into bowls, and sprinkle evenly with tofu and green onions. Yield: 6 servings (serving size: about 1 cup).

CALORIES 61 (37% from fat); FAT 2.5g (sat 0.4g, mono 0.6g, poly 1.4g); PROTEIN 4.7g; CARB 5.1g; FIBER 1.3g; CHOL 0mg; IRON 2.5mg; SODIUM 712mg; CALC 151mg

Bagel Roll
(pictured on page 168)

This rice-on-the-outside roll has everything good from a salmon-topped bagel inside. Use the remaining nori to make the nori strips for Tuna Nigiri (recipe on page 151).

  3 tablespoons chopped green onions
  9 tablespoons (4½ ounces) block-style light cream cheese
1½ teaspoons prepared wasabi
  6 nori (seaweed) sheets
4½ cups cooked Sushi Rice (recipe on page 149)
  2 cups thinly sliced smoked salmon (about 12 ounces)

1. Combine first 3 ingredients. Cut off top quarter of nori sheets along short end; reserve for another use. Place 1 nori sheet, shiny side down, on a sushi mat covered with plastic wrap, with long end toward you. Pat ¾ cup rice over nori with moist hands, leaving a 1-inch border on one long end of nori.
2. Gently flip nori sheet. Spread 1½ tablespoons cream cheese mixture along top third of shiny side of nori; top with ⅓ cup salmon.
3. Lift edge of nori closest to you; fold over filling. Lift bottom edge of sushi mat; roll toward top edge, pressing firmly on sushi roll. Continue rolling to top edge; press mat to seal sushi roll. Repeat with remaining ingredients. Slice each roll into 8 pieces. Yield: 6 servings (serving size: 8 pieces).

CALORIES 341 (23% from fat); FAT 7.7g (sat 3.9g, mono 3.8g, poly 0.8g); PROTEIN 17.1g; CARB 48g; FIBER 2.8g; CHOL 29mg; IRON 3.1mg; SODIUM 769mg; CALC 43mg

How to Roll Sushi

1. *The rice is sticky, so moisten your hands in a bowl of equal parts water and rice vinegar before pressing rice onto nori.*

2. *If you prefer rice on outside (as shown here in making the Bagel Roll), gently flip nori sheet. Position sheet slightly past mat edge closest to you. Fold nori edge closest to you over filling.*

3. *Pick up bamboo mat edge closest to you, and roll rice-covered nori tightly over filling.*

4. *Gently squeeze sushi roll to form a tight, round roll.*

Shrimp Maki
(pictured on page 168)

  6 nori (seaweed) sheets
4½ cups cooked Sushi Rice (recipe on page 149)
1½ cups cooked medium shrimp, peeled, deveined, and halved (about ¾ pound)
12 strips julienne-cut carrot
12 (¼-inch-thick) slices peeled avocado (about 1½ medium)
  6 green onion tops (about 7-inch length)
  1 cucumber, peeled, halved lengthwise, seeded, and cut into 12 (7-inch) julienne-cut strips

1. Cut off top quarter of nori sheets along short end; reserve for another use. Place 1 nori sheet, shiny side down, on a sushi mat covered with plastic wrap, with long end toward you. Pat ¾ cup rice over nori with moist hands, leaving a 1-inch border on one long end of nori.
2. Arrange ¼ cup shrimp, 2 carrot strips, 2 slices avocado, 1 green onion top, and 2 cucumber strips along top third of rice-covered nori.
3. Lift edge of nori closest to you; fold over filling. Lift bottom edge of sushi mat; roll toward top edge, pressing firmly on sushi roll. Continue rolling to top edge; press mat to seal sushi roll. Let rest, seam side down, 5 minutes. Repeat

How to Form Nigiri

1. *Shape rice into a rectangle.*

2. *Place topping and rice across middle joints of fingers, palm turned up; close hand to gently press topping and rice together.*

3. *After pressing topping and rice together, you may need to use your other hand to finish shaping rice to fit snugly against topping.*

procedure with remaining ingredients. Slice each roll into 8 pieces with a sharp knife. Yield: 6 servings (serving size: 8 pieces).

CALORIES 367 (21% from fat); FAT 8.7g (sat 1.5g, mono 5g, poly 1.3g); PROTEIN 17.8g; CARB 53.6g; FIBER 6.1g; CHOL 111mg; IRON 5mg; SODIUM 377mg; CALC 54mg

3. Wrap 1 nori strip around center of nigiri, ending underneath rice. Repeat with remaining ingredients. Yield: 8 servings (serving size: 1 nigiri).

CALORIES 100 (4% from fat); FAT 0.4g (sat 0.1g, mono 0.1g, poly 0.1g); PROTEIN 7.8g; CARB 15.4g; FIBER 0.5g; CHOL 13mg; IRON 1mg; SODIUM 159mg; CALC 6mg

freeze according to manufacturer's instructions. Spoon ice cream into a freezer-safe container; cover and freeze 2 hours or until firm. Yield: 6 servings (serving size: ½ cup).

CALORIES 143 (12% from fat); FAT 1.9g (sat 1.1g, mono 0.6g, poly 0.1g); PROTEIN 3g; CARB 29.7g; FIBER 0g; CHOL 7mg; IRON 0.9mg; SODIUM 28mg; CALC 73mg

Tuna Nigiri

1 (8-ounce) ahi tuna fillet
¼ teaspoon salt
⅛ teaspoon freshly ground black pepper
2 cups cooked Sushi Rice (recipe on page 149)
1 teaspoon prepared wasabi
8 (1 x ½-inch) strips nori (seaweed)

1. Heat a medium nonstick skillet over medium-high heat. Sprinkle tuna with salt and pepper. Add tuna to pan; cook 1 minute on each side or until desired degree of doneness. Cut tuna into 8 strips; cool.
2. Shape ¼ cup rice into a rectangle about the size of 1 tuna strip. Place 1 tuna strip across middle joints of fingers, palm side up. Spread ⅛ teaspoon wasabi over tuna strip; top with shaped rice. Close hand, and gently press rice and tuna together.

Green Tea Ice Cream

The lemon and tea mixture needs to be chilled before adding the milk so the ice cream base doesn't separate.

1½ cups water
¾ cup sugar
2 tablespoons loose Chinese gunpowder green tea or green tea (about 3 tea bags)
4 teaspoons fresh lemon juice
1¼ cups whole milk

1. Combine water and sugar in a small saucepan; bring to a boil, stirring until sugar dissolves. Add tea; cover and steep 5 minutes. Strain tea mixture through a fine sieve into a bowl; discard tea leaves. Stir in lemon juice; chill completely.
2. Stir in milk. Pour mixture into freezer can of an ice-cream freezer, and

Sushi Kits

Get a kit that provides rice, nori, pickled ginger, sesame seeds, soy sauce, sushi rice vinegar, wasabi, a bamboo rolling mat, a bamboo rice spoon, chopsticks, and instructions. Then all you'll need in order to make sushi is the filling.
•**Sushi Starter Kit** from Sushi Foods; $19.99, 888-817-8744 or www.sushifoods.com
•**Sushi-Making Kit** from Sushi Chef; $37.95 or www.localflavor.com

How to Shape Temaki

1. *Spread rice on bottom half of nori, and place filling on rice diagonally, beginning in lower right corner of nori.*

2. *Lift bottom left corner of nori over filling, and gently roll in opposite direction to begin forming a cone shape.*

3. *Fold top half of nori over rolled filling, pressing gently to seal and finish cone.*

Vegetable Temaki

You can use any combination of vegetables to vary this sushi.

  2 cups cooked Sushi Rice (recipe on page 149)
  4 nori (seaweed) sheets, cut in half
  1 teaspoon prepared wasabi
24 snow pea pods, steamed
  1 red bell pepper, cut into 16 strips
  1 avocado, peeled and cut into 8 wedges

1. Spread ¼ cup rice on bottom half of 1 nori sheet. Spread ⅛ teaspoon wasabi diagonally over rice, starting at lower right corner.

2. Arrange 3 snow peas, 2 pepper strips, and 1 avocado wedge over wasabi. Lift left lower corner of nori over vegetable mixture, pressing gently. Wrap top half of nori over vegetable mixture, pressing gently to form a cone shape. Repeat with remaining ingredients. Yield: 8 servings (serving size: 1 temaki).

CALORIES 120 (30% from fat); FAT 4g (sat 0.6g, mono 2.4g, poly 0.5g); PROTEIN 2.6g; CARB 19g; FIBER 2.3g; CHOL 0mg; IRON 1.4mg; SODIUM 87mg; CALC 16mg

cooking light profile

Second Nature

Kathryn Kincannon finds a place where home and career meld gracefully.

Kathryn Kincannon, director of Lake Placid Lodge—a rustic luxury hotel in Adirondack Park—is grateful to have a job that is second nature to her. "Here at the lodge, we provide an escape for people that nourishes and revives," she says. This "reviving" is something she also cultivates in her own life. It's difficult to distinguish where her job ends and her personal life begins.

Kathryn eats little meat, and loosely calls herself a vegetarian. "I love anything soy," she says. Speaking of soy, here is one of Kathryn's personal favorite tofu dishes. It can also be found on the lodge menu.

Sesame-Crusted Tofu Sticks with Vegetable Sauté

Kathryn set out to lighten the lodge menu with recipes like this one. Double-breading the tofu sticks gives them a crisp exterior. Look for ABC sauce in Asian markets.

TOFU:
  ½ teaspoon salt
  ¼ teaspoon black pepper
  1 large egg
  1 large egg white
  1 cup dry breadcrumbs
  ¼ cup all-purpose flour
  2 tablespoons sesame seeds
  1 (15-ounce) package extra-firm tofu, drained and cut into 18 sticks
  2 tablespoons dark sesame oil, divided

VEGETABLES:
  1 (6-ounce) can pineapple juice
Cooking spray
  ½ cup chopped shallots
  1 garlic clove, minced
  ½ pound shiitake mushroom caps (about 10 mushrooms)
  2 cups (2-inch) sliced green onions
  1 cup cherry tomatoes, halved
  1 tablespoon chopped fresh thyme
  2 tablespoons balsamic vinegar
  1 tablespoon Japanese sweet and sour sauce (such as ABC sauce; optional)

1. To prepare tofu, combine first 4 ingredients in a shallow dish. Combine breadcrumbs, flour, and sesame seeds in a shallow dish.

2. Dip tofu, one piece at a time, in egg mixture; dredge in breadcrumb mixture. Return tofu to egg mixture; dredge in breadcrumb mixture.

3. Heat 1 tablespoon oil in a large non-stick skillet over medium-high heat. Add half of tofu; cook 4 minutes, turning to brown all sides. Remove from pan. Repeat procedure with 1 tablespoon oil and remaining tofu. Keep warm.

4. To prepare vegetables, pour pineapple juice into pan. Bring to a boil; cook until juice is reduced to ¼ cup (about 5 minutes). Remove from pan.

5. Heat pan coated with cooking spray over medium-high heat. Add shallots, garlic, and mushrooms; sauté 4 minutes, stirring occasionally. Add green onions, tomatoes, and thyme, and cook 1 minute. Stir in pineapple juice and balsamic vinegar, and cook 30 seconds.

6. Arrange about ½ cup vegetable mixture on each of 6 plates. Top each serving with 3 tofu sticks, and drizzle with ½ teaspoon sweet and sour sauce, if desired. Serve immediately. Yield: 6 servings.

CALORIES 253 (29% from fat); FAT 8.1g (sat 1.4g, mono 3g, poly 3.1g); PROTEIN 12.5g; CARB 32.9g; FIBER 3g; CHOL 36mg; IRON 3.5mg; SODIUM 846mg; CALC 119mg

lighten up

Zucchini Unloaded

Our cake makeover liberates a Seattle reader from the burden of her bounty.

Dorene Farnham planted too much zucchini. So to deplete the bounty, she decided to bake chocolate zucchini cake. But Dorene knew this mouth-watering cake didn't have a place in her healthy diet and asked us for help.

With our revisions, the cake has about one-third fewer calories and less than half the fat of the original. Still, the cake remains tender, moist, and very chocolaty.

BEFORE	AFTER
SERVING SIZE	
1 slice	
CALORIES PER SERVING	
422	281
FAT	
24.2g	9.5g
PERCENT OF TOTAL CALORIES	
51%	30%

Chocolate Zucchini Cake

When you're testing the cake for doneness, insert the wooden pick in several different places. You may hit a melted chocolate chip, which might make you think the cake isn't done.

CAKE:
Cooking spray
1 tablespoon all-purpose flour
¾ cup granulated sugar
½ cup packed brown sugar
½ cup (4 ounces) block-style fat-free cream cheese, softened
⅓ cup vegetable oil
2 large eggs
2 large egg whites
1 teaspoon vanilla extract
2½ cups all-purpose flour
½ cup unsweetened cocoa
2 teaspoons baking powder
½ teaspoon baking soda
½ teaspoon salt
½ teaspoon ground cinnamon
¾ cup fat-free buttermilk
2 cups shredded zucchini
⅔ cup semisweet chocolate chips
¼ cup chopped walnuts

GLAZE:
¾ cup powdered sugar
3 tablespoons unsweetened cocoa
8 teaspoons fat-free milk
2 tablespoons semisweet chocolate chips
1 teaspoon instant coffee granules
½ teaspoon vanilla extract

1. Preheat oven to 350°.

2. To prepare cake, coat a 12-cup Bundt pan with cooking spray; dust pan with 1 tablespoon flour.

3. Place granulated and brown sugars, cream cheese, and oil in a large bowl, and beat with a mixer at medium speed until well blended (about 5 minutes). Add eggs and egg whites, 1 at a time, beating well after each addition. Beat in 1 teaspoon vanilla extract.

4. Lightly spoon 2½ cups flour into dry measuring cups, and level with a knife. Combine 2½ cups flour, cocoa, and next 4 ingredients in a medium bowl, stirring well with a whisk.

5. Add flour mixture and buttermilk alternately to sugar mixture, beginning and ending with flour mixture. Stir in zucchini, ⅔ cup chocolate chips, and walnuts. Pour batter into prepared pan. Bake at 350° for 1 hour or until a wooden pick inserted in cake comes out clean. Cool in pan 10 minutes on a wire rack; remove from pan. Cool completely on wire rack.

6. To prepare glaze, combine ¾ cup powdered sugar and 3 tablespoons cocoa in a small bowl; stir with a whisk. Combine milk, 2 tablespoons chocolate chips, coffee, and ½ teaspoon vanilla extract in a 1-cup glass measure. Microwave at MEDIUM 45 seconds or until chocolate melts, stirring after 20 seconds. Combine powdered sugar mixture and chocolate mixture, stirring with a whisk. Drizzle glaze over cake. Yield: 16 servings (serving size: 1 slice).

CALORIES 281 (30% from fat); FAT 9.5g (sat 2.4g, mono 4.2g, poly 2.4g); PROTEIN 6.6g; CARB 45.6g; FIBER 2.6g; CHOL 27mg; IRON 2.2mg; SODIUM 241mg; CALC 96mg

. . . And Ready in Just About 20 Minutes

Sometimes, all it takes to give a simple dish ethnic flair is one or two ingredients.

Latin ingredients—bottled salsa, cilantro, and sofrito—season grilled fish and picadillo. And for a taste of Italy, pesto blends into a sandwich spread, and prosciutto adds punch to a pasta dish.

Turkey Pesto Sandwiches

Nothing beats homemade pesto when creating a homemade pasta sauce. But when you need only a small amount to accent a sandwich spread, such as the one we use with these turkey pesto sandwiches, bottled pesto works well and will save you lots of time. This sandwich is also great when served with a fresh fruit salad.

¼ cup fat-free mayonnaise
1 tablespoon commercial pesto
1 teaspoon fresh lemon juice
½ teaspoon dried oregano
⅛ teaspoon black pepper
4 (2-ounce) French bread rolls
2 cups trimmed arugula
8 ounces thinly sliced cooked turkey breast
8 (¼-inch-thick) slices tomato
4 (1-ounce) slices part-skim mozzarella cheese

1. Preheat broiler.
2. Combine first 5 ingredients.
3. Cut rolls in half horizontally; spread mayonnaise mixture evenly over cut sides of rolls. Divide arugula, turkey, and tomato slices evenly among bottom halves of rolls; top each with 1 cheese slice. Place bottom halves of rolls on a baking sheet. Broil 2 minutes or until cheese melts. Cover with top halves of rolls. Yield: 4 servings.

CALORIES 358 (26% from fat); FAT 10.5g (sat 4.8g, mono 4g, poly 0.8g); PROTEIN 31.2g; CARB 34.1g; FIBER 0.8g; CHOL 65mg; IRON 2.9mg; SODIUM 705mg; CALC 309mg

Walnut Pizza with Arugula and Yellow Tomatoes

You can also use red tomatoes and spinach for this salad-topped pizza.

2 (7-inch) individual refrigerated pizza shells (such as Mama Mary's)
2 tablespoons coarsely chopped walnuts
½ cup (2 ounces) reduced-fat feta cheese
1 tablespoon fat-free milk
1 teaspoon chopped fresh or ¼ teaspoon dried oregano
¼ teaspoon black pepper
1 cup trimmed arugula
1 cup shredded roasted chicken breast
1 cup chopped yellow tomato
¼ cup chopped red onion
1 teaspoon white balsamic vinegar
⅛ teaspoon black pepper

1. Bake pizza shells according to package directions, omitting fat.
2. While pizza shells bake, heat a small skillet over medium-high heat. Add walnuts; cook 3 minutes or until lightly browned, stirring constantly. Place walnuts, feta, milk, oregano, and ¼ teaspoon pepper in a food processor; pulse to combine.
3. Combine arugula and remaining 5 ingredients; toss well. Divide walnut mixture evenly between pizza shells; spread evenly. Divide arugula mixture evenly between shells. Yield: 2 servings (serving size: 1 pizza).

CALORIES 307 (32% from fat); FAT 10.4g (sat 2.8g, mono 1.8g, poly 4.8g); PROTEIN 11.9g; CARB 37g; FIBER 4.1g; CHOL 24mg; IRON 1.4mg; SODIUM 486mg; CALC 94mg

Fettuccine with Prosciutto and Asparagus

Serve with a tossed garden salad or sliced tomatoes sprinkled with basil and feta.

3 cups (1-inch) diagonally cut asparagus
1 (9-ounce) package fresh fettuccine
1 tablespoon olive oil
1 cup chopped onion
2 teaspoons bottled minced garlic
½ cup chopped prosciutto (about 2 ounces)
2 teaspoons balsamic vinegar
½ teaspoon salt
⅛ teaspoon crushed red pepper
⅛ teaspoon black pepper
¼ cup (1 ounce) preshredded fresh Parmesan cheese

1. Cook asparagus and pasta in boiling water 3 minutes or until pasta is done. Drain asparagus and pasta in a colander over a bowl, reserving ½ cup cooking liquid.
2. Wipe pan dry with a paper towel. Heat oil in pan over medium heat. Add onion and garlic; cook 2 minutes, stirring frequently. Add prosciutto; cook 2 minutes, stirring frequently. Stir in asparagus and pasta, reserved cooking liquid, vinegar, salt, red pepper, and black pepper; toss well. Sprinkle with Parmesan cheese. Yield: 4 servings (serving size: 1¼ cups).

CALORIES 335 (27% from fat); FAT 10g (sat 3.4g, mono 4.3g, poly 1.2g); PROTEIN 17.7g; CARB 44.6g; FIBER 5.4g; CHOL 64mg; IRON 3.4mg; SODIUM 722mg; CALC 211mg

Grilled Grouper with Plantains and Salsa Verde

Choose a yellow, underripe plantain. To peel a plantain, cut off the top and bottom, make a lengthwise cut through the skin, and peel. While the plantain cooks, squeeze the lime juice and mince the cilantro. If your grill pan is large enough, cook the plantain and fish at the same time. Serve with rice tossed with chopped green onions.

Olive oil-flavored cooking spray
1 underripe plantain
¼ teaspoon salt, divided
2 (6-ounce) grouper fillets (about
   ½ inch thick)
1 tablespoon fresh lime juice
1 tablespoon minced fresh cilantro
½ cup bottled green salsa
2 tablespoons reduced-fat sour
   cream
Chopped cilantro (optional)

1. Heat a large grill pan coated with cooking spray over medium-high heat.
2. Cut plantain in half lengthwise; cut each half crosswise into 2 pieces. Spray plantain pieces with cooking spray; grill 4 minutes on each side or until golden and slightly soft. Sprinkle with ⅛ teaspoon salt.
3. Drizzle fish with juice; sprinkle with ⅛ teaspoon salt and minced cilantro. Grill 4 minutes on each side or until fish flakes easily when tested with a fork. Top fish with salsa and sour cream, and serve with plantain pieces. Garnish with chopped cilantro, if desired. Yield: 2 servings (serving size: 1 fillet, ¼ cup salsa, 1 tablespoon sour cream, and 2 plantain pieces).

CALORIES 307 (12% from fat); FAT 4g (sat 1.4g, mono 0.4g, poly 0.6g); PROTEIN 35.7g; CARB 33.1g; FIBER 2.7g; CHOL 68mg; IRON 2.3mg; SODIUM 702mg; CALC 80mg

Pan-Seared Salmon with Mushrooms and Spinach

Serve this dish with French bread or rosemary focaccia.

Cooking spray
4 (6-ounce) salmon fillets (about
   1 inch thick)
½ teaspoon salt, divided
¼ teaspoon black pepper
1 teaspoon olive oil
1 tablespoon thinly sliced
   shallots
1½ cups presliced mushrooms
2 cups fresh spinach
1 teaspoon grated lemon rind
1 teaspoon fresh lemon juice

1. Heat a large nonstick skillet coated with cooking spray over medium-high heat. Sprinkle fish with ¼ teaspoon salt and pepper. Add fish to pan; cook 5 minutes on each side or until fish flakes easily when tested with a fork. Remove fish from pan, and keep warm.
2. Add oil and shallots to pan; sauté 1 minute. Add mushrooms in a single layer; cook 2 minutes (do not stir). Cook 2 minutes, stirring frequently. Add spinach, and cook 30 seconds or until spinach wilts. Remove from heat; stir in ¼ teaspoon salt, rind, and juice. Serve over fish. Yield: 4 servings (serving size: 1 fillet and ¼ cup spinach mixture).

CALORIES 298 (43% from fat); FAT 14.4g (sat 3.3g, mono 6.5g, poly 3.3g); PROTEIN 37.8g; CARB 2.8g; FIBER 0.7g; CHOL 87mg; IRON 1.7mg; SODIUM 394mg; CALC 52mg

Lemon-Shallot Scallops

Shallots are more subtle in flavor than onions, but you can substitute the white parts of green onions for shallots. Serve on a bed of mixed greens with a side dish of pasta.

2 teaspoons olive oil
1½ pounds sea scallops
½ teaspoon salt
¼ teaspoon black pepper
2 teaspoons butter
3 tablespoons minced shallots
½ teaspoon bottled minced
   garlic
¼ cup dry white wine
1 tablespoon fresh lemon juice
2 tablespoons finely chopped fresh
   parsley
Lemon wedges (optional)

1. Heat oil in a large nonstick skillet over medium-high heat. Sprinkle scallops with salt and pepper. Add scallops to pan, and sauté 2 minutes on each side. Remove cooked scallops from pan, and keep warm.
2. Melt butter in pan. Add shallots and garlic; sauté 30 seconds. Add wine and juice; cook 1 minute. Return scallops to pan; toss to coat. Remove from heat; sprinkle with parsley. Serve with lemon wedges, if desired. Yield: 4 servings (serving size: ½ cup).

CALORIES 204 (24% from fat); FAT 5.4g (sat 1.8g, mono 1.7g, poly 0.6g); PROTEIN 28.9g; CARB 6g; FIBER 0.2g; CHOL 61mg; IRON 0.8mg; SODIUM 581mg; CALC 49mg

Turkey Picadillo

Look for bottled sofrito in the Latin section of your supermarket.

1 (3½-ounce) bag boil-in-bag rice
¼ teaspoon salt, divided
1 pound ground turkey breast or
   lean ground beef
¼ cup golden raisins
¼ teaspoon dried oregano
⅛ teaspoon ground cumin
½ cup water
1 tablespoon cider vinegar
1 teaspoon capers, drained
1 teaspoon olive oil
1 (6-ounce) jar prepared sofrito
   (such as Goya)
1 tablespoon chopped fresh flat-leaf
   parsley
Parsley sprigs (optional)

1. Prepare rice according to package directions; stir in ⅛ teaspoon salt.
2. While rice cooks, cook ground turkey in a large nonstick skillet over medium-high heat until browned, stirring to crumble. Stir in ⅛ teaspoon salt, raisins, oregano, and cumin; cook 3 minutes, stirring frequently. Stir in water and next 4 ingredients; cook 5 minutes or until slightly thick. Remove from heat. Stir in chopped parsley. Serve over rice. Garnish with parsley sprigs, if desired. Yield: 4 servings (serving size: about ¾ cup picadillo and ½ cup rice).

CALORIES 403 (22% from fat); FAT 10g (sat 1.7g, mono 2.9g, poly 4.9g); PROTEIN 36.5g; CARB 39.8g; FIBER 2g; CHOL 70mg; IRON 2.3mg; SODIUM 712mg; CALC 39mg

Recipe for Stress Relief

Need a good meal after a tough day? A California reader shares her recipe.

Gail Greminger of Torrance, California, doesn't let cooking stress her out. Instead, she prepares Psycho Chicken, one of her favorite recipes.

"This dish was born of one of those 'What do I do with the chicken?' moments," Gail says. She mixed a little of this and that, slashed and seasoned, and popped the chicken in the oven. This technique stems from her Cuban roots. Her mother told Gail tales of her grandmother's garlic-laden cooking: meats pricked with the tip of a knife, then flavors infused into the openings.

Psycho Chicken

(pictured on page 165)

    1   (3½-pound) whole chicken
    1   tablespoon cider vinegar
 1½   teaspoons dried thyme
  ¼   teaspoon salt
  ¼   teaspoon black pepper
    3   garlic cloves, minced
  ½   cup dry white wine

1. Preheat oven to 325°.
2. Remove and discard giblets and neck. Rinse chicken; pat dry. Trim excess fat. Starting at neck cavity, loosen skin from breast and drumsticks by inserting fingers, gently pushing between skin and meat. With a knife, slash chicken every 2 inches, making ½-inch-deep slits.
3. Combine vinegar, thyme, salt, pepper, and garlic; rub under loosened skin and over breast and drumsticks. Lift wing tips up and over back; tuck under chicken. Place breast side up on a broiler pan. Pour wine over chicken.
4. Bake at 325° for 1 hour and 45 minutes or until thermometer registers 180°, basting occasionally with drippings. Let stand 10 minutes. Discard skin. Yield: 5 servings (serving size: about 3 ounces chicken).

CALORIES 139 (20% from fat); FAT 3.1g (sat 0.8g, mono 0.9g, poly 0.8g); PROTEIN 23.2g; CARB 1.3g; FIBER 0.3g; CHOL 74mg; IRON 1.6mg; SODIUM 204mg; CALC 21mg

Grilled Lamb Chops with Tomato-Onion Sauce

"This sauce is a nice combination of sweet and savory flavors. It is very versatile, complements any grilled meat, and even tastes good over plain white rice. Have the onions, garlic, and tomatoes chopped and close by because the cooking happens quickly, and you shouldn't take your eyes off the pan."

—Susan Stewart, Plainview, New York

    8   (3-ounce) lamb rib chops, trimmed
        Cooking spray
    1   teaspoon olive oil
    1   cup chopped onion
    2   garlic cloves, minced
  ¼   cup apple cider
    2   cups grape or cherry tomatoes
    1   teaspoon dried rosemary, crushed
  ¼   teaspoon salt
  ¼   teaspoon black pepper
        Dash of saffron threads (optional)

1. Prepare grill or preheat broiler.
2. Place lamb on grill rack or broiler pan coated with cooking spray; cook 5 minutes on each side or until a meat thermometer registers 145° (or until desired degree of doneness). Keep warm.
3. Heat oil in a small saucepan over medium-high heat. Add onion; sauté 5 minutes or until golden. Add garlic; sauté 1 minute, stirring constantly. Add apple cider; cook until liquid almost evaporates, scraping pan to loosen browned bits. Add tomatoes; reduce heat, and simmer 5 minutes. Add rosemary, salt, pepper, and saffron, if desired; cook 1 minute. Serve with lamb. Yield: 4 servings (serving size: 2 lamb chops and ½ cup sauce).

CALORIES 254 (44% from fat); FAT 12.6g (sat 4.2g, mono 5.3g, poly 1.3g); PROTEIN 24.9g; CARB 10g; FIBER 1.9g; CHOL 77mg; IRON 2.6mg; SODIUM 229mg; CALC 33mg

Fettuccine with Zucchini and Mint

"I noticed that Italians eat pasta with vegetables, so I decided to try zucchini. Sometimes I add fresh tomatoes and pine nuts."
—Leonora Morales, Santiago, Chile

    1   teaspoon butter
    8   cups (½-inch) cubes zucchini (about 2 pounds)
    4   garlic cloves, minced
  ¼   cup chopped fresh mint
  ½   teaspoon salt
  ¾   teaspoon freshly ground black pepper, divided
    2   (9-ounce) packages fresh fettuccine
 1½   tablespoons olive oil
  ¼   cup (1 ounce) grated fresh Parmesan cheese

1. Melt butter in a large nonstick skillet over medium-high heat. Add zucchini and garlic; sauté 4 minutes or until tender. Stir in chopped mint, salt, and ¼ teaspoon pepper.
2. Cook pasta according to package directions, omitting salt and fat. Combine zucchini mixture, pasta, and oil, tossing to coat. Sprinkle with cheese and ½ teaspoon pepper. Yield: 6 servings (serving size: about 1½ cups).

CALORIES 258 (20% from fat); FAT 5.7g (sat 1.3g, mono 2.9g, poly 0.9g); PROTEIN 9.2g; CARB 42.4g; FIBER 7.1g; CHOL 45mg; IRON 2.4mg; SODIUM 312mg; CALC 64mg

Gazpacho

"Gazpacho is a great dish for summer."
—Judy Jacks Berman, Overland Park, Kansas

    3   cups chopped tomato (about 1 pound)
 2¼   cups chopped peeled cucumber (about ½ pound)
    1   cup chopped red bell pepper
    1   cup chopped green bell pepper
  ½   cup chopped celery
  ½   cup chopped green onions
    2   teaspoons chili powder
    1   garlic clove, minced
    3   cups tomato juice
        Lime wedges (optional)

1. Combine first 8 ingredients in a large bowl; toss well. Place half of tomato mixture in a food processor; process until smooth. Pour pureed tomato mixture into a large bowl. Repeat procedure with remaining tomato mixture. Add juice to pureed tomato mixture; stir to combine. Cover and chill. Garnish with lime wedges, if desired. Yield: 5 servings (serving size: about 1½ cups).

NOTE: Gazpacho can be made up to 3 days ahead. Refrigerate in an airtight container. Stir well before serving.

CALORIES 75 (8% from fat); FAT 0.7g (sat 0.1g, mono 0.1g, poly 0.3g); PROTEIN 2.9g; CARB 17.5g; FIBER 3.8g; CHOL 0mg; IRON 1.7mg; SODIUM 559mg; CALC 40mg

Italian White Beans

"As a working mother and vegetarian, I'm always experimenting with quick, healthy meals. My husband is especially fond of this dish, which I based loosely on a fat-laden bacon and white bean dish in an old Italian cookbook. I serve it over soft polenta with Parmesan."
—Denise Agosto, Cherry Hill, New Jersey

1½ tablespoons olive oil
1 cup finely chopped onion
⅛ teaspoon crushed red pepper
4 garlic cloves, minced
1 bay leaf
1 tablespoon water
1 (16-ounce) can Great Northern or navy beans, rinsed and drained
2 teaspoons white wine vinegar
¼ teaspoon salt
⅛ teaspoon black pepper

1. Heat oil in a large nonstick skillet over medium-high heat. Add onion; sauté 3 minutes. Add red pepper, garlic, and bay leaf; sauté 3 minutes. Stir in water and beans. Cook 3 minutes or until thoroughly heated. Stir in vinegar, salt, and black pepper. Discard bay leaf. Yield: 4 servings (serving size: ½ cup).

CALORIES 178 (28% from fat); FAT 5.6g (sat 0.8g, mono 3.8g, poly 0.7g); PROTEIN 8.1g; CARB 25g; FIBER 5.9g; CHOL 0mg; IRON 2mg; SODIUM 593mg; CALC 61mg

Broccoli Salad

"This is my standard recipe that I bring to summer picnics. No matter how much I make, the bowl is always emptied."
—Gwenn Larson, Edina, Minnesota

4 cups small broccoli florets (about 1½ pounds)
1½ cups seedless green grapes, halved
1 cup chopped celery
1 cup raisins
¼ cup salted sunflower seed kernels
⅓ cup light mayonnaise
¼ cup plain fat-free yogurt
3 tablespoons sugar
1 tablespoon white vinegar

1. Combine first 5 ingredients in a large bowl.
2. Combine mayonnaise and remaining 3 ingredients, stirring with a whisk. Pour dressing over broccoli mixture, and toss well. Chill 1 hour. Yield: 8 servings (serving size: about 1 cup).

CALORIES 175 (29% from fat); FAT 5.7g (sat 0.8g, mono 1.4g, poly 3g); PROTEIN 3.4g; CARB 31g; FIBER 3.5g; CHOL 4mg; IRON 1.2mg; SODIUM 148mg; CALC 55mg

Chicken, Eggplant, and Tomato Curry

"I like to serve this with rice, and sprinkle some extra crushed red pepper over the top. It's a delicious, hearty, and satisfying meal. I enjoy how easy it is to prepare."
—Mary Bayramian, Laguna Beach, California

1 tablespoon curry powder
1 teaspoon salt
1 teaspoon paprika
8 (4-ounce) skinless, boneless chicken breast halves
3 teaspoons olive oil, divided
5 cups coarsely chopped eggplant (about 1 pound)
1⅔ cups thinly sliced onion
1½ cups (¼-inch-thick) slices green bell pepper
¾ cup tomato juice
1 teaspoon crushed red pepper
1 garlic clove, minced
4 cups hot cooked rice

1. Combine curry powder, salt, and paprika in a shallow dish. Dredge chicken in curry mixture.
2. Heat 1½ teaspoons oil in a large non-stick skillet over medium heat. Add half of chicken; cook 5 minutes on each side or until browned. Remove chicken from pan. Repeat procedure with 1½ teaspoons oil and remaining chicken.
3. Add eggplant, onion, and bell pepper to pan; cook 3 minutes or until vegetables are crisp-tender, stirring frequently. Return chicken to pan. Add tomato juice, red pepper, and garlic; bring to a boil. Cover, reduce heat, and simmer 35 minutes or until chicken is done. Serve with rice. Yield: 8 servings (serving size: 1 chicken breast half, about ⅓ cup vegetables, and ½ cup rice).

CALORIES 310 (11% from fat); FAT 3.8g (sat 0.7g, mono 1.8g, poly 0.7g); PROTEIN 30.3g; CARB 37.3g; FIBER 3.1g; CHOL 66mg; IRON 1.8mg; SODIUM 451mg; CALC 41mg

Green Bean Salad with Vidalia Onion and Mint

"I enjoy serving this as a side dish in the summer. I garnish it with extra mint before serving."
—Lisa Roche, Torrington, Connecticut

4 cups (1-inch) cut green beans (about 1 pound)
1 cup canned kidney beans, rinsed and drained
¾ cup chopped Vidalia or other sweet onion
2 tablespoons chopped fresh mint
4 teaspoons olive oil
1 tablespoon balsamic vinegar
2 teaspoons Dijon mustard
¼ teaspoon onion powder
¼ teaspoon black pepper
⅛ teaspoon salt
⅛ teaspoon garlic powder
1 tablespoon chopped fresh parsley

1. Steam green beans, covered, 5 minutes or until crisp-tender. Rinse green beans with cold water; drain. Combine green beans, kidney beans, onion, and mint in a medium bowl.

Continued

2. Combine oil and next 6 ingredients, stirring with a whisk. Pour vinaigrette over green bean mixture, and toss well. Chill 1 hour. Sprinkle with parsley. Yield: 6 servings (serving size: 1 cup).

CALORIES 113 (28% from fat); FAT 3.5g (sat 0.4g, mono 2.3g, poly 0.4g); PROTEIN 4.9g; CARB 17.2g; FIBER 6.9g; CHOL 0mg; IRON 1mg; SODIUM 97mg; CALC 38mg

inspired vegetarian

The Well-Rounded Plate

Solve the protein problem: Spread it around with these four exciting menus.

As vegetarians, we often seek alternative foods to stand in for that slab of protein in the center of the plate (aka meat)—foods that make us feel comfortable and confident that we are indeed getting a square meal. Few choices fit this description: tofu, tempeh, and *seitan* (wheat gluten). Beyond those, we tend to smother vegetables with cheese and opt for egg-based casseroles or pies. And, of course, there's the all-purpose bean. On special occasions, we may turn to time-consuming stuffed vegetables or filled doughs.

But the best way to ensure proper nourishment and get the greatest pleasure is to create a well-rounded plate. The four dinners we feature here go beyond eggs, beans, and cheese.

Whichever menu you choose, there will be plenty to please—and nourish—everyone at your table.

A Taste of Thailand

Coconut milk, tofu, and roasted peanuts deliver the protein. Briefly cooked crisp asparagus tossed in zesty vinaigrette makes a satisfying accompaniment.

Pad Thai with Tofu

Asparagus with Ginger Vinaigrette

search myclar2003.com for all our menus

Pad Thai with Tofu

This vegetarian version of Thailand's classic dish is spicy. If you prefer it mild, use only ½ teaspoon hot sauce.

SAUCE:

¼ cup low-sodium soy sauce
2 tablespoons rice vinegar
1 to 2 tablespoons hot sauce
1 tablespoon mirin (sweet rice wine)
1 tablespoon maple syrup

NOODLES:

1 teaspoon vegetable oil
2 cups thinly sliced shiitake mushroom caps (about 5 ounces)
1 cup grated carrot
1 garlic clove, minced
8 ounces extra-firm tofu, drained and cut into ½-inch cubes
1 cup light coconut milk
2 cups shredded romaine lettuce
1 cup fresh bean sprouts
1 cup (1-inch) sliced green onion tops
1 cup chopped fresh cilantro
⅓ cup dry-roasted peanuts
8 ounces uncooked wide rice stick noodles (Banh Pho), cooked and drained
5 lime wedges

1. To prepare sauce, combine first 5 ingredients, stirring with a whisk.
2. To prepare noodles, heat oil in a large nonstick skillet over medium-high heat. Add mushrooms, carrot, and garlic; sauté 2 minutes. Add sauce and tofu; cook 1 minute. Stir in coconut milk, and cook 2 minutes. Stir in lettuce and next 5 ingredients; cook 1 minute. Serve with lime wedges. Yield: 5 servings (serving size: 2 cups).

WINE NOTE: With sweetness from mirin and maple syrup and heat from hot sauce, this spicy Pad Thai would swamp the flavor of many wines, making them taste blank and a little bitter. There's one grape variety, however, that's more than capable of standing up to this dramatic dish: Viognier. A great example is the 2000 Cline Viognier from Sonoma County ($18). Wildly evocative of roses, gardenias, and honeysuckle, it's also packed with delicious fruit flavors, including peach, lemon, and just a hint of grapefruit.

CALORIES 385 (29% from fat); FAT 12.5g (sat 3g, mono 4g, poly 4.2g); PROTEIN 13.5g; CARB 55.8g; FIBER 4.6g; CHOL 0mg; IRON 7.1mg; SODIUM 868mg; CALC 365mg

Asparagus with Ginger Vinaigrette

When asparagus is out of season in the winter and fall, use fresh green beans or broccoli.

1½ tablespoons rice vinegar
2 teaspoons sesame seeds, toasted
2 teaspoons grated peeled fresh ginger
2 teaspoons vegetable oil
1 teaspoon minced shallots
½ teaspoon sea salt
½ teaspoon low-sodium soy sauce
½ teaspoon honey
¼ teaspoon dried rosemary, crushed
¼ teaspoon black pepper
5 cups (1-inch) diagonally cut asparagus (about 2 pounds), steamed and chilled

1. Combine first 10 ingredients, stirring with a whisk. Combine vinegar mixture and asparagus; toss well. Yield: 5 servings (serving size: 1 cup).

CALORIES 72 (28% from fat); FAT 2.2g (sat 0.4g, mono 0.4g, poly 1.2g); PROTEIN 4.2g; CARB 2.8g; FIBER 3.9g; CHOL 0mg; IRON 3.4mg; SODIUM 252mg; CALC 40mg

Casserole Dinner

Robust Grits Casserole with White Beans and Rosemary makes a beautiful centerpiece for a buffet or an easy carry-along to a potluck. Every element of the casserole can be made up to two days ahead and refrigerated (assemble and bake just before serving). Hearts of Romaine Salad with Creamy Soy Dressing complements the casserole's Mediterranean flavors, and provides refreshing crunch and added protein.

Grits Casserole with White Beans and Rosemary

Hearts of Romaine Salad with Creamy Soy Dressing

Grits Casserole with White Beans and Rosemary

Fresh breadcrumbs and Parmesan cheese create a savory crumb topping.

- 4 (1-ounce) slices French bread or other firm white bread, cubed
- ½ cup (2 ounces) grated fresh Parmesan cheese
- 2 tablespoons finely chopped fresh parsley
- 7 cups boiling water, divided
- 3 ounces sun-dried tomatoes (packed without oil), chopped
- 1 tablespoon olive oil
- 2 cups vertically sliced red onion
- 1 tablespoon chopped fresh rosemary
- ⅛ teaspoon crushed red pepper
- 2 garlic cloves, minced
- 1½ teaspoons sea salt, divided
- ¼ teaspoon black pepper
- 1 (19-ounce) can cannellini beans or other white beans, drained
- 1½ cups uncooked regular grits
- 2 tablespoons butter
- Cooking spray

1. Place bread in a food processor; pulse 10 times or until coarse crumbs form to measure 1 cup. Combine breadcrumbs, cheese, and parsley in a small bowl; set aside.

2. Combine 3 cups boiling water and sun-dried tomatoes in a bowl; let stand 10 minutes or until soft. Drain tomatoes over a bowl, reserving 1 cup liquid.

3. Heat oil in a nonstick skillet over medium-high heat. Add onion, rosemary, crushed red pepper, and garlic; sauté 3 minutes. Add tomatoes and reserved 1 cup liquid. Bring to a boil; cook 7 minutes or until most of liquid evaporates. Add ½ teaspoon salt, black pepper, and beans.

4. Preheat oven to 400°.

5. Combine 4 cups boiling water, 1 teaspoon salt, grits, and butter in a large saucepan. Cook 8 minutes over medium heat, stirring constantly. Pour grits mixture into an 11 x 7-inch baking dish coated with cooking spray. Spoon tomato mixture evenly over grits; top with breadcrumb mixture. Bake at 400° for 20 minutes or until golden. Yield: 8 servings.

CALORIES 303 (22% from fat); FAT 7.4g (sat 3.4g, mono 2.9g, poly 0.9g); PROTEIN 10.2g; CARB 47.2g; FIBER 5.2g; CHOL 13mg; IRON 2.5mg; SODIUM 781mg; CALC 146mg

Hearts of Romaine Salad with Creamy Soy Dressing

Silken tofu gives this dressing its creamy texture and is a great substitute for the raw eggs that are often used in Caesar salads. Leftover dressing will keep in the refrigerator for up to a week.

- 2 tablespoons fresh lemon juice
- 2 tablespoons water
- 1 teaspoon Dijon mustard
- ¼ teaspoon sea salt
- 2 ounces firm silken tofu
- 1 garlic clove, minced
- 2 teaspoons extra-virgin olive oil
- 1 tablespoon finely chopped fresh parsley
- 12 cups torn romaine lettuce (about 2 hearts)
- 3 tablespoons grated fresh Parmesan cheese

1. Combine first 6 ingredients in a food processor; process until smooth. With processor on, slowly pour oil through food chute; process until well blended. Pour tofu mixture into a small bowl; stir in parsley.

2. Combine romaine lettuce and tofu mixture in a large bowl, and toss to combine. Arrange 1½ cups salad on each of 8 plates, and top each serving with about 1 teaspoon Parmesan cheese. Yield: 8 servings.

CALORIES 40 (52% from fat); FAT 2.3g (sat 0.7g, mono 1.1g, poly 0.3g); PROTEIN 2.8g; CARB 2.7g; FIBER 1.5g; CHOL 2mg; IRON 1.1mg; SODIUM 139mg; CALC 67mg

Sautéed Escarole with Pine Nuts and Raisins

Your pan will be full with the fresh escarole, so toss it carefully with tongs. The volume reduces quickly when cooked.

- 1½ teaspoons olive oil
- ⅓ cup raisins
- 2 tablespoons pine nuts
- ¾ teaspoon crushed red pepper
- 4 garlic cloves, minced
- ½ cup vegetable broth
- 1 pound escarole, coarsely chopped (about 2 heads)
- ¼ teaspoon sea salt
- 6 lemon wedges

1. Heat oil in a Dutch oven over medium-high heat. Add raisins, nuts, pepper, and garlic; sauté 2 minutes or until nuts are golden brown, stirring constantly.

2. Add broth and escarole; cook 3 minutes or until wilted. Stir in salt. Serve with lemon wedges. Yield: 6 servings (serving size: about ¾ cup).

CALORIES 98 (29% from fat); FAT 3.2g (sat 0.5g, mono 1.4g, poly 0.9g); PROTEIN 3.9g; CARB 16.5g; FIBER 7.7g; CHOL 0mg; IRON 2.3mg; SODIUM 226mg; CALC 122mg

Roasted Root Vegetables

Balsamic vinegar adds a subtle sweetness.

3½ cups coarsely chopped carrot
(about 1½ pounds)
3 cups coarsely chopped parsnip
(about 1 pound)
1¾ cups coarsely chopped peeled
turnips (about ½ pound)
2 tablespoons olive oil
1 teaspoon brown sugar
½ teaspoon sea salt
2 red onions, each cut into 8 wedges
2 tablespoons chopped fresh parsley
1 tablespoon balsamic vinegar
¼ teaspoon freshly ground black
pepper

1. Preheat oven to 450°.
2. Combine first 7 ingredients in a shallow roasting pan; toss well. Bake at 450° for 1 hour, stirring after 30 minutes. Add parsley, vinegar, and pepper, tossing to coat. Yield: 6 servings (serving size: about 1 cup).

CALORIES 175 (26% from fat); FAT 5.1g (sat 0.7g, mono 3.4g, poly 0.6g); PROTEIN 2.9g; CARB 31.9g; FIBER 6.7g; CHOL 0mg; IRON 1.3mg; SODIUM 267mg; CALC 80mg

Braised Lentils

Cloves infuse the braising liquid—and thus the lentils—with savory, spicy notes.

3 whole cloves
1 small onion, peeled
2 cups water
1½ cups petite green lentils
¼ cup chopped green onions
2 tablespoons sherry
2 tablespoons extra-virgin olive oil
2 teaspoons minced peeled fresh
ginger
¼ teaspoon freshly ground black
pepper
3 garlic cloves, minced
1 bay leaf
1 (14½-ounce) can vegetable broth
¼ teaspoon sea salt

1. Insert cloves into onion. Combine onion, water, and next 9 ingredients in a large saucepan. Bring to a boil; cover, reduce heat, and simmer 30 minutes or until lentils are tender. Remove onion and bay leaf with a slotted spoon; discard. Stir in salt; cook 2 minutes. Yield: 6 servings (serving size: about ¾ cup).

CALORIES 215 (22% from fat); FAT 5.3g (sat 0.7g, mono 3.4g, poly 0.6g); PROTEIN 14.3g; CARB 29.5g; FIBER 5.3g; CHOL 0mg; IRON 4.5mg; SODIUM 394mg; CALC 32mg

Three-Grain Pilaf

Quinoa, a grain that looks like round sesame seeds, contains more protein than other grains.

2 tablespoons butter
½ cup finely chopped green onions
1 cup uncooked basmati rice
½ cup uncooked quinoa
½ cup uncooked millet
3 cups vegetable broth
¼ teaspoon sea salt

1. Melt butter in a large nonstick skillet over medium heat. Add onions; cook 2 minutes. Add rice, quinoa, and millet; cook 3 minutes, stirring frequently. Stir in broth and salt. Bring to a boil; cover, reduce heat, and simmer 25 minutes. Yield: 6 servings (serving size: 1 cup).

CALORIES 275 (20% from fat); FAT 6.1g (sat 2.5g, mono 1.2g, poly 0.3g); PROTEIN 7.8g; CARB 50.9g; FIBER 2.4g; CHOL 10mg; IRON 2.4mg; SODIUM 636mg; CALC 16mg

Tex-Mex Taco Supper

This unique combo brims with contrasting colors, flavors, and textures. Savory black beans with seitan provide a solid protein base to go with crisp taco shells, spicy Avocado Salsa, and marinated vegetables.

Black Bean Tacos with Avocado Salsa

Escabèche

Black Bean Tacos with Avocado Salsa

Seitan has a neutral flavor and a chewy, meatlike texture. Look for it in the refrigerated sections of health food stores or Asian markets. It may also be labeled wheat gluten.

2 teaspoons olive oil
¾ cup chopped onion
½ teaspoon dried oregano
2 garlic cloves, minced
1 jalapeño pepper, seeded and
minced
1 tablespoon dry sherry
1 tablespoon low-sodium soy sauce
1 (15-ounce) can black beans,
undrained
1 (8-ounce) package seitan (wheat
gluten), finely chopped
½ teaspoon black pepper
12 taco shells
2 cups shredded romaine lettuce
Avocado Salsa

1. Heat oil in a large nonstick skillet over medium heat. Add onion, oregano, garlic, and jalapeño; cook 8 minutes, stirring frequently. Stir in sherry, soy sauce, beans, and seitan; bring to a boil. Cook 7 minutes or until liquid almost evaporates. Sprinkle with black pepper.
2. Prepare taco shells according to package directions. Spoon about ⅓ cup bean mixture into each shell; top each taco with about 2½ tablespoons lettuce and about 2½ tablespoons Avocado Salsa. Yield: 6 servings (serving size: 2 tacos).

(Totals include Avocado Salsa) CALORIES 283 (30% from fat); FAT 9.3g (sat 1.2g, mono 5.7g, poly 1.6g); PROTEIN 20.4g; CARB 30g; FIBER 7.6g; CHOL 0mg; IRON 2.8mg; SODIUM 792mg; CALC 58mg

AVOCADO SALSA:

1 cup finely chopped tomato
½ cup chopped fresh cilantro
½ cup chopped peeled avocado
3 tablespoons fresh lime juice
2 tablespoons finely chopped red
onion
¼ teaspoon sea salt
1 garlic clove, minced
1 jalapeño pepper, seeded and
minced

1. Combine all ingredients in a bowl; lightly mash with a fork. Yield: 2 cups (serving size: about ¼ cup).

CALORIES 24 (56% from fat); FAT 1.5g (sat 0.2g, mono 0.9g, poly 0.2g); PROTEIN 0.5g; CARB 2.7g; FIBER 0.9g; CHOL 0mg; IRON 0.2mg; SODIUM 75mg; CALC 5mg

Escabèche

A Spanish dish, escabèche traditionally features cooked fish. The vegetables in this vegetarian adaptation marinate in a tart lemon mixture.

  ¼ cup fresh lemon juice
  1 tablespoon extra-virgin olive oil
  ½ teaspoon sugar
  ¼ teaspoon sea salt
  ¼ teaspoon black pepper
  2 garlic cloves, minced
  1 jalapeño pepper, seeded and
     minced
 12 cups water
  5 cups coarsely chopped green
     cabbage
  1 cup (3-inch) julienne-cut peeled
     jícama
  1 cup (3-inch) julienne-cut peeled
     carrot
  1 cup (3-inch) strips red bell pepper
  1 cup coarsely chopped fresh
     cilantro
  ⅓ cup thinly sliced radishes
  2 tablespoons thinly sliced green
     onions

1. Combine first 7 ingredients in a small bowl, stirring with a whisk.
2. Bring 12 cups water to a boil in a stockpot. Add cabbage; cook 5 minutes or until tender. Drain and plunge cabbage into ice water; drain. Place cabbage in a large bowl. Add jícama and remaining 5 ingredients. Drizzle with juice mixture; toss well to coat. Cover and chill 1 hour. Yield: 6 servings (serving size: about ⅔ cup).

CALORIES 71 (31% from fat); FAT 2.6g (sat 0.4g, mono 1.7g, poly 0.3g); PROTEIN 1.9g; CARB 11.8g; FIBER 4.3g; CHOL 0mg; IRON 0.9mg; SODIUM 276mg; CALC 52mg

Deconstructing the Cream Pie

Its silky style suits a summer table.

We gave six of our favorite pies a nutritional makeover; here's what we learned in the process:

The Crust

Most of the recipes featured here use pastry crust. (See our Piecrust recipe below.) Great pastry relies on fat to deliver tender texture and delicate flavor; specifically, vegetable shortening creates flakiness, and butter lends richness. We've added just enough of each to yield a peerless crust with minimal fat. While the actual difference in fat and calories between our pastry and the store-bought variety is small, the difference in flavor is great. (We think purchased crusts are a bit salty.)

The Filling

The filling, which requires the most attention, should hold its shape when sliced but shouldn't be too firm. Whether thickened with flour or cornstarch (we've used both), the best custards are made with 2% or whole milk. Using fat-free milk or juice alone will yield a thin custard. Just a dab of butter adds richness and flavor. Some egg yolks are necessary for consistency; using egg substitute or egg whites by themselves won't work.

The Topping

For food safety reasons we use Italian meringues rather than the traditional (uncooked) variation. Italian meringues are made by whipping egg whites with cooked sugar syrup. This procedure heats the whites to 238°, which renders them safe to eat. Meringues are delicate and will disintegrate or "weep" over time, so add them just before serving. If you choose to use whipped topping instead, add it before chilling.

Piecrust

This recipe makes a 9- or 10-inch crust.

 1½ cups all-purpose flour
  2 tablespoons sugar
  ¼ teaspoon salt
  3 tablespoons butter
  2 tablespoons vegetable shortening
  4 tablespoons ice water
Cooking spray

1. Preheat oven to 400°.
2. Lightly spoon flour into dry measuring cups; level with a knife. Combine flour, sugar, and salt; cut in butter and shortening with a pastry blender or 2 knives until mixture resembles coarse meal. Sprinkle surface with ice water, 1 tablespoon at a time; toss with a fork until moist and crumbly (do not form a ball).

3. Press mixture gently into a 4-inch circle on plastic wrap; cover. Chill 15 minutes. Slightly overlap 2 lengths of plastic wrap on a slightly damp surface. Unwrap and place chilled dough on plastic wrap. Cover dough with 2 additional lengths of overlapping plastic wrap. Roll dough, still covered, into a 13-inch circle. Place dough in freezer 5 minutes or until plastic wrap can be easily removed.
4. Remove top sheets of plastic wrap; fit dough, plastic wrap side up, into a deep-dish pie plate coated with cooking spray. Remove remaining plastic wrap. Fold edges under; flute. Pierce bottom and sides of dough with a fork; bake at 400° for 15 minutes. Cool on a wire rack. Yield: 1 piecrust (10 servings).

CALORIES 113 (48% from fat); FAT 6g (sat 2.7g, mono 2.1g, poly 0.8g); PROTEIN 1.8g; CARB 13g; FIBER 0.5g; CHOL 9mg; IRON 0.8mg; SODIUM 65mg; CALC 1mg

How to Make an Italian Meringue

1. *(A) Beat egg whites until soft peaks form.*

(B) Overbeating—incorporating too much air—will cause them to separate.

2. *Combine sugar and water in a saucepan. Bring to a boil. Using a candy thermometer, cook until 238° (or soft ball stage). Do not stir.*

3. *Slowly pour sugar syrup into egg whites, beating with a mixer at high speed until syrup is thoroughly incorporated. Meringue should look smooth and glossy.*

Coconut Cream Pie

This pie takes a brief turn under the broiler to brown the peaks of the Italian meringue.

CRUST:

1 (10-inch) Piecrust (recipe on page 161) or ½ (15-ounce) package refrigerated pie dough (such as Pillsbury)

FILLING:

¼ cup all-purpose flour
½ cup sugar
⅛ teaspoon salt
2 large eggs
¾ cup 2% reduced-fat milk
¾ cup light coconut milk
¼ teaspoon coconut extract
¼ teaspoon vanilla extract

MERINGUE:

3 large egg whites
⅔ cup sugar
¼ cup water
1 tablespoon flaked sweetened coconut, toasted

1. Prepare and bake Piecrust in a 10-inch deep-dish pie plate. Cool completely on a wire rack.

2. To prepare filling, lightly spoon flour into a dry measuring cup; level with a knife. Combine flour, ½ cup sugar, salt, and eggs in a large bowl; stir well with a whisk.

3. Heat milk and coconut milk over medium-high heat in a small, heavy saucepan to 180° or until tiny bubbles form around edge (do not boil). Gradually add hot milk mixture to sugar mixture, stirring constantly with a whisk. Place mixture in pan; cook over medium heat until thick and bubbly (about 10 minutes), stirring constantly.

4. Remove from heat. Spoon custard into a bowl; place bowl in a large ice-filled bowl 10 minutes or until custard comes to room temperature, stirring occasionally. Remove bowl from ice. Stir in extracts; spoon mixture into prepared crust. Cover and chill 8 hours or until firm.

5. Preheat broiler.

6. To prepare meringue, place egg whites in a large bowl; beat with a mixer at high speed until soft peaks form.

Combine ⅔ cup sugar and water in a saucepan; bring to a boil. Cook, without stirring, until candy thermometer registers 238°. Pour hot sugar syrup in a thin stream over egg whites, beating at high speed until stiff peaks form.

7. Spread meringue over chilled pie; sprinkle with coconut. Broil 1 minute or until meringue is lightly browned; cool 5 minutes on a wire rack. Serve immediately. Yield: 10 servings (serving size: 1 wedge).

CALORIES 281 (30% from fat); FAT 9.3g (sat 5.6g, mono 2.6g, poly 0.4g); PROTEIN 5.3g; CARB 45.6g; FIBER 0.6g; CHOL 63mg; IRON 1.4mg; SODIUM 208mg; CALC 28mg

Mango-Lime Icebox Pie
(pictured on page 166)

Look for mango nectar in the Latin foods section of your supermarket.

CRUST:

1 (9-inch) Piecrust (recipe on page 161) or ½ (15-ounce) package refrigerated pie dough (such as Pillsbury)

FILLING:

1 cup mango nectar
¾ cup sugar
½ cup fresh lime juice (about 4 limes)
¼ cup cornstarch
¼ cup fresh orange juice
2 large eggs
2½ tablespoons butter
2 teaspoons grated lime rind

MERINGUE:

3 large egg whites
⅛ teaspoon salt
½ cup sugar
¼ cup water
Grated lime rind (optional)

1. Prepare and bake Piecrust in a 9-inch pie plate. Cool piecrust completely on a wire rack.

2. To prepare filling, combine nectar and next 5 ingredients in a large saucepan, stirring with a whisk. Bring to a boil over medium heat, stirring constantly. Cook mixture 1 minute, stirring constantly.

3. Remove from heat; stir in butter and 2 teaspoons rind. Spoon mango mixture into a bowl; place bowl in a large ice-filled bowl 10 minutes or until mango mixture comes to room temperature, stirring occasionally. Remove bowl from ice; spoon mango mixture into prepared crust. Cover pie, and chill 8 hours or until firm.

4. To prepare meringue, place egg whites and salt in a large bowl; beat with a mixer at high speed until soft peaks form. Combine ½ cup sugar and water in a saucepan; bring to a boil. Cook, without stirring, until candy thermometer registers 238°. Pour hot sugar syrup in a thin stream over egg whites, beating at high speed until stiff peaks form. Spread meringue over filling; garnish with rind, if desired. Yield: 9 servings (serving size: 1 wedge).

CALORIES 267 (30% from fat); FAT 9g (sat 3g, mono 3.3g, poly 2g); PROTEIN 3.4g; CARB 44.4g; FIBER 0.5g; CHOL 56mg; IRON 0.3mg; SODIUM 190mg; CALC 14mg

Custard Basics

1. *Heat milk (or other liquid) to 180°; slowly add it to egg mixture. This tempers, or heats, egg mixture without overcooking it. Once you return custard to stove, stir it with a whisk for smoothness.*
2. *Cook custard until thick and bubbly even if you exceed time stated in recipe. Cornstarch must boil 1 minute. Undercooked custard is thin and tastes starchy.*

3. *Place bowl of hot custard in a bowl of ice to cool quickly. Filling sets better if cooled completely when spooned into crust.*

Buttered Rum-Raisin Cream Pie

We've used dark rum for rich flavor, but light rum will work fine. The pie filling should be cooled completely before the whipped topping is added.

CRUST:

1   (9-inch) Piecrust (recipe on page 161) or ½ (15-ounce) package refrigerated pie dough (such as Pillsbury)

FILLING:

2   cups golden raisins
¼   to ⅓ cup dark rum
½   cup sugar
3   tablespoons cornstarch
¼   teaspoon salt
2   large eggs
1½ cups 2% reduced-fat milk
3½ tablespoons butter
1   teaspoon vanilla extract
1½ cups frozen fat-free whipped topping, thawed

1. Prepare and bake Piecrust in a 9-inch pie plate. Cool completely on a wire rack.

2. Combine raisins and rum in a small microwave-safe bowl; microwave at HIGH 1 minute or until raisins are plump. Set aside.

3. Combine sugar, cornstarch, salt, and eggs in a large bowl; stir well with a whisk.

4. Heat milk over medium-high heat in a small, heavy saucepan to 180° or until tiny bubbles form around edge (do not boil). Gradually add hot milk to sugar mixture, stirring constantly with a whisk. Place mixture in pan; cook over medium heat until thick and bubbly (about 10 minutes), stirring constantly. Remove from heat; stir in butter.

5. Spoon custard into a bowl; place bowl in a large ice-filled bowl 10 minutes or until custard comes to room temperature, stirring occasionally. Remove bowl from ice. Stir in raisins and vanilla; spoon into prepared crust. Spread whipped topping evenly over filling. Loosely cover and chill 8 hours or until firm. Yield: 10 servings (serving size: 1 wedge).

CALORIES 309 (29% from fat); FAT 10g (sat 3.9g, mono 3.5g, poly 1.9g); PROTEIN 4.2g; CARB 50.4g; FIBER 2.4g; CHOL 56mg; IRON 0.8mg; SODIUM 223mg; CALC 67mg

Chocolate Silk Pie
(pictured on page 167)

CRUST:

1   (10-inch) Piecrust (recipe on page 161) or ½ (15-ounce) package refrigerated pie dough (such as Pillsbury)

FILLING:

⅓   cup all-purpose flour
½   cup sugar
½   cup unsweetened cocoa
¼   teaspoon salt
1¾ cups 2% reduced-fat milk
4   ounces semisweet chocolate, chopped

MERINGUE:

5   large egg whites
¼   teaspoon salt
1¼ cups sugar
⅔   cup water
Grated chocolate (optional)

Continued

1. Prepare and bake Piecrust in a 10-inch deep-dish pie plate. Cool completely on a wire rack.

2. To prepare filling, lightly spoon flour into a dry measuring cup; level with a knife. Combine flour, ½ cup sugar, cocoa, and ¼ teaspoon salt in a medium saucepan; stir with a whisk. Gradually stir in milk. Bring to a boil over medium heat, stirring constantly. Reduce heat; cook 2 minutes or until thick and bubbly, stirring constantly.

3. Remove from heat; add chopped chocolate, stirring until chocolate melts. Spoon chocolate mixture into a bowl; place bowl in a large ice-filled bowl 10 minutes or until chocolate mixture comes to room temperature, stirring occasionally. Remove bowl from ice.

4. To prepare meringue, place egg whites and ¼ teaspoon salt in a large bowl; beat with a mixer at high speed until soft peaks form. Combine 1¼ cups sugar and water in a saucepan; bring to a boil. Cook, without stirring, until candy thermometer registers 238°. Pour hot sugar syrup in a thin stream over egg whites, beating at high speed until stiff peaks form. Fold 2 cups meringue into chocolate mixture.

5. Spread chocolate mixture into prepared crust. Spread remaining meringue over chocolate mixture. Chill 8 hours; garnish with grated chocolate, if desired. Yield: 10 servings (serving size: 1 wedge).

CALORIES 314 (26% from fat); FAT 9.1g (sat 3.4g, mono 2.1g, poly 1.6g); PROTEIN 6g; CARB 55.8g; FIBER 2.2g; CHOL 4mg; IRON 1.4mg; SODIUM 257mg; CALC 58mg

Peanut Butter-Banana Cream Pie

(pictured on cover and page 166)

CRUST:

    1   cup vanilla wafer cookies (about 20 cookies)
    ⅓   cup packed brown sugar
    2½ tablespoons butter, melted
        Cooking spray

FILLING:

    ¾   cup packed brown sugar
    ½   cup (4 ounces) ⅓-less-fat cream cheese
    ½   cup reduced-fat peanut butter
    ½   teaspoon vanilla extract
    1   (8-ounce) container frozen fat-free whipped topping, thawed
    1½ cups sliced banana (about 2 bananas)
    ¼   cup fat-free chocolate sundae syrup

1. Preheat oven to 350°.

2. To prepare crust, place cookies in a food processor; process until finely ground. Add ⅓ cup brown sugar and butter; pulse 2 or 3 times or just until combined. Press into bottom and up sides of a 9-inch pie plate coated with cooking spray. Bake at 350° for 10 minutes; cool completely on a wire rack.

3. To prepare filling, place ¾ cup brown sugar, cream cheese, peanut butter, and vanilla in a bowl; beat with a mixer at medium speed until smooth. Fold in whipped topping. Arrange banana in bottom of prepared crust. Spread peanut butter mixture over banana; drizzle with syrup. Cover and freeze 8 hours; let stand at room temperature 15 minutes before serving. Yield: 10 servings (serving size: 1 wedge).

CALORIES 300 (29% from fat); FAT 9.6g (sat 3.5g, mono 3.5g, poly 1.4g); PROTEIN 5.4g; CARB 49g; FIBER 1.5g; CHOL 12mg; IRON 1mg; SODIUM 199mg; CALC 41mg

Praline Cream Pie

Make sure the custard cools completely before spooning it over the praline layer.

CRUST:

    1   cup vanilla wafer cookies (about 20 cookies)
    2   tablespoons brown sugar
    1   tablespoon butter, melted
        Cooking spray

PRALINE:

    ¼   cup packed brown sugar
    ¼   cup half-and-half
    2   tablespoons butter
    ½   cup sifted powdered sugar

FILLING:

    ½   cup granulated sugar
    ¼   cup cornstarch
    ¼   teaspoon salt
    1   large egg
    1¾ cups whole milk
    ½   teaspoon vanilla extract

1. Preheat oven to 350°.

2. To prepare crust, place cookies in a food processor; process until finely ground. Add 2 tablespoons brown sugar and 1 tablespoon butter; pulse 2 or 3 times or just until combined. Press crumb mixture into bottom and up sides of a 9-inch pie plate coated with cooking spray. Bake at 350° for 10 minutes; cool completely on a wire rack.

3. To prepare praline, combine ¼ cup brown sugar, half-and-half, and 2 tablespoons butter in a small saucepan. Bring to a boil over medium-high heat, stirring occasionally. Cook 3 minutes without stirring. Remove from heat; add powdered sugar, stirring with a whisk. Spoon praline mixture into prepared crust; chill 30 minutes or until completely cool.

4. To prepare filling, combine granulated sugar, cornstarch, salt, and egg in a medium bowl; stir well with a whisk. Heat milk over medium-high heat in a small, heavy saucepan to 180° or until tiny bubbles form around edge (do not boil). Gradually add hot milk to egg mixture, stirring constantly with a whisk. Place mixture in pan, and bring mixture to a boil, stirring constantly. Cook 1 minute, stirring constantly.

5. Remove from heat. Spoon custard into a bowl; place bowl in a large ice-filled bowl 15 minutes or until custard comes to room temperature, stirring occasionally. Remove bowl from ice. Stir in vanilla; spoon mixture evenly over chilled praline layer. Cover and chill 8 hours or until firm. Yield: 8 servings (serving size: 1 wedge).

CALORIES 261 (31% from fat); FAT 9g (sat 4.8g, mono 2.8g, poly 0.3g); PROTEIN 3.2g; CARB 42.7g; FIBER 0.2g; CHOL 50mg; IRON 0.7mg; SODIUM 191mg; CALC 91mg

Psycho Chicken,
page 156

Lemon-Macerated Okra and Olives,
page 171

Peanut Butter-Banana Cream Pie,
page 164

Mango-Lime Icebox Pie,
page 162

Chocolate Silk Pie, page 163

Shrimp Maki and Bagel
Rolls, page 150

Prosciutto-Wrapped
Shrimp with Lemon
Couscous, page 172

Common Ground

Support local farmers and join a community-supported agricultural farm.

Thousands of people have joined community-supported agricultural farms (CSAs) since they began in Japan in the mid-1960s. A group of Japanese homemakers saw agricultural acreage dwindle as farms turned into housing developments, driving farmers out of business and food prices up. Their concerns led them to approach a farm family and offer a contract that would let them share the farmer's risk.

In the United States the late Robyn Van En is credited with launching the CSA movement in 1985 at her Indian Line Farm in western Massachusetts. Before long, Indian Line's CSA fed 300 people for 43 weeks of the year—from just five acres of land. Today, there are more than 1,000 CSAs all over the country.

The CSA principle is simple: Subscribers pay for a seasonal share, usually enough for two to four adults, at the beginning of the season, when the farmer must pay for seed, fertilizer, and other supplies. Then, over the course of the subscription, members share in the rewards—as well as the risks. Relieved of economic uncertainty, the farmer can concentrate on good stewardship for the land in his care.

Fresh Herbed Heirloom Tomatoes and Goat Cheese Crostini

Basil and parsley are pureed with lemon juice and oil in a flavorful drizzle for fresh tomatoes.

- ¼ cup chopped fresh basil
- ¼ cup chopped fresh parsley
- 2 tablespoons water
- 2 tablespoons fresh lemon juice
- 1 teaspoon extra-virgin olive oil
- 8 (¼-inch-thick) slices diagonally cut French bread baguette
- 4 teaspoons goat cheese
- 20 (¼-inch-thick) slices tomato
- ½ teaspoon kosher salt
- ½ teaspoon freshly ground black pepper

1. Preheat oven to 350°.
2. Place first 5 ingredients in a blender; process until smooth.
3. Place baguette slices in a single layer on a baking sheet. Bake at 350° for 7 minutes or until crisp. Spread ½ teaspoon cheese over each slice.
4. Divide tomatoes evenly among 4 salad plates. Drizzle each serving with 1 tablespoon herbed oil. Sprinkle each with ⅛ teaspoon salt and ⅛ teaspoon pepper. Garnish each with 2 crostini. Yield: 4 servings.

CALORIES 110 (34% from fat); FAT 4.1g (sat 1.2g, mono 1.6g, poly 1g); PROTEIN 3.3g; CARB 16.5g; FIBER 2.3g; CHOL 2mg; IRON 1.2mg; SODIUM 350mg; CALC 25mg

Fresh Peach Croustades

Summer peaches and mint adorn crisp, buttery puff pastry in this simple dessert. Look for puff pastry in the freezer section.

- ¼ cup sugar
- ¼ cup water
- ¼ cup small mint leaves
- 2 cups sliced peeled peaches
- 1 sheet puff pastry

1. Preheat oven to 400°.
2. Combine sugar and water in a small saucepan. Bring to a boil; cook 1 minute or until sugar dissolves. Cool completely. Place sugar mixture and mint in a blender; process until smooth. Combine mint mixture and sliced peaches in a medium bowl.
3. Cut 4 (2-inch) circles in puff pastry using a sharp round cookie cutter. Roll each circle of dough into a 4-inch circle on a floured surface. Place on a baking sheet. Bake at 400° for 12 minutes or until golden brown. Top with peach mixture. Yield: 4 servings (serving size: 1 croustade and ½ cup peach mixture).

WINE NOTE: The 1999 Inniskillin Riesling Icewine from the Niagara Peninsula of Canada is the liquid essence of peaches, and it makes an otherworldly match for this dessert. Great dessert wines are expensive—a half bottle of this Riesling is $65—but they're so rich you don't need much; a half bottle will serve eight.

CALORIES 166 (30% from fat); FAT 5.5g (sat 1.4g, mono 3.1g, poly 0.8g); PROTEIN 1.8g; CARB 28.8g; FIBER 2.3g; CHOL 0mg; IRON 1.1mg; SODIUM 37mg; CALC 17mg

Cold Cucumber Soup with Cherry Tomato Confetti

Sweet cherry tomatoes float atop tangy, creamy cucumber soup for a refreshing lunch or light supper that's easy to prepare.

- ½ cup chopped fresh cilantro
- ¼ cup chopped onion
- ¼ cup fresh lime juice
- ¼ cup fat-free buttermilk
- ¼ cup reduced-fat sour cream
- ½ teaspoon salt
- ½ teaspoon freshly ground black pepper
- 5 cucumbers (about 2½ pounds), peeled, halved lengthwise, seeded, and coarsely chopped
- 1 jalapeño pepper, halved and seeded
- 1 cup cherry tomatoes, halved

1. Place first 9 ingredients in a food processor; process until smooth. Top with tomatoes. Yield: 4 servings (serving size: 1 cup soup and ¼ cup tomatoes).

CALORIES 74 (29% from fat); FAT 2.4g (sat 1.3g, mono 0g, poly 0.2g); PROTEIN 3.2g; CARB 11.9g; FIBER 2.5g; CHOL 8mg; IRON 0.7mg; SODIUM 329mg; CALC 85mg

Steamed Japanese Eggplant with Spicy Green Onion-Ginger Sauce

Small Japanese eggplants are cut into "sticks" and barely steamed for a crisp-tender side dish that's good with fish. This is best served immediately.

12 ounces Japanese eggplant, cut into 3 x ½-inch sticks (about 5 cups)
⅓ cup minced green onions
2 tablespoons low-sodium soy sauce
2 tablespoons rice vinegar
1 teaspoon grated peeled fresh ginger
1 teaspoon extra-virgin olive oil
1 teaspoon chile paste with garlic
¼ cup cilantro leaves (optional)

1. Steam eggplant, covered, 2 minutes or until crisp-tender.
2. Combine onions and next 5 ingredients in a small bowl; stir well. Divide eggplant evenly among 4 plates; drizzle with sauce. Garnish with cilantro leaves, if desired. Yield: 4 servings (serving size: 1 cup eggplant sticks and 1 tablespoon sauce).

CALORIES 45 (26% from fat); FAT 1.3g (sat 0.2g, mono 0.9g, poly 0.2g); PROTEIN 1.5g; CARB 8g; FIBER 3.1g; CHOL 0mg; IRON 0.5mg; SODIUM 291mg; CALC 11mg

Fingerling Potato and Prosciutto Salad

This salad, which also works with red potatoes, is best served immediately.

1 pound fingerling potatoes, halved lengthwise
1 tablespoon white wine vinegar
¼ cup finely chopped shallots
¼ cup chopped fresh flat-leaf parsley
3 tablespoons crème fraîche
1 teaspoon chopped fresh sage
½ teaspoon kosher salt
½ teaspoon freshly ground black pepper
3 ounces very thin slices prosciutto, finely chopped

1. Place potatoes in a medium saucepan; cover with water. Bring to a boil; reduce heat, and simmer 15 minutes or until tender. Drain. Stir in vinegar. Cover and chill.
2. Combine potato mixture and remaining ingredients in a large bowl; toss gently to coat. Yield: 4 servings (serving size: 1 cup).

CALORIES 109 (26% from fat); FAT 5.9g (sat 3.1g, mono 2.1g, poly 0.5g); PROTEIN 8.1g; CARB 31.9g; FIBER 3g; CHOL 21mg; IRON 2.3mg; SODIUM 574mg; CALC 45mg

Roasted Pepper and Rosemary Relish

Serve this versatile relish on crostini or tossed in salad or pasta.

3 orange, red, or yellow bell peppers
2 teaspoons red wine vinegar
1 teaspoon chopped fresh rosemary
1 teaspoon extra-virgin olive oil
½ teaspoon freshly ground black pepper
¼ teaspoon salt

1. Preheat broiler.
2. Cut bell peppers in half lengthwise; discard seeds and membranes. Place pepper halves, skin sides up, on a foil-lined baking sheet; flatten with hand. Broil 15 minutes or until blackened. Place in a zip-top plastic bag; seal. Let stand 20 minutes. Peel and cut into 1-inch pieces.

3. Combine bell pepper and remaining ingredients in a small bowl; toss well. Cover and chill 30 minutes. Yield: 4 servings (serving size: ½ cup).

CALORIES 42 (30% from fat); FAT 1.4g (sat 0.2g, mono 0.9g, poly 0.2g); PROTEIN 1.1g; CARB 7.6g; FIBER 1.3g; CHOL 0mg; IRON 0.6mg; SODIUM 149mg; CALC 14mg

Spring Vegetable Couscous

You can also make this great side with carrots, spinach, zucchini, or any other fresh vegetables.

4 small beets (about 6 ounces)
½ cup fresh green peas
½ cup (1-inch) diagonally cut asparagus
½ cup chopped yellow squash
3 cups cooked couscous
½ cup quartered radishes
½ cup (2 ounces) crumbled feta cheese
2 tablespoons extra-virgin olive oil
1 tablespoon fresh lemon juice
1 tablespoon finely chopped fresh parsley
1 tablespoon chopped fresh mint
½ teaspoon kosher salt
½ teaspoon freshly ground black pepper

1. Leave roots and 1-inch stems on beets; scrub with a brush. Place in a medium saucepan; cover with water. Bring to a boil; cover, reduce heat, and simmer 15 minutes or until tender. Drain and rinse with cold water. Drain; cool. Trim off beet roots; rub off skins. Cut into quarters.
2. Steam peas, asparagus, and squash, covered, 3 minutes or until crisp-tender. Combine beets, peas, asparagus, squash, and remaining ingredients in a large bowl. Yield: 6 servings (serving size: 1 cup).

CALORIES 172 (30% from fat); FAT 5.7g (sat 1.9g, mono 3g, poly 0.5g); PROTEIN 5.9g; CARB 24.7g; FIBER 3.2g; CHOL 8mg; IRON 1mg; SODIUM 292mg; CALC 69mg

Lemon-Macerated Okra and Olives

(pictured on page 165)

Offer these zesty tidbits in place of peanuts or pretzels at your next party. Or combine with bread, cheese, artichokes, and cold shrimp for an antipasto platter.

- 3 cups small okra pods
- ½ cup kalamata olives
- 1 tablespoon grated lemon rind
- ¼ cup fresh lemon juice
- 2 tablespoons extra-virgin olive oil
- ½ teaspoon kosher salt
- ½ teaspoon crushed red pepper
- 2 garlic cloves, thinly sliced
- 2 bay leaves
- 2 thyme sprigs

1. Combine all ingredients in a large zip-top plastic bag, and seal. Marinate in refrigerator 48 to 72 hours, turning bag occasionally. Strain okra mixture through a sieve over a bowl, discarding marinade, bay leaves, and thyme sprigs. Yield: 14 servings (serving size: ¼ cup).

CALORIES 29 (65% from fat); FAT 2.1g (sat 0.3g, mono 1.6g, poly 0.2g); PROTEIN 0.5g; CARB 2.4g; FIBER 0.8g; CHOL 0mg; IRON 0.2mg; SODIUM 105mg; CALC 20mg

Grilled Corn and Vidalia Onion Salsa

Try serving this salsa with fish.

- 4 ears corn
- 1 Vidalia onion or other sweet onion, cut into ½-inch-thick slices
- Cooking spray
- ¼ cup finely chopped fresh cilantro
- 1¼ cups chopped seeded yellow tomato
- 3 tablespoons rice vinegar
- ½ teaspoon kosher salt
- ½ teaspoon crushed red pepper
- ½ teaspoon freshly ground black pepper

1. Prepare grill or preheat broiler.
2. Place corn on grill rack or broiler pan; cook 20 minutes or until corn is lightly browned, turning every 5 minutes. Cool. Cut kernels from ears of corn to measure 3 cups. Place onion on grill rack or broiler pan coated with cooking spray; cook 5 minutes on each side. Cool onion, and chop.
3. Combine corn, onion, and remaining ingredients in a large bowl; toss well. Yield: 4 servings (serving size: 1 cup).

CALORIES 102 (12% from fat); FAT 1.4g (sat 0.2g, mono 0.4g, poly 0.6g); PROTEIN 3.8g; CARB 22.5g; FIBER 3.8g; CHOL 0mg; IRON 0.9mg; SODIUM 255mg; CALC 13mg

happy endings

Sweet on Dad

Pastry Chef Gale Gand does her dad proud with lightened treats aimed straight for his heart.

Gale Gand was named the James Beard Foundation's outstanding pastry chef last year for the luscious desserts she produces at Tru, her Chicago restaurant. She's also coauthor of three cookbooks and host of the Food Network's daily television show *Sweet Dreams*. In a month when doting daughters honor dads everywhere, we thought it fitting to feature the low-fat, healthful desserts that she makes for her father.

Blueberry Angel Food Cake

Everyone likes angel food cake, almost no one is allergic to it, and it provides a light, sweet ending to what is too often a sloth-inducing meal. Fresh blueberries color the cake purple, and a citrusy glaze gives it a festive feeling.

CAKE:

- 1½ cups granulated sugar, divided
- 1 cup sifted cake flour
- 12 large egg whites (about 1½ cups)
- 1¼ teaspoons cream of tartar
- ½ teaspoon salt
- 1 teaspoon vanilla extract
- 1½ cups fresh or frozen blueberries
- 2 tablespoons sifted cake flour
- 1 tablespoon grated lemon rind

GLAZE:

- 1 cup powdered sugar
- 3 tablespoons fresh lemon juice

1. Preheat oven to 375°.
2. Sift together ½ cup granulated sugar and 1 cup flour.
3. In a large bowl, beat egg whites with a mixer at high speed until foamy. Add cream of tartar and salt; beat until soft peaks form. Add 1 cup granulated sugar, 2 tablespoons at a time, beating until stiff peaks form.
4. Sift flour mixture over egg white mixture, ¼ cup at a time; fold in. Fold in vanilla and blueberries.
5. Combine 2 tablespoons flour and lemon rind; toss to coat. Sprinkle over egg white mixture; fold in.
6. Spoon batter into an ungreased 10-inch tube pan, spreading evenly. Break air pockets by cutting through batter with a knife. Bake at 375° for 40 minutes or until cake springs back when lightly touched. Invert pan; cool completely. Loosen cake from sides of pan using a narrow metal spatula. Invert cake onto a serving plate.
7. To prepare glaze, combine powdered sugar and lemon juice in a small bowl; stir well with a whisk. Drizzle over cooled cake. Yield: 8 servings (serving size: 1 slice).

CALORIES 297 (1% from fat); FAT 0.2g (sat 0g, mono 0.1g, poly 0.1g); PROTEIN 6.6g; CARB 68.2g; FIBER 1g; CHOL 0mg; IRON 1.1mg; SODIUM 232mg; CALC 8mg

Bananas and Ginger en Papillotte

En papillotte (the technique of wrapping food in paper and baking it in the oven to steam) is usually used for fish, but Gale brings it into the dessert arena.

- 3 tablespoons lemon juice
- 2 tablespoons brown sugar
- 2 tablespoons honey
- 2 teaspoons chopped pistachios
- 2 teaspoons butter, melted
- 1 teaspoon grated orange rind
- ½ teaspoon minced peeled fresh ginger
- 4 large firm bananas

Continued

1. Preheat oven to 350°.
2. Combine first 7 ingredients in a bowl.
3. Slice each banana in half lengthwise; slice in half crosswise.
4. Cut 4 (10-inch) circles of parchment paper. Fold each circle in half; open each. Place 4 pieces of banana near fold of 1 circle; top with 1 tablespoon juice mixture. Fold paper over filling; seal edges with narrow folds. Repeat procedure with remaining parchment, banana, and juice mixture. Place packets on baking sheets.
5. Bake at 350° for 5 minutes or until packets are slightly puffy and contents are thoroughly heated. Place on plates; cut open. Serve immediately. Yield: 4 servings (serving size: 1 packet).

CALORIES 226 (27% from fat); FAT 6.9g (sat 3.9g, mono 2.1g, poly 0.5g); PROTEIN 1.6g; CARB 43.9g; FIBER 2.2g; CHOL 16mg; IRON 0.6mg; SODIUM 63mg; CALC 18mg

Vanilla-Roasted Strawberries

Ripe strawberries sprinkled with a few drops of rich, salty-sweet balsamic vinegar is a classic summer dessert in Italy. The combination requires perfectly ripe strawberries and flawlessly aged balsamic—hard things for ordinary mortals to get on an ordinary day. So, here's Gale's realist's rendition. Roast strawberries with vanilla, butter, and sugar to tenderize and sweeten them, then borrow a technique from the savory side of the kitchen by simmering the pan juices with wine and vinegar. The result is fragrant, fruity, rich, and light all at once.

  2 tablespoons unsalted butter
  1 vanilla bean, split lengthwise
 24 strawberries, tops removed
  2 tablespoons light brown sugar
  3 tablespoons dry red wine
 1½ tablespoons balsamic vinegar
  1 tablespoon chilled unsalted butter,
     cut into small pieces

1. Preheat oven to 400°.
2. Melt 2 tablespoons butter in a 9-inch baking pan in oven. Scrape seeds from vanilla bean into melted butter; combine. Place strawberries, cut sides down, in pan; sprinkle with sugar. Tuck vanilla halves between berries in bottom of pan. Bake at 400° for 10 minutes or until berries are soft. Cool 20 minutes.
3. Remove berries from pan, and transfer pan juices to a small skillet. Add wine and vinegar to pan; bring to a simmer over medium heat. Remove from heat; whisk in chilled butter. Drizzle sauce over berries. Serve immediately. Yield: 4 servings (serving size: 6 strawberries and 2 tablespoons sauce).

CALORIES 135 (51% from fat); FAT 7.7g (sat 4.8g, mono 2.2g, poly 0.3g); PROTEIN 0.9g; CARB 16.7g; FIBER 3g; CHOL 21mg; IRON 0.8mg; SODIUM 5mg; CALC 25mg

back to the best

Prosciutto-Wrapped Shrimp with Lemon Couscous

When you think of maple syrup, you may not envision seafood and chili powder as suitable companions. Yet they're exactly what make this dish, which appeared in our March 2000 magazine, one of our favorites.

The prosciutto adds intense saltiness to balance the sweetness in the sauce. If you haven't tried prosciutto, this is a worthy application; a little goes a long way, and it's a great accompaniment to shrimp.

Special Projects Editor Mary Creel likes that the tails are left on the shrimp. "There's something about having to lick the glaze off your fingers when you pull the tail off that adds to the sensory pleasure of eating the shrimp," she says.

The lemony zing of the couscous rounds out the complex flavors of this dish.

Prosciutto-Wrapped Shrimp with Lemon Couscous

(pictured on page 168)

  3 tablespoons maple syrup
  2 tablespoons bourbon
  1 tablespoon teriyaki sauce
  2 teaspoons Dijon mustard
  ½ teaspoon chili powder
 24 jumbo shrimp (about 1½ pounds)
  6 very thin slices prosciutto or ham
     (about 3½ ounces)
Cooking spray
Lemon Couscous

1. Preheat broiler.
2. Combine first 5 ingredients in a bowl, stirring with a whisk. Peel shrimp, leaving tails intact. Add shrimp to maple syrup mixture, tossing to coat. Remove shrimp from bowl; discard marinade.
3. Cut each prosciutto slice lengthwise into 4 strips. Wrap 1 strip around each shrimp. Thread 6 shrimp onto each of 4 (8-inch) skewers. Place skewers on a broiler pan coated with cooking spray; broil 3 minutes on each side or until done. Serve over Lemon Couscous. Yield: 4 servings (serving size: 6 shrimp and ½ cup couscous).

(Totals include Lemon Couscous) CALORIES 305 (12% from fat); FAT 4.2g (sat 1.2g, mono 1.4g, poly 0.9g); PROTEIN 36.1g; CARB 27.2g; FIBER 1.4g; CHOL 263mg; IRON 5.2mg; SODIUM 927mg; CALC 67mg

LEMON COUSCOUS:
 1¼ cups water
  ¾ cup uncooked couscous
  ¼ cup sliced green onions
  2 tablespoons finely chopped fresh
     parsley
  2 tablespoons orange juice
  1 teaspoon grated lemon rind
  1 tablespoon fresh lemon juice
  ¼ teaspoon salt
  ⅛ teaspoon black pepper

1. Bring water to a boil in a saucepan; gradually stir in couscous. Remove from heat; cover and let stand 5 minutes. Fluff. Stir in onions and remaining ingredients. Yield: 4 servings (serving size: ½ cup).

CALORIES 102 (3% from fat); FAT 0.3g (sat 0g, mono 0g, poly 0g); PROTEIN 3.7g; CARB 21.8g; FIBER 1.3g; CHOL 0mg; IRON 0.8mg; SODIUM 151mg; CALC 9mg

All About Herbs

How to use fresh herbs to create lively dishes.

What would pesto be without basil, or salsa sans cilantro? Whether used by the pinch or by the bunch, fresh herbs pull a recipe together by infusing the dish with unparalleled aromas and flavors.

Spiced Carrot Soup with Cilantro

Coriander, cumin, and turmeric give this soup Indian flavor. Pungent cilantro balances the spices.

1 tablespoon olive oil
2 cups chopped yellow onion
3 garlic cloves, minced
2 teaspoons ground coriander seeds
1 teaspoon paprika
1 teaspoon ground cumin
½ teaspoon ground turmeric
6 cups fat-free, less-sodium chicken broth
¼ teaspoon salt
¼ teaspoon freshly ground black pepper
2 pounds peeled baby carrots
¾ cup coarsely chopped fresh cilantro, divided
½ cup half-and-half
¼ cup honey
¼ cup (1-inch) sliced fresh chives

1. Heat olive oil in a Dutch oven over medium-high heat. Add onion and garlic; sauté 5 minutes or until tender. Add coriander, paprika, cumin, and turmeric; sauté 2 minutes. Add broth, salt, pepper, and carrots; bring to a boil. Reduce heat, and simmer 30 minutes or until carrots are very tender. Let stand 5 minutes.
2. Place half of carrot mixture in a blender; process until smooth. Pour pureed carrot mixture into a large bowl. Repeat procedure with remaining carrot mixture. Place pureed carrot mixture in pan; stir in ½ cup cilantro, half-and-half, and honey. Cook over low heat 5 minutes or until thoroughly heated. Combine ¼ cup cilantro and chives. Sprinkle over soup. Yield: 8 servings (serving size: about 1 cup soup and 1 tablespoon chive mixture).

CALORIES 153 (22% from fat); FAT 3.7g (sat 1.3g, mono 1.8g, poly 0.3g); PROTEIN 4.8g; CARB 26.1g; FIBER 4.7g; CHOL 8mg; IRON 1mg; SODIUM 461mg; CALC 66mg

Crispy Salmon with Herb Salad

Salmon fillets rest atop fresh herbs tossed with a light lemon dressing. Because they're left whole, use small basil and mint leaves; if you have only large leaves, tear them in half. Refrigerate the herb mixture before preparing the salmon so it won't wilt.

1½ cups arugula leaves
¾ cup fresh flat-leaf parsley leaves
½ cup fresh cilantro leaves
½ cup small fresh basil leaves
¼ cup small fresh mint leaves
1 tablespoon fresh lemon juice
1 tablespoon extra-virgin olive oil
½ teaspoon salt, divided
½ teaspoon freshly ground black pepper, divided
1 garlic clove, minced
Cooking spray
6 (6-ounce) salmon fillets, skinned
6 lemon wedges

1. Combine first 5 ingredients in a large bowl. Cover and refrigerate.

2. Combine juice, oil, ¼ teaspoon salt, ¼ teaspoon pepper, and garlic, stirring with a whisk.
3. Heat a large nonstick skillet coated with cooking spray over medium heat. Sprinkle salmon fillets with ¼ teaspoon salt and ¼ teaspoon pepper. Add fillets to pan; cook 9 minutes or until fish flakes easily when tested with a fork, turning once. Combine arugula mixture and juice mixture; toss well to coat. Place ½ cup herb salad on each of 6 plates; top each serving with 1 fillet. Serve with lemon wedges. Yield: 6 servings.

CALORIES 303 (49% from fat); FAT 16.4g (sat 2.8g, mono 8.4g, poly 3.3g); PROTEIN 35.4g; CARB 1.4g; FIBER 0.6g; CHOL 111mg; IRON 1.4mg; SODIUM 286mg; CALC 35mg

Summer Chicken Salad with Garden Herbs

This recipe leaves you with a bonus: homemade chicken stock. Four cups of rotisserie or leftover chicken, however, will work as a time-saver.

1 (3½-pound) whole chicken
¼ cup chopped fresh chives
3 tablespoons white wine vinegar
2 tablespoons capers
4 teaspoons extra-virgin olive oil
2 teaspoons chopped fresh thyme
1 teaspoon chopped fresh oregano
½ teaspoon salt
½ teaspoon freshly ground black pepper
1 garlic clove, minced

1. Remove and discard giblets and neck from chicken. Rinse with cold water. Place chicken in a stockpot; cover with water, and bring to a boil. Reduce heat, and simmer 50 minutes or until tender. Drain, reserving broth for another use. Cool chicken completely. Remove skin from chicken; discard skin. Remove chicken from bones; discard bones and fat. Chop chicken into bite-sized pieces.
2. Combine chives and remaining 8 ingredients. Add chicken; toss well to coat. Yield: 6 servings (serving size: ⅔ cup).

CALORIES 172 (29% from fat); FAT 5.6g (sat 1.1g, mono 2.9g, poly 0.9g); PROTEIN 28.4g; CARB 0.5g; FIBER 0.3g; CHOL 83mg; IRON 1.2mg; SODIUM 392mg; CALC 23mg

If you have trouble finding quinoa, substitute rice.

Thai Tenderloin Salad

Quinoa pilaf*

**Lemon-Basil Sorbet
(recipe on page 176)**

*Heat 2 teaspoons sesame oil in a small saucepan over medium-high heat. Add ½ cup chopped onion, 2 teaspoons bottled fresh ground ginger, and 2 minced garlic cloves; sauté 4 minutes. Add ¾ cup quinoa; sauté 1 minute. Stir in 1⅓ cups fat-free, less-sodium chicken broth. Bring to a boil; cover, reduce heat, and simmer 20 minutes or until done. Cool; fluff with a fork. Stir in ⅓ cup golden raisins, 3 tablespoons chopped peanuts, 2 tablespoons chopped fresh mint, 1 tablespoon chopped fresh cilantro, and 2 tablespoons fresh lime juice.

search myclar2003.com for all our menus

Thai Tenderloin Salad

Grilled flank steak can substitute for the tenderloin, if you prefer.

  1 pound beef tenderloin, trimmed
Cooking spray
  3 tablespoons lime juice
  2 tablespoons fish sauce
  1 teaspoon sugar
  ¼ teaspoon ground red pepper
  6 cups thinly sliced romaine lettuce
  1 cup thinly sliced red onion
  1 cup thinly sliced red bell pepper
  1 cup thinly sliced peeled cucumber
  ⅓ cup coarsely chopped green onions
  1 jalapeño pepper, seeded and minced
  1 cup cilantro sprigs
  ¾ cup chopped fresh mint

1. Prepare grill.
2. Place beef on grill rack coated with cooking spray; grill 6 minutes on each side or until desired degree of doneness. Cover and let stand 10 minutes. Cut beef diagonally across grain into thin slices.
3. Combine juice, fish sauce, sugar, and ground red pepper in a large bowl. Add beef, lettuce, and next 5 ingredients; toss well. Add cilantro and mint; toss gently. Yield: 4 servings (serving size: 1½ cups).

CALORIES 236 (34% from fat); FAT 9g (sat 3.3g, mono 3.3g, poly 0.5g); PROTEIN 27g; CARB 11.5g; FIBER 3.7g; CHOL 71mg; IRON 4.6mg; SODIUM 717mg; CALC 66mg

Seared Scallops with Parsley-Thyme Relish

Thyme, parsley, and shallots make savory partners for scallops and watercress.

RELISH:
  ¼ cup finely chopped shallots
  3 tablespoons chopped fresh flat-leaf parsley
  1 teaspoon grated lemon rind
  2 tablespoons fresh lemon juice
  2 teaspoons extra-virgin olive oil
  1 teaspoon chopped fresh thyme
  ¼ teaspoon salt
  ¼ teaspoon freshly ground black pepper

SCALLOPS:
1½ pounds sea scallops
  ¼ teaspoon salt
  ¼ teaspoon freshly ground black pepper
  1 tablespoon extra-virgin olive oil, divided
  4 cups trimmed watercress
  4 lemon wedges

1. To prepare relish, combine first 8 ingredients in a bowl; toss well.
2. To prepare scallops, sprinkle scallops with ¼ teaspoon salt and ¼ teaspoon pepper. Heat 1½ teaspoons oil in a large nonstick skillet over medium-high heat. Add half of scallops to pan; cook 2 minutes on each side or until done. Remove from pan. Repeat procedure with 1½ teaspoons oil and remaining scallops. Arrange scallops over watercress; top with relish. Serve with lemon wedges. Yield: 4 servings (serving size: 5 ounces sea scallops, 1 cup watercress, 1 tablespoon relish, and 1 lemon wedge).

CALORIES 217 (29% from fat); FAT 7g (sat 0.9g, mono 4.2g, poly 1g); PROTEIN 29.8g; CARB 7.9g; FIBER 1g; CHOL 56mg; IRON 1mg; SODIUM 584mg; CALC 96mg

Pork Roulade with Lemon and Sage

A roulade is a thin cut of meat that's rolled around a filling and sliced before serving. Braising is an unusual technique for roulade, but ensures moistness and creates a flavorful sauce. Sage's slightly musty fragrance and flavor pair well with pork.

  2 (1-pound) pork tenderloins, trimmed
  ⅔ cup chopped fresh flat-leaf parsley
  ¼ cup chopped fresh sage
  2 tablespoons grated lemon rind
  2 garlic cloves, minced
  1 teaspoon salt, divided
  ½ teaspoon freshly ground black pepper, divided
  1 tablespoon olive oil
  1 cup Sauvignon Blanc or other dry white wine
  1 (14-ounce) can fat-free, less-sodium chicken broth
  1 teaspoon fresh lemon juice
  4 cups hot cooked orzo (about 2 cups uncooked rice-shaped pasta)
  8 lemon wedges
Sage leaves (optional)

1. Slice tenderloins lengthwise, cutting to, but not through, other side. Open halves, laying tenderloins flat. Slice each half lengthwise, cutting to, but not through, other side; open flat. Place plastic wrap over tenderloins; pound to ½-inch thickness using a meat mallet or rolling pin.
2. Combine parsley, sage, rind, and garlic. Sprinkle ½ teaspoon salt and ¼ teaspoon pepper over tenderloins. Spread half of parsley mixture over each tenderloin, leaving a ½-inch border around outside edges. Roll up tenderloins jelly roll fashion, starting with long sides. Secure at 2-inch intervals with twine. Sprinkle ½ teaspoon salt and ¼ teaspoon pepper over tenderloins. Place tenderloins in a large zip-top plastic bag, and seal. Refrigerate at least 1 hour.
3. Heat oil in a large nonstick skillet over medium-high heat. Add tenderloins; cook 5 minutes, turning to brown on all sides. Add wine; cook 2 minutes.

Add broth, and bring to a boil. Cover, reduce heat, and simmer 20 minutes.

4. Remove tenderloins from pan; keep warm. Cook broth mixture until reduced to 1 cup (about 10 minutes). Stir in juice. Remove twine from tenderloins. Cut tenderloins crosswise into ¾-inch-thick slices. Drizzle with sauce. Serve with orzo and lemon wedges. Garnish with sage leaves, if desired. Yield: 8 servings (serving size: 3 ounces pork, 2 tablespoons sauce, ½ cup orzo, and 1 lemon wedge).

WINE NOTE: Pork pairs as easily with white wines as it does with reds. In this roulade, however, the mix of sage, parsley, and lemon rind calls for a wine that has a green herbal flavor all its own. Sauvignon Blanc is a great ingredient with which to braise the roulade; it's also great to drink once the dish is done. A terrific choice: Geyser Peak Sauvignon Blanc 2000 from Sonoma County ($10). It's fresh and zingy with just the right green snap.

CALORIES 338 (23% from fat); FAT 8.6g (sat 2.5g, mono 4.1g, poly 1.1g); PROTEIN 29.7g; CARB 33.5g; FIBER 1.4g; CHOL 75mg; IRON 3.5mg; SODIUM 451mg; CALC 33mg

Pasta with Basil, Arugula, and Walnut Pesto

This is no ordinary pesto. The classic basil version is enhanced with peppery, smoky arugula and the freshness of parsley.

    2   cups basil leaves
    2   cups arugula leaves
    ¼   cup fresh flat-leaf parsley leaves
    3   tablespoons walnuts
    3   tablespoons olive oil
    4   garlic cloves, peeled
    ¾   cup (3 ounces) grated Parmigiano-
        Reggiano cheese
    ⅓   cup fat-free, less-sodium chicken
        broth
    ¾   teaspoon salt
    ½   teaspoon freshly ground black
        pepper
    8   cups hot cooked linguine (about
        1 pound uncooked pasta)

1. Place first 6 ingredients in a food processor; pulse 7 or 8 times or until mixture forms a smooth paste. Add cheese, broth, salt, and pepper; pulse until combined. Combine pesto and pasta in a large bowl, tossing to coat. Yield: 6 servings (serving size: 1⅓ cups).

WINE NOTE: Many Italian white wines are good choices for herb and vegetable pasta dishes like this one. You can serve a Pinot Grigio with this dish, but another fun choice would be a delicious white that's wildly popular in northern Italy: Tocai Friulano. Try the Livio Felluga Tocai Friulano 2000 from the region known as Friuli-Venezia Giulia (about $23). It's dry and just a touch spicy, with exotic meadowy and peppery aromas.

CALORIES 356 (37% from fat); FAT 14.6g (sat 3.5g, mono 6.4g, poly 2.5g); PROTEIN 14.1g; CARB 44.9g; FIBER 3.2g; CHOL 10mg; IRON 3mg; SODIUM 685mg; CALC 212mg

Lebanese Layered Salad

This tangy salad can be served chilled or at room temperature. Make at least a day ahead, so the bulgur will soften and absorb the lemon juice.

    1   cup uncooked medium bulgur
    ¾   cup fresh lemon juice (about 4
        large lemons)
    2   tablespoons extra-virgin olive oil
    1¾ teaspoons salt, divided
    3   garlic cloves, minced
    2   cups finely chopped red onion
    5   cups chopped tomato
    ½   cup chopped fresh parsley
    ½   cup chopped fresh mint
    ¼   cup chopped fresh dill
    2   cups chopped seeded peeled
        cucumber
    1   cup chopped red bell pepper
    ¼   teaspoon freshly ground black
        pepper

1. Place bulgur in a large bowl. Combine juice, oil, 1 teaspoon salt, and garlic in a small bowl; stir well with a whisk. Drizzle juice mixture over bulgur. Layer onion, tomato, parsley, mint, dill, cucumber, and bell pepper evenly over bulgur mixture. Sprinkle with ¾ teaspoon salt and black pepper. Cover with plastic wrap; refrigerate at least 24 hours or up to 48 hours before serving. Yield: 8 servings (serving size: 1 cup).

CALORIES 148 (26% from fat); FAT 4.2g (sat 0.6g, mono 2.6g, poly 0.6g); PROTEIN 4.3g; CARB 26.9g; FIBER 6.1g; CHOL 0mg; IRON 1.6mg; SODIUM 532mg; CALC 40mg

---

Brown-Bag Lunch Menu
serves 8

Creamy Zucchini Soup with Mixed Herbs

Tomato salad*

Fresh fruit

*Combine 6 cups chopped tomato, ¾ cup chopped peeled avocado, ⅓ cup chopped red onion, ¼ cup chopped fresh parsley, 2 tablespoons capers, and 1 tablespoon fresh lemon juice; toss gently. Pack croutons separately, and add them to soup just before eating.

Creamy Zucchini Soup with Mixed Herbs

Parsley, tarragon, and chives are tossed with a light dressing and floated atop the soup on crostini. Pureeing the soup gives it body. Use extra caution when blending hot ingredients by holding a towel over the blender lid.

    1   tablespoon olive oil, divided
    1½ cups chopped onion
    2   garlic cloves, minced
    9   cups (1-inch) sliced zucchini
        (about 2½ pounds)
    5   cups fat-free, less-sodium chicken
        broth
    ½   teaspoon salt
    ½   teaspoon freshly ground black
        pepper
    16 (¼-inch-thick) slices French bread
        baguette (about 4 ounces)
    Cooking spray
    1   garlic clove, halved
    ¾   cup fresh flat-leaf parsley leaves
    3   tablespoons fresh tarragon leaves
    3   tablespoons chopped fresh
        chives
    1   teaspoon fresh lemon juice
    ⅛   teaspoon salt
    ⅛   teaspoon black pepper

Continued

1. Heat 1½ teaspoons oil in a Dutch oven over medium-high heat. Add onion and minced garlic; sauté 5 minutes or until tender. Add zucchini, broth, ½ teaspoon salt, and ½ teaspoon pepper; bring to a boil. Reduce heat, and simmer 25 minutes or until zucchini is very tender. Let stand 5 minutes.

2. Preheat oven to 400°.

3. Place half of zucchini mixture in a blender; process until smooth. Pour pureed zucchini mixture into a large bowl. Repeat procedure with remaining zucchini mixture. Place pureed zucchini mixture in pan. Cook over low heat 5 minutes or until thoroughly heated. Keep warm.

4. Place bread slices in a single layer on a baking sheet. Coat bread with cooking spray. Bake at 400° for 5 minutes or until toasted. Rub bread with cut sides of garlic clove.

5. Place parsley, tarragon, and chives in a small bowl. Combine 1½ teaspoons oil, juice, ⅛ teaspoon salt, and ⅛ teaspoon pepper. Pour over parsley mixture; toss well.

6. Spoon 1 cup soup into each of 8 bowls. Divide parsley mixture evenly over toasted bread slices. Top each serving with 2 bread slices. Serve immediately. Yield: 8 servings.

CALORIES 125 (25% from fat); FAT 3.5g (sat 0.5g, mono 1.7g, poly 1g); PROTEIN 5.5g; CARB 19.2g; FIBER 3.4g; CHOL 0mg; IRON 1.4mg; SODIUM 558mg; CALC 45mg

Making the Cut

An effective tool for chopping herbs is a *mezzaluna*, a curved blade that chops as you rock it from side to side on a cutting board.

Skewers of Rosemary Chicken and Zucchini

Soak wooden skewers in lemon juice 30 minutes before grilling. This prevents charring during grilling, and it infuses the food with more flavor from the inside out.

- 2 tablespoons grated lemon rind
- 1½ tablespoons chopped fresh rosemary
- 2 tablespoons extra-virgin olive oil, divided
- 2 teaspoons minced garlic, divided
- 1½ pounds skinless, boneless chicken breast, cut into ¾-inch pieces
- 2 tablespoons fresh lemon juice
- ¾ teaspoon salt
- ½ teaspoon black pepper
- 1¼ pounds zucchini, cut into ¾-inch pieces
- Cooking spray

1. Place rind, rosemary, 1 tablespoon oil, and 1 teaspoon garlic in a large zip-top plastic bag. Add chicken; seal bag, and refrigerate 1 hour.

2. Prepare grill.

3. Combine 1 tablespoon oil, 1 teaspoon garlic, juice, salt, and pepper, stirring with a whisk.

4. Thread chicken and zucchini alternately onto each of 12 (12-inch) skewers. Place kebabs on grill rack coated with cooking spray, and grill 12 minutes or until chicken is done, turning once. Drizzle with juice mixture. Yield: 6 servings (serving size: 2 skewers).

CALORIES 183 (30% from fat); FAT 6.1g (sat 1g, mono 3.7g, poly 0.8g); PROTEIN 27.4g; CARB 4.1g; FIBER 1.4g; CHOL 66mg; IRON 1.4mg; SODIUM 370mg; CALC 38mg

Lemon-Basil Sorbet

Don't stuff basil leaves into the measuring cup. Pack them loosely; then tear them in half.

- 3 cups loosely packed fresh basil leaves, torn
- 1½ cups sugar
- 1½ cups water
- ½ cup light-colored corn syrup
- 2 cups fresh lemon juice (about 2 pounds lemons)

1. Combine first 4 ingredients in a saucepan. Bring to a boil; cook 3 minutes or until sugar dissolves. Remove from heat; chill. Strain basil mixture through a sieve into a bowl, pressing basil with back of a spoon to remove as much liquid as possible. Discard basil. Combine sugar mixture and juice.

2. Pour lemon-basil mixture into freezer can of an ice-cream freezer; freeze according to manufacturer's instructions. Spoon sorbet into a freezer-safe container; cover and freeze 1 hour or until firm. Remove sorbet from freezer 10 minutes before serving. Yield: 10 servings (serving size: ½ cup).

CALORIES 175 (0% from fat); FAT 0g; PROTEIN 0.2g; CARB 46.7g; FIBER 0.2g; CHOL 0mg; IRON 0mg; SODIUM 21mg; CALC 4mg

Keeping Fresh Herbs Fresh

- Loosely wrap herbs in a damp paper towel, then seal in a zip-top plastic bag filled with air. Refrigerate for up to five days. Check herbs daily, as some of them lose their flavor after a couple of days.
- Store herbs bouquet-style when in bunches: Place herbs, stems down, in a jar with water covering 1 inch of stem ends, enclose in a large zip-top plastic bag, and change water every other day. Most herbs will keep for up to a week this way.
- Many supermarkets carry herb plants in their produce sections. Snip off as much as you need, and the plant will last for weeks or even months.
- To revive limp herbs, trim ½ inch off stems, and place in ice water for a couple of hours.
- Wash herbs just before using; pat dry with a paper towel.
- In most cases, heat kills the flavor of fresh herbs, so they're best when added to a dish at the end.

search myclar2003.com for all our tips

july

Roadside Attractions

Buying locally grown produce from the back of a farmer's truck is one of summer's sweetest pleasures.

If you're lucky, you know the joy of happening upon a local farmer selling fruits and vegetables from a fully loaded tailgate. In midsummer, there might be watermelons and peaches in the South, and tomatoes, corn, green beans, zucchini, and eggplant in the upper Midwest and New England. A farmer might sell mangoes, avocados, and Meyer lemons in the West, and chiles and bell peppers in the Southwest.

Unfortunately, the farmer who sells on the roadside is as endangered as the cowboy. The guy on the side of the road sells from one spot for a while, then moves on to another. He'll sell until he's out of whatever he's selling, and then he'll be done and gone. That being so, the best thing you can do is buy from him when you see him. Enjoy the profound pleasure of eating locally grown food, and let yourself feel rooted in the place you live.

Cucumber-Feta Salsa with Pita Crisps

The salsa is great as an appetizer with pita crisps or as a condiment in a grilled chicken pita.

PITA CRISPS:
  3 (8-inch) pitas, split in half horizontally
  Cooking spray
  ¼ teaspoon salt

SALSA:
  1 cup (4 ounces) crumbled feta cheese
  2 tablespoons fresh lemon juice
  ¼ teaspoon freshly ground black pepper
  1½ cups cubed seeded peeled cucumber
  1 cup finely chopped red onion
  3 tablespoons chopped fresh mint
  3 tablespoons chopped fresh dill
  8 lemon wedges

1. Preheat oven to 350°.
2. To prepare pita crisps, cut each pita half into 8 wedges. Arrange wedges in a single layer on a baking sheet coated with cooking spray. Lightly coat pita wedges with cooking spray, and sprinkle with salt. Bake at 350° for 10 minutes or until crisp.
3. To prepare salsa, combine feta cheese, lemon juice, and pepper; partially mash with a fork. Stir in cucumber, onion, mint, and dill. Serve salsa with pita crisps and lemon wedges. Yield: 8 servings (serving size: 6 pita crisps, 6 tablespoons salsa, and 1 lemon wedge).

CALORIES 135 (23% from fat); FAT 3.5g (sat 2.2g, mono 0.7g, poly 0.3g); PROTEIN 5.3g; CARB 20.9g; FIBER 1.6g; CHOL 13mg; IRON 1.3mg; SODIUM 394mg; CALC 110mg

Grilled Tomato Sandwiches

(pictured on page 204)

  12 (¾-inch-thick) slices tomato
  ½ teaspoon salt, divided
  12 (1-ounce) slices sourdough bread
  Cooking spray
  1 tablespoon balsamic vinegar
  ¼ teaspoon freshly ground black pepper
  6 tablespoons low-fat mayonnaise
  1 teaspoon fresh lemon juice
  1 garlic clove, minced
  3 cups trimmed arugula

1. Prepare grill.
2. Sprinkle tomato slices with ⅛ teaspoon salt. Place slices, salted sides down, on paper towels. Let stand 10 minutes. Repeat procedure on other side of slices.
3. Place tomato slices and bread slices on grill rack coated with cooking spray; grill 2 minutes, turning once. Sprinkle tomato slices with ¼ teaspoon salt, vinegar, and pepper.
4. Combine mayonnaise, juice, and garlic in a bowl. Spread 1 tablespoon mayonnaise mixture on each of 6 bread slices; top each with 2 tomato slices, ½ cup arugula, and 1 bread slice. Serve immediately. Yield: 6 servings (serving size: 1 sandwich).

CALORIES 215 (14% from fat); FAT 3.3g (sat 0.6g, mono 1g, poly 1.2g); PROTEIN 6.5g; CARB 41.1g; FIBER 3.5g; CHOL 0mg; IRON 2.3mg; SODIUM 697mg; CALC 68mg

Green Bean and Cherry Tomato Salad

Use assorted colors of cherry tomatoes in this vibrant salad.

  1¼ pounds green beans, trimmed
  1¼ pounds cherry tomatoes, quartered
  1 teaspoon chopped fresh oregano
  2 tablespoons red wine vinegar
  1 tablespoon minced shallots
  2½ teaspoons extra-virgin olive oil
  ½ teaspoon salt
  ¼ teaspoon freshly ground black pepper

1. Cook beans in boiling water 7 minutes or until tender. Drain. Place beans, tomatoes, and oregano in a large bowl; toss gently to combine.
2. Combine vinegar and shallots, stirring with a whisk. Let vinegar mixture stand 10 minutes. Add oil, salt, and pepper to vinegar mixture, stirring with a whisk until well blended. Pour vinaigrette over bean mixture; toss well. Yield: 8 servings (serving size: 1 cup).

CALORIES 51 (30% from fat); FAT 1.7g (sat 0.2g, mono 1.1g, poly 0.3g); PROTEIN 1.9g; CARB 8.7g; FIBER 3.2g; CHOL 0mg; IRON 1.1mg; SODIUM 158mg; CALC 32mg

Watermelon and Mango Salad with Citrus Dressing

5 cups cubed seedless watermelon
1½ cups cubed peeled ripe mango
3 tablespoons orange juice
1 teaspoon grated lime rind
1 tablespoon fresh lime juice
2 teaspoons honey
6 mint leaves, cut into thin strips

1. Combine watermelon and mango in a large bowl. Combine orange juice, rind, lime juice, and honey, stirring with a whisk. Drizzle over fruit mixture; toss gently to coat. Sprinkle with mint. Yield: 4 servings (serving size: 1½ cups).

CALORIES 107 (2% from fat); FAT 0.2g (sat 0.1g, mono 0.1g, poly 0g); PROTEIN 1.1g; CARB 31.9g; FIBER 2.4g; CHOL 0mg; IRON 0.6mg; SODIUM 8mg; CALC 21mg

Grilled Salmon with Corn and Pepper Relish

Marinating the salmon with lemon rind and oil subtly infuses the fish with the essence of citrus—ideal with the light, fresh relish topping.

4 teaspoons olive oil, divided
1 (6-inch) lemon rind strip
6 (6-ounce) skinless salmon fillets
1 cup fresh corn kernels (about 2 ears)
1 cup chopped yellow bell pepper
1 cup chopped red bell pepper
1 cup chopped green bell pepper
1 cup finely chopped red onion
3 tablespoons red wine vinegar
2 tablespoons chopped fresh parsley
½ teaspoon salt, divided
½ teaspoon freshly ground black pepper, divided
2 garlic cloves, minced
Cooking spray

1. Place 2 teaspoons oil, rind, and salmon in a large zip-top plastic bag. Seal and marinate in refrigerator at least 1 hour or overnight.
2. Prepare grill.
3. Combine corn and next 6 ingredients in a bowl. Stir in 2 teaspoons oil, ¼

teaspoon salt, ¼ teaspoon black pepper, and garlic.
4. Sprinkle salmon with ¼ teaspoon salt and ¼ teaspoon black pepper. Place salmon on grill rack coated with cooking spray; grill 4 minutes on each side or until fish flakes easily when tested with a fork. Serve with relish. Yield: 6 servings (serving size: 1 salmon fillet and about ¾ cup relish).

CALORIES 274 (28% from fat); FAT 8.5g (sat 1.3g, mono 3.3g, poly 2.7g); PROTEIN 35.8g; CARB 13.3g; FIBER 2.6g; CHOL 88mg; IRON 2mg; SODIUM 314mg; CALC 40mg

Roasted Eggplant Dip

When you find yourself with a windfall of fresh eggplant, make this versatile dip, which will keep in the refrigerator for up to two weeks.

2 (1-pound) eggplants, peeled and cut into 1-inch cubes
3¼ teaspoons salt, divided
2 tablespoons olive oil, divided
¼ teaspoon freshly ground black pepper
Cooking spray
¾ cup water
2 teaspoons paprika
1 teaspoon ground cumin
⅛ teaspoon ground red pepper
3 garlic cloves, minced
1 tablespoon chopped fresh flat-leaf parsley
3 tablespoons fresh lemon juice
24 (½-inch-thick) slices diagonally cut French bread baguette, toasted or grilled (about 12 ounces)

1. Preheat oven to 375°.
2. Place eggplant in a large bowl; sprinkle with 1 tablespoon salt. Toss gently to coat. Let stand 30 minutes. Rinse eggplant with cold water. Drain; pat dry.
3. Combine eggplant, ⅛ teaspoon salt, 1 tablespoon oil, and black pepper in a bowl, tossing gently to coat. Arrange eggplant mixture in a single layer on a baking sheet coated with cooking spray. Bake at 375° for 55 minutes or until eggplant is golden brown, turning occasionally.

4. Place eggplant mixture in a large bowl; mash with a potato masher. Stir in ⅛ teaspoon salt, ¾ cup water, paprika, cumin, red pepper, and garlic.
5. Heat 1 tablespoon oil in a large nonstick skillet over medium-low heat. Add eggplant mixture; cook 20 minutes or until liquid almost evaporates, stirring occasionally. Stir in parsley and juice. Serve with bread. Yield: 12 servings (serving size: 2 bread slices and about 3 tablespoons eggplant mixture).

CALORIES 162 (30% from fat); FAT 5.4g (sat 0.9g, mono 2.5g, poly 1.7g); PROTEIN 3.3g; CARB 26.2g; FIBER 3.6g; CHOL 0mg; IRON 0.9mg; SODIUM 270mg; CALC 13mg

Green Beans and Potatoes Tossed with Pesto

You can also use pecans or walnuts in this pesto, if you prefer.

2 cups loosely packed fresh basil leaves
⅓ cup (about 1½ ounces) grated fresh Parmesan cheese
¼ cup fat-free, less-sodium chicken broth
1 tablespoon pine nuts
1 tablespoon olive oil
½ teaspoon salt
¼ teaspoon freshly ground black pepper
1 garlic clove, minced
¾ pound green beans, trimmed and cut into 1½-inch pieces
1¼ pounds red potatoes, each cut into 6 wedges

1. Combine first 8 ingredients in a food processor; process until smooth.
2. Bring water to a boil in a large saucepan. Add green beans, and cook 4 minutes or until tender. Remove beans from pan with a slotted spoon, and place in a large bowl. Add potatoes to pan, and cook 6 minutes or until tender. Drain. Add pesto and potatoes to beans, and toss to coat. Yield: 6 servings (serving size: 1 cup).

CALORIES 148 (30% from fat); FAT 5g (sat 1.6g, mono 2.5g, poly 0.7g); PROTEIN 6.5g; CARB 20.8g; FIBER 4.1g; CHOL 5mg; IRON 2.6mg; SODIUM 339mg; CALC 140mg

Corn and Smoked Mozzarella Pizza

(pictured on page 201)

For a very crispy crust, bake on a pizza stone.

- 2 ears shucked corn
- Cooking spray
- 2 tablespoons olive oil, divided
- ¼ teaspoon crushed red pepper
- 1 garlic clove, minced
- 1 package dry yeast (about 2¼ teaspoons)
- ¾ cup warm water (100° to 110°), divided
- 2¼ cups all-purpose flour, divided
- 2 tablespoons 1% low-fat milk
- 1¼ teaspoons salt, divided
- 2 tablespoons cornmeal, divided
- 1 cup (4 ounces) shredded smoked mozzarella
- 1 cup very thinly sliced red onion
- 2 tablespoons chopped chives
- 1½ teaspoons grated lime rind

1. Prepare grill or preheat broiler.
2. Place corn on grill rack or broiler pan coated with cooking spray; cook 10 minutes, turning occasionally. Cool. Cut kernels from corn to measure 1 cup; set aside.
3. Place 1 tablespoon oil and red pepper in a small bowl; microwave at HIGH 30 seconds. Stir in garlic; set aside.
4. Dissolve yeast in ¼ cup warm water in a large bowl; let stand 20 minutes. Lightly spoon flour into dry measuring cups; level with a knife. Add 1 tablespoon oil, ½ cup warm water, 2 cups flour, milk, and ¾ teaspoon salt to yeast mixture; stir until well blended.
5. Turn dough out onto a floured surface. Knead until smooth and elastic (about 10 minutes); add enough of remaining flour, 1 tablespoon at a time, to prevent dough from sticking to hands (dough will feel tacky).
6. Place dough in a large bowl coated with cooking spray, turning to coat top. Cover and let rise in a warm place (85°), free from drafts, 40 minutes or until doubled in size. (Press two fingers into dough. If indentation remains, dough has risen enough.) Punch dough down; cover and let rest 5 minutes.
7. Preheat oven to 500°.
8. Divide dough in half; roll each half into a 9-inch circle on a floured surface. Place each on a pizza pan or baking sheet coated with cooking spray and sprinkled with 1 tablespoon cornmeal. Crimp edges of dough with fingers to form a rim.
9. Brush dough portions evenly with oil mixture, and sprinkle with cheese. Top evenly with corn and onion, and sprinkle with ½ teaspoon salt. Bake at 500° for 8 minutes or until golden. Sprinkle pizzas with chives and lime rind.
10. Cut each pizza into quarters. Yield: 4 servings (serving size: 2 slices).

CALORIES 473 (27% from fat); FAT 14.4g (sat 5.2g, mono 5.3g, poly 1.2g); PROTEIN 15.5g; CARB 70.2g; FIBER 4.5g; CHOL 23mg; IRON 4.3mg; SODIUM 788mg; CALC 194mg

Chilled Cucumber Soup with Cilantro and Cumin

Try this light, cool soup as a prelude to a spicy, Latin-inspired meal. With yogurt and milk as its foundation, it's also packed with calcium—a serving has about as much as one cup of milk.

- 1 teaspoon ground cumin
- 3 cups plain low-fat yogurt
- 2 cups shredded seeded peeled cucumber
- 2 cups 1% low-fat milk
- 3 tablespoons chopped fresh cilantro
- 3 tablespoons fresh lemon juice
- 2 teaspoons extra-virgin olive oil
- ½ teaspoon salt
- ¼ teaspoon freshly ground black pepper
- 2 garlic cloves, minced
- 1 tablespoon fresh cilantro leaves

1. Cook cumin in a small skillet over medium heat 1 minute or until toasted.
2. Combine cumin, yogurt, and next 8 ingredients in a large bowl. Cover and chill 1 hour. Sprinkle each serving with ½ teaspoon cilantro leaves. Yield: 6 servings (serving size: about 1 cup).

CALORIES 135 (30% from fat); FAT 4.5g (sat 2g, mono 2g, poly 0.3g); PROTEIN 9.5g; CARB 14.6g; FIBER 0.5g; CHOL 11mg; IRON 0.4mg; SODIUM 324mg; CALC 335mg

Eggplant and Tomato Gratin

Japanese eggplants are longer and more narrow than the globe eggplants most of us are familiar with, so the slices are more manageable in the gratin. But in a pinch, you can use globe eggplants.

- 1 pound Japanese eggplant, cut diagonally into ¼-inch-thick slices
- Cooking spray
- ¼ teaspoon salt
- ½ cup (2 ounces) grated fresh Parmesan cheese
- 2 teaspoons chopped fresh oregano
- ¼ teaspoon freshly ground black pepper
- 4 garlic cloves, minced
- 6 plum tomatoes, cut into ¼-inch-thick slices
- 2 medium zucchini, cut into ¼-inch-thick slices

1. Preheat oven to 375°.
2. Arrange eggplant slices in a single layer on a baking sheet coated with cooking spray. Coat slices with cooking spray; sprinkle with salt. Bake at 375° for 16 minutes, turning eggplant over after 8 minutes. Combine cheese, oregano, pepper, and garlic in a bowl.
3. Arrange half of eggplant slices in an 8-inch square baking dish coated with

cooking spray. Arrange half of tomato slices over eggplant slices. Top with half of zucchini slices; sprinkle with half of cheese mixture. Repeat layers with remaining eggplant slices, tomato slices, zucchini slices, and cheese mixture.

4. Bake, covered, at 375° for 1 hour. Uncover and bake an additional 10 minutes or until vegetables are tender and cheese is golden brown. Yield: 8 servings.

CALORIES 87 (29% from fat); FAT 2.8g (sat 1.6g, mono 0.8g, poly 0.2g); PROTEIN 5.5g; CARB 11.2g; FIBER 4g; CHOL 6mg; IRON 0.9mg; SODIUM 257mg; CALC 140mg

Bread Salad with Tomatoes, Herbs, and Ricotta Salata

Ricotta salata is a versatile, mild, and slightly sweet cheese.

    8 (1-ounce) slices sourdough bread
   ⅓ cup water
   ¼ cup red wine vinegar
    1 teaspoon extra-virgin olive oil
   ¼ teaspoon salt
   ¼ teaspoon freshly ground black pepper
    1 cup (4 ounces) crumbled ricotta salata
    2 tablespoons chopped fresh basil
    2 tablespoons chopped fresh chives
    1 tablespoon chopped fresh mint
    1 teaspoon chopped fresh oregano
    1 teaspoon chopped fresh thyme
    4 cups cherry tomatoes, halved (about 2 pints)
    1 cup diced red onion

1. Sprinkle bread with water; let stand 2 minutes. Carefully squeeze moisture from bread. Tear into 1-inch pieces. Let stand on paper towels 20 minutes.

2. Combine vinegar, oil, salt, and pepper, stirring with a whisk. Combine ricotta and next 5 ingredients in a large bowl. Add bread, tomatoes, and onion to ricotta mixture. Drizzle with vinaigrette; toss gently to coat. Yield: 6 servings (serving size: 1⅔ cups).

CALORIES 193 (29% from fat); FAT 6.3g (sat 3.2g, mono 2g, poly 0.6g); PROTEIN 7.3g; CARB 28.2g; FIBER 2.8g; CHOL 17mg; IRON 1.7mg; SODIUM 548mg; CALC 137mg

Shrimp Salad with Mango and Avocado

Fanning the mango and avocado slices around the salad makes this dish look fancy.

    4 quarts water
   2¼ pounds large shrimp, peeled and deveined
   ½ cup thinly sliced red onion
    3 tablespoons chopped fresh cilantro
    2 teaspoons grated lime rind
    2 tablespoons fresh lime juice
    1 tablespoon extra-virgin olive oil
   ½ teaspoon salt
   ¼ teaspoon freshly ground black pepper
    1 jalapeño pepper, seeded and minced
    2 peeled ripe mangoes, each cut into 6 wedges
    1 peeled avocado, seeded and cut into 12 wedges
    6 cilantro sprigs (optional)

1. Bring water to a boil in a large Dutch oven. Add shrimp; cook 2 minutes or until done. Drain and rinse with cold water. Chill.

2. Combine onion and next 7 ingredients in a large bowl. Add shrimp; toss to coat.

3. Spoon ¾ cup shrimp mixture into center of each of 6 salad plates. Arrange 2 mango slices and 2 avocado slices spokelike around each serving. Garnish with cilantro sprigs, if desired. Yield: 6 servings.

CALORIES 257 (29% from fat); FAT 8.3g (sat 1.6g, mono 4.6g, poly 1.5g); PROTEIN 23.3g; CARB 24.4g; FIBER 2.6g; CHOL 202mg; IRON 3.9mg; SODIUM 431mg; CALC 64mg

Peach Cooler

    3 cups coarsely chopped peeled peaches (about 1 pound)
   1½ cups water, divided
   ¾ cup sugar
    2 tablespoons fresh lemon juice
    2 tablespoons white rum

1. Combine chopped peaches and ½ cup water in a blender or food processor; process until smooth. Press peach mixture through a fine sieve into a bowl; discard solids.

2. Combine 1 cup water and sugar in a medium saucepan; bring to a boil. Remove from heat. Stir in peach mixture, juice, and rum. Pour mixture into an 8-inch square baking dish; cover and freeze 4 hours or until firm.

3. Place mixture in a food processor; process until slushy. Freeze 3 hours. Soften slightly in refrigerator 30 minutes before serving. Yield: 8 servings (serving size: ⅔ cup).

CALORIES 109 (0% from fat); FAT 0.1g (sat 0g, mono 0g, poly 0.1g); PROTEIN 0.5g; CARB 26.1g; FIBER 0.8g; CHOL 0mg; IRON 0.1mg; SODIUM 0mg; CALC 4mg

dinner tonight

Burger Sequels

The humble burger is the original star of American grilling. Try these sensational sequels.

Italian Burger Menu
serves 6

Italian Burgers

Chickpea-artichoke salad*

Strawberries with mascarpone cheese

*Combine 1 cup halved grape tomatoes; ½ cup finely chopped celery; ¼ cup finely chopped red onion; 1 (15½-ounce) can chickpeas, drained; and 1 (6-ounce) jar marinated artichoke hearts, undrained, in a large bowl. Cover and chill until ready to serve.

Game Plan

1. Prepare grill or preheat broiler
2. Slice bell peppers and onion for burgers
3. While peppers and onion cook:
   • Prepare patties
   • Grate cheese for burgers
4. While burgers cook:
   • Prepare salad
   • Halve strawberries

search myclar2003.com for all our menus

Continued

Italian Burgers

These messy, robust burgers are just as delicious and satisfying as a meatball sub.

TOTAL TIME: 41 MINUTES

QUICK TIP: To remove sausage from its casing, cut the casing lengthwise with kitchen scissors.

Cooking spray
- 4 cups red bell pepper strips
- 2 cups green bell pepper strips
- 2 cups vertically sliced onion
- 1½ cups fat-free Italian herb pasta sauce (such as Muir Glen)
- 12 ounces hot turkey Italian sausage
- 12 ounces ground turkey breast
- 6 (2-ounce) whole wheat hamburger buns
- ¾ cup (3 ounces) shredded sharp provolone cheese

1. Prepare grill or preheat broiler.
2. Heat a large nonstick skillet coated with cooking spray over medium-high heat. Add bell peppers and onion; sauté 10 minutes. Add pasta sauce, and cook 1 minute or until thoroughly heated. Keep warm.
3. Remove casings from sausage. Combine sausage and turkey in a large bowl. Divide mixture into 6 equal portions, shaping each into a ½-inch-thick patty.
4. Place patties on a grill rack or broiler pan coated with cooking spray; cook 4 minutes on each side or until done.
5. Place 1 patty on bottom half of each bun; top each patty with ⅔ cup bell pepper mixture, 2 tablespoons cheese, and top half of a bun. Yield: 6 servings.

CALORIES 428 (27% from fat); FAT 13g (sat 4.6g, mono 3.9g, poly 2.4g); PROTEIN 34.7g; CARB 42.1g; FIBER 5.6g; CHOL 93mg; IRON 4.4mg; SODIUM 860mg; CALC 233mg

Greek-Style Burger Menu
serves 8

Lamb Burgers with Fennel Salad

Greek potatoes*

Baby carrots with commercial hummus

*Combine 2 tablespoons olive oil, 1 tablespoon fresh lemon juice, 1 teaspoon bottled minced garlic, ½ teaspoon salt, ½ teaspoon dried oregano, and ¼ teaspoon black pepper in a small bowl, stirring with a whisk. Arrange 3 pounds quartered small red potatoes in an 11 x 7-inch baking dish; drizzle with oil mixture, tossing to coat. Cover with plastic wrap; vent. Microwave at HIGH 15 minutes or until potatoes are tender.

Game Plan

1. Prepare grill or preheat broiler
2. Prepare fennel salad
3. Prepare potatoes
4. While potatoes cook, prepare burgers and baby carrots

Lamb Burgers with Fennel Salad

A crunchy yet creamy mixture of fennel, sour cream, yogurt, and mint tops these Greek-style burgers served in pitas. Seasoned feta and olives flavor the patties.

TOTAL TIME: 40 MINUTES

QUICK TIP: Use a mandoline or food processor to slice the fennel thinly and easily.

SALAD:
- 2 cups thinly sliced fennel bulb (about 1 [8-ounce] bulb)
- ½ cup fat-free sour cream
- ½ cup plain fat-free yogurt
- ¼ cup finely chopped red onion
- 2 tablespoons chopped fresh mint
- 1 tablespoon grated lemon rind
- 1 tablespoon honey
- ¼ teaspoon salt
- ¼ teaspoon black pepper
- 1 garlic clove, minced

BURGERS:
- ½ cup (2 ounces) crumbled feta cheese with basil and garlic
- ¼ cup chopped pimiento-stuffed olives
- 2 tablespoons Greek seasoning (such as McCormick)
- ¼ teaspoon salt
- 1 pound lean ground lamb
- 1 pound ground turkey breast
- Cooking spray
- 4 (6-inch) pitas, cut in half

1. Prepare grill or preheat broiler.
2. To prepare salad, combine first 10 ingredients.
3. To prepare burgers, combine cheese and next 5 ingredients in a large bowl. Divide mixture into 8 equal portions, shaping each into a ½-inch-thick patty.
4. Place patties on a grill rack or broiler pan coated with cooking spray; cook 4 minutes on each side or until done. Cut patties in half. Place 2 patty halves and ¼ cup salad in each pita half. Yield: 8 servings.

CALORIES 316 (30% from fat); FAT 10.7g (sat 4.6g, mono 4.1g, poly 0.9g); PROTEIN 29g; CARB 24.7g; FIBER 1.5g; CHOL 81mg; IRON 2.1mg; SODIUM 616mg; CALC 133mg

Comfort Burger Menu
serves 6

Meat Loaf Burgers with Caramelized Onions

Corn on the cob

Quick peach crisp*

*Arrange 1 (29-ounce) can sliced peaches in light syrup, drained, in an 8-inch square baking dish. Combine ¾ cup crushed gingersnaps and 2 tablespoons brown sugar; sprinkle over peaches. Bake at 400° for 15 minutes.

Game Plan

1. Prepare grill or preheat broiler
2. While onions cook:
- Chop bell pepper and celery
- Crush crackers
- Cook corn on the cob
3. While bell pepper and celery cook, measure and combine remaining ingredients for burgers
4. While burgers cook, assemble and bake peach crisp

Meat Loaf Burgers with Caramelized Onions

Meat loaf is shaped into individual burgers that are just as comforting as their namesake. The burgers are delicate, so take extra care when flipping them.

TOTAL TIME: 40 MINUTES

QUICK TIP: To crush crackers (or cookies), place them in a large zip-top plastic bag, and pound with a meat mallet or rolling pin.

ONIONS:

1 teaspoon olive oil
4½ cups vertically sliced red onion (about 2 medium onions)
¼ teaspoon salt
1 tablespoon sugar
2 tablespoons balsamic vinegar

BURGERS:

Cooking spray
1 cup finely chopped green bell pepper
1 cup finely chopped celery
1 cup crushed whole wheat crackers (about 20 crackers)
⅓ cup ketchup, divided
½ teaspoon dried thyme
¼ teaspoon salt
1 pound ground sirloin
1 large egg, lightly beaten
12 (1¼-ounce) slices rye bread, toasted

1. Prepare grill or preheat broiler.
2. To prepare onions, heat oil in a large nonstick skillet over medium-high heat. Add onion and ¼ teaspoon salt; sauté 12 minutes or until golden brown. Stir in sugar and vinegar; cook 30 seconds. Remove from pan.
3. To prepare burgers, heat pan coated with cooking spray over medium-high heat. Add bell pepper and celery; sauté 3 minutes or until tender.
4. Combine bell pepper mixture, crackers, ¼ cup ketchup, thyme, ¼ teaspoon salt, beef, and egg in a large bowl. Divide mixture into 6 equal portions, shaping each into a ½-inch-thick patty.
5. Place patties on a grill rack or broiler pan coated with cooking spray; cook 5 minutes. Carefully turn patties over;

brush with 4 teaspoons ketchup. Cook 5 minutes or until done.
6. Place 1 patty on each of 6 bread slices. Top each patty with ¼ cup onion mixture and 1 bread slice. Yield: 6 servings.

CALORIES 419 (29% from fat); FAT 13.4g (sat 4.3g, mono 6g, poly 1.3g); PROTEIN 23.1g; CARB 51.8g; FIBER 6.6g; CHOL 86mg; IRON 4.2mg; SODIUM 906mg; CALC 92mg

---

Burgers with a Kick Menu

serves 8

Chicken-Chorizo Burgers with Avocado Mayonnaise

Green salad

Pineapple-coconut coolers*

*Combine 2 cups ice, 1 cup light coconut milk, and 2 cups pineapple sherbet in a blender; process until smooth.

Game Plan

1. Prepare grill or preheat broiler
2. Prepare and refrigerate avocado mayonnaise
3. Prepare burgers
4. While burgers cook:
• Prepare salad
• Toast onion rolls
• Prepare pineapple-coconut coolers

search myclar2003.com for all our menus

Chicken-Chorizo Burgers with Avocado Mayonnaise

Bite-sized pieces of corn tortillas act as a binder in these sausage and chicken burgers.

TOTAL TIME: 39 MINUTES

QUICK TIP: Dampen your hands with cool water to prevent the meat from sticking to them as you form the patties.

MAYONNAISE:

⅓ cup fat-free mayonnaise
¼ cup fresh cilantro leaves
2 tablespoons fresh lime juice
¼ teaspoon salt
½ ripe peeled avocado, seeded

BURGERS:

½ pound Spanish chorizo sausage (such as Usinger's)
¼ teaspoon salt
5 (6-inch) corn tortillas, torn into bite-sized pieces
1½ pounds skinless, boneless chicken breast, coarsely chopped
1 jalapeño pepper, seeded and chopped
Cooking spray
8 (2-ounce) onion rolls, toasted
8 (¼-inch-thick) slices tomato

1. Prepare grill or preheat broiler.
2. To prepare mayonnaise, combine first 5 ingredients in a food processor; pulse 10 times or until combined. Cover and chill mayonnaise mixture.
3. To prepare burgers, remove casings from sausage. Place sausage, salt, tortillas, chicken, and jalapeño in food processor; process 30 seconds or until mixture is coarsely ground. Divide mixture into 8 equal portions, shaping each into a ½-inch-thick patty.
4. Place patties on a grill rack or broiler pan coated with cooking spray; cook 7 minutes on each side or until done.
5. Cut rolls in half horizontally; spread 1½ tablespoons mayonnaise mixture over top half of each roll. Place tomato slices on bottom halves of rolls; top each with 1 patty and top half of roll. Yield: 8 servings.

CALORIES 385 (29% from fat); FAT 12.6g (sat 4.4g, mono 4.8g, poly 2.3g); PROTEIN 29.2g; CARB 39.5g; FIBER 3g; CHOL 63mg; IRON 2.8mg; SODIUM 735mg; CALC 111mg

Potato Salad Perfected

Five variations on a theme for the must-have side dish at summer get-togethers.

At virtually any summertime gathering, potato salad is there. But what constitutes "potato salad" is open to interpretation. About the only thing most of the recipes share is potatoes.

Farm Stand Potato Salad

Summer's bounty from the local farm stand inspired this salad, made with fingerling potatoes, crisp sugar snap peas, crunchy broccoli, and a colorful confetti of bell peppers. Vary this recipe by substituting your favorite summer vegetables.

DRESSING:

  3 tablespoons fresh lemon juice
  2 tablespoons olive oil
  1 tablespoon country-style Dijon mustard
  1 teaspoon minced fresh or ¼ teaspoon dried thyme
  ½ teaspoon salt
  ½ teaspoon celery seeds

SALAD:

1¾ pounds fingerling potatoes
  1 cup sugar snap peas, trimmed
  1 cup broccoli florets
  ¼ cup finely chopped red bell pepper
  ¼ cup finely chopped green bell pepper
  ¼ cup finely chopped yellow bell pepper
  ¼ cup chopped green onions

1. To prepare dressing, combine first 6 ingredients, stirring with a whisk.
2. To prepare salad, place potatoes in a saucepan, and cover with water. Bring to a boil. Reduce heat, and simmer 10 minutes or until tender. Remove potatoes from pan with a slotted spoon. Add peas and broccoli florets to pan. Cook 1 minute; drain.

3. Cut potatoes into ¼-inch-thick slices. Combine potatoes, peas, broccoli, bell peppers, and green onions in a large bowl. Add dressing; toss well. Yield: 8 servings (serving size: 1 cup).

CALORIES 120 (29% from fat); FAT 3.8g (sat 0.5g, mono 2.6g, poly 0.4g); PROTEIN 3.1g; CARB 19.8g; FIBER 2.6g; CHOL 0mg; IRON 1.9mg; SODIUM 204mg; CALC 29mg

Potato Salad 101

(pictured on page 201)

An all-American necessity at summer get-togethers and reunions, this creamy, old-fashioned potato salad uses pickle relish, eggs, and mustard.

  2 pounds small all-purpose white or red potatoes
  3 tablespoons white vinegar
  1 tablespoon canola oil
  ½ cup chopped celery
  ½ cup finely chopped red onion
  2 tablespoons sweet pickle relish, drained
  3 hard-cooked large eggs, chopped
  ¾ cup low-fat mayonnaise
  2 tablespoons prepared mustard
  ½ teaspoon salt
  ¼ teaspoon freshly ground black pepper

1. Place potatoes in a saucepan, and cover with water. Bring to a boil. Reduce heat; simmer 10 minutes or until tender. Drain. Cool and peel. Cut potatoes into ½-inch cubes. Place potatoes in a large bowl; sprinkle with vinegar and oil. Add celery, onion, pickle relish, and eggs; toss gently.
2. Combine mayonnaise, mustard, salt, and pepper. Spoon mayonnaise mixture over potato mixture; toss gently to coat. Cover and chill 1 to 24 hours. Yield: 7 servings (serving size: about 1 cup).

CALORIES 215 (26% from fat); FAT 6.1g (sat 1.1g, mono 2.5g, poly 2g); PROTEIN 4.9g; CARB 35.9g; FIBER 1.9g; CHOL 91mg; IRON 0.9mg; SODIUM 536mg; CALC 26mg

---

Preparing Potato Salad

- Use low- to medium-starch potatoes for salads; high-starch potatoes absorb water readily and do not hold their shape. Low- to medium-starch potatoes include Red Bliss, Yukon Gold, all-purpose white, Fingerling, and White Rose.
- Select potatoes of the same size so they cook uniformly. Cover the potatoes with cold water, bring to a boil, and cook until done. Test for doneness with a knife, which lets in less water than a fork. When they're ready, the knife will go in easily.
- Cooking potatoes with the skin on will preserve their shape and add flavor.
- Most potato salads benefit from a short chilling in the refrigerator.

search myclar2003.com for all our menus

Hot German Potato Salad

A classic potato salad gets its unique flavor from bacon and a piquant vinaigrette.

  2 pounds small red potatoes
  6 tablespoons white wine vinegar, divided
Cooking spray
  ½ cup finely chopped red onion
  4 ounces turkey kielbasa, diced
  ½ cup fat-free, less-sodium chicken broth
  3 bacon slices, cooked and crumbled
  1 teaspoon caraway seeds
  ½ teaspoon salt
  ¼ teaspoon freshly ground black pepper
  ½ cup minced fresh parsley

1. Place potatoes in a saucepan; cover with water. Bring to a boil. Reduce heat; simmer 10 minutes or until tender. Drain; cool slightly. Cut potatoes in half lengthwise; cut halves crosswise into ¼-inch-thick slices. Place potatoes in a large bowl; sprinkle with 2 tablespoons vinegar.
2. Heat a large nonstick skillet coated with cooking spray over medium heat.

Add onion and kielbasa to pan; cook 3 minutes or until onion is tender. Add ¼ cup vinegar, broth, and bacon. Bring to a boil; cook 1 minute. Stir in caraway seeds, salt, and pepper.

3. Pour vinegar mixture over potato slices; toss gently. Sprinkle with parsley. Serve immediately. Yield: 6 servings (serving size: 1 cup).

CALORIES 195 (30% from fat); FAT 6.4g (sat 2.2g, mono 2.9g, poly 1.1g); PROTEIN 8.6g; CARB 27g; FIBER 2.1g; CHOL 20mg; IRON 1.2mg; SODIUM 559mg; CALC 21mg

Herbed Potato Salad

Dill, parsley, and onion combine with yogurt and sour cream to make a pungent, creamy dressing. Because it travels well, this flavorful potato salad is wonderful for potlucks and picnics.

    2 pounds Yukon gold potatoes
    3 tablespoons white wine vinegar
    ½ cup plain low-fat yogurt
    ¼ cup reduced-fat sour cream
    1 tablespoon canola oil
    ½ cup finely chopped red onion
    2 tablespoons chopped fresh parsley
    1 tablespoon chopped fresh dill
    ½ teaspoon salt
    ¼ teaspoon freshly ground black
       pepper
    1 garlic clove, minced

1. Place potatoes in a saucepan, and cover with water. Bring to a boil. Reduce heat; simmer 15 minutes or until tender. Drain. Cool slightly and peel. Cut potatoes in half lengthwise; cut halves crosswise into ¼-inch-thick slices. Place potatoes in a large bowl; sprinkle with vinegar.

2. Combine yogurt and sour cream in a medium bowl, stirring with a whisk until smooth. Add oil; stir with a whisk. Add onion and remaining 5 ingredients; stir with a whisk. Add yogurt mixture to potato mixture; toss gently to coat. Cover and chill 1 to 24 hours. Yield: 6 servings (serving size: about 1 cup).

CALORIES 168 (21% from fat); FAT 4g (sat 1.2g, mono 1.4g, poly 0.8g); PROTEIN 4.2g; CARB 30.1g; FIBER 2.6g; CHOL 6mg; IRON 0.6mg; SODIUM 221mg; CALC 66mg

Southwestern Potato Salad

Those whose preferences lean toward the spicy will love this salad. Adjust the heat by increasing or decreasing the amount of jalapeño and chipotle chile.

    1 (7-ounce) can chipotle chiles in
       adobo sauce
    2 pounds small red potatoes
       Cooking spray
  1½ cups fresh corn kernels (about
       3 ears)
    ½ cup chopped celery
    ½ cup finely chopped red onion
    ½ cup chopped red bell pepper
    ¼ cup chopped fresh cilantro
    1 (15-ounce) can black beans, rinsed
       and drained
    1 jalapeño pepper, seeded and finely
       chopped
    ¼ cup fresh lime juice
    3 tablespoons canola oil
    ¾ teaspoon salt
    ¼ teaspoon freshly ground black
       pepper

1. Remove 1 chipotle chile from can. Chop chile to measure 2 teaspoons. Reserve remaining chiles and adobo sauce for another use.

2. Place potatoes in a saucepan, and cover with water. Bring to a boil. Reduce heat; simmer 10 minutes or until tender. Drain; cool. Cut potatoes into ¼-inch cubes. Place cooked potatoes in a large bowl.

3. Heat a large nonstick skillet coated with cooking spray over medium-high heat. Add corn; sauté 5 minutes or until lightly browned. Add corn, celery, and next 5 ingredients to potatoes; toss gently.

4. Combine 2 teaspoons chopped adobo chile, lime juice, oil, salt, and black pepper, stirring with a whisk. Drizzle lime juice mixture over potato mixture, and toss gently. Cover and chill 1 to 24 hours. Yield: 8 servings (serving size: about 1 cup).

CALORIES 209 (25% from fat); FAT 5.8g (sat 0.4g, mono 3.1g, poly 1.8g); PROTEIN 5.1g; CARB 37.9g; FIBER 5.7g; CHOL 0mg; IRON 2.3mg; SODIUM 413mg; CALC 33mg

Double Take

Find your favorites in these top-rated recipes submitted by readers over the years.

Reader Recipes has always been one of our most popular columns. Like neighbors sharing a cup of coffee, it invites us into your kitchens. And it gives you a chance to hear from other readers, who share tips, shortcuts, recipes, and family tidbits and history.

In planning which recipes to include in this section, we talked a great deal about what Americans are eating now. We soon realized that this popular column mirrors the diversity of food enjoyed across the country. To demonstrate and celebrate this diversity, we've chosen seven of our favorite reader recipes from over the years. We hope you enjoy these standout dishes as much as we have.

Grilled Mahimahi Skewers with Pineapple-Mandarin Sauce

Robin Monahan of Fountain Valley, California, serves these with rice. Use a sweet white wine like Riesling if you can't find mirin.

—July/August 1999

    ½ cup chopped onion
    ⅓ cup honey
    ½ cup dry red wine
    2 tablespoons balsamic vinegar
    2 tablespoons pineapple juice
    1 tablespoon low-sodium soy sauce
    1 tablespoon mirin (sweet rice wine)
    2 cups diced fresh pineapple
  1½ pounds mahimahi steaks, cut into
       24 (1-inch) pieces
   24 (1-inch) cubes fresh pineapple
   24 (1-inch) pieces green bell pepper
    1 tablespoon chopped fresh or 1
       teaspoon dried rubbed sage
    ¼ teaspoon salt
    ¼ teaspoon black pepper
       Cooking spray

Continued

1. Heat a medium nonstick skillet over medium heat. Combine onion and honey in pan; cook 12 minutes or until golden brown, stirring occasionally. Add red wine and next 4 ingredients; cook 10 minutes, stirring occasionally. Stir in diced pineapple; cook 5 minutes. Keep warm.
2. Prepare grill.
3. Thread 3 mahimahi pieces, 3 pineapple cubes, and 3 bell pepper pieces alternately onto each of 8 (12-inch) skewers. Sprinkle with sage, salt, and black pepper.
4. Place kebabs on a grill rack coated with cooking spray; grill kebabs 8 minutes or until fish is done, turning once. Serve with pineapple sauce. Yield: 4 servings (serving size: 2 kebabs and ½ cup pineapple sauce).

CALORIES 392 (18% from fat); FAT 7.8g (sat 2g, mono 2.7g, poly 1.9g); PROTEIN 35.1g; CARB 47.7g; FIBER 2.7g; CHOL 66mg; IRON 2.8mg; SODIUM 427mg; CALC 34mg

Anzac Biscuits

Australia native Sandy Bennett of Waldport, Oregon, submitted this favorite recipe from her homeland. Cane syrup is thicker and sweeter than corn syrup and can be found in cans, next to the jellies and other syrups or in Caribbean markets.
—March 1996

     1   cup all-purpose flour
     1   cup regular oats
     1   cup packed brown sugar
    ½   cup shredded sweetened coconut
    ½   teaspoon baking soda
    ¼   cup butter, melted
     3   tablespoons water
     2   tablespoons golden cane syrup or light-colored corn syrup
    Cooking spray

1. Preheat oven to 325°.
2. Lightly spoon flour into a dry measuring cup; level with a knife. Combine flour, oats, sugar, coconut, and baking soda in a bowl; stir well. Add butter, water, and syrup; stir well. Drop by level tablespoons 2 inches apart onto baking sheets coated with cooking spray.
3. Bake at 325° for 12 minutes or until cookies are almost set. Remove from oven; cool on pans 2 to 3 minutes or until firm. Remove cookies from pans; cool completely on wire racks. Yield: 2 dozen (serving size: 1 cookie).

CALORIES 92 (26% from fat); FAT 2.7g (sat 1.7g, mono 0.7g, poly 0.2g); PROTEIN 1g; CARB 17g; FIBER 0.5g; CHOL 5mg; IRON 0.6mg; SODIUM 55mg; CALC 10mg

Monkey Bread

Sent to us by Rita M. Newton of Waukon, Iowa, this recipe calls for frozen bread dough, so making it is easy. Place a baking sheet on the bottom rack of your oven to catch any drips while the bread bakes.
—January/February 1995

    1¼   cups granulated sugar, divided
    ¼   cup packed brown sugar
    ¼   cup 1% low-fat milk
     1   tablespoon butter
    1¾   teaspoons ground cinnamon, divided
     2   (1-pound) loaves frozen white bread dough, thawed
    Cooking spray

1. Combine 1 cup granulated sugar, brown sugar, milk, butter, and 1¼ teaspoons cinnamon in a small saucepan. Bring to a boil; cook 1 minute. Remove sugar syrup from heat; cool 10 minutes.
2. Combine ¼ cup granulated sugar and ½ teaspoon cinnamon in a shallow dish; stir well. Cut each loaf of dough into 24 equal portions. Roll each portion in sugar mixture; layer dough balls in a 12-cup Bundt pan coated with cooking spray. Pour sugar syrup over dough; cover and let rise in a warm place (85°), free from drafts, 35 minutes or until dough has doubled in size.
3. Preheat oven to 350°.
4. Uncover dough, and bake at 350° for 25 minutes or until lightly browned. Immediately loosen edges of bread with a knife. Place a plate upside down on top of pan; invert bread onto plate. Drizzle any remaining syrup over bread. Yield: 24 servings (serving size: 2 rolls).

CALORIES 159 (13% from fat); FAT 2.3g (sat 0.5g, mono 0.8g, poly 0.8g); PROTEIN 4.1g; CARB 32.4g; FIBER 1.3g; CHOL 1mg; IRON 1.5mg; SODIUM 218mg; CALC 16mg

Spicy Supper Menu
serves 9

Serve curry over rice and with green beans.

Indian Chicken Curry

Garlic green beans*

*Heat a nonstick saucepan over medium-high heat; sauté 4 sliced garlic cloves 2 minutes. Add 6 cups fat-free, less-sodium chicken broth and 2 pounds fresh green beans; simmer 20 minutes.

search myclar2003.com for all our menus

Indian Chicken Curry

Mikey Thomas of Florida told us that she inherited this recipe when she married.
—April 2000

     2   teaspoons ground red pepper
     2   teaspoons curry powder
     2   teaspoons chili powder
     1   teaspoon salt
     1   teaspoon ground coriander seeds
     1   teaspoon ground ginger
     1   teaspoon ground cumin
     1   teaspoon ground cinnamon
     3   tablespoons butter
     1   cup chopped onion
     2   garlic cloves, minced
     1   pound skinless, boneless chicken breast, cut into 1-inch pieces
     1   (8-ounce) carton plain fat-free yogurt
     1   (6-ounce) can tomato paste
     5   cups cubed peeled baking potato (about 2½ pounds)
     4   cups water
    4½   cups hot cooked basmati rice
    ⅔   cup chopped tomato

1. Combine first 8 ingredients. Melt butter in a Dutch oven over medium heat. Add onion and garlic; cook 5 minutes, stirring frequently. Stir in spice mixture; cook 5 minutes, stirring frequently. Add chicken; cook 10 minutes, stirring frequently.
2. Combine yogurt and tomato paste; stir with a whisk. Add yogurt mixture, potato, and water to pan. Bring to a boil. Cover, reduce heat, and simmer 1 hour, stirring occasionally. Serve over rice; top

with tomato. Yield: 9 servings (serving size: 1 cup curry mixture, ½ cup rice, and about 1 tablespoon tomato).

CALORIES 315 (15% from fat); FAT 5.2g (sat 2.7g, mono 1.4g, poly 0.5g); PROTEIN 18.2g; CARB 49g; FIBER 3g; CHOL 40mg; IRON 3.1mg; SODIUM 377mg; CALC 96mg

Chocolate Cinnamon Rolls

Gloria Wiech from Frontenac, Minnesota, adapted this recipe from one given to her by a coworker.

—April 1996

 1 package dry yeast (about 2¼ teaspoons)
 2 tablespoons granulated sugar
 1¼ cups warm fat-free milk (100° to 110°)
 ¼ cup butter, melted
 ½ teaspoon vanilla extract
 1 large egg, lightly beaten
 4 cups bread flour, divided
 ⅓ cup unsweetened cocoa
 ½ teaspoon salt
 Cooking spray
 1 egg white, lightly beaten
 ¼ cup granulated sugar
 1 teaspoon ground cinnamon
 1 cup sifted powdered sugar
 2 tablespoons fat-free milk
 1 teaspoon vanilla extract

1. Dissolve yeast and 2 tablespoons granulated sugar in 1¼ cups milk in a large bowl; let stand 5 minutes. Add butter, ½ teaspoon vanilla, and egg; stir well. Lightly spoon flour into dry measuring cups; level with a knife. Stir 3½ cups flour, cocoa, and salt into yeast mixture to form a soft dough.
2. Turn dough out onto a lightly floured surface. Knead until smooth and elastic (about 10 minutes); add enough of remaining flour, 1 tablespoon at a time, to prevent dough from sticking to hands.
3. Place dough in a large bowl coated with cooking spray, turning to coat top. Cover and let rise in a warm place (85°), free from drafts, 45 minutes or until dough has doubled in size. (Press two fingers into dough. If indentation remains, dough has risen enough.)

4. Punch dough down. Turn out onto a lightly floured surface; roll into a 16 x 8-inch rectangle. Brush egg white over entire surface. Combine ¼ cup sugar and cinnamon; sprinkle over dough. Starting at long side, roll up tightly, jelly roll fashion; pinch seam to seal (do not seal ends).
5. Cut roll into 16 (1-inch) slices. Arrange slices, cut sides up, in a 13 x 9-inch baking pan coated with cooking spray. Cover and let rise 30 minutes or until doubled in size.
6. Preheat oven to 350°.
7. Bake rolls at 350° for 20 minutes. Combine powdered sugar, 2 tablespoons milk, and 1 teaspoon vanilla; stir well. Drizzle over rolls. Yield: 16 servings (serving size: 1 roll).

CALORIES 188 (17% from fat); FAT 3.5g (sat 2g, mono 1.1g, poly 0.2g); PROTEIN 5.9g; CARB 35.4g; FIBER 1.5g; CHOL 21mg; IRON 1.8mg; SODIUM 122mg; CALC 33mg

Spicy Soba Noodles with Chicken in Peanut Sauce

This creation became Kate Sackett's signature dish among her friends and family in Seattle.

—September 2000

 1 carrot, peeled
 2 cups fat-free, less-sodium chicken broth, divided
 ⅓ cup reduced-fat peanut butter
 1 tablespoon chopped peeled fresh ginger
 1 tablespoon low-sodium soy sauce
 2 tablespoons honey
 1 to 2 teaspoons crushed red pepper
 1 garlic clove, minced
 1 pound skinless, boneless chicken breast
 5 cups cooked soba (about 10 ounces uncooked buckwheat noodles)
 6 tablespoons sliced green onions
 6 tablespoons chopped unsalted, dry-roasted peanuts

1. Shave carrot lengthwise into thin strips using a vegetable peeler.
2. Combine ⅓ cup broth, peanut butter, ginger, soy sauce, honey, pepper, and garlic; stir with a whisk until smooth.

3. Place chicken in a large saucepan; add 1⅔ cups broth. Bring to a boil. Reduce heat, and simmer 4 minutes or until chicken is done. Remove from heat; let stand 20 minutes. Drain; cut chicken into 2-inch pieces. Combine carrot, peanut sauce, chicken, and noodles in a large bowl; toss to coat. Sprinkle with onions and peanuts. Yield: 6 servings (serving size: 1 cup).

CALORIES 398 (26% from fat); FAT 11.4g (sat 2.1g, mono 5.2g, poly 3.6g); PROTEIN 29.5g; CARB 43.4g; FIBER 4.3g; CHOL 44mg; IRON 1.9mg; SODIUM 477mg; CALC 40mg

Chicken Marsala

Jean M. Converse of Elsinore, California, couldn't find a recipe for chicken Marsala that suited her tastes so she invented this one.

—September 1996

 ½ cup dry Marsala wine
 1 teaspoon cornstarch
 ½ teaspoon dried tarragon
 ⅛ teaspoon salt
 ¼ cup Italian-seasoned breadcrumbs
 2 tablespoons grated Parmesan cheese
 ⅛ teaspoon garlic powder
 4 (4-ounce) skinless, boneless chicken breast halves
 2 teaspoons olive oil
 2 cups hot cooked angel hair (about 4 ounces uncooked pasta)

1. Combine first 4 ingredients in a 1-cup glass measure, stirring with a whisk until blended.
2. Combine breadcrumbs, cheese, and garlic powder in a shallow dish; stir well with a whisk. Dredge chicken in breadcrumb mixture.
3. Heat oil in a large nonstick skillet over medium-high heat. Add chicken; cook 4 minutes on each side or until done.
4. Microwave wine mixture at HIGH 30 seconds or until slightly thick, stirring once. Arrange chicken over pasta; top with sauce. Yield: 4 servings (serving size: 1 chicken breast half, ½ cup pasta, and about 2 tablespoons sauce).

CALORIES 306 (20% from fat); FAT 6.7g (sat 1.8g, mono 3g, poly 1g); PROTEIN 31.9g; CARB 27.1g; FIBER 1.2g; CHOL 74mg; IRON 2.2mg; SODIUM 382mg; CALC 63mg

When Cultures Combine

When immigrants arrive, they bring their kitchens with them—and American cuisine becomes more diverse and enriched.

In 2000 more than 10 percent of the country's population was born elsewhere, the highest proportion since 1930, says the U.S. Census Bureau. Natives of Mexico, Cuba, El Salvador, and the Dominican Republic accounted for more than half of all immigrants. Those born in Asian countries, including China, the Philippines, Vietnam, and Korea, accounted for a quarter. And each group has brought with it their own culinary influences that they've incorporated into "American" foods. Here are some typical American dishes—with an Asian twist. (For all recipes that call for Thai chile sauce, we used Sriracha, a smooth, fiery sauce that's often packaged in a convenient squeeze bottle.)

Lemongrass-Scented Crab Cakes with Mango Relish

Maryland crab cakes take on a distinctive Asian flavor with the addition of aromatic lemongrass and cilantro. Lemongrass has the shape of green onions, but only the pale bottom part should be used. The sweet, colorful relish is a fitting complement to the citrus-spiked cakes. Keep cooked crab cakes warm in a 200° oven while you prepare the rest.

CRAB CAKES:

- 3 (1-ounce) slices white bread
- ¼ cup finely chopped green onions
- ¼ cup finely chopped onion
- ¼ cup low-fat mayonnaise
- 2 tablespoons chopped fresh cilantro
- 2 teaspoons grated lime rind
- 2 tablespoons fresh lime juice
- 1 tablespoon fish sauce
- 2 teaspoons chopped peeled fresh lemongrass
- 1 large egg white, lightly beaten
- 1 pound lump crabmeat, drained and shell pieces removed
- 4 teaspoons peanut oil, divided

RELISH:

- 1¼ cups finely chopped peeled mango (about 1 large mango)
- ½ cup finely chopped red bell pepper
- ¼ cup finely chopped red onion
- 1 tablespoon fresh lime juice
- 2 teaspoons sugar
- ⅛ teaspoon salt
- ⅛ teaspoon ground red pepper

1. To prepare crab cakes, place bread in a food processor; pulse 10 times or until coarse crumbs form to measure 1½ cups. Combine breadcrumbs, green onions, and next 9 ingredients in a bowl. Cover and refrigerate 1 hour.

2. Divide crab mixture into 8 equal portions, shaping each into a ½-inch-thick patty. Heat 2 teaspoons oil in a large nonstick skillet over medium heat. Add 4 patties, and cook 3 minutes. Carefully turn patties over; cook 3 minutes or until golden. Repeat procedure with 2 teaspoons oil and remaining patties.

3. To prepare relish, combine mango and remaining 6 ingredients in a bowl. Serve with crab cakes. Yield: 4 servings (serving size: 2 crab cakes and ½ cup relish).

WINE NOTE: With the sweet fruity mango relish, these crab cakes call for an equally fresh and fruity white wine. A great bet: Thomas Fogarty Gewürztraminer from Monterey, California (the 2000 is about $14).

CALORIES 288 (26% from fat); FAT 8.3g (sat 1.4g, mono 2.9g, poly 2.7g); PROTEIN 22.4g; CARB 30.9g; FIBER 2.3g; CHOL 92mg; IRON 1.8mg; SODIUM 936mg; CALC 130mg

Rice Noodle Salad with Vegetables and Tofu

(pictured on page 203)

Rice noodle salads are found on almost every Vietnamese restaurant menu. The addition of sautéed summer squash, red bell pepper, and tofu gives the dish added texture and flavor. Look for baked tofu in health food stores or in the produce section of large supermarkets.

- 4 ounces rice sticks
- 6 tablespoons rice wine vinegar
- ¼ cup chopped fresh mint
- ¼ cup low-sodium soy sauce
- 3 tablespoons sugar
- 2 tablespoons chopped dry-roasted peanuts
- 2 serrano chiles, halved lengthwise, seeded, and thinly sliced
- 2 garlic cloves, minced
- 2 teaspoons dark sesame oil
- 2 cups yellow squash, halved lengthwise and thinly sliced (about 8 ounces)
- 2 cups thinly sliced red bell pepper rings
- 1¼ cups zucchini, halved lengthwise and thinly sliced (about 6 ounces)
- 3 cups sliced green cabbage
- 2 cups fresh bean sprouts
- ½ cup chopped green onions
- 12 ounces baked tofu, cubed

1. Cook rice sticks according to package directions.

2. Combine vinegar and next 6 ingredients. Combine half of vinegar mixture and rice noodles in a large bowl.

3. Heat oil in a large nonstick skillet over medium-high heat. Add squash, bell pepper, and zucchini; sauté 4 minutes. Add cabbage and remaining 3 ingredients; sauté 3 minutes. Arrange noodle mixture on a platter; top with tofu mixture. Drizzle with remaining vinegar mixture. Yield: 6 servings (serving size: 1⅔ cups).

CALORIES 253 (23% from fat); FAT 6.6g (sat 1.1g, mono 1.9g, poly 2.6g); PROTEIN 11.7g; CARB 37.9g; FIBER 4.9g; CHOL 0mg; IRON 2.9mg; SODIUM 540mg; CALC 252mg

Beef-Barley Pho

Beef and barley soup is a staple American comfort food; *pho*—beef and rice noodle soup—is the Vietnamese equivalent. Barley adds an interesting twist, as well as heartiness, to this anise-flavored soup. Charring the onion and ginger in a dry skillet gives the broth a deep flavor.

    2 cups sliced onion
    4 (⅛-inch) slices unpeeled fresh
       ginger
    5 cups low-salt beef broth
    2 tablespoons sugar
    2 tablespoons fish sauce
    5 star anise
    3 whole cloves
    4 cups water
    ½ cup uncooked pearl barley
   Cooking spray
    3 (4-ounce) beef tenderloin steaks,
       trimmed
    1 cup fresh bean sprouts
    ½ cup vertically sliced onion
    ½ cup chopped green onions
   12 fresh basil leaves
    4 lime wedges
   Chopped seeded serrano chiles
       (optional)

1. Combine 2 cups onion and ginger in a heavy skillet over high heat. Cook 4 minutes or until charred, stirring frequently. Remove from heat. Combine onion mixture, broth, and next 4 ingredients in a large saucepan. Bring to a boil; cover, reduce heat, and simmer 30 minutes. Strain broth mixture through a sieve into a large bowl, reserving liquid; discard solids. Return broth to pan; set aside.
2. Bring water to a boil in a large saucepan. Add barley. Cover, reduce heat, and simmer 35 minutes or until done. Drain.

3. Heat a large nonstick skillet coated with cooking spray over medium-high heat. Add steaks; cook 4 minutes on each side or until desired degree of doneness. Remove from pan; cut steaks diagonally across grain into thin slices.
4. Bring broth to a boil. Spoon ½ cup barley into each of 4 bowls, and ladle ⅔ cup boiling broth over barley in each bowl. Divide beef, bean sprouts, ½ cup onion, green onions, and basil evenly among bowls. Serve with lime wedges and chiles, if desired. Yield: 4 servings.

CALORIES 315 (23% from fat); FAT 8.2g (sat 2.9g, mono 3.2g, poly 0.8g); PROTEIN 28g; CARB 31.2g; FIBER 5.2g; CHOL 54mg; IRON 3.9mg; SODIUM 787mg; CALC 32mg

Grilled Shrimp with Vietnamese Coleslaw

Packaged coleslaw is spruced up with a tangy Asian dressing. If you can't find an English cucumber, which is virtually seedless, seed a regular cucumber and use it instead.

    4 cups packaged coleslaw
    ½ cup English cucumber, halved
       lengthwise and thinly sliced
    ½ cup thinly sliced red bell pepper
    ¼ cup finely chopped onion
    3 tablespoons chopped fresh mint
    3 tablespoons fresh lime juice
   1½ tablespoons sugar
    1 tablespoon fish sauce
    ¾ teaspoon crushed red pepper
    ¼ teaspoon kosher salt
   1½ pounds large shrimp, peeled and
       deveined
   Cooking spray

1. Prepare grill or preheat broiler.
2. Combine first 10 ingredients in a large bowl; toss well.
3. Thread shrimp onto 4 (12-inch) skewers. Place kebabs on a grill rack or broiler pan coated with cooking spray; cook 3 minutes on each side or until shrimp are done. Serve with coleslaw. Yield: 4 servings (serving size: 1 cup coleslaw and 1 kebab).

CALORIES 233 (13% from fat); FAT 3.3g (sat 0.6g, mono 0.5g, poly 1.3g); PROTEIN 36.3g; CARB 13.8g; FIBER 2.5g; CHOL 259mg; IRON 4.7mg; SODIUM 737mg; CALC 131mg

Honey and Coconut-Marinated Cornish Hens

Cornish hens become more tender and flavorful when they soak in a sweet and spicy marinade. The marinade's also used for basting.

    2 (1¼-pound) Cornish hens
    ¼ cup chopped fresh cilantro
    ¼ cup chopped peeled fresh
       lemongrass
    ¼ cup light coconut milk
    3 tablespoons honey
    2 tablespoons fish sauce
    1 tablespoon grated peeled fresh
       ginger
    1 tablespoon Thai chile sauce
    2 garlic cloves
    1 tablespoon honey

1. Remove and discard giblets and necks from hens. Rinse hens with cold water; pat dry. Split hens in half lengthwise. Remove skin; trim excess fat.
2. Place cilantro and next 7 ingredients in a blender; process until smooth. Pour mixture into a large zip-top plastic bag. Add hen halves; seal and marinate in refrigerator 12 hours or overnight.
3. Preheat oven to 400°.
4. Remove hen halves from bag, reserving marinade. Place reserved marinade in a small saucepan. Bring to a boil; cook 1 minute, stirring frequently. Remove from heat.
5. Place hen halves, meaty sides up, on a broiler pan. Insert a meat thermometer into meaty part of a thigh, making sure not to touch bone. Bake at 400° for 30 minutes, basting frequently with reserved marinade. Brush 1 tablespoon honey over hens, and bake an additional 20 minutes or until thermometer registers 180°. Yield: 4 servings (serving size: 1 hen half).

WINE NOTE: This sweet-spicy rendition of Cornish hens calls for a clean, dry white wine with plenty of body. Try a light, crisp French Mâcon Farges (all Mâcons are 100 percent Chardonnay). Henri Perrusset makes a terrific one (the 1999 is about $15).

CALORIES 253 (20% from fat); FAT 5.6g (sat 1.7g, mono 1.6g, poly 1.2g); PROTEIN 29.8g; CARB 21g; FIBER 0.1g; CHOL 132mg; IRON 1.5mg; SODIUM 788mg; CALC 24mg

Spice-Rubbed Pork Tenderloin with Mango Sambal

Sambal is a generic name for any paste-like condiment made with chiles. Authentic versions tend to be extremely hot. This Malaysian-influenced mango sambal works well with the Southern-style barbecue spice rub. The vinegar gives the condiment a flavor that's reminiscent of a North Carolina mop sauce.

PORK:
- 1 teaspoon brown sugar
- ¾ teaspoon chili powder
- ¾ teaspoon paprika
- ½ teaspoon salt
- ½ teaspoon onion powder
- ½ teaspoon ground cumin
- ¼ teaspoon garlic powder
- ¼ teaspoon dried thyme
- 1 (1-pound) pork tenderloin, trimmed
- Cooking spray

SAMBAL:
- 1 cup chopped peeled mango (about 1 mango)
- 2 teaspoons rice wine vinegar
- 2 teaspoons fish sauce
- 1½ teaspoons sugar
- 1 serrano chile, seeded and finely chopped

1. Preheat oven to 425°.

2. To prepare pork, combine first 8 ingredients in a small bowl. Rub pork tenderloin with spice mixture; refrigerate 20 minutes.

3. Place pork on a broiler pan coated with cooking spray. Bake at 425° for 20 minutes or until meat thermometer registers 160°. Let stand 5 minutes; cut into ¼-inch-thick slices.

4. To prepare sambal, combine mango and remaining 4 ingredients. Serve sambal with pork. Yield: 4 servings (serving size: 3 ounces pork and ¼ cup sambal).

CALORIES 208 (28% from fat); FAT 6.5g (sat 2.2g, mono 2.8g, poly 0.8g); PROTEIN 24g; CARB 13.2g; FIBER 1.6g; CHOL 75mg; IRON 2.1mg; SODIUM 573mg; CALC 21mg

Vietnamese Clam Chowder

This chowder takes its cue from New England with its use of potatoes, celery, and onion—but the similarities end there. Flavored with lemongrass, ginger, and fish sauce, this brothy version with coconut milk has an authentically assertive flavor.

- 1 fresh lemongrass stalk, peeled
- 1 teaspoon butter
- 2 cups peeled baking potato, cut into ½-inch pieces
- 1 cup chopped onion
- ½ cup chopped celery
- 1 tablespoon grated peeled fresh ginger
- 2 garlic cloves, minced
- 1½ tablespoons fish sauce
- 1 tablespoon sugar
- 2 (8-ounce) bottles clam juice
- ¾ cup chopped zucchini
- 2 (6½-ounce) cans chopped clams, drained
- 2 serrano chiles, thinly sliced
- ⅔ cup light coconut milk
- ¼ cup fresh lime juice
- 2 tablespoons chopped fresh cilantro

1. Cut lemongrass stalk in half crosswise; coarsely crush using a meat mallet or rolling pin.

2. Melt butter in a large saucepan over medium heat. Add potato, onion, celery, ginger, and garlic; cook 5 minutes or until celery and onion are tender, stirring occasionally. Stir in lemongrass, fish sauce, sugar, and clam juice. Bring to a boil; reduce heat, and simmer, uncovered, 10 minutes or until potato is tender.

3. Stir in zucchini, clams, and chiles. Bring to a boil; cook 2 minutes. Stir in coconut milk, lime juice, and cilantro; remove from heat. Remove lemongrass; discard. Yield: 4 servings (serving size: about 1⅓ cups).

CALORIES 201 (17% from fat); FAT 3.9g (sat 2.1g, mono 0.5g, poly 0.3g); PROTEIN 12.5g; CARB 27g; FIBER 2.6g; CHOL 30mg; IRON 11.3mg; SODIUM 817mg; CALC 75mg

Curried Beef Stew

A green onion paste is sautéed to release its flavor in this Singapore-inspired dish. Serve with basmati rice.

PASTE:
- ½ cup chopped green onions
- 3 tablespoons fresh orange juice
- 2 tablespoons minced peeled fresh ginger
- 1 tablespoon Thai chile sauce
- 4 garlic cloves, peeled
- 2 serrano chiles, seeded and finely chopped

STEW:
- Cooking spray
- 1 pound beef stew meat
- 1 teaspoon vegetable oil
- 1 tablespoon curry powder
- 1 (3-inch) cinnamon stick
- 1 bay leaf
- 3 tablespoons low-sodium soy sauce
- 1 (14¼-ounce) can low-salt beef broth
- 2 cups (1-inch) cubed peeled sweet potato
- 1½ cups (1-inch-thick) sliced carrot
- 1 cup (1-inch-thick) sliced celery
- 1 (8-ounce) package presliced mushrooms
- ½ cup light coconut milk

1. To prepare paste, combine first 6 ingredients in a blender; process until smooth. Spoon into a bowl.

2. To prepare stew, heat a Dutch oven coated with cooking spray over medium-high heat. Add beef; cook 5 minutes, browning on all sides. Remove from pan. **3.** Reduce heat to low; add oil to pan. Add paste; cook 2 minutes, stirring frequently. Add curry, cinnamon, and bay leaf; cook 30 seconds, stirring constantly. Stir in beef, soy sauce, and broth. Increase heat to medium-high. Bring to a boil; cover, reduce heat, and simmer 1 hour. **4.** Add sweet potato, carrot, celery, and mushrooms. Bring to a boil; cover, reduce heat, and simmer 50 minutes or until beef and vegetables are tender. Remove from heat; stir in coconut milk. Discard cinnamon stick and bay leaf. Yield: 4 servings (serving size: 1½ cups).

WINE NOTE: The classic meaty flavors of the beef juxtaposed with the piquant complex seasonings call for a fairly powerful red wine with a full body and a bit of spiciness. One that fits the bill: Bradford Mountain "Grist Vineyard" Zinfandel from the Dry Creek Valley of California. The 1999 ($30) would be magnificent with this stew.

CALORIES 358 (30% from fat); FAT 11.8g (sat 4.4g, mono 4.4g, poly 1g); PROTEIN 28.5g; CARB 34.6g; FIBER 6.1g; CHOL 71mg; IRON 5mg; SODIUM 556mg; CALC 74mg

Catfish Po'boy with Hoisin-Peanut Sauce

A hoisin-peanut sauce stands in for the traditional rémoulade in this take on the New Orleans classic.

SAUCE:

1 teaspoon dark sesame oil
2 tablespoons chopped onion
1 teaspoon minced peeled fresh ginger
3 tablespoons hoisin sauce
1 tablespoon creamy peanut butter
1 tablespoon fresh lime juice
¼ teaspoon sugar

CATFISH:

¼ cup Thai chile sauce
2 garlic cloves, minced
4 (6-ounce) farm-raised catfish fillets
Cooking spray

REMAINING INGREDIENTS:

4 (2½-ounce) hoagie rolls, split and lightly toasted
2 cups shredded napa (Chinese) cabbage

1. To prepare sauce, heat oil in a small saucepan over medium heat. Add onion and ginger; cook 2 minutes, stirring frequently. Reduce heat to low. Add hoisin sauce, peanut butter, lime juice, and sugar; cook 3 minutes, stirring frequently. Remove from heat; set aside. **2.** Prepare grill or preheat broiler. **3.** To prepare catfish, combine chile sauce and garlic in a large zip-top plastic bag. Add catfish; seal and marinate in refrigerator 30 minutes, turning bag occasionally. **4.** Remove fish from bag; discard marinade. Place fish on a grill rack or broiler pan coated with cooking spray. Cook 10 minutes or until fish flakes easily when tested with a fork. **5.** Spread 1 tablespoon sauce over bottom half of each hoagie roll; top each with ½ cup cabbage, 1 catfish fillet, and top half of roll. Serve immediately. Yield: 4 servings.

CALORIES 401 (27% from fat); FAT 12.1g (sat 4.1g, mono 3.5g, poly 3.2g); PROTEIN 30.1g; CARB 43.7g; FIBER 3.2g; CHOL 74mg; IRON 1.8mg; SODIUM 722mg; CALC 121mg

---

Here, There, and Everywhere

The best proof that Asian cuisines have become mainstream is as close as your own grocery store. You'll find a large selection of Asian ingredients—fish sauce, rice wine vinegar, Thai chile sauce, coconut milk, hoisin sauce—in the ethnic foods aisle. If your supermarket doesn't carry the items you need, Asian markets will. Or you can order ingredients from www.ethnicgrocer.com.

search myclar2003.com for all our tips

...And Ready In Just About 20 Minutes

Summer means fresh ingredients, and they're the pick of this month's crop of recipes.

Pasta with Herbed Goat Cheese and Cherry Tomatoes

The herbed goat cheese melts to form a creamy sauce.

12 ounces uncooked angel hair pasta
6 tablespoons (3 ounces) garlic and herb-flavored goat cheese
⅓ cup chopped fresh basil
¼ teaspoon salt
¼ teaspoon black pepper
1 tablespoon olive oil
1½ teaspoons bottled minced garlic
2 cups grape or cherry tomatoes, halved (about 1 pint)
⅔ cup fat-free, less-sodium chicken broth

1. Cook pasta according to package directions, omitting salt and fat. Drain; place in a large bowl, and keep warm. **2.** While pasta cooks, heat oil in a large nonstick skillet over medium-high heat. Add garlic; sauté 30 seconds. Add tomatoes; cook 2 minutes, stirring frequently. Add broth; cook 1 minute. Remove from heat. Add goat cheese, basil, salt, and pepper to pasta; stir until well blended. Add tomato mixture to pasta mixture; toss gently to combine. Yield: 4 servings (serving size: about 1½ cups).

CALORIES 372 (28% from fat); FAT 11.5g (sat 4.9g, mono 4g, poly 0.6g); PROTEIN 16.5g; CARB 51.8g; FIBER 2.5g; CHOL 17mg; IRON 3.1mg; SODIUM 627mg; CALC 75mg

Seared Tuna Sandwiches with Balsamic Onions

Balsamic vinegar gives the onions a rich, sweet flavor.

  2 teaspoons butter
  2 cups vertically sliced onion
1½ tablespoons balsamic vinegar
  ¼ teaspoon dried thyme
  1 tablespoon all-purpose flour
  ½ teaspoon salt
  ¼ teaspoon garlic powder
  ¼ teaspoon black pepper
  4 (6-ounce) tuna steaks (about
      ½ inch thick)
Cooking spray
  4 teaspoons Dijon mustard
  4 (2-ounce) whole wheat hamburger
      buns
  4 curly leaf lettuce leaves
  4 (¼-inch-thick) slices tomato

1. Melt butter in a medium skillet over medium-high heat. Add onion; sauté 5 minutes. Stir in vinegar and thyme; cover and cook 5 minutes, stirring occasionally.
2. While onion cooks, combine flour, salt, garlic powder, and pepper in a shallow dish. Dredge fish in flour mixture. Heat a large nonstick skillet coated with cooking spray over medium-high heat. Add fish; cook 3 minutes on each side or until desired degree of doneness.
3. Spread 1 teaspoon mustard over top half of each bun. Layer 1 lettuce leaf, 1 fish steak, 1 tomato slice, and ¼ cup onion mixture on bottom half of each bun. Top with top halves of buns. Yield: 4 servings (serving size: 1 sandwich).

CALORIES 402 (17% from fat); FAT 7.8g (sat 2.5g, mono 2.8g, poly 1.4g); PROTEIN 46.2g; CARB 35.5g; FIBER 3.8g; CHOL 82mg; IRON 4mg; SODIUM 701mg; CALC 158mg

Think Fast

To quickly caramelize the sliced onions for Seared Tuna Sandwiches with Balsamic Onions (recipe above), cover the pan so the onions "sweat," or release moisture. They cook in their own juice, don't need as much fat, and require less stirring. This method gives you hands-off time to prep the rest of the meal.

Spiced Pepper-Crusted Filet Mignon with Asparagus

Brandy and spices make a flavorful paste to rub on the beef.

  1 teaspoon bottled minced garlic
  ½ teaspoon olive oil
  ½ teaspoon salt, divided
12 ounces fresh asparagus, trimmed
  1 tablespoon cracked black pepper
  2 teaspoons brandy
  ½ teaspoon garlic powder
  4 (4-ounce) beef tenderloin steaks
      (about 1 inch thick)
Cooking spray

1. Preheat broiler.
2. Combine minced garlic, oil, ¼ teaspoon salt, and asparagus in a large bowl, tossing gently to coat.
3. Combine ¼ teaspoon salt, pepper, brandy, and garlic powder; rub evenly over steaks. Place steaks on a broiler pan coated with cooking spray; broil 6 minutes. Turn steaks over; add asparagus to pan. Broil 5 minutes or until desired degree of doneness. Yield: 4 servings (serving size: 1 steak and 3 ounces asparagus).

CALORIES 269 (39% from fat); FAT 11.6g (sat 4.1g, mono 4.5g, poly 0.5g); PROTEIN 34.9g; CARB 4.7g; FIBER 1.2g; CHOL 95mg; IRON 5.1mg; SODIUM 367mg; CALC 36mg

Herbed Pork with Sautéed Wild Mushrooms

If you don't have steak seasoning, use 1 teaspoon cracked black pepper. Serve over brown rice, or with instant polenta and Parmesan cheese.

  1 teaspoon vegetable oil
Cooking spray
  3 cups sliced shiitake mushroom caps
1½ teaspoons steak seasoning
      (such as McCormick Grill Mates)
  1 teaspoon dried thyme
  4 (4-ounce) boneless center-cut loin
      pork chops (about ¾ inch thick)
  1 cup fat-free, less-sodium chicken
      broth
  2 teaspoons cornstarch

1. Heat oil in a large nonstick skillet coated with cooking spray over medium-high heat. Add mushrooms; sauté 3 minutes or until tender. Remove mushrooms from pan.
2. Rub steak seasoning and thyme over pork. Add pork to pan; cook 3 minutes on each side or until done. Combine broth and cornstarch, stirring with a whisk. Add mushrooms and broth mixture to pan. Bring to a boil; cook 1 minute or until slightly thickened. Yield: 4 servings (serving size: 1 pork chop and about ⅓ cup sauce).

CALORIES 181 (27% from fat); FAT 5.5g (sat 1.6g, mono 2.1g, poly 1.2g); PROTEIN 27.4g; CARB 4.2g; FIBER 0.9g; CHOL 78mg; IRON 1.8mg; SODIUM 415mg; CALC 31mg

Orange Mandarin Chicken

Serve with Asian noodles—such as soba, somen, or udon—and steamed snow peas.

  2 teaspoons dark sesame oil
  4 (4-ounce) skinless, boneless
      chicken breast halves
  ½ teaspoon salt
  ¼ teaspoon black pepper
  1 (11-ounce) can mandarin oranges
      in light syrup, undrained
  ½ cup chopped green onions
  1 tablespoon finely chopped seeded
      jalapeño pepper
  1 teaspoon bottled minced garlic
  ½ cup fat-free, less-sodium chicken
      broth
  1 tablespoon low-sodium soy
      sauce
  2 teaspoons cornstarch

1. Heat oil in a large nonstick skillet over medium-high heat. Sprinkle chicken with salt and pepper. Add chicken to pan; cook 4 minutes on each side or until browned.
2. While chicken cooks, drain oranges in a colander over a bowl, reserving 2 tablespoons liquid. Add oranges, 2 tablespoons liquid, onions, jalapeño, and garlic to pan. Reduce heat; simmer 2 minutes. Combine broth, soy sauce, and cornstarch, and add to pan. Bring to a boil; cook 1 minute or until slightly

thickened. Yield: 4 servings (serving size: 1 chicken breast half and 6 tablespoons sauce).

CALORIES 212 (16% from fat); FAT 3.8g (sat 0.7g, mono 1.3g, poly 1.3g); PROTEIN 27.2g; CARB 15.2g; FIBER 0.7g; CHOL 66mg; IRON 1.9mg; SODIUM 562mg; CALC 27mg

Tequila Shrimp

The fresh flavors of cilantro and lime in the rice balance the shrimp's spicy seasonings.

1 (3½-ounce) bag boil-in-bag long-grain rice
½ teaspoon salt, divided
¼ teaspoon ground red pepper
¼ teaspoon chili powder
⅛ teaspoon ground cumin
⅛ teaspoon black pepper
1½ pounds peeled and deveined large shrimp
2 tablespoons vegetable oil, divided
2 teaspoons bottled minced garlic
¼ cup tequila
2 tablespoons minced fresh cilantro, divided
1 tablespoon fresh lime juice
Lime wedges (optional)

1. Cook rice according to package directions, omitting salt and fat.
2. While rice cooks, combine ¼ teaspoon salt and next 4 ingredients in a large zip-top plastic bag; add shrimp. Seal and shake to coat.
3. Heat 1 tablespoon oil in a large skillet over medium-high heat. Add shrimp; cook 3 minutes, turning once. Add garlic; sauté 1 minute. Add tequila and 1 tablespoon cilantro; cook 1 minute.
4. Combine ¼ teaspoon salt, 1 tablespoon oil, 1 tablespoon cilantro, and lime juice; pour over rice, tossing to coat. Serve shrimp over rice mixture. Serve with lime wedges, if desired. Yield: 4 servings (serving size: 4 ounces shrimp and ½ cup rice mixture).

CALORIES 419 (22% from fat); FAT 10.1g (sat 1.6g, mono 2.1g, poly 5.2g); PROTEIN 37.5g; CARB 31.5g; FIBER 0.6g; CHOL 259mg; IRON 4.4mg; SODIUM 548mg; CALC 104mg

Chicken with Summer Squash and Lemon-Chive Sauce

While the chicken cooks, mix the sauce ingredients. Tent cooked chicken with foil to keep it warm. Serve with quinoa or egg noodles to complete the meal.

2 teaspoons vegetable oil
4 (4-ounce) skinless, boneless chicken breast halves
¼ teaspoon salt
¼ teaspoon black pepper
2 cups ½-inch cubed yellow squash
1½ cups ½-inch cubed zucchini
1 cup fat-free, less-sodium chicken broth
1 tablespoon chopped fresh chives
½ teaspoon grated lemon rind
1 tablespoon fresh lemon juice
2 teaspoons cornstarch
2 teaspoons honey mustard

1. Heat oil in a large nonstick skillet over medium-high heat. Sprinkle chicken with salt and pepper; add chicken to pan. Cook 4 minutes on each side; remove from pan. Keep warm.
2. Reduce heat to medium. Add squash and zucchini to pan, and cook 2 minutes, stirring frequently. Return chicken to pan.
3. Combine broth and remaining 5 ingredients in a small bowl, stirring with a whisk. Add broth mixture to pan. Cover, reduce heat to medium-low, and cook 3 minutes. Yield: 4 servings (serving size: 1 chicken breast half and ½ cup squash mixture).

CALORIES 181 (20% from fat); FAT 4g (sat 0.8g, mono 0.9g, poly 1.8g); PROTEIN 28.1g; CARB 6.6g; FIBER 2.3g; CHOL 66mg; IRON 1.4mg; SODIUM 395mg; CALC 38mg

All Fired Up

In the land of enchantment, folks seriously enjoy their chiles. So can you—without getting burned.

In America you find all kinds of chile peppers. Texans are fond of their bullet-shaped jalapeños and broad-shouldered poblanos. Caribbean cooks in Miami adore the superhot habanero. In Louisiana, cayenne and Tabasco peppers are abundant. And in California, the market stalls overflow with pasillas, Fresnos, and Caribes. But in New Mexico, there is only one pepper—the New Mexico chile. When they pick it green, they call it the long green chile. When it's ripe, it becomes the long red chile. Here is a sampling of recipes featuring this one-of-a-kind New Mexican pepper.

Roasted Anaheim Chiles

Roasted chiles are ideal for making ahead and are easy to store. They'll keep for up to two weeks in the refrigerator and three months in the freezer. Don't worry if you can't get every shred of peel off the peppers.

5 Anaheim chiles (about 10 ounces)

1. Preheat broiler.
2. Cut chiles in half lengthwise; discard seeds and membranes. Place chile halves, skin sides up, on a foil-lined baking sheet; flatten with hand. Broil 15 minutes or until blackened.
3. Place in a zip-top plastic bag; seal. Let stand 15 minutes. Peel and chop. Cover and refrigerate. Yield: 1 cup (serving size: ¼ cup).

CALORIES 19 (5% from fat); FAT 0.1g (sat 0g, mono 0g, poly 0.1g); PROTEIN 0.6g; CARB 4.6g; FIBER 1.3g; CHOL 0mg; IRON 0.3mg; SODIUM 1mg; CALC 6mg

Green Chile Sauce

This sauce combines tangy tomatillos with roasted chiles. If you're unable to get fresh tomatillos, omit the ½ teaspoon salt and use 1 (11-ounce) can tomatillos, rinsed and drained, plus 2 tablespoons lime juice.

  7 large tomatillos (about 12 ounces)
  1 cup fat-free, less-sodium chicken broth
  ⅓ cup chopped fresh cilantro
  ⅓ cup chopped Roasted Anaheim Chiles (recipe on page 193)
  ¼ cup chopped onion
  ½ teaspoon salt
  ¼ teaspoon black pepper
  2 garlic cloves, chopped

1. Discard husks and stems of tomatillos. Cook tomatillos in boiling water 10 minutes or until tender. Drain.
2. Place tomatillos, broth, and remaining ingredients in a blender; process until mixture is smooth. Yield: 3 cups (serving size: ¼ cup).

CALORIES 18 (20% from fat); FAT 0.4g (sat 0.1g, mono 0.1g, poly 0.2g); PROTEIN 0.9g; CARB 3.2g; FIBER 1.1g; CHOL 0mg; IRON 0.3mg; SODIUM 138mg; CALC 6mg

New Mexican Red Chile Sauce

New Mexico chile powder gives this sauce an authentic spicy, slightly bitter flavor. You can get a similar flavor by substituting 7 tablespoons top-quality sweet paprika mixed with 1 tablespoon ground red pepper. Don't use commercial chili powder in its place, though. (See the box titled New Mexican Chile Powder on page 195.) Serve with meat, vegetables, or as enchilada sauce.

  ½ teaspoon vegetable oil
  ½ cup finely chopped onion
  ½ cup New Mexico chile powder
  1 garlic clove, minced
  1 cup canned crushed tomatoes
  3 tablespoons honey
  1 teaspoon ground cumin
  ¼ teaspoon black pepper
  1 (14½-ounce) can vegetable broth

1. Heat oil in a large saucepan over medium-high heat. Add onion; sauté 4 minutes. Add chile powder and garlic; sauté 1 minute. Stir in tomatoes and remaining ingredients. Bring to a boil; reduce heat, and simmer 10 minutes. Yield: 3 cups (serving size: ¼ cup).

CALORIES 43 (27% from fat); FAT 1.3g (sat 0.2g, mono 0.3g, poly 0.4g); PROTEIN 1.2g; CARB 8.9g; FIBER 2.1g; CHOL 0mg; IRON 0.9mg; SODIUM 208mg; CALC 20mg

Huevos Rancheros

Have your eggs the way you like them best: with red sauce, green sauce, or both. You can use white, yellow, or blue corn tortillas.

  4 (6-inch) corn tortillas
    Cooking spray
  1 cup chopped onion
  ½ cup chopped green bell pepper
  3 garlic cloves, minced
  ¼ cup canned chopped green chiles
  2 teaspoons New Mexico chile powder
  1 teaspoon ground cumin
  1 teaspoon dried oregano
  ½ teaspoon hot sauce
  1 (14.5-ounce) can diced tomatoes, undrained
  4 large eggs
  ¼ cup New Mexican Red Chile Sauce (recipe at left) or Green Chile Sauce (recipe at left)
  ¼ cup (1 ounce) shredded Monterey Jack cheese
  2 teaspoons chopped fresh cilantro

1. Preheat oven to 350°.
2. Coat tortillas with cooking spray; place on a baking sheet. Bake at 350° for 12 minutes or until crisp.
3. Heat a large nonstick skillet coated with cooking spray over medium-high heat. Add onion, bell pepper, and garlic; sauté 3 minutes. Add green chiles and next 5 ingredients. Bring to a boil; cook 3 minutes or until thick.
4. Heat a large nonstick skillet coated with cooking spray over medium-low heat. Add eggs to pan; cook 3 minutes or until done.
5. Place 1 tortilla on each of 4 plates. Top each tortilla with ½ cup tomato mixture

and 1 egg. Spoon 1 tablespoon New Mexican Red Chile Sauce or Green Chile Sauce over each serving; sprinkle each serving with 1 tablespoon cheese and ½ teaspoon cilantro. Yield: 4 servings.

CALORIES 222 (35% from fat); FAT 8.6g (sat 3.1g, mono 2.8g, poly 1.3g); PROTEIN 11.7g; CARB 26.7g; FIBER 5.5g; CHOL 219mg; IRON 2.5mg; SODIUM 376mg; CALC 174mg

Green Chile and Chicken Enchiladas

Instead of being rolled like most enchiladas, these end up as two layered tortilla stacks, which are then cut in half to serve four. This is a distinctive New Mexican tradition.

  ½ teaspoon vegetable oil
  1 cup chopped onion
  2 garlic cloves, minced
  1 cup shredded cooked chicken breast (about 6 ounces)
  ¼ teaspoon salt
  ¼ teaspoon black pepper
  2 cups Green Chile Sauce (recipe at left)
    Cooking spray
  6 (6-inch) corn tortillas
  ¼ cup (1 ounce) crumbled feta cheese

1. Preheat oven to 350°.
2. Heat oil in a nonstick skillet over medium-high heat. Add onion; sauté 4 minutes or until tender. Add garlic; sauté 1 minute. Combine onion mixture, chicken, salt, and pepper.
3. Spread ¼ cup Green Chile Sauce over bottom of an 11 x 7-inch baking dish coated with cooking spray. Arrange 2 tortillas over sauce; top evenly with half of chicken mixture and ½ cup Green Chile Sauce. Repeat layers, ending with tortillas. Spread remaining sauce over tortillas. Sprinkle with cheese.
4. Bake at 350° for 20 minutes or until thoroughly heated. Cut each tortilla stack in half. Yield: 4 servings (serving size: ½ tortilla stack).

CALORIES 227 (21% from fat); FAT 5.3g (sat 1.8g, mono 1.3g, poly 1.4g); PROTEIN 18.4g; CARB 27.6g; FIBER 4.7g; CHOL 42mg; IRON 1.7mg; SODIUM 543mg; CALC 131mg

New Mexican Chile Powder

Granny Smith-Green Chile Salsa

In New Mexico, apples are often paired with green chiles to create a tart and hot combination. This salsa perks up tacos or grilled pork.

    2   large tomatillos (about 4 ounces)
    1   cup chopped Granny Smith apple
    ½   cup chopped onion
    ½   cup chopped Roasted Anaheim
        Chiles (recipe on page 193)
    3   tablespoons chopped fresh cilantro
    3   tablespoons fresh lime juice
    ¼   teaspoon salt
    ¼   teaspoon white pepper

1. Discard husks and stems of tomatillos. Cook tomatillos in boiling water 10 minutes or until tender. Drain.
2. Place tomatillos in a blender; process until smooth. Combine tomatillo puree, apple, and remaining ingredients. Yield: 2 cups (serving size: ⅓ cup).

CALORIES 42 (11% from fat); FAT 0.5g (sat 0.1g, mono 0.1g, poly 0.3g); PROTEIN 1.6g; CARB 9.5g; FIBER 3.4g; CHOL 0mg; IRON 0.5mg; SODIUM 108mg; CALC 16mg

Christmas Chilaquiles

This Mexican entrée was invented to use up leftovers, earning it the reputation of a working person's dish. This version gets its name because it's served with both red and green chile sauces.

    Cooking spray
    2   cups fresh corn kernels (about
        4 ears)
    2   cups (¼-inch) diced zucchini
    1   cup chopped red bell pepper
    1   cup chopped onion
    ½   cup chopped Roasted Anaheim
        Chiles (recipe on page 193)
    1   teaspoon dried oregano
    3   garlic cloves, minced
    2   ounces baked tortilla chips
        (about 2 cups)
    1   cup (4 ounces) shredded part-skim
        Oaxaca cheese or Monterey Jack
        cheese
    2   cups Green Chile Sauce (recipe on
        page 194)
    2   cups New Mexican Red Chile
        Sauce (recipe on page 194)

1. Preheat oven to 350°.
2. Heat a large nonstick skillet coated with cooking spray over medium-high heat. Add corn, zucchini, bell pepper, and onion; sauté 6 minutes or until browned. Add chopped chiles, oregano, and garlic; sauté 2 minutes.
3. Arrange half of tortilla chips in a single layer in bottom of an 11 x 7-inch baking dish coated with cooking spray. Spread half of corn mixture evenly over tortilla chips. Top with ½ cup cheese. Repeat layers.
4. Bake at 350° for 10 minutes. Top each serving with ¼ cup Green Chile Sauce and ¼ cup New Mexican Red Chile Sauce. Yield: 8 servings.

CALORIES 195 (30% from fat); FAT 6.5g (sat 2.9g, mono 1.6g, poly 1g); PROTEIN 8.4g; CARB 31.1g; FIBER 6.9g; CHOL 15mg; IRON 1.9mg; SODIUM 411mg; CALC 139mg

Posole

This Mexican soup's signature ingredients are pork and hominy. Look for hominy—corn from which the hull and germ have been removed—near the canned corn or in the Mexican food section of your supermarket.

    1   (1½-pound) pork shoulder steak or
        Boston Butt pork roast, trimmed
    1   cup chopped onion
    3   garlic cloves, minced
    ⅔   cup chopped Roasted Anaheim
        Chiles (recipe on page 193)
    1   tablespoon New Mexico chile
        powder
    1   teaspoon ground coriander seeds
    1   teaspoon ground cumin
    1   teaspoon dried oregano
    ½   teaspoon salt
    1   (29-ounce) can white hominy,
        drained
    1   (14-ounce) can fat-free,
        less-sodium chicken broth
    1   (14¼-ounce) can low-salt beef
        broth
    ¾   cup crushed baked tortilla chips
    6   tablespoons thinly sliced radishes
    6   tablespoons finely chopped onion
    ¼   cup chopped fresh cilantro
    6   lime wedges

1. Heat a Dutch oven over medium-high heat. Add pork; cook 2 minutes on each side or until browned. Add onion and garlic; sauté 2 minutes. Stir in chiles and next 8 ingredients. Bring to a boil; cover, reduce heat, and simmer 1½ hours or until pork is tender.
2. Remove pork from pan; remove meat from bone. Chop pork; return pork to pan. Serve with chips and remaining ingredients. Yield: 6 servings (serving size: 1⅓ cups soup, 2 tablespoons crushed chips, 1 tablespoon radishes, 1 tablespoon finely chopped onion, 2 teaspoons cilantro, and 1 lime wedge).

CALORIES 263 (29% from fat); FAT 8.5g (sat 2.6g, mono 3.4g, poly 1.4g); PROTEIN 23.3g; CARB 23.2g; FIBER 6.1g; CHOL 61mg; IRON 2.6mg; SODIUM 641mg; CALC 60mg

Santa Fe Red Chile Enchiladas

This classic presentation features chile sauce, tortillas, and shredded pork layered and baked with cheese.

Cooking spray
- 8 ounces boneless center-cut loin pork chops (about ¼ inch thick)
- ½ teaspoon vegetable oil
- 1 cup chopped onion
- 3 garlic cloves, minced
- 1 teaspoon dried oregano
- ¼ teaspoon salt
- ⅛ teaspoon black pepper
- 1¾ cups New Mexican Red Chile Sauce (recipe on page 194)
- 6 (6-inch) corn tortillas
- ¼ cup (1 ounce) shredded reduced-fat sharp cheddar cheese

1. Preheat oven to 350°.
2. Heat a large nonstick skillet coated with cooking spray over medium-high heat. Add pork; cook 1½ minutes on each side or until done. Remove pork; shred with 2 forks.
3. Add oil to pan; heat over medium-high heat. Add onion; sauté 4 minutes or until tender. Add garlic; sauté 1 minute. Remove from heat; stir in shredded pork, oregano, salt, and pepper.
4. Spread ¼ cup New Mexican Red Chile Sauce over bottom of an 11 x 7-inch baking dish coated with cooking spray. Arrange 2 tortillas over sauce; top evenly with half of pork mixture and ½ cup sauce. Repeat layers, ending with tortillas. Spread remaining sauce over tortillas. Sprinkle with cheese.
5. Bake at 350° for 20 minutes or until thoroughly heated. Cut each tortilla stack in half. Yield: 4 servings (serving size: ½ tortilla stack).

CALORIES 294 (28% from fat); FAT 9.1g (sat 2.8g, mono 2.9g, poly 1.7g); PROTEIN 19.7g; CARB 37.6g; FIBER 6.4g; CHOL 38mg; IRON 2.7mg; SODIUM 605mg; CALC 195mg

Family Matters

From one-day gatherings to weekend jubilees, reunions bring families together to celebrate life, love, and fabulous food.

You see them at train stations and airports all summer, decked out in their brightly colored t-shirts emblazoned with family names. A scan of faces reveals resemblance; these are among thousands of Americans who celebrate kinship at family reunions. Family reunions are opportunities for folks to gather around a table and celebrate bonds that are theirs alone. Try some of this traditional reunion fare at your next family get-together.

Buffet Menu
serves 8

Serve this tangy chicken with veggies and soft polenta for a casual summer meal.

Chicken Thighs with Thyme and Lemon

Grilled vegetables*

Polenta

*Toss 3 quartered onions and 3 quartered bell peppers with 2 teaspoons olive oil. Grill 12 minutes. Add 2 pounds asparagus; grill 5 minutes.

search myclar2003.com for all our menus

Chicken Thighs with Thyme and Lemon

For a healthier alternative to traditional fried chicken, try this simple grilled dish.

- 2½ tablespoons honey
- ½ teaspoon grated lemon rind
- 1½ cups fresh lemon juice (about 6 lemons)
- ¼ cup chopped fresh or 1 tablespoon dried thyme
- 1 tablespoon olive oil
- 16 skinless, boneless chicken thighs (about 3 pounds)
- ½ teaspoon salt
- ¼ teaspoon black pepper
Cooking spray

1. Place first 5 ingredients in a large zip-top plastic bag. Add chicken; seal bag. Chill 2 hours, turning occasionally.
2. Prepare grill or preheat broiler.
3. Remove chicken from bag; discard marinade. Sprinkle chicken with salt and pepper. Place chicken on grill rack or broiler pan coated with cooking spray; cook 5 minutes on each side or until done. Yield: 8 servings (serving size: 2 thighs).

CALORIES 212 (30% from fat); FAT 7.1g (sat 1.6g, mono 2.9g, poly 1.5g); PROTEIN 27.4g; CARB 9.8g; FIBER 0.4g; CHOL 115mg; IRON 1.7mg; SODIUM 266mg; CALC 23mg

Roasted Sweet Onion Dip

Serve this dip with pita chips or carrot sticks. Making the recipe a day ahead allows the flavors to meld.

- 2 large Vidalia or other sweet onions, peeled and quartered
- 1 tablespoon olive oil
- 1 teaspoon salt, divided
- 1 whole garlic head
- ⅓ cup low-fat sour cream
- ¼ cup chopped fresh parsley
- 1 tablespoon fresh lemon juice

1. Preheat oven to 425°.
2. Place onion in a large bowl; drizzle with oil. Sprinkle with ½ teaspoon salt; toss to coat. Remove white papery skin from garlic head (do not peel or separate

cloves). Wrap in foil. Place onion and garlic on a baking sheet. Bake at 425° for 1 hour; cool 10 minutes. Chop onion. Separate garlic cloves; squeeze to extract pulp. Discard skins.

3. Combine onion, garlic, ½ teaspoon salt, sour cream, parsley, and juice in a large bowl. Cover and chill 1 hour. Yield: 8 servings (serving size: about ¼ cup).

CALORIES 66 (34% from fat); FAT 2.5g (sat 0.8g, mono 1.3g, poly 0.2g); PROTEIN 1.7g; CARB 10.3g; FIBER 1.5g; CHOL 3.3mg; IRON 0.4mg; SODIUM 308mg; CALC 42mg

Baked Ham with Guava Glaze

What would a reunion be without a ham? This one uses guava jelly, found in the ethnic or jelly section of your market, to create a beautiful brown crust on the ham. You can substitute passion-fruit jelly or orange marmalade. Peach-Apricot Salsa (recipe at right) makes a great accompaniment.

    1   (5-pound) bone-in, less-sodium
        ham
    Cooking spray
    2   teaspoons whole cloves (optional)
    ¾   cup guava jelly
    2   tablespoons dark rum
    1   tablespoon peach nectar
    1   tablespoon Dijon mustard

1. Preheat oven to 350°.
2. Trim fat and rind from ham. Score ham in a diamond pattern. Place ham on a broiler pan coated with cooking spray. Bake at 350° for 1 hour.
3. Stud ham with cloves, if desired. Combine jelly, rum, nectar, and mustard. Brush ham with jelly mixture. Bake an additional 30 minutes or until meat thermometer registers 140°, basting once. Place ham on a platter; cover with foil. Let stand 10 minutes before slicing. Yield: 20 servings (serving size: about 3 ounces ham).

CALORIES 166 (27% from fat); FAT 4.9g (sat 1.6g, mono 2.3g, poly 0.5g); PROTEIN 18.5g; CARB 10.2g; FIBER 0g; CHOL 47mg; IRON 1.3mg; SODIUM 882mg; CALC 8mg

Orzo Salad

Pasta salad is always a reliable family reunion choice. It's portable and goes with everything from fried chicken to ham. This version can be served chilled or at room temperature.

    3   cups hot cooked orzo (about 1½
        cups uncooked rice-shaped pasta)
    1   cup frozen green peas, thawed
    ¾   cup (3 ounces) crumbled feta
        cheese
    ¼   cup chopped parsley
    3   tablespoons balsamic vinegar
    2   tablespoons extra-virgin olive oil
    ½   teaspoon salt
    ¼   teaspoon black pepper
    1   garlic clove, minced

1. Combine all ingredients in a large bowl, and toss well to coat. Cover bowl, and chill 1 hour. Yield: 8 servings (serving size: ½ cup).

CALORIES 213 (27% from fat); FAT 6.4g (sat 2.2g, mono 3.1g, poly 0.6g); PROTEIN 7.4g; CARB 31.3g; FIBER 2.1g; CHOL 10mg; IRON 2mg; SODIUM 305mg; CALC 71mg

Peach-Apricot Salsa

Pair this salsa with ham, pork, chicken, or fish. Fresh orange juice can stand in for the peach nectar.

    2   cups chopped peeled peaches
    ½   cup finely chopped red onion
    ¼   cup finely chopped dried apricots
    1   tablespoon chopped fresh cilantro
    1   tablespoon fresh lemon juice
    1   tablespoon balsamic vinegar
    1   tablespoon peach nectar
    2   jalapeño peppers, finely chopped
        and seeded

1. Combine all ingredients. Cover and chill 1 hour. Yield: 2¼ cups (serving size: about ¼ cup).

CALORIES 35 (3% from fat); FAT 0.1g (sat 0g, mono 0g, poly 0.1g); PROTEIN 0.6g; CARB 8.9g; FIBER 1.3g; CHOL 0mg; IRON 0.3mg; SODIUM 1mg; CALC 7mg

A Cool Drink

    6   cups cold water
    4   cups fresh orange juice (about 10
        oranges)
    1   cup fresh lime juice (about 6 limes)
    ⅔   cup sugar
    ¼   cup grenadine
    4   teaspoons orange-flower water
        (optional)
    20 lime slices (optional)

1. Combine first 6 ingredients in a pitcher; stir until sugar dissolves. Chill. Serve over ice; garnish with lime slices, if desired. Yield: 10 servings (serving size: 1 cup).

CALORIES 124 (1% from fat); FAT 0.2g (sat 0g, mono 0.1g, poly 0.1g); PROTEIN 0.8g; CARB 31.5g; FIBER 0.3g; CHOL 0mg; IRON 0.2mg; SODIUM 5mg; CALC 14mg

Crustless Smoked Salmon Quiche with Dill

Serve this warm from the oven as an appetizer or for breakfast. Leftovers are good served cold.

    1¼ cups fat-free evaporated milk
    ¼   cup fat-free sour cream
    1   teaspoon Dijon mustard
    4   large egg whites
    1   large egg
    ½   cup (2 ounces) shredded Gouda
        cheese
    ½   cup thinly sliced green onions
    ¼   cup thinly sliced smoked salmon,
        chopped (about 2 ounces)
    2   tablespoons chopped fresh dill
    ½   teaspoon black pepper
    Cooking spray

1. Preheat oven to 350°.
2. Combine first 5 ingredients in a large bowl, stirring with a whisk. Stir in cheese, onions, salmon, dill, and pepper. Pour egg mixture into a 9-inch pie plate coated with cooking spray. Bake at 350° for 35 minutes. Let stand 15 minutes. Yield: 8 servings.

CALORIES 95 (28% from fat); FAT 3g (sat 1.5g, mono 1g, poly 0.2g); PROTEIN 8.8g; CARB 7.5g; FIBER 0.2g; CHOL 37mg; IRON 0.3mg; SODIUM 223mg; CALC 171mg

Sweet Corn Bread with Mixed Berries and Berry Coulis

Corn bread lovers will also love this dessert, which stars sweet corn bread in place of the traditional shortcake. You can use frozen berries in the sauce, but fresh are best for the topping. Garnish with mint sprigs, if desired.

SAUCE:

- ½ cup fresh or thawed frozen raspberries
- ½ cup fresh or thawed frozen blueberries
- ½ cup fresh or thawed frozen blackberries
- 2 tablespoons water
- 2½ teaspoons granulated sugar

TOPPING:

- 1 cup fresh raspberries
- 1 cup fresh blueberries
- 1 cup fresh blackberries
- 2 tablespoons dark brown sugar
- ¼ teaspoon orange-flower water (optional)
- ⅛ teaspoon grated orange rind

CORN BREAD:

- ¾ cup all-purpose flour
- ¾ cup yellow cornmeal
- ⅓ cup granulated sugar
- 2 teaspoons baking powder
- ½ teaspoon salt
- ¾ cup 2% reduced-fat milk
- 2 tablespoons butter, melted
- 1 tablespoon vegetable oil
- 1 large egg
- Cooking spray

REMAINING INGREDIENT:

- ½ cup frozen fat-free whipped topping, thawed

1. To prepare sauce, combine first 5 ingredients in a food processor; process until smooth. Strain berry mixture through a fine sieve over a bowl, reserving liquid; discard solids. Cover and chill.

2. To prepare topping, combine 1 cup each raspberries, blueberries, and blackberries in a large bowl. Add brown sugar, orange-flower water, if desired, and orange rind; toss gently to combine. Cover and chill.

3. Preheat oven to 425°.

4. To prepare corn bread, lightly spoon flour into a dry measuring cup, and level with a knife. Combine flour and next 4 ingredients in a large bowl, stirring with a whisk. Add milk, butter, oil, and egg; stir with a whisk.

5. Pour batter into an 8-inch square baking pan coated with cooking spray. Bake at 425° for 15 minutes or until corn bread is lightly browned and a wooden pick inserted in center comes out clean. Cool in pan 10 minutes on a wire rack; remove from pan. Cool completely on wire rack. Cut corn bread into 9 squares.

6. Spoon about 1 tablespoon sauce onto each of 9 plates, and top with 1 corn bread square. Top each corn bread square with about ¼ cup fresh berry topping. Spoon about 1 tablespoon whipped topping over each serving. Yield: 9 servings.

CALORIES 218 (24% from fat); FAT 5.6g (sat 2.3g, mono 1.5g, poly 1.3g); PROTEIN 4g; CARB 38g; FIBER 2.5g; CHOL 32mg; IRON 1.2mg; SODIUM 286mg; CALC 106mg

Grilled Corn with Lime Butter

Grilling and topping with lime-flavored butter elevates common corn on the cob. You can make the lime butter up to two days ahead and refrigerate. Melt the butter before brushing it over the grilled corn.

- 1½ tablespoons butter, melted
- ¼ teaspoon grated lime rind
- 1½ tablespoons fresh lime juice
- ¼ teaspoon salt
- ¼ teaspoon ground red pepper
- 8 ears shucked corn
- Cooking spray

1. Prepare grill or preheat broiler.

2. Combine first 5 ingredients in a small bowl.

3. Place corn on grill rack or broiler pan coated with cooking spray. Cook 10 minutes, turning frequently. Remove from heat; brush corn with butter mixture. Yield: 8 servings.

CALORIES 103 (28% from fat); FAT 3.2g (sat 1.5g, mono 0.9g, poly 0.6g); PROTEIN 2.6g; CARB 19.6g; FIBER 2.2g; CHOL 6mg; IRON 0.5mg; SODIUM 108mg; CALC 3mg

inspired vegetarian

A Fresh Plate

Plan your Fourth of July festivities around summer's best produce.

The beauty of summer lies in the simple act of creating scrumptious, mouth-watering feasts with perfectly ripe, locally grown produce. And nothing gets your creative juices flowing like a trip to the farm stand.

Simple preparations save time in the kitchen, leaving more time to take advantage of those long, sunny days. In particular, when you plan your Fourth of July spread, think of chilled salads or dishes you can serve at room temperature. All of the following dishes are portable, and we've provided tips for make-ahead components and last-minute assembly of ingredients that will leave you plenty of time to unwind and enjoy the evening's fireworks.

Fourth of July Menu

Rosemary Focaccia

Tomato, Basil, and Fresh Mozzarella Salad

Fresh Cranberry Beans with Lemon and Olive Oil

Millet Salad with Sweet Corn and Avocado

Summer Fruit Salad with Lemon-and-Honey Syrup

Fresh Corn Cake with Raspberries

search myclar2003.com for all our menus

Rosemary Focaccia

Homemade bread makes a meal special. The dough is a bit sticky, but resist the temptation to add more flour.

SPONGE:
- 1 teaspoon honey
- 1 package dry yeast (about 2¼ teaspoons)
- 1¼ cups warm water (100° to 110°)
- 1½ cups all-purpose flour
- 2 tablespoons extra-virgin olive oil

DOUGH:
- 1 cup all-purpose flour
- ½ cup whole wheat flour
- 1 teaspoon salt
- 1 teaspoon chopped fresh rosemary
- Cooking spray

TOPPING:
- 1 tablespoon olive oil
- 1 tablespoon fresh rosemary leaves
- ½ teaspoon kosher salt

1. To prepare sponge, dissolve honey and yeast in warm water in a large bowl; let stand 5 minutes. Lightly spoon 1½ cups all-purpose flour into dry measuring cups; level with a knife. Add 1½ cups all-purpose flour and 2 tablespoons oil to yeast mixture, stirring until well combined. Cover and let rise in a warm place (85°), free from drafts, 1 hour.

2. To prepare dough, lightly spoon 1 cup all-purpose flour and whole wheat flour into dry measuring cups; level with a knife. Stir 1 cup all-purpose flour, whole wheat flour, 1 teaspoon salt, and chopped rosemary into yeast mixture; beat with a mixer at medium speed 6 minutes or until dough is smooth and elastic (dough will be sticky). Cover and let rise in a warm place (85°), free from drafts, 1½ hours or until doubled in size (dough will be wet).

3. Preheat oven to 400°.

4. Scrape dough into a 15 x 10-inch jelly roll pan coated with cooking spray. Gently press dough into a 12 x 8-inch rectangle. Brush dough with 1 tablespoon oil; sprinkle with rosemary leaves and kosher salt. Cover; let rest 30 minutes. Bake at 400° for 25 minutes or until golden brown. Cool 5 minutes. Yield: 10 servings.

CALORIES 175 (23% from fat); FAT 4.5g (sat 0.6g, mono 3.1g, poly 0.5g); PROTEIN 4.4g; CARB 29.2g; FIBER 1.9g; CHOL 0mg; IRON 1.9mg; SODIUM 330mg; CALC 8mg

Tomato, Basil, and Fresh Mozzarella Salad

In this classic salad, infused vegetable broth provides the base for a basil sauce that can stand in for the traditional pesto or vinaigrette.

BASIL SAUCE:
- 1 cup loosely packed fresh basil leaves
- ⅓ cup vegetable broth
- ¼ cup balsamic vinegar
- 1 teaspoon sea salt

SALAD:
- 12 (¼-inch-thick) slices yellow tomato (1½ pounds)
- 12 (¼-inch-thick) slices red tomato (1½ pounds)
- ½ cup (2 ounces) shredded fresh mozzarella cheese
- 1 teaspoon freshly ground black pepper
- ½ cup thinly sliced fresh basil

1. To prepare basil sauce, cook 1 cup basil leaves in boiling water 15 seconds; drain. Plunge basil into ice water; drain and pat dry. Combine basil and broth in a blender; process until smooth. Let mixture stand 2 hours at room temperature. Strain through a fine sieve into a bowl; discard solids. Add vinegar and salt, stirring with a whisk.

2. To prepare salad, arrange yellow and red tomato slices alternately on a large platter. Drizzle with basil sauce; sprinkle with cheese and pepper. Top with sliced basil. Serve immediately. Yield: 8 servings (serving size: 3 tomato slices, about 1 tablespoon basil sauce, and 1 tablespoon cheese).

CALORIES 60 (32% from fat); FAT 2.1g (sat 1.1g, mono 0.6g, poly 0.3g); PROTEIN 3.2g; CARB 8.4g; FIBER 2g; CHOL 6mg; IRON 1.2mg; SODIUM 369mg; CALC 70mg

Fresh Cranberry Beans with Lemon and Olive Oil

Fresh cranberry beans are available at farmers' markets and farm stands. Once shelled, they freeze well. Just blanch them briefly in boiling water; drain, cool, and freeze in zip-top plastic bags. If you can't find them in your area, substitute another fresh shelled bean, such as fava or baby lima beans. Fresh beans need little embellishment beyond olive oil and sea salt.

- 4 cups water
- 2 teaspoons sea salt
- 3 pounds fresh shelled cranberry beans (about 7¾ cups)
- ¼ cup fresh lemon juice
- 2 tablespoons chopped fresh cilantro
- 2 tablespoons extra-virgin olive oil
- ½ teaspoon freshly ground black pepper

1. Bring water and salt to a boil in a stockpot. Add beans. Reduce heat, and simmer 15 minutes or until beans are tender. Drain.

2. Combine lemon juice and remaining 3 ingredients in a small bowl; stir well with a whisk. Combine juice mixture and beans, tossing to coat. Serve at room temperature or chilled. Yield: 8 servings (serving size: about 1 cup).

CALORIES 264 (14% from fat); FAT 4.2g (sat 0.7g, mono 2.6g, poly 0.6g); PROTEIN 16g; CARB 42.4g; FIBER 7.6g; CHOL 0mg; IRON 3.6mg; SODIUM 290mg; CALC 87mg

Fava Beans

Fava beans are most associated with Mediterranean and Middle Eastern cuisines, where they appear in salads, falafel, or soups. The protein-rich beans range in color from yellow to green to tan to nearly black.

Find fava (sometimes called broad beans) at most grocery stores, or grow them yourself—they're easy and adaptable.

Substitute them for cranberry beans in Fresh Cranberry Beans with Lemon and Olive Oil (recipe above).

Millet Salad with Sweet Corn and Avocado

Millet is a popular grain in Asia and Africa. Pan roasting brings out its nutty character. This is a great make-ahead recipe since the millet will continue to absorb flavor as it sits. If you make this salad a day ahead, stir in the avocado just before serving.

```
1    cup uncooked millet, rinsed and
     drained
4    cups water
1    teaspoon sea salt, divided
4    cups fresh corn kernels (about
     8 ears)
⅓    cup chopped fresh cilantro
⅓    cup fresh lime juice
2    tablespoons chopped green
     onions
1    tablespoon extra-virgin olive oil
1½   teaspoons ground cumin
3    to 4 jalapeño peppers, seeded and
     finely chopped
4    cups chopped tomato
1    diced peeled avocado
```

1. Heat a large nonstick skillet over medium heat. Add millet; cook 10 minutes or until fragrant and toasted, stirring frequently. Add water and ½ teaspoon salt; bring to a boil. Cover, reduce heat, and simmer 20 minutes or until water is almost absorbed. Stir in corn kernels; cook, covered, 5 minutes. Remove millet mixture from pan, and cool to room temperature.

2. Combine ½ teaspoon salt, cilantro, and next 5 ingredients. Add cilantro mixture to millet mixture, tossing to combine. Gently stir in tomato and avocado. Cover and chill 30 minutes. Yield: 8 servings (serving size: 1¼ cups).

CALORIES 242 (26% from fat); FAT 6.9g (sat 1.1g, mono 3.6g, poly 1.1g); PROTEIN 7.2g; CARB 45.7g; FIBER 7.1g; CHOL 0mg; IRON 3mg; SODIUM 316mg; CALC 20mg

Summer Fruit Salad with Lemon-and-Honey Syrup

You can also use plums, nectarines, or berries in this recipe. Chop the fruit ahead of time, and store it in a zip-top plastic bag in the refrigerator. Toss the fruit with the syrup one hour before serving.

SYRUP:
```
1    cup water
⅓    cup honey
2    tablespoons fresh lemon juice
½    teaspoon vanilla extract
```

SALAD:
```
3    cups chopped peeled cantaloupe
2    cups seedless grapes
1½   cups sweet cherries, pitted and
     halved (about ½ pound)
1½   cups chopped peeled peaches
     (about 2 peaches)
6    fresh figs, quartered
4    apricots, quartered and pitted
     (about ½ pound)
½    cup chopped fresh mint
```

1. To prepare syrup, combine first 4 ingredients in a small saucepan. Bring to a boil; reduce heat to medium, and cook until mixture is reduced to ¼ cup (about 15 minutes).

2. To prepare salad, place cantaloupe and next 5 ingredients in a large bowl. Pour syrup over fruit; toss gently to coat. Cover and chill 1 hour, stirring occasionally. Toss with mint just before serving. Yield: 8 servings (serving size: 1 cup).

CALORIES 149 (5% from fat); FAT 0.8g (sat 0.1g, mono 0.1g, poly 0.2g); PROTEIN 1.9g; CARB 37.7g; FIBER 3.5g; CHOL 0mg; IRON 0.7mg; SODIUM 8mg; CALC 36mg

Fresh Corn Cake with Raspberries

Pureed fresh corn adds unique sweetness to this dessert. Tossing the fresh raspberries with a small amount of flour prevents them from sinking to the bottom of the cake.

```
     Cooking spray
1    cup fresh corn kernels (about
     2 ears)
6    tablespoons unsalted butter,
     melted and cooled
⅓    cup water
2    teaspoons fresh lemon juice
2    teaspoons vanilla extract
2    large eggs
2    cups all-purpose flour
1¼   cups granulated sugar
2    teaspoons baking powder
1    teaspoon salt
½    teaspoon baking soda
2    cups fresh raspberries
2    tablespoons all-purpose flour
1    tablespoon powdered sugar
     (optional)
```

1. Preheat oven to 325°.

2. Coat a 9-inch round cake pan with cooking spray, and line bottom of pan with wax paper. Coat wax paper with cooking spray.

3. Combine corn and next 5 ingredients in a blender or food processor; process until smooth.

4. Lightly spoon 2 cups flour into dry measuring cups; level with a knife. Combine 2 cups flour and next 4 ingredients in a large bowl; stir well with a whisk. Add corn mixture to flour mixture, stirring just until combined.

5. Toss raspberries with 2 tablespoons flour; fold into batter. Pour batter into prepared pan. Bake at 325° for 1 hour or until a wooden pick inserted in center comes out clean. Cool in pan 10 minutes on a wire rack. Remove from pan, and carefully peel off wax paper. Cool completely on wire rack. Sprinkle with powdered sugar, if desired. Yield: 10 servings (serving size: 1 wedge).

CALORIES 291 (26% from fat); FAT 8.3g (sat 4.7g, mono 2.5g, poly 0.6g); PROTEIN 4.6g; CARB 52.1g; FIBER 2.8g; CHOL 61mg; IRON 1.7mg; SODIUM 481mg; CALC 67mg

Potato Salad 101, page 184

Corn and Smoked Mozzarella
Pizza, page 180

Triple-Berry Crisps with
Meringue Streusel, page 210

Potato-Peanut Cakes, page 209

Rice Noodle Salad with Vegetables and Tofu, page 188

Texas Sheet Cake, page 205

Grilled Tomato Sandwiches,
page 178

Texas Sheet Cake

If you have a Texas-sized crowd to feed this summer, our Texas Sheet Cake will fill the bill.

This easy-to-make treat is so rich and fudgy, some people mistake it for brownies. The recipe first appeared in the March 2000 issue of *Cooking Light* magazine.

No one's quite sure how it got its name, but Beverly Bundy, food editor at the *Fort Worth Star-Telegram*, thinks it has something to do with size. "I've never done a genealogical study of the cake," she says, "but my assumption is that it's called a 'Texas' sheet cake because, as we say in Fort Worth, it's as big as Dallas."

Texas Sheet Cake

(pictured on page 204)

CAKE:
Cooking spray
2 teaspoons all-purpose flour
2 cups all-purpose flour
2 cups granulated sugar
1 teaspoon baking soda
1 teaspoon ground cinnamon
¼ teaspoon salt
¾ cup water
½ cup butter
¼ cup unsweetened cocoa
½ cup low-fat buttermilk
1 teaspoon vanilla extract
2 large eggs

ICING:
6 tablespoons butter
⅓ cup fat-free milk
¼ cup unsweetened cocoa
3 cups powdered sugar
¼ cup chopped pecans, toasted
2 teaspoons vanilla extract

1. Preheat oven to 375°.
2. To prepare cake, coat a 15 x 10-inch jelly roll pan with cooking spray; dust with 2 teaspoons flour.

3. Lightly spoon 2 cups flour into dry measuring cups; level with a knife. Combine 2 cups flour and next 4 ingredients in a large bowl; stir well with a whisk.
4. Combine water, ½ cup butter, and ¼ cup cocoa in a small saucepan; bring to a boil, stirring frequently. Remove from heat; pour into flour mixture. Beat with a mixer at medium speed until well blended. Add buttermilk, 1 teaspoon vanilla, and eggs; beat well.
5. Pour batter into prepared pan; bake at 375° for 17 minutes or until a wooden pick inserted in center comes out clean. Place on a wire rack.
6. To prepare icing, combine 6 tablespoons butter, milk, and ¼ cup cocoa in a medium saucepan; bring to a boil, stirring constantly. Remove from heat; gradually stir in powdered sugar, pecans, and 2 teaspoons vanilla. Spread over hot cake. Cool completely on wire rack. Yield: 20 servings (serving size: 1 slice).
NOTE: You can also make this recipe in a 13 x 9-inch baking pan. Bake at 375° for 22 minutes.

CALORIES 298 (30% from fat); FAT 10g (sat 5.5g, mono 3.2g, poly 0.7g); PROTEIN 3.1g; CARB 49.8g; FIBER 0.5g; CHOL 44mg; IRON 1.1mg; SODIUM 188mg; CALC 25mg

America's Sweethearts

Here, the Lighten Up column takes a different approach. Instead of featuring a reader recipe, we polled the staff about their favorite American desserts.

Our top five choices are familiar ones: strawberry shortcake, apple pie, brownies, blueberry cobbler, and New York cheesecake. Here, they're presented in lightened versions, of course. As a starting point, we gathered classic recipes from traditional American cookbooks. Then we went to work.

Apple Pie

The slurry (a mixture of flour and water that's whisked together) is the secret to keeping the low-fat crust tender.

CRUST:
2 cups all-purpose flour, divided
6 tablespoons ice water
1 teaspoon cider vinegar
2 tablespoons powdered sugar
½ teaspoon salt
7 tablespoons vegetable shortening

FILLING:
8 cups thinly sliced peeled Braeburn apples (about 8 medium)
1 tablespoon fresh lemon juice
⅔ cup sugar
3 tablespoons all-purpose flour
½ teaspoon ground cinnamon
½ teaspoon ground nutmeg
⅛ teaspoon salt

REMAINING INGREDIENTS:
Cooking spray
1 large egg white, lightly beaten
1 tablespoon sugar

1. Preheat oven to 450°.
2. To prepare crust, lightly spoon 2 cups flour into dry measuring cups; level with a knife. Combine ½ cup flour, ice water, and vinegar, stirring with a whisk until well blended to form a slurry. Combine 1½ cups flour, powdered sugar, and ½ teaspoon salt in a large bowl; cut in shortening with a pastry blender or 2 knives until mixture resembles coarse meal. Add slurry; toss with a fork until flour mixture is moist.
3. Divide dough in half. Gently press each half into a 4-inch circle on 2 sheets of overlapping heavy-duty plastic wrap; cover with 2 additional sheets of overlapping plastic wrap. Roll 1 dough half, still covered, into a 12-inch circle. Roll other dough half, still covered, into an 11-inch circle. Chill dough 10 minutes or until plastic wrap can be easily removed.
4. To prepare filling, combine apple and lemon juice in a large bowl. Combine ⅔ cup sugar and next 4 ingredients in a
Continued

small bowl. Sprinkle sugar mixture over apples; toss well to coat.

5. Remove top 2 sheets of plastic wrap from 12-inch dough circle; fit dough, plastic wrap side up, into a 9-inch deep-dish pie plate coated with cooking spray, allowing dough to extend over edge. Remove remaining plastic wrap. Spoon filling into dough; brush edges of dough lightly with water.

6. Remove top 2 sheets of plastic wrap from 11-inch dough circle; place, plastic wrap side up, over filling. Remove remaining plastic wrap. Press edges of dough together. Fold edges under, and flute. Cut 4 (1-inch) slits into top of pastry using a sharp knife. Brush top and edges of pie with egg white; sprinkle with 1 tablespoon sugar.

7. Place pie on a baking sheet; bake at 450° for 15 minutes. Reduce oven temperature to 350° (do not remove pie from oven), and bake an additional 40 minutes or until golden. Cool on a wire rack. Yield: 10 servings (serving size: 1 wedge).

CALORIES 293 (29% from fat); FAT 9.6g (sat 2.4g, mono 4g, poly 2.5g); PROTEIN 3.3g; CARB 50.1g; FIBER 2.5g; CHOL 0mg; IRON 1.4mg; SODIUM 153mg; CALC 10mg

BEFORE	AFTER
APPLE PIE	
1 wedge	
CALORIES PER SERVING	
373	293
FAT	
19.6g	9.6g
PERCENT OF TOTAL CALORIES	
47%	29%

Strawberry Shortcake

Strawberry shortcake probably originated with American colonists' appreciation of a Native American dish of wild strawberries pounded into corn bread. The colonists created their own version by splitting the common biscuit in half, generously buttering it, and filling it with berries and whipped cream. We followed their lead but reduced the amount of butter and switched from whipping cream to fat-free whipped topping. While our dessert has one-third fewer calories and two-thirds less fat than the original, it still has a tender, moist shortcake and plenty of creamy topping.

Strawberry Shortcake

Due to its lower fat content, this shortcake can overcook and crumble quickly, so watch it carefully in the oven—don't allow it to brown.

STRAWBERRIES:
4 cups sliced strawberries
¼ cup sugar

SHORTCAKE:
2 cups all-purpose flour
¼ cup sugar
2 teaspoons baking powder
1 teaspoon grated lemon rind
½ teaspoon salt
¼ teaspoon baking soda
6 tablespoons chilled butter, cut into small pieces
⅔ cup fat-free buttermilk
½ teaspoon vanilla extract
Cooking spray
1 large egg white, lightly beaten
1½ teaspoons turbinado sugar or granulated sugar

REMAINING INGREDIENTS:
2 cups frozen fat-free whipped topping, thawed
Whipped topping (optional)
Whole strawberry (optional)

1. To prepare strawberries, combine sliced strawberries and ¼ cup sugar; cover and chill 1 hour.

2. Preheat oven to 400°.

3. To prepare shortcake, lightly spoon flour into dry measuring cups; level with a knife. Combine flour and next 5 ingredients in a large bowl, stirring with a whisk. Cut in butter with a pastry blender or 2 knives until mixture resembles coarse meal. Combine buttermilk and vanilla; add to flour mixture, stirring just until moist (dough will be sticky).

4. Turn dough out onto a lightly floured surface; knead lightly 4 times with floured hands. Pat dough into an 8-inch circle on a baking sheet coated with cooking spray. Brush top with egg white; sprinkle with 1½ teaspoons sugar.

5. Bake at 400° for 15 minutes or until a wooden pick inserted in center comes out clean. Cool 10 minutes on a wire rack. Carefully split shortcake in half horizontally using a serrated knife; cool layers separately on wire racks.

6. Place bottom half of shortcake, cut side up, on a serving plate. Drain strawberries, reserving juice; drizzle juice over bottom half of shortcake. Spread 2 cups whipped topping over shortcake layer; arrange drained strawberries over whipped topping. Top with remaining shortcake layer, cut side down. Garnish with whipped topping and whole strawberry, if desired. Yield: 10 servings (serving size: 1 wedge).

CALORIES 246 (27% from fat); FAT 7.4g (sat 4.4g, mono 2.1g, poly 0.5g); PROTEIN 4g; CARB 40.3g; FIBER 2.2g; CHOL 19mg; IRON 1.6mg; SODIUM 348mg; CALC 90mg

BEFORE	AFTER
STRAWBERRY SHORTCAKE	
1 wedge	
CALORIES PER SERVING	
384	246
FAT	
26g	7.4g
PERCENT OF TOTAL CALORIES	
61%	27%

Blueberry Cobbler

FILLING:

6 cups fresh blueberries
⅓ cup sugar
2 tablespoons cornstarch
1 teaspoon grated lemon rind

TOPPING:

1⅓ cups all-purpose flour
2 tablespoons sugar
¾ teaspoon baking powder
¼ teaspoon salt
¼ teaspoon baking soda
5 tablespoons chilled butter, cut into small pieces
1 cup fat-free sour cream
3 tablespoons 2% reduced-fat milk
1 teaspoon sugar

1. Preheat oven to 350°.
2. To prepare filling, combine first 4 ingredients in an 11 x 7-inch baking dish.
3. To prepare topping, lightly spoon flour into dry measuring cups; level with a knife. Combine flour and next 4 ingredients in a large bowl, stirring with a whisk. Cut in butter with a pastry blender or 2 knives until mixture resembles coarse meal. Stir in sour cream to form a soft dough.
4. Drop dough by spoonfuls onto blueberry filling to form 8 dumplings. Brush dumplings with milk; sprinkle with 1 teaspoon sugar. Place baking dish on a jelly roll pan. Bake at 350° for 50 minutes or until filling is bubbly and dumplings are lightly browned. Yield: 8 servings.

CALORIES 288 (26% from fat); FAT 8.3g (sat 4.9g, mono 2.2g, poly 0.5g); PROTEIN 4.7g; CARB 50.8g; FIBER 3.5g; CHOL 23mg; IRON 1.3mg; SODIUM 265mg; CALC 90mg

Fudgy Brownies

1 cup sugar
2 large eggs
1 tablespoon hot water
2 teaspoons instant coffee granules
¼ cup butter, melted
1 teaspoon vanilla extract
1 cup all-purpose flour
⅔ cup unsweetened cocoa
¼ teaspoon salt
Cooking spray
1 tablespoon powdered sugar (optional)

1. Preheat oven to 325°.
2. Place sugar and eggs in a large bowl; beat with a mixer at high speed until thick and pale (about 5 minutes). Combine hot water and coffee granules, stirring until coffee granules dissolve. Add coffee mixture, butter, and vanilla to sugar mixture; beat at low speed until combined.
3. Lightly spoon flour into a dry measuring cup; level with a knife. Combine flour, cocoa, and salt, stirring with a whisk. Gradually add flour mixture to sugar mixture, stirring just until moist (batter will be thick).
4. Spread batter into an 8-inch square baking pan coated with cooking spray. Bake at 325° for 23 minutes or until brownies spring back when touched lightly in center. Cool in pan on a wire rack. Garnish brownies with powdered sugar, if desired. Yield: 16 servings (serving size: 1 brownie).

CALORIES 121 (30% from fat); FAT 4.1g (sat 2.3g, mono 1.3g, poly 0.2g); PROTEIN 2.4g; CARB 20.6g; FIBER 1.4g; CHOL 34mg; IRON 1mg; SODIUM 75mg; CALC 10mg

New York Cheesecake

Because we wanted the height of a traditional New York-style cheesecake, we baked this in a springform pan with high (3-inch) sides. If you're not sure about the dimensions of your pan, use a ruler to measure the inside of the pan. To prevent cracks and ensure a creamy texture, the cheesecake needs to cool gradually in the closed oven for one hour.

CRUST:

⅔ cup all-purpose flour
3 tablespoons sugar
2 tablespoons chilled butter, cut into small pieces
1 tablespoon ice water
Cooking spray

FILLING:

4 cups fat-free cottage cheese
2 cups sugar
2 (8-ounce) blocks ⅓-less-fat cream cheese, softened
¼ cup all-purpose flour
½ cup fat-free sour cream
1 tablespoon grated lemon rind
1 tablespoon vanilla extract
¼ teaspoon salt
5 large eggs

1. Preheat oven to 400°.
2. To prepare crust, lightly spoon ⅔ cup flour into a dry measuring cup; level with a knife. Place ⅔ cup flour and 3 tablespoons sugar in a food processor; pulse 2 times or until combined. Add butter; pulse 6 times or until mixture resembles coarse meal. With processor on, slowly pour ice water through food chute, processing just until blended (do not allow dough to form a ball).
3. Firmly press mixture into bottom of a 9 x 3-inch springform pan coated with cooking spray. Bake at 400° for 10 minutes or until lightly browned; cool on a wire rack.
4. Reduce oven temperature to 325°.
5. To prepare filling, strain cottage cheese through a cheesecloth-lined sieve for 10 minutes; discard liquid. Place cottage cheese in food processor; process until smooth.

Continued

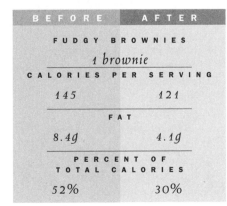

BEFORE	AFTER
BLUEBERRY COBBLER	
1 serving	
CALORIES PER SERVING	
356	288
FAT	
16.5g	8.3g
PERCENT OF TOTAL CALORIES	
42%	26%

BEFORE	AFTER
FUDGY BROWNIES	
1 brownie	
CALORIES PER SERVING	
145	121
FAT	
8.4g	4.1g
PERCENT OF TOTAL CALORIES	
52%	30%

6. Place 2 cups sugar and cream cheese in a large bowl, beat with a mixer at medium speed until smooth. Lightly spoon ¼ cup flour into a dry measuring cup; level with a knife. Add ¼ cup flour, sour cream, and remaining 4 ingredients to cream cheese mixture; beat well. Add cottage cheese, stirring until well blended. Pour cheese mixture into prepared crust.

7. Bake at 325° for 1 hour and 30 minutes or until almost set. Turn oven off. Cool cheesecake in closed oven 1 hour. Remove cheesecake from oven; run a knife around outside edge. Cool to room temperature. Cover and chill at least 8 hours. Yield: 16 servings (serving size: 1 wedge).

NOTE: You can also make cheesecake in a 10 x 2½-inch springform pan. Bake at 300° for 1 hour and 30 minutes or until almost set. Turn oven off. Cool cheesecake in closed oven 30 minutes.

CALORIES 291 (30% from fat); FAT 9.8g (sat 5.7g, mono 3g, poly 0.5g); PROTEIN 12.9g; CARB 37.7g; FIBER 0.2g; CHOL 98mg; IRON 0.7mg; SODIUM 410mg; CALC 93mg

BEFORE	AFTER
NEW YORK CHEESECAKE	
1 wedge	
CALORIES PER SERVING	
531	291
FAT	
44.5g	9.8g
PERCENT OF TOTAL CALORIES	
75%	30%

Salmon on the Sound

Entertaining is a breeze with this traditional, yet spirited, Northwestern menu by Seattle chef Christine Keff.

Christine Keff, chef-owner of Flying Fish and Fandango (two highly acclaimed Seattle restaurants) shares her innovative approach to regional cuisine in the following menu for a Northwest-inspired salmon bake. Salmon is the star of the show, and its flavors are enhanced by Keff's take on traditional accompaniments. The menu features the best foods of the season, simply prepared, in a uniquely American context.

Salmon Menu

Chef Keff celebrates the versatility of salmon by matching it with fresh, peak-of-season produce.

Grilled Salmon with Charred Tomato Salsa or **Mango-Coconut Salsa**

Seattle Black Beans

Fresh Corn Custards

Potato-Peanut Cakes

Triple-Berry Crisps with Meringue Streusel

search myclar2003.com for all our menus

Grilled Salmon with Charred Tomato Salsa

This dish is most flavorful when prepared with wild Pacific salmon, which is redder in color than its milder Atlantic cousin. For a more exotic dish, pair the salmon with Mango-Coconut Salsa (recipe on page 209).

    4 tomatoes (about ½ pound)
    2 jalapeño peppers
    2 poblano chiles
    1 small onion, peeled
    ¼ cup minced fresh cilantro
    2 teaspoons olive oil
    ½ teaspoon salt
    ½ teaspoon black pepper
    6 (6-ounce) salmon fillets
Thyme sprigs (optional)

1. Preheat broiler.

2. Place first 4 ingredients on a broiler pan, and broil 10 minutes or until tomatoes are tender and onion is slightly blackened. Cool 5 minutes.

3. Core tomatoes, and discard cores. Coarsely chop tomatoes, peppers, chiles, and onion; place in a bowl. Add cilantro, oil, salt, and black pepper; toss gently.

4. Prepare grill.

5. Place salmon, skin side down, on grill rack. Grill 10 minutes or until fish flakes easily when tested with a fork. Top each fillet with about 2 tablespoons salsa; garnish with thyme, if desired. Yield: 6 servings (serving size: 1 fillet and about 2 tablespoons salsa).

WINE NOTE: Salmon's "meatiness" makes it one fish that works extremely well with certain red wines—especially Pinot Noir. If the salmon is grilled or broiled as it is here, Pinot Noir's earthiness is a perfect complement to the sweet char. Try the lush Melville Estate "Clone 115 Indigène" Pinot Noir from the Santa Ynez Valley of California (the 1999 is $35).

CALORIES 309 (43% from fat); FAT 14.9g (sat 3.3g, mono 6.8g, poly 3.4g); PROTEIN 37g; CARB 5g; FIBER 1.6g; CHOL 87mg; IRON 1.7mg; SODIUM 279mg; CALC 36mg

Mango-Coconut Salsa

Serve this with the grilled salmon (recipe on page 208) in place of the salsa.

    1   poblano chile
    ½   cup thinly sliced radishes
    ¼   cup flaked, sweetened coconut
    2   tablespoons fresh lime juice
    1   tablespoon olive oil
    2   teaspoons minced fresh cilantro
    1   garlic clove, minced
    2   cups cubed peeled ripe mango
        (about 2 large)
    Cilantro sprigs (optional)

1. Preheat broiler.
2. Place chile on a foil-lined baking sheet, and broil 10 minutes or until blackened, turning occasionally. Place blackened chile in a zip-top plastic bag, and seal. Let stand 15 minutes. Peel and cut chile in half lengthwise. Discard seeds and membrane. Finely chop.
3. Combine chile, radishes, and next 5 ingredients in a medium bowl. Cover and marinate in refrigerator 30 minutes or overnight. Stir in mango. Garnish with cilantro sprigs, if desired. Yield: 5 servings (serving size: 1 salmon fillet and 6 tablespoons salsa).

CALORIES 328 (35% from fat); FAT 12.6g (sat 3.5g, mono 5.2g, poly 3.3g); PROTEIN 37g; CARB 19g; FIBER 2.5g; CHOL 89mg; IRON 2.1mg; SODIUM 207mg; CALC 94mg

Seattle Black Beans

Get a head start by cooking the beans the day before you make this dish.

    3   cups dried black beans
    6   cups fat-free, less-sodium chicken
        broth
    ½   cup water
    ½   teaspoon black pepper
    ¼   teaspoon salt
    2   bacon slices
    1   cup thinly sliced celery
    ½   cup finely chopped onion
    ½   cup finely chopped carrot
    ½   teaspoon dried thyme
    ½   teaspoon ground cumin
    2   garlic cloves, minced

1. Sort and wash beans; place in a large Dutch oven. Cover with water to 2 inches above beans; cover and let stand 8 hours. Drain beans.
2. Return beans to pan; stir in broth, water, pepper, and salt. Bring to a boil; reduce heat, and simmer, uncovered, 2 hours or until tender.
3. Cook bacon in a large nonstick skillet over medium heat until crisp. Remove bacon from pan; crumble. Add celery and remaining 5 ingredients to pan; cook 5 minutes. Add to bean mixture; simmer 10 minutes. Sprinkle with bacon. Yield: 10 servings (serving size: about ⅔ cup).

CALORIES 254 (12% from fat); FAT 3.5g (sat 1.2g, mono 1.3g, poly 0.7g); PROTEIN 15g; CARB 39g; FIBER 9.5g; CHOL 3mg; IRON 3.2mg; SODIUM 378mg; CALC 83mg

Fresh Corn Custards

Coat the ramekins generously with cooking spray to ensure the custards will release easily from the molds.

    3   cups fresh corn kernels (about 6
        ears), divided
    2   cups 2% reduced-fat milk
    ½   teaspoon salt
    ¼   teaspoon black pepper
    4   large eggs, lightly beaten
    Cooking spray
    Chopped fresh chives (optional)

1. Preheat oven to 350°.
2. Bring 2 cups corn and milk to a simmer in a large saucepan over medium heat; cook 20 minutes, and cool. Pour corn mixture into a blender or food processor; process until smooth. Strain mixture through a sieve over a large bowl. Discard solids. Add salt, pepper, and eggs to corn mixture; stir well with a whisk.
3. Divide 1 cup corn evenly among 6 (6-ounce) ramekins generously coated with cooking spray, and top each with ⅓ cup corn mixture.
4. Place ramekins in a 13 x 9-inch baking pan, and add hot water to pan to a depth of 1 inch. Bake at 350° for 30 minutes or until center barely moves when ramekin is touched. Remove ramekins from pan, and cool 5 minutes on a wire rack. Invert custards onto serving plates. Garnish with fresh chives, if desired. Yield: 6 servings (serving size: 1 custard).

CALORIES 181 (30% from fat); FAT 6.1g (sat 2.2g, mono 2.1g, poly 1.0g); PROTEIN 9.6g; CARB 25g; FIBER 1g; CHOL 147mg; IRON 1mg; SODIUM 291mg; CALC 118mg

Potato-Peanut Cakes

(pictured on page 203)

Fresh sweet corn teams with buttery Yukon gold potatoes and chopped peanuts in these patties.

    ¾   pound Yukon gold potatoes
    1   bacon slice
    1   cup fresh corn kernels (about 2 ears)
    ¼   cup finely chopped onion
    ¼   cup finely chopped red bell pepper
    1   teaspoon chopped fresh thyme
    ¼   cup sliced green onions
    ¼   cup chopped peanuts
    ½   teaspoon salt
    1   large egg, lightly beaten
    Cooking spray
    Chopped fresh thyme (optional)

1. Place potatoes in a saucepan; cover with water. Bring to a boil; reduce heat, and simmer 15 minutes or until tender. Drain and cool. Shred potatoes into a large bowl.

Continued

2. Cook bacon in a large nonstick skillet over medium heat until crisp. Remove bacon from pan; crumble. Add corn, chopped onion, chopped bell pepper, and chopped thyme to drippings in pan; cook 4 minutes or until onion is tender.

3. Combine potato, bacon, corn mixture, green onions, peanuts, salt, and egg; stir with a fork until well blended.

4. Coat a nonstick griddle or large nonstick skillet with cooking spray. For each cake, spoon about ⅓ cup potato mixture onto hot griddle or skillet; flatten slightly with a spatula. Cook 5 minutes on each side or until golden brown. Garnish with thyme, if desired. Yield: 8 servings (serving size: 1 cake).

CALORIES 110 (40% from fat); FAT 4.9g (sat 1.1g, mono 2.2g, poly 1.2g); PROTEIN 3.9g; CARB 14g; FIBER 1.9g; CHOL 28mg; IRON 1mg; SODIUM 183mg; CALC 16mg

Triple-Berry Crisps with Meringue Streusel
(pictured on page 202)

This fresh berry dessert uses a baked meringue that's crumbled and stirred into the streusel. The filling uses crystallized ginger and orange rind for a decidedly tart flavor that contrasts with the sweet topping. Because the meringue needs to sit in the oven at least 12 hours, make it a day before serving. Or make our same-day Almond Streusel variation (recipe at right). At her restaurant, Flying Fish, Keff serves the crisps in small skillets, but we tested them in ramekins as well. You can also make a single crisp in a 13 x 9-inch baking dish. For a real treat, serve with ice cream.

STREUSEL:
- 3 large egg whites
- 6 tablespoons granulated sugar
- ¼ cup sliced almonds
- ¼ cup flaked sweetened coconut
- ¼ teaspoon ground cinnamon
- ⅓ cup all-purpose flour
- ¼ cup packed brown sugar
- 1 tablespoon grated lemon rind
- ½ teaspoon ground nutmeg
- ¼ teaspoon ground cinnamon
- 1½ tablespoons chilled butter, cut into small pieces

FILLING:
- 4 cups blueberries
- 2 cups blackberries
- 2 cups raspberries
- ½ cup orange juice
- ¼ cup cornstarch
- ¼ cup packed brown sugar
- 3 tablespoons chopped crystallized ginger
- 2 tablespoons finely grated orange rind
- Cooking spray

1. Preheat oven to 200°.

2. To prepare streusel, place egg whites in a large bowl; beat with a mixer at high speed until foamy (about 30 seconds). Gradually add granulated sugar, 1 tablespoon at a time, beating until stiff peaks form (about 2 minutes). Gently fold in almonds, coconut, and ¼ teaspoon cinnamon. Spread as evenly as possible onto a parchment-lined 15 x 10-inch jelly roll pan.

3. Bake at 200° for 2½ hours. Turn oven off; cool meringue in closed oven at least 12 hours or until completely dry. Remove meringue from paper. Crumble into ¼-inch pieces.

4. Lightly spoon flour into a dry measuring cup; level with a knife. Combine flour and next 4 ingredients in a bowl; cut in butter with a pastry blender or 2 knives until mixture resembles coarse meal. Stir in meringue pieces.

5. Preheat oven to 350°.

6. To prepare filling, combine blueberries and next 7 ingredients in a bowl; toss well. Spoon ½ cup filling into each of 12 (6-ounce) ramekins or custard cups coated with cooking spray. Top each with ⅓ cup meringue streusel mixture. Place ramekins on a baking sheet; bake at 350° for 10 minutes or until bubbly. Serve warm or at room temperature. Yield: 12 servings (serving size: 1 ramekin).

NOTE: You can also make this dessert in a 13 x 9-inch baking dish. (Bake 30 minutes or until bubbly.) Or use small skillets like the one pictured on page 202, which we found at Williams-Sonoma. (Bake 25 minutes.) The recipe makes enough to fill 6 skillets, 2 servings per skillet.

CALORIES 175 (17% from fat); FAT 3.4g (sat 1.5g, mono 1.1g, poly 0.4g); PROTEIN 2.6g; CARB 35.6g; FIBER 4.2g; CHOL 4mg; IRON 1.2mg; SODIUM 40mg; CALC 37mg

Variation:

TRIPLE-BERRY CRISPS WITH ALMOND STREUSEL

If you're in a hurry, try this simpler, traditional streusel topping—made with butter, flour, and sugar.

ALMOND STREUSEL:
- ¾ cup all-purpose flour
- ½ cup packed brown sugar
- ½ teaspoon salt
- 4½ tablespoons chilled butter, cut into small pieces
- ¾ cup regular oats
- ⅓ cup sliced almonds

1. To prepare streusel, lightly spoon flour into a dry measuring cup; level with a knife. Place flour, sugar, and salt in a food processor; pulse 2 times or until combined. Add chilled butter; pulse 6 times or until mixture resembles coarse meal. Add oats and almonds; pulse 2 times. Sprinkle over berry filling; bake according to recipe directions (recipe at left).

CALORIES 247 (28% from fat); FAT 7.6g (sat 3g, mono 2.7g, poly 0.9g); PROTEIN 4g; CARB 43.7g; FIBER 3.8g; CHOL 12mg; IRON 2mg; SODIUM 151mg; CALC 49mg

august

Take Two from the Grill

Jump-start tomorrow's dinner by grilling additional food tonight.

Each of these six menus lets you grill tonight and enjoy another supper tomorrow. All offer extraordinarily bold flavors just off the grill, and the seasonings continue to contribute the next day.

Grilling Menu 1

Tonight: Mediterranean Grilled Chicken

Tomorrow: Chicken-Arugula Focaccia Sandwiches

Mediterranean Grilled Chicken

Serve with skewers of eggplant, tomatoes, onions, bell peppers, and zucchini—the key ingredients of Provence's ratatouille. To prepare the skewers, brush vegetables with olive oil, sprinkle with salt, and grill for 6 minutes, turning once. Save 2 cooked chicken breast halves for the Chicken-Arugula Focaccia Sandwiches (recipe at right).

- 6 bone-in chicken breast halves (about 3 pounds)
- 3 tablespoons Rosemary-Garlic Rub (recipe at right)
- 6 rosemary sprigs
- 6 thyme sprigs
- ½ teaspoon freshly ground black pepper
- Cooking spray

1. Loosen skin from chicken by inserting fingers, gently pushing between skin and meat. Rub Rosemary-Garlic Rub evenly over breast meat. Place 1 rosemary sprig and 1 thyme sprig between skin and meat of each breast half. Gently press skin to secure. Cover and refrigerate 4 hours.
2. Prepare grill.
3. Sprinkle chicken with pepper. Place chicken, skin sides down, on grill rack coated with cooking spray. Grill 25 minutes or until done, turning occasionally. Discard skin before serving. Yield: 6 servings (serving size: 1 chicken breast half).
NOTE: Store cooked chicken in refrigerator for up to 2 days.
WINE NOTE: Pair this dish with a dry rosé to emphasize the herbal flavors of Provence. Although the United States imports many dry rosés from the South of France, none are widely distributed. Just ask your wine clerk to recommend a good producer from Tavel, Provence's famous rosé village.

(Totals include Rosemary-Garlic Rub) CALORIES 167 (10% from fat); FAT 1.9g (sat 0.5g, mono 0.5g, poly 0.4g); PROTEIN 34.3g; CARB 1g; FIBER 0.1g; CHOL 86mg; IRON 1.2mg; SODIUM 151mg; CALC 28mg

Rosemary-Garlic Rub

Try this rub on chicken or pork, or stir it into mayonnaise or yogurt for a sandwich spread. One recipe makes enough for Mediterranean Grilled Chicken (recipe at left) and the Chicken-Arugula Focaccia Sandwiches (recipe at right).

- 2 tablespoons chopped fresh rosemary
- 2 tablespoons plain fat-free yogurt
- ½ teaspoon grated lemon rind
- 1 tablespoon fresh lemon juice
- 1 teaspoon minced fresh thyme
- ¼ teaspoon salt
- 3 garlic cloves, crushed

1. Combine all ingredients. Yield: ¼ cup (serving size: about 1 teaspoon).
NOTE: Store rub in refrigerator for up to 3 days.

CALORIES 3 (0% from fat); FAT 0g; PROTEIN 0.2g; CARB 0.6g; FIBER 0.1g; CHOL 0mg; IRON 0mg; SODIUM 41mg; CALC 8mg

Chicken-Arugula Focaccia Sandwiches

Leftover Mediterranean Grilled Chicken (recipe at left) is paired with a zesty yogurt sauce. If your bakery has fresh focaccia, use it instead of a commercial brand.

- 3 tablespoons plain fat-free yogurt
- 1 tablespoon Rosemary-Garlic Rub (recipe at left)
- 2 Mediterranean Grilled Chicken breast halves (recipe at left)
- 1 teaspoon lemon juice
- 1 teaspoon extra-virgin olive oil
- ⅛ teaspoon salt
- ⅛ teaspoon black pepper
- 3 cups trimmed arugula
- 1 (8.8-ounce) loaf rosemary focaccia (such as Alessi), cut in half horizontally and toasted
- ½ cup thinly sliced red onion
- ¼ cup chopped pitted kalamata olives

1. Combine yogurt and Rosemary-Garlic Rub.
2. Remove Mediterranean Grilled Chicken from bones; thinly slice. Combine juice, oil, salt, and pepper; drizzle over arugula, tossing to coat.
3. Spread yogurt mixture over cut sides of bread. Arrange arugula, sliced chicken, onion, and olives over bottom half of loaf; cover with top half of loaf. Cut into 4 wedges. Yield: 4 servings.

(Totals include Rosemary-Garlic Rub and Mediterranean Grilled Chicken) CALORIES 328 (27% from fat); FAT 9.7g (sat 2.1g, mono 5.3g, poly 2g); PROTEIN 23.5g; CARB 36.5g; FIBER 1.9g; CHOL 43mg; IRON 2.6mg; SODIUM 702mg; CALC 88mg

Tenderloin with Grilled Antipasto Vegetables

Round out this meal with a loaf of crusty bread served with red pepper jelly or flavored olive oil. The recipes for Chile-Garlic Vinaigrette (recipe at right) and Grilled Antipasto Vegetables (recipe at right) yield enough for this dish and the Garlicky Vegetable Pasta Salad (recipe at right), which you can quickly toss together later.

½ teaspoon salt
½ teaspoon freshly ground black pepper
¼ teaspoon dried thyme
⅛ teaspoon garlic powder
1½ pounds beef tenderloin, trimmed
Cooking spray
2½ tablespoons Chile-Garlic Vinaigrette (recipe at right)
4 cups trimmed arugula
8 cups Grilled Antipasto Vegetables (recipe at right)
¼ cup (1 ounce) shaved Parmesan cheese

1. Prepare grill.
2. Combine first 4 ingredients; rub over beef. Place beef on grill rack coated with cooking spray; grill 6 minutes on all 4 sides or until desired degree of doneness. Cover loosely; let stand 5 minutes.
3. Drizzle Chile-Garlic Vinaigrette over arugula; toss gently to coat. Cut beef across grain into thin slices. Arrange beef, Grilled Antipasto Vegetables, and arugula on a platter; top with cheese. Yield: 6 servings (serving size: 3 ounces beef, 1⅓ cups Grilled Antipasto Vegetables, ⅔ cup arugula, and 2 teaspoons cheese).

(Totals include Chile-Garlic Vinaigrette and Grilled Antipasto Vegetables) CALORIES 343 (35% from fat); FAT 13.2g (sat 4.4g, mono 5.7g, poly 0.9g); PROTEIN 33.5g; CARB 26.5g; FIBER 9.3g; CHOL 74mg; IRON 6mg; SODIUM 587mg; CALC 183mg

Chile-Garlic Vinaigrette

Use this vinaigrette to dress Grilled Antipasto Vegetables (recipe below), Garlicky Vegetable Pasta Salad (recipe at right), and the arugula in Tenderloin with Grilled Antipasto Vegetables (recipe at left).

1 tablespoon chopped serrano chile
¾ teaspoon salt
6 garlic cloves, crushed
3 tablespoons red wine vinegar
2 tablespoons water
2 tablespoons fresh lemon juice
1½ tablespoons extra-virgin olive oil
1½ tablespoons anchovy paste

1. Combine first 3 ingredients in a mortar; mash to a paste with a pestle. Combine garlic paste mixture, vinegar, and remaining ingredients in a small bowl, stirring with a whisk. Yield: ¾ cup (serving size: 1 tablespoon).
NOTE: Store vinaigrette in refrigerator for up to 1 week.

CALORIES 21 (73% from fat); FAT 1.7g (sat 0.2g, mono 1.2g, poly 0.2g); PROTEIN 0.3g; CARB 1.1g; FIBER 0.1g; CHOL 1mg; IRON 0.7mg; SODIUM 266mg; CALC 8mg

Grilled Antipasto Vegetables

This colorful recipe appears with tenderloin one night and in pasta salad the next.

4 red bell peppers, halved and seeded
4 red onions, each peeled and cut into 6 wedges
Cooking spray
2 teaspoons olive oil
6 (4-inch) portobello caps
2 pounds asparagus
⅓ cup Chile-Garlic Vinaigrette (recipe above)

1. Prepare grill.
2. Coat bell peppers and onions with cooking spray. Place bell peppers and onions on grill rack coated with cooking spray; grill 15 minutes or until peppers are blackened, turning occasionally. Place peppers in a zip-top plastic bag; seal. Let stand 15 minutes.

3. Chop onions into 1-inch pieces; place in a large bowl. Peel and slice peppers into ½-inch strips; add to onions.
4. Combine oil, mushrooms, and asparagus; toss well to coat. Place mushrooms and asparagus on grill rack; grill 3 minutes on each side or until tender.
5. Chop mushrooms into 1-inch pieces; add to onion mixture. Slice asparagus diagonally into 1½-inch pieces; add to onion mixture. Drizzle Chile-Garlic Vinaigrette over mixture; toss to coat. Yield: 11 cups (serving size: 1 cup).
NOTE: Store cooked vegetables in refrigerator for up to 3 days.

(Totals include Chile-Garlic Vinaigrette) CALORIES 102 (19% from fat); FAT 2.2g (sat 0.3g, mono 1.3g, poly 0.4g); PROTEIN 5.7g; CARB 18.9g; FIBER 6.8g; CHOL 0mg; IRON 1.9mg; SODIUM 157mg; CALC 72mg

Garlicky Vegetable Pasta Salad

The flavors of this robust pasta salad parlay well into a picnic or alfresco lunch. Toss the vegetables with the pasta when they're hot off the grill or after they've chilled. The vinaigrette that flavors the vegetables also dresses the pasta salad.

4 cups cooked fusilli (about 8 ounces uncooked short twisted pasta)
3 cups Grilled Antipasto Vegetables (recipe at left)
¾ cup (3 ounces) crumbled feta cheese
½ cup chopped fresh basil
¼ cup Chile-Garlic Vinaigrette (recipe at left)
3 tablespoons chopped pitted kalamata olives

1. Combine all ingredients in a large bowl, tossing gently. Yield: 4 servings (serving size: about 1¾ cups).

(Totals include Grilled Antipasto Vegetables and Chile-Garlic Vinaigrette) CALORIES 405 (28% from fat); FAT 12.5g (sat 4.2g, mono 6.2g, poly 1.3g); PROTEIN 15.2g; CARB 60.1g; FIBER 6.8g; CHOL 20mg; IRON 4.7mg; SODIUM 854mg; CALC 190mg

Lemongrass Beef

Horseradish mashed potatoes

Mango relish*

*Combine 4 cups finely chopped peeled mango, 1 cup chopped peeled avocado, ½ cup finely chopped red onion, 2 tablespoons chopped fresh mint, 1 tablespoon finely chopped serrano chile, 2 tablespoons fresh lime juice, 2 teaspoons honey, and ¼ teaspoon salt.

Grilling Menu 3

Tonight: Lemongrass Beef

Tomorrow: Vietnamese Summer Rolls

Lemongrass Beef

- 2 pounds sirloin tip roast
- ½ cup chopped peeled fresh lemongrass
- ⅓ cup chopped shallots
- 3 tablespoons fish sauce
- 1½ tablespoons sugar
- 1 teaspoon dark sesame oil
- 1 teaspoon peanut oil
- ¼ teaspoon salt
- 6 garlic cloves, crushed
- 2 serrano chiles, seeded and chopped
- Cooking spray

1. Cover roast with plastic wrap; freeze 30 minutes. Remove beef from freezer, and cut beef horizontally into ⅛-inch-thick slices.
2. Combine lemongrass and next 8 ingredients in a food processor; process until smooth (about 1 minute). Combine beef and lemongrass mixture in a large zip-top plastic bag. Seal and marinate in refrigerator 2 to 4 hours.
3. Prepare grill.
4. Remove beef from bag; discard marinade. Place beef on grill rack coated with cooking spray; grill 1 minute on each side or until desired degree of doneness. Yield: 8 servings.
NOTE: Store cooked beef in refrigerator for up to 2 days.

CALORIES 158 (29% from fat); FAT 5.1g (sat 1.7g, mono 2g, poly 0.4g); PROTEIN 24.8g; CARB 2g; FIBER 0.1g; CHOL 69mg; IRON 2.8mg; SODIUM 353mg; CALC 10mg

Vietnamese Summer Rolls

Summer rolls are wrapped in softened rice paper. This version takes advantage of chilled Lemongrass Beef (recipe at left).

SAUCE:
- ¼ cup rice vinegar
- 1 tablespoon water
- 1½ teaspoons sugar
- 1 teaspoon dark sesame oil
- 1 teaspoon chile paste with garlic
- ½ teaspoon salt

ROLLS:
- 8 (8-inch) round sheets rice paper
- 8 Boston lettuce leaves
- ½ cup cooked bean threads (cellophane noodles)
- ½ cup fresh bean sprouts
- ½ cup julienne-cut seeded peeled cucumber
- ½ cup julienne-cut carrot
- ½ cup fresh mint leaves
- ½ cup fresh cilantro leaves
- 6 ounces Lemongrass Beef (recipe at left), cut into 16 (1-inch-wide) strips

1. To prepare sauce, combine first 6 ingredients in a small bowl, stirring well with a whisk.
2. To prepare rolls, add cold water to a large, shallow dish to a depth of 1 inch. Place 1 rice paper sheet in dish of water; let stand 2 minutes or until soft.
3. Place softened rice paper sheet on a flat surface. Place 1 lettuce leaf on bottom third of sheet. Top with 1 tablespoon each of noodles, sprouts, cucumber, carrot, mint, and cilantro; add 2 Lemongrass Beef strips.
4. Fold sides of rice paper sheet over filling; roll up jelly roll fashion. Gently press seam to seal; place, seam side down, on a serving platter (cover with a damp cloth to keep from drying). Repeat procedure with remaining rice paper sheets, lettuce leaves, noodles, vegetables, herbs, and beef. Serve with sauce. Yield: 4 servings (serving size: 2 summer rolls and about 1½ tablespoons sauce).

(Totals include Lemongrass Beef) CALORIES 230 (16% from fat); FAT 4g (sat 1g, mono 1.5g, poly 0.7g); PROTEIN 14.8g; CARB 34g; FIBER 1.1g; CHOL 34mg; IRON 2.3mg; SODIUM 443mg; CALC 43mg

Grilling Menu 4

Tonight: Citrus Tuna; Thyme Potatoes

Tomorrow: Chopped Niçoise Salad

Citrus Tuna

Serve with Thyme Potatoes (recipe on page 215) or linguine tossed with bottled olive tapenade. Or for a vegetable side, grill fennel wedges brushed with olive oil for 5 minutes and toss with orange slices and chopped olives. Make at least 1 extra recipe of Thyme Potatoes while grilling the tuna, and reserve it along with 2 cooked tuna steaks for the Chopped Niçoise Salad (recipe on page 215).

- 1 cup fresh orange juice (about 3 oranges)
- ½ cup fresh lemon juice (about 3 lemons)
- ½ cup fresh lime juice (about 4 limes)
- 3 tablespoons sugar
- 4 garlic cloves, minced
- 1 tablespoon freshly ground black pepper
- 1 teaspoon salt
- 1 teaspoon fennel seeds, crushed
- 6 (6-ounce) tuna steaks (about ¾ inch thick)
- Cooking spray

1. Prepare grill.
2. Combine first 5 ingredients in a medium saucepan. Bring to a boil; cook until reduced to ½ cup (about 20 minutes). Remove from heat; cool slightly.
3. Combine pepper, salt, and fennel seeds; rub over both sides of fish. Place fish on grill rack coated with cooking spray; grill 3 minutes on each side. Turn fish; brush with half of orange juice glaze. Grill 1 minute. Turn fish; brush with remaining orange juice glaze. Grill 1 minute or until fish is medium-rare or desired degree of doneness. Yield: 6 servings (serving size: 1 tuna steak).
NOTE: Store cooked tuna in refrigerator for up to 1 day.
WINE NOTE: Try Kumeu River Pinot Gris from New Zealand. The 2000 is $15.

CALORIES 295 (25% from fat); FAT 8.2g (sat 2.1g, mono 2.7g, poly 2.4g); PROTEIN 38.9g; CARB 15.7g; FIBER 0.7g; CHOL 63mg; IRON 2.2mg; SODIUM 379mg; CALC 33mg

Thyme Potatoes

Multiply this recipe to make as many servings as you need. Make an individual foil pack for each serving. While the grill is hot, prepare an extra serving of potatoes to reserve for the Chopped Niçoise Salad (recipe below).

½ pound small red potatoes, quartered
1½ teaspoons olive oil
1 teaspoon minced fresh thyme
¼ teaspoon salt
⅛ teaspoon freshly ground black pepper

1. Prepare grill.
2. Combine all ingredients, tossing to coat. Cut 2 (12-inch) sheets of aluminum foil. Arrange potato mixture in a single layer on 1 sheet of foil. Place remaining sheet of foil over potato mixture; seal edges. Place foil packet on grill rack. Grill 8 minutes or until potatoes are tender. Yield: 1 serving (serving size: 1 cup).
NOTE: Store cooked potatoes in refrigerator for up to 2 days.

CALORIES 262 (24% from fat); FAT 7g (sat 1g, mono 5g, poly 0.7g); PROTEIN 4.3g; CARB 46.7g; FIBER 4.5g; CHOL 0mg; IRON 2.6mg; SODIUM 486mg; CALC 29mg

Chopped Niçoise Salad

In Nice, green beans, tuna, and olives make a classic summer salad. The tuna and potatoes are cooked ahead of time, so this is a snap to toss together.

DRESSING:
1½ tablespoons fresh lemon juice
1 tablespoon water
1 tablespoon fat-free cottage cheese or sour cream
1 teaspoon Worcestershire sauce
1 teaspoon red wine vinegar
1 teaspoon extra-virgin olive oil
1 teaspoon anchovy paste
¼ teaspoon salt
¼ teaspoon freshly ground black pepper
1 garlic clove, peeled

SALAD:
1 cup (1-inch) cut green beans
4 cups mixed salad greens
1 cup Thyme Potatoes (recipe at left)
2 tablespoons chopped pitted kalamata olives
2 Citrus Tuna steaks, broken into 1-inch chunks (recipe on page 214)

1. To prepare dressing, combine first 10 ingredients in a blender or food processor; process until smooth.
2. To prepare salad, cook beans in boiling water 1 minute or until crisp-tender. Rinse beans with cold water, and drain well. Combine beans and remaining 4 ingredients in a large bowl. Pour dressing over tuna mixture, and toss gently to combine. Yield: 4 servings (serving size: 1½ cups).

(Totals include Thyme Potatoes and Citrus Tuna) CALORIES 269 (30% from fat); FAT 9.1g (sat 1.7g, mono 4.9g, poly 1.8g); PROTEIN 22.6g; CARB 25.1g; FIBER 3.7g; CHOL 32mg; IRON 3.1mg; SODIUM 668mg; CALC 75mg

---

Grilling Menu 5

Tonight: Hoisin-Marinated Pork Chops

Tomorrow: Grilled Pork and Rice Noodle Salad

Hoisin-Marinated Pork Chops

Marinate chops for at least 8 hours. Reserve 4 cooked pork chops for Grilled Pork and Rice Noodle Salad (recipe at right).

¼ cup low-sodium soy sauce
¼ cup hoisin sauce
¼ cup honey
1 teaspoon crushed red pepper
2 garlic cloves, minced
8 (4-ounce) boneless center-cut loin pork chops (about ¾ inch thick)
Cooking spray

1. Combine first 5 ingredients in a zip-top plastic bag; add pork chops. Seal; marinate in refrigerator 8 hours or overnight.
2. Prepare grill.

3. Remove pork from bag; discard marinade. Place pork on grill rack coated with cooking spray; grill 3 minutes on each side or until done. Yield: 8 servings (serving size: 1 pork chop).
NOTE: Store cooked pork in refrigerator for up to 2 days.

CALORIES 188 (30% from fat); FAT 6.2g (sat 2.1g, mono 2.8g, poly 0.7g); PROTEIN 25.1g; CARB 6.7g; FIBER 0.2g; CHOL 62mg; IRON 1mg; SODIUM 249mg; CALC 27mg

Grilled Pork and Rice Noodle Salad

The fresh herbs in this Vietnamese staple, called *bun*, make a refreshing salad.

⅔ cup boiling water
¼ cup sugar
⅓ cup fresh lime juice
3 tablespoons fish sauce
2 teaspoons chile paste with garlic
1 garlic clove, minced
½ pound uncooked rice sticks (rice-flour noodles)
2 cups mixed salad greens
2 cups julienne-cut cucumber (about ¾ pound)
1½ cups julienne-cut carrot (about ½ pound)
1 cup fresh bean sprouts
½ cup chopped fresh mint
½ cup chopped fresh basil
4 Hoisin-Marinated Pork Chops (recipe at left), thinly sliced
¼ cup chopped dry-roasted peanuts

1. Combine boiling water and sugar, stirring until sugar dissolves. Add juice, fish sauce, chile paste, and garlic. Cool.
2. Prepare noodles according to package directions; drain. Combine noodles, greens, and next 6 ingredients in a large bowl. Add juice mixture; toss well. Sprinkle with peanuts. Yield: 6 servings (serving size: 1½ cups).

(Totals include Hoisin-Marinated Pork Chops) CALORIES 370 (16% from fat); FAT 6.7g (sat 1.8g, mono 3g, poly 1.3g); PROTEIN 22.6g; CARB 55.4g; FIBER 3.6g; CHOL 42mg; IRON 2.6mg; SODIUM 947mg; CALC 82mg

Margarita Grouper Fillets

(pictured on page 222)

These fillets marinate in lime juice and tequila—the makings of a margarita. Serve with yellow rice or black beans. Grouper is delicate, so turn the fillets carefully to keep them intact. Save 2 cooked fillets for Fish Tacos (recipe at right).

- 6 (6-ounce) grouper fillets
- ¾ teaspoon salt, divided
- ¼ cup fresh cilantro leaves
- ¼ cup chopped onion
- 3 tablespoons fresh lime juice
- 1 tablespoon sugar
- 1 tablespoon finely chopped seeded serrano chile
- 1 tablespoon tequila
- 1 tablespoon vegetable oil
- 1 garlic clove, chopped
  Cooking spray
  Chopped fresh chives (optional)
  Lime wedges (optional)

1. Place fillets in a single layer in a 13 x 9-inch baking dish, and sprinkle with ¼ teaspoon salt. Combine ½ teaspoon salt, cilantro, and next 7 ingredients in a blender or food processor, and process until smooth. Pour cilantro mixture over fillets, and turn to coat. Marinate in refrigerator 30 minutes, turning once.
2. Prepare grill.
3. Remove fish from dish; discard marinade. Place fish on grill rack coated with cooking spray; grill 5 minutes on each side or until fish flakes easily when tested with a fork. Garnish fish with chopped chives and lime wedges, if desired. Yield: 6 servings (serving size: 1 grouper fillet).
NOTE: Store cooked fillets in refrigerator for up to 1 day.

CALORIES 197 (18% from fat); FAT 4g (sat 0.7g, mono 0.9g, poly 1.9g); PROTEIN 33.1g; CARB 3.6g; FIBER 0.2g; CHOL 63mg; IRON 1.6mg; SODIUM 326mg; CALC 50mg

Fish Tacos

Serve with chopped tomatoes, onions, jalapeño peppers, bell peppers, and cilantro.

DRESSING:
- 1½ tablespoons reduced-fat sour cream
- 1 tablespoon minced fresh cilantro
- 1½ teaspoons fresh lime juice
- ½ teaspoon red wine vinegar

TACOS:
- 4 (6-inch) corn tortillas
- 2 Margarita Grouper Fillets, flaked (recipe at left)
- ½ cup vertically sliced red onion
- 1 lime, quartered

1. To prepare dressing, combine first 4 ingredients, stirring well with a whisk.
2. To prepare tacos, place tortillas in a zip-top plastic bag; microwave at HIGH 40 seconds. Divide Margarita Grouper Fillets and onion evenly over half of each tortilla; drizzle each with about 2 teaspoons dressing. Fold tortillas in half. Serve with lime wedges. Yield: 2 servings (serving size: 2 tacos and 2 lime wedges).

(Totals include Margarita Grouper Fillets) CALORIES 342 (17% from fat); FAT 6.3g (sat 1.7g, mono 1.1g, poly 2.2g); PROTEIN 37.2g; CARB 34.2g; FIBER 4.4g; CHOL 69mg; IRON 2.6mg; SODIUM 418mg; CALC 177mg

lighten up

A Pie Worth Remembering

A Brooklyn reader weeps with joy over the improvement to her mother's onion pie.

Tara McCarthy, 31, of Brooklyn, New York, thinks our makeover of her late mother's signature dish—Onion Pie—is a miracle. "It's miraculous how similar to the original it tastes," Tara says. We also asked her to try the lightened version with milder Vidalia onions, which don't produce the tears she associates so vividly with the dish. In the following recipe we used regular white onions but offer Vidalias as a sweeter substitute.

	BEFORE	AFTER
SERVING SIZE		*1 wedge*
CALORIES PER SERVING	295	177
FAT	22.1g	4.8g
PERCENT OF TOTAL CALORIES	67%	24%

Onion Pie

This custardy, savory pie makes a great brunch or light supper served with a spinach salad.

- 1 cup low-fat baking mix (such as reduced-fat Bisquick)
- ⅓ cup 2% reduced-fat milk
  Cooking spray
- 1 tablespoon butter
- 2 cups chopped onion
- 1 (8-ounce) block fat-free cream cheese, softened
- 1 large egg
- ½ cup 2% reduced-fat milk
- ½ teaspoon salt
  Dash of hot sauce

1. Preheat oven to 350°.
2. Combine baking mix and ⅓ cup milk. Lightly coat hands with cooking spray. Press dough into bottom and up sides of a 9-inch pie plate coated with cooking spray.
3. Melt butter in a large nonstick skillet over medium heat. Add onion; cook 5 minutes or until tender (do not brown), stirring occasionally. Spoon onion into prepared crust.
4. Place cream cheese and egg in a medium bowl; beat with a mixer at medium speed until smooth. Stir in ½ cup milk, salt, and hot sauce. Pour cream cheese mixture over onion. Bake at 350° for 45 minutes or until set. Let stand 10 minutes before serving. Yield: 6 servings (serving size: 1 wedge).

CALORIES 177 (24% from fat); FAT 4.8g (sat 2.1g, mono 1.1g, poly 0.2g); PROTEIN 10.1g; CARB 22.8g; FIBER 1.2g; CHOL 46mg; IRON 1mg; SODIUM 660mg; CALC 191mg

Book a Cook

Personal chefs offer fresh meals for the harried—at an affordable price and in a variety of ways.

Here, we've featured recipes from three talented personal chefs: Linder Hunt of Best Kept Secret personal chef service in Cincinnati, Ohio; Janet Neyrinck of Free Range Chef in Alexandria, Kentucky; and Trinket Shaw of TV Dinners in Birmingham, Alabama.

Roasted Vegetable Rolls

Personal chef Linder Hunt usually serves these colorful rolls at parties, but some of her clients enjoy them with salad for a light dinner. If you're short on time, use refrigerated bread dough. Or for convenience, make the dough in your bread machine.

DOUGH:

- 1 tablespoon sugar
- 1 package dry yeast (about 2¼ teaspoons)
- 1 cup warm water (100° to 110°)
- 3 cups all-purpose flour, divided
- 1 teaspoon salt
- Cooking spray

FILLING:

- 1 cup finely chopped onion
- 1 cup finely chopped carrot
- 1 cup finely chopped red potato
- 1 cup finely chopped broccoli
- ¾ cup finely chopped red bell pepper
- 1 tablespoon olive oil
- 2 tablespoons grated fresh Parmesan cheese
- ½ cup (2 ounces) crumbled goat cheese
- 1 teaspoon chopped fresh thyme
- ¼ teaspoon salt
- ¼ teaspoon black pepper

1. To prepare dough, dissolve sugar and yeast in warm water in a large bowl; let stand 5 minutes. Lightly spoon flour into dry measuring cups; level with a knife. Stir 2½ cups flour and 1 teaspoon salt into yeast mixture. Turn dough out onto a floured surface. Knead until smooth and elastic (about 10 minutes); add enough of remaining flour, 1 tablespoon at a time, to prevent dough from sticking to hands (dough will feel tacky).
2. Place dough in a large bowl coated with cooking spray, turning to coat top. Cover and let rise in a warm place (85°), free from drafts, 45 minutes or until doubled in size. (Press two fingers into dough. If indentation remains, dough has risen enough.) Punch dough down; cover and let rest 5 minutes.
3. Preheat oven to 400°.
4. To prepare filling, combine onion and next 5 ingredients in a 13 x 9-inch baking dish; toss to coat. Bake at 400° for 20 minutes or until vegetables are lightly browned. Remove from oven; cool slightly. Stir in Parmesan.
5. Reduce oven temperature to 350°.
6. Divide dough into 2 portions; roll each portion into a 14 x 8-inch rectangle. Working with 1 portion at a time, spread half of vegetables onto dough, leaving a 1-inch border. Top with ¼ cup goat cheese; sprinkle with ½ teaspoon thyme, ⅛ teaspoon salt, and ⅛ teaspoon black pepper. Beginning at a long side, roll up dough tightly, jelly roll fashion; fold edges under, and pinch seam and ends to seal. Repeat procedure with remaining dough, vegetables, goat cheese, thyme, salt, and pepper.
7. Place rolls, seam sides down, on a baking sheet coated with cooking spray. Coat rolls with cooking spray. Bake at 350° for 30 minutes or until golden. Let rest 10 minutes; slice into 2-inch rounds. Yield: 2 rolls, 6 rounds each (serving size: 1 round).

WINE NOTE: Serve this dish with snappy Sauvignon Blanc. Try Honig, from the Napa Valley. The 2000 is about $14.

CALORIES 176 (17% from fat); FAT 3.3g (sat 1.4g, mono 1.3g, poly 0.3g); PROTEIN 5.8g; CARB 30.8g; FIBER 2.2g; CHOL 5mg; IRON 2mg; SODIUM 296mg; CALC 45mg

Shrimp and Orzo Pilaf

Linder Hunt likes serving this easy entrée with Raspberry-Asparagus Medley (recipe on page 218), grilled fruit kebabs, or cold soup. Rice-shaped orzo pasta soaks up the flavor of the chicken broth it's cooked in. Toasted almonds provide contrast to the smooth texture of the orzo. If you don't have sun-dried tomato sprinkles, chop regular sun-dried tomatoes to measure ¼ cup.

- 4 cups fat-free, less-sodium chicken broth
- 1 pound uncooked orzo (rice-shaped pasta)
- 1 tablespoon butter
- 3 garlic cloves, minced
- 1½ pounds medium shrimp, peeled and deveined
- 1 cup finely chopped carrot
- 1 cup chopped red bell pepper
- 1 cup chopped green bell pepper
- ¼ cup sun-dried tomato sprinkles
- 1 teaspoon salt
- ¼ teaspoon black pepper
- ½ cup sliced almonds, toasted and divided

1. Bring broth to a boil in a large Dutch oven; stir in orzo. Reduce heat; simmer 5 minutes, stirring frequently. Remove from heat, and cover.
2. Melt butter in a large nonstick skillet over medium-high heat. Add garlic; sauté 1 minute. Add shrimp; sauté 2 minutes. Add carrot and next 5 ingredients; cook 2 minutes or until shrimp are done and vegetables are tender, stirring frequently. Stir in ¼ cup almonds. Combine shrimp mixture and orzo; sprinkle with ¼ cup almonds. Yield: 8 servings (serving size: 1¼ cups).

CALORIES 381 (17% from fat); FAT 7g (sat 1.6g, mono 2.6g, poly 1.8g); PROTEIN 28g; CARB 50.1g; FIBER 3.4g; CHOL 133mg; IRON 4.7mg; SODIUM 688mg; CALC 83mg

Raspberry-Asparagus Medley

Linder Hunt serves this side dish on a bed of greens or with pork tenderloin flavored with balsamic vinegar, rosemary, and garlic.

    2 tablespoons raspberry preserves
    1 tablespoon white wine vinegar
 1½ teaspoons Dijon mustard
    ⅛ teaspoon salt
    ½ teaspoon grated lemon rind
 2½ cups (1-inch) sliced asparagus
       (about 1 pound)
 1½ cups fresh raspberries
    2 tablespoons finely chopped
       pecans, toasted

1. Combine first 4 ingredients in a small saucepan; bring to a boil. Remove from heat; stir in rind.
2. Cook asparagus in boiling water 2 minutes or until crisp-tender. Drain and plunge into ice water; drain. Combine preserves mixture, asparagus, and raspberries in a bowl; toss gently to coat. Sprinkle with pecans. Yield: 6 servings (serving size: about ½ cup).

CALORIES 65 (30% from fat); FAT 2.2g (sat 0.2g, mono 1.1g, poly 0.7g); PROTEIN 2.3g; CARB 10.8g; FIBER 3.9g; CHOL 0mg; IRON 1mg; SODIUM 82mg; CALC 27mg

---

Brown-Bag Lunch Menu
serves 6
Tomato-Basil Tart
Green salad
Strawberries and mint*

*Combine 6 cups quartered strawberries, 2 tablespoons sugar, 1 tablespoon chopped fresh mint, and 2 tablespoons fresh orange juice.

search myclar2003.com for all our menus

Tomato-Basil Tart

Janet Neyrinck often leaves this quichelike main dish with clients as a gift. It pairs well with a simple green salad for a light lunch or brunch. It's a great make-ahead dish because it's good served cold, at room temperature, or hot. Salting the tomato slices extracts excess water so the tart won't get soggy. If your tomatoes are watery after cooking, blot them with a paper towel.

    1 (11-ounce) can refrigerated soft
       breadstick dough
       Cooking spray
    8 plum tomatoes
 1½ teaspoons salt
    1 cup loosely packed basil leaves
    ¾ cup (3 ounces) shredded
       part-skim mozzarella cheese
    ⅔ cup fat-free ricotta cheese
    ½ cup (2 ounces) grated fresh
       Parmesan cheese
    ¼ teaspoon black pepper
    2 large egg whites
    2 teaspoons olive oil

1. Preheat oven to 425°.
2. Unroll dough, separating into strips. Working on a flat surface, coil 1 strip of dough around itself in a spiral pattern. Add second strip of dough to end of first strip, pinching ends to seal; continue coiling remaining dough. Let rest 10 minutes.
3. Roll dough into a 12-inch circle; fit into bottom and up sides of a 9-inch round removable-bottom tart pan coated with cooking spray. Cover dough with foil; arrange pie weights or dried beans on foil. Bake at 425° for 15 minutes; remove weights and foil. Bake an additional 5 minutes or until edges are lightly browned.
4. Reduce oven temperature to 350°.
5. Core and slice tomatoes into ¼-inch-thick slices. Sprinkle tomatoes with salt; place tomato slices, salt sides down, on several layers of paper towels. Cover with additional paper towels. Let stand 10 minutes, pressing down occasionally.
6. Place basil, cheeses, pepper, and egg whites in a blender or food processor; process until smooth. Spread cheese mixture over crust. Arrange tomato slices

---

over cheese mixture; brush with oil. Bake at 350° for 40 minutes or until cheese mixture is set. Let stand 10 minutes before serving. Yield: 6 servings (serving size: 1 wedge).

CALORIES 283 (30% from fat); FAT 9.3g (sat 3.9g, mono 3.5g, poly 1.5g); PROTEIN 15.5g; CARB 32.5g; FIBER 1.8g; CHOL 19mg; IRON 2.1mg; SODIUM 863mg; CALC 273mg

---

Minted Pea Soup

This recipe by Janet Neyrinck takes advantage of green peas. Adding sour cream produces a creamy texture and a bit of tang.

    2 cups fresh or frozen green peas
    1 cup chopped romaine lettuce
    1 cup fat-free, less-sodium chicken
       broth
    ½ cup finely chopped onion
    ½ cup 1% low-fat milk
    ½ cup reduced-fat sour cream
    3 tablespoons chopped fresh mint
    ¼ teaspoon salt
    ¼ teaspoon white pepper

1. Combine first 4 ingredients in a medium saucepan; bring to a boil. Stir in milk; reduce heat, and simmer, uncovered, 15 minutes or until vegetables are very tender.
2. Place pea mixture in a blender; let stand 5 minutes. Process until smooth. Stir in sour cream and remaining ingredients. Yield: 4 servings (serving size: ¾ cup).

CALORIES 133 (30% from fat); FAT 4.4g (sat 2.6g, mono 1.2g, poly 0.3g); PROTEIN 7.4g; CARB 16.4g; FIBER 4.3g; CHOL 17mg; IRON 1.3mg; SODIUM 298mg; CALC 116mg

---

Try New Things Menu
serves 10
Lamb Shanks Hestia with Cucumber Raita
Steamed green beans
Tabbouleh*

*Combine 6 cups cooked bulgur, 2 cups chopped tomato, 1 cup chopped fresh parsley, ¾ cup finely chopped red onion, ⅓ cup chopped fresh mint, ¼ cup fresh lemon juice, and 2 tablespoons olive oil. Chill 1 hour.

Lamb Shanks Hestia with Cucumber Raita

Janet Neyrinck once lived in an apartment above a Greek restaurant. On Sunday nights, she would join her friends and the restaurant owners for dinner in the back room of the restaurant. This earthy meal of braised lamb shanks in a richly flavored sauce—named for the Greek goddess of the hearth—was born during one of those occasions. *Raita* (RAH-ee-tah) is a traditional Indian salad of yogurt and chopped vegetables.

    4 lamb shanks (about 1¼ pounds each)
    Cooking spray
 1½ cups chopped onion
    6 garlic cloves, minced
    1 cup dry Marsala or Madeira
    1 cup low-salt beef broth
    1 cup tomato sauce
    1 teaspoon dried rosemary
  ¼ teaspoon salt
  ¼ teaspoon black pepper
    1 (3-inch) cinnamon stick
    1 cup golden raisins
    Cucumber Raita
    Mint sprigs (optional)

1. Preheat oven to 350°.
2. Rinse lamb with cold water; pat dry.
3. Heat a large oven-proof Dutch oven coated with cooking spray over medium-high heat. Add 2 lamb shanks; cook 10 minutes, browning on all sides. Remove from pan. Repeat procedure with remaining lamb; remove from pan.
4. Add onion and garlic to pan; sauté 2 minutes. Add Marsala; cook 2 minutes, stirring frequently. Add broth and next 5 ingredients. Return lamb to pan; bring mixture to a simmer. Cover pan, and bake at 350° for 1 hour.
5. Remove from oven; stir in raisins. Cover and bake an additional 45 minutes or until lamb is tender. Remove cinnamon stick; discard. Serve lamb with pan sauce and Cucumber Raita. Garnish with mint sprigs, if desired. Yield: 10 servings (serving size: 3 ounces lamb, about ⅓ cup sauce, and 2 tablespoons Cucumber Raita).

(Totals include Cucumber Raita) CALORIES 282 (25% from fat); FAT 7.9g (sat 2.9g, mono 3.3g, poly 0.6g); PROTEIN 33.6g; CARB 18.9g; FIBER 1.7g; CHOL 95mg; IRON 3.1mg; SODIUM 336mg; CALC 81mg

CUCUMBER RAITA:
Pressing the shredded cucumber removes excess water so the sauce isn't diluted.

  ¾ cup shredded peeled cucumber
    1 cup plain low-fat yogurt
    1 tablespoon chopped fresh mint
  ⅛ teaspoon salt
  ⅛ teaspoon white pepper

1. Place cucumber in a colander, pressing until barely moist. Combine cucumber, yogurt, and remaining ingredients. Cover and chill. Yield: 10 servings (serving size: 2 tablespoons).

CALORIES 19 (19% from fat); FAT 0.4g (sat 0.3g, mono 0.1g, poly 0g); PROTEIN 1.5g; CARB 2.4g; FIBER 0.2g; CHOL 1mg; IRON 0.1mg; SODIUM 47mg; CALC 49mg

Spring Vegetable and Herb Purses

These individually wrapped packets are a fun way to serve vegetables. Janet Neyrinck originally created this dish for a beer-and-food pairing party she threw. She likes to roast the purses on a bed of kosher or rock salt for an attractive presentation. If you can't find pattypan squash or fingerling potatoes, substitute sliced yellow squash and quartered new potatoes.

    1 cup (1-inch) sliced asparagus
  ¾ cup baby carrots, halved
  ¾ cup thinly sliced peeled sweet potato
  ⅔ cup yellow pattypan squash, quartered
  ⅔ cup fingerling potatoes, halved
    2 tablespoons chopped fresh basil
    2 teaspoons olive oil
    1 tablespoon chopped fresh mint
    1 teaspoon garam masala
  ¼ teaspoon salt
  ⅛ teaspoon black pepper
    8 sheets frozen phyllo dough, thawed
    Cooking spray

1. Preheat oven to 350°.
2. Combine first 11 ingredients in a large bowl; toss well to combine.
3. Place 1 phyllo sheet on a large cutting board or work surface (cover remaining dough to keep from drying); coat with cooking spray. Top with a second phyllo sheet; coat with cooking spray. Cut in half to form 2 (11 x 8-inch) rectangles. Spoon about ½ cup vegetables into center of each rectangle. Gather 4 corners of each phyllo rectangle, and crimp to seal, forming a purse; lightly coat with cooking spray. Repeat procedure with remaining phyllo sheets, vegetables, and cooking spray.
4. Place purses on a baking sheet coated with cooking spray. Bake at 350° for 30 minutes or until edges begin to brown. Yield: 8 servings (serving size: 1 purse).

CALORIES 102 (22% from fat); FAT 2.5g (sat 0.5g, mono 1.4g, poly 0.4g); PROTEIN 2.7g; CARB 17.7g; FIBER 1.8g; CHOL 0mg; IRON 1.2mg; SODIUM 173mg; CALC 19mg

Mediterranean Chicken with Potatoes

This is one of Trinket Shaw's most popular dishes. She delivers it fully cooked and ready to be popped in the microwave for a quick reheat. The potatoes are roasted in the oven to give them a deep, caramelized flavor before they're tossed with the other ingredients. A Greek salad makes a great accompaniment.

    4 teaspoons minced garlic, divided
    1 tablespoon olive oil
    1 teaspoon salt, divided
  ½ teaspoon black pepper, divided
  ¼ teaspoon dried thyme
  12 small red potatoes, halved (about 1½ pounds)
    Cooking spray
    2 pounds skinless, boneless chicken breast, cut into bite-sized pieces
    1 cup vertically sliced red onion
  ¾ cup dry white wine
  ¾ cup fat-free, less-sodium chicken broth
  ½ cup chopped pepperoncini peppers
  ¼ cup pitted kalamata olives, halved
    2 cups chopped plum tomato
    2 tablespoons chopped fresh basil
    1 (14-ounce) can artichoke hearts, drained and quartered
  ½ cup (2 ounces) grated fresh Parmesan cheese
    Thyme sprigs (optional)

Continued

1. Preheat oven to 400°.

2. Combine 2 teaspoons garlic, oil, ¼ teaspoon salt, ¼ teaspoon black pepper, thyme, and potatoes on a jelly roll pan coated with cooking spray. Bake at 400° for 30 minutes or until tender.

3. Heat a large Dutch oven coated with cooking spray over medium-high heat. Sprinkle chicken with ½ teaspoon salt and ¼ teaspoon black pepper. Add half of chicken to pan; sauté 5 minutes or until browned. Remove chicken from pan. Repeat procedure with remaining chicken; remove from pan.

4. Add onion to pan; sauté 5 minutes. Stir in wine, scraping pan to loosen browned bits. Bring wine to a boil; cook until reduced to ⅓ cup (about 2 minutes). Add potatoes, chicken, broth, pepperoncini, and olives; cook 3 minutes, stirring occasionally. Stir in 2 teaspoons garlic, ¼ teaspoon salt, tomato, basil, and artichokes; cook 3 minutes or until thoroughly heated. Sprinkle with cheese. Garnish with thyme sprigs, if desired. Yield: 8 servings (serving size: 1¼ cups).

CALORIES 331 (20% from fat); FAT 7.3g (sat 2.1g, mono 3.7g, poly 0.9g); PROTEIN 33.5g; CARB 32.5g; FIBER 3.6g; CHOL 71mg; IRON 2.9mg; SODIUM 897mg; CALC 124mg

Overnight Oatmeal Muffins

Personal chef Trinket Shaw serves these versatile muffins with just about everything on her menu. The buttermilk and oats soak together overnight, which gives these muffins a creamy texture. Use any dried fruit in place of the blueberries—or none at all.

    1   cup regular oats
    2   cups low-fat buttermilk
    1⅔ cups whole wheat flour
    ¾   cup packed dark brown
        sugar
    2   tablespoons vegetable oil
    1   teaspoon baking powder
    1   teaspoon baking soda
    1   teaspoon salt
    2   large eggs, lightly beaten
    ⅔   cup dried blueberries
    Cooking spray

1. Combine oats and buttermilk in a medium bowl; cover and refrigerate overnight.

2. Preheat oven to 350°.

3. Lightly spoon flour into dry measuring cups; level with a knife. Place buttermilk mixture, flour, and next 6 ingredients in a large bowl; beat with a mixer at medium speed until smooth. Fold in blueberries.

4. Spoon ¼ cup batter into each of 24 muffin cups coated with cooking spray. Bake at 350° for 15 minutes or until muffins spring back when touched lightly in center. Remove muffins from pans immediately; place on a wire rack. Yield: 24 servings (serving size: 1 muffin).

CALORIES 105 (19% from fat); FAT 2.2g (sat 0.5g, mono 0.6g, poly 0.9g); PROTEIN 3.1g; CARB 19.4g; FIBER 1.7g; CHOL 19mg; IRON 0.9mg; SODIUM 201mg; CALC 49mg

Easy Entertaining Menu
serves 4

Make the salsa and blanch the peas ahead of time; add the avocado to the salsa and sauté the peas just before serving. You can use shrimp instead of scallops, if you prefer.

Citrus-Glazed Scallops with Avocado Salsa

White rice

Sautéed sugar snap peas*

*Snap ends from 1 pound sugar snap peas. Cook in boiling water 1 minute or until crisp-tender; drain. Melt 1 tablespoon butter in a nonstick skillet over medium-high heat; sauté 2 minced garlic cloves 1 minute. Add peas and ¼ teaspoon salt; sauté 2 minutes.

search myclar2003.com for all our menus

Citrus-Glazed Scallops with Avocado Salsa

A favorite on Trinket Shaw's menu, this dish is great hot or cold.

SCALLOPS:

    1½ pounds large sea scallops, cut in
        half horizontally
    ¼   teaspoon salt
    ¼   teaspoon black pepper

GLAZE:

    ¼   cup fresh lime juice
    ¼   cup fresh orange juice
    2   tablespoons fresh lemon juice
    1   tablespoon grated peeled fresh
        ginger
    2   tablespoons honey
    1   teaspoon olive oil
    ¼   teaspoon ground red pepper
    1   garlic clove, crushed
    ½   cup chopped green onions
    ¼   cup finely chopped fresh cilantro

SALSA:

    ½   cup chopped seeded plum tomato
    ½   cup diced peeled avocado
    ¼   cup finely chopped red onion
    1   tablespoon finely chopped fresh
        cilantro
    1   tablespoon chopped jalapeño pepper
    1   tablespoon fresh lime juice
    ½   teaspoon olive oil
    ⅛   teaspoon salt
    ⅛   teaspoon black pepper
    1   garlic clove, crushed

REMAINING INGREDIENT:

    8   Bibb lettuce leaves (optional)

1. To prepare scallops, heat a large nonstick skillet over medium-high heat. Combine first 3 ingredients in a bowl; toss well. Add scallops to pan; cook 2 minutes on each side or until browned. Remove from pan; keep warm.

2. To prepare glaze, combine ¼ cup lime juice and next 7 ingredients in a small bowl; stir with a whisk. Add juice mixture to pan. Cook 7 minutes or until glaze becomes shiny and begins to thicken. Drizzle citrus glaze over scallops; add green onions and ¼ cup cilantro. Toss well.

3. To prepare salsa, combine chopped tomato and next 9 ingredients; toss well. Serve on Bibb lettuce leaves, if desired. Yield: 4 servings (serving size: ⅔ cup scallops and ¼ cup salsa).

WINE NOTE: German Riesling would be sensational. Try a Riesling labeled Kabinett from Fritz Haag, Selbach-Oster, or Joh. Jos. Prüm (about $15–$20).

CALORIES 262 (21% from fat); FAT 6.1g (sat 0.9g, mono 3.1g, poly 1g); PROTEIN 29.8g; CARB 22.5g; FIBER 2.2g; CHOL 56mg; IRON 1mg; SODIUM 503mg; CALC 56mg

Corn and Roasted Pepper Salad
(with chicken), page 237

Summer Farfalle Salad with Smoked Salmon,
page 236

Margarita Grouper Fillets,
page 216

Gazpacho with Roasted Peppers,
page 238

Thai Steak Salad, page 232

A Month of Sundaes

Simple sauces and customized ice creams give you options galore for sweet summer treats.

When you think sundae, you probably think hot fudge. That's a good thought; hot fudge is one of our favorites. But sundae options abound. And you can diversify dessert at home without the heavy wooden bucket, the messy rock salt, or the cranking.

We've picked the best light commercial ice creams and come up with easy stir-ins so you can have premium varieties at plain vanilla prices. You won't find most of these flavor combinations in your supermarket—but if you do, we bet they aren't light. To complement these frozen creations, choose from five easy sauces that taste much fresher than store-bought.

Here's everything you could possibly need for 31 days of bliss—custom-made, low-fat ice creams; easy, flavorful sauces; and suggestions for putting them together.

Crunchy Mocha	**Banana Pudding**	**The Thanksgiving**	**Grasshopper**	**Extreme Strawberry**	**Cold Toddy**	**Fire and Ice**
Mocha Ice Cream* with granola	*Vanilla ice cream with chopped banana, crushed vanilla wafers, and low-fat whipped topping*	*Sweet Potato Pie Ice Cream* with crushed gingersnaps*	*Vanilla ice cream with mini chocolate chips and a splash of crème de menthe*	*Strawberry sorbet with Fresh Strawberry Sauce**	*Maple-Bourbon Ice Cream* with grated lemon rind*	*Vanilla ice cream sprinkled with cayenne pepper*
How 'Bout S'More	**Chocolate Rapture**	**Solid Gold**	**Tropical Breeze**	**Autumn Delight**	**Easter Sundae**	**The Elvis**
S'More Ice Cream* with Warm Chocolate Sauce*	*Mocha Ice Cream* with Warm Chocolate Sauce**	*Dulce de Leche Ice Cream* with Butterscotch Sauce* and butterscotch morsels*	*Piña Colada Sherbet* with Pineapple Sauce* and toasted coconut*	*Spicy Lemon Sorbet* with Easy Fruit Compote**	*Strawberry frozen yogurt with marshmallows and jelly beans*	*Peanut Butter-Banana Ice Cream* with low-fat whipped topping*
Hot Stuff	**Margaritaville**	**Double-Chocolate Malt**	**The Waffler**	**Classic Banana Split**	**Almond Bliss**	**Trick-or-Treat**
Vanilla ice cream with Red Hots and crushed peppermint candies	*Lime sherbet with crushed pretzels and a splash of tequila*	*Malted Chocolate Ice Cream* with Warm Chocolate Sauce* and toasted pecans*	*Vanilla ice cream with crushed waffle cone bits and Butterscotch Sauce**	*Vanilla ice cream with bananas, Warm Chocolate Sauce*, Butterscotch Sauce*, Fresh Strawberry Sauce*, low-fat whipped topping, nuts, and a cherry*	*Vanilla ice cream with crushed amaretti cookies, sliced almonds, and a splash of amaretto*	*Sweet Potato Pie Ice Cream* with candy corn and pecans*
Tiramisu	**Bar None**	**Ultimate Cheesecake**	**Coconut Crème Caramel**	**Orange Ice**	**Apple Pie**	**Berry Good**
Mocha Ice Cream* with a dollop of mascarpone cheese and Warm Chocolate Sauce*	*Vanilla ice cream with Warm Chocolate Sauce* and brownie chunks*	*Strawberry Cheesecake Frozen Yogurt* with Fresh Strawberry Sauce* and graham cracker crumbs*	*Dulce de Leche Ice Cream* with caramel sauce and toasted coconut*	*Vanilla ice cream with orange sherbet*	*Vanilla ice cream with apple pie filling and cooked piecrust bits*	*Raspberry sorbet with fresh raspberries and Fresh Strawberry Sauce**
Packed with Peanuts	**Newly Minted**	**Golden Crunch**				
Peanut Butter-Banana Ice Cream* with crumbled Snickers	*Chocolate ice cream with Junior Mints*	*Dulce de Leche Ice Cream* with toffee bits*				** Recipe included*

Warm Chocolate Sauce

(pictured on page 224)

- ⅔ cup 2% reduced-fat milk
- ½ cup dark corn syrup
- ¼ cup sugar
- ¼ cup unsweetened cocoa
- Dash of salt
- 2½ ounces semisweet baking chocolate, chopped
- 1½ tablespoons butter
- 1 teaspoon vanilla extract

1. Combine first 5 ingredients in a saucepan over medium-high heat, stirring with a whisk. Bring to a boil. Reduce heat to medium; cook 3 minutes, stirring frequently. Remove from heat. Add chocolate, butter, and vanilla; stir until chocolate melts. Yield: 1¾ cups (serving size: 2 tablespoons).

CALORIES 99 (29% from fat); FAT 3.2g (sat 1.9g, mono 1.1g, poly 0.1g); PROTEIN 1g; CARB 19g; FIBER 1g; CHOL 2mg; IRON 0.5mg; SODIUM 40mg; CALC 21mg

Fresh Strawberry Sauce

(pictured on page 224)

- 1 cup ripe strawberries
- ⅓ cup water
- ⅓ cup sugar
- 1½ teaspoons cornstarch
- 1½ teaspoons fresh lemon juice or balsamic vinegar
- 2 cups finely chopped strawberries

1. Mash 1 cup strawberries. Combine mashed strawberries and water in a small saucepan; bring to a boil. Cook 5 minutes, stirring occasionally. Press through a sieve into a bowl; reserve ½ cup strawberry liquid (add enough water to measure ½ cup, if necessary). Discard pulp.
2. Combine sugar and cornstarch in pan. Add strawberry liquid; stir well. Bring to a boil; cook 1 minute, stirring constantly. Reduce heat; cook 2 minutes. Remove from heat; stir in lemon juice. Cool slightly. Stir in chopped strawberries. Yield: 2 cups (serving size: 2 tablespoons).

CALORIES 25 (4% from fat); FAT 0.1g (sat 0g, mono 0g, poly 0.1g); PROTEIN 0.2g; CARB 6.2g; FIBER 0.6g; CHOL 0mg; IRON 0.1mg; SODIUM 0mg; CALC 4mg

Butterscotch Sauce

(pictured on page 224)

- 3 tablespoons butter
- 1¼ cups packed brown sugar
- ⅓ cup 2% reduced-fat milk
- ¼ cup dark corn syrup
- ¼ cup half-and-half
- 1 teaspoon vanilla extract

1. Melt butter in a saucepan over medium-high heat. Add sugar, milk, and syrup; bring to a boil. Reduce heat to medium; cook 5 minutes, stirring frequently.
2. Remove from heat; let stand 5 minutes. Gradually stir in half-and-half and vanilla. Yield: 1½ cups (serving size: 2 tablespoons).

CALORIES 142 (22% from fat); FAT 3.5g (sat 2.2g, mono 1.1g, poly 0.1g); PROTEIN 0.4g; CARB 28.1g; FIBER 0g; CHOL 11mg; IRON 0.5mg; SODIUM 55mg; CALC 35mg

Pineapple Sauce

- 3 cups coarsely chopped pineapple
- 2 tablespoons brown sugar
- ¼ teaspoon vanilla extract

1. Place all ingredients in a food processor, and pulse 10 times or until finely chopped. Cover and chill. Yield: 1¾ cups (serving size: 2 tablespoons).

CALORIES 24 (4% from fat); FAT 0.1g (sat 0g, mono 0g, poly 0.1g); PROTEIN 0.1g; CARB 6g; FIBER 0.4g; CHOL 0mg; IRON 0.2mg; SODIUM 1mg; CALC 4mg

Easy Fruit Compote

- 1 cup water
- 3 tablespoons honey
- 3 whole cloves
- 1 (3-inch) cinnamon stick
- 1 (3-inch) lemon rind strip
- 1 (7-ounce) bag dried mixed fruit bits (such as Sun-Maid)

1. Combine first 5 ingredients in a microwave-safe bowl. Microwave at HIGH 6 minutes. Remove cloves, cinnamon stick, and rind with a slotted spoon, and discard.
2. Add fruit bits to liquid; microwave at

HIGH 1½ minutes. Cover and let stand 20 minutes. Yield: 2 cups (serving size: 2 tablespoons).

CALORIES 49 (0% from fat); FAT 0g; PROTEIN 0.3g; CARB 12.3g; FIBER 0.6g; CHOL 0mg; IRON 0.4mg; SODIUM 6mg; CALC 6mg

Strawberry Cheesecake Frozen Yogurt

- 4 cups strawberry fat-free frozen yogurt
- 1 cup fat-free sour cream
- 1 (8-ounce) block ⅓-less-fat cream cheese, softened
- 1 cup powdered sugar
- ½ teaspoon vanilla extract

1. Place a large bowl in freezer. Let yogurt stand at room temperature 45 minutes or until softened.
2. Place sour cream and cream cheese in a bowl. Beat with a mixer at medium speed 1 minute or until well blended. Gradually add sugar, beating well. Beat in vanilla.
3. With a rubber spatula or stand mixer, combine softened yogurt and cheese mixture in chilled bowl. Cover; freeze to desired consistency. Yield: 12 servings (serving size: ½ cup).

CALORIES 181 (23% from fat); FAT 4.7g (sat 3g, mono 1.3g, poly 0.1g); PROTEIN 5.6g; CARB 28.8g; FIBER 0g; CHOL 16mg; IRON 0.1mg; SODIUM 144mg; CALC 144mg

Strawberry-White Fudge Crunch Frozen Yogurt

- 4 cups strawberry fat-free frozen yogurt
- 1 cup white fudge-covered pretzels, broken into pieces
- ½ cup vanilla-flavored baking chips

1. Place a large bowl in freezer. Let yogurt stand at room temperature 45 minutes or until softened.
2. With a rubber spatula or stand mixer, combine softened yogurt, pretzel pieces, and baking chips in chilled bowl. Cover; freeze to desired consistency. Yield: 8 servings (serving size: ½ cup).

CALORIES 226 (21% from fat); FAT 5.2g (sat 2.9g, mono 1.5g, poly 0.3g); PROTEIN 5.4g; CARB 38.8g; FIBER 0.4g; CHOL 2mg; IRON 0.2mg; SODIUM 150mg; CALC 179mg

Peanut Butter-Banana Ice Cream

4 cups vanilla low-fat ice cream
1 cup mashed ripe banana (about 2 small bananas)
¼ cup chunky peanut butter

1. Place a large bowl in freezer. Let ice cream stand at room temperature 45 minutes or until softened.
2. Combine banana and peanut butter in a small bowl; mash with a fork until well blended. With a rubber spatula or stand mixer, combine softened ice cream and banana mixture in chilled bowl. Cover and freeze to desired consistency. Yield: 8 servings (serving size: ½ cup).

CALORIES 183 (30% from fat); FAT 6.1g (sat 1.8g, mono 1.9g, poly 1.2g); PROTEIN 5.2g; CARB 27.3g; FIBER 2.2g; CHOL 5mg; IRON 0.2mg; SODIUM 84mg; CALC 105mg

Malted Chocolate Ice Cream

4 cups chocolate low-fat ice cream
1 cup chocolate malted milk balls, crushed
½ cup chocolate malted milk powder

1. Place a large bowl in freezer. Let ice cream stand at room temperature 45 minutes or until softened.
2. With a rubber spatula or stand mixer, combine softened ice cream, milk balls, and milk powder in chilled bowl. Cover; freeze to desired consistency. Yield: 8 servings (serving size: ½ cup).

CALORIES 271 (27% from fat); FAT 8.1g (sat 5.1g, mono 2.5g, poly 0.3g); PROTEIN 4.7g; CARB 48.2g; FIBER 0.5g; CHOL 18mg; IRON 0.9mg; SODIUM 168mg; CALC 131mg

Mocha Ice Cream

4 cups chocolate low-fat ice cream
¼ cup Kahlúa (coffee-flavored liqueur)
1 tablespoon instant coffee granules
2 ounces bittersweet chocolate, finely chopped

1. Place a large bowl in freezer. Let ice cream stand at room temperature 45 minutes or until softened.
2. Combine liqueur and coffee granules in a small bowl. Microwave at HIGH 30 seconds; stir until coffee dissolves. Cool.
3. With a rubber spatula or stand mixer, combine softened ice cream, coffee mixture, and chopped chocolate in chilled bowl. Cover and freeze to desired consistency. Yield: 8 servings (serving size: ½ cup).

CALORIES 206 (30% from fat); FAT 6.9g (sat 4.5g, mono 1.5g, poly 0.2g); PROTEIN 3.6g; CARB 30.5g; FIBER 0.6g; CHOL 15mg; IRON 0.4mg; SODIUM 101mg; CALC 101mg

S'More Ice Cream

4 cups chocolate low-fat ice cream
1 cup miniature marshmallows
1 cup honey-flavored bear-shaped graham crackers (about 48 cookies)

1. Place a large bowl in freezer. Let ice cream stand at room temperature 45 minutes or until softened.
2. With a rubber spatula or stand mixer, combine softened ice cream, marshmallows, and graham crackers in chilled bowl. Cover and freeze to desired consistency. Yield: 9 servings (serving size: ½ cup).

CALORIES 170 (26% from fat); FAT 5g (sat 2.8g, mono 1.2g, poly 0.1g); PROTEIN 3.2g; CARB 29.8g; FIBER 0g; CHOL 13mg; IRON 0.3mg; SODIUM 133mg; CALC 89mg

Sweet Potato Pie Ice Cream

4 cups vanilla low-fat ice cream
½ (15-ounce) package refrigerated pie dough (such as Pillsbury)
Cooking spray
1½ cups mashed cooked sweet potato, cooled
3 tablespoons brown sugar
½ teaspoon pumpkin pie spice

1. Place a large bowl in freezer. Let ice cream stand at room temperature 45 minutes or until softened.
2. Preheat oven to 450°.
3. Cut pie dough round in half. Place half of dough on a baking sheet coated with cooking spray; reserve remaining dough for another use. Bake dough at 450° for 10 minutes or until lightly browned. Cool completely on a wire rack. Break crust into small pieces.
4. Place sweet potato, sugar, and spice in a bowl; mash with a fork until well blended. With a rubber spatula or stand mixer, combine softened ice cream, piecrust pieces, and sweet potato mixture in chilled bowl. Cover and freeze to desired consistency. Yield: 8 servings (serving size: ½ cup).

CALORIES 228 (22% from fat); FAT 5.6g (sat 2.4g, mono 1.6g, poly 0.4g); PROTEIN 3.9g; CARB 39.7g; FIBER 2.1g; CHOL 8mg; IRON 0.3mg; SODIUM 101mg; CALC 116mg

Maple-Bourbon Ice Cream

4 cups vanilla low-fat ice cream
¼ cup maple syrup
2 tablespoons bourbon
¼ teaspoon ground cinnamon

1. Place a large bowl in freezer. Let ice cream stand at room temperature 45 minutes or until softened.
2. With a rubber spatula or stand mixer, combine softened ice cream, syrup, bourbon, and cinnamon in chilled bowl. Cover and freeze to desired consistency. Yield: 6 servings (serving size: ½ cup).

CALORIES 193 (13% from fat); FAT 2.7g (sat 1.3g, mono 0.8g, poly 0.1g); PROTEIN 4g; CARB 34.4g; FIBER 1.4g; CHOL 7mg; IRON 0.2mg; SODIUM 61mg; CALC 143mg

Dulce de Leche Ice Cream

1 (14-ounce) can fat-free sweetened condensed milk
4 cups vanilla low-fat ice cream

1. Preheat oven to 400°.
2. Pour milk into a 9-inch pie plate; cover with foil. Place pie plate in a shallow roasting pan. Add hot water to pan to a depth of halfway up the sides of pie plate. Bake milk at 400° for 1½ hours, adding additional water as needed. Remove pie plate from water. Uncover; stir milk with a whisk until smooth. Cool.

Continued

3. Place a large bowl in freezer. Let ice cream stand at room temperature 45 minutes or until softened.
4. With a rubber spatula or stand mixer, combine softened ice cream and milk in chilled bowl. Cover and freeze to desired consistency. Yield: 8 servings (serving size: ½ cup).

CALORIES 248 (8% from fat); FAT 2.1g (sat 1g, mono 0.6g, poly 0.1g); PROTEIN 7.4g; CARB 48.9g; FIBER 1g; CHOL 8mg; IRON 0mg; SODIUM 97mg; CALC 239mg

Piña Colada Sherbet

    4 cups pineapple sherbet
    ½ cup cream of coconut
    ¼ cup white rum
    2 tablespoons fresh lime juice

1. Place a large bowl in freezer. Let sherbet stand at room temperature 45 minutes or until softened.
2. With a rubber spatula or stand mixer, combine softened sherbet and remaining ingredients in chilled bowl. Cover; freeze to desired consistency. Yield: 9 servings (serving size: ½ cup).

CALORIES 171 (16% from fat); FAT 3.1g (sat 2.2g, mono 0.9g, poly 0g); PROTEIN 0.9g; CARB 32.8g; FIBER 0g; CHOL 3mg; IRON 0mg; SODIUM 33mg; CALC 54mg

Spicy Lemon Sorbet

    3 cups lemon sorbet
    2 tablespoons finely chopped
       crystallized ginger
    ¼ teaspoon white pepper

1. Place a large bowl in freezer. Let sorbet stand at room temperature 45 minutes or until softened.
2. With a rubber spatula or stand mixer, combine softened sorbet, ginger, and pepper in chilled bowl. Cover; freeze to desired consistency. Yield: 6 servings (serving size: ½ cup).

CALORIES 124 (0% from fat); FAT 0g; PROTEIN 0g; CARB 32g; FIBER 0.5g; CHOL 0mg; IRON 0mg; SODIUM 5mg; CALC 2mg

All About Beef

From tenderloin to short ribs, roast, broil, grill, and braise your way to great entrées.

Grilled Sirloin Skewers with Peaches and Peppers

Sirloin is the most popular steak in the country for home cooking. (Filet mignon is the most popular restaurant steak.) The sweetness of peaches and red bell peppers contrasts nicely with the cumin-rubbed steak and parsley-garlic sauce.

KEBABS:

    1½ tablespoons ground cumin
    1½ tablespoons cracked black pepper
    2¾ teaspoons kosher salt
     2 pounds boneless sirloin steak, cut
        into 48 (1-inch) pieces
     4 peaches, each cut into 8 wedges
     2 small red onions, each cut into 8
        wedges
     2 large red bell peppers, each cut
        into 8 (1-inch) pieces
   Cooking spray

SAUCE:

    ½ cup chopped fresh parsley
    ¼ cup red wine vinegar
     1 teaspoon olive oil
    ¼ teaspoon kosher salt
    ¼ teaspoon cracked black pepper
     3 garlic cloves, minced
   Parsley sprigs (optional)

1. Prepare grill.
2. To prepare kebabs, combine first 7 ingredients; toss well. Thread 3 steak pieces, 2 peach wedges, 1 onion wedge, and 1 bell pepper piece alternately onto each of 16 (12-inch) skewers. Place on grill rack coated with cooking spray; grill 6 minutes or until tender, turning occasionally. Place on a platter; cover loosely with foil. Let stand 5 minutes.

3. To prepare sauce, combine chopped parsley and next 5 ingredients, stirring with a whisk. Spoon over kebabs. Garnish with parsley sprigs, if desired. Yield: 8 servings (serving size: 2 kebabs).

CALORIES 217 (30% from fat); FAT 7.2g (sat 2.4g, mono 3g, poly 0.4g); PROTEIN 25.5g; CARB 12.4g; FIBER 3.2g; CHOL 69mg; IRON 3.8mg; SODIUM 768mg; CALC 38mg

Roasted Beef Tenderloin with Merlot Shallot Sauce

The center cut used here, also called chateaubriand, is the most tender part of the tenderloin.

TENDERLOIN:

   Cooking spray
    ⅓ cup finely chopped fresh sage
     3 tablespoons minced garlic
     1 tablespoon cracked black pepper
     2 teaspoons kosher salt
     1 (2½-pound) center-cut beef
        tenderloin

SAUCE:

    ⅓ cup finely chopped shallots
    1½ cups Merlot or other dry red wine
    1½ cups low-salt beef broth
     1 teaspoon butter
     3 tablespoons chopped fresh parsley
    ¼ teaspoon kosher salt

1. Preheat oven to 350°.
2. To prepare tenderloin, heat a large nonstick skillet coated with cooking spray over medium-high heat. Combine sage, garlic, pepper, and 2 teaspoons salt; rub over tenderloin. Add tenderloin to pan; cook 6 minutes, lightly browning on all sides.

3. Insert a meat thermometer into thickest portion of tenderloin. Cover handle of pan with foil. Bake at 350° for 25 minutes, until thermometer registers 140° (medium-rare) or desired degree of doneness. Place tenderloin on a cutting board; cover loosely with foil. Let stand 15 minutes. (Temperature of tenderloin will increase 5° upon standing.)

4. To prepare sauce, heat pan coated with cooking spray over medium-high heat. Add shallots; sauté 3 minutes or until tender. Stir in wine. Bring to a boil; cook until reduced to ¾ cup (about 4 minutes). Stir in broth; cook until reduced to 1¼ cups (about 6 minutes). Add butter, stirring until melted. Stir in parsley and ¼ teaspoon salt. Serve with tenderloin. Yield: 10 servings (serving size: 3 ounces tenderloin and 2 tablespoons sauce).

CALORIES 216 (34% from fat); FAT 8.2g (sat 3.1g, mono 3.1g, poly 0.4g); PROTEIN 25.3g; CARB 3.1g; FIBER 0.3g; CHOL 72mg; IRON 3.6mg; SODIUM 495mg; CALC 28mg

London Broil with Texas Toast and Red Onion Jam

The round, or upper part of the leg, includes three muscles: top round, eye round, and bottom round. Only top round is tender enough to cook as steak. Often labeled London broil (as is flank steak), it's a somewhat chewy cut with great flavor, best served in thin slices. You can also use flank steak or sirloin for this recipe.

STEAK:

½ cup balsamic vinegar
2 tablespoons brown sugar
1 tablespoon Dijon mustard
3 garlic cloves, crushed
1 (2-pound) top round steak, trimmed (about 1½ inches thick)
½ teaspoon kosher salt
½ teaspoon cracked black pepper
Cooking spray

JAM:

1 tablespoon olive oil
8 cups sliced red onion (about 1½ pounds)
¼ cup balsamic vinegar
2 tablespoons brown sugar
2 tablespoons minced peeled fresh ginger
6 garlic cloves, minced
1 tablespoon thinly sliced fresh basil
½ teaspoon kosher salt
½ teaspoon cracked black pepper

TOAST:

8 (1½-ounce) slices sourdough bread
2 tablespoons butter, melted
1 garlic clove, crushed

1. To prepare steak, place first 4 ingredients in a large zip-top plastic bag; add steak. Seal and marinate in refrigerator 2 hours, turning occasionally.

2. Preheat broiler.

3. Remove steak from bag; discard marinade. Sprinkle steak with ½ teaspoon salt and ½ teaspoon pepper. Place steak on a broiler pan coated with cooking spray. Broil 10 minutes on each side (medium-rare) or until desired degree of doneness. Place steak on a cutting board; cover loosely with foil. Let stand 10 minutes. Cut steak across grain into thin slices.

4. To prepare jam, heat oil in a Dutch oven over medium-high heat. Add onion; cook 20 to 25 minutes or until deep golden brown, stirring frequently. Add ¼ cup vinegar, 2 tablespoons sugar, ginger, and 6 minced garlic cloves; cook 2 minutes or until liquid almost evaporates. Stir in basil, ½ teaspoon salt, and ½ teaspoon pepper.

5. Preheat oven to 350°.

6. To prepare toast, place bread slices on a large baking sheet. Bake at 350° for 8 minutes or until lightly browned. Combine butter and 1 crushed garlic clove; brush over toast. Serve steak with toast and jam. Yield: 8 servings (serving size: 3 ounces steak, 1 toast slice, and ¼ cup red onion jam).

CALORIES 398 (25% from fat); FAT 11g (sat 3.8g, mono 4.6g, poly 0.8g); PROTEIN 35.8g; CARB 40.1g; FIBER 4.5g; CHOL 84mg; IRON 4.3mg; SODIUM 549mg; CALC 68mg

---

The Skinny on Beef

Here's how cuts of beef stack up against one another. We've included our favorite lean cuts, as well as higher-fat cuts for reference. Figures are for 3 ounces of Choice-grade cooked meat, trimmed of all visible fat.

Cut	Calories	Fat
Bottom round	164	6.6g
Brisket	207	11.7g
Chuck arm pot roast	186	7.4g
Eye of round	149	4.8g
Flank steak	176	8.6g
Ground beef (regular)	248	16.5g
Ground beef (80% lean)	228	15.0g
Ground beef (85% lean)	204	12.0g
Ground beef (90% lean)	169	9.0g
Porterhouse steak	190	10.9g
Prime rib	215	12.8g
Sirloin tip roast	170	7.6g
Short ribs	196	11.6g
T-bone steak	217	14.4g
Tenderloin	180	8.6g
Top round	176	4.9g
Top sirloin	170	6.6g

search myclar2003.com for all our tips

Beef 101

Knowing more about particular foods can add depth and versatility to your cooking. Here, we answer the most common questions we receive about America's favorite red meat.

What are the food staff's favorite cuts?
Two cuts show up repeatedly. Tenderloin is the most tender, luxurious cut you can buy, and it's very lean. Roasted whole, it's the ideal entrée for a special dinner. Cut into filets and pan-seared, it's a superb supper for two. Cut into cubes, it makes outstanding kebabs on the grill.

Flank steak is one of those tough-but-superflavorful cuts, and it has a little more fat than tenderloin. Sear flank steak quickly and slice thinly, or braise slowly and shred. Its flat shape and coarse grain absorb flavors quickly, making it a good candidate for marinades.

What should you look for when buying meat?
Beef should have a cherry red or—if it's vacuum-packed—a dark, purplish-red color; avoid meat with gray or brown blotches. The visible fat should be very white. Seek a moist surface and a fresh smell. Avoid packaged meat with a lot of liquid in the tray—that's usually a sign the meat has been frozen and thawed.

Grades of beef: What do they mean, and what should you look for?
USDA grading has nothing to do with food safety; it's a measure of taste. The two most important factors in grading are the age of the animal and the marbling in the meat. Beef can be given one of eight grades, but only the top three—Prime, Choice, and Select—are sold in supermarkets and butcher shops. Restaurants buy up most of the Prime meat, so supermarkets sell mostly Choice and Select. Look for Choice when tenderness and juiciness matter most, such as for oven roasts or thick steaks for grilling. For pot roast or stew meat, Select is fine.

How long can you keep beef in the refrigerator or freezer?
Tightly wrapped and refrigerated, raw beef will last three to four days (ground beef, one to two days). At that point, it should be cooked or frozen. Cooked, it will keep in the refrigerator three to four days longer; frozen, it's best used within two months.

Which cuts are most tender, and are these tender cuts lean?
Generally speaking, the parts of a steer that are exercised the least—those from the rib and the loin—produce the most tender, lean cuts of meat.

From the rib, we get standing rib roast ("Prime rib," if you can get Prime grade) and rib eye steaks—all tender but generally higher in fat. From the loin come the leanest, most tender, and most expensive cuts of all: beef tenderloin roast along with Porterhouse, T-bone, filet mignon, and New York strip steaks.

If rib and loin cuts are the most tender and leanest, then why eat anything else? Flavor. Chefs and food experts agree that the parts of the animal that are exercised the most produce the most flavorful meat. If you're willing to accept a little chewiness in the name of flavor, try rump roast for Sunday dinner; it offers taste you just can't get from tenderloin.

How do you tenderize tough cuts of beef?
The most effective way is low, slow, moist heat (see Moist vs. Dry Heat on page 232). Braising and stewing break down the connective tissues and marbled fat, creating juicy, fork-tender meat with outstanding flavor. Just about any cut from the chuck or bottom round, as well as brisket, short ribs, and oxtails, makes great stews and braises.

Don't count on marinades to make chewy steaks tender. Marinating is great for adding flavor, but high-acid mixtures will only soften the surface, turning it mushy before the liquid can penetrate the meat. The best way to treat flavorful, chewy steaks—especially top round, skirt, flank, or even sirloin—is to sear quickly over high heat, as rare as you're willing to go (overcooking increases toughness). Slice thinly across the grain before serving.

How long should beef marinate to sufficiently absorb flavor?
A few hours will transfer flavor without making the surface of the meat mushy. Low-acid mixtures like teriyaki sauce can remain on for up to 48 hours, but don't let beef sit in a high-acid liquid, like lime juice, for more than an hour or two.

What is pot roast?
A great pot roast is the best way to convince people that inexpensive, tough cuts can be just as delicious as more expensive tender ones. Choosing the right roast is easy: Pick top blade roast (also called 7-bone roast because the blade bone resembles the number 7), boneless shoulder roast, arm pot roast, or chuck eye roast. Bottom round and rump roast are also recommended for pot roast. Besides choosing the right cut, a few steps ensure a juicy, flavorful pot roast:
• Searing browns the meat well; a good crusty exterior creates flavors that spread throughout the dish.
• Use a covered pot that will hold the meat snugly, so that liquid will come halfway up the sides and the top half of the roast will be bathed in steam as it cooks.
• Cook the roast a day ahead. All braises and stews taste better the second day, and chilling allows you to skim off excess fat before reheating.

Why do recipes tell you to let meat rest before you cut it?
As a roast cooks, external heat drives its juices toward the center. Once the meat comes out of the oven and cools slightly, the juices are reabsorbed and redistributed, so they won't run out as freely when you carve.

Traditional Yankee Pot Roast

Any roast from the chuck, which is the shoulder section (arm, 7-bone, or blade), will make great pot roast. Since the shoulder gets lots of exercise, it's riddled with fibrous tissue that melts during slow cooking—keeping the meat moist and ensuring rich, beefy flavor.

 2 teaspoons olive oil
 1 (4-pound) boneless chuck roast, trimmed
 1 tablespoon kosher salt
 1 tablespoon cracked black pepper
 2 cups coarsely chopped onion
 2 cups low-salt beef broth
 ¼ cup ketchup
 2 tablespoons Worcestershire sauce
 1 cup chopped plum tomato
 1¼ pounds small red potatoes
 1 pound carrots, peeled and cut into 1-inch pieces
 2 tablespoons fresh lemon juice
 Chopped fresh parsley (optional)

1. Preheat oven to 300°.
2. Heat oil in a large oven-proof Dutch oven over medium-high heat. Sprinkle roast with salt and pepper. Add roast to pan, browning on all sides (about 8 minutes). Remove from pan. Add onion to pan; sauté 8 minutes or until browned. Return roast to pan. Combine broth, ketchup, and Worcestershire; pour over roast. Add tomato; bring to a simmer.
3. Cover and bake at 300° for 2½ hours or until tender. Add potatoes and carrots; cover and bake an additional 30 minutes or until vegetables are tender. Stir in lemon juice. Garnish with parsley, if desired. Yield: 10 servings (serving size: 3 ounces beef and about ½ cup vegetables).

CALORIES 290 (26% from fat); FAT 8.4g (sat 2.8g, mono 3.7g, poly 0.5g); PROTEIN 32.9g; CARB 20g; FIBER 3g; CHOL 92mg; IRON 4.3mg; SODIUM 756mg; CALC 36mg

Real Texas Chili

In the Lone Star state, purists insist that chili has no beans. Any beef stew meat will work in this dish: top or bottom round, rump roast, or chuck.

 Cooking spray
 2 pounds beef stew meat
 ½ teaspoon kosher salt
 ½ teaspoon cracked black pepper
 3 cups chopped onion
 1 tablespoon cumin seeds
 3 tablespoons finely chopped jalapeño pepper
 6 garlic cloves, minced
 1 cup dry red wine
 ¼ cup white vinegar
 2 tablespoons chili powder
 2 tablespoons dried oregano
 1 (14¼-ounce) can low-salt beef broth
 1 (12-ounce) can beer
 ½ cup chopped fresh cilantro
 ½ cup chopped onion
 ½ cup fat-free sour cream

1. Heat a large Dutch oven coated with cooking spray over medium-high heat. Sprinkle beef with salt and pepper. Place half of beef in pan; cook 8 minutes or until browned. Remove from pan. Repeat procedure with remaining beef; remove from pan.
2. Add 3 cups onion to pan; sauté 5 minutes or until lightly browned. Add cumin, jalapeño, and garlic; sauté 1 minute. Add wine, scraping pan to loosen browned bits. Return cooked beef to pan.
3. Stir in vinegar and next 4 ingredients; bring to a boil. Cover, reduce heat, and simmer 1½ hours or until beef is tender, stirring occasionally. Uncover and simmer 1 hour, stirring occasionally. Stir in cilantro. Serve with ½ cup onion and sour cream. Yield: 8 servings (serving size: about 1 cup chili, 1 tablespoon sour cream, and 1 tablespoon onion).

CALORIES 268 (30% from fat); FAT 9g (sat 3.3g, mono 3.7g, poly 0.6g); PROTEIN 25.1g; CARB 13.8g; FIBER 2.7g; CHOL 72mg; IRON 4.3mg; SODIUM 218mg; CALC 85mg

Doneness: A Matter of Taste

Doneness is an issue of personal preference. One person's medium-rare may seem very rare to someone else, and those who prefer their meat well-done should be allowed to enjoy it that way.

According to the USDA, beef steaks and roasts should be cooked to a minimum of 145 degrees. For ground beef, the minimum is 160 degrees. *Cooking Light* follows the USDA temperature guidelines, but if you like your beef rare, cook it to a lower temperature than the recipes direct. Remember that ground beef should *always* be cooked to 160 degrees.

It's important to know when the meat has reached the desired degree of doneness. For larger cuts of meat, use a thermometer (preferably one that's an instant-read), and remove the meat from the oven when it's slightly more rare than you like it. After a roast comes out of the oven, its internal temperature will continue to rise by 5 to 20 degrees. The higher the cooking temperature, the greater the carryover.

Though using a thermometer is the only way to truly know how done meat is, for steaks, the "nick, peek, and cheat" method works well: Nick the meat with a sharp knife and take a peek inside to check its doneness. Don't worry about juices escaping when you cut into the meat; the small amount you'll lose is preferable to under- or overcooking your steak. As you become more experienced, you will be able to determine whether a steak's done just by touching it.

When braising, the only tool you need to check for doneness is a large fork. Plunge the fork into the center of the meat, and try to lift it: If the meat slides off the fork, it's done; if it hangs onto the fork, cook it longer.

search myclar2003.com for all our tips

Moist vs. Dry Heat

Generally, it's best to cook tender cuts with dry heat, and tough cuts with moist heat.

Dry-Heat Methods

Roast large tender cuts of beef. Roasting refers to cooking meat without added liquid. It's the gentlest dry-heat method, perfect for roasts from the rib and loin (and a few cuts from the chuck and round, too).

Sauté small tender cuts. Sauté quickly on the stove over direct, intense heat. Sautéing best suits small pieces of any tender cut like sirloin, tenderloin, or top blade steak.

Grill or broil small tender cuts. Grill on a rack with the heat source below the food; broil on a rack with the heat source above the food. These methods are best for relatively small tender cuts like rib, loin, or flank steak.

Moist-Heat Methods

Braise large tough cuts of beef. Sear the meat to crusty dark brown, then add a small amount of liquid. Cover the pan, and cook it low and slow on the stove or in the oven until the meat is fork-tender. Because boiling water can't rise above 212 degrees, braising ensures steady, gentle heat. Pot roast and short ribs are classic examples of braised meats.

Stew small tough cuts of beef. Stewing is similar to braising, but with more liquid and smaller pieces of meat. Chunks of beef are browned very well, a few at a time, and then covered completely with seasoned liquid in a pot. The liquid regulates the cooking temperature of the meat and forms the sauce.

Chipotle-Sweet Potato Shepherd's Pie

If you prefer, use Yukon gold or regular baking potatoes.

TOPPING:

1 (7-ounce) can chipotle chiles in adobo sauce
2¼ pounds peeled sweet potatoes, cut into 1-inch pieces
1 cup 2% reduced-fat milk
1 teaspoon kosher salt
¼ teaspoon cracked black pepper

FILLING:

2 pounds ground sirloin
Cooking spray
2 cups chopped onion
1 cup chopped carrot
3 garlic cloves, minced
1 cup frozen green peas, thawed
½ cup crushed tomatoes
¼ cup chopped fresh parsley
3 tablespoons steak sauce (such as A-1)
2 tablespoons tomato paste
½ teaspoon cracked black pepper

1. Preheat oven to 400°.

2. To prepare topping, remove 1 chile and 2 teaspoons sauce from can; reserve remaining chiles and sauce for another use. Coarsely chop 1 chile.

3. Place potatoes in a saucepan; cover with water. Bring to a boil; cook 15 minutes or until very tender. Drain. Place potatoes, chopped chile, 2 teaspoons adobo sauce, milk, salt, and ¼ teaspoon pepper in a large bowl. Beat with a mixer at medium speed until smooth.

4. To prepare filling, cook beef in a large nonstick skillet over medium-high heat until browned, stirring to crumble. Remove from pan; drain.

5. Heat pan coated with cooking spray over medium-high heat. Add onion, carrot, and garlic; sauté 8 minutes or until tender. Return beef to pan; stir in peas and remaining 5 ingredients. Cook 2 minutes.

6. Spoon beef mixture into a 3-quart casserole; top with sweet potato mixture, spreading evenly. Bake at 400° for 30 minutes or until thoroughly heated. Yield: 8 servings.

CALORIES 408 (29% from fat); FAT 13.2g (sat 5.2g, mono 5.6g, poly 0.7g); PROTEIN 28.3g; CARB 43.4g; FIBER 6.3g; CHOL 84mg; IRON 3.7mg; SODIUM 480mg; CALC 105mg

---

Thai Steak Salad
(pictured on page 223)

Flank steak is widely available and easy to recognize by its long, flat shape and distinctive longitudinal grain. Cutting across the grain breaks up the muscle fibers for more tender slices.

DRESSING:

⅓ cup fresh lime juice (about 3 limes)
1½ tablespoons brown sugar
1 tablespoon grated peeled fresh ginger
1 tablespoon Thai fish sauce
1 to 2 teaspoons chile paste with garlic

STEAK:

Cooking spray
1 (1½-pound) flank steak, trimmed
1 tablespoon cracked black pepper

SALAD:

3 cups trimmed watercress (about 2 bunches)
1 cup thinly sliced red cabbage
1 cup loosely packed fresh basil leaves
1 cup loosely packed fresh mint leaves
½ cup loosely packed fresh cilantro leaves
½ cup julienne-cut carrot
2 tablespoons finely chopped unsalted, dry-roasted peanuts

1. To prepare dressing, combine first 5 ingredients; stir well with a whisk.

2. To prepare steak, heat a large nonstick skillet or grill pan coated with cooking spray over medium-high heat. Rub both sides of steak with pepper. Add steak to pan; cook 6 minutes on each side or until desired degree of doneness. Remove from pan; place on a cutting board. Cover loosely with foil; let stand 5 minutes. Cut steak diagonally across grain into thin slices. Place steak in a bowl. Drizzle with half of dressing, and toss well.

3. To prepare salad, combine watercress and next 5 ingredients in a large bowl. Drizzle with remaining dressing, and toss well. Divide salad evenly among 6

plates; arrange steak evenly over salad. Sprinkle each serving with 1 teaspoon peanuts. Yield: 6 servings.

CALORIES 230 (40% from fat); FAT 10.3g (sat 4g, mono 4.2g, poly 0.9g); PROTEIN 25.1g; CARB 9.5g; FIBER 2g; CHOL 57mg; IRON 3.3mg; SODIUM 327mg; CALC 68mg

Balsamic-Braised Short Ribs with Horseradish Mashed Potatoes

Short ribs are the meaty ends of the rib bones. Choose cuts from the chuck, which are the most flavorful, or from the rib, which are a bit leaner. Packages labeled "short ribs" in the supermarket are likely to come from the chuck.

RIBS:
Cooking spray
4 pounds beef short ribs, trimmed
1 teaspoon kosher salt, divided
1 teaspoon freshly ground black pepper, divided
2 cups finely chopped red onion
¼ cup minced garlic (about 12 cloves)
2 cups low-salt beef broth
1 cup dry red wine
¾ cup balsamic vinegar
⅓ cup packed brown sugar
2 cups chopped plum tomato

POTATOES:
2½ pounds baking potatoes, peeled and cut into quarters
¾ cup warm 1% low-fat milk
2 tablespoons fat-free sour cream
1½ tablespoons prepared horseradish
1 teaspoon kosher salt
½ teaspoon freshly ground black pepper

1. Preheat oven to 300°.
2. To prepare ribs, heat a large oven-proof Dutch oven coated with cooking spray over medium-high heat. Sprinkle ribs with ½ teaspoon salt and ½ teaspoon pepper. Add half of ribs to pan; cook 8 minutes or until browned, turning occasionally. Remove from pan. Repeat procedure with remaining ribs; remove from pan.
3. Add onion to pan; sauté 8 minutes or until lightly browned. Add garlic; sauté 1 minute. Return ribs to pan. Add broth, wine, vinegar, sugar, and tomato; bring to a simmer.
4. Cover and bake at 300° for 1½ hours or until tender. Cool slightly. Refrigerate 8 hours or overnight.
5. Skim fat from surface of broth mixture; discard fat. Cook over medium heat 30 minutes or until thoroughly heated. Stir in ½ teaspoon salt and ½ teaspoon pepper.
6. To prepare mashed potatoes, place potato in a large saucepan; cover with water. Bring to a boil; cook 20 minutes or until very tender. Drain. Combine potato, milk, and remaining 4 ingredients in a large bowl. Mash potato mixture with a potato masher. Serve with ribs and cooking liquid. Yield: 7 servings (serving size: 3 ounces beef, about ¾ cup mashed potatoes, and ⅓ cup cooking liquid).

CALORIES 463 (26% from fat); FAT 13.4g (sat 5.6g, mono 5.7g, poly 0.7g); PROTEIN 27.2g; CARB 53.5g; FIBER 4.2g; CHOL 64mg; IRON 4mg; SODIUM 649mg; CALC 100mg

reader recipes

Home Improvement

A do-it-yourself-minded reader remodels an old Southern favorite.

When Becky Taylor of Athens, Georgia, isn't renovating her kitchen, she loves to create new dishes for her husband.

One recipe is a takeoff on a traditional Southern dish, shrimp and grits. "I replaced the grits with mashed potatoes, added crawfish, fresh corn, and some other ingredients to create Crawfish and Corn over Smoked Gouda Potatoes," she says. "The combination just seemed to work."

The result is an all-purpose dish. "My friends and family love the flavor, and I love it because it is so simple," Becky says. To dress up the meal, Becky serves it with homemade bread or rolls.

Crawfish and Corn over Smoked Gouda Potatoes

Use shrimp in place of crawfish, if desired.

POTATOES:
6 cups cubed peeled baking potato (about 1½ pounds)
⅔ cup 1% low-fat milk
¼ teaspoon salt
¼ teaspoon black pepper
¾ cup (3 ounces) shredded smoked Gouda cheese

CRAWFISH:
2 tablespoons butter
1 cup chopped onion
4 garlic cloves, minced
1½ cups fresh corn kernels (about 3 ears)
½ teaspoon salt
½ teaspoon paprika
¼ teaspoon ground red pepper
¼ teaspoon dried thyme
¼ teaspoon black pepper
1 (16-ounce) package frozen cooked and peeled crawfish meat, thawed
½ cup chopped green onions
Fresh thyme sprigs (optional)

1. To prepare potatoes, place potato in a saucepan; cover with water. Bring to a boil; reduce heat, and simmer 20 minutes or until tender. Drain. Return potato to pan; add milk, ¼ teaspoon salt, and ¼ teaspoon black pepper. Mash potato mixture with a potato masher to desired consistency. Stir in cheese. Keep warm.
2. To prepare crawfish, melt butter in a large nonstick skillet over medium-high heat. Add onion and garlic; sauté 5 minutes. Stir in corn; sauté 2 minutes. Add ½ teaspoon salt and next 5 ingredients; sauté 5 minutes or until thoroughly heated. Remove from heat; stir in green onions. Serve crawfish mixture over mashed potatoes. Garnish with thyme sprigs, if desired. Yield: 4 servings (serving size: about 1¼ cups crawfish mixture and 1 cup mashed potatoes).

CALORIES 454 (28% from fat); FAT 14.1g (sat 8g, mono 3.9g, poly 1.2g); PROTEIN 30.3g; CARB 53.4g; FIBER 6.1g; CHOL 171mg; IRON 2.2mg; SODIUM 781mg; CALC 263mg

Best BBQ Chicken Ever

—Shelley Gronick, Kelowna, BC, Canada

  2 tablespoons butter
  ½ cup ketchup
  ¼ cup fresh lemon juice
  ¼ cup low-sodium soy sauce
  ¼ teaspoon black pepper
  ¼ teaspoon hot sauce
  6 (4-ounce) skinless, boneless
     chicken breast halves
Cooking spray

1. Melt butter in a medium saucepan over medium-low heat. Add ketchup and next 4 ingredients; bring to a boil. Partially cover; cook until reduced to ⅔ cup (about 15 minutes), stirring frequently.
2. Prepare grill.
3. Place chicken on grill rack coated with cooking spray. Grill 12 minutes or until done, turning and basting with ⅓ cup sauce after 8 minutes; serve with remaining ⅓ cup sauce. Yield: 6 servings (serving size: 1 chicken breast half and about 1 tablespoon sauce).

CALORIES 157 (29% from fat); FAT 5g (sat 2.7g, mono 1.4g, poly 0.4g); PROTEIN 20.6g; CARB 7.4g; FIBER 0.4g; CHOL 60mg; IRON 1mg; SODIUM 693mg; CALC 17mg

Peasant Stew

—Heather Mader, Portland, Oregon

  1 teaspoon ground cumin
  ¼ teaspoon salt
  ¼ teaspoon black pepper
  6 chicken thighs (about 1½ pounds),
     skinned
  1 cup chopped onion
  1 (14.5-ounce) can Mexican-style
     stewed tomatoes with jalapeño
     peppers and spices, undrained
  1 (4.5-ounce) can chopped green
     chiles, undrained
  1 (15-ounce) can pinto beans, rinsed
     and drained
  1 (15-ounce) can kidney beans,
     rinsed and drained
  ¼ cup minced fresh cilantro
  ¼ cup reduced-fat sour cream

1. Combine cumin, salt, and pepper; sprinkle over chicken.
2. Place chicken in an electric slow cooker; stir in onion, tomatoes, and chiles. Cover with lid; cook on high-heat setting 3 hours. Stir in beans. Cover; cook on high-heat setting 1 hour.
3. Place 1 chicken thigh in each of 6 soup bowls; ladle 1¼ cups stew into each bowl. Top each serving with 2 teaspoons cilantro and 2 teaspoons sour cream. Yield: 6 servings.

CALORIES 214 (16% from fat); FAT 3.9g (sat 1.4g, mono 0.9g, poly 0.9g); PROTEIN 21.5g; CARB 23.7g; FIBER 6g; CHOL 61mg; IRON 3mg; SODIUM 773mg; CALC 85mg

Party Pineapple Chicken

"This recipe makes a great edible centerpiece for a luau and is easy to prepare."
—Alyssa Fisher, Spokane, Washington

  1⅓ cups pineapple juice
  ⅓ cup low-sodium teriyaki sauce
  ¼ teaspoon salt
  ¼ teaspoon black pepper
  2 pounds skinless, boneless
     chicken breast; cut into 1-inch
     cubes
Cooking spray

1. Combine first 4 ingredients in a large zip-top plastic bag; add chicken breast. Seal and marinate in refrigerator 2 hours or overnight.
2. Prepare grill.
3. Remove chicken from bag, reserving ½ cup marinade. Bring reserved marinade to a boil in a small saucepan over medium-high heat; cook 1 minute.
4. Thread chicken onto 12 (12-inch) skewers; place skewers on grill rack coated with cooking spray. Grill 12 minutes or until done, turning and basting with reserved marinade once. Yield: 6 servings (serving size: 2 skewers).

CALORIES 169 (8% from fat); FAT 1.5g (sat 0.4g, mono 0.4g, poly 0.3g); PROTEIN 27.3g; CARB 10.3g; FIBER 0.1g; CHOL 66mg; IRON 1mg; SODIUM 454mg; CALC 22mg

back to the best

Lemon-Garlic Chicken Thighs

A satisfying weeknight meal, this recipe calls for everyday ingredients you're likely to have on hand.

Pair this tender chicken with a simple starchy side, such as roasted potatoes, to offset the slightly elevated fat content, as we did in the September 1998 issue of *Cooking Light* magazine. You'll have a deliciously healthful dinner with little effort.

Lemon-Garlic Chicken Thighs

  ¼ cup fresh lemon juice
  2 tablespoons molasses
  2 teaspoons Worcestershire sauce
  4 garlic cloves, chopped
  8 chicken thighs, skinned (about 2
     pounds)
Cooking spray
  ¼ teaspoon salt
  ¼ teaspoon black pepper
Lemon wedges (optional)
Parsley sprigs (optional)

1. Combine first 4 ingredients in a dish; add chicken. Cover and marinate in refrigerator 1 hour, turning occasionally.
2. Preheat oven to 425°.
3. Remove chicken from dish; reserve marinade. Arrange chicken in a shallow roasting pan coated with cooking spray. Pour reserved marinade over chicken; sprinkle with salt and pepper.
4. Bake at 425° for 20 minutes; baste chicken with marinade. Bake an additional 20 minutes or until chicken is done. Serve with lemon wedges, and garnish with parsley, if desired. Yield: 4 servings (serving size: 2 chicken thighs).

CALORIES 258 (40% from fat); FAT 11.6g (sat 3.3g, mono 4.4g, poly 2.6g); PROTEIN 27.3g; CARB 9.9g; FIBER 0.1g; CHOL 98mg; IRON 1.9mg; SODIUM 268mg; CALC 43mg

Pasta Salads

With a quick cook, a cool rinse, and an easy toss, you can have these pasta dishes on the table in minutes.

search myclar2003.com for all our menus

Penne Pasta Salad Menu
serves 4

Chicken-Penne Salad with Green Beans

Mozzarella toasts*

Mixed berries dolloped with vanilla yogurt

*Place 4 (½-inch-thick) diagonally cut slices French bread baguette on a baking sheet. Sprinkle each bread slice with 1 tablespoon shredded part-skim mozzarella cheese. Bake at 350° for 12 minutes or until bread is golden and cheese is melted.

Game Plan

1. While water for pasta comes to a boil and oven preheats for toasts:
- Prepare toasts
- Trim and cut green beans
- Shred chicken

2. While pasta and beans cook:
- Slice onion and bell pepper
- Chop basil and parsley
- Prepare dressing
- Prepare berries

Chicken-Penne Salad with Green Beans

To quickly prepare the beans, trim just the stem ends, leaving the tapered blossom ends intact. Line up 5 or 6 beans at a time and cut them roughly the same length as the pasta.

TOTAL TIME: 36 MINUTES

QUICK TIP: Use 2 forks to shred the chicken breast. The texture of shredded chicken allows it to hold the dressing more easily.

  2 cups uncooked penne (tube-shaped pasta)
  2 cups (1-inch) cut green beans (about ½ pound)
  2 cups shredded cooked chicken breast
  ½ cup vertically sliced red onion
  ¼ cup chopped fresh basil
1½ teaspoons chopped fresh flat-leaf parsley
  1 (7-ounce) bottle roasted red bell pepper, drained and cut into thin strips
  2 tablespoons extra-virgin olive oil
  2 tablespoons red wine vinegar
  1 tablespoon cold water
  ½ teaspoon salt
  ½ teaspoon bottled minced garlic
  ¼ teaspoon black pepper

1. Cook pasta in boiling water 7 minutes. Add green beans; cook 4 minutes. Drain and rinse with cold water; drain.

2. Combine pasta mixture, chicken, and next 4 ingredients in a large bowl, tossing gently to combine.

3. Combine oil and remaining 5 ingredients in a small bowl, stirring with a whisk. Drizzle over pasta mixture; toss gently to coat. Yield: 4 servings (serving size: 2 cups).

CALORIES 384 (23% from fat); FAT 9.7g (sat 1.8g, mono 5.7g, poly 1.5g); PROTEIN 26.9g; CARB 47.8g; FIBER 2.6g; CHOL 49mg; IRON 3.2mg; SODIUM 866mg; CALC 59mg

Orzo Pasta Salad Menu
serves 4

Orzo Salad with Chickpeas, Dill, and Lemon

Sliced romaine with mint*

Garlic breadsticks

*Combine 4 cups thinly sliced romaine lettuce and ½ cup chopped fresh mint in a bowl. Combine 1 tablespoon fresh lemon juice, 2 teaspoons olive oil, and ⅛ teaspoon salt in a small bowl, stirring with a whisk. Drizzle over salad; toss to combine.

Game Plan

1. While water for pasta comes to a boil and oven preheats for breadsticks:
- Slice green onions
- Chop dill
- Drain chickpeas

2. While pasta cooks:
- Bake breadsticks
- Prepare romaine salad
- Prepare dressing for orzo salad

Orzo Salad with Chickpeas, Dill, and Lemon

If you're not a big dill fan, use half the amount. Quick-cooking couscous can replace the orzo.

TOTAL TIME: 30 MINUTES

QUICK TIP: To get more juice from a lemon, be sure it's at room temperature. Then, before juicing, roll it across the countertop while applying pressure with the palm of your hand.

  1 cup uncooked orzo (rice-shaped pasta)
  ½ cup thinly sliced green onions
  ½ cup (2 ounces) crumbled feta cheese
  ¼ cup chopped fresh dill
  1 (19-ounce) can chickpeas (garbanzo beans), drained
  3 tablespoons fresh lemon juice
1½ tablespoons extra-virgin olive oil
  1 tablespoon cold water
  ½ teaspoon salt
  ½ teaspoon bottled minced garlic

Continued

1. Cook pasta according to package directions, omitting salt and fat. Drain and rinse with cold water; drain.

2. Combine pasta, onions, cheese, dill, and chickpeas in a large bowl, tossing gently to combine.

3. Combine juice and remaining 4 ingredients in a small bowl, stirring with a whisk. Drizzle over pasta mixture; toss gently to coat. Yield: 4 servings (serving size: 1¼ cups).

CALORIES 327 (29% from fat); FAT 10.4g (sat 2.9g, mono 5.1g, poly 1.8g); PROTEIN 10.8g; CARB 47.6g; FIBER 4.9g; CHOL 13mg; IRON 3mg; SODIUM 641mg; CALC 107mg

---

Bow Tie Pasta Salad Menu
serves 6

Summer Farfalle Salad with Smoked Salmon

Artichoke-Parmesan cream cheese with crackers*

Sliced peaches

*Combine ¾ cup tub-style light cream cheese, ¼ cup chopped canned artichoke hearts, 3 tablespoons grated Parmesan cheese, and ¼ teaspoon garlic salt. Serve with crackers.

Game Plan

1. While water for pasta comes to a boil:
- Halve cherry tomatoes
- Chop dill
- Prepare artichoke-Parmesan cream cheese

2. While pasta cooks:
- Prepare dressing for salad
- Cut salmon
- Slice peaches

search myclar2003.com for all our menus

Summer Farfalle Salad with Smoked Salmon
(pictured on page 222)

Substitute leftover cooked salmon for the sliced smoked salmon, if you prefer.

TOTAL TIME: 35 MINUTES

QUICK TIP: Look for sliced smoked salmon near the gourmet cheeses or in the seafood department. Freeze leftover salmon for later use—sprinkle on scrambled eggs or add to a toasted bagel with light cream cheese.

    3   cups uncooked farfalle
        (bow tie pasta)
    2   cups cherry tomatoes, halved
    ¼   cup chopped fresh dill
    1   (6-ounce) bag baby spinach
    1   teaspoon grated lemon rind
    2   tablespoons fresh lemon juice
    2   tablespoons cold water
    1½ tablespoons extra-virgin
        olive oil
    ½   teaspoon salt
    ¼   teaspoon black pepper
    4   ounces (about 8 slices) smoked
        salmon, cut into thin strips

1. Cook pasta according to package directions, omitting salt and fat. Drain and rinse with cold water; drain.

2. Combine pasta, tomatoes, dill, and spinach in a large bowl, tossing gently.

3. Combine lemon rind and next 5 ingredients in a small bowl, stirring with a whisk. Drizzle over pasta mixture; toss gently to coat. Top with salmon. Yield: 6 servings (serving size: 2 cups).

CALORIES 206 (23% from fat); FAT 5.3g (sat 0.9g, mono 3.1g, poly 1.1g); PROTEIN 9.8g; CARB 31.4g; FIBER 2.7g; CHOL 4mg; IRON 2.3mg; SODIUM 603mg; CALC 43mg

---

How Her Garden Grows

A Seattle woman leaves the corporate world to cultivate her dream job—teaching gardening.

Relying on her former marketing expertise, Cindy Combs launched Gardening Getaways—how-to workshops for gardeners held in various locales.

An accomplished cook who thrives on fresh produce and grains, she occasionally creates gardening menus for her "students." Here's just a sample recipe of what you might find at one of her Gardening Getaways.

Gardener's Ratatouille

Chop all the vegetables the same size for even cooking. Serve as a side dish, or as a vegetarian entrée with rosemary focaccia.

    2   teaspoons olive oil
    1   cup chopped onion
    3   cups chopped plum tomato
        (about 1 pound)
    2   cups chopped peeled eggplant
    1½ cups chopped zucchini
    1   cup chopped green bell pepper
    1   garlic clove, minced
    1   tablespoon chopped fresh oregano
    1   tablespoon chopped fresh basil
    1   tablespoon chopped fresh parsley
    ½   teaspoon salt
    ¼   teaspoon black pepper

1. Heat oil in a large skillet over medium-high heat. Add onion; sauté 3 minutes or until tender, stirring frequently. Add tomato and next 4 ingredients. Cover, reduce heat, and simmer 30 minutes, stirring occasionally.

2. Stir in oregano and remaining ingredients; cook, uncovered, 5 minutes or until most of liquid evaporates. Yield: 4 servings (serving size: about ¾ cup).

CALORIES 91 (30% from fat); FAT 3g (sat 0.4g, mono 1.8g, poly 0.5g); PROTEIN 2.8g; CARB 16g; FIBER 4.6g; CHOL 0mg; IRON 1.2mg; SODIUM 308mg; CALC 37mg

Roasting Bell Peppers

Precise pointers to prepare perfect peppers.

Roasting Rudiments

- A typical baking sheet will hold 8 flattened, large bell pepper halves.
- The key step in roasting bell peppers is to seal them in a bag immediately after taking them out of the oven. The steam produced in the bag makes the skins slide off easily.
- If you're roasting 1 large or 2 small bell peppers, steam the peppers in the foil you used to line the baking sheet. Larger amounts need to be transferred to large zip-top plastic bags.
- One large roasted bell pepper will yield about ½ cup when chopped.

Roasted Bell Peppers

Red, yellow, and orange bell peppers are virtually identical in flavor and are interchangeable. Green peppers aren't as sweet.

  4 large bell peppers (about 2 pounds)

1. Preheat broiler.
2. Cut bell peppers in half lengthwise; discard seeds and membranes. Place pepper halves, skin sides up, on a foil-lined baking sheet; flatten with hand. Broil 20 minutes or until thoroughly blackened.
3. Immediately place peppers in a large zip-top plastic bag; seal. Let stand 20 minutes. Peel peppers; discard skins. Chop peppers according to recipe directions. Yield: 4 servings (serving size: 1 pepper).

CALORIES 44 (6% from fat); FAT 0.3g (sat 0.1g, mono 0g, poly 0.2g); PROTEIN 1.5g; CARB 10.6g; FIBER 3.1g; CHOL 0mg; IRON 0.8mg; SODIUM 3mg; CALC 15mg

Pizza with Roasted Peppers, Caramelized Onions, and Olives

  1 teaspoon olive oil
Cooking spray
  2 cups vertically sliced Vidalia or other sweet onion
  1 cup julienne-cut Roasted Bell Peppers (recipe at left)
  ¼ cup chopped pitted kalamata olives
  1 (14.5-ounce) can Italian-style diced tomatoes, drained
  1 (10-ounce) Italian cheese-flavored thin pizza crust (such as Boboli)
  ½ cup (2 ounces) shredded provolone cheese

1. Preheat oven to 450°.
2. Heat oil in a large nonstick skillet coated with cooking spray over medium heat. Add onion; cook 12 minutes or until browned, stirring occasionally. Remove from heat; stir in peppers, olives, and tomatoes.
3. Place pizza crust on a baking sheet. Spread onion mixture over pizza crust, leaving a ½-inch border, and top with cheese. Bake at 450° for 12 minutes or until cheese melts. Yield: 4 servings.

CALORIES 342 (30% from fat); FAT 11.6g (sat 4.2g, mono 4g, poly 0.6g); PROTEIN 13.1g; CARB 46.3g; FIBER 3.4g; CHOL 10mg; IRON 2.8mg; SODIUM 968mg; CALC 352mg

Barley Pilaf with Roasted Peppers and Snow Peas

This recipe provides a hearty alternative to rice pilaf and goes well with beef, chicken, or pork. Use a mix of roasted red and yellow peppers for the best appearance.

  1 teaspoon olive oil
  ⅓ cup finely chopped celery
  2 tablespoons finely chopped onion
  1⅓ cups vegetable broth
  ⅔ cup uncooked quick-cooking barley
  ½ cup (½-inch) diagonally cut snow peas
  6 tablespoons finely chopped Roasted Bell Peppers (recipe at left)
  ⅛ teaspoon black pepper

1. Heat oil in a medium saucepan over medium-high heat. Add celery and onion; sauté 3 minutes or until tender. Add broth; bring to a boil. Stir in barley; cover, reduce heat, and simmer 15 minutes or until tender.
2. Stir in peas, bell peppers, and black pepper; remove from heat. Cover and let stand 5 minutes. Yield: 4 servings (serving size: about ⅔ cup).

CALORIES 113 (17% from fat); FAT 2.1g (sat 0.3g, mono 0.9g, poly 0.4g); PROTEIN 3.9g; CARB 22.2g; FIBER 3.4g; CHOL 0mg; IRON 0.9mg; SODIUM 344mg; CALC 19mg

Corn and Roasted Pepper Salad
(pictured on page 221)

Use any combination of peppers in this salad. Serve with chicken breasts sprinkled with salt, black pepper, and paprika, and sautéed seven minutes on each side.

  2 cups fresh corn kernels (about 4 ears)
  1 cup chopped Roasted Bell Peppers (recipe at left)
  ⅔ cup chopped seeded plum tomato
  ¼ cup minced shallots
  2 tablespoons finely chopped fresh flat-leaf parsley
  2 teaspoons minced seeded jalapeño pepper
  ½ teaspoon grated lime rind
  2 tablespoons fresh lime juice
  2 teaspoons extra-virgin olive oil
  ½ teaspoon salt
  ⅛ teaspoon black pepper
Flat-leaf parsley sprigs (optional)

1. Combine first 6 ingredients in a large bowl. Combine lime rind and remaining 4 ingredients in a small bowl, stirring with a whisk. Drizzle lime juice mixture over corn mixture, and toss well. Garnish with parsley sprigs, if desired. Yield: 6 servings (serving size: ½ cup salad).

CALORIES 72 (28% from fat); FAT 2.2g (sat 0.3g, mono 1.3g, poly 0.5g); PROTEIN 2.2g; CARB 13g; FIBER 2.2g; CHOL 0mg; IRON 0.6mg; SODIUM 206mg; CALC 10mg

Chicken Stew with Sweet Peppers

2 teaspoons olive oil
1 cup finely chopped onion
¾ pound skinless, boneless chicken breast, cut into bite-sized pieces
3 cups chopped zucchini
1 cup finely chopped carrot
⅓ cup canned chopped green chiles, drained
¾ teaspoon dried oregano
½ teaspoon ground cumin
¼ teaspoon salt
¼ teaspoon black pepper
2 garlic cloves, minced
1 (15.5-ounce) can Great Northern beans, drained
1 (14-ounce) can fat-free, less-sodium chicken broth
1 cup chopped Roasted Bell Peppers (recipe on page 237)
4 teaspoons chopped fresh cilantro

1. Heat oil in a Dutch oven over medium-high heat. Add onion and chicken; sauté 5 minutes or until lightly browned. Add zucchini and next 9 ingredients; bring to a boil. Cover, reduce heat, and simmer 30 minutes or until vegetables are tender.
2. Add peppers; cook, uncovered, 10 minutes, stirring occasionally. Sprinkle with cilantro. Yield: 4 servings (serving size: 1½ cups).
NOTE: Store stew in refrigerator for up to 2 days. Reheat in a saucepan over medium heat until thoroughly heated; sprinkle with cilantro before serving.

CALORIES 262 (14% from fat); FAT 4.1g (sat 0.7g, mono 2g, poly 0.7g); PROTEIN 28.3g; CARB 28.8g; FIBER 7.8g; CHOL 49mg; IRON 3mg; SODIUM 455mg; CALC 96mg

Mediterranean Salsa

You can serve this as a side dish or on top of toasted baguette slices as an appetizer. Any assortment of sweet roasted bell peppers works in this recipe.

1½ cups chopped seeded tomato
1 cup finely chopped zucchini
½ cup finely chopped Roasted Bell Peppers (recipe on page 237)
2 tablespoons finely chopped red onion
1 tablespoon finely chopped fresh basil
1 tablespoon finely chopped fresh flat-leaf parsley
2 teaspoons fresh lemon juice
2 teaspoons extra-virgin olive oil
1½ teaspoons capers
¼ teaspoon salt
⅛ teaspoon black pepper
1 garlic clove, minced

1. Combine all ingredients in a large bowl. Yield: 6 servings (serving size: ½ cup).
NOTE: Store salsa in the refrigerator for up to 2 days.

CALORIES 33 (46% from fat); FAT 1.7g (sat 0.2g, mono 1.1g, poly 0.2g); PROTEIN 0.8g; CARB 4.4g; FIBER 1.3g; CHOL 0mg; IRON 0.5mg; SODIUM 124mg; CALC 11mg

---

Storing Peppers

Store unwashed, uncut fresh peppers in a plastic bag in the refrigerator. They will keep for at least a week, depending on how fresh they were when you purchased them. Because red peppers are softer and more mature than green peppers, they do not keep as well. Once cut, peppers are especially short lived.

Although you can roast peppers one at a time over a stovetop flame, broiling several at once is far more efficient. Roasted peppers can be refrigerated in a covered bowl for up to five days. Before using, drain any liquid and blot peppers with paper towels.

search myclar2003.com for all our tips

Gazpacho with Roasted Peppers
(pictured on page 223)

Because this tomato-based soup is red, use a combination of yellow, orange, and green peppers for the prettiest color.

3 cups chopped seeded peeled tomato (about 1½ pounds)
⅓ cup finely chopped red onion
3 large basil leaves
1 garlic clove, minced
1 cup finely chopped peeled cucumber, divided
1½ cups tomato juice
½ cup finely chopped Roasted Bell Peppers (recipe on page 237)
2 tablespoons red wine vinegar
1 teaspoon Worcestershire sauce
1 teaspoon extra-virgin olive oil
½ teaspoon salt
¼ teaspoon black pepper
4 teaspoons chopped fresh flat-leaf parsley

1. Combine first 4 ingredients in a food processor; add ¾ cup cucumber. Pulse 5 times or until coarsely pureed.
2. Combine pureed tomato mixture, juice, and next 6 ingredients; stir well. Cover and refrigerate 3 hours or until chilled.
3. Sprinkle with ¼ cup cucumber and parsley. Yield: 4 servings (serving size: about 1 cup).
NOTE: Store soup in refrigerator for up to 2 days. Stir and sprinkle with parsley before serving.

CALORIES 72 (23% from fat); FAT 1.8g (sat 0.3g, mono 0.9g, poly 0.4g); PROTEIN 2.5g; CARB 14.2g; FIBER 2.8g; CHOL 0mg; IRON 1.6mg; SODIUM 651mg; CALC 31mg

september

Party Favors

Learn how to entertain with ease—making things perfect
for your guests, and manageable for you.

On the next few pages we offer ideas and recipes to simplify your next gathering and secure your reputation as a star enter- tainer. From stylish table setting ideas to fabulous menus to minute-by-minute game plans, we'll show you how to kindle the sparks that make an evening glow. Every idea and recipe is specially designed to subtract the stress from your next party.

A Party with Style

Cooking Light *Senior Photo Stylist Lydia DeGaris-Pursell shares her secrets for an alfresco dinner.*

Stick with what you know. Start with a menu to equal your capabilities. Expand on dishes you're comfortable making. For her, that's pasta.

Less is more at the table. A casual table setting will set the tone for the affair, put your friends at ease, and make your life simpler.

Be flexible about location. Use a room of your house other than the dining room, such as the living room. Or head outside. She decided on her back deck for her casual alfresco affair.

Wine Suggestions

• Serve the antipasto and flatbread with a light, snappy white like Pino and Toi from Maculan. A blend of Pinot Grigio, Pinot Bianco, Tocai, and Chardonnay, the 2001 is $10.

• For the pasta, move on to a fresh herbal-laced white. The 2001 Meridian Sauvignon Blanc is $8.

• End the evening by serving the Pumpkin Spice-Cream with small glasses of tawny port. The rich, nutty, and languorously smooth Taylor Fladgate 20-Year-Old Tawny Port is $45.

Alfresco Dinner Menu

Fresh Tomato Soup

Rosemary-Scented Flatbread with Black Grapes with dipping oils

Baby Vegetable Antipasto

Roasted Pepper, Kalamata, and Prosciutto Pasta

Pumpkin Spice-Cream

Fresh Tomato Soup

Prepare the soup through step 2 up to a day ahead. Reheat over medium-low heat, and stir in the basil, lemon rind, and butter just before serving.

    1   teaspoon olive oil
    1   cup chopped onion
    6   cups chopped plum tomato
        (about 1½ pounds)
    3   (14-ounce) cans fat-free,
        less-sodium chicken broth
    2   garlic cloves, crushed
    7   cups chopped seeded peeled plum
        tomato (about 1¾ pounds)
    ¼   teaspoon salt
    ¼   teaspoon black pepper
    3   tablespoons thinly sliced fresh
        basil
    1   teaspoon grated lemon rind
    1   teaspoon butter

1. Heat oil in a large saucepan over medium-high heat. Add onion; sauté 4 minutes or until tender. Add 6 cups tomato; cook 2 minutes. Reduce heat to low; stir in broth and garlic. Simmer, covered, 30 minutes.

2. Uncover; simmer 45 minutes or until reduced to about 6 cups. Strain broth mixture through a sieve into a large bowl; discard solids. Return broth to pan. Stir in 7 cups tomato, salt, and pepper; bring to a boil. Reduce heat; simmer, uncovered, 10 minutes.

3. Remove soup from heat. Stir in basil, rind, and butter. Yield: 6 servings (serving size: about 1 cup).

CALORIES 64 (27% from fat); FAT 1.9g (sat 0.6g, mono 0.8g, poly 0.3g); PROTEIN 3.9g; CARB 8.5g; FIBER 1.9g; CHOL 2mg; IRON 0.8mg; SODIUM 496mg; CALC 12mg

Rosemary-Scented Flatbread with Black Grapes

Blue or red grapes will also work well in this recipe as long as they're fresh and firm. Be sure not to overwork the dough when incorporating the grapes. They won't disperse well at first, but they'll spread properly when you shape the dough. Serve with one or more of the dipping oils on page 241.

    3¼   cups all-purpose flour, divided
      1   teaspoon sugar
      1   package dry yeast (about 2¼
          teaspoons)
    1¼   cups warm water (100° to 110°)
      ½   cup white cornmeal
    1¼   teaspoons salt, divided
    1½   teaspoons chopped fresh rosemary
    2½   teaspoons olive oil, divided
          Cooking spray
      1   cup seedless black grapes,
          quartered and divided
          Rosemary sprig (optional)

1. Lightly spoon flour into dry measuring cups, and level with a knife. Dissolve sugar and yeast in 1¼ cups warm water in a large bowl. Stir in 1 cup flour. Cover loosely with plastic wrap, and let stand 30 minutes.

2. Add 2 cups flour, cornmeal, 1 teaspoon salt, chopped rosemary, and 1½ teaspoons oil to yeast mixture; stir until a soft dough forms.

3. Turn dough out onto a floured surface. Knead until smooth and elastic (about 8 minutes); add enough of remaining flour, 1 tablespoon at a time, to prevent dough from sticking to hands (dough will feel tacky).

4. Place dough in a large bowl coated with cooking spray, turning to coat top. Cover and let rise in a warm place (85°), free from drafts, 1 hour or until doubled in size. (Press two fingers into dough. If indentation remains, dough has risen enough.)

5. Punch dough down, and turn out onto a lightly floured surface. Arrange ⅔ cup grapes over dough, and knead gently 4 or 5 times or just until grapes are incorporated into dough. Let rest 5 minutes.

6. Press dough into a 15 x 10-inch rectangle. Place on a large baking sheet coated with cooking spray. Brush surface of dough with 1 teaspoon oil. Cover and let rise 30 minutes or until doubled in size.

7. Preheat oven to 475°.

8. Uncover dough. Make indentations in top of dough using handle of a wooden spoon or your fingertips. Sprinkle surface of dough with ⅓ cup grapes; gently press grapes into dough. Sprinkle with ¼ teaspoon salt. Bake at 475° for 20 minutes or until golden. Garnish with rosemary sprig, if desired. Yield: 12 servings.

CALORIES 164 (8% from fat); FAT 1.4g (sat 0.2g, mono 0.8g, poly 0.3g); PROTEIN 4.4g; CARB 33g; FIBER 1.6g; CHOL 0mg; IRON 2mg; SODIUM 246mg; CALC 8mg

Sage, Bay, and Garlic Dipping Oil

Bay and sage permeate this garlicky oil, infusing it with wonderful earthy, woodsy flavors.

½ cup olive oil
2 garlic cloves, crushed
2 fresh sage leaves
1 bay leaf

1. Combine all ingredients in a small, heavy saucepan. Cook over medium-low heat until thermometer registers 180°. Reduce heat to low, and cook 20 minutes (do not allow temperature to rise above 200°). Cool to room temperature. Strain oil mixture through a sieve into a bowl, and discard solids. Yield: ½ cup (serving size: 2 teaspoons).

CALORIES 80 (100% from fat); FAT 9g (sat 1.2g, mono 6.6g, poly 0.8g); PROTEIN 0g; CARB 0g; FIBER 0g; CHOL 0mg; IRON 0mg; SODIUM 0mg; CALC 0mg

Basil Dipping Oil

2 cups chopped fresh basil leaves (about 2 [¾-ounce] packages)
½ cup olive oil

1. Combine basil and oil in a small, heavy saucepan. Cook over medium-low heat until thermometer registers 180°. Reduce heat to low; cook 20 minutes (do not allow temperature to rise above 200°). Cool to room temperature. Strain oil mixture through a sieve into a bowl; discard solids. Yield: ½ cup (serving size: 2 teaspoons).

CALORIES 80 (100% from fat); FAT 9g (sat 1.2g, mono 6.6g, poly 0.8g); PROTEIN 0g; CARB 0g; FIBER 0g; CHOL 0mg; IRON 0mg; SODIUM 0mg; CALC 0mg

Three-Pepper Dipping Oil

½ cup olive oil
1 pepperoncini pepper, halved lengthwise
1 whole dried hot red chile, crushed
2 whole black peppercorns

1. Combine all ingredients in a small, heavy saucepan. Cook over medium-low heat until thermometer registers 180°. Reduce heat to low, and cook 20 minutes (do not allow temperature to rise above 200°). Cool to room temperature. Strain oil mixture through a sieve into a bowl, and discard solids. Yield: ½ cup (serving size: 2 teaspoons).

CALORIES 80 (100% from fat); FAT 9g (sat 1.2g, mono 6.6g, poly 0.8g); PROTEIN 0g; CARB 0g; FIBER 0g; CHOL 0mg; IRON 0mg; SODIUM 0mg; CALC 0mg

Baby Vegetable Antipasto

Immediately place the prepared vegetables in the marinade so they won't discolor.

MARINADE:
3 tablespoons white wine vinegar
1 tablespoon chopped fresh flat-leaf parsley
1 tablespoon chopped fresh basil
2 teaspoons extra-virgin olive oil
½ teaspoon salt
Dash of sugar
Dash of freshly ground black pepper
1 garlic clove, crushed

VEGETABLES:
8 baby artichokes (about 1½ pounds)
20 small red potatoes (about 12 ounces)
3 bunches baby carrots with tops (about 1½ pounds), peeled
2 bunches small radishes with tops (about 1½ pounds)
1 cup torn radicchio
1 head Belgian endive, separated into leaves (about 4 ounces)

REMAINING INGREDIENTS:
20 pitted ripe olives
3 ounces fresh mozzarella cheese, torn into bite-sized pieces
Continued

Take a Dip

Serve one or more of these oils with the Rosemary-Scented Flatbread with Black Grapes (recipe on page 240). Pour them into small, wide bowls to facilitate dipping, and garnish each oil with its seasonings. Cooking the oil gently infuses it with flavor.

If the temperature rises above 200°, though, the oil may develop a bitter flavor, so watch the thermometer closely. Refrigerate oils up to a week in glass containers. Toss leftover oil with pasta or use it in salad dressing.

1. To prepare marinade, combine first 8 ingredients in a small bowl, and stir well with a whisk.

2. To prepare vegetables, working with 1 artichoke at a time, cut off stem to the base. Remove bottom leaves and tough outer leaves, leaving tender heart and bottom; trim about 1 inch from top of artichoke. Steam artichokes, covered, 20 minutes or until tender; cool to room temperature. Cut artichokes in half lengthwise. Remove fuzzy thistle from bottom with a spoon.

3. Steam potatoes, covered, 6 minutes or until tender. Cool to room temperature.

4. Trim carrot stems to 2 inches. Steam carrots, covered, 20 seconds. Plunge into ice water; drain well.

5. Trim radish tops to 1 inch.

6. Place artichokes, potatoes, carrots, radishes, radicchio, and endive in a large bowl. Drizzle with marinade; toss gently to coat. Cover and marinate in refrigerator 2 hours.

7. Arrange vegetables on a platter; top with olives and cheese. Yield: 10 servings (serving size: about 1¼ cups).

CALORIES 127 (30% from fat); FAT 4.2g (sat 1.5g, mono 1.9g, poly 0.4g); PROTEIN 6.4g; CARB 19.5g; FIBER 6g; CHOL 7mg; IRON 2.1mg; SODIUM 386mg; CALC 127mg

---

Home Plates

For most settings, neutral plates are a smart investment. Whether you choose off-white plates from a restaurant supply store or have some custom made, plain dinnerware is a versatile choice. Cream-colored plates allow you to change bowls with the seasons. Black works for fall, red for winter, and turquoise for summer. Clear glassware with simple, traditional shapes is adaptable enough to go formal or informal.

search myclar2003.com for all our tips

Roasted Pepper, Kalamata, and Prosciutto Pasta

(pictured on page 259)

Wide, flat pappardelle pasta creates a refined presentation: Its cascading quality gives the dish more height. If you can't find pappardelle, substitute a short pasta, such as cavatappi or penne.

- 3 red bell peppers (about 1½ pounds)
- 1 yellow bell pepper
- ⅓ cup pitted kalamata olives, quartered
- 2 tablespoons capers
- 2 tablespoons extra-virgin olive oil
- ½ teaspoon grated lemon rind
- 1½ teaspoons fresh lemon juice
- ¼ teaspoon salt
- ⅛ teaspoon freshly ground black pepper
- ⅓ cup chopped fresh flat-leaf parsley
- 4 ounces prosciutto, cut into ⅛-inch strips
- 6 cups hot cooked pappardelle pasta (about 12 ounces uncooked pasta)
- 6 tablespoons (1½ ounces) shaved Parmigiano-Reggiano cheese
- Parsley sprigs (optional)

1. Preheat broiler.
2. Cut bell peppers in half lengthwise; discard seeds and membranes. Place pepper halves, skin sides up, on a foil-lined baking sheet; flatten with hand. Broil 10 minutes or until blackened. Place in a zip-top plastic bag; seal. Let stand 10 minutes. Peel and cut into thin strips.
3. Combine olives and next 6 ingredients in a bowl. Add bell pepper and chopped parsley; toss gently to combine.
4. Cook prosciutto in a large nonstick skillet over medium heat 3 minutes or until crisp; remove from pan. Add bell pepper mixture to pan; cook over low heat 3 minutes or until heated.
5. Place pasta in a large bowl. Add bell pepper mixture and prosciutto; toss gently to combine. Sprinkle with cheese. Garnish with parsley sprigs, if desired. Yield: 6 servings (serving size: 1¼ cups pasta mixture and 1 tablespoon cheese).

CALORIES 343 (29% from fat); FAT 11.2g (sat 2.8g, mono 6.3g, poly 1.4g); PROTEIN 14.5g; CARB 46.2g; FIBER 4.3g; CHOL 16mg; IRON 3mg; SODIUM 707mg; CALC 111mg

---

Pumpkin Spice-Cream

Spiced with cinnamon, ginger, and nutmeg, this make-ahead dessert tastes like pumpkin pie; crumbled biscotti adds a crisp crunch. This will keep in the freezer for up to four days.

- 1½ cups 1% low-fat milk, divided
- 2 tablespoons dark brown sugar
- 2 large egg yolks
- 1 (14-ounce) can fat-free sweetened condensed milk
- 1 teaspoon vanilla extract
- ¼ teaspoon ground nutmeg
- ⅛ teaspoon ground ginger
- ⅛ teaspoon ground cinnamon
- Dash of salt
- 1 cup canned pumpkin
- 1 (8-ounce) carton reduced-fat sour cream
- 2 commercial biscotti, crumbled (about ¾ cup)

1. Combine 1 cup 1% milk and sugar in a medium, heavy saucepan, and heat to 180° or until tiny bubbles form around edge (do not boil). Remove from heat.
2. Place egg yolks in a bowl. Gradually add hot milk mixture to egg yolks, stirring constantly with a whisk. Place mixture in pan. Cook over medium heat until mixture coats a metal spoon (about 4 minutes), stirring constantly. Strain custard through a sieve into a bowl; discard solids.
3. Combine ½ cup 1% milk, condensed milk, and next 5 ingredients in a medium bowl. Stir in pumpkin. Gradually add custard, stirring with a whisk. Cover and chill at least 8 hours.
4. Combine ½ cup pumpkin mixture and sour cream, stirring well with a whisk. Add sour cream mixture to chilled pumpkin mixture, and stir until well blended. Pour mixture into freezer can of an ice-cream freezer, and freeze according to manufacturer's instructions.
5. Spoon ice cream into a freezer-safe container; fold in crumbled biscotti. Cover and freeze 1 hour or until firm. Yield: 8 servings (serving size: ½ cup).

CALORIES 263 (22% from fat); FAT 6.3g (sat 3.2g, mono 1.8g, poly 0.6g); PROTEIN 8.7g; CARB 43g; FIBER 1.1g; CHOL 74mg; IRON 0.9mg; SODIUM 204mg; CALC 258mg

The Supper Club Challenge

Try this supper club menu at your next group gathering. It's sure to be a hit.

Supper Club Menu

Marinated Spanish Olives

Watercress-Bibb Salad with Apples and Blue Cheese

Gruyère, Arugula, and Prosciutto-Stuffed Chicken Breasts with Caramelized Shallot Sauce

Baked Rice with Butternut Squash

Cloverleaf Honey-Wheat Rolls

Harvest Pear Crisp

Marinated Spanish Olives

Make and refrigerate up to a week ahead.

- 24 large unpitted Spanish olives
- 2 tablespoons sherry vinegar
- 1 tablespoon extra-virgin olive oil
- 2 teaspoons coriander seeds, crushed
- 1 teaspoon dried thyme
- 1 teaspoon dried rosemary, crushed
- ½ teaspoon crushed red pepper
- 2 garlic cloves, thinly sliced
- Rosemary sprigs (optional)

1. Combine first 8 ingredients in a bowl. Cover and marinate in refrigerator at least 8 hours. Serve at room temperature. Garnish with rosemary sprigs, if desired. Yield: 6 servings (serving size: 4 olives).

CALORIES 49 (66% from fat); FAT 3.6g (sat 0.1g, mono 2g, poly 1.4g); PROTEIN 0.2g; CARB 3.1g; FIBER 0.2g; CHOL 0mg; IRON 0.4mg; SODIUM 322mg; CALC 13mg

---

Wine Suggestions

- Start dinner with Cava. Try Freixenet's Cordon Negro Brut, $9.
- Serve Benziger Fumé Blanc from Sonoma County with the chicken. The 2000 is $13.
- For dessert try a late harvest Riesling from California, like the Geyser Peak Late Harvest Riesling Reserve. A half bottle of the 2000 is $19.

Watercress-Bibb Salad with Apples and Blue Cheese

Prepare dressing up to three days ahead, refrigerate in a jar, and shake well before tossing.

DRESSING:
- 3 tablespoons apple juice
- 1 tablespoon cider vinegar
- 1 tablespoon finely chopped shallots
- 2 teaspoons Dijon mustard
- 1 teaspoon vegetable oil
- ¼ teaspoon salt
- ¼ teaspoon freshly ground black pepper

SALAD:
- 7 cups torn Bibb lettuce
- 2½ cups trimmed watercress
- 2 cups thinly sliced Granny Smith apple (about ½ pound)
- ¼ cup (1 ounce) crumbled blue cheese

1. To prepare dressing, combine first 7 ingredients in a jar. Cover tightly; shake vigorously. Refrigerate at least 2 hours.
2. To prepare salad, combine lettuce and remaining 3 ingredients in a bowl. Add dressing; toss well. Yield: 6 servings (serving size: about 1½ cups).

CALORIES 61 (35% from fat); FAT 2.4g (sat 1g, mono 0.2g, poly 0.6g); PROTEIN 2.2g; CARB 9.2g; FIBER 1.7g; CHOL 3mg; IRON 0.4mg; SODIUM 210mg; CALC 52mg

---

Gruyère, Arugula, and Prosciutto-Stuffed Chicken Breasts with Caramelized Shallot Sauce

Stuffing the chicken a day ahead and refrigerating it makes it easier to sauté. See our technique for stuffing the chicken breasts on page 244.

CHICKEN:
- 6 (4-ounce) skinless, boneless chicken breast halves
- 6 (½-ounce) slices prosciutto
- 6 (½-ounce) slices Gruyère cheese
- 1½ cups trimmed arugula
- ½ teaspoon salt
- ½ teaspoon black pepper
- 3 tablespoons all-purpose flour
- 1 tablespoon olive oil

SAUCE:
- 1 cup thinly sliced shallots
- 2 teaspoons tomato paste
- 2 cups dry white wine
- 2¼ cups fat-free, less-sodium chicken broth
- 1½ teaspoons water
- 1 teaspoon cornstarch

1. Preheat oven to 350°.
2. To prepare chicken, place each breast half between 2 sheets of heavy-duty plastic wrap; pound to ¼-inch thickness using a meat mallet or rolling pin. Discard plastic wrap. Top each half with 1 slice prosciutto, 1 slice cheese, and ¼ cup arugula, leaving a ¼-inch border around edges. Fold in half, pinching edges together to seal; sprinkle with salt and pepper. (Chicken can be prepared up to a day ahead, and refrigerated.)
3. Dredge chicken in flour, shaking off excess. Heat oil in a large nonstick skillet over medium-high heat. Add chicken; cook 5 minutes on each side. Place chicken in a shallow baking pan; bake at 350° for 5 minutes or until done. Keep warm.
4. To prepare sauce, add shallots to skillet; sauté 4 minutes over medium-high heat or until browned. Add tomato paste; cook 1 minute, stirring constantly. Stir in wine; bring to a boil over high heat. Cook until reduced to 1 cup (about 6 minutes).
Continued

How to Stuff Chicken Breasts

Three simple steps make the Gruyère, Arugula, and Prosciutto-Stuffed Chicken Breasts a snap to prepare. See recipe on page 243.

1. *Pound chicken between two sheets of plastic wrap to keep work surface clean.*

2. *Leave a ¼-inch border around edges so filling won't spill out during cooking.*

3. *No toothpicks required. Simply press edges of chicken breast together to seal.*

Add broth; bring to a boil. Cook until reduced by half (about 8 minutes).

5. Combine water and cornstarch in a small bowl; stir with a fork until smooth. Add cornstarch mixture to sauce; bring to a boil. Cook 1 minute, stirring constantly. Yield: 6 servings (serving size: 1 chicken breast half and about ¼ cup sauce).

CALORIES 300 (29% from fat); FAT 9.8g (sat 4g, mono 4g, poly 0.9g); PROTEIN 29.7g; CARB 9.7g; FIBER 0.5g; CHOL 75mg; IRON 1.7mg; SODIUM 562mg; CALC 189mg

Baked Rice with Butternut Squash

Prepare the squash up to two days ahead.

1 butternut squash (about 1½ pounds)
2 cups fat-free, less-sodium chicken broth
1 cup water
1 tablespoon chopped fresh or 1 teaspoon dried rubbed sage
1 teaspoon olive oil
1 cup chopped onion
2 garlic cloves, minced
1 cup uncooked Arborio or other short-grain rice
¼ cup dry white wine
1 teaspoon chopped fresh or ¼ teaspoon dried thyme
½ teaspoon salt
¼ teaspoon black pepper
Cooking spray
¼ cup (1 ounce) grated fresh Parmesan cheese
Thyme sprigs (optional)

1. Preheat oven to 350°.
2. Place squash on a baking sheet. Bake at 350° for 30 minutes or until tender; cool. Peel squash; cut in half lengthwise. Discard seeds and membranes; cut into ½-inch cubes. Increase oven temperature to 400°.
3. Bring broth, water, and sage to a simmer in a medium saucepan (do not boil). Heat oil in a large nonstick skillet over medium-high heat. Add onion; sauté 6 minutes. Add garlic; sauté 2 minutes. Add rice; sauté 1 minute. Stir in squash, broth mixture, wine, chopped thyme, salt, and pepper; cook 5 minutes, stirring occasionally.
4. Place rice mixture in a 13 x 9-inch baking dish coated with cooking spray. Bake at 400° for 30 minutes. Stir mixture gently. Sprinkle with cheese; bake an additional 5 minutes or until cheese melts. Garnish with fresh thyme sprigs, if desired. Yield: 6 servings (serving size: about 1 cup).

CALORIES 186 (11% from fat); FAT 2.2g (sat 1g, mono 0.7g, poly 0.1g); PROTEIN 5.4g; CARB 35.1g; FIBER 2.1g; CHOL 4mg; IRON 0.9mg; SODIUM 244mg; CALC 112mg

Cloverleaf Honey-Wheat Rolls

Bake these rolls up to a day ahead; store at room temperature in a zip-top plastic bag, or freeze them for later. Wrap the rolls in foil, and reheat at 350° for 10 minutes or until warm.

1 package dry yeast (about 2¼ teaspoons)
1 cup warm water (100° to 110°)
2 cups bread flour, divided
1 cup whole wheat flour
3 tablespoons honey
2½ tablespoons butter, melted
1 teaspoon salt
Cooking spray
1 tablespoon water
1 large egg

1. Dissolve yeast in 1 cup warm water in a large bowl; let stand 5 minutes. Lightly spoon flours into dry measuring cups; level with a knife. Add 1½ cups bread flour, whole wheat flour, honey, butter, and salt to yeast mixture; stir until well blended. Add ¼ cup bread flour; stir until a soft dough forms.
2. Turn dough out onto a floured surface. Knead until smooth and elastic (about 8 minutes); add enough of remaining bread flour, 1 tablespoon at a time, to prevent dough from sticking to hands (dough will feel tacky).
3. Place dough in a large bowl coated with cooking spray, turning to coat top. Cover and let rise in a warm place (85°), free from drafts, 1 hour or until doubled in size. (Press two fingers into dough. If indentation remains, dough has risen enough.) Punch dough down; cover and let rest 5 minutes.
4. Coat 12 muffin cups with cooking spray. Divide dough into 12 equal portions. Working with 1 portion at a time, divide each portion into 3 pieces; shape each piece into a ball (cover remaining

dough to prevent it from drying). Place 3 balls in each muffin cup. Cover and let rise 25 minutes or until doubled in size.

5. Preheat oven to 425°.

6. Uncover dough. Combine 1 tablespoon water and egg; brush over rolls. Bake at 425° for 12 minutes or until lightly browned. Serve warm. Yield: 1 dozen (serving size: 1 roll).

CALORIES 152 (18% from fat); FAT 3g (sat 1.6g, mono 0.9g, poly 0.2g); PROTEIN 5.1g; CARB 27.3g; FIBER 2g; CHOL 24mg; IRON 1.5mg; SODIUM 206mg; CALC 4mg

Harvest Pear Crisp

(pictured on page 258)

Cinnamon-spiced pears bake under a crunchy streusel topping in this easy dessert. Assemble the dish ahead of time, and put it in the oven when guests arrive. Or bake it earlier in the day, and serve it at room temperature. Serve with low-fat vanilla ice cream.

    6 cups Anjou or Bartlett pears, cored
       and cut lengthwise into ½-inch-
       thick slices (about 3 pounds)
    1 tablespoon fresh lemon juice
    ⅓ cup granulated sugar
    1 tablespoon cornstarch
    1½ teaspoons ground cinnamon, divided
    ⅓ cup all-purpose flour
    ½ cup packed brown sugar
    ½ teaspoon salt
    3 tablespoons chilled butter, cut into
       small pieces
    ⅓ cup regular oats
    ¼ cup coarsely chopped walnuts

1. Preheat oven to 375°.

2. Combine pears and lemon juice in a 2-quart baking dish; toss gently to coat. Combine granulated sugar, cornstarch, and 1 teaspoon cinnamon; stir with a whisk. Add cornstarch mixture to pear mixture; toss well to coat.

3. Lightly spoon flour into a dry measuring cup; level with a knife. Place flour, ½ teaspoon cinnamon, brown sugar, and salt in a food processor; pulse 2 times or until combined. Add chilled butter; pulse 6 times or until mixture resembles coarse meal. Add oats and chopped walnuts; pulse 2 times. Sprinkle flour mixture evenly over pear mixture.

4. Bake at 375° for 40 minutes or until pears are tender and topping is golden brown. Cool 20 minutes on a wire rack; serve warm or at room temperature. Yield: 8 servings.

CALORIES 285 (24% from fat); FAT 7.7g (sat 3g, mono 1.8g, poly 2.2g); PROTEIN 2.4g; CARB 55.5g; FIBER 5.1g; CHOL 12mg; IRON 1.2mg; SODIUM 197mg; CALC 42mg

Fancy Finger Foods

Pull out all the stops with these impressive party nibbles.

When you're hosting a celebration and want to impress, nothing gets a party—or the appetites—going like hors d'oeuvres. Each of the colorful bites here will delight the palate with intense, focused flavors and contrasting textures. And not only are they impressive, but they're also meatless.

Appetizer Party Buffet

Truffle-Scented Risotto in Phyllo

Roasted Cauliflower Skewers with Sweet Peppers and Cumin

Curried Chickpea Canapés with Ginger-Carrot Butter

Tempeh Satay with Curried Cashew Sauce

Spiced Red Lentil Dip with Pita Crisps

Hiziki Caviar with Lemon Tofu Cream and Chives

Herbed Ricotta Won Tons with Spicy Tomato Sauce

search myclar2003.com for all our menus

Truffle-Scented Risotto in Phyllo

We loved the subtle flavor imparted by the white truffle oil. If you don't have truffle oil, add a little extra Parmesan. Look for phyllo cups in the freezer section of your grocery store, if you'd rather not make your own.

    2   teaspoons olive oil
    ⅓   cup finely chopped onion
    1   teaspoon minced fresh thyme
    1   garlic clove, minced
    ½   cup uncooked Arborio rice
    2   tablespoons dry white wine
    1½ cups water
    ½   teaspoon fine sea salt
    2   tablespoons grated fresh Parmesan
        cheese
    2   teaspoons butter
    1   teaspoon white truffle oil
    ¼   teaspoon black pepper
    6   sheets frozen phyllo dough,
        thawed
Cooking spray
    2   tablespoons chopped fresh parsley

1. Heat olive oil in a large nonstick skillet over medium-high heat. Add onion; sauté 3 minutes. Add thyme and garlic; sauté 1 minute. Stir in rice; sauté 1 minute. Stir in wine; cook 1 minute or until liquid is nearly absorbed, stirring constantly. Add water and salt; bring to a boil. Cover, reduce heat, and simmer 18 minutes. Remove from heat. Stir in cheese, butter, truffle oil, and pepper. Cool completely.

2. Preheat oven to 375°.

3. Place 1 phyllo sheet on a large cutting board or work surface (cover remaining dough to keep from drying); lightly coat sheet with cooking spray. Repeat layers with remaining phyllo sheets and cooking spray, ending with phyllo. Gently press phyllo layers together. Lightly coat top phyllo sheet with cooking spray. Cut phyllo layers into 24 (1½-inch) squares using a sharp knife or pizza cutter.

4. Carefully place 1 layered square in each of 24 miniature muffin cups coated with cooking spray; gently press squares
Continued

into pan to form cups. Bake at 375° for 5 minutes or until crisp. Remove phyllo cups from pan. Fill each cup with 1 tablespoon risotto. Sprinkle cups evenly with parsley. Yield: 12 servings (serving size: 2 phyllo cups).

CALORIES 88 (28% from fat); FAT 2.7g (sat 0.9g, mono 1.4g, poly 0.3g); PROTEIN 1.9g; CARB 13.1g; FIBER 0.5g; CHOL 3mg; IRON 0.5mg; SODIUM 168mg; CALC 22mg

Roasted Cauliflower Skewers with Sweet Peppers and Cumin

Roasting cauliflower amplifies its flavor.

    3 tablespoons fresh lemon juice
    1 tablespoon extra-virgin olive oil
    1 teaspoon fine sea salt
    1 teaspoon ground cumin
    1 teaspoon ground coriander seeds
    ½ teaspoon cumin seeds
    ½ teaspoon crushed red pepper
   30 cauliflower florets (about 1 medium head)
    1 large yellow bell pepper, cut into 15 (1-inch) squares
    1 large red bell pepper, cut into 15 (1-inch) squares
    ½ cup chopped fresh cilantro

1. Preheat oven to 450°.
2. Combine first 7 ingredients in a large bowl, stirring with a whisk. Add cauliflower and bell pepper squares; toss gently to coat.
3. Spoon vegetables into a single layer on a jelly roll pan. Bake at 450° for 25 minutes or until lightly browned and crisp-tender, stirring after 15 minutes. Cool completely; stir in cilantro.
4. Thread 1 cauliflower floret and 1 bell pepper square onto each of 30 (6-inch) skewers. Yield: 15 servings (serving size: 2 skewers).

CALORIES 25 (40% from fat); FAT 1.1g (sat 0.1g, mono 0.7g, poly 0.1g); PROTEIN 1g; CARB 3.6g; FIBER 1.5g; CHOL 0mg; IRON 0.4mg; SODIUM 167mg; CALC 15mg

Curried Chickpea Canapés with Ginger-Carrot Butter

These canapés are made with chickpea flour, but you can also make them with polenta or grits.

CANAPÉS:
    1 cup chickpea flour
  2⅔ cups cold water
    ¾ teaspoon fine sea salt
       Cooking spray
    1 tablespoon curry powder

BUTTER:
  2⅓ cups thinly sliced carrot
    2 cups water
    1 tablespoon butter
    1 tablespoon honey
    2 teaspoons minced peeled fresh ginger
    1 tablespoon fresh lemon juice
    ¼ teaspoon fine sea salt
    ⅛ teaspoon white pepper

REMAINING INGREDIENTS:
    2 tablespoons sliced almonds, toasted
    2 tablespoons finely chopped fresh cilantro

1. To prepare canapés, lightly spoon flour into a dry measuring cup; level with a knife. Combine flour, 2⅔ cups water, and ¾ teaspoon salt in a medium saucepan, stirring with a whisk. Bring to a boil, stirring constantly. Cover, reduce heat, and simmer 20 minutes. Uncover and stir with a whisk until smooth. Pour into an 11 x 7-inch baking dish coated with cooking spray; sprinkle evenly with curry powder. Chill 1 hour or until firm.
2. Preheat oven to 375°.
3. Cut chickpea mixture into 40 (1-inch) squares; place on a jelly roll pan coated with cooking spray. Bake at 375° for 20 minutes or until golden. Cool.
4. To prepare butter, combine carrot and next 4 ingredients in a saucepan. Bring to a boil. Cover, reduce heat, and simmer 7 minutes or until carrot is tender. Increase heat to medium-high; uncover and cook 12 minutes or until liquid evaporates.
5. Combine carrot mixture, lemon juice, ¼ teaspoon salt, and pepper in a food

processor; process until smooth. Place carrot butter in a zip-top plastic bag; seal. Snip a small hole in 1 corner of bag; pipe about 1 teaspoon carrot butter onto each canapé. Sprinkle canapés evenly with almonds and cilantro. Yield: 20 servings (serving size: 2 canapés).

CALORIES 36 (30% from fat); FAT 1.2g (sat 0.4g, mono 0.4g, poly 0.1g); PROTEIN 1.2g; CARB 5.5g; FIBER 0.8g; CHOL 2mg; IRON 0.5mg; SODIUM 127mg; CALC 13mg

Tempeh Satay with Curried Cashew Sauce

Tempeh and cashews stand in for the traditional chicken and peanuts in this classic Indonesian dish.

TEMPEH:
    ¼ cup rice vinegar
    ¼ cup low-sodium soy sauce
    ¼ cup mirin (sweet rice wine)
    2 teaspoons minced peeled fresh ginger
    2 teaspoons vegetable oil
    1 garlic clove, crushed
    1 pound tempeh, cut into 40 cubes

SAUCE:
       Cooking spray
    1 cup chopped onion
    2 teaspoons minced peeled fresh ginger
    ¼ teaspoon fine sea salt
    2 garlic cloves, chopped
    2 teaspoons curry powder
    ½ teaspoon ground turmeric
    1 cup water
    2 tablespoons chopped cashews
    1 tablespoon fresh lemon juice

1. To prepare tempeh, combine first 6 ingredients in a large nonstick skillet; add tempeh, tossing lightly to coat. Bring to a boil. Cover, reduce heat to low, and simmer 15 minutes.
2. Uncover tempeh mixture, and increase heat to medium-high. Cook 4 minutes or until golden brown, turning frequently. Cool.
3. To prepare sauce, heat a small saucepan coated with cooking spray over medium-high heat. Add chopped onion,

2 teaspoons ginger, salt, and 2 garlic cloves; sauté 5 minutes. Stir in curry powder and turmeric; sauté 1 minute. Add water. Bring to a boil, and cook 1 minute. Cool 5 minutes.

4. Pour onion mixture into a blender, and add cashews and lemon juice. Process until smooth. Place a toothpick in each tempeh cube. Serve with warm cashew sauce. Yield: 20 servings (serving size: 2 tempeh cubes and about 2 teaspoons sauce).

CALORIES 50 (32% from fat); FAT 1.8g (sat 0.4g, mono 0.3g, poly 0.7g); PROTEIN 4g; CARB 4.1g; FIBER 1.7g; CHOL 0mg; IRON 0.7mg; SODIUM 241mg; CALC 32mg

Spiced Red Lentil Dip with Pita Crisps

You can use green or brown lentils, but the dip won't be as pretty.

DIP:
- 1 cup dried small red lentils
- 1 bay leaf
- 1 tablespoon olive oil
- 1 cup finely chopped onion
- 2 tablespoons pine nuts
- 1 tablespoon tomato paste
- 1 teaspoon fine sea salt
- 1 teaspoon ground coriander seeds
- ½ teaspoon ground cumin
- ½ teaspoon ground caraway seeds
- ⅛ teaspoon ground red pepper
- 3 garlic cloves, minced
- 3 tablespoons fresh lemon juice

PITA CRISPS:
- 4 (6-inch) pitas, each cut into 5 wedges
- Cooking spray
- ⅛ teaspoon fine sea salt
- ⅛ teaspoon freshly ground black pepper

1. Preheat oven to 350°.

2. To prepare dip, place lentils and bay leaf in a saucepan; cover with water to 2 inches above lentils. Bring to a boil. Cover, reduce heat, and simmer 8 minutes or until tender. Drain well. Discard bay leaf.

3. Heat oil in a small nonstick skillet over medium-high heat. Add onion and nuts; sauté 5 minutes or until nuts are lightly browned. Stir in tomato paste and next 6 ingredients; cook 5 minutes, stirring occasionally. Stir in juice. Combine lentils and onion mixture in a food processor; process until smooth.

4. To prepare pita crisps, coat 1 side of each pita wedge with cooking spray; sprinkle wedges evenly with ⅛ teaspoon salt and black pepper. Arrange wedges in a single layer on a baking sheet. Bake at 350° for 20 minutes or until golden. Yield: 10 servings (serving size: about ¼ cup dip and 2 pita crisps).

CALORIES 159 (15% from fat); FAT 2.6g (sat 0.4g, mono 1.4g, poly 0.6g); PROTEIN 7.4g; CARB 27g; FIBER 3.9g; CHOL 0mg; IRON 2mg; SODIUM 395mg; CALC 46mg

Hiziki Caviar with Lemon Tofu Cream and Chives

Look for *hiziki*, a black ribbonlike seaweed, in Asian markets; substitute dried nori seaweed sheets if hiziki isn't available. If your knife skills are rusty, preshredded carrots will do nicely for the garnish. Use the leftover tofu cream as a dip for crudités.

CAVIAR:
- 1 ounce dried hiziki seaweed
- 1 teaspoon dark sesame oil
- ½ teaspoon vegetable oil
- ⅔ cup water
- 1½ tablespoons low-sodium soy sauce
- 1 garlic clove, minced

REMAINING INGREDIENTS:
- 1 lemon
- 48 sesame-flavored rice crackers
- ½ cup Lemon Tofu Cream
- 48 pieces (1-inch) sliced fresh chives
- 48 pieces matchstick-cut carrot

1. To prepare caviar, place seaweed in a large bowl; cover with hot water to 2 inches above seaweed. Cover and let stand 30 minutes or until soft. Drain. Rinse with cold water, and drain. Place seaweed in a food processor; process until minced.

2. Heat oils in a large nonstick skillet over medium heat. Add seaweed; cook 3 minutes, stirring occasionally. Add ⅔ cup water, soy sauce, and garlic; bring to a boil. Reduce heat; simmer 6 minutes or until liquid evaporates.

3. To prepare remaining ingredients, peel lemon, and cut lengthwise into 6 wedges. Cut each wedge crosswise into 8 pieces to yield 48 triangles.

4. Place 1 teaspoon seaweed caviar on each cracker. Place Lemon Tofu Cream in a small zip-top plastic bag; seal. Snip a small hole in 1 corner of bag; pipe about ½ teaspoon tofu cream on each cracker. Place 1 lemon triangle, 1 chive piece, and 1 carrot piece on each cracker. Yield: 16 servings (serving size: 3 crackers).

(Totals include Lemon Tofu Cream) CALORIES 40 (20% from fat); FAT 0.9g (sat 0.1g, mono 0.3g, poly 0.5g); PROTEIN 1.1g; CARB 7g; FIBER 0.5g; CHOL 0mg; IRON 0.6mg; SODIUM 127mg; CALC 16mg

LEMON TOFU CREAM:
- 1 (2-inch) piece peeled fresh ginger
- 2 tablespoons fresh lemon juice
- 1 tablespoon vegetable oil
- ½ teaspoon fine sea salt
- 8 ounces firm silken tofu, drained

1. Finely grate ginger; place ginger on several layers of damp cheesecloth. Gather edges of cheesecloth together; squeeze over a small bowl to extract 1 teaspoon ginger juice.

2. Combine ginger juice, lemon juice, oil, salt, and tofu in a food processor; process until smooth. Yield: 1 cup (serving size: 2 tablespoons).

CALORIES 34 (66% from fat); FAT 2.5g (sat 0.3g, mono 0.6g, poly 1.4g); PROTEIN 2g; CARB 1.1g; FIBER 0.1g; CHOL 0mg; IRON 0.3mg; SODIUM 154mg; CALC 10mg

Selecting Seaweed

The salty Japanese seaweed *hiziki* (also called *nijiki*) comes in two different forms. You may find it in sheets, but we prefer the long black ribbons. Either works fine in Hiziki Caviar with Lemon Tofu Cream and Chives (recipe at left).

search myclar2003.com for all our tips

Herbed Ricotta Won Tons with Spicy Tomato Sauce

Habanero peppers are fiery, so wear gloves while chopping them. To tame the sauce, substitute a jalapeño or poblano pepper. You can make the won tons ahead of time, freeze them, and bake just before serving.

WON TONS:

1 cup part-skim ricotta cheese
¼ cup blanched almonds, toasted
½ teaspoon all-purpose flour
½ cup chopped fresh mint
2 tablespoons grated fresh Parmesan cheese
2 tablespoons fresh flat-leaf parsley leaves
2 tablespoons finely chopped fresh chives
1 tablespoon grated lemon rind
½ teaspoon fine sea salt
¼ teaspoon freshly ground black pepper
1 large egg white
1 garlic clove, chopped
30 won ton wrappers
Cooking spray
1 large egg white, lightly beaten

SAUCE:

1 (28-ounce) can whole tomatoes, drained
1 teaspoon olive oil
⅔ cup chopped onion
2 teaspoons finely grated orange rind
1 teaspoon sugar
1 habanero pepper, finely chopped
2 tablespoons chopped fresh basil

1. To prepare won tons, place colander in a 2-quart glass measure or medium bowl. Line colander with 2 layers of cheesecloth, allowing cheesecloth to extend over edges of bowl. Spoon ricotta into colander. Gather edges of cheesecloth together; tie securely. Refrigerate 1 hour. Gently squeeze cheesecloth bag to remove excess liquid; discard liquid. Spoon ricotta into a food processor.
2. Preheat oven to 350°.
3. Place almonds and flour in a spice or coffee grinder, and process until finely ground. Set aside 3 tablespoons almond mixture; add remaining almond mixture, mint, and next 8 ingredients to food processor. Process until smooth.
4. Working with 1 won ton wrapper at a time (cover remaining wrappers with a damp towel to keep them from drying), spoon about 2 teaspoons ricotta mixture into center of each wrapper. Moisten edges of dough with water; bring 2 opposite corners together. Press edges together to seal, forming a triangle.
5. Place won tons on 2 baking sheets lined with parchment paper and coated with cooking spray. Brush won tons with lightly beaten egg white; sprinkle with reserved almond mixture.
6. Bake at 350° for 15 minutes or until lightly browned. Cool won tons 5 minutes on a wire rack.
7. To prepare sauce, place tomatoes in food processor; process until finely chopped. Heat oil in a large nonstick skillet over medium-high heat. Add onion, and sauté 3 minutes. Stir in orange rind, sugar, and habanero pepper; sauté 2 minutes. Reduce heat to medium. Stir in tomatoes and basil; cook 10 minutes, stirring occasionally. Serve with won tons. Yield: 15 servings (serving size: 2 won tons and about 1 tablespoon sauce).

CALORIES 120 (29% from fat); FAT 3.9g (sat 2.2g, mono 1g, poly 0.4g); PROTEIN 5.8g; CARB 15.5g; FIBER 1.9g; CHOL 10mg; IRON 1.3mg; SODIUM 456mg; CALC 111mg

A Feast for the Eyes

These plating tips make your food look as good as it tastes.

We asked two of our experts in the *Cooking Light* Test Kitchens—chef and former restaurant owner Sam Brannock, and food stylist Kellie Gerber Kelley—to provide some ways to make your dinner plates eye-catching. Here's how to make the following recipes as stunning to the eye as they are to your palate. See Add Pizzazz to Your Plate on page 251 for more ideas.

Crispy Salmon with Risotto and Slow-Roasted Tomatoes

(pictured on page 260)

Slow-roasting the tomatoes helps them develop a sweet, earthy flavor. For a rich and satisfying meal, just add a green salad.

PLATING TIP: Break a childhood rule—it's OK for foods to touch. Layer and stack the tomatoes, risotto, and salmon to increase height and showcase shapes and colors.

ROASTED TOMATOES:

Cooking spray
9 plum tomatoes, halved
1 tablespoon olive oil
½ teaspoon sea salt
½ teaspoon chopped fresh thyme
½ teaspoon freshly ground black pepper
4 garlic cloves, minced

RISOTTO:

4½ cups fat free, less-sodium chicken broth
1 tablespoon olive oil
2¼ cups (½-inch-thick) sliced leek
1½ cups uncooked Arborio rice
⅓ cup dry white wine
6 cups torn arugula or spinach
½ cup half-and-half
¼ cup (1 ounce) grated fresh Parmesan cheese
¼ teaspoon sea salt
¼ teaspoon freshly ground black pepper

SALMON:

2 teaspoons olive oil
6 (5-ounce) salmon fillets, skinned
½ teaspoon sea salt
½ teaspoon chopped fresh thyme
¼ teaspoon freshly ground black pepper

GARNISH:

Thyme sprigs (optional)

1. Preheat oven to 350°.
2. To prepare tomatoes, coat a foil-lined baking sheet with cooking spray. Place tomatoes, cut sides up, on baking sheet.

Drizzle with 1 tablespoon oil; sprinkle with ½ teaspoon salt, ½ teaspoon thyme, ½ teaspoon pepper, and garlic. Bake at 350° for 1½ hours or until very soft and slightly shriveled, turning tomatoes occasionally.

3. To prepare risotto, bring broth to a simmer in a medium saucepan (do not boil). Keep warm over low heat.

4. Heat 1 tablespoon oil in a large saucepan over medium-high heat. Add leek, and sauté 3 minutes or until tender. Add rice; cook 1½ minutes, stirring constantly. Stir in wine; cook 30 seconds or until liquid is nearly absorbed. Stir in 1 cup broth; cook 3 minutes or until liquid is nearly absorbed, stirring frequently.

5. Add remaining broth, ½ cup at a time, stirring frequently until each portion of broth is absorbed before adding next (about 25 minutes). Stir in arugula and next 4 ingredients.

6. To prepare salmon, heat 2 teaspoons oil in a large nonstick skillet over medium-high heat. Sprinkle salmon with ½ teaspoon salt, ½ teaspoon thyme, and ¼ teaspoon pepper. Place fillets, skin sides up, in pan; cook 5 minutes. Turn fillets over, and cook 2 minutes or until fish flakes easily when tested with a fork.

7. Arrange 3 tomato halves, cut sides up, in a spoke-like pattern in center of each of 6 plates. Mound ⅔ cup risotto in center of each plate (leaving about a 1½-inch edge of tomatoes uncovered). Arrange fillets on risotto. Garnish with thyme sprigs, if desired. Yield: 6 servings.

CALORIES 569 (30% from fat); FAT 18.8g (sat 5.2g, mono 9.4g, poly 2.9g); PROTEIN 36.9g; CARB 58.1g; FIBER 3.1g; CHOL 81mg; IRON 2.4mg; SODIUM 992mg; CALC 186mg

Bourbon and Brown Sugar Flank Steak with Garlic-Chive Mashed Potatoes

Pork tenderloin will also work in this recipe.

PLATING TIP: Slicing the meat thinly reveals the gradation in its color and allows you to fan it along or atop the potatoes. Drizzle the sauce on the plate to keep it from getting lost on the meat.

STEAK:

- ¼ cup packed dark brown sugar
- ¼ cup minced green onions
- ¼ cup bourbon
- ¼ cup low-sodium soy sauce
- ¼ cup Dijon mustard
- ½ teaspoon freshly ground black pepper
- ¼ teaspoon Worcestershire sauce
- 1 (2-pound) flank steak, trimmed
  Cooking spray
- ½ teaspoon cornstarch

POTATOES:

- 3 pounds small red potatoes
- 6 garlic cloves, peeled
- ½ cup reduced-fat sour cream
- ⅓ cup 2% reduced-fat milk
- 2½ tablespoons butter
- 1 teaspoon salt
- ¼ teaspoon freshly ground black pepper
- ¼ cup chopped fresh chives

GARNISH:

- 8 fresh chives, cut into 1-inch pieces

1. To prepare steak, combine first 7 ingredients in a large zip-top plastic bag; add steak. Seal and marinate in refrigerator 8 hours or overnight, turning bag occasionally. Remove steak from bag, reserving marinade.

2. Prepare grill.

3. Place steak on grill rack coated with cooking spray; grill 5 minutes on each side or until desired degree of doneness. Let stand 10 minutes. Cut diagonally across grain into thin slices.

4. Combine reserved marinade and cornstarch in a saucepan. Bring to a boil; cook 1 minute, stirring constantly.

5. To prepare potatoes, place potatoes and garlic in a large Dutch oven; cover with water. Bring to a boil. Reduce heat; simmer 30 minutes or until tender. Drain.

6. Return potatoes and garlic to pan, and place over medium heat. Add sour cream, milk, butter, salt, and ¼ teaspoon pepper. Mash potato mixture to desired consistency with a potato masher. Stir in chopped chives. Mound ¾ cup potatoes on each of 8 plates; arrange 3 ounces steak around each serving of potatoes.

Drizzle 1 tablespoon sauce on each plate; sprinkle with chive pieces. Yield: 8 servings.

WINE NOTE: A great wine match for this dish is the powerfully structured yet superjuicy Stag's Leap Winery Merlot from the Napa Valley. The 1998 is about $31.

CALORIES 456 (30% from fat); FAT 15.4g (sat 7.4g, mono 4.9g, poly 0.8g); PROTEIN 29.1g; CARB 45.9g; FIBER 3.7g; CHOL 77mg; IRON 4.8mg; SODIUM 887mg; CALC 84mg

Crepes with Bananas and Hazelnut-Chocolate Sauce

Don't worry if all your crepes don't turn out perfectly; there's enough batter to allow for a few mistakes.

PLATING TIP: Sloshing the sauce over the crepes may be traditional, but it isn't particularly attractive. Spoon the sauce onto the plate to prevent it from discoloring the delicate crepes. A dusting of powdered sugar finishes the dish.

CREPES:

- 1 cup all-purpose flour
- 1 tablespoon granulated sugar
- ¼ teaspoon salt
- 1½ cups fat-free milk
- 2 large eggs, lightly beaten
  Cooking spray

SAUCE:

- ¼ cup hazelnut-chocolate spread (such as Nutella)
- 2 tablespoons fat-free milk
- ¼ teaspoon vanilla extract
- 2 large firm unpeeled bananas (about 1¾ pounds)
  Powdered sugar (optional)

1. To prepare crepes, lightly spoon flour into a dry measuring cup; level with a knife. Place flour, granulated sugar, and salt in a medium bowl; stir with a whisk. Combine 1½ cups milk and eggs, stirring with a whisk. Add milk mixture to flour mixture, stirring with a whisk just until smooth. Cover batter; chill 15 minutes.

2. Heat a 10-inch nonstick skillet coated with cooking spray over medium-high

Continued

heat. Remove pan from heat. Pour a scant ¼ cup batter into pan; quickly tilt pan in all directions so batter covers pan with a thin film. Cook about 1 minute.

3. Carefully lift edge of crepe with a spatula. Crepe is ready to turn when it can be shaken loose from pan and underside is lightly browned. Turn crepe over; cook 30 seconds.

4. Place crepe on a towel; keep warm. Repeat procedure until all batter is used. Stack crepes between single layers of wax paper or paper towels to prevent sticking.

5. To prepare sauce, combine hazelnut-chocolate spread, 2 tablespoons milk, and vanilla in a small saucepan over medium heat, stirring with a whisk until smooth. Keep warm.

6. Peel bananas, and cut in half lengthwise; cut each half crosswise into 2 pieces.

7. Heat a large nonstick skillet coated with cooking spray over medium-high heat. Arrange 4 banana pieces in a single layer in pan. Cook 1 minute or until lightly browned. Turn pieces over; cook 1 minute. Remove banana pieces from pan; keep warm. Repeat procedure with remaining banana pieces.

8. Place 1 banana piece in center of each crepe; fold sides and ends over, and place, seam side down, on clean surface.

9. Spoon about 1 tablespoon sauce onto each of 4 plates, spreading to cover center of plates. Arrange 2 crepes on each plate; sprinkle with powdered sugar, if desired. Serve immediately. Yield: 4 servings.

CALORIES 312 (22% from fat); FAT 7.6g (sat 1.8g, mono 4.3g, poly 0.9g); PROTEIN 9.6g; CARB 51.6g; FIBER 3.3g; CHOL 81mg; IRON 2mg; SODIUM 148mg; CALC 141mg

---

Yellow Pepper Soup with Cilantro Puree

Peas add body and sweetness to the puree. If you can't find crème fraîche, substitute sour cream.

PLATING TIP: A table knife transforms ordinary dollops into sensual swirls.

SOUP:
- 1 teaspoon butter
- 1½ cups chopped onion
- 1 cup chopped fennel bulb
- 1 teaspoon curry powder
- 1 teaspoon grated peeled fresh ginger
- 2 garlic cloves, chopped
- ⅓ cup dry white wine
- 3¼ cups coarsely chopped yellow bell pepper (about 1¼ pounds)
- 3 cups fat-free, less-sodium chicken broth
- 1½ cups chopped peeled Granny Smith apple (about ½ pound)
- 1 cup cubed peeled Yukon gold or red potato
- ¼ teaspoon salt
- 2 tablespoons fresh lemon juice

PUREE:
- ⅓ cup frozen green peas, thawed
- ⅓ cup fresh cilantro leaves
- 3 tablespoons fat-free, less-sodium chicken broth
- 1 tablespoon mirin (sweet rice wine)
- 1 teaspoon vegetable oil
- Dash of salt

REMAINING INGREDIENT:
- 2 tablespoons crème fraîche

1. To prepare soup, melt butter in a Dutch oven over medium-high heat. Add onion and fennel, and sauté 3 minutes. Add curry, ginger, and garlic; sauté 1 minute. Stir in white wine; cook 1 minute or until liquid almost evaporates. Add bell pepper and next 4 ingredients; bring to a boil. Reduce heat; simmer 20 minutes. Cool.

2. Place half of soup in a blender; process until smooth. Pour into a bowl. Repeat procedure with remaining soup. Chill at least 2 hours. Stir in juice.

3. To prepare puree, place peas and next 5 ingredients in a blender; process until smooth.

4. Pour ¾ cup soup into each of 6 bowls. Make 3 dollops with 3 teaspoons puree on each serving. Using tip of a knife, swirl each dollop into a "V" shape. Dollop 1 teaspoon crème fraîche in center of each serving. Yield: 6 servings.

CALORIES 138 (18% from fat); FAT 2.7g (sat 1.1g, mono 0.7g, poly 0.7g); PROTEIN 4.2g; CARB 23g; FIBER 4.5g; CHOL 4mg; IRON 1mg; SODIUM 392mg; CALC 40mg

---

Beet, Jícama, and Watercress Salad

Ruby red beets, creamy white jícama, emerald watercress, and sunny tangerines make a stunning salad. Since the vinaigrette for the jícama and tangerines needs to stand 30 minutes, prepare it while the beets cool. If you can't find tangerines, use small orange sections instead.

PLATING TIP: Arranging the jícama and tangerines around the greens and beets lets them share the spotlight.

- 2½ pounds beets with tops
- 5 teaspoons white balsamic vinegar, divided
- 1 teaspoon extra-virgin olive oil
- ½ teaspoon freshly ground black pepper, divided
- ¼ teaspoon salt, divided
- ⅓ cup thinly sliced red onion
- ¼ cup fresh orange juice
- 2½ cups (½-inch) diced peeled jícama
- ⅓ cup tangerine sections
- 2 cups trimmed watercress

1. Preheat oven to 425°.

2. Leave root and 1 inch stem on beets; scrub with a brush. Wrap each beet in foil. Place on a baking sheet. Bake at 425° for 45 minutes or until tender. Cool. Trim off roots and stems; rub off skin. Cut beets into ½-inch slices. Cut each slice into quarters. Combine beets, 1 teaspoon vinegar, oil, ¼ teaspoon pepper, and ⅛ teaspoon salt.

3. Combine 4 teaspoons vinegar, ¼ teaspoon pepper, ⅛ teaspoon salt, onion, and juice; let stand 30 minutes. Stir in jícama and tangerine.

4. Arrange ½ cup watercress on each of 4 plates. Mound ¾ cup beet mixture in center of each plate. Arrange ¾ cup jícama mixture around beets. Serve immediately. Yield: 4 servings.

CALORIES 147 (10% from fat); FAT 1.7g (sat 0.3g, mono 1g, poly 0.3g); PROTEIN 4.4g; CARB 30.9g; FIBER 10.2g; CHOL 0mg; IRON 2.2mg; SODIUM 306mg; CALC 70mg

Tuna Summer Rolls

Seasoned sushi rice replaces traditional rice noodles in these summer rolls. Use shrimp in place of tuna to vary the recipe.

PLATING TIP: Slicing the summer rolls diagonally gives a preview of the brightly colored ingredients tucked inside. Stand one half up to make the serving look more dramatic and add height to the plate.

ROLLS:

    1 cup uncooked sushi rice or
       short-grain rice
 1¼ cups water
    2 tablespoons minced peeled fresh
       ginger
    2 tablespoons mirin (sweet rice
       wine)
    2 teaspoons minced jalapeño
       pepper
    2 teaspoons minced shallots
    1 teaspoon sugar
    1 teaspoon fish sauce
  ¼ teaspoon salt
    1 tablespoon low-sodium soy sauce
    1 teaspoon sugar
    1 (½-pound) tuna steak
    8 (8-inch) round sheets rice paper
    2 cups trimmed watercress

SAUCE:

  ¼ cup white vinegar
    1 tablespoon sugar
    1 tablespoon fish sauce
 1½ teaspoons minced shallots
    1 teaspoon minced jalapeño pepper

1. To prepare rolls, rinse rice thoroughly in a sieve. Drain well. Bring 1¼ cups water to a boil in a medium saucepan; add rice. Cover, reduce heat, and simmer 20 minutes or until liquid is absorbed. Remove from heat, and let stand 5 minutes. Stir in ginger and next 6 ingredients.

2. Combine soy sauce and 1 teaspoon sugar; brush over tuna. Marinate in refrigerator 10 minutes. Heat a nonstick skillet over medium-high heat. Add tuna to pan; cook 1½ minutes on each side or until desired degree of doneness. Cut tuna into 8 (¼-inch-thick) slices.

3. Add hot water to a large, shallow dish to a depth of 1 inch. Place 1 rice paper sheet in dish. Let stand 30 seconds or just until soft.

4. Place softened sheet on a flat surface. Arrange ¼ cup watercress to cover half of sheet, leaving a ½-inch border. Top with ⅓ cup rice mixture; spread evenly. Arrange 1 tuna slice over rice. Fold sides of sheet over filling; starting with filled side, roll up jelly roll fashion. Repeat procedure with remaining rice paper sheets, watercress, rice mixture, and tuna. Cut each roll in half diagonally.

5. To prepare sauce, combine vinegar and remaining 4 ingredients. Arrange 2 roll halves on each of 8 plates; serve 2¼ teaspoons sauce with each serving. Yield: 8 servings.

CALORIES 149 (3% from fat); FAT 0.5g (sat 0.1g, mono 0.1g, poly 0.1g); PROTEIN 9.1g; CARB 25.6g; FIBER 0.7g; CHOL 13mg; IRON 1.1mg; SODIUM 388mg; CALC 24mg

Add Pizzazz to Your Plate

Here are some presentation pointers from food stylist Kellie Gerber Kelley:

1. Heavily patterned china distracts your guests' focus from the food. In general, the more complex and colorful the finished dish is, the more it needs a simple plate. Plain white or off-white dishes really showcase food.

2. Stacking or piling portions gives an illusion of a bigger serving and showcases colors and textures. If the bottom layer is rice, polenta, or mashed potatoes, so much the better: Pale foods, like white dishes, act as a neutral backdrop for your supper's star.

3. Soups and stews benefit from a scattering of chopped herbs, rather than sprigs.

4. Garnish your finished dish with some of the fresh herbs you used to prepare it. If you know you want to garnish with herbs, go through the packet and pick out the prettiest sprigs first. Wrap them in a damp paper towel, and keep them in the refrigerator until needed. And remember, citrus zest, grated or julienned, is also a fine garnish.

5. Use your vegetable peeler to shave Parmesan cheese into thin shards for entrées, or to shave chocolate for desserts. Ribbons of vegetables, made in the same way, are terrific for soups. Cucumber ribbons on gazpacho look especially summery and cool.

6. Dust sweets with powdered sugar, cocoa, or cinnamon; use paprika on savory dishes. The key is to sift the ingredient through a small sieve.

7. Whatever your dessert, berries make it better. If you put fresh berries on a store-bought dessert, it looks homemade—they add color and the idea of freshness. Herbs can garnish desserts, too. Mint can go on almost anything.

8. Pooling dessert sauces on plates provides a canvas for a dazzling dessert. Put a thick sauce in a squeeze bottle to make squiggles or dots.

Say Cheese for Dessert

A lucky reader wins the chance to preview top dessert recipes for the Big Cheese Sweeps.

Hope Philbrick of Marietta, Georgia, was the lucky winner chosen at random from more than 37,000 entries in the Big Cheese Sweeps, a contest sponsored by the American Dairy Association and *Cooking Light*. She won an all-expenses-paid trip to the magazine's offices in Birmingham, Alabama. While there, she attended taste testing and previewed the cheese desserts created especially for *Cooking Light* readers by the chefs who make up the dairy association's advisory board. Here are some of the recipes she had the pleasure to sample.

Petite Crème Citrus Bread Pudding with Passionfruit Caramel Sauce

Chef Paul Grosz favors a simple, homey approach in his presentation, which he demonstrates in this bread pudding.

PUDDING:

- 2 cups fresh orange juice
- 1 tablespoon grated lemon rind
- ¼ cup fresh lemon juice
- 1 tablespoon grated lime rind
- 1 teaspoon dried thyme
- 8 large egg whites
- 5 cups (1-inch) cubed French bread
- Cooking spray
- 6 (1-ounce) slices petite crème cheese or Brie cheese

SAUCE:

- 1¾ cups sugar
- 1 cup passionfruit puree
- ⅓ cup fresh orange juice
- Thyme sprigs (optional)

1. To prepare pudding, combine first 6 ingredients in a large bowl, stirring with a whisk. Stir in bread cubes. Cover and chill 30 minutes.

2. Preheat oven to 350°.

3. Place bread mixture in an 8-inch square baking dish coated with cooking spray; top with cheese. Bake, uncovered, at 350° for 40 minutes or until set and lightly browned. Let stand 10 minutes before serving.

4. To prepare sauce, combine sugar and puree in a large saucepan. Cook over medium-high heat until candy thermometer registers 238°. Remove from heat; gradually stir in ⅓ cup orange juice. Serve warm with pudding. Garnish with thyme sprigs, if desired. Yield: 10 servings (serving size: 1 piece pudding and about 1 tablespoon sauce).

NOTE: Passionfruit puree and petite crème cheese are available in specialty food stores. You can make your own puree with fresh passionfruit. Puree the pulp of a dozen passionfruit in a food processor for about 1 cup. You can also order petite crème cheese from The Great American Cheese Collection; call 773-779-5055.

CALORIES 296 (20% from fat); FAT 6.6g (sat 3.8g, mono 1.7g, poly 0.3g); PROTEIN 6.3g; CARB 55.7g; FIBER 3.6g; CHOL 19mg; IRON 37mg; SODIUM 1.1mg; CALC 180mg

Pears with Teleme and Fig Compote

The flavor of Teleme (TEHL-uh-may) cheese is a cross between those of crème fraîche and Brie. Raymond Hook, a cheese specialist who developed this recipe, recommends Brie as an acceptable substitute.

- 1 cup tawny port or other sweet red wine
- 1 (8-ounce) package dried figs
- 2 red Bartlett or Anjou pears, each cut into 12 slices
- 6 (½-ounce) slices Teleme cheese

1. Combine port and figs in a small saucepan; cook, covered, over low heat 45 minutes or until tender. Remove from heat; let stand 20 minutes.

2. Arrange 4 pear slices on each of 6 dessert plates; top each serving with 1 cheese slice. Divide fig compote evenly among plates. Yield: 6 servings.

CALORIES 179 (23% from fat); FAT 4.6g (sat 2.6g, mono 1.3g, poly 0.4g); PROTEIN 4.4g; CARB 33.9g; FIBER 5.4g; CHOL 14mg; IRON 1.2mg; SODIUM 96mg; CALC 90mg

Panna Cotta with Vermont Blue Cheese and Roasted Stone Fruit

Panna cotta is a light, silky Italian custard. Its delicate, sweet flavor is a blank slate that showcases chef Felino Samson's spirited cooking style. He emphasizes harmonic but bold flavors with roasted stone fruit and blue cheese.

- 2 cups pear nectar
- 3 (¼-ounce) envelopes unflavored gelatin
- 2 cups whole milk
- Cooking spray
- 1 cup pitted sweet cherries
- ¼ cup tawny port or other sweet red wine
- 3 tablespoons honey
- 4 plums, each cut into 4 wedges (about 1 pound)
- 3 peaches, each peeled and cut into 6 wedges (about 1 pound)
- 1 cup (4 ounces) crumbled Vermont or other blue cheese

1. Strain pear nectar through a fine sieve over a small bowl, and discard solids. Sprinkle gelatin over strained pear nectar, and let stand 1 minute.

2. Place milk in a medium saucepan; stir in gelatin mixture. Cook over medium-low heat until gelatin dissolves, stirring constantly. Pour evenly into 8 (4-ounce) ramekins or muffin cups coated with cooking spray. Chill 2 hours or until set.

3. Preheat oven to 400°.

4. Combine cherries and next 4 ingredients in a 13 x 9-inch baking dish coated with cooking spray, tossing to coat. Bake at 400° for 20 minutes or until tender, stirring once. Cool.

5. Loosen edges of panna cottas with a knife or rubber spatula. Place a dessert plate, upside down, on top of each ramekin; invert onto plates. Spoon about ½ cup roasted fruit around each panna cotta. Sprinkle each serving with 2 tablespoons cheese. Yield: 8 servings.

CALORIES 213 (28% from fat); FAT 6.7g (sat 4.1g, mono 1.9g, poly 0.3g); PROTEIN 8g; CARB 30.6g; FIBER 2g; CHOL 19mg; IRON 0.4mg; SODIUM 236mg; CALC 158mg

Crispy Phyllo Napoleons with Berkshire Blue Cheese, Nectarines, and Pears

Chef Michael Maddox fuses tradition and fresh ideas in this inspired update of the classic French pastry dessert.

COMPOTE:
2½ cups diced nectarine or apricot
2 cups diced Bartlett or Anjou pear
¼ cup granulated sugar
¼ cup packed brown sugar
2 (3-inch) cinnamon sticks
1 (4-inch) piece vanilla bean, split lengthwise

PHYLLO NAPOLEONS:
3 large sheets frozen phyllo dough, thawed
2 tablespoons butter, melted
6 tablespoons powdered sugar
¼ cup ground hazelnuts
Cooking spray

REMAINING INGREDIENTS:
6 ounces Berkshire blue cheese, crumbled
½ cup fat-free caramel sundae syrup

1. To prepare compote, combine first 6 ingredients in a large saucepan; bring to a boil. Reduce heat; simmer, uncovered, 35 minutes or until liquid almost evaporates. Cool completely. Discard cinnamon sticks and vanilla bean.
2. Preheat oven to 350°.
3. To prepare phyllo Napoleons, line a large baking sheet with parchment paper. Place 1 phyllo sheet on parchment paper, and lightly brush with butter. Sprinkle with 2 tablespoons powdered sugar and 4 teaspoons hazelnuts. Repeat layers twice.
4. Using a sharp knife or pizza cutter, cut phyllo stack into 24 (3 x 2½-inch)

rectangles. Cover phyllo with parchment paper. Coat bottom of another baking sheet with cooking spray; place, coated side down, on top of phyllo.
5. Bake at 350° for 12 minutes or until golden. Carefully remove top baking sheet and parchment paper; cool phyllo rectangles on bottom baking sheet on a wire rack.
6. Place 1 phyllo rectangle on each of 8 dessert plates. Top each rectangle with 1½ tablespoons compote and about 1 tablespoon crumbled blue cheese. Repeat layers with remaining phyllo rectangles, compote, and cheese, ending with phyllo rectangles. Drizzle each serving with 1 tablespoon caramel syrup. Serve immediately. Yield: 8 servings.
NOTE: Use a pizza cutter to slice through sheets of phyllo dough without ripping and tearing. Covering rectangles with another baking sheet keeps them flat and crispy while they bake.

CALORIES 328 (32% from fat); FAT 11.9g (sat 6.2g, mono 3.5g, poly 0.9g); PROTEIN 7.2g; CARB 50.3g; FIBER 2.3g; CHOL 23mg; IRON 0.8mg; SODIUM 400mg; CALC 161mg

Aged Cheddar with Apple Wedges and Cider Reduction

Chef Sarah Stegner re-creates the classic fruit, cheese, and nut combination with an easy apple syrup and toasted nut bread.

2 cups apple cider
2 teaspoons chilled butter
8 (1-ounce) slices walnut or other nut bread, toasted and halved
½ pound Shelburne Farms or other aged cheddar cheese, thinly sliced
2 Granny Smith apples, cored and each cut into 16 slices

1. Bring cider to a boil in a large saucepan; cook until reduced to ½ cup (about 15 minutes). Remove from heat. Add butter; stir with a whisk until butter melts.
2. Place 2 bread halves on each of 8 dessert plates. Divide cheese slices evenly among bread halves. Place 2 apple slices on each bread half. Drizzle

1 tablespoon cider reduction around each serving. Yield: 8 servings.

CALORIES 257 (43% from fat); FAT 12.4g (sat 7.2g, mono 3.7g, poly 0.3g); PROTEIN 9.4g; CARB 28g; FIBER 1.6g; CHOL 32mg; IRON 0.2mg; SODIUM 305mg; CALC 206mg

Apple Domes with Bravo Farm Special Reserve Cheddar

Chef Hiro Sone's cuisine is distinctly eclectic, and his choice of ingredients reflects the bounty of his Napa Valley home.

½ cup cold water
2 tablespoons sugar
2 (¼-ounce) envelopes unflavored gelatin
1⅓ cups Champagne or sparkling wine
¾ cup diced peeled Granny Smith apple
Cooking spray
3 ounces Bravo Farm Special Reserve cheddar cheese or other aged cheddar cheese, sliced
1 Granny Smith apple, cored and cut into 16 slices

1. Combine cold water and sugar in a small saucepan. Sprinkle gelatin over sugar mixture; let stand 1 minute. Place pan over medium-low heat; cook until sugar and gelatin dissolve, stirring constantly. Remove mixture from heat; cool slightly. Stir in Champagne.
2. Spoon 3 tablespoons diced apple into each of 4 (4-ounce) ramekins or custard cups coated with cooking spray. Pour wine mixture evenly over diced apple. Chill 2 hours or until set.
3. Loosen edges of domes with a knife or rubber spatula. Place a dessert plate, upside down, on top of each ramekin; invert onto plates. Serve with cheddar cheese and apple slices. Yield: 4 servings (serving size: 1 apple dome, ¾ ounce cheese, and 4 apple slices).
NOTE: You can also remove the domes from the ramekins by quickly dipping the cups in hot water and then running a knife around the edges.

CALORIES 206 (31% from fat); FAT 7.2g (sat 4.5g, mono 2g, poly 0.3g); PROTEIN 8.5g; CARB 15.5g; FIBER 1.3g; CHOL 22mg; IRON 0.5mg; SODIUM 55mg; CALC 166mg

Soup Nights at Martha's

This children's book author brings neighbors together in a weekly ritual of sharing.

The invitation reads: "Bring a loaf and/or a jug of wine, or simply thou and thine. We will provide soup and paperware and drinks. Come one Thursday. Come all Thursdays. No RSVP required."

Not knowing how many guests are coming or what they're bringing might seem like an invitation for disaster. But Martha Freeman and her husband face the unknown every Thursday evening from October through March, when they host "Soup Night" at their home in State College, Pennsylvania. Mushroom soup is her guests' favorite. Try it for yourself, or share it with friends by starting your own soup night.

Mushroom Soup

Adding bread thickens the soup. Because she enjoys its earthy flavor, Martha adds 1 tablespoon brewer's yeast with the parsley and garlic.

 2 cups boiling water
 1 (2-ounce) package dried porcini mushrooms
 2 tablespoons olive oil
 4 cups sliced yellow onion
 5 tablespoons chopped fresh flat-leaf parsley, divided
 6 garlic cloves, minced
 1 cup dry white wine
 4 cups chopped portobello caps (about 8 ounces)
 3 (8-ounce) packages presliced button mushrooms
 4 cups water
 2 (14½-ounce) cans vegetable broth
 4 (1-ounce) slices French bread
 ½ teaspoon black pepper
 ¼ cup half-and-half
 ¼ cup fat-free sour cream

1. Combine boiling water and porcini in a bowl. Cover and let stand 30 minutes or until tender.
2. Heat oil in a stockpot over medium-high heat. Add onion; sauté 5 minutes. Add 2 tablespoons parsley and garlic; sauté 5 minutes. Add wine; bring to a boil. Cook 5 minutes. Add portobello and button mushrooms; cook 15 minutes, stirring occasionally.
3. Add porcini mixture, 4 cups water, broth, and bread; bring to a boil. Reduce heat; simmer 30 minutes. Stir in pepper; let stand 5 minutes.
4. Place one-fourth of mushroom mixture in a food processor or blender; process until smooth. Pour soup into a large bowl. Repeat procedure with remaining mushroom mixture.
5. Combine half-and-half and sour cream. Ladle about 2 cups soup into each of 7 bowls. Top each serving with about 1 tablespoon sour cream mixture; sprinkle with about 1 teaspoon parsley. Yield: 7 servings.

CALORIES 230 (26% from fat); FAT 6.7g (sat 1.3g, mono 3.5g, poly 0.8g); PROTEIN 9.7g; CARB 30.5g; FIBER 5.4g; CHOL 4mg; IRON 4mg; SODIUM 629mg; CALC 72mg

Scrumptious Scones

We help a favorite scone recipe get on the right track.

With two teenagers and two working parents, the Dorien household in Croton on Hudson, New York, is a busy place. But Ham and Cheese Scones suit the tight timetable: They're great for breakfast, lunch, a light dinner, or a snack. Susan Dorien, a railroad conductor, liked keeping them on hand, but they were so heavy she felt she shouldn't make them too often.

The new version has less than half the fat of the original—but lots of ham and great cheese flavor. And we're happy to report that the new scones are a big hit. All of the family is on board with the lightened version.

Ham and Cheese Scones

Pair with salad or soup for a light meal.

 2 cups all-purpose flour
 1 tablespoon baking powder
 2 teaspoons sugar
 ¼ teaspoon salt
 ¼ teaspoon ground red pepper
 3 tablespoons chilled butter, cut into small pieces
 ¾ cup (3 ounces) shredded reduced-fat extra-sharp cheddar cheese
 ¾ cup finely chopped 33%-less-sodium ham (about 3 ounces)
 ¾ cup fat-free buttermilk
 2 large egg whites
Cooking spray

1. Preheat oven to 400°.
2. Lightly spoon flour into dry measuring cups; level with a knife. Combine flour, baking powder, sugar, salt, and pepper in a large bowl; cut in butter with a pastry blender or 2 knives until mixture resembles coarse meal. Stir in cheese and ham. Combine buttermilk and egg whites, stirring with a whisk. Add to flour mixture, stirring just until moist.
3. Turn dough out onto a lightly floured surface; knead lightly 4 or 5 times with floured hands. Pat dough into an 8-inch circle on a baking sheet coated with cooking spray. Cut dough into 8 wedges, cutting into but not through dough. Bake at 400° for 20 minutes or until lightly browned. Yield: 8 servings (serving size: 1 wedge).

CALORIES 217 (30% from fat); FAT 7.2g (sat 4.1g, mono 1.6g, poly 0.4g); PROTEIN 10.4g; CARB 27.1g; FIBER 0.9g; CHOL 26mg; IRON 1.8mg; SODIUM 519mg; CALC 235mg

BEFORE	AFTER
SERVING SIZE	
1 wedge	
CALORIES PER SERVING	
285	217
FAT	
15.2g	7.2g
PERCENT OF TOTAL CALORIES	
48%	30%

The Accidental Squash

It's all downhill—in ease and versatility—when you cook with butternut squash.

Senior Food Editor Jill Melton refers to the steep ravine behind her house as Death Valley. One day last year, she pitched half of a butternut squash into it and several months later saw a baby squash vine.

Butternut squash is the easiest of all the winter squashes to cook, because its smooth skin pares away with a potato peeler, and its pulp cooks relatively fast. It seems to have fewer seeds than the rest of the winter squash, and there's no mistaking it at the supermarket.

Soon Jill's crop will be ready to harvest. Rest assured she'll throw at least one back into Death Valley, with high hopes for next year.

Roasted Butternut Squash with Herbes de Provence

Herbes de Provence is a combination of dried herbs, including rosemary, lavender, thyme, marjoram, and sage. If you're roasting in a stainless pan, use a metal spatula to turn the butternut squash so you scrape up all the flavorful browned edges.

　6　cups (1½-inch) cubed peeled butternut squash (about 2½ pounds)
　1　tablespoon olive oil
1½　teaspoons dried herbes de Provence
　¾　teaspoon kosher salt
　½　teaspoon freshly ground black pepper
　2　medium onions, each cut into 8 wedges (about ¾ pound)
Cooking spray

1. Preheat oven to 425°.
2. Place first 6 ingredients in a shallow roasting pan coated with cooking spray;

toss well. Bake at 425° for 30 minutes or until tender and lightly browned, stirring occasionally. Yield: 4 servings (serving size: 1 cup).

CALORIES 125 (27% from fat); FAT 3.8g (sat 0.5g, mono 2.5g, poly 0.5g); PROTEIN 3.6g; CARB 22.5g; FIBER 4.2g; CHOL 0mg; IRON 1.3mg; SODIUM 362mg; CALC 75mg

Butternut Squash Ravioli with Pancetta and Sage

Serve the ravioli with a green salad and baguette slices with our Sage, Bay, and Garlic Dipping Oil (recipe on page 241).

　¼　cup dried porcini mushrooms (about ¼ ounce)
1½　tablespoons olive oil
　⅔　cup chopped pancetta (about 2½ ounces)
　1　cup mashed cooked butternut squash (about 1 pound uncooked)
　5　tablespoons dry breadcrumbs
　¼　cup (1 ounce) grated fresh Parmesan cheese
　2　teaspoons grated lemon rind
　¼　teaspoon salt
　⅛　teaspoon ground nutmeg
　1　large egg, lightly beaten
　40　won ton wrappers
　2　teaspoons chopped fresh sage
　¼　teaspoon freshly ground black pepper

1. Pour boiling water over mushrooms in a bowl. Cover and let stand 30 minutes or until tender. Drain mushrooms, and squeeze to remove excess moisture. Chop mushrooms.
2. Heat oil in a medium saucepan over medium-high heat. Add pancetta; cook until crisp. Remove half of pancetta from pan with a slotted spoon, and place in a medium bowl, reserving remaining pancetta and drippings in pan. Add mushrooms, squash, and next 6 ingredients to bowl, stirring to combine.
3. Place 1 won ton wrapper on work surface (cover remaining wrappers with a damp towel to keep them from drying), and spoon about 1 tablespoon squash mixture into center of wrapper. Brush edges of wrapper with water, and top

with another wrapper, stretching top wrapper slightly to meet edges of bottom wrapper. Press edges together firmly with fingers, and cut edges with a 2½-inch round cutter. Repeat procedure with remaining won ton wrappers and squash mixture.
4. Fill a large Dutch oven with water; bring to a simmer. Add half of ravioli; cook 3 minutes or until done (do not boil). Remove ravioli with a slotted spoon. Keep warm. Repeat procedure with remaining ravioli.
5. Reheat remaining pancetta and drippings over medium-low heat; drizzle over ravioli. Sprinkle with sage and pepper. Yield: 4 servings (serving size: 5 ravioli).

CALORIES 389 (27% from fat); FAT 11.6g (sat 3.1g, mono 6g, poly 1.5g); PROTEIN 18.4g; CARB 52.5g; FIBER 4.6g; CHOL 74mg; IRON 5.3mg; SODIUM 961mg; CALC 171mg

Butternut Squash and Rosemary Gratin

A gratin is a dish topped with cheese and baked until browned. The piney flavor of rosemary complements the sweet butternut squash and sharp cheeses.

　3　cups mashed cooked butternut squash (about 3 pounds uncooked)
　¼　cup (1 ounce) grated fresh Parmesan cheese, divided
　½　teaspoon kosher salt
　½　to ¾ teaspoon chopped fresh rosemary
　¼　teaspoon freshly ground black pepper
Cooking spray
　¼　cup (1 ounce) shredded Asiago or provolone cheese

1. Preheat oven to 450°.
2. Combine squash, 2 tablespoons Parmesan, salt, rosemary, and pepper. Spoon mixture into a 1½-quart baking dish coated with cooking spray; sprinkle with 2 tablespoons Parmesan and Asiago. Bake at 450° for 20 minutes. Yield: 4 servings (serving size: ¾ cup).

CALORIES 129 (28% from fat); FAT 4g (sat 2.5g, mono 1.1g, poly 0.2g); PROTEIN 6.2g; CARB 19.9g; FIBER 5.2g; CHOL 11mg; IRON 1.3mg; SODIUM 427mg; CALC 230mg

Quinoa with Butternut Squash and Red Bell Pepper

Serve this dish with grilled chicken or pork.

  1 tablespoon olive oil
  1 cup coarsely chopped peeled butternut squash
 ⅔ cup chopped red bell pepper
 ⅓ cup finely chopped onion
1½ teaspoons finely chopped seeded jalapeño pepper
  1 garlic clove, minced
1⅓ cups fat-free, less-sodium chicken broth
  1 cup uncooked quinoa
 ½ teaspoon kosher salt
1½ tablespoons thinly sliced green onions

1. Heat oil in a large saucepan over medium-high heat. Add squash and next 4 ingredients; sauté 4 minutes. Stir in broth, quinoa, and salt; bring to a boil.
2. Cover, reduce heat, and simmer 20 minutes or until liquid is absorbed. Sprinkle quinoa mixture with green onions. Yield: 4 servings (serving size: 1 cup).

CALORIES 225 (24% from fat); FAT 6g (sat 0.7g, mono 3.2g, poly 1.3g); PROTEIN 7.4g; CARB 37g; FIBER 4.5g; CHOL 0mg; IRON 4.4mg; SODIUM 397mg; CALC 50mg

Butternut Squash Pudding

  2 cups mashed cooked butternut squash (about 2 pounds uncooked)
 ½ cup half-and-half
 ⅓ cup maple syrup
  2 teaspoons finely chopped crystallized ginger
 ½ teaspoon ground cinnamon
 ¼ teaspoon ground nutmeg
  3 large egg yolks
  3 large egg whites
  1 tablespoon sugar
Cooking spray
 ¼ cup graham cracker crumbs

1. Preheat oven to 350°.
2. Combine first 7 ingredients in a large bowl; stir with a whisk until blended.
3. Place egg whites in a large bowl; beat with a mixer at high speed until foamy. Gradually add sugar, beating until stiff peaks form. Stir one-fourth of egg white mixture into squash mixture; gently fold in remaining egg white mixture.
4. Spoon mixture into an 8-inch square baking dish coated with cooking spray. Sprinkle with crumbs. Bake at 350° for 40 minutes or until set. Yield: 6 servings (serving size: ½ cup).

CALORIES 177 (26% from fat); FAT 5.2g (sat 2.2g, mono 1.8g, poly 0.6g); PROTEIN 4.9g; CARB 28.4g; FIBER 2.5g; CHOL 116mg; IRON 1.5mg; SODIUM 77mg; CALC 84mg

Shrimp and Butternut Squash in Coconut Milk Broth

Use a pound of firm water-packed tofu, drained and cut into ½-inch cubes, in place of the shrimp for a vegetarian dish.

 ¾ cup fat-free, less-sodium chicken broth or water
1½ teaspoons brown sugar
  1 teaspoon kosher salt
 ¼ teaspoon crushed red pepper
 ¼ teaspoon freshly ground black pepper
  1 (14-ounce) can light coconut milk
  2 cups (¾-inch) cubed peeled butternut squash
  1 cup (1 x ¼-inch) julienne-cut red bell pepper
  1 pound large shrimp, peeled, deveined, and halved lengthwise
  2 cups hot cooked basmati rice
 ¼ cup fresh lime juice
  3 tablespoons minced fresh cilantro

1. Combine first 6 ingredients in a large saucepan, stirring with a whisk. Stir in squash and bell pepper; bring to a boil. Reduce heat, and simmer 10 minutes or until squash is just tender.
2. Stir in shrimp; bring to a boil. Cook 1 minute or until shrimp are done, stirring occasionally. Stir in rice, lime juice, and cilantro. Yield: 4 servings (serving size: about 1¾ cups).

CALORIES 294 (19% from fat); FAT 6.1g (sat 3.6g, mono 0.2g, poly 0.5g); PROTEIN 18.5g; CARB 41.8g; FIBER 3.9g; CHOL 135mg; IRON 4.6mg; SODIUM 848mg; CALC 85mg

Alaska Molasses Cookies, page 266

Black-and-White Cake Cookies, page 267

Double Chocolate Cookies, page 268

Chocolate Chip Meringues, page 267

Harvest Pear Crisp, page 245

Korean-Style Pork Tenderloin,
page 270

Roasted Pepper, Kalamata, and
Prosciutto Pasta, page 242

Rice and Feta Stuffed Baby Eggplant, page 273

Crispy Salmon with Risotto and Slow-Roasted Tomatoes, page 248

All About Fish

Here's how to select, store, and cook the most popular varieties.

Many of us grew up with the notion of fish based on school-cafeteria fish sticks and frozen breaded fish fillets. But today the variety of fish at the market is so broad, there is a fish to suit anyone's palate. Fresh fish varies enormously, from assertive salmon to subtle tilapia; from buttery, delicate halibut to meaty tuna and swordfish. Arctic char, mahimahi, amberjack, and pompano are a few of the lesser-known varieties, but they're now more widely available and ready to add to your repertoire.

Still, it can be daunting to stand in front of the fish case and see so many kinds. That's why we've given you plenty of information on how to select the freshest fish possible, store it, and cook it. You'll find a lot of new choices, and learn how to best take advantage of them.

Of the many varieties of fish, we chose 11 based on their flavor, availability, ease of cooking, and popularity. Seasons affect availability, but you should be able to get most of these fish at some point during the year. Technology and transportation now allow people in the middle of the country to buy fresh ocean fish, people on the Atlantic to buy Pacific fish, and vice versa.

Arctic Char with Bouillabaisse Broth

Bouillabaisse is the inspiration for this flavorful broth. Try this recipe with salmon if you can't find arctic char.

- 2   teaspoons olive oil, divided
- 1   cup finely chopped onion
- 1   cup finely chopped fennel bulb
- 3   tablespoons finely chopped shallots
- ¾   teaspoon saffron threads, crushed
- ½   teaspoon chopped fresh thyme
- ½   teaspoon aniseed
- 2   garlic cloves, minced
- 2   cups water
- 2   tablespoons tomato paste
- 1   (8-ounce) bottle clam juice
- 2   cups cubed peeled Yukon gold potato (about 12 ounces)
- 1   (½-pound) fennel bulb, cut into 8 wedges
- 4   (6-ounce) arctic char or salmon fillets
- ½   teaspoon salt
- ¼   teaspoon freshly ground black pepper

1. Heat 1 teaspoon oil in a large saucepan over medium heat. Add onion and next 6 ingredients; cook 7 minutes or until tender, stirring frequently. Stir in water, tomato paste, and clam juice; bring to a boil. Reduce heat, and simmer 45 minutes.

2. Strain mixture through a sieve over a bowl; discard solids. Return mixture to pan; bring to a boil. Add potato; cook 5 minutes. Add fennel wedges; cook 4 minutes. Remove potato mixture from heat, and keep warm.

3. Heat 1 teaspoon oil in a large nonstick skillet over medium-high heat. Sprinkle fish with salt and pepper. Add fish to pan; cook 3 minutes on each side or until fish flakes easily when tested with a fork. Yield: 4 servings (serving size: 1 fillet, ½ cup potatoes, 2 fennel wedges, and ¼ cup broth).

CALORIES 371 (33% from fat); FAT 13.4g (sat 2.2g, mono 7g, poly 2.7g); PROTEIN 37.5g; CARB 24.7g; FIBER 4.3g; CHOL 96mg; IRON 4.1mg; SODIUM 607mg; CALC 128mg

Fennel-Marinated Halibut with Fennel Tzatziki

Tzatziki is a yogurt-based Greek condiment that traditionally contains cucumber. Using fennel in place of cucumber adds sweetness and a mild licorice flavor to the sauce. Fennel seeds impart a slightly nutty flavor to the marinade. Substitute snapper if you can't find fresh halibut.

- 1   teaspoon grated lemon rind
- 1   tablespoon fresh lemon juice
- 1   tablespoon extra-virgin olive oil
- 2   teaspoons fennel seeds, crushed
- ⅛   teaspoon freshly ground black pepper
- ½   teaspoon salt, divided
- 4   (6-ounce) halibut fillets
- 1   cup plain low-fat yogurt
- ½   cup shredded fennel bulb
- 2   teaspoons chopped fennel fronds
- 1   garlic clove, minced
- Cooking spray

1. Combine first 5 ingredients and ¼ teaspoon salt in a large zip-top plastic bag; add fish. Seal and marinate in refrigerator 1 hour, turning occasionally.

2. Preheat broiler.

3. Spoon yogurt onto several layers of heavy-duty paper towels; spread to ½-inch thickness. Cover with additional paper towels; let stand 5 minutes. Scrape into a bowl using a rubber spatula. Add ¼ teaspoon salt, shredded fennel bulb, chopped fennel fronds, and garlic. Cover and refrigerate.

4. Remove fish from bag; discard marinade. Place fish on a broiler pan coated with cooking spray. Broil 8 minutes or until fish flakes easily when tested with a fork. Serve with yogurt sauce. Yield: 4 servings (serving size: 1 fillet and 2 tablespoons sauce).

CALORIES 239 (24% from fat); FAT 6.5g (sat 1.4g, mono 2.8g, poly 1.4g); PROTEIN 37.6g; CARB 5.9g; FIBER 0.6g; CHOL 56mg; IRON 1.6mg; SODIUM 358mg; CALC 202mg

Buying and Storing Fish

Fresh Fillets or Steaks

This is the easiest and best way to buy fish. Don't be afraid to ask at the fish counter when the fish came in, and don't buy anything more than one day old—especially if you don't plan to cook it that night. Look for fish that is blemish-free and neither slick nor soggy. Fresh fish will be firm and spring back when touched. The fish should smell subtly of the water from which it came. If it has a "fishy" smell, it's not fresh. Avoid fish displayed directly on ice, since the contact can cause quality to deteriorate; ask if there is more in the back. Buying fish that has been frozen at sea is your next best alternative.

Frozen Fish

When possible, purchase vacuum-packed frozen fish, and look for "once frozen" on the label. Avoid any fish that has symptoms of freezer burn, such as brown or dry edges. Defrost frozen fish in the refrigerator overnight.

Whole Fresh Fish

This is the most economical way to purchase fish. When you buy a whole fish, look for clear, glossy eyes; shiny, red gills; and a firm body, free of any dark blemishes. The tail should not be dried out or curled. Ask the fishmonger to fillet the fish and portion it for you. (Most *Cooking Light* recipes call for 6-ounce raw fillets or steaks, which yield 4½-ounce portions.) Cook what you need and freeze the rest. Ask for the bones so you can make fish stock for soups and stews—the bones will freeze, and the stock will, too.

Storing Fish

Buy fish on your way out of the store, take it directly home, and cook (or freeze) it within 24 hours. Keep the fish as cold as possible until you are ready to cook it by storing it in the coldest part of your refrigerator.

Buffalo-Style Catfish Strips with Ranch Dressing

The inspiration for this appetizer is Buffalo chicken wings. We breaded and baked catfish strips, then drizzled them with a spicy sauce. If you don't like spicy foods, omit the hot pepper sauce. Products labeled "hot sauce" generally have less heat and stronger vinegar flavor than those labeled "hot pepper sauce," which are intensely hot and should be used sparingly.

    2   tablespoons all-purpose flour
    1   teaspoon garlic powder
    1   teaspoon paprika
    ½   teaspoon onion powder
    ½   teaspoon salt
    ⅛   teaspoon ground red pepper
    2   large egg whites, lightly beaten
 1½   cups coarsely crushed cornflakes
    1   pound catfish fillets, cut into
        ½-inch-thick strips
Cooking spray
    ⅓   cup hot sauce (such as Crystal)
    1   teaspoon hot pepper sauce (such as
        Tabasco)
    ½   teaspoon Worcestershire sauce
    1   tablespoon butter
    ½   cup fat-free ranch dressing
    4   celery stalks, cut into ¼ x 3-inch
        sticks
    4   carrots, cut into ¼ x 3-inch sticks

1. Preheat oven to 400°.
2. Combine first 6 ingredients in a shallow dish, stirring with a whisk. Place egg whites in a shallow dish. Place cornflakes in a shallow dish. Working with 1 fish strip at a time, dredge each strip in flour mixture. Dip in egg whites; dredge in cornflakes. Place on a baking sheet coated with cooking spray.
3. Lightly coat fish strips with cooking spray. Bake at 400° for 10 minutes or until done, turning once.
4. Combine hot sauce, pepper sauce, and Worcestershire in a small saucepan; bring to a boil. Reduce heat, and simmer 1 minute. Remove from heat; stir in butter. Drizzle hot sauce mixture over fish. Serve with ranch dressing, celery, and carrots. Yield: 8 servings (serving size:

about 2 ounces fish, ½ celery stalk, ½ carrot, and 1 tablespoon dressing).

CALORIES 183 (30% from fat); FAT 6.2g (sat 2g, mono 2.5g, poly 1.1g); PROTEIN 12.5g; CARB 19.2g; FIBER 2g; CHOL 31mg; IRON 3mg; SODIUM 618mg; CALC 34mg

Potato Cod Cakes with Dijon Tartar Sauce

Shape the cakes up to 8 hours ahead; cover and refrigerate until you're ready to cook them. Have the cod steamed at the market to save time. If you can't find *panko*, coarse Japanese breadcrumbs, substitute fresh breadcrumbs.

SAUCE:
    ½   cup fat-free mayonnaise
    3   tablespoons finely chopped
        onion
    3   tablespoons sweet pickle relish
    4   teaspoons Dijon mustard
    2   teaspoons fresh lemon juice

CAKES:
    1   cup cubed peeled baking potato
 1½   cups panko or fresh breadcrumbs
    ½   cup thinly sliced green onions
    ⅓   cup finely chopped red bell pepper
    3   tablespoons chopped fresh parsley
    1   teaspoon salt
    1   teaspoon dried oregano
    ¼   teaspoon freshly ground black
        pepper
    2   large eggs, lightly beaten
 1½   pounds cod fillets, cooked
    1   garlic clove, minced
    2   tablespoons vegetable oil, divided
Cooking spray

GARNISH:
Flat-leaf parsley sprigs (optional)

1. Preheat oven to 350°.
2. To prepare sauce, combine first 5 ingredients in a small bowl. Cover; refrigerate.
3. To prepare cakes, place potato in a large glass bowl; cover with plastic wrap. Microwave at HIGH 5 minutes or until tender. Mash potato with a potato masher; cool.
4. Add breadcrumbs and next 9 ingredients to potato; stir well. Divide mixture

into 12 equal portions, shaping each into a ½-inch-thick patty.

5. Heat 1 tablespoon oil in a large nonstick skillet over medium-high heat. Add half of cakes; cook 2 minutes on each side. Place cakes on a baking sheet coated with cooking spray. Repeat procedure with remaining oil and cakes.

6. Bake cakes at 350° for 10 minutes. Serve with sauce. Garnish with parsley sprigs, if desired. Yield: 6 servings (serving size: 2 cakes and 2 tablespoons sauce).

CALORIES 254 (28% from fat); FAT 7.8g (sat 1g, mono 3.9g, poly 2.2g); PROTEIN 24.5g; CARB 21.3g; FIBER 1.7g; CHOL 113mg; IRON 1.4mg; SODIUM 869mg; CALC 43mg

West Indies Mahimahi

A bit sweet, tangy, and spicy, this marinade is reminiscent of Jamaican jerk seasoning.

  ¼ cup fresh lime juice
  ¼ cup fresh orange juice
  3 tablespoons chopped fresh cilantro
  3 tablespoons low-sodium soy sauce
  2 tablespoons honey
  2 teaspoons vegetable oil
  ¾ teaspoon ground allspice
  ¾ teaspoon ground cumin
  2 finely chopped seeded jalapeño peppers
  2 garlic cloves, peeled
  2 green onions, chopped
  4 (6-ounce) mahimahi fillets
  Cooking spray

1. Combine first 11 ingredients in a blender or food processor; process until smooth. Place fish in a shallow dish; pour marinade over fish. Cover and marinate in refrigerator 30 minutes, turning once.

2. Prepare grill or preheat broiler.

3. Remove fish from dish, reserving marinade. Place fish on grill rack or broiler pan coated with cooking spray. Cook 5 minutes on each side or until fish flakes easily when tested with a fork, basting frequently with reserved marinade. Yield: 4 servings.

CALORIES 218 (15% from fat); FAT 3.6g (sat 0.7g, mono 0.7g, poly 1.6g); PROTEIN 31.4g; CARB 14.6g; FIBER 0.8g; CHOL 120mg; IRON 2.4mg; SODIUM 548mg; CALC 40mg

---

Fish Substitutions

Fish divide easily into three categories: delicate-, medium-, and firm-fleshed. These categories reflect how fish respond to cooking methods and which substitutions work.

	If a recipe calls for:	You can substitute:
Delicate Treat delicate fish with care when you cook them; they flake easily and have a soft texture when cooked. These fish are traditionally sold as fillets, and they're best prepared by poaching, braising, pan-frying, or baking.	sole/flounder cod	turbot, plaice, fluke, all varieties of sole/flounder orange roughy (mild)
Medium These fish flake easily, but with more resistance than delicate fish, and are firmer when cooked. They're the most versatile fish to cook and can be used when your recipe specifies "or other flaky white fish." They're best prepared by baking, broiling, braising, pan-frying, or grilling.	arctic char mahimahi red snapper tilapia	steelhead trout, salmon grouper, monkfish halibut, walleye (sweet, delicate), all varieties of snapper bass (fresh water), pike, tilefish
Firm These fish don't flake easily when cooked and have a meaty texture. They're best prepared over high heat—by grilling or sautéing, for example.	pompano tuna	amberjack, catfish swordfish, trigger fish (mildly sweet)

Broiled Tilapia with Thai Coconut-Curry Sauce

Tilapia's mild flavor allows the bold flavors in the brothy sauce to shine.

  1 teaspoon dark sesame oil, divided
  2 teaspoons minced peeled fresh ginger
  2 garlic cloves, minced
  1 cup finely chopped red bell pepper
  1 cup chopped green onions
  2 teaspoons red curry paste
  1 teaspoon curry powder
  ½ teaspoon ground cumin
  4 teaspoons low-sodium soy sauce
  1 tablespoon brown sugar
  ½ teaspoon salt, divided
  1 (14-ounce) can light coconut milk
  2 tablespoons chopped fresh cilantro
  4 (6-ounce) tilapia fillets
  Cooking spray
  3 cups hot cooked basmati rice
  4 lime wedges

1. Preheat broiler.

2. Heat ½ teaspoon oil in a large nonstick skillet over medium heat. Add ginger and garlic; cook 1 minute. Add pepper and onions; cook 1 minute. Stir in curry paste, curry powder, and cumin; cook 1 minute. Add soy sauce, sugar, ¼ teaspoon salt, and coconut milk; bring to a simmer (do not boil). Remove from heat; stir in cilantro.

3. Brush fish with ½ teaspoon oil; sprinkle with ¼ teaspoon salt. Place fish on a baking sheet coated with cooking spray. Broil 7 minutes or until fish flakes easily when tested with a fork. Serve fish with sauce, rice, and lime wedges. Yield: 4 servings (serving size: 1 fillet, ½ cup sauce, ¾ cup rice, and 1 lime wedge).

CALORIES 506 (30% from fat); FAT 17.1g (sat 5.9g, mono 6g, poly 2.5g); PROTEIN 29g; CARB 56.6g; FIBER 3.1g; CHOL 82mg; IRON 2.7mg; SODIUM 616mg; CALC 47mg

The Most Popular Fish Varieties

Amberjack

Full flavor and firm flesh make amberjack, which stands up to more assertive flavors, ideal to grill, pan-fry, or broil. It's available in fillets or steaks year-round, especially in the South, since it comes primarily from the Gulf of Mexico. One 4½-ounce serving has 135 calories and 2.3 grams of fat.

Arctic char (farmed freshwater)

Arctic char, most often sold in fillets, has a distinctive pink flesh, with a rich flavor similar to salmon and steelhead trout. You can substitute arctic char for salmon in almost any recipe, and vice versa. Like salmon, this fish lends itself to most any cooking method. A 4½-ounce serving of arctic char has 234 calories and 10.1 grams of fat.

Catfish (farmed freshwater)

Farmed catfish is available fresh year-round and accounts for close to 99 percent of the catfish sold in the United States. Catfish's sweet flavor and firm texture make it ideal for grilling, roasting, pan-frying, and braising. It can also substitute for other firm-flesh fish, such as pompano. A 4½-ounce serving of catfish has 194 calories and 10.2 grams of fat.

Cod

The darling of New England, cod is a flaky white fish with mild, sweet flavor—so mild, in fact, those who are wary of seafood tend to gravitate to it. Cod is often used to make fish cakes and fish sticks (along with pollock) and frequently appears in chowders and stews. Now rebounding from shortages in the Atlantic, cod is plentiful year-round. A 4½-ounce serving has 134 calories and 1.1 grams of fat.

Halibut

Popular because of its mild flavor, this flaky white fish should be prepared with subtle flavors that won't overwhelm its delicacy. The Atlantic halibut fishery is virtually extinct, but Pacific halibut is plentiful and is available fresh from March to November. It's sold frozen the rest of the year. A 4½-ounce serving of halibut has 179 calories and 3.8 grams of fat.

Mahimahi

Originally called dolphinfish, the Hawaiian name mahimahi was adopted to end confusion that it is related to the dolphin. Popular because of its versatility, mahimahi pairs well with fruits and spicy sauces. It grills, broils, pan-fries, and braises beautifully. A 4½-ounce serving of mahimahi has 139 calories and 1.2 grams of fat.

Pompano

Pompano has a delicate, sweet flavor. While there is no season for pompano, catch limits affect its availability; catfish makes a suitable substitute when pompano is scarce. Grill, broil, or pan-fry pompano. A 4½-ounce serving has 269 calories and 15.5 grams of fat.

Red snapper

The most prized member of the large snapper family is American red snapper, which has a pronounced sweet flavor, similar to shrimp. Many varieties of snapper are available year-round, and though they may not be quite as sweet as American red snapper, they are excellent substitutions. A 4½-ounce serving has 163 calories and 2.2 grams of fat.

Salmon

Most of what we get at the market is farmed Atlantic salmon. While wild Atlantic salmon is virtually extinct, wild Pacific salmon is still available. As salmon farming has become an increasingly bigger business, the fish has become more affordable. Salmon averages $4 to $6 a pound at the grocery. The high fat content of salmon keeps it moist when cooked by almost any method—you can pan-fry, grill, roast, steam, poach, or smoke it. A 4½-ounce serving of farmed coho salmon has 224 calories and 10.5 grams of fat.

Sole/Flounder

Although sole are actually members of the flounder family, the words sole and flounder are often used interchangeably. (You're likely to see flounder at the fish market, and sole on restaurant menus.) Sauté this flaky white fish with lemon and a little butter

to enhance its delicate flavor. It's harvested year-round, but turbot, plaice, or fluke (sometimes called summer flounder) substitute well. A 4½-ounce serving of sole/flounder has 149 calories and 2 grams of fat.

Swordfish

Popular for its mild flavor and meaty texture, fresh swordfish appears in markets year-round, usually as steak, and is best pan-fried or grilled. A 4½-ounce serving has 198 calories and 6.6 grams of fat.

Tilapia (farmed freshwater)

Tilapia has a firm texture and mild flavor (some argue that it has almost none) that make it a great canvas on which to paint layers of flavor. Like cod, this is a great fish for people who say they don't like fish. Readily available year-round, tilapia can be pan-fried, broiled, baked, or braised in a flavorful broth or sauce. A 4½-ounce serving has 106 calories and about 1 gram of fat.

Trout (farmed freshwater)

Trout's flavor ranges from subtle and mild to sweet. Most of the trout sold at markets is rainbow trout, although you'll also see such other varieties as brook trout. At its best, trout is subtle; prepare it simply to avoid masking its flavor. A 4½-ounce serving has 243 calories and 10.8 grams of fat.

Tuna

The many species of tuna vary in flavor and texture. Costly sashimi-grade tuna—so named because this is the best quality for sushi and sashimi—has a clean, subtle flavor, a delicate texture, and is higher in fat. The tuna most widely available in grocery stores tends to be meatier, with a more assertive flavor. The fish is ideal for grilling or searing, which caramelizes the outside and leaves the interior moist. Many chefs think tuna is best seared on the outside and left almost raw inside. It is less forgiving than other fish, and when overcooked can be dry and tough. Tuna is sold fresh and frozen year-round. A 4½-ounce serving of yellowfin tuna has 178 calories and 1.6 grams of fat.

Snapper Tacos with Chipotle Cream

The fish cooks on top of vegetables in one skillet. Break fish into chunks to finish filling.

½ cup fat-free sour cream
⅛ teaspoon salt
1 canned chipotle chile in adobo sauce, seeded and minced
1½ cups chopped onion, divided
1½ cups chopped tomato, divided
2 tablespoons butter
1 teaspoon ground cumin
½ teaspoon salt
½ teaspoon ground cinnamon
4 garlic cloves, minced
3 tablespoons chopped fresh cilantro
1 pound red snapper fillets, skinned
1 teaspoon grated lime rind
2 tablespoons fresh lime juice
4 (8-inch) fat-free flour tortillas

1. Combine first 3 ingredients; set aside. Combine ½ cup onion and ½ cup tomato; set aside.
2. Melt butter in a large nonstick skillet over medium heat. Add 1 cup onion, 1 cup tomato, cumin, ½ teaspoon salt, cinnamon, and garlic; cook 5 minutes, stirring frequently. Stir in cilantro. Arrange fish over onion mixture in pan; cover and cook 3 minutes. Turn fish; cover and cook 2 minutes. Break fish into chunks. Stir in rind and juice; cook 2 minutes. Remove from heat.
3. Warm tortillas according to package directions. Fill each tortilla with ½ cup fish mixture and ¼ cup reserved onion mixture; top each serving with 2 tablespoons chipotle cream. Fold in half or roll up. Yield: 4 servings (serving size: 1 taco).

CALORIES 340 (21% from fat); FAT 7.8g (sat 4g, mono 2g, poly 0.9g); PROTEIN 28.1g; CARB 38.1g; FIBER 3.3g; CHOL 56mg; IRON 2mg; SODIUM 896mg; CALC 108mg

Asian Seared Tuna Salad

SALAD:

2 tablespoons low-sodium soy sauce
2 tablespoons rice vinegar
1 tablespoon mirin (sweet rice wine)
1 tablespoon honey
2 teaspoons grated peeled fresh ginger
1 teaspoon dark sesame oil
3 cups shredded napa (Chinese) cabbage
3 cups gourmet salad greens
1 cup diagonally cut snow peas
½ cup chopped green onions
½ cup shredded carrot
2 teaspoons sesame seeds, toasted

TUNA:

1 teaspoon dark sesame oil
¾ teaspoon five-spice powder
¼ teaspoon salt
⅛ teaspoon freshly ground black pepper
1½ pounds yellowfin tuna steaks (about 1 inch thick)

GARNISH:

1 teaspoon sesame seeds, toasted

1. To prepare salad, combine first 6 ingredients in a small bowl. Combine cabbage and next 5 ingredients in a large bowl.
2. To prepare tuna, heat 1 teaspoon oil in a large nonstick skillet over medium-high heat. Combine five-spice powder, salt, and pepper; rub over tuna. Add tuna to pan; cook 2 minutes on each side or until desired degree of doneness. Let stand 2 minutes. Cut into ½-inch cubes.
3. Drizzle cabbage mixture with soy sauce mixture; toss to combine. Place 2 cups salad on each of 4 plates; top each serving with ½ cup tuna cubes. Sprinkle 1 teaspoon sesame seeds evenly over salads. Yield: 4 servings.

CALORIES 249 (14% from fat); FAT 3.9g (sat 0.7g, mono 1.1g, poly 1.5g); PROTEIN 32.6g; CARB 16.2g; FIBER 3.8g; CHOL 57mg; IRON 6.1mg; SODIUM 490mg; CALC 89mg

Pan-Fried Sole with Cucumber and Tomato Salsa

2 cups quartered cherry tomatoes
¾ cup finely chopped cucumber
⅓ cup finely chopped yellow bell pepper
3 tablespoons chopped fresh basil
2 tablespoons capers
1½ tablespoons finely chopped shallots
1 tablespoon balsamic vinegar
2 teaspoons grated lemon rind
1 teaspoon salt, divided
¼ teaspoon freshly ground black pepper, divided
1 tablespoon olive oil
4 (6-ounce) sole fillets, skinned

1. Combine first 8 ingredients in a bowl; stir in ½ teaspoon salt and ⅛ teaspoon black pepper.
2. Heat oil in a large nonstick skillet over medium-high heat. Sprinkle fish with ½ teaspoon salt and ⅛ teaspoon black pepper. Add fish to pan; cook 1½ minutes on each side or until fish flakes easily when tested with a fork. Serve with salsa. Yield: 4 servings (serving size: 1 fillet and ½ cup salsa).

CALORIES 175 (27% from fat); FAT 5.3g (sat 0.9g, mono 2.8g, poly 0.9g); PROTEIN 25.2g; CARB 6.5g; FIBER 1.6g; CHOL 61mg; IRON 1.1mg; SODIUM 826mg; CALC 40mg

Baked Citrus-Herb Salmon

Ask your fishmonger to remove the pin bones from the salmon. Toss the leftover salmon with pasta or salad.

Cooking spray
1 (3½-pound) salmon fillet
1 teaspoon sea salt
½ teaspoon freshly ground black pepper
2 tablespoons grated lemon rind
1 tablespoon grated orange rind
10 fresh chives
4 thyme sprigs
4 oregano sprigs
4 tarragon sprigs
10 (⅛-inch-thick) slices lemon (about 1 lemon)

Continued

1. Preheat oven to 450°.
2. Line a shallow roasting pan with foil; coat foil with cooking spray.
3. Sprinkle salmon with salt and pepper. Combine lemon and orange rinds; spread over fish. Arrange chives, thyme, oregano, and tarragon horizontally across fish. Arrange lemon slices on top of herbs.
4. Place fish on prepared pan. Cover with foil; seal. Bake at 450° for 30 minutes or until fish flakes easily when tested with a fork. Serve warm or at room temperature. Yield: 10 servings (serving size: about 4 ounces).

WINE NOTE: Try Pinot Gris from New Zealand. Two great producers are Huia (the 2001 is about $17) and Kumeu River (the 2001 is about $15).

CALORIES 213 (41% from fat); FAT 9.8g (sat 2.3g, mono 4.3g, poly 2.3g); PROTEIN 28.9g; CARB 0.4g; FIBER 0.2g; CHOL 75mg; IRON 0.5mg; SODIUM 292mg; CALC 17mg

Pompano with Tropical Barbecue Glaze

The sweet-tart barbecue sauce will keep in the refrigerator for up to a week.

  1   cup mango nectar
  ¼ cup apricot preserves
  3   tablespoons honey
  2   teaspoons grated lime rind
  2   tablespoons fresh lime juice
  2   teaspoons minced peeled fresh ginger
  1   teaspoon ground cumin
  ¼ teaspoon ground cinnamon
  1   jalapeño pepper, seeded and finely chopped
  ¾ teaspoon salt, divided
1½ pounds pompano
  ⅛ teaspoon freshly ground black pepper
     Cooking spray

1. Prepare grill or preheat broiler.
2. Combine first 9 ingredients and ¼ teaspoon salt in a small saucepan; bring to a boil. Reduce heat, and simmer 18 minutes or until thick, stirring frequently.
3. Sprinkle fish with ½ teaspoon salt and pepper; place on grill rack or broiler pan coated with cooking spray, skin side up. Cook 5 minutes. Turn fish; brush with sauce. Cook 4 minutes or until fish flakes easily when tested with a fork. Yield: 4 servings.

CALORIES 410 (35% from fat); FAT 15.8g (sat 5.8g, mono 4.3g, poly 1.9g); PROTEIN 30.8g; CARB 37g; FIBER 1.2g; CHOL 82mg; IRON 1.3mg; SODIUM 548mg; CALC 73mg

Zesty Swordfish Kebabs

  3   tablespoons low-sodium soy sauce
  2   tablespoons chopped fresh rosemary
  1   tablespoon grated lemon rind
  2   tablespoons fresh lemon juice
1½ tablespoons extra-virgin olive oil
  2   teaspoons grated orange rind
  1   tablespoon fresh orange juice
  2   teaspoons honey
  1   teaspoon grated peeled fresh ginger
  ½ teaspoon salt
  ¼ teaspoon freshly ground black pepper
  5   garlic cloves, chopped
1½ pounds swordfish steaks, cut into 1-inch pieces
  ¾ cup (2-inch) sliced green onions
12 (1-inch) pieces red bell pepper
     Cooking spray

1. Combine first 12 ingredients in a large zip-top plastic bag; add fish. Seal and marinate in refrigerator 30 minutes, turning once.
2. Prepare grill.
3. Remove fish from bag; discard marinade. Thread fish, green onions, and bell pepper alternately onto each of 4 (10-inch) skewers. Place on grill rack coated with cooking spray; grill 8 minutes or until desired degree of doneness, turning once. Yield: 4 servings (serving size: 1 kebab).

CALORIES 248 (28% from fat); FAT 7.8g (sat 2g, mono 3.4g, poly 1.7g); PROTEIN 33.8g; CARB 9.7g; FIBER 1.6g; CHOL 64mg; IRON 2mg; SODIUM 711mg; CALC 38mg

Better by the Batch

Our favorite cookie recipes from readers are great for a no-fuss, festive dessert plate.

Martina Webb, of Sterling Heights, Michigan, credits her husband and young son with the idea for her molasses cookie recipe. "When my husband, Mark, would return from a business trip, he always brought my son, Alex, the cookie that was served with lunch on the airplane," she remembers. "They were often molasses cookies, which Alex thought were called 'Alaska' cookies. Those cookies soon became his favorite."

About that same time, Martina read a story in *Cooking Light* about using drained applesauce as a fat substitute. From her experiments came Alaska Molasses Cookies, which were an instant hit with 6-year-old Alex.

Alaska Molasses Cookies
(pictured on page 257)

If you can't find whole wheat pastry flour, increase the all-purpose flour to 1¾ cups and use ¼ cup whole wheat flour.

  ½ cup applesauce
1¼ cups sugar, divided
  6   tablespoons butter, softened
  ¼ cup dark molasses
  1   large egg
  1   cup all-purpose flour
  1   cup whole wheat pastry flour
  2   teaspoons baking soda
  1   teaspoon ground cinnamon
  ½ teaspoon salt
  ½ teaspoon ground ginger
  ½ teaspoon ground cloves
     Cooking spray

1. Spoon applesauce onto several layers of heavy-duty paper towels; spread to ½-inch thickness. Cover with additional paper towels; let stand 5 minutes. Scrape into a bowl using a rubber spatula.

2. Combine applesauce, 1 cup sugar, and butter; beat with a mixer at medium speed until well blended (about 3 minutes). Add molasses and egg; beat well.

3. Lightly spoon flours into dry measuring cups; level with a knife. Combine flours and next 5 ingredients, stirring well with a whisk. Gradually add flour mixture to sugar mixture, beating until blended. Cover and freeze dough 30 minutes or until firm.

4. Preheat oven to 375°.

5. With moist hands, shape dough into 32 (1-inch) balls. Roll balls in ¼ cup sugar. Place 3 inches apart on baking sheets coated with cooking spray. Bake at 375° for 8 to 10 minutes. Cool on pans 5 minutes. Remove from pans; cool completely on wire racks. Yield: 32 cookies (serving size: 1 cookie).

CALORIES 88 (25% from fat); FAT 2.4g (sat 1.4g, mono 0.7g, poly 0.1g); PROTEIN 1.2g; CARB 16g; FIBER 0.7g; CHOL 12mg; IRON 0.7mg; SODIUM 141mg; CALC 16mg

Black-and-White Cake Cookies

(pictured on page 257)

"These large, cakelike cookies are covered half in chocolate and half in white frosting."
—Sylvia Lee, Chapel Hill, North Carolina

COOKIES:

1½ cups all-purpose flour
1½ teaspoons baking powder
½ teaspoon salt
⅔ cup applesauce
1 cup granulated sugar
¼ cup butter, softened
1½ teaspoons vanilla extract
2 large egg whites

FROSTING:

1½ cups powdered sugar, divided
3 tablespoons 2% reduced-fat milk, divided
¼ teaspoon almond extract
2 tablespoons unsweetened cocoa

1. Preheat oven to 375°.

2. To prepare cookies, lightly spoon flour into dry measuring cups; level with

a knife. Combine flour, baking powder, and salt, stirring with a whisk.

3. Place applesauce in a fine sieve; let stand 15 minutes.

4. Combine drained applesauce, granulated sugar, and butter in a large bowl; beat with a mixer at medium speed 2 minutes or until well blended. Beat in vanilla and egg whites. Add flour mixture; beat at low speed until blended.

5. Drop dough by level tablespoons 2 inches apart onto parchment-lined baking sheets. Bake at 375° for 10 minutes or until set (not browned). Cool on pans 2 minutes or until firm. Remove from pans; cool completely on wire racks.

6. To prepare frosting, combine ¾ cup powdered sugar, 1 tablespoon milk, and almond extract in a bowl, stirring well with a whisk until smooth. Working with 1 cookie at a time, hold cookie over bowl, and spread about 1 teaspoon white frosting over half of cookie (scrape excess frosting from edges). Let stand 10 minutes or until frosting is set.

7. Combine ¾ cup powdered sugar and cocoa in a bowl. Gradually add 2 tablespoons milk, stirring with a whisk until smooth. Working with 1 cookie at a time, hold cookie over bowl, and spread about 1 teaspoon chocolate frosting over other half of cookie (scrape excess frosting from edges). Let stand 10 minutes or until frosting is set. Yield: 2 dozen cookies (serving size: 1 cookie).

CALORIES 106 (17% from fat); FAT 2g (sat 1.2g, mono 0.6g, poly 0.1g); PROTEIN 1.3g; CARB 21.4g; FIBER 0.4g; CHOL 5mg; IRON 0.4mg; SODIUM 100mg; CALC 14mg

Chocolate Chip Meringues

(pictured on page 257)

"These cookies will keep for a week in an airtight container."
—Catharine Grimes, New York City, New York

3 large egg whites
¼ teaspoon cream of tartar
⅛ teaspoon salt
¾ cup sugar
¼ cup unsweetened cocoa, divided
½ cup semisweet chocolate minichips
¼ teaspoon vanilla extract

1. Preheat oven to 250°.

2. Cover a baking sheet with parchment paper; secure with masking tape.

3. Place egg whites, cream of tartar, and salt in a large bowl; beat with a mixer at high speed until foamy. Combine sugar and 3 tablespoons cocoa, stirring with a whisk. Gradually add sugar mixture to egg white mixture, 1 tablespoon at a time, beating at medium speed until stiff peaks form. Gently fold in minichips and vanilla.

4. Spoon mixture into a pastry bag fitted with a ½-inch round tip, or a large zip-top plastic bag with 1 corner snipped to form a ½-inch opening. Pipe 30 (2-inch-round) mounds ¼ inch apart onto prepared baking sheet. Bake at 250° for 1½ hours.

5. Turn oven off; cool meringues in closed oven 1 hour. Carefully remove meringues from paper. Using a fine sieve, dust meringues with 1 tablespoon cocoa. Yield: 30 cookies (serving size: 1 cookie).

CALORIES 26 (42% from fat); FAT 1.2g (sat 0.7g, mono 0.1g, poly 0.1g); PROTEIN 0.7g; CARB 3.1g; FIBER 0.2g; CHOL 0mg; IRON 0.2mg; SODIUM 15mg; CALC 3mg

Low-Fat Cookie Tips

1. Freezing the cookie dough is a crucial step, so don't omit it. In three recipes, we direct you to freeze the dough at various stages. This does two things: It makes sticky dough easier to handle, and it controls spreading in the oven.

2. Beating the egg white mixture to just the right consistency is crucial for the success of the meringues. The goal is stiff peaks. You can tell if you have reached the right stage by lifting the beaters out of the mixture; at the stiff peak stage, the egg whites stand up straight and don't fall over.

search myclar2003.com for all our tips

Crisp Pecan Cookies

"Pecan sandies have always been one of my favorite cookies, and these are reminiscent of them. I always keep pecans in the freezer so I can make this recipe for something sweet after dinner."

—Catherine Hall, Birmingham, Alabama

  1 cup all-purpose flour
  ½ teaspoon baking powder
  ¼ teaspoon salt
  1 cup packed brown sugar
  5 tablespoons butter, softened
  1 teaspoon vanilla extract
  1 large egg white
  3 tablespoons pecans, toasted and finely chopped
  ⅓ cup powdered sugar, divided
Cooking spray

1. Lightly spoon flour into a dry measuring cup; level with a knife. Combine flour, baking powder, and salt, stirring with a whisk.
2. Combine brown sugar and butter in a bowl, and beat with a mixer at high speed until light and fluffy. Add vanilla and egg white, and beat 1 minute. Stir in flour mixture and chopped pecans. Refrigerate dough 30 minutes.
3. Preheat oven to 350°.
4. Place ¼ cup powdered sugar in a small bowl. With moist hands, shape dough into 30 (½-inch) balls. Roll balls in ¼ cup powdered sugar. Place 2 inches apart on baking sheets coated with cooking spray. Place pans in freezer 10 minutes.
5. Bake at 350° for 12 minutes or until cookies are golden. Cool on pans 2 minutes. Remove from pans; cool completely on wire racks. Using a fine sieve, sprinkle 4 teaspoons powdered sugar over cookies. Yield: 30 cookies (serving size: 1 cookie).

CALORIES 69 (33% from fat); FAT 2.5g (sat 1.2g, mono 0.9g, poly 0.2g); PROTEIN 0.6g; CARB 11.6g; FIBER 0.2g; CHOL 5mg; IRON 0.4mg; SODIUM 50mg; CALC 10mg

Double Chocolate Cookies

(pictured on page 257)

"I borrowed this recipe from my mother-in-law and added the white chocolate chips and dried cherries. We think they are even better than the original. You can use dried cranberries if you prefer."

—Christy Milton, Amarillo, Texas

  1¼ cups all-purpose flour
  ½ teaspoon baking powder
  ¼ teaspoon salt
  5 tablespoons butter, softened
  ½ cup granulated sugar
  ½ cup packed brown sugar
  1½ teaspoons vanilla extract
  1 large egg white
  ⅓ cup dried tart cherries
  ¼ cup semisweet chocolate chunks
  2½ tablespoons premium white chocolate chips
Cooking spray

1. Preheat oven to 350°.
2. Lightly spoon flour into dry measuring cups; level with a knife. Combine flour, baking powder, and salt, stirring with a whisk.
3. Combine butter and sugars in a large bowl; beat with a mixer at medium speed until well blended. Add vanilla and egg white; beat 1 minute. Stir in flour mixture, cherries, chocolate chunks, and chocolate chips.
4. Drop by level tablespoons 2 inches apart onto baking sheets coated with cooking spray. Place pans in freezer 5 minutes. Bake at 350° for 10 minutes or until lightly browned. Cool on pans 2 minutes. Remove from pans; cool completely on wire racks. Yield: 2 dozen cookies (serving size: 1 cookie).

CALORIES 98 (30% from fat); FAT 3.3g (sat 2g, mono 1g, poly 0.1g); PROTEIN 1g; CARB 16.6g; FIBER 0.4g; CHOL 7mg; IRON 0.5mg; SODIUM 63mg; CALC 12mg

dinner tonight

Marvelous Marinades

Whether by quick dip or overnight soak, marinades provide a head start to tender, flavorful entrées.

Tandoori Chicken

Although it's not cooked in a tandoor oven, this vibrant entrée has all the flavors of the traditional Indian dish, thanks to a long marinating time.

TOTAL TIME: 23 MINUTES (DOES NOT INCLUDE MARINATING)

  ¾ cup coarsely chopped onion
  1 teaspoon coarsely chopped peeled fresh ginger
  2 garlic cloves, peeled
  ½ cup plain low-fat yogurt
  1 tablespoon fresh lemon juice
  1 teaspoon paprika
  1 teaspoon ground cumin
  1 teaspoon ground coriander seeds
  ½ teaspoon salt
  ½ teaspoon chili powder
  ¼ teaspoon black pepper
  Dash of ground nutmeg
  4 (4-ounce) skinless, boneless chicken breast halves
  Cooking spray

1. Place first 3 ingredients in a food processor; process until finely chopped. Add yogurt and next 8 ingredients; pulse 4 times or until blended.
2. Make 3 diagonal cuts ¼ inch deep across top of each chicken breast half. Combine chicken and yogurt mixture in a large zip-top plastic bag. Seal and marinate in refrigerator 8 hours or overnight, turning occasionally.
3. Prepare grill or preheat broiler.
4. Remove chicken breast halves from bag; discard marinade. Place chicken on grill rack or broiler pan coated with cooking spray; cook 6 minutes on each side or until done. Yield: 4 servings (serving size: 1 chicken breast half).

CALORIES 146 (12% from fat); FAT 1.9g (sat 0.6g, mono 0.4g, poly 0.4g); PROTEIN 27.4g; CARB 3.4g; FIBER 0.7g; CHOL 67mg; IRON 1.1mg; SODIUM 234mg; CALC 50mg

---

Marinade Menu 2
serves 4

Salmon with Orange-Fennel Sauce

Rice pilaf*

Sautéed snow peas

*Heat 2 teaspoons olive oil over medium-high heat in a large nonstick skillet. Add 1 cup chopped onion; sauté 5 minutes or until tender. Stir in 1 cup uncooked long-grain rice; sauté 1 minute. Add 2 cups water, ½ teaspoon salt, ¼ teaspoon dried thyme, and ⅛ teaspoon black pepper; bring to a boil. Cover, reduce heat, and simmer 20 minutes or until water is absorbed. Sprinkle with 1 tablespoon chopped fresh parsley.

Game Plan

1. Prepare marinade
2. While fish marinates:
  • Preheat broiler for fish
  • Cook rice pilaf
3. While fish cooks:
  • Cook reserved marinade
  • Sauté snow peas
  • Chop parsley for rice pilaf

Salmon with Orange-Fennel Sauce

Be careful not to marinate longer than 20 minutes; as in ceviche, the citrus marinade can "cook" the fish. Crush the fennel seeds with a mortar and pestle, or place them in a zip-top plastic bag on a cutting board and crush with a heavy pan.

TOTAL TIME: 40 MINUTES (INCLUDES MARINATING)

QUICK TIP: Prepare the marinade up to one day in advance; refrigerate in an airtight container.

  2 teaspoons grated orange rind
  ½ cup fresh orange juice
  1 teaspoon chopped fresh rosemary
  1 teaspoon fennel seeds, crushed
  4 (6-ounce) salmon fillets (about 1 inch thick)
  Cooking spray
  ¼ teaspoon salt
  ⅛ teaspoon black pepper

1. Combine first 4 ingredients in a large zip-top plastic bag; add fish. Seal and marinate in refrigerator 20 minutes, turning once.
2. Preheat broiler.
3. Remove fish from bag, reserving marinade. Place fish, skin sides down, on a broiler pan coated with cooking spray; sprinkle with salt and pepper. Broil 10 minutes or until fish flakes easily when tested with a fork.
4. Bring reserved marinade to a boil in a small saucepan. Reduce heat, and simmer 3 minutes. Serve sauce with fish. Yield: 4 servings (serving size: 1 fillet and about 1 tablespoon sauce).

CALORIES 244 (39% from fat); FAT 10.7g (sat 2.5g, mono 4.7g, poly 2.5g); PROTEIN 31.3g; CARB 3.8g; FIBER 0.4g; CHOL 80mg; IRON 0.7mg; SODIUM 214mg; CALC 28mg

---

Marinade Menu 3
serves 6

Korean-Style Pork Tenderloin

Buttered spaghetti squash*

Sautéed broccolini

*Cut 1 (3-pound) spaghetti squash in half lengthwise; discard seeds. Place squash halves, cut sides down, in a baking dish; add ¼ cup water to dish. Cover with heavy-duty plastic wrap; vent. Microwave at HIGH 15 minutes or until squash is tender when pierced with a fork. Scrape inside of squash with a fork to remove spaghetti-like strands. Toss squash strands with 1 tablespoon butter, 2 teaspoons sugar, 1 teaspoon grated lemon rind, ¼ teaspoon salt, and ¼ teaspoon black pepper.

Game Plan

1. Prepare marinade, and marinate pork 8 hours or overnight
2. While oven heats for pork:
  • Microwave spaghetti squash
3. While pork cooks:
  • Cook reserved marinade
  • Scrape squash, and toss with seasonings
  • Sauté broccolini

search myclar2003.com for all our menus

Continued

Korean-Style Pork Tenderloin

(pictured on page 258)

Nutty, slightly sweetened spaghetti squash and tender, sweet broccolini complement the pork and its zesty marinade.

TOTAL TIME: 31 MINUTES (DOES NOT INCLUDE MARINATING)

QUICK TIP: To mince ginger easily, place a small, peeled piece in a garlic press and squeeze.

⅓ cup low-sodium soy sauce
3 tablespoons rice vinegar
2 tablespoons sugar
1 tablespoon minced peeled fresh ginger
1 tablespoon dark sesame oil
¼ teaspoon crushed red pepper
4 garlic cloves, minced
1½ pounds pork tenderloin, trimmed
Cooking spray

1. Combine first 7 ingredients in a large zip-top plastic bag; add pork. Seal and marinate in refrigerator 8 hours or overnight, turning occasionally.
2. Preheat oven to 425°.
3. Heat a large ovenproof skillet coated with cooking spray over medium-high heat. Remove pork from bag, reserving marinade. Add pork to pan; cook 6 minutes, browning on all sides.
4. Place pan in oven; bake at 425° for 15 minutes or until meat thermometer registers 160° (medium) or until desired degree of doneness. Let stand 5 minutes before slicing.
5. Bring reserved marinade to a boil in a small saucepan. Reduce heat, and simmer 5 minutes.
6. Cut pork into ¼-inch-thick slices; serve with sauce. Yield: 6 servings (serving size: 3 ounces pork and about 1 tablespoon sauce).

CALORIES 184 (30% from fat); FAT 6.2g (sat 1.7g, mono 2.7g, poly 1.4g); PROTEIN 24.7g; CARB 6.2g; FIBER 0.2g; CHOL 74mg; IRON 1.7mg; SODIUM 531mg; CALC 12mg

Marinade Menu 4
serves 4

Flank Steak Marinated with Shallots and Pepper

Corn and sugar snap salad*

Mashed sweet potatoes

*Combine 1½ cups fresh or thawed frozen corn kernels, 1½ cups chopped fresh sugar snap peas, ¼ cup chopped green onions, 2 tablespoons chopped fresh cilantro, and 2 teaspoons chopped seeded jalapeño pepper. Combine 1 tablespoon fresh lime juice, 1 teaspoon vegetable oil, ¼ teaspoon salt, and ¼ teaspoon black pepper, stirring with a whisk; drizzle over salad. Toss to combine.

Game Plan

1. Prepare marinade, and marinate steak 8 hours or overnight
2. While grill or broiler heats for steak:
 • Bring water to a boil for potatoes
 • Prepare corn salad
3. While steak cooks:
 • Cook potatoes
 • Cook corn (optional)

Flank Steak Marinated with Shallots and Pepper

TOTAL TIME: 17 MINUTES (DOES NOT INCLUDE MARINATING)

QUICK TIP: If the corn you have for the salad is less than the freshest, grill it alongside the steak for the same amount of time, turning occasionally.

¼ cup chopped shallots
¼ cup red wine vinegar
2 tablespoons balsamic vinegar
1 teaspoon coarsely ground black pepper, divided
1 (1-pound) flank steak, trimmed
¼ teaspoon salt
Cooking spray

1. Combine first 3 ingredients in a large zip-top plastic bag; add ½ teaspoon pepper and steak. Seal and marinate in refrigerator 8 hours or overnight, turning occasionally.
2. Prepare grill or preheat broiler.
3. Remove steak from bag; discard marinade. Sprinkle steak with ½ teaspoon pepper and salt. Place steak on grill rack or broiler pan coated with cooking spray; cook 6 minutes on each side or until desired degree of doneness. Cut steak diagonally across grain into thin slices. Yield: 4 servings (serving size: 3 ounces).

CALORIES 184 (42% from fat); FAT 8.6g (sat 3.7g, mono 3.5g, poly 0.4g); PROTEIN 23.2g; CARB 1.8g; FIBER 0.2g; CHOL 57mg; IRON 2.5mg; SODIUM 220mg; CALC 12mg

classics

Pesto Aplenty

Got a bumper crop of basil? Turn it into freezer-friendly pesto and enjoy the taste of summer throughout the winter.

Our pesto has half the fat and calories of a typical recipe. The powerful flavor makes quite an impression, so a little goes a long way. You'll be using less than a tablespoon per serving for these recipes.

Classic Pesto

2 tablespoons coarsely chopped walnuts or pine nuts
2 garlic cloves, peeled
3 tablespoons extra-virgin olive oil
4 cups basil leaves (about 4 ounces)
½ cup (2 ounces) grated fresh Parmesan cheese
¼ teaspoon salt

1. Drop nuts and garlic through food chute with food processor on; process until minced. Add oil; pulse 3 times. Add basil, cheese, and salt; process until finely minced, scraping sides of bowl once. Yield: ¾ cup (serving size: 1 tablespoon).

CALORIES 58 (82% from fat); FAT 5.3g (sat 1.3g, mono 3g, poly 0.8g); PROTEIN 2.1g; CARB 0.9g; FIBER 0.6g; CHOL 3mg; IRON 0.5mg; SODIUM 125mg; CALC 72mg

Pesto Pizza with Butternut Squash

Top pizza with a trio of flavors—sweet squash, piquant pesto, and mild, buttery cheese.

  6 (¼-inch-thick) slices peeled butternut squash or pumpkin (about ½ pound)
  2 teaspoons sugar
  ¾ teaspoon olive oil
Cooking spray
  ½ cup (2 ounces) shredded fontina or Gouda cheese
Pizza Dough
  1 (14.5-ounce) can finely chopped tomatoes, drained
  ½ teaspoon dried oregano
  ¼ cup Classic Pesto (recipe on page 270)
  ½ cup (2 ounces) grated fresh Romano or Parmesan cheese

1. Preheat oven to 400°.
2. Combine first 3 ingredients in a medium bowl. Place squash mixture on a baking sheet coated with cooking spray. Bake at 400° for 20 minutes or until squash is tender.
3. Increase oven temperature to 450°.
4. Sprinkle fontina over dough, leaving a ½-inch border; top with squash mixture, tomatoes, and oregano. Drop Classic Pesto by level teaspoons onto mixture; sprinkle with Romano. Bake at 450° for 20 minutes or until lightly browned. Yield: 6 servings (serving size: 1 slice).

(Totals include Pizza Dough) CALORIES 310 (30% from fat); FAT 10.4g (sat 4.5g, mono 4.1g, poly 1.1g); PROTEIN 12.4g; CARB 42.3g; FIBER 2.8g; CHOL 23mg; IRON 3mg; SODIUM 511mg; CALC 242mg

PIZZA DOUGH:
  1 package dry yeast (about 2¼ teaspoons)
  ⅔ cup warm water (100° to 110°)
  2 cups all-purpose flour, divided
  1 tablespoon cornmeal
  ½ teaspoon salt
Cooking spray

1. Dissolve yeast in warm water in a large bowl; let stand 5 minutes. Lightly spoon flour into dry measuring cups; level with a knife. Add 1¾ cups flour, cornmeal, and salt to yeast mixture, stirring to form a soft dough.
2. Turn dough out onto a lightly floured surface. Knead dough until smooth and elastic (about 5 minutes); add enough of remaining flour, 1 tablespoon at a time, to prevent dough from sticking to hands.
3. Place dough in a large bowl coated with cooking spray, turning to coat top. Cover and let rise in a warm place (85°), free from drafts, 40 minutes or until doubled in size. (Press two fingers into dough. If indentation remains, dough has risen enough.)
4. Punch dough down. Cover and let rest 5 minutes. Roll into a 12-inch circle on a lightly floured surface. Place dough on a 12-inch pizza pan or baking sheet coated with cooking spray. Crimp edges of dough with your fingers to form a rim. Top and bake dough according to recipe directions. Yield: 1 (12-inch) pizza crust.

CALORIES 968 (3% from fat); FAT 3.6g (sat 0.5g, mono 0.6g, poly 1.5g); PROTEIN 29.2g; CARB 200.2g; FIBER 9.1g; CHOL 0mg; IRON 13.1mg; SODIUM 1,177mg; CALC 43mg

Roasted Pepper, Tomato, and Feta Sandwich with Pesto Mayonnaise

Adding mayonnaise to our pesto creates a mild, creamy spread that's great on nearly any sandwich.

  1 yellow bell pepper
  1 (8-ounce) loaf French bread
Pesto Mayonnaise
  ½ cup (2 ounces) crumbled feta cheese
  8 (¼-inch-thick) slices tomato
  4 (⅛-inch-thick) slices red onion, separated into rings

1. Preheat broiler.
2. Cut bell pepper in half lengthwise; discard seeds and membranes. Place pepper halves, skin sides up, on a foil-lined baking sheet; flatten with hand. Broil 15 minutes or until blackened. Place in a zip-top plastic bag; seal. Let stand 15 minutes. Peel and cut each piece in half.
3. Cut loaf in half horizontally. Spread Pesto Mayonnaise evenly over bottom half of loaf; sprinkle with feta. Arrange bell pepper, tomato, and onion over bottom half of loaf; top with remaining half. Cut loaf into 4 sandwiches. Yield: 4 servings (serving size: 1 sandwich).

(Totals include Pesto Mayonnaise) CALORIES 256 (28% from fat); FAT 8.1g (sat 3.2g, mono 3g, poly 1.3g); PROTEIN 8.8g; CARB 37.3g; FIBER 3.2g; CHOL 14mg; IRON 2.2mg; SODIUM 713mg; CALC 157mg

PESTO MAYONNAISE:
  2 tablespoons light mayonnaise
  2 tablespoons Classic Pesto (recipe on page 270)
  ⅛ teaspoon salt
  ⅛ teaspoon black pepper

1. Combine all ingredients in a small bowl. Yield: ¼ cup (serving size: 1 tablespoon).
NOTE: Pesto Mayonnaise will keep for up to 5 days in the refrigerator when stored in an airtight container.

CALORIES 42 (69% from fat); FAT 3.2g (sat 0.7g, mono 1.6g, poly 0.7g); PROTEIN 1.1g; CARB 2.5g; FIBER 0.3g; CHOL 2mg; IRON 0.3mg; SODIUM 206mg; CALC 36mg

Potato, Mushroom, and Pesto Omelet

We packed this omelet so full that it's too thick to fold in half. Serve it open faced with fresh fruit and muffins.

  4 large egg whites
  1 large egg
  ⅛ teaspoon salt
  ⅛ teaspoon black pepper
Cooking spray
  1 cup thinly sliced mushrooms
  ¼ cup finely chopped red bell pepper
  ½ cup diced peeled baking potato, cooked
  1 tablespoon Classic Pesto (recipe on page 270)

1. Combine first 4 ingredients in a medium bowl, stirring with a whisk.
2. Heat a small nonstick skillet coated with cooking spray over medium-high
Continued

heat. Add mushrooms and bell pepper; sauté 5 minutes. Pour egg mixture into pan; top with potato (do not stir). Cover, reduce heat to medium-low, and cook 8 minutes or until center is set.

3. Spread Classic Pesto over omelet. Loosen omelet with a spatula, and cut in half. Slide omelet halves onto plates. Yield: 2 servings.

CALORIES 146 (36% from fat); FAT 5.9g (sat 1.5g, mono 2.6g, poly 1g); PROTEIN 12.7g; CARB 10.8g; FIBER 1.7g; CHOL 112mg; IRON 1.7mg; SODIUM 345mg; CALC 56mg

Pasta Tossed with Shrimp, Vegetables, and Pesto

This summery pasta can easily become a complete meal; just add salad and bread.

1½ cups diagonally sliced snow peas
1½ cups julienne-cut yellow squash
2 teaspoons olive oil
¾ pound large shrimp, peeled and deveined
½ cup fat-free, less-sodium chicken broth
4 cups hot cooked farfalle (about 3 cups uncooked bow tie pasta)
1½ cups cherry tomatoes, halved
¼ cup (1 ounce) crumbled feta cheese
¼ cup Classic Pesto (recipe on page 270)
1 tablespoon lemon juice
½ teaspoon salt
⅛ teaspoon black pepper

1. Bring water to a boil in a saucepan; add snow peas and squash. Cook 45 seconds or until crisp-tender; drain.
2. Heat oil in a large nonstick skillet over medium heat. Add shrimp; cook 3 minutes or until done. Add snow pea mixture and broth. Cover and cook 30 seconds or until thoroughly heated.
3. Combine shrimp mixture, pasta, and remaining ingredients in a large bowl; toss well. Yield: 6 servings (serving size: 1⅓ cups).

CALORIES 293 (26% from fat); FAT 8.6g (sat 2.8g, mono 3.8g, poly 1.4g); PROTEIN 18g; CARB 35.8g; FIBER 3.2g; CHOL 75mg; IRON 4mg; SODIUM 475mg; CALC 148mg

Tomato Soup with Chickpeas and Pesto

1 tablespoon olive oil
1½ cups vertically sliced onion
1 cup finely chopped celery
2 cups water
¼ teaspoon salt
¼ teaspoon black pepper
3 (5.5-ounce) cans low-sodium vegetable juice
1 (28-ounce) can finely chopped tomatoes, undrained
1 (15½-ounce) can chickpeas (garbanzo beans), drained
⅓ cup uncooked ditalini (very short tube-shaped macaroni)
⅓ cup Classic Pesto (recipe on page 270)

1. Heat oil in a Dutch oven over medium heat. Add onion and celery. Cover and cook 15 minutes, stirring occasionally. Add water and next 5 ingredients; bring to a boil. Add pasta. Cover, reduce heat; simmer 20 minutes. Stir in Classic Pesto. Yield: 6 servings (serving size: 1½ cups).

CALORIES 218 (29% from fat); FAT 7.1g (sat 1.5g, mono 4g, poly 1.3g); PROTEIN 8.8g; CARB 29.3g; FIBER 4.6g; CHOL 3mg; IRON 3.2mg; SODIUM 581mg; CALC 144mg

Basmati Rice with Corn and Pesto

2 teaspoons olive oil
2 cups sliced mushrooms
1 cup sliced green onions
2 cups uncooked basmati rice
¾ cup water
¼ teaspoon salt
¼ teaspoon black pepper
2 (14-ounce) cans fat-free, less-sodium chicken broth
1 (10-ounce) package frozen whole-kernel corn, thawed and drained
3 tablespoons Classic Pesto (recipe on page 270)

1. Heat oil in a Dutch oven over medium-high heat. Add mushrooms and onions; sauté 3 minutes. Add rice; sauté 2 minutes. Add water, salt, pepper, and broth; bring to a boil. Cover, reduce

heat, and simmer 20 minutes or until liquid is absorbed.
2. Stir in corn. Cover and cook 5 minutes. Remove from heat; stir in Classic Pesto. Yield: 8 servings (serving size: ¾ cup).

CALORIES 247 (14% from fat); FAT 3.7g (sat 0.8g, mono 2.1g, poly 0.6g); PROTEIN 7.2g; CARB 46.5g; FIBER 2.2g; CHOL 1mg; IRON 2.7mg; SODIUM 367mg; CALC 52mg

Chicken Chili with Pesto

2 teaspoons vegetable oil
¾ cup finely chopped onion
¾ pound skinless, boneless chicken breast, cut into bite-sized pieces
1½ cups finely chopped carrot
¾ cup finely chopped red bell pepper
¾ cup thinly sliced celery
¼ cup canned chopped green chiles
¾ teaspoon dried oregano
½ teaspoon ground cumin
¼ teaspoon salt
⅛ teaspoon black pepper
1 (16-ounce) can cannellini beans or other white beans, rinsed and drained
1 (14-ounce) can fat-free, less-sodium chicken broth
3 tablespoons Classic Pesto (recipe on page 270)

1. Heat oil in a Dutch oven over medium-high heat. Add onion and chicken; sauté 5 minutes. Add carrot, bell pepper, and celery; sauté 4 minutes. Add chiles and next 6 ingredients; bring to a boil.
2. Cover, reduce heat, and simmer 25 minutes. Stir in Classic Pesto. Yield: 4 servings (serving size: 1¼ cups).
NOTE: The chili and pesto can be made ahead and frozen for up to 3 months. Prepare and freeze 3 tablespoons Classic Pesto. Prepare the chili without Classic Pesto, and spoon into a freezer-safe container. Cool completely in refrigerator; cover and freeze. Thaw chili and pesto in refrigerator. Place chili in a large skillet; cook over medium-low heat until thoroughly heated, stirring occasionally. Stir in Classic Pesto.

CALORIES 327 (23% from fat); FAT 8.5g (sat 1.8g, mono 3.4g, poly 2.5g); PROTEIN 30.3g; CARB 30.7g; FIBER 5.9g; CHOL 52mg; IRON 4.1mg; SODIUM 769mg; CALC 134mg

Eggplant Confidential

Eggplants come in an assortment of colors, sizes, and shapes. Here's how to use them all.

Extremely versatile, eggplants respond to a variety of cooking methods. Braise or stew the garden variety, since, like tofu, it's bland and easily takes on other more assertive flavors. Dry heat, such as grilling and broiling, concentrates the eggplant's flavor and transforms its texture to a creamy consistency. Long, thin Japanese eggplants are best suited for broiling or pan-frying, because their dry, firm flesh is excellent for high-heat cooking.

Asian-Inspired Menu
serves 4

Grilled ginger flank steak*

Miso-Garlic Broiled Eggplant

Jasmine rice

*Combine ¼ cup low-sodium soy sauce, 2 tablespoons minced peeled fresh ginger, 2 tablespoons rice vinegar, 1 tablespoon honey, and 3 minced garlic cloves in a zip-top plastic bag. Add 1 (1-pound) flank steak; refrigerate 1 hour. Grill steak 6 minutes on each side.

Miso-Garlic Broiled Eggplant

Serve this as an appetizer or a side dish.

¼ cup mirin (sweet rice wine)
3 tablespoons yellow miso (soybean paste)
2 teaspoons grated peeled fresh ginger
1 teaspoon dark sesame oil
½ teaspoon crushed red pepper
2 garlic cloves, minced
4 Japanese eggplants, cut diagonally into ½-inch-thick slices (about 1 pound)
Cooking spray
1 tablespoon sesame seeds
¼ cup thinly sliced green onions

1. Preheat broiler.
2. Combine first 6 ingredients, stirring with a whisk. Arrange eggplant slices on a baking sheet coated with cooking spray. Spread mirin mixture evenly over eggplant slices, and sprinkle with sesame seeds. Broil 8 minutes or until topping is golden. Place eggplant slices on a platter, and sprinkle with onions. Yield: 4 servings.

CALORIES 115 (26% from fat); FAT 3.3g (sat 0.5g, mono 1.1g, poly 1.5g); PROTEIN 3.3g; CARB 16.1g; FIBER 4g; CHOL 0mg; IRON 1.1mg; SODIUM 475mg; CALC 46mg

Roasted Eggplant and Garlic Soup

This is a great make-ahead recipe. Keep it refrigerated for up to three days, then reheat and garnish with yogurt and cilantro just before serving.

1 (1-pound) eggplant, cut in half lengthwise
Cooking spray
10 garlic cloves, unpeeled
1 teaspoon coriander seeds
½ teaspoon cumin seeds
2 teaspoons olive oil
1 cup chopped onion
¼ teaspoon black pepper
1½ tablespoons all-purpose flour
¼ cup water
1 (14½-ounce) can vegetable broth
1 tablespoon balsamic vinegar
2 tablespoons plain low-fat yogurt
2 teaspoons minced fresh cilantro

1. Preheat oven to 450°.
2. Place eggplant, cut sides down, in a baking pan coated with cooking spray; add garlic. Bake at 450° for 30 minutes or until eggplant is tender; cool. Scrape pulp from eggplant skins; discard skins. Squeeze cloves to extract garlic pulp; discard skins.
3. Place coriander and cumin seeds in a spice or coffee grinder; process until finely ground. Heat oil in a medium saucepan over medium heat. Add spice mixture, onion, and pepper; cook 5 minutes or until onion is tender, stirring frequently. Add flour; cook 2 minutes, stirring constantly. Add water and vegetable broth, scraping pan to loosen browned bits. Bring to a boil. Cool 5 minutes.
4. Combine eggplant pulp, garlic pulp, and broth mixture in a blender, and process until smooth. Return pureed mixture to pan. Bring to a simmer over medium-high heat, and cook 3 minutes, stirring frequently. Stir in balsamic vinegar. Ladle 1½ cups soup into each of 2 bowls. Top each serving with 1 tablespoon yogurt and 1 teaspoon cilantro. Yield: 3 cups.

CALORIES 214 (27% from fat); FAT 6.5g (sat 0.8g, mono 3.4g, poly 0.6g); PROTEIN 7.5g; CARB 37.1g; FIBER 2.7g; CHOL 1mg; IRON 1.6mg; SODIUM 899mg; CALC 99mg

Rice and Feta-Stuffed Baby Eggplant

(pictured on page 260)

2 cups chopped tomato
¼ cup dry white wine
½ teaspoon sugar
1 teaspoon sea salt, divided
6 baby eggplants (about 1¼ pounds), cut in half lengthwise
2 teaspoons olive oil
1 cup finely chopped onion
1 cup finely chopped yellow bell pepper
2 garlic cloves, minced
2 tablespoons finely chopped fresh basil
1 jalapeño pepper, seeded and finely chopped
1 cup cooked brown basmati rice
½ cup (2 ounces) crumbled feta cheese
1 tablespoon finely chopped fresh parsley
Parsley sprigs (optional)

1. Preheat oven to 375°.
2. Combine tomato, wine, sugar, and ¼ teaspoon salt in a 13 x 9-inch baking dish; spread evenly.
3. Scoop pulp from eggplant halves, leaving ¼-inch-thick shells. Chop pulp. Sprinkle inside surfaces of shells with ¼ teaspoon salt.

Continued

4. Heat oil in a large nonstick skillet over medium-high heat. Add onion, bell pepper, garlic, and ½ teaspoon salt; sauté 3 minutes. Stir in eggplant pulp, basil, and jalapeño; cover, reduce heat, and cook over low heat 10 minutes or until eggplant is tender. Remove from heat; stir in rice, cheese, and chopped parsley.

5. Spoon about ¼ cup eggplant mixture into each eggplant shell, pressing gently; place shells, cut sides up, over tomato mixture in baking dish. Cover and bake at 375° for 15 minutes. Uncover; bake an additional 15 minutes or until shells are tender. Spoon about 1½ tablespoons tomato mixture over each eggplant half. Garnish with parsley sprigs, if desired. Yield: 4 servings (serving size: 3 eggplant halves).

CALORIES 256 (28% from fat); FAT 8.1g (sat 3.5g, mono 3g, poly 0.9g); PROTEIN 7.9g; CARB 40.1g; FIBER 3.7g; CHOL 17mg; IRON 1.6mg; SODIUM 810mg; CALC 132mg

---

To Salt or Not?

Salting draws excess water from the eggplant, which, in turn, helps collapse the internal cell structure. This firms the flesh, and prevents it from absorbing too much oil. (If you've cooked with eggplant before, you know that it acts like a sponge and can soak up large amounts of oil.) By drawing out liquid, salting decreases bitterness, since the liquid contains the bitter substances. If your eggplant is fresh and in season, there's no need to salt. If it's out of season, salting certainly can't hurt. Follow these steps for salting eggplant:

• Slice eggplant into desired shape; toss with coarse salt.

• Leave in colander to drain 30 minutes to 1 hour.

• Squeeze out or pat off liquid; rinse well. Pat dry.

search myclar2003.com for all our tips

Eggplant Sandwiches with Spinach and Fontina

Eggplant stands in for bread in this savory and intriguing dish. Dredging the eggplant in polenta adds crunch.

    2 (1-pound) eggplants, peeled and
       cut into 28 (½-inch-thick) slices
    1 teaspoon sea salt, divided
    1 cup water
    1 (10-ounce) package fresh spinach
       Cooking spray
 1½ cups finely chopped onion
    ½ teaspoon crushed red pepper
    2 garlic cloves, minced
    1 tablespoon fresh lemon juice
    ¼ teaspoon black pepper
    ½ cup (2 ounces) shredded fontina
       cheese
    2 tablespoons grated fresh Parmesan
       cheese
    ¼ cup fat-free milk
    3 large egg whites, lightly beaten
    1 cup dry polenta
    4 teaspoons olive oil
  14 lemon wedges

1. Preheat broiler.

2. Sprinkle eggplant with ½ teaspoon salt. Place half of eggplant on a baking sheet; broil 5 minutes on each side or until lightly browned. Repeat procedure with remaining eggplant.

3. Bring water to a boil in a large Dutch oven. Add spinach; cover and cook 2 minutes or until wilted. Drain well. Place spinach on several layers of paper towels; cover with additional paper towels. Let stand 5 minutes, pressing down occasionally. Coarsely chop spinach.

4. Heat a medium skillet coated with cooking spray over medium heat. Add onion, red pepper, and garlic; cook 4 minutes or until onion is tender, stirring occasionally. Stir in lemon juice; cook 30 seconds or until liquid evaporates. Combine onion mixture and chopped spinach in a bowl; stir in ½ teaspoon salt and black pepper.

5. Combine fontina and Parmesan in a small bowl. Working with 1 eggplant slice at a time, spread about 2½ tablespoons spinach mixture evenly over each of 14 eggplant slices; sprinkle each with

---

about 2 teaspoons cheese mixture. Cover with remaining eggplant slices, and gently press together.

6. Combine milk and egg whites in a medium bowl, stirring with a whisk. Working with 1 sandwich at a time, brush both sides of each sandwich with milk mixture, and dredge in polenta.

7. Heat 2 teaspoons oil in a large nonstick skillet over medium-high heat. Add half of sandwiches; cook 5 minutes on each side or until browned. Repeat procedure with 2 teaspoons oil and remaining sandwiches. Serve with lemon wedges. Yield: 7 servings (serving size: 2 sandwiches and 2 lemon wedges).

CALORIES 236 (30% from fat); FAT 7.9g (sat 2.5g, mono 2.1g, poly 0.5g); PROTEIN 11g; CARB 34.9g; FIBER 5.3g; CHOL 11mg; IRON 3.5mg; SODIUM 695mg; CALC 214mg

---

Lentils with Eggplant and Garam Masala

Store the remaining Garam Masala in an airtight container in the freezer for up to six months. Use it to season tofu, couscous, and steamed vegetables.

    2 teaspoons olive oil
    1 cup chopped onion
 1½ teaspoons Garam Masala
    1 cup chopped tomato
    1 teaspoon ground turmeric
    1 teaspoon grated peeled fresh
       ginger
    2 garlic cloves, minced
    1 (1-pound) eggplant, peeled and
       chopped
    4 cups water
    1 cup dried lentils
 1½ teaspoons salt
    2 bay leaves
    2 cups chopped zucchini
 4½ cups hot cooked basmati rice

1. Heat oil in a Dutch oven over medium-high heat. Add onion and Garam Masala; sauté 3 minutes or until onion is tender. Stir in tomato, turmeric, ginger, garlic, and eggplant; sauté 7 minutes or until eggplant is tender.

2. Add water, lentils, salt, and bay leaves to pan; bring to a boil. Cover, reduce heat, and simmer 15 minutes. Stir in zucchini; bring to a boil. Reduce heat, and simmer 10 minutes or until zucchini is tender. Discard bay leaves. Serve over rice. Yield: 6 servings (serving size: 1¼ cups lentil mixture and ¾ cup rice).

(Totals include Garam Masala) CALORIES 447 (7% from fat); FAT 3.3g (sat 0.6g, mono 1.5g, poly 0.8g); PROTEIN 17g; CARB 90.6g; FIBER 12.4g; CHOL 0mg; IRON 4.5mg; SODIUM 587mg; CALC 56mg

GARAM MASALA:

    2   tablespoons coriander seeds
    2   tablespoons cumin seeds
    2   tablespoons black peppercorns
  1½   teaspoons whole cloves
   ¾   teaspoon cardamom seeds
    1   (1-inch) cinnamon stick

1. Heat a medium skillet over medium heat; add all ingredients. Cook 2 minutes or until toasted, stirring frequently. Place spice mixture in a spice or coffee grinder; process until finely ground. Yield: about ⅓ cup.

CALORIES 27 (33% from fat); FAT 1g (sat 0.6g, mono 0.2g, poly 0.1g); PROTEIN 0.9g; CARB 4.4g; FIBER 1.7g; CHOL 0mg; IRON 2.2mg; SODIUM 6mg; CALC 58mg

Sweet and Sour Eggplant with Ricotta Salata

Ricotta salata is a dry, aged cheese that's more like Parmesan than fresh ricotta. Use sheep's milk feta or Pecorino Romano to substitute if you can't find ricotta salata. Serve this dish with couscous.

    2   teaspoons olive oil
    1   cup sliced shallots
    3   cups (1-inch) pieces red bell pepper
    3   tablespoons golden raisins
   ¾   teaspoon sea salt
   ¼   teaspoon crushed red pepper
    2   garlic cloves, minced
    1   (1-pound) eggplant, cut into (1-inch) cubes
    1   cup water
    2   tablespoons red wine vinegar
  1½   tablespoons honey
   ¼   cup chopped fresh parsley
    3   ounces ricotta salata, crumbled

1. Heat oil in a large nonstick skillet over medium-high heat. Add shallots; sauté 2 minutes or until lightly browned. Add bell pepper; sauté 2 minutes. Add raisins and next 4 ingredients; sauté 6 minutes or until eggplant is tender.
2. Add water, vinegar, and honey to pan; bring to a boil. Reduce heat, and simmer 2 minutes. Remove from pan. Sprinkle with parsley and cheese. Yield: 4 servings (serving size: 1 cup).

CALORIES 201 (25% from fat); FAT 5.5g (sat 2.2g, mono 2.5g, poly 0.5g); PROTEIN 6g; CARB 35.4g; FIBER 3.1g; CHOL 11mg; IRON 1.9mg; SODIUM 465mg; CALC 90mg

Eggplant and Chickpea Dip with Mint

Serve with toasted pita wedges.

    1   whole garlic head
    1   (1-pound) eggplant, cut in half lengthwise
    3   tablespoons fresh lemon juice
    2   tablespoons sesame seeds, toasted
    1   tablespoon chopped fresh mint
    1   tablespoon extra-virgin olive oil
    1   teaspoon sea salt
   ¼   teaspoon ground red pepper
    1   (15½-ounce) can chickpeas (garbanzo beans), drained

1. Preheat oven to 450°.
2. Remove white papery skin from garlic head (do not peel or separate cloves); wrap in foil. Bake at 450° for 45 minutes, and cool 10 minutes. Separate cloves; squeeze to extract garlic pulp. Discard skins.
3. While garlic roasts, place eggplant, cut sides down, in a baking pan. Add water to a depth of ¼ inch. Bake at 450° for 30 minutes or until tender, and cool 10 minutes.
4. Scrape pulp from eggplant skins; discard skins. Place eggplant, garlic pulp, lemon juice, and remaining ingredients in a food processor; process until smooth, scraping sides of bowl. Yield: 2½ cups (serving size: ¼ cup).

CALORIES 84 (20% from fat); FAT 1.9g (sat 0.2g, mono 1.1g, poly 0.3g); PROTEIN 2.5g; CARB 12.3g; FIBER 1.7g; CHOL 0mg; IRON 3.4mg; SODIUM 336mg; CALC 25mg

back to the best

Chicken with 40 Cloves of Garlic

Don't let the amount of garlic in this dish scare you away.

This recipe (which first appeared in the December 1996 issue of *Cooking Light* magazine) is as versatile as it is flavorful. Use all drumsticks, all thighs, or mix it up. Serve with French bread.

Chicken with 40 Cloves of Garlic

  2½   cups chopped onion
    1   teaspoon dried tarragon
    6   parsley sprigs
    4   celery stalks, each cut into 3 pieces
    8   chicken thighs, skinned (about 2¾ pounds)
    8   chicken drumsticks, skinned (about 1¾ pounds)
   ½   cup dry vermouth or white wine
  1½   teaspoons salt
   ¼   teaspoon black pepper
        Dash of ground nutmeg
   40   garlic cloves, unpeeled (about 4 heads)
        Tarragon sprigs (optional)
        French bread (optional)

1. Preheat oven to 375°.
2. Combine first 4 ingredients in a 4-quart casserole. Arrange chicken pieces over vegetable and herb mixture. Drizzle with vermouth, and sprinkle with salt, pepper, and nutmeg. Nestle garlic around chicken. Cover casserole with aluminum foil and casserole lid.
3. Bake at 375° for 1½ hours. Garnish with tarragon sprigs, and serve with French bread, if desired. Yield: 8 servings (serving size: 1 thigh, 1 drumstick, ¼ cup vegetable and herb mixture, and 5 garlic cloves).

CALORIES 294 (24% from fat); FAT 7.8g (sat 2g, mono 2.4g, poly 2g); PROTEIN 43.1g; CARB 11g; FIBER 1.6g; CHOL 165mg; IRON 2.7mg; SODIUM 641mg; CALC 73mg

. . . And Ready in Just about 20 Minutes

These timesaving recipes bring the flavor of exotic classics to the table in a fraction of their usual time.

In less than 20 minutes, you can have *chili con carne* (Spanish for chili with meat), or chicken *cacciatore* (Italian for hunter). There's also *panzanella*—an Italian bread salad with onions, tomatoes, and cucumbers tossed with a vinaigrette. Or choose beef with sour-cream sauce—named for Russian Count Paul Stroganov. Now that you know these dishes' derivations, you can use the serving suggestions to quickly pronounce them *dinner*.

Chicken Thighs Cacciatore

Serve over pasta with a garden salad and Italian bread.

   3 tablespoons all-purpose flour
   ½ teaspoon salt
   ½ teaspoon dried thyme
   ½ teaspoon fennel seeds
   ¼ teaspoon black pepper
   1 pound skinless, boneless chicken thighs
   1 teaspoon olive oil
Cooking spray
   2 cups frozen pepper stir-fry (such as Birds Eye)
   1 cup frozen chopped onion
   ½ cup dry red wine
   2 (14.5-ounce) cans diced tomatoes, drained
   1 bay leaf

1. Combine first 5 ingredients in a large zip-top plastic bag; add chicken. Seal bag, and shake to coat.
2. Heat oil in a large nonstick skillet coated with cooking spray over medium-high heat. Add chicken; cook 5 minutes or until browned, turning once. Add pepper stir-fry and remaining ingredients; cover and cook 8 minutes.
3. Uncover and cook 3 minutes or until thick. Discard bay leaf. Yield: 4 servings (serving size: 1¼ cups).

CALORIES 223 (24% from fat); FAT 5.9g (sat 1.3g, mono 2.3g, poly 1.3g); PROTEIN 25.2g; CARB 17.7g; FIBER 4g; CHOL 94mg; IRON 2.6mg; SODIUM 568mg; CALC 55mg

Chili con Carne with Beans

Serve over rice or with corn bread twists.

   1 cup chopped onion
   4 teaspoons chili powder
   1 tablespoon ground cumin
   1 teaspoon bottled minced garlic
   ¼ teaspoon ground red pepper
   1 pound ground sirloin
   1½ cups canned crushed tomatoes
   ½ teaspoon salt
   1 (14.5-ounce) can diced tomatoes with green pepper, celery, and onion
   1 (19-ounce) can kidney beans, rinsed and drained

1. Cook first 6 ingredients in a large nonstick skillet over medium-high heat until beef is browned, stirring to crumble. Add crushed tomatoes, salt, and diced tomatoes; bring to a boil.
2. Cook 4 minutes, stirring occasionally. Add beans; cook 2 minutes or until thoroughly heated. Yield: 4 servings (serving size: 1½ cups).

CALORIES 403 (30% from fat); FAT 13.5g (sat 4.8g, mono 5.4g, poly 0.7g); PROTEIN 32g; CARB 38.8g; FIBER 14g; CHOL 75mg; IRON 3.9mg; SODIUM 824mg; CALC 65mg

---

Convenient Product

In soup, stew, and other saucy dishes, frozen chopped onions are a great time-saver. No need to thaw first.

search myclar2003.com for all our tips

Simple Seared Scallops

These sea scallops are crisp and glazed outside, tender and moist inside. Serve with orzo tossed with chopped tomato, feta cheese, basil, salt, and black pepper.

   3 tablespoons all-purpose flour
   ½ teaspoon salt
   ½ teaspoon dried marjoram
   1½ pounds sea scallops
   2 teaspoons olive oil
   ½ cup dry white wine
   1 tablespoon balsamic vinegar
Parsley sprigs (optional)

1. Combine first 3 ingredients in a large zip-top plastic bag; add scallops. Seal bag, and shake to coat.
2. Heat oil in a large nonstick skillet over medium-high heat. Add scallops; cook 3 minutes on each side or until done. Remove from pan; keep warm.
3. Add wine and vinegar to pan; cook 3 minutes or until slightly thick, stirring with a whisk. Stir in scallops; remove from heat. Garnish with parsley sprigs, if desired. Yield: 4 servings (serving size: about 5 ounces scallops).

CALORIES 211 (15% from fat); FAT 3.6g (sat 0.4g, mono 1.7g, poly 0.6g); PROTEIN 29.2g; CARB 9.2g; FIBER 0.2g; CHOL 56mg; IRON 1mg; SODIUM 567mg; CALC 46mg

Tortellini with Spinach and Cherry Tomatoes

Use any flavored tortellini or ravioli in this recipe.

   1 (9-ounce) package fresh three-cheese tortellini
   2 teaspoons olive oil
   2 teaspoons bottled minced garlic
   ½ to ¾ teaspoon crushed red pepper
   2 cups cherry tomatoes, halved
   ¼ cup fat-free, less-sodium chicken broth or vegetable broth
   1 tablespoon chopped fresh basil
   ¼ teaspoon salt
   1 (6-ounce) package fresh baby spinach

1. Cook tortellini according to package directions, omitting salt and fat.
2. While tortellini cooks, heat oil in a large nonstick skillet over medium-high heat. Add garlic and red pepper; sauté 30 seconds.
3. Add tomatoes, broth, basil, salt, and spinach to pan; cook 2 minutes or until spinach wilts. Stir in tortellini; cook 1 minute. Yield: 4 servings (serving size: 1½ cups).

CALORIES 254 (26% from fat); FAT 7.4g (sat 3.1g, mono 1.7g, poly 0.4g); PROTEIN 11.6g; CARB 34.8g; FIBER 2.8g; CHOL 24mg; IRON 2.4mg; SODIUM 395mg; CALC 207mg

Soft Chicken Tacos

Everyone loves tacos. If you're making this for children, choose a milder salsa. Serve with a tomato-and-onion salad.

    2 cups shredded roasted skinless, boneless chicken breast
    ½ cup chopped fresh cilantro
    ½ cup bottled chipotle salsa (such as Frontera)
    8 (6-inch) flour tortillas
    1 cup chopped tomato
    ½ cup (2 ounces) preshredded reduced-fat cheddar cheese
    ½ cup diced peeled avocado
    ¼ cup fat-free sour cream

1. Combine first 3 ingredients in a medium bowl, tossing well to combine. Spoon about ⅓ cup chicken mixture onto each tortilla; microwave each taco at HIGH 30 seconds or until warm.
2. Top each taco with 2 tablespoons tomato, 1 tablespoon cheese, 1 tablespoon avocado, and 1½ teaspoons sour cream; fold in half. Yield: 4 servings (serving size: 2 tacos).

CALORIES 404 (28% from fat); FAT 12.4g (sat 4g, mono 4g, poly 1.6g); PROTEIN 33g; CARB 40.2g; FIBER 3.5g; CHOL 69mg; IRON 3.4mg; SODIUM 623mg; CALC 193mg

---

Think Fast

Speed up the cooking time when you prepare pork tenderloin by cutting it crosswise into ½-inch-thick medallions. This will shave off about 5 minutes. Plus, the pork pieces will look glamorous fanned across the plate beside your side dish of choice.

Glazed Pork

Try this saucy pork over couscous cooked in chicken broth and sprinkled with parsley.

    1 pound pork tenderloin, trimmed
    2 tablespoons brown sugar, divided
    1 tablespoon all-purpose flour
    ½ teaspoon salt
    ½ teaspoon ground cumin
    ¼ teaspoon ground cardamom
    ⅛ teaspoon ground red pepper
    ¼ cup raisins
    ¼ cup orange juice
    3 tablespoons balsamic vinegar
    2 tablespoons capers
    1 tablespoon olive oil

1. Cut pork crosswise into 16 pieces.
2. Combine 1 tablespoon sugar, flour, salt, cumin, cardamom, and pepper; rub evenly over pork.
3. Combine 1 tablespoon sugar, raisins, juice, vinegar, and capers, stirring until sugar dissolves.
4. Heat oil in a large nonstick skillet over medium-high heat. Add pork; cook

---

2 minutes. Turn pork over; cook 1 minute. Add vinegar mixture, and cook 1 minute or until sauce thickens and pork is done. Yield: 4 servings (serving size: 4 pork pieces and 2 tablespoons sauce).

CALORIES 234 (25% from fat); FAT 6.5g (sat 1.5g, mono 3.8g, poly 0.6g); PROTEIN 27.9g; CARB 15.5g; FIBER 1g; CHOL 67mg; IRON 2.1mg; SODIUM 482mg; CALC 20mg

Pizza Panzanella Salad

Use a bottled Greek or Caesar dressing instead of making a vinaigrette to save even more time.

    1 (1-pound) Italian cheese-flavored pizza crust (such as Boboli)
    2 cups torn romaine lettuce
    1 cup cherry tomatoes, halved
    ½ cup thinly sliced red onion
    2 tablespoons chopped pitted kalamata olives
    1 small cucumber, halved lengthwise and thinly sliced
    1 (15-ounce) can navy beans, drained
    1 (7-ounce) bottle roasted red bell peppers, drained and chopped
    1 (4-ounce) package crumbled feta cheese
    2 tablespoons red wine vinegar
    2 teaspoons extra-virgin olive oil
    1 teaspoon dried dill
    1 teaspoon fennel seeds
    ¼ teaspoon salt
    ¼ teaspoon black pepper

1. Preheat oven to 450°.
2. Place pizza crust on a baking sheet; bake at 450° for 8 minutes. Cut crust into 1-inch pieces.
3. While crust bakes, combine lettuce and next 7 ingredients in a large bowl. Combine vinegar and remaining 5 ingredients, stirring with a whisk.
4. Add crust pieces to lettuce mixture; toss gently. Drizzle vinaigrette over salad; toss gently to coat. Yield: 6 servings (serving size: 2 cups).

CALORIES 336 (30% from fat); FAT 11.3g (sat 4.7g, mono 4.4g, poly 1.1g); PROTEIN 15.5g; CARB 47.3g; FIBER 4.6g; CHOL 14mg; IRON 3.2mg; SODIUM 953mg; CALC 304mg

Beef Stroganoff

Broccoli or Brussels sprouts are both good accompaniments to this pasta dish.

  4 cups uncooked medium egg noodles (about 8 ounces)
  1 cup beef broth
  1 tablespoon Worcestershire sauce
  1 teaspoon balsamic vinegar
  2 teaspoons tomato paste
  1 teaspoon salt, divided
  ¼ teaspoon black pepper, divided
Cooking spray
  1 pound boneless sirloin steak (about ½ inch thick)
  1 cup chopped onion
  1 (8-ounce) package presliced mushrooms
  3 tablespoons all-purpose flour
  ½ cup reduced-fat sour cream
  ¼ cup chopped fresh parsley

1. Cook pasta according to package directions, omitting salt and fat.
2. While pasta cooks, combine broth, Worcestershire, vinegar, tomato paste, ½ teaspoon salt, and ⅛ teaspoon pepper in a medium bowl, stirring with a whisk.
3. Heat a Dutch oven coated with cooking spray over medium-high heat. Sprinkle beef with ½ teaspoon salt and ⅛ teaspoon pepper. Add beef to pan; cook 3½ minutes on each side or until desired degree of doneness. Remove beef from pan.
4. Add onion and mushrooms to pan; sauté 3 minutes or until mushrooms are tender. Stir in flour; cook 1 minute, stirring constantly. Stir in broth mixture; cook 1 minute or until slightly thick, stirring constantly.
5. Cut beef into thin strips; return to pan. Stir in pasta, sour cream, and parsley; cook 1 minute or until thoroughly heated. Yield: 5 servings (serving size: 1½ cups).

CALORIES 398 (24% from fat); FAT 10.7g (sat 4.5g, mono 3.8g, poly 1g); PROTEIN 31.5g; CARB 43.3g; FIBER 2.7g; CHOL 117mg; IRON 5.6mg; SODIUM 774mg; CALC 80mg

Beef Tenderloin with Mustard-Tarragon Cream Sauce

Serve with quartered red potatoes tossed with olive oil, minced garlic, pepper, and salt, and cooked, covered, in the microwave for about 15 minutes.

Cooking spray
  6 (4-ounce) beef tenderloin steaks, trimmed (1 inch thick)
  ½ teaspoon salt, divided
  ¼ teaspoon black pepper
  ¼ cup dry white wine
  1½ teaspoons sugar
  1 tablespoon Dijon mustard
  ¼ cup fat-free sour cream
  1½ teaspoons finely chopped fresh tarragon
Tarragon sprigs (optional)

1. Heat a large nonstick skillet coated with cooking spray over medium-high heat. Sprinkle steaks with ¼ teaspoon salt and pepper. Add steaks to pan; cook 3 minutes on each side or until desired degree of doneness. Remove from pan; keep warm.
2. Add wine, sugar, and mustard to pan; bring to a boil. Cook 1 minute, stirring constantly. Remove from heat. Stir in ¼ teaspoon salt, sour cream, and chopped tarragon. Spoon sauce over warm steaks. Garnish with tarragon sprigs, if desired. Yield: 6 servings (serving size: 1 steak and 1 tablespoon sauce).

CALORIES 213 (46% from fat); FAT 11g (sat 4.2g, mono 4.3g, poly 0.5g); PROTEIN 23.8g; CARB 3.2g; FIBER 0g; CHOL 73mg; IRON 3.1mg; SODIUM 318mg; CALC 27mg

Roasted Chicken, Avocado, and Grapefruit Salad

Look for grapefruit sections in jars near the refrigerated fruit juices in your supermarket's produce department. Serve this fresh main-dish salad with crusty French bread for an easy and light lunch or supper.

  1 (24-ounce) jar unsweetened red grapefruit sections, undrained
  2 tablespoons chopped fresh cilantro
  2 tablespoons plain fat-free yogurt
  1 tablespoon honey
  1½ teaspoons Dijon mustard
  ⅛ teaspoon salt
  8 cups fresh baby spinach
  3 cups shredded roasted skinless, boneless chicken breast
  ½ peeled avocado, cut into 8 wedges

1. Drain grapefruit in a colander over a bowl, reserving ½ cup juice. Combine reserved ½ cup juice, cilantro, and next 4 ingredients, stirring with a whisk.
2. Arrange 2 cups spinach on each of 4 plates. Top each serving with ½ cup grapefruit sections, ¾ cup chicken, and 2 avocado wedges. Drizzle 2 tablespoons dressing over each serving. Yield: 4 servings.

CALORIES 309 (24% from fat); FAT 8.3g (sat 1.7g, mono 3.8g, poly 1.4g); PROTEIN 37.8g; CARB 22.8g; FIBER 2.8g; CHOL 89mg; IRON 4.8mg; SODIUM 304mg; CALC 168mg

october

All About Poultry

From chicken to quail, enjoy the variety and pleasing flavors of poultry.

Osso Buco-Style Chicken Thighs

Chicken thighs stand in well for veal shanks in osso buco; their higher-fat content, compared to other chicken parts, lets them hold up to long cooking or braising times.

CHICKEN:

- 1 tablespoon olive oil, divided
- 6 chicken thighs (about 2 pounds), skinned
- ¾ teaspoon salt, divided
- ¼ teaspoon black pepper
- 2 cups chopped onion
- ¾ cup cubed carrot
- ¾ cup coarsely chopped celery
- 2 garlic cloves, minced
- ¾ cup dry white wine
- 5 cups chopped tomato (about 2 pounds)
- 1 teaspoon dried basil
- 1 teaspoon dried rosemary

POLENTA:

- 2 cups 1% low-fat milk
- 1 (14-ounce) can fat-free, less-sodium chicken broth
- 1 cup uncooked instant polenta
- ¾ cup (3 ounces) grated fresh Gruyère cheese
- ¼ teaspoon salt

GREMOLATA:

- 3 tablespoons chopped fresh parsley
- 2 teaspoons grated lemon rind
- 1 garlic clove, minced

1. To prepare chicken, heat 2 teaspoons oil in a large nonstick skillet over medium-high heat. Sprinkle chicken with ¼ teaspoon salt and pepper. Add chicken to pan; cook 4 minutes on each side or until browned. Remove chicken from pan.

2. Heat 1 teaspoon oil in pan over medium-high heat. Add onion, carrot, celery, and 2 garlic cloves. Cover and cook 5 minutes or until tender, stirring occasionally. Stir in wine, scraping pan to loosen browned bits. Stir in ½ teaspoon salt, tomato, basil, and rosemary; bring to a boil. Cover, reduce heat to medium-low, and cook 15 minutes.

3. Return chicken to pan. Cover and simmer 35 minutes or until chicken is done. Uncover and cook 5 minutes or until tomato mixture thickens.

4. To prepare polenta, combine milk and broth in a medium saucepan; bring to a boil. Remove from heat; gradually add instant polenta, stirring constantly with a whisk. Cover and cook over medium-low heat 2 minutes. Remove from heat; stir in cheese and ¼ teaspoon salt.

5. To prepare gremolata, combine parsley, rind, and 1 garlic clove. Serve chicken mixture over polenta; sprinkle with gremolata. Yield: 6 servings (serving size: ¾ cup polenta, 1 chicken thigh, ⅔ cup tomato mixture, and about 1½ teaspoons gremolata).

WINE NOTE: A fairly rich, well-structured red like a bold California Merlot fits the bill for this dish (try Markham Merlot; the 2000 is $22). Or go all-Italian, and try the Nottola Vino Nobile di Montepulciano "Vigna del Fattore" (about $25 for the 1997). This wine features aromas of violets, dried leaves, and vanilla, and flavors that suggest dried cherries, dried cranberries, tea, and almonds.

CALORIES 412 (29% from fat); FAT 13.4g (sat 4.8g, mono 4.9g, poly 2.2g); PROTEIN 33.6g; CARB 40.8g; FIBER 6.9g; CHOL 108mg; IRON 3.5mg; SODIUM 763mg; CALC 314mg

Quail with Grapes and Grappa

(pictured on page 294)

Grappa is an Italian liquor distilled from grape pressings left over after winemaking; cognac is a good substitute. Use red and green grapes for an attractive presentation. Serve with steamed green beans and wild rice tossed with toasted hazelnuts.

- 1½ cups seedless green grapes
- 8 (4-ounce) quail, skinned
- ½ teaspoon salt
- ½ teaspoon black pepper
- 8 (1-inch) rosemary sprigs
- 8 (1-inch) thyme sprigs
- 2 teaspoons olive oil
- 1¼ cups fat-free, less-sodium chicken broth, divided
- ¼ cup finely chopped prosciutto (about 1 ounce)
- 3 tablespoons grappa (Italian brandy) or cognac
- 1½ tablespoons minced shallots
- Whole rosemary sprigs (optional)
- Whole thyme sprigs (optional)

1. Cut ½ cup grapes in half lengthwise.

2. Sprinkle quail with salt and pepper. Place 1 (1-inch) rosemary sprig and 1 (1-inch) thyme sprig into cavity of each quail.

3. Heat oil in a large nonstick skillet over medium-high heat. Add quail; cook 3 minutes on each side or until browned. Arrange quail, breast sides up, in pan; add ½ cup broth. Partially cover, reduce heat to medium-low, and cook 25 minutes or until done. Place quail on a platter; cover loosely with foil.

4. Add ¼ cup broth, prosciutto, grappa, and shallots to pan; cook over medium-high heat 1½ minutes or until shallots are tender, scraping pan to loosen browned bits. Stir in ½ cup broth and whole and halved grapes; cook 2 minutes or until grapes are thoroughly heated. Pour grape mixture over quail; garnish with whole rosemary and thyme sprigs, if desired. Yield: 4 servings (serving size: 2 quail and about ⅓ cup sauce).

CALORIES 355 (29% from fat); FAT 11.6g (sat 3.1g, mono 4.4g, poly 2.6g); PROTEIN 43.1g; CARB 11.8g; FIBER 0.7g; CHOL 133mg; IRON 8.7mg; SODIUM 636mg; CALC 34mg

Turkey Cutlets with Roasted Peppers and Mozzarella

Because turkey cutlets (often labeled "filets") are very lean, cook at medium heat or lower to keep them moist and tender. Butter adds a rich finish to the sauce. Serve with pasta tossed with a little butter and garlic.

- 1 large red bell pepper, cut into 4 wedges
- 2 teaspoons olive oil
- 4 (½-inch-thick) turkey breast cutlets (about 1 pound)
- 2 teaspoons chopped fresh sage
- ½ teaspoon salt
- ¼ teaspoon black pepper
- ½ cup (2 ounces) shredded part-skim mozzarella cheese
- ¼ cup dry Marsala or Madeira
- ¼ cup fat-free, less-sodium chicken broth
- 2 teaspoons butter
- Sage leaves (optional)

1. Preheat broiler.

2. Place bell pepper wedges, skin sides up, on a foil-lined baking sheet; flatten with hand. Broil 10 minutes or until blackened. Place in a zip-top plastic bag; seal. Let stand 10 minutes; peel.

3. Heat oil in a large nonstick skillet over medium heat. Sprinkle turkey with chopped sage, salt, and pepper. Add turkey to pan; cook 2½ minutes on each side or until browned. Top each cutlet with 1 bell pepper piece and 2 tablespoons cheese. Add Marsala and broth to pan. Cover and cook 45 seconds or until cheese melts. Remove turkey from pan with a slotted spoon.

4. Bring Marsala mixture to a boil; cook until reduced to ¼ cup (about 1½ minutes). Remove from heat; add butter, stirring with a whisk until well blended. Serve with turkey; garnish with sage leaves, if desired. Yield: 4 servings (serving size: 1 turkey cutlet and 1 tablespoon sauce).

CALORIES 239 (30% from fat); FAT 8g (sat 3.5g, mono 3.3g, poly 0.7g); PROTEIN 32.6g; CARB 4.8g; FIBER 0.9g; CHOL 83mg; IRON 1.6mg; SODIUM 490mg; CALC 121mg

Poultry Varieties

Chicken

Whole chickens are marketed by weight. Broiler-fryers are about 7 weeks old, and weigh 3 to 4 pounds. They're good for making stock and will work in any recipe that calls for a cut-up fryer. Roasters, at 3 to 5 months old, weigh 4 to 7 pounds. If you want to bake a whole chicken, look for a roaster—they have the highest meat-to-bone ratio. Stewing hens, at 10 months to 1½ years old, are tough and best for chicken and dumplings or soup; when roasted, they're tough.

Cornish game hens are actually a cross between Cornish game roosters and White Rock hens; despite the gender-specific name, both male and female birds are sold. At a month old, they weigh about 1½ to 2 pounds. Roasting works best for these petite birds.

Chicken parts come packaged in many ways in today's markets. We use boneless, skinless chicken breasts a great deal. Try chicken tenders, which save prep and cooking time. For long simmering in dishes that feature hearty flavors, use thighs—either bone-in or skinless, boneless thighs. Their slightly higher-fat content and firmer flesh help them stand up to longer cooking. You'll be hard-pressed to find recipes in *Cooking Light* that use wings because they are high in fat. Wings are usually inexpensive, however, and can be used to make stock, since you'll skim the fat anyway.

Turkey

Whole turkeys are often sold by the sex of the bird. Hens weigh up to 16 pounds, while toms weigh more. There is no flavor difference; figure about 1 pound (including skin and bones) per person to allow for seconds and leftovers.

Turkey cuts have come a long way. Newer ones include skinless, boneless turkey breast halves (sometimes labeled "turkey London broil"); turkey cutlets (often labeled "turkey breast filets"), a fine substitute for veal in a scaloppine; and turkey tenderloins. Turkey breast is very lean, so keep a close eye on these cuts to avoid overcooking.

Ground turkey comes in several types, so read the label to be sure you get what you want. The leanest (about 3% fat) is white meat only, with no skin. It's labeled "ground turkey breast." Regular "ground turkey" is made from white and dark meat with some skin and is about 10% fat (similar to ground round). Frozen ground turkey is usually all dark meat with skin and is 15% fat, similar to ground sirloin. Italian turkey sausage is a fine way to get Mediterranean flavor with low fat (about 10% fat for the turkey version, compared to an average 30% for pork). You'll find it in both mild and spicy versions.

Duck

Like turkey, duck is now frequently sold in parts. Your gourmet market, for example, may carry boned duck breast and leg quarters. The quarters are great for ragouts (remove the skin before cooking, and skim the fat from the broth). Duck skin is thick and fatty, but duck meat has little marbling and is only about 2% fat. Whole duck at supermarkets is usually of the Pekin variety. You can usually find whole duck or duck parts in the freezer case.

Boneless duck breast (often sold by its French name, *magret*) usually comes from the Moulard duck, a cross of the Pekin and Muscovy varieties. In preparing duck breast, think of it as the steak of the poultry world: Cook it past medium-rare, and you'll lose flavor and compromise its texture. Duck is the only poultry that *Cooking Light* recommends serving medium-rare.

Quail

These dainty birds (weighing only about 8 ounces each) have mild flesh that's well suited to bold flavors. Whole birds and semiboned birds are both available. Look for quail in your supermarket's freezer section or at specialty butcher shops.

Grilled Chicken with Whiskey-Ginger Marinade

Hot cooked rice

Honey-balsamic roasted squash*

*Combine 2 tablespoons balsamic vinegar, 2 tablespoons honey, ½ teaspoon salt, and 2 minced garlic cloves in a large bowl, stirring until honey dissolves. Add 2 cups peeled chopped acorn squash and 1 cup chopped onion, tossing to coat. Bake at 425° for 25 minutes or until golden brown. Toss with 2 tablespoons chopped green onions.

Grilled Chicken with Whiskey-Ginger Marinade

- 4 (4-ounce) skinless, boneless chicken breast halves
- ⅓ cup bourbon
- ⅓ cup low-sodium soy sauce
- 3 tablespoons brown sugar
- 2 tablespoons hoisin sauce
- 1 teaspoon grated lime rind
- 2 tablespoons fresh lime juice
- 2 teaspoons grated peeled fresh ginger
- 2 teaspoons dark sesame oil
- ¼ teaspoon crushed red pepper
- 2 garlic cloves, minced
- Cooking spray
- 1 tablespoon water
- ½ teaspoon cornstarch
- 1 teaspoon sesame seeds, toasted

1. Place each chicken breast half between 2 sheets of heavy-duty plastic wrap; pound to ½-inch thickness using a meat mallet or rolling pin.
2. Combine bourbon and next 9 ingredients. Reserve ⅓ cup bourbon mixture. Pour remaining mixture into a zip-top plastic bag; add chicken. Seal bag, and marinate chicken in refrigerator 1 hour, turning occasionally.
3. Preheat grill to medium-hot using both burners.
4. Turn left burner off (leave right burner on). Remove chicken from bag; discard marinade. Coat grill rack with cooking spray. Place chicken on grill rack over right burner; grill 2 minutes on

each side or until browned. Move chicken to grill rack over left burner. Cover and cook 5 minutes or until done. Cut each breast diagonally into thin strips; place chicken on a platter. Cover loosely with foil.
5. Combine water and cornstarch, stirring well with a whisk. Place reserved ⅓ cup bourbon mixture in a small saucepan; stir in cornstarch mixture. Bring to a boil; cook 15 seconds, stirring constantly. Drizzle sauce over chicken; sprinkle with sesame seeds. Yield: 4 servings (serving size: 1 chicken breast half, about 1 tablespoon sauce, and ¼ teaspoon sesame seeds).

CALORIES 202 (16% from fat); FAT 3.6g (sat 0.7g, mono 1.1g, poly 1.1g); PROTEIN 27.3g; CARB 7.1g; FIBER 0.3g; CHOL 66mg; IRON 1.3mg; SODIUM 610mg; CALC 27mg

Game Hens with Pesto Rub and Roasted Potatoes

Use kitchen shears or a sharp knife to split the hens.

- 4 cups loosely packed fresh basil leaves
- ⅓ cup (about 1½ ounces) grated fresh Parmesan cheese
- 1 tablespoon water
- 1 tablespoon olive oil
- ¼ teaspoon salt
- ⅛ teaspoon black pepper
- 2 garlic cloves, chopped
- 4 (22-ounce) Cornish hens
- Cooking spray
- 7 cups small red potatoes, quartered (about 2 pounds)
- 1 tablespoon olive oil
- ½ teaspoon salt
- ¼ teaspoon black pepper
- 1 cup fat-free, less-sodium chicken broth
- 1 tablespoon water
- 1 teaspoon cornstarch
- Basil sprigs (optional)

1. Preheat oven to 375°.
2. Combine first 7 ingredients in a food processor; process until smooth.
3. Remove and discard giblets and necks from hens. Rinse hens with cold water;

pat dry. Starting at neck cavity, loosen skin from breast and drumsticks by inserting fingers, gently pushing between skin and meat. Rub pesto under loosened skin. Gently press skin to secure. Lift wing tips up and over back; tuck under hens.
4. Place hens on a broiler pan coated with cooking spray. Insert a meat thermometer into meaty part of a thigh, making sure not to touch bone.
5. Combine potatoes and next 3 ingredients, tossing well to coat. Arrange potatoes around hens; bake at 375° for 45 minutes or until thermometer registers 180° and potatoes are tender.
6. Remove hens and potatoes from pan, and cover loosely with foil. Let stand 10 minutes. Discard skin. Cut hens in half, and cover loosely with foil.
7. Place a zip-top plastic bag inside a 2-cup glass measure. Pour pan drippings into bag; let stand 10 minutes (fat will rise to top). Seal bag, and carefully snip off 1 bottom corner. Drain drippings into pan, stopping before fat layer reaches opening; discard fat.
8. Place pan over medium-high heat. Stir in broth, scraping pan to loosen browned bits. Combine 1 tablespoon water and cornstarch, stirring well with a whisk. Add to pan. Bring to a boil; cook until reduced to ½ cup (about 3 minutes). Serve sauce with hens and potatoes. Garnish with basil sprigs, if desired. Yield: 8 servings (serving size: ½ hen, about ¾ cup potatoes, and 1 tablespoon sauce).

CALORIES 299 (27% from fat); FAT 9g (sat 2.4g, mono 4.2g, poly 1.4g); PROTEIN 28.9g; CARB 25g; FIBER 3.1g; CHOL 113mg; IRON 2.8mg; SODIUM 434mg; CALC 120mg

Take It Off

Remove the skin from a whole bird before cooking, and you reduce its fat grams by about half. However, the skin adds moisture and protects lean meat from drying out. You'll get the best results by cooking the poultry with the skin on, then removing it before serving—the fat savings are still substantial. Rub flavorings under the skin. When it's removed, some seasoning will cling to the meat.

Duck Breast with Pineapple-Cherry Chutney

When you're looking for an elegant and quick recipe, consider this entrée with Asian flavors. If your supermarket doesn't carry fresh duck breast, look for duck breast in the freezer section. Serve with stir-fried bok choy and steamed jasmine rice.

CHUTNEY:
- 2 cups (¾-inch) cubed fresh pineapple
- ¾ cup pineapple juice
- ⅓ cup dried tart cherries
- 2 tablespoons brown sugar
- 2 tablespoons balsamic vinegar
- 1 tablespoon minced peeled fresh ginger
- 1 tablespoon minced shallots
- ⅛ teaspoon crushed red pepper
- 1 garlic clove, minced

DUCK:
- Cooking spray
- 1 pound boneless duck breast halves, skinned
- ¾ teaspoon salt
- ¾ teaspoon five-spice powder

REMAINING INGREDIENT:
- 2 tablespoons chopped fresh cilantro

1. To prepare chutney, combine first 9 ingredients in a saucepan; bring to a boil over medium-high heat. Cook 10 minutes or until syrupy, stirring frequently; remove from heat.

2. To prepare duck, heat a large, heavy skillet coated with cooking spray over high heat. Sprinkle duck with salt and five-spice powder. Add duck to pan; cook 4 minutes. Turn duck over. Reduce heat to medium, and cook 6 minutes or until desired degree of doneness. Place duck on a cutting board; cover loosely with foil. Let stand 5 minutes. Cut duck into ¼-inch-thick diagonal slices.

3. Add chutney and cilantro to pan; cook over medium heat 1 minute, scraping pan to loosen browned bits. Serve with duck. Yield: 4 servings (serving size: 3 ounces duck and 3 tablespoons chutney).

CALORIES 278 (17% from fat); FAT 5.2g (sat 1.5g, mono 1.4g, poly 0.8g); PROTEIN 23.7g; CARB 33g; FIBER 2.3g; CHOL 87mg; IRON 5.9mg; SODIUM 514mg; CALC 32mg

Roast Chicken Provençale

Look for herbes de Provence, a combination of dried herbs (basil, lavender, marjoram, rosemary, sage, savory, and thyme), in the spice section of supermarkets.

- 2 tablespoons dried herbes de Provence
- 2 tablespoons fresh lemon juice
- 2 teaspoons kosher salt
- ½ teaspoon black pepper
- 3 garlic cloves, minced
- 1 (7-pound) roasting chicken
- 1 small onion, quartered
- Cooking spray
- ⅓ cup Sauvignon Blanc or other dry white wine
- ⅔ cup fat-free, less-sodium chicken broth
- 1 tablespoon chilled butter, cut into small pieces

1. Preheat oven to 400°.

2. Combine first 5 ingredients in a small bowl; mash to a paste consistency.

3. Remove and discard giblets and neck from chicken. Rinse chicken with cold water; pat dry. Trim excess fat. Starting at neck cavity, loosen skin from breast and drumsticks by inserting fingers, gently pushing between skin and meat.

4. Rub seasoning mixture under loosened skin. Place onion in body cavity. Lift wing tips up and over back; tuck under chicken. Tie legs together with string.

5. Place chicken, breast side up, on a broiler pan coated with cooking spray. Insert a meat thermometer into breast, making sure not to touch bone. Bake at 400° for 1 hour and 20 minutes or until thermometer registers 180°. Remove chicken from pan. Cover with foil, and let stand 10 minutes. Discard skin.

6. Place a zip-top plastic bag inside a 2-cup glass measure. Pour pan drippings into bag; let stand 5 minutes (fat will rise to top). Seal bag; carefully snip off 1 bottom corner of bag. Drain drippings into pan, stopping before fat layer reaches opening; discard fat.

7. Place pan over medium-high heat. Stir in wine, scraping pan to loosen browned bits. Add broth; bring to a boil. Cook until reduced to ⅔ cup (about 3 minutes). Remove from heat; add butter, stirring with a whisk until well blended. Serve sauce with chicken. Yield: 12 servings (serving size: about 4 ounces chicken and about 1 tablespoon sauce).

CALORIES 204 (37% from fat); FAT 8.4g (sat 2.6g, mono 3.1g, poly 1.7g); PROTEIN 28.2g; CARB 1g; FIBER 0.3g; CHOL 86mg; IRON 1.7mg; SODIUM 433mg; CALC 25mg

A Few Words About Safety

Storing: Refrigerate raw poultry for up to 2 days and cooked poultry for up to 3 days. Raw skinless, boneless chicken can marinate in the refrigerator for up to 8 hours; raw chicken pieces with skin and bone can marinate for up to 1 day. Freeze uncooked poultry for up to 6 months and cooked poultry for up to 3 months.

Thawing: You can thaw frozen poultry in the refrigerator, in cold water, or in the microwave. Allow about 5 hours per pound of frozen poultry to thaw in the refrigerator. For the cold water method, submerge the poultry—still in its wrapping—in a sink or pot of cold water, and change the water every 30 minutes until it's thawed. Follow your microwave's directions for safe thawing.

Handling: Wash your hands well with hot water and plenty of soap before and after handling poultry. Use hot water and soap to wash the cutting board and any utensils that come in contact with the meat. Be careful when you rinse poultry; you may splash water from the poultry onto a clean area.

Cooking: To prevent food-borne illnesses, poultry must be cooked to 180°. For whole birds, use an instant-read thermometer inserted in the thickest part of the thigh to confirm the temperature. Pierce poultry parts with the tip of a knife—the flesh should be opaque, and the juices clear when it's done.

For more guidance on poultry, call the USDA Meat and Poultry Hotline (800-535-4555).

search myclar2003.com for all our tips

Cajun Oven-Fried Chicken

Panko, fresh crunchy Japanese bread-crumbs, can be found at Asian markets.

 ⅓ cup low-fat buttermilk
 1 tablespoon salt-free Cajun
  seasoning (such as Spice Hunter)
 ½ teaspoon salt
 1 cup panko (Japanese breadcrumbs)
 2 chicken breast halves (about 1
  pound), skinned
 2 chicken drumsticks (about ½
  pound), skinned
 2 chicken thighs (about ½ pound),
  skinned
 Cooking spray

1. Preheat oven to 400°.
2. Combine first 3 ingredients in a shallow dish. Place panko in a shallow dish. Dip chicken, one piece at a time, into buttermilk mixture; dredge in panko.
3. Place chicken on a baking sheet lined with parchment paper. Lightly coat chicken with cooking spray. Bake at 400° for 40 minutes or until done, turning after 20 minutes. Yield: 4 servings (serving size: 1 breast half or 1 thigh and 1 drumstick).

CALORIES 206 (16% from fat); FAT 3.7g (sat 1g, mono 1g, poly 0.8g); PROTEIN 31.7g; CARB 9g; FIBER 0.3g; CHOL 95mg; IRON 1.2mg; SODIUM 439mg; CALC 39mg

reader recipes

Monday Night Special

Spice up TV night with this casserole.

 Tracy Carr, 29, created La Bamba Casserole while she was in graduate school at Mississippi State University. "My friends and I gathered weekly at my house to watch television on Monday nights. One night, I just threw some ingredients together that I had on hand, and La Bamba Casserole was born," she says.

 Tracy likes to serve her casserole with Mexican corn bread and a green salad. She says the dish is perfect for hearty and picky eaters alike, and it's easy to adapt.

La Bamba Casserole

(pictured on page 293)

 1 (5.25-ounce) can whole green
  chiles, drained
 Cooking spray
 1 pound ground turkey breast
 1 cup chopped onion
 2 teaspoons chili powder
 ½ teaspoon ground cumin
 ¼ teaspoon salt
 2 garlic cloves, minced
 1 (10-ounce) can diced tomatoes and
  green chiles, undrained
 2 cups frozen whole-kernel corn,
  thawed
 1 (16-ounce) can fat-free refried beans
1½ cups (6 ounces) shredded cheddar
  cheese
 1 cup chopped tomato
 ½ cup chopped green onions

1. Preheat oven to 375°.
2. Cut chiles in half lengthwise. Arrange chiles in a single layer in an 8-inch square baking dish coated with cooking spray.
3. Heat a large nonstick skillet coated with cooking spray over medium-high heat. Add turkey and next 5 ingredients; sauté 5 minutes, stirring to crumble. Add diced tomatoes; cook 5 minutes or until liquid evaporates.
4. Spoon turkey mixture over chiles. Top with corn. Carefully spread beans over corn. Sprinkle cheese over beans. Bake at 375° for 30 minutes. Let stand 5 minutes; top with chopped tomato and green onions. Yield: 6 servings (serving size: 1⅓ cups).

CALORIES 344 (28% from fat); FAT 10.7g (sat 6.3g, mono 2.9g, poly 0.8g); PROTEIN 32.2g; CARB 30.7g; FIBER 7.4g; CHOL 77mg; IRON 3.2mg; SODIUM 902mg; CALC 269mg

Tomato Chutney

"This recipe for tomato chutney was taught to me by my mother. It's been a favorite since childhood. An easy, everyday sauce, the chutney's best features are that it's light and that it's a good accompaniment to steamed rice and any curry."
   —Veenu Chopra, New Delhi, India

 Cooking spray
 2 cups finely chopped onion
 ½ teaspoon finely chopped garlic
 ½ teaspoon finely chopped peeled
  fresh ginger
 4 cups chopped seeded peeled
  tomato
 ¼ cup raisins
 2 tablespoons sugar
 2 teaspoons ground coriander
  seeds
 1 teaspoon finely chopped fresh mint
 1 teaspoon finely chopped fresh
  cilantro
 ½ teaspoon salt
 ½ teaspoon paprika
 ¼ teaspoon ground red pepper

1. Heat a large nonstick skillet coated with cooking spray over medium-high heat. Add onion, garlic, and ginger; sauté 6 minutes or until onion begins to brown. Add tomato and remaining ingredients, stirring well to combine.
2. Bring to a simmer; cook 17 minutes or until liquid almost evaporates (chutney will be thick). Yield: 9 servings (serving size: ¼ cup).

CALORIES 59 (6% from fat); FAT 0.4g (sat 0.1g, mono 0.1g, poly 0.1g); PROTEIN 1.3g; CARB 13.6g; FIBER 2.1g; CHOL 0mg; IRON 0.7mg; SODIUM 140mg; CALC 18mg

Cheese Enchilada Casserole

"I adapted this recipe to make a casserole when I couldn't get the tortillas to stay rolled up for enchiladas. It's a supereasy dish and is always welcome at my house."
   —Lisa Boyle, Evansville, Indiana

 1 cup (4 ounces) shredded reduced-
  fat extra-sharp cheddar cheese
 1 cup chopped tomato
 1 cup fat-free cottage cheese
 ⅓ cup sliced green onions
 2 teaspoons chili powder
 2 garlic cloves, minced
 9 (6-inch) corn tortillas
 Cooking spray
 1 cup taco sauce (such as Ortega)
 ¼ cup shredded Monterey Jack
  cheese

1. Preheat oven to 375°.

2. Combine first 6 ingredients in a medium bowl. Arrange 3 tortillas in bottom of an 11 x 7-inch baking dish coated with cooking spray. Spread half of cheese mixture over tortillas. Repeat procedure with 3 tortillas and remaining cheese mixture; top with 3 tortillas.

3. Pour taco sauce over tortillas; sprinkle with Monterey Jack cheese. Bake at 375° for 20 minutes or until cheese melts. Yield: 4 servings.

CALORIES 299 (18% from fat); FAT 6g (sat 2.8g, mono 1.7g, poly 0.9g); PROTEIN 19.1g; CARB 42.3g; FIBER 4.3g; CHOL 15mg; IRON 1.4mg; SODIUM 1029mg; CALC 332mg

Pad Thai

"One of our favorite dishes with tofu is Pad Thai. We were eating it out so often, I had to create my own recipe."

—Charlotte Pence, Nashville, Tennessee

    4 ounces uncooked wide rice sticks
       (rice-flour noodles)
    ¼ cup cider vinegar
    ¼ cup low-sodium soy sauce
    3 tablespoons brown sugar
    2 tablespoons water
    1 teaspoon red curry paste
    3 garlic cloves, minced
       Cooking spray
 1½ cups chopped reduced-fat firm tofu
       (about 8 ounces)
    ⅛ teaspoon salt
    ⅛ teaspoon ground red pepper
    ⅛ teaspoon black pepper
    1 cup chopped onion
    ¾ cup chopped broccoli
    ½ cup chopped carrot
    1 large egg, lightly beaten
    1 tablespoon fresh lime juice
    ¼ cup chopped dry-roasted peanuts

1. Place noodles in a large bowl. Add boiling water to cover; let stand 10 minutes or until tender. Drain.

2. Combine vinegar and next 5 ingredients in a small bowl, stirring with a whisk.

3. Heat a large nonstick skillet coated with cooking spray over medium-high heat. Sprinkle tofu with salt, red pepper,

and black pepper. Add tofu to pan; sauté 8 minutes or until lightly browned. Remove from pan. Add onion, broccoli, and carrot to pan; sauté 4 minutes or until tender. Remove from pan. Add egg to pan; stir-fry 20 seconds or until soft-scrambled, stirring constantly.

4. Return tofu and onion mixture to pan. Stir in noodles and vinegar mixture; cook 1 minute or until thoroughly heated, stirring constantly. Remove from heat. Stir in juice; sprinkle with peanuts. Yield: 4 servings (serving size: 1 cup).

CALORIES 263 (23% from fat); FAT 6.6g (sat 1.1g, mono 2.9g, poly 2g); PROTEIN 11.9g; CARB 40.8g; FIBER 2.7g; CHOL 53mg; IRON 2.4mg; SODIUM 691mg; CALC 71mg

Bon Voyage Chicken

"My husband and I travel quite a bit. We recently went on a cruise for a week and had to clean out the refrigerator. I tossed its contents together and came up with this recipe. This is a very simple dish that I like to serve with Caesar salad and bread. Even our three-year-old loves it."

—Beth Gallagher, Mableton, Georgia

    1 tablespoon olive oil
 1½ cups red bell pepper strips
    2 cups chopped cooked chicken
       breast (about 2 breasts)
    1 tablespoon minced garlic
    1 teaspoon chopped fresh oregano
    1 (14.5-ounce) can diced tomatoes with
       Italian Herbs (such as Contadina)
    2 cups hot cooked ziti or penne
       (about 4 ounces uncooked
       tube-shaped pasta)
    ½ teaspoon freshly ground black
       pepper
    ¼ cup thinly sliced fresh basil
    ¼ cup (1 ounce) grated fresh
       Parmesan cheese

1. Heat oil in a large skillet over medium-high heat. Add bell pepper; sauté 4 minutes or until crisp-tender. Add chicken, garlic, and oregano; sauté 2 minutes. Add tomatoes; reduce heat, and simmer 10 minutes, stirring occasionally.

2. Add pasta and black pepper, stirring well. Place about 1½ cups pasta mixture

into each of 4 bowls; top each serving with 1 tablespoon basil and 1 tablespoon Parmesan. Yield: 4 servings.

CALORIES 312 (25% from fat); FAT 8.6g (sat 2.5g, mono 4g, poly 1.7g); PROTEIN 29.6g; CARB 27.6g; FIBER 2.7g; CHOL 65mg; IRON 2.5mg; SODIUM 362mg; CALC 136mg

Breakfast Pizza

"The 'fat' version of this recipe was given to me by a friend. I've come up with a lighter version that gets rave reviews. One slice is very filling, and when served with fresh fruit, it makes a great Sunday morning breakfast."

—DeDe Cappellino, Rochester, New York

    1 (8-ounce) can reduced-fat
       refrigerated crescent dinner roll
       dough
       Cooking spray
  12 ounces turkey breakfast sausage
    1 cup frozen shredded hash brown
       potatoes, thawed
    1 cup (4 ounces) shredded fat-free
       cheddar cheese
    ¼ cup fat-free milk
    ½ teaspoon salt
    ⅛ teaspoon black pepper
    1 (8-ounce) carton egg substitute
    2 tablespoons grated fresh Parmesan
       cheese

1. Preheat oven to 375°.

2. Separate dough into triangles. Press triangles together to form a single round crust on a 12-inch pizza pan coated with cooking spray. Crimp edges of dough with fingers to form a rim.

3. Cook sausage in a large nonstick skillet over medium heat until browned, stirring to crumble. Drain.

4. Top prepared dough with sausage, potatoes, and cheddar cheese. Combine milk, salt, pepper, and egg substitute, stirring with a whisk. Carefully pour milk mixture over sausage mixture. Sprinkle with Parmesan. Bake at 375° for 25 minutes or until crust is browned. Yield: 8 servings (serving size: 1 wedge).

CALORIES 203 (28% from fat); FAT 6.4g (sat 1.8g, mono 1.9g, poly 1.6g); PROTEIN 15.4g; CARB 20.3g; FIBER 0.4g; CHOL 13.2mg; IRON 1.5mg; SODIUM 771mg; CALC 239mg

Oven-Puffed Pancake with Fresh Raspberries

—Jane Shapton, Tustin, California

⅓ cup all-purpose flour
⅓ cup soy milk
2 tablespoons granulated sugar
3 large eggs, lightly beaten
Cooking spray
1 cup fresh raspberries
1 teaspoon powdered sugar

1. Preheat oven to 425°.
2. Lightly spoon flour into a dry measuring cup; level with a knife. Combine flour, soy milk, granulated sugar, and eggs in a bowl, stirring with a whisk until smooth. Pour mixture into a medium nonstick ovenproof skillet coated with cooking spray. Wrap handle of pan with foil.
3. Bake at 425° for 18 minutes or until puffy and golden. Top with raspberries; sprinkle with powdered sugar. Serve immediately. Yield: 4 servings (serving size: 1 wedge).

CALORIES 146 (27% from fat); FAT 4.4g (sat 1.2g, mono 1.5g, poly 0.7g); PROTEIN 6.6g; CARB 20.2g; FIBER 2.4g; CHOL 159mg; IRON 1.4mg; SODIUM 59mg; CALC 52mg

Tortitas de Maiz

"Tortitas de Maiz are like polenta but sweeter. You can serve them with syrup or sprinkle with powdered sugar."
—Barbara O'Ferrall, El Centro, California

1 cup water
1 cup 2% reduced-fat milk
½ cup sugar
2 tablespoons butter
¼ teaspoon salt
1½ cups yellow cornmeal
1 tablespoon vanilla extract
3 large eggs, lightly beaten
Cooking spray

1. Combine first 5 ingredients in a medium saucepan; bring to a boil. Gradually add cornmeal, stirring constantly with a whisk. Remove from heat; cool 10 minutes. Add vanilla and eggs, stirring well with a whisk.

2. Heat a nonstick skillet coated with cooking spray over medium-high heat. Spoon about ⅓ cup batter into pan. Cook 2½ minutes on each side or until golden brown. Repeat procedure with remaining batter. Yield: about 9 servings (serving size: 1 cake).

CALORIES 192 (24% from fat); FAT 5.1g (sat 2.5g, mono 1.6g, poly 0.5g); PROTEIN 5g; CARB 30.7g; FIBER 1.7g; CHOL 80mg; IRON 0.5mg; SODIUM 127mg; CALC 43mg

Chicken-Pasta-Mushroom Dish

—Helen Engelhart, North Saint Paul, Minnesota

1 tablespoon olive oil
8 skinless, boneless chicken thighs (about 2 pounds)
2 cups sliced mushrooms
1 cup chopped onion
2 garlic cloves, minced
¾ cup dry white wine
¾ cup fat-free, less-sodium chicken broth
1 teaspoon dried thyme
½ teaspoon salt
2 bay leaves
⅔ cup 1% low-fat milk
2 tablespoons all-purpose flour
4 cups hot cooked ziti or penne (about ½ pound uncooked tube-shaped pasta)

1. Heat oil in a large nonstick skillet over medium-high heat. Add chicken; sauté 5 minutes on each side. Remove from pan.
2. Add mushrooms, onion, and garlic to pan; sauté 5 minutes. Return chicken to pan. Add wine, broth, thyme, salt, and bay leaves; bring to a boil. Cover, reduce heat, and simmer 30 minutes. Discard bay leaves.
3. Combine milk and flour, stirring with a whisk. Stir milk mixture into pan; bring to a boil. Reduce heat; simmer 3 minutes or until thick, stirring often. Stir in pasta. Yield: 4 servings (serving size: 2 chicken thighs and 1 cup pasta mixture).

CALORIES 474 (26% from fat); FAT 13.6g (sat 3.2g, mono 5.4g, poly 2.8g); PROTEIN 51.3g; CARB 27.3g; FIBER 2g; CHOL 191mg; IRON 4mg; SODIUM 536mg; CALC 99mg

dinner tonight

Roasts in Minutes

Think it takes all day to cook a roast? Mere minutes are all you need.

Pork Tenderloin Menu
serves 4

Pork Tenderloin Studded with Rosemary and Garlic

Caramelized carrots*

Boiled red potatoes

*Combine 1 pound baby carrots, 1 tablespoon low-sodium soy sauce, 2 teaspoons brown sugar, 2 teaspoons olive oil, ¼ teaspoon salt, and ¼ teaspoon black pepper. Arrange in a single layer on a baking sheet coated with cooking spray; place in oven on rack below pork. Bake at 475° for 15 minutes or until tender, turning once.

Game Plan

1. While oven heats:
• Trim and make slits in pork
• Rub pork with rosemary mixture
• Bring water to a boil for potatoes
2. While pork roasts:
• Prepare carrots
• Place carrots in oven during final 15 minutes of pork's cooking time
• Boil potatoes

search myclar2003.com for all our menus

Pork Tenderloin Studded with Rosemary and Garlic

TOTAL TIME: 35 MINUTES

2 tablespoons finely chopped fresh rosemary
4 garlic cloves, minced
1 (1-pound) pork tenderloin, trimmed
½ teaspoon salt
¼ teaspoon black pepper
Cooking spray

1. Preheat oven to 475°.
2. Combine rosemary and garlic. Make several ½-inch-deep slits in pork; place about half of rosemary mixture in slits. Rub pork with remaining rosemary mixture; sprinkle with salt and pepper. Place pork on a jelly roll pan coated with cooking spray. Insert a meat thermometer into thickest portion of pork.
3. Bake at 475° for 20 minutes or until thermometer registers 160° (slightly pink) or to desired degree of doneness. Let stand 5 minutes, and cut into ¼-inch-thick slices. Yield: 4 servings (serving size: 3 ounces).

CALORIES 147 (26% from fat); FAT 4.2g (sat 1.4g, mono 1.6g, poly 0.4g); PROTEIN 24.2g; CARB 1.5g; FIBER 0.1g; CHOL 67mg; IRON 1.6mg; SODIUM 342mg; CALC 23mg

Cornish Hens Menu
serves 4

Orange-Ginger Glazed Cornish Hens

Oven-roasted green beans*

Long-grain and wild rice blend

*Combine 1 pound green beans (trimmed), 2 teaspoons olive oil, ½ teaspoon salt, and ⅛ teaspoon black pepper. Arrange in a single layer on a baking sheet coated with cooking spray; place in oven on rack below hens. Bake at 475° for 10 minutes or until tender, turning once. Remove from oven; toss with 2 teaspoons fresh lemon juice.

Game Plan

1. While oven heats:
   • Prepare glaze
   • Split and skin hens
   • Bring water to a boil for rice
2. While hens roast:
   • Cook rice
   • Prepare green beans
   • Place beans in oven during final 10 minutes of hens' cooking time

Orange-Ginger Glazed Cornish Hens

TOTAL TIME: 45 MINUTES

QUICK TIP: Line your pan with foil for easy cleanup. Don't worry if the sweet glaze burns on the foil; it won't burn on the hens. Cooking the hens and green beans in the oven together saves time and ensures that everything will be ready at once.

¾ cup fresh orange juice (about 3 oranges)
2 tablespoons minced peeled fresh ginger
2 tablespoons honey
1 tablespoon low-sodium soy sauce
1 tablespoon water
2 teaspoons cornstarch
2 (1½-pound) Cornish hens, skinned and halved
Cooking spray
½ teaspoon salt
½ teaspoon ground ginger

1. Preheat oven to 475°.
2. Combine first 4 ingredients in a small saucepan; bring to a boil. Combine water and cornstarch in a small bowl, stirring with a whisk. Add to juice mixture in pan, stirring with a whisk. Cook 2 minutes or until thick and glossy, stirring constantly.
3. Place hen halves, meaty sides up, on a foil-lined jelly roll pan coated with cooking spray; sprinkle hen halves with salt and ground ginger. Spoon juice mixture evenly over hen halves.
4. Insert a meat thermometer into meaty part of a thigh, making sure not to touch bone. Bake at 475° for 25 minutes or until thermometer registers 180°. Yield: 4 servings (serving size: 1 hen half).

CALORIES 188 (18% from fat); FAT 3.8g (sat 1g, mono 1.2g, poly 0.9g); PROTEIN 22.5g; CARB 15.6g; FIBER 0.3g; CHOL 99mg; IRON 1mg; SODIUM 487mg; CALC 19mg

Sirloin Steak Menu
serves 4

Cumin-Coriander Sirloin Steak

Sweet potato spears*

Collard greens

*Peel 1½ pounds sweet potato; cut lengthwise into ½-inch wedges. Combine potato wedges, 1 tablespoon olive oil, ½ teaspoon salt, ¼ teaspoon dried thyme, ¼ teaspoon black pepper, and ⅛ teaspoon ground nutmeg. Arrange in a single layer on a baking sheet coated with cooking spray; place in oven on bottom rack. Bake at 450° for 25 minutes or until tender, turning once.

Game Plan

1. While oven heats:
   • Prepare sweet potatoes
   • Prepare spice rub for steak
   • Trim steak, and coat with spice rub
2. While potatoes roast:
   • Preheat cast-iron skillet
   • Place steak in oven during final 14 minutes of potatoes' cooking time
   • Prepare collard greens

Cumin-Coriander Sirloin Steak

TOTAL TIME: 21 MINUTES

QUICK TIP: Cooking the steak in a preheated cast-iron skillet seasons the steak without having to first brown it on the stovetop.

Cooking spray
1 tablespoon brown sugar
½ teaspoon salt
½ teaspoon ground cumin
½ teaspoon ground coriander seeds
¼ teaspoon ground red pepper
1 pound boneless sirloin steak (about 1¼ inches thick), trimmed

1. Preheat oven to 450°.
2. Coat an 8-inch cast-iron skillet with cooking spray. Place pan in a 450° oven 5 minutes.
3. Combine brown sugar and next 4 ingredients; rub over both sides of steak. Place steak in preheated pan.

Continued

4. Bake at 450° for 7 minutes on each side or until desired degree of doneness. Let stand 5 minutes. Cut steak diagonally across grain into thin slices. Yield: 4 servings (serving size: 3 ounces).

CALORIES 198 (39% from fat); FAT 8.6g (sat 3.4g, mono 3.6g, poly 0.3g); PROTEIN 25.1g; CARB 3.7g; FIBER 0.3g; CHOL 76mg; IRON 2.9mg; SODIUM 350mg; CALC 17mg

Chicken Thighs Menu
serves 4

Chicken Thighs with Roasted Apples and Garlic

Browned Brussels sprouts*

Dinner rolls

*Heat 1 tablespoon olive oil in a large nonstick skillet over medium heat. Add 1½ pounds Brussels sprouts (trimmed and halved), ¼ teaspoon salt, and 3 thinly sliced garlic cloves; cook 15 minutes or until lightly browned, stirring occasionally. Stir in 2 teaspoons balsamic vinegar; cook 1 minute.

Game Plan

1. While oven heats for chicken:
- Prepare apple mixture
- Skin chicken thighs
2. While chicken roasts:
- Prepare and cook Brussels sprouts
- Warm dinner rolls

Chicken Thighs with Roasted Apples and Garlic

TOTAL TIME: 43 MINUTES
QUICK TIP: Look for bone-in chicken thighs that are already skinned.

    5 cups chopped peeled Braeburn
       apple (about 1½ pounds)
    1 teaspoon chopped fresh sage
   ¼ teaspoon ground cinnamon
   ⅛ teaspoon ground nutmeg
    4 garlic cloves, chopped
   ½ teaspoon salt, divided
Cooking spray
    8 chicken thighs (about 2 pounds),
       skinned
   ¼ teaspoon black pepper

1. Preheat oven to 475°.
2. Combine first 5 ingredients. Add ¼ teaspoon salt; toss well to coat. Spread apple mixture on a jelly roll pan coated with cooking spray.
3. Sprinkle chicken with ¼ teaspoon salt and pepper, and arrange on top of apple mixture. Bake at 475° for 25 minutes or until chicken is done and apple is tender. Remove chicken from pan; keep warm.
4. Partially mash apple mixture with a potato masher, and serve with chicken. Yield: 4 servings (serving size: 2 thighs and about ⅔ cup apple mixture).

CALORIES 257 (20% from fat); FAT 5.7g (sat 1.4g, mono 1.6g, poly 1.4g); PROTEIN 25.9g; CARB 26.6g; FIBER 3.5g; CHOL 107mg; IRON 1.7mg; SODIUM 405mg; CALC 30mg

classics

Warming Italian Ragùs

These rich, flavorful pasta sauces are the perfect antidote to cold weather.

Seafood Ragù with Cavatappi

Use mussels or scallops in place of the clams or shrimp.

    2 tablespoons olive oil, divided
 1½ cups finely chopped red onion
    2 teaspoons minced garlic cloves
   ½ teaspoon crushed red pepper
    1 cup dry red wine
 1½ cups canned crushed plum tomatoes
    3 tablespoons minced fresh flat-leaf
       parsley, divided
   ½ teaspoon salt
   24 littleneck clams
   16 medium shrimp, peeled and
       deveined (about ½ pound)
    1 pound skinless halibut fillets, cut
       into ½-inch pieces
   ½ cup water
    4 cups hot cooked cavatappi (about
       10 ounces uncooked pasta)

1. Heat 1 tablespoon oil in a large Dutch oven over medium heat. Add onion, garlic, and pepper; cover and cook 10 minutes or until tender, stirring occasionally.
2. Add wine; bring to a boil. Reduce heat; simmer, uncovered, 10 minutes or until liquid almost evaporates. Stir in tomatoes, 2 tablespoons parsley, and salt; bring to a boil. Cover, reduce heat, and simmer 10 minutes.
3. Add clams. Cover and cook 2 minutes. Stir in shrimp and fish. Increase heat to medium-high; cook 2 minutes. Add water. Cover, reduce heat, and simmer 5 minutes or until clams open. Discard any unopened shells. Add 1 tablespoon oil and pasta; toss to coat. Sprinkle with 1 tablespoon parsley. Yield: 6 servings (serving size: 1½ cups).

CALORIES 361 (22% from fat); FAT 8.7g (sat 1.2g, mono 4.2g, poly 1.9g); PROTEIN 37.8g; CARB 31.3g; FIBER 3g; CHOL 154mg; IRON 9.2mg; SODIUM 390mg; CALC 113mg

Ragù Alla Bolognese with Fettuccine

This recipe is adapted from the classic ragùs of Italy's Emilia-Romagna region.

    1 tablespoon olive oil
    1 cup finely chopped onion
    1 cup finely chopped celery
   ½ cup finely chopped carrot
    5 ounces ground veal
    5 ounces ground pork
    5 ounces ground round
    1 cup dry white wine
   ½ teaspoon salt
   ½ teaspoon black pepper
   ¼ teaspoon ground nutmeg
    1 bay leaf
    1 (14-ounce) can fat-free,
       less-sodium chicken broth
    1 (10¾-ounce) can tomato
       puree
    1 cup whole milk
    2 tablespoons minced fresh flat-leaf
       parsley
    2 (9-ounce) packages fresh fettuccine,
       cooked and drained
    2 tablespoons grated fresh Parmesan
       cheese
Parsley sprigs (optional)

1. Heat oil in a large Dutch oven over medium heat. Add onion, celery, and carrot; cover. Cook 8 minutes, stirring occasionally. Remove onion mixture from pan.
2. Add veal, pork, and beef to pan; cook over medium heat until browned, stirring to crumble. Add wine, salt, pepper, nutmeg, and bay leaf; bring to a boil. Cook 5 minutes. Add onion mixture, broth, and tomato puree; bring to a simmer. Cook 1 hour, stirring occasionally.
3. Stir in milk and minced parsley; bring to a boil. Reduce heat, and simmer 40 minutes. Discard bay leaf. Add pasta, and toss to coat. Sprinkle evenly with cheese. Garnish with parsley sprigs, if desired. Yield: 8 servings (serving size: 1½ cups).

CALORIES 369 (29% from fat); FAT 11.8g (sat 4.2g, mono 4.8g, poly 1.4g); PROTEIN 21.4g; CARB 44g; FIBER 4.2g; CHOL 87mg; IRON 3.7mg; SODIUM 546mg; CALC 117mg

Ragù Finto with Cheese Polenta

RAGÙ:
- 2 cups boiling water, divided
- ½ cup dried porcini mushrooms (about ½ ounce)
- 1 cup sun-dried tomatoes, packed without oil (about 2 ounces)
- 1 tablespoon olive oil
- 1½ cups finely chopped red onion
- 1 tablespoon minced garlic cloves
- 5 cups finely chopped cremini mushrooms (about 1 pound)
- 2 teaspoons minced fresh or ½ teaspoon dried rosemary
- ½ teaspoon salt
- ¼ teaspoon crushed red pepper
- 1 cup dry red wine
- 2 tablespoons minced fresh flat-leaf parsley

POLENTA:
- ¾ cup yellow cornmeal
- ¼ teaspoon salt
- 1½ cups water
- 1½ cups fat-free milk
- ½ cup (2 ounces) shredded Gruyère cheese
- 2 tablespoons grated fresh Parmesan cheese

1. To prepare ragù, combine 1 cup boiling water and porcinis in a bowl; cover and let stand 15 minutes. Drain porcinis through a sieve over a bowl, reserving soaking liquid. Discard porcini stems; finely chop porcini caps.
2. Combine 1 cup boiling water and sun-dried tomatoes in a bowl. Cover and let stand 15 minutes. Drain and finely chop tomatoes.
3. Heat oil in a Dutch oven over medium heat. Add onion and garlic; cover and cook 10 minutes, stirring occasionally. Add creminis, rosemary, salt, and red pepper. Cover and cook 5 minutes. Uncover and cook 5 minutes or until liquid almost evaporates.
4. Add chopped porcini caps, reserved soaking liquid, chopped tomatoes, wine, and parsley; bring to a boil. Reduce heat; simmer 12 minutes.
5. To prepare polenta, place cornmeal and salt in a large saucepan. Gradually add 1½ cups water and milk, stirring constantly with a whisk; bring to a boil. Reduce heat to medium; cook 5 minutes, stirring frequently.
6. Remove from heat; stir in Gruyère. Serve with ragù; sprinkle with Parmesan. Yield: 4 servings (serving size: about 1 cup ragù, 1 cup polenta, and 1½ teaspoons Parmesan).

CALORIES 334 (28% from fat); FAT 10.3g (sat 4g, mono 4.5g, poly 1.1g); PROTEIN 17.8g; CARB 46g; FIBER 6.2g; CHOL 20mg; IRON 3.4mg; SODIUM 905mg; CALC 361mg

Try New Things Menu
serves 8

Abruzzese Lamb and Red Pepper Ragù with Penne

Roasted vegetables

Wilted spinach with pine nuts*

*Melt 2 teaspoons butter in a large skillet over medium-high heat. Add 2 (10-ounce) packages fresh spinach, trimmed, and 2 minced garlic cloves; sauté 2 minutes. Stir in ⅓ cup raisins, 2 tablespoons pine nuts, and ½ teaspoon salt.

search myclar2003.com for all our menus

Abruzzese Lamb and Red Pepper Ragù with Penne

Abruzzese refers to a style of cooking from Italy's Abruzzo region, which is east of Rome. Tomatoes and chile peppers are abundant in traditional dishes; we've substituted crushed red pepper for this recipe.

- 1 tablespoon olive oil
- 2 cups finely chopped red onion
- 1½ cups chopped yellow bell pepper
- 1½ cups chopped red bell pepper
- 4 teaspoons minced garlic cloves
- 12 ounces lean ground lamb
- 1 cup dry red wine
- 1 cup canned crushed tomatoes
- ¼ cup chopped fresh flat-leaf parsley, divided
- 1 teaspoon salt
- ½ teaspoon crushed red pepper
- 4 bay leaves
- 1 (14-ounce) can fat-free, less-sodium chicken broth
- 8 cups hot cooked penne (about 1 pound uncooked tube-shaped pasta or other short pasta)
- ½ cup (2 ounces) grated fresh pecorino Romano cheese

1. Heat oil in a large Dutch oven over medium heat. Add onion, bell peppers, and garlic. Cover and cook 12 minutes, stirring occasionally. Remove onion mixture from pan.
2. Add lamb to pan; cook over medium heat until browned, stirring to crumble. Drain. Wipe drippings from pan with a paper towel. Return onion mixture and lamb to pan. Add wine; bring to a boil. Cook 10 minutes or until liquid almost evaporates.
3. Add tomatoes, 3 tablespoons parsley, salt, crushed red pepper, bay leaves, and broth; bring to a boil. Reduce heat; simmer 10 minutes. Discard bay leaves. Add pasta and cheese; toss to coat. Sprinkle with 1 tablespoon parsley. Yield 8 servings (serving size: 1½ cups).

CALORIES 368 (26% from fat); FAT 10.6g (sat 4g, mono 4.4g, poly 1.5g); PROTEIN 18.8g; CARB 50.8g; FIBER 4.1g; CHOL 35mg; IRON 3mg; SODIUM 520mg; CALC 110mg

Falling for Soup

Pair hearty main-dish soup with bread for a satisfying supper.

Soulful Soup Supper 1

Curried Butternut Soup
&
Dried Pear and Cardamom Scones

Curried Butternut Soup

(pictured on page 295)

You can make this rich soup with any kind of squash, or even sweet potatoes.

     8 cups cubed peeled butternut
        squash (about 2 pounds)
   Cooking spray
     1 tablespoon butter
     2 cups chopped peeled Granny
        Smith apple (about ¾ pound)
  1½ cups finely chopped onion
     ½ cup thinly sliced celery
     1 bay leaf
     2 teaspoons curry powder
     1 garlic clove, minced
     3 (14-ounce) cans fat-free,
        less-sodium chicken broth
     ⅛ teaspoon salt
     ½ cup (2 ounces) grated extra-sharp
        white cheddar cheese

1. Preheat oven to 400°.

2. Arrange squash in a single layer on a foil-lined baking sheet coated with cooking spray. Bake at 400° for 45 minutes or until tender.

3. Melt butter in a Dutch oven over medium-high heat. Add apple, onion, celery, and bay leaf; sauté 10 minutes. Stir in curry powder and garlic; cook 1 minute, stirring constantly. Add squash, broth, and salt; stir well.

4. Reduce heat to medium-low; simmer, uncovered, 30 minutes. Discard bay leaf. Partially mash mixture with a potato masher until thick and chunky; stir well with a spoon. Top each serving with cheese. Yield: 4 servings (serving size: 1½ cups soup and 2 tablespoons cheese).

CALORIES 270 (27% from fat); FAT 8.2g (sat 4.5g, mono 2.3g, poly 0.5g); PROTEIN 10.4g; CARB 42.7g; FIBER 9.8g; CHOL 23mg; IRON 1.9mg; SODIUM 783mg; CALC 221mg

Dried Pear and Cardamom Scones

(pictured on page 295)

Scones are most tender when handled minimally. Have ingredients ready, and use a soft touch when mixing and patting the dough.

  1½ cups all-purpose flour
     ½ cup whole wheat flour
     ¼ cup sugar
     2 teaspoons baking powder
     ½ teaspoon salt
     ⅛ teaspoon ground cardamom
     3 tablespoons chilled butter, cut into
        small pieces
   10 tablespoons low-fat buttermilk
     1 teaspoon grated lemon rind
     1 teaspoon vanilla extract
     1 large egg, lightly beaten
     1 cup chopped dried pears
     2 teaspoons all-purpose flour
   Cooking spray
     1 large egg white, lightly beaten

1. Preheat oven to 350°.

2. Lightly spoon 1½ cups all-purpose flour and whole wheat flour into dry measuring cups; level with a knife. Combine flours, sugar, baking powder, salt, and cardamom in a large bowl; cut in butter with a pastry blender or 2 knives until mixture resembles coarse meal.

3. Combine buttermilk, rind, vanilla, and 1 egg in a medium bowl; stir in dried pears. Add buttermilk mixture to flour mixture, stirring just until moist (dough will be sticky).

4. Turn dough out onto a lightly floured surface. Dust top of dough with 2 teaspoons all-purpose flour, and pat into an 8-inch circle. Cut dough into 8 wedges; arrange wedges ½ inch apart on a baking sheet coated with cooking spray. Brush egg white over wedges. Bake at 350° for 25 minutes or until golden. Serve warm. Yield: 8 servings.

CALORIES 228 (23% from fat); FAT 5.7g (sat 3.1g, mono 1.6g, poly 0.4g); PROTEIN 5.7g; CARB 39.5g; FIBER 2.6g; CHOL 39mg; IRON 1.8mg; SODIUM 349mg; CALC 105mg

Soulful Soup Supper 2

Potato-Kale Soup with Gruyère
&
Walnut and Rosemary Loaves

Potato-Kale Soup with Gruyère

Use fresh spinach in place of kale, if you prefer.

     2 tablespoons butter
  1½ cups finely chopped onion
     1 garlic clove, minced
     7 cups fat-free, less-sodium chicken
        broth
     4 cups coarsely chopped peeled Yukon
        gold potato (about 1½ pounds)
     ¼ teaspoon salt
     1 bay leaf
     6 cups chopped fresh kale (about ¾
        pound)
     1 teaspoon dried basil
     9 tablespoons (about 2 ounces)
        shredded Gruyère cheese

1. Melt butter in a large saucepan over medium heat. Add onion; cook 8 minutes or until tender, stirring frequently. Add garlic; cook 30 seconds, stirring constantly. Stir in broth, potato, salt, and bay leaf; bring to a boil. Cover, reduce heat, and simmer 15 minutes or until potato is tender.

2. Stir in kale and basil. Cover and simmer 10 minutes or until kale is tender. Discard bay leaf. Partially mash potatoes with a potato masher until thick and chunky. Top with cheese. Yield: 6 servings (serving size: 1⅔ cups soup and 1½ tablespoons cheese).

CALORIES 239 (29% from fat); FAT 7.8g (sat 4.4g, mono 2.2g, poly 0.6g); PROTEIN 11.7g; CARB 32g; FIBER 3.9g; CHOL 21mg; IRON 2.2mg; SODIUM 733mg; CALC 215mg

Walnut and Rosemary Loaves

Not only is this bread great with soups, it's also excellent for sandwiches.

    2 cups warm 1% low-fat milk
       (100° to 110°)
    ¼ cup warm water (100° to 110°)
    3 tablespoons sugar
    2 tablespoons butter, melted
    2 teaspoons salt
    2 packages dry yeast (about 4½
       teaspoons)
 5½ cups all-purpose flour, divided
    1 cup chopped walnuts
    3 tablespoons coarsely chopped
       fresh rosemary
    1 large egg, lightly beaten
 Cooking spray
    1 tablespoon yellow cornmeal
    1 tablespoon 1% low-fat milk
    1 large egg, lightly beaten

1. Combine first 5 ingredients in a large bowl, stirring with a whisk. Add yeast, stirring with a whisk; let stand 5 minutes. Lightly spoon flour into dry measuring cups; level with a knife. Add 2 cups flour to yeast mixture, stirring with a whisk. Cover and let rise in a warm place (85°), free from drafts, 15 minutes.

2. Add 2½ cups flour, walnuts, rosemary, and 1 egg, stirring with a whisk. Turn dough out onto a lightly floured surface. Knead until smooth and elastic (about 10 minutes), adding enough of remaining flour, ¼ cup at a time, to prevent dough from sticking to hands.

3. Place dough in a large bowl coated with cooking spray, turning to coat top. Cover and let rise in a warm place (85°), free from drafts, 1 hour or until doubled in size. (Lightly press two fingers into dough. If indentation remains, dough has risen enough.)

4. Preheat oven to 400°.

5. Punch dough down; turn dough out onto a lightly floured surface. Divide dough in half, shaping each portion into a round. Place loaves on a baking sheet dusted with cornmeal. Cover and let rise 30 minutes or until doubled in size.

6. Combine 1 tablespoon milk and 1 egg, stirring with a whisk; brush over loaves. Make 3 diagonal cuts ¼-inch-deep across top of each loaf using a sharp knife.

7. Place loaves in oven; reduce oven temperature to 375°, and bake 40 minutes or until bottom of each loaf sounds hollow when tapped. Let stand 20 minutes before slicing. Yield: 2 loaves, 12 servings per loaf (serving size: 1 slice).

CALORIES 170 (28% from fat); FAT 5.2g (sat 1.2g, mono 1g, poly 2.6g); PROTEIN 5.2g; CARB 25.7g; FIBER 1.3g; CHOL 21mg; IRON 1.7mg; SODIUM 222mg; CALC 39mg

---

Soulful Soup Supper 3
Mexican Ham and Bean Soup
&
Oatmeal Molasses Bread

Mexican Ham and Bean Soup

A perfectly sweet partner for this filling soup is our Oatmeal Molasses Bread (recipe at right).

    1 pound dried pinto beans
    8 cups fat-free, less-sodium chicken
       broth
    2 cups chopped onion
    2 cups water
 1½ cups cubed smoked ham steak
       (about 8 ounces)
    1 tablespoon chili powder
    2 teaspoons ground cumin
    2 teaspoons dried oregano
    3 bay leaves
    3 garlic cloves, crushed
    1 (14.5-ounce) can diced tomatoes,
       undrained
    1 chipotle chile (or dried ancho or
       pasilla chile)
    ½ cup (2 ounces) shredded Manchego
       cheese or Monterey Jack cheese
    ½ cup minced fresh cilantro

1. Sort and wash beans; place in a large Dutch oven. Cover with water to 2 inches above beans; bring to a boil. Cook 2 minutes; remove from heat. Cover and let stand 1 hour. Drain.

2. Combine beans, broth, and next 8 ingredients in a Dutch oven; bring to a boil. Partially cover; reduce heat to medium-low. Simmer 1½ hours or until beans are tender.

3. Stir in tomatoes and chile; simmer 30 minutes. Discard bay leaves and chile. Ladle soup into 8 bowls. Top with cheese; sprinkle with cilantro. Yield: 8 servings (serving size: 1½ cups soup, 1 tablespoon cheese, and 1 tablespoon cilantro).

CALORIES 303 (12% from fat); FAT 4.2g (sat 1.8g, mono 1.3g, poly 0.5g); PROTEIN 20.3g; CARB 46.8g; FIBER 16.1g; CHOL 22mg; IRON 4.3mg; SODIUM 958mg; CALC 153mg

Oatmeal Molasses Bread

This dark quick bread takes only a minute to knead and doesn't require rising time. The dough will be sticky and wet as you knead it. The loaves brown quickly and may appear done before they really are.

    2 cups fat-free buttermilk
    ½ cup regular oats
    ¼ cup unsulfured molasses
    2 tablespoons vegetable oil
 2¾ cups all-purpose flour
    1 cup whole wheat flour
    2 tablespoons sugar
 1½ teaspoons salt
    1 teaspoon baking powder
    1 teaspoon baking soda
    1 cup raisins
    1 tablespoon yellow cornmeal

1. Preheat oven to 400°.

2. Combine first 4 ingredients in a medium bowl. Lightly spoon flours into dry measuring cups; level with a knife. Combine flours, sugar, salt, baking powder, and baking soda in a large bowl; make a well in center of mixture.

3. Add buttermilk mixture to flour mixture, stirring just until moist; stir in raisins. Stir with a wooden spoon until
Continued

dough pulls together in a shaggy mass. Let rest 2 minutes.

4. Turn half of dough out onto a lightly floured surface. Knead dough 1 minute with floured hands (dough will feel tacky); shape dough into a 6-inch round loaf. Place on a baking sheet dusted with cornmeal. Repeat procedure with remaining dough. Make 3 diagonal cuts ¼-inch-deep across top of each loaf using a sharp knife.

5. Bake at 400° for 20 minutes. Reduce oven temperature to 375° (do not remove loaves from oven); bake an additional 15 minutes or until bottom of each loaf sounds hollow when tapped. Let stand 15 minutes before slicing. Yield: 2 loaves, 12 servings per loaf (serving size: 1 slice).

CALORIES 126 (11% from fat); FAT 1.5g (sat 0.2g, mono 0.3g, poly 0.8g); PROTEIN 3.4g; CARB 25.2g; FIBER 1.6g; CHOL 0mg; IRON 1.3mg; SODIUM 243mg; CALC 50mg

cooking light profile

Grape Expectations

Lack of expertise didn't stop Susan and Earl Samson from embracing the challenges of winemaking. Now they reap the rewards.

In the 15 years since they bought Sakonnet Vineyards and Winery in Little Compton, Rhode Island, the Samsons have become experts on wine production, from growing grapes to purchasing bottles and corks to creating optimal storage conditions.

They've even learned a thing or two about pairing food and wine. Here's one recipe Susan has developed which is great served with a Sakonnet wine.

Grilled Tuna with Basil Butter and Fresh Tomato Sauce

Boston-based chef Jasper White's Grilled Swordfish with Basil Butter and Tomato Sauce inspired Susan's recipe.

BASIL BUTTER:

¾ cup fresh basil leaves
2 tablespoons butter, softened
1 tablespoon fresh lemon juice
¼ teaspoon salt
2 garlic cloves, minced

SAUCE:

2 teaspoons olive oil
½ cup finely chopped red onion
2 garlic cloves, minced
3 cups grape or cherry tomatoes, halved
½ cup dry white wine
3 tablespoons capers
2 tablespoons balsamic vinegar
¼ teaspoon sugar
¼ cup chopped fresh flat-leaf parsley

TUNA:

4 (6-ounce) tuna steaks (about 1 inch thick)
½ teaspoon salt
¼ teaspoon black pepper
Cooking spray
4 basil leaves (optional)

1. Prepare grill or preheat broiler.

2. To prepare basil butter, combine first 5 ingredients in a food processor; process until smooth, scraping sides as needed. Set aside.

3. To prepare sauce, heat oil in a saucepan over medium-high heat. Add onion and 2 garlic cloves; sauté 3 minutes. Add tomatoes; sauté 2 minutes. Stir in wine, capers, vinegar, and sugar; bring to a boil. Reduce heat; simmer 5 minutes, stirring occasionally. Stir in parsley. Set aside.

4. To prepare tuna, sprinkle tuna with ½ teaspoon salt and pepper. Place tuna on a grill rack or broiler pan coated with cooking spray. Cook 5 minutes on each side or until desired degree of doneness. Serve with sauce and basil butter. Garnish with basil leaves, if desired. Yield: 4 servings (serving size: 1 tuna steak, ¾ cup sauce, and about 1 tablespoon basil butter).

CALORIES 323 (28% from fat); FAT 10.2g (sat 4.4g, mono 3.7g, poly 1.1g); PROTEIN 41.8g; CARB 10.9g; FIBER 2.4g; CHOL 92mg; IRON 2.7mg; SODIUM 770mg; CALC 72mg

back to the best

Squash-Rice Casserole

Ordinary pantry ingredients combine to create a dish that's a grassroots favorite.

First featured in a November 2000 story, this casserole recipe was adapted from the family cookbook of retired *Cooking Light* staffer Joyce Swisdak.

Squash-Rice Casserole

8 cups sliced zucchini (about 2½ pounds)
1 cup chopped onion
½ cup fat-free, less-sodium chicken broth
2 cups cooked rice
1 cup (4 ounces) shredded reduced-fat sharp cheddar cheese
1 cup fat-free sour cream
¼ cup (1 ounce) grated fresh Parmesan cheese, divided
¼ cup Italian-seasoned breadcrumbs
1 teaspoon salt
¼ teaspoon black pepper
2 large eggs, lightly beaten
Cooking spray

1. Preheat oven to 350°.

2. Combine first 3 ingredients in a Dutch oven; bring to a boil. Cover, reduce heat, and simmer 20 minutes or until tender. Drain; partially mash with a potato masher.

3. Combine zucchini mixture, rice, cheddar cheese, sour cream, 2 tablespoons Parmesan cheese, breadcrumbs, salt, pepper, and eggs in a bowl; stir gently. Spoon into a 13 x 9-inch baking dish coated with cooking spray; sprinkle with 2 tablespoons Parmesan cheese. Bake at 350° for 30 minutes or until bubbly.

4. Preheat broiler. Broil 1 minute or until lightly browned. Yield: 8 servings (serving size: 1 cup).

CALORIES 197 (25% from fat); FAT 5.5g (sat 2.7g, mono 1.5g, poly 0.4g); PROTEIN 12.7g; CARB 24g; FIBER 1.4g; CHOL 65mg; IRON 1.5mg; SODIUM 623mg; CALC 209mg

La Bamba Casserole, page 284

Baked Potato Soup, page 311

Mixed Apple Salad over Greens,
page 303

Quail with Grapes and Grappa,
page 280

Curried Butternut Soup and Dried Pear and
Cardamom Scones, page 290

Tofu Vegetable Hot Pot,
page 308

Pancetta and Swiss Chard with Soft Polenta,
page 298

296   October

Two of a Kind

Polenta and grits have corn in common, as well as delicious versatility.

Polenta is Italian, and as uptown as an Armani suit. Grits are strictly domestic, and as down-home as blue jeans. Here are recipes for each from two chefs who have affectionate recollections about each.

Grist for the Mill

Both grits and polenta are made from dried corn kernels; the difference lies in how those kernels are milled. When the corn is ground, the coarser particles become grits, while the finer granules are used for polenta.

Polenta

Polenta is a New World food introduced to Italy by Venetian traders in the mid-17th century. Before the introduction of corn, porridges of chestnut flour and barley were staples. But because corn grew well in its adopted land and the dried grain stored well, too, polenta eventually held central importance in the Italian kitchen. Preparing polenta is something of a ritual—it's often made daily—and even today cooks are judged by the lightness and quality of their polenta.

In these recipes, we used whole grain yellow cornmeal—which yields a richly flavored and textured polenta. We liked the whole grain cornmeal from Hodgson

Mill (www.hodgsonmill.com) and from Arrowhead Mill. Look for both brands in your grocery store, near the flour.

Grits

Stone-ground grits, our choice for these recipes, have a chunkier texture and more "corny" flavor than quick grits. Though they do take longer to cook than their counterpart—and need more stirring to release the starch and soften the grains—stone-ground grits are worth the effort.

Finding them may take some initiative, as well. Coarse stone-ground grits aren't reliably available in supermarkets, but you can find them in specialty food markets, or by contacting mills directly. Our favorite grits come from Nora Mill Granary (www. noramill.com or 800-927-2375), Anson Restaurant (www.ansonrestaurant.com), and War Eagle Mill (www.wareaglemill.com). If you like finer grits, try Adam's Whole Heart Grits (800-239-4233).

Homemade Polenta

To make polenta yourself, remember two simple ratios: one part cornmeal to three parts liquid for firm polenta, and one part cornmeal to five or six parts liquid for soft polenta.

You can eat soft polenta alone or with browned butter, or use it as a bed for a

quick sauté of pancetta and broccoli rabe. Firm polenta is good served sliced, as a side dish. This is also the polenta to cut into diamonds, rectangles, or small croutons, which can then be sprinkled with cheese and roasted, or brushed with oil and grilled, fried, or sautéed.

search myclar2003.com for all our tips

Apple Crostata

Here's an Italian twist on an American cobbler. Michael Chiarello, Italian chef, connoisseur, and host of PBS's Michael Chiarello's Napa, suggests a baking sheet underneath the crostata to catch any juices that bubble over the topping.

TOPPING:

- ¾ cup pastry or all-purpose flour
- ⅓ cup whole grain yellow cornmeal
- ¼ cup granulated sugar
- ¾ teaspoon baking powder
- ⅛ teaspoon ground nutmeg
- Dash of salt
- ¼ cup chilled butter, cut into small pieces
- 2 tablespoons egg substitute

FILLING:

- ½ cup golden raisins
- ¼ cup brandy
- ⅔ cup granulated sugar
- ⅔ cup packed brown sugar
- 1 tablespoon grated orange rind
- 1½ teaspoons grated lemon rind
- ½ teaspoon salt
- ¼ teaspoon ground cinnamon
- ¼ teaspoon black pepper
- 4 cups cubed Granny Smith apple (about 1½ pounds)
- 2 tablespoons fresh lemon juice
- Cooking spray
- 3 tablespoons balsamic vinegar

1. To prepare topping, lightly spoon flour into a dry measuring cup; level with a knife. Combine flour and next 5 ingredients in a food processor; pulse 2 times or until combined. Add butter; pulse 6 times or until mixture resembles sand.

2. Place flour mixture in a large bowl; make a well in center of mixture. Add egg substitute to flour mixture; stir until well blended.

3. Preheat oven to 375°.

4. To prepare filling, combine raisins and brandy in a large bowl; let stand 15 minutes. Drain; discard liquid. Return raisins to bowl. Add ⅔ cup granulated sugar and next 6 ingredients to raisins; toss well. Combine apple and juice in a small bowl. Add to raisin mixture; toss to combine.

Continued

5. Spoon apple mixture into an 11 x 7-inch baking dish coated with cooking spray; sprinkle topping evenly over apple mixture. Bake at 375° for 40 minutes or until topping is crisp and golden brown. Serve warm with a drizzle of balsamic vinegar. Yield: 9 servings (serving size: 1 piece crostata and 1 teaspoon balsamic vinegar).

CALORIES 311 (16% from fat); FAT 5.4g (sat 3.6g, mono 0g, poly 0.1g); PROTEIN 2.3g; CARB 62.5g; FIBER 2.6g; CHOL 13mg; IRON 1.2mg; SODIUM 216mg; CALC 45mg

Pancetta and Swiss Chard with Soft Polenta

(pictured on page 296)

Bitter greens make a great companion for the polenta. Choose kale, broccoli rabe, or mustard greens in place of the chard.

      2 ounces pancetta, cut into ¼-inch
         pieces
   Cooking spray
      2 tablespoons minced garlic
   1½ cups fat-free, less-sodium chicken
         broth
      1 tablespoon chopped fresh or
         1 teaspoon dried thyme
      8 cups coarsely chopped Swiss chard
      ¼ teaspoon sea salt
      ¼ teaspoon black pepper
      2 cups Soft Polenta
      ¼ cup (1 ounce) shaved fresh Parmesan

1. Cook pancetta in a large skillet coated with cooking spray over medium heat until crisp (about 10 minutes). Remove pancetta from pan.
2. Add garlic to drippings in pan; sauté 30 seconds. Add broth and thyme; bring to a boil. Cook until mixture is reduced to ¾ cup (about 5 minutes).
3. Add chard, salt, and pepper, tossing to coat. Cover, reduce heat, and simmer 3 minutes or until chard is tender. Serve over Soft Polenta; top with pancetta and Parmesan. Yield: 4 servings (serving size: ½ cup chard mixture, ½ cup polenta, and 1 tablespoon Parmesan).

(Totals include Soft Polenta) CALORIES 322 (29% from fat); FAT 10.5g (sat 5.9g, mono 2.9g, poly 0.5g); PROTEIN 23.5g; CARB 35.9g; FIBER 1g; CHOL 37mg; IRON 2mg; SODIUM 955mg; CALC 392mg

SOFT POLENTA:
To create a dish that is smooth, rich, and fast, include equal parts cornmeal and semolina, a coarse flour made from hard durum wheat. The semolina ensures that the milk won't separate. Stir the broth and milk as it comes to a boil to prevent the mixture from spilling over the edge of the pan.

   1½ cups fat-free, less-sodium chicken
         broth
   1½ cups 2% reduced-fat milk
      5 tablespoons yellow cornmeal
      5 tablespoons semolina
      ½ teaspoon grated whole nutmeg
      ¼ teaspoon salt
      ¼ cup (1 ounce) shredded fontina
         cheese
      ¼ cup (1 ounce) grated fresh
         Parmesan cheese

1. Combine broth and milk in a large saucepan; bring to a boil, stirring frequently with a whisk. Add cornmeal, semolina, nutmeg, and salt, stirring constantly with a whisk until cornmeal and semolina begin to absorb liquid (about 2 minutes). Reduce heat to low; cook 20 minutes, stirring frequently. Stir in cheeses. Yield: 4 servings (serving size: ½ cup).
NOTE: The polenta can be made ahead and reheated. Add ¼ to ½ cup water or broth to the polenta, then cover and microwave until thoroughly heated. Whisk before serving to break up any lumps.

CALORIES 206 (27% from fat); FAT 6.2g (sat 3.7g, mono 1.7g, poly 0.2g); PROTEIN 11g; CARB 25.2g; FIBER 0.9g; CHOL 21mg; IRON 0.7mg; SODIUM 532mg; CALC 227mg

Polenta Croutons

Toss these in a salad or enjoy them as a snack. To vary the flavor, add cheeses or herbs. Spray your knife with cooking spray between cuts to slice the polenta easily.

   3½ cups water
      ¾ teaspoon sea salt
      ¾ cup whole grain yellow cornmeal
      ½ cup half-and-half
   Cooking spray

1. Bring water and salt to a boil in a large saucepan. Add cornmeal, stirring constantly with a whisk until cornmeal begins to absorb liquid (about 2 minutes). Reduce heat to low; cook 20 minutes, stirring frequently. Stir in half-and-half; cook 15 minutes, stirring frequently.
2. Spoon cornmeal mixture into an 8-inch square baking dish coated with cooking spray. Using a spatula coated with cooking spray, spread into an even layer. Chill, uncovered, 30 minutes or until completely cool.
3. Preheat oven to 400°.
4. Turn polenta out onto a dry surface; cut into ½-inch cubes. Place polenta cubes on a baking sheet coated with cooking spray. Bake at 400° for 45 minutes, turning once with a spatula. Cool on a wire rack. Yield: 6 servings (serving size: ½ cup).

CALORIES 100 (18% from fat); FAT 2g (sat 1.3g, mono 0.7g, poly 0g); PROTEIN 2g; CARB 16.7g; FIBER 0.5g; CHOL 10mg; IRON 0.7mg; SODIUM 298mg; CALC 20mg

Caponata with Polenta Crostini

Michael Chiarello serves this caponata on crisp squares of polenta as an appetizer.

      1 red bell pepper
      1 tablespoon olive oil, divided
   5½ cups (½-inch) cubed peeled
         eggplant (about 1 pound)
      ¼ teaspoon sea salt
      ¼ teaspoon black pepper
   1½ cups diced onion
      1 tablespoon minced garlic
      1 tablespoon chopped fresh thyme
      1 teaspoon anchovy paste
      ¼ cup balsamic vinegar
      1 tablespoon capers
      1 tablespoon chopped fresh flat-leaf
         parsley
   Polenta Crostini

1. Preheat broiler.
2. Cut bell pepper in half lengthwise; discard seeds and membranes. Place halves, skin sides up, on a foil-lined baking sheet; flatten with hand. Broil 15 minutes or until blackened.

3. Place in a heavy-duty zip-top plastic bag; seal. Let stand 15 minutes. Peel; cut into ½-inch squares.

4. Heat 1 teaspoon oil in a large nonstick skillet over medium-high heat. Add eggplant; cook 6 minutes or until browned, stirring frequently. Add salt and black pepper; stir well. Remove from pan.

5. Add 2 teaspoons oil and onion to pan; cook 3 minutes or until onion begins to brown, stirring frequently. Add garlic, thyme, and anchovy paste; cook 2 minutes, stirring frequently. Add vinegar; cook 30 seconds. Add eggplant and capers; stir well. Remove from heat.

6. Stir in bell pepper and parsley. Cool to room temperature before serving. Serve with Polenta Crostini. Yield: 10 servings (serving size: about 3 tablespoons caponata and 2 crostini).

(Totals include Polenta Crostini) CALORIES 83 (35% from fat); FAT 3.2g (sat 1g, mono 1.7g, poly 0.3g); PROTEIN 3.7g; CARB 10.5g; FIBER 2.2g; CHOL 3mg; IRON 0.6mg; SODIUM 309mg; CALC 67mg

POLENTA CROSTINI:

  3 cups fat-free, less-sodium chicken broth
  1 teaspoon extra-virgin olive oil
  ⅓ cup whole grain yellow cornmeal
  ⅓ cup (1½ ounces) grated fresh Parmesan cheese
  Cooking spray

1. Bring broth and oil to a boil in a small saucepan. Add cornmeal; stir constantly with a whisk until cornmeal begins to absorb liquid (about 2 minutes). Reduce heat to low; cook 25 minutes, stirring frequently. Remove from heat; stir in cheese.

2. Spoon cornmeal mixture into a 2-quart baking dish coated with cooking spray. Using a spatula coated with cooking spray, spread into an even layer. Cool to room temperature; cover and chill overnight.

3. Preheat oven to 400°.

4. Cut polenta into 20 pieces. Arrange in a single layer on a baking sheet coated with cooking spray. Bake at 400° for 30 minutes, turning after 15 minutes. Cool to room temperature on a wire rack. Yield: 10 servings (serving size: 2 crostini).

CALORIES 41 (37% from fat); FAT 1.7g (sat 0.8g, mono 0.7g, poly 0.1g); PROTEIN 2.8g; CARB 3.6g; FIBER 0.3g; CHOL 3mg; IRON 0.2mg; SODIUM 205mg; CALC 51mg

Grilled Grits with Chicken-Apple Sausages

You can use any chicken and apple sausage, but Aidell's minisausages look handsome on the serving platter. Order them at www.aidells.com.

GRITS:

  5 cups water
  ¾ teaspoon kosher salt
  1 cup stone-ground yellow grits
  ½ cup (2 ounces) grated fresh Parmesan cheese
  ¼ teaspoon white pepper
  ¼ teaspoon hot pepper sauce
  Cooking spray

TOMATO SAUCE:

  2 teaspoons olive oil
  2 cups finely chopped onion
  1 cup thinly sliced celery
  6 fennel seeds
  2 garlic cloves, minced
  1 (28-ounce) can whole tomatoes, undrained
  ¼ teaspoon dried marjoram
  6 basil leaves
  2 bay leaves
  2 dried chile peppers, lightly crushed

REMAINING INGREDIENT:

  12 (½-ounce) chicken-apple sausages (such as Aidell's)

1. To prepare grits, bring water and salt to a boil in a large saucepan; gradually stir in grits. Reduce heat; simmer 30 minutes or until thick, stirring frequently. Remove from heat; stir in cheese, white pepper, and pepper sauce.

2. Spread grits into a 15 x 10-inch jelly roll pan coated with cooking spray; cool completely on a wire rack. Cover with plastic wrap; chill 30 minutes.

3. To prepare tomato sauce, heat oil in a large nonstick skillet over medium-high heat. Add onion and celery; sauté 5 minutes or until onion is tender. Add fennel seeds and garlic; sauté 2 minutes. Reduce heat to medium-low. Add tomatoes, marjoram, basil, bay leaves, and chiles; cook 20 minutes, stirring frequently. Discard bay leaves.

4. Prepare grill pan.

5. Invert pan containing grits onto cutting board; cut grits into 12 squares. Place squares on grill pan coated with cooking spray, and grill 3 minutes on each side or until lightly browned and thoroughly heated. Remove from pan; keep warm.

6. Place sausages in pan; grill 8 minutes, turning occasionally. Arrange 3 grits squares in each of 4 bowls. Top each serving with 3 sausages and ¼ cup sauce. Yield: 4 servings.

CALORIES 368 (30% from fat); FAT 12.4g (sat 4.5g, mono 5g, poly 1.9g); PROTEIN 17.3g; CARB 47.7g; FIBER 4.6g; CHOL 49mg; IRON 2.4mg; SODIUM 939mg; CALC 254mg

Cornmeal Pound Cake

Frank Stitt, the 2001 winner of the James Beard Award for Best Chef in the Southeast, recommends serving this cake with strawberries and peaches.

  Cooking spray
  1 tablespoon stone-ground white cornmeal
  2 cups sugar, divided
  ⅔ cup butter, softened
  1 teaspoon grated lemon rind
  1 teaspoon vanilla extract
  5 large egg yolks
  1 cup low-fat sour cream
  2 cups all-purpose flour
  ½ cup stone-ground white cornmeal
  ½ cup stone-ground white grits
  ½ teaspoon salt
  ½ teaspoon baking soda
  5 large egg whites

1. Preheat oven to 325°.

2. Coat a 10-inch tube pan with cooking spray; dust with 1 tablespoon cornmeal.

3. Place 1¾ cups sugar, butter, rind, and vanilla in a large bowl; beat with a mixer at medium speed until light and fluffy. Add egg yolks, 1 at a time, beating well after each addition. Beat in sour cream.

4. Lightly spoon flour into dry measuring cups; level with a knife. Combine flour, ½ cup cornmeal, grits, salt, and baking soda in a medium bowl; stir well

Continued

with a whisk. Add flour mixture to sugar mixture, stirring to combine.

5. Beat egg whites with a mixer at high speed until foamy. Gradually add ¼ cup sugar, 1 tablespoon at a time, beating until stiff peaks form. Gently stir one-fourth of egg white mixture into batter; gently fold in remaining egg white mixture. Spoon batter into prepared pan.

6. Bake at 325° for 50 minutes or until a wooden pick inserted in cake comes out clean. Cool in pan 15 minutes on a wire rack; remove from pan. Cool cake completely on wire rack. Yield: 16 servings (serving size: 1 slice).

CALORIES 294 (30% from fat); FAT 9.9g (sat 6.6g, mono 0.6g, poly 0.2g); PROTEIN 4.7g; CARB 47g; FIBER 0.6g; CHOL 91mg; IRON 1.2mg; SODIUM 203mg; CALC 28mg

Baked Grits with Country Ham, Wild Mushrooms, Fresh Thyme, and Parmesan

This is an adaptation of a signature appetizer at Frank Stitt's Highlands Bar and Grill in Birmingham, Alabama.

GRITS:

5 cups water
1 teaspoon kosher salt
1¼ cups stone-ground yellow grits
¼ cup (1 ounce) grated Parmigiano-Reggiano cheese
¼ teaspoon white pepper
1 large egg, lightly beaten
Cooking spray

SAUCE:

½ cup finely chopped shallots
½ cup dry white wine
½ cup fat-free, less-sodium chicken broth, divided
¼ cup sherry vinegar
1 bay leaf
1 dried chile pepper, crushed
1 teaspoon cornstarch
2 tablespoons butter
1 tablespoon whipping cream
2 tablespoons grated Parmigiano-Reggiano cheese
1 teaspoon fresh lemon juice
¼ teaspoon black pepper

REMAINING INGREDIENTS:

1 ounce country ham, cut into julienne strips
2½ cups (½-inch) sliced shiitake mushroom caps
1 tablespoon minced shallots
1 teaspoon water
3 thyme sprigs
Additional thyme sprigs (optional)

1. Preheat oven to 325°.

2. To prepare grits, bring 5 cups water and salt to a boil in a large saucepan; gradually stir in grits. Reduce heat; simmer 30 minutes or until thick, stirring constantly. Remove from heat; stir in ¼ cup cheese and white pepper. Stir in egg.

3. Spoon ½ cup grits mixture into each of 8 (4-ounce) ramekins or custard cups coated with cooking spray. Place ramekins in a 13 x 9-inch baking pan; add hot water to pan to a depth of 1 inch. Bake at 325° for 20 minutes. Remove ramekins from pan; cool completely on a wire rack.

4. To prepare sauce, bring ½ cup shallots, wine, ¼ cup broth, vinegar, bay leaf, and chile to a boil in a small saucepan over medium heat; cook until reduced to 1 tablespoon liquid (about 6 minutes). Strain mixture through a sieve over a bowl; discard solids. Return liquid to pan.

5. Combine ¼ cup broth and cornstarch. Add cornstarch mixture to pan; bring to a boil. Cook 1 minute, stirring constantly. Reduce heat to low; add butter and cream, stirring with a whisk until well blended. Stir in 2 tablespoons cheese, juice, and black pepper.

6. Cook ham in a large nonstick skillet coated with cooking spray over medium heat 1 minute. Add mushrooms, 1 tablespoon shallots, 1 teaspoon water, and 3 thyme sprigs; sauté 3 minutes or just until mushrooms are tender.

7. Loosen edges of grits with a knife or rubber spatula. Place a plate, upside down, on top of each ramekin; invert onto plates. Spoon 1 tablespoon sauce onto each plate; sprinkle ham mixture evenly among plates. Garnish with thyme sprigs, if desired. Yield: 8 servings.

WINE NOTE: Match this grits dish with a full-bodied Chardonnay (Chardonnay has an uncanny ability to taste great with anything based on corn). Try Grant Burge "Barossa Vines" Chardonnay from Australia (the 2001 is $12). If you're in the mood for red wine, opt for something with a smooth, dense texture to parallel the texture of the grits. The Baron Philippe de Rothschild Syrah 2000 from the Vin de Pays d'Oc, France (about $10), has pure juicy red fruit flavors laced with a touch of black pepper, and is soft and sensual.

CALORIES 197 (29% from fat); FAT 6.3g (sat 3.9g, mono 1.1g, poly 0.2g); PROTEIN 7.1g; CARB 28.8g; FIBER 1.8g; CHOL 43mg; IRON 0.9mg; SODIUM 456mg; CALC 97mg

Comfort Food Menu
serves 8

These grits received our highest rating. Savor it with a roasted pork or chicken.

Creamy Grits with Sweet Corn

Stewed turnip greens

Garlic-pepper pork tenderloin*

*Combine 1 teaspoon salt, 1 teaspoon freshly cracked black pepper, 2 teaspoons olive oil, and 3 minced garlic cloves; brush 2 (1-pound) pork tenderloins, trimmed, with spice mixture. Bake at 425° for 20 minutes or until meat thermometer registers 160°. Let stand 5 minutes.

search myclar2003.com for all our menus

Creamy Grits with Sweet Corn

This recipe by Frank Stitt uses ground corn grits with fresh corn, creating layers of flavor. These grits are a nice medium for rabbit, smoked fish, or country ham. They can also sub for mashed potatoes.

5 cups water
1 teaspoon kosher salt
1 cup stone-ground yellow grits
½ cup (2 ounces) grated fresh Parmesan cheese
¼ cup (1 ounce) shredded white cheddar cheese
¼ teaspoon hot pepper sauce
⅛ teaspoon ground white pepper
1½ teaspoons butter
1 cup fresh corn kernels (about 2 ears)
¼ cup sliced green onions

1. Bring water and salt to a boil in a large saucepan; gradually stir in grits. Reduce heat; simmer 30 minutes or until thick and tender, stirring frequently.

2. Remove from heat; stir in cheeses, pepper sauce, and white pepper. Cover.

3. Melt butter in a large nonstick skillet over medium-high heat. Add corn; sauté 4 minutes or until lightly browned. Add corn and onions to grits mixture, stirring well. Yield: 8 servings (serving size: ½ cup).

CALORIES 141 (25% from fat); FAT 3.9g (sat 2.3g, mono 0.8g, poly 0.2g); PROTEIN 5.7g; CARB 20.8g; FIBER 1.2g; CHOL 10mg; IRON 0.4mg; SODIUM 386mg; CALC 112mg

sound bites

Cabbage Come Lately

Time to turn over a new leaf and eat more of what's good—and good for you.

Vegetable-Bean Soup

This soup offers a warm, comforting start to an autumn meal.

- 1 tablespoon olive oil
- 1½ cups thinly sliced leek (about 2 large)
- 1 cup finely chopped carrot
- 1 cup thinly sliced celery
- 4 cups fat-free, less-sodium chicken broth
- 2 cups finely chopped baking potato (about ¾ pound)
- 1 cup water
- ½ teaspoon salt
- ½ teaspoon dried rosemary
- ¼ teaspoon black pepper
- 2 garlic cloves, minced
- 1 (15.8-ounce) can Great Northern beans or other white beans, drained
- 1 (14.5-ounce) can no-salt-added stewed tomatoes, undrained
- 4 cups thinly sliced napa (Chinese) cabbage (about 1 pound)
- ⅔ cup chopped fresh flat-leaf parsley

1. Heat oil in a large Dutch oven over medium heat. Add leek, carrot, and celery; cook 8 minutes or until tender, stirring occasionally. Stir in broth and next 8 ingredients; bring to a boil.

2. Reduce heat; simmer 20 minutes or until vegetables are tender. Stir in cabbage; cover and cook 1 minute or until cabbage wilts. Stir in parsley. Yield: 9 servings (serving size: 1 cup).

CALORIES 136 (12% from fat); FAT 1.8g (sat 0.3g, mono 1.2g, poly 0.3g); PROTEIN 6.3g; CARB 24.8g; FIBER 3.1g; CHOL 0mg; IRON 2.5mg; SODIUM 458mg; CALC 97mg

Tofu Fried Rice with Cabbage

Cook and chill the rice the night before, so it will be ready ahead of time.

- 1 tablespoon vegetable oil
- 1 (12.3-ounce) package extra-firm light tofu, drained and cut into ½-inch cubes
- 3 cups thinly sliced napa (Chinese) cabbage (about ¾ pound)
- 3 cups chilled cooked long-grain rice
- 3 tablespoons low-sodium soy sauce
- 2 teaspoons dark sesame oil
- ½ cup frozen green peas, thawed
- 2 tablespoons thinly sliced green onions
- ¼ teaspoon salt

1. Heat vegetable oil in a large nonstick skillet over medium-high heat. Add tofu; cook 9 minutes or until golden brown, stirring occasionally. Remove from pan.

2. Add cabbage to pan; cook 45 seconds or until cabbage wilts, stirring constantly. Stir in rice, soy sauce, and sesame oil. Reduce heat, and cook 2 minutes or until hot, stirring occasionally. Stir in tofu, peas, onions, and salt; cook 3 minutes or until thoroughly heated, stirring occasionally. Yield: 5 servings (serving size: 1 cup).

CALORIES 226 (22% from fat); FAT 5.6g (sat 1g, mono 1.7g, poly 2.7g); PROTEIN 9.3g; CARB 34.4g; FIBER 1.1g; CHOL 0mg; IRON 2.4mg; SODIUM 518mg; CALC 95mg

Braised Red Cabbage with Sausage and Apples

The cabbage picks up salty and sweet flavors from the sausage and apples. Serve with toasted sourdough bread.

- 1 teaspoon vegetable oil
- 6 ounces turkey Italian sausage (about 2 links)
- 1 cup thinly sliced red onion
- 6 cups thinly sliced red cabbage (about 1½ pounds)
- 1½ cups finely chopped peeled Granny Smith apple
- ⅔ cup apple juice
- 2 tablespoons dark brown sugar
- 2 tablespoons red wine vinegar
- ¼ teaspoon salt
- ¼ teaspoon dried thyme
- ⅛ teaspoon black pepper
- 1 bay leaf

1. Heat oil in a large nonstick skillet over medium-high heat. Remove casings from sausage. Add sausage and onion to pan; cook 4 minutes or until sausage is browned, stirring to crumble. Add cabbage and remaining ingredients; bring to a boil.

2. Cover, reduce heat, and simmer 20 minutes or until cabbage is tender, stirring occasionally. Discard bay leaf. Yield: 3 servings (serving size: 1⅔ cups).

CALORIES 238 (28% from fat); FAT 7.5g (sat 2.1g, mono 2.6g, poly 2.6g); PROTEIN 12.6g; CARB 32.7g; FIBER 4.7g; CHOL 48mg; IRON 2.1mg; SODIUM 556mg; CALC 93mg

---

Preparing Cabbage

Start by removing and discarding the tough outer leaves. Unlike loose-leafed mustard and kale, cabbage comes tightly wound, so it doesn't pick up grit from the garden. A quick rinse is sufficient.

Cabbage Gremolata

Parsley, lemon rind, and garlic—the typical ingredients found in the Italian garnish gremolata—give this side dish a fresh flavor.

  2 teaspoons butter
  1 tablespoon minced shallots
  1 garlic clove, minced
  6 cups thinly sliced green cabbage
     (about 1½ pounds)
  2 tablespoons fresh lemon juice
  2 tablespoons finely chopped fresh
     parsley
  2 teaspoons grated lemon rind
  ¼ teaspoon salt
  ⅛ teaspoon black pepper

1. Melt butter in a large nonstick skillet over medium-high heat. Add shallots and garlic; cook 3 minutes or until tender, stirring frequently. Add cabbage and juice. Cover and cook over medium heat 10 minutes, stirring occasionally.
2. Remove from heat; stir in parsley and remaining ingredients. Serve immediately. Yield: 4 servings (serving size: ¾ cup).

CALORIES 63 (33% from fat); FAT 2.3g (sat 1.2g, mono 0.6g, poly 0.2g); PROTEIN 2.3g; CARB 10.8g; FIBER 4.2g; CHOL 5mg; IRON 1.1mg; SODIUM 198mg; CALC 88mg

---

Leafy Distinctions

Savoy
The crinkled leaves of Savoy cabbage are mild. It's a good choice for salads and one of the best cabbages for cooking.

Napa
Sometimes you'll see rounded shapes, but napa cabbage is usually elongated and similar in appearance to romaine lettuce. It is thin and delicate and has a mild flavor.

Red
Other than its ruby red to purple color, this cabbage is very similar to green cabbage.

Green
This is the most common form of cabbage. The waxy outer leaves are dark green, and the inner leaves vary from white to pale green.

Curried Cabbage

The pungent flavors of turmeric, mustard, and curry go well with grilled pork loin or lamb.

  1 tablespoon vegetable oil
  ½ cup minced shallots
  2 garlic cloves, minced
  2 tablespoons whole-grain Dijon
     mustard
  2 teaspoons curry powder
  1 teaspoon ground turmeric
 12 cups thinly sliced green cabbage
     (about 3 pounds)
  ¼ cup fat-free, less-sodium chicken
     broth
  ¼ cup rice vinegar
  ½ teaspoon salt
  ¼ teaspoon black pepper

1. Heat oil in a large nonstick skillet over medium-high heat. Add shallots and garlic; sauté 2 minutes. Add mustard, curry, and turmeric; cook 1 minute, stirring constantly. Stir in cabbage and remaining ingredients; cook 5 minutes or until tender, stirring frequently. Yield: 8 servings (serving size: ⅔ cup).

CALORIES 58 (36% from fat); FAT 2.3g (sat 0.4g, mono 0.7g, poly 1g); PROTEIN 1.8g; CARB 8.4g; FIBER 2.8g; CHOL 0mg; IRON 1mg; SODIUM 244mg; CALC 58mg

---

Cabbage with Zucchini and Sesame Seeds

The flavors of the soy sauce, chile paste, and sesame seeds make this a good side for an Asian-inspired meal.

  1 tablespoon sesame seeds
  1 teaspoon olive oil
  3 cups finely chopped zucchini
  6 cups thinly sliced Savoy cabbage
     (about 1½ pounds)
  ¼ cup rice vinegar
  ¼ cup low-sodium soy sauce
  1 teaspoon chile paste with garlic
  ⅛ teaspoon black pepper
  1 tablespoon chopped fresh mint
     (optional)

---

1. Toast sesame seeds in a large skillet over medium heat 3 minutes or until lightly browned, shaking pan frequently. Remove from pan.
2. Heat oil in pan over medium-high heat. Add zucchini; cook 3 minutes or until tender, stirring frequently. Add cabbage and next 4 ingredients. Cover, reduce heat to medium, and cook 6 minutes or until tender, stirring occasionally. Remove from heat; stir in sesame seeds and mint, if desired. Serve immediately. Yield: 4 servings (serving size: 1 cup).

CALORIES 75 (30% from fat); FAT 2.5g (sat 0.4g, mono 1.3g, poly 0.7g); PROTEIN 4.4g; CARB 10.9g; FIBER 1.4g; CHOL 0mg; IRON 1.5mg; SODIUM 535mg; CALC 76mg

---

Cabbage with Green Onions and Caraway

Serve with corned beef or pork chops.

  6 cups thinly sliced green cabbage
     (about 1½ pounds)
  1 cup finely chopped peeled cucumber
  ½ cup thinly sliced green onions
  2 tablespoons water
  ½ teaspoon caraway seeds
  ¼ teaspoon salt
  ⅛ teaspoon black pepper
  ¼ cup dry vermouth or dry white wine

1. Heat a large nonstick skillet over medium heat. Add first 7 ingredients. Cover and cook 10 minutes or until cabbage wilts, stirring occasionally. Add vermouth; cook 2 minutes. Yield: 4 servings (serving size: 1 cup).

CALORIES 40 (7% from fat); FAT 0.3g (sat 0.1g, mono 0g, poly 0.2g); PROTEIN 2.1g; CARB 5g; FIBER 1.6g; CHOL 0mg; IRON 1.2mg; SODIUM 220mg; CALC 127mg

The Apple of Our Eye

Red Delicious, Golden Delicious, and Granny Smiths used to be the standard. But today, newer varieties share space with the old standbys.

We picked common supermarket varieties of apples, and gathered our Test Kitchens staff and food editors to size them up. We used our favorites in these recipes, but recommend using varieties you like best for each dish. After all, beauty is in the eye of the beholder.

Jackson Pollock Candied Apples

Named for the abstract expressionist's signature paint-splattered canvases, these apples make great Halloween treats. Green Granny Smiths go well, but use any apple. Look for wooden sticks at craft supply stores, or use forks instead.

- 6 Granny Smith apples
- 3 ounces bittersweet chocolate, coarsely chopped
- 2½ ounces premium white baking chocolate (such as Baker's), coarsely chopped

1. Wash and dry apples; remove stems. Insert a wooden stick into stem end of each apple.
2. Place bittersweet chocolate in a glass bowl; microwave at HIGH 1 minute or until melted, stirring every 20 seconds until smooth. Working with 1 apple at a time, hold apple over bowl. Using a spoon, drizzle apple with about 2 teaspoons bittersweet chocolate. Place apple, stick side up, on a baking sheet covered with wax paper. Repeat procedure with remaining apples.
3. Place white chocolate in a glass bowl; microwave at HIGH 1 minute or until melted, stirring every 15 seconds until smooth. Working with 1 apple at a time, hold apple over bowl. Using a spoon, drizzle apple with about 1½ teaspoons white chocolate. Place apple, stick side up, on baking sheet covered with wax paper. Repeat procedure with remaining apples. Chill apples until ready to serve. Yield: 6 servings (serving size: 1 apple).

CALORIES 260 (30% from fat); FAT 8.7g (sat 5g, mono 2.5g, poly 0.4g); PROTEIN 1.9g; CARB 48.4g; FIBER 7.8g; CHOL 2mg; IRON 0.8mg; SODIUM 11mg; CALC 38mg

Mixed Apple Salad over Greens

(pictured on page 294)

DRESSING:
- ¼ cup fresh lemon juice
- 2 tablespoons honey
- 1 teaspoon olive oil
- Dash of salt
- Dash of freshly ground black pepper

SALAD:
- 2 cups chopped Granny Smith apple
- 2 cups chopped Cameo or Braeburn apple
- ¼ cup (1 ounce) crumbled blue cheese
- 2 bacon slices, cooked and crumbled
- 4 cups mixed salad greens

1. To prepare dressing, combine first 5 ingredients; stir well with a whisk.
2. To prepare salad, combine apples, cheese, and bacon. Drizzle dressing over mixture; toss gently. Serve over greens. Yield: 4 servings (serving size: about 1 cup apple mixture and 1 cup greens).

CALORIES 163 (29% from fat); FAT 5.3g (sat 2.1g, mono 2.2g, poly 0.5g); PROTEIN 3.7g; CARB 28.7g; FIBER 4.3g; CHOL 8mg; IRON 1.1mg; SODIUM 201mg; CALC 78mg

Open-Faced Turkey with Apple and Havarti

Substitute nutty fontina or mild Muenster for the Havarti, if you prefer.

- 4 (2-ounce) slices country or peasant bread
- 4 teaspoons low-fat mayonnaise
- 4 teaspoons Dijon mustard
- 1 cup trimmed arugula
- 4 (⅛-inch-thick) slices red onion
- 12 ounces thinly sliced deli turkey
- 2 Pink Lady or Cameo apples, each cored and cut crosswise into 8 (¼-inch-thick) slices
- ½ cup (2 ounces) grated Havarti cheese
- Coarsely ground black pepper (optional)

1. Preheat broiler with oven rack in middle position.
2. Spread each bread slice with 1 teaspoon mayonnaise and 1 teaspoon mustard. Layer each slice with ¼ cup arugula, 1 onion slice, 3 ounces turkey, 4 apple slices, and 2 tablespoons cheese.
3. Place sandwiches on a baking sheet; broil 4 minutes or until cheese is bubbly. Remove from heat; sprinkle with pepper, if desired. Serve immediately. Yield: 4 servings (serving size: 1 sandwich).

CALORIES 427 (30% from fat); FAT 14.1g (sat 6.2g, mono 4.5g, poly 1.6g); PROTEIN 29.9g; CARB 44.2g; FIBER 5.7g; CHOL 69mg; IRON 4.8mg; SODIUM 634mg; CALC 141mg

---

Pick a Beauty

Look for vibrantly colored apples that are firm and free of bruises. They should smell fresh, not musty. Skins should be tight and smooth. Though you may like to display apples in a fruit bowl, don't. Storing at room temperature can make them mealy. Store them in a plastic bag in the refrigerator for up to 6 weeks. Apples emit ethylene, a gas that hastens ripening; the plastic bag will prevent them from accelerating the ripening of other produce in your refrigerator.

search myclar2003.com for all our tips

---

12 Common Apple Varieties

Variety	Flavor/Texture (Raw)	Flavor/Texture (Cooked)	Best Applications
Braeburn	sweet, spicy, tart/crisp	slightly muted/juicy, crisp	raw and cooked
Cameo	complex, deep/juicy, hearty	not as good as raw/ juicy, holds texture well	raw and cooked
Empire	aromatic but slightly bland/crisp	flat/does not hold texture well	raw
Fuji	sweet, ciderlike/crisp	flat/dry	raw
Gala	very sweet/crisp	lemony/crunchy-chewy	raw
Golden Delicious	wildflower, honey, grassy/juicy	cloying/soft	raw
Granny Smith	very tart, lemony/very crisp	mellowed tartness/juicy, firm	cooked
Jonagold	tangy, sweet, gingery/pearlike	flat/squishy	raw
McIntosh	wine-cherry, old-fashioned apple flavor/a bit mealy	honey/falls apart	raw
Pink Lady	complex, perfumy, tangy/very firm	tangy/dry, crunchy	raw and cooked
Red Delicious	sugary with thick, bitter skin/ semifirm	sweet, flat/mushy	raw
Rome	slightly sweet/a bit dry	very sweet/soft, cooks down a lot	cooked

Baked Apple Rings with Caramel Sauce

4 Golden Delicious apples, peeled and cored
¾ cup plus 2 tablespoons all-purpose flour
1 tablespoon granulated sugar
¼ teaspoon salt
Dash of freshly grated nutmeg
⅓ cup apple cider
2 large egg whites, lightly beaten
Cooking spray
¼ cup fat-free caramel sundae syrup
Powdered sugar (optional)

1. Preheat oven to 400°.
2. Cut apples crosswise into ½-inch slices. Set aside 8 largest slices; reserve remaining apple for another use.
3. Lightly spoon flour into dry measuring cups; level with a knife. Combine flour, granulated sugar, salt, and nutmeg in a medium bowl. Stir in cider and egg whites (batter will be thick).
4. Heat a large nonstick skillet coated with cooking spray over medium-high heat. Dip 4 apple slices in batter, and place in pan. Cook apple slices 2 minutes on each side or until lightly browned. Arrange cooked apple slices on a baking sheet coated with cooking spray; lightly coat apple slices with cooking spray. Repeat procedure with remaining apple slices.
5. Bake apple slices at 400° for 10 minutes or until edges are crisp. Drizzle each of 4 plates with 1 tablespoon caramel sauce; top with 2 apple slices. Sprinkle with powdered sugar, if desired. Serve immediately. Yield: 4 servings (serving size: 2 apple slices and 1 tablespoon caramel sauce).

CALORIES 205 (2% from fat); FAT 0.5g (sat 0.1g, mono 0g, poly 0.2g); PROTEIN 3.7g; CARB 46.2g; FIBER 2.4g; CHOL 0mg; IRON 1.1mg; SODIUM 151mg; CALC 20mg

Apple Slaw

The vinaigrette goes well with pork chops or ham. Cameo, Fuji, or Gala apples will also work well.

VINAIGRETTE:
⅓ cup packed brown sugar
⅓ cup cider vinegar
1½ tablespoons vegetable oil
¼ teaspoon salt
¼ teaspoon freshly ground black pepper

SLAW:

- 2½ cups chopped Pink Lady or other sweet apple
- 1 (12-ounce) package broccoli slaw
- 1 (3-ounce) package dried tart cherries
- 2 tablespoons unsalted sunflower seed kernels

1. To prepare vinaigrette, combine first 5 ingredients in a small bowl, stirring well with a whisk.

2. To prepare slaw, combine apple, broccoli slaw, and dried cherries. Drizzle with vinaigrette; toss well to combine. Sprinkle with sunflower seeds; chill for up to 3 hours. Yield: 8 servings (serving size: 1 cup).

CALORIES 125 (29% from fat); FAT 4g (sat 0.5g, mono 2.1g, poly 1.1g); PROTEIN 2.1g; CARB 24.9g; FIBER 2.7g; CHOL 0mg; IRON 0.9mg; SODIUM 91mg; CALC 33mg

Marinated Grilled Apples with Mint

Serve these highly flavored apple rings as a side with pork or chicken. We liked this recipe with Granny Smiths. For a dessert version, use Pink Lady apples, and serve with low-fat ice cream.

- ⅔ cup fresh orange juice
- 1 tablespoon chopped fresh mint
- 2 tablespoons honey
- 1 teaspoon vanilla extract
- ½ teaspoon ground ginger
- ¼ teaspoon black pepper
- 3 Granny Smith apples, cored and each cut crosswise into 4 (½-inch) slices
- Cooking spray

1. Combine first 6 ingredients in a large zip-top plastic bag. Add apple slices; seal and marinate in refrigerator 1 to 2 hours, turning bag occasionally.

2. Prepare grill.

3. Remove apple from bag, reserving marinade. Place apple slices on grill rack coated with cooking spray; grill 3 minutes on each side, turning and basting frequently with reserved marinade. Arrange apple slices on a platter; drizzle with any remaining marinade. Yield: 4 servings (serving size: 3 apple slices).

CALORIES 116 (4% from fat); FAT 0.5g (sat 0.1g, mono 0g, poly 0.1g); PROTEIN 0.6g; CARB 29.3g; FIBER 3g; CHOL 0mg; IRON 0.4mg; SODIUM 1mg; CALC 14mg

Apple Soup with Pound Cake Croutons

Serve this thick, creamy soup either hot or cold for brunch or dessert. Thin with more cider, if you like. Hold a potholder or towel firmly over the blender lid so you don't burn yourself while pureeing the apple mixture.

CROUTONS:

- 1 (10.75-ounce) loaf reduced-fat pound cake (such as Sara Lee)

SOUP:

- 1 cup apple cider
- 1 cup dry white wine
- ½ cup sugar
- ½ cup water
- Dash of ground cloves
- Dash of ground allspice
- 3 Granny Smith apples, peeled, cored, and quartered
- 3 Braeburn apples, peeled, cored, and quartered
- 1 (3-inch) cinnamon stick
- ½ cup half-and-half

1. Preheat oven to 375°.

2. To prepare croutons, cut 8 (½-inch) crosswise slices from cake; reserve remaining cake for another use. Cut each slice diagonally into 2 pieces. Place cake pieces on a baking sheet. Bake at 375° for 8 minutes or until lightly browned; turn after 4 minutes. Cool completely on a wire rack.

3. To prepare soup, combine cider and next 8 ingredients in a large Dutch oven; bring to a boil. Reduce heat to medium-low; simmer, uncovered, 30 minutes or until apples are very tender. Remove cinnamon stick; discard.

4. Place half of apple mixture in a blender or food processor; let stand 5 minutes. Cover tightly; process until smooth. Pour pureed apple mixture into a large bowl. Repeat procedure with remaining apple mixture.

5. Place pureed mixture in pan; stir in half-and-half. Cook over low heat 5 minutes or until heated, stirring occasionally. Yield: 8 servings (serving size: ½ cup soup and 2 croutons).

CALORIES 263 (20% from fat); FAT 5.9g (sat 2.2g, mono 1.7g, poly 0.3g); PROTEIN 2.3g; CARB 46.8g; FIBER 1.8g; CHOL 32mg; IRON 0.7mg; SODIUM 143mg; CALC 32mg

Rustic Applesauce

A combination of sweet Braeburns and tart Granny Smiths gives this applesauce a pleasant balance. Mashing the apples creates a chunky sauce; for a smoother version, process part or all of the apple mixture in a food processor or blender. Crème fraîche gives the sauce a smooth, rich finish; substitute full-fat sour cream if your market doesn't carry it.

- 4 cups cubed peeled Braeburn or Pink Lady apple
- 4 cups cubed peeled Granny Smith apple
- ½ cup packed brown sugar
- 2 teaspoons grated lemon rind
- 3 tablespoons fresh lemon juice
- 1 teaspoon ground cinnamon
- 1 teaspoon vanilla extract
- Dash of salt
- 2 tablespoons crème fraîche

1. Combine first 8 ingredients in a Dutch oven over medium heat. Cook 25 minutes or until apples are tender, stirring occasionally.

2. Remove from heat; mash to desired consistency with a fork or potato masher. Stir in crème fraîche. Serve warm or chilled. Yield: 7 servings (serving size: about ½ cup).

CALORIES 140 (12% from fat); FAT 1.8g (sat 1g, mono 0.5g, poly 0.2g); PROTEIN 0.3g; CARB 32.5g; FIBER 2.3g; CHOL 3mg; IRON 0.5mg; SODIUM 30mg; CALC 31mg

Cheese Fondue with Apples

We recommend Pink Lady apples, which don't discolor as quickly as other apples, for this fondue. Use your favorite apple, or a combination of a few varieties; just toss the apple wedges with 2 teaspoons lemon juice to prevent browning. Kirsch, a type of cherry brandy, traditionally finishes cheese fondues, but you can substitute white wine.

    ¼ cup all-purpose flour
    ¾ cup (3 ounces) shredded
       Emmenthaler or Swiss cheese
    ⅛ teaspoon ground nutmeg
    1 garlic clove, halved
    ¾ cup fat-free, less-sodium chicken
       broth
    ¼ cup dry white wine
    1 teaspoon kirsch (cherry brandy)
    3 Pink Lady apples, each cored and
       cut into 9 wedges

1. Lightly spoon flour into a dry measuring cup; level with a knife. Combine flour, cheese, and nutmeg, tossing well.
2. Rub cut sides of garlic on inside of a medium, heavy saucepan. Add broth and wine to pan; bring to a simmer over medium heat.
3. Add one-third cheese mixture to pan; stir with a whisk until combined. Repeat procedure with remaining cheese mixture. Reduce heat to medium-low. Cook 5 minutes or until smooth; stir frequently.
4. Remove cheese mixture from heat; stir in kirsch. Pour mixture into a fondue pot. Keep warm over low flame. Serve with apple wedges. Yield: 9 servings (serving size: 3 apple wedges and about 2 tablespoons fondue).

CALORIES 84 (32% from fat); FAT 3g (sat 1.8g, mono 0.7g, poly 0.2g); PROTEIN 3.4g; CARB 9.9g; FIBER 1.3g; CHOL 9mg; IRON 0.3mg; SODIUM 80mg; CALC 101mg

Choucroute Garni

Choucroute garni is French for "garnished sauerkraut." This dish is just that, with hearty pork tenderloin, bacon, and turkey sausage. Use a good dark beer (such as stout) for extra flavor.

    5 cups sliced Braeburn apple
    6 whole black peppercorns
    6 juniper berries, lightly crushed
    2 bacon slices, chopped
    1 (32-ounce) jar sauerkraut, rinsed
       and drained
    1 (14-ounce) package smoked
       turkey sausage, cut into 8 equal
       pieces
    1 (12-ounce) bottle dark beer
    1 pound pork tenderloin, trimmed
       Cooking spray
    ¼ teaspoon salt
    ¼ teaspoon black pepper

1. Combine first 7 ingredients in a Dutch oven; bring to a boil. Cover, reduce heat, and simmer 30 minutes. Remove from heat, and keep warm.
2. While sauerkraut mixture is cooking, cut pork crosswise into 8 equal slices. Place each slice between 2 sheets of heavy-duty plastic wrap; flatten each piece to ¼-inch thickness using a meat mallet or rolling pin. Lightly coat both sides of pork slices with cooking spray, and sprinkle both sides of pork with salt and pepper.
3. Heat a large nonstick skillet over medium-high heat. Add half of pork; sauté 2 minutes on each side or until pork loses its pink color. Remove from heat, and keep warm. Repeat procedure with remaining pork. Serve pork with sauerkraut mixture. Yield: 8 servings (serving size: 1 pork slice, 1 sausage piece, and about ½ cup sauerkraut mixture).

CALORIES 247 (30% from fat); FAT 8.2g (sat 2.8g, mono 3.4g, poly 1.2g); PROTEIN 19.2g; CARB 21g; FIBER 4.4g; CHOL 59mg; IRON 2mg; SODIUM 950mg; CALC 55mg

The Braeburn Apple

If we had to pick the perfect apple—the most outstanding apple for eating and cooking—our Test Kitchens staff would have to choose the Braeburn. It's decidedly our favorite all-purpose apple. Great both raw and cooked, this rich, juicy apple deserves the notoriety as the best. However, the lovely Pink Lady would be our second choice.

search myclar2003.com for all our tips

Chicken with Apple-Cream Sauce

Skinless, boneless chicken breasts are dressed up with a creamy, sweet-savory sauce. Don't be alarmed if the sauce separates after you add the apples and half-and-half; it will become smooth as it simmers.

    1 tablespoon olive oil
    4 (4-ounce) skinless, boneless
       chicken breast halves
    ¾ teaspoon salt
    ½ teaspoon dried thyme
    ½ teaspoon black pepper
    ⅔ cup apple cider
    3 cups thinly sliced peeled Braeburn
       apple
    ¾ cup half-and-half

1. Heat oil in a large nonstick skillet over medium-high heat. Sprinkle chicken with salt, thyme, and pepper. Add chicken to pan; cook 5 minutes on each side or until done. Remove chicken from pan; keep warm.
2. Add cider to pan, scraping pan to loosen browned bits. Reduce heat to medium-low; cook until reduced to ⅓ cup (about 5 minutes).
3. Add apple and half-and-half; simmer over low heat 10 minutes or until sauce thickens and apple is tender, stirring occasionally. Serve sauce with chicken immediately. Yield: 4 servings (serving size: 1 chicken breast half and ½ cup sauce).

CALORIES 285 (30% from fat); FAT 9.6g (sat 3.9g, mono 4.3g, poly 0.7g); PROTEIN 28.1g; CARB 19.2g; FIBER 2.4g; CHOL 88mg; IRON 1.2mg; SODIUM 540mg; CALC 70mg

Apple Cobbler

This cobbler comes together quickly with the help of packaged pie dough. Tart Granny Smith apples—our favorite for baking—remain firm and pleasantly sharp after cooking. You could also experiment with Rome or Braeburn apples.

    8   cups sliced peeled Granny Smith
        apple (about 2¾ pounds)
    ⅓   cup apple cider
    ¼   cup all-purpose flour
    ½   cup packed brown sugar
    ½   teaspoon ground cinnamon
    1   tablespoon chilled butter, cut into
        small pieces
    ½   (15-ounce) package refrigerated
        pie dough (such as Pillsbury)
    1   teaspoon water
    1   large egg white, lightly beaten
    1   tablespoon turbinado sugar or
        granulated sugar

1. Preheat oven to 350°.
2. Arrange apple in an 11 x 7-inch baking dish. Drizzle cider over apple.
3. Lightly spoon flour into a dry measuring cup; level with a knife. Combine flour, brown sugar, and cinnamon; cut in butter with a pastry blender or 2 knives until mixture resembles coarse meal. Sprinkle flour mixture over apple mixture.
4. Roll dough into a 12 x 8-inch rectangle. Place dough over apple mixture; fold edges under, and flute. Cut 3 slits in top of dough to allow steam to escape.
5. Combine water and egg white, stirring well with a whisk. Brush dough with egg white mixture; sprinkle evenly with turbinado sugar. Bake at 350° for 40 minutes or until crust is golden brown. Yield: 8 servings.

CALORIES 275 (29% from fat); FAT 8.8g (sat 3.8g, mono 3.6g, poly 0.9g); PROTEIN 1.5g; CARB 48.5g; FIBER 2.3g; CHOL 9mg; IRON 0.6mg; SODIUM 129mg; CALC 21mg

inspired vegetarian

A Soy Story

Having grown in popularity and availability, soy finds a home in more and more recipes.

Vegetable Tagine with Baked Tempeh

Don't let the long ingredient list for this recipe intimidate you—the deliciously spicy blend of seasonings makes this dish an autumn standout.

TAGINE:
    1   teaspoon cumin seeds
    1   teaspoon caraway seeds
    1   teaspoon coriander seeds
    ½   teaspoon paprika
    ½   teaspoon black peppercorns
    1   (1-inch) piece cinnamon stick
    2   teaspoons extra-virgin olive oil
    2   cups finely chopped onion
    ¾   cup finely chopped carrot
    ½   cup finely chopped celery
    ½   teaspoon sea salt
    2   garlic cloves, peeled
    2   cups (½-inch) cubed peeled sweet
        potato
    2   cups chopped green cabbage
    1½ cups water
    1   cup finely chopped yellow squash
    1   cup finely chopped zucchini
    1   cup finely chopped peeled tomato
    1   tablespoon fresh lemon juice

TEMPEH:
    ⅔   cup water
    6   tablespoons fresh lemon juice
    ⅓   cup finely chopped fresh flat
        leaf parsley
    2   teaspoons ground cumin
    2   teaspoons paprika
    ½   teaspoon sea salt
    ½   teaspoon ground red pepper
    4   garlic cloves, minced
    1   pound tempeh, cut into ½-inch
        cubes

REMAINING INGREDIENTS:
    2   cups hot cooked couscous
    4   teaspoons minced fresh cilantro
        (optional)

1. To prepare tagine, combine first 6 ingredients in a spice or coffee grinder; process until finely ground.
2. Heat oil in a large Dutch oven over medium heat. Add onion and next 4 ingredients; cook 5 minutes, stirring occasionally. Cover, reduce heat to low, and cook 20 minutes.
3. Stir in cumin mixture, sweet potato, and next 5 ingredients; bring to a boil. Reduce heat; simmer, uncovered, 30 minutes or until thick. Stir in 1 tablespoon lemon juice.
4. To prepare tempeh, preheat oven to 350°.
5. Combine ⅔ cup water and next 7 ingredients in a large bowl. Add tempeh, and toss well to coat. Arrange tempeh mixture in a single layer in an 11 x 7-inch baking dish. Cover with foil.
6. Bake at 350° for 35 minutes. Uncover and bake an additional 5 minutes or until liquid is absorbed. Serve tempeh over tagine and couscous; sprinkle with cilantro, if desired. Yield: 4 servings (serving size: 4 ounces tempeh, ¾ cup tagine, and ½ cup couscous).

CALORIES 507 (29% from fat); FAT 16.1g (sat 3g, mono 5.3g, poly 5.1g); PROTEIN 29.5g; CARB 69.3g; FIBER 16.3g; CHOL 0mg; IRON 6.4mg; SODIUM 642mg; CALC 262mg

---

Today's Soy

Over the years we've developed ingenious ways to transform tofu and tempeh into some of America's favorite foods—cheesecake, ice cream, pudding, creamy dips and dressings, burgers, cutlets, and even Alfredo sauce. But today, we're incorporating soy in a much broader style of cuisine. Many people now rely on tofu, tempeh, or edamame to deliver protein and on miso or soy sauce as flavoring agents in meatless dishes. One thing to remember is that tofu and edamame *carry* flavor while miso and tempeh *add* flavor to dishes.

Edamame with Mustard Vinaigrette

1½ tablespoons red wine vinegar
1 tablespoon Dijon mustard
½ teaspoon sea salt
1 teaspoon extra-virgin olive oil
1 pound frozen shelled edamame, thawed
1 cup thinly sliced red onion
½ cup finely chopped celery
1 tablespoon chopped fresh parsley

1. Combine first 3 ingredients in a large bowl, stirring with a whisk. Add oil, stirring with a whisk until well combined.
2. Cook edamame in boiling water 4 minutes. Add onion and celery; cook 1 minute. Drain well. Add edamame mixture to vinaigrette; toss well to coat. Stir in parsley. Chill 1 hour. Yield: 6 servings (serving size: about ½ cup).

CALORIES 124 (30% from fat); FAT 4.1g (sat 0.5g, mono 1.2g, poly 1.6g); PROTEIN 8.6g; CARB 12.4g; FIBER 0.7g; CHOL 0mg; IRON 1.9mg; SODIUM 295mg; CALC 44mg

Teriyaki Tofu Steaks with Soba Noodles

Look for water-packed when you need tofu to hold its shape. Weighting the tofu with a plate for at least 20 minutes releases water, giving it a firmer texture.

1 pound water-packed extra-firm tofu, drained
¼ cup mirin (sweet rice wine)
¼ cup low-sodium soy sauce
2 tablespoons sake (rice wine)
2 tablespoons rice vinegar
2 tablespoons honey
1 tablespoon dark sesame oil
1 tablespoon finely chopped peeled fresh ginger
½ teaspoon crushed red pepper
1 garlic clove, minced
½ cup vegetable broth
4 heads baby bok choy (about 1½ pounds), each cut in half lengthwise
4 cups cooked soba noodles (about 1 pound uncooked buckwheat noodles)
¼ cup thinly sliced green onions
2 teaspoons sesame seeds, toasted

1. Place tofu between several layers of paper towels. Place a heavy plate on top of tofu, and let stand 20 minutes. Cut tofu crosswise into 4 pieces.
2. Combine mirin and next 8 ingredients in a bowl, stirring with a whisk.
3. Heat a large nonstick skillet over medium-high heat. Add tofu pieces; pour mirin mixture over tofu. Bring to a boil; cook 4 minutes. Turn tofu pieces over; cook 3 minutes. Remove from heat, and keep warm.
4. Bring broth to a boil in a Dutch oven. Add bok choy; cover and cook 2 minutes or until crisp-tender. Drain.
5. Place 1 cup noodles on each of 4 plates; top each serving with 1 tofu piece. Spoon about 1 tablespoon sauce over each tofu piece; sprinkle each serving with 1 tablespoon onions and ½ teaspoon sesame seeds. Arrange 2 bok choy halves on each plate. Yield: 4 servings.

CALORIES 331 (19% from fat); FAT 6.9g (sat 1g, mono 2.1g, poly 3.2g); PROTEIN 18.3g; CARB 47.5g; FIBER 3.6g; CHOL 0mg; IRON 4mg; SODIUM 848mg; CALC 244mg

Tofu-Carrot-Ginger Dressing with Miso

This dressing is as good on salads as in a marinade. Any silken tofu will work in this recipe.

½ cup grated carrot
½ cup silken tofu
2 tablespoons yellow miso (soybean paste)
2 tablespoons fresh lemon juice
1 tablespoon rice vinegar
1 tablespoon vegetable oil
2 teaspoons chopped peeled fresh ginger
1 teaspoon honey
¼ teaspoon sea salt
1 garlic clove, crushed

1. Place all ingredients in a blender or food processor, and process until smooth. Yield: 1¼ cups (serving size: 2 tablespoons).

CALORIES 33 (52% from fat); FAT 1.9g (sat 0.3g, mono 0.4g, poly 1.1g); PROTEIN 1.1g; CARB 2.9g; FIBER 0.4g; CHOL 0mg; IRON 0.2mg; SODIUM 186mg; CALC 9mg

Tofu Vegetable Hot Pot

(pictured on page 296)

Tame this fiery soup by seeding the chile. If you love heat, try using two chiles.

1 teaspoon vegetable oil
Cooking spray
1 cup thinly sliced shallots
1 tablespoon matchstick-cut peeled fresh ginger
1 teaspoon ground turmeric
1 serrano chile, thinly sliced
1 garlic clove, minced
1½ cups shredded green cabbage
1 cup sliced shiitake mushroom caps (about 3 ounces)
½ cup (¼-inch-thick) diagonally cut carrot
1 cup water
¼ cup low-sodium soy sauce
½ teaspoon sea salt
1 (14-ounce) can light coconut milk
1 pound water-packed firm tofu, drained and cut into 1-inch cubes
2 tomatoes, cut into 1-inch-thick wedges
½ cup torn fresh basil leaves
¼ cup (1-inch) sliced green onions
2 cups hot cooked jasmine rice
4 lime wedges

1. Heat oil in a large nonstick saucepan coated with cooking spray over medium-high heat. Add shallots; sauté 2 minutes. Reduce heat to medium. Add ginger, turmeric, chile, and garlic; cook 1 minute, stirring constantly. Add cabbage, mushroom, and carrot; cook 2 minutes, stirring occasionally.
2. Stir in water, soy sauce, salt, and coconut milk; bring to a boil. Add tofu. Reduce heat; simmer 5 minutes. Add tomato; simmer 3 minutes. Stir in basil and onions. Serve over rice with lime wedges. Yield: 4 servings (serving size: 2 cups soup, ½ cup rice, and 1 lime wedge).

CALORIES 407 (23% from fat); FAT 10.2g (sat 4.3g, mono 1.2g, poly 2.7g); PROTEIN 14.5g; CARB 63.3g; FIBER 4.8g; CHOL 0mg; IRON 4.4mg; SODIUM 933mg; CALC 87mg

... And Ready in Just About 20 Minutes

To punch up the flavor of a dish in no time, use strongly seasoned prepared ingredients.

Scallops on Lemony Watercress

To get a nicely browned crust on the scallops, pat them dry with paper towels before you sauté them.

2 teaspoons olive oil, divided
1½ pounds sea scallops
½ teaspoon salt, divided
¼ teaspoon paprika
1 tablespoon grated lemon rind
1 tablespoon chopped fresh parsley
2 tablespoons fresh lemon juice
2 teaspoons sugar
2 teaspoons bottled minced garlic
¼ teaspoon coarsely ground black pepper
8 cups trimmed watercress (about 2½ bunches)

1. Heat 1 teaspoon oil in a large nonstick skillet over medium-high heat. Sprinkle scallops with ¼ teaspoon salt and paprika. Add scallops to pan; cook 3 minutes on each side or until done. Combine rind and parsley; sprinkle over scallops. Keep warm.
2. Combine 1 teaspoon oil, ¼ teaspoon salt, lemon juice, sugar, garlic, and pepper. Place watercress in a large bowl; drizzle with lemon juice mixture, tossing gently to coat. Serve scallops over watercress mixture. Yield: 4 servings (serving size: 2 cups watercress mixture and about 4 ounces scallops).

CALORIES 192 (17% from fat); FAT 3.7g (sat 0.5g, mono 1.9g, poly 0.7g); PROTEIN 30.3g; CARB 8.6g; FIBER 1.9g; CHOL 56mg; IRON 0.8mg; SODIUM 593mg; CALC 130mg

Steak Salad

Try fat-free sun-dried tomato vinaigrette on this salad. Serve with Texas toast.

½ teaspoon garlic powder
¼ teaspoon salt
¼ teaspoon black pepper
1 pound boneless sirloin steak
Cooking spray
12 cups torn romaine lettuce
8 (¼-inch-thick) slices tomato
4 (¼-inch-thick) slices red onion, separated into rings
2 tablespoons crumbled blue cheese
½ cup fat-free balsamic vinaigrette

1. Preheat broiler.
2. Combine first 3 ingredients; rub over both sides of steak. Place steak on a broiler pan coated with cooking spray; broil 4 minutes on each side or until desired degree of doneness.
3. While steak cooks, arrange 3 cups lettuce and 2 tomato slices on each of 4 plates; arrange onion slices over tomato.
4. Cut steak across grain into ¼-inch-thick slices; arrange evenly over onion. Sprinkle each serving with 1½ teaspoons cheese. Drizzle each serving with 2 tablespoons vinaigrette. Yield: 4 servings.

CALORIES 259 (30% from fat); FAT 8.5g (sat 3.5g, mono 3.3g, poly 0.5g); PROTEIN 29g; CARB 15.8g; FIBER 2.6g; CHOL 80mg; IRON 3.8mg; SODIUM 672mg; CALC 65mg

Tuna Puttanesca

¼ cup chopped pimiento-stuffed olives
1 tablespoon capers
2 teaspoons bottled minced garlic
1 teaspoon fresh lemon juice
1 teaspoon anchovy paste
⅛ teaspoon crushed red pepper
1 (14.5-ounce) can diced tomatoes, drained
1 tablespoon olive oil
4 (6-ounce) tuna steaks
½ teaspoon salt
¼ teaspoon black pepper
¼ cup chopped fresh parsley

1. Combine first 7 ingredients.

2. Heat oil in a large nonstick skillet over medium-high heat. Sprinkle tuna with salt and black pepper. Add fish to pan; cook 2 minutes on each side or until desired degree of doneness. Remove fish from pan; keep warm.
3. Add tomato mixture to pan; cook until thoroughly heated (about 2 minutes). Stir in parsley. Pour sauce over fish. Yield: 4 servings (serving size: 1 tuna steak and ¼ cup sauce).

CALORIES 236 (23% from fat); FAT 6.1g (sat 1.2g, mono 3.5g, poly 0.9g); PROTEIN 38.6g; CARB 5.1g; FIBER 1.7g; CHOL 81mg; IRON 3.1mg; SODIUM 801mg; CALC 85mg

Pork and Pineapple Tacos

Serve with refried black beans sprinkled with shredded cheese.

¾ cup chopped onion
½ cup minced fresh cilantro
1 teaspoon vegetable oil
1 teaspoon chipotle chile pepper powder (such as McCormick)
1 teaspoon chili powder
½ teaspoon salt
1 pound pork tenderloin, trimmed and coarsely chopped
1 (15¼-ounce) can pineapple tidbits in juice, undrained
6 (6-inch) flour tortillas
¾ cup salsa verde (such as Herdez)

1. Combine onion and cilantro; set aside.
2. Heat oil in a large nonstick skillet over medium-high heat. Combine chipotle powder, chili powder, salt, and pork. Add to pan; sauté 4 minutes or until browned. Remove from pan.
3. Add pineapple to pan; bring to a boil. Cook 5 minutes or until slightly thickened. Stir in pork mixture; cook 1 minute or until pork is done.
4. Warm tortillas according to package directions. Spoon about ⅔ cup pork mixture down center of each tortilla. Top each serving with 2 tablespoons onion mixture and 2 tablespoons salsa; roll up. Yield: 6 servings (serving size: 1 taco).

CALORIES 310 (21% from fat); FAT 7.3g (sat 1.9g, mono 3.2g, poly 1.3g); PROTEIN 20.9g; CARB 40.7g; FIBER 3.2g; CHOL 49mg; IRON 3.1mg; SODIUM 677mg; CALC 37mg

Shrimp with Sweet Pea Sauce

This sauce is also great with lamb.

2 teaspoons olive oil
20 peeled and deveined jumbo shrimp (about 1½ pounds)
½ teaspoon salt, divided
¼ teaspoon black pepper
1 cup fat-free, less-sodium chicken broth
1 teaspoon bottled minced garlic
1 (10-ounce) package frozen petite green peas
¼ cup fresh mint leaves
2 tablespoons butter
2 teaspoons white wine vinegar

1. Heat oil in a large nonstick skillet over medium-high heat. Sprinkle shrimp with ¼ teaspoon salt and pepper. Add shrimp to pan; cook 4 minutes, turning once. Remove from pan; keep warm.
2. Add broth, garlic, and peas to pan; simmer 3 minutes. Combine ¼ teaspoon salt, pea mixture, mint, and butter in a blender; process until smooth. Add vinegar; pulse to combine. Spoon ⅓ cup pea sauce onto each of 4 plates; top each serving with 5 shrimp. Yield: 4 servings.

CALORIES 300 (29% from fat); FAT 9.8g (sat 4g, mono 3.4g, poly 0.5g); PROTEIN 38.7g; CARB 12.8g; FIBER 3.5g; CHOL 16mg; IRON 4.5mg; SODIUM 542mg; CALC 147mg

Catfish Po'Boys

2 tablespoons fat-free milk
1 pound catfish fillets, cut into 2½-inch pieces
½ teaspoon salt
¼ cup yellow cornmeal
1 tablespoon Cajun seasoning (such as McCormick)
2 teaspoons vegetable oil
2 tablespoons fat-free mayonnaise
1 tablespoon white wine vinegar
1 tablespoon fat-free sour cream
1½ teaspoons sugar
Dash of crushed red pepper
2 cups bagged broccoli coleslaw
4 (2½-ounce) hoagie rolls with sesame seeds, toasted

1. Combine milk and catfish in a large bowl, tossing gently to coat. Remove fish from bowl; shake off excess milk. Sprinkle fish with salt. Combine cornmeal and Cajun seasoning in a large zip-top plastic bag. Add fish to bag. Seal and shake to coat.
2. Heat oil in a large nonstick skillet over medium-high heat. Add fish; cook 3 minutes on each side or until fish flakes easily when tested with a fork.
3. While fish cooks, combine mayonnaise and next 4 ingredients in a medium bowl. Add broccoli coleslaw; toss well to coat. Spoon ½ cup slaw mixture onto bottom half of each roll. Arrange fish evenly over slaw, and top with top halves of rolls. Yield: 4 servings.

CALORIES 442 (30% from fat); FAT 14.7g (sat 3.2g, mono 6.4g, poly 3.8g); PROTEIN 26g; CARB 50.2g; FIBER 3.4g; CHOL 54mg; IRON 3.6mg; SODIUM 818mg; CALC 144mg

Chickpea and Spinach Curry

In less than 10 minutes, this fiber-rich dish is ready for dinner. Serve with warm pitas or over basmati rice. You can top with a dollop of low-fat plain yogurt to contrast the earthy spices.

1 cup coarsely chopped onion
1½ tablespoons bottled ground fresh ginger (such as Spice World)
1 teaspoon olive oil
1½ teaspoons sugar
1½ teaspoons red curry powder (such as McCormick)
1 (19-ounce) can chickpeas (garbanzo beans), rinsed and drained
1 (14.5-ounce) can diced tomatoes, undrained
4 cups fresh spinach
½ cup water
¼ teaspoon salt

1. Combine onion and ginger in a food processor; pulse until minced.
2. Heat oil in a large nonstick skillet over medium-high heat. Add onion mixture, sugar, and curry to pan; sauté 3 minutes. Add chickpeas and tomatoes; simmer 2 minutes. Stir in spinach, water, and salt; cook 1 minute or until spinach wilts. Yield: 3 servings (serving size: 1⅓ cups).

CALORIES 247 (15% from fat); FAT 4g (sat 0.6g, mono 1.6g, poly 0.9g); PROTEIN 11.1g; CARB 45g; FIBER 8.4g; CHOL 1mg; IRON 5mg; SODIUM 857mg; CALC 194mg

lighten up

Potato Soup Makeover

A nip here, a tuck there, and this soup has a whole new look.

The recipe for Baked Potato Soup, from the Abilene Junior League cookbook just seemed too thick and rich to Elayne J. Watson, a Mary Kay Cosmetics sales director from Abilene, Texas. There were good reasons: It included more than a quarter-pound of butter, six cups of whole milk, 12 slices of bacon, five ounces of cheese, and a cup of sour cream. But with a few changes from *Cooking Light*, the soup was transformed into a true beauty. It still tastes indulgent, and has plenty of crunchy bacon on top—despite its 226 fewer calories and about 72 percent less fat per serving.

Lazy Day Lunch Menu
serves 8
Baked Potato Soup
Green salad*
Orange sections

*Combine 8 cups mixed salad greens, 1 cup halved cherry tomatoes, ½ cup thinly sliced red onion, ¼ cup (1 ounce) crumbled feta cheese, and 3 tablespoons toasted slivered almonds in a large bowl. Toss greens mixture with ¼ cup Italian vinaigrette just before serving.

search myclar2003.com for all our menus

Baked Potato Soup

(pictured on page 293)

All the flavors of a loaded baked potato come together in this rich, creamy soup.

4 baking potatoes (about 2½ pounds)
⅔ cup all-purpose flour
6 cups 2% reduced-fat milk
1 cup (4 ounces) reduced-fat shredded extra-sharp cheddar cheese, divided
1 teaspoon salt
½ teaspoon black pepper
1 cup reduced-fat sour cream
¾ cup chopped green onions, divided
6 bacon slices, cooked and crumbled

1. Preheat oven to 400°.
2. Pierce potatoes with a fork; bake at 400° for 1 hour or until tender. Cool. Peel potatoes; coarsely mash. Discard skins.
3. Lightly spoon flour into a dry measuring cup; level with a knife. Place flour in a large Dutch oven; gradually add milk, stirring with a whisk until blended. Cook over medium heat until thick and bubbly (about 8 minutes). Add mashed potatoes, ¾ cup cheese, salt, and pepper, stirring until cheese melts. Remove from heat.
4. Stir in sour cream and ½ cup onions. Cook over low heat 10 minutes or until thoroughly heated (do not boil). Sprinkle each serving with cheese, onions, and bacon. Yield: 8 servings (serving size: about 1½ cups soup, 1½ teaspoons cheese, 1½ teaspoons onions, and about 1 tablespoon bacon).

CALORIES 329 (30% from fat); FAT 10.8g (sat 5.9g, mono 3.5g, poly 0.7g); PROTEIN 13.6g; CARB 44.5g; FIBER 2.8g; CHOL 38mg; IRON 1.1mg; SODIUM 587mg; CALC 407mg

happy endings

Sweets with Spirit

A kiss of liqueur enhances the taste of these desserts.

Orange Cream Tart

CRUST:

40 reduced-fat vanilla wafers (about 5 ounces)
2 tablespoons butter, melted
1 large egg white
Cooking spray

FILLING:

2 cups 1% low-fat milk, divided
⅔ cup sugar
3 tablespoons cornstarch
⅛ teaspoon salt
1 large egg, lightly beaten
2 tablespoons Grand Marnier (orange-flavored liqueur)
1 tablespoon butter
2 teaspoons grated orange rind
1 teaspoon vanilla extract
1½ cups frozen reduced-calorie whipped topping, thawed
1 tablespoon chopped pistachios

1. Preheat oven to 350°.
2. To prepare crust, place cookies in a food processor; pulse until crumbs form to measure 1¼ cups. Add melted butter and egg white; pulse until moist.
3. Spoon crumb mixture into a 9-inch round removable-bottom tart pan coated with cooking spray; press into bottom and up sides of pan. Bake at 350° for 9 minutes or until golden brown; cool on a wire rack.
4. To prepare filling, combine ½ cup milk, sugar, cornstarch, salt, and egg in a large bowl; stir with a whisk. Heat 1½ cups milk in a heavy saucepan over medium-high heat to 180° or until tiny bubbles form around edge (do not boil). Remove from heat. Gradually add hot milk to sugar mixture; stir constantly with a whisk.

5. Place mixture in pan. Cook over medium heat until thick (about 3 minutes), stirring constantly. Reduce heat to low; cook 2 minutes, stirring constantly. Remove from heat; stir in liqueur, 1 tablespoon butter, rind, and vanilla. Pour into prepared crust; cover surface with plastic wrap. Chill 8 hours or until set. Remove plastic wrap. Spread whipped topping over filling. Sprinkle with nuts. Yield: 8 servings (serving size: 1 wedge).

CALORIES 275 (29% from fat); FAT 8.8g (sat 4.9g, mono 2.3g, poly 0.4g); PROTEIN 4.1g; CARB 42.1g; FIBER 0.2g; CHOL 41mg; IRON 0.6mg; SODIUM 194mg; CALC 82mg

Tropical Fruit Ambrosia with Rum

¼ cup sugar
¼ cup water
2 tablespoons white rum
2 tablespoons fresh lime juice
2 cups cubed peeled ripe mango (about 2 mangoes)
2 cups cubed peeled kiwifruit (about 6 kiwifruit)
2 tablespoons flaked sweetened coconut, toasted

1. Combine sugar and water in a small saucepan. Bring to a boil, and cook 1 minute or until sugar dissolves. Remove from heat; stir in rum and lime juice. Cool completely.
2. Combine mango and kiwifruit; add rum syrup, tossing gently. Sprinkle with coconut. Yield: 4 servings (serving size: 1 cup fruit and 1½ teaspoons coconut).

CALORIES 185 (7% from fat); FAT 1.4g (sat 0.7g, mono 0.2g, poly 0.3g); PROTEIN 1.4g; CARB 41.3g; FIBER 4.6g; CHOL 0mg; IRON 0.6mg; SODIUM 14mg; CALC 33mg

When Quality Counts

- Use a less-expensive brand when the alcohol will be cooked.
- Use premium brands when the spirit is added after cooking. Opting for Grand Marnier rather than a less expensive orange liqueur will make a big difference in the overall flavor of the dessert.

Date-Nut Pudding Cake with Vanilla Sauce

1 cup all-purpose flour
¾ cup granulated sugar
2 teaspoons baking powder
⅛ teaspoon salt
½ cup fat-free milk
2 tablespoons bourbon
2 tablespoons vegetable oil
1 teaspoon vanilla extract
¾ cup chopped pitted dates
3 tablespoons coarsely chopped walnuts, toasted
Cooking spray
⅔ cup packed brown sugar
1¼ cups boiling water
Vanilla Sauce

1. Preheat oven to 350°.
2. Lightly spoon flour into a dry measuring cup; level with a knife. Combine flour, granulated sugar, baking powder, and salt in a large bowl; stir with a whisk. Combine milk, bourbon, oil, and vanilla in a bowl. Add to flour mixture, stirring just until moist. Stir in dates and nuts.
3. Spoon batter into an 8-inch square baking pan coated with cooking spray. Sprinkle brown sugar over batter. Pour boiling water over batter (do not stir). Bake at 350° for 30 minutes or until cake springs back when touched lightly in center (cake will not test clean when a wooden pick is inserted in center). Cut into squares. Serve each square with about 2 tablespoons warm Vanilla Sauce. Yield: 9 servings.

(Totals include Vanilla Sauce) CALORIES 322 (18% from fat); FAT 6.3g (sat 1.3g, mono 1.4g, poly 3.1g); PROTEIN 4.2g; CARB 62g; FIBER 1.7g; CHOL 27mg; IRON 1.4mg; SODIUM 181mg; CALC 151mg

VANILLA SAUCE:
1⅓ cups 1% low-fat milk
3 tablespoons sugar
2 teaspoons cornstarch
1 large egg yolk
1½ teaspoons vanilla extract
1 teaspoon butter

1. Combine first 4 ingredients in top of a double boiler; stir with a whisk. Cook over simmering water until slightly thick (about 15 minutes), stir constantly with a whisk. Remove from heat; add vanilla and butter, stirring until smooth. Place plastic wrap on surface of sauce; chill. Yield: 1¼ cups (serving size: 2 tablespoons).

CALORIES 41 (26% from fat); FAT 1.2g (sat 0.6g, mono 0.4g, poly 0.1g); PROTEIN 1.4g; CARB 5.9g; FIBER 0g; CHOL 24mg; IRON 0.1mg; SODIUM 21mg; CALC 43mg

Apple Streusel Cake with Almonds

STREUSEL:
2 tablespoons all-purpose flour
2 tablespoons brown sugar
⅛ teaspoon ground cinnamon
1 tablespoon butter
2 tablespoons sliced almonds

CAKE:
¾ cup granulated sugar
¼ cup (2 ounces) ⅓-less-fat cream cheese, softened
¼ cup butter, softened
2 tablespoons amaretto (almond-flavored liqueur)
1 teaspoon vanilla extract
¼ teaspoon almond extract
1 large egg
1¼ cups all-purpose flour
½ teaspoon baking powder
¼ teaspoon baking soda
¼ teaspoon salt
¾ cup low-fat buttermilk
Cooking spray
1½ cups thinly sliced peeled Braeburn apple (about ¾ pound)

1. Preheat oven to 350°.
2. To prepare streusel, combine first 3 ingredients in a medium bowl; cut in 1 tablespoon butter with a pastry blender or 2 knives until mixture resembles coarse meal. Stir in almonds.
3. To prepare cake, beat granulated sugar, cream cheese, and ¼ cup butter in a large bowl with a mixer at medium speed until smooth. Add amaretto, extracts, and egg, beating well.
4. Lightly spoon flour into dry measuring cups; level with a knife. Combine flour, baking powder, baking soda, and salt in a medium bowl, stirring well with a whisk. Add flour mixture and butter-milk alternately to egg mixture, beginning and ending with flour mixture.
5. Pour batter into a 9-inch round cake pan coated with cooking spray; sharply tap pan once on counter to remove air bubbles. Arrange apple slices over batter; sprinkle with streusel.
6. Bake at 350° for 45 minutes or until a wooden pick inserted in center comes out clean. Cool in pan 10 minutes on a wire rack; remove from pan. Cool completely on wire rack. Cut into wedges. Yield: 9 servings (serving size: 1 wedge).

CALORIES 277 (31% from fat); FAT 9.5g (sat 5.3g, mono 3g, poly 0.6g); PROTEIN 4.4g; CARB 43.8g; FIBER 1.9g; CHOL 47mg; IRON 1.3mg; SODIUM 249mg; CALC 56mg

Mocha Fudge Brownies

BROWNIES:
Cooking spray
1 ounce semisweet chocolate, chopped
3½ tablespoons butter
1 cup sugar
½ cup unsweetened cocoa
1 tablespoon instant coffee granules
2 tablespoons Kahlúa (coffee-flavored liqueur)
2 teaspoons vanilla extract
1 large egg white, lightly beaten
1 large egg, lightly beaten
¾ cup all-purpose flour
¼ teaspoon baking powder
¼ teaspoon baking soda
¼ teaspoon salt

GLAZE:
2 tablespoons sugar
1 tablespoon water
1 tablespoon dark corn syrup
2 teaspoons butter
1 ounce semisweet chocolate, chopped
1 teaspoon Kahlúa (coffee-flavored liqueur)

1. Preheat oven to 350°.
2. To prepare brownies, coat an 8-inch square baking pan with cooking spray (do not coat sides of pan); set aside.
3. Combine 1 ounce chocolate and 3½ tablespoons butter in a microwave-safe bowl. Cover and microwave at HIGH 1 minute or until chocolate almost melts.

Stir until completely melted. Stir in 1 cup sugar and next 6 ingredients.

4. Lightly spoon flour into dry measuring cups; level with a knife. Combine flour, baking powder, baking soda, and salt in a large bowl; stir well with a whisk. Add chocolate mixture; stir just until moist. Spread into prepared pan.

5. Bake at 350° for 22 minutes or until a wooden pick inserted in center comes out almost clean. Cool in pan on a wire rack.

6. To prepare glaze, combine 2 tablespoons sugar, water, syrup, and 2 teaspoons butter in a small microwave-safe bowl. Microwave at HIGH 40 seconds or until sugar dissolves, stirring once. Add 1 ounce chocolate and 1 teaspoon liqueur, stirring until chocolate melts. Spread over brownies; cool 20 minutes or until glaze is set. Yield: 16 servings (serving size: 1 brownie).

CALORIES 146 (32% from fat); FAT 5.2g (sat 3g, mono 1.7g, poly 0.2g); PROTEIN 2.1g; CARB 24.1g; FIBER 1.2g; CHOL 21mg; IRON 0.9mg; SODIUM 105mg; CALC 14mg

sidetracked

Simply Smashing Mashed Potatoes

Here are some of our superlative spuds.

Basic Mashed Potatoes

  3 pounds cubed peeled baking potato
  ½ cup 2% reduced-fat milk
  ½ cup fat-free, less-sodium chicken broth
  3 tablespoons reduced-fat sour cream
  1 teaspoon salt
  ½ teaspoon black pepper
  ¼ cup butter, softened

1. Place potato in a saucepan, and cover with water. Bring to a boil. Reduce heat; simmer 15 minutes or until tender.

2. Drain and return potato to pan. Add milk and broth; mash to desired consistency. Cook 2 minutes or until thoroughly heated, stirring constantly. Stir in sour cream, salt, and pepper. Top with butter. Yield: 8 servings (serving size: about ¾ cup).

CALORIES 162 (30% from fat); FAT 5.4g (sat 3.4g, mono 1.4g, poly 0.2g); PROTEIN 3.7g; CARB 25.4g; FIBER 2.2g; CHOL 15mg; IRON 1mg; SODIUM 306mg; CALC 32mg

Corn and Smoked Mozzarella Mashed Potatoes

Serve these sweet, smoky potatoes with spice-rubbed chicken or flank steak. If you can't find smoked mozzarella, try smoked Gouda or smoked cheddar.

    Cooking spray
  3 cups fresh corn kernels (about 6 ears)
2½ pounds red potatoes, quartered
  ¾ cup 2% reduced-fat milk
  ½ cup (2 ounces) shredded smoked mozzarella cheese
  3 tablespoons butter, softened
  ¼ cup chopped fresh cilantro
  1 tablespoon fresh lime juice
  ¾ teaspoon salt
  ½ teaspoon freshly ground black pepper

1. Heat a large nonstick skillet coated with cooking spray over medium-high heat. Add corn; sauté 5 minutes or until lightly browned. Cool.

2. Place potato in a saucepan, and cover with water. Bring to a boil. Reduce heat; simmer 15 minutes or until tender.

3. Drain and return potato to pan. Add milk, cheese, and butter; mash to desired consistency. Cook 2 minutes or until thoroughly heated, stirring constantly. Stir in corn, cilantro, and remaining ingredients. Yield: 8 servings (serving size: about ¾ cup).

CALORIES 240 (27% from fat); FAT 7.2g (sat 4.1g, mono 2.1g, poly 0.6g); PROTEIN 7.2g; CARB 39.7g; FIBER 4g; CHOL 19mg; IRON 1.5mg; SODIUM 325mg; CALC 77mg

Mashing Potatoes
Whether you prefer your potatoes chunky or silky, potato mashers give you a multitude of options. They're your best bet if you like the texture of the skin in your mashed potatoes. We tested all these recipes with a potato masher since most people have one.

Whipping Potatoes
An electric mixer whips potatoes in an instant, but a food processor will over-mix potatoes and make them gummy.

Ricing Potatoes
Loved by food purists, potato ricers and food mills make smooth mashed potatoes. These do double duty, peeling and mashing at the same time. Look for ricers and food mills at specialty cookware stores.

Smoked Salmon and Chive Mashed Potatoes

Serve these potatoes with eggs Benedict for a fantastic brunch. Add fresh fruit to finish the menu.

2½ pounds cubed peeled baking potato
⅓ cup 2% reduced-fat milk
2 tablespoons butter, softened
3 ounces ⅓-less-fat cream cheese, softened
2 tablespoons chopped fresh chives
2 tablespoons capers
1 tablespoon chopped fresh dill
¼ teaspoon freshly ground black pepper
4 ounces smoked salmon, finely chopped

1. Place potato in a saucepan, and cover with water. Bring to a boil. Reduce heat; simmer 15 minutes or until tender.
2. Drain and return potato to pan. Add milk, butter, and cream cheese; mash to desired consistency. Cook 2 minutes or until thoroughly heated, stirring constantly. Stir in chives and remaining ingredients. Yield: 8 servings (serving size: about ⅔ cup).

CALORIES 184 (27% from fat); FAT 5.5g (sat 3.3g, mono 1.2g, poly 0.3g); PROTEIN 7g; CARB 26.9g; FIBER 2.4g; CHOL 17mg; IRON 1.3mg; SODIUM 442mg; CALC 39mg

Pesto Mashed Potatoes

Brilliant green pesto dresses Parmesan-laced potatoes in a side dish similar to the one served at chef Bobby Flay's New York City restaurant, Bolo. Just drizzle the pesto over the potatoes; if you stir it in thoroughly, you'll have green mashed potatoes.

PESTO:
1½ cups loosely packed fresh basil leaves
½ cup chopped fresh parsley
¼ cup fat-free, less-sodium chicken broth
2½ tablespoons extra-virgin olive oil

POTATOES:
2½ pounds cubed peeled baking potato
½ cup (2 ounces) grated fresh Parmesan cheese
½ cup 2% reduced-fat milk
½ cup fat-free, less-sodium chicken broth
¾ teaspoon salt
½ teaspoon black pepper

1. To prepare pesto, combine first 4 ingredients in a blender; process until smooth, scraping sides.
2. To prepare potatoes, place potato in a saucepan, and cover with water. Bring to a boil. Reduce heat; simmer 15 minutes or until tender.
3. Drain and return potato to pan. Add cheese and remaining 4 ingredients; mash to desired consistency. Cook 2 minutes or until thoroughly heated, stirring constantly. Drizzle each serving with 1 tablespoon pesto. Yield: 8 servings (serving size: about ¾ cup).

CALORIES 190 (30% from fat); FAT 6.4g (sat 1.9g, mono 3.2g, poly 0.4g); PROTEIN 6.2g; CARB 28.5g; FIBER 2.8g; CHOL 7mg; IRON 1.6mg; SODIUM 312mg; CALC 103mg

Mashed Potatoes with Roasted Garlic Butter

Make the garlic butter ahead and refrigerate it for up to 3 days.

GARLIC BUTTER:
2 whole garlic heads
¼ cup butter, softened
1 tablespoon finely chopped shallots
2 teaspoons finely chopped fresh rosemary

POTATOES:
2½ pounds cubed Yukon gold or red potato
⅓ cup fat-free, less-sodium chicken broth
¼ cup buttermilk
2 tablespoons chopped fresh parsley
1 teaspoon salt
½ teaspoon freshly ground black pepper

1. Preheat oven to 350°.
2. To prepare garlic butter, remove white papery skin from garlic heads (do not peel or separate cloves). Wrap each head separately in foil. Bake at 350° for 45 minutes; cool 10 minutes.
3. Separate cloves; squeeze to extract garlic pulp. Discard skins. Combine garlic pulp, butter, shallots, and rosemary.
4. To prepare potatoes, place potato in a saucepan, and cover with water. Bring to a boil. Reduce heat; simmer 15 minutes or until tender.
5. Drain and return potato to pan. Add broth and buttermilk; mash to desired consistency. Cook 2 minutes or until thoroughly heated, stirring constantly. Stir in garlic butter, parsley, salt, and pepper. Yield: 8 servings (serving size: about ⅔ cup).

CALORIES 181 (30% from fat); FAT 6.1g (sat 3.7g, mono 1.7g, poly 0.3g); PROTEIN 3.9g; CARB 28.8g; FIBER 2.4g; CHOL 16mg; IRON 1.4mg; SODIUM 375mg; CALC 39mg

Caramelized Onion and Horseradish Mashed Potatoes

Horseradish and Dijon mustard flavor these potatoes. Pair them with steak or tuna.

¼ cup butter, divided
4 cups chopped onion
2 teaspoons brown sugar
1 tablespoon white balsamic vinegar (optional)
2½ pounds cubed peeled baking potato
½ cup whole milk
¼ cup Dijon mustard
2 tablespoons prepared horseradish
1 tablespoon fresh lemon juice
1 tablespoon light mayonnaise
½ teaspoon salt

1. Melt 1 tablespoon butter in a medium nonstick skillet over medium-high heat. Add onion and sugar; sauté 10 minutes or until caramelized. Remove from heat; stir in vinegar, if desired.
2. Place potato in a saucepan, and cover with water. Bring to a boil. Reduce heat; simmer 15 minutes or until tender.

3. Drain and return potato to pan. Add 3 tablespoons butter and milk to pan; mash to desired consistency. Cook 2 minutes or until thoroughly heated, stirring constantly.

4. Combine mustard and remaining 4 ingredients in a bowl, stirring with a whisk until blended. Add mustard mixture and onion mixture to potato mixture, stirring to combine. Yield: 10 servings (serving size: about ¾ cup).

CALORIES 186 (30% from fat); FAT 6.3g (sat 3.3g, mono 1.7g, poly 0.4g); PROTEIN 3.9g; CARB 30.4g; FIBER 2.9g; CHOL 15mg; IRON 1.3mg; SODIUM 353mg; CALC 45mg

Chipotle Mashed Sweet Potatoes

These potatoes are a great accompaniment with spice-rubbed pork tenderloin.

2½ pounds cubed peeled sweet potato
½ cup half-and-half
3 tablespoons butter, softened
2 tablespoons fresh lime juice
1 (7-ounce) can chipotle chiles in adobo sauce
½ cup packed brown sugar
¾ teaspoon salt
¾ teaspoon ground cinnamon, divided

1. Place sweet potato in a saucepan, and cover with water. Bring to a boil. Reduce heat; simmer 15 minutes or until tender.

2. Drain and return sweet potato to pan. Add half-and-half, butter, and juice; mash to desired consistency. Cook 2 minutes or until thoroughly heated, stirring constantly.

3. Remove 2 chiles from can, and chop; reserve remaining chiles and adobo sauce for another use. Stir chopped chiles, brown sugar, salt, and ½ teaspoon cinnamon into potato mixture. Sprinkle with ¼ teaspoon cinnamon. Yield: 8 servings (serving size: about ⅔ cup).

CALORIES 264 (22% from fat); FAT 6.4g (sat 3.8g, mono 1.8g, poly 0.4g); PROTEIN 3g; CARB 49.4g; FIBER 4.4g; CHOL 19mg; IRON 1.2mg; SODIUM 328mg; CALC 65mg

---

Tips from the Test Kitchen

• Warm the milk or broth before you mash it with the potatoes to reduce lumps.

• Our recipes direct you to cube the potatoes before you cook them. You can cook them whole, if you prefer; it just takes longer.

• After you drain the potatoes, take a moment to place the pan over low heat, then shake the potatoes in the pan to dry them before mashing. If your pan is stainless, mash the potatoes right in the pan over low heat to keep them warm.

• Russet and thin-skinned white potatoes have a fluffy, dry texture and often require slightly more liquid for creamy results. If you have a potato ricer, use it with these spuds.

• Waxy red potatoes and Yukon golds make good chunky smashed potatoes. Peel them before or after cooking, or leave the skin on for rustic appeal.

• If your menu includes gravy or jus, keep your mashed potatoes simple.

search myclar2003.com for all our tips

Bacon and Cheddar Mashed Potatoes

Tailor the flavors to suit your preferences by using Swiss cheese instead of cheddar and prosciutto instead of bacon.

2½ pounds cubed peeled baking potato
1 cup (4 ounces) shredded extra-sharp cheddar cheese
1 cup 2% reduced-fat milk
½ cup chopped green onions
2 tablespoons reduced-fat sour cream
½ teaspoon salt
½ teaspoon freshly ground black pepper
4 bacon slices, cooked and crumbled (drained)

1. Place potato in a saucepan, and cover with water. Bring to a boil. Reduce heat; simmer 15 minutes or until tender.

---

2. Drain and return potato to pan. Add cheese and milk; mash to desired consistency. Cook 2 minutes or until thoroughly heated, stirring constantly. Stir in onions and remaining ingredients. Yield: 8 servings (serving size: about ¾ cup).

CALORIES 214 (30% from fat); FAT 7.1g (sat 4.1g, mono 2.1g, poly 0.4g); PROTEIN 8.9g; CARB 29.6g; FIBER 2.6g; CHOL 22mg; IRON 1.4mg; SODIUM 330mg; CALC 157mg

Hummus Mashed Potatoes

Flavored with hummus, these mashed potatoes pair nicely with kebabs, lamb stew, or chicken with Greek seasoning. Tahini—a thick paste made from ground sesame seeds—is a common ingredient in Middle Eastern cooking and is available at most supermarkets.

¾ cup fat-free, less-sodium chicken broth
¼ cup tahini (sesame-seed paste)
3 tablespoons fresh lemon juice
1 teaspoon extra-virgin olive oil
½ teaspoon salt
¼ teaspoon ground red pepper
2 garlic cloves, peeled
1 (15-ounce) can chickpeas (garbanzo beans), rinsed and drained
2 pounds cubed peeled red potato
1 tablespoon extra-virgin olive oil
Lemon wedges (optional)

1. Combine first 8 ingredients in a food processor, and process until smooth, scraping sides.

2. Place potato in a saucepan, and cover with water. Bring to a boil. Reduce heat; simmer 15 minutes or until tender.

3. Drain and return potato to pan. Stir in broth mixture, and mash to desired consistency. Cook 2 minutes or until thoroughly heated, stirring constantly. Drizzle potato mixture with 1 tablespoon olive oil, and garnish with lemon wedges, if desired. Yield: 10 servings (serving size: about ¾ cup).

CALORIES 185 (30% from fat); FAT 6.1g (sat 0.9g, mono 2.8g, poly 2g); PROTEIN 5.6g; CARB 28.8g; FIBER 4.1g; CHOL 0mg; IRON 1.5mg; SODIUM 260mg; CALC 30mg

Butter Me Up!

With just the touch of a button, you can create fresh nut butters that add complexity and depth to sweet and savory dishes.

When we learned about research demonstrating the health benefits of eating nuts (see Go Nuts on page 320), we knew there had to be better ways to reap the benefits than chowing down on peanut butter sandwiches.

So we asked one of our favorite recipe developers, Lorrie Hulston Corvin, to come up with creative recipes using nuts. The project excited her, she said, because it was a challenge: *Cooking Light* wanted more than nuts sprinkled on top of something else.

Her solution? Processing nuts into butters, which are then used to flavor, thicken, and replace dairy cream in traditional recipes. "Nut butters are seldom mentioned in Western cooking, but they're often a staple in other countries," Lorrie says. "Peanut sauces are common in Thai dishes, and peanut stew is a traditional African dish, but Americans are most likely to think just of peanut butter cookies and sandwiches."

Lorrie has come up with ways to change that perception, using almonds, pecans, cashews, walnuts, hazelnuts, pistachios, peanuts, and macadamias in surprising ways, both sweet and savory: Hazelnut butter thickens a lamb stew, walnut butter shows up in an apple tart, and macadamia butter appears in cookies. "The more you experiment with these adaptable nut butters, the more you'll love them," Lorrie says.

Thai Noodles with Peanut Sauce

- 8 ounces uncooked rice noodles
- ½ cup roasted peanuts
- 1 cup vegetable broth
- 2 tablespoons brown sugar
- 1 tablespoon grated peeled fresh ginger
- 1 teaspoon red curry paste
- ¾ teaspoon salt
- 1 garlic clove, minced
- 1 tablespoon rice wine vinegar
- 1½ pounds medium shrimp, peeled and deveined
- 1 large red bell pepper, cut into thin strips
- ¾ cup finely chopped seeded peeled cucumber
- ¼ cup sliced green onions
- ¼ cup chopped fresh basil
- 2 tablespoons chopped dry-roasted peanuts
- 1 lime, cut into 6 wedges

1. Cook noodles in boiling water 6 minutes. Rinse and drain. Keep warm.

2. Place ½ cup peanuts in a food processor; process until smooth (about 2 minutes), scraping sides of bowl once.

3. Combine peanut butter, broth, and next 5 ingredients in a large skillet; bring to a boil. Reduce heat; simmer 1 minute. Pour broth mixture into a blender or food processor; let stand 5 minutes. Process until smooth. Stir in vinegar.

4. Cook shrimp in boiling water 2 minutes or until done; drain.

5. Combine noodles, shrimp, bell pepper, cucumber, onions, and basil in a large bowl. Add peanut sauce; toss gently to coat. Sprinkle with chopped nuts; serve with lime wedges. Yield: 6 servings (serving size: 1⅓ cups noodle mixture, 1 teaspoon chopped nuts, and 1 lime wedge).

CALORIES 369 (24% from fat); FAT 9.9g (sat 1.4g, mono 4.1g, poly 3.2g); PROTEIN 30.7g; CARB 39.1g; FIBER 1.9g; CHOL 172mg; IRON 4.3mg; SODIUM 633mg; CALC 87mg

Macadamia Butter Cookies with Dried Cranberries

These cookies are as humble as peanut butter cookies but not as crumbly. The dough is somewhat sticky; chilling it briefly makes handling easier.

- ⅔ cup macadamia nuts
- ½ cup granulated sugar
- ½ cup packed light brown sugar
- 1 teaspoon vanilla extract
- 1 large egg
- 1¼ cups all-purpose flour
- ½ teaspoon baking soda
- ¼ teaspoon salt
- ⅛ teaspoon ground nutmeg
- ½ cup sweetened dried cranberries, chopped
- 1 tablespoon granulated sugar

1. Preheat oven to 375°.

2. Place nuts in a food processor; process until smooth (about 2 minutes), scraping sides of bowl once. Combine macadamia butter, ½ cup granulated sugar, and brown sugar in a large bowl; beat with a mixer at medium speed. Add vanilla and egg; beat well.

3. Lightly spoon flour into dry measuring cups; level with a knife. Combine flour, baking soda, salt, and nutmeg, stirring with a whisk. Add flour mixture to sugar mixture; beat at low speed just until combined (mixture will be very thick). Stir in cranberries. Chill 10 minutes.

4. Divide chilled dough into 30 equal portions; roll each portion into a ball. Place 1 tablespoon granulated sugar in a small bowl. Lightly press each ball into sugar. Place 15 balls, sugar side up, on each of 2 baking sheets covered with parchment paper.

5. Gently press top of each cookie with a fork. Dip fork in water; gently press top of each cookie again to form a criss-cross pattern.

6. Bake cookies, 1 baking sheet at a time, at 375° for 9 minutes or until golden. Remove cookies from pans; cool on wire racks. Yield: 30 servings (serving size: 1 cookie).

CALORIES 76 (30% from fat); FAT 2.5g (sat 0.4g, mono 1.8g, poly 0.1g); PROTEIN 1g; CARB 13.2g; FIBER 0.6g; CHOL 7mg; IRON 0.5mg; SODIUM 44mg; CALC 7mg

Nut Butter Primer

Cashew: The smooth butter forms after about 2 minutes of processing. It's ideal for sandwiches. Try it with avocado and other vegetables in a pita, or substitute it for tahini when you make hummus.

Almond: Roasted whole almonds have skins that will fleck the butter. When the almonds start to come away from the sides of the food processor, the butter is ready. Slivered, toasted almonds take about 3½ minutes to form a butter, but roasted whole almonds have additional oil and will be ready in just 2½ minutes. This mild, sweet butter is adaptable in sweet and savory dishes. Try almond butter on a sandwich with apples and Brie or Gouda cheese.

Macadamia: Hands down, this is our favorite nut butter—we actually licked the spoon. Because of macadamias' high fat content, the nuts grind into a butter too thin for spreading on bread in just 2

minutes. Chill to thicken it. Its buttery flavor is great for desserts.

Hazelnut: This grainy, thick butter with brown specks is fruity and naturally sweet. Processing the nuts takes about 2½ minutes. Bags of chopped nuts have few skins, so don't worry about removing them. If nuts are whole, toast them in a 400° oven for 5 minutes or until they start to look shiny and the skins begin to loosen. Rub them in a dishtowel to remove skins. Mix a 1 to 1 ratio of chocolate syrup and hazelnut butter for a delicious spread that's great on toasted honey wheat bread with bananas or on apple wedges.

Pecan: With a rich, hearty flavor that stands up well, pecan butter is great over meats. Pecans process into butter in about 1 minute. The loose paste spreads easily, but skins give it a slightly bitter aftertaste, so it's best to use it in recipes.

Peanut: Use plain roasted peanuts, rather than dry-roasted peanuts, which are seasoned with paprika, garlic, and onion powder. This smooth nut butter has distinctive fresh peanut flavor, and the nuts take about 2 minutes to process. It's lighter in color than commercial peanut butters and is grainier than commercial hydrogenated brands.

Pistachio: A very dry, crumbly butter, it's best combined with something else, like softened cream cheese. Cream cheese—pistachio spread is nice on French or egg bread. It takes about 3½ to 4 minutes to grind into butter. It tends to clump during processing.

Walnut: Like pecan butter, this soft, oily butter is ready in about 1 minute. It, too, has a bitter aftertaste from the skins, making it good for recipes but not on sandwiches. Walnut halves are expensive, so look for pieces.

search myclar2003.com for all our tips

Chocolate Lava Cakes with Pistachio Cream

These flourless chocolate cakes are as rich as a restaurant dessert, but they're made with a fraction of the fat and no dairy butter. When these cakes bake, the gooey filling causes the center to sink in.

1 cup shelled dry-roasted pistachios
1¾ cups granulated sugar, divided
¼ cup unsweetened cocoa
2 large eggs, lightly beaten
5 large egg whites, lightly beaten
2 ounces bittersweet chocolate, coarsely chopped
½ teaspoon baking powder
½ teaspoon vanilla extract
Cooking spray
1 cup 2% reduced-fat milk
Dash of salt
Powdered sugar (optional)

1. Place pistachios in a food processor; process until a crumbly paste forms (about 3½ minutes), scraping sides of bowl once (makes about ½ cup).

2. Remove ¼ cup pistachio butter from processor, and place in top of a double boiler. Add 1¼ cups granulated sugar, cocoa, eggs, and egg whites to double boiler; stir well with a whisk. Add chocolate; cook over simmering water until chocolate melts and sugar dissolves

(about 3 minutes). Remove from heat; add baking powder and vanilla. Stir with a whisk until smooth. Spoon batter into 12 muffin cups coated with cooking spray. Chill 2 hours.

3. Add ½ cup granulated sugar to ¼ cup pistachio butter remaining in food processor; pulse 4 times or until combined. Add milk and salt; process until smooth. Strain mixture through a sieve into a small saucepan; discard solids. Bring to a boil. Reduce heat; simmer 4 minutes or until thick. Remove from heat; pour into a bowl. Cover and chill.

4. Preheat oven to 450°.

5. Bake cakes at 450° for 9 minutes or until almost set (centers will not be firm). Cool in pan 5 minutes. Invert each cake onto a dessert plate; drizzle with sauce. Garnish with powdered sugar, if desired. Yield: 12 servings (serving size: 1 cake and 2 teaspoons sauce).

CALORIES 232 (30% from fat); FAT 7.7g (sat 2.2g, mono 3.1g, poly 1.5g); PROTEIN 6.1g; CARB 37.2g; FIBER 2g; CHOL 37mg; IRON 0.9mg; SODIUM 73mg; CALC 51mg

Fettuccine with Cashew Cream

Delicious, easy, and fast—and much better for you than a creamy sauce like Alfredo. Cashew cream (a mixture of water and cashew nut butter) replaces the traditional heavy cream in this recipe, with no loss of richness and an improved fat profile. In a typical fettuccine Alfredo, 60 percent of the fat is saturated; less than a quarter of the fat in the cashew cream is saturated.

½ cup roasted cashews
1¼ cups water
Cooking spray
3 garlic cloves, minced
4 cups hot cooked fettuccine (about 8 ounces uncooked pasta)
¼ cup (1 ounce) grated fresh Parmesan cheese
¼ teaspoon freshly ground black pepper
⅛ teaspoon salt

1. Place cashews in a food processor; process until smooth (about 2 minutes), scraping sides of bowl once. With processor on, add water; process until smooth, scraping sides of bowl once.
2. Place cashew cream in a small saucepan over medium-high heat. Bring to a boil, stirring occasionally with a whisk. Reduce heat; simmer 1 minute or until cream is thick.
3. Heat a large nonstick skillet coated with cooking spray over medium-high heat. Add garlic; sauté 30 seconds. Stir in cashew cream, pasta, cheese, pepper, and salt; cook until thoroughly heated. Yield: 4 servings (serving size: about 1⅓ cups).

CALORIES 378 (35% from fat); FAT 14.7g (sat 3.6g, mono 7g, poly 1.9g); PROTEIN 14.7g; CARB 51g; FIBER 2.7g; CHOL 6mg; IRON 3.5mg; SODIUM 388mg; CALC 128mg

Chicken with Pecan Cream and Mushrooms

A simple chicken sauté gets an elegant makeover. You can also serve it with rice or orzo to soak up the sauce. This sauce is also great made with roasted almond butter.

¾ cup coarsely chopped pecans, toasted
1 cup water
1¼ teaspoons salt, divided
6 (4-ounce) skinless, boneless chicken breast halves
1 teaspoon freshly ground black pepper
Cooking spray
¼ cup finely chopped shallots
1 (8-ounce) package presliced mushrooms
4 cups cooked egg noodles
Chopped fresh parsley (optional)

1. Place pecans in a food processor; process until smooth (about 1 minute), scraping sides of bowl once. With processor on, add water and ¾ teaspoon salt; process until smooth, scraping sides of bowl once.
2. Sprinkle chicken with ½ teaspoon salt and pepper.
3. Heat a large nonstick skillet coated with cooking spray over medium-high heat. Add chicken; sauté 3 minutes on each side or until done. Remove chicken from pan; keep warm.
4. Add shallots and mushrooms to pan; sauté 3 minutes or until mushrooms are tender. Stir in pecan cream; bring to a boil. Cook 1½ minutes. Place ⅔ cup noodles on each of 6 plates. Top each serving with 1 chicken breast half and ⅓ cup sauce. Garnish with parsley, if desired. Yield: 6 servings.

CALORIES 378 (30% from fat); FAT 12.8g (sat 1.6g, mono 6.5g, poly 3.8g); PROTEIN 33.9g; CARB 31.2g; FIBER 3.7g; CHOL 101mg; IRON 3.4mg; SODIUM 573mg; CALC 32mg

Lamb Stew with Hazelnut Butter and Dates

Ground hazelnuts flavor and thicken this sweet, rich stew. Dried fruits add sweetness to the flavor, so cut back on the dates if you want a more savory stew. Serve over couscous or rice.

⅔ cup coarsely chopped hazelnuts, toasted
Cooking spray
1½ pounds lean lamb stew meat, cubed
2½ cups chopped onion
¾ teaspoon salt
¼ teaspoon ground cinnamon
¼ teaspoon ground allspice
¼ teaspoon crushed red pepper
3 garlic cloves, crushed
2 (14-ounce) cans fat-free, less-sodium chicken broth
2½ cups (½-inch) cubed peeled turnips (about 1 pound)
2½ cups small red potatoes, halved (about 1 pound)
1½ cups baby carrots, peeled
½ cup whole pitted dates, chopped
2 cups water
1½ cups frozen green peas

1. Place hazelnuts in a food processor; process until smooth (about 2½ minutes), scraping sides of bowl once.
2. Heat a large Dutch oven coated with cooking spray over high heat. Add lamb; cook 5 minutes, browning on all sides. Reduce heat to medium-high. Add onion and next 5 ingredients; sauté 7 minutes or until onion is lightly browned.
3. Add hazelnut butter and broth to pan; stir well, scraping pan to loosen browned bits. Stir in turnips, potatoes, carrots, dates, and 2 cups water; bring to a boil.
4. Reduce heat to medium. Cover and simmer 15 minutes. Uncover and simmer 1 hour and 20 minutes, or until lamb is tender and sauce has thickened. Stir in peas; simmer 5 minutes. Yield: 8 servings (serving size: about 1 cup).

CALORIES 361 (29% from fat); FAT 11.8g (sat 2.5g, mono 6.7g, poly 1.4g); PROTEIN 28.4g; CARB 36.7g; FIBER 608g; CHOL 69mg; IRON 3.8mg; SODIUM 518mg; CALC 65mg

Apple and Walnut Cream Tart

The nuts are toasted to deepen the color of the slightly gray walnut butter.

⅔ cup coarsely chopped walnuts
½ cup sugar
¼ cup 2% reduced-fat milk
⅛ teaspoon salt
1 large egg, lightly beaten
2 tablespoons sugar
½ teaspoon ground cinnamon
Cooking spray
6 sheets frozen phyllo dough, thawed
1 tablespoon butter
5 cups sliced peeled Granny Smith apple (about 2 pounds)
⅓ cup raisins
3 tablespoons sugar

1. Preheat oven to 400°.
2. Place walnuts in a single layer on a jelly roll pan. Bake at 400° for 5 minutes or until toasted; cool. Reduce oven temperature to 350°.
3. Place walnuts in a food processor; process until smooth (about 1 minute), scraping sides of bowl once.
4. Combine walnut butter, ½ cup sugar, milk, salt, and egg; stir well with a whisk.
5. Combine 2 tablespoons sugar and cinnamon. Coat a 9-inch pie plate with cooking spray. Working with 1 phyllo sheet at a time, coat sheet with cooking spray; sprinkle with 1 teaspoon cinnamon mixture.
6. Fold phyllo sheet in half lengthwise to form a 13 x 8½-inch rectangle. Gently press folded phyllo sheet into prepared pan, allowing ends to extend over edges; coat phyllo with cooking spray. Repeat procedure with remaining phyllo sheets and cinnamon mixture, arranging folded phyllo sheets in a crisscross pattern. Fold edges of phyllo under.
7. Melt butter in a large nonstick skillet over medium-high heat. Add apple; sauté 5 minutes or until lightly browned. Add raisins and 3 tablespoons sugar; cook 2 minutes, stirring occasionally.
8. Cool apple mixture slightly; arrange in pan on phyllo crust. Pour egg mixture over apples. Bake at 350° for 50 minutes or until center is set. Cool 15 minutes before serving. Yield: 10 servings (serving size: 1 wedge).

CALORIES 209 (30% from fat); FAT 7g (sat 1.6g, mono 1g, poly 3.7g); PROTEIN 2.9g; CARB 36g; FIBER 1.7g; CHOL 25mg; IRON 0.8mg; SODIUM 103mg; CALC 23mg

Smokey Turkey Almond Mole

Serve this saucy dish over rice tossed with chopped green onions. You can also use cooked chicken. If you like your mole really hot, use a whole chipotle chile. This freezes well, so make a double batch and save half for later.

½ cup roasted almonds
½ teaspoon vegetable oil
2 dried Anaheim chiles, stemmed, seeded, and chopped
1 cup chopped onion
1 garlic clove, crushed
1 (7-ounce) can chipotle chiles in adobo sauce
1½ cups fire-roasted crushed tomatoes (such as Muir Glen)
1 tablespoon sugar
½ teaspoon ground cumin
¼ teaspoon salt
⅛ teaspoon ground cloves
2 (6-inch) corn tortillas, torn into small pieces
1 (14½-ounce) can vegetable broth
1 tablespoon white wine vinegar
3 cups chopped cooked turkey breast
Cilantro sprigs (optional)

1. Place almonds in a food processor; process until smooth (about 2½ minutes), scraping sides of bowl once. Set aside.
2. Heat oil in a large nonstick skillet over medium-high heat. Add Anaheim chiles; sauté 1 minute or until softened. Add onion and garlic; sauté 4 minutes or until onion is lightly browned.
3. Remove 1 chipotle chile from can; cut chile in half. Add 1 chile half to onion mixture. Reserve remaining chiles and adobo sauce for another use. Add tomatoes and next 6 ingredients to onion mixture; bring to a boil. Reduce heat; simmer 15 minutes, stirring occasionally.
4. Spoon mixture into food processor; process until smooth. Return mixture to pan; stir in almond butter and vinegar. Cook 1 minute. Stir in turkey. Garnish with cilantro, if desired. Yield: 4 servings (serving size: 1 cup).

CALORIES 366 (30% from fat); FAT 12.1g (sat 1.3g, mono 6.2g, poly 3g); PROTEIN 40.7g; CARB 25.9g; FIBER 6.2g; CHOL 94mg; IRON 4.2mg; SODIUM 737mg; CALC 117mg

Butters in a Nutshell

Making nut butters: Just grind nuts in a food processor until they form a paste. Some nut butters will be creamy; others, a bit grainy. The higher the fat, the smoother the butter will be.

Commercial vs. fresh: We'd planned on using commercial nut butters for these recipes, but after a side-by-side tasting with homemade butters, we abandoned that idea. Homemade nut butters taste much better but are more perishable than commercial varieties, so make them in small batches. Store homemade butters covered in the refrigerator for up to a month. To make spreading easier, let nut butters return to room temperature. As a general rule, there is a 2 to 1 ratio of nuts used to the nut butter yield (1 cup nuts will make ½ cup nut butter, for example). To toast nuts, spread them on a baking sheet, and bake at 400° for 5 minutes.

Making nut creams: Whisk about 1 cup water into ¼ cup nut butter to create a nut cream, a good substitute for heavy cream in pasta sauces and desserts. Start with neutral-flavored cashew or almond butter, then branch out to more flavorful nuts.

search myclar2003.com for all our tips

Vegetarian West African Soup

This hearty one-dish meal is packed with fiber and can be ready in less than an hour.

⅔ cup roasted peanuts
2 teaspoons vegetable oil
2 cups chopped onion
6 cups (1-inch) cubed peeled sweet potato
1 tablespoon ground cumin
½ teaspoon black pepper
¼ teaspoon salt
2 (15½-ounce) cans chickpeas (garbanzo beans), drained
2 (14½-ounce) cans vegetable broth
1 (28-ounce) can diced tomatoes, undrained
Flat-leaf parsley sprigs (optional)

1. Place peanuts in a food processor; process until smooth (about 2 minutes), scraping sides of bowl once.
2. Heat oil in a Dutch oven over medium-high heat. Add onion; sauté 7 minutes or until lightly browned. Add peanut butter, potato, and next 6 ingredients; bring to a boil. Reduce heat; simmer, uncovered, 30 minutes or until potato is tender. Garnish with parsley, if desired. Yield: 8 servings (serving size: 1½ cups).

CALORIES 477 (18% from fat); FAT 9.4g (sat 1.3g, mono 3.5g, poly 3.3g); PROTEIN 13g; CARB 89.7g; FIBER 13.1g; CHOL 0mg; IRON 3.2mg; SODIUM 904mg; CALC 110mg

Chicken Pasanda

Yogurt combines with cashew cream to replace heavy cream in this fragrant and traditional Pakistani dish. The spicy chicken is accompanied with fresh pineapple and the mellow cashew-yogurt sauce. Use the pita wedges to scoop up the remaining sauce.

½ cup roasted cashews
2 cups plain low-fat yogurt
1 cup coarsely chopped onion
¼ cup fresh lemon juice
2 tablespoons chopped peeled fresh ginger
2 jalapeño peppers, seeded
2½ teaspoons ground coriander seeds
¾ teaspoon ground cardamom
¾ teaspoon ground cinnamon
½ teaspoon black pepper
¼ teaspoon ground cloves
1 teaspoon salt, divided
6 (4-ounce) skinless, boneless chicken breast halves, cut into thirds
2 teaspoons vegetable oil
1 cup cubed fresh pineapple
2 tablespoons chopped cashews, roasted
2 tablespoons chopped fresh cilantro
4 (6-inch) pitas, each cut into 6 wedges

1. Place ½ cup cashews in a food processor; process until smooth (about 2 minutes), scraping sides of bowl once. Add yogurt; process until well blended. Remove from processor; set aside.
2. Combine onion, juice, ginger, and jalapeño in a blender or food processor; process until finely chopped.
3. Combine coriander and next 4 ingredients in a large zip-top plastic bag; add ½ teaspoon salt and chicken. Seal bag, and shake to coat.
4. Heat oil in a large nonstick skillet over medium-high heat; add chicken pieces. Cook 4 minutes on each side or until done. Remove chicken from pan, and keep warm.
5. Add onion mixture to pan. Reduce heat to medium; cook 3 minutes or until liquid evaporates, stirring frequently. Add ½ teaspoon salt and yogurt mixture to pan; cook 3 minutes or until heated, stirring frequently.
6. Spoon ½ cup yogurt mixture onto each of 6 plates. Top each serving with 3 chicken pieces. Sprinkle each serving with about 2½ tablespoons pineapple, 1 teaspoon chopped cashews, and 1 teaspoon cilantro. Arrange 4 pita wedges on each plate. Yield: 6 servings.

CALORIES 368 (27% from fat); FAT 11g (sat 2.5g, mono 4.5g, poly 2.5g); PROTEIN 27.7g; CARB 40.3g; FIBER 2.9g; CHOL 51mg; IRON 3.2mg; SODIUM 708mg; CALC 206mg

november

All About Grains

Don't know barley from bulgur? Here's a guide to versatile grains, from amaranth to wheat berries.

Most of us know that grains are good for us but have difficulty naming more than two or three. And if the most common side dishes you serve with chicken are pasta and potatoes, maybe a lesson in grains is in order. Here, we offer some simple recipes and tips on where to find and how to cook grains, and explore a few of the most versatile—from the everyday (wheat) to the exotic (quinoa).

Bulgur and Lamb Meatballs in Tomato Sauce

Refrigerating the meat mixture makes it easier to handle and helps the meatballs hold their shape. You can use fine or medium bulgur in this recipe. Serve with rice.

MEATBALLS:

2 cups water
1 cup uncooked bulgur
1 cup chopped fresh parsley
2 tablespoons chopped fresh dill
¾ teaspoon salt
½ teaspoon freshly ground black pepper
10 ounces lean ground lamb
2 large egg whites, lightly beaten
2 garlic cloves, minced

SAUCE:

2 teaspoons olive oil
1 cup finely chopped onion
1 garlic clove, minced
½ cup dry red wine
½ cup water
⅛ teaspoon ground cinnamon
1 (28-ounce) can diced tomatoes, undrained

1. To prepare meatballs, soak bulgur in 2 cups water 2 minutes; drain through a fine sieve. Combine bulgur, parsley, and next 6 ingredients. Cover and chill 30 minutes. Shape lamb mixture into 18 (1-inch) meatballs; cover and chill 30 minutes.

2. To prepare sauce, heat oil in a Dutch oven over medium heat. Add onion; cook 5 minutes, stirring occasionally. Add 1 minced garlic clove; cook 3 minutes, stirring frequently. Add wine; bring to a boil. Cook 2 minutes. Stir in ½ cup water, cinnamon, and tomatoes.

3. Add meatballs; bring to a boil. Cover, reduce heat, and simmer 10 minutes. Turn meatballs; cover and cook 10 minutes. Yield: 6 servings (serving size: 3 meatballs and about 1⅓ cups sauce).

CALORIES 309 (38% from fat); FAT 13g (sat 5g, mono 5.7g, poly 1g); PROTEIN 14.2g; CARB 32.4g; FIBER 5.7g; CHOL 34mg; IRON 4.4mg; SODIUM 515mg; CALC 55mg

---

Buying and Storing Grains

In the past, you would have had to go to a health or natural foods store to buy these grains, but now you can find many of them at the supermarket. Arrowhead Mills and Bob's Red Mill are two commonly available brands. Grains—especially whole ones—have oils that eventually turn rancid. Shop at stores where the turnover seems high, and buy only what you plan to use within a few months. If you have space, it's best to refrigerate grains, but you still can't keep them forever. You can tell if they've lost their freshness by their smell—old grains, including flours, will have a stale odor.

Wheat Berry Bread

This is a hearty sandwich bread. Cooked wheat berries add texture, and the wheat bran gives the surface a nice rustic finish. The recipe makes two loaves, so you can freeze one for later.

3 cups water
¾ cup uncooked wheat berries
1 package dry yeast (about 2¼ teaspoons)
1 cup 2% reduced-fat milk
2 tablespoons dark honey (such as buckwheat)
2½ teaspoons salt
3 cups bread flour, divided
2 cups whole wheat flour
1 cup amaranth flour
Cooking spray
2 tablespoons bread flour
2 tablespoons wheat bran

1. Combine water and wheat berries in a saucepan; bring to a boil. Cover, reduce heat, and simmer 1 hour or until tender. Drain wheat in a colander over a bowl, reserving 1 cup cooking liquid; set wheat berries aside.

2. Let reserved cooking liquid stand until warm (100° to 110°). Stir yeast into cooking liquid.

3. Combine milk, honey, and salt in a small, heavy saucepan, stirring with a whisk until honey and salt dissolve. Heat milk mixture over medium heat until warm (100° to 110°). Add milk mixture to yeast mixture, stirring with a whisk; let stand 5 minutes.

4. Lightly spoon 3 cups bread flour, whole wheat flour, and amaranth flour into dry measuring cups; level with a knife. Stir 2½ cups bread flour, whole wheat flour, and amaranth flour into yeast mixture.

5. Turn dough out onto a floured surface. Knead until smooth and elastic (about 10 minutes); add up to ½ cup bread flour, 1 tablespoon at a time, to prevent dough from sticking to hands (dough will feel tacky).

6. Place dough in a large bowl coated with cooking spray, turning to coat top. Cover and let rise in a warm place (85°), free from drafts, 1 hour or until doubled in size. (Press two fingers into dough. If indentation remains, dough has risen enough.)

7. Punch dough down; cover and let rest 5 minutes. Coat two 9 x 5-inch loaf pans with cooking spray; dust each with 1 tablespoon bread flour.

8. Divide dough in half. Working with 1 portion at a time (cover remaining dough to keep from drying), knead half of wheat berries into dough; place dough in prepared pan. Sprinkle dough with 1 tablespoon wheat bran. Repeat procedure with remaining dough, wheat berries, and wheat bran. Cover and let rise 45 minutes or until doubled in size.

9. Preheat oven to 375°.

10. Bake at 375° for 45 minutes or until golden. Cool loaves in pans 10 minutes on a wire rack; remove from pans. Cool completely on wire rack. Yield: 2 loaves, 9 slices per loaf (serving size: 1 slice).

CALORIES 198 (6% from fat); FAT 1.4g (sat 0.3g, mono 0.2g, poly 0.4g); PROTEIN 7.2g; CARB 39.8g; FIBER 3.9g; CHOL 1mg; IRON 3.6mg; SODIUM 334mg; CALC 37mg

Grano with Mushrooms and Greens

Grano is the polished form of durum wheat, so its flavor is similar to that of pasta. You may substitute pearl barley.

- 2½ cups fat-free, less-sodium chicken broth
- 1½ tablespoons olive oil
- 1⅓ cups chopped onion
- 3¼ cups chopped mushrooms (about 1 [8-ounce] package)
- 1 cup grano
- ½ cup dry white wine
- 6 cups chopped kale
- ½ teaspoon salt
- 2 garlic cloves, minced
- 2 tablespoons chopped fresh parsley
- 1 tablespoon chopped fresh marjoram
- 1 tablespoon butter
- ¼ teaspoon freshly ground black pepper

1. Bring broth to a simmer in a small saucepan.

2. Heat oil in a Dutch oven over medium heat. Add onion; cook 5 minutes, stirring occasionally. Add mushrooms; cook 3 minutes, stirring occasionally. Stir in grano and wine; cook until liquid almost evaporates (about 2 minutes), stirring frequently. Stir in broth. Cover, reduce heat, and simmer 25 minutes.

3. Add kale, salt, and garlic; cook 6 minutes or until kale is tender, stirring frequently. Add parsley and remaining ingredients. Yield: 5 servings (serving size: 1 cup).

CALORIES 215 (26% from fat); FAT 6.3g (sat 1.7g, mono 3.1g, poly 0.7g); PROTEIN 9.2g; CARB 33.9g; FIBER 3.9g; CHOL 5mg; IRON 2.9mg; SODIUM 436mg; CALC 108mg

Rye Berry Salad with Orange Vinaigrette

Any of the whole grains—or a mix of them—will work in this salad. Substitute raisins if you don't have currants.

- 3 cups water
- 1 cup uncooked rye berries or wheat berries
- 1 cup hot water
- 3 tablespoons dried currants
- 1½ cups finely chopped celery
- ¼ cup chopped fresh parsley
- ¾ teaspoon salt, divided
- ¼ teaspoon freshly ground black pepper
- ¼ cup finely chopped shallots
- 1 tablespoon grated orange rind
- 1 tablespoon fresh orange juice
- 2 teaspoons Champagne vinegar or white wine vinegar
- 2 tablespoons olive oil

1. Combine 3 cups water and rye berries in a saucepan; bring to a boil. Cover, reduce heat, and simmer 1 hour. Drain.

2. Combine 1 cup hot water and currants in a small bowl; let stand 30 minutes. Drain well.

3. Combine rye berries, currants, celery, parsley, ½ teaspoon salt, and pepper.

4. Combine ¼ teaspoon salt, shallots, rind, juice, and vinegar in a small bowl, stirring well. Let stand 5 minutes. Stir in oil with a whisk. Pour shallot mixture over rye mixture; toss well to coat. Yield: 6 servings (serving size: about ⅔ cup).

CALORIES 174 (27% from fat); FAT 5.3g (sat 0.6g, mono 3.3g, poly 0.4g); PROTEIN 4.8g; CARB 29.3g; FIBER 5.2g; CHOL 0mg; IRON 1.8mg; SODIUM 329mg; CALC 41mg

Oats and Buttermilk Snack Cake

Soaking steel-cut oats in buttermilk softens them but still preserves a nice crunch. This cake makes a great afternoon snack or—with a maple syrup glaze—dessert.

- 1½ cups buttermilk
- ½ cup steel-cut oats
- ½ cup oat flour
- 1 cup all-purpose flour
- 1 teaspoon baking powder
- ½ teaspoon baking soda
- ½ teaspoon salt
- ⅔ cup packed brown sugar
- ¼ cup butter, softened
- 1½ teaspoons vanilla extract
- 1 large egg
- Cooking spray
- 1 tablespoon powdered sugar (optional)

1. Combine buttermilk and oats; cover and refrigerate 8 hours.

2. Preheat oven to 375°.

3. Lightly spoon flours into a dry measuring cup; level with a knife. Combine flours, baking powder, baking soda, and salt, stirring with a whisk.

4. Place brown sugar and butter in a large bowl; beat with a mixer at medium speed until light and fluffy. Add vanilla and egg; beat until well blended. Stir in oat mixture; beat until well blended. Add flour mixture, beating just until moist.

5. Spoon batter into a 13 x 9-inch baking pan coated with cooking spray. Bake at 375° for 30 minutes or until a wooden pick inserted in center comes out clean. Cool 10 minutes in pan on a wire rack. Cut into squares. Garnish with powdered sugar, if desired. Yield: 12 servings (serving size: 1 square).

CALORIES 176 (27% from fat); FAT 5.2g (sat 2.8g, mono 1.5g, poly 0.4g); PROTEIN 4.1g; CARB 28.9g; FIBER 1.4g; CHOL 29mg; IRON 1.3mg; SODIUM 266mg; CALC 69mg

A Guide to Grains

Amaranth [AM-ah-ranth] was a principal food of the Aztecs. It has a slightly peppery, molasses-like flavor with a faint nuttiness. The grains (or seeds) are tiny and shiny, and can be yellow and black. They're so small that they seem almost lost when served alone as a side dish. But amaranth is good as a thickener in soups because, when cooked, it has a slightly gummy texture, like okra. Try amaranth flour, along with wheat berries, in Wheat Berry Bread (recipe on page 322).

Barley is best known as an ingredient in beer and soup. Creamy and possessing a fairly neutral flavor when cooked, pearl barley is easy to serve in place of rice; because it's so starchy, pearl barley can be treated just like Arborio rice for risotto. Whole barley, with its protective layer of bran intact, plumps nicely when cooked. Barley flour, when toasted, has a strong nutty flavor; try adding it to breads. A great source of fiber, ½ cup of pearl barley offers more than 12 grams.

Bulgur is familiar to many of us through the Middle Eastern dishes *tabbouleh* and *kibbeh*. Bulgur is wheat that has been steamed whole, dried, then cracked. So bulgur is essentially precooked and quick to prepare. It comes in three grinds—fine, medium, and coarse. Fine and medium bulgurs are used for tabbouleh, and the coarse is good in pilafs. Bulgur, especially fine bulgur, needs only to be soaked to become tender, but it can also be cooked pilaf-style. You can find bulgur in Middle Eastern markets as well as natural foods stores.

Grano [gra-NO] is probably unfamiliar to most Americans, since it's a new product in the United States. *Grano* (Italian for "grain") is essentially polished durum wheat (a variety of wheat used to make pasta), and most reminiscent of barley. It has a golden hue and an appealing chewiness when cooked. Because the bran has been removed, the starch is more accessible, which means you can cook grano as you would Arborio rice for risotto. Or you can simmer it without stirring, which leaves the grains intact. It provides a nice combination of texture and neutral flavor. Use grano in soups, stews, salads, and other dishes in which you might use a small pasta such as orzo. Grano has yet to appear on supermarket shelves, but is available at www.sunnylandmills.com.

Kamut [kah-MOOT] is a primitive high-protein variety of wheat and takes its name from the ancient Egyptian word for wheat. Kamut berries are about twice the size of, but similar in flavor and texture to, wheat berries. Substitute kamut for wheat berries, and buy kamut flour to use in place of or alongside wheat flour. Spelt, another primitive form of wheat similar to kamut, has become fashionable among restaurant chefs. Both kamut and spelt contain a more digestible form of gluten than that found in wheat, so people with an intolerance to wheat are often able to eat these grains.

Oats are most widely available in rolled form. Steel-cut oats are cracked whole grain oats; when cooked, they're chewy. They're also called Irish oatmeal. A good source of fiber, ½ cup of steel-cut oats has 7.5 grams. You may also see oat groats or whole grain oats.

Quinoa [KEEN-wah] tastes wonderful and has a nice crunch. It's a good alternative to rice because of its lightness. Make more than you need for a recipe because the leftovers are so useful. (Try it for breakfast with maple syrup and milk, add it to pancake and muffin batter, or mix it with potatoes for croquettes.) The tiny beige-colored seeds, about the size of pellets of couscous, cook in about 20 minutes. The only special handling required with quinoa is to give it a good rinse before cooking; otherwise, the grains can be bitter. A good source of protein and fiber, ½ cup of quinoa has 14 grams of protein and 6 grams of fiber.

Rye is most commonly seen as flour. Also available are whole rye berries, which are green and work nicely in salads. Rye berries are a lot like wheat berries, kamut berries, and other whole grains—chewy and neutral in flavor, they hold their shape when cooked. Like wheat berries, they can be added to breads. Rye is now often available rolled as well. Rolled rye cooks quickly and makes tasty breakfast cereals. Rye ferments easily, so it's not surprising that it's used to make whiskey.

Wheat is the world's largest cereal grass crop, with thousands of varieties. Wheat berries are simply whole grain wheat. They're big, chewy, and take about an hour to cook. Once cooked, they can go in salads, soups, and in mixed-grain dishes. They're also great kneaded into bread, providing welcome texture. Wheat bran, the exterior layer of the grain, is rich in fiber.

search myclar2003.com for all our tips

Beef, Beer, and Barley Stew

You can use barley groats rather than pearl barley in this stew. Substitute rutabagas, parsnips, or other root vegetables of your choice for the carrots and turnips.

- 2 tablespoons olive oil
- 1 pound beef stew meat
- 1 teaspoon salt, divided
- ¼ teaspoon black pepper
- 3 cups coarsely chopped onion
- 2 bay leaves
- 2 thyme sprigs
- 2 tablespoons tomato paste
- 2 cups (1½-inch-thick) slices carrot
- 2 cups chopped peeled turnips (about 1 pound)
- ¾ cup uncooked pearl barley
- 5 garlic cloves, minced and divided
- 2 (8-ounce) packages mushrooms, quartered
- 3 cups water
- 3 cups low-salt beef broth
- 2 tablespoons Worcestershire sauce
- 1 (12-ounce) bottle dark beer (such as Guiness Stout)
- 3 small beets
- 3 tablespoons chopped fresh parsley
- 1 teaspoon thyme leaves
- 2 tablespoons prepared horseradish

1. Heat oil in a stockpot over medium-high heat. Sprinkle beef with ½ teaspoon salt and pepper. Add beef to pan; sauté 10 minutes or until browned. Remove from pan. Add onion, bay leaves, and thyme sprigs to pan. Cover, reduce heat, and cook 10 minutes, stirring occasionally.
2. Uncover; stir in tomato paste. Increase heat to medium-high. Add carrot, turnips, barley, 4 garlic cloves, and mushrooms; sauté 3 minutes. Add beef, ½ teaspoon salt, water, broth, Worcestershire, and beer; bring to a boil. Reduce heat; simmer, covered, 1½ hours. Discard bay leaves and thyme sprigs.
3. While stew is simmering, trim beets, leaving root and 1 inch stem on each; scrub with a brush. Place in a medium saucepan, and cover with water; bring to a boil. Cover, reduce heat, and simmer 35 minutes or until tender. Drain; rinse with cold water. Drain; cool. Leave root and stem on beets; rub off skins. Cut each beet into 6 wedges.
4. Combine parsley, thyme leaves, and 1 garlic clove. Ladle about 2 cups stew into each of 6 bowls. Top each serving with 3 beet wedges, about 1½ teaspoons parsley mixture, and 1 teaspoon horseradish. Yield: 6 servings.

CALORIES 379 (27% from fat); FAT 11.4g (sat 2.9g, mono 6g, poly 1.1g); PROTEIN 24.5g; CARB 45.2g; FIBER 10.2g; CHOL 47mg; IRON 4.8mg; SODIUM 654mg; CALC 85mg

Quinoa and Potato Croquettes

Serve this meatless main dish with coleslaw. If you can't find panko, use fresh breadcrumbs.

- 1 (10-ounce) baking potato
- 2 cups water
- 1 cup uncooked quinoa, rinsed
- ½ teaspoon salt
- 4 teaspoons vegetable oil, divided
- ½ cup thinly sliced green onions
- ⅓ cup chopped fresh cilantro
- 1 jalapeño pepper, seeded and finely chopped
- 1 teaspoon ground cumin
- ½ teaspoon dried oregano
- ½ teaspoon freshly ground black pepper
- 2 garlic cloves, minced
- ½ cup 1% low-fat cottage cheese, drained
- 3 tablespoons grated extra-sharp cheddar cheese
- 1 large egg, lightly beaten
- 1 cup panko (Japanese breadcrumbs)

1. Pierce potato with a fork; place on paper towels in microwave oven. Microwave at HIGH 5 minutes or until fork pierces potato easily, turning potato after 3 minutes. Wrap in a towel; let stand 5 minutes. Peel and mash potato.
2. Bring 2 cups water to a boil in a saucepan; add quinoa and salt. Cook 15 minutes; drain.
3. Heat 1 teaspoon oil in a large nonstick skillet over medium-high heat. Add onions, cilantro, and jalapeño; sauté 1 minute. Add cumin, oregano, black pepper, and garlic; sauté 1 minute. Combine potato, quinoa, onion mixture, cottage cheese, and cheddar cheese in a bowl, stirring well. Let stand 5 minutes; stir in egg.
4. Shape into 10 patties. Carefully dredge each patty in panko. Place on a baking sheet. Cover and chill 10 minutes.
5. Heat 1½ teaspoons oil in skillet over medium heat. Add 5 patties to pan; cook 2 minutes on each side or until golden brown. Keep warm. Repeat procedure with remaining oil and patties. Yield: 5 servings (serving size: 2 croquettes).

CALORIES 346 (23% from fat); FAT 8.9g (sat 1.9g, mono 1.8g, poly 3.1g); PROTEIN 13g; CARB 53.6g; FIBER 4.1g; CHOL 48mg; IRON 3.8mg; SODIUM 450mg; CALC 85mg

Kamut, Lentil, and Chickpea Soup

Substitute spelt, grano, or wheat berries for the kamut.

- ¾ cup kamut berries, rinsed
- 2 cups boiling water
- 2 tablespoons olive oil
- 2 cups finely chopped onion
- 1 cup finely chopped carrot
- ¾ cup chopped fresh parsley
- ½ cup thinly sliced celery
- 1 tablespoon chopped fresh tarragon
- 2 teaspoons chopped fresh thyme
- 2 garlic cloves, minced
- 4 (14-ounce) cans fat-free, less-sodium chicken broth
- 2 bay leaves
- ⅓ cup dried lentils
- ¼ teaspoon black pepper
- 1 (15-ounce) can chickpeas (garbanzo beans), rinsed and drained
- 2 teaspoons chopped celery leaves (optional)

Continued

1. Place kamut in a small bowl. Carefully pour boiling water over kamut. Let stand 30 minutes; drain.
2. Heat oil in a stockpot over medium heat. Add onion and next 5 ingredients; cook 10 minutes, stirring occasionally. Add garlic; cook 2 minutes, stirring often.
3. Add kamut, broth, and bay leaves to onion mixture; bring to a boil. Cover, reduce heat, and simmer 30 minutes. Add lentils and pepper; cook 20 minutes or until lentils are tender. Discard bay leaves. Add chickpeas; simmer 2 minutes. Garnish with celery leaves, if desired. Yield: 5 servings (serving size: about 1⅔ cups).

CALORIES 298 (21% from fat); FAT 7g (sat 1g, mono 4.3g, poly 1.2g); PROTEIN 15.2g; CARB 44.4g; FIBER 9.2g; CHOL 0mg; IRON 3.8mg; SODIUM 824mg; CALC 76mg

---

Processing Grains

When we refer to grains, we mean grains in their most natural form. To put this into perspective, it helps to know how grains are processed.

Whole grains and **groats** are interchangeable terms for **unrefined grains.** Because the bran, endosperm, and germ are intact, they're higher in fiber and minerals than other forms. Whole grains take longer to cook than refined forms. Examples of whole grains include wheat berries, whole grain rye, and buckwheat groats.

Polished grains include pearl barley and brown rice. These grains have been refined. This makes them less chewy and quicker to cook than whole grains.

Cracked grains, such as bulgur and steel-cut oats, result when grains are ground into smaller pieces. Some cracked grains are derived from whole grains, others from refined grains.

Flakes are sliced whole grains or cracked grains that have been steamed and rolled. Rolled oats are probably the most familiar, but you'll also find rolled barley, wheat, and rye.

Flour is grain that has been milled to a powder. Whole wheat flour is the product of processing whole wheat berries.

Buckwheat Pilaf with Pecans

Unlike wheat berries, rye berries, and kamut, buckwheat groats cook quickly and are light in texture. Sauté them with egg whites to ensure that the grains stay separate and to keep them from dissolving into one another. Serve this pilaf with roasted chicken, pork, or any other dish with which you'd serve rice pilaf.

1 (14-ounce) can fat-free, less-sodium chicken broth
1½ cups uncooked kasha (buckwheat groats)
2 large egg whites, lightly beaten
2 tablespoons butter, divided
1 teaspoon salt, divided
½ cup matchstick-cut carrots
¼ cup chopped pecans
1 cup sliced mushrooms
1 cup chopped green onions
2 cups hot cooked brown basmati rice
3 tablespoons chopped fresh parsley
1 teaspoon chopped fresh thyme
½ teaspoon freshly ground black pepper

1. Bring broth to a simmer in a large saucepan (do not boil). Keep warm over low heat.
2. Heat a large nonstick skillet over medium heat. Combine kasha and egg whites in a bowl; add to skillet. Cook 3 minutes or until grains are dry and separate, stirring constantly.
3. Add kasha mixture, 1 tablespoon butter, and ½ teaspoon salt to broth; bring to a boil. Cover, reduce heat, and simmer 10 minutes or until liquid is absorbed. Remove from heat; let stand 5 minutes.
4. Melt 1 tablespoon butter in skillet over medium heat. Add carrots and pecans; cook 3 minutes, stirring frequently. Add mushrooms and onions; cook 3 minutes, stirring occasionally.
5. Combine kasha mixture, carrot mixture, ½ teaspoon salt, rice, and remaining ingredients in a large bowl, stirring well. Yield: 8 servings (serving size: 1 cup).

CALORIES 234 (25% from fat); FAT 6.9g (sat 2.3g, mono 2.5g, poly 0.9g); PROTEIN 7.8g; CARB 38g; FIBER 4.3g; CHOL 9mg; IRON 2mg; SODIUM 376mg; CALC 65mg

---

dinner tonight

Fish Fare

Versatile, quick-cooking fish offers a welcome respite from the season's usual fare.

Miso-Glazed Salmon Menu
serves 4
Miso-Glazed Salmon
Wasabi mashed potatoes*
Steamed bok choy

*Place 2 pounds cubed red potato in a large saucepan; cover with water. Bring to a boil; cook 15 minutes or until tender. Drain. Place potato, ¼ cup fat-free, less-sodium chicken broth, ¼ cup reduced-fat sour cream, 2 tablespoons butter, 1 teaspoon wasabi paste, ½ teaspoon salt, and ¼ teaspoon black pepper in a bowl. Mash to desired consistency.

Game Plan

1. While water comes to a boil for potato and oven heats for fish:
 • Prepare miso mixture for fish
 • Combine flavorings for mashed potatoes in a large bowl
2. While potato and fish cook:
 • Steam bok choy
 • Chop chives

Miso-Glazed Salmon

A sweet-salty miso, brown sugar, and soy sauce glaze caramelizes in about 10 minutes as it cooks atop this rich, meaty salmon.

TOTAL TIME: 17 MINUTES

¼ cup packed brown sugar
2 tablespoons low-sodium soy sauce
2 tablespoons hot water
2 tablespoons miso (soybean paste)
4 (6-ounce) salmon fillets (about 1 inch thick)
Cooking spray
1 tablespoon chopped fresh chives

1. Preheat broiler.
2. Combine first 4 ingredients, stirring with a whisk. Arrange fish in a shallow baking dish coated with cooking spray. Spoon miso mixture evenly over fish.
3. Broil 10 minutes or until fish flakes easily when tested with a fork, basting twice with miso mixture. Sprinkle with chives. Yield: 4 servings.

CALORIES 297 (33% from fat); FAT 10.9g (sat 2.5g, mono 4.7g, poly 2.8g); PROTEIN 32.4g; CARB 15.7g; FIBER 0.3g; CHOL 80mg; IRON 1mg; SODIUM 742mg; CALC 29mg

---

Creole Cod Menu
serves 4
Creole Cod

Steamed fingerling potatoes

Warm cabbage slaw*

*Heat 2 teaspoons olive oil in a large nonstick skillet over medium-high heat. Add 1 (16-ounce) package coleslaw and ½ teaspoon salt; sauté 3 minutes or until coleslaw wilts. Remove from heat. Stir in 2 tablespoons chopped green onions, 1 tablespoon sugar, 3 tablespoons cider vinegar, and 1 tablespoon capers.

Game Plan

1. While water comes to a boil for potatoes and oven heats for fish:
 • Prepare Creole mixture for fish
 • Juice lemon for fish
2. While fish bakes, steam potatoes and prepare slaw

Creole Cod

The mildness of cod takes well to bold flavorings such as Dijon mustard and Creole seasoning. Lemon juice, added after cooking, brightens the flavor.

TOTAL TIME: 22 MINUTES

QUICK TIP: If you can't find Creole seasoning, make your own: Combine 1 tablespoon paprika with 1 teaspoon each of salt, onion powder, garlic powder, dried oregano, ground red pepper, and black pepper. Store in an airtight container.

2 teaspoons olive oil
2 teaspoons Dijon mustard
½ teaspoon salt
½ teaspoon Creole seasoning blend (such as Spice Island)
4 (6-ounce) cod fillets (about 1 inch thick)
Cooking spray
1 tablespoon fresh lemon juice
Chopped fresh parsley (optional)

1. Preheat oven to 400°.
2. Combine first 4 ingredients; brush evenly over fish.
3. Place fish on a foil-lined baking sheet coated with cooking spray. Bake at 400° for 17 minutes or until fish flakes easily when tested with a fork. Drizzle juice evenly over fish; garnish with parsley, if desired. Yield: 4 servings.

CALORIES 148 (21% from fat); FAT 3.5g (sat 0.4g, mono 1.9g, poly 0.6g); PROTEIN 27.2g; CARB 0.8g; FIBER 0.1g; CHOL 55mg; IRON 0.5mg; SODIUM 523mg; CALC 16mg

---

Grouper and Vegetables Menu
serves 4
Pan-Roasted Grouper with Provençale Vegetables

Spinach-mushroom salad*

French bread

*Combine 6 cups torn spinach, 1 cup sliced mushrooms, and ½ cup thinly sliced red onion. Combine ⅓ cup fat-free ranch dressing, ¼ cup (1 ounce) grated fresh Parmesan cheese, and ½ teaspoon freshly ground black pepper; spoon over salad. Toss gently to combine.

Game Plan

1. While oven heats:
 • Prepare vegetable mixture for fish
 • Wash spinach for salad
2. While vegetable mixture bakes, prepare fish
3. While fish and vegetables bake, prepare salad

search myclar2003.com for all our menus

Pan-Roasted Grouper with Provençale Vegetables

Use a broiler pan for both components of this recipe. The fennel-tomato mixture cooks in the bottom of the pan, helping to steam the fish on the rack above.

TOTAL TIME: 32 MINUTES

QUICK TIP: For easier pitting of the olives, mash each olive with the flat side of a knife—the pit will easily dislodge.

2 cups thinly sliced fennel bulb (about 1 medium bulb)
2 tablespoons fresh orange juice
16 picholine olives, pitted and chopped
1 (28-ounce) can whole tomatoes, drained and coarsely chopped
½ teaspoon salt, divided
½ teaspoon black pepper, divided
Cooking spray
2 teaspoons olive oil
1 garlic clove, minced
4 (6-ounce) grouper fillets (about 1 inch thick)

1. Preheat oven to 450°.
2. Combine first 4 ingredients. Add ¼ teaspoon salt and ¼ teaspoon pepper; toss well. Spoon mixture into bottom of a broiler pan coated with cooking spray. Bake at 450° for 10 minutes; stir once.
3. Combine ¼ teaspoon salt, ¼ teaspoon pepper, oil, and garlic; brush evenly over fish. Remove pan from oven. Place fish on rack of pan coated with cooking spray; place rack over fennel mixture.
4. Bake at 450° for 10 minutes or until fish flakes easily when tested with a fork. Yield: 4 servings (serving size: 1 grouper fillet and ¾ cup fennel mixture).

CALORIES 247 (25% from fat); FAT 6.9g (sat 0.7g, mono 3.4g, poly 2.1g); PROTEIN 33.6g; CARB 11.5g; FIBER 2.8g; CHOL 60mg; IRON 2.6mg; SODIUM 898mg; CALC 91mg

Halibut with Charmoula

Couscous tossed with
golden raisins

Frozen yogurt with spiced
honey and walnuts*

*Place ½ cup honey and ¼ teaspoon
pumpkin-pie spice in a microwave-safe
bowl. Microwave at HIGH 30 seconds or
until warm. Spoon ½ cup vanilla fat-free
frozen yogurt into each of 4 bowls, and
top each serving with 2 tablespoons
spiced honey and 1½ teaspoons chopped
toasted walnuts.

Game Plan

1. While oven heats for fish, prepare
sauce
2. While fish bakes:
- Prepare couscous
- Scoop frozen yogurt into bowls,
and place in freezer
- Toast walnuts for dessert
- Combine honey and spice
(microwave after dinner)

search myclar2003.com for all our menus

Halibut with Charmoula

Charmoula is a traditional Moroccan herb
sauce used to season or marinate fish.
TOTAL TIME: 23 MINUTES

SAUCE:
- 1 tablespoon olive oil
- 1 teaspoon paprika
- ½ teaspoon salt
- ½ teaspoon ground cumin
- ½ teaspoon black pepper
- 2 garlic cloves
- 1 cup loosely packed fresh flat-leaf parsley leaves
- 1 cup loosely packed fresh cilantro leaves
- 2 tablespoons capers
- 2 teaspoons grated lemon rind
- ¼ cup fresh lemon juice

FISH:
- 4 (6-ounce) halibut fillets (about 1 inch thick)
- ¼ teaspoon salt
- ¼ teaspoon black pepper
- Cooking spray

GARNISH:
Parsley sprigs (optional)

1. Preheat oven to 350°.
2. To prepare sauce, combine first 6 ingredients in a food processor; process until garlic is finely chopped. Add parsley leaves, cilantro, capers, rind, and juice; pulse until herbs are coarsely chopped.
3. To prepare fish, sprinkle fish with ¼ teaspoon salt and ¼ teaspoon pepper. Place fish on a foil-lined baking sheet coated with cooking spray.
4. Bake at 350° for 15 minutes or until fish flakes easily when tested with a fork. Serve fish with sauce. Garnish with parsley sprigs, if desired. Yield: 4 servings (serving size: 1 halibut fillet and 1 tablespoon sauce).

CALORIES 234 (29% from fat); FAT 7.6g (sat 1.1g, mono 3.8g, poly 1.6g); PROTEIN 36.6g; CARB 3.8g; FIBER 1.3g; CHOL 54mg; IRON 2.9mg; SODIUM 701mg; CALC 118mg

lighten up

Carrot Soufflé, by Popular Demand

We've revamped a favorite holiday side dish for the multitudes who asked.

Lighten Up usually sticks to a one-reader, one-recipe format. But since we received so many pleas to lighten this dish, we decided against singling out just one reader for the before-and-after. Here's the lightened version of the holiday favorite, Carrot Soufflé. While this dish isn't a true soufflé, it does have a soufflé-like consistency. It's similar to sweet potato casserole, a dish popular with both kids and adults.

BEFORE	AFTER
SERVING SIZE	
½ cup	
CALORIES PER SERVING	
289	187
FAT	
13.6g	5.1g
PERCENT OF TOTAL CALORIES	
42%	25%

Carrot Soufflé

Because this dish contains no beaten egg whites, it's not a true soufflé—the name is derived from its light, airy texture. Similar in color and flavor to sweet potato casserole, it pairs well with ham or turkey.

- 7 cups chopped carrot (about 2 pounds)
- ⅔ cup granulated sugar
- ¼ cup fat-free sour cream
- 3 tablespoons all-purpose flour
- 2 tablespoons butter, melted
- 1 teaspoon baking powder
- 1 teaspoon vanilla extract
- ¼ teaspoon salt
- 3 large eggs, lightly beaten
- Cooking spray
- 1 teaspoon powdered sugar

1. Preheat oven to 350°.
2. Cook carrot in boiling water 15 minutes or until very tender; drain. Place carrot in a food processor; process until smooth. Add granulated sugar and next 7 ingredients; pulse to combine.
3. Spoon mixture into a 2-quart baking dish coated with cooking spray. Bake at 350° for 40 minutes or until puffed and set. Sprinkle with powdered sugar. Yield: 8 servings (serving size: ½ cup).

CALORIES 187 (25% from fat); FAT 5.1g (sat 2.5g, mono 1.6g, poly 0.5g); PROTEIN 4.2g; CARB 32.3g; FIBER 3.5g; CHOL 88mg; IRON 1.1mg; SODIUM 233mg; CALC 86mg

Celery Salad, page 361

Sourdough Stuffing with Apples and Ham, page 349

Cranberry, Apple, and Walnut Relish, page 350

Herbed Turkey with Roasted Garlic Gravy, page 348

Green Beans with Caramelized Onions, page 350

Oat Bran Muffins,
page 337

Cider-Glazed Carrots,
page 335

Rosemary-Lemon Cornish Hens with
Roasted Potatoes, page 361

Pumpkin Cake with Cream Cheese
Glaze, page 336

Pecan and Date Pie,
page 336

In the Best Tradition

This classic holiday menu features your favorite dishes.

Y ou've got a few minutes to make one last check of the table before the turkey comes out of the oven. There's your grandmother's gravy boat, the one she used every Thanksgiving when you were little, and your mother's cut-glass jelly dish. In half an hour the table will be ringed with the people you love most, all talking at the same time and all delighting in this homey and familiar menu.

Thanksgiving with the Family Menu
serves 12

Brined Maple Turkey with Cream Gravy

Old-Fashioned Mashed Potatoes

New England Sausage Stuffing with Chestnuts

Cider-Glazed Carrots

Roasted Brussels Sprouts with Ham and Garlic

Cranberry-Fig Relish

Potato Rolls

Pecan and Date Pie

Pumpkin Cake with Cream Cheese Glaze

Brined Maple Turkey with Cream Gravy

Brining makes for a juicier bird, and the subtle flavors of the brine soak into the turkey. Kosher salt works well for the brine because it dissolves more easily than table salt. If you have the time and refrigerator space, the brining procedure is worthwhile. If not, the turkey will still be quite good.

BRINE:
- 8 quarts water
- ¾ cup kosher salt
- ¾ cup maple syrup
- 3 tablespoons black peppercorns
- 8 garlic cloves, crushed
- 1 lemon, thinly sliced

TURKEY:
- 1 (12-pound) fresh or thawed frozen turkey
- 1 cup cola
- ½ cup maple syrup
- 2 tablespoons minced fresh thyme
- 1 tablespoon dried rubbed sage
- 1 tablespoon poultry seasoning
- ½ teaspoon black pepper
- 4 garlic cloves, chopped
- 2 onions, quartered
- Cooking spray

GRAVY:
- 1 (14-ounce) can fat-free, less-sodium chicken broth
- 1 cup whole milk
- 2 tablespoons cornstarch
- ¼ teaspoon salt
- ¼ teaspoon black pepper

1. To prepare brine, combine first 6 ingredients in a stockpot; stir until salt dissolves.

2. To prepare turkey, remove and reserve giblets and neck from turkey. Rinse turkey with cold water; pat dry. Trim excess fat. Add turkey to pot, turning to coat. Cover and refrigerate 24 hours, turning occasionally.

3. Preheat oven to 375°.

4. Bring cola and ½ cup syrup to a boil in a small saucepan; cook 1 minute.

5. Combine thyme, sage, seasoning, and ½ teaspoon pepper. Remove turkey from brine; pat dry. Starting at neck cavity, loosen skin from breast and drumsticks by inserting fingers, gently pushing between skin and meat. Rub thyme mixture under loosened skin; sprinkle inside body cavity. Place chopped garlic and onions in body cavity. Tie ends of legs together with twine. Lift wing tips up and over back; tuck under turkey.

6. Place turkey on a broiler pan coated with cooking spray. Insert a meat thermometer into meaty part of a thigh, making sure not to touch bone. Bake at 375° for 45 minutes. Pour cola mixture over turkey; cover with foil. Bake an additional 1 hour and 45 minutes or until thermometer registers 180°. Remove turkey from pan, reserving drippings for gravy. Place turkey on a platter. Cover loosely with foil; let stand 10 minutes. Remove twine. Discard skin.

7. To prepare gravy, while turkey bakes, combine reserved giblet and neck and broth in a saucepan; bring to a boil. Cover, reduce heat, and simmer 45 minutes. Strain mixture through a colander into a bowl, discarding solids.

8. Place a zip-top plastic bag inside a 2-cup glass measure. Pour pan drippings into bag; let stand 10 minutes (fat will rise to top).

9. Seal bag; carefully snip off 1 bottom corner of bag. Drain drippings into broiler pan, stopping before fat layer reaches opening; discard fat. Add broth mixture. Place broiler pan on stovetop over medium heat, scraping pan to loosen browned bits. Combine milk and cornstarch in a small bowl, stirring well with a whisk; add to pan. Bring to a boil; cook 1 minute, stirring mixture constantly.

Continued

10. Strain gravy through a sieve into a bowl; discard solids. Stir in ¼ teaspoon salt and ¼ teaspoon pepper. Yield: 12 servings (serving size: 6 ounces turkey and about ¼ cup gravy).

WINE NOTE: The sweet and savory flavors of this old-fashioned turkey dinner call for a soft, rich Zinfandel with a lot of berry flavors. Try Ridge "Geyserville" Zinfandel 1999 (Sonoma County, California; $30). If your budget is a bit more modest, try Bogle "Old Vine" Zinfandel 2000 (California; $11).

CALORIES 375 (25% from fat); FAT 10.5g (sat 3.6g, mono 2.5g, poly 2.8g); PROTEIN 51.7g; CARB 15.7g; FIBER 0.2g; CHOL 140mg; IRON 3.6mg; SODIUM 809mg; CALC 91mg

Old-Fashioned Mashed Potatoes

Nothing fancy here—just good, basic mashed potatoes that are great as is or topped with the gravy from the turkey (recipe on page 333). For extra flavor, sprinkle with chopped chives.

  5 pounds cubed peeled baking potato
  ¾ cup warm 2% reduced-fat milk
  2 tablespoons butter
1½ teaspoons salt
  ¾ teaspoon black pepper

1. Place potato in a medium saucepan; cover with water. Bring to a boil. Reduce heat; simmer 15 minutes or until tender; drain.
2. Combine milk, butter, salt, and pepper in a large bowl. Add potato; let stand 5 minutes or until butter melts.
3. Beat potato mixture with a mixer at medium speed until smooth. Yield: 12 servings (serving size: about ¾ cup).

CALORIES 169 (13% from fat); FAT 2.4g (sat 1.4g, mono 0.7g, poly 0.2g); PROTEIN 3.4g; CARB 34.2g; FIBER 3g; CHOL 6mg; IRON 0.6mg; SODIUM 329mg; CALC 33mg

---

Thanksgiving Countdown

Up to one month ahead:
• Make and freeze Potato Rolls.

Up to five days ahead:
• Prepare and refrigerate Cranberry-Fig Relish (stir in the toasted pecans just before serving).

The morning before:
• Place turkey in brine.

The day before:
• Julienne and cook carrots; refrigerate in a zip-top plastic bag.
• Trim and halve Brussels sprouts; refrigerate in a zip-top plastic bag.
• Make and toast breadcrumbs for Brussels sprouts; store at room temperature in an airtight container or zip-top plastic bag.
• Make Pumpkin Cake with Cream Cheese Glaze (garnish with orange wedges before serving).

Thanksgiving morning:
• Make Pecan and Date Pie.
• Boil cola-syrup mixture for turkey.

• Peel and cube potatoes. Place in a saucepan; cover with cold water.
• Toast chestnuts and bread cubes for stuffing.

A few hours before:
• Put turkey in oven (tent cooked turkey with foil to keep warm).
• Simmer broth mixture for gravy while turkey bakes.
• Thaw rolls at room temperature.

Last minute:
• Finish gravy; keep warm.
• Prepare mashed potatoes.
• Prepare Cider-Glazed Carrots.
• Cook stuffing and Brussels sprouts together in oven.
• Garnish cake with orange slices, if desired.
• Toast pecans and stir into Cranberry-Fig Relish.
• Heat thawed rolls in oven during last 12 minutes of cooking time for the stuffing and Brussels sprouts.

New England Sausage Stuffing with Chestnuts

If you've never made stuffing with chestnuts, give it a try. Here, their sweetness contrasts with the savory sausage. You can also use fresh chestnuts, if you prefer.

  1 cup coarsely chopped bottled chestnuts
  1 (16-ounce) loaf French bread, cut into 1-inch cubes
  6 ounces mild pork sausage
  3 cups chopped onion
  2 cups chopped celery
1½ cups fat-free, less-sodium chicken broth
  1 tablespoon dried rubbed sage
  1 teaspoon dried thyme
  ½ teaspoon salt
  ½ teaspoon black pepper
    Cooking spray

1. Preheat oven to 375°.
2. Arrange chopped chestnuts and bread cubes in a single layer on a jelly roll pan. Bake at 375° for 10 minutes or until lightly browned.
3. Cook sausage in a large nonstick skillet over medium-high heat 4 minutes or until browned, stirring to crumble. Add onion and celery; sauté 6 minutes or until tender. Add broth, scraping pan to loosen browned bits.
4. Combine bread mixture, sausage mixture, sage, thyme, salt, and pepper, tossing to combine. Spoon into a 13 x 9-inch baking pan coated with cooking spray; cover with foil. Bake at 375° for 20 minutes. Uncover and bake an additional 10 minutes or until golden brown. Yield: 12 servings (serving size: about ⅔ cup).

CALORIES 214 (30% from fat); FAT 7.2g (sat 2.4g, mono 3.2g, poly 1.2g); PROTEIN 6.4g; CARB 30.6g; FIBER 3g; CHOL 10mg; IRON 1.5mg; SODIUM 498mg; CALC 55mg

Cider-Glazed Carrots

(pictured on page 330)

Cider vinegar gives these carrots the flavor of an apple cider reduction, but in a fraction of the time. To get a head start, boil the carrots a day ahead. Refrigerate them in a zip-top plastic bag, then sauté just before serving.

 9 cups (3-inch) julienne-cut carrot
    (about 2½ pounds)
 ¼ cup packed brown sugar
 2 tablespoons butter
 2 tablespoons cider vinegar
 ½ teaspoon dry mustard
 ½ teaspoon paprika
 ¼ teaspoon salt
 ¼ teaspoon celery seeds
 1 tablespoon chopped fresh
    parsley

1. Place carrot in a large saucepan; cover with water. Bring to a boil. Reduce heat; simmer 1 minute or until tender. Drain.
2. Combine brown sugar and next 6 ingredients in a large nonstick skillet over low heat; cook until butter melts, stirring frequently. Bring to a boil.
3. Reduce heat to medium; add carrot. Cook 3 minutes or until glazed and thoroughly heated, stirring constantly. Sprinkle with chopped parsley; toss to combine. Yield: 12 servings (serving size: about ⅔ cup).

CALORIES 75 (26% from fat); FAT 2.2g (sat 1.2g, mono 0.6g, poly 0.2g); PROTEIN 1g; CARB 14g; FIBER 2.8g; CHOL 5mg; IRON 0.6mg; SODIUM 103mg; CALC 31mg

Roasted Brussels Sprouts with Ham and Garlic

Roasting brings out the best in Brussels sprouts. It lightly caramelizes their edges but keeps them tender inside. Don't trim too much from the stem ends of the sprouts, since they may fall apart. Country ham imparts saltiness to the dish; if it's unavailable in your market, substitute regular ham. Freeze leftover toasted breadcrumbs for up to 6 months; use them to top macaroni and cheese and casseroles.

 1 (1-ounce) slice white bread
 3 pounds Brussels sprouts, trimmed
    and halved
 ¼ cup finely chopped country ham
    (about 1 ounce)
 2 tablespoons fresh lemon juice
 1 teaspoon olive oil
 ½ teaspoon salt
 3 garlic cloves, thinly sliced
    Cooking spray
 2 tablespoons grated fresh Parmesan
    cheese

1. Preheat oven to 425°.
2. Place bread in a food processor; pulse 2 times or until crumbly. Sprinkle crumbs on a baking sheet; bake at 425° for 5 minutes or until golden. Reduce oven temperature to 375°. Set aside 3 tablespoons breadcrumbs, reserving remaining breadcrumbs for another use.
3. Combine sprouts and next 5 ingredients in a 3-quart baking dish coated with cooking spray, tossing to coat. Bake at 375° for 30 minutes or until sprouts are tender and lightly browned on edges, stirring twice.
4. Combine 3 tablespoons breadcrumbs and Parmesan cheese; sprinkle over sprouts. Serve immediately. Yield: 12 servings (serving size: ¾ cup).

CALORIES 58 (19% from fat); FAT 1.2g (sat 0.4g, mono 0.5g, poly 0.2g); PROTEIN 4.4g; CARB 9.6g; FIBER 3.6g; CHOL 2mg; IRON 1.4mg; SODIUM 211mg; CALC 57mg

Cranberry-Fig Relish

Toasted pecans add a pleasing crunch to this fruity condiment. If you make it a few days ahead, leave out the nuts until just before serving so they'll remain crunchy. Leftovers are great on a turkey sandwich with horseradish or cream cheese.

 1 cup fresh orange juice (about
    4 oranges)
 ¾ cup chopped dried figs
 ½ cup dry red wine
 ½ cup granulated sugar
 ¼ cup packed brown sugar
 1 (12-ounce) package fresh
    cranberries
 ⅓ cup chopped pecans, toasted

1. Combine first 3 ingredients in a medium saucepan; bring to a boil. Cover, reduce heat, and simmer 10 minutes.
2. Add sugars and cranberries. Cook over medium heat 10 minutes or until mixture is slightly thick and berries pop, stirring occasionally. Cool slightly. Stir in pecans. Cover and chill. Yield: 12 servings (serving size: ¼ cup).

CALORIES 128 (18% from fat); FAT 2.6g (sat 0.2g, mono 1.4g, poly 0.8g); PROTEIN 1g; CARB 27.4g; FIBER 3g; CHOL 0mg; IRON 0.6mg; SODIUM 4mg; CALC 30mg

Potato Rolls

Adding potato to the dough creates a light texture. Bake these rolls up to 1 month ahead. Cool completely, wrap in heavy-duty aluminum foil, and freeze. Thaw completely, and reheat (still wrapped in foil) at 375° for 12 minutes or until warm. Try using the leftover rolls to make miniature sandwiches with turkey and relish.

 2 cups cubed peeled baking potato
 4 teaspoons sugar, divided
 1 package dry yeast (about 2¼
    teaspoons)
 4¼ cups bread flour, divided
 3 tablespoons butter, melted
 1½ teaspoons salt
 1 large egg, lightly beaten
    Cooking spray
 2 tablespoons bread flour

1. Place potato in a medium saucepan; cover with water. Bring to a boil. Reduce heat; simmer 15 minutes or until tender. Drain in a colander over a bowl, reserving 1 cup cooking liquid. Mash potatoes with a fork.
2. Cool reserved cooking liquid to 105° to 115°. Stir in 1 teaspoon sugar and yeast. Let stand 5 minutes.
3. Lightly spoon 4¼ cups flour into dry measuring cups; level with a knife. Combine mashed potato, yeast mixture, 1 tablespoon sugar, 4 cups flour, butter, salt, and egg in a large bowl, stirring until well blended.
4. Turn dough out onto a floured surface. Knead until smooth and elastic
Continued

(about 10 minutes); add up to ¼ cup flour, 1 tablespoon at a time, to prevent dough from sticking to hands (dough will feel tacky).

5. Place dough in a large bowl coated with cooking spray, turning to coat top. Cover and let rise in a warm place (85°), free from drafts, 45 minutes or until doubled in size. (Press two fingers into dough. If indentation remains, dough has risen enough.) Punch dough down; cover and let rest 10 minutes.

6. Divide dough in half; divide each half into 12 equal portions. Working with 1 portion at a time (cover remaining dough to keep from drying), shape each portion into a 2-inch-long oval on a floured surface. Roll up tightly, starting with a long edge, pressing firmly to eliminate air pockets; pinch seam and ends to seal. Place rolls, seam side down, on 2 baking sheets coated with cooking spray, placing 12 rolls on each.

7. Sift 2 tablespoons flour over rolls to lightly coat. Cover rolls, and let rise 45 minutes or until doubled in size.

8. Preheat oven to 350°.

9. Bake at 350° for 10 minutes with 1 baking sheet on bottom rack and 1 baking sheet on second rack from top. Rotate baking sheets; bake an additional 10 minutes or until rolls are browned on bottom, lightly browned on top, and sound hollow when tapped. Remove from pans; cool on wire racks. Yield: 24 servings (serving size: 1 roll).

CALORIES 121 (16% from fat); FAT 2.1g (sat 1g, mono 0.6g, poly 0.3g); PROTEIN 3.6g; CARB 21.6g; FIBER 0.9g; CHOL 13mg; IRON 1.2mg; SODIUM 165mg; CALC 7mg

Pecan and Date Pie

(pictured on page 332)

The unexpected addition of dates to this classic pie gives the filling more body and a smooth sweetness. Don't use packaged chopped dates, which are rolled in sugar. Instead, use moist and sticky whole dates. Coat your knife with cooking spray for easy chopping.

CRUST:

1 cup all-purpose flour, divided
3 tablespoons ice water
1 teaspoon fresh lemon juice
2 tablespoons powdered sugar
¼ teaspoon salt
¼ cup vegetable shortening
Cooking spray

FILLING:

½ cup whole pitted dates, chopped
⅓ cup chopped pecans
1 cup dark corn syrup
½ cup packed brown sugar
3 tablespoons all-purpose flour
1 teaspoon vanilla extract
¼ teaspoon salt
4 large eggs

1. Preheat oven to 325°.

2. To prepare crust, lightly spoon 1 cup flour into a dry measuring cup; level with a knife. Combine ¼ cup flour, water, and juice, stirring with a whisk until well blended to form a slurry.

3. Combine ¾ cup flour, powdered sugar, and ¼ teaspoon salt; cut in shortening with a pastry blender or 2 knives until mixture resembles coarse meal. Add slurry; toss with a fork until mixture is moist. Slightly overlap 2 sheets of heavy-duty plastic wrap. Gently press dough into a 4-inch circle on plastic wrap; cover with 2 additional sheets of overlapping plastic wrap. Roll dough, still covered, into a 12-inch circle; freeze 10 minutes.

4. Remove top 2 sheets of plastic wrap; let dough stand 1 minute or until pliable. Fit dough, plastic-wrap side up, into a 9-inch pie plate coated with cooking spray. Remove remaining plastic wrap. Press dough into bottom and up sides of pan. Fold edges under; flute.

5. To prepare filling, sprinkle dates and pecans over crust. Combine syrup and remaining 5 ingredients in a large bowl; beat with a mixer at medium speed until well blended. Pour into prepared crust. Bake at 325° for 55 minutes or until a knife inserted 1 inch from edge comes out clean. Cool on a wire rack. Yield: 10 servings (serving size: 1 wedge).

CALORIES 321 (29% from fat); FAT 10.2g (sat 2.2g, mono 4.7g, poly 2.5g); PROTEIN 4.6g; CARB 55.8g; FIBER 1.5g; CHOL 85mg; IRON 1.5mg; SODIUM 198mg; CALC 33mg

Pumpkin Cake with Cream Cheese Glaze

(pictured on page 332)

The oranges are optional, but they add a burst of freshness to the cake. If you make the cake a day ahead, garnish with orange wedges shortly before serving. You can also bake the cake in a Bundt pan, but reduce the oven temperature to 325°.

CAKE:

1½ cups granulated sugar
½ cup butter, softened
¾ cup egg substitute
1 teaspoon vanilla extract
1 (15-ounce) can pumpkin
3 cups sifted cake flour
1 teaspoon baking powder
1 teaspoon baking soda
1 teaspoon ground cinnamon
½ teaspoon salt
¼ teaspoon ground ginger
¼ teaspoon ground nutmeg
Cooking spray

GLAZE:

½ cup powdered sugar
½ cup (4 ounces) ⅓-less-fat cream cheese, softened
½ teaspoon vanilla extract
3 tablespoons fresh orange juice

GARNISH:

Fresh orange sections (optional)

1. Preheat oven to 350°.

2. To prepare cake, place granulated sugar and butter in a large bowl; beat with a mixer at medium speed until well blended (about 5 minutes). Add egg substitute, ¼ cup at a time, beating well after each addition. Beat in 1 teaspoon vanilla and pumpkin.

3. Combine flour and next 6 ingredients, stirring well with a whisk. Fold flour mixture into pumpkin mixture.

4. Spoon batter into a 10-inch tube pan coated with cooking spray. Bake at 350° for 55 minutes or until a wooden pick inserted in cake comes out clean. Cool in pan 10 minutes on a wire rack. Remove from pan; place on wire rack.

5. To prepare glaze, place powdered sugar and cream cheese in a bowl; beat with a mixer at medium speed until well blended. Beat in ½ teaspoon vanilla. Add orange juice, 1 tablespoon at a time, beating well after each addition. Drizzle glaze over warm cake. Cool completely on wire rack. Garnish with orange sections, if desired. Yield: 16 servings (serving size: 1 slice).

CALORIES 236 (29% from fat); FAT 7.5g (sat 4.6g, mono 1.7g, poly 0.3g); PROTEIN 3.9g; CARB 38.8g; FIBER 1.5g; CHOL 21mg; IRON 1.8mg; SODIUM 295mg; CALC 41mg

reader recipes

Marvelous Muffins

These muffins are worth waking up to.

With flaxseed, carrot, apple, orange, and raisins, Oat Bran Muffins are more than just your typical breakfast muffin. Sharon Pederson of Vancouver Island, British Columbia, created this recipe as a way to incorporate better nutrition into her husband's snacks. You can easily double the recipe, and freeze some for later.

Oat Bran Muffins
(pictured on page 330)

    1   cup all-purpose flour
    1   cup whole wheat flour
 1¾   cups oat bran
   ¾   cup packed brown sugar
   ⅓   cup nonfat dry milk
   ¼   cup flaxseed
    4   teaspoons ground cinnamon
    2   teaspoons baking soda
    2   teaspoons baking powder
   ½   teaspoon salt
    2   cups shredded carrot
    2   cups chopped Granny Smith apple
    1   cup raisins
    1   cup fat-free milk
   ¼   cup canola oil
    2   teaspoons vanilla extract
    3   large egg whites
    1   thin-skinned orange, unpeeled and
        quartered
Cooking spray

1. Preheat oven to 375°.
2. Lightly spoon flours into dry measuring cups; level with a knife. Combine flours and next 8 ingredients in a large bowl, stirring well with a whisk. Stir in carrot, apple, and raisins.
3. Combine milk, oil, vanilla, egg whites, and orange in a blender or food processor; process until smooth. Make a well in center of flour mixture. Add milk mixture; stir just until moist.
4. Spoon 3 tablespoons batter into each of 28 muffin cups coated with cooking spray. Bake in batches at 375° for 20 minutes or until muffins are browned and spring back when touched lightly in center. Remove muffins from pans immediately, and place on a wire rack. Yield: 28 muffins (serving size: 1 muffin).

CALORIES 114 (22% from fat); FAT 2.8g (sat 0.3g, mono 1.3g, poly 0.8g); PROTEIN 3.5g; CARB 22.6g; FIBER 3g; CHOL 0mg; IRON 1.1mg; SODIUM 188mg; CALC 61mg

Angel Hair Pasta Delight

"When I created this recipe, I had recently discovered Asiago cheese and loved the flavor. It really makes a difference when added to a simple dish, and a little goes a long way."

—Somer Little, Palm Desert, California

    2   teaspoons olive oil
 1½   cups chopped Vidalia or other
        sweet onion
    3   garlic cloves, minced
   ¼   cup water
    1   (10-ounce) package fresh spinach,
        chopped
    2   cups chopped plum tomato
    2   cups chopped cooked chicken
        breast (about ½ pound)
   ¼   cup chopped cooked bacon (about
        2 slices)
    3   tablespoons balsamic vinegar
    4   cups hot cooked angel hair
        (about 8 ounces uncooked pasta)
   ¼   cup (1 ounce) shredded Asiago
        cheese

1. Heat oil in a large nonstick skillet over medium-high heat. Add onion; sauté 2 minutes. Add garlic; sauté 1 minute. Add water and spinach; cover and cook 2 minutes or until spinach wilts.
2. Stir in tomato, chicken, bacon, and vinegar; cook 1 minute or until thoroughly heated. Serve over pasta; sprinkle with cheese. Yield: 4 servings (serving size: 1 cup spinach mixture, 1 cup pasta, and 1 tablespoon cheese).

CALORIES 350 (21% from fat); FAT 8.1g (sat 2.4g, mono 2.6g, poly 0.8g); PROTEIN 26.4g; CARB 44.7g; FIBER 4.7g; CHOL 42mg; IRON 4.4mg; SODIUM 433mg; CALC 153mg

Garlic Chicken Pizza

"The first time I had a slice of garlic pizza in a restaurant in Juneau, Alaska, I knew I'd have to create my own version. After experimenting with the ingredients for more than five years, I finally came up with the ideal mix. I like Boboli crust the best, and these three cheeses work well together. I make this for my friends about once a month."

—Linda Salter, Richmond Hill, Georgia

    2   tablespoons red wine vinegar
 1½   tablespoons Dijon mustard
    4   garlic cloves, minced
    1   (16-ounce) Italian cheese-flavored
        pizza crust (such as Boboli)
 1½   cups shredded cooked chicken
        breast (about 8 ounces)
    1   cup chopped plum tomato
    1   cup chopped mushrooms
   ¾   cup (3 ounces) shredded part-skim
        mozzarella cheese
   ¼   cup (1 ounce) crumbled feta cheese
   ¼   cup (1 ounce) finely shredded
        fresh Parmesan cheese
   ¼   cup chopped green onions

1. Preheat oven to 400°.
2. Combine first 3 ingredients, stirring well with a whisk. Place crust on a baking sheet; brush vinegar mixture over crust. Top with chicken, tomato, and mushrooms; sprinkle with cheeses and green onions.
3. Bake at 400° for 15 minutes or until cheeses melt. Yield: 8 servings (serving size: 1 slice).

CALORIES 263 (27% from fat); FAT 7.8g (sat 3.6g, mono 2.8g, poly 0.9g); PROTEIN 19.9g; CARB 27.1g; FIBER 0.5g; CHOL 36mg; IRON 2.1mg; SODIUM 563mg; CALC 296mg

Parsley Red Potatoes

"This recipe is simple, economical, and delicious. It makes a colorful side dish for my roasted chicken. I serve steamed broccoli or carrots to finish out the meal."

—Susan Brooks, Arlington, Virginia

2 teaspoons olive oil
1 garlic clove, minced
2 cups small red potatoes, quartered
1½ tablespoons chopped fresh parsley
¼ teaspoon salt
Dash of crushed red pepper

1. Heat oil in a medium nonstick skillet over medium heat. Add garlic; cook 1 minute, stirring frequently. Add potato; cook 18 minutes or until tender, stirring frequently. Stir in parsley, salt, and pepper. Yield: 2 servings (serving size: 1 cup).

CALORIES 162 (26% from fat); FAT 4.7g (sat 0.7g, mono 3.3g, poly 0.5g); PROTEIN 3.3g; CARB 27.7g; FIBER 2.5g; CHOL 0mg; IRON 1.4mg; SODIUM 304mg; CALC 18mg

Todd's Chicken Fajitas

"I love to prepare foods that create a sense of celebration through their flavors and presentation. This recipe satisfies my love of Mexican food. It's a mouthwatering blend of flavors that complement one another."

—Todd Ehardt, Cheyenne, Wyoming

¼ cup low-sodium soy sauce
¼ cup Worcestershire sauce
3 tablespoons chopped fresh cilantro
¼ teaspoon black pepper
4 garlic cloves, crushed
1 (12-ounce) can light beer
4 (4-ounce) skinless, boneless chicken breast halves
Cooking spray
1½ cups (½-inch-thick) slices green bell pepper
1 cup (½-inch-thick) slices onion
4 (10-inch) flour tortillas
½ cup bottled salsa
¼ cup (1 ounce) shredded reduced-fat extra-sharp cheddar cheese
¼ cup fat-free sour cream

1. Combine first 6 ingredients in a large zip-top plastic bag; add chicken. Seal and marinate in refrigerator 8 hours or overnight, turning occasionally.
2. Prepare grill.
3. Remove chicken from bag; discard marinade. Place chicken on grill rack coated with cooking spray; grill 4 minutes on each side or until done. Cut chicken diagonally into thin strips. Place bell pepper and onion slices on grill rack; grill 2 minutes on each side or until lightly browned.
4. Warm tortillas according to package directions. Working with 1 tortilla at a time, place one-fourth of chicken strips, bell pepper, and onion in center of each tortilla. Top each serving with 2 tablespoons salsa, 1 tablespoon cheese, and 1 tablespoon sour cream; roll up. Yield: 4 servings.

CALORIES 316 (18% from fat); FAT 6.5g (sat 2.6g, mono 1.2g, poly 2g); PROTEIN 26.8g; CARB 33.5g; FIBER 1.7g; CHOL 56mg; IRON 3mg; SODIUM 847mg; CALC 146mg

Caribbean Rice

"This recipe was born when I was tossing around ideas for different side dishes for when we grilled. It's wonderful with jerk-style meats and with seafood because the sweetness of the coconut milk works well with the spices."

—Raquel Muszynski, Phoenix, Arizona

1¼ cups fat-free, less-sodium chicken broth
1 cup light coconut milk
1 cup long-grain parboiled rice (such as Uncle Ben's)
1 teaspoon olive oil
1 cup chopped onion
1¾ cups (¼-inch) cubed peeled butternut squash
1 teaspoon chopped fresh or ¼ teaspoon dried thyme
½ teaspoon salt
½ teaspoon ground turmeric
¼ teaspoon freshly ground black pepper
1 (15-ounce) can black beans, rinsed and drained

1. Bring broth and coconut milk to a boil in a medium saucepan over medium-high heat; add rice. Cover, reduce heat, and simmer 20 minutes or until liquid is absorbed. Remove from heat; keep warm.
2. Heat oil in a large nonstick skillet over medium-high heat. Add onion; sauté 5 minutes.
3. Reduce heat to medium. Add squash; cook 8 minutes or until tender, stirring occasionally. Stir in thyme and remaining 4 ingredients; cook 3 minutes or until thoroughly heated, stirring occasionally. Add rice to squash mixture, stirring to combine. Yield: 6 servings (serving size: about 1 cup).

CALORIES 186 (14% from fat); FAT 2.9g (sat 1.5g, mono 0.7g, poly 0.1g); PROTEIN 5.3g; CARB 36.8g; FIBER 3.3g; CHOL 0mg; IRON 2.3mg; SODIUM 502mg; CALC 32mg

Moo Shu Chicken with Vegetables

"My husband and I love stir-fried foods. I decided it's quicker to shred the vegetables instead of hand-chopping them."

—Heidi Smid, Travelers Rest, South Carolina

1 teaspoon dark sesame oil, divided
3 tablespoons hoisin sauce
3 tablespoons low-sodium soy sauce
2 tablespoons water
1 tablespoon orange marmalade
1½ teaspoons fresh lemon juice
1 teaspoon oyster sauce
½ teaspoon chicken-flavored bouillon granules
1 garlic clove, minced
½ pound skinless, boneless chicken breast, cut into bite-sized pieces
1½ cups chopped mushrooms
1½ cups very thinly presliced green cabbage
1 cup shredded carrot
1 cup shredded zucchini
6 (6-inch) fat-free flour tortillas

1. Combine ½ teaspoon oil, hoisin, and next 7 ingredients; stir well with a whisk.
2. Heat ½ teaspoon oil in a large nonstick skillet over medium-high heat. Add chicken; sauté 4 minutes or until done. Add

Add hoisin mixture to pan; cook 1 minute, stirring frequently. Add mushrooms, cabbage, carrot, and zucchini; cook 3 minutes, stirring occasionally.

3. Warm tortillas according to package directions. Spoon about ½ cup chicken mixture down center of each tortilla; roll up. Yield: 6 servings.

CALORIES 182 (10% from fat); FAT 2g (sat 0.3g, mono 0.5g, poly 0.7g); PROTEIN 12.8g; CARB 28.5g; FIBER 4g; CHOL 22mg; IRON 1mg; SODIUM 754mg; CALC 28mg

---

Casserole Supper Menu

Butternut Squash and Parsnip Baked Pasta

Kale with Lemon-Balsamic Butter (recipe on page 345)

Maple-Glazed Rutabaga (recipe on page 358)

Butternut Squash and Parsnip Baked Pasta

"This meatless dish combines two autumn vegetables that I love. It's warming, spicy, and very satisfying. It's homey enough to serve on weeknights and festive enough to serve during the holidays."

—A. Shvets, Urbana, Illinois

 1   tablespoon olive oil
 1   cup finely chopped onion
 ¼   teaspoon crushed red pepper
 2   garlic cloves, minced
 2   cups (½-inch) cubed peeled butternut squash
 1   cup chopped parsnip
 1   tablespoon chopped fresh or 1 teaspoon dried rubbed sage
 1   tablespoon chopped fresh or 1 teaspoon dried parsley
 ½   teaspoon salt, divided
 ½   teaspoon black pepper, divided
 ¼   teaspoon ground nutmeg
 ¼   teaspoon ground allspice
 2   cups uncooked penne pasta
 ½   cup (2 ounces) grated fresh Parmesan cheese, divided
 Cooking spray
 1½ tablespoons butter
 2   tablespoons all-purpose flour
 1   cup 1% low-fat milk

1. Preheat oven to 375°.

2. Heat oil in a large nonstick skillet over medium-high heat. Add onion, red pepper, and garlic; sauté 3 minutes. Add squash and parsnip; sauté 10 minutes. Stir in sage, parsley, ¼ teaspoon salt, ¼ teaspoon black pepper, nutmeg, and allspice; remove from heat.

3. Cook pasta according to package directions, omitting salt and fat. Drain in a colander over a bowl, reserving 1 cup cooking liquid. Combine squash mixture, pasta, and ¼ cup cheese in an 11 x 7-inch baking dish coated with cooking spray, tossing gently.

4. Melt butter in a medium saucepan over medium heat. Add flour; cook 3 minutes, stirring constantly with a whisk. Add milk; cook 5 minutes, stirring constantly with a whisk. Gradually add reserved cooking liquid; cook 2 minutes or until thick, stirring constantly with a whisk. Add ¼ teaspoon salt and ¼ teaspoon pepper.

5. Pour milk mixture over pasta mixture; sprinkle with ¼ cup cheese. Bake at 375° for 30 minutes or until lightly browned. Yield: 4 servings (serving size: 2 cups).

CALORIES 437 (28% from fat); FAT 13.4g (sat 6.1g, mono 5.1g, poly 1g); PROTEIN 16.5g; CARB 63.6g; FIBER 5.3g; CHOL 25mg; IRON 3.1mg; SODIUM 607mg; CALC 297mg

---

in season

Grand Berries

They're fresh for the holidays, but cranberries are at their best when cooked.

If you've ever popped a fresh cranberry into your mouth, you've experienced the very definition of tart. Unlike other fruits, cranberries need to be cooked to release their full flavor and to absorb that of other ingredients—one of which is usually sugar.

If you grew up believing that cranberries were only for the holidays—and only came molded into a cylinder—these great recipes will change your mind. You'll want to make these dishes spotlighting the berry year-round.

Lamb Stew with Carrots, Zucchini, and Cranberries

Cranberries certainly don't grow in North Africa, but this tagine-style stew reflects the Moroccan custom of combining fruit with lamb.

 1   teaspoon olive oil
 Cooking spray
 1½   pounds boneless leg of lamb, trimmed and cut into 1-inch pieces
 1½   cups finely chopped onion
 2   tablespoons water
 2   cups (¼-inch) diagonally cut carrot
 1⅔   cups water
 ¾   teaspoon ground cinnamon
 ¾   teaspoon ground ginger
 ½   teaspoon salt
 ¼   teaspoon coarsely ground black pepper
 1   (10½-ounce) can beef consommé
 2   tablespoons honey
 1½   pounds zucchini, cut into 1-inch cubes (about 4 cups)
 1   cup fresh cranberries
 4½   cups hot cooked couscous

1. Heat oil in a large Dutch oven coated with cooking spray over medium-high heat. Add lamb; cook 5 minutes or until browned, turning occasionally. Remove lamb from pan. Add onion and 2 tablespoons water to pan. Reduce heat; simmer 3 minutes, scraping pan to loosen browned bits.

2. Return lamb to pan. Add carrot and next 6 ingredients; bring to a boil. Cover, reduce heat, and simmer 1 hour and 10 minutes or until lamb is tender.

3. Add honey and zucchini; cover and simmer 15 minutes, stirring occasionally. Add cranberries. Cover and simmer 3 minutes or until cranberries pop. Serve stew over couscous. Yield: 6 servings (serving size: 1 cup lamb stew and ¾ cup couscous).

CALORIES 393 (18% from fat); FAT 7.7g (sat 2.5g, mono 3.4g, poly 0.7g); PROTEIN 32.1g; CARB 48.9g; FIBER 6.6g; CHOL 73mg; IRON 3.4mg; SODIUM 533mg; CALC 67mg

Cranberry Sauce with Apple Cider

Apple cider stands in for water to add dimension to this cranberry sauce. It's great with pork or turkey. Try some as a relish on a sandwich made with leftovers.

- 1 cup sugar
- 1 cup apple cider or apple juice
- 1 (12-ounce) package fresh cranberries

1. Combine all ingredients in a medium saucepan; bring to a boil over medium-high heat. Reduce heat; simmer 10 minutes or until cranberries pop, stirring occasionally. Chill. Yield: 8 servings (serving size: ¼ cup).

CALORIES 135 (0% from fat); FAT 0g; PROTEIN 0.3g; CARB 35g; FIBER 1.8g; CHOL 0mg; IRON 0.1mg; SODIUM 1mg; CALC 3mg

---

Cranberries' Health Benefits

Cranberries have tannins, compounds that keep bacteria from binding to cells, preventing them from multiplying and causing infections. Tannins are also antioxidants that bond with free radicals—compounds that damage the body—and reduce their energy level so they're less harmful. Antioxidants may help prevent certain cancers and contribute to cardiovascular health. Studies indicate that on a per-serving basis, cranberry juice, sweetened dried cranberries, cranberry sauce, and cooked cranberries have comparable amounts of tannins. "With antiadhesion and antioxidant capabilities, cranberries have a dual-action [health] formula that most foods don't have," says Amy Howell, Ph.D., a research scientist at the Marucci Center for Blueberry and Cranberry Research at Rutgers University in Chatsworth, New Jersey.

Earthy Entertaining Menu

Pork Medallions with Cranberries and Apples

Rye Berry Salad with Orange Vinaigrette (recipe on page 323)

Roasted Cauliflower (recipe on page 356)

Molasses Cake with Lemon Cream Cheese Frosting (recipe on page 356)

search myclar2003.com for all our menus

Pork Medallions with Cranberries and Apples

Serve with nutty wild rice or a blend of white and wild rice.

- ½ cup apple juice
- ½ cup fat-free, less-sodium chicken broth
- 1 tablespoon brown sugar
- 1½ teaspoons cornstarch
- ½ teaspoon salt
- ¼ teaspoon dried rubbed sage
- ⅛ teaspoon coarsely ground black pepper
- 1 (1-pound) pork tenderloin, trimmed
- 1 tablespoon all-purpose flour
- 4 teaspoons olive oil, divided
- Cooking spray
- ½ cup finely chopped onion
- 1 cup thinly sliced peeled Rome apple
- ¾ cup fresh cranberries
- Fresh sage sprigs (optional)

1. Combine first 7 ingredients in a small bowl, stirring well with a whisk.
2. Cut pork crosswise into 8 pieces. Place each piece between 2 sheets of heavy-duty plastic wrap; flatten each piece to ¾-inch thickness using a meat mallet or rolling pin. Dredge each pork piece in flour.
3. Heat 3 teaspoons oil in a large nonstick skillet coated with cooking spray over medium-high heat. Add pork; cook 2½ minutes on each side or until browned. Remove pork from pan.

---

4. Add 1 teaspoon oil to pan. Add onion; cover, reduce heat, and cook 5 minutes or until golden brown, stirring frequently. Return pork to pan; add juice mixture, apple, and cranberries. Bring to a simmer; cover and cook 3 minutes or until cranberries pop and pork is done, stirring occasionally. Garnish with sage sprigs, if desired. Yield: 4 servings (serving size: 2 pork medallions and ⅓ cup fruit mixture).

CALORIES 262 (30% from fat); FAT 8.7g (sat 2g, mono 5.1g, poly 0.9g); PROTEIN 24.8g; CARB 20.9g; FIBER 2.2g; CHOL 74mg; IRON 1.8mg; SODIUM 409mg; CALC 20mg

---

Cranberry-Orange Tart

CRUST:
- 1½ cups all-purpose flour
- 2 tablespoons sugar
- ⅛ teaspoon salt
- 6 tablespoons chilled butter, cut into small pieces
- ⅓ cup ice water
- Cooking spray

FILLING:
- ⅓ cup orange juice
- 2½ tablespoons cornstarch
- 1 cup sugar
- ¼ cup orange marmalade
- 2 tablespoons chopped walnuts, toasted
- 1 tablespoon grated orange rind
- 1 (12-ounce) package fresh cranberries

1. Preheat oven to 425°.
2. To prepare crust, lightly spoon flour into dry measuring cups; level with a knife. Combine flour, 2 tablespoons sugar, and salt in a bowl; cut in butter with a pastry blender or 2 knives until mixture resembles coarse meal.
3. Sprinkle surface with ice water, 1 tablespoon at a time, and toss with a fork until moist and crumbly (do not form a ball). Gently press mixture into a 4-inch circle on plastic wrap. Cover and chill 15 minutes.
4. Slightly overlap 2 lengths of plastic wrap on slightly damp surface. Unwrap and place chilled dough on plastic wrap.

Cover dough with 2 additional lengths of overlapping plastic wrap. Roll dough, still covered, into a 14-inch circle. Place dough in freezer 5 minutes or until plastic wrap can be easily removed.

5. Remove plastic wrap; fit dough into a 10-inch round removable-bottom tart pan coated with cooking spray. Fold edges under or flute decoratively.

6. To prepare filling, combine juice and cornstarch in a large bowl; stir well with a whisk. Stir in 1 cup sugar and remaining 4 ingredients. Pour mixture into prepared pan.

7. Bake at 425° for 20 minutes. Reduce oven temperature to 350° (do not remove tart from oven); bake an additional 35 minutes or until crust is lightly browned. Cool completely on a wire rack. Yield: 10 servings.

CALORIES 274 (27% from fat); FAT 8.2g (sat 4.4g, mono 2.2g, poly 1.1g); PROTEIN 2.5g; CARB 49.4g; FIBER 2.2g; CHOL 19mg; IRON 1.1mg; SODIUM 105mg; CALC 14mg

Cranberry Scones

Scones are best served soon after baking.

1¾ cups all-purpose flour
½ cup granulated sugar
¼ cup yellow cornmeal
2 teaspoons baking powder
¼ teaspoon baking soda
¼ teaspoon salt
2 tablespoons chilled butter, cut into small pieces
½ cup halved fresh cranberries
½ cup low-fat buttermilk
½ teaspoon grated orange rind
1 large egg, lightly beaten
Cooking spray
1 teaspoon powdered sugar

1. Preheat oven to 375°.

2. Lightly spoon flour into dry measuring cups; level with a knife. Combine flour and next 5 ingredients in a bowl; cut in butter with a pastry blender or 2 knives until mixture resembles coarse meal. Add cranberries, tossing to coat.

3. Combine buttermilk, rind, and egg; add to flour mixture, stirring just until moist (dough will be sticky).

4. Turn dough out onto a lightly floured surface, and knead lightly 5 times with floured hands. Pat dough into a 7-inch circle on a baking sheet coated with cooking spray. Cut dough into 10 wedges, cutting into but not completely through dough. Bake at 375° for 30 minutes or until golden. Sift powdered sugar over scones; serve warm. Yield: 10 servings (serving size: 1 scone).

CALORIES 168 (17% from fat); FAT 3.2g (sat 1.7g, mono 0.9g, poly 0.3g); PROTEIN 3.7g; CARB 31.2g; FIBER 1.1g; CHOL 28mg; IRON 1.4mg; SODIUM 231mg; CALC 75mg

Cranberry Quick Bread with Raisins and Hazelnuts

The batter is a pale tan, but the finished bread is a rich golden brown. The fruit in this easy quick bread helps it stay moist. You can use chopped walnuts in place of the hazelnuts.

1⅓ cups all-purpose flour
⅔ cup whole wheat flour
1 cup sugar
1 teaspoon baking powder
½ teaspoon baking soda
¼ teaspoon salt
¾ cup apple juice
3 tablespoons vegetable oil
1 teaspoon grated orange rind
1 large egg, lightly beaten
1⅓ cups chopped fresh cranberries
⅓ cup golden raisins
¼ cup chopped hazelnuts
Cooking spray

1. Preheat oven to 350°.

2. Lightly spoon flours into dry measuring cups; level with a knife. Combine flours and next 4 ingredients in a large bowl; make a well in center of mixture. Combine juice, oil, rind, and egg; add to flour mixture, stirring just until moist. Fold in cranberries, raisins, and hazelnuts.

3. Spoon batter into a 9 x 5-inch loaf pan coated with cooking spray. Bake at 350° for 50 minutes or until a wooden pick inserted in center comes out clean. Cool 10 minutes in pan on a wire rack; remove from pan. Cool completely on

wire rack. Yield: 16 servings (serving size: 1 slice).

CALORIES 162 (23% from fat); FAT 4.2g (sat 0.6g, mono 1.6g, poly 1.8g); PROTEIN 2.6g; CARB 29.6g; FIBER 1.6g; CHOL 13mg; IRON 1mg; SODIUM 112mg; CALC 27mg

That's the Way the Berry Bounces

How can you tell if a cranberry is good? Before machines took over the job of checking for quality, people used to roll cranberries down stairs. The soft, undesirable berries didn't have the oomph to make it down; the fresh ones made it to the bottom.

For fun at home, play along by dropping one onto the counter or floor. It should bounce like a rubber ball. Not feeling so playful? Top-quality cranberries float.

Wild Rice and Cranberry Salad

The dressing can be made ahead and stored, covered, in the refrigerator for a couple of days.

DRESSING:

¾ cup chopped fresh cranberries
¼ cup cranberry juice cocktail
1 tablespoon sugar
2 garlic cloves, minced
3 tablespoons cider vinegar
1½ tablespoons olive oil
1 teaspoon kosher salt
1 teaspoon freshly ground black pepper

SALAD:

2 cups cooked wild rice (about ½ cup uncooked)
1 cup cooked orzo (about ½ cup uncooked rice-shaped pasta)
½ cup finely chopped yellow bell pepper
½ cup finely chopped red bell pepper
½ cup thinly sliced green onions
2 tablespoons chopped fresh parsley
Continued

1. To prepare dressing, combine first 4 ingredients in a small saucepan. Bring to a boil; cook 2 minutes. Remove from heat. Stir in vinegar, oil, salt, and black pepper. Chill.

2. To prepare salad, combine wild rice and remaining 5 ingredients in a large bowl. Drizzle dressing over rice mixture, tossing to coat. Yield: 6 servings (serving size: ⅔ cup).

CALORIES 134 (26% from fat); FAT 3.8g (sat 0.5g, mono 2.5g, poly 0.5g); PROTEIN 3.4g; CARB 22.9g; FIBER 1.5g; CHOL 0mg; IRON 1mg; SODIUM 320mg; CALC 17mg

---

Caring for Cranberries

- Look for round, plump cranberries with smooth skin.
- A 12-ounce bag (the most common size) yields 3 cups whole or 2½ cups chopped berries.
- Store cranberries in the refrigerator for up to 1 month, or in the freezer for up to 9 months.
- Don't wash the berries until just before using them to keep them at their best.
- The best way to chop cranberries is to use a food processor—they tend to roll away from you when you use a knife.
- Don't bother to defrost frozen berries before using in a recipe.

search myclar2003.com for all our tips

---

resources

Turkey with an Accent

Give your Thanksgiving leftovers exciting, worldly flavors.

Traditional Thanksgiving fare is the very definition of American comfort food. But that doesn't mean your post-holiday meals made from the leftover turkey can't assume a bit of international intrigue.

Turkey Vatapa

Vatapa is a rustic Brazilian stew, a fiery blend with beer, coconut milk, and ground peanuts as its base. Made with leftover turkey, it's a snap to prepare. Vatapa can be made up to 2 days in advance; keep it covered in the refrigerator. It will thicken as it sits; just add a little water. Seed the jalapeño pepper to tame its heat.

    1   teaspoon peanut oil
    ½   cup finely chopped onion
    3   garlic cloves, minced
    1   tablespoon minced peeled fresh
        ginger
    1   jalapeño pepper, minced
    1   cup water
    1   (28-ounce) can no-salt-added
        diced tomatoes, undrained
    1   (12-ounce) can light beer
    ¼   cup unsalted, dry-roasted peanuts
    3   cups chopped skinned cooked
        turkey
    ½   cup light coconut milk
    ½   cup finely chopped fresh parsley
    ½   cup finely chopped fresh cilantro
    1   tablespoon fresh lime juice
    ½   teaspoon salt
    ½   teaspoon black pepper
    Cilantro sprigs (optional)

1. Heat oil in a Dutch oven over medium-high heat. Add onion and garlic; sauté 2 minutes. Add ginger and jalapeño; sauté 30 seconds. Stir in water, tomatoes, and beer; bring to a boil. Cover, reduce heat, and simmer 20 minutes.

2. Place peanuts in a spice or coffee grinder; process until finely ground. Add ground peanuts, turkey, and coconut milk to pan, stirring to combine. Increase heat to medium. Bring mixture to a simmer; cook 5 minutes, stirring occasionally. Stir in parsley and next 4 ingredients. Garnish with cilantro sprigs, if desired. Yield: 6 servings (serving size: 1⅓ cups).

CALORIES 195 (30% from fat); FAT 6.4g (sat 1.8g, mono 2.3g, poly 1.7g); PROTEIN 19.9g; CARB 11.8g; FIBER 3.3g; CHOL 56mg; IRON 2.3mg; SODIUM 301mg; CALC 55mg

Turkey Pot Stickers

Dim sum, a popular dining tradition in China's Canton province, consists of many small dishes—including bite-sized dumplings like these. You can assemble these ahead and cook them just before serving. If you can't find gyoza skins, you can substitute won ton wrappers.

DIPPING SAUCE:

    2   tablespoons water
    2   tablespoons rice vinegar
    2   tablespoons low-sodium soy sauce
    ½   teaspoon dark sesame oil
    2   garlic cloves, minced

DUMPLINGS:

    1   cup sliced shiitake mushroom caps
    ½   cup sliced green onions
    ¼   cup sliced carrot
    2   tablespoons minced peeled fresh
        ginger
    2   tablespoons rice vinegar
    3   large egg whites, lightly beaten
    2   cups chopped skinned cooked
        turkey
    24 (4-inch) gyoza skins
    2   teaspoons vegetable oil, divided
    ½   cup water, divided

1. To prepare dipping sauce, combine first 5 ingredients, stirring well with a whisk.

2. To prepare dumplings, place mushrooms, onions, carrot, ginger, and vinegar in a food processor; pulse until coarsely chopped, scraping sides. Combine mushroom mixture and egg whites in a large bowl; add turkey, stirring until combined.

3. Working with 1 gyoza skin at a time (cover remaining skins to keep from drying), spoon about 1 tablespoon turkey mixture on center of each skin. Moisten edges of skin with water. Fold in half, pinching edges together to seal. Place dumplings on a baking sheet (cover loosely with a towel to keep from drying).

4. Heat 1 teaspoon vegetable oil in a large nonstick skillet over medium-high heat. Arrange half of dumplings in pan; cover and cook 5 minutes or until lightly browned. Turn dumplings; add ¼ cup water. Cover and simmer 5 minutes. Remove from pan; keep warm.

5. Wipe pan dry with a paper towel. Repeat procedure with remaining vegetable oil, dumplings, and water. Serve warm with dipping sauce. Yield: 8 servings (serving size: 3 pot stickers and about 2 teaspoons dipping sauce).

CALORIES 144 (16% from fat); FAT 2.5g (sat 0.5g, mono 0.5g, poly 1g); PROTEIN 12.7g; CARB 16.5g; FIBER 0.9g; CHOL 30mg; IRON 1.6mg; SODIUM 332mg; CALC 25mg

Turkey Pizza

Provolone and mozzarella are traditional pizza cheeses, but you can use any combination of your favorites.

    1   teaspoon olive oil
    1   cup chopped onion
    3   garlic cloves, minced
1¾   cups canned crushed tomatoes
    ⅛   teaspoon salt
    ⅛   teaspoon crushed red pepper
    ¼   cup chopped fresh parsley
    2   tablespoons chopped fresh basil
    1   (10-ounce) can refrigerated pizza
         crust dough
    Cooking spray
    2   cups chopped skinned cooked
         turkey
    ½   cup (2 ounces) shredded provolone
         cheese
    ½   cup (2 ounces) shredded part-skim
         mozzarella cheese

1. Preheat oven to 400°.
2. Heat oil in a large nonstick skillet over medium-high heat. Add onion and garlic; sauté 4 minutes. Stir in tomatoes, salt, and pepper; bring to a boil. Reduce heat; simmer 15 minutes or until thick, stirring occasionally. Stir in parsley and basil. Remove from heat, and cool completely.
3. Roll dough into a 10-inch circle on a lightly floured surface. Place dough on a (12-inch) pizza pan or baking sheet coated with cooking spray. Crimp edges of dough with fingers to form a rim.
4. Spread tomato mixture over crust, leaving a ¼-inch border. Top with turkey; sprinkle with cheeses. Bake at 400° for 10 minutes or until golden. Yield: 6 servings (serving size: 1 slice).

CALORIES 275 (27% from fat); FAT 8.3g (sat 3.2g, mono 2.8g, ~-¹, 0.9g); PROTEIN 21.5g; CARB 28.8g; FIBER 1.8g; CHOL 49mg; IRON 2.6mg; SODIUM 641mg; CALC 172mg

Turkey Picadillo

Turkey matches well with the flavorful ingredients of this Cuban dish: tomato, chiles, cinnamon, and cumin. Serve with baked tortilla chips.

    1   teaspoon olive oil
    ¼   cup finely chopped onion
    1   garlic clove, minced
    1   cup chopped tomato
    2   tablespoons canned chopped green
         chiles
    1   tablespoon dark brown
         sugar
    ½   teaspoon ground cinnamon
    ½   teaspoon ground cumin
    ½   teaspoon black pepper
    ¼   teaspoon salt
    2   tablespoons golden raisins
    2   tablespoons capers
    1   tablespoon red wine vinegar
    1   tablespoon dry sherry
    2   cups chopped skinned cooked
         turkey
    8   (6-inch) corn tortillas

1. Heat oil in a large skillet over medium heat. Add onion and garlic; cook 2 minutes, stirring occasionally. Add tomato and chiles; cook 1 minute, stirring frequently. Stir in brown sugar, cinnamon, cumin, black pepper, and salt; cook 30 seconds, stirring constantly.
2. Reduce heat to low. Stir in raisins, capers, vinegar, and sherry; cook 3 minutes or until thoroughly heated, stirring frequently. Stir in turkey. Remove from heat.
3. Warm tortillas according to package directions. Spoon about ⅓ cup turkey mixture onto each tortilla; fold in half. Yield: 4 servings (serving size: 2 filled tortillas).

CALORIES 258 (14% from fat); FAT 4.1g (sat 0.8g, mono 1.5g, poly 1.2g); PROTEIN 20.8g; CARB 35.1g; FIBER 4g; CHOL 55mg; IRON 2.6mg; SODIUM 434mg; CALC 120mg

Yucatán Turkey Lime Soup

This peppery soup is a local favorite at the weekly market in Merida, the capital of Mexico's Yucatán province. There, this luscious, simple broth is usually ladled over goat meat or chicken. It's equally delicious with turkey. Serve with warm corn tortillas.

  12   garlic cloves, crushed
    4   (14-ounce) cans fat-free,
         less-sodium chicken broth
    4   whole cloves
    2   large onions, each trimmed and
         quartered
    1   jalapeño pepper, quartered
    3   cups chopped skinned cooked
         turkey
    ¼   cup chopped fresh cilantro
    ¼   cup fresh lime juice
    4   lime wedges (optional)

1. Combine first 5 ingredients in a Dutch oven over medium-high heat; bring to a simmer. Cover and cook 30 minutes. Strain broth through a colander into a bowl; discard solids.
2. Return broth to pan; stir in turkey, cilantro, and lime juice. Cook over low heat 5 minutes or until thoroughly heated. Garnish with lime wedges, if desired. Yield: 4 servings (serving size: about 1¾ cups).

CALORIES 217 (28% from fat); FAT 6.7g (sat 2.8g, mono 0.7g, poly 1g); PROTEIN 32.4g; CARB 6.3g; FIBER 0.4g; CHOL 99mg; IRON 1.9mg; SODIUM 304mg; CALC 64mg

Cold Soba Noodles with Turkey

Soba noodles are a traditional component of Japanese cuisine. The brown noodles, which are made from buckwheat flour, contrast nicely with the red bell pepper, shredded carrot, and green onion.

DRESSING:

    ¼   cup rice vinegar
1½   tablespoons low-sodium soy sauce
    1   teaspoon minced peeled fresh
         ginger
    4   teaspoons sesame oil

Continued

SALAD:

- 6 ounces uncooked soba noodles
- 3 cups chopped skinned cooked turkey
- 1½ cups thinly sliced red bell pepper
- 1 cup shredded carrot
- ½ cup thinly sliced green onions
- ¼ cup chopped fresh cilantro
- 2½ tablespoons chopped unsalted, dry-roasted peanuts

1. To prepare dressing, combine first 4 ingredients in a small bowl, stirring well with a whisk.

2. To prepare salad, cook soba noodles according to package directions, omitting salt and fat. Drain and rinse with cold water.

3. Combine noodles, turkey, and remaining 5 ingredients in a large bowl. Drizzle dressing over salad, tossing gently to coat. Serve immediately. Yield: 4 servings (serving size: 2 cups).

CALORIES 371 (25% from fat); FAT 10.1g (sat 1.9g, mono 3.8g, poly 3.6g); PROTEIN 33.3g; CARB 39.2g; FIBER 2.6g; CHOL 83mg; IRON 3.3mg; SODIUM 746mg; CALC 48mg

inspired vegetarian

Blending Old and New

This satisfying holiday dinner takes the spirit of the season to heart.

The melting-pot spirit is the true beauty of the Thanksgiving table. After all, the meal itself is a result of indigenous foodstuffs of the New World prepared in the traditional techniques of the old, forming a uniquely American cuisine. So how do we who have chosen a vegetarian lifestyle continue in this great tradition? We simply do what our forebears did—make our own hybrid. With that in mind, you'll find that this vegetarian Thanksgiving menu satisfies the longing for deep, earthy flavors, which are the hallmark of a great autumn meal. Meanwhile, it incorporates new cultural influences into the fold, mixing Italian, Mexican, and even Asian ingredients.

Vegetarian Thanksgiving Menu
serves 10

Romaine Salad with Lemon-Parmesan Dressing

Roasted Squash Stuffed with Corn Bread Dressing

Kale with Lemon-Balsamic Butter

Roasted Cipollini Onions

Easy Savory Gravy

Smashed Potatoes, Parsnips, and Turnips

Sweet Potato Tart with Pecan Crust

search myclar2003.com for all our menus

Romaine Salad with Lemon-Parmesan Dressing

Oil-packed sun-dried tomatoes add depth and flavor to this salad.

- 2 tablespoons grated fresh Parmesan cheese
- 2 tablespoons fresh lemon juice
- 1 tablespoon extra-virgin olive oil
- 1 tablespoon Dijon mustard
- ¼ teaspoon black pepper
- ⅛ teaspoon salt
- 1 garlic clove, halved
- 18 cups torn romaine lettuce
- 5 oil-packed sun-dried tomato halves, drained and chopped

1. Combine first 6 ingredients in a small bowl, stirring with a whisk.

2. Rub garlic halves on the inside of a salad bowl; discard. Add lettuce and tomatoes to bowl. Drizzle dressing over salad, tossing well to coat. Yield: 10 servings (serving size: about 1¾ cups).

CALORIES 38 (54% from fat); FAT 2.3g (sat 0.5g, mono 1.3g, poly 0.3g); PROTEIN 2.4g; CARB 3.3g; FIBER 1.8g; CHOL 1mg; IRON 1.2mg; SODIUM 102mg; CALC 57mg

---

Roasted Squash Stuffed with Corn Bread Dressing

You can make the Maple Corn Bread ahead and toast it. Roast the squash and refrigerate it up to 2 days. All you'll have to do on Thanksgiving Day is assemble the dish and bake it.

- 7½ cups (½-inch) cubed Maple Corn Bread
  Cooking spray
- 5 acorn squash (about 1 pound each)
- 4 cups boiling water, divided
- 1 cup dried cranberries
- ¼ cup dried currants
- 2 teaspoons olive oil
- 1 cup finely chopped onion
- 1 cup finely chopped celery
- 1 cup finely chopped carrot
- 2 tablespoons chopped fresh sage
- 3 garlic cloves, minced
- 1 cup vegetable broth
- ¼ cup chopped pecans, toasted
- 2 tablespoons finely chopped fresh parsley
- ¾ teaspoon fine sea salt
- ¼ teaspoon black pepper

1. Preheat oven to 400°.

2. Arrange corn bread cubes in a single layer on a jelly roll pan coated with cooking spray. Bake at 400° for 30 minutes or until corn bread is toasted, stirring twice. Set aside.

3. Decrease oven temperature to 350°.

4. Cut each squash in half lengthwise, and discard seeds and membranes. Place squash, cut sides down, in a 13 x 9-inch baking pan. Coat squash with cooking spray. Pour 2 cups of boiling water over squash. Cover and bake at 350° for 20 minutes. Remove squash from pan.

5. Place cranberries, currants, and 2 cups boiling water in a bowl. Cover and let stand 30 minutes. Drain.

6. Heat oil in a large nonstick skillet over medium-high heat. Add onion; sauté 5 minutes. Add celery, carrot, sage, and garlic; sauté 3 minutes.

7. Combine corn bread cubes, cranberry mixture, onion mixture, broth, and remaining 4 ingredients in a bowl, tossing to coat.

8. Spoon about 1½ cups dressing mixture into each squash half. Place squash halves in pan, cut sides up.

9. Bake at 350° for 30 minutes or until tip of a knife pierces squash easily. Yield: 10 servings (serving size: 1 stuffed squash half).

(Totals include Maple Corn Bread) CALORIES 398 (23% from fat); FAT 10.2g (sat 4.1g, mono 3.8g, poly 1.6g); PROTEIN 6.5g; CARB 74.2g; FIBER 7.7g; CHOL 16mg; IRON 3.8mg; SODIUM 732mg; CALC 198mg

MAPLE CORN BREAD:

  1 teaspoon vegetable oil
1½ cups all-purpose flour
  ¾ cup masa harina
  ¾ cup yellow cornmeal
  1 tablespoon baking powder
  1 teaspoon fine sea salt
1½ cups water
  ⅓ cup maple syrup
  5 tablespoons butter, melted
  1 jalapeño pepper, finely chopped

1. Preheat oven to 350°.

2. Coat a 9-inch cast iron skillet with oil. Place in oven 10 minutes.

3. Lightly spoon flour and masa harina into dry measuring cups; level with a knife. Combine flour, masa harina, cornmeal, baking powder, and salt in a large bowl, stirring well with a whisk.

4. Combine water and remaining 3 ingredients in a small bowl, stirring with a whisk. Add water mixture to flour mixture, stirring until moist. Spoon batter into preheated pan.

5. Bake at 350° for 25 minutes or until a wooden pick inserted in center comes out clean. Remove corn bread from pan; cool completely on a wire rack. Yield: 12 servings.

CALORIES 184 (27% from fat); FAT 5.6g (sat 3.1g, mono 1.6g, poly 0.6g); PROTEIN 3g; CARB 31.5g; FIBER 1.2g; CHOL 13mg; IRON 1.4mg; SODIUM 342mg; CALC 62mg

Kale with Lemon-Balsamic Butter

If you like spicy foods, add a dash of crushed red pepper.

  4 (1-pound) bunches kale
  4 quarts water
  3 tablespoons butter
  ½ cup raisins
  3 tablespoons fresh lemon juice
  3 tablespoons balsamic vinegar
  ¾ teaspoon fine sea salt
  ¼ teaspoon freshly ground black pepper

1. Remove stems and center ribs from kale. Wash and pat dry. Coarsely chop to measure 24 cups. Bring water to a boil in an 8-quart stockpot. Add kale; cover and cook 3 minutes. Drain well; place kale in a bowl.

2. Melt butter in a small skillet over medium-high heat; cook 3 minutes or until lightly browned. Stir in raisins, juice, and vinegar; cook 30 seconds, stirring constantly with a whisk. Pour butter mixture over kale. Sprinkle with salt and pepper; toss well to coat. Yield: 10 servings (serving size: about 1 cup).

CALORIES 151 (28% from fat); FAT 4.7g (sat 2.3g, mono 1.1g, poly 0.7g); PROTEIN 6.3g; CARB 25.5g; FIBER 4.9g; CHOL 9mg; IRON 3.4mg; SODIUM 289mg; CALC 252mg

Roasted Cipollini Onions

Cipollini (chip-oh-LEE-nee) are sometimes called wild onions. If you can't find them in the supermarket or an Italian market, substitute pearl onions. Briefly blanching the onions makes them easy to peel. The cooking liquid takes on a beautiful yellow hue from the peel; save it to add to rice or soup.

  2 quarts water
  4 pounds Cipollini onions
  4 rosemary sprigs
  1 cup dry red wine
  ½ cup low-sodium soy sauce
  ⅓ cup balsamic vinegar
  2 tablespoons olive oil
  2 tablespoons honey
Rosemary sprigs (optional)

1. Preheat oven to 475°.

2. Bring water to a boil in a stockpot. Add onions; cook 30 seconds. Drain; cool. Peel onions; arrange in a single layer on a jelly roll pan. Top with 4 rosemary sprigs.

3. Combine wine and next 4 ingredients, stirring with a whisk. Pour wine mixture over onions. Bake at 475° for 30 minutes, turning twice.

4. Remove onions from pan with a slotted spoon. Carefully pour cooking liquid into a small saucepan; bring to a boil. Reduce heat; simmer 3 minutes or until mixture is the consistency of a thin syrup. Pour over onions; toss well to coat. Garnish with rosemary sprigs, if desired. Yield: 10 servings (serving size: about ⅓ cup).

CALORIES 187 (15% from fat); FAT 3.1g (sat 0.4g, mono 2g, poly 0.2g); PROTEIN 3.3g; CARB 32.5g; FIBER 1.2g; CHOL 0mg; IRON 1mg; SODIUM 522mg; CALC 54mg

Easy Savory Gravy

This gravy is thickened with a lightly browned roux, which adds richness. Soy sauce gives it a hearty flavor.

  2 tablespoons olive oil
  6 tablespoons all-purpose flour
  2 (14½-ounce) cans vegetable broth
  ¼ cup low-sodium soy sauce
  ½ teaspoon black pepper

1. Heat oil in a saucepan over medium heat. Add flour; cook 5 minutes or until lightly browned and fragrant, stirring constantly with a whisk. (If flour browns too quickly, remove pan from heat; stir constantly until it cools.)

2. Gradually add broth to pan, stirring constantly with a whisk. Stir in soy sauce and pepper; cook until thick (about 15 minutes), stirring frequently. Yield: 12 servings (serving size: about ¼ cup).

CALORIES 42 (54% from fat); FAT 2.5g (sat 0.3g, mono 1.7g, poly 0.2g); PROTEIN 1.3g; CARB 4.1g; FIBER 0.1g; CHOL 0mg; IRON 0.2mg; SODIUM 493mg; CALC 0mg

Smashed Potatoes, Parsnips, and Turnips

You can make this ahead, but it may thicken as it sits. Reserve ½ cup of cooking liquid; just before serving, gradually stir it into the mixture until it's the desired consistency.

 5 cups cubed peeled Yukon gold or red potato (about 2 pounds)
 3 cups chopped parsnip (about 1 pound)
 3 cups chopped peeled turnip (about 1 pound)
 ¼ cup butter
 1 tablespoon prepared horseradish
 1½ teaspoons fine sea salt
 ½ teaspoon black pepper

1. Place first 3 ingredients in a Dutch oven; cover with water. Bring to a boil. Reduce heat; simmer 15 minutes or until tender. Drain.
2. Stir in butter and remaining ingredients; mash mixture with a potato masher to desired consistency. Yield: 10 servings (serving size: about ¾ cup).

CALORIES 160 (28% from fat); FAT 4.9g (sat 2.9g, mono 1.4g, poly 0.3g); PROTEIN 2.9g; CARB 27.5g; FIBER 3.9g; CHOL 12mg; IRON 1.1mg; SODIUM 437mg; CALC 39mg

Sweet Potato Tart with Pecan Crust

Be sure to look for pure maple syrup to use in this recipe. It adds just a hint of sweetness that doesn't overpower the other flavors of the tart. You can make this dessert up to 2 days ahead; keep it refrigerated until you're ready to serve it to your guests.

CRUST:
 1 cup whole wheat pastry flour
 ¼ cup pecans
 ⅛ teaspoon salt
 3½ tablespoons chilled butter, cut into small pieces
 2 tablespoons maple syrup
 Cooking spray

FILLING:
 ½ cup maple syrup
 2 tablespoons cornstarch
 1½ cups mashed cooked sweet potatoes
 ¾ cup soft silken tofu, drained
 1½ teaspoons finely chopped peeled fresh ginger
 1½ teaspoons grated orange rind
 ¾ teaspoon vanilla extract
 ¼ teaspoon ground cinnamon
 ⅛ teaspoon ground nutmeg

SYRUP:
 ½ cup maple syrup

1. Preheat oven to 350°.
2. To prepare crust, lightly spoon flour into a dry measuring cup; level with a knife. Place flour, pecans, and salt in a food processor; process until pecans are finely ground. Add butter; pulse 4 times or until mixture resembles coarse meal.
3. With processor on, slowly add 2 tablespoons syrup through food chute, processing just until combined (do not form a ball). Place dough on a lightly floured surface; knead lightly 4 or 5 times (dough will be sticky).
4. Place dough in a 9-inch round removable-bottom tart pan lightly coated with cooking spray. Place a sheet of plastic wrap over dough; press dough into bottom and up sides of pan. Discard plastic wrap. Pierce bottom and sides of dough with a fork; bake at 350° for 15 minutes or until lightly browned. Cool on a wire rack.
5. To prepare filling, combine ½ cup syrup and cornstarch. Place syrup mixture, sweet potato, and next 6 ingredients in a food processor; process until smooth, scraping sides. Spoon mixture into prepared crust, spreading evenly. Bake at 350° for 50 minutes or until set. Cool on a wire rack.
6. Place ½ cup syrup in a heavy saucepan; bring to a boil. Cook until reduced to ⅓ cup; remove from heat. Cool and drizzle about 1½ teaspoons over each serving. Yield: 10 servings.

CALORIES 264 (25% from fat); FAT 7.3g (sat 2.8g, mono 2.5g, poly 1.2g); PROTEIN 4g; CARB 46.6g; FIBER 3.4g; CHOL 11mg; IRON 1.6mg; SODIUM 81mg; CALC 45mg

...And Ready in Just About 20 Minutes

Many of these recipes use pantry items—such as bottled garlic and ginger, dried herbs, and ground peppers—to make glazes and sauces for quick, flavorful entrées.

Polenta Gratin with Mushrooms and Fontina

Match this comforting meatless main dish with focaccia and a spinach salad.

 1 (16-ounce) tube of polenta, cut into ¼-inch-thick slices
 Cooking spray
 1 (8-ounce) package presliced mushrooms
 1 teaspoon bottled minced garlic
 ¼ teaspoon salt
 ⅓ cup sun-dried tomato Alfredo sauce (such as Classico)
 ¼ cup chopped fresh basil
 ¼ cup (1 ounce) shredded fontina cheese

1. Preheat oven to 500°.
2. Arrange polenta slices in an 11 x 7-inch baking dish coated with cooking spray, allowing slices to overlap.
3. Heat a medium nonstick skillet coated with cooking spray over medium-high heat. Add mushrooms; cook 2 minutes, stirring frequently. Stir in garlic and salt. Cover, reduce heat, and cook 2 minutes. Stir in Alfredo sauce and basil.
4. Spoon mushroom mixture evenly over polenta. Top with cheese. Bake at 500° for 7 minutes or until thoroughly heated. Yield: 3 servings.

CALORIES 221 (30% from fat); FAT 7.4g (sat 3.9g, mono 1.7g, poly 1.2g); PROTEIN 8.3g; CARB 28.7g; FIBER 4.2g; CHOL 29mg; IRON 2.4mg; SODIUM 739mg; CALC 82mg

Orange Teriyaki Salmon

Mixing the sauce ingredients in the baking dish makes cleanup a cinch for this simple recipe.

    3   tablespoons orange juice
    2   tablespoons low-sodium soy sauce
    1   tablespoon rice vinegar
    1   tablespoon honey
    2   teaspoons bottled ground fresh
        ginger (such as Spice World)
    1   teaspoon bottled minced garlic
    4   (6-ounce) salmon fillets (about
        1 inch thick)

1. Preheat oven to 450°.
2. Combine first 6 ingredients in an 8-inch square baking dish, stirring with a whisk. Add fish to baking dish; spoon sauce over fish.
3. Bake at 450° for 15 minutes or until fish flakes easily when tested with a fork, basting occasionally with sauce. Yield: 4 servings (serving size: 1 fillet).

CALORIES 299 (39% from fat); FAT 13.1g (sat 3.1g, mono 5.7g, poly 3.2g); PROTEIN 36.8g; CARB 6.6g; FIBER 0.1g; CHOL 87mg; IRON 0.8mg; SODIUM 347mg; CALC 25mg

Barley-Mushroom Pilaf

Use vegetable broth to make this dish vegetarian. Serve with roasted asparagus.

    3   cups fat-free, less-sodium chicken
        broth
   ⅓   cup dried porcini mushrooms,
        chopped (about ⅓ ounce)
  1½   cups uncooked quick-cooking
        barley
    2   tablespoons olive oil
    3   cups quartered shiitake mushroom
        caps (about 8 ounces)
    2   cups chopped onion
   ¾   teaspoon salt
   ½   teaspoon dried rosemary
    1   (8-ounce) package presliced
        mushrooms
   ¼   cup dry Marsala
    2   teaspoons sherry vinegar

1. Combine broth and porcini in a large saucepan. Bring to a boil; stir in barley.

Cover, reduce heat, and simmer 12 minutes or until tender.
2. While barley cooks, heat oil in a Dutch oven over medium-high heat. Add shiitake, onion, salt, rosemary, and presliced mushrooms; sauté 5 minutes. Stir in Marsala; cook 1 minute. Stir in barley mixture and vinegar; cook 2 minutes or until thoroughly heated, stirring frequently. Yield: 4 servings (serving size: 1½ cups).

CALORIES 415 (19% from fat); FAT 8.7g (sat 1.3g, mono 5.2g, poly 1.5g); PROTEIN 15.3g; CARB 66.6g; FIBER 15g; CHOL 0mg; IRON 4.6mg; SODIUM 805mg; CALC 46mg

Asian Chicken and Cabbage

    2   tablespoons hoisin sauce
    1   teaspoon bottled minced
        garlic
    1   teaspoon bottled ground fresh
        ginger (such as Spice World)
    4   (4-ounce) skinless, boneless chicken
        breast halves
        Cooking spray
    1   teaspoon vegetable oil
   ½   cup chopped onion
    4   cups packaged coleslaw
    1   teaspoon dark sesame oil
   ½   teaspoon salt
   ½   teaspoon black pepper

1. Preheat broiler.
2. Combine first 3 ingredients; spread evenly over both sides of chicken. Place chicken on a broiler pan coated with cooking spray; broil 6 minutes on each side or until done.
3. While chicken cooks, heat vegetable oil in a large skillet over medium-high heat. Add onion; sauté 2 minutes. Add coleslaw; sauté 1 minute or until coleslaw begins to wilt.
4. Place coleslaw mixture in a medium bowl. Add sesame oil, salt, and pepper, tossing to coat. Serve coleslaw mixture with chicken. Yield: 4 servings (serving size: 1 chicken breast half and ½ cup coleslaw mixture).

CALORIES 189 (16% from fat); FAT 4.3g (sat 0.7g, mono 1.1g, poly 1.6g); PROTEIN 27.8g; CARB 9.5g; FIBER 2.1g; CHOL 66mg; IRON 1.4mg; SODIUM 505mg; CALC 52mg

Tomato-Basil Pizza

    1   (10-ounce) Italian cheese-flavored
        thin pizza crust (such as Boboli)
  1¼   cups (5 ounces) shredded part-skim
        mozzarella cheese, divided
    1   pound plum tomatoes, cut into
        ¼-inch-thick slices
   ½   cup chopped fresh basil
    1   teaspoon dried Italian seasoning
    2   teaspoons balsamic vinegar

1. Preheat oven to 450°.
2. Place pizza crust on a baking sheet; sprinkle with ½ cup cheese, leaving a ½-inch border. Arrange tomato slices over cheese; sprinkle with basil. Sprinkle with seasoning; drizzle with vinegar. Top with ¾ cup cheese.
3. Bake at 450° for 10 minutes or until cheese melts. Cut into 8 wedges. Yield: 4 servings (serving size: 2 wedges).

CALORIES 305 (29% from fat); FAT 9.8g (sat 4.9g, mono 1.7g, poly 0.3g); PROTEIN 17.2g; CARB 36.9g; FIBER 2.2g; CHOL 20mg; IRON 2.8mg; SODIUM 549mg; CALC 436mg

Sausage and Chicken Gumbo

    1   (3½-ounce) bag boil-in-bag rice
    2   tablespoons all-purpose flour
    1   tablespoon vegetable oil
    1   cup frozen chopped onion
    1   cup frozen chopped green bell
        pepper
    1   cup frozen cut okra
    1   cup chopped celery
    1   teaspoon bottled minced garlic
   ½   teaspoon dried thyme
   ¼   teaspoon ground red pepper
    2   cups chopped roasted skinless,
        boneless chicken breasts (about
        2 breasts)
    8   ounces turkey kielbasa, cut into
        1-inch pieces
    1   (14½-ounce) can diced tomatoes
        with peppers and onion
    1   (14-ounce) can fat-free,
        less-sodium chicken broth

1. Cook rice according to package directions, omitting salt and fat.

Continued

2. While rice cooks, combine flour and oil in a Dutch oven; sauté over medium-high heat 3 minutes. Add onion and next 6 ingredients; cook 3 minutes or until tender, stirring frequently.

3. Stir in chicken, kielbasa, tomatoes, and broth; cook 6 minutes or until thoroughly heated. Serve over rice. Yield: 4 servings (serving size: 1½ cups gumbo and ½ cup rice).

CALORIES 369 (28% from fat); FAT 11.3g (sat 2.7g, mono 4.8g, poly 3g); PROTEIN 29.4g; CARB 37g; FIBER 3g; CHOL 77mg; IRON 2.2mg; SODIUM 949mg; CALC 92mg

Beef Tenderloin with Mushroom Gravy

Gradually add the hot mushroom mixture to the cold sour cream to keep the two from separating.

    Cooking spray
    4   (4-ounce) beef tenderloin steaks,
        trimmed (½ inch thick)
    ½   teaspoon black pepper
    ¼   teaspoon salt
    1   cup presliced mushrooms
    ½   cup finely chopped onion
    1   teaspoon bottled minced garlic
    ½   cup low-salt beef broth
    ⅓   cup fat-free sour cream
    2   tablespoons minced fresh parsley

1. Heat a large nonstick skillet coated with cooking spray over medium-high heat. Sprinkle steaks with pepper and salt. Add steaks to pan; cook 3 minutes on each side or until desired degree of doneness. Remove from pan.

2. Add mushrooms, onion, and garlic to pan; sauté 5 minutes. Stir in broth; bring to a boil. Cover, reduce heat, and simmer 3 minutes.

3. Place sour cream in a medium bowl. Gradually add mushroom mixture to sour cream, stirring constantly with a whisk. Stir in parsley. Serve gravy with steak. Yield: 4 servings (serving size: 1 steak and ¼ cup gravy).

CALORIES 210 (33% from fat); FAT 7.8g (sat 2.9g, mono 2.9g, poly 0.4g); PROTEIN 26.2g; CARB 6.7g; FIBER 0.7g; CHOL 75mg; IRON 3.6mg; SODIUM 237mg; CALC 45mg

Thanksgiving Dinner, Ready When You Are

Your celebration will be leisurely if you follow our make-ahead tips.

Thanksgiving, Made Ahead Menu
serves 10
Herbed Turkey with Roasted Garlic Gravy
Sherried Mushroom Soup
Streuseled Sweet Potato Casserole
Sourdough Stuffing with Apples and Ham
Cranberry, Apple, and Walnut Relish
Green Beans with Caramelized Onions
Vanilla Cheesecake with Cherry Topping

search myclar2003.com for all our menus

Make-Ahead Tips

Up to two months ahead:
Make the cheesecake up to two months ahead and freeze it. Before freezing, though, chill the cooled cheesecake in the pan for 2 hours; then wrap pan in heavy-duty plastic wrap. Thaw cheesecake in the refrigerator. Or make both the cheesecake and topping up to 3 days ahead, and store—separately—in the refrigerator.

Two weeks ahead:
Assemble the sweet potato mixture and sprinkle with the streusel, then freeze the casserole. Thaw it in the refrigerator and bake as directed. Or cook just the potatoes a day ahead, mash and refrigerate, and proceed with the recipe as directed (starting with the addition of half-and-half) the day you're serving the dish.

Four days ahead: Make the broth for the mushroom soup up to four days ahead and refrigerate. Just before serving, add the shiitakes, sherry, and chives, and heat.

Herbed Turkey with Roasted Garlic Gravy

(pictured on page 329)

Make the garlic-herb rub up to a day ahead and rub under the skin of the turkey, then let the turkey chill. After you cook the turkey, cover it with foil to keep it warm while you bake the sweet potato casserole and sourdough stuffing.

GARLIC-HERB RUB:
    1   cup fresh flat-leaf parsley leaves
    ¼   cup fresh sage leaves
    ¼   cup fresh rosemary leaves
    ¼   cup fresh thyme leaves
    12 garlic cloves

TURKEY:
    1   whole garlic head
    1   (15-pound) fresh or frozen turkey,
        thawed
    Cooking spray

ROASTED GARLIC GRAVY:
    2   (14-ounce) cans fat-free,
        less-sodium chicken broth
    ¼   cup all-purpose flour

1. Preheat oven to 325°.

2. To prepare garlic-herb rub, place first 5 ingredients in a food processor; process until finely minced.

3. To prepare turkey, remove white papery skin from garlic head (do not peel or separate the cloves). Wrap garlic head in foil. Set aside.

4. Remove and discard giblets and neck from turkey. Rinse turkey with cold water; pat dry. Trim excess fat. Starting at neck cavity, loosen skin from breast and drumsticks by inserting fingers, gently pushing between skin and meat. Spread garlic-herb rub under loosened skin, and rub over breast and drumsticks. Gently press skin to secure. Lift wing tips up and over back; tuck under turkey.

5. Place turkey on a broiler pan coated with cooking spray. Insert a meat thermometer into meaty part of a thigh, making sure not to touch bone. Bake at 325° for 1 hour. Add garlic head to pan; bake an additional 2 hours or until thermometer registers 180°. Set garlic head aside. Place turkey on a platter, reserving pan drippings; let stand 20 minutes. Discard skin.

6. To prepare gravy, place a zip-top plastic bag inside a 4-cup glass measure. Pour pan drippings into bag; let stand 10 minutes (fat will rise to top). Seal bag; carefully snip off 1 bottom corner of bag. Drain drippings into glass measure, stopping before fat layer reaches opening (you should have about ⅔ cup). Reserve 1 tablespoon fat; discard remaining fat. Add enough broth to drippings to measure 3 cups; reserve remaining broth for another use.

7. Separate roasted garlic cloves; squeeze to extract garlic pulp. Discard skins. Heat reserved fat in a medium saucepan over medium heat. Add garlic pulp and flour; cook 30 seconds or until lightly browned, stirring constantly with a whisk. Gradually add broth mixture, stirring with a whisk until blended. Bring to a boil over high heat, stirring constantly. Remove from heat. Yield: 15 servings (serving size: 6 ounces turkey and about 3 tablespoons gravy).

CALORIES 299 (23% from fat); FAT 7.5g (sat 2.4g, mono 1.8g, poly 2.1g); PROTEIN 50.6g; CARB 3.9g; FIBER 0.4g; CHOL 148mg; IRON 3.8mg; SODIUM 232mg; CALC 58mg

Sherried Mushroom Soup

BROTH:

2 tablespoons butter
1 tablespoon chopped fresh thyme
1 pound shallots, coarsely chopped
6 (14-ounce) cans fat-free, less-sodium chicken broth
2 ounces dried porcini mushrooms

REMAINING INGREDIENTS:

2 cups thinly sliced shiitake mushroom caps (about 4 ounces mushrooms)
¾ cup dry sherry
3 tablespoons chopped fresh chives

1. To prepare broth, melt butter in a Dutch oven over medium heat. Add thyme and shallots; cook 10 minutes or until shallots are golden brown. Stir in broth and porcini mushrooms; bring to a boil. Reduce heat; simmer, uncovered, 1 hour. Strain broth mixture through a sieve into a bowl; discard solids.

2. Return broth to pan. Stir in shiitake mushrooms and sherry; cook 10 minutes over low heat. Stir in chives. Serve immediately. Yield: 12 servings (serving size: about ½ cup).

CALORIES 52 (35% from fat); FAT 2g (sat 1.2g, mono 0.6g, poly 0.1g); PROTEIN 3g; CARB 2.5g; FIBER 0.2g; CHOL 5mg; IRON 0.4mg; SODIUM 401mg; CALC 4mg

Streuseled Sweet Potato Casserole

Add ⅛ teaspoon ground red pepper if you want to add a bit of heat to this sweet dish.

14 cups (1-inch) cubed peeled sweet potato (about 5 pounds)
½ cup half-and-half
½ cup maple syrup
1 teaspoon vanilla extract
¾ teaspoon salt
1 large egg, lightly beaten
Cooking spray
½ cup all-purpose flour
½ cup packed brown sugar
¼ cup chilled butter, cut into small pieces
½ cup chopped pecans

1. Preheat oven to 375°.

2. Place potato in a Dutch oven; cover with water. Bring to a boil. Reduce heat; simmer 12 minutes or until tender. Drain.

3. Combine half-and-half and next 4 ingredients in a large bowl, stirring with a whisk. Add potato to egg mixture; beat with a mixer at medium speed until smooth. Spoon potato mixture into a 13 x 9-inch baking dish coated with cooking spray.

4. Combine flour and sugar in a food processor; pulse to combine. Add butter; pulse until mixture resembles coarse meal. Stir in pecans; sprinkle over potato mixture.

5. Cover and bake at 375° for 15 minutes. Uncover and bake an additional 25 minutes or until topping is browned and potatoes are thoroughly heated. Yield: 18 servings (serving size: about ½ cup).

CALORIES 250 (23% from fat); FAT 6.3g (sat 2.4g, mono 2.5g, poly 1g); PROTEIN 3.3g; CARB 46.1g; FIBER 2.7g; CHOL 22mg; IRON 1.2mg; SODIUM 149mg; CALC 49mg

Sourdough Stuffing with Apples and Ham

(pictured on page 329)

Prepare the onion mixture up to 3 days ahead. Cover and store in the refrigerator. You can also toast the bread up to 3 days ahead; store it in an airtight container. Before serving, combine the onion mixture and bread, then add the broth and bake.

1 (1-pound) loaf sourdough bread, cut into ½-inch cubes (about 12 cups)
2 tablespoons butter
2 cups vertically sliced red onion
2 cups thinly sliced celery
2 cups chopped 33%-less-sodium ham (about 10 ounces)
2 cups diced peeled Braeburn apple
½ teaspoon dried thyme
½ teaspoon poultry seasoning
½ teaspoon freshly ground black pepper
¼ teaspoon salt
1 (14-ounce) can fat-free, less-sodium chicken broth
Cooking spray

Continued

1. Preheat oven to 350°.
2. Arrange bread cubes in single layers on 2 baking sheets. Bake at 350° for 18 minutes or until toasted. Remove from oven.
3. Increase oven temperature to 375°.
4. Melt butter in a large nonstick skillet over medium-high heat. Add onion and celery; sauté 4 minutes or until tender. Add ham and next 5 ingredients; sauté 2 minutes.
5. Combine onion mixture and bread, tossing gently to combine. Add broth; toss gently to coat. Spoon mixture into a 13 x 9-inch baking dish coated with cooking spray.
6. Cover and bake at 375° for 10 minutes. Uncover and bake an additional 35 minutes or until golden brown. Yield: 12 servings (serving size: about 1 cup).

CALORIES 179 (25% from fat); FAT 4.5g (sat 1.9g, mono 1.7g, poly 0.5g); PROTEIN 9.1g; CARB 25.4g; FIBER 2.2g; CHOL 18mg; IRON 1.5mg; SODIUM 609mg; CALC 45mg

Cranberry, Apple, and Walnut Relish

(pictured on page 329)

Make this relish up to 3 days ahead, then store it in the refrigerator. Walnuts add richness.

1   cup sugar
½   cup cranberry-apple juice
1   pound fresh cranberries
4   cups diced peeled Granny Smith apple (about 1 pound)
⅔   cup coarsely chopped walnuts

1. Combine sugar, juice, and cranberries in a large saucepan; bring to a boil over medium-high heat. Reduce heat; simmer 15 minutes or until cranberries pop and mixture thickens.
2. Remove from heat; stir in apple and walnuts. Spoon into a bowl; cool. Cover and chill at least 4 hours. Yield: 4 cups (serving size: ⅓ cup).

CALORIES 121 (25% from fat); FAT 3.3g (sat 0.2g, mono 0.7g, poly 2.1g); PROTEIN 1.5g; CARB 23.2g; FIBER 2.1g; CHOL 0mg; IRON 0.3mg; SODIUM 2mg; CALC 7mg

Green Beans with Caramelized Onions

(pictured on page 329)

Prepare the onions up to 2 days ahead, and refrigerate. Add them to the green beans in a last-minute sauté just before serving. The onions are thawed ahead to reduce the liquid that can splatter in the hot pan.

2   tablespoons olive oil, divided
2   (16-ounce) packages frozen pearl onions, thawed
1   tablespoon sugar
1   teaspoon salt, divided
2   pounds green beans, trimmed
½   teaspoon black pepper

1. Heat 1 tablespoon oil in a large nonstick skillet over medium heat. Pat onions dry with paper towels; add to pan. Increase heat to medium-high; sauté onions 5 minutes. Add sugar and ½ teaspoon salt; sauté 15 minutes or until onions are tender and golden brown. Spoon into a bowl.
2. Heat 1 tablespoon oil in pan over medium-high heat. Add beans; sauté 8 minutes or until crisp-tender. Add onions, ½ teaspoon salt, and pepper; cook 2 minutes or until mixture is thoroughly heated. Yield: 10 servings (serving size: 1 cup).

CALORIES 89 (29% from fat); FAT 2.9g (sat 0.4g, mono 2g, poly 0.3g); PROTEIN 2.5g; CARB 15.4g; FIBER 4.6g; CHOL 0mg; IRON 1.4mg; SODIUM 249mg; CALC 67mg

Vanilla Cheesecake with Cherry Topping

We use the entire vanilla bean, so none of it is wasted. The seeds flavor the cheesecake, and the bean halves flavor the topping.

CRUST:
¾   cup graham cracker crumbs
¼   cup sugar
2   tablespoons butter, melted
2   teaspoons water
Cooking spray

FILLING:
3   (8-ounce) blocks fat-free cream cheese, softened
2   (8-ounce) blocks ⅓-less-fat cream cheese, softened
1   cup sugar
3   tablespoons all-purpose flour
¼   teaspoon salt
1   (8-ounce) carton fat-free sour cream
4   large eggs
2   teaspoons vanilla extract
1   vanilla bean, split lengthwise

TOPPING:
⅔   cup tawny port or other sweet red wine
½   cup sugar
2   (10-ounce) bags frozen pitted dark sweet cherries
2   tablespoons fresh lemon juice
4   teaspoons cornstarch
4   teaspoons water

1. Preheat oven to 400°.
2. To prepare crust, combine first 3 ingredients, tossing with a fork. Add 2 teaspoons water; toss with a fork until moist and crumbly. Gently press mixture into bottom and 1½ inches up sides of a 9-inch springform pan coated with cooking spray. Bake at 400° for 5 minutes; cool on a wire rack.
3. Reduce oven temperature to 325°.
4. To prepare filling, beat cheeses with a mixer at high speed until smooth. Combine 1 cup sugar, flour, and salt, stirring with a whisk. Add to cheese mixture; beat well. Add sour cream; beat well. Add eggs, 1 at a time, beating well after each addition. Stir in vanilla extract. Scrape seeds from vanilla bean; stir seeds into cheese mixture, reserving bean halves.
5. Pour cheese mixture into prepared pan; bake at 325° for 1 hour and 15 minutes or until cheesecake center barely moves when pan is touched. Remove cheesecake from oven, and run a knife around outside edge. Cool to room temperature. Cover and chill at least 8 hours.
6. To prepare topping, combine port, ½ cup sugar, cherries, and reserved vanilla bean halves in a large saucepan; bring to

a boil. Cook 5 minutes or until cherries are thawed and mixture is syrupy. Remove vanilla bean halves; discard.

7. Combine juice, cornstarch, and 4 teaspoons water, stirring with a whisk until well blended. Stir cornstarch mixture into cherry mixture; bring to a boil. Reduce heat; simmer 3 minutes or until mixture is slightly thickened and shiny. Remove from heat; cool to room temperature. Cover and chill. Serve over cheesecake. Yield: 16 servings (serving size: 1 slice cheesecake and about 2 tablespoons topping).

CALORIES 324 (30% from fat); FAT 10.7g (sat 6.1g, mono 3.2g, poly 0.7g); PROTEIN 12.2g; CARB 42.8g; FIBER 1g; CHOL 83mg; IRON 0.8mg; SODIUM 458mg; CALC 134mg

great starts

We Break for Coffee Cake

These simple-to-make cakes are suited to many occasions. Bake one and see.

In the spirit of the holidays, we've chosen some of our favorite coffee cake recipes. Bake one, invite the neighbors over, and make time to catch up. Stash one in the freezer to serve when guests arrive on your doorstep. Better yet, make several and give them away. Coffee cakes are versatile enough to serve as breakfast pastry, brunch accompaniment, light dessert—or midnight snack for Santa.

We gave these recipes a seasonal spin by adding fruits and nuts. The nuts are toasted to bring out their flavors, then paired with everything from fresh apples to raspberry jam. To save time, we use baking powder and soda for leavening, which means the cakes don't require long rising times. And we kept the embellishments simple—last-minute dustings of powdered sugar, streusels, or stir-together icings in place of fussy frostings.

Sour Cream Raspberry Swirl Loaf

This cake freezes well for up to 2 months.

⅓ cup seedless raspberry jam
3 tablespoons chopped walnuts, toasted
1½ cups all-purpose flour
1 teaspoon baking powder
¼ teaspoon baking soda
⅛ teaspoon salt
¾ cup sugar
¼ cup butter, softened
2 teaspoons grated lemon rind
1⅛ teaspoons vanilla extract, divided
1 large egg
1 large egg white
¾ cup fat-free sour cream
Cooking spray
¼ cup sifted powdered sugar
1½ teaspoons 2% reduced-fat milk

1. Preheat oven to 350°.

2. Combine raspberry jam and walnuts in a small bowl.

3. Lightly spoon flour into dry measuring cups; level with a knife. Combine flour, baking powder, baking soda, and salt in a bowl, stirring with a whisk. Combine sugar, butter, lemon rind, 1 teaspoon vanilla, egg, and egg white in a large bowl; beat with a mixer at medium speed until well blended. Add flour mixture and sour cream alternately to sugar mixture, beginning and ending with flour mixture.

4. Spread half of batter into an 8 x 4-inch loaf pan coated with cooking spray. Spoon raspberry mixture over top, leaving a ¼-inch border. Spread remaining batter over raspberry mixture.

5. Bake at 350° for 55 minutes or until a wooden pick inserted in center comes out clean. Cool in pan 10 minutes on a wire rack; remove from pan. Cool completely on wire rack. Combine ⅛ teaspoon vanilla , powdered sugar, and milk in a small bowl, stirring well with a whisk. Drizzle over loaf. Yield: 12 servings (serving size: 1 slice).

CALORIES 184 (26% from fat); FAT 5.4g (sat 2.6g, mono 1.6g, poly 0.9g); PROTEIN 3.2g; CARB 31.2g; FIBER 0.7g; CHOL 28mg; IRON 1.2mg; SODIUM 155mg; CALC 53mg

Cherry-Almond Cake

Find almond paste in the baking section of your grocery store.

1 cup all-purpose flour
1 teaspoon baking powder
⅛ teaspoon salt
⅛ teaspoon ground cloves
⅔ cup granulated sugar
3½ tablespoons butter, softened
3 tablespoons fat-free cream cheese
2 tablespoons almond paste
¼ teaspoon almond extract
1 large egg
⅓ cup 1% low-fat milk
Cooking spray
2 tablespoons chopped almonds, toasted
2 tablespoons granulated sugar
1 (14.5-ounce) can pitted tart red cherries in water, drained
1 teaspoon powdered sugar

1. Preheat oven to 350°.

2. Lightly spoon flour into a dry measuring cup; level with a knife. Combine flour, baking powder, salt, and cloves in a bowl, stirring with a whisk. Combine ⅔ cup granulated sugar and next 5 ingredients in a large bowl; beat with a mixer at medium speed until blended.

3. Add flour mixture and milk alternately to sugar mixture, beginning and ending with flour mixture. Pour batter into a 9-inch round cake pan coated with cooking spray.

4. Combine almonds and 2 tablespoons granulated sugar; sprinkle over batter. Arrange cherries on top. Bake at 350° for 50 minutes or until a wooden pick inserted in center comes out clean. Cool in pan 10 minutes on a wire rack; remove from pan. Sift powdered sugar over top of cake. Yield: 12 servings (serving size: 1 wedge).

CALORIES 191 (24% from fat); FAT 5.1g (sat 2.4g, mono 1.6g, poly 0.4g); PROTEIN 3.7g; CARB 26.8g; FIBER 1.8g; CHOL 27mg; IRON 2.3mg; SODIUM 137mg; CALC 61mg

Apple Cake with Almonds

We tested this dish with Braeburn apples, but Granny Smith also will work.

- 5 tablespoons butter, divided
- 2 cups chopped peeled cooking apple
- 1½ cups all-purpose flour
- 1½ teaspoons baking powder
- ⅛ teaspoon salt
- 1 cup granulated sugar
- ½ cup (4 ounces) block-style fat-free cream cheese
- 1¼ teaspoons vanilla extract, divided
- ½ teaspoon almond extract
- ½ cup 1% low-fat milk
- 1 large egg, lightly beaten
- 1 large egg white, lightly beaten
- Cooking spray
- 2 tablespoons sliced almonds, toasted
- ⅓ cup sifted powdered sugar
- 2 teaspoons water

1. Preheat oven to 350°.
2. Melt 1 tablespoon butter in a large nonstick skillet over medium-high heat. Add apple; cook 5 minutes or until tender.
3. Lightly spoon flour into dry measuring cups; level with a knife. Combine flour, baking powder, and salt in a bowl, stirring with a whisk. Combine ¼ cup butter, granulated sugar, cream cheese, 1 teaspoon vanilla, and almond extract in a large bowl; beat with a mixer at medium speed until blended.
4. Combine milk, egg, and egg white. Add flour mixture and milk mixture alternately to cream cheese mixture, beginning and ending with flour mixture. Stir in apple. Pour batter into a 9-inch round cake pan coated with cooking spray. Sprinkle with almonds.
5. Bake at 350° for 55 minutes or until a wooden pick inserted in center comes out clean. Cool in pan 10 minutes on a wire rack; remove from pan.
6. Combine ¼ teaspoon vanilla, powdered sugar, and water in a small bowl. Drizzle over cake. Serve cake warm or at room temperature. Yield: 12 servings (serving size: 1 wedge).

CALORIES 225 (25% from fat); FAT 6.2g (sat 3.4g, mono 2g, poly 0.5g); PROTEIN 4.4g; CARB 38.5g; FIBER 1.3g; CHOL 32mg; IRON 1mg; SODIUM 201mg; CALC 74mg

Blueberry Buckle with Walnuts and Ginger

CRUMBS:

- 2 tablespoons all-purpose flour
- 2 tablespoons brown sugar
- ⅛ teaspoon ground cinnamon
- 1 tablespoon butter
- 2 tablespoons chopped walnuts, toasted

CAKE:

- 1¼ cups all-purpose flour
- 1¼ teaspoons baking powder
- ⅛ teaspoon salt
- ½ cup granulated sugar
- ⅓ cup packed brown sugar
- 3½ tablespoons butter, softened
- 1½ teaspoons grated peeled fresh ginger
- 1 teaspoon vanilla extract
- 1 large egg
- ½ cup 1% low-fat milk
- Cooking spray
- 2 cups frozen blueberries
- 1½ teaspoons powdered sugar

1. Preheat oven to 350°.
2. To prepare crumbs, combine first 3 ingredients in a small bowl; cut in 1 tablespoon butter with a pastry blender or 2 knives until mixture resembles coarse meal. Stir in walnuts.
3. To prepare cake, lightly spoon 1¼ cups flour into dry measuring cups; level with a knife. Combine 1¼ cups flour, baking powder, and salt in a bowl, stirring with a whisk. Combine granulated sugar and next 5 ingredients in a large bowl; beat with a mixer at medium speed until well blended. Add flour mixture and milk alternately to butter mixture, beginning and ending with flour mixture.
4. Pour batter into a 9-inch round cake pan coated with cooking spray. Sprinkle with blueberries and crumbs. Bake at 350° for 1 hour or until a wooden pick inserted in center comes out clean. Cool in pan 10 minutes on a wire rack; remove from pan. Sift powdered sugar over cake. Serve cake warm or at room temperature. Yield: 12 servings (serving size: 1 wedge).

CALORIES 189 (29% from fat); FAT 6g (sat 3g, mono 1.6g, poly 0.9g); PROTEIN 2.7g; CARB 31.8g; FIBER 1.2g; CHOL 30mg; IRON 1mg; SODIUM 134mg; CALC 57mg

Orange Yogurt Cake with Golden Raisins and Pistachios

CRUMBS:

- 2 tablespoons all-purpose flour
- 2 tablespoons brown sugar
- 1 tablespoon butter, cut into small pieces and softened
- 2 tablespoons chopped pistachios

CAKE:

- ¼ cup (2 ounces) block-style ⅓-less-fat cream cheese, softened
- 2 tablespoons orange marmalade
- 1¼ cups all-purpose flour
- ½ teaspoon baking powder
- ¼ teaspoon baking soda
- ⅛ teaspoon salt
- ¾ cup granulated sugar
- ¼ cup butter, softened
- 2 teaspoons grated orange rind
- 1 teaspoon vanilla extract
- 1 large egg
- ¾ cup fat-free plain yogurt
- 3 tablespoons golden raisins
- Cooking spray

1. Preheat oven to 350°.
2. To prepare crumbs, combine 2 tablespoons flour and brown sugar in a medium bowl; cut in 1 tablespoon butter with a pastry blender or 2 knives until mixture resembles coarse meal. Stir in pistachios.
3. To prepare cake, combine cream cheese and marmalade in a small bowl; set aside. Lightly spoon 1¼ cups flour into dry measuring cups, and level with a knife. Combine 1¼ cups flour, baking powder, baking soda, and salt in a bowl, stirring with a whisk. Combine granulated sugar and next 4 ingredients in a large bowl; beat with a mixer at medium speed until well blended. Add flour mixture and yogurt alternately to egg mixture, beginning and ending with flour mixture. Stir in raisins.
4. Pour batter into a 9-inch round cake pan coated with cooking spray; spread evenly. Spread cream cheese mixture over batter. Sprinkle crumbs over cream cheese mixture.
5. Bake at 350° for 50 minutes or until cake is golden brown and starts to pull away from sides of pan. Cool in pan 10

minutes on a wire rack; remove from pan. Serve cake warm or at room temperature. Yield: 12 servings (serving size: 1 wedge).

CALORIES 195 (28% from fat); FAT 6g (sat 3.2g, mono 1.9g, poly 0.5g); PROTEIN 4g; CARB 31.8g; FIBER 0.7g; CHOL 31mg; IRON 0.9mg; SODIUM 163mg; CALC 67mg

Banana Coffee Cake with Macadamia Nuts and Coconut

Cooking spray
1⅓ cups all-purpose flour
½ teaspoon salt
½ teaspoon baking powder
¼ teaspoon baking soda
1 cup mashed ripe banana (about 2 large bananas)
¾ cup granulated sugar
3 tablespoons vegetable oil
1 teaspoon vanilla extract
¼ teaspoon ground nutmeg
1 large egg
¼ cup packed dark brown sugar
1 tablespoon water
2 teaspoons butter
2 tablespoons chopped macadamia nuts, toasted
2 tablespoons flaked sweetened coconut

1. Preheat oven to 350°.
2. Coat a 9-inch round cake pan with cooking spray; line bottom of pan with wax paper. Coat wax paper with cooking spray.
3. Lightly spoon flour into dry measuring cups; level with a knife. Combine flour, salt, baking powder, and baking soda in a bowl, stirring with a whisk. Combine banana and next 5 ingredients in a bowl; beat with a mixer at medium speed 1 minute or until well blended. Add flour mixture to banana mixture, and beat until blended. Pour batter into prepared pan.
4. Bake at 350° for 30 minutes or until a wooden pick inserted in center comes out clean. Cool in pan 10 minutes on a wire rack; remove from pan. Carefully peel off wax paper.
5. Combine brown sugar, water, and butter in a small saucepan; bring to a boil. Cook 1 minute, stirring constantly.

Remove from heat; stir in nuts and coconut. Spread over cake. Serve cake warm. Yield: 12 servings (serving size: 1 wedge).

CALORIES 189 (28% from fat); FAT 5.8g (sat 1.4g, mono 1.9g, poly 2.1g); PROTEIN 2.3g; CARB 32.6g; FIBER 1g; CHOL 19mg; IRON 0.9mg; SODIUM 159mg; CALC 22mg

Pineapple Coffee Cake with Toasted Pecans

Cooking spray
1 (8-ounce) can crushed pineapple in juice, undrained
1¼ cups all-purpose flour
¾ teaspoon baking powder
¼ teaspoon baking soda
⅛ teaspoon salt
¾ cup granulated sugar
¼ cup butter, softened
1 teaspoon vanilla extract
1 large egg
½ cup low-fat buttermilk
2 tablespoons chopped pecans, toasted
½ cup sifted powdered sugar

1. Preheat oven to 350°.
2. Coat a 9-inch round cake pan with cooking spray; line bottom with wax paper. Coat wax paper with cooking spray.
3. Drain pineapple in a colander over a bowl, reserving 1 tablespoon juice.
4. Lightly spoon flour into dry measuring cups; level with a knife. Combine flour, baking powder, baking soda, and salt, stirring with a whisk. Combine granulated sugar, butter, vanilla, and egg in a large bowl; beat with a mixer at medium speed until well blended. Add flour mixture and buttermilk alternately to sugar mixture, beginning and ending with flour mixture. Stir in pineapple and pecans. Pour batter into prepared pan.
5. Bake at 350° for 30 minutes or until a wooden pick inserted in center comes out clean. Cool in pan 10 minutes on a wire rack; remove from pan. Carefully peel off wax paper. Combine powdered sugar and reserved 1 tablespoon juice, stirring with a whisk; drizzle over cake. Yield: 12 servings (serving size: 1 wedge).

CALORIES 177 (27% from fat); FAT 5.4g (sat 2.7g, mono 1.8g, poly 0.5g); PROTEIN 2.4g; CARB 30.1g; FIBER 0.6g; CHOL 29mg; IRON 0.8mg; SODIUM 138mg; CALC 34mg

back to the best

Hot Maple Soufflés

This dessert has become a holiday favorite at Cooking Light.

The recipe by Quebecois chef Daniel Vézina originally appeared in a November 1998 *Cooking Light* magazine story that highlights French-Canadian cooking.

Hot Maple Soufflés

1 tablespoon butter, softened
2 tablespoons granulated sugar
3 tablespoons bourbon
3 tablespoons maple syrup
1 cup maple syrup
4 large egg whites
⅛ teaspoon salt
1 teaspoon baking powder
1 tablespoon sifted powdered sugar

1. Preheat oven to 425°.
2. Coat 6 (10-ounce) ramekins with butter; sprinkle evenly with granulated sugar. Combine bourbon and 3 tablespoons syrup in a small microwave-safe bowl; microwave at HIGH 1½ minutes or until mixture boils. Pour about 1 tablespoon bourbon mixture into each prepared ramekin.
3. Cook 1 cup syrup in a medium, heavy saucepan over medium-high heat 8 minutes or until candy thermometer registers 250°.
4. Beat egg whites and salt with a mixer at medium speed until foamy. Pour hot maple syrup in a thin stream over egg whites, beating at medium speed, then at high speed, until stiff peaks form. Add baking powder; beat well.
5. Spoon evenly into ramekins; place on a jelly roll pan. Bake at 425° for 13 minutes or until puffy and set. Sprinkle with powdered sugar. Serve immediately. Yield: 6 servings.

CALORIES 212 (8% from fat); FAT 2g (sat 0.4g, mono 0.8g, poly 0.6g); PROTEIN 2.3g; CARB 47.8g; FIBER 0g; CHOL 0mg; IRON 0.8mg; SODIUM 193mg; CALC 89mg

Variations on the Theme

Add new flavors to your table with this eclectic bill of fare.

If you're tired of the same old same old, you may be thankful for some new serving ideas. Contemporary ingredients turn up in Greens with Roasted Corn and Pepper Salad, Blue Corn Bread Dressing, and sautéed duck, yet this whole menu is grounded in tradition, moving smoothly from Mushroom Turnovers to Mincemeat Charlottes. It's familiar enough to feel friendly, but adventurous enough to impress even the most jaded palate.

Thanksgiving with a Twist Menu
serves 8

Mushroom Turnovers

Greens with Roasted Corn and Pepper Salad

Sautéed Duck Breast with Cherry-Pistachio Salsa

Blue Corn Bread Dressing

Roasted Asparagus with Balsamic-Shallot Butter

Molasses Cake with Lemon Cream Cheese Frosting or **Mincemeat Charlottes**

search myclar2003.com for all our menus

Mushroom Turnovers

This recipe makes a great appetizer for a potluck supper any time of year. The turnovers can be made ahead, frozen, and baked just before serving.

PASTRY:
- 2 cups all-purpose flour
- ¾ cup (6 ounces) block-style fat-free cream cheese
- 6 tablespoons chilled butter, cut into small pieces
- 1 teaspoon salt
- 6 tablespoons ice water

FILLING:
- 1 pound mushrooms, coarsely chopped
- Cooking spray
- ¼ cup minced shallots
- ⅛ teaspoon salt
- ⅛ teaspoon black pepper
- 2 tablespoons chopped fresh basil

ADDITIONAL INGREDIENTS:
- 2 teaspoons water
- 1 large egg white, lightly beaten

1. To prepare pastry, lightly spoon flour into dry measuring cups; level with a knife. Combine flour, cream cheese, butter, and 1 teaspoon salt in a food processor; pulse 4 times or until mixture resembles coarse meal. With processor on, add ice water through food chute, processing until dough forms a ball. Gently press mixture into a 4-inch circle on plastic wrap. Cover pastry, and chill 15 minutes.

2. To prepare filling, place mushrooms in food processor, and process until finely chopped. Heat a large nonstick skillet coated with cooking spray over medium-high heat. Add shallots; cook 1 minute or until soft. Stir in mushrooms, ⅛ teaspoon salt, and pepper. Cook 10 minutes or until most of liquid evaporates, stirring frequently. Remove from heat; stir in basil. Cool completely.

3. Preheat oven to 350°.

4. Combine 2 teaspoons water and egg white in a small bowl, and stir well with a whisk.

5. Divide dough into 24 equal portions. Shape each portion into a ball; chill. Working with 1 portion at a time, roll each dough ball into a 4-inch circle on a lightly floured surface. Lightly brush with egg white mixture. Spoon about 2 teaspoons mushroom filling onto half of each circle. Fold dough over filling; press edges together with a fork to seal. Brush egg white mixture over pastries. Place 1 inch apart on a baking sheet lined with parchment paper.

6. Bake at 350° for 20 minutes or until lightly browned. Let stand 5 minutes before serving. Yield: 24 servings (serving size: 1 turnover).

CALORIES 71 (38% from fat); FAT 3g (sat 1.8g, mono 0.9g, poly 0.1g); PROTEIN 2.6g; CARB 9.3g; FIBER 0.8g; CHOL 9mg; IRON 0.8mg; SODIUM 190mg; CALC 8mg

Greens with Roasted Corn and Pepper Salad

Roast the corn up to 2 days ahead. Combine the corn with all but the greens and pine nuts an hour before dinner, then finish assembling the salad just before serving.

- 1 cup frozen corn kernels, thawed
- 5 ounces bottled roasted red bell peppers, drained and chopped
- ½ cup chopped green onions
- 1 jalapeño pepper, seeded and finely chopped
- ¼ cup low-fat sour cream
- 3 tablespoons white wine vinegar
- 1 teaspoon salt
- 2 (10-ounce) packages Italian-blend salad greens (about 12 cups)
- 3 tablespoons pine nuts, toasted

1. Preheat broiler.

2. Place corn on a foil-lined baking sheet. Broil 12 minutes or until lightly browned, stirring once. Cool.

3. Combine corn, bell peppers, onions, and jalapeño pepper in a large bowl. Combine sour cream, vinegar, and salt, stirring with a whisk. Add sour cream mixture to corn mixture, tossing to coat; chill 1 hour.

4. Divide greens evenly among 8 plates; top each serving with about ⅓ cup corn mixture and about 1 teaspoon pine nuts. Yield: 8 servings.

CALORIES 73 (37% from fat); FAT 3g (sat 0.9g, mono 0.8g, poly 1g); PROTEIN 3.6g; CARB 10g; FIBER 3.7g; CHOL 3mg; IRON 1.7mg; SODIUM 324mg; CALC 60mg

Sautéed Duck Breast with Cherry-Pistachio Salsa

Duck breasts cook more quickly than turkey and you can easily adjust this recipe for the number of guests you'll have. Look for boneless duck breasts in the freezer section of your supermarket. You can substitute chicken if you don't like duck.

1½ cups dried sweet or tart cherries (about 8 ounces)
1½ cups boiling water
1 dried chipotle chile
½ cup shelled dry-roasted pistachios, coarsely chopped
⅓ cup finely chopped red onion
¼ cup chopped fresh cilantro
2 tablespoons fresh lime juice
1 teaspoon chili powder
1 teaspoon honey
1 jalapeño pepper, seeded and finely chopped
1¼ teaspoons salt, divided
1 teaspoon black pepper
8 (6-ounce) boneless duck breast halves, skinned
1 teaspoon vegetable oil
Cooking spray

1. Combine first 3 ingredients in a large bowl; let stand 30 minutes. Drain well; discard chile. Combine cherries, pistachios, and next 6 ingredients. Stir in ¼ teaspoon salt.

2. Sprinkle 1 teaspoon salt and pepper over duck. Heat oil in a large nonstick skillet coated with cooking spray over medium-high heat. Add duck; sauté 6 minutes on each side or until desired degree of doneness. Serve with salsa. Yield: 8 servings (serving size: 1 duck breast half and about ⅓ cup salsa).

WINE NOTE: From mushrooms to duck, this menu is full of earthy flavors and touches of spice. Saintsbury's Pinot Noir 2000 (Carneros, California; $24) has the aroma of chocolate cherries and spiced tea, and flavors evocative of cherry compote, strawberry jam, licorice, vanilla, and exotic spices—just the ticket for the duck. And with dessert, try tawny port, with flavors of vanilla, brown sugar, and roasted nuts. Taylor Fladgate 10-year-old tawny port is $26.

CALORIES 354 (29% from fat); FAT 11.4g (sat 2.7g, mono 4g, poly 2.4g); PROTEIN 37.1g; CARB 23.1g; FIBER 3.3g; CHOL 131mg; IRON 8.4mg; SODIUM 469mg; CALC 32mg

Blue Corn Bread Dressing

We used blue cornmeal for this dressing. If you can't find it, yellow cornmeal will work fine.

Cooking spray
1 tablespoon all-purpose flour
⅓ cup sugar
5 tablespoons butter, softened
5 large eggs
½ cup fat-free buttermilk
1 cup all-purpose flour
1 cup blue cornmeal
2 teaspoons baking powder
1 teaspoon baking soda
1 teaspoon salt
5 (14-ounce) cans fat-free, less-sodium chicken broth
1 teaspoon olive oil
1 cup finely chopped onion
1 cup frozen corn kernels, thawed
7 ounces bottled roasted red bell peppers, drained and chopped
8 cups (1-inch) cubed French bread (about 8 ounces)
¾ cup chopped green onions
Cooking spray

1. Preheat oven to 450°.

2. Coat a 13 x 9-inch baking pan with cooking spray, and dust with 1 tablespoon flour.

3. Place sugar and butter in a bowl; beat with a mixer at medium speed until well blended. Add eggs, 1 at a time, beating well after each addition. Stir in buttermilk.

Lightly spoon 1 cup flour into a dry measuring cup; level with a knife. Combine flour, cornmeal, baking powder, baking soda, and salt, stirring well with a whisk. Add flour mixture to buttermilk mixture, stirring until moist.

4. Pour batter into prepared baking pan. Bake at 450° for 20 minutes or until a wooden pick inserted in center comes out clean. Cool completely. Cut corn bread into 1-inch cubes.

5. Reduce oven temperature to 350°.

6. Bring broth to a boil in a large saucepan; cook until reduced to 5 cups (about 30 minutes). Heat oil in a large nonstick skillet over medium-high heat. Add 1 cup onion; sauté 3 minutes. Add corn and bell pepper; sauté 3 minutes.

7. Combine onion mixture, corn bread, French bread, and green onions in a large bowl, stirring to combine. Add broth, tossing to coat. Spoon mixture into a 13 x 9-inch baking pan coated with cooking spray. Bake at 350° for 40 minutes or until set. Yield: 8 servings.

CALORIES 216 (30% from fat); FAT 7.2g (sat 3.5g, mono 2.1g, poly 0.6g); PROTEIN 7.6g; CARB 30.7g; FIBER 1.5g; CHOL 79mg; IRON 1.5mg; SODIUM 534mg; CALC 62mg

Roasted Asparagus with Balsamic-Shallot Butter

Make the butter ahead, if you like. Roast the asparagus and toss it with the butter just before serving.

3 tablespoons finely chopped shallots
2 tablespoons butter, melted
2 tablespoons balsamic vinegar
1 teaspoon chopped fresh thyme
¾ teaspoon salt
½ teaspoon grated lemon rind
2 pounds asparagus spears
Cooking spray

1. Combine first 6 ingredients, stirring well with a whisk.

2. Preheat oven to 450°.

3. Snap off tough ends of asparagus. Arrange asparagus in a single layer on a jelly roll pan coated with cooking spray. Cover with foil; bake at 450° for 5
Continued

minutes. Uncover and bake an additional 10 minutes or until asparagus is crisp-tender. Pour butter mixture over asparagus, toss gently to coat. Serve immediately. Yield: 8 servings.

CALORIES 56 (50% from fat); FAT 3.1g (sat 1.9g, mono 0.9g, poly 0.2g); PROTEIN 2.7g; CARB 6.2g; FIBER 1.8g; CHOL 8mg; IRON 1.1mg; SODIUM 253mg; CALC 28mg

Molasses Cake with Lemon Cream Cheese Frosting

You can make this cake up to 2 days ahead and keep it chilled.

CAKE:
Cooking spray
2 cups sifted cake flour
1 teaspoon baking soda
1 teaspoon ground cinnamon
½ teaspoon salt
1 cup fat-free buttermilk
¾ cup molasses
½ cup granulated sugar
6 tablespoons butter, melted
1 tablespoon minced peeled fresh ginger
1 large egg, lightly beaten

FROSTING:
½ cup powdered sugar
1 tablespoon grated lemon rind
1 (8-ounce) block ⅓-less-fat cream cheese, softened

1. Preheat oven to 350°.
2. To prepare cake, coat a 9-inch square baking pan with cooking spray; line bottom of pan with wax paper. Coat wax paper with cooking spray.
3. Sift together flour, baking soda, cinnamon, and salt.
4. Place buttermilk and next 5 ingredients in a large bowl; beat with a mixer at medium speed until well blended. Add flour mixture to buttermilk mixture, stirring just until combined.
5. Spoon batter into prepared pan. Bake at 350° for 35 minutes or until a wooden pick inserted in center comes out clean. Cool in pan 10 minutes on a wire rack. Loosen cake from sides of pan with a narrow metal spatula; remove from pan. Peel off wax paper; cool completely on a wire rack.
6. To prepare frosting, place powdered sugar, lemon rind, and cream cheese in a bowl; beat with a mixer at medium speed until smooth. Spread frosting over top of cake. Cut into squares. Yield: 12 servings.

CALORIES 253 (29% from fat); FAT 8.2g (sat 4.9g, mono 1.9g, poly 0.3g); PROTEIN 4.6g; CARB 41.7g; FIBER 0.4g; CHOL 41mg; IRON 4mg; SODIUM 369mg; CALC 147mg

Mincemeat Charlottes

This dessert is delicious served warm with low-fat vanilla ice cream. You can substitute apple juice for cognac.

1 (9-ounce) package condensed mincemeat (such as Borden's)
Cooking spray
1 tablespoon sugar
24 slices very thin white bread, divided
1 cup chopped peeled apple
¼ cup butter, melted
¼ cup cognac

1. Preheat oven to 350°.
2. Reconstitute mincemeat according to package directions to yield 2 cups. Lightly coat 8 (6-ounce) ramekins with cooking spray; evenly dust ramekins with sugar.
3. Place 16 bread slices on a cutting board or work surface. Cut 16 bread circles with a (2-inch) round cutter; discard bread trimmings. Place 1 circle in bottom of each ramekin; reserve remaining circles.
4. Trim crusts from 8 bread slices. Cut each slice into 3 (3 x 1-inch) rectangles. Then cut each in half to produce 6 (1½ x 1-inch) rectangles. Line sides of each ramekin with 6 rectangles, arranged vertically, side by side. Press rectangles gently to fit.
5. Combine mincemeat, apple, butter, and cognac. Place about ⅓ cup mincemeat mixture in each ramekin; top each with 1 remaining bread circle, pressing circles gently onto mincemeat filling. Place ramekins on a baking sheet. Bake at 350° for 30 minutes or until golden.

Remove from oven; cool on baking sheet 5 minutes. Place a dessert plate, upside down, on top of each ramekin; invert onto plates. Serve warm. Yield: 8 servings.

CALORIES 303 (23% from fat); FAT 7.7g (sat 3.6g, mono 2.2g, poly 1.2g); PROTEIN 4.1g; CARB 53.6g; FIBER 2.3g; CHOL 16mg; IRON 1.4mg; SODIUM 499mg; CALC 57mg

sidetracked

Cinderella Vegetables

It's time to invite the overlooked but utterly delicious vegetables to your table.

Roasted Cauliflower

2 teaspoons olive oil
2 onions, quartered
5 garlic cloves, halved
4 cups cauliflower florets (about 1½ pounds)
Cooking spray
1 tablespoon water
1 tablespoon Dijon mustard
½ teaspoon salt
¼ teaspoon freshly ground black pepper
1 tablespoon chopped fresh flat-leaf parsley

1. Preheat oven to 500°.
2. Heat oil in a large skillet over medium heat. Add onion and garlic; cook 5 minutes or until browned, stirring frequently. Remove from heat.
3. Place onion mixture and cauliflower in a roasting pan coated with cooking spray. Combine water and mustard; pour over vegetable mixture. Toss to coat; sprinkle with salt and pepper. Bake at 500° for 20 minutes or until golden brown, stirring occasionally. Sprinkle with parsley. Yield: 4 servings (serving size: 1 cup).

CALORIES 94 (30% from fat); FAT 3.1g (sat 0.4g, mono 1.8g, poly 0.5g); PROTEIN 4.5g; CARB 15.4g; FIBER 5.4g; CHOL 0mg; IRON 1.1mg; SODIUM 408mg; CALC 63mg

Potato, Celeriac, and Green Onion Gratin

To get a head start, place the sliced potato and celeriac in a large bowl of cold water mixed with a little lemon juice (to prevent discoloration). Pat the slices dry with paper towels before arranging them in the baking dish. You can use Swiss cheese in place of Jarlsberg, if you prefer.

¾ teaspoon salt
½ teaspoon dried marjoram
½ teaspoon black pepper
6 cups thinly sliced baking potato (about 2 pounds)
Cooking spray
1 (2-pound) celeriac (celery root), peeled, quartered lengthwise, and thinly sliced
1 cup thinly sliced leek (about 2 medium)
1 cup thinly sliced green onion
1 cup (4 ounces) shredded reduced-fat Jarlsberg cheese
½ cup fat-free, less-sodium chicken broth
½ cup dry sherry
½ cup dry breadcrumbs
2 tablespoons chopped fresh parsley
1 tablespoon grated fresh Parmesan cheese
1 tablespoon olive oil

1. Preheat oven to 375°.
2. Combine first 3 ingredients.
3. Arrange 2 cups potato slices in a 13 x 9-inch baking dish coated with cooking spray. Arrange half of celeriac slices over potato slices. Top with ½ cup leek, ½ cup onions, and ½ cup Jarlsberg cheese. Sprinkle with one-third of marjoram mixture. Repeat procedure with 2 cups potato slices; remaining celeriac slices, leek, onions, and Jarlsberg cheese; and one-third of marjoram mixture.
4. Top with 2 cups potato slices. Pour broth and sherry over potato mixture; sprinkle with remaining marjoram mixture. Cover and bake at 375° for 1 hour or until tender.
5. Combine breadcrumbs and remaining 3 ingredients; sprinkle over potato mixture. Bake, uncovered, an additional 20 minutes or until lightly browned. Let stand 10 minutes before serving. Yield: 8 servings (serving size: 1 cup).

CALORIES 227 (14% from fat); FAT 3.4g (sat 1g, mono 1.7g, poly 0.5g); PROTEIN 9.3g; CARB 39.8g; FIBER 4.6g; CHOL 6mg; IRON 2.9mg; SODIUM 461mg; CALC 229mg

Peeling Celeriac

1. *Cut off top and bottom, squaring off bottom so celeriac will sit securely on cutting board.*

2. *Using a sharp knife, cut around sides to remove outer layer.*

Curried Celeriac Slaw with Dried Cherries

½ cup dried tart cherries
½ cup finely chopped red onion
3 tablespoons plain fat-free yogurt
3 tablespoons fat-free sour cream
1 tablespoon Dijon mustard
1 teaspoon curry powder
1 teaspoon olive oil
½ teaspoon sugar
½ teaspoon salt
3 cups shredded peeled celeriac (about 1 pound celery root)

1. Combine all ingredients except celeriac in a large bowl, stirring with a whisk. Add celeriac; toss well to coat. Cover and chill 2 hours. Yield: 4 servings (serving size: about ⅔ cup).

CALORIES 138 (14% from fat); FAT 2.2g (sat 0.4g, mono 1.1g, poly 0.4g); PROTEIN 3.9g; CARB 32.3g; FIBER 3.6g; CHOL 2mg; IRON 1.4mg; SODIUM 486mg; CALC 101mg

Parsnip and Portobello Casserole

Mushrooms, sweet parsnips, and cheese are an unusual yet pleasing combination. Serve with roast beef.

6 ounces portobello mushroom caps
⅔ cup chopped sugar-cured ham (about 3 ounces)
1 cup chopped yellow onion
2 tablespoons minced shallots
⅔ cup fat-free, less-sodium chicken broth
2½ cups shredded parsnip (about 1 pound)
¼ teaspoon black pepper
½ cup (2 ounces) shredded Gouda cheese
Cooking spray
¼ cup dry breadcrumbs
2 tablespoons chopped fresh parsley

1. Preheat oven to 375°.
2. Remove brown gills from undersides of portobello mushrooms using a spoon; discard gills. Chop mushroom caps to measure 3½ cups.
3. Heat a large skillet over medium-high heat. Add chopped ham; sauté 2 minutes, stirring frequently. Add onion and shallots; sauté 5 minutes or until tender. Add mushroom and broth; cook 5 minutes, stirring frequently. Add parsnip and pepper; cook 5 minutes, stirring frequently.
4. Remove from heat; stir in cheese. Spoon mixture into a 2-quart baking dish coated with cooking spray. Combine breadcrumbs and parsley; sprinkle over mushroom mixture. Bake at 375° for 10 *Continued*

minutes or until golden brown. Yield: 4 servings (serving size: ¾ cup).

CALORIES 227 (24% from fat); FAT 6g (sat 3.3g, mono 0.2g, poly 0.1g); PROTEIN 11.6g; CARB 33.5g; FIBER 3.9g; CHOL 24mg; IRON 1.8mg; SODIUM 407mg; CALC 174mg

Maple-Glazed Rutabaga

Sweet maple syrup complements earthy, slightly bitter rutabaga. Serve with pork tenderloin or ham.

  ¼ cup maple syrup
1½ teaspoons butter, melted
  7 cups (½-inch) cubed peeled rutabaga (about 2 medium)
  ¼ teaspoon salt
  ¼ teaspoon black pepper
Cooking spray

1. Preheat oven to 425°.
2. Combine syrup and butter in a large bowl, stirring with a whisk. Add rutabaga, salt, and pepper; toss to coat. Spread rutabaga mixture on a jelly roll pan coated with cooking spray.
3. Bake at 425° for 35 minutes or until rutabaga is tender, stirring occasionally. Yield: 4 servings (serving size: 1 cup).

CALORIES 153 (12% from fat); FAT 2g (sat 1.1g, mono 0.5g, poly 0.3g); PROTEIN 3g; CARB 33.5g; FIBER 6.2g; CHOL 5mg; IRON 1.5mg; SODIUM 212mg; CALC 131mg

Turnip and Rutabaga Stir-Fry

  2 teaspoons vegetable oil
  2 teaspoons minced peeled fresh ginger
  2 garlic cloves, minced
  2 cups (3-inch) julienne-cut peeled turnip (about ½ pound)
  2 cups (3-inch) julienne-cut peeled rutabaga (about ½ pound)
  1 cup sugar snap peas, trimmed and each cut in half lengthwise
  ¼ cup fat-free, less-sodium chicken broth
  3 tablespoons low-sodium soy sauce
  2 teaspoons cornstarch
  2 teaspoons mirin (sweet rice wine)

1. Heat oil in a large nonstick skillet over medium-high heat. Add ginger and garlic; stir-fry 30 seconds. Add turnip and rutabaga; stir-fry 1 minute or until crisp-tender. Add sugar snap peas; stir-fry 30 seconds.
2. Combine broth, soy sauce, cornstarch, and mirin in a small bowl; add to pan. Bring to a boil; cook 1 minute, stirring constantly. Yield: 4 servings (serving size: ¾ cup).

CALORIES 96 (23% from fat); FAT 2.5g (sat 0.4g, mono 0.6g, poly 1.4g); PROTEIN 3.3g; CARB 15.7g; FIBER 3.7g; CHOL 0mg; IRON 1mg; SODIUM 514mg; CALC 72mg

happy endings

Warm Desserts for Cold Nights

For a rich, creamy dessert that's great straight from the oven, try these easy bread puddings.

When you need a dessert that will please holiday guests of all ages, consider bread pudding. Assemble it ahead of time, refrigerate, and then pop it in the oven just before dinner. By the time you're ready for dessert, the bread pudding will be at its best—steaming hot, fresh from the oven.

Blueberry Bread Puddings with Lemon Curd

Tart lemon curd tops individual bread puddings laced with berries. Fresh blueberries also work well in this recipe. Prepare the lemon curd while the puddings bake.

PUDDINGS:
1¼ cups 2% reduced-fat milk
  ½ cup sugar
1½ teaspoons grated lemon rind
  3 large eggs, lightly beaten
4½ cups (½-inch) cubed French bread (about 8 ounces)
    Cooking spray
1½ cups frozen blueberries

LEMON CURD:
  ⅓ cup sugar
  1 large egg, lightly beaten
  ¼ cup fresh lemon juice
  2 teaspoons butter

1. To prepare puddings, combine first 4 ingredients in a large bowl, stirring well with a whisk. Add bread, tossing gently to coat. Cover and chill 30 minutes or up to 4 hours.
2. Preheat oven to 350°.
3. Divide half of bread mixture evenly among 8 (6-ounce) ramekins or custard cups coated with cooking spray; sprinkle evenly with ¾ cup berries. Divide remaining bread mixture among ramekins; top with ¾ cup berries.
4. Cover each ramekin with foil. Place ramekins in a 13 x 9-inch baking pan; add hot water to pan to a depth of 1 inch. Bake, covered, at 350° for 15 minutes. Uncover and bake an additional 15 minutes or until a knife inserted in center comes out clean.
5. To prepare lemon curd, combine ⅓ cup sugar and 1 egg in a small saucepan over medium heat, stirring with a whisk. Cook 2 minutes or until sugar dissolves and mixture is light in color, stirring constantly. Stir in lemon juice and butter; cook 2 minutes or until mixture coats back of a spoon, stirring constantly with a whisk.
6. Place saucepan in a large ice-filled bowl 5 minutes or until lemon curd cools to room temperature. Serve lemon curd over warm bread puddings. Yield: 8 servings (serving size: 1 bread pudding and 1 tablespoon lemon curd).

CALORIES 240 (20% from fat); FAT 5.2g (sat 2g, mono 1.8g, poly 0.7g); PROTEIN 7.1g; CARB 41.9g; FIBER 1.7g; CHOL 112mg; IRON 1.2mg; SODIUM 234mg; CALC 84mg

Cinnamon Bread Puddings with Caramel Syrup

This recipe is easy because it starts with cinnamon-swirl bread, reducing the need to add other flavorings. Commercial caramel syrup saves time, too. Baking the pudding in muffin cups creates individual servings.

1⅓ cups 2% reduced-fat milk
½ cup sugar
3 large eggs, lightly beaten
1 (1-pound) loaf cinnamon-swirl bread, cut into 1-inch cubes
Cooking spray
⅔ cup fat-free caramel sundae syrup

1. Combine first 3 ingredients in a large bowl, stirring well with a whisk. Add bread, tossing gently to coat. Cover and chill 30 minutes or up to 4 hours.
2. Preheat oven to 350°.
3. Divide bread mixture evenly among 11 muffin cups coated with cooking spray. Bake at 350° for 30 minutes or until a knife inserted in center comes out clean. Serve warm with syrup. Yield: 11 servings (serving size: 1 bread pudding and about 1 tablespoon syrup).

CALORIES 251 (20% from fat); FAT 5.6g (sat 1.5g, mono 2.9g, poly 0.2g); PROTEIN 7.1g; CARB 46.3g; FIBER 3g; CHOL 60mg; IRON 1.3mg; SODIUM 255mg; CALC 52mg

Bread Pudding Tidbits

• Assemble and refrigerate the pudding up to 4 hours in advance.
• Let the bread stand at least 30 minutes after tossing it with the custard mixture to ensure that every drop of liquid is absorbed, yielding a creamier texture. Because most recipes use egg-and-milk custards, this soak needs to take place in the refrigerator.
• If you're using stale bread, add ¼ cup more liquid (milk or water, depending on the recipe). How do you define stale bread? It doesn't compress when you cut it.
• Most of these puddings cook in a water bath, which surrounds delicate custard-based dishes with gentle heat to keep the custard from breaking.
• Use a 13 x 9-inch metal baking pan or a large roasting pan for the water bath.
• Bread puddings are best served warm from the oven; they don't reheat well.

search myclar2003.com for all our tips

New Orleans Bread Pudding with Bourbon Sauce

Raisin-studded bread pudding and buttery, bourbon-spiked sauce combine in this time-honored dessert.

PUDDING:
¼ cup raisins
2 tablespoons bourbon
1¼ cups 2% reduced-fat milk
½ cup sugar
1 tablespoon vanilla extract
½ teaspoon ground cinnamon
¼ teaspoon ground nutmeg
Dash of salt
3 large eggs, lightly beaten
4½ cups (½-inch) cubed French bread (about 8 ounces)
Cooking spray

SAUCE:
½ cup sugar
¼ cup light-colored corn syrup
¼ cup butter
¼ cup bourbon

1. To prepare pudding, combine raisins and 2 tablespoons bourbon in a bowl. Let stand 30 minutes. Drain mixture in a sieve over a bowl, reserving liquid.
2. Combine reserved liquid, milk, and next 6 ingredients in a large bowl, stirring well with a whisk. Add bread, tossing gently to coat. Spoon mixture into an 8-inch square baking dish coated with cooking spray. Sprinkle evenly with raisins, pressing gently into bread mixture. Cover with foil; chill 30 minutes or up to 4 hours.
3. Preheat oven to 350°.
4. Place dish in a 13 x 9-inch baking pan; add hot water to pan to a depth of 1 inch. Bake, covered, at 350° for 20 minutes. Uncover and bake an additional 10 minutes or until a knife inserted in center comes out clean.
5. To prepare sauce, combine ½ cup sugar, corn syrup, and butter in a small saucepan over medium heat. Bring to a simmer; cook 1 minute, stirring constantly. Remove from heat; stir in ¼ cup bourbon. Serve each bread pudding

piece warm with about 1 tablespoon sauce. Yield: 9 servings.

CALORIES 309 (24% from fat); FAT 8.2g (sat 4.3g, mono 2.7g, poly 0.6g); PROTEIN 5.6g; CARB 47.6g; FIBER 1g; CHOL 87mg; IRON 1.1mg; SODIUM 272mg; CALC 74mg

Indian Bread Pudding with Cardamom Sauce

The flavors of rose-flower water and cardamom are typical in Indian and Middle Eastern desserts. The bread cooks in a mixture of milk and sugar, but without eggs—so it's not as creamy as a typical bread pudding. Instead, it's topped with a rich custard sauce.

PUDDING:
9 (1-ounce) slices white bread
2 tablespoons butter, melted
Cooking spray
1 cup evaporated fat-free milk
3 tablespoons sugar
¼ teaspoon rose-flower water (optional)

SAUCE:
2 tablespoons sugar
2 large egg yolks, lightly beaten
1 cup whole milk
⅛ teaspoon ground cardamom
1 tablespoon finely chopped pistachios

1. Preheat oven to 400°.
2. To prepare pudding, trim crusts from bread. Arrange bread slices in a single layer on a baking sheet; brush with melted butter. Bake at 400° for 8 minutes or until toasted.
3. Remove bread from oven; cool 5 minutes on a wire rack. Cut each slice into 4 squares. Arrange squares in overlapping rows in an 11 x 7-inch baking dish coated with cooking spray.
4. Combine evaporated milk, 3 tablespoons sugar, and rose-flower water, if desired, stirring well with a whisk. Pour mixture evenly over bread. Cover with foil; chill 30 minutes or up to 4 hours.
5. Preheat oven to 350°.
6. Bake pudding, covered, at 350° for 15 minutes.

Continued

7. To prepare sauce, combine 2 tablespoons sugar and egg yolks in a medium bowl, stirring well with a whisk. Heat whole milk in a small, heavy saucepan over medium heat to 180° or until tiny bubbles form around edge (do not boil). Gradually add hot milk to egg yolk mixture, stirring constantly with a whisk.

8. Place mixture in pan; cook over low heat 6 minutes or until mixture coats back of a spoon, stirring constantly with a whisk. Remove from heat; stir in cardamom.

9. Place pan in a large ice-filled bowl 5 minutes or until sauce cools to room temperature, stirring occasionally.

10. Arrange 6 warm bread pudding squares on each of 6 dessert plates. Top each serving with about 2½ tablespoons sauce and ½ teaspoon pistachios. Yield: 6 servings.

CALORIES 272 (29% from fat); FAT 8.7g (sat 3.8g, mono 2.5g, poly 0.6g); PROTEIN 9g; CARB 41.9g; FIBER 2.6g; CHOL 90mg; IRON 1.2mg; SODIUM 352mg; CALC 191mg

Capirotada
Mexican Bread Pudding

Unlike bread puddings with custard bases, *capirotada* typically features layers of nuts, cheese, dried fruit, and bread drizzled with cinnamon-infused sugar syrup. And because there's no custard, there's no need for a water bath.

1¼ cups packed dark brown sugar
1¼ cups water
 2 (3-inch) cinnamon sticks
4½ cups (½-inch) cubed French bread
       (about 8 ounces)
 ¼ cup golden raisins
 ¼ cup slivered almonds, toasted
 2 tablespoons butter, cut into small
       pieces
   Cooking spray
 ¾ cup (3 ounces) shredded Monterey
       Jack cheese

1. Combine first 3 ingredients in a medium saucepan; bring to a boil. Reduce heat; simmer 10 minutes. Discard cinnamon sticks.

2. Combine bread, raisins, almonds, and butter in a large bowl. Drizzle with warm sugar syrup, tossing gently to coat. Spoon mixture into an 8-inch square baking dish coated with cooking spray. Top with cheese. Cover with foil; chill 30 minutes or up to 4 hours.

3. Preheat oven to 350°.

4. Bake at 350° for 20 minutes. Uncover and bake an additional 15 minutes or until cheese is golden brown. Serve warm. Yield: 8 servings.

CALORIES 313 (27% from fat); FAT 9.3g (sat 4.4g, mono 3.6g, poly 0.9g); PROTEIN 5.8g; CARB 52.6g; FIBER 1.4g; CHOL 19mg; IRON 1.6mg; SODIUM 289mg; CALC 140mg

Pumpkin Bread Pudding

Toasted pecans and maple syrup adorn this dessert that's reminiscent of pumpkin pie. Using egg-rich *challah* bread rather than French bread yields a richer flavor.

1¼ cups 2% reduced-fat milk
 ½ cup sugar
 ½ teaspoon pumpkin-pie
       spice
 3 large eggs, lightly beaten
 1 (15-ounce) can pumpkin
4½ cups (½-inch) cubed challah or
       other egg bread (about 8 ounces)
   Cooking spray
 ½ cup maple syrup
 ¼ cup chopped pecans, toasted

1. Combine first 5 ingredients in a large bowl, stirring well with a whisk. Add bread, tossing gently to coat. Spoon mixture into an 8-inch square baking dish coated with cooking spray. Cover mixture with foil, and chill 30 minutes or up to 4 hours.

2. Preheat oven to 350°.

3. Place dish in a 13 x 9-inch baking pan; add hot water to pan to a depth of 1 inch. Bake, covered, at 350° for 25 minutes. Uncover and bake an additional 10 minutes or until a knife inserted in center comes out clean. Serve each bread pudding piece warm with about 1 tablespoon syrup and 1½ teaspoons pecans. Yield: 8 servings.

CALORIES 273 (23% from fat); FAT 7g (sat 1.7g, mono 3.1g, poly 1.4g); PROTEIN 7.5g; CARB 46.1g; FIBER 3.3g; CHOL 97mg; IRON 1.8mg; SODIUM 186mg; CALC 117mg

Chocolate-Hazelnut Bread Pudding

Vanilla ice cream melts over the warm bread pudding to form a sauce. If you have whole hazelnuts, toast them at 350° for 8 to 10 minutes, or until the skins are loosened. To rub off the papery skins, roll the nuts in a clean dish towel. Then chop as needed.

1⅓ cups 2% reduced-fat milk
 ½ cup sugar
 ¼ cup unsweetened
       cocoa
 1 ounce unsweetened chocolate,
       chopped
 2 large egg whites, lightly beaten
 1 large egg, lightly beaten
 ¼ cup Frangelico (hazelnut-flavored
       liqueur)
 ¾ teaspoon vanilla extract
 ⅛ teaspoon salt
4½ cups (½-inch) cubed French bread
       (about 8 ounces)
   Cooking spray
 2 tablespoons chopped hazelnuts
 2 cups vanilla low-fat ice cream

1. Combine first 4 ingredients in a medium saucepan. Cook over medium-low heat 3 minutes or until chocolate melts, stirring constantly (do not boil).

2. Combine egg whites and egg in a large bowl; gradually add hot milk mixture to egg mixture, stirring constantly with a whisk. Stir in liqueur, vanilla, and salt. Add bread, tossing gently to coat.

3. Spoon mixture into an 8-inch square baking dish coated with cooking spray. Cover with foil; chill 30 minutes or up to 4 hours.

4. Preheat oven to 350°.

5. Sprinkle hazelnuts evenly over pudding. Place dish in a 13 x 9-inch baking pan; add hot water to pan to a depth of 1 inch. Bake, covered, at 350° for 30 minutes. Uncover and bake an additional 5 minutes or until a knife inserted in center comes out clean. Serve each bread pudding piece warm with ¼ cup ice cream. Yield: 8 servings.

CALORIES 277 (22% from fat); FAT 6.7g (sat 2.8g, mono 2.4g, poly 0.5g); PROTEIN 8.2g; CARB 44.8g; FIBER 3g; CHOL 32mg; IRON 1.5mg; SODIUM 275mg; CALC 133mg

Bountiful Harvest

For these Wisconsin farmers, growing cranberries is a labor of love.

Mary Brazeau Brown, 50, and her husband, Philip, run Glacial Lake Cranberries in Wisconsin Rapids, Wisconsin. Though central Wisconsin is best known for its dairy farms, it also is an area proud of its cranberry harvest. Wisconsin is actually the nation's top cranberry-growing state. Of Mary and Philip's 6,000-acre spread, 330 acres are devoted to cranberry production with wetland and a forestry-management program accounting for the balance. Mary and Philip practice holistic cranberry farming and offer you one of their favorite chutney recipes to try for yourself.

Cranberry Chutney

Slivered almonds add crunch to Mary's favorite chutney, which she serves with shrimp or chicken. For more cranberry recipes, see Grand Berries (recipes begin on page 339).

4 cups fresh cranberries
2 cups packed brown sugar
1 cup raisins
1 cup water
½ cup slivered almonds, toasted
¼ cup fresh lemon juice
1 teaspoon salt
1 teaspoon grated onion
⅛ teaspoon ground cloves

1. Combine all ingredients in a large saucepan, and bring to a boil. Reduce heat, and simmer 35 minutes or until thickened. Yield: 3½ cups (serving size: ¼ cup).

CALORIES 199 (11% from fat); FAT 2.5g (sat 0.2g, mono 1.6g, poly 0.6g); PROTEIN 1.4g; CARB 44.2g; FIBER 2.2g; CHOL 0mg; IRON 1.2mg; SODIUM 184mg; CALC 47mg

Table for Two

Enjoy a feast tailored to fit a duo.

When you wish to celebrate a cozy Thanksgiving à deux, you may face a dilemma: A 12-pound turkey is too big. Enter Cornish hens: perfect poultry for a pair. And you'll enjoy marking the holiday with the rest of this equally streamlined menu.

An Intimate Thanksgiving Menu

Celery Salad

Rosemary-Lemon Cornish Hens with Roasted Potatoes

Swiss Chard with Garlic and Oregano

Maple-Glazed Winter Squash

Pear-Cranberry Sauce

Apple Crumble with Golden Raisins

search myclar2003.com for all our menus

Celery Salad

(pictured on page 329)

A cool, crisp salad adds crunch and contrast to the menu. You can also use dried cranberries and walnuts.

¾ cup sliced celery
⅓ cup dried sweet cherries
⅓ cup frozen green peas, thawed
3 tablespoons chopped fresh parsley
1½ tablespoons fat-free mayonnaise
1½ tablespoons plain low-fat yogurt
1 tablespoon chopped pecans, toasted
1½ teaspoons fresh lemon juice
⅛ teaspoon salt
⅛ teaspoon black pepper

1. Combine all ingredients; chill. Yield: 2 servings (serving size: about ⅔ cup).

CALORIES 160 (21% from fat); FAT 3.7g (sat 0.4g, mono 1.7g, poly 1.3g); PROTEIN 4.1g; CARB 27.5g; FIBER 4.5g; CHOL 0mg; IRON 1.3mg; SODIUM 332mg; CALC 71mg

Rosemary-Lemon Cornish Hens with Roasted Potatoes

(pictured on page 331)

Vary this recipe by using thyme in place of rosemary.

2 teaspoons crushed dried rosemary
½ teaspoon salt, divided
¼ teaspoon black pepper, divided
2 (1¼-pound) Cornish hens
½ lemon, halved
Cooking spray
2 cups cubed Yukon gold or red potato
2 teaspoons olive oil

1. Preheat oven to 375°.
2. Combine rosemary, ¼ teaspoon salt, and ⅛ teaspoon pepper.
3. Remove and discard giblets from hens. Rinse hens with cold water; pat dry. Remove skin; trim excess fat. Working with 1 hen at a time, place 1 lemon piece in cavity of hen; tie ends of legs together with twine. Lift wing tips up and over back; tuck under hen. Repeat procedure with remaining hen and lemon piece. Rub hens with rosemary mixture. Place hens, breast sides up, on a broiler pan coated with cooking spray.
4. Toss potato with oil; sprinkle with ¼ teaspoon salt and ⅛ teaspoon pepper. Arrange potato around hens.
5. Insert a meat thermometer into meaty part of a thigh, making sure not to touch bone. Remove twine from legs. Bake at 375° for 1 hour or until thermometer registers 180°. Yield: 2 servings (serving size: 1 hen and about ¾ cup potatoes).

CALORIES 372 (28% from fat); FAT 11.4g (sat 2.4g, mono 5.5g, poly 2.1g); PROTEIN 41.8g; CARB 24.1g; FIBER 2.7g; CHOL 180mg; IRON 3mg; SODIUM 702mg; CALC 47mg

Swiss Chard with Garlic and Oregano

After you rinse and drain the chard, there should be just enough water clinging to the leaves for it to wilt.

10 cups coarsely chopped Swiss chard (about 10 ounces)
 1 teaspoon olive oil
 1 garlic clove, minced
 ¼ teaspoon dried oregano
 ⅛ teaspoon salt
Dash of black pepper
 2 teaspoons red wine vinegar

1. Rinse Swiss chard with cold water; drain well.
2. Heat oil in a large nonstick skillet over medium-high heat. Add garlic, and sauté 1 minute or until slightly golden. Add chard. Cover and cook 1 minute or until chard begins to wilt. Stir in oregano, salt, and pepper. Cover and cook 5 minutes or until tender, stirring occasionally. Remove from heat; stir in vinegar. Yield: 2 servings (serving size: about ½ cup).

CALORIES 51 (46% from fat); FAT 2.6g (sat 0.4g, mono 1.7g, poly 0.3g); PROTEIN 2.7g; CARB 6.1g; FIBER 2.4g; CHOL 0mg; IRON 2.8mg; SODIUM 454mg; CALC 80mg

Maple-Glazed Winter Squash

Cook the squash in the same roasting pan as the Cornish hens and potatoes to save time. Arrange the squash on the front of the pan so you can easily brush it with the syrup mixture when you open the oven door. Save the remaining squash to cube for soup or risotto, or to roast and serve later.

 1 (1¾-pound) butternut squash
Cooking spray
 4 teaspoons maple syrup
 1 teaspoon butter

1. Preheat oven to 375°.
2. Cut squash 1 inch above bulb; save stem section for another use. Cut bulb in half lengthwise. Remove and discard seeds and membranes. Place squash halves, cut sides up, on a broiler pan coated with cooking spray; place 2 teaspoons maple syrup and ½ teaspoon butter in each squash half.
3. Bake at 375° for 1 hour or until squash is tender, brushing cut sides with syrup mixture every 20 minutes. Yield: 2 servings (serving size: 1 squash half).

CALORIES 86 (21% from fat); FAT 2g (sat 1.2g, mono 0.6g, poly 0.1g); PROTEIN 0.8g; CARB 17.9g; FIBER 2.4g; CHOL 5mg; IRON 0.7mg; SODIUM 24mg; CALC 45mg

Pear-Cranberry Sauce

 ⅓ cup fresh cranberries
 3 tablespoons water
 2 Bartlett pears, peeled and coarsely chopped
 1 tablespoon sugar
 ¼ teaspoon grated orange rind

1. Combine first 3 ingredients in a small saucepan. Cover and cook over medium-low heat 25 minutes or until cranberries pop, stirring occasionally.
2. Remove from heat; stir in sugar and rind. Cool to room temperature. Yield: 2 servings (serving size: about ⅓ cup).

CALORIES 118 (5% from fat); FAT 0.6g (sat 0.1g, mono 0.1g, poly 0.2g); PROTEIN 0.5g; CARB 30.4g; FIBER 2.9g; CHOL 0mg; IRON 0.3mg; SODIUM 0mg; CALC 13mg

Apple Crumble with Golden Raisins

Baked apple—sweetened with raisins, orange juice, and cinnamon—is graced with a simple crumb topping. For a sweeter flavor, try Braeburn apples.

 2 tablespoons all-purpose flour
 2 tablespoons granulated sugar, divided
 1 tablespoon brown sugar
 1 tablespoon chilled butter, cut into small pieces
1½ cups diced peeled Granny Smith apple
 2 tablespoons fresh orange juice
 1 tablespoon golden raisins
 ½ teaspoon fresh lemon juice
 ⅛ teaspoon ground cinnamon
Cooking spray

1. Preheat oven to 375°.
2. Combine flour, 1 tablespoon granulated sugar, and brown sugar in a medium bowl. Cut in butter with a pastry blender or 2 knives until mixture resembles coarse meal.
3. Combine 1 tablespoon granulated sugar, apple, and next 4 ingredients, tossing well. Divide apple mixture evenly between 2 (6-ounce) ramekins coated with cooking spray. Sprinkle evenly with flour mixture. Bake at 375° for 30 minutes or until golden brown. Yield: 2 servings.

CALORIES 223 (25% from fat); FAT 6.2g (sat 3.7g, mono 1.7g, poly 0.4g); PROTEIN 1.3g; CARB 43.1g; FIBER 2.4g; CHOL 16mg; IRON 0.7mg; SODIUM 61mg; CALC 17mg

december

All About Winter Fruit

These fruits will brighten your table and excite your palate.

Just when it seems the fruit section of produce markets will be barren for the cold months ahead, exotic winter fruits enter—and with them, hope. But these specialty fruits look different from those we know so well, and it's not always obvious how to eat or cook with them. Here's the lowdown on six of winter's most delicious: blood oranges, clementines, kumquats, persimmons, pomegranates, and quinces. Learn how to choose, store, and best enjoy each one. Once you're more familiar with them, you'll never dread the less bountiful produce shelves of winter again.

Persimmon and Fennel Salad

The easiest way to peel persimmons is to cut the fruit into wedges and remove the peel from each wedge with a paring knife. We prefer nonastringent Fuyu persimmons in this salad. Serve with roasted pork or chicken.

- 2 tablespoons finely chopped shallots
- 2 tablespoons red wine vinegar
- 2 teaspoons sugar
- 1½ teaspoons olive oil
- ½ teaspoon salt
- ¼ teaspoon freshly ground black pepper
- 3 cups thinly sliced fennel bulb (about 1 large bulb)
- ¼ cup chopped fresh chives
- 4 persimmons, each cut into 6 wedges and peeled
- ¼ cup (1 ounce) crumbled goat cheese

1. Combine first 6 ingredients in a large bowl, stirring well with a whisk. Add fennel, chives, and persimmons; toss gently to coat. Divide fennel mixture evenly among 4 plates. Top each serving with 1 tablespoon cheese. Yield: 4 servings.

CALORIES 103 (30% from fat); FAT 3.4g (sat 1.3g, mono 1.6g, poly 0.2g); PROTEIN 2.6g; CARB 17.5g; FIBER 2.1g; CHOL 3mg; IRON 1.4mg; SODIUM 355mg; CALC 55mg

Seared Scallops with Pomegranate Sauce

Look for pomegranate juice at markets specializing in Middle Eastern foods, or make fresh juice by squeezing the fruit as you would an orange.

- 2 large pomegranates, halved crosswise
- ¼ cup balsamic vinegar
- 2 tablespoons low-sodium soy sauce
- ⅛ teaspoon freshly ground black pepper
- Dash of ground red pepper
- 1½ pounds sea scallops
- 2 teaspoons vegetable oil
- ¼ teaspoon salt
- ¼ teaspoon sugar
- ⅛ teaspoon freshly ground black pepper
- 3 cups trimmed watercress (about 1 bunch)
- ¾ cup pomegranate seeds (about 1 pomegranate)

1. Squeeze juice from pomegranate halves using a citrus reamer or juicer to measure 1 cup. Combine juice, vinegar, soy sauce, ⅛ teaspoon black pepper, and red pepper in a small saucepan; bring to a boil. Reduce heat; simmer until reduced by half (about 15 minutes), stirring frequently. Keep warm.

2. Rinse scallops; pat dry. Heat oil in a cast iron skillet over medium-high heat. Sprinkle scallops with salt, sugar, and ⅛ teaspoon black pepper. Add scallops to pan; cook 2 minutes on each side or until done.

3. Arrange ½ cup watercress on each of 6 plates; divide scallops evenly among plates. Drizzle each serving with about 1 tablespoon sauce; sprinkle with 2 tablespoons seeds. Yield: 6 servings.

CALORIES 175 (14% from fat); FAT 2.7g (sat 0.2g, mono 1g, poly 0.8g); PROTEIN 20.2g; CARB 17.9g; FIBER 0.7g; CHOL 37mg; IRON 0.7mg; SODIUM 592mg; CALC 53mg

Pepper-Crusted Beef Tenderloin with Kumquat Marmalade

Kumquats, carrot juice, Dijon mustard, and rice vinegar create a piquant accompaniment for peppered beef tenderloin. Try the kumquat marmalade with pork or chicken as well.

- 1½ cups vertically sliced onion
- ½ cup halved, seeded, and vertically sliced kumquats
- ½ cup carrot juice or orange juice
- 1 tablespoon Dijon mustard
- ¼ teaspoon salt
- 2 thyme sprigs
- 1 bay leaf
- 2 teaspoons rice vinegar
- 2 teaspoons olive oil
- 1½ to 2 tablespoons freshly ground mixed peppercorns or black peppercorns
- 4 (4-ounce) beef tenderloin steaks, trimmed (about ¾ inch thick)
- ½ teaspoon salt

1. Combine first 7 ingredients in a small saucepan; bring to a boil. Reduce heat; simmer 15 minutes or until liquid almost evaporates, stirring occasionally. Remove from heat. Discard thyme sprigs and bay leaf. Stir in rice vinegar, and cool.

2. Heat oil in a large nonstick skillet over medium-high heat. Place pepper in a shallow dish. Dredge steaks in pepper; sprinkle evenly with ½ teaspoon salt. Add beef to pan; cook 3 minutes on each side or until desired degree of doneness. Serve with marmalade. Yield: 4 servings (serving size: 1 steak and about ¼ cup marmalade).

CALORIES 211 (29% from fat); FAT 6.9g (sat 1.9g, mono 3.3g, poly 0.4g); PROTEIN 23.8g; CARB 17.1g; FIBER 3.4g; CHOL 60mg; IRON 4.1mg; SODIUM 611mg; CALC 62mg

Spiced Shrimp Skewers with Clementine Salsa

Don't be intimidated by the long list of ingredients—more than half are spices. Serve this dish with cooked rice to balance the earthy-flavored shrimp and fiery-sweet salsa.

SHRIMP:
- ½ teaspoon ground cinnamon
- ½ teaspoon paprika
- ¼ teaspoon salt
- ¼ teaspoon ground ginger
- ¼ teaspoon ground coriander seeds
- ¼ teaspoon ground cumin
- ⅛ teaspoon ground red pepper
- ⅛ teaspoon freshly ground black pepper

Dash of ground nutmeg
- 36 jumbo shrimp (about 2½ pounds), peeled and deveined

Cooking spray

SALSA:
- 6 cups clementine sections (about 6 clementines)
- 1½ cups chopped peeled jícama
- 1 cup finely chopped red onion
- 1 tablespoon minced peeled fresh ginger
- 1 tablespoon fresh lime juice
- 1 tablespoon extra-virgin olive oil
- 2 teaspoons chopped fresh thyme
- ½ teaspoon salt
- ¼ teaspoon freshly ground black pepper
- 2 serrano chiles, seeded and finely chopped

1. To prepare shrimp, combine first 9 ingredients in a large bowl; stir well. Add shrimp, tossing well to coat. Cover and marinate in refrigerator 4 hours.
2. Preheat grill or grill pan.

3. Thread 3 shrimp onto each of 12 (6-inch) skewers. Place skewers on grill rack or grill pan coated with cooking spray; cook 3 minutes on each side or until shrimp are done.
4. To prepare salsa, combine clementine and remaining 9 ingredients, stirring well. Serve salsa with shrimp. Yield: 6 servings (serving size: 2 skewers and about ⅔ cup salsa).

CALORIES 135 (22% from fat); FAT 3.3g (sat 0.5g, mono 1.8g, poly 0.6g); PROTEIN 9.7g; CARB 15.9g; FIBER 3.3g; CHOL 64mg; IRON 1.5mg; SODIUM 360mg; CALC 49mg

Rice Pudding with Pomegranate Syrup

You can serve this versatile dessert warm just after cooking, or make it ahead of time, refrigerate, and serve chilled.

PUDDING:
- 3½ cups 2% reduced-fat milk, divided
- ½ cup uncooked Arborio rice or other short-grain rice
- ⅓ cup sugar
- 1 tablespoon butter
- 1 large egg, lightly beaten
- 1 teaspoon vanilla extract

SYRUP:
- 2 large pomegranates, halved crosswise
- ¼ cup sugar
- 6 tablespoons pomegranate seeds

1. To prepare pudding, combine 3 cups milk, rice, ⅓ cup sugar, and butter in a medium saucepan; bring to a boil. Reduce heat; simmer, uncovered, 10 minutes, stirring occasionally. Remove mixture from heat.
2. Combine ½ cup milk and egg, stirring with a whisk. Gradually stir about one-fourth of warm rice mixture into egg mixture; add to pan, stirring constantly. Simmer, uncovered, 30 minutes or until rice is tender, stirring occasionally. Remove from heat; stir in vanilla.
3. To prepare syrup, squeeze juice from pomegranate halves using a citrus reamer or juicer to measure 1 cup. Combine juice and ¼ cup sugar in a small

saucepan; bring to a boil. Reduce heat; simmer until reduced to ⅓ cup (about 20 minutes), stirring frequently.
4. Drizzle syrup evenly over pudding, and sprinkle with seeds. Yield: 6 servings (serving size: ½ cup pudding, about 1 tablespoon syrup, and 1 tablespoon seeds).

CALORIES 296 (18% from fat); FAT 5.9g (sat 3.2g, mono 1.8g, poly 0.2g); PROTEIN 7.7g; CARB 53.1g; FIBER 0.7g; CHOL 52mg; IRON 0.5mg; SODIUM 131mg; CALC 171mg

White Chocolate Sorbet with Warm Clementine Sauce

Clementine juice flavors the sorbet, and sections are added to the sauce. Juice the clementines just as you would oranges.

SORBET:
- ½ cup clementine juice (about 5 clementines)
- 5 ounces premium white chocolate, chopped
- 2½ cups water
- ¾ cup sugar
- ½ cup fresh lemon juice
- ¼ teaspoon vanilla extract

SAUCE:
- 1 tablespoon water
- 1 teaspoon cornstarch
- ½ cup clementine juice (about 5 clementines)
- ¼ cup water
- 2 teaspoons sugar
- 1 teaspoon fresh lemon juice
- 3 cups clementine sections (about 3 clementines)

1. To prepare sorbet, bring ½ cup clementine juice to a boil in a small saucepan. Reduce heat; simmer until reduced to ¼ cup (about 12 minutes).
2. Place chocolate in a large bowl. Combine 2½ cups water and ¾ cup sugar in a small saucepan; bring to a boil. Cook 1 minute; remove from heat. Pour over chocolate; let stand 2 minutes. Stir gently with a whisk until smooth. Add reduced clementine juice, ½ cup lemon juice,

Continued

and vanilla to chocolate mixture, stirring well. Cool completely.

3. Pour mixture into freezer can of ice-cream freezer; freeze according to manufacturer's instructions. Spoon sorbet into a freezer-safe container; cover and freeze 1 hour or until firm.

4. To prepare sauce, combine 1 tablespoon water and cornstarch in a small bowl, stirring well with a whisk. Combine ½ cup clementine juice, ¼ cup water, 2 teaspoons sugar, and 1 teaspoon lemon juice in a small saucepan; bring to a simmer. Add cornstarch mixture to juice mixture, and bring to a boil. Cook 1 minute or until thickened, stirring constantly.

5. Remove from heat, and gently stir in clementine sections. Cover and let stand 2 minutes. Serve sauce warm with sorbet. Yield: 5 servings (serving size: about ⅓ cup sorbet and about ½ cup sauce).

CALORIES 320 (26% from fat); FAT 9.2g (sat 5.5g, mono 2.6g, poly 0.3g); PROTEIN 2.4g; CARB 59.6g; FIBER 0.2g; CHOL 6mg; IRON 0.2mg; SODIUM 27mg; CALC 75mg

Quince Upside-Down Tart

This dessert is similar to *tarte Tatin*, the classic upside-down apple tart from France.

1½	tablespoons butter
¼	cup sugar, divided
2½	pounds quince, cored, peeled, and thinly sliced (about 5 quince)
¼	cup honey
3	tablespoons fresh lemon juice
½	(15-ounce) package refrigerated pie dough (such as Pillsbury)

1. Melt butter in a 10-inch cast iron or large, heavy skillet over medium heat. Stir in 3 tablespoons sugar; remove from heat. Arrange quince slices spokelike on top of butter mixture, working from center of pan to edge.

2. Combine 1 tablespoon sugar, honey, and juice, stirring well with a whisk. Drizzle mixture evenly over quince slices. Cover pan with foil; cook over medium heat 30 minutes.

3. Remove pan from heat; carefully remove foil. Cool 10 minutes.

4. Preheat oven to 400°.

5. Roll dough into an 11-inch circle; place over quince mixture. Tuck edges of crust into sides of pan. Cut 2 small slits in top of dough to allow steam to escape. Bake at 400° for 20 minutes or until lightly browned. Let stand 5 minutes. Place a plate upside down on top of pan, and invert onto plate. Serve warm. Yield: 9 servings (serving size: 1 wedge).

CALORIES 246 (30% from fat); FAT 8.2g (sat 3.8g, mono 2.5g, poly 1.5g); PROTEIN 1g; CARB 44.6g; FIBER 21.9g; CHOL 10mg; IRON 0.9mg; SODIUM 121mg; CALC 16mg

Blood Orange Layer Cake

CAKE:

Cooking spray
4	large eggs
¼	teaspoon vanilla extract
⅛	teaspoon salt
½	cup granulated sugar
1	cup all-purpose flour, sifted

FILLING:

1	(16-ounce) carton plain yogurt
2	tablespoons honey
½	teaspoon vanilla extract
⅓	cup whipping cream
¼	cup sifted powdered sugar
5	cups blood orange sections (about 3 blood oranges)
2	tablespoons chopped fresh mint

SYRUP:

1	cup blood orange juice (about 2 blood oranges)
¼	cup granulated sugar

GARNISH:

Mint sprigs (optional)

1. Preheat oven to 375°.

2. To prepare cake, coat an 8-inch round cake pan with cooking spray; line bottom of pan with wax paper. Coat wax paper with cooking spray.

3. Combine eggs, ¼ teaspoon vanilla, and salt in a large bowl, and beat with a mixer at high speed 2 minutes. Gradually add ½ cup granulated sugar, beating until egg mixture is thick and pale (about 3 minutes). Gently fold flour into egg

mixture, ¼ cup at a time. Spoon batter into prepared pan.

4. Bake at 375° for 20 minutes or until cake springs back when touched lightly in center. Cool in pan 10 minutes on a wire rack; remove from pan. Cool completely on wire rack.

5. To prepare filling, place a colander in a 2-quart glass measure or medium bowl. Line colander with 4 layers of cheesecloth, allowing cheesecloth to extend over outside edges. Spoon yogurt into colander. Cover loosely with plastic wrap; refrigerate 12 hours.

6. Spoon yogurt cheese into a large bowl; discard liquid. Add honey and ½ teaspoon vanilla to yogurt, stirring well with a whisk.

7. Combine cream and powdered sugar in a medium bowl, and beat with a mixer at high speed until soft peaks form. Gently stir one-fourth of cream mixture into yogurt mixture; gently fold in remaining cream mixture. Cover mixture, and chill 15 minutes.

8. Arrange orange sections in a single layer on several layers of paper towels, and let stand 5 minutes. Reserve half of sections; roughly chop remaining sections. Combine chopped orange sections and chopped mint. Cover and chill.

9. To prepare syrup, combine juice and ¼ cup granulated sugar in a small saucepan; bring to a boil over medium-high heat, stirring constantly with a whisk. Reduce heat; simmer until reduced to ¼ cup (about 15 minutes). Remove from heat; cool.

10. Split cake in half horizontally using a serrated knife; place bottom layer, cut side up, on a plate. Brush with 2 tablespoons syrup. Spread with half of yogurt mixture, leaving a ¼-inch border. Sprinkle chopped orange mixture evenly over yogurt mixture.

11. Top with remaining cake layer, cut side down. Brush top layer with remaining syrup; spread with remaining yogurt mixture. Top cake with reserved whole orange sections; garnish with mint sprigs, if desired. Yield: 12 servings (serving size: 1 slice).

CALORIES 240 (25% from fat); FAT 6.7g (sat 3.4g, mono 2g, poly 0.3g); PROTEIN 6.1g; CARB 41.9g; FIBER 0.4g; CHOL 101mg; IRON 1.1mg; SODIUM 77mg; CALC 101mg

Winter Fruit Varieties

Blood Orange

Somewhat expensive, the blood orange is prized for its bright citrus flavor as much as for its color. Moro, a variety usually available from December through March, is less acidic than common oranges.

The fruit's skin may be pitted or smooth, and blood oranges are usually smaller than traditional oranges. They keep refrigerated for 2 to 4 weeks. When cooking with the blood orange, consider different ways to highlight its beautiful color. Squeeze the fresh juice, or use the peeled sections as a garnish.

Clementine

Unlike naval oranges, clementines peel effortlessly and have no seeds. They're in the Mandarin family of fruits, but are smaller and juicier.

Clementines flood the supermarkets in December and January, but their season seems to start earlier and stretch later every year. They'll keep refrigerated for a week. The simplest way to enjoy clementines: Peel and eat.

Kumquat

These 2-inch oblong fruits are golden orange and can be served whole or chopped. The juicy fruit has an intense sour-orange flavor, which is why you'll often see them candied, pickled, or preserved. Kumquats can thicken sauces, and are often prepared to accompany roasted meats and game. The name of the fruit comes from its native China, where kumquat translates as golden orange.

Kumquats are in season as early as October and as late as June, but they're most plentiful from December through April. Buy only firm fruit. Store them at room temperature if you plan to eat them within a few days; keep them for up to 2 weeks when refrigerated. You can eat kumquats whole, seeds included. The piquant flavor is a nice addition to chutneys and marmalades paired with beef, pork, or chicken. Use them whole and uncooked to garnish holiday platters and grace ornamental fruit bowls.

Persimmon

There are two distinct categories of persimmons—astringent and nonastringent. We recommend the Fuyu variety for our Persimmon and Fennel Salad (recipe on page 364). It's a nonastringent persimmon shaped like a tomato. This and all other nonastringent varieties are firm when ripe and have a sweet-spicy flavor.

Hachiya persimmons are the most common astringent (or tannic) variety, and must be soft and ripe when eaten, or they'll make you pucker. Both Hachiyas and Fuyus are delicious raw. Fuyus can be eaten like apples. Hachiyas are rather messy, but—when ripe—are worth the effort. Cut a Hachiya in half, and eat the soft fruit right out of the skin.

Look for persimmons from October through December. Fuyus should be crisp, smooth, and hard, like apples. Avoid ones that are green, broken-skinned, or mushy. Unlike many other fruits, black marks on the skin don't affect the flesh. Depending on ripeness, Fuyus keep refrigerated for up to a month. Hachiya persimmons keep 1 to 3 days in the refrigerator.

Pomegranate

You'll find hundreds of seeds in a pomegranate that are surrounded by ruby-red pulp, which has an intense sweet-tart flavor. Pomegranates were originally the basis for grenadine syrup, and are still used to make pomegranate molasses.

The seeds provide a tart, crisp addition to salads and creamy desserts. The flesh that surrounds the seeds, though, is encased in an inedible, bitter membrane. To remove the seeds intact, cut the fruit in half and turn the skin inside out.

Pomegranates are available from late August through December. Look for heavy, large, and richly colored fruit, which yield the most juice and the highest proportion of pulp to membrane. The skin should be uniform, free of blemishes, thin, and tough. Refrigerate whole pomegranates for up to 3 months, and freeze the seeds in an airtight container for up to 3 months. For a colorful bolt of sweet-tart flavor, sprinkle the seeds on salads, roasts, ice cream, or pies.

Quince

Leaving a few quinces out on the table will infuse your home with a wonderful aroma. Slow cooking yields a pale apricot-colored, firm-textured fruit that tastes like a cross between an apple and a pear, with slight pineapple flavors. Quinces are often used in the United States to make jams and jellies because of their high pectin content, but in much of the Middle East and northern Africa, quinces are more commonly cooked in stews and with roasts. They stay firm through long, slow cooking and develop beautiful color.

Available from September through December, quinces bruise very easily, but can be kept in the refrigerator for as long as 2 to 3 months. A noticeable perfume is the best indicator of ripeness. Peel and core them just as you would an apple or a pear.

For More Information

Specialty produce importer Frieda's (www.friedas.com) has a large selection of exotic fruits and vegetables for sale. You'll also find useful tips on availability and storage at the web site.

One of the most comprehensive books on the subject is *Uncommon Fruits and Vegetables* by Elizabeth Schneider. Schneider details flavors, then guides you through selecting, storing, and preparing each item.

Fast Lane Pizza

Feed yourself well during the hectic holidays with these fast, inventive pizzas.

BBQ Chicken Pizza Menu
serves 6

BBQ Chicken Pizza

Quick coleslaw*

Corn on the cob

*Combine 2 tablespoons white vinegar, 3 tablespoons low-fat mayonnaise, ½ teaspoon black pepper, and ⅛ teaspoon ground red pepper in a large bowl, stirring with a whisk. Add 1 (10-ounce) package angel hair slaw; toss well to coat.

Game Plan

1. While oven heats:
- Chop chicken, tomato, and onions
- Shred cheese

2. While pizza bakes:
- Prepare coleslaw
- Boil corn

search myclar2003.com for all our menus

BBQ Chicken Pizza

We love the contrast of flavors provided by sweet tomato chutney, savory chicken, and sharp cheddar cheese.
TOTAL TIME: 26 MINUTES

- 1 (10-ounce) Italian cheese-flavored thin pizza crust (such as Boboli)
- ¾ cup tomato chutney
- 2 cups chopped roasted skinless, boneless chicken breast (about 2 breasts)
- ⅔ cup chopped plum tomato
- ¾ cup (3 ounces) shredded extra-sharp white cheddar cheese
- ⅓ cup chopped green onions

1. Preheat oven to 450°.
2. Place crust on a baking sheet. Bake at 450° for 3 minutes. Remove from oven; spread chutney over crust, leaving a ½-inch border.
3. Top chutney with chicken. Sprinkle tomato, cheese, and onions evenly over chicken. Bake at 450° for 9 minutes or until cheese melts. Cut pizza into 6 wedges. Yield: 6 servings (serving size: 1 wedge).
NOTE: If you can't find tomato chutney, make your own. Combine 2 cups chopped plum tomato, 3 tablespoons brown sugar, 3 tablespoons cider vinegar, ⅛ teaspoon Jamaican jerk seasoning, and 1 minced garlic clove in a small saucepan; bring to a boil. Reduce heat to medium; cook 20 minutes or until thickened.

CALORIES 300 (26% from fat); FAT 8.5g (sat 3.9g, mono 2.9g, poly 1g); PROTEIN 21.3g; CARB 35.2g; FIBER 1.2g; CHOL 48mg; IRON 1.7mg; SODIUM 622mg; CALC 247mg

---

Meaty, Cheesy Pizza Menu
serves 6

Steak and Blue Cheese Pizza

Romaine salad with garlic-balsamic vinaigrette*

Raspberry sorbet

*Combine 1 tablespoon balsamic vinegar, 2 teaspoons extra-virgin olive oil, ½ teaspoon Dijon mustard, ¼ teaspoon salt, ⅛ teaspoon black pepper, and 1 minced garlic clove, stirring well with a whisk. Drizzle vinaigrette over 6 cups torn romaine lettuce; toss gently to coat.

Game Plan

1. While oven heats:
- Prepare onion mixture
- Cook steak
- Prepare mayonnaise mixture

2. While pizza bakes, prepare salad

Steak and Blue Cheese Pizza

Bake the topping in stages to keep the steak from overcooking.
TOTAL TIME: 27 MINUTES

QUICK TIP: Covering the onion-mushroom mixture for the first few minutes in the skillet helps it cook faster.

Cooking spray
- 2 cups vertically sliced onion
- 1 (8-ounce) package presliced mushrooms
- ¾ teaspoon salt, divided
- 1 (8-ounce) boneless sirloin steak, trimmed
- ¼ teaspoon coarsely ground black pepper
- 3 (7-inch) refrigerated individual pizza crusts (such as Mama Mary's)
- 2 tablespoons low-fat mayonnaise
- 1½ teaspoons prepared horseradish
- ⅓ cup (about 1½ ounces) crumbled blue cheese

1. Preheat oven to 450°.
2. Heat a large nonstick skillet coated with cooking spray over medium-high heat. Add onion and mushrooms; cover and cook 3 minutes. Uncover and cook 5 minutes, stirring occasionally. Stir in ¼ teaspoon salt; remove onion mixture from pan.
3. Sprinkle steak with ½ teaspoon salt and pepper. Add steak to pan; cook over medium-high heat 3 minutes on each side or until desired degree of doneness. Let stand 5 minutes; cut steak diagonally across grain into thin slices.
4. Place crusts on a baking sheet. Bake at 450° for 3 minutes. Remove cooked crusts from oven.
5. Combine mayonnaise and horseradish; spread each crust with about 2 teaspoons mayonnaise mixture. Arrange onion mixture evenly over crusts; bake at 450° for 2 minutes. Divide steak and cheese evenly among pizzas; bake an additional 2 minutes or until cheese melts. Cut each pizza in half. Yield: 6 servings (serving size: 1 pizza half).

CALORIES 323 (30% from fat); FAT 10.8g (sat 3.7g, mono 3.3g, poly 3.3g); PROTEIN 12.4g; CARB 38.6g; FIBER 4.2g; CHOL 31mg; IRON 2.3mg; SODIUM 599mg; CALC 91mg

Pizza Margherita Menu
serves 4

Quick Pizza Margherita

Lemon broccoli*

Chocolate wafer cookies

*Combine 2 teaspoons fresh lemon juice, 1 teaspoon extra-virgin olive oil, ½ teaspoon salt, ⅛ teaspoon black pepper, and 1 minced garlic clove in a large bowl, stirring with a whisk. Add 4 cups hot cooked broccoli florets and ¼ cup very thinly sliced red onion; toss gently to coat.

Game Plan

1. While oven heats:
- Slice tomatoes
- Prepare dough

2. While crust bakes:
- Combine oil and vinegar for pizza
- Shred cheese
- Slice basil

3. While pizza bakes, prepare broccoli

Quick Pizza Margherita

Baking the dough before topping it with tomato keeps the crust crisp. Be sure to use fresh mozzarella, which comes packed in water and can be found with other gourmet cheeses.

TOTAL TIME: 30 MINUTES

QUICK TIP: If you're having trouble shaping the dough, let it rest for 5 minutes and it will become more elastic.

- 1 (10-ounce) can refrigerated pizza crust dough
- Cooking spray
- 1 teaspoon extra-virgin olive oil, divided
- 1 garlic clove, halved
- 5 plum tomatoes, thinly sliced (about ¾ pound)
- 1 cup (4 ounces) shredded fresh mozzarella cheese
- 1 teaspoon balsamic vinegar
- ½ cup thinly sliced fresh basil
- ⅛ teaspoon salt
- ⅛ teaspoon black pepper

1. Preheat oven to 400°.

2. Unroll dough onto a baking sheet coated with cooking spray; pat into a 13 x 11-inch rectangle. Bake at 400° for 8 minutes. Remove crust from oven, and brush with ½ teaspoon oil. Rub crust with cut sides of garlic.

3. Arrange tomato slices on crust, leaving a ½-inch border; sprinkle evenly with cheese. Bake at 400° for 12 minutes or until cheese melts and crust is golden.

4. Combine ½ teaspoon oil and vinegar, stirring with a whisk.

5. Sprinkle pizza evenly with sliced basil, salt, and pepper. Drizzle vinegar mixture evenly over pizza. Cut pizza into 8 pieces. Yield: 4 servings (serving size: 2 pieces).

CALORIES 298 (30% from fat); FAT 10g (sat 4.6g, mono 3.5g, poly 1.4g); PROTEIN 12.2g; CARB 38.6g; FIBER 2.1g; CHOL 22mg; IRON 2.6mg; SODIUM 595mg; CALC 175mg

Peppery Pizza Menu
serves 4

Sausage, Pepper, and Onion Pizza

Pickle spears

Strawberry-anise sundaes*

*Bring ¼ cup light-colored corn syrup, 2 tablespoons sugar, 2 teaspoons fresh lemon juice, and ⅛ teaspoon salt to a boil in a small saucepan. Cook 1 minute or until sugar dissolves, stirring constantly. Remove from heat; stir in 1 tablespoon anise-flavored liqueur. Place ½ cup vanilla low-fat ice cream in each of 4 bowls. Top each serving with ¼ cup sliced strawberries; drizzle each serving with about 1 tablespoon anise syrup.

Game Plan

1. While oven heats:
- Prepare pizza topping
- Cut French bread in half

2. While pizza bakes, prepare anise syrup for dessert

Sausage, Pepper, and Onion Pizza

This recipe uses mild turkey Italian sausage and, for a little heat, a touch of crushed red pepper. Use hot turkey Italian sausage if you want more kick.

TOTAL TIME: 26 MINUTES

- Cooking spray
- 1½ cups vertically sliced onion
- 1 cup green bell pepper strips
- 2 (4-ounce) links mild turkey Italian sausage
- ¼ teaspoon crushed red pepper
- 1 (14.5-ounce) can diced tomatoes, undrained
- 1 (8-ounce) loaf French bread, cut in half horizontally
- 1 cup (4 ounces) shredded part-skim mozzarella cheese

1. Preheat oven to 450°.

2. Heat a large nonstick skillet coated with cooking spray over medium-high heat. Add onion and bell pepper strips, and sauté 6 minutes or until tender.

3. Remove casings from sausage. Add sausage to pan, and cook 5 minutes or until lightly browned, stirring to crumble. Add red pepper and tomatoes, and cook 5 minutes or until mixture thickens.

4. Spread sausage mixture evenly over cut sides of bread, and sprinkle evenly with cheese. Place bread halves on a baking sheet. Bake at 450° for 5 minutes or until cheese melts. Cut each pizza in half. Yield: 4 servings (serving size: 1 piece).

CALORIES 375 (29% from fat); FAT 12g (sat 5.1g, mono 4.2g, poly 2.2g); PROTEIN 24.6g; CARB 42g; FIBER 4.9g; CHOL 63mg; IRON 2.7mg; SODIUM 967mg; CALC 280mg

Rising from History

Let these 19th-century yeast bread recipes become one of your family heirlooms.

Spanish Buns

This is a light-textured, sweet yeast bread that's cut into squares. It's ideal for serving with hot tea or coffee. According to historian William Woys Weaver, this recipe is referred to as "Spanish" because it's similar to a cake made in Latin America. It has a fairly strong nutmeg flavor, but you can cut the nutmeg in half if you'd like. These buns are extremely easy to make since there's no kneading involved. They just need a few minutes of vigorous stirring with a wooden spoon.

>   3   cups all-purpose flour, divided
>   ¾   cup sugar
>   1   teaspoon salt
>   1   teaspoon freshly grated whole or
>   ground nutmeg
>   1   package quick-rise yeast (about
>   2¼ teaspoons)
>   1   cup warm 1% low-fat milk
>   (100° to 110°)
>   ½   cup butter, melted
>   4   large eggs
>   2   teaspoons vanilla extract
>   Cooking spray
>   1   tablespoon powdered sugar

1. Lightly spoon flour into dry measuring cups; level with a knife. Combine 2 cups flour, sugar, salt, nutmeg, and yeast in a large bowl. Add milk and butter, stirring with a wooden spoon until smooth. Add eggs, 1 at a time, beating well after each addition. Stir in vanilla. Add 1 cup flour, stirring until smooth.

2. Scrape batter into a 13 x 9-inch baking pan coated with cooking spray. Coat dough with cooking spray. Cover and let rise in a warm place (85°), free from drafts, 1 hour or until doubled in size

(batter should become bubbly on surface).

3. Preheat oven to 350°.

4. Bake at 350° for 30 minutes or until golden brown and a toothpick inserted in center comes out clean. Cool in pan on a wire rack. Sprinkle with powdered sugar. Cut in squares. Yield: 16 servings (serving size: 1 square).

CALORIES 203 (33% from fat); FAT 7.5g (sat 4.2g, mono 2.3g, poly 0.5g); PROTEIN 4.8g; CARB 29g; FIBER 0.8g; CHOL 70mg; IRON 1.4mg; SODIUM 229mg; CALC 29mg

Rice Bread

>   1½   cups water
>   ½   cup basmati rice
>   1¼   cups warm water (100° to 110°)
>   6   cups all-purpose flour, divided
>   1   package quick-rise yeast (about
>   2¼ teaspoons)
>   2   teaspoons salt
>   Cooking spray

1. Combine 1½ cups water and rice in a medium saucepan over medium-high heat; bring to a boil. Cover, reduce heat, and simmer 20 minutes or until liquid is absorbed. Spoon rice into a large bowl; cool to room temperature. Stir in 1¼ cups warm water.

2. Lightly spoon flour into dry measuring cups; level with a knife. Add 2 cups flour and yeast to rice mixture; stir well to combine. Cover with plastic wrap; let stand 1 hour (batter should become very bubbly and almost double in size).

3. Add 2 cups flour and salt to batter; stir with a wooden spoon 1 minute or until well combined.

4. Scrape dough onto a heavily floured surface; sprinkle dough with 1 cup flour. Knead until smooth and elastic (about 8 minutes); add enough of remaining flour, 1 tablespoon at a time, to prevent dough from sticking to hands (dough will feel tacky).

5. Divide dough in half. Working with 1 portion at a time (cover remaining dough to keep from drying), roll each portion into a 14 x 7-inch rectangle on a lightly floured surface. Roll up each rectangle tightly, starting with a short edge,

pressing firmly to eliminate air pockets; pinch seam and ends to seal. Place each roll, seam side down, in an 8 x 4-inch loaf pan coated with cooking spray.

6. Lightly coat loaves with cooking spray; cover and let rise in a warm place (85°), free from drafts, 1 hour or until doubled in size.

7. Preheat oven to 375°.

8. Bake at 375° for 45 minutes or until loaves are lightly browned and sound hollow when tapped. Cool in pans on wire racks. Yield: 2 loaves, 12 slices per loaf (serving size: 1 slice).

CALORIES 129 (3% from fat); FAT 0.5g (sat 0.1g, mono 0.1g, poly 0.2g); PROTEIN 3.7g; CARB 27g; FIBER 1.1g; CHOL 0mg; IRON 1.6mg; SODIUM 196mg; CALC 6mg

Thirded Bread

Before wheat became cheap and plentiful in the late 1860s, bread was often made with readily available rye flour and cornmeal. As a result, it was low in gluten and very dense. Sometimes wheat flour was added, which accounts for the moniker. This bread is great for sandwiches and makes marvelous toast.

>   1   cup stone-ground yellow
>   cornmeal
>   1½   cups water
>   1½   cups 1% low-fat milk
>   ¼   cup unsalted butter, cut into
>   pieces
>   ½   cup molasses
>   3½   cups all-purpose flour, divided
>   1½   cups whole wheat flour
>   1   cup stone-ground rye flour (such
>   as Hodgson Mill)
>   1   tablespoon salt
>   2   packages quick-rise yeast (about
>   4½ teaspoons)
>   Cooking spray

1. Combine first 3 ingredients in a large, heavy saucepan; bring to a boil over medium heat, stirring occasionally. Cook 2 minutes, stirring frequently with a whisk. Remove from heat; add butter, stirring until melted. Stir in molasses. Let stand 15 minutes or until warm (100° to 110°).

2. Lightly spoon flours into dry measuring cups; level with a knife. Combine 3 cups all-purpose flour, whole wheat flour, rye flour, salt, and yeast in a large bowl. Add warm cornmeal mixture to flour mixture, stirring with a wooden spoon until combined.

3. Turn dough out onto a lightly floured surface. Knead until smooth and elastic (about 8 minutes); add enough of remaining flour, 1 tablespoon at a time, to prevent dough from sticking to hands (dough will feel tacky).

4. Place dough in a large bowl coated with cooking spray, turning to coat top. Cover dough, and let rise in a warm place (85°), free from drafts, 1½ hours or until doubled in size. (Press two fingers into dough. If indentation remains, dough has risen enough.) Punch dough down. Cover and let rest 5 minutes.

5. Divide dough in half. Working with 1 portion at a time (cover remaining dough to keep from drying), roll each portion into a 14 x 7-inch rectangle on a lightly floured surface. Roll up each rectangle tightly, starting with a short edge, pressing firmly to eliminate air pockets; pinch seam and ends to seal. Place each roll, seam side down, in an 8 x 4-inch loaf pan coated with cooking spray.

6. Lightly coat loaves with cooking spray; cover and let rise 1 hour or until doubled in size.

7. Preheat oven to 375°.

8. Bake at 375° for 40 minutes or until loaves are lightly browned and sound hollow when tapped. Remove loaves from pans, and cool completely on wire racks. Yield: 2 loaves, 12 slices per loaf (serving size: 1 slice).

CALORIES 169 (14% from fat); FAT 2.7g (sat 1.4g, mono 0.7g, poly 0.3g); PROTEIN 4.5g; CARB 32.3g; FIBER 2.5g; CHOL 6mg; IRON 1.8mg; SODIUM 324mg; CALC 39mg

Pennsylvania Dutch Tea Rolls

These sweet, buttery rolls historically served with afternoon tea are just as at home with Sunday night's chicken dinner.

Bread Making's Past

Many people consider making bread from scratch a lot of work. Consider how daunting a task it was in the 19th century. Commercial yeast wasn't available until 1868, so the cook had to make yeast herself from a yeast stock she obtained from a friend or local brewery. But the yeast was finicky, and a recipe's success or failure hinged on the potency of the yeast and how well it performed on any given day. Often, a baker had to start over.

Making bread was a once-a-week activity, and the cook had to fit it in with her other time-consuming chores. One technique she used to save time was the "sponge" method. The night before baking, she made a batterlike dough with the yeast and some flour, then let it sit overnight. By the morning, after the yeast had formed millions of carbon dioxide bubbles and imparted its unique flavor to the mixture, the lively sponge was ready to be transformed into bread dough. The cook added several pounds of flour to the sponge and laboriously kneaded it by hand into a supple, stretchable mass.

Once the cook made her dough, she set it aside to rise while she readied the stove for baking. It took about two hours for a wood-burning oven built alongside the fireplace to get hot enough. By the 1830s, the cast iron range was a standard fixture in many home kitchens. This range used far less fuel than the wood-burning stove, it heated more quickly, and its temperature could be regulated somewhat by manipulating a system of dampers and flues.

Today, we turn on our ovens without a second thought. And while we now have dependable ovens and scientifically formulated dry yeasts—both of which guarantee we can make good bread relatively quickly—we've found that breads made using the old-fashioned sponge method taste better than those made without it. Even a sponge allowed to rise for just an hour adds a fine depth of flavor, so use this traditional technique to make most of your yeast breads.

search myclar2003.com for all our tips

5¼ cups all-purpose flour, divided
1⅓ cups warm 1% low-fat milk (100° to 110°)
1 package quick-rise yeast (about 2¼ teaspoons)
½ cup sugar
¼ cup butter, melted and cooled to room temperature
1 teaspoon salt
1 large egg, lightly beaten
Cooking spray
3 tablespoons 1% low-fat milk
1½ teaspoons poppy seeds

1. Lightly spoon flour into dry measuring cups, and level with a knife. Combine 2 cups flour, warm milk, and yeast in a large bowl. Cover mixture with plastic wrap, and let stand 1½ hours (batter should become very bubbly and almost triple in size).

2. Add 3 cups flour, sugar, butter, salt, and egg; stir with a wooden spoon 3 minutes or until well combined. Turn dough out onto a lightly floured surface. Knead until smooth and elastic (about 8 minutes); add enough of remaining flour, 1 tablespoon at a time, to prevent dough from sticking to hands (dough will feel tacky).

3. Place dough in a large bowl coated with cooking spray, turning to coat top. Cover and let rise in a warm place (85°), free from drafts, 1½ hours or until doubled in size. (Lightly press two fingers into dough. If indentation remains, dough has risen enough.)

Continued

4. Turn dough out onto a lightly floured surface; lightly dust dough with flour, and pat into an 10 x 8-inch rectangle. Divide dough by making 3 lengthwise cuts and 4 crosswise cuts to form 20 equal pieces; shape each piece into a ball. Place balls in a 13 x 9-inch baking pan coated with cooking spray.

5. Lightly coat dough with cooking spray. Cover with plastic wrap, and let rise in a warm place (85°), free from drafts, 1 hour or until doubled in size.

6. Preheat oven to 375°.

7. Brush 3 tablespoons milk lightly over dough; sprinkle with poppy seeds. Bake at 375° for 20 minutes or until browned. Cool rolls in pan 5 minutes. Serve rolls warm, or cool completely on a wire rack. Yield: 20 servings (serving size: 1 roll).

CALORIES 173 (17% from fat); FAT 3.2g (sat 1.7g, mono 0.9g, poly 0.3g); PROTEIN 4.6g; CARB 31.3g; FIBER 1g; CHOL 18mg; IRON 1.7mg; SODIUM 154mg; CALC 31mg

lighten up

A Better Brunch

After trying to lighten her family's favorite morning casserole, a Minnesota reader turns to us for guidance.

Cheesy Brunch Casserole found its way to Mary Ann McCann's family more than 20 years ago and has been a favorite ever since. But it was loaded with fat. So after several attempts to lighten it herself, Mary Ann—from Rosemount, Minnesota—asked for our help. Overall we removed about 200 calories from each serving and cut the fat by about 74 percent.

Mary Ann says she likes the casserole because it's so easy to throw together—and to vary. She sometimes makes it with leftover ham instead of sausage, and has even made a meatless version during Lent. It's a great recipe for the holiday season, when feeding guests becomes a priority. Unlike many breakfast casseroles or stratas, this cheesy dish doesn't need to soak overnight before cooking—just assemble and bake right away.

BEFORE	AFTER
SERVING SIZE	
1 wedge	
CALORIES PER SERVING	
496	298
FAT	
34.7g	9.6g
PERCENT OF TOTAL CALORIES	
63%	29%

Cheesy Brunch Casserole

Because herb-seasoned stuffing mix is the base of this casserole, you have to add only a touch of seasoning. If you'd prefer a bit of heat, substitute hot turkey Italian sausage.

  1 pound turkey Italian sausage
  5 cups herb-seasoned stuffing mix (such as Pepperidge Farm)
    Cooking spray
  ½ cup fat-free, less-sodium chicken broth
  2 tablespoons butter, melted
1½ cups (6 ounces) shredded reduced-fat extra-sharp cheddar cheese
  2 cups 2% reduced-fat milk
  ½ teaspoon onion powder
  ½ teaspoon freshly ground black pepper
  2 (8-ounce) cartons egg substitute

1. Preheat oven to 325°.

2. Remove casings from sausage. Cook sausage in a large nonstick skillet over medium-high heat until browned, stirring to crumble. Drain. Place sausage in a large bowl; add stuffing mix, tossing to combine.

3. Place stuffing mixture in a 13 x 9-inch baking dish coated with cooking spray. Drizzle stuffing mixture with broth and butter; sprinkle with cheese. Combine milk and remaining 3 ingredients, stirring with a whisk; pour milk mixture over stuffing mixture.

4. Bake at 325° for 40 minutes or until set. Let casserole stand 5 minutes before serving. Yield: 9 servings.

CALORIES 298 (29% from fat); FAT 9.6g (sat 4g, mono 3.6g, poly 1.3g); PROTEIN 19.8g; CARB 31.5g; FIBER 2.9g; CHOL 50mg; IRON 2.8mg; SODIUM 986mg; CALC 284mg

superfast

. . .And Ready in Just About 20 Minutes

Whether you crave familiar foods or new flavor combinations for dinner, there's plenty to choose from here.

Chicken soup is always a quick family favorite, but adventurous tastes will be satisfied by Ginger Shrimp with Carrot Couscous or Curried Chicken and Chickpeas. So be conservative or stretch your boundaries. Either way, dinner preparation will take less than 20 minutes out of your day.

Baja Fish Tacos

The cabbage slaw adds a nice crunch and peppery bite to the delicate fish tacos.

  2 tablespoons taco seasoning
  1 tablespoon fresh lime juice
  1 tablespoon fresh orange juice
  1 pound mahimahi or other firm whitefish fillets, cut into bite-sized pieces
  1 tablespoon vegetable oil
  2 cups presliced green cabbage
  ½ cup chopped green onions
  ½ cup reduced-fat sour cream
  8 (6-inch) corn tortillas
  8 lime wedges

1. Combine first 3 ingredients in a medium bowl. Add fish; toss to coat.

2. Heat oil in a large nonstick skillet over medium-high heat. Add fish; sauté 5 minutes or until fish is done.

3. Combine cabbage, onions, and sour cream in a medium bowl.

4. Warm tortillas according to package directions. Spoon about ¼ cup cabbage mixture down center of each tortilla. Divide fish evenly among tortillas; fold in half. Serve with lime wedges. Yield: 4 servings (serving size: 2 fish tacos and 2 lime wedges).

CALORIES 327 (26% from fat); FAT 9.4g (sat 3.3g, mono 1.3g, poly 2.8g); PROTEIN 26g; CARB 35.8g; FIBER 4.6g; CHOL 98mg; IRON 2.4mg; SODIUM 624mg; CALC 182mg

Curried Chicken and Chickpeas

Spinach sold in microwave-safe bags makes cooking it a snap. Place any other kind of bagged spinach in a microwave-safe container before cooking.

Cooking spray
¾ teaspoon salt, divided
½ teaspoon bottled minced garlic
1 pound chicken breast tenders, cut into 1-inch pieces
2 teaspoons curry powder
1 cup chopped plum tomato
1 cup fat-free, less-sodium chicken broth
1 teaspoon hot chile sauce (such as Sriracha)
1 (15½-ounce) can chickpeas (garbanzo beans), drained
1 cup water
1 teaspoon olive oil
¾ cup uncooked couscous
1 (10-ounce) microwaveable package fresh spinach
4 lemon wedges (optional)

1. Heat a large nonstick skillet coated with cooking spray over medium-high heat. Combine ½ teaspoon salt, garlic, and chicken, tossing to coat. Add chicken mixture to pan; sauté 3 minutes or until browned. Stir in curry powder; cook 1 minute. Add tomato, broth, chile sauce, and chickpeas; bring to a simmer. Cover and cook 8 minutes.

2. While chicken mixture cooks, place ¼ teaspoon salt, 1 cup water, and oil in a medium saucepan; bring to a boil.

Gradually stir in couscous; remove from heat. Cover and let stand 5 minutes. Fluff couscous with a fork.

3. While couscous stands, poke holes in spinach bag. Microwave at HIGH 2 minutes. Garnish with lemon wedges, if desired. Yield: 4 servings (serving size: 1 cup chicken mixture, about ½ cup couscous, and ½ cup spinach).

CALORIES 436 (13% from fat); FAT 6.5g (sat 1.1g, mono 3.2g, poly 1.3g); PROTEIN 38.6g; CARB 55.1g; FIBER 8.3g; CHOL 66mg; IRON 4.8mg; SODIUM 924mg; CALC 126mg

Chicken, Sausage, and Rice Soup

Make a meal of this comforting soup by adding crackers or warm bread.

4 ounces hot turkey Italian sausage
2 (2½-ounce) skinless, boneless chicken thighs, cut into ½-inch pieces
Cooking spray
1½ cups frozen chopped onion
2 thyme sprigs
⅓ cup chopped celery
⅓ cup chopped carrot
2 (14-ounce) cans fat-free, less-sodium chicken broth
1 (3½-ounce) bag boil-in-bag brown rice
1 tablespoon chopped fresh parsley
¼ teaspoon salt
⅛ teaspoon black pepper

1. Remove casings from sausage. Combine sausage and chicken in a large saucepan coated with cooking spray over high heat; cook 2 minutes, stirring to crumble sausage. Add onion and thyme sprigs; cook 2 minutes, stirring occasionally. Add celery, carrot, and broth; bring to a boil.

2. Remove rice from bag; stir into broth mixture. Cover, reduce heat to medium, and cook 7 minutes or until rice is tender. Discard thyme sprigs. Stir in parsley, salt, and pepper. Yield: 4 servings (serving size: 1½ cups).

CALORIES 245 (19% from fat); FAT 5.2g (sat 1.5g, mono 1.8g, poly 1.5g); PROTEIN 18.4g; CARB 30g; FIBER 3.4g; CHOL 56mg; IRON 1.6mg; SODIUM 754mg; CALC 35mg

Penne with Zucchini and Feta

For variety, try yellow squash and any other short pasta.

8 ounces uncooked penne (tube-shaped pasta)
1 tablespoon olive oil
½ teaspoon dried oregano
2 medium zucchini, halved lengthwise and sliced
2 garlic cloves, crushed
¾ cup fat-free, less-sodium chicken broth
½ teaspoon grated lemon rind
1½ tablespoons fresh lemon juice
¼ teaspoon black pepper
⅔ cup (about 2½ ounces) crumbled feta cheese

1. Cook pasta according to package directions, omitting salt and fat.

2. While pasta cooks, heat oil in a large skillet over medium-high heat. Add oregano, zucchini, and garlic; sauté 3 minutes. Stir in broth, rind, juice, and pepper. Add pasta and cheese; toss well. Serve immediately. Yield: 4 servings (serving size: 1½ cups).

CALORIES 260 (30% from fat); FAT 8.7g (sat 3.3g, mono 3.4g, poly 0.4g); PROTEIN 10g; CARB 37.3g; FIBER 3.6g; CHOL 17mg; IRON 2.1mg; SODIUM 398mg; CALC 118mg

Pork with Port Wine and Raisin Sauce

Serve with white rice tossed with chopped green onions.

½ cup port or other sweet red wine
⅓ cup raisins
2 teaspoons honey
1 teaspoon olive oil
4 (4-ounce) boneless loin pork chops
½ teaspoon salt, divided
¼ teaspoon black pepper
½ cup fat-free, less-sodium chicken broth

Continued

1. Combine first 3 ingredients.

2. Heat oil in a large skillet over medium-high heat. Sprinkle pork with ¼ teaspoon salt and pepper; cook 4 minutes on each side or until done. Remove from pan.

3. Add ¼ teaspoon salt and broth to pan, scraping pan to loosen browned bits. Add raisin mixture; cook over high heat until reduced to ½ cup (about 6 minutes). Serve over pork. Yield: 4 servings (serving size: 1 pork chop and 2 tablespoons sauce).

CALORIES 256 (19% from fat); FAT 5.3g (sat 1.6g, mono 2.7g, poly 0.6g); PROTEIN 26.3g; CARB 17.4g; FIBER 1g; CHOL 78mg; IRON 1.4mg; SODIUM 428mg; CALC 31mg

Sherry-Glazed Salmon with Collard Greens

This sauce is slightly sweet and is nicely countered by the bitter greens. Line your pan with foil for easy cleanup.

¼ cup dry sherry
2 tablespoons brown sugar
1 tablespoon low-sodium soy sauce
⅛ teaspoon five-spice powder
1 teaspoon cider vinegar
4 (6-ounce) salmon fillets, skinned (about 1 inch thick)
Cooking spray
½ cup water
½ cup fat-free, less-sodium chicken broth
1½ teaspoons olive oil
½ teaspoon fresh lemon juice
½ teaspoon bottled minced garlic
¼ teaspoon salt
⅛ teaspoon black pepper
1 (1-pound) bag chopped collard greens

1. Preheat oven to 375°.

2. Combine first 4 ingredients in a small saucepan; bring to a boil, stirring occasionally. Cook until reduced to 3 tablespoons (about 5 minutes). Remove from heat; stir in vinegar.

3. Arrange fish on a broiler pan coated with cooking spray. Brush fish with half of sherry mixture. Bake at 375° for 5 minutes; brush fish with remaining sherry mixture. Bake an additional 5 minutes or until fish flakes easily when tested with a fork.

4. While fish bakes, combine water and next 6 ingredients in a large skillet over medium-high heat; bring to a simmer. Add greens; cover, reduce heat to medium, and cook 10 minutes or until tender. Yield: 4 servings (serving size: 1 salmon fillet and ¾ cup greens).

CALORIES 354 (39% from fat); FAT 15.2g (sat 3.4g, mono 6.9g, poly 3.5g); PROTEIN 39.6g; CARB 11.9g; FIBER 4.1g; CHOL 87mg; IRON 1.1mg; SODIUM 442mg; CALC 193mg

Chicken Spinach Salad with Spicy Vinaigrette

Use bagged spinach and matchstick carrots to cut down on the preparation time. Cooked shrimp also works in this dish.

8 ounces uncooked bean threads (cellophane noodles)
½ cup rice vinegar
2 tablespoons sugar
2 tablespoons low-sodium soy sauce
2 tablespoons peanut oil
4 teaspoons chile paste with garlic
½ teaspoon sesame oil
2 cups shredded roasted skinless, boneless chicken breast
4 cups fresh baby spinach
1 cup julienne-cut carrot
¼ cup finely chopped dry-roasted peanuts

1. Cook noodles according to package directions, omitting salt and fat. Drain and rinse with cold water. Drain well.

2. While noodles cook, combine rice vinegar and next 5 ingredients in a large bowl.

3. Add noodles and chicken to vinegar mixture; toss to coat. Arrange 1 cup spinach and ¼ cup carrot on each of 4 plates. Top each serving with 1½ cups chicken mixture; sprinkle each serving with 1 tablespoon peanuts. Yield: 4 servings.

CALORIES 494 (27% from fat); FAT 14.6g (sat 2.6g, mono 6.5g, poly 4.5g); PROTEIN 25.5g; CARB 63.4g; FIBER 2.8g; CHOL 60mg; IRON 3.4mg; SODIUM 490mg; CALC 68mg

Ginger Shrimp with Carrot Couscous

Carrot juice, rich in beta-carotene, gives the couscous vibrant color and packs this dish with more than 100 percent of the daily recommended amount of vitamin A. The juice is reduced to concentrate the flavor.

1 tablespoon vegetable oil, divided
1 (12-ounce) can carrot juice, divided
¾ cup uncooked couscous
¼ cup fresh lime juice
2 to 3 teaspoons minced seeded jalapeño pepper
2 teaspoons grated peeled fresh ginger
¼ teaspoon salt
¼ cup sliced green onions
4 cups gourmet salad greens
1½ pounds cooked, peeled, and deveined medium shrimp

1. Combine 1 teaspoon oil and 1 cup carrot juice in a medium saucepan; bring to a boil. Gradually stir in couscous. Remove from heat. Cover and let stand 5 minutes.

2. While couscous stands, bring remaining carrot juice to a boil in a small saucepan; cook until reduced to ¼ cup (about 2½ minutes). Remove from heat; stir in 2 teaspoons oil, lime juice, jalapeño, ginger, and salt.

3. Fluff couscous with a fork; stir in ¼ cup reduced carrot juice mixture and onions. Combine remaining carrot juice mixture, greens, and shrimp in a bowl, tossing gently to coat. Yield: 4 servings (serving size: about ½ cup couscous mixture and 1½ cups shrimp mixture).

CALORIES 403 (13% from fat); FAT 5.8g (sat 1.1g, mono 1.2g, poly 3g); PROTEIN 42.7g; CARB 43.4g; FIBER 4.2g; CHOL 332mg; IRON 6.9mg; SODIUM 572mg; CALC 133mg

Renaissance Man

Miami bookstore owner Mitchell Kaplan mixes his love of food and words.

Marinated pork sizzles on the grill, chilled sangria flows freely, and the sultry sound of salsa music floats above crowded patio tables on a warm Miami evening. Shuffling around in his signature rumpled khakis, Mitchell Kaplan, 47, strokes his beard and gently whispers to a waiter, "Everything going ok?"

It could be a scene from a trendy restaurant. But it's actually Books and Books, one of the few thriving independent bookstores in Florida.

The faint aroma of fresh garlic and herbs is as much a part of the atmosphere as the 100,000 books that line the floor-to-ceiling shelves. Kaplan added the café in part so that he could include the sensuality of savory foods in otherwise cerebral gatherings. "I didn't want the clichéd bookstore menu of coffee and croissants," he says. "I wanted to serve food that stands up on its own and has real quality—food that's fresh, healthy, and well prepared." Here's one recipe now.

Creamy Hummus

This vegetarian appetizer served in the restaurant at Books and Books is made for garlic lovers. You can use less garlic if you prefer. Serve with pita wedges.

¾   cup water
½   cup tahini (sesame-seed paste)
6   garlic cloves, peeled
6   tablespoons fresh lemon
      juice
1   tablespoon extra-virgin olive oil
1   teaspoon ground cumin
½   teaspoon salt
¼   teaspoon black pepper
2   (19-ounce) cans chickpeas
      (garbanzo beans), rinsed and
      drained

1. Place first 3 ingredients in a food processor; process until smooth. Add juice and remaining ingredients; process until smooth, scraping sides of bowl occasionally. Yield: 4 cups (serving size: 1 tablespoon).

CALORIES 34 (40% from fat); FAT 1.5g (sat 0.2g, mono 0.6g, poly 0.6g); PROTEIN 1.2g; CARB 4.3g; FIBER 0.9g; CHOL 0mg; IRON 0.3mg; SODIUM 69mg; CALC 8mg

A Keeper

A zesty tomato sauce blankets this seafood entrée.

No stranger to the kitchen, east Texan Ricki McMillian knows a good recipe when she tastes one. A registered dietitian, Ricki appreciates delicious low-calorie, heart-healthy recipes, and her Grouper Veracruz is no exception.

This recipe is easy enough for a quick weeknight meal and tasty enough to serve to guests. Ricki says you can use any other firm white fish, such as catfish or tilapia. And, she says, the dish travels well, so it's terrific for taking to potlucks.

Grouper Veracruz

Serve this dish over hot cooked rice.

4   (6-ounce) grouper fillets
      (¾ inch thick)
Cooking spray
1   tablespoon olive oil
2   cups chopped onion
1   teaspoon ground cumin
1   garlic clove, minced
¼   cup water
3   tablespoons fresh orange juice
2   tablespoons chopped fresh cilantro
2   tablespoons chopped pitted green
      olives
2   tablespoons tomato paste
1   tablespoon fresh lime juice
1   tablespoon capers
1   (10-ounce) can diced tomatoes and
      green chiles, undrained

1. Preheat oven to 400°.
2. Place fish in a 13 x 9-inch baking dish coated with cooking spray.
3. Heat oil in a large nonstick skillet over medium-high heat. Add onion; sauté 3 minutes. Add cumin and garlic; sauté 1½ minutes. Add water and remaining 7 ingredients; bring to a boil. Reduce heat, and simmer 3 minutes or until slightly thick. Pour tomato mixture over fish.
4. Bake at 400° for 20 minutes or until fish flakes easily when tested with a fork. Yield: 4 servings (serving size: 1 grouper fillet and ½ cup sauce).

CALORIES 258 (24% from fat); FAT 7g (sat 0.9g, mono 4g, poly 1.3g); PROTEIN 35g; CARB 13.7g; FIBER 2.8g; CHOL 63mg; IRON 2.3mg; SODIUM 663mg; CALC 87mg

Puttanesca-Style Chicken

"This recipe was inspired by my love for the puttanesca sauces I've enjoyed in restaurants over the years. The basic ingredients include garlic, onion, black olives, and seasonings. It's pretty easy, and the reason I've made the recipe so often is that I usually have all of the ingredients I need to make it on hand."

—Lois Smith, Reseda, California

¼   cup Italian-seasoned breadcrumbs
½   teaspoon salt
⅛   teaspoon black pepper
4   (4-ounce) skinless, boneless
      chicken thighs
1   tablespoon olive oil
2   cups thinly sliced onion
1   garlic clove, minced
2   tablespoons capers
2   tablespoons chopped pitted
      kalamata olives
1   (12-ounce) bottle beer
2   cups cooked medium egg noodles
      (about 1½ cups uncooked pasta)

1. Combine breadcrumbs, salt, and pepper in a zip-top plastic bag; seal and shake well to combine. Add chicken; seal and shake well to coat.
2. Heat oil in a large nonstick skillet over medium-high heat. Add chicken; *Continued*

sauté 2 minutes on each side or until browned. Remove chicken from pan.

3. Add onion to pan; sauté 2 minutes or until tender. Add garlic; sauté 1 minute. Add capers, olives, and beer; cook 1 minute or until liquid almost evaporates, stirring frequently.

4. Return chicken to pan. Cover, reduce heat, and simmer 20 minutes.

5. Increase heat to medium; cook, uncovered, 5 minutes. Serve chicken over noodles. Yield: 4 servings (serving size: 1 chicken thigh, ½ cup noodles, and ¼ cup sauce).

CALORIES 374 (26% from fat); FAT 10.8g (sat 2.1g, mono 5.4g, poly 2g); PROTEIN 28.3g; CARB 34.3g; FIBER 3.5g; CHOL 121mg; IRON 3mg; SODIUM 820mg; CALC 50mg

Turkey Breakfast Sausage

—Diane Gardner, Reston, Virginia

    1   tablespoon olive oil
    ½   cup finely chopped onion
    ½   cup shredded peeled Fuji
        or Braeburn apple
    1   garlic clove, minced
    1   tablespoon chopped fresh
        or 1 teaspoon dried thyme
    1   tablespoon chopped fresh
        or 1 teaspoon dried rubbed sage
    1   teaspoon salt
    ½   teaspoon black pepper
    2   pounds ground turkey breast
    Cooking spray

1. Heat oil in a nonstick skillet over medium-high heat. Add onion and apple; sauté 3 minutes. Add garlic; sauté 30 seconds. Remove from pan; cool completely.

2. Combine onion mixture, thyme, sage, salt, pepper, and turkey; stir well to combine. Divide mixture into 24 equal portions; shape each into a ½-inch-thick patty.

3. Heat a large nonstick skillet coated with cooking spray over medium heat. Add half of patties; cook 3 minutes on each side or until done. Keep warm. Repeat procedure with remaining patties. Yield: 8 servings (serving size: 3 patties).

CALORIES 155 (15% from fat); FAT 2.5g (sat 0.5g, mono 1.4g, poly 0.4g); PROTEIN 28.1g; CARB 3.4g; FIBER 0.7g; CHOL 70mg; IRON 1.5mg; SODIUM 349mg; CALC 23mg

Tofu Fruit Smoothies

—Sonja Johnson, Washington, D.C.

    1   cup frozen mixed berries
    ½   cup white grape juice
    1   tablespoon honey
    1   firm ripe banana, peeled and sliced
    1   (12.3-ounce) package light silken
        tofu (such as Mori-Nu)

1. Place all ingredients in a blender; process until smooth. Yield: 3 servings (serving size: about ¾ cup).

CALORIES 145 (7% from fat); FAT 1.2g (sat 0.3g, mono 0.2g, poly 0.6g); PROTEIN 8g; CARB 27.6g; FIBER 2g; CHOL 0mg; IRON 1.6mg; SODIUM 101mg; CALC 61mg

Strawberry Cheesecake

"This is my family's favorite—I make it for birthdays. I revised the original recipe by using low-fat cottage cheese and cream cheese, and I added the strawberries."
—Jeannie Mullinax, Cookeville, Tennessee

    ¾   cup graham cracker crumbs
        (about 5 cookie sheets)
    Cooking spray
    2   cups 1% low-fat cottage cheese
    ¼   cup all-purpose flour
    2   cups (16 ounces) light cream
        cheese, softened
    ½   cup sugar
    2   teaspoons vanilla extract
    2   large egg whites
    1   large egg
    ½   cup strawberries
    1   teaspoon water

1. Preheat oven to 450°.

2. Press graham cracker crumbs into bottom of a 9-inch springform pan coated with cooking spray.

3. Place cottage cheese in a blender; process until smooth. Lightly spoon flour into a dry measuring cup; level with a knife. Combine flour, cream cheese, and sugar in a bowl; beat with a mixer at low speed until smooth. Beat in cottage cheese and vanilla. Add egg whites and egg, 1 at a time, beating well after each addition. Pour into prepared pan.

4. Combine strawberries and water in a blender, and process until smooth. Swirl strawberry mixture into cheese mixture using tip of a knife.

5. Bake at 450° for 15 minutes. Reduce oven temperature to 250° (do not remove cheesecake from oven); bake an additional 45 minutes or until cheesecake center barely moves when pan is touched.

6. Remove cheesecake from oven; run a knife around outside edge. Cool to room temperature. Cover and chill at least 8 hours. Cut into wedges. Yield: 10 servings (serving size: 1 wedge).

CALORIES 201 (26% from fat); FAT 5.9g (sat 3g, mono 0.7g, poly 0.5g); PROTEIN 12.7g; CARB 22.9g; FIBER 0.5g; CHOL 39mg; IRON 0.7mg; SODIUM 424mg; CALC 66mg

Pasta with White Beans and Kale

"I created this recipe one night after digging through my refrigerator. I found leftover pasta, home-cooked cannellini beans, and some kale from the farmers' market. I tossed them together with sautéed garlic, fresh parsley, and feta cheese. Not only is the dish super easy, but it is also loaded with folic acid."

—Nancy Harvey,
Battle Ground, Washington

    1   tablespoon olive oil
    3   garlic cloves, minced
    10 cups chopped kale (about 1
        pound)
    ½   cup fat-free, less-sodium chicken
        broth
    ¾   teaspoon salt
    ¼   teaspoon black pepper
    3   cups hot cooked whole wheat
        penne (about 1½ cups uncooked
        tube-shaped pasta)
    1   tablespoon fresh lemon
        juice
    1   (19-ounce) can cannellini beans
        or other white beans, rinsed
        and drained
    ¼   cup coarsely chopped fresh
        flat-leaf parsley
    ¼   cup (1 ounce) crumbled feta
        cheese

1. Heat oil in a large nonstick skillet over medium-high heat. Add garlic; sauté 1 minute. Add kale, broth, salt, and pepper, stirring to combine. Cover, reduce heat to medium, and simmer 5 minutes or until kale wilts, stirring occasionally.

2. Add pasta, juice, and beans to pan, stirring to combine; cook 1 minute or until mixture is thoroughly heated.

3. Divide pasta mixture evenly among 4 plates; sprinkle each serving with 1 tablespoon parsley and 1 tablespoon cheese. Yield: 4 servings (serving size: 2 cups).

CALORIES 325 (19% from fat); FAT 6.7g (sat 1.7g, mono 3g, poly 1.3g); PROTEIN 13.6g; CARB 54.5g; FIBER 6.8g; CHOL 6mg; IRON 3.9mg; SODIUM 793mg; CALC 233mg

inspired vegetarian

One-Dish Wonders

Just a single pot can yield hearty, warming dinners.

Beet Risotto with Greens, Goat Cheese, and Walnuts

Before you sauté the onion, toast the walnuts in the Dutch oven until they're fragrant.

- 2 teaspoons olive oil
- 1 cup chopped onion
- 1 cup Arborio rice
- 1 tablespoon minced peeled fresh ginger
- 2 teaspoons finely chopped fresh rosemary
- ½ cup dry white wine
- 3 cups finely chopped peeled beets
- ½ cup water
- ¼ teaspoon fine sea salt
- 1 (14½-ounce) can vegetable broth
- 6 cups finely sliced Swiss chard
- ½ cup (2 ounces) crumbled goat cheese
- ¼ cup chopped walnuts, toasted

1. Heat oil in a Dutch oven over medium-high heat. Add onion; sauté 3 minutes. Add rice, ginger, and rosemary; sauté 1 minute. Add wine; cook 3 minutes or until liquid is nearly absorbed, stirring constantly.

2. Add beets, water, salt, and broth; bring to a boil. Cover, reduce heat, and simmer 20 minutes or until beets are tender, stirring occasionally.

3. Stir in chard; cook 5 minutes. Add cheese, stirring until blended. Sprinkle each serving with 1 tablespoon walnuts. Yield: 4 servings (serving size: 1½ cups).

CALORIES 412 (30% from fat); FAT 13.7g (sat 4.9g, mono 4g, poly 3.6g); PROTEIN 14.1g; CARB 57.5g; FIBER 4.1g; CHOL 14mg; IRON 2.1mg; SODIUM 611mg; CALC 92mg

Tempeh and Wild Mushroom Fricassee

Fricassee often refers to a thick and chunky meat-based stew. Tempeh stands in for the meat in this recipe.

- Cooking spray
- 12 ounces tempeh, cut into ½-inch cubes
- ¼ cup dry white wine
- 2 tablespoons low-sodium soy sauce
- 4 cups thinly sliced leek (about 4 large)
- 2 cups sliced button mushrooms
- 2 cups sliced cremini mushrooms
- 2 cups chopped shiitake mushroom caps (about 4 ounces)
- 2 (4-inch) portobello mushroom caps, gills removed, chopped
- 1 tablespoon all-purpose flour
- ⅓ cup celery leaves
- 2 thyme sprigs
- 1 parsley sprig
- ½ cup thinly sliced garlic (about 20 cloves)
- 1 (14½-ounce) can vegetable broth
- 1 tablespoon fresh lemon juice
- ¼ teaspoon fine sea salt
- ¼ teaspoon freshly ground black pepper
- 2 tablespoons chopped fresh parsley
- 1 tablespoon grated lemon rind (optional)

1. Heat a Dutch oven coated with cooking spray over medium-high heat. Add tempeh; sauté 8 minutes or until golden brown. Add wine and soy sauce; cook 15 seconds or until liquid almost evaporates. Remove tempeh from pan.

2. Add leek and mushrooms to pan; sauté 5 minutes. Stir in flour; cook 1 minute, stirring frequently. Tie celery leaves, thyme sprigs, and parsley sprig together securely with string. Add herbs, garlic, and broth to pan; bring to a boil. Add tempeh, stirring well. Cover, reduce heat, and simmer 15 minutes.

3. Uncover and cook 3 minutes or until thick. Discard herbs. Stir in lemon juice, salt, and pepper; sprinkle with parsley. Garnish each serving with ½ teaspoon lemon rind, if desired. Yield: 6 servings (serving size: 1 cup).

CALORIES 317 (30% from fat); FAT 10.4g (sat 2g, mono 2.6g, poly 3.6g); PROTEIN 23.7g; CARB 37.8g; FIBER 8.6g; CHOL 0mg; IRON 6.2mg; SODIUM 898mg; CALC 206mg

Asian Root Vegetable Stew

Kombu, a dried dark seaweed, is available in Asian specialty markets. If you can't find it, add ¼ teaspoon salt instead. This stew is good served over hot cooked rice.

- 1 tablespoon vegetable oil
- 2 cups chopped onion
- 2 pounds extra-firm tofu, drained and cut into 1-inch cubes
- 6 cups water
- 1 cup (1-inch) cubed peeled daikon radish
- 1 cup (1-inch-thick) slices parsnip
- 1 cup (1-inch) cubed peeled rutabaga
- 1 cup (1-inch-thick) slices carrot
- ¼ cup low-sodium soy sauce
- 2 tablespoons mirin (sweet rice wine)
- 6 dried shiitake mushrooms (about ⅓ ounce)
- 1 (3-inch-square) piece kombu seaweed
- 6 tablespoons water
- ¼ cup cornstarch
- 2 teaspoons dark sesame oil
- ¼ cup chopped green onions

Continued

1. Heat vegetable oil in a Dutch oven over medium heat. Add 2 cups onion, and cook 5 minutes, stirring occasionally. Add tofu; cook 5 minutes or until golden brown, stirring frequently.

2. Add 6 cups water, daikon, and next 7 ingredients; bring to a boil. Cover, reduce heat, and simmer 35 minutes.

3. Combine 6 tablespoons water and cornstarch, stirring with a whisk. Stir cornstarch mixture into stew; bring to a boil. Cook 2 minutes, stirring constantly. Discard kombu. Stir in sesame oil; sprinkle with green onions. Yield: 5 servings (serving size: about 2⅓ cups).

CALORIES 276 (28% from fat); FAT 8.5g (sat 1.2g, mono 2.1g, poly 4.5g); PROTEIN 16.5g; CARB 33.5g; FIBER 5.1g; CHOL 0mg; IRON 3.6mg; SODIUM 873mg; CALC 123mg

Pasta with Chickpeas and Vegetables

We liked chickpeas, but you can use any kind of canned bean.

  12 cups water
   3 cups peeled, halved lengthwise,
        and thinly sliced butternut squash
   2 cups small cauliflower florets
   1 cup (1-inch-thick) diagonally
        cut carrot
   2 red onions, cut into 1-inch-thick
        wedges
   8 ounces uncooked penne
        (tube-shaped pasta)
  2½ cups cherry tomatoes, halved
   2 tablespoons olive oil
   1 tablespoon ground cumin
   ½ teaspoon crushed red pepper
   4 garlic cloves, sliced
   3 thyme sprigs
   1 (15½-ounce) can chickpeas
        (garbanzo beans), drained
   ½ cup dry white wine
   ½ teaspoon fine sea salt
   ¼ teaspoon black pepper
   ½ cup chopped fresh parsley

1. Bring water to a boil in a large stockpot or Dutch oven. Add squash, cauliflower, carrot, and onion, and cook 2 minutes. Remove vegetables with a slotted spoon; drain well.

2. Return water to a boil. Add pasta; cook 10 minutes or until done. Drain in a colander over a bowl, reserving ½ cup cooking liquid.

3. Return vegetables to pan; add tomatoes and next 6 ingredients. Cook 2 minutes over medium-high heat, stirring occasionally. Add reserved cooking liquid and wine; cook 15 minutes or until squash is tender, stirring occasionally. Discard thyme sprigs.

4. Add pasta, salt, and pepper to pan; stir to combine. Sprinkle with parsley. Yield: 5 servings (serving size: about 2½ cups).

CALORIES 398 (18% from fat); FAT 8g (sat 1.1g, mono 4.4g, poly 1.6g); PROTEIN 12.5g; CARB 69.6g; FIBER 10.4g; CHOL 0mg; IRON 4.3mg; SODIUM 450mg; CALC 123mg

Vegetable Chickpea Bouillabaisse

   2 leeks
   2 small fennel bulbs with stalks
   6 cups water, divided
   ½ cup dry white wine
   2 teaspoons fennel seeds
   1 tablespoon olive oil
   1 teaspoon fine sea salt
   3 garlic cloves, thinly sliced
   4 cups (1-inch) cubed peeled
        butternut squash
   2 cups cubed peeled baking potato
        (about 12 ounces)
   2 tablespoons fresh lemon juice
   ¼ teaspoon saffron threads, crushed
   1 (15½-ounce) can chickpeas
        (garbanzo beans), drained
   1 (14½-ounce) can plum tomatoes,
        undrained and chopped
   ¼ teaspoon black pepper
   2 tablespoons chopped fresh parsley
   8 (1-ounce) slices sourdough bread,
        toasted
   1 cup (4 ounces) shredded Gruyère
        cheese

1. Remove and discard roots, outer leaves, and tops from leeks. Cut off dark leaves, leaving 6 inches of bulb; reserve dark leaves and bulbs. Remove stalks from fennel bulbs; reserve stalks and bulbs.

2. Combine dark leaves of leek, fennel stalks, 4 cups water, wine, and fennel seeds in a Dutch oven; bring to a boil. Reduce heat; simmer 25 minutes. Drain broth through a colander over a large bowl; discard solids.

3. Cut reserved leek bulbs in half lengthwise. Cut each half crosswise into thin slices. Rinse with cold water; drain. Cut reserved fennel bulbs into thin slices.

4. Add oil to pan; heat over medium heat. Add sliced leek and salt; cook 5 minutes, stirring occasionally. Add garlic; cook 2 minutes, stirring frequently. Add broth, sliced fennel, 2 cups water, squash, and next 5 ingredients; bring to a boil. Partially cover, reduce heat, and simmer 35 minutes. Stir in pepper; sprinkle with parsley.

5. Preheat broiler.

6. Place bread on a baking sheet; sprinkle each slice with 2 tablespoons cheese. Broil 1 minute or until cheese melts. Serve with soup. Yield: 8 servings (serving size: 1½ cups soup and 1 bread slice).

CALORIES 336 (21% from fat); FAT 8g (sat 3.1g, mono 3.1g, poly 1g); PROTEIN 12.5g; CARB 54.2g; FIBER 7.8g; CHOL 15mg; IRON 3.9mg; SODIUM 754mg; CALC 280mg

Tomato Goat Cheese Strata

Similar to a frittata, this savory bread pudding starts on the stovetop and finishes in the oven. Using a large cast iron skillet will help you get a crisp, brown crust.

   1 cup 2% reduced-fat milk
   3 tablespoons chopped fresh
        parsley
   5 large egg whites, lightly beaten
   3 large eggs, lightly beaten
   2 teaspoons olive oil
   2 cups thinly sliced onion
   1 tablespoon chopped fresh
        sage
   2 garlic cloves, sliced
   ½ teaspoon crushed red pepper
   1 (28-ounce) can diced tomatoes
        with basil, garlic, and oregano,
        undrained
   8 cups (1-inch) cubed sourdough
        bread (about 8 ounces)
   ¾ cup (3 ounces) crumbled goat
        cheese

1. Preheat oven to 450°.
2. Combine first 4 ingredients in a bowl, stirring well with a whisk.
3. Heat oil in a large cast iron or oven-proof skillet over high heat. Add onion; sauté 2 minutes. Add chopped sage and sliced garlic; sauté 1 minute. Add pepper and tomatoes, stirring well. Bring to a boil, and cook 1 minute. Stir bread into tomato mixture; top with cheese. Pour egg mixture over tomato mixture (pan will be very full).
4. Carefully place pan in oven, and bake at 450° for 25 minutes or until egg is set. Let stand 5 minutes. Cut strata into 4 wedges. Yield: 4 servings (serving size: 1 wedge).

CALORIES 415 (30% from fat); FAT 13.9g (sat 5.7g, mono 5.2g, poly 1.4g); PROTEIN 23g; CARB 50.3g; FIBER 5.4g; CHOL 174mg; IRON 3.9mg; SODIUM 880mg; CALC 246mg

Wheat Berry, Black Bean, and Vegetable Stew

Look for black soy beans in the organic section of major supermarkets. If you can't find them, substitute canned black beans or shelled edamame.

 1   cup uncooked wheat berries (hard winter wheat)
 2   cups hot water
 4   cups water
 1   teaspoon fine sea salt
 1   tablespoon olive oil
 1   cup chopped onion
 4   cups sliced cremini mushrooms
 ½   cup sliced celery
 ½   cup sliced carrot
 1   tablespoon chopped fresh rosemary
 2   cups chopped Savoy cabbage
 ½   teaspoon freshly ground black pepper
 1   (14.5-ounce) can no-salt-added whole tomatoes, undrained and chopped
 1   (15-ounce) can no-salt-added black soy beans, drained
 2   tablespoons chopped fresh parsley

1. Combine wheat berries and 2 cups hot water in a bowl; let stand 1 hour.

2. Drain wheat berries through a sieve over a bowl; reserve 1½ cups of soaking liquid.
3. Combine wheat berries, 4 cups water, and salt in a Dutch oven; bring to a boil. Reduce heat; simmer 30 minutes. Remove from pan.
4. Add oil to pan; heat over medium-high heat. Add onion; sauté 5 minutes. Add mushrooms, celery, carrot, and rosemary; sauté 5 minutes.
5. Add reserved soaking liquid and wheat berry mixture to pan; bring to a boil. Stir in cabbage and pepper. Cover, reduce heat, and simmer 20 minutes, stirring occasionally.
6. Add tomatoes; simmer 10 minutes or until wheat berries are tender, stirring occasionally. Add soy beans; bring to a boil. Cook 10 minutes or until thick. Stir in parsley. Yield: 4 servings (serving size: 1½ cups).

CALORIES 333 (16% from fat); FAT 5.9g (sat 0.7g, mono 2.6g, poly 0.8g); PROTEIN 17.9g; CARB 56.9g; FIBER 14.5g; CHOL 0mg; IRON 5.6mg; SODIUM 620mg; CALC 133mg

back to the best

Oven-Roasted Sweet Potatoes and Onions

Five ingredients plus a little chopping equal one fabulous side dish.

This short and simple recipe, which first appeared in the April 1997 issue of *Cooking Light*, combines kitchen staples, yet its taste is sublimely robust. The gently flavored onions and potatoes develop a richer, more complex sweetness as they caramelize, and that sweetness is balanced by the sharp garlic-pepper seasoning.

This recipe possesses two other virtues we appreciate: It dirties only one dish, and it's pretty much hands-off cooking. Try serving it alongside roasted chicken, pork loin, or ham at holiday gatherings, and you'll see why it's a staff favorite.

Oven-Roasted Sweet Potatoes and Onions

 4   peeled sweet potatoes, cut into 2-inch pieces (about 2¼ pounds)
 2   Oso Sweet or other sweet onions, cut into 1-inch pieces (about 1 pound)
 2   tablespoons extra-virgin olive oil
 ¾   teaspoon garlic-pepper blend (such as McCormick)
 ½   teaspoon salt

1. Preheat oven to 425°.
2. Combine all ingredients in a 13 x 9-inch baking dish, tossing to coat.
3. Bake at 425° for 35 minutes or until tender, stirring occasionally. Yield: 6 servings (serving size: 1 cup).

CALORIES 247 (19% from fat); FAT 5.1g (sat 0.7g, mono 3.4g, poly 0.6g); PROTEIN 3.6g; CARB 47.8g; FIBER 6.5g; CHOL 0mg; IRON 1.2mg; SODIUM 255mg; CALC 53mg

Sweet Potatoes in Season

There are two main varieties of sweet potato that are available commercially. The pale sweet potato has a thin, light yellow skin and a pale yellow flesh. It's not as sweet as its darker counterpart, which has a thick, dark orange skin and bright orange flesh.

You should be able to find fresh sweet potatoes at any time during the year, though they may be more readily available in the cooler months. And you can always find canned and frozen sweet potatoes erroneously labeled as yams.

For optimal storage, keep your sweet potatoes in a dark, dry, and cool environment (around 55 degrees) for up to 3 or 4 weeks. They keep best when not stored in the refrigerator, so if you can't manage a naturally low temperature for them, try to use your supply within a week.

And never underestimate the nutritional worth of these vegetables. Sweet potatoes are a good source of vitamins A and C.

search myclar2003.com for all our tips

The *Cooking Light* Holiday Cookbook

Like you, we're always in search of new recipes around this time of year. It's when we feel most called upon to produce fabulous yet familiar foods, to combine the excitement of the new with the comfort of custom.

That's a tall order—but one we've done our best to fill in the pages that follow. From appetizers to desserts, there are recipes here for every occasion—be it a quick post-shopping lunch, Christmas Eve dinner, or impromptu family brunch. And we've mixed things up to keep everyone happy, from the hard-core traditionalist to the culinary adventurer. There are eight menus to help you plan your special meals, along with plenty of make-ahead tips that will allow you to join the party (not just cook for it). We've even included a section on presents from the kitchen— food, we think, is a personal gift that's always appreciated. This year's cookbook is our gift to you.

Appetizers and Beverages

Whether your guests prefer familiar flavors or lean toward the exotic, these starters and sippers will satisfy everyone's appetite.

Wasabi Bloody Marys

Prepared horseradish typically adds heat to this drink, but we've opted for wasabi paste— the green Japanese version of horseradish. Garnish with a pickled asparagus stalk or green bean, or serve with pickled okra.

- ½ cup fresh lime juice
- 1½ tablespoons wasabi paste
- 6 cups low-sodium vegetable juice
- 3 tablespoons Worcestershire sauce
- 1¼ teaspoons hot pepper sauce
- ¾ teaspoon salt
- 1½ cups vodka

1. Combine lime juice and wasabi; stir with a whisk until wasabi dissolves.

2. Combine wasabi mixture, vegetable juice, Worcestershire, pepper sauce, and salt in a pitcher. Chill thoroughly.

3. Stir in vodka. Serve over ice. Yield: 8 servings (serving size: about 1 cup).

CALORIES 166 (0% from fat); FAT 0g; PROTEIN 1.6g; CARB 11.3g; FIBER 1.8g; CHOL 0mg; IRON 1.2mg; SODIUM 395mg; CALC 43mg

Mini Black Bean Cakes with Green Onion Cream and Avocado Salsa

Seasoned black beans kick up the Southwestern flavor; the sour cream topping tempers the heat.

CAKES:
- ½ cup bottled salsa
- 2 teaspoons ground cumin
- 2 (19-ounce) cans seasoned black beans (such as La Costeña), rinsed and drained
- 1 cup dry breadcrumbs, divided
- ¼ cup thinly sliced green onions
- ½ teaspoon salt
- Cooking spray

TOPPINGS:
- ½ cup reduced-fat sour cream
- ¼ cup thinly sliced green onions
- ¼ cup diced peeled avocado
- ¼ cup chopped plum tomato
- 1 teaspoon fresh lime juice

1. Preheat oven to 375°.

2. To prepare cakes, combine first 3 ingredients in a food processor; process until smooth. Stir in ½ cup breadcrumbs, ¼ cup green onions, and salt.

3. Divide mixture into 24 equal portions, shaping each into a ½-inch-thick patty. Place ½ cup breadcrumbs in a shallow dish. Dredge patties in breadcrumbs. Place patties on a baking sheet coated with cooking spray. Bake at 375° for 14 minutes, turning after 7 minutes.

4. To prepare toppings, combine sour cream and ¼ cup green onions in a small bowl. Combine avocado, tomato, and juice in a small bowl. Top each patty with 1 teaspoon green onion cream and 1 teaspoon avocado salsa. Yield: 12 servings (serving size: 2 cakes).

CALORIES 99 (25% from fat); FAT 2.8g (sat 1g, mono 0.5g, poly 0.2g); PROTEIN 3.8g; CARB 16.3g; FIBER 0.7g; CHOL 5mg; IRON 1.6mg; SODIUM 421mg; CALC 61mg

Spicy Thyme and
Garlic Oil, page 402

Red Onion Marmalade,
page 403

Roast Lamb with Rosemary and Garlic,
page 389

Challah, page 392

Espresso Crème Brûlée, page 399

Baked Feta with Marinara

If you can find them, use fire-roasted diced tomatoes (such as Muir Glen); just add a pinch of basil, a pinch of oregano, and a minced garlic clove. Toasted sourdough bread and rosemary focaccia are also good accompaniments.

    1   teaspoon fresh lemon juice
    ¼   teaspoon crushed red pepper
    2   garlic cloves, minced
    1   (14.5-ounce) can diced tomatoes
        with basil, garlic, and oregano,
        drained
    1   (4-ounce) package crumbled feta
        cheese
        Cooking spray
    32 (½-inch-thick) slices diagonally
        cut French bread baguette (about 1
        pound), toasted

1. Preheat oven to 350°.
2. Combine first 4 ingredients in a bowl. Sprinkle feta evenly into a 6-inch gratin dish or small shallow baking dish coated with cooking spray. Top with tomato mixture. Bake at 350° for 20 minutes. Serve as a spread with bread slices. Yield: 16 servings (serving size: 2 bread slices and 2 tablespoons spread).

CALORIES 107 (20% from fat); FAT 2.4g (sat 1.3g, mono 0.3g, poly 0.2g); PROTEIN 4.1g; CARB 16.9g; FIBER 1g; CHOL 6mg; IRON 1mg; SODIUM 352mg; CALC 72mg

Hot White Chocolate with Ginger

Ginger gives this sweet beverage a refreshing bite.

    ⅔   cup chopped peeled fresh ginger
    ½   cup sugar
    ¼   cup water
    8   cups fat-free milk
    1   cup chopped premium white
        baking chocolate (about 4 ounces;
        such as Ghiradelli)

1. Combine ginger, sugar, and water in a large saucepan; cook over medium-high heat until sugar dissolves and mixture is golden (about 5 minutes), stirring

frequently. Remove from heat; cool slightly.
2. Add milk and chocolate, stirring with a whisk. Heat over medium-low heat to 180° or until bubbles form around edge of pan, stirring frequently (do not boil). Strain mixture through a sieve into a bowl; discard solids. Yield: 8 servings (serving size: 1 cup).

CALORIES 210 (21% from fat); FAT 5g (sat 3g, mono 1.4g, poly 0.2g); PROTEIN 9.2g; CARB 32.8g; FIBER 0g; CHOL 7mg; IRON 0.1mg; SODIUM 139mg; CALC 331mg

Vietnamese Rolls with Peanut Dipping Sauce

Crunchy vegetables pair with hoisin-seasoned chicken in this refreshing appetizer. You can make the sauce and chicken mixture a few hours ahead, but assemble the rolls just before serving so they don't dry out.

SAUCE:
    ½   cup seasoned rice vinegar
    ¼   cup honey
    ¼   teaspoon salt
    ⅓   cup finely chopped roasted peanuts

ROLLS:
    1   tablespoon peanut oil
    4   teaspoons minced peeled fresh
        ginger
    4   garlic cloves, minced
    1   pound skinless, boneless chicken
        breast, cut into ¼-inch-wide strips
    ⅓   cup hoisin sauce
    1   teaspoon hot chile sauce (such as
        Sriracha)
    12 (8-inch) round sheets rice paper
    3   cups thinly sliced romaine lettuce
    36 (2-inch) julienne-cut seeded peeled
        cucumber strips
    36 (2-inch) julienne-cut red bell pepper
        strips
    36 mint leaves

1. To prepare sauce, combine first 3 ingredients in a small bowl, stirring until honey dissolves. Stir in peanuts.
2. To prepare rolls, heat oil in a large nonstick skillet over medium-high heat. Add ginger, garlic, and chicken; sauté 5

minutes. Combine chicken mixture, hoisin sauce, and chile sauce; chill.
3. Add hot water to a large, shallow dish to a depth of 1 inch. Place 1 rice paper sheet in dish. Let stand 30 seconds or just until soft. Place sheet on a flat surface. Arrange ¼ cup lettuce over half of sheet, leaving a 1-inch border. Top lettuce with ¼ cup chicken mixture, 3 cucumber strips, 3 bell pepper strips, and 3 mint leaves. Fold sides of sheet over filling and, starting with filled side, roll up jelly-roll fashion. Gently press seam to seal. Place roll, seam side down, on a serving platter (cover to keep from drying).
4. Repeat procedure with remaining sheets, lettuce, chicken mixture, cucumber strips, bell pepper strips, and mint leaves. Cut each roll in half diagonally. Serve rolls with sauce. Yield: 12 servings (serving size: 1 roll and about 1½ tablespoons sauce).

CALORIES 176 (23% from fat); FAT 4.5g (sat 0.7g, mono 1.8g, poly 1.3g); PROTEIN 11.9g; CARB 22.9g; FIBER 2g; CHOL 22mg; IRON 1.4mg; SODIUM 422mg; CALC 39mg

Wild Mushroom and Artichoke Dip

    1   teaspoon olive oil
    2   cups sliced shiitake mushroom
        caps (about 4 ounces)
    1   (6-ounce) package presliced
        portobello mushrooms, chopped
    ½   cup low-fat mayonnaise
    ¼   cup (1 ounce) grated fresh
        Parmesan cheese
    ¼   cup finely chopped celery
    ¼   cup finely chopped onion
    ¼   cup thinly sliced green onions
    2   tablespoons chopped fresh parsley
    1   teaspoon garlic powder
    1   teaspoon black pepper
    ¾   teaspoon salt
    ¼   teaspoon ground red pepper
    1   (14-ounce) can artichoke hearts,
        drained and coarsely chopped
    1   (8-ounce) block ⅓-less-fat cream
        cheese
    1   (8-ounce) block fat-free cream
        cheese
        Cooking spray

Continued

1. Preheat oven to 350°.

2. Heat oil in a large nonstick skillet over medium-high heat. Add mushrooms; sauté 5 minutes or until tender. Combine mushrooms, mayonnaise, and remaining ingredients except cooking spray in a large bowl, stirring until well blended.

3. Spoon mixture into a 2-quart casserole coated with cooking spray. Bake at 350° for 30 minutes or until thoroughly heated. Yield: 5 cups (serving size: ¼ cup).

CALORIES 66 (30% from fat); FAT 2.2g (sat 1g, mono 0.3g, poly 0.1g); PROTEIN 4.5g; CARB 7.6g; FIBER 1.2g; CHOL 6mg; IRON 0.2mg; SODIUM 377mg; CALC 50mg

Spicy Rum Punch

Add the ginger beer and rum just before serving so the punch will be fizzy. Ginger beer, which actually contains no alcohol, tastes like a spicy ginger ale.

¼ cup chopped crystallized ginger
2 tablespoons black peppercorns
6 star anise
4 (3-inch) cinnamon sticks
2 (64-ounce) bottles cranberry-pineapple juice drink (such as Ocean Spray)
2 cups dark rum
4 (12-ounce) bottles ginger beer (such as Stewart's)

1. Combine first 5 ingredients in a large Dutch oven; bring to a boil. Remove from heat; let stand 30 minutes.

2. Strain cranberry mixture through a fine sieve into a bowl; discard solids. Chill thoroughly. Stir in rum and ginger beer just before serving. Yield: 20 servings (serving size: about ¾ cup).

CALORIES 205 (0% from fat); FAT 0g; PROTEIN 0.2g; CARB 38.2g; FIBER 0.2g; CHOL 0mg; IRON 0.1mg; SODIUM 4mg; CALC 13mg

Spiced Parmesan Cheese Crisps

About 15 minutes after you start this recipe, you can start munching on this crunchy snack. You can also make these up to a day ahead and store them in an airtight container. They're great with Wild Mushroom and Artichoke Dip (recipe on page 385).

10 egg roll wrappers
Cooking spray
2 large egg whites, lightly beaten
1 cup (4 ounces) grated fresh Parmesan cheese
1 teaspoon dried oregano
1 teaspoon dried basil
½ teaspoon ground red pepper

1. Preheat oven to 425°.

2. Place egg roll wrappers in a single layer on baking sheets coated with cooking spray. Lightly brush with egg whites; cut each wrapper into 8 wedges. Combine cheese and remaining 3 ingredients; sprinkle evenly over wedges. Bake at 425° for 5 minutes or until lightly browned. Yield: 80 crisps (serving size: 4 crisps).

CALORIES 75 (24% from fat); FAT 2g (sat 1.1g, mono 0.5g, poly 0.1g); PROTEIN 4.3g; CARB 9.6g; FIBER 0.4g; CHOL 6mg; IRON 0.7mg; SODIUM 203mg; CALC 88mg

Soups and Salads

A welcome addition to the dinner table, soups and salads can also be the main attraction for lunch or a snack.

Endive, Sweet Lettuce, and Cashew Salad

2 tablespoons minced shallots
2 tablespoons honey
1 tablespoon sherry vinegar
2 teaspoons walnut oil
½ teaspoon salt
8 cups torn green leaf lettuce
4 cups sliced Belgian endive (about 3 heads)
2 tablespoons roasted unsalted cashews, coarsely chopped

1. Combine first 5 ingredients; stir with a whisk. Add lettuce, endive, and cashews; toss to coat. Serve immediately. Yield: 8 servings (serving size: about 1¼ cups).

CALORIES 55 (35% from fat); FAT 2.1g (sat 0.3g, mono 0.8g, poly 0.9g); PROTEIN 1.3g; CARB 9.2g; FIBER 2g; CHOL 0mg; IRON 0.4mg; SODIUM 173mg; CALC 40mg

Arugula, Fennel, and Parmesan Salad

3 tablespoons fresh lemon juice
2 teaspoons sugar
1 teaspoon olive oil
½ teaspoon salt
¼ teaspoon black pepper
4 cups thinly sliced fennel bulb (about 2 bulbs)
1 cup thinly sliced red onion
8 cups trimmed arugula
½ cup (2 ounces) shaved fresh Parmesan cheese

1. Combine first 5 ingredients in a small bowl, stirring with a whisk. Combine fennel and onion in a large bowl; drizzle with dressing, tossing gently to coat.

2. Arrange 1 cup arugula on each of 8 plates. Top each serving with about ¾ cup fennel mixture and 1 tablespoon cheese. Yield: 8 servings.

CALORIES 62 (38% from fat); FAT 2.6g (sat 1.3g, mono 1g, poly 0.2g); PROTEIN 3.8g; CARB 7g; FIBER 2g; CHOL 5mg; IRON 0.7mg; SODIUM 289mg; CALC 141mg

Warm Spinach Salad with Mushroom Vinaigrette

    6   cups fresh spinach
 1½   cups torn radicchio
    2   tablespoons (½-inch) sliced green
        onions
    ½   pound shiitake mushrooms
    ½   teaspoon olive oil
    1   tablespoon finely chopped fresh or
        1 teaspoon dried rubbed sage
 1½   teaspoons finely chopped fresh or
        ½ teaspoon dried thyme
    2   garlic cloves, minced
 3½   tablespoons sherry vinegar
    ⅛   teaspoon salt
    ⅛   teaspoon black pepper
 1½   teaspoons balsamic vinegar
    2   hard-cooked large eggs, quartered
        lengthwise

1. Combine first 3 ingredients in a large bowl.

2. Remove and discard stems from mushrooms, reserving caps. Heat oil in a large nonstick skillet over medium-high heat. Add mushroom caps; sauté 5 minutes. Reduce heat to medium. Add sage, thyme, and garlic; sauté 3 minutes. Stir in sherry vinegar, salt, and pepper; bring to a boil. Remove from heat.

3. Pour mushroom mixture over spinach mixture, tossing well to coat. Drizzle with balsamic vinegar. Place about 1 cup salad on each of 4 plates; top each serving with 2 egg quarters. Yield: 4 servings.

CALORIES 105 (30% from fat); FAT 3.5g (sat 0.9g, mono 1.4g, poly 0.5g); PROTEIN 6g; CARB 11.9g; FIBER 2.2g; CHOL 106mg; IRON 2.6mg; SODIUM 160mg; CALC 71mg

Chicken-Apple Crunch Salad

    2   cups cubed cooked chicken breast
    1   cup chopped Granny Smith apple
    ½   cup chopped celery
    ¼   cup raisins
    2   tablespoons chopped green onions
    ⅓   cup low-fat mayonnaise
    1   tablespoon reduced-fat sour cream
    1   teaspoon fresh lemon juice
    ¼   teaspoon salt
    ¼   teaspoon freshly ground black
        pepper
    ⅛   teaspoon ground cinnamon

1. Combine first 5 ingredients in a large bowl. Combine mayonnaise and remaining 5 ingredients, stirring well with a whisk. Add mayonnaise mixture to chicken mixture, tossing well to coat. Yield: 4 servings (serving size: 1 cup).

CALORIES 207 (19% from fat); FAT 4.4g (sat 1.2g, mono 1.2g, poly 1.4g); PROTEIN 22.4g; CARB 18.4g; FIBER 1.1g; CHOL 61mg; IRON 1.2mg; SODIUM 402mg; CALC 32mg

Turkey Mole Soup

Mole [MOH-lay] is a rich, spicy, and slightly sweet sauce that is served with poultry in many Mexican dishes. Look for it with the Hispanic ingredients in your supermarket.

    1   teaspoon olive oil
 1¼   pounds ground turkey
    1   cup chopped onion
    1   cup chopped green bell pepper
    2   tablespoons chili powder
    4   garlic cloves, minced
    ¼   cup bottled mole (such as La Costeña)
    2   (14-ounce) cans fat-free,
        less-sodium chicken broth
    ½   cup raisins
    ½   teaspoon salt
    ½   teaspoon black pepper
    1   (19-ounce) can black beans, drained
    1   (14.5-ounce) can diced tomatoes,
        undrained
    1   (4.5-ounce) can chopped green
        chiles, undrained
    3   (6-inch) corn tortillas, cut into
        ¼-inch strips
    ½   cup chopped fresh cilantro

1. Heat oil in a Dutch oven over medium heat. Add turkey; cook 5 minutes or until browned, stirring to crumble. Add onion, bell pepper, chili powder, and garlic; cook 5 minutes, stirring frequently. Combine mole and chicken broth, stirring with a whisk. Add broth mixture, raisins, and next 5 ingredients to turkey mixture, stirring to combine; bring to a boil. Cover, reduce heat, and simmer 20 minutes.

2. Preheat oven to 425°.

3. Place tortilla strips on a baking sheet. Bake at 425° for 5 minutes or until golden brown.

4. Spoon 1¼ cups soup into each of 8 bowls. Divide tortilla strips evenly among servings. Top each serving with 1 tablespoon cilantro. Yield: 8 servings.

CALORIES 281 (28% from fat); FAT 8.8g (sat 1.7g, mono 2.7g, poly 2g); PROTEIN 19.5g; CARB 30.6g; FIBER 7.1g; CHOL 56mg; IRON 3.4mg; SODIUM 926mg; CALC 89mg

Cream of Mushroom Soup with Sherry

    2   teaspoons olive oil
    2   cups chopped onion
    1   cup thinly sliced carrot
    ⅔   cup chopped celery
    8   cups sliced button mushrooms
        (about 1½ pounds)
    4   cups sliced shiitake mushroom
        caps (about 7 ounces)
    2   garlic cloves, minced
    1   cup water
    1   teaspoon dried rubbed sage
    ¼   teaspoon salt
    ¼   teaspoon black pepper
    4   (14-ounce) cans fat-free,
        less-sodium chicken broth
    6   tablespoons half-and-half
    ¼   cup dry sherry
    ¼   cup chopped fresh
        parsley

1. Heat oil in a Dutch oven over medium-high heat. Add onion, carrot, and celery; sauté 6 minutes or until tender. Reduce heat to medium; add mushrooms and garlic. Cook 7 minutes or until mushrooms are tender, stirring frequently.
Continued

Add water, sage, salt, pepper, and broth; bring to a simmer. Cover and simmer 25 minutes. Remove from heat; cool 5 minutes. **2.** Place half of mushroom mixture in a blender; process until smooth. Pour pureed soup into a large bowl. Repeat procedure with remaining mushroom mixture. Return soup to pan. Stir in half-and-half and sherry; cook over low heat 5 minutes or until thoroughly heated, stirring frequently. Sprinkle each serving with 1 teaspoon parsley. Yield: 12 servings (serving size: 1 cup).

CALORIES 71 (24% from fat); FAT 1.9g (sat 0.7g, mono 0.8g, poly 0.2g); PROTEIN 4.7g; CARB 8.4g; FIBER 1.9g; CHOL 3mg; IRON 1.2mg; SODIUM 321mg; CALC 26mg

Winter Vegetable Soup

Potatoes, squash, and white beans combine for a substantial main-dish soup. Pancetta is Italian cured bacon. If you can't find it, 2 strips of smoked bacon will work.

    1   teaspoon olive oil
    2   ounces pancetta, chopped
    1   cup chopped onion
    3   garlic cloves, minced
    2   cups cubed peeled acorn squash
    2   cups chopped peeled red potato
    ½   cup chopped celery
    ½   cup chopped carrot
    1   teaspoon dried basil
    ¼   teaspoon ground cinnamon
    ¼   teaspoon dried thyme
    1   (28-ounce) can whole tomatoes,
        drained and chopped
    2   (14-ounce) cans fat-free,
        less-sodium chicken broth
    4   cups chopped kale
    1   (15.5-ounce) can navy beans or
        other small white beans, rinsed
        and drained

1. Heat oil in a Dutch oven over medium-high heat. Add pancetta; sauté 3 minutes. Add chopped onion and garlic; sauté 3 minutes. Add squash and next 6 ingredients, stirring to combine; cook 4 minutes, stirring occasionally. Add tomatoes; cook 2 minutes. **2.** Stir in broth; bring to a boil. Reduce heat; simmer 8 minutes. Add kale; simmer

5 minutes. Add beans; simmer 4 minutes or until potato and kale are tender. Yield: 4 servings (serving size: about 2 cups).

CALORIES 349 (27% from fat); FAT 10.4g (sat 3.3g, mono 4.6g, poly 1.4g); PROTEIN 14.4g; CARB 55g; FIBER 10.5g; CHOL 10mg; IRON 4.2mg; SODIUM 1,076mg; CALC 213mg

Pumpkin Soup

Pumpkin and sweet potato add vibrant color to this curry-spiced first course.

    1   tablespoon butter
    1   cup chopped onion
    3   tablespoons all-purpose flour
    ½   teaspoon curry powder
    ¼   teaspoon ground cumin
    ¼   teaspoon ground nutmeg
    2   garlic cloves, crushed
    1   cup (½-inch) cubed peeled sweet
        potato
    ¼   teaspoon salt
    2   (14-ounce) cans fat-free,
        less-sodium chicken broth
    1   (15-ounce) can pumpkin
    1   cup 1% low-fat milk
    1   tablespoon fresh lime juice
    2   tablespoons chopped fresh chives
        (optional)

1. Melt butter in a Dutch oven over medium-high heat. Add onion; sauté 3 minutes. Stir in flour and next 4 ingredients; sauté 1 minute. Add sweet potato, salt, broth, and pumpkin; bring to a boil. Reduce heat; simmer, partially covered, 20 minutes or until potato is tender, stirring occasionally. Remove from heat; cool 10 minutes. **2.** Place half of pumpkin mixture in a blender or food processor; process until smooth. Pour pureed soup into a large bowl. Repeat procedure with remaining pumpkin mixture. Return soup to pan; stir in milk. Cook over medium heat 6 minutes or until thoroughly heated, stirring frequently (do not boil). Remove from heat; stir in juice. Garnish with chives, if desired. Yield: 6 servings (serving size: 1 cup).

CALORIES 121 (21% from fat); FAT 2.8g (sat 1.6g, mono 0.7g, poly 0.2g); PROTEIN 5.1g; CARB 19.7g; FIBER 3.5g; CHOL 7mg; IRON 1.5mg; SODIUM 565mg; CALC 85mg

Main Dishes

Though steeped in tradition, these entrées are anything but ordinary.

Holiday Feast Menu
serves 12

Slide the table apart, put in the extra leaves, and enjoy this classic celebratory dinner with your extended family.

**Cream of Mushroom Soup
with Sherry
(recipe on page 387)**

**Roast Beef with Horseradish-
Mustard Sauce**

Mashed potatoes

Sautéed zucchini

**Challah
(recipe on page 392)**

**Grand Marnier Soufflé with
Vanilla Sauce
(recipe on page 401)***

*Double the recipe to serve 12.

search myclar2003.com for all our menus

Roast Beef with Horseradish-Mustard Sauce

Let roast beef star in your special meal by matching it with simple sides such as mashed potatoes and sautéed zucchini. A dry rub of coriander, pepper, salt, and garlic encrusts the roast. Use leftover roast and sauce along with Swiss cheese to make great sandwiches on toasted sourdough.

ROAST BEEF:
    2   tablespoons ground coriander seeds
    1   tablespoon cracked black pepper
    2   teaspoons kosher salt
    5   garlic cloves, crushed
    1   (3-pound) sirloin tip roast, trimmed
    Cooking spray

SAUCE:
    ¾   cup prepared horseradish
    ½   cup stone-ground mustard
    ¼   cup white vinegar

1. Preheat oven to 450°.

2. To prepare roast beef, combine first 4 ingredients; rub over roast. Place roast on a broiler pan coated with cooking spray. Insert a meat thermometer into thickest portion of roast. Bake at 450° for 20 minutes.

3. Reduce oven temperature to 300° (do not remove roast from oven); bake an additional 40 minutes or until thermometer registers 140° (medium-rare) or desired degree of doneness. Place roast on a cutting board; cover loosely with foil. Let stand 15 minutes. (Temperature of roast will increase 5° upon standing.) Cut roast across grain into thin slices.

4. To prepare sauce, combine horseradish, mustard, and vinegar. Serve with roast beef. Yield: 12 servings (serving size: 3 ounces beef and 2 tablespoons sauce).

WINE NOTE: Roast beef calls for a big, soft wine of substance. Such wines often cost a fortune, but this stellar Syrah is a steal: Penfolds "Thomas Hyland" Shiraz from South Australia costs just $15. (Shiraz is the Aussie name for the French grape Syrah).

CALORIES 203 (36% from fat); FAT 8.1g (sat 2.8g, mono 3.1g, poly 0.4g); PROTEIN 24.9g; CARB 5.3g; FIBER 2.4g; CHOL 70mg; IRON 2.9mg; SODIUM 575mg; CALC 37mg

Shrimp and Tomatoes with Cheese Grits

Cooking the grits in a combination of milk and chicken broth gives them a rich flavor and creamy texture.

    Cooking spray
    1 cup chopped green bell pepper
    1½ pounds medium shrimp, peeled
       and deveined
    1½ cups chopped plum tomato
    ½ cup sliced green onions
    1½ cups fat-free milk
    1 (14-ounce) can fat-free,
       less-sodium chicken broth
    1 cup uncooked quick-cooking grits
    1 cup (4 ounces) shredded reduced-
       fat sharp cheddar cheese
    1 tablespoon Worcestershire
       sauce

1. Heat a large nonstick skillet coated with cooking spray over medium-high heat. Add bell pepper and shrimp; sauté 7 minutes or until shrimp are done. Add tomato and onions; cook 3 minutes, stirring frequently. Remove mixture from heat; keep warm.

2. Bring milk and broth to a boil in a large saucepan over medium-high heat; gradually stir in grits. Cover, reduce heat to low, and simmer 5 minutes or until thick, stirring occasionally. Add cheese and Worcestershire, stirring until cheese melts. Serve shrimp mixture over grits. Yield: 6 servings (serving size: ⅔ cup shrimp mixture and ⅔ cup grits).

CALORIES 329 (16% from fat); FAT 6g (sat 2.5g, mono 1.4g, poly 1g); PROTEIN 35.3g; CARB 32.8g; FIBER 1.9g; CHOL 187mg; IRON 4.2mg; SODIUM 508mg; CALC 311mg

Apple-Stuffed Pork Chops

Port, dried fruit, and pistachios embellish the stuffing for these meaty pork chops. Tart Granny Smith apple provides a nice foil for the sweet dried plums and port wine, but you can use your favorite apple or pear in its place.

    2 cups chopped peeled Granny
       Smith apple
    ⅔ cup chopped pitted dried plums
    ¼ cup chopped pistachios
    2 tablespoons chopped fresh or
       2 teaspoons dried thyme
    2 teaspoons brown sugar
    5 tablespoons port or other sweet
       red wine, divided
    8 (6-ounce) lean bone-in center-cut
       pork chops (about ¾ inch thick),
       trimmed
    1 teaspoon salt, divided
    ½ teaspoon black pepper
       Cooking spray
    3 tablespoons all-purpose flour
    1 (14-ounce) can fat-free,
       less-sodium chicken broth

1. Combine first 5 ingredients. Stir in 2 tablespoons port.

2. Cut a horizontal slit through thickest portion of each pork chop to form a pocket. Stuff about ¼ cup apple mixture into each pocket. Sprinkle pork evenly with ½ teaspoon salt and pepper.

3. Heat a large nonstick skillet coated with cooking spray over medium-high heat; add 4 pork chops. Cook 7 minutes on each side or until done. Remove pork from pan; keep warm. Repeat procedure with remaining pork.

4. Combine ½ teaspoon salt and flour, stirring with a whisk. Gradually add 3 tablespoons port and broth, stirring with a whisk. Add to pan, scraping pan to loosen browned bits. Bring to a simmer over low heat; cook 5 minutes or until thick, stirring constantly. Serve sauce with pork. Yield: 8 servings (serving size: 1 pork chop and about 3 tablespoons sauce).

CALORIES 242 (29% from fat); FAT 7.7g (sat 2.3g, mono 3.5g, poly 1g); PROTEIN 23.6g; CARB 18.5g; FIBER 2g; CHOL 58mg; IRON 1.4mg; SODIUM 429mg; CALC 44mg

Roast Lamb with Rosemary and Garlic

(pictured on page 382)

This roast cooks with just a simple rub of rosemary and garlic; coarse salt goes on the second the lamb emerges from the oven.

    1 (3-pound) rolled boned leg of
       lamb, trimmed
    1 tablespoon chopped fresh rosemary
    3 garlic cloves, minced
    1 teaspoon kosher or sea salt

1. Preheat oven to 450°.

2. Secure roast at 1-inch intervals with heavy string. Rub surface of roast with rosemary and garlic. Place roast on rack of a broiler pan or roasting pan; insert a meat thermometer into thickest portion of roast. Bake at 450° for 1 hour and 15 minutes or until thermometer registers 140° (medium-rare) to 155° (medium).

3. Sprinkle roast with salt. Place roast on a cutting board; cover loosely with foil. Let stand 10 minutes. (Temperature of roast will increase 5° upon standing.) Remove string before slicing. Yield: 8 servings (serving size: 3 ounces).

CALORIES 165 (36% from fat); FAT 6.6g (sat 2.4g, mono 2.9g, poly 0.4g); PROTEIN 24.2g; CARB 0.5g; FIBER 0g; CHOL 76mg; IRON 1.9mg; SODIUM 293mg; CALC 12mg

Fire and Spice Ham

1 (5½- to 6-pound) 33%-less-sodium smoked, fully cooked ham half
Cooking spray
½ cup red pepper jelly
½ cup pineapple preserves
¼ cup packed brown sugar
¼ teaspoon ground cloves

1. Preheat oven to 425°.
2. Trim fat and rind from ham half. Score outside of ham in a diamond pattern. Place ham on a broiler pan coated with cooking spray. Combine jelly and remaining 3 ingredients, stirring with a whisk until well blended. Brush about one-third of jelly mixture over ham.
3. Bake at 425° for 5 minutes. Reduce oven temperature to 325° (do not remove ham from oven); bake an additional 45 minutes, basting with jelly mixture every 15 minutes. Transfer to a serving platter; let stand 15 minutes before slicing. Yield: 18 servings (serving size: about 3 ounces).

WINE NOTE: Ham accented with brown sugar and preserves needs a wine to balance the sweetness. One option is a sparkling wine or Champagne (which many people unfortunately view only as an aperitif). In this case, a creamy but crisp sparkler will provide just the right counterpoint. Try the lively Mirabelle Brut from California (about $16).

CALORIES 188 (23% from fat); FAT 4.9g (sat 1.6g, mono 2.3g, poly 0.5g); PROTEIN 18.4g; CARB 16.8g; FIBER 0g; CHOL 47mg; IRON 1.4mg; SODIUM 865mg; CALC 10mg

Moroccan Turkey with Cranberry Couscous

TURKEY:

2 teaspoons ground cumin
1 teaspoon ground coriander seeds
¾ teaspoon salt
½ teaspoon ground ginger
½ teaspoon garlic powder
½ teaspoon dried oregano
¼ teaspoon ground cinnamon
¼ teaspoon black pepper
2 (1¼-pound) skinless, boneless turkey breast halves
Cooking spray

COUSCOUS:

1 cup fresh orange juice
1 cup dried cranberries
1 tablespoon olive oil
8 garlic cloves, sliced
⅔ cup finely chopped onion
⅔ cup finely chopped red bell pepper
1 cup water
2 teaspoons curry powder
1 teaspoon salt
1 (14-ounce) can fat-free, less-sodium chicken broth
2 cups uncooked couscous
½ cup chopped fresh basil
½ cup chopped fresh cilantro
4 teaspoons grated lemon rind
⅓ cup chopped peeled lemon sections

1. Preheat oven to 400°.
2. To prepare turkey, combine first 8 ingredients; rub over turkey. Place turkey on a broiler pan coated with cooking spray; insert a meat thermometer into thickest portion of a breast. Bake at 400° for 55 minutes or until thermometer registers 180°. Let stand 10 minutes before slicing.
3. To prepare couscous, bring orange juice to a boil in a small saucepan. Stir in cranberries. Remove from heat; let stand 30 minutes. Drain cranberries in a colander over a bowl, reserving juice.
4. Heat oil in a large saucepan over medium-high heat. Add sliced garlic; sauté 1 minute. Add onion and bell pepper; sauté 2 minutes. Stir in reserved juice, water, curry, 1 teaspoon salt, and broth; bring to a boil. Gradually stir in couscous; remove from heat. Cover and let stand 5 minutes.
5. Fluff couscous with a fork. Add cranberries, basil, cilantro, rind, and lemon sections, tossing gently to combine. Cut each turkey breast into ½-inch-thick slices. Serve turkey with couscous. Yield: 10 servings (serving size: 3 ounces turkey and about ¾ cup couscous).

CALORIES 339 (7% from fat); FAT 2.8g (sat 0.5g, mono 1.2g, poly 0.5g); PROTEIN 33.8g; CARB 42.7g; FIBER 3.9g; CHOL 70mg; IRON 2.5mg; SODIUM 548mg; CALC 49mg

Chicken and Wild Rice with Smoked Sausage

On hectic days, nothing beats a one-pot entrée. Artichoke hearts and black olives jazz up this rice-based dish. All you need is a simple salad to complete the meal.

Cooking spray
1 pound skinless, boneless chicken breast, cut into bite-sized pieces
1 (14-ounce) package reduced-fat smoked sausage (such as Healthy Choice), cut into ½-inch-thick slices
4 cups (½-inch-thick) slices portobello mushroom caps (about 8 ounces)
2 cups chopped onion
2 garlic cloves, minced
2 (14-ounce) cans fat-free, less-sodium chicken broth
2 (6.2-ounce) packages fast-cooking recipe long-grain and wild rice (such as Uncle Ben's)
½ cup chopped green onions
1 (14-ounce) can quartered artichoke hearts, drained
1 (2¼-ounce) can sliced ripe olives

1. Heat a Dutch oven coated with cooking spray over medium-high heat. Add chicken; sauté 4 minutes or until done. Remove from pan; keep warm.

2. Recoat pan with cooking spray. Add sausage; sauté 5 minutes or until browned. Add mushrooms, 2 cups onion, and garlic; sauté 3 minutes. Add broth and rice, omitting seasoning packets; bring to a boil. Cover, reduce heat, and simmer 20 minutes or until liquid is absorbed.

3. Stir in chicken, green onions, artichokes, and olives. Cook 3 minutes or until thoroughly heated. Yield: 8 servings (serving size: 1½ cups).

CALORIES 340 (9% from fat); FAT 3.3g (sat 0.7g, mono 1.4g, poly 0.8g); PROTEIN 27.7g; CARB 48.4g; FIBER 4.6g; CHOL 51mg; IRON 2.7mg; SODIUM 895mg; CALC 57mg

Mediterranean Spinach Strata

This make-ahead dish is great for brunch, lunch, or dinner. Substitute Parmesan, Romano, or sharp provolone cheese for the Asiago, if you prefer.

  2 (8-ounce) loaves French bread baguette, cut into 1-inch-thick slices
Cooking spray
  1 cup chopped onion
  4 garlic cloves, minced
  1 (8-ounce) package presliced mushrooms
  1 tablespoon all-purpose flour
  2 (7-ounce) bags baby spinach
  ½ teaspoon salt, divided
  ½ teaspoon black pepper, divided
  3 cups thinly sliced plum tomato (about 1 pound)
  1 (4-ounce) package crumbled feta cheese
  ¾ cup (3 ounces) grated Asiago cheese, divided
  3 cups fat-free milk
  2 tablespoons Dijon mustard
1½ teaspoons dried oregano
  5 large eggs, lightly beaten
  4 large egg whites, lightly beaten

1. Preheat oven to 350°.

2. Place bread slices in a single layer on a baking sheet. Bake at 350° for 12 minutes or until lightly browned.

3. Heat a large nonstick skillet coated with cooking spray over medium-high heat. Add onion, garlic, and mushrooms; sauté 5 minutes or until tender. Sprinkle flour over mushroom mixture; cook 1 minute, stirring constantly. Add 1 bag of spinach, and cook 3 minutes or until spinach wilts. Add remaining spinach, and cook 3 minutes or until spinach wilts. Stir in ¼ teaspoon salt and ¼ teaspoon pepper.

4. Place half of bread slices in bottom of a 13 x 9-inch baking dish coated with cooking spray. Spread spinach mixture over bread. Top with tomato slices; sprinkle evenly with feta and half of Asiago cheese. Arrange remaining bread slices over cheese. Combine ¼ teaspoon salt, ¼ teaspoon pepper, milk, and remaining 4 ingredients, stirring well with a whisk. Pour over bread; sprinkle with remaining Asiago cheese. Cover and chill 8 hours or overnight.

5. Preheat oven to 350°.

6. Uncover strata; bake at 350° for 40 minutes or until lightly browned and set. Serve warm. Yield: 10 servings.

CALORIES 297 (29% from fat); FAT 9.5g (sat 4.4g, mono 2.8g, poly 1g); PROTEIN 17.9g; CARB 36g; FIBER 3.1g; CHOL 125mg; IRON 3.5mg; SODIUM 720mg; CALC 332mg

Breads

From the big family gathering to breakfast for company, meals are more special when fresh-baked bread is on the menu.

Crusty Rye Loaf

This bread is a great choice for corned beef, roast beef, or pastrami sandwiches slathered with grainy mustard and topped with Swiss cheese. The sponge can be made ahead and refrigerated for up to 24 hours, but bring it back to room temperature before making the bread. For a unique presentation, you can monogram the bread: Cut a ½-inch-wide initial into parchment paper, then place the stencil on the loaf and sift several tablespoons of flour over the initial. Remove the stencil, and bake the loaf as directed.

SPONGE:

  1 package dry yeast (about 2¼ teaspoons)
  ⅔ cup warm water (100° to 110°)
  ½ cup rye flour—medium
  ¼ cup bread flour

BREAD:

  2 cups bread flour
  ½ cup rye flour—medium
  ½ cup water
  2 teaspoons caraway seeds
1¼ teaspoons salt
  2 tablespoons bread flour
Cooking spray

1. To prepare sponge, dissolve yeast in warm water in a large bowl; let stand 5 minutes. Lightly spoon ½ cup rye flour and ¼ cup bread flour into dry measuring cups; level with a knife. Add ½ cup rye flour and ¼ cup bread flour to yeast mixture, stirring with a whisk. Cover and let stand in a warm place (85°), free from drafts, 2 hours.

2. To prepare bread, lightly spoon 2 cups bread flour and ½ cup rye flour into dry measuring cups; level with a knife. Add 2 cups bread flour, ½ cup rye flour, ½ cup water, caraway seeds, and salt to sponge; beat with a mixer at medium speed until smooth.

3. Turn dough out onto a lightly floured surface. Knead until smooth and elastic (about 10 minutes); add 2 tablespoons bread flour, 1 tablespoon at a time, to prevent dough from sticking to hands.

4. Shape dough into a round loaf; place loaf on a baking sheet coated with cooking spray. Cover and let rise 1½ hours or until doubled in size. (Press two fingers into dough. If indentation remains, dough has risen enough.)

5. Preheat oven to 425°.

6. Uncover and pierce loaf 1 inch deep in several places with a wooden pick. (Stencil an initial on bread, if monogramming.) Bake at 425° for 30 minutes or until loaf is browned on bottom and sounds hollow when tapped. Let stand 20 minutes before slicing. Yield: 12 servings (serving size: 1 slice).

CALORIES 131 (5% from fat); FAT 0.7g (sat 0.1g, mono 0.1g, poly 0.3g); PROTEIN 4.3g; CARB 26.7g; FIBER 2.2g; CHOL 0mg; IRON 1.5mg; SODIUM 246mg; CALC 9mg

Challah

(pictured on page 383)

This traditional Jewish bread has a moist, rich texture and is often braided.

  ½ teaspoon sugar
  1 package dry yeast (about 2¼ teaspoons)
  ¾ cup warm water (100° to 110°)
  ¼ cup vegetable oil
  1 large egg, lightly beaten
  3⅓ cups all-purpose flour
  1¼ teaspoons salt
  Cooking spray
  2 teaspoons water
  1 large egg yolk, lightly beaten

1. Dissolve sugar and yeast in warm water in a large bowl; let stand 5 minutes. Add oil and 1 egg, stirring with a whisk. Lightly spoon flour into dry measuring cups; level with a knife. Add flour and salt to yeast mixture; beat with a mixer at medium speed until smooth.

2. Turn dough out onto a lightly floured surface. Knead until smooth and elastic (about 10 minutes). Place dough in a large bowl coated with cooking spray, turning to coat top. Cover and let rise in a warm place (85°), free from drafts, 1 hour or until doubled in size. (Press two fingers into dough. If indentation remains, dough has risen enough.)

3. Punch dough down; shape into a ball. Return dough to bowl; cover and let rise 1 hour or until doubled in size.

4. Punch dough down; turn dough out onto a lightly floured surface. Cover and let rest 15 minutes.

5. Divide dough into 3 equal portions. Working with 1 portion at a time (cover remaining dough to keep from drying), shape each portion into a 15-inch rope. Place ropes lengthwise on a baking sheet coated with cooking spray (do not stretch); pinch ends together at one end to seal. Braid ropes, and pinch loose ends together to seal. Cover and let rise 1 hour or until doubled in size.

6. Preheat oven to 375°.

7. Uncover dough. Combine 2 teaspoons water and egg yolk; brush over braid. Bake at 375° for 35 minutes or until loaf is browned on bottom and sounds hollow when tapped. Remove from pan; cool on a wire rack. Yield: 16 servings (serving size: 1 slice).

CALORIES 124 (30% from fat); FAT 4.1g (sat 0.7g, mono 1g, poly 2.1g); PROTEIN 3.2g; CARB 19.5g; FIBER 0.7g; CHOL 27mg; IRON 1.4mg; SODIUM 188mg; CALC 3mg

Tomato and Eggplant Focaccia

Lightly coat your hands with cooking spray to prevent the dough from sticking as you knead it.

DOUGH:

  1 package dry yeast (about 2¼ teaspoons)
  1⅓ cups warm water (100° to 110°)
  4 cups all-purpose flour, divided
  3 tablespoons chopped fresh basil
  1 tablespoon olive oil
  1 teaspoon salt
  Cooking spray

TAPENADE:

  2 tablespoons olive oil, divided
  1 garlic clove, minced
  1 cup finely chopped peeled eggplant
  2 tablespoons chopped fresh basil
  2 teaspoons capers
  ⅛ teaspoon salt
  ⅛ teaspoon black pepper
  16 kalamata olives, pitted and chopped
  5 plum tomatoes, thinly sliced (about 1 pound)

1. To prepare dough, dissolve yeast in warm water in a large bowl. Lightly spoon flour into dry measuring cups; level with a knife. Add 3½ cups flour, 3 tablespoons basil, 1 tablespoon oil, and 1 teaspoon salt to yeast mixture; stir just until moist.

2. Turn dough out onto a lightly floured surface. Knead until smooth and elastic (about 10 minutes); add enough of remaining flour, 1 tablespoon at a time, to prevent dough from sticking to hands.

3. Place in a large bowl coated with cooking spray, turning to coat top. Cover and let rise in a warm place (85°), free from drafts, 1 hour or until doubled in size.

4. Punch dough down; cover and let rest 5 minutes. Divide dough in half. Working with 1 portion at a time (cover remaining dough to keep from drying), roll each half into a 10-inch circle on a pizza pan or baking sheet coated with cooking spray. Cover and let rise 30 minutes or until doubled in size.

5. Preheat oven to 425°.

6. To prepare tapenade, heat 1 tablespoon oil in a nonstick skillet over medium-low heat. Add garlic; cook 30 seconds. Add eggplant; cook 8 minutes or until tender, stirring occasionally. Place eggplant mixture in a food processor. Add 1 tablespoon oil, 2 tablespoons basil, and next 4 ingredients; pulse 1 minute, scraping sides of bowl once.

7. Uncover dough. Spread ¼ cup tapenade over each focaccia. Arrange tomato slices evenly over tapenade. Spread remaining tapenade over tomatoes. Bake at 425° for 20 minutes or until crust is golden brown. Yield: 2 focaccia, 8 servings per focaccia (serving size: 1 wedge).

CALORIES 149 (21% from fat); FAT 3.4g (sat 0.5g, mono 2.3g, poly 0.4g); PROTEIN 3.7g; CARB 25.6g; FIBER 1.5g; CHOL 0mg; IRON 1.8mg; SODIUM 217mg; CALC 12mg

Whole Grain Cornsticks

You can prepare these in muffin tins, but the cast iron cornstick pan yields a crisper crust.

  ¾ cup whole wheat flour
  ¾ cup yellow cornmeal
  3 tablespoons grated fresh Parmesan cheese
  2 teaspoons baking powder
  1½ teaspoons chili powder
  1 teaspoon salt
  ¾ cup plus 2 tablespoons fat-free milk
  2 tablespoons olive oil
  2 tablespoons honey
  1 large egg, lightly beaten
  ¾ cup frozen whole-kernel corn, thawed
  ⅓ cup minced red onion
  2 tablespoons minced jalapeño pepper
  Cooking spray

1. Preheat oven to 425°.

2. Lightly spoon flour into a dry measuring cup; level with a knife. Combine flour and next 5 ingredients in a large bowl. Make a well in center of mixture. Combine milk, oil, honey, and egg. Add to flour mixture, stirring just until moist. Fold in corn, onion, and jalapeño.

3. Place a cast iron cornstick pan in a 425° oven for 5 minutes. Remove from oven; immediately coat with cooking spray. Spoon batter into pan. Bake at 425° for 18 minutes or until lightly browned. Remove from pan immediately; serve warm. Yield: 1 dozen (serving size: 1 cornstick).

CALORIES 120 (27% from fat); FAT 3.6g (sat 0.8g, mono 2.1g, poly 0.4g); PROTEIN 4g; CARB 19g; FIBER 2g; CHOL 19mg; IRON 0.7mg; SODIUM 325mg; CALC 96mg

Apple "Fritters"

Apple-filled balls of dough are placed in muffin pans, baked, and then drizzled with a glaze to replicate classic apple fritters. Braeburn or Pink Lady apples are a good substitute for the tangier Granny Smiths. The apple juice in the glaze gives these a double dose of apple flavor.

FILLING:

1 tablespoon butter
3 cups chopped peeled Granny Smith apple (about 1 pound)
½ cup apple juice
2 tablespoons granulated sugar
1 teaspoon ground cinnamon

DOUGH:

2 packages dry yeast (about 4½ teaspoons)
1 cup warm 1% low-fat milk (100° to 110°)
5 cups all-purpose flour, divided
⅔ cup granulated sugar
3 tablespoons butter, melted
1 teaspoon salt
2 large eggs, lightly beaten
Cooking spray

GLAZE:

1½ cups powdered sugar
4 teaspoons butter, melted
1 tablespoon apple juice
⅛ teaspoon ground cinnamon

1. To prepare filling, melt 1 tablespoon butter in a large nonstick skillet over medium-high heat. Add apple; sauté 3 minutes. Add ½ cup apple juice, 2 tablespoons granulated sugar, and 1 teaspoon cinnamon. Reduce heat to medium-low; simmer 3 minutes or until liquid is almost absorbed. Remove from heat; cool.

2. To prepare dough, dissolve yeast in warm milk in a large bowl. Let stand 5 minutes or until foamy. Lightly spoon flour into dry measuring cups; level with a knife. Add 3½ cups flour, ⅔ cup granulated sugar, 3 tablespoons melted butter, salt, and eggs to yeast mixture, stirring until smooth. Add 1 cup flour; stir until a soft dough forms.

3. Turn dough out onto a lightly floured surface. Knead until smooth and elastic (about 10 minutes); add enough of remaining flour, 1 tablespoon at a time, to prevent dough from sticking to hands (dough will feel tacky).

4. Place dough in a large bowl coated with cooking spray, turning to coat top. Cover and let rise in a warm place (85°), free from drafts, 1½ hours or until doubled in size. (Press two fingers into dough. If indentation remains, dough has risen enough.)

5. Punch dough down. Cover and let rest 5 minutes. Divide dough into 24 equal portions. Working with 1 portion at a time (cover remaining dough to keep from drying), roll each portion into a 3-inch circle on a lightly floured surface. Spoon about 2 teaspoons filling into center of dough; gather dough over filling to form a ball, pinching seam to seal. Place balls, seam side down, in muffin cups coated with cooking spray. Cover and let rise 40 minutes or until doubled in size.

6. Preheat oven to 400°.

7. Uncover dough; bake at 400° for 20 minutes or until lightly browned. Remove from pan; cool on a wire rack.

8. To prepare glaze, combine powdered sugar and remaining 3 ingredients; drizzle over rolls. Yield: 2 dozen (serving size: 1 roll).

CALORIES 191 (16% from fat); FAT 3.4g (sat 1.8g, mono 1g, poly 0.3g); PROTEIN 3.9g; CARB 36.4g; FIBER 1.3g; CHOL 25mg; IRON 1.4mg; SODIUM 136mg; CALC 21mg

Pumpkin Muffins

These spicy muffins are good for a quick breakfast on the run or to include in bag lunches. A combination of brown sugar and granulated sugar creates a crunchy topping that contrasts with the moist, tender muffins.

2¾ cups all-purpose flour
1 cup granulated sugar
1 tablespoon baking powder
1 teaspoon baking soda
1 teaspoon ground cinnamon
½ teaspoon salt
1 cup canned pumpkin
¾ cup fat-free sour cream
⅓ cup fat-free milk
¼ cup vegetable oil
1 teaspoon vanilla extract
1 large egg, lightly beaten
1 large egg white, lightly beaten
Cooking spray
1 tablespoon granulated sugar
1½ teaspoons brown sugar

1. Preheat oven to 375°.

2. Lightly spoon flour into dry measuring cups; level with a knife. Combine flour and next 5 ingredients in a medium bowl, stirring with a whisk. Make a well in center of mixture.

3. Combine pumpkin and next 6 ingredients; add to flour mixture, stirring just until moist. Spoon batter into 18 muffin cups coated with cooking spray.

4. Combine 1 tablespoon granulated sugar and brown sugar; sprinkle over muffins.

5. Bake at 375° for 25 minutes or until muffins spring back when touched lightly in center. Remove muffins from pans immediately; cool on a wire rack. Yield: 18 servings (serving size: 1 muffin).

CALORIES 164 (19% from fat); FAT 3.5g (sat 0.6g, mono 0.8g, poly 1.9g); PROTEIN 3.5g; CARB 29.7g; FIBER 1g; CHOL 12mg; IRON 1.2mg; SODIUM 269mg; CALC 78mg

Olive and Asiago Rolls

You can substitute Parmesan for Asiago
and use green olives, if you prefer.

1   tablespoon sugar
1   package dry yeast (about 2¼
    teaspoons)
¾   cup warm water (100° to 110°)
3⅔ cups bread flour
½   cup whole wheat flour
¾   cup 1% low-fat milk
2   tablespoons chopped fresh
    oregano
1   teaspoon salt
1   teaspoon olive oil
Cooking spray
3   tablespoons chopped pitted
    kalamata olives
1   tablespoon water
1   large egg white, lightly beaten
½   cup (2 ounces) grated Asiago cheese

1. Dissolve sugar and yeast in warm
water in a large bowl; let stand 5 minutes. Lightly spoon flours into dry measuring cups; level with a knife. Add
flours, milk, and next 3 ingredients to
yeast mixture; beat with a mixer at
medium speed until smooth.
2. Turn dough out onto a lightly floured
surface. Knead until smooth and elastic
(about 10 minutes).
3. Place dough in a large bowl coated
with cooking spray, turning to coat top.
Cover and let rise in a warm place (85°),
free from drafts, 45 minutes or until
doubled in size. (Press two fingers into
dough. If indentation remains, dough
has risen enough.)

4. Punch dough down. Cover and let
rest 5 minutes. Turn dough out onto a
lightly floured surface. Arrange olives
over dough; knead gently 4 or 5 times
or until olives are incorporated into
dough. Cover and let rest 10 minutes.
5. Punch dough down. Divide dough
into 16 equal portions. Working with 1
portion at a time (cover remaining
dough to keep from drying), roll each
portion into a 2-inch ball. Place on baking sheets coated with cooking spray.
Cover and let rise 30 minutes or until
doubled in size. Cut a ¼-inch-deep "X"
in top of each roll.
6. Preheat oven to 375°.
7. Combine 1 tablespoon water and egg
white; brush over rolls. Bake at 375° for
18 minutes or until golden brown. Remove from oven; immediately sprinkle
with cheese. Serve warm. Yield: 16 rolls
(serving size: 1 roll).

CALORIES 161 (15% from fat); FAT 2.7g (sat 0.9g, mono 1.1g,
poly 0.4g); PROTEIN 6.1g; CARB 27.5g; FIBER 1.3g; CHOL 4mg;
IRON 1.6mg; SODIUM 212mg; CALC 58mg

Strawberry Yogurt Scones

Serve fresh from the oven with hot tea.

1½ cups all-purpose flour
⅔   cup whole wheat flour
½   cup sugar
2   teaspoons baking powder
½   teaspoon baking soda
¼   teaspoon salt
¾   cup chopped strawberries
⅔   cup strawberry fat-free
    yogurt
3   tablespoons butter, melted
½   teaspoon grated orange rind
1   large egg white, lightly beaten
Cooking spray
2   teaspoons sugar

1. Preheat oven to 400°.
2. Lightly spoon flours into dry measuring cups; level with a knife. Combine
flours, ½ cup sugar, baking powder,
baking soda, and salt in a large bowl.
Combine strawberries, yogurt, butter,
rind, and egg white; add to flour mixture, stirring just until moist.

3. Turn dough out onto a lightly floured
surface; knead lightly 4 times with
floured hands. Pat into an 8-inch circle
on a baking sheet coated with cooking
spray. Cut into 12 wedges, cutting into
but not through dough; sprinkle with 2
teaspoons sugar. Bake at 400° for 20
minutes or until lightly browned. Yield:
12 scones (serving size: 1 scone).

CALORIES 152 (20% from fat); FAT 3.3g (sat 1.9g, mono 0.9g,
poly 0.3g); PROTEIN 3.6g; CARB 27.7g; FIBER 1.5g; CHOL 8mg;
IRON 1.1mg; SODIUM 227mg; CALC 78mg

Sweet Potato-Streusel Quick Bread

To make this quick bread even quicker, we
used the microwave to cook the potato and
soften the butter for the streusel topping.
Use an electric knife to get clean slices.
Serve with the Chicken-Apple Crunch Salad
(recipe on page 387) for an easy lunch.

1   large sweet potato (about 12 ounces)
2   teaspoons butter
⅓   cup chopped pecans
2   tablespoons dark brown sugar
1½ cups all-purpose flour
½   cup whole wheat flour
¾   cup packed dark brown sugar
2   teaspoons baking powder
1   teaspoon ground cinnamon
¾   teaspoon salt
¼   teaspoon ground nutmeg
⅔   cup fresh orange juice
3   tablespoons vegetable oil
1   large egg, lightly beaten
Cooking spray

1. Preheat oven to 350°.
2. Pierce potato with a fork; place on a
paper towel in microwave oven. Microwave at HIGH 7 minutes, turning
after 4 minutes. Wrap potato in paper
towel; let stand 5 minutes. Peel potato;
mash to measure 1 cup.
3. Place butter in a small microwave-
safe bowl. Microwave at MEDIUM 20
seconds or until soft. Stir in pecans and
2 tablespoons sugar.
4. Lightly spoon flours into dry measuring
cups; level with a knife. Combine flours,
brown sugar, and next 4 ingredients in

a large bowl, stirring with a whisk. Add mashed sweet potato, juice, oil, and egg, stirring until well blended.

5. Spoon batter into an 8 x 4-inch loaf pan coated with cooking spray. Drop pecan mixture by spoonfuls over top of loaf; gently press into batter.

6. Bake at 350° for 1 hour or until a wooden pick inserted in center comes out clean. Cool in pan 5 minutes on a wire rack. Remove from pan; cool completely on wire rack. Yield: 16 servings (serving size: 1 slice).

CALORIES 174 (28% from fat); FAT 5.4g (sat 1g, mono 1.9g, poly 2.2g); PROTEIN 2.8g; CARB 29.5g; FIBER 1.5g; CHOL 15mg; IRON 1.2mg; SODIUM 187mg; CALC 57mg

Orange-Cranberry Bubble Bread

This simple breakfast bread relies on refrigerated biscuit dough.

½ cup dried cranberries
⅓ cup sugar
1½ teaspoons grated orange rind
6 ounces ⅓-less-fat cream cheese, softened
2 (10-count) cans refrigerated buttermilk biscuit dough
Cooking spray
2 tablespoons butter, melted
¼ cup packed brown sugar

1. Preheat oven to 350°.
2. Combine first 4 ingredients.
3. Working with 1 biscuit at a time (cover remaining biscuits to keep from drying), pat each biscuit into a 3-inch circle. Spoon about 1 teaspoon cream cheese mixture into center of each circle; gather dough over filling to form a ball, pinching seam to seal.
4. Place filled biscuits, seam sides up, in a 13 x 9-inch baking pan coated with cooking spray. Drizzle melted butter over biscuits; sprinkle with brown sugar.
5. Bake at 350° for 40 minutes or until lightly browned. Yield: 20 servings (serving size: 1 biscuit).

CALORIES 141 (29% from fat); FAT 4.5g (sat 2.3g, mono 1.1g, poly 0.1g); PROTEIN 2.7g; CARB 22.6g; FIBER 0.6g; CHOL 11mg; IRON 0.9mg; SODIUM 280mg; CALC 11mg

Side Dishes

Complement your entrées and create an impressive array of festive meals with these accompaniments.

Roasted Potatoes with Tangy Watercress Sauce

Add watercress, basil, and mint to a yogurt base for a fragrant, fresh-tasting sauce you can make up to 2 days ahead. Serve alongside chicken, beef, or lamb. You can also use the sauce as a dip for vegetables.

SAUCE:
1½ cups plain fat-free yogurt
1 cup trimmed watercress
⅓ cup light mayonnaise
¼ cup chopped green onions
3 tablespoons chopped fresh basil
1 tablespoon chopped fresh mint
1 teaspoon balsamic vinegar
¼ teaspoon salt
⅛ teaspoon freshly ground black pepper

POTATOES:
3 pounds small red potatoes, quartered
1½ tablespoons olive oil
1 teaspoon freshly ground black pepper
½ teaspoon salt
Cooking spray

1. Preheat oven to 450°.
2. To prepare sauce, place first 9 ingredients in a food processor or blender; process until smooth, scraping sides. Cover and chill.
3. To prepare potatoes, combine potatoes and next 3 ingredients in a jelly roll pan or shallow roasting pan coated with cooking spray, tossing to coat. Bake at 450° for 35 minutes or until tender, stirring occasionally. Serve with sauce. Yield: 8 servings (serving size: 1 cup potatoes and 2 tablespoons sauce).

CALORIES 210 (26% from fat); FAT 6.1g (sat 0.9g, mono 1.9g, poly 0.3g); PROTEIN 6.6g; CARB 33.2g; FIBER 3.1g; CHOL 4mg; IRON 2.6mg; SODIUM 347mg; CALC 123mg

Maple-Roasted Acorn Squash

The syrup brings out the natural sweetness in the squash. And while the squash roasts, the sugars caramelize, intensifying the flavor. The darker the syrup, the richer the flavor.

6 acorn squash (about 1 pound each)
⅓ cup maple syrup
2 tablespoons extra-virgin olive oil
1 teaspoon kosher salt
½ teaspoon freshly ground black pepper
Cooking spray

1. Preheat oven to 425°.
2. Cut each squash in half lengthwise. Discard seeds and membranes. Cut each half crosswise into 1-inch-thick slices; peel. Combine syrup, oil, salt, and pepper in a large bowl, stirring well. Add squash; toss to coat.
3. Place squash in a 13 x 9-inch baking dish coated with cooking spray. Bake at 425° for 25 minutes or until tender, stirring every 10 minutes. Yield: 9 servings (serving size: about 1 cup).

CALORIES 170 (20% from fat); FAT 3.7g (sat 0.6g, mono 2.3g, poly 0.6g); PROTEIN 4.4g; CARB 34.6g; FIBER 4.9g; CHOL 0mg; IRON 1.9mg; SODIUM 222mg; CALC 102mg

Cinnamon Stewed Apples

A terrific companion for ham or pork, this recipe can be doubled easily, and will keep in the refrigerator for about a week. The sauce is somewhat thin just after cooking, but it will thicken upon standing.

6 cups chopped peeled Granny Smith apple (about 2 pounds)
½ cup packed brown sugar
¼ cup apple juice
1 teaspoon ground cinnamon
⅛ teaspoon ground nutmeg
⅛ teaspoon salt

1. Combine all ingredients in a large, heavy saucepan. Cover and cook over medium-low heat 45 minutes or until
Continued

apple is tender, stirring occasionally. Let stand 5 minutes. Yield: 2 cups (serving size: ¼ cup).

CALORIES 121 (3% from fat); FAT 0.4g (sat 0.1g, mono 0g, poly 0.1g); PROTEIN 0.2g; CARB 31.3g; FIBER 2.3g; CHOL 0mg; IRON 0.4mg; SODIUM 42mg; CALC 19mg

Tree Trimming Party Menu
serves 6

Warm up with lightly spiced hot chocolate, put up your favorite decorations, and then sit down to this casual supper.

Hot White Chocolate with Ginger (recipe on page 385)

Spicy Swiss Chard with Lemon

Whole Grain Cornsticks (recipe on page 392)

Chicken and Wild Rice with Smoked Sausage (recipe on page 390)

Coffee Cupcakes (recipe on page 397)

WINE NOTE: Artichokes and smoky sausage are notoriously tough on wine—both can swamp delicate flavors. But Beaujolais really stands up to both foods. Plus, in France, Beaujolais is a favorite wine with chicken. Georges Duboeuf makes excellent Beaujolais. Consider the ones known as Fleurie, Moulin-a-Vent, or Morgon; each costs about $13.

search myclar2003.com for all our menus

Spicy Swiss Chard with Lemon

Although 16 cups seems like a large amount of chard, it will cook down. Three simple ingredients—crushed red pepper, garlic, and fresh lemon juice—round out the flavor.

　2　teaspoons olive oil
　16　cups trimmed Swiss chard (about 2 pounds)
　¼　to ½ teaspoon crushed red pepper
　3　garlic cloves, minced
　1　tablespoon fresh lemon juice
　⅛　teaspoon salt

1. Heat oil in a large Dutch oven over medium-high heat. Add chard; sauté 1 minute or until slightly wilted. Stir in pepper and garlic. Cover and cook 4 minutes or until tender, stirring occasionally. Uncover and cook 3 minutes or until liquid evaporates. Stir in juice and salt. Yield: 6 servings (serving size: ½ cup).

CALORIES 43 (38% from fat); FAT 1.8g (sat 0.3g, mono 1.2g, poly 0.2g); PROTEIN 2.6g; CARB 6g; FIBER 2.3g; CHOL 0mg; IRON 2.6mg; SODIUM 345mg; CALC 74mg

Spinach and Gruyère Soufflé

Gruyère, which has a nutty, slightly sweet flavor, is an aged Swiss cheese that's commonly made in France. Substitute Swiss, Jarlsberg, or Asiago if you can't find Gruyère.

　Cooking spray
　3　tablespoons dry breadcrumbs, divided
　¼　cup finely chopped onion
　2　tablespoons all-purpose flour
　¼　teaspoon salt
　¼　teaspoon freshly ground black pepper
　⅛　teaspoon ground red pepper
　Dash of ground nutmeg
　1　cup fat-free milk, divided
　1　large egg yolk, lightly beaten
　6　tablespoons (1½ ounces) finely grated Gruyère cheese
　1　(10-ounce) package frozen chopped spinach, thawed, drained, and squeezed dry
　6　large egg whites, lightly beaten
　¼　teaspoon cream of tartar

1. Preheat oven to 400°.
2. Coat a 1-quart soufflé dish with cooking spray; sprinkle with 1 tablespoon breadcrumbs.
3. Heat a medium saucepan coated with cooking spray over medium-high heat. Add onion; sauté 2 minutes or until tender. Remove from heat. Add flour, salt, peppers, and nutmeg, stirring well. Gradually add ½ cup milk, stirring with a whisk until well blended. Stir in ½ cup milk. Cook over medium heat 2 minutes or until thick and bubbly, stirring constantly with a whisk. Remove from heat.

4. Place egg yolk in a bowl. Gradually add milk mixture to egg yolk, stirring constantly with a whisk. Return mixture to pan. Cook 1 minute or until thick. Remove from heat; stir in cheese and spinach. Cool 5 minutes.
5. Place egg whites and cream of tartar in a large bowl; beat with a mixer at high speed until stiff peaks form. Gently stir one-fourth of egg white mixture into milk mixture; gently fold in remaining egg white mixture and 2 tablespoons breadcrumbs. Spoon into prepared dish. Bake at 400° for 30 minutes or until soufflé is puffy and set. Serve immediately. Yield: 6 servings.

CALORIES 109 (29% from fat); FAT 3.5g (sat 1.6g, mono 1.1g, poly 0.3g); PROTEIN 9.8g; CARB 9.6g; FIBER 1.8g; CHOL 44mg; IRON 1.4mg; SODIUM 261mg; CALC 187mg

Broccolini with Pepper Dressing

Broccolini is a cross between broccoli and Chinese kale. It has long, thin, edible stalks topped with tiny buds that resemble broccoli florets. The flavor is reminiscent of broccoli, but with a peppery bite. Substitute broccoli or asparagus if you can't find broccolini.

　⅓　cup finely chopped red bell pepper
　2　tablespoons finely chopped shallots
　2　tablespoons rice vinegar
　1　tablespoon fresh lime juice
　1　tablespoon sugar
　2　teaspoons minced peeled fresh ginger
　1　teaspoon vegetable oil
　½　teaspoon salt
　¼　teaspoon crushed red pepper
　1　pound broccolini, trimmed

1. Combine first 9 ingredients in a bowl; toss well.
2. Steam broccolini, covered, 5 minutes or until crisp-tender; drain. Spoon pepper dressing over broccolini. Yield: 4 servings (serving size: 1 cup broccolini and 2 tablespoons pepper dressing).

CALORIES 60 (24% from fat); FAT 1.6g (sat 0.2g, mono 0.3g, poly 0.9g); PROTEIN 3.5g; CARB 10.5g; FIBER 3g; CHOL 0mg; IRON 1.1mg; SODIUM 325mg; CALC 57mg

Brussels Sprouts with Pecans

The sprouts take just a brief turn in the pan; slicing them cuts down on their cooking time. The dish's sweet, buttery flavors mellow the bite of the Brussels sprouts.

2 teaspoons butter
1 cup chopped onion
4 garlic cloves, thinly sliced
8 cups halved and thinly sliced Brussels sprouts (about 1½ pounds)
½ cup fat-free, less-sodium chicken broth
1½ tablespoons sugar
½ teaspoon salt
8 teaspoons coarsely chopped pecans, toasted

1. Melt butter in a large nonstick skillet over medium-high heat. Add onion and garlic; sauté 4 minutes or until lightly browned. Stir in Brussels sprouts; sauté 2 minutes. Add broth and sugar; cook 5 minutes or until liquid almost evaporates, stirring frequently. Stir in salt. Sprinkle with pecans. Yield: 8 servings (serving size: about ⅔ cup).

CALORIES 82 (33% from fat); FAT 3g (sat 0.8g, mono 1.3g, poly 0.7g); PROTEIN 3.6g; CARB 12.6g; FIBER 3.9g; CHOL 3mg; IRON 1.3mg; SODIUM 207mg; CALC 45mg

Cranberry Salsa

The sweet-tart flavor of this fresh salsa sparks simple chicken, turkey, or pork. You can make it up to 2 days before serving.

2 cups fresh cranberries
1½ cups coarsely chopped orange sections (about 3 oranges)
⅓ cup chopped red onion
⅓ cup fresh orange juice
3 tablespoons sugar
2 tablespoons chopped fresh cilantro
¼ teaspoon salt
1 jalapeño pepper, seeded and finely chopped

1. Place cranberries in a food processor; pulse 2 or 3 times or until coarsely chopped. Combine cranberries, orange sections, and remaining ingredients in a large bowl, tossing gently to combine. Cover and chill. Yield: 3 cups (serving size: ¼ cup).

CALORIES 36 (3% from fat); FAT 0.1g (sat 0g, mono 0g, poly 0.1g); PROTEIN 0.4g; CARB 9.2g; FIBER 1.3g; CHOL 0mg; IRON 0.1mg; SODIUM 50mg; CALC 13mg

Risotto with Mushrooms and Parmesan

You can use any fresh mushrooms, such as shiitake or portobello, in this recipe.
MAKE-AHEAD TIP: Prepare the risotto, reserving a cup of the broth mixture and leaving the rice slightly undercooked. Cool and refrigerate for up to 2 days. Reheat the risotto just before serving, adding the remaining liquid and fully cooking the rice.

2 cups water
1 (14½-ounce) can vegetable broth
4 teaspoons olive oil, divided
2 cups chopped cremini mushrooms (about 6 ounces)
½ cup chopped onion
1½ cups Arborio rice or other medium-grain rice
1 cup dry white wine
½ cup (2 ounces) grated fresh Parmesan cheese
¼ cup chopped fresh parsley
2 tablespoons chopped fresh basil
¼ to ½ teaspoon crushed red pepper
¼ teaspoon salt
¼ teaspoon black pepper

1. Bring water and broth to a simmer in a saucepan (do not boil). Keep warm over low heat.
2. Heat 2 teaspoons oil in a medium saucepan over medium-high heat. Add mushrooms; sauté 5 minutes or until tender. Remove mushrooms from pan.
3. Heat 2 teaspoons oil in pan over medium-high heat. Add onion; sauté 2 minutes or until tender. Add rice; cook 1 minute, stirring constantly. Stir in wine; cook 2 minutes or until liquid is nearly absorbed, stirring constantly.
4. Add broth mixture, ½ cup at a time, stirring constantly until each portion of broth mixture is absorbed before adding the next (about 20 minutes). Stir in mushrooms, cheese, and remaining ingredients. Yield: 7 servings (serving size: about ¾ cup).

CALORIES 276 (16% from fat); FAT 5g (sat 1.7g, mono 2.5g, poly 0.3g); PROTEIN 8.2g; CARB 41.9g; FIBER 1.7g; CHOL 5mg; IRON 0.9mg; SODIUM 475mg; CALC 123mg

Desserts

From homey cupcakes to an elegant soufflé, these sweet treats will crown a variety of menus.

Coffee Cupcakes

If you'd prefer a single-layer cake to cupcakes, use a 9-inch square baking pan or round cake pan. Bake the cake at 350° for 25 minutes or until a wooden pick inserted in the center comes out clean.

CUPCAKES:
2 tablespoons boiling water
4 teaspoons instant espresso granules or 8 teaspoons instant coffee granules
⅓ cup low-fat buttermilk
1¼ cups all-purpose flour
½ teaspoon baking soda
¼ teaspoon salt
¾ cup granulated sugar
5 tablespoons butter, softened
2 teaspoons vanilla extract
2 large eggs

ESPRESSO SYRUP:
¼ cup granulated sugar
¼ cup water
2 tablespoons instant espresso granules or ¼ cup instant coffee granules
2 tablespoons light-colored corn syrup
¼ teaspoon vanilla extract
2 tablespoons powdered sugar

Continued

1. Preheat oven to 350°.

2. To prepare cupcakes, combine 2 tablespoons boiling water and 4 teaspoons espresso, stirring until espresso dissolves. Stir in buttermilk.

3. Lightly spoon flour into dry measuring cups; level with a knife. Combine flour, baking soda, and salt, stirring well with a whisk.

4. Place ¾ cup granulated sugar, butter, and 2 teaspoons vanilla in a large bowl; beat with a mixer at medium speed until well blended (about 5 minutes). Add eggs, 1 at a time, beating well after each addition. Add flour mixture and buttermilk mixture alternately to sugar mixture, beginning and ending with flour mixture.

5. Spoon batter into 12 muffin cups lined with paper liners. Bake at 350° for 20 minutes or until a wooden pick inserted in center comes out clean. Cool cupcakes in pan 10 minutes on a wire rack; remove from pan.

6. To prepare syrup, combine ¼ cup granulated sugar, ¼ cup water, 2 tablespoons espresso, corn syrup, and ¼ teaspoon vanilla in a small saucepan; bring to a boil. Reduce heat; simmer 3 minutes. Pierce cupcake tops several times with a wooden skewer. Brush espresso syrup evenly over cupcakes. Cool completely on wire rack. Sprinkle with powdered sugar. Yield: 1 dozen (serving size: 1 cupcake).

CALORIES 192 (27% from fat); FAT 5.8g (sat 3.3g, mono 1.8g, poly 0.4g); PROTEIN 3g; CARB 31.8g; FIBER 0.4g; CHOL 49mg; IRON 0.9mg; SODIUM 173mg; CALC 19mg

Chocolate Pound Cake with Chocolate-Pistachio Glaze

CAKE:

3 cups all-purpose flour
½ cup unsweetened cocoa
1 teaspoon baking powder
¼ teaspoon salt
2¼ cups granulated sugar
¾ cup butter, softened
3 large eggs
2 teaspoons vanilla extract
1¼ cups fat-free milk
Cooking spray

GLAZE:

¾ cup powdered sugar
3 tablespoons unsweetened cocoa
2 tablespoons fat-free milk
½ teaspoon vanilla extract
2 tablespoons chopped pistachios

1. Preheat oven to 325°.

2. To prepare cake, lightly spoon flour into dry measuring cups; level with a knife. Combine flour, ½ cup cocoa, baking powder, and salt in a small bowl, stirring with a whisk.

3. Place granulated sugar and butter in a large bowl; beat with a mixer at medium speed until well blended (about 5 minutes). Add eggs, 1 at a time, beating well after each addition. Beat in 2 teaspoons vanilla. Add flour mixture and 1¼ cups milk alternately to sugar mixture, beginning and ending with flour mixture.

4. Spoon batter into a 12-cup Bundt pan coated with cooking spray. Bake at 325° for 40 minutes or until a wooden pick inserted in cake comes out clean. Cool in pan 10 minutes on a wire rack; remove from pan. Cool completely on wire rack.

5. To prepare glaze, combine powdered sugar and 3 tablespoons cocoa. Add 2 tablespoons milk and ½ teaspoon vanilla; stir with a whisk until smooth. Drizzle over cool cake; sprinkle with pistachios. Yield: 18 servings (serving size: 1 slice).

CALORIES 290 (30% from fat); FAT 9.6g (sat 5.4g, mono 3g, poly 0.6g); PROTEIN 4.7g; CARB 48.2g; FIBER 1.8g; CHOL 56mg; IRON 1.7mg; SODIUM 159mg; CALC 53mg

Sweet Potato Cheesecake

Canned sweet potatoes and packaged graham cracker crumbs are great time-savers. For the smoothest, most velvety texture, puree the potatoes completely so there are no lumps.

CRUST:

2 cups graham cracker crumbs (about 12 cookie sheets)
3 tablespoons sugar
2 tablespoons butter, melted
1 tablespoon water
Cooking spray

FILLING:

½ cup vanilla fat-free yogurt
2 (8-ounce) blocks ⅓-less-fat cream cheese, softened
2 (8-ounce) blocks fat-free cream cheese, softened
⅓ cup all-purpose flour
1¼ cups sugar
1 tablespoon vanilla extract
1 tablespoon light molasses
¾ teaspoon ground cinnamon
½ teaspoon ground ginger
¼ teaspoon salt
¼ teaspoon ground nutmeg
3 large eggs
2 (15-ounce) cans sweet potatoes, drained

1. Preheat oven to 350°.

2. To prepare crust, combine first 4 ingredients, tossing with a fork until well blended. Press into bottom of a 9-inch springform pan coated with cooking spray. Bake at 350° for 10 minutes; cool on a wire rack. Reduce oven temperature to 325°.

3. To prepare filling, place yogurt and cheeses in a large bowl; beat with a mixer at high speed until smooth. Lightly spoon flour into a dry measuring cup; level with a knife. Add flour and next 7 ingredients to cheese mixture; beat well. Add eggs, 1 at a time, beating well after each addition.

4. Place sweet potatoes in a food processor; process until smooth. Add sweet potatoes to cheese mixture, stirring until well blended.

5. Pour cheese mixture into prepared crust. Bake at 325° for 1 hour and 20 minutes or until cheesecake center barely moves when pan is touched. Turn oven off. Cool cheesecake in closed oven 1 hour.

6. Remove cheesecake from oven; run a knife around outside edge. Cool to room temperature. Cover and chill at least 8 hours. Yield: 16 servings (serving size: 1 wedge).

CALORIES 310 (29% from fat); FAT 10.1g (sat 5.5g, mono 3.2g, poly 1g); PROTEIN 10.3g; CARB 44g; FIBER 1.6g; CHOL 67mg; IRON 1.2mg; SODIUM 434mg; CALC 134mg

Two Ways to Brûlée

1 Using a torch

1. *Carefully sift sugar, using a small sieve, over each custard. This disperses sugar evenly.*

2

2. *Torch sugar immediately after it's sifted onto custards or it will start to dissolve into custards. Hold torch about 2 inches away and work from side to side until all sugar is melted and caramelized.*

1 On the stovetop

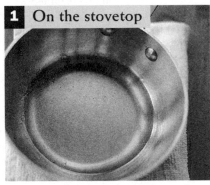

1. *In a small saucepan or skillet, cook sugar over medium heat until golden (about 5 to 8 minutes).*

2

2. *Working quickly, evenly drizzle sugar topping over cold custards. Using a rubber spatula coated with cooking spray, spread caramel evenly to form a thin layer. Work quickly because caramel will set.*

Tips to Great Espresso Crème Brûlée

- For the most intense coffee flavor, use strong coffee beans. If you don't have espresso beans, French roast or dark roast coffee beans will work best.
- For the best flavor, steep the beans in the milk for 30 minutes. For a more subtle coffee flavor, steep them 15 minutes.
- You can make the custards in almost any small oven-proof dishes. Just make sure they are shallow, to provide ample surface area for the sugar shell.
- We tested both a small kitchen torch and a propane torch. The larger propane torch is more powerful and melts the sugar faster, but the kitchen torch works equally well. You can buy a kitchen torch at cookware stores, or order one from Cooking.com. Propane torches are available at most hardware stores.
- Serve the crème brûlée within an hour of melting the sugar. Wait any longer, and the hard sugar shells will become soft as they start to dissolve into the custards.

Espresso Crème Brûlée
(pictured on page 384)

Expect a crowd in the kitchen when you crown the custards with their burnt-sugar shells. To do so, we recommend using a small kitchen torch. It's easy to use, and the torch procedure doesn't take as long as the stovetop method (although we give you instructions for that, too). Cold custards stand up well to the heat of the torch, so it's best to make them 1 to 2 days ahead. Although any kind of coffee beans work, the darker the bean the more intense the flavor.

- 2 cups 2% reduced-fat milk
- 1 cup whole espresso coffee beans
- ¾ cup nonfat dry milk
- 3 tablespoons sugar, divided
- 1 teaspoon vanilla extract
- Dash of salt
- 4 large egg yolks, lightly beaten
- ¼ cup sugar

1. Combine 2% milk, espresso beans, dry milk, and 2 tablespoons sugar in a medium saucepan. Heat mixture over medium heat to 180° or until tiny bubbles form around edge (do not boil), stirring occasionally. Remove milk mixture from heat. Cover and steep 30 minutes.

2. Preheat oven to 300°.

3. Strain milk mixture through a sieve into a bowl; discard solids. Stir in vanilla.

4. Combine 1 tablespoon sugar, salt, and egg yolks in a medium bowl, stirring well with a whisk.

5. Gradually add milk mixture to egg mixture, stirring constantly with a whisk. Divide mixture evenly among 4 (4-ounce) ramekins, custard cups, or shallow baking dishes. Place ramekins in a 13 x 9-inch baking pan, and add hot water to pan to a depth of 1 inch.

6. Bake at 300° for 25 minutes or until center barely moves when ramekin is touched. Remove ramekins from pan; cool completely on a wire rack. Cover and chill at least 4 hours or overnight.

7. Sift 1 tablespoon sugar evenly over each custard. Holding a kitchen blow torch about 2 inches from top of each custard, heat sugar, moving torch back and forth, until sugar is completely
Continued

melted and caramelized (about 1 minute). Serve immediately or within 1 hour. Yield: 4 servings (serving size: 1 crème brûlée).

NOTE: If you don't have a kitchen blow torch, you can make the sugar topping on the stovetop. Place ¼ cup sugar and 1 tablespoon water in a small, heavy saucepan. Cook over medium heat 5 to 8 minutes or until golden. (Resist the urge to stir, since doing so may cause the sugar to crystallize.) Immediately pour the sugar mixture evenly over cold custards, spreading to form a thin layer.

CALORIES 262 (26% from fat); FAT 7.7g (sat 3.2g, mono 2.7g, poly 0.7g); PROTEIN 11.3g; CARB 36g; FIBER 0g; CHOL 225mg; IRON 0.6mg; SODIUM 215mg; CALC 315mg

---

Cocktail Party Menu
serves 12

Vietnamese Rolls with Peanut Dipping Sauce (recipe on page 385)

Mini Black Bean Cakes with Green Onion Cream and Avocado Salsa (recipe on page 380)

Baked Feta with Marinara (recipe on page 385)

Shrimp cocktail

Vanilla Cheesecake with Rum Raisin Syrup

Wine, beer, and spirits

search myclar2003.com for all our menus

Vanilla Cheesecake with Rum Raisin Syrup

CRUST:
- ⅔ cup reduced-fat vanilla wafer crumbs (about 20 cookies)
- 1 large egg white, lightly beaten
- Cooking spray

FILLING:
- 1 (12-ounce) carton 1% low-fat cottage cheese
- 1 (8-ounce) block ⅓-less-fat cream cheese, softened
- ⅔ cup sugar
- 2 tablespoons cornstarch
- 1 teaspoon vanilla extract
- 1 large egg

SYRUP:
- ¾ cup dark rum
- ½ cup raisins
- ¼ cup sugar
- 2 tablespoons water, divided
- 1 teaspoon cornstarch

1. Preheat oven to 325°.
2. To prepare crust, combine crumbs and egg white, tossing with a fork until moist. Press into bottom of an 8-inch springform pan coated with cooking spray. Bake at 325° for 5 minutes or until lightly browned; cool on a wire rack.
3. To prepare filling, place cottage cheese in a food processor; process until smooth (about 2 minutes), scraping sides of bowl once. Add cream cheese, and process until smooth. Add ⅔ cup sugar, 2 tablespoons cornstarch, vanilla, and egg; pulse just until combined. Pour batter into prepared crust.
4. Bake at 325° for 30 minutes. Reduce oven temperature to 300° (do not remove cheesecake from oven); bake an additional 20 minutes or until center of cheesecake barely moves when pan is touched. Remove cheesecake from oven; run a knife around outside edge. Cool to room temperature. Cover and chill at least 8 hours.
5. To prepare syrup, combine rum and raisins in a microwave-safe bowl; microwave at HIGH 2 minutes. Cover with plastic wrap; let stand 10 minutes.
6. Combine ¼ cup sugar and 1 tablespoon water in a small saucepan over medium heat; cook, without stirring, 5 minutes or until golden. Combine 1 teaspoon cornstarch and 1 tablespoon water, stirring with a whisk. Stir rum mixture and cornstarch mixture into sugar mixture; bring to a boil. Cook 1 minute. Serve syrup chilled or at room temperature with cheesecake. Yield: 12 servings (serving size: 1 cheesecake wedge and about 1½ tablespoons syrup).

CALORIES 203 (25% from fat); FAT 5.6g (sat 3.1g, mono 1.6g, poly 0.2g); PROTEIN 6.6g; CARB 27.9g; FIBER 0.3g; CHOL 33mg; IRON 0.5mg; SODIUM 223mg; CALC 41mg

---

Frozen White Chocolate and Hazelnut Mousse

Place a freezer-safe container in the freezer before you start the recipe; a chilled container helps preserve a light, fluffy texture.

- 2 large egg yolks, lightly beaten
- 3 tablespoons water
- 1 teaspoon butter
- 2 ounces premium white baking chocolate, finely chopped
- ¼ cup Frangelico (hazelnut-flavored liqueur)
- ½ teaspoon cream of tartar
- Dash of salt
- 6 large egg whites
- ¾ cup sugar
- ⅔ cup water
- 1½ cups frozen fat-free whipped topping, thawed
- 3 tablespoons chopped hazelnuts, toasted

1. Place egg yolks in a medium bowl. Combine 3 tablespoons water, butter, and chocolate in a large, heavy saucepan over medium heat, stirring constantly until chocolate melts. Gradually add chocolate mixture to egg yolks, stirring constantly with a whisk. Return chocolate mixture to pan; cook over medium heat until thick (about 3 minutes), stirring constantly. Remove from heat, and stir in liqueur. Cool slightly.
2. Place cream of tartar, salt, and egg whites in a large bowl; beat with a mixer at high speed until foamy. Combine sugar and ⅔ cup water in a saucepan; bring to a boil. Cook, without stirring, until candy thermometer registers 238°. Gradually pour hot sugar syrup in a thin stream into egg white mixture, beating at high speed until stiff peaks form (5 to 7 minutes).
3. Gently stir one-fourth of egg white mixture into chocolate mixture; gently fold in remaining egg white mixture. Fold in whipped topping and hazelnuts. Spoon mixture into a chilled freezer-safe container; freeze 8 hours or overnight. Yield: 8 servings (serving size: about ¾ cup).

CALORIES 207 (25% from fat); FAT 5.7g (sat 2.2g, mono 2.5g, poly 0.5g); PROTEIN 4.2g; CARB 30g; FIBER 0.3g; CHOL 56mg; IRON 0.3mg; SODIUM 81mg; CALC 25mg

Banana Layer Cake with Cream Cheese Frosting

Mashed banana adds more than just flavor to this cake; it also keeps the layers moist.

CAKE:
Cooking spray
  2 cups all-purpose flour
  1 teaspoon baking powder
  ¾ teaspoon baking soda
  ⅛ teaspoon salt
  1⅓ cups granulated sugar
  ⅓ cup vegetable oil
  1¼ teaspoons vanilla extract
  2 large egg whites
  1 large egg
  1 cup mashed ripe banana
  ½ cup low-fat buttermilk

FROSTING:
  ⅔ cup (about 5 ounces) ⅓-less-fat cream cheese
  1 teaspoon vanilla extract
  3 cups powdered sugar

REMAINING INGREDIENTS:
  2 tablespoons finely chopped pecans, toasted
  2 tablespoons flaked sweetened coconut, toasted

1. Preheat oven to 350°.
2. To prepare cake, coat 2 (8-inch) round cake pans with cooking spray; line bottoms with wax paper. Coat wax paper with cooking spray.
3. Lightly spoon flour into dry measuring cups; level with a knife. Combine flour, baking powder, baking soda, and salt in a small bowl, stirring well with a whisk. Place granulated sugar, oil, 1¼ teaspoons vanilla, egg whites, and egg in a large bowl; beat with a mixer at medium speed until well blended. Add banana; beat well. Add flour mixture and buttermilk alternately to sugar mixture, beginning and ending with flour mixture.
4. Pour batter into prepared pans. Bake at 350° for 35 minutes or until a wooden pick inserted in center comes out clean. Cool in pans 10 minutes on wire racks; remove from pans. Peel off wax paper; cool completely on wire racks.

5. To prepare frosting, place cream cheese and 1 teaspoon vanilla in a large bowl; beat with a mixer at medium speed until fluffy. Add powdered sugar; beat at low speed until smooth.
6. Place 1 cake layer on a plate; spread with ½ cup icing, and top with other cake layer. Spread remaining icing over top and sides of cake. Sprinkle pecans and coconut over top of cake. Store cake loosely covered in refrigerator. Yield: 16 servings (serving size: 1 slice).

CALORIES 307 (24% from fat); FAT 8.2g (sat 2.5g, mono 2.2g, poly 3g); PROTEIN 3.9g; CARB 55.6g; FIBER 0.9g; CHOL 20mg; IRON 0.9mg; SODIUM 165mg; CALC 38mg

Grand Marnier Soufflé with Vanilla Sauce

A creamy vanilla custard sauce tops this ethereally light soufflé, which is delicately flavored with orange liqueur.

SAUCE:
  2 large egg yolks, lightly beaten
  1 cup whole milk
  2½ tablespoons sugar
  1 teaspoon vanilla extract
Dash of salt

SOUFFLÉ:
Cooking spray
  1 tablespoon sugar
  3 large egg yolks, lightly beaten
  3 tablespoons all-purpose flour
  ⅔ cup 2% reduced-fat milk
  ¼ cup sugar
  1 tablespoon butter
  3 tablespoons Grand Marnier (orange-flavored liqueur)
  2 teaspoons vanilla extract
  5 large egg whites
  ½ teaspoon cream of tartar
  ⅛ teaspoon salt
  2 tablespoons sugar

1. To prepare sauce, place 2 egg yolks in a medium bowl. Combine whole milk and 2½ tablespoons sugar in a small, heavy saucepan over medium heat; heat to 180° or until tiny bubbles form around edge (do not boil).

2. Gradually add hot milk mixture to 2 egg yolks, stirring constantly with a whisk. Return mixture to pan; cook over medium heat until thick and bubbly (about 3 minutes), stirring constantly. Remove from heat. Stir in 1 teaspoon vanilla and dash of salt. Pour into a glass bowl; cover and chill.
3. Preheat oven to 375°.
4. To prepare soufflé, coat a 1½-quart soufflé dish with cooking spray; sprinkle with 1 tablespoon sugar.
5. Place 3 egg yolks in a medium bowl; set aside. Place flour in a small, heavy saucepan; gradually add 2% milk, stirring with a whisk. Stir in ¼ cup sugar; add butter. Cook over medium heat until thick (about 5 minutes), stirring constantly. Gradually add hot milk mixture to 3 egg yolks, stirring constantly with a whisk. Return mixture to pan; cook over medium heat until thick and bubbly (about 3 minutes), stirring constantly. Stir in liqueur and 2 teaspoons vanilla; cook 1 minute, stirring constantly. Remove from heat.
6. Place egg whites, cream of tartar, and ⅛ teaspoon salt in a large bowl; beat with a mixer at high speed until soft peaks form. Gradually add 2 tablespoons sugar, 1 tablespoon at a time, beating until stiff peaks form. Gently stir one-fourth of egg white mixture into warm milk mixture; gently fold in remaining egg white mixture.
7. Spoon into prepared soufflé dish. Place soufflé dish in a 9-inch square baking pan; add hot water to pan to a depth of 1 inch. Bake at 375° for 30 minutes or until puffy and set. Spoon about 3 tablespoons sauce over each serving. Serve immediately. Yield: 6 servings.

CALORIES 242 (30% from fat); FAT 8.1g (sat 3.7g, mono 2.7g, poly 0.8g); PROTEIN 7.9g; CARB 30g; FIBER 0.1g; CHOL 190mg; IRON 0.7mg; SODIUM 179mg; CALC 104mg

Gifts from the Kitchen

This year, surprise your friends with a homemade specialty.

• Apricot-Cream Cheese Braid

DOUGH:
- ½ cup granulated sugar
- ⅓ cup butter
- ½ teaspoon salt
- 1 (8-ounce) carton light sour cream
- 2 packages dry yeast (about 4½ teaspoons)
- ½ cup warm water (100° to 110°)
- 2 large eggs, lightly beaten
- 4 cups all-purpose flour

FILLING:
- ⅔ cup apricot preserves
- ¼ cup granulated sugar
- 1 teaspoon vanilla extract
- 2 (8-ounce) blocks ⅓-less-fat cream cheese, softened
- 1 large egg, lightly beaten
- Cooking spray

GLAZE:
- 1½ cups sifted powdered sugar
- 2 tablespoons fat-free milk
- 1 teaspoon vanilla extract

1. To prepare dough, combine first 4 ingredients in a saucepan over medium heat, stirring until sugar dissolves. Remove from heat; cool. Dissolve yeast in warm water in a large bowl; let stand 5 minutes. Stir in sour cream mixture and 2 eggs. Lightly spoon flour into dry measuring cups; level with a knife. Gradually stir flour into sour cream mixture (dough will be soft and sticky). Cover dough; chill 8 hours or overnight.

2. To prepare filling, combine preserves and next 4 ingredients in a medium bowl; beat with a mixer at medium speed until well blended.

3. Divide dough into 4 equal portions. Turn each portion out onto a lightly floured surface; knead lightly 4 or 5 times. Roll each portion into a 12 x 8-inch rectangle. Spread one-fourth of filling over each portion, leaving a ½-inch border. Starting at a long side, carefully roll up each portion jelly-roll fashion; pinch seam and ends to seal.

4. Place 2 loaves on each of 2 baking sheets coated with cooking spray. Cut 4 (¼-inch-deep) "X"s in top of each loaf with scissors. Cover and let rise in a warm place (85°), free from drafts, 25 minutes or until doubled in size.

5. Preheat oven to 375°.

6. Place 1 baking sheet in oven (cover remaining loaves to keep from drying). Bake at 375° for 15 minutes or until lightly browned. Repeat procedure with remaining loaves. Cool loaves slightly.

7. To prepare glaze, combine powdered sugar, milk, and 1 teaspoon vanilla, stirring with a whisk. Drizzle warm loaves with glaze. Yield: 4 loaves, 10 slices per loaf (serving size: 1 slice).

CALORIES 145 (31% from fat); FAT 5g (sat 3g, mono 1.5g, poly 0.3g); PROTEIN 3.3g; CARB 21.6g; FIBER 0.5g; CHOL 30mg; IRON 0.8mg; SODIUM 102mg; CALC 26mg

Spicy Thyme and Garlic Oil

(pictured on page 381)

Pour the oil into a decorative glass bottle, then package it with a fresh baguette, a small dipping bowl for the oil, and some colorful napkins in a beautiful basket for a memorable gift. Be careful not to let the oil temperature rise above 220°; too much heat could ruin the flavor.

- 1 cup extra-virgin olive oil
- ½ teaspoon crushed red pepper
- 4 garlic cloves, halved
- 2 bay leaves, crumbled
- 1 (4-inch) thyme sprig

1. Combine all ingredients in a small, heavy saucepan. Cook over medium-low heat until thermometer registers 200°. Reduce heat to low; cook 20 minutes (do not allow temperature to rise above 220°). Cool to room temperature.

2. Strain oil mixture through a sieve into a bowl; discard solids. Store in refrigerator. Yield: 1 cup (serving size: 1 tablespoon).

NOTE: Store in the refrigerator in a glass container for up to 1 week.

CALORIES 119 (100% from fat); FAT 13.5g (sat 1.8g, mono 10g, poly 1.1g); PROTEIN 0g; CARB 0g; FIBER 0g; CHOL 0mg; IRON 0.1mg; SODIUM 0mg; CALC 0mg

Peppered Peanut Brittle

Pepper adds an unexpected bit of heat to the brittle, but you can omit it. To wrap, place pieces of brittle in clear food-safe cellophane bags, then tie with ribbon.

- Cooking spray
- 1½ cups sugar
- ⅓ cup light-colored corn syrup
- 3 tablespoons water
- 1½ teaspoons vanilla extract
- 1 teaspoon fresh lemon juice
- ½ teaspoon salt
- 1½ cups roasted peanuts
- 1 teaspoon baking soda
- 1 teaspoon butter
- ½ teaspoon crushed red pepper
- ¼ teaspoon cracked black pepper
- ⅛ teaspoon ground red pepper

1. Coat a large jelly roll pan with cooking spray.
2. Combine sugar and next 5 ingredients in a large saucepan; bring to a boil over medium-high heat. Cook 10 minutes or until sugar dissolves and candy thermometer registers 325°, stirring occasionally. Remove mixture from heat; stir in peanuts and remaining ingredients. (Baking soda will cause mixture to bubble and become opaque.)
3. Quickly pour mixture into prepared pan, spreading to edges. Let stand 1 hour; break into pieces. Yield: about 1¼ pounds (serving size: about 1 ounce).

NOTE: Store the peanut brittle in an airtight container for up to 2 weeks.

CALORIES 105 (32% from fat); FAT 3.7g (sat 0.6g, mono 1.8g, poly 1.1g); PROTEIN 1.7g; CARB 17.6g; FIBER 0.6g; CHOL 0mg; IRON 0.2mg; SODIUM 166mg; CALC 4mg

Red Onion Marmalade

(pictured on page 381)

Recommend this as a spread on rosemary focaccia or as a sauce for pork tenderloin.

    2 tablespoons olive oil
    8 cups thinly sliced red onion (about 2 pounds)
    1 teaspoon fresh thyme leaves
    1 bay leaf
    ¾ teaspoon fine sea salt
    3 garlic cloves, minced
    1 cup Cabernet Sauvignon or other dry red wine
    ¼ cup packed brown sugar
    2 tablespoons balsamic vinegar
    ¼ teaspoon freshly ground black pepper

1. Heat oil in a large nonstick skillet over medium heat. Add onion, thyme, and bay leaf. Cover and cook 25 minutes, stirring occasionally.
2. Stir in salt and garlic; cook, uncovered, 2 minutes, stirring frequently. Stir in wine, brown sugar, and vinegar; bring to a boil. Reduce heat; simmer 12 minutes or until liquid almost evaporates and becomes syrupy.
3. Remove from heat; stir in pepper. Cool to room temperature. Discard bay leaf. Yield: 3 cups (serving size: ¼ cup).

NOTE: Store in the refrigerator for up to 1 week.

CALORIES 77 (28% from fat); FAT 2.4g (sat 0.3g, mono 1.7g, poly 0.2g); PROTEIN 1g; CARB 10.5g; FIBER 1.4g; CHOL 0mg; IRON 0.4mg; SODIUM 149mg; CALC 22mg

Golden Vanilla Syrup

For a gift, attach your favorite pancake recipe. This syrup is also good drizzled over ice cream or pound cake.

    1 vanilla bean, split lengthwise
    2 cups granulated sugar
    1½ cups water
    ⅓ cup fresh lemon juice, strained
    1 tablespoon light brown sugar

1. Scrape seeds from vanilla bean; place seeds and bean in a small bowl.
2. Combine granulated sugar and remaining 3 ingredients in a medium saucepan. Bring to a boil over medium-high heat, stirring until sugar dissolves. Reduce heat; simmer 5 minutes. Remove from heat. Add vanilla bean and seeds, stirring gently. Cool syrup to room temperature.
3. Pour syrup and vanilla bean into a glass container. Cover and chill. Yield: 2¼ cups (serving size: 2 tablespoons).

NOTE: Store in the refrigerator for up to 1 month.

CALORIES 89 (0% from fat); FAT 0g; PROTEIN 0g; CARB 23.1g; FIBER 0g; CHOL 0mg; IRON 0mg; SODIUM 1mg; CALC 1mg

Caramel Popcorn

Let the popcorn cool completely before dividing it into holiday tins for giving.

    Cooking spray
    1 cup packed dark brown sugar
    ½ cup light-colored corn syrup
    ⅓ cup butter
    1 tablespoon light molasses
    1½ teaspoons vanilla extract
    ½ teaspoon baking soda
    ½ teaspoon salt
    12 cups popcorn (popped without salt or fat)

1. Preheat oven to 250°.
2. Coat a large jelly roll pan with cooking spray.
3. Combine sugar, corn syrup, butter, and molasses in a medium saucepan; bring to a boil over medium heat. Cook 5 minutes; stir once. Remove from heat; stir in vanilla, baking soda, and salt. Place popcorn in a large bowl; pour sugar mixture over popcorn in a steady stream; stir to coat.
4. Spread popcorn mixture into prepared pan. Bake at 250° for 1 hour, stirring every 15 minutes.
5. Remove from oven; stir to break up any large clumps. Cool 15 minutes. Serve warm or at room temperature. Yield: 18 servings (serving size: ⅔ cup).

NOTE: Store in an airtight container for up to 1 week.

CALORIES 126 (26% from fat); FAT 3.6g (sat 2.2g, mono 1.1g, poly 0.2g); PROTEIN 0.7g; CARB 23.9g; FIBER 0.8g; CHOL 9mg; IRON 0.4mg; SODIUM 151mg; CALC 15mg

Gingerbread Squares

Place these moist squares in a parchment paper-lined gift box.

    1¼ cups all-purpose flour
    1 teaspoon ground ginger
    1 teaspoon ground cinnamon
    ½ teaspoon baking soda
    ½ cup granulated sugar
    ½ cup low-fat buttermilk
    ½ cup molasses
    ⅓ cup butter, melted
    1 large egg, lightly beaten
    Cooking spray
    1 tablespoon powdered sugar

1. Preheat oven to 350°.
2. Lightly spoon flour into dry measuring cups; level with a knife. Combine flour, ginger, cinnamon, and baking soda, stirring with a whisk.
3. Combine granulated sugar and next 4 ingredients in a large bowl, stirring with a whisk. Stir in flour mixture. Pour batter into a 9-inch square baking pan coated with cooking spray.
4. Bake at 350° for 25 minutes or until a wooden pick inserted in center
Continued

comes out clean. Cool in pan on a wire rack. Sprinkle gingerbread with powdered sugar. Yield: 25 servings (serving size: 1 [1¾-inch] square).

CALORIES 84 (30% from fat); FAT 2.8g (sat 1.6g, mono 0.8g, poly 0.2g); PROTEIN 1.1g; CARB 14g; FIBER 0.2g; CHOL 15mg; IRON 0.7mg; SODIUM 61mg; CALC 22mg

Lemon-Coconut Bar Cookies

Slip these tart cookies into a box lined with wax paper. Or keep them in the pan, and make that part of your gift.

COOKIES:
- 1 cup all-purpose flour
- 2 tablespoons granulated sugar
- ¼ cup chilled butter, cut into small pieces
- Cooking spray
- 1 cup packed brown sugar
- 3 tablespoons fresh lemon juice
- 2 large eggs, lightly beaten
- ½ cup flaked sweetened coconut

GLAZE:
- ⅔ cup powdered sugar
- 1 teaspoon grated lemon rind
- 2 tablespoons fresh lemon juice

1. Preheat oven to 350°.
2. To prepare cookies, lightly spoon flour into a dry measuring cup; level with a knife. Combine flour and granulated sugar in a bowl; cut in butter with a pastry blender or 2 knives until mixture resembles coarse meal.
3. Press mixture into a 9-inch square baking pan coated with cooking spray. Bake at 350° for 10 minutes.
4. Combine brown sugar, 3 tablespoons juice, and eggs in a medium bowl, stirring with a whisk. Stir in coconut; pour evenly into pan. Bake an additional 25 minutes or until set.
5. To prepare glaze, combine powdered sugar, rind, and 2 tablespoons juice, stirring with a whisk. Spread glaze evenly over cookies. Cool completely in pan on a wire rack. Cut cookies into squares.

Yield: 25 servings (serving size: 1 [1¾-inch] square).

CALORIES 95 (27% from fat); FAT 2.8g (sat 1.7g, mono 0.7g, poly 0.2g); PROTEIN 1.1g; CARB 17g; FIBER 0.2g; CHOL 22mg; IRON 0.5mg; SODIUM 31mg; CALC 11mg

Gingered Fig Preserves

The preserves need to be refrigerated, so store in clear glass containers with secure lids. Include a note on the gift tag to keep the preserves chilled. Also include these serving suggestions: "Spread preserves on toasted nut bread and serve with Brie, or make sandwiches using the preserves and cashew butter."

- 1¾ cups water
- 1 cup sugar
- ½ cup fresh orange juice (about 1 large orange)
- 3 tablespoons fresh lemon juice
- 3 (1-inch) pieces peeled fresh ginger
- 1 pound dried Calimyrna figs, stemmed
- ½ cup chopped crystallized ginger (about 3 ounces)
- 2 teaspoons grated orange rind

1. Combine first 6 ingredients in a large saucepan. Bring to a boil over medium-high heat, stirring until sugar dissolves. Cover, reduce heat to low, and simmer 25 minutes or until figs are tender.
2. Stir in crystallized ginger and rind. Cook, uncovered, over medium heat 30 minutes or until mixture is syrupy, stirring occasionally.
3. Remove mixture from heat, and cool 10 minutes. Discard fresh ginger pieces. Place mixture in a food processor, and process until smooth. Store in refrigerator. Yield: about 3 cups (serving size: 2 tablespoons).
NOTE: Store in the refrigerator for up to 2 weeks.

CALORIES 96 (3% from fat); FAT 0.3g (sat 0.1g, mono 0.1g, poly 0.1g); PROTEIN 0.6g; CARB 24.5g; FIBER 2.2g; CHOL 0mg; IRON 1.2mg; SODIUM 4mg; CALC 36mg

HOW TO USE IT AND WHY Glance at the end of any *Cooking Light* recipe, and you'll see how committed we are to helping you make the best of today's light cooking. With six chefs, four registered dietitians, three home economists, and a computer system that analyzes every ingredient we use, *Cooking Light* gives you authoritative dietary detail like no other magazine. We go to such lengths so you can see how our recipes fit into your healthful eating plan. If you're trying to lose weight, the calorie and fat figures will probably help most. But if you're keeping a close eye on the sodium, cholesterol, and saturated fat in your diet, we provide those numbers, too. And because many women don't get enough iron or calcium, we can also help there, as well. Finally, there's a fiber analysis for those of us who don't get enough roughage.

Here's a helpful guide to put our nutrition analysis numbers into perspective. Remember, one size doesn't fit all, so take your lifestyle, age, and circumstances into consideration when determining your nutrition needs. For example, pregnant or breast-feeding women need more protein, calories, and calcium. And men over 50 need 1,200mg of calcium daily, 200mg more than the amount recommended for younger men.

IN OUR NUTRITIONAL ANALYSIS, WE USE THESE ABBREVIATIONS:

sat	saturated fat	**CHOL**	cholesterol
mono	monounsaturated fat	**CALC**	calcium
poly	polyunsaturated fat	**g**	gram
CARB	carbohydrates	**mg**	milligram

Your Daily Nutrition Guide

	WOMEN AGES 25 TO 50	WOMEN OVER 50	MEN OVER 24
Calories	2,000	2,000 or less	2,700
Protein	50g	50g or less	63g
Fat	65g or less	65g or less	88g or less
Saturated Fat	20g or less	20g or less	27g or less
Carbohydrates	304g	304g	410g
Fiber	25g to 35g	25g to 35g	25g to 35g
Cholesterol	300mg or less	300mg or less	300mg or less
Iron	18mg	8mg	8mg
Sodium	2,400mg or less	2,400mg or less	2,400mg or less
Calcium	1,000mg	1,200mg	1,000mg

The nutritional values used in our calculations either come from The Food Processor, Version 7.5 (ESHA Research), or are provided by food manufacturers.

Menu Index

A topical guide to all the menus that appear in Cooking Light Annual Recipes 2003.
See page 426 for the General Recipe Index.

Dinner Tonight

**Indian-Seasoned
Soup Menu** (page 27)
serves 4
Spicy Mulligatawny
Pita wedges
Ice cream with sautéed pears

Bean Soup Supper (page 28)
serves 5
North Woods Bean Soup
Country apple coleslaw
Pumpernickel bread with honey butter

Quick and Cheesy Soup Menu (page 28)
serves 6
Broccoli and Cheese Soup
Broiled plum tomatoes
Baked potatoes

Classic Soup Supper Menu (page 29)
serves 4
Tomato-Basil Soup
Cheese toast
Green salad

Hungarian Menu (page 69)
serves 4
Chicken Paprikash-Topped Potatoes
Garlic breadsticks
Roasted Brussels sprouts

French Menu (page 69)
serves 4
Tarragon Chicken-in-a-Pot Pies
Green salad
Caramel-coconut sundaes

Classic Russian Menu (page 70)
serves 4
Dilled Pork Stroganoff
Dinner rolls
Herbed green peas

A Taste of Germany Menu (page 70)
serves 4
Spicy Pork and Sauerkraut Sandwiches
Vegetables with roasted garlic dip
Strawberry sorbet

Diner-Style Breakfast (page 79)
serves 4
Lumberjack Hash
Honeyed citrus salad
Corn bread twists

Pancake Breakfast Menu (page 79)
serves 6
Whole Wheat Buttermilk
Pancakes
Fresh fruit salad
Chai tea

Southwestern Breakfast Menu (page 80)
serves 2
Southwestern Omelet
Quick quesadillas
Pineapple juice

French-Style Breakfast (page 80)
serves 4
Croque Monsieur
Berry smoothies

Beef Noodle Bowl Menu (page 126)
serves 5
Udon-Beef Noodle Bowl
Steamed edamame (fresh soybeans)
Gingered won ton chips with
ice cream

Thai Noodle Menu (page 127)
serves 6
Shrimp Pad Thai
Spicy cucumber salad
Lemon sorbet

Asian Flair Menu (page 127)
serves 5
Chicken and Noodles with
Peanut Sauce
Asian slaw
Steamed broccoli spears

Vegetarian Noodle Menu (page 128)
serves 4
Curried Noodles with Tofu
Sesame-scented snow peas and carrots
Green tea

Summer on a Plate Menu (page 146)
serves 4
Tuscan Panzanella
Eggplant Napoleons
Lemon sorbet

Easy Salad Supper Menu (page 147)
serves 4
Fennel-Grapefruit Salad with
Chicken
Peppered fontina breadsticks
Fresh melon

Busy Night Salad Menu (page 147)
serves 4
Warm Sesame Shrimp and Eggplant Salad
Seasoned jasmine rice
Mango slices topped with crystallized ginger

Greek Salad Menu (page 148)
serves 4
Chicken Souvlaki Salad
Greek pita wedges
Vanilla low-fat ice cream topped with
cinnamon and honey

Italian Burger Menu (page 181)
serves 6
Italian Burgers
Chickpea-artichoke salad
Strawberries with mascarpone cheese

Greek-Style Burger Menu (page 182)
serves 8
Lamb Burgers with Fennel Salad
Greek potatoes
Baby carrots with commercial hummus

Comfort Burger Menu (page 182)
serves 6
Meat Loaf Burgers with Caramelized Onions
Corn on the cob
Quick peach crisp

Burgers with a Kick Menu (page 183)
serves 8
Chicken-Chorizo Burgers with
Avocado Mayonnaise
Green salad
Pineapple-coconut coolers

Penne Pasta Salad Menu (page 235)
serves 4
Chicken-Penne Salad with Green Beans
Mozzarella toasts
Mixed berries dolloped with vanilla yogurt

Orzo Pasta Salad Menu (page 235)
serves 4
Orzo Salad with
Chickpeas, Dill, and Lemon
Sliced romaine with mint
Garlic breadsticks

Bow Tie Pasta Salad Menu (page 236)
serves 6
Summer Farfalle Salad with Smoked Salmon
Artichoke-Parmesan cream cheese with crackers
Sliced peaches

Marinade Menu 1 (page 268)
serves 4
Tandoori Chicken
Tabbouleh
Pita wedges

Marinade Menu 2 (page 269)
serves 4
Salmon with Orange-Fennel Sauce
Rice pilaf
Sautéed snow peas

Marinade Menu 3 (page 269)
serves 6
Korean-Style Pork Tenderloin
Buttered spaghetti squash
Sautéed broccolini

Marinade Menu 4 (page 270)
serves 4
Flank Steak Marinated with
Shallots and Pepper
Corn and sugar snap salad
Mashed sweet potatoes

Pork Tenderloin Menu (page 286)
serves 4
Pork Tenderloin Studded with
Rosemary and Garlic
Caramelized carrots
Boiled red potatoes

Cornish Hens Menu (page 287)
serves 4
Orange-Ginger Glazed
Cornish Hens
Oven-roasted green beans
Long-grain and wild rice blend

Sirloin Steak Menu (page 287)
serves 4
Cumin-Coriander
Sirloin Steak
Sweet potato spears
Collard greens

Chicken Thighs Menu (page 288)
serves 4
Chicken Thighs with
Roasted Apples and Garlic
Browned Brussels sprouts
Dinner rolls

Miso-Glazed Salmon Menu (page 326)
serves 4
Miso-Glazed Salmon
Wasabi mashed potatoes
Steamed bok choy

Creole Cod Menu (page 327)
serves 4
Creole Cod
Steamed fingerling potatoes
Warm cabbage slaw

Grouper and Vegetables Menu (page 327)
serves 4
Pan-Roasted Grouper with
Provençale Vegetables
Spinach-mushroom salad
French bread

Moroccan Halibut Menu (page 328)
serves 4
Halibut with Charmoula
Couscous tossed with golden raisins
Frozen yogurt with spiced honey and walnuts

BBQ Chicken Pizza Menu (page 368)
serves 6
BBQ Chicken Pizza
Quick coleslaw
Corn on the cob

Meaty, Cheesy Pizza Menu (page 368)
serves 6
Steak and Blue Cheese Pizza
Romaine salad with garlic-balsamic vinaigrette
Raspberry sorbet

Pizza Margherita Menu (page 369)
serves 4
Quick Pizza Margherita
Lemon broccoli
Chocolate wafer cookies

Peppery Pizza Menu (page 369)
serves 4
Sausage, Pepper, and Onion Pizza
Pickle spears
Strawberry-anise sundaes

Simple Suppers

Simple Supper Menu (page 18)
serves 8
Watercress Salad with Fennel and Citrus
Lemon couscous
Pan-grilled chicken breast
Orange sherbet

Come in from the Cold Menu (page 25)
serves 5
Fisherman's Seafood Stew
Baguette
Angel food cake with citrus compote

Sunday Dinner Menu (page 40)
serves 6
Mussels with Fennel
Quick Coq au Vin
Goat Cheese, Roasted Garlic,
and Tomato Croutes

Hearty Weeknight Menu (page 40)
serves 6
Quick Coq au Vin
Tarragon red potatoes
Brussels sprouts

Saturday Dinner Menu (page 42)
serves 6
Lamb Shanks on Cannellini Beans
Chicory and Roasted Beet Salad with
Blue Cheese Dressing

Family Night Menu (page 46)
serves 4
Caribbean Vegetables
Buttermilk mashed potatoes
Whole roasted chicken

Sunday Supper Menu (page 48)
serves 10
Fiery Chipotle Baked Beans
Tangy turnip greens
Roasted pork tenderloins

Casual Supper Menu (page 78)
serves 5
Baked pork chops
Spiced Braised Carrots with
Olives and Mint
Mashed potatoes

South of the Border Menu (page 116)
serves 5
Creamy Spinach and Mushroom Enchiladas
Spanish rice
Black beans

Casual Supper Menu (page 134)
serves 8
Polenta with Fontina and Spinach
Balsamic grilled asparagus
Grilled pork tenderloin

**Power-Packed Antioxidant
Dinner Menu** (page 137)
serves 4
Wine
Cumin-Dusted Salmon Fillets
Curried Barley with Raisins and Almonds
Spinach sautéed with garlic
Blueberry and Peach Cobbler

Easy Roasting Menu (page 144)
serves 4
Roasted Pork with Honeyed Grape Sauce
Roasted asparagus with feta
Couscous

Garden Fresh Menu (page 170)
serves 4
Fingerling Potato and Prosciutto Salad
Cucumber and melon salad
Tomato-arugula sandwiches

Summer's Best Menu (page 180)
serves 8
Eggplant and Tomato Gratin
Angel hair pasta with fresh herbs
Green salad
Breadsticks

Spicy Supper Menu (page 186)
serves 9
Indian Chicken Curry
Garlic green beans

Quick & Colorful Menu (page 238)
serves 4
Chicken Stew with Sweet Peppers
Couscous
Maple-roasted baby carrots

Fresh Summer Menu (page 250)
serves 6
Yellow Pepper Soup with Cilantro Puree
Tomato sandwiches
Dilled cucumber salad

Spicy Supper Menu (page 265)
serves 4
Snapper Tacos with Chipotle Cream
Black bean and corn salad
Baked tortilla chips

Simple Dinner Menu (page 277)
serves 4
Glazed Pork
Couscous
Plum salsa

Soulful Soup Supper 1 (page 290)
serves 4
Curried Butternut Soup
Dried Pear and Cardamom Scones

Soulful Soup Supper 2 (page 290)
serves 6
Potato-Kale Soup with Gruyère
Walnut and Rosemary Loaves

Soulful Soup Supper 3 (page 291)
serves 8
Mexican Ham and Bean Soup
Oatmeal Molasses Bread

Comfort Food Menu (page 300)
serves 8
Creamy Grits with Sweet Corn
Stewed turnip greens
Garlic-pepper pork tenderloin

Casserole Supper Menu (page 339)
serves 4
Butternut Squash and Parsnip Baked Pasta
Kale with Lemon-Balsamic Butter
Maple-Glazed Rutabaga

Breakfast and Lunch Menus

Brown-Bag Lunch Menu (page 30)
serves 6
Cuban Beans and Rice Salad
Pineapple salsa
Baked tortilla chips

Brown-Bag Lunch Menu (page 51)
serves 6
Red Onion Focaccia
Fresh fruit
Spicy chicken salad

Brown-Bag Lunch Menu (page 106)
serves 4
Tomato soup
Whole Wheat Mushroom Croutons
Roast beef sandwich

Brunch Menu (page 110)
serves 4
Raspberry-Orange Sunrises
Apple-Oat Muffins
Sliced Mangoes with Crystallized Ginger
Spinach and Tomato Strata
or Tofu Breakfast Burritos

Brown-Bag Lunch Menu (page 114)
serves 9
Garlicky Red Lentil Dal
Pitas
Chickpea, olive, and feta salad

Power-Packed Antioxidant Breakfast Menu (page 137)
serves 4
Toasted whole wheat bagels with peanut butter
Strawberry-Kiwi Smoothie
Green tea

Power-Packed Antioxidant Lunch and Snack Menu (page 137)
serves 6
Turkey, Swiss cheese, and asparagus wrap
Chopped Vegetable Salad with Garlic Dressing
Carrots, broccoli, and cauliflower with ranch dressing
Pistachios

Brown-Bag Lunch Menu (page 175)
serves 8
Creamy Zucchini Soup with Mixed Herbs
Tomato salad
Fresh fruit

Brown-Bag Lunch Menu (page 200)
serves 8
Millet Salad with Sweet Corn and Avocado
Chilled minty pea soup
Fresh fruit

Brown-Bag Lunch Menu (page 218)
serves 6
Tomato-Basil Tart
Green salad
Strawberries and mint

Brown-Bag Lunch Menu (page 268)
serves 4
Chilled tomato soup
Green salad with blue cheese
Crisp Pecan Cookies

Lazy Day Lunch Menu (page 310)
serves 8
Baked Potato Soup
Green salad
Orange sections

Shoppers' Lunch Menu (page 394)
serves 4
Olive and Asiago Rolls
Winter Vegetable Soup
Warm Spinach Salad with Mushroom Vinaigrette

Gift-Opening Breakfast Menu (page 402)
serves 10
Orange juice
Apricot-Cream Cheese Braid
Canadian bacon
Fresh fruit

Casual Entertaining

Casual Company Menu (page 41)
serves 6
Cabbage Remoulade
Olive Bread
Bouillabaisse

Eats for Eight Menu (page 86)
serves 8
Broiled salmon fillets
Potato Gratin with
Baby Carrots and Asiago
Arugula-apple salad with pecorino

Company is Coming Menu (page 125)
serves 6
Shrimp Skewers with Romesco Sauce
Salad with goat cheese and Dijon dressing
Couscous with chopped green onions

Buffet Menu (page 196)
serves 8
Chicken Thighs with Thyme and Lemon
Grilled vegetables
Polenta

Easy Entertaining Menu (page 220)
serves 4
Citrus-Glazed Scallops with Avocado Salsa
White rice
Sautéed sugar snap peas

Alfresco Dinner Menu (page 240)
serves 6
Fresh Tomato Soup
Rosemary-Scented Flatbread with Black
Grapes with dipping oils
Baby Vegetable Antipasto
Roasted Pepper, Kalamata, and
Prosciutto Pasta
Pumpkin Spice-Cream

Supper Club Menu (page 243)
serves 6
Marinated Spanish Olives
Watercress-Bibb Salad with Apples and
Blue Cheese
Gruyère, Arugula, and
Prosciutto-Stuffed Chicken Breasts with
Caramelized Shallot Sauce
Baked Rice with Butternut Squash
Cloverleaf Honey-Wheat Rolls
Harvest Pear Crisp

Appetizer Party Buffet (page 245)
serves 10-15
Truffle-Scented Risotto in Phyllo
Roasted Cauliflower Skewers with
Sweet Peppers and Cumin
Curried Chickpea Canapés with
Ginger-Carrot Butter
Tempeh Satay with Curried Cashew Sauce
Spiced Red Lentil Dip with Pita Crisps
Hiziki Caviar with Lemon Tofu Cream
and Chives
Herbed Ricotta Won Tons with
Spicy Tomato Sauce

Entertaining Menu (page 317)
serves 12
Grilled salmon
Citrus couscous
Chocolate Lava Cakes with Pistachio Cream

Hearty Autumn Menu (page 325)
serves 6
Beef, Beer, and Barley Stew
Roasted Cipollini Onions
Wild Rice and Cranberry Salad
Sweet Potato Tart with Pecan Crust

Earthy Entertaining Menu (page 340)
serves 4
Pork Medallions with Cranberries and Apples
Rye Berry Salad with Orange Vinaigrette
Roasted Cauliflower
Molasses Cake with Lemon Cream
Cheese Frosting

Open House Buffet Menu (page 386)
serves 18
Spicy Rum Punch
Wild Mushroom and Artichoke Dip
Spiced Parmesan Cheese Crisps
Apple "Fritters"
Tea sandwiches
Chocolate Pound Cake with
Chocolate-Pistachio Glaze
Sugar cookies

Cocktail Party Menu (page 400)
serves 12
Vietnamese Rolls with Peanut Dipping Sauce
Mini Black Bean Cakes with
Green Onion Cream and Avocado Salsa
Baked Feta with Marinara
Shrimp cocktail
Vanilla Cheesecake with Rum Raisin Syrup
Wine, beer, and spirits

Special Occasions

Chinese New Year's Feast for Eight
(page 12)
serves 8
New Year's Dumpling Delight
Longevity Noodles
Lion's Head Meatballs
in Spicy Coconut Sauce
Chicken-Ginseng Soup
Orange-Ginger Shrimp Skewers
Steamed Fish with Ginger-Wine Sauce
Vegetarians' Delight
New Year's Rice Cake

Fourth of July Menu (page 198)
serves 8
Rosemary Focaccia
Tomato, Basil, and Fresh Mozzarella Salad
Fresh Cranberry Beans
with Lemon and Olive Oil
Millet Salad with Sweet Corn and Avocado
Summer Fruit Salad
with Lemon-and-Honey Syrup
Fresh Corn Cake with Raspberries

Thanksgiving with the Family Menu
(page 333)
serves 12
Brined Maple Turkey with Cream Gravy
Old-Fashioned Mashed Potatoes
New England Sausage Stuffing
with Chestnuts
Cider-Glazed Carrots
Roasted Brussels Sprouts
with Ham and Garlic
Cranberry-Fig Relish
Potato Rolls
Pecan and Date Pie
Pumpkin Cake with Cream Cheese Glaze

Thanksgiving, Made Ahead Menu
(page 348)
serves 10
Herbed Turkey with Roasted Garlic Gravy
Sherried Mushroom Soup
Streuseled Sweet Potato Casserole
Sourdough Stuffing with
Apples and Ham
Cranberry, Apple, and Walnut Relish
Green Beans with
Caramelized Onions
Vanilla Cheesecake with Cherry Topping

Thanksgiving with a Twist Menu
(page 354)
serves 8
Mushroom Turnovers
Greens with Roasted Corn and Pepper
Salad
Sautéed Duck Breast with
Cherry-Pistachio Salsa
Blue Corn Bread Dressing
Roasted Asparagus with
Balsamic-Shallot Butter
Molasses Cake with Lemon Cream Cheese
Frosting or Mincemeat Charlottes

An Intimate Thanksgiving Menu
(page 361)
serves 2
Celery Salad
Rosemary-Lemon Cornish Hens with
Roasted Potatoes
Swiss Chard with Garlic and Oregano
Maple-Glazed Winter Squash
Pear-Cranberry Sauce
Apple Crumble with Golden Raisins

New Year's Day Brunch Menu (page 386)
serves 8
Wasabi Bloody Marys
Endive, Sweet Lettuce, and Cashew Salad
Mediterranean Spinach Strata
Mixed citrus fruits
Banana Layer Cake with
Cream Cheese Frosting

Holiday Feast Menu (page 388)
serves 12
Cream of Mushroom Soup with Sherry
Roast Beef with
Horseradish-Mustard Sauce
Mashed potatoes
Sautéed zucchini
Challah
Grand Marnier Soufflé with Vanilla Sauce

Christmas Dinner Menu (page 390)
serves 8
Arugula, Fennel, and Parmesan Salad
Fire and Spice Ham
Wild rice pilaf
Brussels Sprouts with Pecans
Cinnamon Stewed Apples
Dinner rolls
Sweet Potato Cheesecake

Tree Trimming Party Menu (page 396)
serves 6
Hot White Chocolate with Ginger
Spicy Swiss Chard with Lemon
Whole Grain Cornsticks
Chicken and Wild Rice
with Smoked Sausage
Coffee Cupcakes

Recipe Title Index

An alphabetical listing of every recipe title that appeared
in the magazine in 2002. See page 426 for the General Recipe Index.

Month-by-Month Index

A month-by-month listing of every food story with recipe titles that appeared in the magazine in 2002. See page 426 for the General Recipe Index.

General Recipe Index

*A listing by major ingredient, food category, and/or regular column
for every recipe that appeared in the magazine in 2002.*

Credits

CONTRIBUTING RECIPE DEVELOPERS:

Patricia Baird
Melanie Barnard
Peter Berley
Jack Bishop
David Bonom
Jennifer Brulé
Maureen Callahan
Viviana Carballo
Michael Chiarello
Holly Clegg
Katherine Cobbs
Jim Coleman
Ying Chang Compestine
Martha Condra
Kathryn Conrad
Lorrie Hulston Corvin
Leslie DeDominic
Cynthia DePersio
David DiResta
Susan Dosier

Melissa Dupree
Linda West Eckhardt
Amy Farges
Jim Fobel
Dorothy Foltz-Gray
Gale Gand
Paul Grosz
Ken Haedrich
Jessica B. Harris
Tamar Haspel
Giuliano Hazan
Raymond Hook
Lia Mack Huber
Linder Hunt
Patsy Jamieson
Christine Keff
Jean Kressy
Barbara Lauterbach
Jeanne Lemlin
Karen A. Levin
Susan Herrmann Loomis
Karen MacNeil
Michael Maddox

Deborah Madison
Elaine Magee
Domenica Marchetti
Don Mauer
Alice Medrich
Joan Nathan
Janet Neyrinck
Greg Patent
Jean Patterson
Marge Perry
Steven Raichlen
Leslie Revsin
Victoria Abbott Riccardi
Elizabeth Riely
Rick Rodgers
Richard Ruben
Julia Dowling Rutland
Todd-Michael St. Pierre
Felino Samson
Sharon Sanders
Mark Scarbrough
Chris Schlesinger
Trinket Shaw

Marie Simmons
Nina Simonds
Allen Smith
Hiro Sone
Sarah Stegner
Frank Stitt
Elizabeth Taliaferro
Daniel Vézina
Robin Vitetta-Miller
Robb Walsh
Robyn Webb
Bruce Weinstein
Joanne Weir
Laura Werlin
Karen Wilcher
Lisa Zwirn

CONTRIBUTING PHOTO STYLISTS:

Mary Catherine Muir, page 130
    Raspberry-Orange Sunrises
Fonda Shaia, page 3
    Pennsylvania Dutch Tea Rolls